Handbook of Data Analysis

Advisory Board for the Handbook of Data Analysis

Handbook of Data Analysis

Melissa Hardy and Alan Bryman

FARNBOROUGH COLLEGE OF TECHNOLOGY
LEARNING RESOURCE CENTRE

SAGE Publications
London • Thousand Oaks • New Delhi

Editorial arrangement and Introduction by
Melissa Hardy and Alan Bryman

Chapter 1 © Melissa Hardy and Alan Bryman 2004
Chapter 2 © Alan Bryman and Duncan Cramer 2004
Chapter 3 © Melissa Hardy 2004
Chapter 4 © Lawrence Hazelrigg 2004
Chapter 5 © Mortaza Jamshidian 2004
Chapter 6 © Mary Maynard 2004
Chapter 7 © Dennis Smith 2004
Chapter 8 © Ross M. Stolzenberg 2004
Chapter 9 © Melissa Hardy and John Reynolds 2004
Chapter 10 © James Jaccard and Tonya Dodge 2004
Chapter 11 © J. Scott Long and Simon Cheng 2004
Chapter 12 © Douglas L. Anderton and Eric
    Cheney 2004
Chapter 13 © Nancy Brandon Tuma 2004
Chapter 14 © Trond Petersen 2004
Chapter 15 © Guang Guo and John Hipp 2004
Chapter 16 © Paul Allison 2004
Chapter 17 © Heather MacIndoe and Andrew
    Abbott 2004

Chapter 18 © Vincent Kang Fu, Christopher
    Winship and Robert D. Mare 2004
Chapter 19 © Jodie B. Ullman and
    Peter M. Bentler 2004
Chapter 20 © William Browne and Jon Rasbash 2004
Chapter 21 © Christopher Winship and
    Michael Sobel 2004
Chapter 22 © Ronald L. Breiger 2004
Chapter 23 © Raymond M. Lee and
    Nigel G. Fielding 2004
Chapter 24 © Roberto P. Franzosi 2004
Chapter 25 © Peter K. Manning 2004
Chapter 26 © Steven E. Clayman and
    Virginia Teas Gill 2004
Chapter 27 © Jonathan Potter 2004
Chapter 28 © Nick Pidgeon and Karen
    Henwood 2004
Chapter 29 © Barbara Czarniawska 2004
Chapter 30 © Sara Delamont and Paul
    Atkinson 2004

First published 2004

SAGE Publications Ltd
1 Oliver's Yard
55 City Road
London EC1Y 1SP

SAGE Publications Inc.
2455 Teller Road
Thousand Oaks, California 91320

SAGE Publications India Pvt Ltd
B-42, Panchsheel Enclave
Post Box 4109
New Delhi 110 017

British Library Cataloguing in Publication data

A catalogue record for this book is available from
the British Library

ISBN 0 7619 6652 8

Library of Congress control number available

Typeset by C&M Digitals (P) Ltd., Chennai, India
Printed in Great Britain by The Cromwell Press Ltd, Trowbridge, Wiltshire

Contents

Preface

As is the case with any edited text, this book represents the culmination of exchanges with authors past and present. We are fortunate to have persuaded so many well-established data analysts to contribute chapters. Their investment of time and thought is reflected in the quality of the discussions that fill these pages. We are most appreciative of the support and assistance we received from Sage and would like to give special thanks to Chris Rojek, Kay Bridger and Ian Antcliff. We would like to thank Richard Leigh for his meticulous copyediting, which has greatly improved the book. We would also like to thank the members of our Advisory Board and several colleagues who provided us with advice on chapters, Chardie Baird who helped manage the multiple drafts and reviews, and our spouses for their support and encouragement.

Our intention was to put together a set of resource chapters that described major techniques of data analysis and addressed noteworthy issues involved in their application. The list of techniques included here is not exhaustive, but we did try to cover a wide range of approaches while providing reference to an even broader set of methods. With that in mind, we decided to include techniques appropriate to data of different sorts, including survey data, textual data, transcripts of conversations, and longitudinal information. Regardless of the format of the original data, analysis requires researchers to develop coding schemes, classification protocols, definitional rules, and procedures for ensuring reliability in the application of all of these tools. How researchers organize the information they will use in their analyses should be informed by theoretical concerns. Even so, this process of organization is also one of creation and, as such, it can be accomplished in a variety of ways and analyzed by different approaches.

Data analysts must concern themselves with the criteria they use to sort between the systematic component of their observations and the stochastic elements, or random influences, that are also reflected in these observations. The randomness of events is something we acknowledge, but we often behave as though we can exert considerable control over the way our lives unfold.

That point is often driven home in unanticipated ways. During the time we dedicated to the production of this book, we made frequent adjustments to modify a once reasonable schedule that had become impossible to meet. These unanticipated events reflect the fabric of people's lives, and forecasting life's events that would occur a year or two into the future was sometimes tragically inaccurate. Prominent among our initial list of authors were Lee Lillard and Aage Sørensen, both greatly respected by the scientific community, admired by their peers, and loved by their friends and families. Both men died unexpectedly while this volume was under way.

We make note here of the substantial contributions they made to this field of inquiry and to this volume through their published work, their teaching, and their involvement in too many discussions of these issues to count.

Melissa Hardy and Alan Bryman

Notes on Contributors

Andrew Abbott is the Gustavus F. and Ann M. Swift Distinguished Service Professor in the Department of Sociology and the College at the University of Chicago. Known for his ecological theories of occupations, Abbott has also pioneered algorithmic analysis of social sequence data. His recent books include studies of academic disciplines and publication (*Department and Discipline*, 1999) and of fractal patterns in social and cultural structures (*Chaos of Disciplines*, 2001), as well as a collection of theoretical and methodological essays in the Chicago pragmatist and ecological tradition (*Time Matters*, 2001). He is currently writing on social science heuristics and developing a major research project on the life course. Abbott is also a past Editor of the *American Journal of Sociology*.

Paul Allison is Professor of Sociology at the University of Pennsylvania where he teaches graduate methods and statistics. He is the author of *Missing Data* (2001), *Logistic Regression Using the SAS*® *System* (1999), *Multiple Regression: A Primer* (1999), *Survival Analysis Using the SAS*® *System* (1995), *Event History Analysis* (1984), and numerous articles on regression analysis, log-linear analysis, logit analysis, latent variable models, missing data, and inequality measures. He is a member of the editorial board of *Sociological Methods and Research*. A former Guggenheim Fellow, Allison received the 2001 Lazarsfeld Award for distinguished contributions to sociological methodology.

Douglas L. Anderton is Professor of Sociology at the University of Massachusetts Amherst, Director of the Social and Demographic Research Institute and a Fellow of the American Statistical Association. His research emphasizes quantitative-historical analysis of population and environment interactions. He is the author of over fifty journal articles and has co-authored several books, including: *Demography: Study of Human Populations* (2001), *Population of the United States* (1998), *Fertility on the Frontier* (1993), and an edited series, *Readings in Population Research Methodology* (1997). He is currently an editor of the ASA Rose Monograph Series in policy studies.

Paul Atkinson is Research Professor in Sociology at Cardiff University, UK. He is co-director of the ESRC Research Centre on Social and Economic Aspects of Genomics. His main research interests are the sociology of medical knowledge and the development of qualitative research methods. His publications include: *Ethnography: Principles in Practice* (with Martyn Hammersley), *The Clinical Experience, The Ethnographic Imagination, Understanding Ethnographic Texts, Medical Talk and Medical Work, Fighting Familiarity* (with Sara Delamont), *Making Sense of Qualitative Data* (with Amanda Coffey), *Sociological Readings and Re-readings, Interactionism* (with William Housley) and *Key Themes in Qualitative Research* (with Sara Delamont and Amanda Coffey). He was one of the editors of the *Handbook of*

Ethnography. Together with Sara Delamont he edits the journal *Qualitative Research*. His recent ethnographic study of an international opera company will be published in 2004 as *Everyday Arias*.

Peter M. Bentler is Professor of Psychology and Statistics at University of California, Los Angeles, and former Chair of the Department of Psychology, and has over 400 publications in methodology, psychometrics, and statistics as well as in applied fields such as personality, attitudes, drug abuse, health, sexuality and related topics. He has been an elected president of the Society of Multivariate Experimental Psychology, the Psychometric Society, and the Division of Evaluation, Measurement, and Statistics of the American Psychological Association (APA). He is also a recipient of the Distinguished Scientific Contributions Award from the APA Division of Evaluation, Measurement, and Statistics.

Ronald L. Breiger is Professor of Sociology, University of Arizona. With Linton Freeman, he edits the journal *Social Networks*. His interests include social network analysis, stratification, mathematical models, theory, and measurement issues in cultural and institutional analysis. He has recently written with Philippa Pattison on lattices and dimensional representation of network structures, with David Stark and Szabolcz Kemény on ownership patterns among banks and firms in Hungary, and with John Mohr on the dual aggregation of social categories.

William Browne is a Lecturer in the School of Mathematical Sciences, University of Nottingham. He received his doctorate from the University of Bath in 1998 for his research on Monte Carlo Markov chain methods and multilevel modeling. He was formerly a member of the team at the University of London Institute of Education responsible for the development of the leading multilevel modeling software package MLwiN. He has written several papers in both statistical methodology and statistical applications in areas including education, medicine, demography, and ecology.

Alan Bryman is Professor of Social Research, Department of Social Sciences, Loughborough University. His main research interests lie in the fields of social research methodology, leadership, theme parks and the theming process more generally, and human–animal relations. He is particularly interested in the integration of quantitative and qualitative research. He has written several books, including *Quantity and Quality in Social Research* (1988), *Disney and His Worlds* (1995), and *Social Research Methods* (2001). He is the editor of the Understanding Social Research series for Open University Press and is co-editor of the forthcoming Sage *Encyclopedia of Social Science Research Methods*.

Eric Cheney is a Ph.D. candidate at the University of Massachusetts Amherst. His research interests include economic sociology, organizations, social networks, statistics, and quantitative methodology. He is currently completing his dissertation on the topic of social structure and economic exchange.

Simon Cheng is an Assistant Professor in the Department of Sociology at the University of Connecticut. His substantive research is in race and ethnicity, family–school relationships, and political-economic development, where he has recently published articles in *Sociology of Education, Social Forces,* and other journals. His dissertation, 'Standing in the middle of interracial relations: The educational experiences of children from multiracial backgrounds', examines differences between biracial and monoracial families in a variety of family and student outcomes. He is also studying the small-sample behavior of tests of the independence of irrelevant alternatives assumption in the multinomial logit model.

Steven E. Clayman is Professor of Sociology and is affiliated with the Communication Studies Program at the University of California Los Angeles. His research concerns the intersection of talk, interaction, and mass communication. He has studied broadcast news interviews, presidential press conferences, newspaper editorial conferences, the dynamics of quotability, and collective audience behavior in political speeches and debates. His articles have appeared in *American Sociological Review, American Journal of Sociology, Language in Society, Journal of Communication,* and *Media, Culture, and Society.* He is the author (with John Heritage) of *The News Interview: Journalists and Public Figures on the Air.*

Duncan Cramer is Reader of Psychological Health, Department of Social Sciences, Loughborough University. He received his doctorate in 1973 from the Institute of Psychiatry in London. His main research interests and publications lie in the fields of close relationships, personality, psychological health, counselling, and psychotherapy. He has authored or co-authored a number of books, including *Personality and Psychotherapy* (1992), *Close Relationships* (1998), and *Fundamental Statistics for Social Research* (1998). From 1995 to 2000 he was Joint Editor of the *British Journal of Medical Psychology* and is currently again an Associate Editor of the journal, which in 2002 was renamed *Psychology and Psychotherapy.*

Barbara Czarniawska holds a Skandia Chair of Management Studies at Gothenburg Research Institute, School of Economics and Commercial Law, Göteborg University, Sweden. Her research focuses on complex organizing processes, most recently big city management. In terms of methodological approach, she combines institutional theory with the narrative approach. She has published in the area of business and public administration in Polish, her native language, as well as in Swedish, Italian and English, her most recent publications being *Narrating the Organization: Dramas of Institutional Identity* (1997), *A Narrative Approach to Organization Studies* (1998), *Writing Management* (1999), and *A Tale of Three Cities* (2002). She is a member of the Swedish Royal Academy of Sciences and the Swedish Royal Engineering Academy.

Sara Delamont is Reader in Sociology at Cardiff University. She was the first woman to be president of the British Education Research Association, and the first woman Dean of Social Sciences at Cardiff. Her research interests are educational ethnography, Mediterranean anthropology, and gender. Her most famous book is *Interaction in the Classroom* (1976 and 1983), her favourites *Knowledgeable Women* (1989) and *Appetites and Identities* (1995). She is co-editor of the journal *Qualitative Research.*

Tonya Dodge is a pre-doctoral student in the Psychology Department at the University of Albany, State University of New York. Her research interests focus on attitudes and decision-making, with a particular interest in attitude ambivalence. She also conducts research on the effects of athletic participation on adolescent risk behavior.

Nigel G. Fielding is Professor of Sociology and co-director of the Institute of Social Research at the University of Surrey, Guildford. He was editor of the *Howard Journal of Criminal Justice* from 1985 to 1998 and is co-editor of the Sage series 'New Technologies for Social Research'. His principal research interests are in policing and in qualitative research methods. He has authored or edited 13 books, 40 journal articles, 40 chapters in edited collections and 141 other publications. Among his books on aspects of method are *Linking Data: The Articulation of Qualitative and Quantitative Methods in Social Research* (with J.L. Fielding, 1986); *Actions and Structure* (ed., 1988); *Using Computers in Qualitative Research* (ed., with R. Lee, 1991) and *Computer Analysis and Qualitative Research* (with R. Lee, 1998). He was recently co-editing a special issue of *Forum Qualitative Sozialforschung* on methodological triangulation.

Roberto P. Franzosi is currently Professor of Sociology and Head of the Department of Sociology at the University of Reading, having previously taught at the University of Wisconsin-Madison (1983–93) and at the University of Oxford, with a fellowship at Trinity College. Franzosi's long-standing research interest has been in the area of social conflict, with several articles and a book (*The Puzzle of Strikes: Class and State Strategies in Postwar Italy*, 1995). Since the early 1980s Franzosi has been involved in the development of a new linguistic- and computer-based approach to content analysis applied to the study of historical processes. His new book *From Words to Numbers* (2004) summarizes his work in the area. Franzosi has served as consulting editor for the *American Journal of Sociology* and he is currently a managing editor for the *Journal of Historical Sociology*.

Vincent Kang Fu is Assistant Professor in the Department of Sociology at the University of Utah. His interests are in race and ethnicity, quantitative methods, demography, marriage, and immigration. He is investigating variation in racial and ethnic intermarriage patterns across regions and among groups in order to understand changes over time in intermarriage. His research has been published in *Demography*.

Virginia Teas Gill is an Associate Professor in the Department of Sociology at Illinois State University. She received her Ph.D. from the University of Wisconsin in 1995. Her major research interest is doctor–patient interaction. Her publications focus on patients' explanations for illness and their requests for medical interventions in primary care clinic visits, and the labeling process in a clinic for childhood developmental disabilities.

Guang Guo is Professor of Sociology, Department of Sociology, University of North Carolina at Chapel Hill. He has published methodological work in the *Journal of the American Statistical Association, Sociological Methodology, Annual Review of Sociology,* and *Behavior Genetics* on event-history analysis, multilevel analysis, and random-effects models for genetically related siblings. He has published substantive work in *American Sociological Review, Social Forces, Sociology of Education, Demography,* and *Population Studies* on child and infant mortality, poverty and children's intellectual development, sibsize and intellectual development, and heritability–environment interactions for intellectual development. His current interest lies mainly in the interactions between environment and heritability using both sibling and DNA data.

Melissa Hardy is Distinguished Professor of Human Development and Sociology and Director of the Gerontology Center at Pennsylvania State University. She received her graduate degree in sociology from Indiana University in 1980. Her current research focuses on pensions and financial security in old age, expectations and achievement, and health policy. She is the author of *Regression with Dummy Variables* (1993), editor of *Studying Aging and Social Change: Conceptual and Methodological Issues* (1997), and co-author of *Ending a Career in the Auto Industry: 30 and Out* (1997).

Lawrence Hazelrigg is now Emeritus Professor, College of Social Sciences, Florida State University, and is engaged in two research projects – a series of studies of risk perception and its correlates/consequences; and a study of historical-cultural differences of the constitution and practice of selfhood. Recent and representative publications include: *Cultures of Nature* (1995); 'Individualism', in *Encyclopedia of Sociology*, 2nd edition (2000); 'Scaling the semantics of satisfaction' (with M.A. Hardy) in *Social Indicators Research* (2000); 'Fueling the politics of age' (with M.A. Hardy) in *American Sociological Review* (1999); and 'Marx and the meter of nature' in *Rethinking Marxism* (1993).

Karen Henwood is a Senior Lecturer in Clinical and Health Psychology, University of East Anglia. A social psychologist by training (Ph.D., University of Bristol), her research addresses the role of culture, difference and life history in the formation of identity and subjectivity. She has undertaken research projects on gender and family relationships, masculinity and the body, and the meanings and non-economic values people attach to their natural environment. With Nick Pidgeon she has explored the role of qualitative methods in psychology and the social sciences. Her published work has appeared in journals such as *British Journal of Psychology, Feminism and Psychology, Theory and Psychology, Journal of Environmental Psychology, Social Science and Medicine* and *British Journal of Social Psychology*. She has recently completed an (ESRC-funded) project on 'masculinities, identities and the transition to fatherhood'.

John Hipp is a graduate student in Sociology at the University of North Carolina at Chapel Hill. His substantive work is concerned with community and urban processes, focusing on how networks and institutions can play a role in helping communities deal with social externalities. He uses both social network and structural equation modeling methodologies to address these questions. He has published in *Social Forces* and *Sociological Methodology*, and is currently exploring modeling nonlinear longitudinal processes within a latent variable framework as a member of the Carolina Structural Equation Modeling research group.

James Jaccard is Distinguished Professor of Psychology at the University at Albany, State University of New York. His primary research interest is in adolescent risk behavior, with an emphasis on understanding adolescent unintended pregnancy and adolescent drunk driving. His work has focused on family-based approaches to dealing with adolescent problem behaviors. He has authored four monographs on the analysis of interaction effects using a wide range of statistical models.

Mortaza (Mori) Jamshidian is Associate Professor of Mathematics, Department of Mathematics, California State University, Fullerton. His main research area is computational statistics. He has made significant contributions in the area of EM estimation, which has numerous applications in missing-data analysis. In particular his papers in acceleration of EM and EM standard error estimation are important contributions. His general work and contributions have included development of computing algorithms in the fields of psychometrics, biostatistics, and general statistical field.

Raymond M. Lee is Professor of Social Research Methods in the Department of Social and Political Science, Royal Holloway University of London. With Nigel Fielding, he is Co-Director of the CAQDAS Networking Project and co-edits the Sage series 'New Technologies for Social Research'. He has written widely on a range of methodological topics, including the problems and issues surrounding research on 'sensitive' topics, research in physically dangerous environments, and the impact of new technologies on the research process. He is the author of *Doing Research on Sensitive Topics* (1993), *Dangerous Fieldwork* (1995), *Computer Analysis and Qualitative Research* (with Nigel Fielding, 1998), and *Unobtrusive Methods in Social Research* (2000).

J. Scott Long is Chancellor's Professor of Sociology at Indiana University, Bloomington. His research focuses on gender differences in the scientific career, aging and labor force participation, and statistical methods. His recent research on the scientific career was published as *From Scarcity to Visibility*. He is past Editor of *Sociological Methods and Research* and the recipient of the American Sociological Association's Paul F. Lazarsfeld Memorial Award for Distinguished Contributions in the Field of Sociological Methodology. He is author of *Confirmatory Factor Analysis, Covariance Structure Analysis, Regression Models for Categorical and Limited Dependent Variables*, and *Regression Models for Categorical and Limited Dependent Variables with Stata* (with Jeremy Freese), as well as several edited volumes.

Heather MacIndoe is a doctoral candidate in the Department of Sociology at the University of Chicago. She received her M.A. degree in sociology from Stanford University and is a former student editor of the *American Journal of Sociology*. Her research interests include formal organizations, social change, philanthropy, and civil society. Her dissertation, 'Organizational alliances and philanthropic support: Social change in Chicago 1970–2000', examines the relationships between philanthropic foundations and the organizations they support across neighborhoods in the city of Chicago.

Peter K. Manning (Ph.D. Duke, 1966, M.A. Oxon., 1982) holds the Elmer V. H. and Eileen M. Brooks Chair in Policing. He has taught at Massachusetts Institute of Technology, Oxford, the University of Michigan, and elsewhere, and was a Fellow of the National Institute of Justice, Balliol and Wolfson Colleges, Oxford, the American Bar Foundation, the Rockefeller Villa (Bellagio), and the Centre for Socio-Legal Studies, Wolfson College, Oxford. Listed in *Who's Who in America*, he has been awarded many contracts and grants, the Bruce W. Smith and the O.W. Wilson Awards from the Academy of Criminal Justice Sciences, and the Charles Horton Cooley Award from the Michigan Sociological Association. The author and editor of some 13 books, including (with Brian Forst) *Privatization of Policing: Two Views* (2000), his research interests include the rationalizing of policing, crime mapping and crime analysis, uses of information technology, and qualitative methods. The second edition of *Narcs' Game* (1979) appeared in 2002, and his monograph, *Policing Contingencies*, in 2003.

Robert D. Mare   is Professor of Sociology at the University of California Los Angeles. His research interests include social mobility and inequality, demography, and quantitative methods. He has done extensive research on intergenerational educational mobility, assortative mating, youth unemployment, and methods for the analysis of categorical data. His recent work focuses on models for residential mobility and residential segregation and on links between educational stratification and marriage markets. His research has appeared in a number of journals, including the *American Sociological Review, American Journal of Sociology,* and *Sociological Methodology.* He is a former editor of *Demography.*

Mary Maynard   is Professor in the Department of Social Policy and Social Work at the University of York, UK, where she was previously Director of the Centre for Women's Studies. She works and writes in the areas of gender, ethnicity, later life, social theory, and social research methodology. She has just completed a project focusing on what empowers older women, from a variety of ethnic groups, in later life.

Trond Petersen   is a Professor at the University of California Berkeley, in the Department of Sociology and Haas School of Business. His research and teaching are in the areas of inequality and social stratification, organizations, human resource management, economic sociology, and quantitative methods. He has also taught at the University of Oslo and previously at Harvard University. Among his recent publications are: 'Offering a job: Meritocracy and social networks' in *American Journal of Sociology* (2000, with Ishak Saporta and Marc-David Seidel); 'Equal pay for equal work? Evidence from Sweden and a comparison with Norway and the U.S.' in *Scandinavian Journal of Economics* (2001, with Eva M. Meyersson Milgrom and Vemund Snartland); and 'The opportunity structure for discrimination' (with Ishak Saporta), to appear in *American Journal of Sociology.*

Nick Pidgeon   is Professor of Psychology and Director of the Centre for Environmental Risk in the School of Environmental Sciences, University of East Anglia. He has research interests in people's perception of risk and its communication, the construction of preferences and risk valuation, the human and organizational causes of major industrial accidents, and risk management. He is co-author of *Man-Made Disasters* (2nd edition, 1997) and *The Social Amplification of Risk* (2003).

Jonathan Potter   is Professor of Discourse Analysis at Loughborough University. He has studied scientific argumentation, descriptions of crowd disorder, current affairs television, racism, and relationship counselling, and is currently studying calls to a child protection helpline. His most recent books include *Representing Reality* (1996), which attempts to provide a systematic overview, integration and critique of constructionist research in social psychology, postmodernism, rhetoric, and ethnomethodology; *Talk and Cognition* (in press, with Hedwig te Molder), in which a range of different researchers consider the implication of studies of interaction for understanding cognition; and *Focus Group Interaction* (in press, with Claudia Puchta), which analyses interaction in market research focus groups. He is co-editor of the journal *Theory and Psychology.*

Jon Rasbash   is a Reader in Statistical Computing at the Institute of Education, University of London. He is the principle author of the MLwiN software package. Jon's interests and publications cover the following areas: development and implementation of algorithms to estimate multilevel models, statistical methodology, the application of multilevel modeling techniques to social science data, and designing user interfaces for statistical modeling software. A publication list is available at http://multilevel.ioe.ac.uk/team/jon. html

John Reynolds   is an Associate Professor of Sociology and an Associate of the Pepper Institute on Aging and Public Policy at Florida State University. His research interests include gender-related trends in higher education, the conditioning effects of social and economic contexts on adults' physical and mental well-being, and quantitative methods. Recent publications include 'Rising college expectations among youth in the U.S.' in *Journal of Human Resources*; 'The contingent meaning of neighborhood stability for residents' psychological well-being' in *American Sociological Review*; and 'Age, depression, and attrition in the National Survey of Families and Households' in *Sociological Methods and Research*.

Dennis Smith   is Professor of Sociology in the Department of Social Sciences at Loughborough University. He has written several articles and books, including *The Rise of Historical Sociology* (1990), *Zygmunt Bauman. Prophet of Postmodernity* (1999), *Norbert Elias and Modern Social Theory* (2000), *Conflict and Compromise. Class Formation in English Society 1830–1914* (1982), *Capitalist Democracy on Trial. The Transatlantic Debate from Tocqueville to the Present* (1991), *Barrington Moore. Violence, Morality and Political Change* (1983), *The Chicago School. A Liberal Critique of Capitalism* (1988), and has been a contributing editor of *Whose Europe? The Turn towards Democracy* (1999) and *The Civilized Organization. Norbert Elias and the Future of Organization Studies* (2002). He is currently completing a book on modernity and humiliation. He is a past vice-president of the European Sociological Association (2001–3), one-time editor of *Sociological Review* and currently editor of *Current Sociology*, journal of the International Sociological Association.

Michael Sobel   is a professor at Columbia University. His research interests include causal inference and new applications of the theory of financial decision-making to the social sciences. He is a previous co-editor of *Sociological Methodology* and a co-editor of the *Handbook of Statistical Modeling for the Social and Behavioral Sciences* (1995).

Ross M. Stolzenberg   is Professor of Sociology at the University of Chicago. He is editor of the journal, *Sociological Methodology*, and his current research concerns the connection between family and labor market processes in stratification systems. He has held academic posts in university programs in social relations, sociology, population dynamics, and applied statistics at Harvard University, Johns Hopkins University and the University of Illinois at Urbana. He has held nonacademic posts at the Rand Corporation, the Graduate Management Admission Council, and as a consultant in complex litigation and other matters. He has served on editorial boards or held editorial postions at seven refereed academic journals.

Nancy Brandon Tuma   obtained her Ph.D. in sociology from Michigan State University in 1972, and is currently a Professor of Sociology at Stanford University. She is a leading sociological methodologist, focusing primarily on the study of change. Best known for her pioneering work on event-history analysis and as co-author of *Social Dynamics: Models and Methods* (1984), she has published studies of life careers and social inequalities in the United States, China, Germany, Poland, the former Soviet Union, and various countries formerly in the Soviet Union. Her current primary research interest is the impact of the transition from socialism on people's life careers. She has served as editor of *Sociological Methodology* and also as associate editor of the *Journal of the American Statistical Association*. In 1994 she received the Lazarsfeld award for her contributions to sociological methodology.

Jodie B. Ullman is an Associate Professor of Psychology at California State University, San Bernardino. She earned her Ph.D. in measurement and psychometrics from the University of California Los Angeles in 1997. Her primary research interests are in applied multivariate statistics with a particular emphasis on structural equation modeling and hierarchical linear modeling. She is particularly interested in applications of complex statistical techniques to substance use questions. Her recent research includes evaluations of the Drug Abuse Resistance Education program, longitudinal examinations of cigarette sales to minors, and reduction of HIV/AIDS risk behaviors in homeless populations.

Christopher Winship is Professor of Sociology in the Kennedy School of Government at Harvard University. He did his undergraduate work in sociology and mathematics at Dartmouth College and received his graduate degree from Harvard in 1977. He is currently doing research on the Ten Point Coalition, a group of black ministers who are working with the Boston police to reduce youth violence; statistical models for causal analysis; the effects of education on mental ability; causes of the racial difference in performance on elite colleges and universities; and changes in the racial differential in imprisonment rates over the past sixty years.

'With the appearance of this handbook, data analysts no longer have to consult dozens of disparate publications to carry out their work. The essential tools for an intelligent telling of the data story are offered here, in thirty chapters written by recognized experts. While quantitative methods are treated, from basic statistics through the general linear model and beyond, qualitative methods are by no means neglected. Indeed, a unique feature of this volume is the careful integration of quantitative and qualitative approaches.' **Michael S. Lewis-Beck, F. Wendell Miller Distinguished Professor of Political Science at the University of Iowa.**

This book, which will rapidly be recognized as a social research bible, provides a peerless guide to key issues in data analysis, from fundamental concerns such as the construction of variables, the characterization of distributions and the notions of inference, to the more advanced topics of causality, models of change and network analysis.

No other book provides a better one-stop account of the field of data analysis. Throughout, the editors encourage readers to develop an appreciation of the range of analytic options available for a wide variety of data structures, so that they can develop a suitable analytic approach to their research questions.

Scholars and students can turn to it for teaching and applied needs with confidence, while specialists will find the provision of up to date expositions on a wide range of techniques invaluable.

Melissa Hardy is Distinguished Professor of Human Development and Family Studies, Sociology, and Demography and Director of the Gerontology Center at The Pennsylvania State University; Alan Bryman is Professor of Social Research, University of Loughborough.

'The book provides researchers with guidance in, and examples of, both quantitative and qualitative modes of analysis, written by leading practitioners in the field. The editors give a persuasive account of the commonalities of purpose that exist across both modes, as well as demonstrating a keen awareness of the different things that each offers the practising researcher.' **Clive Seale, Department of Sociology, Goldsmiths College, London.**

'This is an excellent guide to current issues in the analysis of social science data. I recommend it to anyone who is looking for authoritative introductions to the state of the art. Each chapter offers a comprehensive review and an extensive bibliography and will be invaluable to researchers wanting to update themselves about modern developments.' **Professor Nigel Gilbert, Pro Vice-Chancellor and Professor of Sociology, University of Surrey.**

1

Introduction

Common Threads among Techniques of Data Analysis

MELISSA HARDY AND ALAN BRYMAN

In deciding the mix of topics to include in this *Handbook*, we wanted to provide a wide range of analytic options suited to many different research questions and different data structures. An early decision was to include both 'quantitative' and 'qualitative' techniques in a single volume. Within the current research environment, practitioners can hardly fail to notice the schism that exists between camps of qualitative and quantitative researchers. For some, this division is fundamental, leading them to pay little attention to developments in the 'other' camp. Certainly the assumption has been that practitioners of these different approaches have so little in common that any text on data analysis must choose between the two approaches rather than include both in a single text.

We believe that reinforcing this division is a mistake, especially for those of us who practice in the behavioral and social sciences. Discipline boundaries too often act as intellectual fences beyond which we rarely venture, as if our own field of research is so well defined and so much ours that we can learn nothing from other disciplines that can possibly be of use. Many of us may remember our first forays into literature searches on a given research topic, which we too often

defined in the narrowest of terms, only to learn from our advisors that we had missed mountains of useful publications arrayed across a variety of fields, time periods, and (perhaps) languages. One of the major costs of dividing and subdividing fields into an increasing number of specializations is that we may inadvertently limit the kinds of intellectual exchanges in which we engage. One learns more from attempting to view a subject through a variety of different lenses than from staring at the same page through the same pair of glasses. And so it can be with analytic techniques.

Researchers run the gamut from technical experts who speak in equations and spin out table after table of numerical results to those who have tried to devise an alternative to page enumeration, so averse to 'numbers' were they. Most of us are somewhere in the middle, interested in a particular research question and trying to formulate as systematic and as persuasive an answer as possible.

Both approaches attempt to 'tell a story' from the data. Quantitative researchers generally refer to this process as hypothesis testing or 'modeling' the data to determine whether and to what extent empirical observations can be represented by the motivating theoretical model. Qualitative researchers may or may not invoke models. Whether the method of *analysis* will be quantitative or qualitative is not so much an issue of whether the information/data at hand are organized through classifications, rank-ordered relative to some notion of magnitude, or assessed at the interval or ratio level of measurement. The choice can involve assumptions about the nature of social reality, how it should be studied, the kinds of research questions that are of interest, and how errors of observation, measurement, estimation, and conclusion should be addressed.

Because this is a text in data analysis rather than data collection, each author assumes a certain structure of data and a certain range of research questions. To be sure, many decisions have been made before the researcher begins analysis, although active researchers seldom march through the stages of design, data collection, and data analysis as if they were moving through security checkpoints that allowed mobility in only one direction. Instead, researchers typically move back and forth, as if from room to room, taking what they learn in one room and revisiting what was decided in the previous room, keeping the doors open.

However, if the researcher is relying on secondary data – data collected to serve a broad range of interests, often involving large national samples – key features such as the sampling design and questionnaire must be taken as given, and other types of information – how long it took the respondent to settle on a response, whether the respondent took some care to frame the response within a particular context even though what was recorded was simply a level of agreement with a statement, for example – are not retrievable. Researchers who collect their own data use a variety of sampling procedures and collection tools that are designed to illuminate what they seek to understand and to provide information best suited to their research interests. But once the data are in hand, the evidence that may be required to address the research problem will be limited to interpretations, reconfigurations, or creative combinations of this already collected information.

This distinction between measuring amounts and distinguishing categories is sometimes referred to as the distinction between quantitative and qualitative variables, and it is only one of the arenas in which 'quantity' and 'quality' are counterposed. Another contrast that is made between qualitative and quantitative approaches involves the use of *statistical* methods of analysis, where quantitative implies using statistics and qualitative, in some quarters, means eschewing statistical approaches. But not all research that is classified as quantitative relies only on statistical approaches. Certainly in coding interview information, any researcher must make decisions about the boundaries of classification, must determine 'like' and 'unlike' things, and these decisions are already shaping any analysis that will follow. In similar fashion, not all qualitative researchers reject statistics, although reliance on inferential statistics is not common. Does the fact that a researcher calculates a correlation coefficient or bases a conclusion on differences in the counts of events suddenly toss the research into the quantitative camp? Does it matter, so long as the procedures are systematic and the conclusions are sound?

THE BASICS

We begin the volume with some basic issues that require a researcher's attention. The novice researcher is often dismayed when first using a given data set, since the correspondence between the concepts he or she has in mind is seldom there simply to be plucked from a list. Issues of reliability and validity loom large in the enterprise of analysis, for the conclusions that can be drawn on the basis of an analysis, regardless of how simple or complex, are contingent on the utility of the information on which the analysis is based. It is the instrumentality of measurement – measure as organizing tool that relates observation to concept to theory – that is a common thread of all analysis. Having made that most fundamental recognition, however, we must also note that it is often through debates over procedures of *analysis* that concerns about the limitations of measurement are played out. The value of a measure is its utility for improving our understanding of some social process, whether such a measure emerges through the manual sifting of data, or whether it serves as the framework for data collection.

Defining variables is therefore an exercise in establishing correspondence. Part of our everyday activities involves organizing the steady flow of information that our senses feed to our brains. The manner in which we accomplish this organization is not a random process. Rather, we categorize, we classify, we monitor frequency and intensity, we note repetition, stability, change, and amount of change, along a variety of dimensions. We fudge the boundaries of these categories with phrases such as 'kind of' and 'sort of'. And whereas our classification schemes may be quite functional for our own use, they may not sit well with the schemes others use.

In our everyday conversations we either gloss over disagreements, or we may pursue the issue by defending how we make sense of a situation. But in taking this next step, we move closer to scientific practice, in that our original statement must then be argued on the basis of empirical evidence, rules of assignment, what counts as 'similar' versus 'different', and which traits trump others in making such assignments. In other words, such statements – such classifications – have to be reproducible on the basis of the rules and the evidence alone. Then the issue is how convincing others find our approach.

Once we have defined the terms of our analysis, the temptation for statistical analysts is to move quickly to the most complex procedures, but that step is premature. We can learn much by studying the distributions of the variables we observe. And once we have good basic information on the univariate distributions, we should spend some time examining simple associations among variables, two at a time. Although this stage can be time-consuming, it is essential to gradually build our understanding of the data structures on which more complex associations will rely. These insights prove valuable when one must translate the finding into some reasoned argument that allows others to grasp what has been learned.

THE UTILITY OF STATISTICS

In many of these early chapters, basic statistical procedures are explained and illustrated. As Duncan (1975: 4) noted:

> There are two broad kinds of problems that demand statistical treatment in connection with scientific use of [models] … One is the problem of inference from samples … Statistical methods are needed to contrive optimal estimators and proper tests of hypotheses, and to indicate the degree of precision in our results or the size of the risk we are taking in drawing a particular conclusion from

them. The second, not unrelated, kind of problem that raises statistical issues is the supposition that some parts of the world (not excluding the behavior of scientists themselves, when making fallible measurements) may realistically be described as behaving in a stochastic (chance, probabilistic, random) manner. If we decide to build into our models some assumption of this kind, then we shall need the aid of statistics to formulate appropriate descriptions of the probability distributions.

A major benefit of even 'fallible' measurement as the method of organizing our observations within some comparative framework is that it serves as a tool of standardization, which provides some assurance that both we, as well as others who attempt to replicate our work, can reliably identify equivalences and differences. 'Better' measurement is often taken to mean 'more precise' measurement, but the increase in precision must have utility for the question at hand; otherwise, such efforts simply increase the amount of 'noise' in the measure. For example, a public opinion researcher may decide that she can better capture variability in people's view of a certain taxation policy by moving beyond a Likert scale of agreement or disagreement to a set of possible responses that range from 0 (I see no redeeming value in such a policy) to 100 (I see this policy as the perfect response to the need). In testing this new measurement strategy, however, the researcher may discover that the set of actual responses is far more limited than the options available to respondents and, for the most part, these responses cluster at the deciles (10, 20, 30, …, 90); the respondents effectively reduce the choice set by focusing on multiples of 10 rather than increments of one. However, the researcher may also observe the occasional response of 54 or 32. What is she to make of that additional variability? Can she be confident that the difference between a response of 32 and one of 30 represents a reliable distinction with regard to tax policy? Or is the 32 response perhaps more a reflection of 'a tendency toward non-comformity'?

But this issue of precision/reliability/variability is not in itself a function of a statistical versus a non-statistical approach. The issue of precision, as Duncan notes, is one of assessing the likelihood of erroneous conclusions and the role played by 'chance' in our research activities. Error is inescapable. Error as mistaken observation, error as blunder, error as bias – how do we systematically manage error within the range of techniques available to us? The question at hand is how we manage error when using 'quantitative' or 'qualitative' techniques of analysis.

In sum, any analysis of data, however it proceeds, is a sorting process of information that contains errors – however it was collected. Further, this sorting process by which we sift 'good' information from 'error' also allows us to sort for logical patterns, for example, Y only occurs when X is present, but when X is present, Y does not always occur. And by identifying certain patterns, noting their frequency, determining the contexts under which they occur always, sometimes, or never, we make sense of the data. And that is our goal – to make 'sense' of the data.

SIMILARITIES BETWEEN QUANTITATIVE AND QUALITATIVE DATA ANALYSIS

It is easy to assume that the different preoccupations and inclinations of their respective practitioners mean that as research strategies, quantitative and qualitative research are totally different. Indeed, they *are* different, reflecting as they do distinctive intellectual traditions. However, this does not signal that they are so different they do not share any common features. It is worth reflecting, therefore, on the ways in which quantitative and qualitative data analysis may be said to have common characteristics. In doing so, we begin to raise issues about what data analysis is and also what constitutes a good data analysis, whether quantitative or qualitative.

Both are concerned with data reduction

Although data analysis is something more than data reduction, it is also true to say that paring down and condensing the vast amounts of data that we frequently collect in the course of fieldwork is a major preoccupation of all analysts. Indeed, it would be surprising if this were *not* the case since dictionary definitions of 'analysis', such as that found in *The Concise Oxford Dictionary*, refer to a process of resolving into simpler elements. Therefore, to analyze or to provide an analysis will always involve a notion of reducing the amount of data we have collected so that capsule statements about the data can be provided.

In quantitative research, we are often confronted with a large array of data in the form of many cases and many variables. With small amounts of quantitative data, whether in terms of cases or variables, we may be able to 'see' what is happening. We can sense, for example, the way in which a variable is distributed, such as whether there is bunching at one end of the scale or whether a particular value tends to recur again and again in a distribution. But with increasing numbers of cases and variables our ability to 'see' tails off. We begin to lose sight of what is happening. The simplest techniques that we use to summarize quantitative data, such as frequency tables and measures of central tendency and dispersion, are ways of reducing the amount of data we are handling. They enable us to 'see' our data again, to gain a sense of what the data show. We may want to reduce our data even further. For example, we might employ factor analysis to establish whether we can reduce the number of variables that we are handling.

Similarly with qualitative data, the researcher accumulates a large amount of information. This information can come in several different forms. Ethnographers are likely to amass a corpus of field notes based on their reflections of what they heard or saw. Researchers who use qualitative interviews usually find that they compile a mountain of transcripts of tape-recorded interviews. As Lee and Fielding remark in Chapter 23, the transcription of such interviews is frequently the source of a major bottleneck in qualitative research, because it is so time-consuming to produce. However, transcripts frequently constitute a kind of double bottleneck because, in addition to being time-consuming to generate, they are daunting to analyze. Most approaches to analyzing ethnographic fieldnotes, qualitative interview transcripts, and other qualitative data (such as documents) comprise a coding approach that segments the textual materials in question. Not all approaches to qualitative data analysis entail this approach; for example, narrative analysis, which is discussed in Chapter 29 by Czarniawska, involves a preference for emphasizing the flow in what people say in interviews. But whatever strategy is adopted, the qualitative researcher is keen to break his or her data down so that it is more manageable and understandable. As Lee and Fielding show, the growing use of computer-aided qualitative data analysis software is a means of making that process easier (in terms of the coding, retrieval, and management of data) in much the same way as statistical software can rapidly summarize large quantities of data.

Both are concerned with answering research questions

While the precise nature of the relationship between research questions and data analysis may be different among quantitative and qualitative researchers, both are concerned with answering research questions. In quantitative research, the stipulation of research questions may be highly specific and is often translated into hypotheses which are outlined either at the beginning of an investigation or as we begin to analyze our data. This process is often depicted as indicative of the hypothetico-deductive method with which quantitative research is often associated. Stipulating research questions helps to guide the collection and analyses of data, but having such organizing questions also serves to ensure that the research is about *something* and that the something will make a contribution to our understanding of an issue or topic.

Qualitative researchers are often somewhat circumspect about devising research questions, or perhaps more precisely about the timing of their formulation. In qualitative research there is frequently a preference for an open-ended strategy so that the meaning systems with which participants operate are not closed off by a potentially premature confinement of what should be looked at. In addition, qualitative researchers frequently revel in the flexibility that the open-endedness offers them. Consequently, it is not unusual to find accounts of the qualitative research process which suggest that the investigation did not start with any concrete research questions. Not all qualitative research is like this; many practitioners prefer to begin with the relatively clear focus that research questions provide. Nonetheless, there is a strong tradition among practitioners which enjoins them not to restrict their field of vision too early in the research process by orienting to research questions. Some versions of grounded theory, for example, specifically encourage the deferment of research questions, as Pidgeon and Henwood observe in Chapter 28. But all this is not to say that research questions do not get asked in some versions of qualitative research. Instead, they tend to emerge in the course of an investigation as the researcher gradually narrows the area of interest. The research questions may even be developed into hypotheses, as in grounded theory. Deferring the asking of research questions has the advantage for qualitative researchers of enabling them to develop an understanding of what is important and significant from the perspective of the people they are studying, so that research questions that may be irrelevant to participants are less likely to be asked, if it is the perspective of relevance that matters. It also offers greater flexibility in that interesting insights gleaned while in the field can be used as a springboard for new research questions.

Thus, while the stage at which the formulation of research questions occurs frequently differs between quantitative and qualitative research, and the nature of the research questions may also be somewhat different, data analysis is typically oriented to answering research questions regardless of whether the research strategy is quantitative or qualitative.

Both are concerned with relating data analysis to the research literature

This point is closely related to the previous one but nonetheless deserves separate treatment. An important aspect of any data analysis is to relate the issues that drive and emerge from it to the research literature. With quantitative data analysis, the literature tends to provide an impetus for data analysis, in that it is invariably a key element in the formulation of a set of research questions. Quantitative research papers typically conclude by returning to the literature in order to address such issues as whether a hypothesis deriving from it is confirmed and how far the findings are consistent with it.

With qualitative data analysis, the existing literature may help to inform or at least act as a background to the analysis. This means, for example, that the coding of transcripts or fieldnotes will be partly informed by the literature. Existing categories may be employed as codes. In addition, the qualitative researcher will typically seek to demonstrate the implications of an analysis for the existing literature.

Thus, practitioners of both research strategies are highly attuned to the literature when conducting data analysis. This feature is indicative of the fact that practitioners are equally concerned with making a contribution to theory through their data analysis.

Both are concerned with variation

Variability between cases is central to quantitative data analysis. The goal of quantitative data analysis is to capture the amount of variation in a sample and to explain why that variation exists as it does and/or how it was produced. An attribute on which people (or whatever the nature of the cases) do not vary, and which is therefore a constant rather than a variable, is typically not of great interest to most analysts. Their toolkit of data analysis methods is geared to variability rather than to its absence. As noted above, even the most basic tools of quantitative data analysis – measures of central tendency and dispersion – are concerned to capture the variability that is observed.

But variation is equally important to qualitative researchers when they conduct their analyses. Variation is understood somewhat differently from quantitative research in that it relates to differences one observes but to which one does not necessarily assign a numerical value, but it is nonetheless central as an observation of relative magnitude (e.g., respondents differed more in their opinions on this than on that). In the course of carrying out an analysis of qualitative data, the researcher is likely to be attending to assorted issues that reflect an interest in variation: Why does a particular activity or form of behavior occur in some situations rather than others? Why are some people excluded from participation in certain activities? To what extent do differences in certain kinds of behavior vary because of the different meanings associated with the behavior in certain situations? How and why do people's behavior or meaning attributions vary over time? These are common issues that are likely to arise in the course of qualitative data analysis, and all of them relate in some way to variation and variability. The idea that meaning and behavior need to be understood contextually (e.g., Mishler, 1979) implies that the researcher is forced to consider the implications of contextual variation for his or her findings.

Conversation analysis might be assumed to belie this point about qualitative data analysis in that its emphasis on the ordered nature of talk in interaction could be taken to imply that it is a lack of variation that is of concern. However, the conversation analyst is also concerned with such issues as *preference organization*, which presumes that certain kinds of responses are preferred following an initial utterance and is at least implicitly concerned with the exploration of variation. Similarly, an interest in the use of *repair mechanisms* in conversations would seem to imply a concern with variation and responses to it. Thus, once again, while it is addressed in different ways in quantitative and qualitative data analysis, the exploration of variation is an important component of both strategies.

Further, an initial understanding of patterns of variability may inform the collection of data. In the formal application of sampling theory, populations may be viewed as comprised of different strata, and each stratum may be assigned a different sampling ratio. In this way, the researcher ensures that sufficient variability of important minority characteristics occurs in the sample. Similarly, in deciding where and whom to observe, qualitative researchers may choose sites and/or groups they expect to differ, thereby building into the research design variability of observed behavior and/or observational context.

Both treat frequency as a springboard for analysis

That issues of frequency are important in quantitative data analysis is neither surprising nor illuminating. In the course of quantitative data analysis, the practitioner is bound to be concerned with issues to do with the numbers and proportions of people holding certain views or engaging in different types of behavior. The emphasis on frequency is very much bound up with variation, since establishing frequencies is a common way of expressing variation.

However, frequency is a component of qualitative data analysis as well. There are two ways in which this occurs. Firstly, as some commentators remark when they write up their analyses, qualitative researchers often use quantitative terms, such as 'most', 'many', 'often', and 'sometimes' (Becker, 1958). In many ways, these are very imprecise ways of conveying frequency and, given their ambiguity, it is usually difficult to know what they mean. Qualitative researchers are not alone in this regard, however. In spite of the fact that they use apparently more precise yardsticks for gauging frequency, quantitative researchers also resort to such terms as embellishments of their quantitative findings, although the actual values are generally reported as well. Moreover, when quantitative researchers do employ such terms, they apply to widely different indicators of frequency (Ashmore et al., 1989). Silverman (1985) recommends that qualitative researchers use limited quantification in their analyses rather than rely excessively on vague adjectival terms.

Frequency can be discerned in relation to qualitative data analysis in another way. As Bryman and Burgess (1994) observe, when they code their unstructured data, qualitative researchers are likely to rely on implicit notions of frequency. This can occur in at least two ways. They may be impressed by the frequency with which a theme appears in their transcripts or fieldnotes and may use this as a criterion for deciding whether to apply a code. Themes that occur very infrequently may be less likely to receive a distinct code. In addition, in developing codes into concepts or categories, they may use frequency as a method of deciding which ones are worth cultivating in this way.

Both seek to ensure that deliberate distortion does not occur

Although few social scientists nowadays subscribe to the view that we are objective, value-free observers of the social world, this recognition makes it more important that we proceed in ways that are explicitly defined and therefore replicable. There is evidence in certain quarters of the emergence of avowedly partial research. For example, Lincoln and Guba (1985) recommend that one set of criteria by which research should be judged involves the issue of *authenticity*. This set of criteria relates to the political dimension of research and includes such principles as *catalytic authenticity*, which enjoins researchers to ask whether their research has motivated members to engage in action to change their circumstances, and *tactical authenticity*, which asks whether the research has empowered members to engage in action. In spite of the use of such criteria, which are political in tone and which are a feature of much writing from a feminist standpoint, qualitative researchers have not suggested that the distortion of findings during data analysis should accompany political ambitions. There are plenty of opportunities for researchers to twist findings intentionally during data analysis – whether quantitative or qualitative. However, by and large, they are

committed to presenting an analysis that is faithful to the data. Of course, there is a far greater recognition nowadays that both quantitative and qualitative researchers employ a variety of rhetorical strategies for convincing readers of the authenticity of their analyses (see Bryman, 1998, for a review of some of these writing techniques). However, this is not to suggest that data analysis entails distortion, but that through their writings researchers have to win over their readers to the credibility of what they are trying to say. In essence, what is guarded against in most quantitative and qualitative data analysis is what Hammersley and Gomm (2000) call *willful bias*, that is, consciously motivated misrepresentation.

Both argue the importance of transparency

Regardless of the type of research being conducted, the methodology that is used should not eclipse the data, but should put the data to optimal use. The techniques of analysis should be sufficiently transparent that other researchers familiar with the area can recognize how the data are being collected and tested, and can replicate the outcomes of the analysis procedure. (Journals are now requesting that authors provide copies of their data files when a paper is published so that other researchers can easily reproduce the analysis and then build on or dispute the conclusions of the paper.) Whether they also agree about what those outcomes mean is a different issue. Much of the disagreement that occurs in the research literature is less with analysis-as-process and more with the specification or the context in which the question is being addressed and the interpretation of the findings. In arguing a certain 'story line', a quantitative researcher may try to demonstrate the 'robustness' of findings by showing that certain key results persist when evaluated within a variety of contexts of specifications.

If we take as an exemplar of quantitative research the analysis of national survey data, transparency in the data collection process is generally high. Sampling procedures are well documented; comparative analysis of how the sample compares to the population on known characteristics is reported; the researcher is provided with a codebook and questionnaire that provide details about the questions asked, the range of responses given, and frequency distributions, so researchers can be confident they are reading the data correctly. Improvements in computer technology have made this process considerably easier, faster, and more reliable. In addition, the general availability of software packages to perform a wide range of analyses removes the mystery of what algorithm was used and what calculations were made.

But one issue of 'transparency' in quantitative research involves the use of statistical tools that, from some perspectives, 'distance' the researcher from the data. For example, missing values are imputed, cases are weighted, parameter estimates have confidence intervals that change with each specification, sometimes achieving the status of statistical 'significance' and sometimes falling short. Estimates of effects to the first, second, occasionally third decimal point – how can anyone 'see' the original data behind this screen of computational complexity? But to say that the procedures are sufficiently complex to require computer assistance in their application is *not* to say that they are opaque. The sampling framework that generates the case weights is derived from sampling theory, an ample literature that provides rules for both selection and adjustment, as well as the likely consequence of proceeding other than 'by the rules'. The algorithms on which sample estimates are based are derived from estimation theory, their properties tested through simulations and statistical experiments so that researchers can understand the conditions under which their use will yield desirable and reliable results. The process is neither convoluted nor impenetrable, but it is complex, and it is reasonable to assume that practitioners who use quantitative methods are not always well acquainted with the details of sampling, estimation, or statistical theories that provide the rationale for the practice. To acknowledge that building an understanding of the theoretical foundations for this practice is a challenging task is one thing; to reject this literature because it is challenging is quite another.

With qualitative research, an absence of distance and, until rather recently, limited use of technological innovation for organizing and analyzing information can create a different dilemma for replication. Observational data may rely on one person's recollections as fieldnotes are written; transcriptions of taped interviews or coded segments of videotape

that anyone can evaluate provide more the type of exactitude that many quantitative types find reassuring. And clear rules that govern who, what, and when we observe; justifications for the chosen procedure over alternatives; rules of coding; logical relationships; analytical frameworks; and systematic treatments of data can combine to produce consistent and reproducible findings.

Conversation analysis (Chapter 26) takes a somewhat different line on this issue from most forms of qualitative data analysis, in that practitioners have always exhibited a concern to demonstrate the transparency of their data and of their analysis. Qualitative researchers generally have few guidelines about how to approach their data other than the need to address their research questions through their data. One of the great appeals of grounded theory (Chapter 28) has been that it provides a framework, albeit at a far more general level than statistical techniques provide, for thinking about how to approach qualitative data analysis. It is also worth bearing in mind that one of the arguments frequently employed in favor of computer-assisted qualitative data analysis is that it forces researchers to be more explicit about the way they approach their data, so that, in the process, the transparency of the analytic process may be enhanced.

Indeed, we begin to see here some of the ways in which quantitative and qualitative data analysis differ. Not only is there a difference in most instances in the transparency of the process, but also quantitative data analysts have readily available toolkits for the examination of their data. Conversation analysis comes closer to a toolkit approach than many other forms of qualitative data analysis, although semiotics (see Chapter 25) and to a certain extent discourse analysis (see Chapter 27) come close to providing this kind of facility. A further difference is that in analyzing secondary data, quantitative researchers usually conduct their analyses at the end of the research process, since data collection occurred elsewhere. However, in analyzing primary data, both quantitative and qualitative researchers intersperse data collection with data analysis. Quantitative researchers need to pilot-test their measures to ensure that the information collected meets criteria of both validity and reliability. And many writers on qualitative data analysis, particularly those influenced by grounded theory, advocate that data collection and analysis should be pursued more or less in tandem. As Coffey and Atkinson (1996: 2) suggest: 'We should never collect data without substantial analysis going on simultaneously. Letting data accumulate without preliminary analysis along the way is a recipe for unhappiness, if not total disaster.' Coffey and Atkinson (1996: 2) go on to say that there 'is no single right way to analyze data'. While this comment is made in relation to the analysis of qualitative data, it applies equally well in relation to quantitative data analysis. On the other hand, there are plenty of ways in which data can be wrongly or inappropriately analyzed, and a book such as this will help to steer people away from potential mistakes.

Both must address the question of error

The manner in which quantitative and qualitative approaches manage the effects of error may well be the most central point of difference. Quantitative research can be viewed as an exercise in managing error, since variability-as-observed-difference is both a function of empirically distinct characteristics and error in the empirical process of observing those distinctions. One context in which the utility of statistical information and the acknowledgment of error come into conflict is the courtroom. Statisticians asked to give expert testimony are inevitably asked by opposing counsel whether they are 'certain' of their findings. Regardless of whether they acknowledge a 5% margin for error, a 1% margin for error, or a 0.1% margin for error, they can never say with absolute certainty that 'this' occasion cannot possibly be an error. In contrast, for many years eyewitness testimony was the gold standard of evidence, since a 'good' eyewitness would deny uncertainty, testifying to no doubt, no possibility of error – testifying with certainty. And so they may have believed. But the frequency with which recently utilized DNA evidence is proving exculpatory has given everyone pause. If we cannot trust our own eyes, how can we be sure of anything? One answer is that absolute certainty was always an illusion, whether it was asserted in scientific enterprise or everyday life. Even so, we know many things, and in so knowing, we can accomplish many tasks. And in trying to accomplish, we can learn much more. So if our choice is between drowning in doubt or acting on best

information, we act. Neither judge nor jury can ever be certain, in the sense that they cannot claim that error is impossible; but they can draw conclusions by weighing the evidence. And so they do.

Within the framework of behavioral and social science, both quantitative and qualitative analysts acknowledge that error is an unavoidable aspect of data collection, measurement, coding, and analysis procedures. And both agree that error cannot always be assumed to be random, such that the summary influences of error on our conclusions simply 'cancel out'. Much of the development in quantitative research that has occurred over the past three decades has been oriented toward better managing error. In particular, attention has been focused on developing procedures to address error as a confounding source in the data while preserving the substantive focus and the structural relations of interest. In fact, we can look at the chapters in this text as representing advancements in the analysis of error.

The early chapters on constructing variables, describing distributions, and dealing with missing data involve the exposition of techniques for using already collected bits of information and combining them, reconfiguring them, transforming them in ways that create a better match between the measure and the concept. The variance has been called the 'mean squared error' because it provides the average weighted distance of observations from the midpoint of the distribution. This measure of inequality, of observed difference, provides the problematic for further analysis designed to answer the question: what produced the differences?

Missing data can create problems of error, since the missing information may occur at higher frequency in one or another part of the distribution (creating truncated distributions), or the pattern of missing data may be correlated with other factors. Chapter 4, on inference, underscores the complications introduced by sampling error, or generally by procedures designed to allow statements about the whole using only partial information. What this and other early chapters share is an emphasis on process. Dealing with missing information through some kind of imputation procedure requires that we theorize about the process that created the data gaps in the first place. Why do some people answer this question, while other respondents refuse? What is it about the question, the kind of information the question tries to elicit, and the known characteristics of the respondent that makes 'refusal' more likely?

For example, collecting income information is notoriously difficult. People generally consider their household income or the amount they have saved or invested to be private information. Although respondents often like to offer their opinions, they are less pleased – and sometimes angered – by questions of 'fact' that appear to invade their privacy. But techniques for collecting information in wide categories, coupled with information about relationships among observed characteristics of respondents and the piece of missing information, have allowed improvements in imputations. To ask someone to report last year's gross annual income may elicit a refusal. But to follow up with a question that asks the respondent to report whether it was 'above $50 000' creates a benchmark. Once the respondent supplies that first benchmark, it is often possible to channel them through a progressive series of categories, so that the gross annual income is eventually known to be between $25 000 and $35 000. The exact income is still 'missing', but imputation procedures can now utilize the range of values in which it falls.

In similar fashion, Chapter 4 links the adjustments we make for sampling error (e.g., the building of confidence intervals around estimates by using information on the error of those estimates) to the selection procedures that generated the sample (the part) from the population (the whole). Again, we rely on the theory of probability to move from the population to the sample, and then again to move back from the sample estimate to the population parameter. If the selection process was not according to some known probability process, then probability theory is of no use to us, and we are left with a description of a set of observations that do not generalize to any known population. Later chapters on selection models take these issues further by suggesting approaches that explicitly model mechanisms of sample selection as part of the system of equations testing structural relationships.

The process of constructing variables also introduces error. Are single indicators sufficient? If we combine indicators, what type of weighting scheme should we employ? And even at our best, we realize that there is some slippage between the concepts as abstractions and the variables that we use as the informational repositories of their meaning. But errors in measurement attenuate measures of association, making it more difficult to take that next step of describing underlying processes that produce what we observe. And in trying to represent that process, we are limited to our success in finding information that maps well the conceptual space we have defined. Missing pieces of information – missing for everyone rather than missing selectively – create specification error, which can introduce bias into our conclusions. The chapters on regression, structural equation models, models for categorical data, etc. all address these issues of error that complicate the task of the researcher, providing guidance on proper procedures when we attempt to explain the variability in dependent variables measured in different ways (e.g., by interval scale, by dichotomy, by polytomous classification) and within different levels of complexity (e.g., single equation versus multiple equation models motivated by concerns of endogeneity).

And if we are really interested in the underlying process, don't we need to look at process? In other words, shouldn't we be analyzing longitudinal data, following individuals over time so we know how changes in one aspect of their lives may be linked to subsequent changes in other aspects of their lives? But then we have the complication of correlated errors, since multiple observations on one respondent are likely to be characterized by similar observational errors at each point in time. Or perhaps our longitudinal frame should be the comparison of same-aged people over time to determine whether opinions in the aggregate have changed over time, for example? Further, as social scientists, we know that context is important, that processes may unfold one way under one set of circumstances, but unfold differently under different organizational or institutional constraints. How do we analyze information that describes the individual *within* the organizational context? Over time? These are the issues that event-history models, hierarchical linear models, panel models, latent curve models, and other advanced techniques were designed to address.

The more complicated the questions we ask, the more complicated the error structure with which we must deal, but we are not without tools to tackle these tasks, although the tools become more complicated as well. Any carpenter who wants to saw a board into two pieces has a variety of tools at his or her disposal, the simplest being a handsaw. But to cut designs into the wood, or dovetail a joint, or fit rafters on a double-hipped roof, requires more sophisticated tools to produce the desired outcome.

In qualitative research, error has not been a notion that has great currency. Indeed, some qualitative researchers argue that the very idea of error implies a 'realist' position with which some versions of qualitative research, particularly those influenced by postmodernism (see Chapter 30), are uncomfortable. For these qualitative researchers, it is demonstrating the credibility of findings that is likely to be of roughly equivalent concern (Lincoln and Guba, 1985), although it may be implicit in some notions of validity in qualitative research (e.g., Kirk and Miller, 1986). Demonstrating credibility takes many forms, but a major feature is being able to show a close correspondence between one's data and one's conceptualization, a concern which can be translated into quantitative research as concerns with 'goodness of fit', or how well the theoretical model fits the empirical information.

For those who use statistics, the 'fit' can be assessed as prediction successes versus prediction errors. But interpreting whether a given level of fit, a given value of the statistic, is persuasive evidence of the correctness of the theory is open to dispute. And the terms of dispute on this point are likely to be similar for both qualitative and quantitative researchers. Are your observations consistent with the predictions of the theory? Has the information been properly classified? Have you ignored other things that could change this picture? Do I believe your story? In both types of research, the richer the data, the more persuasive the conceptualization is likely to be.

Moreover, for the qualitative researcher, the emerging concepts must be demonstrably located in the data. The quantitative researcher refers to this as operationalization – whether the empirical variables fit the theoretical concepts. In the process of sorting through the vast amounts of information, many qualitative researchers must inevitably classify, which means they determine categories and group what they observed into 'like' and 'unlike' observations. Is there only one way this can be accomplished? Most researchers from either camp would answer 'no'. So both types of researchers may be accused of

category 'errors', in that someone else working with these same observational data may define groups differently. Disputes such as these are not uncommon.

Has the researcher ignored something 'important' in his or her analysis? Not intentionally, but someone with a different perspective may argue a different 'story' by picking up a feature that the first researcher failed to consider. Quantitative researchers refer to this as specification 'error', which simply means that in developing your story, you have left out something relevant. This error of omission is among the most serious in quantitative research, since it means that the evidence on which you are basing your conclusions is incomplete, and it is difficult to say how the story may change once you take this new twist into account.

These sources of 'error' in qualitative and quantitative research – observational error, classification error, and specification error – can be introduced through the choices made by the researcher, who may fail to pick up important cues from his or her research participants or may misread in conceptual terms what is happening. Thus, even though error is a term that is unlikely to sit easily with the way many, if not most, qualitative researchers envision their work, it is not without merit. A major difference is that the quantitative researcher turns to sampling, measurement, and estimation theory to mathematically formalize how error is assessed and addressed; the qualitative researcher generally relies on rules of logic, but not on mathematics. Both researchers, however, must rely on argument and the strength of evidence they muster from their data to convince others of their story.

The trick for the qualitative researcher is one of balancing a fidelity to the data (in a sense, a commitment to naturalism) with a quest to say something meaningful to one's peers (in other words, to conceptualize and theorize). The advantage of fidelity to the data is that the researcher's emerging conceptual framework will be relatively free of error, but the problem is that it may be difficult to appear to have done anything other than act as a conduit for the world-view of the people who have been studied. The corollary of this position is that qualitative researchers must be wary of conceptualizing to such an extent that there is a loss of contact with the data, so that the credibility of their findings is threatened and therefore error creeps in.

ORGANIZATION OF THE BOOK

It is with the kinds of issues and considerations outlined above that the authors of the chapters in this volume have sought to come to terms. The quantitative–qualitative research distinction partly maps onto the organization of the book, but only partly. On the face of it, qualitative data analysis is covered in Part V. However, content analysis is essentially a quantitative approach to the analysis of unstructured or qualitative data, while the chapters in Part I on feminist issues in data analysis (Chapter 6) and historical analysis (Chapter 7) transcend the distinction in having implications for and elements of both quantitative and qualitative approaches to data analysis. Part I provides some of the foundations of data analysis – the nature of distributions and their analysis; how to construct variables; the nature of observational and statistical inference; what missing data are and their implications; and, as has just been remarked upon, feminist issues and historical analysis.

Part II teaches the reader about the single-equation general linear model, its extensions, and its applicability to particular sorts of research questions. Although called the 'linear' model, it can accommodate a variety of functional forms of relationships, which can be used to test whether an association is monotonic, curvilinear, or proportional, for example.

Part III addresses the issue of studying change. Whereas in cross-sectional analysis we can describe how the outcome is associated with certain characteristics, in longitudinal analysis we introduce the timing of the outcome relative to the timing of changes in the characteristics. Introducing time into the research design creates another layer of complications, which must be addressed through both theory and technique. It also requires a different data structure, which factors time into both the procedures and the content of data collection.

Part IV introduces the reader to some recently developed but well-established approaches to data analysis. Many of these approaches address the issue of endogeneity, which is the complication that some of the factors we view as predictors of a certain outcome are also at least partly determined *within* the same system of relationships. In such circumstances, single-equation models are not sufficient.

Part V, as previously noted, is devoted to the analysis of qualitative data. In Chapter 23, some of the main elements of qualitative data analysis are outlined, along with the issues involved in the use of computer software for the management and analysis of qualitative data. Chapter 24 deals with content analysis, which, although an approach for the analysis of qualitative data, employs an analytic strategy that is very much in tune with quantitative research. Chapters 25–27 deal with approaches to qualitative data analyses that emphasize language and its significance in the construction of social reality. Chapter 28 discusses grounded theory, which has been referred to several times in this introduction and which has become one of the major frameworks for organizing qualitative data analysis. Chapter 29, in presenting narrative analysis, provides a discussion of an approach that is attracting a growing number of adherents and which in many ways provides an alternative to the coding approach to the initial analysis of qualitative data that is characteristic of grounded theory and many other approaches to the analysis of qualitative data. Finally, Chapter 30 provides an outline of the highly influential postmodernist approach, particularly in relation to qualitative data. In many ways, the postmodernist mind-set entails an inversion of many of our cherished beliefs about how social research should be carried out and about how to understand its written products.

SUMMARY

The approaches explicated in this *Handbook* are not exhaustive of the range of approaches available to the researcher. As we explained earlier, we chose to build on basics, yet address some of the most difficult and complicated issues researchers face. Some of the most recent innovations in approaches are, at best, mentioned parenthetically, with reference to other sources of information the interested reader is encouraged to pursue. Our goal is to help readers do 'good research'.

Good research shares some common features. It does not violate ethical guidelines. It is not based on 'fictionalized' data, but rather on information collected according to rules of observation and recording. It describes with fidelity and, at its best, explains how what was observed came to be as it was rather than otherwise. In building this text, we hope to allow interested researchers to learn from one another about a wide range of approaches to data analysis. New techniques are in the process of development; techniques already in use find new advocates and new critics. Here is a place to take up the journey.

REFERENCES

Ashmore, M., Mulkay, M. and Pinch, T. (1989) *Health and Efficiency: A Sociology of Health Economics*. Milton Keynes: Open University Press.

Becker, H.S. (1958) 'Problems of inference and proof in participant observation', *American Sociological Review*, 23: 652–60.

Bryman, A. (1998) 'Quantitative and qualitative research strategies in knowing the social world', in T. May and M. Williams (eds), *Knowing the Social World*. Buckingham: Open University Press.

Bryman, A. and Burgess, R.G. (1994) 'Reflections on qualitative data analysis', in A. Bryman and R.G. Burgess (eds), *Analyzing Qualitative Data*. London: Routledge.

Coffey, A. and Atkinson, P. (1996) *Making Sense of Qualitative Data: Complementary Research Strategies*. Thousand Oaks, CA: Sage.

Duncan, O.D. (1975) *Introduction to Structural Equation Models*. New York: Academic Press.

Hammersley, M. and Gomm, R. (2000) 'Bias in social research', in M. Hammersley (ed.), *Taking Sides in Social Research: Essays in Partisanship and Bias*. London: Routledge.

Kirk, J. and Miller, M.L. (1986) *Reliability and Validity in Qualitative Research*. Newbury Park, CA: Sage.

Lincoln, Y.S. and Guba, E. (1985) *Naturalistic Inquiry*. Beverly Hills, CA: Sage.

Mishler, E. (1979) 'Meaning in context: is there any other kind?', *Harvard Educational Review*, 49: 1–19.

Silverman, D. (1985) *Qualitative Methodology and Sociology: Describing the Social World*. Aldershot: Gower.

PART I

Foundations

2

Constructing Variables

ALAN BRYMAN AND DUNCAN CRAMER

The process of quantitative research is frequently depicted as one in which theory is employed in order to deduce hypotheses which are then submitted to empirical scrutiny. Within the hypothesis will be two or more concepts that will require translation into empirical indicators. These indicators are frequently referred to as *variables* and represent the fundamental focus of all quantitative research. While some writers might question the degree to which quantitative research necessarily follows such a linear progression and indeed how far it is driven by hypotheses (as against simply research questions), there is no doubt that the variable represents a major focus (Bryman, 2001). It constitutes a crucial bridge between conceptualization and findings.

Essentially, the quantitative researcher is concerned to explore variation in observed values among units of analysis and the correlates and causes of variation. All techniques of quantitative data analysis – from the most basic methods to the most advanced – are concerned with capturing variation and with helping us to understand that variation. The variable is crucial because it is the axis along which variation is measured and thereby expressed. Indeed, so central is the variable to the discourse of quantitative research that it has to all intents and purposes become synonymous with the notion of a concept. Variables are, after all, supposed to be measures or indicators that are designed to quantify concepts, but frequently writers of research papers and methodology texts refer to the process of measuring variables. In the process, concepts and variables become almost indistinguishable. The variable is also frequently the focus of attention for critics of quantitative research (e.g., Blumer, 1956), in large part because it is emblematic of the research strategy.

The variable can be usefully contrasted with the idea of a *constant*. The latter occurs when there is no variation in observed values among units of analysis, as when all members of a survey sample reply to a questionnaire item in the same way. Uncovering constants is relatively unusual and is likely to require a somewhat different strategy on the part of the researcher, since techniques of quantitative data analysis are typically concerned with exploring variation rather than its absence.

LEVELS OF MEASUREMENT

One of the most fundamental issues in quantitative data analysis is knowing which types of technique can be used in relation to particular levels of measurement. It is fundamental because each statistical technique presumes that the levels of measurement to which it is being applied are of a certain type or at least meet certain basic preconditions. This means that if a technique is applied to variables which do not meet its underlying assumptions, the resulting calculation will be meaningless. Therefore, being able to distinguish between the different levels of measurement is basic to the art and craft of quantitative data analysis.

Writers often refer to different 'types of variables' as a shorthand for different levels of measurement. As such there is an array of different types of variables or levels of measurement. This array reflects the fact that the four levels of measurement to be discussed are on a continuum of degrees of refinement. There are four types of variables which are typically presented in terms of an ascending scale of refinement: nominal; ordinal; interval; and ratio.

Nominal variable

The *nominal variable*, often also referred to as the *categorical variable*, is the most basic level of measurement. It entails the arbitrary assignment of numbers (a process referred to as *coding*) to the different categories that make up a variable. The different categories simply constitute a classification. We cannot order them in any way – they are simply different. The numbers that are different have no mathematical significance; instead, they act as tags which facilitate the computer processing of the data. Thus, if we asked a question in a social survey on religious affiliation, we would assign a number to each type of affiliation and record each respondent's affiliation with the appropriate number. Similarly, in an experiment on asking questions, Schuman and Presser (1981) asked:

> The next question is on the subject of work. People look for different things in a job. Which of the following five things would you *most* prefer in a job?

The five options which could be chosen were:

1 Work that pays well
2 Work that gives a feeling of accomplishment
3 Work where there is not too much supervision and you make most decisions yourself
4 Work that is pleasant and where the other people are nice to work with
5 Work that is steady with little chance of being laid off

In assigning numbers to each of these five possible answers, all we are doing is supplying a label to each type of response. We can only say that all those answering in terms of the first response differ from those answering in terms of the second, who differ from those answering in terms of the third, and so on.

Sometimes, we have just two categories, such as male/female or pass/fail. Strictly speaking such variables – often referred to as *dichotomous variables* or *binary variables* (e.g., Bryman and Cramer, 2001) – are nominal variables. However, sometimes such variables require a different approach to analysis from nominal variables with more than two categories and are therefore treated by some writers as a separate type of variable.

Ordinal variable

As we have seen, with a nominal variable we can say no more than that people (or whatever the unit of analysis) differ in terms of its constituent categories. If we are able to array the categories in terms of rank order then we have an ordinal variable. Thus, if we asked a sample of people how satisfied they were with their jobs and presented them with the following possible responses, we would have an ordinal variable:

1 Very satisfied
2 Fairly satisfied
3 Neither satisfied nor dissatisfied
4 Fairly dissatisfied
5 Very dissatisfied

In this case, although the numbers attached to each category are merely used to allow the answers to be processed, we can say that each number has a significance that is *relative* to the others, since they are on a scale from 1 (denoting very satisfied) to 5 (denoting very dissatisfied). Each number therefore represents a level of job satisfaction or dissatisfaction. What we cannot say is that, for example, the difference between being very satisfied and fairly satisfied is the same as the difference between being very dissatisfied and fairly dissatisfied. All we can say is that the respondents differ in terms of their levels of job satisfaction, with some respondents being more satisfied than others.

Interval variable

An interval variable is the next highest level of refinement. It shares with an ordinal variable

Table 2.1 *Summary of the characteristics of the four types of variable*

	Is there a true zero point?	Are the distances between categories equal?	Can the categories be rank-ordered?
Ratio variable	Yes	Yes	Yes
Interval variable	No	Yes	Yes
Ordinal variable	No	No	Yes
Nominal variable	No	No	No

the quality of the rank ordering of the categories (which should more properly be called *values*) but differs in that with an interval variable, the distances between the categories are equal across the range of categories. Thus, we can say that the difference between a temperature of 43°F and 44°F is the same as the difference between 24°F and 25°F. As such, the values that an interval variable can take are genuine numbers rather than the scoring or coding process associated with the quantification of the categories of nominal and ordinal variables, where the number system is essentially arbitrary. However, interval variables are relatively unusual in the social sciences, in that most apparently interval variables are in fact ratio variables.

Ratio variable

A ratio variable represents the highest level of measurement. It is similar to an interval variable, but in addition there is a true zero-point. In measurement theory, a true zero point implies an absence of the quality being measured, that is, you cannot have less than none of it. This feature means that not only can we say that the difference between an income of $30 000 a year and an income of $60 000 a year is the same as the difference between an income of $40 000 and an income of $70 000 a year (that is, a difference of $30 000), but also we can say that the income of $60 000 a year is double that of $30 000 a year. This means that we can conduct all four forms of arithmetic on ratio variables. Similar qualities can be discerned in such common variables as age, years in full-time education, size of firm, and so on.

In the social sciences, because most apparently interval variables are ratio variables, it is common for writers to prefer to refer to them as interval/ratio variables (e.g., Bryman and Cramer, 2001). Moreover, the vast majority of statistical techniques which require that the variable in question is at the interval level of measurement can also be used in relation

to ratio variables. Therefore, the crucial distinctions for most purposes are between nominal, ordinal and interval/ratio variables.

Table 2.1 seeks to bring together the key decision-making principles that are involved in deciding how to distinguish between different kinds of variables.

MEASURES AND INDICATORS

A distinction is often drawn between measures and indicators. Measures constitute direct quantitative assessments of variables. For example, we could say that a question on respondents' incomes in a survey would provide us with a measure of the variable income. As such, reported income is a very direct estimate of income. This can be contrasted with a situation in which the quantitative assessment of a variable is or has to be indirect. An example is the previously cited question on job satisfaction. While the question asks directly about job satisfaction, we do not know whether it does in fact tap that underlying variable. In this case, we are using the question as an *indicator* of job satisfaction. Whether it does in fact reflect respondents' levels of job satisfaction is an issue to do with whether it is a *valid* indicator, about which more will be said below. The issue of whether something is an indicator or a measure is not to do with an inherent quality: if respondents' answers to a question on their incomes are employed as a proxy for social class, it becomes an indicator rather than a measure as in the previous illustration.

CODING

A key step in the preparation of data for processing by computer is *coding*. As has already been suggested in relation to nominal and ordinal variables, precisely because these variables are not inherently numerical, they must be transformed into quantities. Illustrations of the coding process have already been provided in relation to Schuman and Presser's (1981) question on work motivation and an imaginary example of a question on job satisfaction. In each case, the numbers chosen are arbitrary. They could just as easily start with zero, or the direction of the coding could be the other way around.

Coding in relation to social surveys arises mainly in relation to two kinds of situations. Firstly, in the course of designing a structured interview or self-administered questionnaire, researchers frequently employ *pre-coded questions*. Such questions include on the instrument itself both the categories from which respondents must choose and the code attached to each answer. Coding then becomes a process of designating on the completed questionnaires which code an answer denotes. The second kind of context arises in relation to the post-coding of open questions. Coding in this context requires that the researcher derives a comprehensive and mutually exclusive set of categories which can denote certain kinds of answer.

What is crucial is that the coding should be such that:

- the list of categories is mutually exclusive so that a code can only apply to one category;
- the list of categories is comprehensive, so that no category or categories have been obviously omitted; and
- whoever is responsible for coding has clear guidelines about how to attach codes so that their coding is consistent (often called *intra-coder reliability*) and so that where more than one person is involved in coding the people concerned are consistent with each other (*inter-coder reliability*).

The first two considerations are concerned with the design of pre-coded questions and with the derivation of categories from open questions. The third consideration points to the need to devise a coding frame which pinpoints the allocation of numbers to categories. In a sense, with pre-coded questions, the coding frame is incorporated into the research instrument. With open questions, the coding frame is crucial in ensuring that a complete list of categories is available and that the relevant codes are designated. In addition, it is likely to be necessary to include a detailed set of instructions for dealing with the uncertainties associated with the categorization of answers to open questions when the appropriate category is not immediately obvious. With techniques like structured observation and content analysis, the design of such instructions – which is often in a form known as a *coding manual* – is a crucial step in the coding of the unstructured data which are invariably the focus of these methods.

A further consideration is that researchers quite often *recode* portions of their data. This means that their analyses suggest that it is likely to be expedient or significant to aggregate some of the codes and hence the categories that the codes stand for. For example, in the coding of unstructured data, the researcher might categorize respondents into, for example, nine or ten categories. For the purposes of presenting a frequency table for that variable, this categorization may be revealing, but if the sample is not large, when a contingency table analysis is carried out (e.g. cross-tabulating the variable by age), the cell frequencies may be too small to provide a meaningful set of findings. In response to this situation, the researcher may group some of the categories of response so that there are just five categories. Such recoding of the data can only be carried out if the recoded categories can be meaningfully combined. There is the risk that the process of recoding in this way might result in combinations that cannot be theoretically justified, but recoding of data is quite common in the analysis of survey and other kinds of data.

SCALE CONSTRUCTION

One of the crucial issues faced in the measurement process in social research is whether to employ just one or more than one (and in fact usually several) indicators of a variable. Employing more than one indicator has the obvious disadvantage of being more costly and time-consuming than relying on one indicator. However, there are certain problems with a dependence on single indicators:

1. A single indicator may fail to capture the full breadth of the concept that it is standing in for. This means that important aspects of the concept are being overlooked. The use of more than one

indicator increases the breadth of the concept that is being measured.

2. In surveys, a single indicator may fail to capture a respondent's attitude to an issue or behaviour. This may be due to a variety of factors, such as lack of understanding or misinterpretation of a question. By using several indicators, the effect of such error may be at least partly offset by answers to other questions which serve as indicators and which are not subject to the same problem.

3. When more than one indicator is employed and the score on each indicator is then combined to form a total score for each respondent (as occurs with the use of summated scales – see below), much greater differentiation between respondents is feasible than when a single indicator is employed. For example, with the imaginary job satisfaction indicator used above, respondents could only be arrayed along a scale from 1 to 5. If more than one indicator is used and scores are aggregated, much finer quantitative distinctions become possible.

In other words, for any single respondent, reliance on a single indicator increases the likelihood of measurement error.

The recognition of the importance of multiple-indicator measures has resulted in a growing emphasis on the construction of scales. There are different approaches to scale construction, but most researchers employ *summated scales*, which entail the use of several items which are aggregated to form a score for each respondent. This allows much finer distinctions between respondents to be made (see point 3 above). One of the most common formats for this type of scale is the *Likert scale*, whereby respondents are presented with a series of statements to which they indicate their levels of agreement or disagreement.

To illustrate this approach to scale construction, consider an attempt by a researcher interested in consumerism to explore (among other issues) the notion of the 'shopaholic'. The following items might be used to form a Likert scale to measure shopaholicism:

1 I enjoy shopping.
Strongly Agree Neither Disagree Strongly
agree   agree   disagree
                   nor
                   disagree

2 I look forward to going shopping.
Strongly Agree Neither Disagree Strongly
agree   agree   disagree
                   nor
                   disagree

3 I shop whenever I have the opportunity.
Strongly Agree Neither Disagree Strongly
agree   agree   disagree
                   nor
                   disagree

4 I avoid going shopping if I can.
Strongly Agree Neither Disagree Strongly
agree   agree   disagree
                   nor
                   disagree

5 When I visit a town or city I don't know well, I always want to see the shops.
Strongly Agree Neither Disagree Strongly
agree   agree   disagree
                   nor
                   disagree

6 Shopping is a chore that I have to put up with.
Strongly Agree Neither Disagree Strongly
agree   agree   disagree
                   nor
                   disagree

Each reply will be scored. Various scoring mechanisms might be envisaged, but let us say that we want 5 to represent the highest level of shopaholicism represented by each answer and 1 the lowest, with 3 representing the neutral position. Notice that two of the items (4 and 6) are 'reverse items'. With the four others agreement implies a penchant for shopping. However, with items 4 and 6, agreement suggests a dislike of shopping. Thus, with items 1, 2, 3 and 5, the scoring from strongly agree to strongly disagree will go from 5 to 1, but with items 4 and 6 it will go from 1 to 5. This reversal of the direction of questioning is carried out because of the need to identify respondents who exhibit *response sets*, which have been defined as 'irrelevant but lawful sources of variance' (Webb et al., 1966: 19). An example of a response set to which Likert and similar scales are particularly prone is *yeasaying* or *naysaying*, whereby respondents consistently answer in the affirmative or negative to a battery of items apparently regardless of their content. Consequently, if a respondent answered strongly agree to all six items, we would probably take the view that he or she is not paying much attention to the content of the items, since the answers are highly inconsistent in their implications.

The scale would have a minimum score for any individual of 6 (presumably indicating a 'shopaphobe') and a maximum of 30 (a total 'shopaholic'). Most will be arrayed on the 23 points in between. A respondent scoring 5, 4, 4, 5, 3, 5, producing a score of 26, would be towards the shopaholic end of the continuum. A further feature of such scales is that essentially they produce ordinal variables. We cannot really say that the difference between a score of 12 and a score of 13 is equal to the difference between a score of 15 and a score of 16. However, most writers are prepared to treat such scales as interval/ratio variables on the grounds that the large number of categories (25 in this case) means that they approximate to a 'true' interval/ratio variable. Certainly, summated scales are routinely treated as though they are interval/ratio variables in journal papers reporting the results of research.

With a Likert scale, respondents indicate their degrees of agreement. While a five-point scale of agreement is employed in the above example, some researchers prefer to use seven-point scales (very strongly agree, strongly agree, agree, etc.) or even longer ones. Other types of response format for summated scales include the binary response format:

I enjoy shopping   Agree   Disagree

the numerical response format:

I enjoy shopping   5   4   3   2   1

(where 5 means Strongly agree and 1 means Strongly disagree)

and the bipolar numerical response format:

I enjoy shopping 7 6 5 4 3 2 1 I hate shopping

Once a scale has been devised and administered, the researcher needs to ask whether the resulting scale measures a single dimension. There are three highly related aspects to this question.

1. Is there an item (or are there items) showing a different pattern of response from those associated with the other constituent items? If there are, the offending item or items need to be eliminated from the scale. One way of checking for this possibility is to search out information on the *item–total correlations*. An inter-item correlation relates scores on each item to scores on the scale overall. If an inter-item correlation is much lower or higher than other inter-item correlations, it becomes a candidate for exclusion from the scale.

2. Is the scale internally reliable? This issue, which will be elaborated upon below, is concerned with the overall internal coherence of the items. Eliminating items which show a different pattern of response from the rest will enhance internal reliability.

3. Does the scale contain more than one dimension? If there are items which show a different pattern of response, it may be that there is a systematic quality to this variation such that the scale is not measuring a single dimension but possibly two or more. When this occurs, the nature of the underlying dimensions needs to be identified and named. Factor analysis is the most appropriate means of exploring this issue and will be given greater attention below.

The second of these aspects is concerned with the more general issue of the reliability of variables, which, along with validity, is a crucial issue in the evaluation of the adequacy of a variable.

RELIABILITY AND VALIDITY OF VARIABLES

Reliability and validity are crucial criteria in the evaluation of variables. In spite of the fact that these two terms are often used interchangeably in everyday speech, they refer to different aspects of the qualities of variables.

Reliability

Reliability is concerned with the consistency of a variable. There are two identifiable aspects of this issue: *external* and *internal reliability*. If a variable is externally reliable it does not fluctuate greatly over time; in other words, it is stable. This means that when we administer our scale of shopaholicism, we can take the view that the findings we obtain are likely to be the same as those we would find the following week. The most obvious examination of external reliability is to test for *test–retest reliability*. This means that sometime after we administer our scale, we readminister it and examine the degree to which respondents' replies are the same for the two sets of data. The chief difficulty with this method is that there are no guidelines about the passage of time that should elapse between the two waves of administration. If the passage of time is too great, test–retest reliability may simply be reflecting change due to intervening events or respondents' maturation. Furthermore, testing for test–retest reliability can become a major data collection exercise in its own right, especially when large samples are involved and when there are several variables to be tested.

Internal reliability is an issue that arises in connection with multiple-indicator variables. If a variable is internally reliable it is coherent. This means that all the constituent indicators are measuring the same thing. There are several methods for assessing internal reliability, one of which – item–total correlations – was briefly mentioned above. A further method is *split-half reliability*. This entails randomly dividing the items making up a scale into two halves and establishing how well the two halves correlate. A correlation below 0.8 would raise doubts about the internal coherence of the scale and perhaps prompt a search for low item–total correlations. In the case of the shopaholicism scale, the scale would be divided into two groups of three items, and respondents' scores on the two groups of items would be assessed. Nowadays, the most common method of estimating internal reliability is *Cronbach's alpha* (α), which is roughly equivalent to the average of all possible split-half reliability coefficients for a scale (Zeller and Carmines, 1980: 56). The usual formula is

$$\alpha = \frac{k}{k-1}\left(1 - \frac{1}{\sigma_x^2}\sum \sigma_i^2\right),$$

where k is the number of items; $\sum \sigma_i^2$ is the sum of the total variances of the items; and σ_x^2 is the variance of the total score (Pedhazur and Schmelkin, 1991: 93). If alpha comes out below 0.8, the reliability of the scale may need to be investigated further. Computer software programs such as SPSS include a facility whereby it is possible to request that the alpha for the scale be computed with a particular item deleted. If there is a sharp rise in the level of alpha when any item is deleted, that item will then become a candidate for exclusion from the scale.

An important consideration in the measurement process is that resulting variables will contain *measurement error* – variation that is separate from true variation in the sample concerned. Such measurement error is an artefact of the measurement instruments employed and their administration. For many researchers, assessing internal reliability is one way in which they can check on the degree of measurement error that exists in summated scales, although it cannot exhaust the range of possible manifestations of such error.

Validity

Validity is concerned with the issue of whether a variable really measures what it is supposed to measure. Can we be sure that our scale of shopaholicism is really to do with shopaholicism and not something else? At the very least, we should ensure that our scale exhibits *face validity*. This will entail a rigorous examination of the wording of the items and an examination of their correspondence with the theoretical literature on consumption. We might also submit our items to judges and invite them to comment on the wording of the items and on the goodness of fit between the items and what we might take shopaholicism to entail. However, face validity is only a first step in validity assessment.

Criterion-related validity assesses a scale in terms of a criterion in terms of which people are known to differ. This form of validity assessment can be viewed in terms of two forms. Firstly, testing for *concurrent validity* relates a variable to a contemporaneous criterion. Thus, we might ask respondents who are completing our shopaholicism scale how frequently they go shopping. If we found that there was no difference between shopaholics and shopaphobes in terms of the frequency with which they go shopping, we might question how well the scale is measuring the underlying concept. Equally, if the two types of shoppers clearly differ, our confidence is enhanced that the scale is measuring what it is supposed to be measuring. Secondly, testing for *predictive validity* relates a variable to a future criterion. Some months after we administer the shopaholicism scale we might recontact our respondents and ask them about the frequency with which they have been shopping in the previous month. Again, we would expect the shopaholicism scale to be able to discriminate between the frequent and occasional shoppers. Alternatively, we might ask our respondents to complete a structured diary in which they report the frequency with which they go shopping and the amounts of time spent on their expeditions.

Testing for *construct validity* entails an examination of the theoretical inferences that might be made about the underlying construct. It means that we would have to stipulate hypotheses concerning the construct (shopaholicism) and then test them. Drawing on theories about the consumer society and consumerism, we might anticipate that shopaholics will be more concerned about the sign value of goods than their use value. Consequently, we might expect they will be more concerned with the purchase of goods with designer labels. We could therefore design some questions concerned with respondents' predilection for designer brands and relate these to findings from our shopaholicism scale. Of course, the problem here is that if the theoretical reasoning is flawed, the association will not be forged and this is clearly not a product of any deficiencies with our scale.

These are the major forms of validity assessment. Other methods, such as *convergent validity*, whereby a different method is employed to measure the same concept, are employed relatively rarely because they constitute major projects in their own right.

One final point on this issue is that validity presupposes reliability. If you have an unreliable variable, it cannot be valid. If a variable is externally unreliable, it fluctuates over time and therefore cannot be providing a true indication of what it is supposed to be measuring. If it is internally unreliable, it is tapping more than one underlying concept and therefore is not a genuine measure of the concept in question.

DUMMY VARIABLES

One way of examining the association between a nominal or categorical variable (such as religious affiliation or nationality) and a non-nominal variable (such as income or life satisfaction) is to code the different categories of the categorical variable in a particular way called dummy coding (Cohen and Cohen, 1983). This procedure will be

Table 2.2   *Life satisfaction in three nationalities*

	American	British	Canadian
	9	8	7
	7	5	7
	6	4	4
Mean	7.33	5.67	6.00

explained in terms of the following example. Suppose we wanted to determine the association between nationality and life satisfaction. To enable the relevant statistics to be computed, a small sample of fictitious data has been created and is presented in Table 2.2.

The categorical variable consists of three nationalities, American, British and Canadian. Each group consists of three people. The non-categorical variable comprises a 10-point measure of life satisfaction varying from 1 to 10, with higher scores representing greater life satisfaction. From the mean score for each nationality, we can see that the Americans have the greatest life satisfaction, followed by the Canadians and then the British. What we are interested in is not the association between particular nationalities and life satisfaction (e.g., being American and life satisfaction) but the association between the general variable reflecting these nationalities and life satisfaction (i.e., the association between nationality and life satisfaction).

The simplest way of expressing the association between the general variable of nationality and life satisfaction is in terms of the statistical coefficient called *eta squared*. Eta squared is the variance in life satisfaction attributed to the variable of nationality as a proportion of the total variance in life satisfaction. It can be worked out from an unrelated one-way analysis of variance. In this case eta squared is 0.194. This method does not involve dummy coding.

The dummy coding of a categorical variable may be used when we want to compare the proportion of variance attributed to that variable with the proportion of variance attributed to non-categorical variables (such as age) together with any other categorical variables (such as marital status). The method usually used to determine these proportions is multiple regression. Multiple regression can be represented by the following regression equation:

$$y = a + b_1 x_1 + b_2 x_2 + \cdots + b_k x_k.$$

The dependent or criterion variable is often designated y and in our example is life satisfaction. The independent or predictor variables are usually signified by x_1 to x_k. One of the predictor variables in our example is nationality. Another predictor might be age. The contribution or weight of each predictor is normally the partial regression coefficient, which is generally symbolized as b_1 to b_k. The a is the intercept and may be referred to as the constant.

Multiple regression assumes that the predictor variables are dichotomous or noncategorical. Dichotomous variables (such as gender) have two categories (female and male) and may be treated as if they are noncategorical in that one category is arbitrarily assumed to be higher than another. For example, females may be coded 1 and males 2. This cannot be done with categorical variables having more than two categories because the numbers will be seen as reflecting an ordinal scale at the very least. For instance, if we coded Americans 1, Britons 2 and Canadians 3, multiple regression will assume that Americans have the highest value and Canadians the lowest, which might not be the case. We cannot order nationalities in terms of their mean score on life satisfaction (with Americans coded 1, Canadians 2 and Britons 3) because this order might not be the same for the other predictor variables (such as age). Consequently, we have to treat the categorical variable as if it were a series of dichotomous variables.

The simplest form of coding is *dummy coding*, where we assign a 1 to the units of analysis belonging to that category and 0 to units not belonging to that category. So, for example, we could code the three nationalities as shown in Table 2.3. Here we use one dummy variable to code all Americans as 1 and all non-Americans as 0. We use another dummy variable to code all Britons as 1 and non-Britons as 0. In this scheme Americans are represented by a 1 on the first dummy variable and a 0 on the second dummy variable. Britons are denoted by a 0 on the first dummy variable and a 1 on the second dummy variable. We do not need a third dummy variable to code Canadians because Canadians are represented by a 0 on both dummy variables. The category denoted by all 0s is sometimes known as the reference category. Thus, only two dummy variables are needed to represent these three categories.

The number of dummy variables required to code a categorical variable is always one

Table 2.3 *Dummy variable coding of three nationalities*

Nationalities	d_1	d_2
American	1	0
British	0	1
Canadian	0	0

less than the number of categories. So, if there are four categories, three dummy variables are necessary. It does not matter which category is denoted by 1s and 0s. In our example, Americans could have been coded 0 0, Britons 1 0 and Canadians 0 1. The results for the dummy variables taken together will be exactly the same. If the reference category is also coded in 1s and 0s, then one less than the total number of dummy variables will be entered into the multiple regression because one of them is redundant. The reference category is represented by the intercept a in the regression equation. So, the multiple regression equation for regressing the criterion of life satisfaction on the dummy coded categorical variable of nationality is:

Life satisfaction = Canadian

(y) (a)

$+ b_1 \times$ American $+ b_2 \times$ British

(b_1x_1) (b_2x_2)

The multiple correlation squared is 0.194, which is the same value as that for eta squared. Dummy coded variables representing a particular categorical variable need to be entered together in a single step in a hierarchical multiple regression analysis.

EFFECTS AND CONTRAST CODING

Two other ways of coding categorical variables are effects and contrast coding. Both these methods will explain exactly the same proportion of variance by the categorical variable as dummy coding. However, the partial regression coefficients may differ insofar as they represent different comparisons. If information on particular comparisons is also needed, the required comparisons have to be specified with the appropriate coding. With dummy coding, the constant is the reference category. In our example on nationality, the unstandardized partial regression coefficient for the first dummy variable essentially compares the mean life satisfaction of Americans with that of Canadians. Similarly,

Table 2.4　*Effects coding of three nationalities*

Nationality	e_1	e_2
American	1	0
British	0	1
Canadian	−1	−1

Table 2.5　*Contrast coding of three nationalities*

Nationality	c_1	c_2
American	1	−½
British	−1	−½
Canadian	0	1

the unstandardized partial regression coefficient for the second dummy variable compares the mean life satisfaction of Britons with that of Canadians. See Cohen and Cohen (1983) for further details.

With effects coding, the constant is the mean of all equally weighted group means, which is produced by coding one of the categories as −1 instead of 0, such as the Canadians as shown in Table 2.4. In this case, the unstandardized partial regression coefficient for the first effects-coded variable compares the mean life satisfaction of Americans with that of all three groups. The unstandardized partial regression coefficient for the second effects-coded variable contrasts the mean life satisfaction of Britons with that of the three nationalities.

Contrast coding enables other kinds of comparisons to be made provided that the comparisons are independent or orthogonal. As with dummy and effects coding, the number of comparisons is always one less than the number of groups. For example, if we wanted to compare Americans with Britons and Americans and Britons combined with Canadians, we would code the groups as indicated in Table 2.5. For the comparisons to be independent, the products of the codes for the new contrast-coded variables have to sum to zero, which they do in this case:

$$1 \times (-½) + (-1) \times (-½) + 0 \times 1$$

$$= -½ + ½ + 0 = 0.$$

FACTOR ANALYSIS

Factor analysis is commonly used to determine the factorial validity of a measure

assessed by several different indices. Factorial validity refers to the extent to which separate indices may be seen as assessing one or more constructs. Indices that measure the same construct are grouped together to form a factor. Suppose, for example, we were interested in determining whether people who said they were anxious were also more likely to report being depressed. We made up three questions for assessing anxiety (A1–A3) and three questions for measuring depression (D1–D3):

> A1 I get tense easily
> A2 I am often anxious
> A3 I am generally relaxed
>
> D1 I often feel depressed
> D2 I am usually happy
> D3 Life is generally dull

Each question is answered on a five-point Likert scale ranging from 'Strongly agree' (coded 1) through 'Neither agree nor disagree' (coded 3) to 'Strongly disagree' (coded 5).

The anxiety questions appear to ask about anxiety and the depression questions seem to be concerned with depression. If people can distinguish anxiety from depression and if people who are anxious tend not to be depressed as well, then answers to the anxiety questions should be more strongly related to each other than to the answers to the depression questions. Similarly, the answers to the depression questions should be more highly associated with each other than with the answers to the anxiety questions. If this turns out to be the case, the three items measuring anxiety may be combined together to form a single index of anxiety, while the three items assessing depression may be aggregated to create a single measure of depression. In other words, the anxiety items should form one factor and the depression items should form another factor.

However, the way the answers to these six questions are actually grouped together may differ from this pattern. At one extreme, each answer may be unrelated to any other answer so that the answers are not grouped together in any way. At the other extreme, all the answers may be related and grouped together, perhaps representing a measure of general distress. In between these two extremes the range of other possible patterns is large. For example, the two positively worded items (A3 and D2) may form one group of related

Table 2.6   Coded answers on a 5-point scale to six questions

Cases	A1(Tense)	A2 (Anxious)	A3 (Relaxed)	D1 (Depressed)	D2 (Happy)	D3 (Dull)
1	5	3	2	3	4	2
2	2	1	4	3	2	4
3	4	3	2	4	1	4
4	3	5	1	2	3	2
5	2	1	5	4	2	4
6	3	2	4	3	4	1

Table 2.7   Triangular correlation matrix for six variables

Variables	A1 (Tense)	A2 (Anxious)	A3 (Relaxed)	D1 (Depressed)	D2 (Happy)	D3 (Dull)
A1 (Tense)	1.00					
A2 (Anxious)	0.51	1.00				
A3 (Relaxed)	−0.66	−0.94	1.00			
D1 (Depressed)	−0.04	−0.61	0.51	1.00		
D2 (Happy)	0.33	0.22	−0.11	−0.59	1.00	
D3 (Dull)	−0.36	−0.45	0.29	0.63	−0.91	1.00

items and the remaining four negatively worded items may comprise another group of related items. We use factor analysis to see how the items group together.

Correlation matrix

The first step in looking at the way the answers are related to each other is to correlate each answer with every other answer. To illustrate our explanation we will use the small sample of fictitious data in Table 2.6. This table shows the coded answers of six people to the six questions on anxiety and depression. So, case number 1 answers 'strongly disagree' to the first question (A1) and 'neither agree nor disagree' to the second question (A2). Correlating the answers of the six cases to the six questions results in the triangular correlation matrix shown in Table 2.7.

Correlations can vary from −1 through 0 to 1. The sign of the correlation indicates the direction of the relationship between two variables. A negative correlation represents high scores on one variable (e.g., 5) being associated with low scores on the other

variable (e.g., 1). For instance, from Table 2.7 we can see that the correlation between the answers to the questions about being anxious (A2) and being relaxed (A3) is −0.94. In other words, people who agree they are anxious have a strong tendency to disagree that they are relaxed (and vice versa). A positive correlation indicates high scores on one variable being associated with high scores on the other variable and low scores on one variable going together with low scores on the other variable. For example, in Table 2.7 we can see that the correlation between the answers to the questions about being tense (A1) and being anxious (A2) is 0.51. In other words, individuals who agree that they are tense have a moderate tendency to agree that they are anxious.

The strength of the association between two variables is indicated by its absolute value (i.e., disregarding the sign of the correlation). The correlation between being anxious and being relaxed (−0.94) is stronger than that between being tense and being anxious (0.51) because it is bigger. Conventionally, correlations in the range of 0.1 to 0.3 are usually described verbally as being weak, small or low; correlations in the range of 0.4 to 0.6 as being moderate or modest; and correlations in the range of 0.7 to 0.9 as being strong, large or high. The correlations in the diagonal of the matrix can be ignored or omitted as they represent the correlation of the variable with itself. This will always be 1.0 as there is a perfect positive relationship between two sets of the same scores.

From Table 2.7 it can be seen that the absolute size of the correlations among the three anxiety answers ranges from 0.51 to 0.94, suggesting that these answers go together. The absolute size of the correlations among the three depression answers ranges from 0.59 to 0.91, indicating that these answers go together. The data were deliberately generated to be associated in this way. In data that have not been so made up, the pattern may be less obvious. Even in these data, the pattern of results is not clear-cut. The absolute size of the correlation between being anxious (A2) and being depressed (D1) is 0.61, larger than the 0.51 between being tense (A1) and being anxious (A2). Furthermore, the correlation between being relaxed (A3) and being depressed (D1) is 0.51, the same as that between being tense (A1) and being anxious (A2). Consequently, it is possible that the answers to D1 may be more closely associated with the three anxiety items than with the other two depression items. Thus, the way the items are grouped may not be sufficiently apparent from simply looking at the correlations among the items. This is more likely to be the case the larger the number of variables. Factor analysis is used to make the way variables are grouped together more obvious.

Factor analysis is a set of statistical procedures that summarize the relationships between the original variables in terms of a smaller set of derived variables called factors. The relationship between the original variable and the factors is expressed in terms of a correlation or *loading*. The larger the absolute size of the correlation, the stronger the association between that variable and that factor. The meaning of a factor is inferred from the variables that correlate most highly with it. Originally, factor analysis was used to *explore* the way in which variables were grouped together. More recently, statistical techniques have been designed to determine whether the factors that have been obtained are similar to or *confirm* those that were either

hypothesized as existing or actually found in another group. Consequently, when developing a series of indices to measure a variable, it may be more appropriate to use an exploratory rather than a confirmatory factor analytic technique. If we want to compare our results with those already obtained, then confirmatory factor analysis may be preferable.

Exploratory factor analysis

There are a number of different procedures for exploratory factor analysis. The two most commonly used are *principal components* and *principal factors* or *axes*. Factor analysis is the term used to describe all methods of analysis but may also refer to the particular technique called principal factors. In principal components all the variance in a variable is analysed. Variance is a measure of the extent to which the values of a variable differ from the mean. In principal components, this variance is set at 1.0 to indicate that all the variance in a variable is to be analysed. This will include any variance that may be due to error rather than to the variable being measured. In principal axes only the variance that the variable shares with all other variables in the analysis is analysed. This shared variance or covariance is known as *communality* and will be less than 1.0. Communality is also sometimes used to refer to the variance in principal components.

Often both procedures will give similar results so that it does not matter which procedure is selected. Tabachnick and Fidell (2001) have suggested that principal components should be used when an empirical summary of the data is required, whereas principal axes should be applied when testing a theoretical model. One problem with principal axes is that the communalities may not always be estimable or may be invalid (e.g., having values greater than 1 or less than 0), thereby requiring one or more variables to be dropped from the analysis. Consequently, we will use principal components to illustrate the explanation of factor analysis.

Initial factors The number of factors initially extracted in an analysis is always the same as the number of variables, as shown in Table 2.8. For each variable, the entries in the table represent its loading or correlation with each factor; the square of each entry is a

Table 2.8 *Initial principal components*

	1	2	3	4	5	6
A1 (Tense)	−0.62	0.39	0.67	−0.13	−0.02	0.00
A2 (Anxious)	−0.84	0.44	−0.23	0.20	0.09	0.00
A3 (Relaxed)	0.79	−0.61	0.10	0.05	0.03	0.00
D1 (Depressed)	0.77	0.26	0.54	0.21	0.04	0.00
D2 (Happy)	−0.69	−0.68	0.24	−0.08	0.11	0.00
D3 (Dull)	0.80	0.53	−0.15	−0.22	0.10	0.00
Eigenvalues	3.42	1.53	0.88	0.16	0.03	0.00
Eigenvalues as proportion of total variance	0.57	0.26	0.15	0.03	0.01	0.00

measure of variance. So, the variance of A1 is −0.62 squared, which is about 0.38. The amount of variance accounted for by a factor is called the *eigenvalue* or latent root, and is the sum of the squares of each entry in a column, that is, the sum of the variances for each variable. The first factor has the highest loadings and extracts or reflects the greatest amount of variance in the variables. It has an eigenvalue of 3.42. Subsequent factors represent decreasing amounts of variance. The second factor has an eigenvalue of 1.53, while the sixth factor has an eigenvalue of 0. The eigenvalues should sum to the number of factors, which in this case is 6 (allowing for rounding error). The variance that each factor accounts for can also be expressed as a proportion of the total variance. Thus, the first factor explains 3.42/6.00 = 0.57 of the total variance, and the second factor 1.53/6.00 = 0.26.

Number of factors to be retained Because the number of factors extracted is always the same as the number of variables that are analysed, we need some criterion for determining which of the smaller factors should be ignored as the bigger ones account for most of the variance. One of the main criteria used is the Kaiser or Kaiser–Guttman criterion, which was suggested by Guttman and adapted by Kaiser. This criterion ignores factors that have eigenvalues of 1 or less. The maximum variance that each variable explains is set at 1, so that factors having eigenvalues of 1 or less explain less variance than that of one variable on average. In other words, according to this criterion, only factors that account for the variance of more than one variable are retained for further analysis.

In our example, only the first two factors have eigenvalues of more than 1, while the other four factors have eigenvalues of 1 or less. Thus, according to this criterion, we would keep the first two factors for further analysis. It should be noted that a cut-off at 1 may be somewhat arbitrary when there are factors which fall close to either side of this value. According to this criterion, a factor with an eigenvalue of 1.01 will be retained while one with an eigenvalue of 0.99 will be dropped, although the difference in the eigenvalues of these two factors is very small. In such cases it may be worthwhile extracting both more and fewer to see whether these factors, when rotated, are more meaningful than those retained according to Kaiser's criterion.

A second criterion is the graphical scree test proposed by Cattell (1966), who suggested that the Kaiser criterion may retain too many factors when there are many variables and too few factors when there are few variables. Child (1990) has specified 'many variables' as more than 50 and 'few' as less than 20. In the scree test the eigenvalue of each factor is represented by the vertical axis of the graph while the factors are arranged in order of decreasing size of eigenvalue along the horizontal axis, as shown in Figure 2.1.

Scree is a geological term for the rubble and boulders lying at the base of a steep slope and obscuring the real base of the slope itself. The number of factors to be extracted is indicated by the number of factors that appear to represent the line of the steep slope itself where the scree starts. The factors forming the slope are seen as being the substantial factors, while those comprising the scree are thought to be small error factors. The number

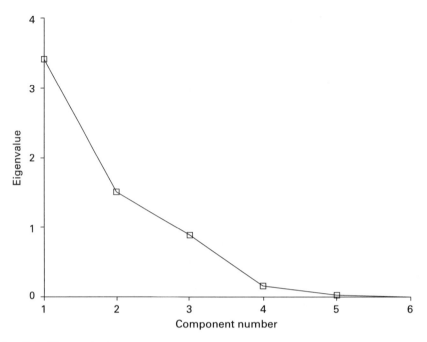

Figure 2.1   *Cattell's scree test*

of the factor identifying the start of the scree indicates the number of factors to be kept.

The scree factors are usually identified by being able to draw a straight line through or very close to their points on the graph. This is not always easy to do, as shown in Figure 2.1. In this case it is unclear whether the scree begins at factors 2, 3 or 4, and so whether the number of factors to be retained for further analysis should be 2, 3 or 4. Thus, one problem with the scree test is that determining where the scree begins may be subjective, as in this example. When this occurs, it may be useful to extract both fewer and more factors around the number suggested by the scree test and to compare their meaningfulness when rotated. If more than one scree can be identified using straight lines, the number of factors to be retained is minimized by selecting the uppermost scree.

Factor rotation   As already explained, the first factor in a factor analysis is designed to represent the largest amount of variance in the variables. In other words, most of the variables will load or correlate most highly with the first factor. If we look at the absolute loadings of the variables on the first factor in Table 2.8, we see that they vary from 0.62 to 0.84. The second factor will reflect the next largest amount of variance. As a consequence, the loadings of the variables on the second factor will generally be lower. We see in Table 2.8 that they range in absolute value from 0.26 to 0.68. The loading of variables on two factors can be plotted on two axes representing those factors, as shown in Figure 2.2. These axes are called reference axes. In Figure 2.2 the horizontal axis represents the first factor and the vertical axis the second factor. The scale on the axes indicates the factor loadings and varies in steps of 0.2 from -1.0 to $+1.0$. The item on anxiousness (A2), for example, has a loading of -0.84 on the first factor and of 0.44 on the second (see Table 2.8).

It may be apparent that the two axes do not run as close as they could to the points representing the variables. If we were to rotate the axes around their origin, then these two axes could be made to pass nearer to these points, as shown in Figures 2.3 and 2.4.

The effect of rotating the axes is generally to increase the loading of a variable on one of the factors and to decrease it on the others, thereby making the factors easier to interpret. For example, in Table 2.9 we can see that the effect of rotating the two axes is to increase the loading of the item on anxiousness from -0.84 to -0.91 on the first rotated

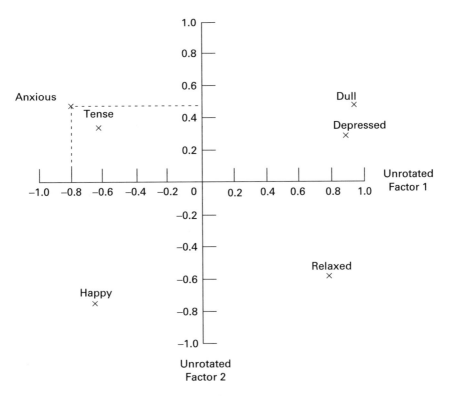

Figure 2.2   *Plotting variables on two unrotated factors*

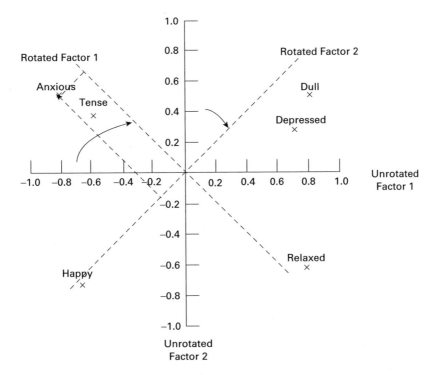

Figure 2.3   *Initial factors orthogonally rotated*

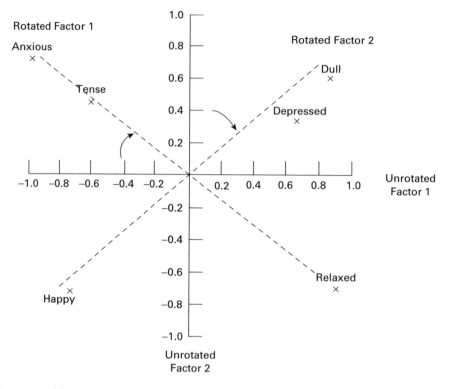

Figure 2.4 *Initial factors obliquely rotated*

Table 2.9 *First two orthogonally rotated principal components*

	1	2
A1 (Tense)	−0.72	−0.15
A2 (Anxious)	−0.91	−0.27
A3 (Relaxed)	0.99	0.11
D1 (Depressed)	0.37	0.72
D2 (Happy)	0.03	−0.96
D3 (Dull)	0.22	0.94
Eigenvalues	2.51	2.43
Eigenvalues as proportion of total variance	0.42	0.41

factor and to decrease it from 0.44 to 0.27 on the second rotated factor.

Axes may be rotated in one of two ways. First, they may be made to remain at right angles to each other, as is the case in Figure 2.3. This is known as *orthogonal* rotation. The factors are independent of or uncorrelated with one another. The advantage of this approach is that the information provided by the factors is not redundant. Knowing the values on one factor (e.g., anxiety) does not

enable one to predict the values of another factor (e.g., depression) as the factors are unrelated. The disadvantage is that the factors may be related to one another in reality and so the factor structure does not accurately represent what occurs.

Second, the factors may be allowed to be related and to vary from being at right angles to one another, as illustrated in Figure 2.4. This is known as *oblique* rotation. The advantage of this method is that the factors may more accurately reflect what occurs in real life. The disadvantage is that if the factors are related, knowledge about the values of one factor may allow one to predict the values of other factors. The results of the two methods may be similar, as in this example.

The most widely used form of orthogonal rotation is *varimax*, which maximizes the variance within a factor by increasing high loadings and decreasing low loadings. The loadings shown in Table 2.9 were derived using this method. Comparing the results of Tables 2.8 and 2.9, we can see that orthogonal rotation has increased the loadings of three variables for the first (A1, A2 and A3) and second factor (D1, D2 and D3). It has decreased the loadings of three variables for the first (D1, D2 and D3) and second factor (A1, A2 and A3). The variables loading highest on the first factor are being relaxed (0.99), not anxious (–0.91) and not tense (–0.72) respectively, indicating that this factor represents anxiety. The variables loading highest on the second factor are not being happy (–0.96), finding life dull (0.94) and being depressed (0.72) respectively, showing that this factor reflects depression. These results suggest that the three items on anxiety (A1, A2 and A3) can be aggregated to measure anxiety and the three items on depression (D1, D2 and D3) can be grouped together to assess depression. Orthogonal rotation also has the effect of spreading the variance across the factors more equally. The variance accounted for by the first factor is 0.57 when unrotated and 0.42 (2.51/6.00) when rotated. For the second factor it is 0.26 when unrotated and 0.41 (2.43/6.00) when rotated.

The results of an oblique rotation using a method called *direct oblimin* are presented in Table 2.10. The findings are similar to those for varimax. The variables loading highest on the first factor are being relaxed (0.99), not anxious (–0.94) and not tense (–0.73), respectively. The variables loading highest on the second factor are finding life dull (0.96), not being happy (–0.95) and being depressed (0.78), respectively. The results indicate that the three anxiety items (A1, A2 and A3) can be combined together, as can the three depression items (D1, D2 and D3). The two factors were found to have a correlation of 0.36 with one another. As negative values on the first factor indicate anxiety and positive values on the second factor depression, the positive correlation between the two factors means that depression is associated with low anxiety. Because the factors are correlated, the proportion of variance explained by each factor cannot be estimated as it is shared between the factors.

Combining items to form indices The results of the factor analysis are used to determine which items should be combined to form the scale for measuring a particular construct. Items loading highly on the relevant factor (e.g., anxiety) and not on the other factors (e.g., depression) should be used to form the scale. The direction of scoring for

Table 2.10 *First two obliquely rotated principal components*

	1	2
A1 (Tense)	–0.73	–0.28
A2 (Anxious)	–0.94	–0.43
A3 (Relaxed)	0.99	0.29
D1 (Depressed)	0.50	0.78
D2 (Happy)	–0.20	–0.95
D3 (Dull)	0.39	0.96

the scale needs to be established. Generally higher scores on the scale should indicate greater quantities of the variable being measured. For example, if the scale is assessing anxiety, it is less confusing if high scores are used to denote high anxiety rather than low anxiety. The numerical codes for the responses may have to be reversed to reflect this. For instance, the numerical codes for the anxiety items A1 and A2 need to be reversed so that strong agreement with these items is recoded as 5. The scale should have adequate alpha reliability. Items not contributing to this should be omitted.

CONCLUSION

In this chapter, we have moved fairly rapidly from some very basic ideas concerning variables to some fairly complex approaches to their creation and assessment. However, in another sense, the entire chapter deals with issues that are fundamental to the analysis of quantitative data, since the variable is the basic reference point. We have explored several ways in which variables are created, both in terms of such strategies as summated scales, which are common in the measurement of attitudes, and in terms of the ways in which analysts seek to refine and improve the quality of variables. Since the variable is fundamental to all quantitative data analysis, the material covered in this chapter constitutes an important starting point for many of the chapters in this book that deal with various aspects of quantitative data analysis.

REFERENCES

Blumer, H. (1956) 'Sociological analysis and the "variable"', *American Sociological Review*, 21, 683–90.
Bryman, A. (2001) *Social Research Methods*. Oxford: Oxford University Press.

Bryman, A. and Cramer, D. (2001) *Quantitative Data Analysis with SPSS Release 10 for Windows: A Guide for Social Scientists*. London: Routledge.

Cattell, R.B. (1966) 'The scree test for the number of factors', *Multivariate Behavioral Research*, 1, 245–76.

Child, D. (1990) *The Essentials of Factor Analysis* (2nd edition). London: Cassell.

Cohen, J. and Cohen, P. (1983) *Applied Multiple Regression/Correlation Analysis for the Behavioral Sciences* (2nd edition). Hillsdale, NJ: Lawrence Erlbaum Associates.

Pedhazur, E.J. and Schmelkin, L.P. (1991) *Measurement, Design and Analysis: An Integrated Approach*. Hillsdale, NJ: Lawrence Erlbaum Associates.

Schuman, H. and Presser, S. (1981) *Questions and Answers in Attitude Surveys: Experiments on Question Form, Wording, and Context*. San Diego, CA: Academic Press.

Tabachnick, B.G. and Fidell, L.S. (2001) *Using Multivariate Statistics* (4th edition). New York: HarperCollins.

Webb, E.J., Campbell, D.T., Schwartz, R.D. and Sechrest, L. (1966) *Unobtrusive Measures: Nonreactive Measures in the Social Sciences*. Chicago: Rand McNally.

Zeller, R.A. and Carmines, E.G. (1980) *Measurement in the Social Sciences: The Link between Theory and Data*. Cambridge: Cambridge University Press.

3

Summarizing Distributions

MELISSA HARDY

Statistical analysis is similar to any number of summarizing activities we perform each day. We describe a book as 'fascinating', a meal as 'delicious', a co-worker as 'kind'. In each case this single word communicates a central feature of the object which it describes, while ignoring much else. But we can expand our descriptions. For example, we can say that the book captured our attention in the first paragraph and held it to the last word, or perhaps that it took a few chapters to get into the story but thereafter was difficult to put down. We can recount the main story line, characterize the protagonist, discuss the use of language, liken it to other novels, and at some point, as a listener who had not read the book, you could gain an understanding of this text. So it is with statistical analysis.

When we work with a data set, our goal is to tell its story – or one of its stories. We use the data to formulate an answer to a question, to illustrate a point, to test a theory. And we need tools by which to accomplish these tasks. Staring at pages and pages of numbers, even numbers already organized into the necessary data matrices, will accomplish little. What we require are shorthand ways to represent the data arrays, a practice that helps us visualize what each variable 'looks like'. In general, we need methods of summarizing the information, and we need techniques of assessing how well and how consistently the summary suits the data. But any summary measure is designed to succinctly portray a specific feature of the data, not to provide a detailed description. Therefore, it is important to choose measures suited to the question at hand and to the nature of the data.

CLASSIFYING, COUNTING, AND MEASURING

The tools that we use must be suited to the type of information we wish to analyze. In the same way that a carpenter learns that different types of saws with different types of blades are best suited to cutting different sorts of materials, so the analyst learns that the first task is to identify the nature of the information at hand. Initially, we can categorize variables into two types: discrete and continuous. Discrete variables can take a finite number of values, whereas continuously measured variables can take on any value within a much more detailed range of possible values. In other words, the possible values for discrete variables are countable;

Table 3.1　*Descriptive statistics for variables in the NLSY79 data extract*

Variable name	Valid N	Mode	Median	Mean	Range	Variance	St. Dev.	Skew	Kurtosis
Gender	8889	1	1	0.5	1	0.25	0.5	_[a]	_[a]
Employment status	8889	1	1	0.84	1	0.134	0.366	_[a]	_[a]
Race/ethnicity	8889	3	_[a]	_[a]	3	_[a]	_[a]	_[a]	_[a]
Marital status	8884	1	_[a]	_[a]	6	_[a]	_[a]	_[a]	_[a]
Gender role attitude	8831	2	2	2.03	3	0.7	0.84	0.6	−0.11
Region of residence	8679	3	_[a]	_[a]	3	_[a]	_[a]	_[a]	_[a]
Age at interview	8889	31	33	32.98	8	5.01	2.24	0.135	0.052
Age at first marriage	6455	21	22	22.92	24	17.335	4.164	0.501	−0.231
Number of pregnancies	4411	2	2	2.34	14	3.09	1.76	0.834	1.234
Number of jobs	8882	6	8	8.8	44	27.78	5.27	1.05	1.784
Tenure at current job	7469	1	158	231.56	1045	49704.23	222.94	1.073	0.306
Highest grade completed	8884	12	12	12.98	20	5.98	2.44	0.172	1.319
Weight	8684	180	166	170.47	400	1548.71	39.35	0.823	1.393
Total net family income	7004	_[b]	33200	40883.12	189918	1.329E+09	36452.78	2.455	7.506
ln(family income)	7004	_[b]	10.41	10.12	12.15	2.6	1.61	−4.337	24.3

[a]Statistic is inappropriate for nominal variables.
[b]Measure is uninformative.

the possible values for continuous measures are not. Because of this difference, the statistical approaches to describing distributions of discrete and continuous measures utilize different branches of mathematics.

Among discrete variables, we also have different possible types. These types include nominal classifications, ordinal classifications, and counts. Continuous variables may be measured on either interval or ratio scales, the difference being that ratio scales have an absolute zero point. To facilitate our discussion of distribution statistics, we will rely on an exemplary data set extracted from the National Longitudinal Survey of Youth (NLSY) that was initiated in 1979. Table 3.1 lists the variables we will use in examples. Most of the variables are from the 1994 wave; a few are taken from the initial wave in 1979. The sample consists of men and women who were initially interviewed when they were aged 14–22. By 1994, the sample members were aged 29–37. In our data extract, respondents are classified by gender and by race/ethnicity. We know their employment status, marital status, and region of residence in 1994. We have one measure of gender attitudes taken in 1979, which

records the level of the respondent's agreement/disagreement with the statement: 'A woman's place is in the home, not the office or the shop.' In 1994, we also know the highest grade of schooling they had completed, the number of jobs they had had, their age at first marriage (if ever married), the number of pregnancies (for the women), and number of weeks of tenure on their primary job (if employed). Finally, we know age at interview, weight, and total net family income. An example of a complete case is a 30-year-old African-American man who completed a bachelor's degree and was married at the age of 24 to a woman from whom he was divorced in 1993; the year 1994 saw him living in Massachusetts and employed in his second job, which he has held for 6 years; he disagreed with the statement that 'A woman's place is in the home', weighed 180 pounds, and had a total net income of $65 350.

Gender, employment, race/ethnicity, region, and marital status are all nominal classifications containing information that allows us to sort cases into categories. Gender and employment are binary items; the remaining variables in this list have several categories.

Our attitude measure is ordinal. The remaining variables are treated as interval or ratio measures.

SINGLE-VARIABLE DISTRIBUTIONS

The most common way to display the pattern of observations for a given variable is to produce a frequency distribution, which displays the values of the observations, relative to the number of times each specific value is observed. In generating this distribution, we often use the standard geometry of the upper right quadrant of a two-dimensional space, which displays all positive values and is bounded below by the x-axis and to the left by the y-axis.[1] Here, the x-axis reports the case-by-case values of the variable, the y-axis the frequency of its observation. If the variable is measured continuously, then the frequency distribution is represented as a smooth curve. If the variable is a classification, then the frequency distribution is often a histogram, which displays vertical columns labeled by the category, rising to the number (frequency) of times it is observed.

Perusal of this simple type of distribution communicates much useful information. We view each value and each frequency relationally, within the full range of observed values (highest to lowest, if quantitative) and relative to how common or uncommon an observation is. In that way, we see the most likely observed value, and the range of possible values. We see the distributional form of each variable. Whereas a variable with a more limited number of possible category responses allows an observer to accurately assess this information through simple visualization, the more precisely a variable is measured, the less easily this is accomplished. With variables quantitatively measured, then, we require mathematics beyond simple counts to provide us with the summary information we desire.

Descriptive statistics

The statistics used to describe a distribution were developed to provide information about four features: a typical or most likely value in the distribution (a value at the midpoint of the distribution or one that is most often observed); the heterogeneity of the distribution (or the extent to which observations have different, perhaps widely different values); the symmetry of the distribution (whether observations are more heavily concentrated at values lower than the most likely value, higher than the most likely value, or equally divided between higher and lower values); and the peakedness of the distribution (or the extent to which observations are heavily concentrated around the most likely observation). The combination of these four types of measures provides a good picture of the entire distribution, which the researcher uses to decide how to proceed with further analysis. Therefore, regardless of the modeling technique or analysis approach that will ultimately be used to address research questions, the first step in analysis must always be to learn about the distributional properties of one's data.

Central tendency In summarizing an observed distribution, the most useful pieces of information tell us the most likely observed value and something about the differences among observed values, referred to as central tendency and dispersion. With classifications, the typical observation belongs to the category most frequently observed. We call this category the *mode* or *modal category*. It may happen that we have two or three categories observed equally frequently and more than any other, in which case we speak of the distribution as being bimodal or trimodal. Figure 3.1 shows the distributions of a subset of our variables.

Consider the bar chart for gender. Although the modal category is 'women', the sample is almost equally divided between men and women. Is it then correct to describe the 'typical' respondent as a woman? If the sample is (all but) equally divided between these two groups, such a description is misleading. If, on the other hand, we drew a simple random sample from a population with 70% women (as is the case at the oldest age ranges), our sample would be primarily older women. Turning to employment, again we have two categories, but in this case more than four of five respondents were employed at the time of interview; only 1422 (or 16%) were not.

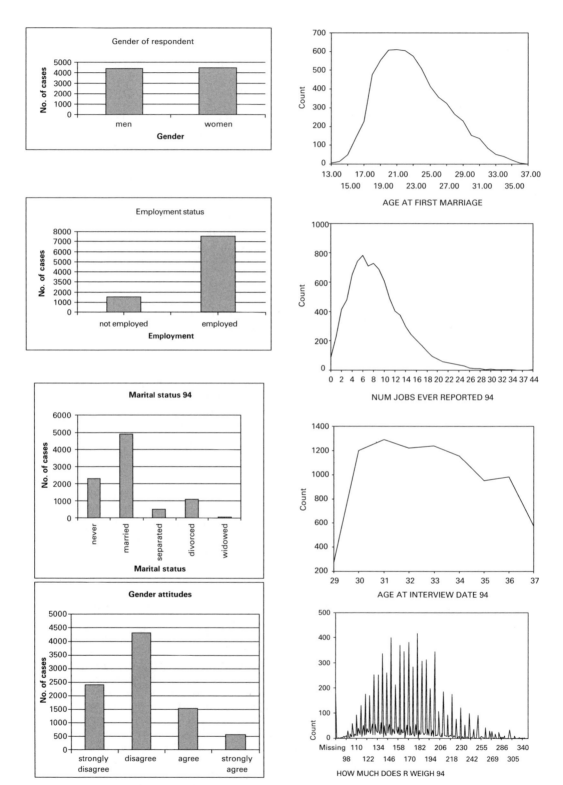

Figure 3.1   *Frequency distributions for binary, multinominal, and continuous variables*

To describe the 'typical' respondent as 'employed' is therefore appropriate. As for marital status, which is reported in five categories, the modal response is currently married at the time of the interview, a status which captures more than half the respondents.

The measure of gender attitudes allows for four responses, ranging from strongly disagree to strongly agree. Here the modal response is 'disagree', which captures almost half the respondents, so the 'typical' respondent disagrees with the statement: 'A woman's place is in the home, not the office or the shop.' Since these responses can be ordered, we can use a second measure of central tendency – the *median*. The median reports the middle value in an ordered array of numbers and is often referred to as the 50th percentile.[2] In this example, if we sorted (in ascending order) the data relative to responses on this question, the first 2420 (or 27.2% of) cases, coded 1, register strong disagreement. The following 4308 respondents (respondents numbered 2421 through 6728) disagreed with the statement. Given that 8831 respondents answered the question, the median value is associated with the 4416th case, 'disagree'.

Variables at a higher level of measurement can be characterized by the median or the mode, but a more useful measure is the *mean*. As precision of measurement increases, the mode becomes less and less useful, since the likelihood that multiple respondents are (precisely) 'the same' declines. In practice, commonality of responses on items that can be measured with precision is more likely a function of 'rounding' in the respondent's reporting.[3] The weight variable provides such an example here. One might have anticipated a symmetric, bell-shaped curve on weight. Instead, we see a set of spikes and toe holds, which undoubtedly result from people reporting their weight as 'roughly' 175, for example, rather than 176.882. The mean, as a measure of central tendency, is appropriate to interval and ratio data. It assumes that the values are meaningful quantities (rather than a shorthand way of denoting particular categories of qualitative information), and the mathematics of its formula uses this information of equally spaced numerical intervals in calculating its value, as in:

$$\bar{X} = \frac{1}{n} \sum_{i=1}^{N} X.$$

Special cases involve binary coded items (i.e., items coded 0 or 1) such as gender and employment status, in our extract. Mean values for these variables are reported in Table 3.1, but the information represented is actually the proportions of cases coded 1 (here, women and employed) rather than 0 on the variable in question. The binary coding transforms the summation into a counting process, which yields the frequency of 1s. The division by N relativizes the frequency for sample size, yielding the relative frequency of the category coded 1, or the proportion of the sample who are women (0.504) or who are employed (0.84).

Mean values for schooling, number of jobs, number of pregnancies, age at interview, age at first marriage, weight, net family income, and tenure are all reported in Table 3.1. In describing our sample, we would say that, on average, our respondents had completed 1 year of college beyond high school, had worked at 9 jobs, were aged 33 at interview, weighed 170 pounds, and had a net family income of $40 883. Women had experienced 2 pregnancies, on average. Among those ever married, the average age at first marriage was just shy of 23. Among those currently working, the average length of time with their primary employer was 232 weeks.[4]

How useful is this information? How accurate a picture do we now have of our sample of respondents? Answers to these questions require additional information about the distributions that the measures of central tendency were meant to describe. Are our respondents a relatively homogeneous group? Or are they widely divergent on the characteristics of interest to us? This is the issue of dispersion or variability.

Dispersion In the case of categorical measures, a measure of dispersion captures how observations are distributed across the various categories. First, we can visually inspect the charts in Figure 3.1 to draw some conclusions. Return to the graph of gender composition. We have two possible categories, and the distribution is virtually bimodal. In other words, we have two groups more or less equal in size. Does that suggest homogeneity (sameness) or heterogeneity (differences) among respondents in the sample? To put it another way, if a case were drawn at random from the sample, how confident are you that you could correctly guess the gender of the respondent? If your response is that you would be no more confident than in calling the toss of a fair coin, you would be correct.

Defining the limits of variability in a categorical measure leads us to the observation that, when all cases belong to a single category, the variance equals zero, which means our 'variable' is in fact a *constant*. But what defines the upper bound of variability? Imagine observations flowing from that single category into the second category, thereby increasing variability. At what point is variance maximized? Within this context, variability increases as the proportion of cases in the two categories moves to equality. Therefore, for gender and employment, we have less variability in employment status, more variability in gender in our sample. Again, since these items are binary, we can express the variance as:

$$s^2 = pqn,$$

where p is the proportion coded 1, q its complement, and n the number of cases. Table 3.1 reflects this difference in variability: the variance for gender is 0.25, for employment 0.13.

The logic of a variance measure is the same when we have more than two categories. Variance is maximized when cases are equally distributed across all categories (the frequency graph of categories is rectangular). The *measure of qualitative variation* allows us to assess the degree of dispersion in nominal distributions. Based on the number of categories and their respective frequencies, the larger the number of categories and the larger the differences in frequencies across categories, the larger the variance. The measure of qualitative variation compares the total number of differences in the distribution to the maximum number of possible differences for the same distribution. Calculation therefore requires an evaluation of observed differences relative to possible differences. The number of observed differences is

$$\text{Total observed differences} = \sum f_i f_j, \quad i \neq j,$$

where f refers to the frequency of categories i, j. We can calculate these differences for gender and for marital status, by way of illustration. For gender, the frequencies are 4409 for men and 4480 for women, so total observed differences are $4409 \times 4480 = 19\,752\,320$. To calculate the maximum number of possible differences (*MPD*), we use the formula

$$MPD = \frac{c(c-1)}{2} \left(\frac{n}{c}\right)^2,$$

where c is the number of categories and n is the number of observations. In the case of gender, we have

$$MPD_{Gender} = \frac{2 \times 1}{2} \left(\frac{8889}{2}\right)^2 = 4444.5^2$$

$$= 19\,753\,580.25.$$

The index of qualitative variation or IQV (Mueller and Schuessler, 1961: 177–9) is defined as the ratio of observed differences to maximum differences. Again, for gender, that ratio is

$$IQV_{Gender} = \frac{19\,752\,320}{19\,953\,580.25} = 0.9999,$$

which tells us that variability in gender in this sample is all but at maximum. Comparison of the value 0.25, which is the variance calculated as previously noted, to the maximum variance possible for a binary item, $0.5 \times 0.5 = 0.25$, shows consistency in the statistics.

Calculating *IQV* when there are more than two categories becomes an increasingly complex exercise, but it follows the same logic. In evaluating *IQV* for marital status, we use the same formula. To determine observed differences, we have 10 elements in the summation:

$$2327 \times 4915 + 2327 \times 513 + 2327 \times 1076$$
$$+ 2327 \times 53 + 4915 \times 513 + 4915 \times 1076$$
$$+ 4915 \times 53 + 513 \times 1076 + 513 \times 53$$
$$+ 1076 \times 53 = 23\,964\,774.$$

For the denominator,

$$MPD = \frac{5 \times 4}{2}\left(\frac{8824}{5}\right)^2 = 10 \times 1776.8^2$$

$$= 31\ 570\ 182.4;$$

therefore,

$$IQV = \frac{23\ 964\ 774}{31\ 570\ 182.4} = 0.76.$$

A second issue raised by measures such as IQV is whether standardization clarifies or confuses the interpretation of the measure. With IQV as well as other like measures, the calculated level of diversity is expressed as a proportion of the maximum possible diversity, given the number of subgroups. Is this form of standardization desirable? Lieberson (1969) notes that when dealing with a single population at a single point in time, a standardized measure is appropriate. Also, if the researcher is making comparisons between different populations with the same number of qualitative subgroups in each population, either the standardized or an unstandardized index may be used. However, if the researcher is comparing two or more populations that differ in the number of qualitative subgroups, an unadjusted measure of diversity is preferable. In general, when the goal is to describe the actual level of diversity in a population, an unadjusted measure is preferred. Lieberson's diversity measure, A_w, is defined as the probability that randomly paired members of a population will differ on a specified characteristic.[5] Holding aside the modifications due to sampling without replacement and the standardization procedure just discussed, A_w is equivalent to the index of qualitative variation (Lieberson, 1969).

To calculate A_w for marital status, which has five categories, we let P_k be the proportion of respondents in the first through fifth statuses, such that $P_1 + P_2 + P_3 + P_4 + P_5 = 1.00$. If we assume sampling with replacement (for simplicity's sake) the proportion of pairs with each possible marital status combination is the square of the sum of the proportions, or $(P_1 + P_2 + P_3 + P_4 + P_5)^2$. Expanding this polynomial gives us the following expression:

$$\begin{aligned}P_1^2 + P_2^2 + P_3^2 + P_4^2 + P_5^2 + 2(P_1P_2 \\ + P_1P_3 + P_1P_4 + P_2P_3 + P_2P_4 + P_2P_5 \\ + P_1P_5 + P_3P_4 + P_3P_5 + P_4P_5) = 1.00.\end{aligned}$$

The proportion of pairs with a common marital status, S, is the sum of the squares for all

marital statuses. In this example, S equals the sum of the first five terms. The proportion of pairs with a different marital status, D, is the sum of the remaining terms, or twice the bracketed expression. Using the same information for marital status from the data set, $S = 0.262^2 + 0.553^2 + 0.058^2 + 0.121^2 + 0.006^2 = 0.3925$, and A_w, the probability of different marital statuses, equals $1.00 - S = 0.6075$.

A final lesson here is that with qualities or characteristics that are classifiable, the more lop-sided the distribution – the higher the proportion of observations that fall in a single category – the less variability we have, and the better a descriptor the mode becomes. The more equally divided observations are across categories, the greater the variability (which is maximized when all categories are equal), and the less efficient is a measure of central tendency as a summary of the distribution.

For interval/ratio variables, we have several measures from which to choose. The simplest is the *range*, which reports the difference between the lowest value and the highest value. For age the range is 8 years, a function of sample design. The range for years of schooling is 20, for weight 400. The range gives us a sense of the magnitude of individual level differences we might observe, but also has some limitations. Suppose, for example, that in this sample we had one person who weighed 450 pounds and that the second highest weight was 300 pounds. A range of 400 suggests a level of variation that may be misleading in this case. A derivative measure, the *interquartile range*, reports the difference between the value associated with the 25th percentile and the 75th percentile. Nevertheless, both these measures use only two data points in the distribution.

For interval/ratio variables, we would prefer a measure that tells us about aggregate variation, a measure that utilizes information on every observation, as the mean does for measures of central tendency. The two most common measures of dispersion are based on deviations from the arithmetic mean of the distribution.[6] A deviation is a measure of difference, in this case the difference between an observed value and the mean. The sign of the deviation, either positive or negative, indicates whether the observation is larger than or smaller than the mean. The magnitude of the value reports how different (in the relevant numerical scale) an observation is from the mean. One of the features of the mean is that the sum of the deviations across all observations must always equal zero. Hence, the mean is often referred to as the center of gravity of a distribution – the balancing point. By using the absolute value of the deviation score, one can calculate the average deviation as:

$$\text{Average deviation} = \frac{1}{n}\sum |(X - \bar{X})|.$$

However, the most common measures of dispersion are the *variance* and the *standard deviation* (which is the square root of the variance). The sample variance is built on the same concept of deviation score, but in this case the deviations are *squared* (an important distinction between the 'average' deviation and the variance/standard deviation), and then summed over all cases and divided by $n - 1$:

$$\text{Variance} = s^2 = \frac{1}{n - 1}\sum(X - \bar{X})^2.$$

Subtracting 1 from n in the denominator is necessary to adjust for degrees of freedom, which is a count of the remaining pieces of information on which you have imposed no linear constraints. Because we use sample statistics to estimate population parameters, we must be vigilant about keeping track of the circumstances in which we must use sample information (in this case, $\bar{X}$) to calculate other sample estimates of parameters.[7] The variance is also referred to as the 'mean squared error' in the context of prediction error. The mean is also the general least-squares estimate of central tendency, which means that the sum of the squared deviations around it (the numerator of the variance formula) is minimized, i.e., smaller than around any other measure of central tendency or any other value in the distribution. Therefore, the mean becomes the 'best' predictor in the absence of any information beyond the variable's distribution.

The standard deviation, s, is found by taking the square root of the variance, which accomplishes a return to the original unit of measurement. Although its value is generally close to that of the *average deviation*, it should not be confused with it in discussions. So, for example, it is *not* correct to say that, given a standard deviation value of 39.35 for weight, respondents differ from mean weight by 39.35 pounds on average.[8]

According to *Chebyshev's theorem*, it is possible to calculate the minimum proportion of observations that will fall within k (where $k > 1$) standard deviations of the mean. The formula for making this calculation, $1 - 1/k^2$, is applicable to *any* distribution, regardless of its shape. For example, at least 75% ($1 - 1/4$) of the observations of a distribution will fall within ±2 standard deviations of the mean. In other words, knowing nothing about the distribution but its mean and standard deviation, one can say that at least 75% of all observations lie with a range of ±2 standard deviations around the mean; at least 89% lie within ±3 standard deviations around the mean; and at least 94% lie within ±4 standard deviations around the mean.

One final measure of dispersion is the *coefficient of variation*, which relativizes the size of the standard deviation to the scale of measurement for the variable by dividing it by the mean:

$$\text{Coefficient of variation} = V = \frac{s}{\bar{X}}.$$

For example, the standard deviation for schooling is 2.44 and the standard deviation for weight is 39.35. How can we make sense of that magnitude of difference? Using the *coefficient of variation*, we have 2.44/12.98 = 0.108 for schooling and 39.35/170.47 = 0.231 for weight. Clearly, the relative dispersion from the mean is larger in the case of weight than it is for schooling, but not nearly as much larger as we may have initially believed. We could also calculate V for number of pregnancies (1.76/2.34 = 0.752) indicating that, although the standard deviations for schooling and pregnancies were fairly close, the dramatically different means suggest that relative variation for pregnancies is much higher.

Shape In addition to the midpoint of a distribution and some notion of the degree of heterogeneity among respondents, information about the shape of the distribution can also be quite useful. Two measures that describe distribution shapes are skewness and kurtosis.

Skewness describes the degree of symmetry in a distribution, where symmetry refers to the balance between the number of observations that are above the mean and the number of observations below the mean. If we have an equal number of observations above and below, and the distribution is unimodal, the distribution is also symmetric. Since equality of the number of observations on either side of the mean is equivalent to saying the mean and median of the distribution are equal, Pearson developed a coefficient of skewness based on the *difference* between the mean $\bar{X}$ and the median $\tilde{X}$:

$$\text{Pearsonian coefficient of skewness} = Sk = \frac{3(\bar{X} - \tilde{X})}{s}.$$

Since the numerator is the simple difference between the two measures of 'average' value, the measure of skewness is signed: a distribution can be either positively skewed or negatively skewed, with the sign indicating which tail of the distribution contains the smaller proportion of observations. The mean is greater than the median when extreme positive values pull the mean in the direction of the right tail. Since the mean, unlike the median, uses information on the specific value, rather than simply noting its rank among other observations, even a relatively small number of very large observed values can shift a distribution away from symmetry.

Another measure of skewness is reported in Table 3.2, which contains the four sample *moments* around the mean of a distribution. The first moment is the midpoint, around which the sum of the deviations equals zero. The second moment is the variance, or mean squared deviation around the mean. The third moment is the average of the cubed deviations around the mean, which measures skewness when divided by the cube of the standard deviation. Since the variance is based on squared deviations around the mean, it must always be positive (with the standard deviation being defined as the positive square root). Cubing the deviations around the mean reintroduces the sign, positive or negative, to the measure.

Imagine a distribution of 1,2,2,3,3,3,4,4,5. The mean, median and mode are all equal to 3. Variance is equal to 1.5. Skewness is equal to 0. Now change the 5 to 10. The median and mode remain 3, but the mean is now 3.56. Variance is 6.78. Skewness is 2.21. We have five observations less than the mean; three observations greater than the mean, and a skewness value that tells us this fact: we have fewer observations to the right of the mean than to the left of the mean.

The frequency distribution of total family income is an example from our data set of a distribution that is positively skewed, with a value of 2.455. Income distributions are frequently skewed, which is to say that if one uses the arithmetic mean of an income distribution as its 'midpoint', one is indeed describing the center of gravity of the distribution. But since the distribution is asymmetrical, that balance point is such that more than half the cases lie below the mean (values lower than the mean are sampled in greater density because they are more likely observations). The relatively rare but very large values to the right of the mean disproportionately influence the 'balance point'. The greater the difference between the median value and the mean value, the more skewed the distribution; the more skewed the distribution, the more necessary it becomes to provide two measures of central tendency. The median will always be the proportional midpoint of the observations, the point above and below which 50% of the cases fall. The mean will be the numerical midpoint of the observed values in the distribution, a different meaning of 'midpoint'. In skewed distributions, that distinction is very important. We could not say, for example, that half the respondents in our sample have family income in excess of \$40 883. We can say, however, that half the respondents in our sample have family income in excess of \$33 200, since this is the median value of the distribution.

Kurtosis tells us whether the distribution is very peaked around the mean, or whether it is relatively flat. It is based on the fourth moment around the mean of a distribution. Since the mean deviations are now raised to the fourth power, measures of kurtosis will always be positive. In addition, by summing the mean deviations raised to the fourth power, observations that are far from the mean receive much more weight than they do in the calculation of the variance. A very peaked unimodal and symmetric distribution with observations compactly distributed around the mean is called leptokurtic ($k > 3$). A flatter unimodal and symmetric distribution with observations more widely dispersed around the mean is called platykurtic ($k < 3$). Mesokurtic describes a distribution that is neither excessively peaked nor excessively flat ($k = 3$).

THE NORMAL DISTRIBUTION

One type of symmetrical distribution is the *normal distribution*[9] or *normal curve*, which is a

Table 3.2 *Relationship between features of a distribution and moments around the mean*

Moments of a random variable

First moment (mean)	$\mu = E\{x\}$
Second moment (variance)	$\sigma^2 = E\{(x - \mu)^2\}$
Third moment (skewness)	$\gamma_1 = \dfrac{1}{\sigma^3} E\{(x - \mu)^3\}$
Fourth moment (kurtosis)	$\gamma_2 = \dfrac{1}{\sigma^4} E\{(x - \mu)^4\}$

Sample moments around the mean

First moment	$m_1 = \dfrac{\sum (X - \bar{X})}{n}$
Second moment	$m_2 = \dfrac{\sum (X - \bar{X})^2}{n}$
Third moment	$m_3 = \dfrac{\sum (X - \bar{X})^3}{n}$
Fourth moment	$m_4 = \dfrac{\sum (X - \bar{X})^4}{n}$

Statistics of a distribution

Arithmetic mean	$\dfrac{\sum X_i}{n}$	Midpoint of the distribution
Variance	$\dfrac{\sum (X_i - \bar{X})^2}{n - 1}$	Measure of dispersion around the mean
Skewness	$\dfrac{m_3}{m_2^{3/2}}$	Measure of symmetry around the mean
Kurtosis	$\dfrac{m_4}{m_2^2}$	Measure of peakedness at the mean

distribution of particular significance in data analysis. The *normal distribution* is both symmetrical and bell-shaped, with the three measures of central tendency (the mean, median, and mode) equal to the same numerical value; skewness is zero; kurtosis is equal to 3. Although, in theory, the normal distribution is asymptotic to the axis, in practice, applications generally have a finite number of observations. The exact shape of the normal distribution is determined by two parameters, the mean and the standard deviation of the distribution; its probability density function (pdf) is defined as:

$$f(X) = \frac{1}{\sigma\sqrt{2\pi}} \, e^{-(1/2)\,[(X - \mu)/\sigma]^2}$$

where μ is the population mean of X, σ is the population standard deviation of X, $\pi = 3.14159...$, and e $= 2.71828....$. This formula allows one to calculate the value of the expected frequency (or density) of observation associated with a given value of x for a normal curve specified by a particular mean and standard deviation.

In estimating probabilities, the normal distribution is particularly useful, since the area under the curve, given by the cumulative density function (cdf), allows us to estimate the probability of a given range of outcomes.

The total area under the curve, ranging from $-\infty$ to $+\infty$, totals 1:

$$\int_{-\infty}^{\infty} f(x)\mathrm{d}x = 1.$$

Because x is continuous and the probability is defined by area, it is not possible to assess the probability of a specific outcome value. Rather, one defines a range of values, which may be small or large depending on the question at hand, to determine the probability:

$$\int_{b}^{a} f(x)\mathrm{d}x = P(a < x \leq b),$$

where $f(x)$ dx is the probability associated with a small interval of a continuous variable, the interval $[a, b]$.

Being able to locate a specific observation in the normal distribution therefore allows one to determine the empirical probability of values less than or greater than the observation of interest. This practice is limited to variables that are measured at the interval/ratio level, with normal distributions. However, since any given normally distributed variable will present its own mean and standard deviation, calculation of these probabilities (through integration of areas under the curve) would be tedious. By making an adjustment to an observed distribution that would set the mean and standard deviation at standard values, we could utilize a single normal distribution, which is, in fact, how we proceed.

This standardization procedure is generally called the *z-transformation*, and it is appropriate to normally distributed interval/ratio variables. Calculating a *z-score*, or transforming the observed empirical distribution into the standardized normal distribution, is accomplished by dividing the unit deviation by the standard deviation:

$$Z = \frac{X - \bar{X}}{s}.$$

This produces a distribution with mean equal to 0 and a standard deviation of 1. By calculating the z-scores, we can immediately view each observation in probabilistic terms.

A positive z-score means the observation is higher than the mean, which automatically signals that the respondent scored higher than at least half the respondents in the sample. How many more than half the sample? Although Chebyshev's theorem could prove useful here, we have more information than that theorem requires. Chebyshev's theorem is silent on the shape of the distribution; therefore, it is applicable to all distributions of all shapes and sizes. We are now working with a particular type of distribution – a normal distribution. Using this additional information, we can be more precise about the proportion of observations that lie within the range of k standard deviations around the mean. The empirical rule can be applied here, allowing us to say that 68.3% of the values will fall between ± 1 standard deviation around the mean; 95.5% will fall between ± 2 standard deviations around the mean; and 99.7% will fall between ± 3 standard deviations around the mean.

The z-transformation allows us to take advantage of tables that report already calculated areas under the normal curve (see the Appendix at the back of the book), rather than having to evaluate integrals in each distinct normal distribution we observe. Since we are dealing with a continuous distribution, the probabilities we can assess must be bounded by two values; we cannot ascertain the probability of observing a specific discrete value. Working through a few examples should make this clear.

Table 3.3 shows a small portion of the z-distribution included in the Appendix. The range of possible values for z lies between $-\infty$ and $+\infty$. Since the variance of the distribution is also 1, the sum of the area under the curve is equal to 1 as well, which is the upper limit of a probability. Given that the curve is symmetric, the mean divides the area in two, with 0.5 between the mean and $+\infty$, and 0.5 between the mean and $-\infty$. Tables that report the area under the normal curve either report the area that lies between the mean and a given z-score or the area that lies between the given z-score and infinity. Both the extract in Table 3.3 and the complete table in the Appendix report the area between the mean and the z-score. Finally, only positive z-scores are reported in the table. Again the symmetry of the curve allows the reader to determine the area between negative z-scores and the mean as easily as between positive z-scores and the mean.

Consider the quantitative portion of the Graduate Record Examination (GRE), one of the exams often required for admission to graduate school in the US. The highest possible score is 800. Suppose in a given year that the mean score was 480, the standard deviation was 100, and your score was 600. You can convert your score to a z-score by dividing 120 by 100, which is 1.2. Your score is 1.2 standard deviations above the mean, so you know you scored better than more than half of those who took the exam. How much better? Consider the extract from the z-distribution in Table 3.3. You find the area associated with your z-score by looking in the row headed 1.2 and the column headed 0.00. The value is 0.3849, which describes the area between the mean, 0, and your score, 1.2 (Figure 3.2 (a)). Add to that the area in the other half of the distribution, 0.5, and you gain the information that you scored better than 88.49% of those taking the exam. To determine the probability that someone picked at random scored better than you, simply subtract 0.8849 from 1: 0.1151 is your answer.

As a second example, consider a score of 350, which converts to a z-score of -1.3. The area between the mean and a z-score of 1.3 is 0.4032, therefore the area between the mean and a z-score of -1.3 is also 0.4032. In this case, 90.32% scored better than 350, and 9.68% scored worse (Figure 3.2 (b)).

As a final example, consider the area under the normal curve that corresponds to the difference between scoring 325 and scoring 628. The corresponding z-scores are -1.55 and 1.48 (Figure 3.2 (c)). The corresponding areas from the table are 0.4394 and 0.4306. Based on that information, we can say that 87% scored between 325 and 628; the probability that someone at random scored better than 628 is 0.0694; the probability that someone at random scored worse than 325 is 0.0606.

Table 3.3 *Extract from the table of the z-distribution*

z	\multicolumn{10}{c}{Second decimal place in z}
	0.00	*0.01*	*0.02*	*0.03*	*0.04*	*0.05*	*0.06*	*0.07*	*0.08*	*0.09*
1.0	0.3413	0.3438	0.3461	0.3485	0.3508	0.3531	0.3554	0.3577	0.3599	0.3621
1.1	0.3643	0.3665	0.3686	0.3708	0.3729	0.3749	0.3770	0.3790	0.3810	0.3830
1.2	0.3849	0.3869	0.3888	0.3907	0.3925	0.3944	0.3962	0.3980	0.3997	0.4015
1.3	0.4032	0.4049	0.4066	0.4082	0.4099	0.4115	0.4131	0.4147	0.4162	0.4177
1.4	0.4192	0.4207	0.4222	0.4236	0.4251	0.4265	0.4279	0.4292	0.4306	0.4319
1.5	0.4332	0.4345	0.4357	0.4370	0.4382	0.4394	0.4406	0.4418	0.4429	0.4441
1.6	0.4452	0.4463	0.4474	0.4484	0.4495	0.4505	0.4515	0.4525	0.4535	0.4545
1.7	0.4554	0.4564	0.4573	0.4582	0.4591	0.4599	0.4608	0.4616	0.4625	0.4633
1.8	0.4641	0.4649	0.4656	0.4664	0.4671	0.4678	0.4686	0.4693	0.4699	0.4706
1.9	0.4713	0.4719	0.4726	0.4732	0.4738	0.4744	0.4750	0.4756	0.4761	0.4767

JOINT DISTRIBUTIONS AND MEASURES OF ASSOCIATION

An understanding of the main features of univariate distributions is an important preface to answering questions of relationships between or among variables. It is this notion of 'relationship' that is often of primary interest. Bivariate relationships can be assessed for different types of variables, thereby generating information about 'total' or 'gross' effects. But the complexity of the research questions we ask often requires us to assess 'partial' or 'net' relationships between variables. So how do we move from the characteristics of single distributions to those of joint distributions? One place to begin is with bivariate distributions.[10]

Bivariate distributions

Interval/ratio variables Given that we ended the last section with z-scores, observed values transformed into values from the standard normal distribution, let us begin this section with two standardized variables, Z_1 and Z_2, which are the z-transformed values for X_1 and X_2. The distributions of Z_1 and Z_2 are standard normal, with mean equal to 0 and variance and standard deviation equal to 1. What does their *bivariate* distribution, or *joint* distribution, look like? Somehow this third distribution must incorporate information from both univariate distributions in such a way that we can make judgments about whether the two variables are related, and if so, how they are related.

What does it mean to say two variables are related? We know what it means to say two people 'are related'. They belong to the same family: if 'closely related' they stem from the same portion of their 'family tree'. If 'distantly related', the branches of their respective nuclear families diverged some number of generations ago. Therefore, a close relationship can indicate a shared genetic structure (in a biological sense) but also shared likes and dislikes, similar attitudes, preferences, behaviors, mannerisms and so on (in a social sense). It also implies a certain predictability, which is the major reason family medical history is collected by physicians. So how do we translate this commonplace notion of 'relationship' to statistics?

Begin with the notion of predictability. How can an observed value for one variable be predicted by the value for the second variable? Suppose these values were equal. Suppose that, for respondent after respondent, the numerical value for Z_1 is the same as the numerical value for Z_2. This situation would allow us to perfectly predict the distribution of Z_2, if we knew Z_1 values, and vice versa, since each pair of observed values contains two identical numbers. To say that we can perfectly reproduce a second distribution by utilizing knowledge of the first distribution is to say that the two variables are related – perfectly related. Can we translate that statement into a statistic? We want to summarize, on a case-by-case basis, how the distributional position of the value of Z_1 corresponds to the distributional position of the value of Z_2. Recall that the variance measures heterogeneity in a univariate distribution by summing the squared mean deviations, case by case, and dividing by $n-1$. Since z-scores are themselves indicators of distributional position (e.g., 1 standard deviation above the mean, 2.3 standard deviations below the mean), the variance of Z_1 and Z_2 would be written as $(\sum Z_1^2)/(n-1)$ and $(\sum Z_2^2)/(n-1)$, respectively.[11] What we want in this case is a measure of the mean difference

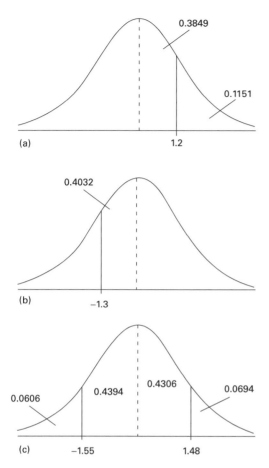

Figure 3.2 *Calculating probabilities of various outcomes using the area under the normal curve*

in the product of relative placement in the two distributions. That measure is named the *covariance* of Z_1 and Z_2 and is given by

$$\mathrm{cov}(Z_1, Z_2) = \frac{\sum Z_1 Z_2}{n - 1}.$$

If we return to our invented data set of nine cases (1,2,2,3,3,3,4,5) and create values on a second variable as 5,10,10,15,15,15, 20,20,25, then transform both distributions to z-scores, we have the two identical distributions in Z_1 and Z_2. Calculating the covariance by summing the products across all cases and dividing by $n - 1$ yields a value of 1 (Table 3.4).

Since we have now linked the value of 1.00 with a 'relationship' of identity, we have also established a limit on the positive value of the covariance between two z-distributions. If we reverse the signs of observed values for Z_2 to produce Z_2^* and repeat the calculation of the covariance, we get a value of –1.00. What does this mean? It means that on a case-by-case basis, the relative position in the distribution of Z_1 is the reverse of, or opposite to, the position of the respondent in Z_2^*. If, as before, we assume these scores to be evaluations of respondents' performances on two tests, we can say, for example, that if the ninth respondent performed better than 94.84% of the sample on measure X_1, he performed worse than 94.84% of the respondents on X_2. If the third respondent performed better than 20.62% of the respondents on X_1, she scored worse than 20.62% of the respondents on X_2.[12] The other limiting value of the covariance between two z-distributed variables is –1.00, which indicates a perfect negative relationship, a predictability of one outcome to its opposite.

But what if we were not using z-scores? What if we were using values in their observed metric? In that case, we would use the more general formula for the covariance, which is

$$\mathrm{cov}(X_1, X_2) = \frac{\sum(X_{1i} - \bar{X}_1)(X_{2i} - \bar{X}_2)}{n - 1}.$$

If we return to the original metrics of X_1 and X_2, our covariance is 7.5. What does that mean? When dealing with various measurement units on different scales, dealing with just the covariance tells us something about how the two variables are related (e.g., whether positive or negative), but the strength of the association is ambiguous, because we lack defined limits for each pair of variables. The advantage of assessing the bivariate distribution of two z-distributed variables is that both distributions have been standardized to means of 0 and standard deviations of 1. In other words, through the z-transformation, we had incorporated into each observation the information of the first and second moments of each univariate distribution, thereby producing a set of values already standardized on this distributional information. Therefore, it seems only reasonable that if we calculate the covariance of two distributions in their original metrics, we then apply some kind of distributional adjustment to

Table 3.4 *Demonstration data for z-scores, covariance and correlation*

Case no.	X_1	X_2	Z_{X1}	Z_{X2}	$Z_{X1}Z_{X2}$
1	1	5	−1.63	−1.63	2.67
2	2	10	−0.82	−0.82	0.67
3	2	10	−0.82	−0.82	0.67
4	3	15	0	0	0
5	3	15	0	0	0
6	3	15	0	0	0
7	4	20	0.82	0.82	0.67
8	4	20	0.82	0.82	0.67
9	5	25	1.63	1.63	2.67
Sum	27	135	0.00	0.00	8.00
Mean	3	15	0	0	
St. Dev.	1.22	6.12	1	1	
Variance	1.5	37.5	1	1	
Skew	0	0	0	0	
Kurtosis	−0.29	−0.29	−0.29	−0.29	
$\sum(X_1-\bar{X}_1)(X_2-\bar{X}_2)$	60	$\sum Z_1 Z_2$	8		
$cov(X_1, X_2)$	7.5	$cov(Z_1, Z_2)$	1		
$r_{X_1 X_2}$	1	$r_{Z_1 Z_2}$	1		

again move us to a standard metric. We need a joint adjustment for the two distributions, and we accomplish that by dividing the covariance by the product of the two standard deviations. So, for example, if we divide the covariance of X_1 and X_2, 7.5, by the product of the two standard deviations, $1.225 \times 6.124 = 7.5$, we reproduce the value of 1.

This standardized measure of the covariance is, in fact, *Pearson's product moment*[13] *correlation coefficient (r)*, one of the most commonly used measures of linear association for interval/ratio variables, and is defined as the ratio of the covariance to the product of the standard deviations. Pearson's r can also be transformed into a *proportional reduction of error* (PRE) measure of association, which returns us to the notion of predictability. PRE measures of association are a special class of measures that indicate how much the error in prediction of one variable can be reduced by knowing the value of the other variable. Since such a proportion must always be positive and because the limiting values of r are −1.00 and +1.00, we know that r itself cannot be a PRE measure. But r^2 is, with a range of 0 to 1: information on a second variable can reduce your prediction errors not at all, can reduce them to zero (100%), or by any amount between the two.

In addition, some measures of association are symmetrical. Symmetrical measures of association assume no causal direction to the relationship, whereas asymmetrical measures

assume that one variable depends on the other. Asymmetrical measures therefore make a distinction between dependent and independent variables, and the mathematical value of the measure incorporates this assumption. Symmetrical measures use the information of both variables in exactly the same way. Reviewing the measures already introduced, we can see that the covariance, r, and r^2 are all symmetrical measures.

We can now return to our data extract and explore the bivariate distributions of our interval/ratio variables. Table 3.5 contains information for the interval/ratio variables, including zero-order[14] (bivariate) correlation coefficients, r, the covariance, and the pairwise number of cases.[15] Among things to note are that r and the covariance always have the same sign; that r ranges between −1 and +1; that larger values of the covariance do not imply larger values of r. On this latter point, note as examples the bivariate relationships between income and weight, between age at first marriage and weight, and between age at interview and weight. The covariance between income and weight is very large (more than 33 000) and the correlation coefficient is quite small (0.023) – about as small as the correlation coefficient between age at interview and weight, which has a covariance less than 2. The correlation between age at first marriage and weight, 0.11, is notably larger (although still not what we would call 'large' in an absolute sense), with a covariance in the teens. The point is that the size of the

Table 3.5 *Zero-order correlation matrix for variable in data extract*

	weight	tenure	no. job	schooling	age (int)	age (fm)	no. preg.	
tenure	0.06							
	519.1							
	7298							
no. jobs	0.024	−0.468						
	5.01	−547.4						
	8677	7464						
schooling	−0.044	0.062	0.096					
	−4.223	33.13	1.242					
	8679	7465	8877					
age (int)	0.021	0.161	−0.118	0.011				
	1.817	80.533	−1.395	0.063				
	8684	7469	8882	8884				
age (fm)	0.11	0.044	0.075	0.325	0.045			
	17.83	41.648	1.623	3.311	0.422			
	6299	5507	6448	6452	6455			
no. preg.	0.039	−0.138	−0.086	−0.293	0.146	−0.268		
	2.494	−50.12	−0.744	−1.253	0.577	−1.855		
	4227	3502	4409	4408	4411	3371		
income	−0.023	0.192	−0.043	0.37	0.079	0.206	−0.108	*r*
	−33023.2	1573591	−8216.5	33031.7	6443	31613.3	−6795.6	covariance
	6882	5950	6998	6999	7004	5250	3514	no. of cases

covariance, being influenced by the scale on which the variable is measured (e.g., the range of values), tells us only the sign of the relationship. If we want a measure of the strength of association, we must use *r*, since it is a standardized measure.

The closer the value of *r* is to its limits, the stronger the relationship; the closer the value of *r* is to zero, the weaker the relationship. But if we want to discuss strength of association in the text of a report, the preference is to use r^2, since it is a PRE measure. For example, the correlation between age at first marriage and schooling is 0.325, which indicates that more than 10% ($0.325^2 = 0.1056$) of the variance in schooling can be explained (accounted for) by age at first marriage. The relationship is positive; therefore, we can say that respondents who married at older ages achieved higher levels of schooling, on average, than those who married at younger ages. The qualification 'on average' is an important component of the statement. We are *not* claiming that if we compared, one by one, those who married at younger ages with those who married at older ages, we would find no case in which the respondent who married at the younger age had more schooling. We are, however, claiming that if you calculate *mean schooling* for each value of age at first marriage, as age at first marriage increases, so would mean schooling. A cruder way of

testing this statement would be to bisect the distribution of age at first marriage into two groups: those who married at age 20 or younger and those who married when they were older than 20. If we do so, we find a mean of 11.9 for those who married 'young' and a mean of 13.52 for those who were 'older' when married. As we can see, the mean for the 'young' group is less than that for those who married later.

Another important caveat is to note that we cannot claim that the level of schooling is *caused* by age at marriage. The causal direction could be the reverse – age at marriage may have led to the level of completed schooling. Or there could be no causal relationship between these two features. Rather, both completed schooling and age at first marriage may be two outcomes of a more complex social process that we have not considered in this simple example. Demonstrating causal relationships requires more than establishing a statistical correlation (see Winship and Sobel, this volume).

Nominal/ordinal variables For variables that are classifications we must rely on a different set of tools to assess relationships. The logic is the same. We are interested in predictability from one set of information to a second, wondering whether having a certain quality makes more or less likely a particular

Table 3.6   *Bivariate distribution of gender and employment status, percentaged by column*

		Gender of respondent		
		Men (0)	Women (1)	Total
Employment status	*Count*	**495**	**925**	**1420**
0	*% within gender*	(11.2)	(20.6)	(16.0)
	Count	**3914**	**3555**	**7469**
1	*% within gender*	(88.8)	(79.4)	(84.0)
Total	*Count*	**4409**	**4480**	**8889**
	% within gender	(100)	(100)	(100)

Source: Author's calculations, using NLSY data

preference, or whether making one choice increases the likelihood of a particular second choice. The bivariate distribution for interval/ratio measures was represented by the covariance. Bivariate distributions of categorical variables are represented through cross-tabulations. Using variables from our data extract, we could ask whether employment rates were different for men and women. Essentially, this is a question of proportions. We know that 49.6% of our sample are men, 50.4% are women, and that 84% are employed and 16% are not. If gender and employment are *not* related, what should we expect? The absence of a relationship suggests uniformity of outcome, that employment among women is no more or less likely than employment among men. In other words, the proportion of respondents who are employed does not depend on (i.e., does not differ by) gender. That suggests that if we limit our attention to women and calculate proportion employed and not employed, we should find the same proportional distribution as for the sample as a whole: 84% and 16%. The same should apply to men.[16] If we produce the joint distribution of gender and employment, we assign each respondent to one of four groups: not employed men, employed men, not employed women, and employed women. Each of these 'groups' is represented by a cell in a 2 × 2 table, as in Table 3.6.

The four shaded cells in the table display the joint distribution of gender by employment. Each cell is associated with a particular pair of categories on the two variables. For example, 495 respondents are both men and not employed; 3555 respondents are both women and employed. Within the body of the table, each respondent is jointly characterized on both variables. The column to the right of the shaded cells and the row below the shaded cells are the marginal distributions of our two original variables. We have 4409 men and 4480 women, 7469 employed persons and 1420 who are not employed. The bottom right cell gives us the total valid cases for these two variables, $n = 8889$.

If the likelihood of employment is not related to respondent's gender, the conditional distribution of employment by gender should be the same as the marginal distribution of employment, ignoring gender. Because we often do not have the same number of observations in each category, we cannot rely on frequencies to tell the story. Instead, we look at the proportional distribution *within categories of gender*. For example, 88.8% (3914/4409) of men are employed compared to 79.4% (3555/4480) of women. In our sample, then, employment is more likely among men than women.

Is there a statistic we can use to quantify that conclusion? There are several. Since this table is 2 × 2, we can use the phi (ϕ) statistic as a measure of association. Calculation of phi depends on a more basic statistic for cross-tabular analyses, chi-square (χ^2).

The chi-square statistic results from a comparison of the observed bivariate distribution with the bivariate distribution we would expect to see if, in fact, gender and employment were not related, that is, under the assumption of independence. Using probability theory, the definition of independence is that the marginal probability equals the conditional probability, as in:

$$\Pr(EMP = 1) = \Pr(EMP = 1 \mid Gender = male)$$
$$= \Pr(EMP = 1 \mid Gender = female).$$

In our example, the empirical probabilities are the same as the proportion of respondents satisfying a particular condition. The probability of employment compared to the probability of employment conditioned on gender is

$$\Pr(EMP = 1) = 0.840,$$

$$\Pr(EMP = 1 \mid Gender = male) = 0.888,$$

$$\Pr(EMP = 1 \mid Gender = female) = 0.794.$$

Clearly these three values are not equal, but can we quantify the extent to which they are different? We can begin by generating the frequencies we would expect if gender and employment were independent. We know what the conditional probabilities would be: 0.84 for men and 0.84 for women. If we have 4409 men and the probability of employment for men were 0.84, how many men would be employed? The answer is 3704.7.[17] Similarly, if we have 4480 women, 84% of whom should be employed (under independence), we should have 3764.3 employed women. We apply the same logic to determine the expected number of not employed persons, 16% of 4409 = 704.3 and 16% of 4480 = 715.7, and we have a complete set of expected frequencies.[18]

We noted earlier in the chapter that a measure of *variance* was a way to quantify differences among mathematical values, differences between the value observed and the value expected (the *mean*) if we had complete homogeneity. Here, we need a measure that will quantify differences between observed and expected (under the condition of independence) frequencies. We calculate the chi-square statistic as follows:

$$X^2 = \sum_{r=1}^{R} \sum_{c=1}^{C} \frac{(f_{obs} - f_{exp})^2}{f_{exp}}$$

where f_{obs} are observed frequencies, f_{exp} are expected frequencies, and the summation is performed across all cells, which is denoted by the double summation indicating across all rows and columns. In our example, X^2 equals 146.909, which allows us to calculate phi as:

$$\phi = \sqrt{\frac{146.909}{8889}} = 0.129.$$

In cases where both variables are dichotomous, ϕ is the equivalent of the correlation coefficient, *r*. Known as a *tetrachoric correlation coefficient*, it describes the relationship between two binary variables, which are observed indicators of an underlying latent variable. The latent variable is assumed to be normally distributed, but unobservable.[19]

The procedure is the same when the bivariate distribution requires more than four cells. However, as the number of cells increases the likelihood that some cells may have a zero or very low frequency increases, which creates a problem for the use of chi-square or any other type of cross-tabular analysis. Small expected frequencies can lead to very large values of chi-square, therefore chi-square should not be used if expected cell frequencies are smaller than 5.

Suppose, for example, we continued to be interested in the relationship between schooling and age at first marriage. Since both are discrete variables, we can look at their joint distribution, cell by cell. But schooling has a range of 20 and age at first marriage a range of 24. Therefore, the joint distribution is defined by a 20 × 24 matrix, or 480 cells. However, we always have the option of combining categories (values), or reclassifying according to some other conceptual scheme. Our interest may be in the effect of marrying at a young age, say age 20 or younger, versus marrying at a later age on completing schooling, with the expectation that marrying at a young age would be linked to less schooling. We can reclassify age at first marriage into two groups, and then compare the two groups' schooling distributions. But one could also argue that the primary interest is in obtaining educational credentials, so we can also reclassify years of completed schooling into five categories: 11 or fewer years, 12 years, 13 to 15 years, 16 years, and 17 or more years. The bivariate distribution of these recoded variables produces a 5 × 2 = 10 cell table.

When we compare the conditional distributions (within columns of age at first marriage) to the marginal distribution of schooling, we see that those who married at 20 or younger are overrepresented among high school dropouts and those with a high school diploma. Those who married later are overrepresented among those who went on to college, received a college degree, and continued postgraduate education. The value of chi-square for this table is 614.413. Because the table is larger than 2 × 2 and both variables are ordinal in their collapsed state, appropriate measures of association include Somer's *d* (0.355), gamma (0.499), Kendall's τ_b (0.277), and Spearman's correlation coefficient (0.303). All these measures rely on paired responses.

Gamma, also known as Goodman and Kruskal's gamma (Goodman and Kruskal,

Table 3.7   *Bivariate distribution of age at first marriage*
(dichotomized) and years of completed schooling,
percentaged by column

| | | Age at first marriage | | |
		≤ 20	> 20	Total
Schooling completed				
<12	Count	435	392	827
	% within age	(21.0)	(8.9)	12.8%
12	Count	1132	1700	2832
	% within age	(54.8)	(38.8)	43.9%
13–15	Count	406	1126	1532
	% within age	(19.6)	(25.7)	23.7%
16	Count	63	716	779
	% within age	(3.0)	(16.3)	12.1%
17+	Count	31	451	482
	% within age	(1.5)	(10.3)	7.5%
Total		2067	4385	6452

$\gamma = 0.499$	Somer's $d = 0.355$	$\tau_b = 0.277$	Spearman's rho $= 0.303$

Source: Author's calculations, using NLSY data

1954), is a symmetric measure of association for ordinal variables based on the number of same-ordered pairs (N_s) and the number of different-ordered pairs (N_d). Tied pairs are not considered in the calculation of gamma. The coefficient is defined as

$$\gamma = \frac{0.5\,(N_s + N_d) - \min\,(N_s, N_d)}{0.5\,(N_s + N_d)}.$$

Calculation of γ requires a return to the table and an accounting of the different types of pairs. We begin in the upper left corner (435), which describes those who married young and have the least schooling. For same-ranked pairs, we move down and to the right in the table, since respondents in the four cells below right all married later and completed more schooling than our initial 435 respondents. Hence, the first element in our summation of same-ranked pairs is 435 $(1700 + 1126 + 716 + 451)$. Pursuing this same logic, we have three remaining elements in the summation: 1132 $(1126 + 716 + 451) + 406$ $(716 + 451) + 63 \times 451$. Altogether, then, we have 4 834 846 same-ordered pairs.

To find the number of different-ordered pairs, we move to the upper right cell, with 392 respondents who married later but completed the lowest level of schooling. For pairs that share this difference in ranking (later on marriage but sooner on stopping school), we look to the cells down and to the left, since they are occupied by those who married younger, yet completed more schooling than our 392 respondents. Our first element in the

different-ordered pairs is therefore 392 $(1132 + 406 + 63 + 31)$. Remaining elements in the summation are determined by moving down one cell in the right-hand column and multiplying by the combined number of respondents in cells to the lower left. The three remaining elements in the summation are therefore 1700 $(406 + 63 + 31) + 1126$ $(63 + 31) + 716 \times 31$, which sums to 1 617 784 different-ordered pairs. We then calculate γ by substituting into the formula, using 1 617 784 for the second term in the numerator (since it is smaller than 4 834 846) and generate a value of 0.4986. Ranging between −1.00 and +1.00, γ also allows a PRE interpretation. A second formula for γ follows the same logic, but combines the information in a somewhat simpler way:

$$\gamma = \frac{N_s - N_d}{N_s + N_d},$$

which, in our example, would give us 3 226 315/6 443 377 = 0.4986.[20]

Kendall's τ_b addresses this limitation by amending the formula for γ by including tied pairs in the denominator:

$$\tau_b = \frac{N_s - N_d}{\sqrt{(N_s + N_d + T_y)\,(N_s + N_d + T_x)}},$$

where T_y and T_x are the number of pairs tied on y and x, respectively. In our example, schooling is y and age at first marriage is x. We find the number of ties on y by multiplying across columns, within rows, such that

$$435 \times 392 + 1132 \times 1700 + 406 \times 1126$$
$$+ 63 \times 716 + 31 \times 451 = 2\,611\,165 = T_y.$$

To find pairs tied on x, we move across rows but within columns, such that

$$435\,(1132 + 406 + 63 + 31) + 1132(406$$
$$+ 63 + 31) + 406\,(63 + 31) + 63 \times 31$$
$$+ 392\,(1700 + 1126 + 716 + 451)$$
$$+ 1700\,(1126 + 716 + 451)$$
$$+ 1126\,(716 + 541)$$
$$+ 716 \times 451 = 8\,416\,351 = T_x.$$

The final calculation for Kendall's τ_b is:

$$\tau_b = \frac{3\,226\,315}{\sqrt{9\,054\,542 \times 14\,859\,728}} = 0.278,$$

which is much closer in value to those reported for Somer's d and for Spearman's rho. Since the tied pairs amend the denominator, the value of τ_b will never be greater than γ, although it may be equal to γ in cases where there are no tied pairs. When tied pairs are present, τ_b will always be smaller than γ, with the difference increasing as the number of tied pairs increases. τ_b is also a symmetrical measure of association, ranging from -1 to $+1$.

Somer's d is a measure of association for ordinal variables, which is also a PRE measure. In this example, it indicates that somewhat more than 7% of the variation in education is accounted for by age at first marriage. Rather than including tied pairs on both x and y, Somer's d adds only pairs tied on y to the denominator, so that the calculation is:

$$d = \frac{3\,226\,315}{9\,054\,542} = 0.355.$$

Spearman's rho measures the degree of monotonic relationship between two ordinal variables. As the number of categories increases, Spearman's rho becomes a more useful measure, since it relies on a comparison of the rank ordering of respondents within the two distributions. Rank orderings that are quite similar produce high positive values of ρ_S; rank orderings that are opposite produce high negative values of ρ_S; and rank orderings that are unrelated produce values close to zero. It is defined by

$$\rho_S = 1 - \frac{6\sum d^2}{n(n^2 - 1)},$$

where n is the number of pairs of observations in the sample and d is the difference in the ranks of each pair (*not* Somer's d). In this example, the value of 0.303 indicates a positive relationship between the two variables (as age at first marriage increases, average schooling completed increases, as well). Also a PRE measure, the squared value indicates that approximately 9% of the variation in schooling is explained by age at first marriage.[21]

Another useful method for comparing the ordered distribution of two groups is calculating *the index of net difference* (Lieberson, 1976). Although researchers often compare means for different groups, or compare medians when the observed distributions are skewed, the index of net difference makes no assumptions about the distributional form for either group involved in the comparison and is most useful when the researcher is interested in a comparison between entire distributions. The Wilcoxon (1945, 1947) rank-sum statistic and its more general forms, the Mann–Whitney U test (for comparisons between two samples of unequal size) and the Kruskal–Wallis H test (for comparisons of more than two samples) were used frequently in the 1960s and 1970s; however, this set of statistics was less useful in comparing distributions with frequent ties (when the pairs have the same ranking within their groups, which occurs more frequently as the number of ordinal categories decreases).

To calculate the index of net difference, we assume two observed occupational distributions, for example, for groups A and B. We then randomly pair observations from these two groups, noting that sometimes the ranking in A exceeds the ranking in B; sometimes the ranking in B exceeds the ranking in A; and sometimes the rankings are equal (tied). We can express these outcomes in terms of probabilities, which sum to 1.00, since they exhaust the set of possible outcomes. The net difference is $ND_{AB} = \Pr(A > B) - \Pr(B > A)$. Ranking in value from $+1$ to -1, ND_{AB} will equal zero if the probabilities are the same. The existence of ties is reflected in the maximum ND_{AB}. If, for example, the $\Pr(A = B) = 0.60$, then the maximum value for $ND_{AB} = \pm 0.40$.

Elaborating relationships

Although bivariate relationships are a good starting point when you begin to analyze your data, many of the research questions we develop are more complex and therefore require *multivariate* rather than bivariate analyses. The remaining chapters in this volume will provide readers with a variety of approaches to more complex questions with different types of data. In this section, we will briefly explore what is meant by *partial* relationships, *intervening* variables, and *interaction*.

In assessing partial relationships, we add at least one more variable to the mix. Our intention is to re-examine the relationship of initial interest under a new set of conditions. The term 'partial' is used because we are interested only in that part of the initial relationship that continues to obtain once these new control variables are introduced. The new set of conditions consists in 'controlling' for the effects of additional variables. When we introduced the term 'relationship', we linked it to the covariance between two variables, which represented their bivariate distribution. As we add variables, it becomes more difficult to think in these terms so long as we try to think of all variables at once. If we knew a way to pull them apart, then perhaps our understanding would improve.

Let us return to our example of age at first marriage and schooling, measured as interval variables. We reported a zero-order correlation between the two of 0.325, which is quite close to the statistical estimates of association we calculated after collapsing the two measures into categories. To introduce partials, we will return to the interval metric and examine the process implied by 'partialling'. In fact, the term 'partialling' is descriptive of what we want to accomplish in terms of the covariance, or the semblance of bivariate distributions we have implied. Suppose we are particularly interested in the relationship between age of first marriage and schooling among women in the sample, and we wonder whether the number of pregnancies experienced could be involved in the earlier relationship we observed. It may be that marrying young need not necessarily interfere with schooling, but marrying young could imply a larger number of pregnancies, and it is the pregnancies that make continued schooling impossible. To address that question, what we want is a measure of association between schooling and age at first marriage (in this example, just for women), controlling for the number of pregnancies they have experienced.

What does it mean to say we want to 'control' for number of pregnancies? In the nomenclature of 'partialling out' the effect of pregnancies, we want to rid the covariance between schooling and age at first marriage of the potentially confounding covariance that is shared with number of pregnancies. Although we have already reported the set of zero-order correlations for the sample, in this case we need to reproduce the same correlations for women only. The zero-order correlation coefficient between schooling and number of pregnancies (–0.2609) tells us that 6.8% of the variance in schooling is shared with number of pregnancies, such that more pregnancies are associated with less schooling. Similarly, the correlation coefficient of age at first marriage and number of pregnancies (–0.2681) indicates that 7.2% of the variation in age at first marriage is explained by (overlaps with) the variation in number of pregnancies, such that younger ages of marriage are associated with more pregnancies, on average. What we want to correlate is the remaining 93.2% of the variance in schooling with the remaining 92.8% of the variation in age at first marriage. Then we can see how that correlation coefficient compares to the zero-order coefficient we calculated. This new correlation coefficient is called a first-order partial because we are controlling for one additional variable.[22]

If we denote pregnancies as *P*, schooling as *S*, and age at first marriage by *AFM*, we can calculate the partial correlation coefficient as

$$r_{S,AFM.P} = \frac{r_{S,AFM} - r_{S,P} r_{AFM,P}}{\sqrt{(1 - r_{S,P}^2)(1 - r_{AFM,P}^2)}}.$$

The notation for the term to the left of the equal sign defines the first-order partial correlation between schooling and age at first marriage, controlling for the number of pregnancies the respondent has experienced. To the right of the equal sign we have a combination of all possible zero-order correlations – those between schooling and age at first marriage, between schooling and pregnancies, and between age at first marriage and pregnancies. Consider the denominator first. When we said earlier that we wanted the remaining 91.4% of the variance in schooling and the 92.8% of the variance that remains in age at first marriage, we were describing the kind of operations performed in the denominator. The expression in the first set of parentheses under the radical sign equals 0.914 (expressed as a proportion rather than a percentage). The expression in the second set equals 0.928. To calculate the remaining joint variation we multiply these two terms. To return to standard units we take the square root of the product. Our denominator is therefore $\sqrt{(0.9319 \times 0.9281)} = 0.9300$.

In the numerator, we begin with the zero-order correlation between schooling and age at first marriage (0.782) and then subtract from it the product of the standardized covariance between schooling and pregnancies and between age at first marriage and pregnancies. Our results are as follows:

$$r_{S,\,AFM.P} = \frac{0.3782 - (-0.2609 \times 0.2681)}{0.9300}$$
$$= \frac{0.3083}{0.9300} = 0.3315.$$

This partial correlation coefficient is slightly smaller – by about 12% – than the zero-order correlation coefficient. The reader can see that the pattern of zero-order relationships between the control variable and the two variables of interest plays the crucial role in whether the partial coefficient is smaller, larger, or even the same sign as the zero-order relationship.

As we have noted before, dichotomous variables coded in binary fashion can be used in statistical procedures such as these, although the interpretation of the coefficient must be adapted to the information they convey. To provide a second illustration, we may ask whether the relationship between age at first marriage and schooling is, in essence, a gender difference. Women may marry younger and complete less schooling than men. Therefore, once gender is controlled, we may find that the relationship between schooling and age at first marriage was spurious. We return to the sample of both men and women who have been married at least once during their lifetimes. The zero-order correlation between schooling and age at first marriage is 0.325, between age at first marriage and gender (with women coded 1) is –0.2116, and between schooling and gender is 0.0183. The latter two correlation coefficients actually give us information about the mean values of age at first marriage and of schooling for men and women. The negative coefficient, –0.2116, suggests that women marry younger than men, on average. The very small coefficient 0.0183 suggests the very slightest difference in favor of

women in terms of completed schooling. But in general, we would conclude that men and women had received about equal amounts of schooling. We can now substitute into the partial formula to determine the correlation between schooling and age at first marriage, controlling for gender,

$$r_{S,\,AFM.\;Gender} = \frac{0.3253 - (-0.2116 \times 0.0183)}{\sqrt{(1 - 0.2116^2)(1 - 0.0183^2)}}$$
$$= 0.3369.$$

What we are calculating is the average correlation coefficient across fixed values of the third variable, the 'control' variable. In this case, the partial is marginally larger than the zero-order, and the reader can identify the circumstances that made this possible.[23]

An important lesson for the reader to take from these examples is that controlling for additional variables does not ensure that bivariate relationships will not change. Compared to the zero-order correlation coefficient, the partial may be larger or smaller by sizeable or trivial amounts, and in some cases the sign of the partial may be different from the sign of the zero-order. You are examining a relationship between two variables under different sets of conditions as control variables are added to the process – much as you can evaluate colors under different lights. In daylight a green cloth may take on a particular green hue, but if the lighting changes, the color of same green cloth may shift more toward blue, or more toward yellow. It is being viewed in amended circumstances that are related to the terms of our perception. Using statistics can be quite the same as such mundane acts.

Partial tables

We can make the same type of assessment of a relationship, while controlling for a third variable, in cross-tabular analyses. If we return to our collapsed versions of age at first marriage and completed schooling, controlling for gender requires that we analyze two tables each with five rows and two columns – one table for men and one table for women. In other words, we examine the relationship between age at first marriage and schooling within gender categories. By doing so, we take a step beyond what we accomplished through the partialling procedure,

Table 3.8 *Bivariate distribution of age at first marriage (dichotomized) and years of completed schooling, conditioned on gender*

		Men			Women		
		Age at first marriage			Age at first marriage		
		≤ 20	> 20	Total	≤ 20	> 20	Total
School <12	*Count*	**167**	**257**	424	**268**	**135**	403
	% within age	(25.9)	(10.8)	14.0%	(18.9)	(6.7)	11.8%
12	*Count*	**359**	**1016**	1375	**773**	**684**	1457
	% within age	(55.6)	(42.6)	45.4%	(54.4)	(34.2)	42.6%
13–15	*Count*	**97**	**538**	635	**309**	**588**	897
	% within age	(15.0)	(22.6)	21.0%	(21.7)	(29.4)	26.2%
16	*Count*	**18**	**333**	351	**45**	**383**	428
	% within age	(2.8)	(14.0)	11.6%	(3.2)	(19.1)	12.5%
17	*Count*	**5**	**240**	245	**26**	**211**	237
	% within age	(0.8)	(10.1)	8.1%	(1.8)	(10.5)	6.9%
Total		646	2384	3030	1421	2001	3422

$$\chi^2 = 224.279 \qquad \chi^2 = 462.423$$
$$\text{Somer's } d = 0.360 \qquad \text{Somer's } d = 0.401$$
$$\text{Gamma} = 0.517 \qquad \text{Gamma} = 0.549$$
$$\tau_b = 0.248 \qquad \tau_b = 0.330$$
$$\text{Spearman's } \rho = 0.271 \qquad \text{Spearman's } \rho = 0.360$$

Source: Author's calculations, using NLSY data

when we simply held to the side the covariance with gender. Here, our 'control' for gender is to examine the *within-gender* relationships. By doing so, we can assess not only whether the relationship was spurious (i.e., whether the relationship 'disappears' once we look within gender categories), but whether the relationship is the same for men and women. This is the question of *interaction*: whether the relationship is the *same or different* across categories of a third variable. In our example, is the relationship between schooling and age at first marriage *the same or different* for men and women? We could speculate, for example, that marrying at a young age could have more profound effects on continued schooling for women than for men. If that is the case, then the relationship should be stronger among women than among men. If there is no interaction, the relationship would be the same for men and women.

By examining the conditional percentage distributions (the within-column percentages) in Table 3.8, it is clear that less schooling is completed by both men and women who married young. We can also see from the marginal distributions on age (the column totals) that proportionately more women than men married at ages up to 20. But the quantification of the strength of the relationship is contained in the statistics at the bottom of the table. In all cases, the values for women are higher than they are for men. The difference is particularly

notable in the values of τ_b and Spearman's rho. Therefore, in the analysis of this table of sample data, we have information consistent with an interaction effect.

Interactions with interval variables Had we wanted to test for an interaction effect using the same variables in interval metric, we could have taken several approaches. The approach most similar to the one above is to calculate the zero-order correlation coefficient separately for men and women. This question is significantly different from the question we asked before. When we controlled for gender, we were asking whether the relationship between completed schooling and age at first marriage was either spurious or indirect. If spurious, we would conclude that the observed bivariate relationship was, in fact, due to some third factor, which was positively correlated with both schooling and age. If an indirect relationship, we might conclude that the effect of early marriage was carried by number of pregnancies, for example, which could intervene between age at first marriage and schooling.

To infer that a control variable actually intervenes in the relationship by linking the independent and dependent variables, we must show that the control variable is associated with both independent and dependent variables. Second, when we control for variation in this third variable, we must show that the original bivariate relationship reduces to or near zero. These are the same conditions as required for concluding that a relationship is spurious. In this, as in many other circumstances, the statistical test may be identical. It is the interpretation that differs. In a spurious relationship, the control variable severs the relationship between independent and dependent variables. An intervening variable clarifies the relationship between independent and dependent variable, often by providing an answer (if only partial) to the question of what mechanism translates early marriage (in our example) to lower levels of schooling.

We noted earlier that the zero-order correlation coefficient between age at first marriage and completed schooling is 0.325, which was calculated for both men and women. Next we calculated the partial correlation coefficient between schooling and age at first marriage, controlling for gender, as 0.337. We noted that, in this case, we were averaging the relationship between schooling and age at first marriage across groups, in this case an average of men and women. Now we are interested in the bivariate relationship between schooling and age at first marriage, calculated within gender groups, separately for men and women. We find $r_{S,AFM}$ for men equals 0.292, and $r_{S,AFM}$ for women equals 0.376. We can reconcile these results with the previous results by noting that the weighted average of these gender-specific rs is, in fact, equal to

$$r_{S,AFM.\,Gender} = \frac{r_{men}\, n_{men} + r_{women}\, n_{women}}{n_{men} + n_{women}}$$
$$= \frac{0.292 \times 3030 + 0.376 \times 3422}{3030 + 3422}$$
$$= 0.337.$$

We can compare the r for men and women and notice that they are different for this sample. Therefore, we again have evidence of an interaction effect – that the relationship between schooling and age at first marriage is stronger for women than for men.

We can approach this same issue by comparing mean schooling by age at first marriage (dichotomized) by gender. By generating a different sort of 2 × 2 table, we can describe both marginal and conditional distributions (Table 3.9). Cell entries will be the

Table 3.9 *Mean number of years of completed schooling, conditioned on age at first marriage (dichotomized) and gender*

	AFM ≤ 20	AFM > 20	
Men	11.68 (0.007 45)	13.30 (0.005 18)	12.96 (0.004 54)
Women	12.00 (0.005 35)	13.79 (0.005 30)	13.05 (0.0041)
	11.90 (0.004 36)	13.52 (0.003 73)	13.00 (0.0030)

Source: Author's calculations, using NLSY data
Note: Standard deviations and number of cases in parentheses

mean value of completed schooling for the designated group. Shaded cells report mean values for gender-by-age groups; normally bordered cells in the far right column report mean years of schooling by gender; normally bordered cells in the bottom row report mean years of schooling by age at first marriage; and the heavily bordered cell at bottom right is the mean years of schooling for all respondents married at least once.

This table allows us to review some of the sample-based conclusions we have drawn so far. If we wonder whether men and women who have been married differ in completed schooling, the statistic we want is one that offers a comparison of the mean values for men and women. The *difference in means* $(\bar{X}_{men} - \bar{X}_{women})$ is therefore the statistic we require, since it quantifies the similarity versus dissimilarity in the two measures. A difference of 0.09 seems trivial, so we conclude that these values are equivalent. If we wondered whether those who married at 20 or younger averaged different amounts of schooling than those who married beyond age 20, we need the statistic $(\bar{X}_{AFM \leq 20} - \bar{X}_{AFM > 20})$, which equals 1.62, a more substantial difference in outcome. Finally, we might ask the question whether the age at first marriage is associated with a smaller difference in completed schooling among men than among women. This question is once again a question of interaction, since we are speculating about the strength (or existence) of a relationship on varying conditions (here, gender). In this case, our statistic is a difference of differences: $(11.68 - 13.30) - (12.00 - 13.79) =$ $1.62 - 1.79 = -0.17$. The difference is larger for women, but not by less than one-fifth of a year, which does not seem to be a very noteworthy difference.

All of these mathematical maneuvers have therefore led us to a crucial decision point: how large is large enough? That question must be answered at two levels. The first level is one that we have been addressing throughout the chapter: is it large enough to matter? In this last exercise, we decided that the gender difference in schooling (0.09) was not large enough to matter, that the age at first marriage difference (1.62) was large enough to consider the two 'different'; and in this last case, that −0.17 was not sufficiently large to believe in the interaction effect. In other words, marrying young cut short completed school in an equivalent way for men and women. The boundaries of 'large' cannot be made uniform across all research settings or across all scales of measurement. Instead, it is a matter of judgment informed by the theory motivating the analysis. That means that people may see it differently, so the researcher is required not only to calculate the statistic, but to interpret it. Interpretation requires argument; arguments are based on concepts; concepts derive from theory. The researcher's work is not completed in the calculation of arrays of numbers. It is the story that is evidenced in the numbers that must be presented persuasively that makes the analysis complete. But to the extent that social researchers are interested in unraveling the processes that produce different outcomes under varying circumstances for persons (or states, or organizations, or families) with varying characteristics, dispositions, and abilities, one way to answer the question of effect size is to turn to significance of another sort.

For example, if you determine that earnings are a function of education, then imagine that you are making the argument for a program that would increase the level of education of some portion of your sample by year of schooling or by credential: How much more would you expect them to earn? In using our estimates to make individual predictions, we introduce wider ranges because of possible error. But if you find yourself believing that a reasonable person would judge the difference in outcome as hardly worth the effort, then your 'effect' is not large enough.

The second level of the question – how large is large enough – is a theoretical question of another source. Based in sampling theory, these are the questions of inferential statistics. Answering this set of questions allows us to go beyond a description of our sample to statements about the population from which it was drawn. These issues will be developed in Chapter 4, in which the reader will be introduced to a new level of distributions which are not directly observed, but which are vital to our ability to make statements about our world. These distributions are distributions of the statistics themselves, and the inferential process is one in which we evaluate our sample statistics within the context of their theoretical distributions. The question of sufficient size is, within that context, a question of the size of the observed statistic relative to the size of the sampling error that irrevocably shadows it. The larger the shadow, the larger the statistic must be for us to note it; the smaller the shadow (the brighter the light), the better we can discern what in numerical magnitude may appear small, but may inform our understanding of the processes we study.

In the latter context, we are concerned that our estimates are sufficiently reliable for us to believe that we have identified a connection between some characteristic and an outcome. Once we are satisfied that the criterion of reliability has been met, we can move on to asking what the consequences of this connection are within a given context. If, for example, we are investigating how much arsenic there is in our drinking water, our first concern must be to provide a reliable quantification of 'how much'. Having done that, the obvious follow-up question is: Is that a little, a lot, too much? This question is answerable only once you establish the context for evaluation. An economic context may be to balance the cost of reducing the level of arsenic with the expected decline in the prevalence of symptoms and illness for human beings. An environmentalist context may be to consider other forms of life in this equation. A parental context may be to switch to bottled water.

Distributional consequences of variable transformations

This discussion is of two parts. The first is to demonstrate how the moments of a univariate distribution and a standardized measure of a bivariate distribution, r, are affected by the addition, subtraction, multiplication, and division by a constant. The second is to illustrate the distributional consequences of some

Table 3.10   *Summary statistics for age at first marriage, and its various transformations*

AFM	Mean	Median	Range	Variance	St. Dev.	Skewness	Kurtosis	$r_{School, AFM}$
original	22.925	22.000	24	17.335	4.1636	0.501	−0.231	0.325
+10	32.925	32.000	24	17.335	4.1636	0.501	−0.231	0.325
−10	12.925	12.000	24	17.335	4.1636	0.501	−0.231	0.325
×10	229.25	220.00	240	1733.54	41.636	0.501	−0.231	0.325
÷10	2.2925	2.200	2.4	0.173	0.4164	0.501	−0.231	0.325
AFM − $\overline{AFM}$	0.000	−0.925	24	17.335	4.1636	0.501	−0.231	0.325
ln(AFM)	3.1161	3.091	1.05	0.032	0.1794	0.100	−0.482	0.339
√AFM	4.7686	4.690	2.48	0.185	0.4301	0.301	−0.417	0.333
Z_{AFM}	0	−0.222	5.764	1.00	1.00	0.501	−0.231	0.325

Source: Author's calculations, using NLSY data

variable transformations commonly used in analysis.

To describe a statistic as scale-invariant means that it is not changed by mathematical transformations. In Table 3.10, we can determine which statistics are scale-invariant and whether changes in remaining statistics can be anticipated. For this exercise, we are using the age at first marriage variable. We begin with age at first marriage (AFM) in its original metric of years of age. This is followed by AFM + 10, AFM − 10, AFM × 10, AFM/10, AFM as a mean deviate, the natural log of AFM, the square root of AFM, and the z-transformation of AFM. The columns of the table are defined by two measures of central tendency (mean, median), three measures of dispersion (range, variance, standard deviation), a measure of symmetry (skewness), a measure of peakedness (kurtosis), and a measure of association, r, with years of completed schooling.

We will withhold discussion of the natural log and square-root transformations for the moment. As for the rest, recall that the mean is based on the value of each observation, therefore increasing or decreasing each observation by a constant or multiplying or dividing by a constant, in this case 10, will have the same effect on the mean. By subtracting the value of the mean, 22.925, from each observation we create unit deviate scores. This transformation is often called 'recentering the distribution', since we shift the number line underlying the distribution to the right by 22.925 years of age. The mean value of the recentered distribution is zero. Calculation of the z-score standardizes these mean deviates relative to the amount of dispersion in the distribution, dividing the mean deviate by the standard deviation. The units of this z-distribution are no longer 'years of age', but

standard deviations, each of which is equal to 4.1636 years of age in this sample distribution. Clearly the mean is not scale-invariant.

Nor is the median. Although it relies only on information of rank ordering, it reports the value of the middle case. Therefore, adding, subtracting, multiplying or dividing the distribution by a constant will yield a median that is mathematically related to the median of the original metric distribution in the same way the transformed observations are related to their original values. Measures of central tendency, therefore, change as the scale of measurement changes, with typical or average values reflecting that measurement scale.

What happens with measures of dispersion? Since two of the three measures of dispersion are based on the mean (that is, they include the mean value in their calculation), we might expect measures of dispersion to also shift with measurement scale. Scale invariance of measures of dispersion depends on what type of transformation is performed. If we simply add or subtract a constant, as we do in rows 2, 3 and 6, we do not alter the shape of the distribution. Even though we have rescaled the values of observation, each observation stands relative to all other observations as it did originally. Therefore, the range, variance and standard deviation are the same for these three distributions.

Not so when we multiply or divide by a constant. In that case, we do alter the relative standing of each observation. Observations that differed by one unit in the original distribution (row 1) differ by 10 units (row 4) or by one-tenth of a unit (row 5). We see this difference reflected in the range, which spans 240 units (row 4) compared to 2.4 units (row 5). When we compare variances, the differences are larger. To the extent that we identify measures of dispersion with heterogeneity or inequality in the distribution, multiplying by a constant, c, increases inequality by a factor of c^2. Therefore, the variance in row 4 is 100 times the variance in row 1, and the variance in row 5 is 0.01 times the variance in row 1. Multiplicative transformations are not uncommon in research. For example, if the researcher begins with a salary distribution at time t, and in each subsequent year workers receive a constant across-the-board wage increase of 3%, the longer the process continues, the greater the differences between the 'best' paid and the 'worst' paid will be. In contrast, if the constant across-the-board raise is $1000, the variance of the distribution will remain the same as the entire wage distribution shifts upward by $1000 each year.

Since the standard deviation is the square root of the variance, it increases or decreases concomitantly with the range, by a factor of c. Within a regression format, we might divide a variable such as 'dollar monthly earnings' by 100 or by 1000, so we would express earnings as hundreds or thousands of dollars. Generally, we do not argue that a $1 difference in earnings will lead to a different outcome, but a $1000 difference in monthly earnings may well make a difference to the quality of life and financial security of the person.

As noted earlier, the z-transformation is designed to produce a variance and standard deviation equal to 1.00, and so it does in this case. The range, 5.764, is equal to the range of the original distribution, 24, divided by the standard deviation of the original distribution, 4.1636, which is to say that the original range of 24 years of age has been transformed to a range of 5.764 standard deviations in age at first marriage.

Perhaps the most surprising results for the reader are in the last three columns. Skewness and kurtosis are the same regardless of adding, subtracting, multiplying, dividing, or z-transforming. Under all these types of distributional amendments, neither the measure of symmetry nor the measure of peakedness changes. One point to take from this part of the illustration is that, although the z-transformation is associated with a standard normal distribution, z-transformed distributions are no different from the original distribution in terms of symmetry. In this example, the illustration of the frequency distribution of age at first marriage indicates a small amount of positive skew. The mean is almost one year 'older' than the median, which suggests that more

observations lie to the left of the mean than to the right: a larger proportion of respondents married at 22.925 or younger than married at older ages. The consistent value of 0.501 for skewness (rather than a value of 0.00) indicates a slight positive skew as well. That degree of asymmetry is retained in the z-transformed distribution. Therefore, one use of the standard normal distribution – calculating probabilities based on the area under the curve – is not quite accurate in this situation.

Finally, how do these transformations affect the bivariate distribution with a second variable? For the transformations we have discussed so far, the answer is 'not at all'. The zero-order correlation coefficient, 0.325, incorporates not only the covariance between AFM, however it is scaled, and schooling, but adjusts for each distribution's dispersion, which is to say that adjustments of multiplication and division cancel each other out.

The remaining two transformations, the natural logarithm and the square root, are among the options in Tukey's (1977) 'ladder of expressions'. We have noted in passing that variables whose distributions are normal (or near normal) can be a precondition for the use of certain statistics. We also noted that the measures of association of interval variables, which we explored in this chapter, are measures of linear association. When analyzing data, it sometimes is necessary to transform variables for the purpose of generating a distribution that more closely approximates the normal distribution. Both the natural logarithm and the square-root transformation reduce the amount of skewness in a distribution, the former more than the latter, as we can see from the table. Taking the natural logarithm compresses the range to 1.05 units, whereas the range for the square-root transformation is more than twice that number. But the logarithm produces greater symmetry, yielding a skewness measure of only 0.10 compared to 0.301 for the square root. The correlation coefficient with schooling is somewhat larger for both these transformed variables, with little difference between them. Nevertheless, the general conclusion is that in this example, the strength of relationship is consistent across all transformations.

Ratios and difference scores

Examples of other common types of variable transformations involve the construction of ratio variables and difference scores. Whereas the previous transformations we discussed resulted in rather predictable changes in measures of central tendency, dispersion, and correlation, this is not the case with either ratio variables or difference scores. Although a wide range of possible expressions exist, some of the more common forms of ratio variables include expressing values as proportions of the whole and expressing values as per-capita measures. One point researchers occasionally forget when defining a ratio variable is that the zero point must be theoretically supportable rather than simply a mathematical artifact of the calculation. Similarly, difference terms have been used in mobility research to measure movement from origin to destination statuses, which were then correlated with the initial (origin) status; and they were used to calculate the association between mobility over two adjacent time periods, e.g., (second job – first job) correlated with (third job – second job).[24]

When calculating correlation coefficients between variables that include one or more ratios, the researcher must exercise caution in interpretation (Fuguitt and Lieberson, 1973). Consider the following examples of correlations between: A/B and B, where A is the number of women employees and B is the total number of employees in the firm; in this case the correlation coefficient is between $A(1/B)$ and B. Or A/C and B/C, where A is gross national product, B is total national debt, and C is population size; here, we can think of correlating $A(1/C)$ and $B(1/C)$. Or A/B and B/C, where A is the number of home owners with paid-off mortgages, B is the number of home owners, and C is the adult population, which again builds inverse terms of $1/B$ and B into the correlation.

In calculating the zero-order correlations in these cases, the fact that variables have common terms creates the potential for spurious correlation[25] and misinterpretation. An important distinction for the researcher to make is whether one's focal interest is on the ratio or difference score – as a measure of some population characteristic – or whether one's primary interest is in the component measures, recognizing the importance of including certain controls in the assessment process. In general, when correlation coefficients are calculated for ratios or difference scores, which contain a common element in both variables, part of the empirical correlation may be attributable to that common element. As Fuguitt and Lieberson (1973: 138, 141) note:

> Since only under … special conditions are ratio or difference-score correlations equivalent to corresponding part or partial correlations, one would seldom be justified in using the former as a substitute for the latter. Problems can be reformulated in terms of component variables, or in any event the relation between the components and the composite variables may be profitably explored.

SUMMARY

In this chapter, we have explored a range of statistics that can be used to describe univariate and bivariate distributions. A major goal of data analysis, however, is to use what we know about a sample to make statements about the population from which the sample was drawn. Taking that next step moves us from descriptive statistics to inferential statistics, which necessarily involves the process of probability. Descriptive statistics can be calculated on any sample, regardless of how it was drawn, to provide an accounting of what was observed. While that information may be interesting, we cannot move beyond *that particular sample* unless we know how that sample was generated. The kind of knowledge required includes the selection processes that resulted in this one particular set of observations. To the extent that the selection processes can be described probabilistically, we can use sample statistics to formulate statements about the population by again invoking probability. It is through that reasoning process, the process of inference, that we learn about our world.

ACKNOWLEDGMENTS

The author wishes to acknowledge the helpful comments of Stanley Lieberson, Lawrence Hazelrigg, Alan Bryman, and John Reynolds, as well as the valuable instruction provided by Karl Schuessler.

NOTES

1 However, negative values of x are possible, depending on what you are measuring or the metric you use. When negative values occur, the frequency

curve must extend to both the right and the left of the y-axis, since the y-axis intersects the x-axis at the point (0, 0).

2 Percentiles locate observations in distributions by dividing an ordered sample of observations into 100 parts. The ith percentile is defined as $(in/100)$, where i is the percentile of interest and n is the number of cases. Here, the 50th percentile would be the value associated with the $50 \times 8831/100 = 4415.5$th case. If we require the value of the 50th percentile for a continuous variable, then we add the values for the 4415th and 4416th cases and divide by 2, so that the value associated with the 50th percentile is the average of these two cases. If instead we require the 50th percentile for a discrete variable, we need the value of the 4416th case in the ranked array. The general procedure is to determine which case occupies the appropriate rank in the data array and then look at the variable's value for that case.

Percentiles are useful measures when we want to know an observation's relative position within an ordered data array. A score that represents the 10th percentile is a score that is higher than 10% of the observations, but less than 90% of the observations. Because percentile values transform the actual score into a value of relative position, percentiles are often used as a way of standardizing observations.

3 For example, those analyzing census data have long noted a tendency to 'round' age to the lower decade marker for those in their 'early' 20s or 30s or 40s.

4 Because both mean and median can be calculated for interval/ratio measures, we can choose which measure of central tendency best suits our data. Because the mean uses all the observed information available – the actual score – we might ask whether circumstances arise when use of the actual score proves misleading. In fact, when we have extreme scores existing at one end (e.g., the 'high' end) or the other end (e.g., the 'low' end) of the distribution, using the actual scores tends to pull the mean in the direction of the extreme scores. Under these circumstances, the mean no longer provides a midpoint in the distribution, and is therefore less desirable as a measure of central tendency than the median.

5 The index A_w is essentially the same as Gini's index of mutability, Bachi's (1956) index of linguistic homogeneity, Simpson's (1949) measure of diversity, the P^* index used by Bell (1954), and the measure of industrial diversification suggested by Gibbs and Martin (1962), with the acknowledgment that some authors prefer to emphasize agreement, as in $(1-A_w)$, rather than diversity, A_w.

6 We specify the arithmetic mean because there are other ways of defining the mean, including the geometric mean and the harmonic mean. Although less often used, both the geometric mean and the harmonic mean can be useful for certain types of problems. For example, the geometric mean can be useful in calculating average rate of change and is appropriate for a set of n positive numbers. It is calculated as the nth root of their product, but is more often expressed in a more tractable mathematical form, the logarithm, since the logarithm of the geometric mean is equal to the mean of the logarithms of the observed values. The harmonic mean is calculated as n divided by the sum of the reciprocals of the observed values. For example, if one spends 6 hours making widgets that take 10 minutes each and one's co-worker spends 6 hours making widgets at 15 minutes each, then the average production of widgets can be found using the harmonic mean: $2/(1/10 + 1/15) = 2/(1/6) = 12$, so the average time to make a widget is 12 minutes, and the average worker should be able to make 5 widgets per hour.

7 This concept will be discussed in Chapter 4 on inference and invoked repeatedly throughout the text. Strictly speaking, since we are concerned in this chapter with descriptive statistics rather than inferential statistics, adjusting for degrees of freedom in calculating the variance is not necessary. The adjustment corrects for the downward bias in the sample estimate of the population variance. Unfortunately, making those types of distinctions generally causes more confusion than understanding, which is why the presentation here foreshadows some of the issues motivating the next chapter.

8 This point often causes confusion, since those learning statistics are often looking for shorthand ways to remember what the different statistics measure. Given that we use 'average' as a synonym for 'mean', the standard deviation is not equal to the 'average' deviation from the mean. Recall that one name for the variance is 'mean squared error', where 'error' is a synonym for 'deviation'. In other words, the standard deviation is the square root of the mean squared error, whereas the 'average deviation' is simply the sum of the unsigned (absolute value of) differences from the mean divided by n. In practice, then, the standard deviation is always larger in value than the average deviation, since the standard deviation gives proportionately more weight to larger deviations from the mean. For our weight variable, for example, the standard deviation is 39.35; the average deviation is 30.80. The difference between the two measures tends to be greater in skewed distributions, as in total net family income, which has a standard deviation of $36 453 and an average deviation of $24 120.

9 It is also referred to as the Gaussian distribution, crediting Karl Gauss (1777–1855) for its discovery, or the normal curve of error. Although Pierre-Simon de Laplace (1749–1827) is credited by some with its discovery, many statisticians now believe that Abraham de Moivre (1667–1754) was the first to grasp the normal distribution, since he published a table of values for the normal curve that are almost identical to those currently published (Kirk, 1972).

10 When a bivariate distribution is mentioned, we are usually referring to a bivariate normal distribution. In a bivariate normal distribution of $X_1 X_2$, the distributions

of both variables, X_1 and X_2, are normal. In addition, for any given value of X_1, the values of X_2 are normally distributed, and vice versa.

11 Note that the formulas for z-transformed variables simplify to these because the mean of a z-distribution equals 0, therefore deviations from the mean are the z-scores themselves.

12 Reference to the areas of the standard normal distribution will allow the reader to reproduce these results.

13 The term 'product moment' derives from the fact that when the correlation coefficient is calculated for z-scores, the numerator is the 'product' of the z-scores, and dividing by $n-1$ produces the *mean* of the products (or the first moment of the distribution of products).

14 The term 'zero-order' applies to bivariate correlation coefficients, also sometimes called 'gross' correlation coefficients, because these measures do not 'control' for the covariance of any additional variables. Notation for the correlation coefficient generally indicates the variables involved in the correlation in the subscript to the correlation symbol, r. Within the subscript, a distinction is made between which variables are being correlated and which, if any, variables are being controlled by placing the variables being controlled after a period. For example, a bivariate correlation between X_1 and X_2 would be represented by r_{12} or r_{21}, since correlations are symmetrical measures of association. A correlation between X_1 and X_3 is r_{13}; however a partial correlation between X_1 and X_2, controlling for X_3, is denoted as $r_{12.3}$. A correlation such as r_{12} is a zero-order correlation coefficient because there are zero variables being controlled and therefore no period nor any variables listed after the period, whereas $r_{12.3}$ is a first-order partial correlation, since one variable, X_3, is being controlled when we assess the relationship between X_1 and X_2. Should we also want to control for X_4, the second-order partial correlation would be represented as $r_{12.34}$.

15 The number of cases differs for each pair of variables because of the patterns of missing data. Chapter 5 on missing data (Jamshidian) provides the reader with strategies for addressing the missing data generated by a variety of processes. In our case, missing data are generated in some variables because of refusals to provide the information (e.g., income); in other cases they could be introduced by a variable transformation (see earlier discussion on calculating the natural logarithm of family income). Finally, some of our missing data occur because the respondent did not exhibit (or is not capable of exhibiting) a specific behavior linked to the measure. For example, someone who is not yet married cannot report an age of first marriage. As a second example, for obvious reasons men were not asked the number of their previous pregnancies. To include information for them on this variable would require us to code zeros for all men, which would create an artificial (and artifactual) lumping of cases at zero, swamping the zero codes for women who have not yet been pregnant. In the first example, the pattern

of missingness is problematic. In the second example, 'filling in' the missing data would create a problem not otherwise present.

16 In fact, if we do find that 84% of women are employed, the same would *have* to hold for men for the marginal distribution (the distribution of the sample as a whole) to hold true. Conversely, it can be demonstrated that when we have two groups grossly unequal in size, such that the number of men is almost the same as the total number of respondents, then the proportions for men and the proportion for the total sample will be almost the same (since the 'part' of the total sample comprised of men is so near to being the 'whole'), and the proportion for women will be freer to vary from the total.

17 Even though we cannot have 7/10 of a person, we generally calculate expected frequencies to at least one decimal place for added precision in the calculation of the chi-square statistic.

18 Notice that in determining cell frequencies expected under the condition of independence, we do not alter the marginal distributions of gender or of employment. We simply rearrange respondents within the cells as we would expect to observe them if, in fact, employment and gender were independent.

19 These issues receive more attention in subsequent chapters on regression, models for categorical variables, and structural equation models.

20 The value of γ is higher than other measures of association, indicating a stronger relationship than other measures suggest. The reason for this discrepancy is that the calculation of γ excludes pairs that are tied, that is, pairs that have the same value on age at first marriage, but a different level of schooling, or pairs that married at different ages, but nevertheless completed the same level of schooling. In other words, the more pairs that are 'tied', the more the value of γ can be inflated by their exclusion. Both Somer's d and Kendall's τ_b address this limitation, but in somewhat different ways.

21 In fact, the value of ρ_S is the same as the product moment correlation calculated on the ranked data, assuming one used the rankings as the values.

22 Again, the caution of unsubstantiated causal interpretations is worth noting.

23 Since the zero-order relationships between the control variable and the two variables of interest were of opposite sign, the numerator becomes larger than the zero-order coefficient was by itself. Couple that with the fact that the denominator cannot be larger than 1, but depending on the strength of the relationships between the control variable and the others, the denominator can be notably less than one, the resultant partial will be larger than the zero-order coefficient.

24 Blau and Duncan (1967: 194–9) were critical of the use of difference-score correlations in mobility research. They argued that it was preferable to state research problems in terms of the component variables.

25 Pearson defined a *spurious correlation* as one that was based on the variances of the individual variables,

even though all component correlations were zero (Fuguitt and Lieberson, 1973).

REFERENCES

Bachi, Roberto (1956) 'A statistical analysis of the revival of Hebrew in Israel', in Roberto Bachi (ed.), *Studies in Economic and Social Sciences*, Scripta Hierosolymitana, Vol. III. Jerusalem: Magnus Press.

Bell, Wendell (1954) 'A probability model for the measurement of ecological segregation', *Social Forces*, 32: 357–64.

Blau, Peter M. and Duncan, Otis D. (1967) *The American Occupational Structure*. New York: Wiley.

Fuguitt, Glenn V. and Lieberson, Stanley (1973) 'Correlation of ratios or difference scores having common terms', *Sociological Methodology*, 5: 128–44.

Gibbs, Jack P. and Martin, Walter T. (1962) 'Urbanization, technology and the division of labor: International patterns', *American Sociological Review*, 27: 667–77.

Goodman, Leo A. and Kruskal, William H. (1954) 'Measure of association for cross classification', *Journal of the American Statistical Association*, 49: 732–64.

Kirk, Roger E. (1972) *Statistical Issues: A Reader for the Behavioral Sciences*. Monterey, CA: Brooks/Cole.

Lieberson, Stanley (1969) 'Measuring population diversity', *American Sociological Review*, 34: 850–62.

Lieberson, Stanley (1976) 'Rank-sum comparisons between groups', *Sociological Methodology*, 7: 276–91.

Mueller, John H. and Schuessler, Karl F. (1961) *Statistical Reasoning in Sociology*. Boston: Houghton Mifflin.

Simpson, E.H. (1949) 'Measurement of diversity', *Nature*, 163: 688.

Tukey, John W. (1977) *Exploratory Data Analysis*. Reading, MA: Addison-Wesley.

Wilcoxon, F. (1945) 'Individual comparisons by ranking methods', *Biometrics Bulletin*, 1: 80–3.

Wilcoxon, F. (1947) 'Probability tables for individual comparisons by ranking methods', *Biometrics* 3: 119–22.

4

Inference

LAWRENCE HAZELRIGG

A goal of data analysis is to produce information that will aid in making decisions about hypothesized states of the world. Information, both as product and as the process that results in that product, involves a number of very basic and unexceptional sorts of action, among which observation, sampling, classification, measurement, estimation, and decision-making itself are simply inescapable. Inseparable from each of those, inference is therefore manifoldly integral to the production of information.

In most general terms, inference is a process of arriving at a conclusion (which, as product of the process, is also called an inference). Standard English usage has distinguished 'infer' from 'imply', in accordance with their Latin roots, at least since the days of Sir Thomas More. An *implication* is a conclusion that follows by necessity from, by involvement in, or by reference to that from which it comes. An *inference* is an inherently more problematic conclusion. If I imply something by a remark I make to you, I cannot be wrong about what I have implied (even if, by some external standard, the logic of my implication is faulty). You, on the other hand, in trying to infer from the remark my implied meaning, may draw an incorrect conclusion (even when the logic of my implication is perfectly sound). By extension, if someone proposes a substantive theory of some patch of reality, that theory entails *by logic* certain specific implications; insofar as the theory is correct, the implications are correct. But anyone's inferences from the meanings of

one's *experiences* to any meaningfulness beneath or behind those experiences are inherently problematic and therefore offer only dubious evidence concerning claims of equipollence between the theory's implications and that to which they refer.

No process is more basic to modern science than inference. But it is also an entirely ordinary activity, the same kind of process whether performed as an action of scientific research or as any 'everyday action'. The difference of this latter distinction is quantitative, not qualitative. Actions of scientific research are supposed to accord by design with core values of modern science. These values include: *empiricism* (knowledge grounded in experience); *experimentalism* (the grounding can be best achieved, when ethically allowable, by systematically manipulating or interfering with components of experience); *scepticism* (because human action, including inference, is inherently fallible, the outcome of even the most carefully reasoned action is always open to doubt); and *publicity* (scientific inquiry is a public good, not the preserve of any private or privileged individual, group, or segment of society, and the self-criticism implied by scepticism can be enforced only when all claims of knowledge *and the processes by which they are produced* are exposed to public scrutiny). These values are not unique to modern science; they are shared by broader cultures of modernity as well. To the extent that there is a difference, it is that the method of modern science urges an even more assiduous, self-conscious practice of those values.

Like any other human activity, inference is historical. This chapter is concerned with inference as its principles and limits are understood today, which is to say a description primarily of theoretical principles pertaining to sets of highly important behaviors in modern society.[1] The account proceeds with a brief review of the conceptual context and development of the problem of inference. Attention then turns sequentially to each of the two most important exercises of inference in scientific research – observational inference and statistical inference. The bulk of the chapter is devoted to statistical inference, but because it would be misleading to leave the impression that inference is only or mainly about 'tests of statistical significance', the discussion proceeds first through an admittedly cursory and incomplete review of issues of observational inference, which are present in any investigation long before the question of 'significance testing' arises. Problems of inference when the range and conditions of observability and the range and conditions of causality do not overlap perfectly continue to be central to scientific inquiry, in sociocultural as well as physical domains (e.g., Kerszberg, 1989; Schaie, 1996: 36; Sobel, 1995). These problems are touched upon in later chapters.

HOW DID NEWTON KNOW THAT?

If modern science and the larger cultures it has increasingly informed were to be characterized by a *single* paradigmatic question, one of the leading candidates would be this: 'What must the world be like, in order that I have the experiences I do have?' It is the question posed by Immanuel Kant, toward the end of the eighteenth century, when explaining Isaac Newton's achievements 100 years earlier (see Kant, 1952). Newton's mathematical encapsulation of the dynamical relationships among bodies as disparate as an apple, a planet, and its moon, across distances then far beyond the ordinary human scale, had been simply astonishing. A statement as spare as $F = k(m_1 m_2 / d^2)$ – in words, that the force of attraction between two objects is directly proportional to their masses, m_1 and m_2, and inversely proportional to the square of the distance d between them (where k is the constant of proportionality) – applied without exception, anywhere at any time, in

places where no human had ever been and at times when humans did not exist. No one had demonstrated any direct experience, in what had been the ordinary sense of 'experience', with such distant bodies and the effects they might have on one another. Yet Newton had demonstrated that the *necessary connection* of the causation of motion (which neither Newton nor anyone else could ever observe) lay not in some property inherent to a body (e.g., *anima, vis, virtus*), nor in a motive force contributed from a source external to the object, but in properties inherent to the *relationship* of conjunctive objects. And, astonishingly, the results of Newton's calculations worked. They made sense, in a unified way, of so many different kinds and scales of experience; and the sense they made could be registered not merely in an idiom of theory but also, and with growing abundance and power, in the practical idioms of experimentation and invention.

Newton's experience of the moon was just that, *an experience*, a set of sense perceptions, and not the moon as it is in itself, independently of any observations of it. An object as it is in itself is necessarily an existence other than in terms of human conception and sense perception; therefore, that existence is permanently beyond the bounds of conception or perception. Neither Newton nor anyone else can validate the congruence of sense perception with *any* object as it is in itself, whether that object be huge or tiny, near or far.[2] And yet Kant had no doubt that Newton's equations were correct. More generally, that is, he did not doubt that experience of a natural object is a consequence not only of the apparatus of experience but also of a reality beyond that apparatus, even though that reality is closed to human experience. Newton could know what he did know, because he could *infer* from a set of effects (his experiences) back to their hidden causes – that is, to answers to the question 'What would cause these effects?'.

The core problem and mandate of modern science were thereby set out, and developments of scientific research and theorization were guided accordingly, for the most part, during the next two centuries. Because Kant's description of the limits of the scientific program explicitly left proposals of 'a science of society' or 'human affairs' stillborn (e.g., Kant, 1974), debates about those limits and what could be delivered within them grew more pressing (e.g., the famous 'methods controversy' of the late nineteenth and early twentieth centuries), even as the sciences of nature flourished and grew ever more powerful (e.g., Stich, 1990; Stigler, 1986).

The inference paradigm of modern science is enormously demanding in its requirements. 'What must reality be, that I have the experiences I do have?' The answer to that question, achieved inferentially, always comes as a mixture of two sorts of ingredient. In principle, we can think of the answer as composed of two discriminable parts, as described below. In practice, the mixture is highly resistant to efforts of separation.

One part refers to the *action* and *apparatus* of human experience – that is, to the incontrovertible fact that, for any actor, it is *I* who am having the experience, here and now, from this standpoint, with these actions and tools of experiencing, all of which is productive of the experience I do have. Insofar as the action and apparatus of experience are productive of effects exclusive of the external causes of experience, an experience contains an 'error component' (classification error, measurement error, sampling error, specification error, as discussed below). While there have been, and are, human beings who claim error-free experiences, few of us are so devoid of scepticism as to imagine that our acts are infallible. The 'error component' is necessarily, though often not obviously, present. It is the part that stems from an observer's decisions and actions. In principle, therefore, it can be directly manipulated, perhaps reduced, and its effects on subsequent decisions managed.

Of course, that is not the part in which we are primarily interested. The more interesting part of the answer – sometimes called the 'true component', but by whatever name necessary unless we are content with the solipsism (and incoherence) of believing that reality as it exists independently of any observer nonetheless conforms perfectly at all times to his or her experiences (and his or hers *alone* insofar as others' experiences disagree) – refers to some part of reality that exists in itself, independently of any actor's conceptions and perceptions, and thus not accessible by any observer. An observer's task is to infer what that reality must be, by subtracting from experience all that is due to the action and apparatus of experiencing, thus leaving what (one can only assume) was an effect of causes beyond the experiencing.

As many scholars after Kant have pointed out in various ways (e.g., Foucault,

1970; Manski, 1995), separating the two components – that is, knowing what part of an experienced effect is due to one component and what part to the other – is for social science inherently very difficult at best and always ends in uncertainty. Why? Because any effort to make the assessment necessarily reproduces the very question it seeks to answer. Even aside from this regressive ('Chinese boxes') problem of frameworks of evidence and proof, there are enormous difficulties. We usually face a *surplus* of answers to the question 'What could cause the effects I experience?'. This aspect of the difficulty of meeting the paradigmatic demands is sometimes treated in terms of 'the problem of identification'. Our ability to construct *plausible* theories of the process that produced a set of experienced effects (minus the part of the experience that is due to the act of experiencing) very often exceeds our ability to theorize with enough specificity to yield at least one *uniquely discriminating implication* of any one of the theories relative to its competitors. Thus, theoretical expectations are often too anemic to be of much help as we try to sort through the plethora of covariations that are our experiences. By the same token, our ability to construct (conceptualize, measure, etc.) experiences with such specificity that they can uniquely discriminate among sufficiently specific theoretical implications is limited by the ever-present 'error component' which is integral to those covariations.

OBSERVATIONAL INFERENCE

The world of my experience simply is as it is. How can it be otherwise? I observe what I observe.[3] How could that be otherwise? Accordingly, 'the world' (i.e., my world of experience) just *is* as I observe it to be.

That attitude has been called 'the egocentric attitude' (which means as well that it is necessarily 'ethnocentric', for any ego's *ethnos*). It has also been called 'the natural attitude', which is taken to mean that in form the attitude is universal, common to all cultures, even though in content it is always local, or specified in and as *a* culture and therefore an *ethnos* (see Schutz, 1967). Understood from the value of scepticism in the particular culture of modern science, this basic attitude of observation must be regarded as prejudicial (by empirical probability, not logical necessity) precisely because it is not sceptical. One can *reflect on* one's observations sceptically, but it is very difficult (perhaps impossible) to *be* sceptical *in* the momentary act of observation itself. Thus, 'even' in actions designed in accordance with scientific methodology, each of us tends to behave as a 'true believer'. The task, from the standpoint of the expectations of modern science, is to try to maintain and utilize the benefits of an attitude of scepticism.[4]

The core of observational inference is classification – classificatory acts. Closely tied to that, because implied by at least one aspect of classification, is measurement. Both classification and measurement are information-bearing and information-producing acts. The aim is to produce information that discriminates with increasing specificity the kinds and quantities of 'things' that populate our realities of experience.

Classification

When I observe, I always observe *something*. I may not know its proper name or even whether it has one, but irreducibly I know it to be *something*, something *I did observe*, at the very least an instance of a category named 'puzzle' or 'the unknown'. Meaning, as general category and as *particular* meaning, is inseparable from observational experience. In any observation I automatically infer the meaning of what I observed (even if that meaning is only the category of 'puzzle', etc.). I simply cannot but accomplish that much, and in the instance of observation it is an irreducible accomplishment. The sceptical attitude of modern science reminds us, however, that this accomplishment is in principle always an at least partly *erroneous* accomplishment, because observational inference is inescapably fallible, no matter what its methodology and technology. It is the enormous importance of coding that recommends healthy scepticism toward its products, even as some of those products inherently limit the force of scepticism (Alston, 1993; Berger, 1972; Cover and Thomas, 1991; Crary, 1990; Mohr, 1998; Stich, 1990).

An illustration presented by Gilbert Ryle in 1968 (see Ryle, 1971) and later used to advantage by Clifford Geertz (1973: 6–7) offers useful guidance (cf. Hazelrigg, 1995: 78–81). Assume that a minute ago you saw a person's right eyelid shut, then open. What

did you observe? Was it a twitch or a wink? Or perhaps a rehearsal of a wink, or even a parody of a rehearsal of a wink? And if truly a wink, was it an ironic wink, a conspiratorial wink, a flirtatious wink, or still another kind? But maybe it was an imitation of a twitch? You saw what you saw (even if it was only the specificity of 'I don't know what that was') – which is to say that the observational experience was located in a classification scheme, most fundamentally the classification scheme that is your language but perhaps also, within that, another, more specialized or 'technical' classification scheme – and it stood out in that scheme as *this kind of thing* (the name of a category in the classification).[5] Note that this is not a process in which first you have an observational experience and then you locate it in the proper classification. Having the observational experience *is* classifying: observation is always observation of *something*. As the Ryle–Geertz illustration is meant to show, a great deal can ride on being correct in the classification, yet any error of observational inference is always incorrigible in the given act of observation.

Careful attention to the problem of observational inference therefore always reminds us of the inseparability of 'theory' and 'observation' (and of either from 'fact') both in the general sense that the act of observational inference is always contingent on the classificatory logic behind one's sense-making skills (e.g., one's language) and in the more specific sense that, because one's research is informed by a particular theory or set of competing theories (or even by a looser conceptual formation such as a 'general theoretical perspective'), expectations implied by that theoretical resource are likely to inform one's observational inferences (e.g., leading to more specific tendencies 'to see what one expects to see').

Measurement

Observational inference is always a qualitative act (i.e., an act of classification). But it is also always quantitative, minimally in this most rudimentary sense (illustrated by Ryle's 'wink') of being able to apply answers to questions of the following sort: 'Did I observe three events of the same kind, one event each of three different kinds, or two events of one kind and a third event of another kind?' To infer kind is necessarily to establish criteria of category membership and therefore countability both within and across categories.

Countability is directly an act of measurement. The criteria by which membership in categories is decided usually include some that have dimensions of quantitative relationship, which is the basis of additional acts of measurement.[6] Thus, measurement depends on characteristics (including 'goodness') of prior substantive classification – which is to say prior substantive theory (Duncan, 1984: 147). It has also long been held that specific acts of measurement depend on the prior existence of a classification of 'levels' or 'scales' of measurement (e.g., Ellis, 1965). An account of this latter, technical sort of classification was given in Chapter 3. Here it will be considered briefly, within the context of some general remarks about the aims and import of measurement.

The aim of measurement is to produce information in extension of that of the prior substantive classification. The common objective of classification and measurement is descriptive specificity of observations – within limits of ethics, available technologies, and basic assumptions about that which is to be observed. Descriptive specificity is achieved by information that can discriminate reliably among alternative descriptions of that which is observed. The ideal is unambiguous, even unique specificity. Short of that ideal, as we always are,[7] we nonetheless prefer information with enough discriminatory power to give confidence that our methodical operations, leading up to and including tests of hypotheses, are consistently and sufficiently supported. Measurement technology has been developed (mostly during the last 150 years) as extensions of the discriminatory power available from classification. These extensions are based on assumptions about properties of that which is to be measured. The classificatory properties of a specific kind of 'thing' (object, event, relation, etc.) support a type of measurement that the properties of another kind of 'thing' might not support. These 'types' comprise a classification of what is more commonly called 'levels of measurement'. Several different classifications are available. The one usually recognized in the social sciences stems from psychometric work by Stevens (1946): nominal, ordinal, interval, and ratio 'levels' of measurement.[8] This classification can be approached in different ways. Here it is interpreted primarily in terms of power of discrimination, using a

distinction between manifest and latent variables.

The statistical theory of measurement assumes, first, that variables are divided into those that can be directly observed ('manifest variables') and those that cannot ('latent variables'); second, that manifest variables can be theorized as the products of latent-variable processes; and third, that the observed value V of a measurement is the sum of two components, the 'true value' V^*, which is a property of the quantitative relationship of that which is observed, and measurement error e, which results from acts of mensural observation. Each of these assumptions involves observational inference. The third assumption will be treated additionally in the next section. For the moment it is important to note two stipulations. If a variable is measurable, then in principle it has at any given moment an exact value,[9] which in principle can be estimated with commensurate exactitude. But because measurement technologies are never infallible, any inference from observed value V to V^* is always vulnerable. Thus, measurement theory and estimation theory partly overlap: V^* remains unknown except insofar as V can be relied on as an estimate of it.

Examples of latent variables include any population parameter and any variable the observation of which is censored (which includes as a special case all future observations). The logic of this concept of 'latency' parallels the logic of the relationship between V^* and V: in the same way that a 'true value' is inferred from an observed value, values of a latent variable can be inferred from values of an observed or manifest variable. So, for example, population parameters can be inferred from corresponding sample statistics (see below); censored observations can be inferred from non-censored observations. The same logic helps us understand the chief dimension of Stevens' classification.

Assume an observable phenomenon X. For the moment, let us specify X as 'being risk-tolerant' and assume that we have observations consisting of person-specific answers to the question 'Are you tolerant of risk?'. Neglecting (in order to simplify the illustration) all but 'Yes' and 'No' answers, we can sort persons into those who are and those who are not 'risk-tolerant', and then count the number of persons in each category. The alternate answers are the values of this manifest variable – a binomial variable, in this case, names of two mutually exclusive categories.

However, one could argue that what has been observed as two names is a manifestation of an underlying or latent variable. What are the mensural properties of this latent variable? One possibility is that it has none beyond the fact that, were direct observation of the variable possible, membership counts could be conducted (of kinds of persons, the 'risk-tolerant' and the 'risk-intolerant'). To the extent that the reports are free of category error relative to the latent variable, counts based on the manifest variable are reliable estimates of counts for the latent variable.

A second possibility is that the latent variable takes more than two values. One can imagine, for instance, that there are not two kinds of people but three – the 'risk-intolerant', the 'somewhat risk-tolerant', and the 'very risk-tolerant'. One can further imagine (from language use) that the three kinds are ordered from 'least tolerant' to 'most tolerant'. Those who are most tolerant are most likely to have said 'Yes' to our query; those who are least tolerant are most likely to have said 'No'; those in the middle category are about equally likely to have given either answer. A third possibility is that not only are there three (or more) ordered kinds of people, as just described, but also that the magnitude of difference between contiguous kinds is constant. Clearly the binomial responses are ignorant of that additional information, too. A fourth possibility is not only that the magnitude of difference is constant from one quantity of risk tolerance to the next, but also that the constant difference is scaled from a fixed, non-arbitrary origin, such that there cannot be less than zero quantity of risk tolerance. These four possibilities are Stevens' nominal, ordinal, interval, and ratio levels of measurement.[10]

Which of those four descriptions is the correct description of the latent variable? The answer must always derive from and be defensible in terms of substantive theory. Given a defensible answer, the task is then to devise a commensurate technique of measurement. Let us assume in this illustration that substantive theory implies that the latent variable has all the properties of a ratio variable. Call it 'propensity to risk tolerance'. Our model of the measurement act assumes that this propensity ranges from zero to some theoretical upper limit on a continuous gradient of repeatedly divisible differences of magnitude, that every person's propensity is locatable on that gradient, but that most (all?)

persons lack the training to detect and/or express those differences at that same ratio level of sensitivity. Let us assume that the best most persons can do is to offer the very large-grained self-descriptions 'risk-tolerant' and 'not risk-tolerant'. Do we, as observers, have a measurement technique that, compatible with the governing theory, can do better than that? If we do (thus the reserved space of the parenthetical 'all' above), how much better?

If our technique enables us to detect an ordering among three or more categories, we have achieved information that discriminates better than does the information of kinds alone. But unless the number of ordered categories begins to approach the number of persons, the discriminatory power of our measure is still weak, since all members of a given category are necessarily treated, by default, as if they were equally risk-tolerant or equally risk-averse. Indeed, for any ordinal distribution there are in principle *infinitely many* underlying frequency distributions that are perfectly compatible with it. Thus, assuming that our substantive theory about variation in risk tolerance is correct, our distribution of measured observations cannot discriminate among a huge number of possible descriptions of how persons compare to one another in 'propensity to risk tolerance'. We simply lose (or never detect) that information. It is of course possible that this censored information is redundant of the information observed in the ordinal observations. But it is also possible that the censored information contains most of the 'action' affecting, or affected by, risk tolerance – in which case our insensitive measurement will have left us ignorant of 'what is really going on' in this patch of reality (Goffman, 1974; cf. Hazelrigg, 2000).

If we can invent a suitable interval-level measure of 'propensity to risk tolerance', our measured observations are vastly more sensitive and give us much more discriminatory power for making decisions about difference. But this invention depends upon still stronger substantive theory – specifically, a theory that describes 'propensity to risk tolerance' in a metric of constant units, which allows us to quantify consistently the differences not only between but also (assuming the units are sufficiently divisible) within the ranked categories. If that level of sensitivity cannot be achieved, our observational inferences are ignorant of the semantic elasticities that suffuse language use. So, for example, if we have ordinal distributions of 'risk tolerance' among persons sampled and observed a year ago and then reobserved today, we simply cannot say whether the person with the highest rank today is any more (or less) risk-tolerant today than a year ago, even if the person's rank a year ago was well below the top. Nor, if some portion of the sampled persons today each reports being more (less) risk-tolerant than a year ago, can we say that they have equally changed or that some have changed more (less) than others. Likewise, two persons simultaneously sampled from what appear to be two different populations, each person having equivalent rank in the respective samples, cannot be compared beyond the fact of their equivalent rank. We simply cannot say whether they are equally risk-tolerant or not. And so forth.

Measurement by constant units ('equal intervals') enables us to make those discriminations. Indeed, all distributions that differ not only by the ranking of observations but also by the addition or subtraction of metric units are individually discriminable. This constitutes an enormous improvement in our ability to discriminate among observations, and thus also in our ability to make much better decisions because of richer information.

Yet the fact remains that, while any given interval-level measured observation is in principle uniquely determined except for origin and scale unit, its measurement distribution cannot be discriminated from an infinitely large number of possible underlying distributions. This limit is due to the fact that an interval-level metric, consisting of constant units that are relative to an *arbitrary* origin or 'zero point', is insensitive to the operations of multiplication and division (plus all operations based upon them, such as powers and roots).[11] In order to discriminate among this infinitely large number of underlying distributions, one needs to have invented a *ratio* metric of 'propensity to risk tolerance' – which presupposes a substantive theory strong enough to support not only the claim of constant or inelastic units of such propensity but also the claim that 'zero-degree propensity' is a definable and, in principle, observable state. Assuming those claims are supported and a suitable measurement technique devised, refinements of the metric can lead to a measurement distribution defined by a fixed origin and metric units that are both constant and indivisibly *discrete* (i.e., 'natural units') – which amounts to a 'cardinal'

or 'absolute' level of measurement (not nominated as such but nonetheless used by Stevens; see Duncan, 1984: 119–55). This returns us to the (seemingly simple) operation of counting a category's membership: each and every instance of a category's finite membership is now discriminated uniquely in a metric distribution of observations.[12]

As numerous scholars have cautioned, there is far too much use in the social sciences of variables the measurement reliability of which 'is either known to be low or is unknown and suspect' (Cohen and Cohen, 1983: 411; also Duncan, 1975: 114, 127; Greene, 1993: 279). Measurement remains one of the most poorly developed parts of the toolkit of the social sciences, especially the measurement of dynamical properties (see Collins and Sayer, 2001). Little wonder that statisticians have concluded that so much statistical inference testing in regression-type analyses lacks basis in adequate substantive knowledge of the phenomenon being studied (Freedman, 1991; see also Lieberson, 1985).

Errors of observational inference

Observational error is descriptive error, of either classification or measurement (or both). Whatever it is that an observer *knows* she or he is observing – whether as a kind of thing, as number of instances of a kind of thing (i.e., counting), or as a measurable property of a kind of thing – the observation can be wrong. Indeed, observational error is *usually* present. Those instances of observation that *are* error-free – and such instances probably do occur – must be detectable, if they are to be differently valued as information, and any means of detection will also be subject to error. This ubiquity (or near-ubiquity) of observational error can be used to advantage, however, for there is no doubt that *this* component of observation is a result of actions by the observer – which means that the observer has access to and, at least in principle, can manipulate the causes of the error. Virtually all of the apparatus of statistics, a set of very powerful tools for information management and decision-making, has been invented and developed within a framework of 'the theory of error'.

The main questions about error are: What kind of error? How much? What can be done to mitigate its effects? In general, error can be divided into two kinds, random and non-random.[13] Random error is not systematic, not predictable, and therefore, *in the (large enough) aggregate*, not damaging (excepting an effect known as 'attenuation error', discussed below). Non-random error, on the other hand, is potentially very damaging, depending on the degree to which it biases estimations and decision-making. Errors that are products of human acts are rarely random, although they sometimes aggregate into quasi-random distributions.

Both random and non-random errors occur in the practice of observational inference and in the practice of statistical inference. The latter, in which error is the principal avenue of activity and success, is treated in the next main section of this chapter (and in other chapters of this *Handbook*). Here the concern is with errors of description. The discussion must be brief and selectively indicative.

Errors of observational inference include most fundamentally 'error of classification' (also called 'category error') – misclassifying that which is observed, such as mistaking a wink for a twitch or vice versa. Since classifications are usually multileveled (categories within categories within categories, etc.), an observational inference that is correct at one level might not be correct at a lower (finer) level. ('Yes, that was a horse – but a cremello, not a palomino.') In any case, category error is virtually never random (not even when one is trying to observe in a new language), and a relatively small number of category errors, depending on where they occur in a distribution of observations, can be severely biasing of analytic decisions.

Something that can be observed ('an observable') can usually be observed in different spatial and temporal contexts. Category error can easily follow from those contextual or framing effects, but it is often not so easy to know in any given instance whether category error *has* occurred.[14] Is the difference in spatial and/or temporal context incidental to the stability of the observable, such that we are in fact observing 'the same thing' in different places and/or times? Or is the difference in context in fact a difference in observables, such that we are observing 'different things'? An important question in the determination of meaning structures, it typically resists clear resolution. Likewise, differences due to observer's perspective are often difficult to parse. A common response to the problem of spatiotemporal coverage of observation is to use multiple observers. This

is often an excellent practice for exactly the same reason that it equally often raises a problem – namely, reconciling the multiple perspectives. We might be highly confident that molecules of H_2O look exactly the same, without exception, regardless of observer's gender (say) or racial category. But we are surely much less confident that what counts as prejudicial discrimination by gender or by racial category is indifferent to the gender or racial category of the observer. (And as for the H_2O example, consider the disagreements of boundary between 'clean water' and 'contaminated water' – an example that illustrates an advantage of the 'grade of membership' approach of classification by 'fuzzy logic', relative to Cartesian logic.) Any human observer is located non-randomly in a socioculturally structured reality and has a non-randomly structured biography in a non-randomly structured history – all of which, manifested in the particular language community, in the particular sense of self-relative-to-world and self-relative-to-other, and so on, cannot but inform an observer's observations. Thus, any sociocultural observable can be observed from multiple perspectives. The determination of meaning structures and thus the determination of category errors are sensitive to the practices by which an observable that varies only incidentally because of perspective is distinguished from perspective-correlated differences between observables. These issues of spatiotemporal and perspectival effects in the action of observation are also important for sampling, as will be discussed below.

Error of observational inference also includes measurement error. The validity of a specific measure is determined by the isomorphic relation of the measure to a specific conceptual location within a classification, whether that location is an entire category, a property listed in the definitive membership characteristics of a specific category, or a relation or property of relation between/among categories. Just as category error can be deeply and extensively damaging to subsequent estimations and decision-making, so, too, can an inadequate fit of measure to that which is purportedly being measured. This fit is judged on conceptual-theoretical grounds. Once the assumption of adequate fit has been assayed and defended, attention turns to measurement reliability, which (as already mentioned) is itself an estimation problem, estimating the (unobservable) 'true value' of a variable by one's actual measured observation of that variable. The 'true value' is purely theoretical, in the sense that it is destined to remain unobserved. We only ever observe (fallible) estimates of it (Duncan, 1975: 101, 150–1).

The statistical model of measurement (thus, of measurement error) is a sampling model.[15] By way of illustration (and following notation used earlier), assume that we know a piece of reality adequately described as

$$Y^* = \beta X^*$$

where β is an exact constant of proportionality (i.e., β is a fixed, not a random, effect). We are assuming no missing variables; Y^* is known to be a function of X^* alone, but we do not know the value of β (i.e., we do not know how much difference in Y^* equates to one unit of difference in X^*). In order to estimate the exact value of β, we must first measure the two variables, and each measurement will include some unknown amount of error, such that

$$Y = Y^* + e_y$$

and

$$X = X^* + e_x,$$

where e_y and e_x are the respective errors of measurement. Thus, in our actual estimations of our model the relation of Y to X will not be exact, so our estimated model becomes

$$Y = bX + (e_y - be_x).$$

We assume that both e_y and e_x are random variables with means of zero.[16] That is, given that Y^* (or X^*) takes exact and stable values, if the value of any given instance of Y^* is measured by exactly the same procedure in an infinite number of repeated independent measurements, the expected value of e_y (i.e., the mean of the distribution of measurement errors) is zero. Thus, given that e_y is a random variable, it is uncorrelated with Y^*, and it is uncorrelated with X^* and e_x. In other words, the ideal is that the executed procedure of measuring Y^* (or X^* or any other variable of interest) should be perfectly neutral (work equally well) with respect to the full range of variation in Y^* and should not be a function of (sensitive to, influenced by) any variable other than Y^*. To the extent that these conditions are satisfied, the error of measurement is randomly distributed around the expected value, zero.

Error of measurement can be estimated as a correlation between two measured values, V_1 and V_2 (the square root of that correlation used as an 'index of reliability'; see Cohen and Cohen, 1983: 67–9). The prototypical case consists of infinitely repeated independent measurement of the same variable. As a practical matter, testing the reliability of a newly devised mensural technique involves repeated application of the technique in a large number of trials that are as uniform in design and independent execution as one can make them. The higher the correlation averaged across pairs of trials, the greater the reliability of the measure. An alternative approach assumes that one already has in stock a highly reliable measure that can be used as a criterion against which to assess another (in some way – ease of use, expense, etc. – arguably better) measure of the same variable. Note that in either case the estimation of measurement error assumes that V is stable during the interim. Mustering a defense of that assumption can be difficult.

The consequences of measurement error vary considerably, depending on whether the error is random or non-random and where it occurs. This is a complex topic, but some general guidelines can be briefly described (cf. Cohen and Cohen, 1983: 69–70, 406–17; Duncan, 1975: 114–18, 1984; Fuller, 1987).

Whereas random error is often neutral in effect, non-random error is by definition biasing and can fatally damage efforts to estimate relationships between/among variables. For example, one of the standard assumptions of ordinary least-squares (OLS) estimation is that specification error (i.e., error in how one's model is specified; see below) is independent of each independent variable. This assumption cannot be exactly satisfied when the measurement error of any of the independent variables is correlated with an unobserved variable (which is necessarily represented in the specification error). While random error in a dependent variable is usually harmless, non-random error in a dependent variable can render OLS coefficients meaningless.

But even random error is not necessarily harmless. It tends to elevate measured variances, which means that correlations between the (unobservable) 'true values' of any two covariates are underestimated. Thus, random error in one or more independent variables tends to shift OLS coefficients toward zero. This problem, known as 'attenuation error', can be especially serious for 'difference scores' or 'change scores' (a variable defined as the difference in a measured variable between two groups, for instance, or as the change in a measured variable). There are procedures (based on the above-mentioned index of reliability) for correcting attenuation. But much care should be exercised, for this is the sort of situation in which 'correction' can yield a result worse than the condition one is trying to correct (Rogosa, 1995).

Whereas the effect of random measurement error in covariates is predictable and relatively harmless (attentuation), in *partialled* independent variables (as in multivariate analysis) the effect is quite unpredictable. Coefficients can be either overestimated or underestimated; even signs can be switched.

In principle, one can explicitly specify the measurement-error components of measured variables as separate variables, using a causal-modeling approach and techniques such as LISREL (an acronym for 'linear structural relationships'). This approach depends on some very strong assumptions, however, buttressed only by correlational evidence (Duncan, 1984: 210). A standard asymptotic solution uses 'instrumental variable' estimation, which assumes that the instrumental variable is highly correlated with the true value of the erroneously measured variable and uncorrelated with the error component. Such instruments are not easily discernable.[17]

STATISTICAL INFERENCE

The relationship of a sample to the population from which it derives is the relationship of a part to its whole. One can infer from a part to its whole – that is, treat an observed part as representative of its (mostly unobserved) whole. Why would one want to do that? The first, easy, and incomplete answer is because it is easier to observe a part than its whole. But strictly speaking, all one ever observes is a part or parts.

This sort of inference is called 'sampling inference' or 'statistical inference'.[18] The latter name points to an important terminological distinction. The observed values of variables in a sample are called 'statistics' or 'statistical characteristics'. The corresponding values for the sampled population, which we do not know but are trying to estimate on the basis of the sample, are called 'parameters' or 'parametric characteristics'. We try to infer the values of specified parameters of a population

from what we believe to be the corresponding statistics of an appropriate sample of observations. The conditions under which a statistic (e.g., the mean, $\bar{X}$) can be taken as a reliable representative of the corresponding parameter (e.g., the population mean, μ) is the core topic of sampling theory and of the portion of estimation theory concerning the properties of inference from a sample to its whole.

Statistical inference is also and more fundamentally the core of a particular kind of decision theory. Sometimes called 'statistical decision theory', it enables us to make decisions under conditions of uncertainty. Virtually all decisions about 'how the world is' in social science research are decisions under conditions of uncertainty. Unlike the case of Newton's laws of motion and gravitational attraction, where information about relationships can in principle be absolutely certain because the relationships themselves are strictly deterministic, information available to social science researchers is almost always uncertain ('stochastic') information[19] because the underlying relationships are 'probabilistic' (stochastic), not strictly deterministic. The importance of that difference in informational properties cannot be overstated. Consider by way of illustration the following puzzle.

Suppose three opaque jars, each containing some large number of marbles, all black marbles in one jar, all white marbles in another, and a mixture of some black and some white marbles in the third, have been mislabeled. What is the smallest number of marbles you can blindly remove in order to put the correct label on each jar? The (perhaps surprising) answer is 'one marble', although this one marble must be selected strategically in order to take advantage of minimized degrees of freedom.[20] Selecting from the jar mislabeled 'Mixed', if the marble is black (white) you know the jar's correct label is 'Black' ('White'). Since degrees of freedom have been exhausted, you immediately know also that the jar mislabeled 'White' ('Black') must contain the mixture.

The lesson usually intended by this puzzle is that even a single item of information, if used to its strategic limit, can solve multiple unknowns. There is another lesson, however, at least equally important. The puzzle can be solved so neatly, by a single draw, *only* because the informational content is completely deterministic. Not only do we know beyond doubt that one jar contains all white marbles, another all black marbles, and the third a mixture of black and white marbles, but we also know beyond doubt – and this is key to the single-draw solution – that each of the jars is mislabeled. But having *certain* information on any relevant variables, much less on all, is highly atypical for social science research. The typical condition is *uncertainty* – in this case, for example, that the jars *might* be mislabeled, or that there is some chance that a white marble (or a gray marble) was mistakenly included with the black marbles. Such are the conditions under which to appreciate the utility of statistical decision theory, arguably the single most powerful device human beings have yet invented for making decisions under conditions of uncertainty. Statistical decision theory enables us (1) to make decisions from the uncertain information of our fallible observations about inherently probabilistic events, processes, or states of being, (2) to choose the kind of error that we are most likely to commit if we do decide wrongly, thus enabling us to minimize the least desired consequence of decisional error, and (3) to estimate the probability that a decision we have made *is* wrong in that least desired way (or in some other way).

This section treats statistical inference as decision theory, as estimation theory, and of course as sampling theory. The treatment is elementary; many important topics, some of them flagged,[21] are not covered. The treatment presupposes that issues of observational inference in the given research project are settled at least temporarily. It assumes measurement at least to the extent of counting observational events within a specified classification, although the elemental principles of statistical inference are relevant whether observations are measured observations or not.[22] The small number of concepts comprising the process of statistical inference are developed in slightly different ways in sampling theory, estimation theory, and decision theory, but they form a single, unified theoretical framework. Thus, the order of presentation in the following discussion should be interpreted more as an unfolding of a texture of mutually implicated ideas than as a step-by-step sequence of successively 'later' ideas added to more 'primary' or 'foundational' ideas.

Sampling

There is nothing unusual about sampling. It is an unavoidable behavior. Being neither spatially nor temporally omnipresent, and experiencing reality necessarily from one's own perspective (even while engaging in actions such as 'taking the perspective of the other'), each of us is always sampling observations. And we tend to infer from what we *have* observed (the sample) to what we largely have not (the population) without much thought about how well founded the inference is. It should be easy to see, however, that the well-foundedness or 'goodness' of that inference, the part–whole relation, is a vital condition of our ability *both* to generalize from what we *have* observed to some larger population *and* to demonstrate publicly and consistently how we can have confidence in that process of inference and generalization.

If our goal is a highly accurate estimate of a population parameter, and our means of gaining it is by observing a sample of observations from that population, then the chances of achieving that highly accurate estimate will depend crucially on the extent to which relevant information contained in the sample is redundant of corresponding information contained in the population of possible observations. If the sample contains precisely all and only the information of the population, then the fact that we can never actually achieve the total population of possible observations is not a source of concern.

If each and every observation in the population of possible observations is equally likely, a sampling of that population can in principle yield perfect redundancy of information. But what is there to learn about a phenomenon that is perfectly homogeneous or randomly distributed in its population of possible observations? In fact, there *are* phenomena that occur with such uniformity that sampling has no relevance. Within the domain of Newtonian mechanics, for instance, the selection of observations of gravitational attraction is *in principle* (but see below) perfectly neutral with respect to spatial, temporal, and perspectival properties of the observational action. On the other hand, phenomena that interest us in the theoretical realms of social science are heterogeneous and non-randomly distributed spatially, temporally, and/or perspectivally. Even the most careful sampling is unlikely to yield perfect redundancy of information. Under the right conditions, however, the information derived from careful sampling can fairly represent the information of the population. More will be said about the meaning of the phrase 'fairly represent' below, in the subsection on estimation. Here, attention is directed to the meaning of those 'right conditions'.

In the nature of the case, we know less, and often much less, about the specified population than we want to know. Usually we do not know enough to make directed choices of which parts of the whole will comprise our sample (as we do, for instance, when standing in front of a rack of doughnuts and ordering a selection of 'one of each kind', on the assumption that all of a given kind do not importantly vary in characteristics of interest).[23] In the face of that much ignorance, we usually revert to a selection mechanism that is in principle neutral with regard to any relevant heterogeneities of the population.[24] Because neutrality is an uncommon human condition, special tools have been invented to aid in achieving it. One such tool is the principle of 'the random draw' or randomized selection (as assumed above in the marble puzzle). The key idea is to select the sample in such a way that each of the population of possible observations has an equal chance of being selected. Actual results of randomized selection only approximate that principle even under the best of circumstances, although the approximations can be quite good. The difficulty stems from our ignorance: in order to achieve equiprobability of selection we can use a table of random numbers (or the random number generator of a computer), but that use requires that each of the population of possible observations be uniquely identified by number or name, and such knowledge is in fact denied to us.[25] We must revert to a second-best solution, known as a 'sampling frame', which is a part of the population of possible observations but might not be (probably is not) a neutrally selected part. The sampling frame is that portion of the population for which unique identifiers (numbers, names) are known.[26] Random sampling (or some other type of probability sampling) is then performed on the sampling frame.

In general, probability sampling is greatly superior to non-probability sampling, for our ability to assess the quantitative aspects of the part–whole relation depends on successful construction of a probability sample. However, there are circumstances under which probability sampling is not feasible – for instance, a research opportunity that will disappear before a probability sample can be constructed. Under such circumstances one

should attempt to maximize variance on the main variables of one's analysis designs, and especially on any variables that will be treated analytically as dependent variables. The importance of capturing the full range of variation, in particular the *unlikely* observations, outweighs the importance of equiprobability. In any heterogeneous population some observables are likelier to catch our attention than are others. That can be due to relative frequency. But it can also be due to other factors, such as availability bias and vividness (Stich, 1990), which deflect attention away from the improbable. The advantage of the equiprobability rule is that it counteracts the observational tendencies that favor the easily available and the vivid. Even in random sampling, however, where the equiprobability rule gives overwhelming weight to relative frequency, it is important to assess coverage of the full range of variation. As an illustration, consider the distribution of household wealth. Only 10% of US households hold nearly three-quarters of all the wealth held by US households, and the majority of that is held by the wealthiest 2% of households (Keister, 2000: Table 3-2). A random sample as large as 5000 or 6000 households – which is quite large even for sample surveys of the US population – will probably include a very small number of the wealthiest households, too few to support generalizations from the sample statistics. Without using a sampling design that assigns very disproportionately high probabilities of observing these households, one will be able to say much about the broad middle range of households which hold modest amounts of wealth, but nearly nothing about the households that account for the lion's share of privately held personal wealth – that is, about the individuals and families who are chief beneficiaries in the process of asset accumulation.

The remainder of this chapter assumes probability sampling – usually simple random sampling, the basis of all probability sampling. The very fact that the core condition of simple random sampling is so unlike the heterogeneous, non-randomly structured character of human life means that it tends to be a difficult and therefore expensive condition to achieve. As the example of household wealth distributions illustrates, a very large simple random sample would be required in order to achieve good representation of the few very wealthy households. Other types of probability sampling (e.g., stratified random sampling, cluster and quota techniques) have been developed to reduce costs and achieve good representation of the uncommon as well as the common elements of a population. Descriptions of these more complex sampling designs are available in a variety of sources (e.g., Kish, 1965; Lohr, 1999; Yamane, 1967). Other specialized topics, for pursuit elsewhere, include bootstrap techniques (useful, for example, when one's analytic problem features a very large number of alternative outcomes only a few of which account for nearly all of the actual outcomes; Horowitz, 1997); Gibbs sampling (useful to simulate posterior distributions from data in Bayesian frameworks, as in Kim and Nelson, 1999, and in other applications involving sequential observations, as in Abbott and Barman, 1997); problems of inference in multistage sampling for multilevel designs (Snijders, 2001); and sampling events and temporal properties of non-stationary or time-variant processes (Tuma and Hannan, 1984: Chs 7–9).[27]

Observations as experimental outcomes

Recall Newton's gravity equation: the force of gravitational attraction, F, is theorized to be a *strictly determined* variable. The equation expressing Newton's theory of gravitational attraction is therefore specified completely and includes no term (commonly designated e) for error of specification. To say that F is strictly determined is to say that variation in F is strictly a function of the three variables, m_1, m_2, and d (as defined above). Those three variables alone, in the specific form of the relationship as described by the equation, account for every scintilla of variation in F, everywhere at all times and regardless of differences in the observer's perspective (per Newtonian mechanics).

Rarely can we theorize with such specificity that the variables of a theory can be expressed as strictly determined. Our governing theories typically lack sufficient specificity to account for all of the variation in a given variable of interest. We rarely have the confidence to claim that we have identified *all* of the determinants of a variable, that our theory describes all of their relationships in proper form and function, and that we have included no extraneous factors. Bear in mind, moreover, that because a governing theory is designed to explain variations in our *experience*

(i.e., our observations of the given variable), determinants of variation in the observed variable will necessarily include not only the causal factors that (by the particular theory) operate independently of observations but also factors of the action of experience itself. Our governing theories often do not sufficiently specify the conditions of variation in measurement error, for example, and our technologies of measurement are often too anemic to match very much theoretical specificity.

The variables we typically work with are stochastic variables, more commonly called 'random variables'. The latter name can lead to confusion: a random variable is *not* called that because its variation is random. Rather, the name refers to the fact that any observation of the variable can be treated as the outcome of an experiment for which all possible outcomes are in principle describable by a probability distribution. By way of illustration, imagine that a hat contains n uniquely numbered tokens. A blind draw from that hat is an experiment in the sense that it has an uncertain outcome. If the outcome of an experiment (a blind draw) is observation of a '6', I know that this observation was only one of n possible outcomes of the experiment; and if the n tokens were in fact independently subject to a strictly random draw, so that no token had a better chance of selection than any other of the n tokens, then I know that the probability of having observed what I did observe is precisely $1/n$.

It should be emphasized that even variables in the domain of Newtonian mechanics can be usefully treated as random variables. Within the Newtonian domain, remember, a governing theory is considered universal; it holds without exception. An implication is that any empirical observation that fails to accord with theoretical expectation is discrepant solely because of error in observation. It was recognition of this 'problem of error' in measured observations (relative to what was regarded as the absolute certainty of theoretical expectation) that stimulated the development of modern statistics as a methodology and technology for modeling probability distributions of error. By the mid-nineteenth century the application of statistical modeling to observations of personal (rather than astronomical) attributes was well under way, led by Adolphe Quetelet. These applications were considerably more challenging, to say the least. Discriminating the

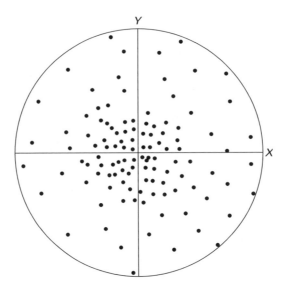

Figure 4.1 *Illustrative plot of attempts to hit target*

part of an observation (or set of observations) that is due to observational error is far more difficult when the other part is not some Platonic certitude but is due to the stochastic nature of that which is observed.

By way of illustration that 'even' a Newtonian variable can be a random variable, consider the task of sending a ballistic missile from a launch site to a target 4000 miles away. In principle all of the force vectors are Newtonian, amenable to exact solution. But the number of force vectors operating over a distance of 4000 miles is huge. It is not reasonable to expect to have measured observations for all the dynamic factors involved in the actual trajectory. Unmeasured variations in Earth's gravitational attraction, in the rate of fuel passing into combustion, in the impulse rate from that combustion, in atmospheric factors during launch and re-entry, and so forth, imply that the actual point of impact will rarely be exactly the intended target. Letting the intended target be a point, draw two lines such that they intersect at right angles on that point, as in Figure 4.1. These two axes are the distance metrics of two random variables, X and Y. Now imagine a very large number of independent repeated efforts to hit that intersection. The actual points of impact will be distributed across the area of a circle centered on that intersection, the density of impacts diminishing with distance

from the intersection. These 'radial distances' are given as $R = (X^2 + Y^2)^{1/2}$, which is random simultaneously in two dimensions. It is *random* because the (X,Y) coordinates of any given impact can be predicted only as an approximation. Each impact will be as a random draw from an entire field of possible points of impact, most of which are clustered near the intended target (the intersection) but a few of which are quite far away. An observation of any specific actual impact can be usefully thought of as the outcome of an experiment (trying to hit the intended target).

So, the values of a random variable follow a probability distribution. Depending on the shape of that probability distribution, values of a given random variable Y can be predicted *in the aggregate*, with an accuracy that can only approximate perfect prediction, from knowledge of one or more other variables X_i that (by particular theory) are determinants of Y. Assume, for example, that Y is annual income at age 35 and that the X_i are a set of determinants such as employment status, occupation, level of relevant skills, and gender. Not only Y but also indeed each of the X_i will be treated as stochastic.[28] Our theory of income determination is surely incompletely specified (e.g., there are missing determinants, some of which I can identify approximately but lack the means to measure, but others of which I have not identified even approximately; and there are unspecified errors of measurement, classification, etc.). Therefore, I cannot precisely predict the income of any 35-year-old person selected at random from the population of such persons (whereas, by contrast, knowledge of individual mass and distance of separation for any two bodies selected at random enables me to predict precisely, within limits of measurement, etc., per Newtonian mechanics, the gravitational attraction between them). For any given person, my prediction will be either correct or (more likely) incorrect.

It should be evident from the foregoing that explanation in the context of random variables is more complex than explanation in the context of strictly deterministic variables. Indeed, the presence of random variables and relations makes the task of demonstrating adequate evidence of *causality* even more difficult (see Chapter 21). In general, adequate evidence of a cause-and-effect relationship is achieved through satisfaction of four criteria. Listed in order of increasing difficulty, these are covariance, temporal sequence, model specification, and process linkage or mechanism. Evidence of covariance is easy to find; the hard part is discriminating the covariances of specific interest from the plethora of other covariances that we experience, many of them having no more meaning or significance than random coincidence. Evidence of temporal sequence consists in a specific temporal relation of events (if X, then Y), which can be variously complicated by lags, feedback loops, simultaneities, and other features of temporality. Newton's third law of motion – for every action, there is an equal and opposed reaction – is unambiguous in the abstract and in the strictly deterministic world of Newtonian mechanics. But in the midst of a world of random variables, determining 'if–then' relationships without ambiguity can be extremely difficult, perhaps impossible.

The third criterion, also probably impossible to satisfy completely, demands that one's model of a process include all relevant variables and exclude all irrelevant variables. Imagine a model specifying that variable Y is a causal function of two other variables, X_1 and X_2. Empirically the model is stated as $Y = f(X_1, X_2, e)$, where f is specified as a particular type of function (e.g., linear, additive) and e is the 'error term' or 'disturbance term' of the specification. Assume I am wrong in my theory that change in Y is caused by change

in X_1 and X_2 alone; assume that one other variable, X_3, is an independent determinant of Y. Where in my model have I represented the part of the variance in Y that is an effect specifically of X_3? It is represented in e, a 'grab bag' of all the factors, including missing variables, that should be specified in the model as separate and explicit determinants of variation in Y.[29] Why did I not include X_3 as an explicit determinant? Probably because of ignorance. Perhaps I did have a vague notion of its role in Y, but not enough to enable me to measure it. Perhaps ethical considerations precluded measurement. The point is, whether by ignorance or technical or ethical limitations, nearly all of the motivating theories in the sociocultural sciences are far from complete as causal explanations of what they purport to explain. The usual situation is that e probably contains several, even many, missing variables. By the same token, while the evidence of covariance and temporal sequence might indicate that, say, X_2 is indeed a determinant, that evidence is far from sufficient. The temporally ordered covariance is real, not an illusion, but it could be causally spurious. As one possibility, for example, Y and X_2 are each a function of some unknown variable, and because X_2 is more sensitive than is Y to the unknown variable, for any effective change in the unknown variable a response in X_2 will occur before a response in Y.

Finally, the fourth criterion: assuming that all determinants are known and specified with correct temporal order, there remains the issue of how it all fits together. That is, what are the correct functional forms of the relationships? Is a given causal relation monotonic or polytonic, symmetrical between ascending and descending functions, variant or invariant by organizational scale, and so on?[30] In sum, what is the operative process by which determinants are orchestrated in such a way as to yield a particular gradient of effects? By analogy, think of the determinants as inputs, and the effects as outputs. One's task is to imagine what happens in the 'black box' of the actual process by which inputs become outputs. In physical analogs one can sometimes peer into the mechanism without unduly altering its operation and observe the process of inputs becoming outputs. To do so in processes of sociocultural phenomena is, where possible technically and acceptable ethically, usually very much harder. The presence of random variables and random-variable relationships complicates the task, sometimes to the point of intractability. Consider, for instance, that under conditions of random-variable modeling one is often faced with what appear to be different but equally valid sets of determinants of some observed effect. In the absence of prior theory strong enough to rule out one of the sets on analytic grounds, and given that *post hoc* accounts of each set can often be plausibly constructed, how is one to decide between the sets? Or how is one to decide if in fact the observed effect *does* occur as a result of two (or more) different processes? The task is further complicated by the fact that dynamics at one level of organizational scale (e.g., individual life course) often aggregate to a higher scale (e.g., group structure) as statics.

Experimental designs – especially designs such as the Solomon multiple-group design with multiple pre-tests (establishing trend lines) and multiple post-tests with different lags (establishing deferrals and decays) – generally afford the best approximations to the four criteria, far better than the approximations afforded by survey techniques, ethnographic methods, and other non-experimental approaches. But even in experimental designs, which achieve their strength in internal validity typically at the cost of reduced external validity,[31] satisfaction of the third and fourth criteria always remains problematic. In the final analysis, 'causality' is a purely theoretical standard which empirically we can only try to approximate – an inherently frustrating task, one cannot help but notice, when the standard to be approximated remains empirically unknown. In view of this seemingly incorrigible limit, it is perhaps understandable that people sometimes prefer the apparent certitudes of a non-sceptical and ego/ethnocentric attitude.

Probability distributions as theoretical models

Central features of the methodology and technology of statistical inference include sets of *theoretical probability distributions* which are used in conjunction with sampling theory. A random variable X, which consists of a series of random events x (the values that X can assume), is completely characterized by its probability mass (if X is discrete), density (if continuous), and distribution functions. Random variables are classified by the types of distribution they follow. Among the most important are the Bernoulli and binomial distributions, the Poisson distribution, the standard normal distribution, and three that derive from the standard normal distribution, a set of t distributions, a set of χ^2 distributions, and a set of F distributions (this F being eponymous for 'Fisher', not 'force').[32] Processes that generate random-variable distributions that approximate those theoretical models are often assigned the same names – for instance, a Bernoulli process, a Poisson process, and so on.

The Bernoulli distribution The probability mass function of a Bernoulli random variable X (named after a late seventeenth-century mathematician, Jacob Bernoulli) is given by

$$P\{X = 0\} = 1 - p,$$
$$P\{X = 1\} = p, \qquad (4.1)$$

where p is the probability that the binary outcome is a 'success' $(0 \leq p \leq 1)$, and the theoretical expectation is

$$E[X] - 1 \cdot P\{X = 1\} + 0 \cdot P\{X = 0\} = p$$

(i.e., the probability that the random variable equals 1).

The binomial distribution If in n independent trials X successes occur, with each success governed by the underlying probability p, then X is a binomial random variable with parameters n and p, and a probability mass function given by

$$P\{X = i\} = \binom{n}{i} p^i (1 - p)^{n-i},$$
$$i = 0, 1, \ldots, n, \qquad (4.2)$$

where $\binom{n}{i} = n!/(i!(n-i)!)$ and $n!$ means $1 \times 2 \times \ldots \times n$. The mean value of the binomial is $\mu = np$. The variance is $\sigma^2 = np(1 - p)$. This distribution dates back to James Bernoulli and Blaise Pascal. A Bernoulli process generates the distribution of probabilities of observing a married (vs. not married) person, for example. If the probability that any adult selected at random is a 'married person' is $p = 0.65$, I can estimate from the binomial distribution the probability of observing 0, 1, 2, 3, 4, ..., n

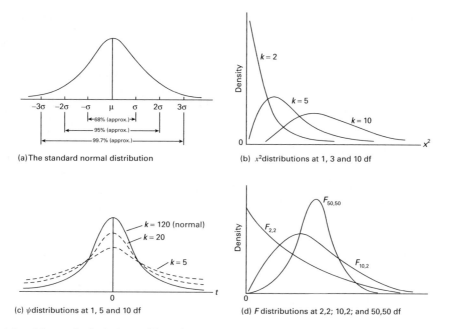

(a) The standard normal distribution

(b) x^2 distributions at 1, 3 and 10 df

(c) ψ distributions at 1, 5 and 10 df

(d) F distributions at 2,2; 10,2; and 50,50 df

Figure 4.2 *Schematic depictions of four theoretical probability distributions*

married persons in n independent observations of adults. As n becomes large, the empirical distribution converges to the theoretical model.

The Poisson distribution A Poisson random variable X, taking one of the values 0, 1, 2 ..., has the single parameter λ (where $\lambda > 0$) and the probability mass function given by

$$P\{X = i\} = e^{-\lambda}\frac{\lambda^i}{i!}, \qquad i = 0, 1, ..., \qquad (4.3)$$

where $e \approx 2.7183$, which is the base of the natural logarithm. The mean is $\mu = \lambda$, as also is the variance $\sigma^2 = \lambda$. Named after Siméon Denis Poisson, who introduced it in 1837, the Poisson distribution is the limiting case of the binomial (i.e., as the binomial $n \to \infty$ and $p \to 0$, with the added assumption that $\lambda = np$). Thus, it is very useful for predicting the prevalence of an observational event that occurs rarely (i.e., as $p \to 0$). For example, a Poisson process generates the distribution of deaths from, say, reactions to injection of an anti-toxin. (If $p = 0.000\ 01$, for instance, what

is the probability of observing 0, 1, 2, 3, ..., n deaths in $n = 20\ 000$ injections?) More generally, uses extend to a variety of Poisson processes of 'birth–death' events.

The normal distribution A random variable X is normally distributed with parameters μ and σ^2 if its density function is

$$f(x) = \frac{1}{\sigma\sqrt{2\pi}}\ e^{-(x-\mu)^2/2\sigma^2}, \qquad -\infty < X < \infty \quad (4.4)$$

(where $\pi \approx 3.141\ 59$). This is the familiar 'normal curve', represented in Figure 4.2(a). Note that the coefficient $(1/\sigma\sqrt{2\pi})$ assumes that the total density integrates to unity, so that the total probability (or 'area under the curve') sums to 1. Also note that $f(x)$ attains maximum value $(1/\sigma\sqrt{2\pi} \approx 0.399/\sigma)$ at $x = \mu$. Furthermore, for any random variable X with mean μ and variance σ^2 it is true that the relationship, $Y = \alpha + \beta X$, is normal with mean $\beta\mu + \alpha$ and variance $\alpha^2\sigma^2$. And any linear combination of two or more normally distributed random variables is itself normally distributed. Thus, if $Y = b_1 X_1 + b_2 X_2$ (where b_1 and b_2 are 'weighting' constants), then if X_1 and X_2 are normally distributed with means μ_1 and μ_2 and variances σ_1^2 and σ_2^2, Y is normally distributed with mean $b_1\mu_1 + b_2\mu_2$ and variance $b_1^2\sigma_1^2 + b_2^2\sigma_2^2$.[33]

The normal frequency distribution was derived by Abraham de Moivre in 1733 as an approximation to the binomial law. This application was developed in 1810–11 by Pierre Simon Laplace as the central limit theorem, which describes a highly generalizable limiting distribution function for sums of independent random variables. A year or two earlier in 1808, when applying the method of least squares to problems of geodesic survey, Carl Friedrich Gauss had developed a statistical theory of measurement errors, which featured 'the Gaussian error curve'. What is commonly known as 'the normal distribution' is a *normalized* Gaussian distribution. That is, because it is tedious to calculate individual values of the density function of a random variable X that can be described as a Gaussian distribution, one instead relates each random-variable distribution to the Gaussian distribution as it has been normalized with mean μ set to zero and variance σ^2 set to one. This normalized metric is referred to as the 'standard normal' or 'unit normal deviate' metric (commonly designated Z). Transformation of the observed Gaussian or normal random variable X into the normalized distribution (i.e., into Z or 'standard scores') is obtained by $Z = (X - \mu)/\sigma$. Thus, all probability statements about X can be written in terms of Z, which is very useful since the density function of Z has been tabulated and appears as an appendix in virtually all textbooks in elementary statistics as a 'table of coordinates and areas under the normal curve' (as in the Appendix at the back of this book).

Note that for increasing n, as p diverges from its limits ($0 < p < 1$) the binomial distribution increasingly converges to the normal distribution. This is highly useful, since calculation of probability values for the binomial becomes very tedious as n becomes large.

The chi-square distributions

If $Z_1, Z_2, ..., Z_k$ are independent standard normal random variables, then the random variable

$$X = Z_1^2 + Z_2^2 + \cdots + Z_k^2 \qquad (4.5)$$

is said to have a chi-square distribution with k degrees of freedom (hereafter designated χ_k^2). Moreover, if X_1 and X_2 are independent chi-square random variables with k_1 and k_2 degrees of freedom, then $X_1 + X_2$ is also chi-square distributed with $k_1 + k_2$ degrees of freedom. The mean of the chi-square distribution is k, and its variance is $2k$.[34] Density functions for $k = 1, 3$, and 10 are depicted in Figure 4.2(b). Note that whereas the distribution is strongly skewed when degrees of freedom are few, the skew diminishes as degrees of freedom increase. For degrees of freedom greater than 100, the random variable

$$(2\chi^2)^{1/2} - (2k-1)^{1/2}$$

can be treated as a standardized normal variable.

The set of chi-square distributions and some associated tests were developed by Karl Pearson just before 1900 and received important clarification by Ronald Fisher in 1922.

The t distributions

If Z and χ_k^2 are independent random variables, then the random variable

$$t_k = \frac{Z}{\sqrt{\chi_k^2/n}} \qquad (4.6)$$

is said to have a t distribution with k degrees of freedom. The mean of the distribution is zero; the variance is $k / (k - 2)$. Density functions for $k = 1, 5$, and 10 are depicted in Figure 4.2(c). Note that the density function for t is symmetrical around zero, and as k increases it rapidly converges to the standard normal density function. As $k \to 0$, the tails of the t distribution become thicker, by comparison to the normal, indicating greater variability.

The set of t distributions are also known as 'Student's t', the eponym being a pseudonym adopted by W.S. Gosset in connection with work he published in 1908. The set of distributions is at least as old as Poisson's treatment of the special case having but a single degree of freedom.

The F distributions

If χ_k^2 and χ_m^2 are independent chi-square random variables with n and m degrees of freedom, then the random variable

$$F_{k,\,m} = \frac{\chi_k^2/k}{\chi_m^2/m} \qquad (4.7)$$

is said to have an *F* distribution with *k* and *m* degrees of freedom. *F* distributions are also known as variance-ratio distributions (see below). Density functions for *F* at three different sets of degrees of freedom are depicted in Figure 4.2(d). Here, too, it is apparent that the normal distribution is increasingly approximated as degrees of freedom increase. The mean of an *F*-distributed variable is $m/(m-2)$ and the variance is

$$\frac{2m^2(k+m-2)}{k(m-2)^2(m-4)}.$$

(The mean is undefined for $m \leq 2$ and the variance is undefined for $m \leq 4$.) This set of distributions, named after Ronald Fisher, is particularly useful in analysis-of-variance problems and in tests of models involving several parameter estimates. Note that the value of *t* for a number of degrees of freedom is equal to $(F_{1,m})^{1/2}$.

The sampling distribution of a statistic

Recall the two examples of drawing tokens from a hat and sending a missile 4000 miles to an intended impact. Both illustrate repeated outcomes in an experiment. In each example we can stipulate (as we did with the token draws) that the repeated outcomes are independent of each other, which means that any given outcome (e.g., a specific token drawn) does not affect the probability of any alternative outcome (a different token being drawn). Independence of observational event is achievable (approximately) with the tokens by returning to the hat a token that has been drawn and mixing all the tokens before making the next draw. This is known as 'sampling with replacement'; without replacement, it should be evident, the probability of each succeeding draw is a function of the draws that have already occurred.[35]

Imagine now a sequence of independent random samplings of observations from a large population of possible observations. The observations could be of tokens, missile impacts, school years completed, or some other variable of interest. Suppose that the variable is body weight of individual human beings. From the population we extract a random sample of size *n*, then measure and record the body weight of each individual. We can summarize most of the information contained in that distribution of measured observations by one of the measures of central tendency – in this case (since we are measuring at an interval level and do not suspect a strongly skewed distribution) the mean. Following replacement, we extract a second random sample of same size *n* and repeat the measurement and recording, ending with a second sample mean. It should be evident that we could in principle repeat that activity a very large number of times. Each of the repetitions is the outcome of an independent experiment on a specific random variable. Now let us add two conditions that are purely theoretical (i.e., could not be empirically enacted): let us assume that we repeat the independent random sampling (each sample of size *n*) an *infinite* number of times and that the repetitions occur instantaneously (thereby excluding the possibility that the observable, body weight, changes during the course of the experiment). We would thus have an infinite number of independent random samples (size *n*) and an infinite number of sample means, all representing the one large population of possible observations.

That infinite number of sample means is itself a distribution (see Figure 4.3). Think of it as a second-order distribution, where 'first-order distribution' refers to each of the observed distributions of body weights. This second-order distribution consists not of individual body weights but of *mean* body weights, one for each of the infinite number of samples.

A moment's reflection on the process just described should confirm that the mean of the infinite number of sample means *necessarily* equals the population mean, μ. This second-order distribution is technically known as *the sampling distribution of the statistic* (here, the statistic being the sample mean). This concept, the sampling distribution of a statistic, is the linchpin of statistical inference. Insofar as any sample of observations (so long as it is a probability sample) has *any* utility beyond itself, it is because of the power of that concept.

Surely, one might think, this utility cannot amount to much if it depends on an infinite repetition. But in fact, while the necessary identity of the expected value of the second-order distribution of means and μ occurs *only* at infinity, as the number of repetitions *n* gets increasingly very large (i.e., as $n \to \infty$) the mean of the sample means increasingly approximates μ. The utility consists in the fact

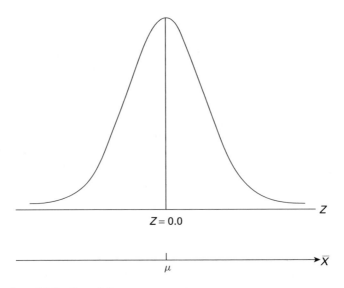

Figure 4.3   *Sampling distribution of the mean*

that as $n \rightarrow \infty$, the sampling distribution of sample means increasingly approximates the normal distribution with mean μ and variance σ^2/n. This property, proven in 1810–11 by Laplace, is known as the central limit theorem. The property holds *regardless of the form of the probability density function of the observed random variable*. In other words, the 'shape' of the distribution of measured observations can diverge greatly from the normal curve – it can be J-shaped, for instance, or L-shaped or U-shaped or M-shaped – and still the sampling distribution of sample means increasingly approaches the normal distribution as the number of samples becomes large. Thus, for any sample mean $\bar{X}$,

$$Z = \frac{\bar{X} - \mu}{\sigma/n^{1/2}} \tag{4.8}$$

is a standardized normal variable.

Errors of statistical inference

Before discussing errors of statistical inference (sampling error), another kind of error will be briefly treated, error that affects sample statistics but is not due to characteristics of the sampling design itself. Commonly described under the heading 'non-sampling error', it consists of *failures* of execution of a probability sample design. In the case of a simple random sample, for instance, each possible observation is equiprobable. But if some observations are excluded in practice, the probability design, and thus the basis of statistical inference, has been brought into question and perhaps damaged to an extent that precludes inference. Exclusions can occur for a number of different reasons: some observables evade observation (e.g., sample members cannot be found or refuse cooperation); other observables are neglected because of observer error (e.g., perceived danger, expense of contact, witting or unwitting prejudicial attitude). Because non-sampling errors are almost always non-random errors, their effect is to bias the sample statistics. Depending on how much is confidently known about the 'missing observations', the bias can be estimated and approximately corrected (Groves, 1999). As the volume of missing observations increases, however, confidence in any such efforts at correction rapidly diminishes.[36]

Errors of statistical inference have to do with the following sampling problem. A random sample is necessarily *one* of the infinite number of samples that is the sampling distribution. But we never know *which* one. The shape of the normal distribution tells us that the large majority of samples in the distribution of samples are in middle range of the distribution; the one sample that we have actually drawn is *probably* among that large majority. (This will be said with greater precision in the section on estimation, below.)

Our goal, when constructing a probability sample, is to design one that well represents the population from which it is drawn. Ideally, $\bar{X} = \mu$. But the one sample we have actually drawn, *no matter how carefully designed and executed*, might still be a sample that very poorly represents the population. Stated graphically, it could be one of the relatively small number of samples that lie in the left or right tail of the normal curve.

A measure of the error of statistical inference is a measure of where, in the sampling distribution of a statistic, the statistic from our one actual sample is probably located. As an illustrative case consider the sample mean. The greater the divergence of $\bar{X}$ from μ, the greater the inferential error committed by inferring the unknown value of μ from the known value of $\bar{X}$. Since μ equals the mean of the sampling distribution of means, it follows that a measure of the divergence of any one of the sample means is given by a measure of the standard deviation of the sampling distribution. That measure is called 'the standard error of the mean' (defined in the first row of Table 4.1). Note that this error is directly proportional to the population standard deviation, σ, and is inversely proportional to the square root of the sample size. The greater the diversity (σ) of a population on a specified variable, the more likely $\bar{X}$ of any given sample diverges from μ. The larger the size of the sample drawn from the population, the more likely $\bar{X}$ converges to μ; but the convergence occurs at a decelerating rate (which means that very large samples are decreasingly cost-efficient).

Formulae for the standard errors of a number of different statistics are recorded in Table 4.1. While these standard errors are now routinely calculated and reported in standard statistical software packages, it is still instructive to examine the algorithms.

Statistical inference and estimation theory

Estimation has been a topic of this chapter from the beginning. When deciding/observing the kind of thing one has just observed, an estimation of fit to some set of criteria of category membership is being made, whether in terms of a Cartesian logic of 'clear and distinct ideas' (kinds) or in terms of a fuzzy-set logic of grades of membership. When deciding/observing the amount of something, whether the countable instances of a kind or the continuous gradient of degrees from zero, an estimation of some otherwise unknowable value is being made. These estimations, qualitative and quantitative, are about description. Here the concern is with generalizing a description – that is, with the use of statistical inference in the estimation of population parameters by sampled observations (i.e., statistics) from that population. The mean of the sampling distribution of a statistic is the reference for a 'point estimate' of a parameter. The standard deviation of the sampling distribution of a statistic – that is, the standard error of the point estimate – is the reference for an 'interval estimate' of that same parameter. The phrase 'interval estimate' means that an interval has been constructed around the point estimate.

It should be evident from the discussion of sampling distributions that a statistic calculated from a probability sample gives us our best single-number estimate (point estimate) of the corresponding parameter. It should also be evident from that discussion that in any given sampling the point estimate of a parameter is unlikely to be exactly on target. For instance, while most of the means in the sampling distribution of means will be in the general vicinity of μ, only a tiny proportion of them will be exactly μ. It follows that we can have little confidence that the mean of our one actual sample, no matter how well designed and carefully executed the sampling, is exactly μ. It also follows, however, that for any given probability sample we can construct an interval, a range of estimates, centered on the point estimate $\bar{X}$ (or any other sample statistic taken as estimate of its corresponding parameter), and thereby increase our confidence that this interval estimate encompasses μ. (Remember, we do not, and in principle will *never*, know beyond doubt the value of a parameter. The aim of inferential statistics is to make the most effective use of the experiences – the observations – we do have in order to *estimate* the value of the parameter.) Finally, it should be evident that we can increase confidence in an interval estimate by increasing the width of the interval around the point estimate, but that we do so at a cost – namely, reduced usefulness of the estimate.

Before turning to the technique of calculating an interval estimate, some properties of estimators will be considered briefly. An *estimator* is a rule or formula for calculating from a sample of observations a point estimate of a

Table 4.1   *Standard errors for selected sampling distributions*

Sampling distribution	Standard error	Comments
Means	$$\sigma_{\bar{X}} = \frac{\sigma}{\sqrt{n}}$$	Even if the population is not normal, the sampling distribution of means is nearly normal for $n \geq 30$. In all cases, $\mu_{\bar{x}} = \mu$.
Proportions	$$\sigma_p = \sqrt{\frac{p(1-p)}{n}} = \sqrt{\frac{pq}{n}}$$	See comments for the sampling distribution of the mean.
Medians	$$\sigma_{\text{med}} = \sigma\sqrt{\frac{\pi}{2n}} = \frac{1.2533\sigma}{\sqrt{n}}$$	The sampling distribution of the median is nearly normal for $n \geq 30$, as the population approaches normality. $\mu_{\text{med}} = \mu$.
Standard deviations	(1) $\sigma_s = \dfrac{\sigma}{\sqrt{2n}}$ (2) $\sigma_s = \sqrt{\dfrac{\mu_4 - \mu_2^2}{4n\mu_4}}$	The sampling distribution is nearly normal for $n \geq 100$. As population approaches normality, (1) applies; if population is not normal, (2) can be used. For $n \geq 100$, $\mu_s \approx \sigma$.
Variances	(1) $\sigma_{s^2} = \sigma^2\sqrt{\dfrac{2}{n}}$ (2) $\sigma_{s^2} = \sqrt{\dfrac{\mu_4 - \mu_2^2}{n}}$	See comments for standard deviations. $\mu_{s^2} = \sigma^2(n-1)/n$, which approaches σ^2 as n becomes large.
First and third quartiles	$$\sigma_{Q_1} = \sigma_{Q_3} = \frac{1.3626\sigma}{\sqrt{n}}$$	See comments for the sampling distribution of the median.
Semi-interquartile range	$$\sigma_Q = \frac{0.7867\sigma}{\sqrt{n}}$$	See comments for the median.

Note: See Table 3.2 for moment designations.

specified parameter. For instance, $\bar{X} = (1/n)\, \Sigma x_i$ is an estimator of μ. It is often the case that two or more estimators can be found to estimate the same parameter (e.g., the mean and median of a sample are alternative estimators of μ). Estimation theory assigns criteria by which to evaluate the 'goodness' of an estimator. These criteria describe properties of the sampling distributions of alternative estimators.

First, an estimator should be *unbiased*, which occurs when the *expected value* of the statistic agrees with the parameter. In other words, the expected value of the estimator always equals the value of the parameter it is estimating. (The emphasis on *expected value* signals that unbiasedness is a property of the sampling distribution, *not* of any specific sample.) Thus, $\bar{X}$ (unlike the median) is an unbiased estimator of μ, because the expected value $E[\bar{X}]$ equals the mean of the sampling

distribution of means, which equals μ. In practical terms, to say that a statistic is an unbiased estimator is to say that if the statistic does not equal its parameter (and it most likely does not) it will be neither more nor less likely to underestimate than to overestimate the parameter. While lack of bias is obviously an important property of an estimator, not all parameters have unbiased estimators.

A second property is *efficiency*. If the sampling distributions of two statistics have the same mean (i.e., expected value), the one with the smaller variance is the more efficient estimator. (Note that efficiency is referring to the standard error of an estimate, which is the standard deviation of a sampling distribution. Thus, the more efficient estimator is the one having the smaller standard error.) Other factors being equal, the most efficient estimator is preferred. However, in any comparison of two alternative estimators the one with the smaller variance might also be a biased estimator. Preference for unbiasedness usually dominates preference for efficiency. Given two unbiased estimators, the one with the smaller variance is preferable.

Whereas the preceding properties pertain to small samples as well as large, this next property of an estimator – *consistency* – is a large-sample (or 'asymptotic') property. An estimator is consistent if it differs from the parameter by an ever smaller amount with increasing probability as sample size n increases. This means that as n increases not only does the sampling distribution of the statistic used as estimator become increasingly centered on the parameter, but also the variance of the sampling distribution becomes increasingly smaller. Thus, as n becomes sufficiently large, the shape of the distribution diverges from the 'bell shape' of the normal curve, as its base becomes increasingly narrow and its vertical axis increasingly elongated. In the limit condition ($n \to \infty$) the distribution collapses to a single point, as the variance drops to zero and the maximum value of $f(x)$ for the normal curve (ordinarily about $0.399/\sigma$) jumps to infinity.

The properties of most parameter estimators used in social science research have already been documented. One should bear in mind that while an estimator that satisfies all three of the properties described above is better than one that does not, there can be trade-offs, such that satisfying one to maximum degree (e.g., maximum efficiency) leads to some sacrifice on another (e.g., some amount of bias). One should also bear in mind that sub-maximal estimators are often better than none at all, so long as one recognizes how, and roughly the degree to which, the estimator is sub-maximal.

Now to the construction of an interval estimate. Recall that the interval is constructed as a function of the standard error of the (point) estimate. Consider as generalized illustration a sample mean $\bar{X}$ and its standard error. We know from previous discussion that the estimator $\bar{X}$ is normally distributed with mean μ and variance σ^2/n. As a result we can use that variance – or more properly its square root, which is the standard error of the mean – to construct an interval around the point estimator. For as we saw in equation (4.8), if μ is set to zero (on the metric

line of the standardized normal distribution), then

$$\bar{X} \pm Z \frac{\sigma}{n^{1/2}} \qquad (4.9)$$

where Z (the standard score) describes any fraction or multiple of the standard error of the mean as the upper and lower limits of an interval estimate of μ. (Recall from Chapter 3 that ordinates of Z demarcate partial areas under the standard normal curve; see Figure 3.2, as well as Figure 4.2(a).)

The following empirical illustrations, a small selection of the many possible applications, are based on data from the National Longitudinal Survey of Youth (NLSY), as described in Chapter 3, and involve three variables: Gender, Schooling (last grade of school completed as of interview in 1994), and age at first marriage as of 1994 (designated as AGEFM).

Let us consider the sample mean of Schooling as an estimate of the mean of Schooling in the sampled population. $\bar{X} = 12.98$ for the sample of 8884 youths (i.e., 8889 minus 5 missing-data cases). The sample standard deviation $s = 2.44$ (with skewness 0.172 and kurtosis 1.32).[37] Assuming no better source of information about the population mean (μ) value of completed grade of schooling among US adults aged 29–37 in 1994, my best point estimate of that value is 12.98.

Recognizing that a best point estimate need not *precisely* equal μ and in fact *could* deviate from μ by some large amount, I convert the point estimate into an interval estimate, thereby increasing the chance that my claim to know the value of μ is both well founded and correct. Obviously that chance can be maximized by setting the bounds of the interval estimate to the full range of possible values. But a claim such as 'μ is between grade zero and grade 25' is both not helpful and extremely wasteful of the (expensive) information obtained by sampling. I want to use this information in a way that optimizes the inevitable trade-off between two goods: the chance that my claim about μ will be helpful (i.e., makes a helpful distinction within the range of possible values) and the chance that my claim about μ is correct (i.e., distinguishes that part of the range that does include the value of μ). In order to achieve this optimum, I next calculate the standard error of the point estimate ($\sigma_{\bar{X}}$), which, as we have seen already, is defined as the ratio of the

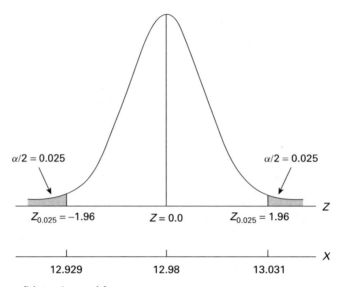

Figure 4.4   *95% confidence interval for a mean*

standard deviation of the population distribution of completed grades of schooling in 1994 (σ) to the square root of the size of my sample (n). Obviously I do not known the value of σ, but I know a good point estimate of it – namely, the sample standard deviation (s = 2.44). Lacking better information, I will use that. Thus, the standard error of the mean is estimated as

$$\hat{\sigma}_{\bar{X}} = 2.44/\,8884^{1/2} = 2.44/94.25 = 0.0259.$$

Notice that this value (0.0259) is quite small relative to the sample mean (12.98). From this fact already I gain confidence in the precision of my sample mean as a reliable estimate of μ. That is, I gain confidence that the sample mean is *a good guess at* (as in the meaning of 'stochastic') the population parameter I want to estimate. But I can be usefully more systematic about that guess and my confidence in it.

Recall from Chapter 3 that in a normal empirical distribution about 68.3 (95.5, 99.7)% of the observations fall within ±1 (2, 3) standard deviation(s) around the mean of the distribution. Shifting from that descriptive context to the inferential context, the same notion of boundedness applies to a sampling distribution. The sample mean is the point estimate of the expected mean of the sampling distribution of means, and about 68.3 (95.5, 99.7)% of the means in the sampling

distribution fall within ±1 (2, 3) standard errors of the expected mean. Thus, following from equation (4.9), bounds can be constructed for $Z = \pm 1$, 2, or 3 – or any other value, such as ±1.96, which is (more precisely than ± 2) the value of Z at the 95% confidence interval:

$$12.98 \pm 1.96(2.44/8884^{1/2}) = 12.98$$
$$\pm\, 1.96 \times 0.0259) = 12.98 \pm 0.051.$$

In other words, I estimate that 95% of the means in the sampling distribution of means lie between 12.929 and 13.031, a very narrow range of values around the sample mean.[38] This is depicted in Figure 4.4, where the point estimate, $\bar{X} = 12.98$, is taken as our best single-number estimate of μ and is therefore equated with the mean of the normal distribution, $\mu_z = 0$. A standard deviation of ± 1.96 standard scores, encompassing 95% of the area under the normal curve, corresponds to the observed-metric interval from 12.929 to 13.031. The area outside those bounds, given as $1 - p = \alpha$, contains 5% of the total area under the curve and is here divided symmetrically, $\alpha = 0.025$ in each tail. The area designated by α, often called 'the critical region', will figure prominently in the next subsection of this chapter.

Notice that, had I used $Z = \pm 2.33$ (the 98% confidence interval) rather than $Z = \pm 1.96$ when calculating the confidence interval, the resulting estimate would have been 12.920 to 13.040. Had I used $Z = \pm1.645$ (the 90% confidence interval), the resulting estimate would have been 12.937 to 13.023. Notice that while the difference from 90% to 95% or, even more, to 98% is suggestive of a substantial improvement, the three intervals around the point estimate differ very little. This is because the standard error of the mean is so small, which in turn is a function of the large sample size and the small size of the sample standard deviation relative to the sample mean.[39] The sample standard deviation is small, we surmise, because the population variance is small. It should be intuitively evident that an estimate of μ in a population in which all members are very similar on X will have a smaller error than will an estimate of μ in a population in which the members are highly diverse on X, all else being equal.

The alternative interval estimates calculated just above invite a return to the question of the meaning of a 'confidence interval' or of 'the level of confidence in an estimate'. The *interval* in question is empirical; it is calculated from sample statistics (mean and standard deviation), as exemplified above. The *probability* value associated with an interval pertains *not* to the particular sample statistics (for they are precisely as calculated) but to the process in which they are used as estimates of the corresponding parameters. Confusion between the two contexts is potentially serious in consequence. Using the present illustration by way of instruction, it should be clear that a sentence such as 'The probability that the value of μ lies between 12.929 and 13.031 is 0.95' is nonsensical. Why nonsensical? Because μ is not a random variable. It is, for any given population, an instantaneously fixed value. Immediately upon my having drawn the sample of observations any confidence interval that I construct necessarily *either does or does not* contain μ. The statement of 'confidence in the estimate' refers to the sample mean and its sampling distribution. It does not in any sense dictate an answer to the question 'What is the value of μ?'. This judgment *always* remains to be made, no matter how many 'confidence intervals' (or, to preview the next section of this chapter, 'significance levels') one wants to construct. The issue (in the vocabulary of 'confidence intervals') is simply that, while my best point estimate of μ is (and, barring new and superior information, will remain) 12.98, I think it likely that this value reflects

some amount of sampling error, and I want to generate as reliably as I can some information about how large that sampling error might be. In the nature of the case, the only information I have is contained in my sample of observations. I do not create any information not already in my sample, but I try to maximize the utility of the information that *is* there. My method of assaying sampling error (and remember, 'guessing' is perfectly substitutable as the operative gerund) is to ask a question of the form 'How likely would be an error of size e?', where e here represents sampling error and is specified as a multiple of $\hat{\sigma}_{\bar{X}}$ (e.g., $\pm1.96\hat{\sigma}_{\bar{X}}$). The size of the multiple has associated with it a probability value *only* in the theoretical context of a sampling distribution. With that context in mind, I can utter sentences such as 'If I could exactly repeat this estimation a very large number of times, I could be confident that only about 5% of the sample means would lie outside the interval between 12.929 and 13.031'. The import of that sentence is considerable. Whereas initially, having just calculated the sample mean, I saw no information from which to make a systematically informed guess about where that mean is located in its sampling distribution ('Is it an unlikely sample mean, located in one of the distributional tails, or is it a highly likely sample mean, thus close to the mean of the distribution of means?'), I am now better prepared to make that judgment. I am more confident now than initially that 12.98 is a highly likely sample mean from the population of youth, and because of *that* gain I am more confident that 12.98 is close to μ. But the confidence I gain is a matter of judgment, not an algorithmic statement.[40]

Before turning to another example of interval estimation, a brief comment about the symmetry of an interval will add insight and perhaps advance the cause of deritualizing usages. Ordinarily an interval estimate is constructed symmetrically about the point estimate: the interval that is stipulated as some preferred probability range (e.g., 95%), once converted from the Z (or t) metric back to the metric of the sample observations, is distributed half to either side of the point estimate. This is appropriate when the point estimator is known to be unbiased (as is $\bar{X}$), and in the absence of any contrary information about the sampled population. However, there are conditions under which the interval may be appropriately distributed more heavily to one side than to the other. Consider a population distribution for X with a possible range from zero to, say, ten. Assume $\bar{X} = 3.8$, with $s = 2.8$ for a random sample $n = 1000$. This implies $\sigma_{\bar{X}} = 0.089$ and, for the 95% confidence interval, 3.8 ± 0.17 (or 3.63 to 3.97). These values appear to be perfectly regular. But let us say you already have reliable information that values of zero and one, while possible, are rare. This information suggests that your sample mean is probably too unlikely – specifically, too far toward the left tail of the sampling distribution. One response would be to sample again. But assume that you cannot (the phenomenon is past, you cannot regain entry to the site, you lack the funds, etc.). An alternative response would be to shift most or all of the interval estimate to the right of the sample mean (e.g., $3.8 - 0.34$, an interval from 3.8 to 4.14). More generally, a 'one-sided' interval would be preferred if interest is in estimating whether, at some level of confidence, μ (or some other parameter) is 'at least as large (small) as' some value or 'no larger (smaller) than' some value, where the stipulated value has substantive empirical (i.e., non-statistical) importance.

Moving on to the importance of sample size, recall my inference that mean Schooling among all adults aged 29–37 in 1994 was 12.98. Because that inference was based on the large number of observations in the NLSY, I could have good confidence that s closely approximated σ. Had the sample size been not 8884 but (say) 30, I could not have had that same confidence. As sample size diminishes, the sampling distribution of the mean and, even more, the sampling distribution of the standard deviation begin to diverge from the normal distribution. The divergence is inconsequentially small, however, until the sample size becomes quite small.[41]

With the shift to a small sample, s becomes a poor approximation to σ, and probably *under*estimates it.[42] For purposes of illustration, I extracted from the 8884 cases a random subsample, $n = 30$. The mean is here 12.80 (which is only 1.4% smaller than 12.98); the standard deviation is 1.92 (which is 21.3% smaller than 2.44). If I substitute these small-sample statistics into the formula used above for calculating an interval estimate (the 95% confidence interval), I obtain

$$12.80 \pm 1.96(1.92/30^{1/2}) = 12.80 \pm 1.96 \times 0.3505 = 12.80 \pm 0.687$$

which implies bounds of 12.113 and 13.487 (rather than 12.929 and 13.031).

Note that this wider interval results from two (partly offsetting) differences – the smaller n and the smaller estimate of σ – which is to say that the standard error of the mean is now considerably larger (0.3505 rather than 0.0259), primarily because of the smaller sample size. There is still another difference that should have been taken into account in that calculation, however, but was not. I retained the assumption that the sampling distribution of the mean is normal, even though with small samples there is greater variability in the sampling distribution. In using the normal distribution when locating the mean associated with the 95% confidence interval in its sampling distribution, I neglected the fact of greater variability. In order to maintain the same conservative posture about sampling error as before, I should switch from Z to the appropriate t distribution, since the set of t distributions allows different amounts of variability in the sampling distribution (the amount depending on the exact size of the sample).[43] With this correction,[44] I determine from a table of t distributions that with $n - 1 = 29$ degrees of freedom the appropriate value of t for the 95% confidence interval is ± 2.045 (rather than ± 1.96, as in the Z distribution); therefore,

$$12.80 \pm 2.045 \, (1.92/29^{1/2}) = 12.80 \pm 2.045 \times 0.3565 = 12.80 \pm 0.729$$

which implies bounds of 12.071 and 13.529. In this instance the difference is quite modest (due to the fact that $\hat{\sigma}_{\bar{X}} = 0.3565$, albeit much larger than before, is still small relative to $\bar{X} = 12.80$).

Sometimes the metric of our observations is not interval or ratio but a count of cases within (ranked or unranked) categories. Accordingly, as a second exercise, assume interest in the fact that 1204 of the 8884 sample members (i.e., 13.6%) had not completed grade 12 as of 1994. This proportion ($\hat{p} = 0.136$) is my best estimate of the actual proportion p in the sampled population, but I want to assess the reliability of that point estimate. The procedural logic of the assessment is exactly the same as it was for the sample mean. First, I calculate the standard error of the sample proportion, which is approximately $\sigma_p = (pq/n)^{1/2}$ (where $q = 1 - p$). As before, since I do not know σ_p (because I do not know the parametric value of p, and therefore of q), I use the sample statistics ($\hat{p}$ and $\hat{q}$) in substitution. Given the large sample size, the Z distribution appropriately represents the sampling distribution.[45] Thus, the 95% confidence interval is

$$0.136 \pm 1.96 \ (0.136 \times 0.864/8884)^{1/2}$$
$$= 0.136 \pm 1.96 \ (0.000 \ 013 \ 2)^{1/2}$$
$$= 0.136 \pm 0.0071,$$

or bounds of 0.1289 and 0.1431.

Determining a confidence interval for a sample proportion (as for a sample mean) is sensitive to variability in the sampling distribution, which increases as sample size declines. With proportions the rate of increase becomes steeper as parametric p approaches either of its limits (zero and one). This characteristic reduces the reliability of the normal estimate of the standard error of a proportion unless that proportion is based on an extremely large sample. An adjustment proposed by Wilson (1927) is a useful response for small samples. Whereas a sample $\hat{p}$ is calculated as the ratio x/n (where $x = 1204$ in the above example, and $n = 8884$), adjusted $\hat{p}^*$ is given as the ratio $(x + 2)/(n + 4)$. It should be clear, however, that whereas either bound of a confidence interval is a random variable, the limits of parametric p are constants and theoretical. Thus, a calculated lower (upper) bound that touches or exceeds zero (one) must be shifted away from that limit.

Because variability in sampling distribution increases more rapidly for $s^2 = npq$ than for $s^2 = (1/n) \sum (x - \bar{X})^2$ as n becomes small, the boundary for 'small' is typically set at 100 rather than 30. At $n = 100$ the t distribution is barely more conservative than the Z distribution. Special tables given in Pearson and Hartley (1954: 195) may be used instead.

The preceding exercises concerned problems of estimation in a single sample. Often we want to compare sample estimates across sampled populations or across multiple samplings of the same population, in which case the statistic of interest is a *difference* (between means, between proportions, between correlation coefficients, etc.). Thus, the sampling distribution is of a difference term, as in $\bar{X}_1 - \bar{X}_2$, which converges to the normal as the number of sampled difference terms increases.[46] Assuming independent large random samples of observations of a variable that is normally distributed for each of the sampled populations, the standard error of the difference $\bar{X}_1 - \bar{X}_2$ is given as

$$\sigma_{\bar{X}_1 - \bar{X}_2} = (\sigma_1^2/n_1 + \sigma_2^2/n_2)^{1/2} \qquad (4.10)$$

and a confidence interval is therefore given as

$$\bar{X}_1 - \bar{X}_2 \pm Z \ \sigma_{\bar{X}_1 - \bar{X}_2}. \qquad (4.11)$$

If the metric is in proportions, the same logic applies for the difference $p_1 - p_2$, with the standard error of the difference approximated by

$$\sigma_{p_1 - p_2} = (p_1 q_1/n_1 + p_2 q_2/n_2)^{1/2} \qquad (4.12)$$

using the sample proportions $\hat{p}$ and $\hat{q}$ ($= 1 - \hat{p}$) as substitutes for the parametric values.

Matters become more complicated if either n_1 or n_2 is small. Strictly speaking, both of the foregoing difference-of-statistic procedures assume not only large samples but also that the variances of the compared populations are equal. The latter (stringent) assumption can be tested by calculating a ratio of the sample variances, s_1^2/s_2^2. The sampling distribution of this 'variance ratio' is the set of F distributions, which vary according to the degree of freedom respectively of the numerator and of the denominator.[47] As can be seen from an inspection of the table of 'percentage points' of the F distribution, the ratio remains close to 1.0 (i.e., close to the $\sigma_1 = \sigma_2$ equality) until either sample size declines to about 120, then increases from 1.0 at an accelerating rate as the sample sizes decline from 120. Thus, with very large samples the assumption of equal variances can be relaxed without much consequence. With small samples the assumption must be observed, however. If $\sigma_1 = \sigma_2 = \sigma$ (i.e., 'common variance'), then for the small-sample context

$$\sigma_{\bar{X}_1 - \bar{X}_2} = \sigma(1/n_1 + 1/n_2)^{1/2} \qquad (4.13)$$

with the assumed common variance estimated as the weighted average of the two sample variances:

$$\sigma \approx s = [[s_1^2 \ (n_1 - 1) + s_2^2 \ (n_2 - 1)] \ / \ (n_1 + n_2 - 2)]^{1/2}.$$

This yields confidence intervals of

$$\bar{X}_1 - \bar{X}_2 \pm t \ [[s_1^2 \ (n_1 - 1) + s_2^2 (n_2 - 1)]/$$
$$[n_1 + n_2 - 2]^{1/2} \ [1/n_1 + 1/n_2]^{1/2}]. \qquad (4.14)$$

where degrees of freedom are defined as $n_1 + n_2 - 2$.

The assumption of independence is important because otherwise the probability of an observation in one sample would be a function of the probability of an observation in the other sample. In some research settings dependence is unavoidable, however. Indeed, a virtue can be made of it, as in a quasi-experimental design in which members of a 'control group' and members of a 'test group' are matched, one by one across groups, on (in principle) all relevant variables except the 'test variable', to which members of the test group alone are exposed. In this way, between-group individual-level variation on each relevant variable except the test variable has been reduced to zero, leaving only variation in effect of the test variable to be manifest in the specified 'post-test' outcome (relative to the corresponding 'pre-test' measurement, if available). Clearly in this design the assumption of independence has been violated, deliberately so. Insofar as exact 'pairwise matching' has been closely approximated – that is, a member of one group and an exactly matching member of the other group form a pair – the variable of interest becomes the *within-pair difference* in the value of the post-test outcome (with the value of the corresponding pre-test measurement, if available, subtracted). Designating that difference as $d_i = x_{1i} - x_{2i}$ for the ith pair, and the number of paired differences as n_d, a confidence interval around the mean can be calculated as

$$\bar{d} \pm t(s_d/n_d^{1/2}) \qquad (4.15)$$

if the distribution of d is normal.

Researchers who rely on large-sample survey data often find themselves in the position of comparing statistics for different groups within the sampled population as if the groups were separately sampled populations. In the NLSY data on education, for instance, it might be of interest to compare mean grade completed as of 1994 by gender: 13.08 for 4477 women and 12.89 for 4407 men (with respective standard deviations of 2.43 and 2.46). Treating the two groups as if they were independently randomly sampled from the populations of all men and all women aged 29–37 in 1994, I could calculate the standard error of the (13.08 – 12.89 = 0.19) difference in means as

$$\hat{\sigma}_{\bar{X}_1 - \bar{X}_2} = (2.43^2/4477 + 2.46^2/4407)^{1/2}$$
$$= (5.90/4477 + 6.05/4407)^{1/2} = 0.052$$

using the sample variances as estimates of the population variances (which estimates, it may be noted, are very nearly equal: 5.90/6.05 = 0.98). From that standard error, I could set the (e.g.) 95% confidence interval as

$$0.19 \pm 1.96 \times 0.052 = 0.19 \pm 0.102$$

which implies an interval from 0.088 to 0.292.

It should be obvious that we cannot assume that the population of women aged 29–37 in 1994 and the population of men in the same age range in 1994 were independently randomly sampled. In this particular instance, as it happens, the outcome for the one actual sample is very probably only slightly different from the outcome of independent samplings of men and women. But there are many other possible cases in which partitioning a single random sample into two (or more) parts in alignment with social groupings and then treating each of the parts as if it were an independent random sampling of one of the social groupings will yield a set of outcomes different from those that would be obtained from actually independent random samplings. The size of the difference tends to increase as the distribution of the groupings diverges from a rectangular distribution.[48]

Let us look at another case. My substantive claim is that educational attainment is lower among those who marry at young ages than among those who do not, regardless of gender. Using the same NLSY data set, I inspect comparative distributions of Schooling (Table 4.2).[49] Comparing the mean for men whose first marriages occurred at or before age 20 to the mean for men whose first marriage occurred after age 20, I estimate that difference to be 1.62 (= 13.30 – 11.68) and the standard error of that estimate to be

$$\hat{\sigma}_{\bar{X}_1 - \bar{X}_2} = (\hat{\sigma}_1^2/n_1 + \hat{\sigma}_2^2/n_2)^{1/2}$$
$$= (2.53^2/2384 + 1.89^2/646)^{1/2} = 0.091,$$

which implies a 95% confidence interval of 1.62 ± 0.178 (i.e., from 1.442 to 1.798). Likewise, the corresponding values for women are an estimated difference in means of 1.79, a standard error of 0.075, and a 95% confidence interval of 1.79 ± 0.147 (i.e., from 1.643 to 1.937). Similarly, I could compare men and women whose first marriages occurred by age 20: the corresponding values would be a difference in means of 0.32, a standard error of 0.092, and a 95% confidence interval of 0.32 ± 0.180 (i.e., from 0.140 to 0.500). And so forth.

Table 4.2 *Completed grade of school, 1994, by gender, marital status, and age at first marriage among US adults aged 29–37 years*

	Men				Women			
	Age at first marriage		Not yet married	All men	Age at first marriage		Not yet married	All women
	≤20	>20			≤20	>20		
<12	0.259	0.108	0.186	0.154	0.189	0.067	0.137	0.122
12	0.556	0.426	0.444	0.451	0.544	0.342	0.391	0.418
13–15	0.150	0.226	0.207	0.209	0.217	0.294	0.255	0.261
16	0.028	0.140	0.102	0.112	0.032	0.191	0.120	0.124
>16	0.008	0.101	0.061	0.075	0.018	0.105	0.096	0.075
Total	1.000	1.000	1.000	1.000	1.000	1.000	1.000	1.000
n	646	2384	1306	4336	1421	2001	976	4398
Row proportion	0.149	0.550	0.301	1.000	0.323	0.455	0.222	1.000
$\bar{X}$	11.68	13.30	12.77	12.89	12.00	13.79	13.21	13.08
s	1.89	2.53	2.38	2.46	2.01	2.37	2.51	2.43

Source: National Longitudinal Survey of Youth.

What conclusions might I draw from such comparisons? One possibility is that men and women do not differ in Schooling even after controlling for the difference in AGEFM. The evidence for this consists of the fact that the 95% confidence interval for the difference in means between men and women whose first marriages occurred by age 20 (just calculated as 0.140 to 0.500) overlaps the 95% confidence interval for the difference in means between men and women whose first marriages occurred after age 20. This evidence is pertinent, to be sure, but it is apparent that it is based on a violation of the assumption of independence, since 'male' and 'female' are analytically interdependent categories which were not sampled separately. How strong is the effect of this assumption violation?

Before considering that question here and in the general case, it will be useful to describe a common error in the interpretation of interval-estimate comparisons, such as the one made just above. Notice that the point estimate (0.49) for the difference in means between men and women whose first marriages occurred after age 20 lies within the range of the 95% confidence interval (0.140 to 0.500) for the difference in means between men and women whose first marriages occurred by age 20. Similarly, I *might* conclude not only that adults whose first marriages occurred by age 20 and adults whose first marriages occurred after age 20 did differ in mean Schooling but also that this difference was probably greater for women than for men – the evidence for this latter

gender comparison being the fact that the 95% confidence interval around the difference-in-means point estimate for women (1.79 ± 1.96 × 0.075, or bounds of 1.643 and 1.937) does not include the difference-in-means point estimate for men (1.62). However, taken at face value this evidentiary base becomes ambiguous, for it is apparent that the 95% confidence interval around the difference-in-means point estimate for *men* (1.62 ± 1.96 × 0.091, or bounds of 1.442 and 1.798) *does* include the difference-in-means point estimate for women (1.79). We seem to be stuck with mutually contrary conclusions. In fact, not; because we have been comparing *unlike* statistics. Point estimates should be compared to point estimates, interval estimates to interval estimates. The correct comparison above is the fact that the two interval estimates, one for men and the other for women, are overlapping.[50]

Now let us consider the generally applicable question about violation of the assumption of independence. In the case of Table 4.2, for instance, it is easy to see that the social processes that sort people (whether by gender or not) into a joint distribution of Schooling and AGEFM are non-random processes. Some intersections of the two distributions (or three, if gender is included) are likelier than others. Recall that random sampling assumes that all of the possible observations are equally likely. Therefore, whereas a random sample (of sufficient size) gives a representation (of sufficient goodness) of a very large finite population (even if that population diverges from the normal distribution), that same degree of 'goodness of representation' will almost surely *not* apply to the unlikely combinations in the joint distributions of two (or more) variables. The reason, as we have repeatedly seen, is that unlikely observations have relatively low absolute frequencies ('small *n*') *and*, because of the small *n*, variances that are more likely underestimated. Thus, any statement that can be made with some degree of confidence about the statistical properties of an entire sample can be made about the statistical properties of portions of that sample but with lower reliability.

What happens when one makes a comparative statement about two (or more) parts of a single random sample on the assumption of independence, when in fact the sort between/among the parts is far from random? Clearly the assumption of independence is not supportable. What consequence does that hold for any conclusions about (for instance) confidence intervals around difference-of-means statistics?

The consequence is *necessarily* that any such interval estimate will be, if different, *wider* (i.e., have wider bounds) than it would have if the dependence were taken into account.[51] If sampling from one population is dependent on sampling from another population (either because of dependent sampling or because the distribution on some variable *X* in one population actually depends on the distribution of *X*, or a strong correlate of *X*, in the other population), the consequence will be that variation in *X* in one sampled population is correlated with variation in *X* in the other sampled population. Now recall that in the formula for the standard error of a difference in means (or proportions), the two sample variances, each weighted by the inverse of the sample size, are added together. But this involves a 'double counting', to the extent of the size of the covariance. (Note that in perfectly matched pairs, where necessarily $s_1^2 = s_2^2$, the double counting is avoided by use of the 'common variance', which is $s_1^2 = s_2^2$.) When calculating (for instance) the error of a difference-in-means estimate under a *counterfactual* assumption of independence, one is treating the sum of the two variances in the denominator of the formula as if the two variances were completely non-redundant of information. But if there is covariation on *X* between the two supposedly independently sampled populations, the variances are *not* completely non-redundant: the extent of the

covariance is the extent of the redundancy. Thus, (1) the value of the denominator will be larger than it would be with that redundancy removed; (2) whatever the (non-zero) size of the numerator of the formula, the quotient will be exaggerated; and (3) for any value of Z (or t) the bounds of the interval estimation will be wider than 'need' be.

Statistical inference and decision theory

In the preceding subsection, statistical information was used to assess sampling error in order to improve the reliability of a point estimate by converting it into an interval estimate. In this next subsection, the same statistical information will be used to decide how the process that has generated our observations might fit some externally generated claims about reality. These decisions are conventionally referred to as 'hypothesis tests'. The same empirical illustrations that were used in the preceding section will be carried forward to this section.

Assume an observed difference either (1) between the statistics – the means of variable X_1, for example, or the correlations of two variables X_1 and X_2 – of two probability samples that are differentiated in space, time, and/or observer perspective (including samples differentiated, at least in principle, by exact replication) or (2) between the statistic of one probability sample and a theoretical expectation of what the corresponding population parameter should be.[52] Of the first sort of observed difference we ask 'Are the two sample statistics different because they are from two different populations, or are they different because of random errors in sampling the same population twice?'. Of the second sort we ask 'Is the sample statistic the same as the result expected by (implied by, predicted by) the theory?'. In either case, the question is basically the same: 'Given that I *have* observed a difference, whether between two empirical facts (two sample statistics) or between one empirical fact and a theoretical expectation, to what source(s) should the difference be attributed?' The immediate candidates are features of the observational act itself, the most basic being category error and measurement error. Let us assume that we are confident that the observed difference is due to more than the combined effects of all errors of classification and measurement.[53] The next candidate is sampling error.

In principle, the observed difference is almost surely due in some part to sampling error, for (as noted before) it is highly unlikely that a statistic from any given sample will precisely equal the corresponding population parameter. The key question is 'What is the probability that the observed difference is due *wholly* to sampling error?'. If our estimate of this probability is sufficiently low, we can have confidence that some part of the observed difference is not due to sampling error. This confidence, when combined with our prior confidence that classification and measurement error are sufficiently low, leads to the conclusion that the observed difference is probably due to factors extraneous to the observational act itself. These factors are sometimes called 'real-world factors', an otherwise nonsensical distinction that is meant to emphasize that the motivating interest of our endeavor is to learn about more than the immediate consequences of our acts of inquiry.

Let us consider again the estimated mean of Schooling, 12.98 (with $s = 2.44$, $n = 8884$, and $\hat{\sigma}_{\bar{x}} = 0.0259$). Assume that in another study of the same sampled population, conducted via a separate sampling by another researcher who measured variables with exactly the same error, the estimated mean is 13.73 (with $s = 2.51$, $n = 2455$, and $\hat{\sigma}_{\bar{x}} = 0.0507$). Should I conclude that this difference in estimates is probably due to sampling error, or should I conclude that one of the estimates is probably better than the other? Already I can say that, given the respective sample statistics, and assuming all else is equal, the first estimate is probably the better, because it is based on a larger sample size which is reflected in the smaller standard error. But in making that conclusion I have assumed that the two estimates do differ other than by probable sampling error. While empirically there is no doubt that 13.73 > 12.98, the issue here is not the empirical difference as such but whether the unknown amount of sampling error in each of the two samplings is large enough to encompass the empirical difference. I should assess probable sampling error before deciding about difference.

In order to make that decision I need a decision rule. The decision rule *could* be ad hoc, but that would be an invitation to error from personal bias.[54] An explicit standard decision rule guards against (indeliberate) influence of personal bias. We have been using decision rules throughout this chapter, usually without remarking on them as such. In the classificatory action of observation, for instance, decision rules sort observations into kinds, either by a Cartesian logic of clear and distinct category boundaries or by a fuzzy-set logic that allows uncertainty at the boundary. Likewise, decision rules are used in measurement actions – for instance, in order to sort observations into the types of arithmetic operations that can be performed. Here, as in the preceding subsection, the decision rules have to do with random errors of sampling.

Recall that when building a confidence interval, I can decide whether the interval should be symmetrical (the usual choice) or asymmetrical, with the interval arrayed mostly or entirely to one side of the point estimate. The same choice is available in the context of deciding between competing hypotheses. Known as the choice between a 'two-tailed' and a 'one-tailed test', this choice should be explicitly part of one's decision rule. The logic is as follows. The basic decision for my difference-of-means test is whether the observed difference (0.75) can or cannot be said to differ from zero, at some level of confidence, once sampling error has been taken into account. This choice between two possible states normally begins (for reasons that will become clear later) with the 'null' state – that is, the state of 'no difference', commonly called 'the null hypothesis', which is formulated as (in the context of the present example)

$$H_0 : \mu_1 = \mu_2.$$

The second of the two states, commonly known as 'the alternative hypothesis', is presence of difference – that is, a difference even after allowance for probable sampling error. This is the 'two-tailed' formulation of the decision rule. By adopting it I am saying 'Any difference, if large enough, counts; I don't care which of the estimated means is bigger or smaller'.

Stated abstractly, either of two states, $A > B$ or $A < B$, equally well satisfies $A \neq B$. In order to discriminate between $A > B$ and $A < B$, I must have information that specifies *direction* of difference. This is analogous to the decision about distributing a confidence interval asymmetrically. In deciding to which side of the point estimate the bulk of the interval should be placed, I rely on information external to my sample statistics. As in the earlier

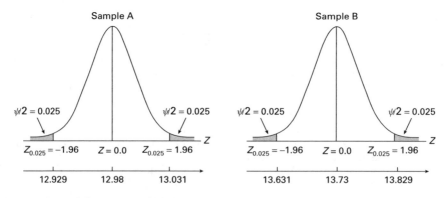

Figure 4.5   *95% confidence intervals for two sample means*

illustration, the information might derive from prior reliable experience. In the context of hypothesis testing, the information can also derive from an implication ('theoretical expectation') of a substantive theory. In any case, when sufficient information about *expected direction* of a difference is available, the decision rule can be formulated as a one-tailed rather than as a two-tailed test. Whatever the source of the information, it should be independent of the sample statistics being used in the test, and it should be specified explicitly as part of the decision rule. These strictures are important because, as will become clear, it is generally easier to conclude in favor of 'difference' in a one-tailed than in a two-tailed test (at any given level of confidence). Note, by the way, that while a two-tailed test is usually constructed symmetrically, this is not by logical necessity. It is conceivable (if unlikely in practice) that one's independent information about direction of difference would justify not a one-tailed test but, say, a one-and-a-half-tailed test (that is, reserving some chance of difference in the unexpected direction).

Let us return to the empirical example and proceed with a two-tailed decision rule. I need to decide whether the observed difference is greater than zero once sampling error has been taken into account, but I do not know the actual amount of sampling error. I do know by the central limit theorem, however, that in general sampling error is distributed normally for means and differences of means.[55] I used this knowledge when constructing confidence intervals, which were simply point estimates with specified

amounts of allowance for sampling error placed around them. I can do exactly the same in my present context of decision-making, as depicted in Figure 4.5. The graph shows the two sample estimates of μ in relation to each other on the same number line of the observed metric (Schooling). My decision rule begins with the null state, which is that the two estimates differ only by sampling error. An equivalent way of making that statement is that the two samples are from one and the same population, not two. Because I am here assuming an interval metric, I can translate each of the sample means into its corresponding value in the Z metric. If I next set a specified confidence interval (e.g., the 95% interval) around each of the sample means, I can determine whether the lower bound of the larger mean (13.73) overlaps the upper bound of the smaller mean (12.98). If they do overlap, I have reason to believe that the observed difference between these means is probably due to sampling error. In the present case, it is clear that there is no overlap: the lower bound of the larger mean (13.631) exceeds the upper bound of the smaller mean (13.031). Based on that evidence, I would conclude that the observed difference is *probably* due to more than sampling error.

A more direct approach to the decision focuses specifically on the difference term (13.73 − 12.98 = 0.75). Rather than place confidence intervals around each mean and then inspect for overlap, we can locate the difference term within *its* own sampling distribution. As before, the first step is to calculate the standard error of the difference of means, which is given as the square root of the sum of inversely weighted variances, the latter estimated by the respective sample variances.[56] Thus,

$$\hat{\sigma}_{\bar{X}_1 - \bar{X}_2} = (s_1^2/n_1 + s_2^2/n_2)^{1/2} = (2.44^2/8884$$
$$+ 2.51^2/2455)^{1/2} = 0.057.$$

The difference term is defined in the general case as

$$(\bar{X}_1 - \bar{X}_2) - D_0$$

as before, except for the addition of D_0. If the null expectation is $\mu_1 = \mu_2$ (i.e., the observed difference in sample means is due to sampling error), $D = 0$. More often than not, we assume the null hypothesis and set D to zero. This need not be the case, of course. If a particular theory strictly implies a specific size (and therefore usually direction) of difference between μ_1 and μ_2, or if prior experience has repeatedly indicated a specific value, one would be justified in proceeding from that value, thus setting D to that value instead of zero. Usually, as in the present case, we assume $D = 0$, because usually neither is our theory so rigorous nor our experience so confident as to support the stronger assumption that $D \neq 0$. Therefore, setting the difference term in ratio to its standard error, we get

$$Z = (\bar{X}_1 - \bar{X}_2)/\hat{\sigma}_{\bar{X}_1 - \bar{X}_2} = 0.75/0.057 = 13.16,$$

which is quite large. Before considering that result, let us make a short detour.

It should be apparent that I *could* have used the standard error of the difference in means to put a confidence interval around the difference term. Had I selected the 95% confidence interval, it would have been

$$0.75 \pm 1.96 \times 0.057 = 0.75 \pm 0.112,$$

or bounds of 0.638 and 0.862. Since 0.75 is our best point estimate of the expected value of the sampling distribution, we set 0.75 (an observed-metric value) equal to zero in the standard-score or Z metric, and the bounds 0.638 and 0.862 are then equal to $Z = -1.96$ and $Z = +1.96$.

But in the more direct approach to hypothesis testing, rather than calculate the confidence interval we algebraically rearrange

$$(\bar{X}_1 - \bar{X}_2) \pm Z \, \hat{\sigma}_{\bar{X}_1 - \bar{X}_2}.$$

to obtain

$$Z = (\bar{X}_1 - \bar{X}_2)/\hat{\sigma}_{\bar{X}_1 - \bar{X}_2}.$$

This standard-score value is then compared to a 'critical value', Z_c, in the table of areas under the standard normal distribution. Z_c is 'critical' because it sets a standard against which to compare the calculated ratio of a difference of means to its standard error. (Note that this ratio is simply a translation of the difference term from its observed metric to the standard-score metric.) The larger that ratio, the greater the confidence we can have in rejecting the null hypothesis – that is, conclude that the observed difference of means is not zero.

The value of Z_c is set by the researcher in advance of the hypothesis test. Some conventional choices of Z_c values are shown in Table 4.3 (an extract from the Appendix at the back of the book). Recall that $\alpha = 1 - p$ and is sometimes called the 'critical region' or 'critical area' of the theoretical distribution. When the standard-score equivalent of an observed statistic is larger than Z_c (smaller than $-Z_c$) that statistic is located in the $\alpha/2$ 'critical area' of the right (left) tail of the distribution (here, the normal distribution).[57] Here, as when setting confidence intervals, there is nothing sacrosanct or magical about these numbers, either Z_c or α. They are entirely conventional choices, and one is free to select a different number. Typically one begins with a value of α that is personally acceptable and that will be acceptable to one's audience (where 'acceptability' is defined in terms of managing errors of decision, a topic treated below). In a one-tailed test, that value of α (e.g., 0.05 or 0.01) describes an area entirely in either the left or the right tail of the normal curve; determination of whether it is the left or the right tail is made not from the sample statistics but from prior information. In a two-tailed test the value of α describes the sum of an area in the left tail and an area in the right tail of the normal curve. Usually these two areas are equal – in which case, if one's preference for α is 0.05 (or 0.01), then 0.025 (or 0.005) will be in each tail.

Returning once again to the empirical example involving (in part) the NLSY data, it is apparent that the standard-score equivalent of the observed difference in means $(Z = 13.16)$ is very far to the right of $Z_c = +1.96$. Thus, if in fact $\mu_1 = \mu_2$, the observed difference in sample means $(13.73 - 12.98 = 0.75)$ would be an extremely unlikely observation. As seen in the Appendix, a standard score as large as 13.16 is *so* unlikely that it is 'off the chart'. Indeed, the probability of observing

Table 4.3 *Rejection regions for some conventional values of α in a standard normal distribution*

α	Two-tailed test	One-tailed test Lower	One-tailed test Upper
0.10	$Z < -1.645$ or $Z > 1.645$	$Z < -1.28$	$Z > 1.28$
0.05	$Z < -1.96$ or $Z > 1.96$	$Z < -1.645$	$Z > 1.645$
0.01	$Z < -2.575$ or $Z > 2.575$	$Z < -2.33$	$Z > 2.33$
0.001	$Z < -3.27$ or $Z > 3.27$	$Z < -3.08$	$Z > 3.08$

$Z > 5.0$ is less than one in 3 million. Hence, we conclude from the hypothesis test that the observed difference is very probably due to more than sampling error. Where does that conclusion leave us? Recall that we began with the assumption of equal measurement and category error across samples. Rarely can we be so confident in that assumption. The observed difference could also be due to non-sampling error – for instance, if one of the samplings was by a relatively poor sampling frame, or if one of the samplings had a higher rate of (non-randomly distributed) refusals of cooperation, and so forth. Recall also that we began with the assumption of two independent samplings of the same population. But if the samplings were separated in time, it is possible that the relevant parameter had changed during the interval. Finally, while we are justifiably highly confident in our conclusion that the observed difference is due to more than sampling error, it is still possible nonetheless (even with Z as large as 13.16) that one of the samples was a fluke, a highly unlikely chance outcome.

Notice what we do *not* do, when concluding that the observed difference was probably due to more than sampling error. We do not partition the observed difference into a part due to sampling error and a part due to other factors (presumably 'real world', if we have ruled out category and measurement error, non-sampling error, etc.). We lack the information that would tell us where to draw that line of partition. Even when *highly* confident that sampling error is not the whole story, we have not somehow removed sampling error from an estimate. Sampling error remains an unknown quantity, integral to a statistic descriptively, inferentially, and in any explanatory uses that we make of it. Remembrance of this incorrigible limitation can help us to avoid some misleading uses of 'significance testing' (see below).

The foregoing empirical example is an instance of what is called a 'two-sample inference test'. With the assumption of independent sampling, one can thus conduct inference tests of the difference between sample-specific statistics (e.g., difference in mean years of schooling). Often, however, one wants instead to compare, within a single sample, estimations for differently specified models having the same dependent variable (where 'same' here includes functional form; e.g., $Y \neq \log Y$). For instance, the model described in Table 4.2 specifies completed schooling as a function of gender, marital status, and (if ever married) age at first marriage. There are embedded within that specification at least six other alternative specifications (ignoring the possibility of interaction terms and issues of functional form). One of these six, for example, treats completed schooling as a function of gender and marital status only, regarding age at first marriage as irrelevant. How does one decide between alternative specifications? Strictly speaking, of course, this is not an issue of sampling inference, and we can easily exceed the power of any inferential tests by overusing the information of one sample as if it came from two or more independent samples. Model selection should be made primarily on theoretical grounds. If one has too little substantive knowledge of the phenomenon to make intelligent choices of theory, then the use of complicated analytic techniques is probably premature. It has nevertheless been common practice to make such comparisons within a sample, on the basis of measures of how well each of two or more alternative specifications fits the data.

The standard 'goodness of fit' measure for a regression-type model has been a statistic called the coefficient of determination, designated as R^2 and defined as

$$R^2 = 1 - \left[\sum e_i^2 / \sum (Y_i - \bar{Y})^2 \right] \qquad (4.16)$$

The numerator is the sum of squared errors from predicting Y_i by the model (commonly called the 'unexplained variation' or the 'residual sum of squares'). The denominator is the sum of squared errors from predicting Y_i by the mean of its distribution (commonly called 'total sum of squares'). Because the numerical value of R^2 never declines and usually increases with increases in the number of parameters of one's model (i.e., the number of predictor variables plus the intercept or 'constant' term), an adjustment for the degrees of freedom associated with the numerator and with the denominator of equation (4.16) is appropriate, especially when comparing models. This *adjusted R^2* is given by

$$1-\left[\sum e_i^2/(n-k)\right]/\left[\sum (Y_i - \bar{Y})^2/(n-1)\right] \qquad (4.17)$$

where n is sample size and k is the number of parameters. The sampling distribution of the R^2 statistic (in either version) is the F distribution.

As sample size becomes very large (i.e., $n >$ 5000) the prospect that any given model will *not* fit the data at any conventional level of probability (e.g., $p < 0.001$) is increasingly remote, and the power of tests based on the F ratio to discriminate among models quickly weakens. In such circumstances investigators who still seek to select among models as if they had each been estimated with independently sampled data switch from an OLS estimation model to a 'maximum likelihood' estimation model. The basic principle of the latter is to choose the parameter estimates that maximize the probability of obtaining the observed sample (a related account is given in Chapter 5). This estimation procedure generates a statistic known as a 'log-likelihood' value. When models are nested (i.e., when restrictions on the parameters of one model are used to define another model), the difference in the respective log-likelihood values is judged as a χ_k^2 distribution with degrees of freedom (k) equal to the difference in the number of parameters in the covariance structures of the models being compared. The Akaike information criterion (AIC) uses the same likelihood values but with greater penalty for number of parameters estimated. Likewise the Bayesian information criterion (BIC), but with still greater penalty. That is, from a direct comparison of log-likelihood values (as in a statistic called 'the likelihood ratio') to AIC to BIC one is making it increasingly difficult to reject the null hypothesis that two models of the process generating a given dependent variable are equivalent in their fit to the data (Gill, 2002: 208–9, 223–5; Raftery, 2001: 9–10).

There are numerous other specialized topics that intersect with sampling inference, on the one hand, and issues of inferring causes from effects, on the other. Some of these topics are treated in later chapters. While the limits of causal inference in social science inquiry are profound – as recent scholars (e.g., Sobel, 1998) have demonstrated in lessons that reconfirm the argument from logic by Kant (1952, 1974) – there is still some room to develop and refine tools of statistical inference that inform modes of inquiry short of those limits.

Let us return once again to the empirical example of a *two-sample* difference in schooling, and consider the troubled practice of interpreting significance tests. As we saw from the earlier calculations, a standard score of $Z = 13.16$ seems very impressive, given that nearly all of the sampling distribution of the statistic is contained within the interval of $Z = \pm 3.00$. Indeed, it *is* impressive, but even so, in the hypothesis test, it tells us *only* that our best decision is to reject the null hypothesis. Had Z been 3.16 instead, our best decision still would have been to reject the null. Furthermore, while the test tells us that the parametric difference (or 'true difference') is very likely larger than zero, it does not tell us how much larger. Our best point estimate of *that* is the observed difference (0.75) with which we started, and if we want a more reliable guess of the magnitude we can switch to an interval estimate, as we did earlier. If a grade of completed schooling is equivalent to 36 weeks, then the difference in means for the two sampled populations is about 27 weeks. Calculated as the 95% confidence interval, the difference is very likely to be at least 23 weeks but less than 31 weeks.

As with confidence intervals, hypothesis tests are sometimes a locus of confusion when interpreting probability values. Again, in any given decisional problem, the null hypothesis either is or is not true; and immediately upon drawing a sample of observations the observed difference either is or is not different from zero. It is nonsensical to say, for example, that 'there is a 95% chance that the null is false' or that 'there is a 95% chance that the true difference is greater than zero', or any of the frequently encountered variations on those statements. The probability value (or the value of α) is properly interpreted as a statement about the sampling distribution of a particular statistic, and from that information a researcher can then decide whether to reject the null hypothesis or not. This judgment must be made in light of the fact that, whatever the probable location of a sample in its sampling distribution, it could yet be a 'bad' sample.

The core issue of interpreting results of hypothesis testing will be considered further, but some other issues must be considered. As already stated, hypothesis tests are usually constructed on the assumption that the null hypothesis is true. The traditional preference for the null as point of reference derives from a logic of negation. Assume I put a penny and a quarter on the table and invite you to make a statement such that (1) if the statement is true, I must give you one of the two coins, although I will not commit in advance to which of the two, or (2) if the statement is false, you get neither coin. Is there a statement that will logically compel me to give you the quarter? There is. But it is not the usual first choice ('You will give me the quarter'); for to that statement my response ('That's false') leaves you nothing. However, if you say 'You will *not* give me the penny', all degrees of freedom have been absorbed, and I am logically compelled to give you the quarter. Consider the implications of this second statement. If false, you would actually be saying that I *will* give you the penny; but I cannot give you *either* coin for a false statement, so it is impossible for the statement to be false. This leaves only that it *is* a true statement; so I must give you a coin, and it must be the quarter.

More generally put, the inferential process of negation enables one to proceed farther through decisional queues by eliminating false hypotheses. If a claim (theory, prior experience) says that one should observe state S under specified conditions, and one does observe S under those conditions, the observation counts only as evidence in favor of the claim, because S could occur for reasons other than those stated in the claim. On the other hand, failure to observe S counts as evidence by which to reject the claim.

Note, however, that this interpretation of 'failure to observe S' presupposes two conditions that are difficult to satisfy: motivation by a theory that has strict implications, and the availability of decisive observations. Unfortunately, very few theories in the social sciences have strict implications. But an underdetermined structure of implications (i.e., 'loose' or 'mushy' implications) cannot discriminate among observations very well.

By the same token, available observations are also underdetermined, which is another way of saying that they are probabilistic. It is sometimes avowed (rightly) that one should never discard a good theory as a result of contrary data, because good theories are too difficult to make. The counterpart for observations is the caution that one should never reject an observation as a result of its apparent unlikeliness (i.e., apparently due to sampling error). As Chebyshev's inequality advises, a rare event can tell us more than an event that is only moderately different from the modal or typical event – assuming, of course, that the rare event is more than a manifestation of our efforts in inquiry – and, by definition, rare events are not often observed.[58] So one should be slow to discard rare-event information even when an inference test indicates that it is probably sampling error.

Despite the gap between aspiration (for theory, if not observations) and capability, the perspective and standard afforded by the inferential logic of negation are still useful to contemporary decision theory. An analogy offers appropriate instruction. In the tradition of Anglo-American jurisprudence a fundamental principle is 'innocence until proven guilty'. The presumption is that any two people, one accused before the bar and the other not, are *equal* legal subjects, both innocent, and the burden of proof to the contrary ('beyond a reasonable doubt') stays with the prosecution. This insistence on a null hypothesis which, if not rejected, automatically stands, is recognition of two conditions. First, 'difference' in matters as important as who has full rights of legal subject and who does not must be decided by extraordinary effort, relative to a prejudice of 'no difference'. Second, there is always some probability that any such decision, once made, was an incorrect decision, although we can never know with certainty that it was (remember, the rule is 'beyond a *reasonable* doubt'). If the decision *is* incorrect, better that it is incorrect because of failure to convict a not-innocent person than that it is incorrect because of conviction of an innocent person. Similarly, a scientific researcher generally prefers not to declare differences that are artifacts of his or her efforts of investigation.

As the preceding analogy illustrates, part of the information that should be evaluated when choosing between (or among) alternative hypotheses is information about the

Table 4.4 *Possible outcomes of decision in a test of the null hypothesis*

Test decision	Null hypothesis is in fact:	
	true	false
Reject null	Error, Type I	Correct decision
Do not reject null	Correct decision	Error, Type II

consequences of being wrong. The state of 'being wrong' (an incorrect decision) and information pertinent to that state are firmly embedded in conditions of uncertainty. In any decision involving random variables we simply can never know with certainty whether we have made a correct or an incorrect decision. What we *can* do, however, is to construct the decision rule in a way that seeks to minimize the probability of being wrong when rejecting the null hypothesis.

Consider the binary logic of a decision about the null hypothesis. My choice is between rejecting the null and not rejecting the null. There are two ways in which my decision can be correct and two ways in which it can be incorrect (see Table 4.4). Because I do not know whether the null is true or not (and will never know that beyond doubt), I can never know beyond doubt whether either decision I make is correct or incorrect. I prefer that it be a correct decision, of course. But since nothing I can do will guarantee a correct decision, it is both reasonable and prudent that I consider the consequences of being wrong. If my decision should be incorrect, which of the two ways of being wrong should I prefer?

There are two answers to that question. One answer is predominant at the conclusion of an investigation, when preparing to publicize findings. Preference should then be given to the decision rule that minimizes Type I error (i.e., minimizes the probability of rejecting a true null hypothesis). During earlier stages of an investigation, however, a researcher might reasonably prefer to minimize Type II error. In general, of course, both types of error should be reduced as much as possible. But for any given sample of size n there tends to be a rather sharp trade-off between the two types of error; minimizing one comes at the cost of an increase in the other.[59]

The probability value associated with Type I error is α ($= 1 - p$), which was introduced and used in the example above. It is commonly referred to as 'the level of significance' of a null hypothesis test. The probability value associated with Type II error is β, and $1 - \beta$ is commonly referred to as 'the power of a test'.[60] Recall that specification of α is a function of a researcher's personal judgment. It could be set at $\alpha = 0.10$, for instance, or 0.20, or even higher, if the researcher is comfortable with the greater probability that an observed difference, having been accorded the status of a 'real difference' by virtue of rejecting the null, is in fact due to sampling error. Setting α at any given level has implications for β, as noted above. Increasing the size of α tends to increase the power of the test (i.e., decrease the probability of Type II error), which means that the test is more likely to detect the presence of difference even at the cost of detecting difference that is due to sampling error. Note that an increase in sample size can both increase power and decrease the probability of Type I error.

During early stages of an investigation, when a researcher is calibrating instruments for the detection of difference, the cost of detecting differences that are artifacts of the detection process itself is relatively low. Results are still privately held, so the risk of a misleading generalization is minimal. On the other hand, that same cost at the conclusion of an investigation becomes the cost of capitalizing on chance results, and *this* cost, while never reducible to zero, is far less acceptable to the extent that it can mislead in potentially damaging ways. Creating differences as if they existed independently of one's inquiry is the type of error that one generally prefers not to foist onto a public.

This preference, too, however, should be maintained explicitly as an element of personal judgment, not as an algorithmic dictation. The earlier analogy to judgments in a court of law illustrates the burden of responsibility with respect to declarations of difference. Here, another analogy illustrates the need for caution when invoking rules about 'the burden of evidence'.

Consider that a state of wellness is generally preferred to a state of illness in personal health. Thus, wellness is the assumed state. A null hypothesis of no difference implies that any person selected at random is in the state of wellness. Illness is the exceptional state, warranting special attention. Along comes

Table 4.5 *Possible outcomes of decision in medical diagnostic test of disease*

Test decision	Actual health condition:	
	well	not well
Has disease	False positive	Correct decision
Disease free	Correct decision	False negative

person NW who claims to be not well. A diagnostician undertakes a test of the null hypothesis relative to one or more alternatives, the kinds of illness suggested on initial presentation. Relative to any given alternative, a diagnostic test can yield one of two possible outcomes (disregarding ambiguities of classification and measurement): a positive result, which recommends rejection of the null hypothesis, and a negative result, which recommends retention of the null. Assuming binary 'real-world' states, the decisional matrix is as shown in Table 4.5. Medical diagnostics are designed to minimize 'false negatives' (i.e., Type II errors), because failure to detect a difference in this situation is usually highly undesirable. The effort to minimize 'false negatives' comes at the cost of 'false positives', especially during early stages of the development and application of the test. Which diagnostic error would you prefer, a 'false negative' or a 'false positive'? Neither is desirable; neither is without consequence. But if a choice must be made, the consequence of a 'false positive' – personal stress while the test is being replicated – is usually less dire than the consequence of a 'false negative'.

Instruments designed to detect difference are calibrated, not surprisingly, in terms of the researcher's prior beliefs or expectations about the possible differences being investigated. Thus, the power of a test is in a sense *leading toward* an expected difference (Cohen, 1988). The common tendency to observe what one expects to observe is good reason to bestow final preference to minimization of Type I error, relative to Type II error. Preferred values of α are usually quite small, and with very large samples (e.g., 8000 rather than 800) the preference should be for even smaller values (e.g., 0.001 or 0.0001) in order to reduce opportunities to capitalize on chance outcomes.[61] But ritualized or unthinking uses of significance tests are not helpful, especially when the ritual displaces reasoned judgment about the meaning of a

hypothesis test. Others have offered many instructive illustrations of the traps and failures that follow from that displacement (e.g., Abelson, 1995; Cliff, 1989; Cohen, 1994).[62] To cite two quick illustrations from Abelson (1995: 76):

> If a sample is divided at the median into high scorers and low scorers, there is no point in showing by a *t* test that the high scorers differ significantly from the low scorers. A somewhat subtler case arises when a trustworthy procedure for random assignment of subjects to experimental conditions seems to go awry, yielding a cluster of smarter or faster (or whatever) subjects in one particular group. In this situation, students are prone to test the significance of the difference between groups. But because the null hypothesis here is that the samples were randomly drawn from the same population, it is true by definition, and needs no data. What has happened is that one of those flukey outcomes that arise from time to time has arisen *this* time. ... chance is lumpy.

A final, still more involved illustration is instructive in a different way. Imagine that you estimate a model that specifies variable Y as a linear additive function of two determinants:

$$Y = a + b_1 X_1 + b_2 X_2,$$

where b_1 and b_2 are measures of the sensitivity of Y to X_1 and X_2, respectively.[63] Your results indicate that the value of b_1 is significant at precisely $\alpha = 0.049$ but that the corresponding probability for the value of b_2 is 0.051, which falls just short of the conventional $\alpha = 0.05$ standard. Because, according to convention, you can be confident that the b_1 estimate is indeed different from zero, you interpret the substantive significance of this result as support for the first hypothesis. But lacking the same confidence that the b_2 estimate differs from zero, you decide to reject the second hypothesis and then probably say nothing more about it. My point is not that these decisions are necessarily wrong. Rather, it is that they are separated by a very thin margin, perhaps thinner than is often realized, and a ritualized dutiful following of procedures can blind us to what it is we are actually trying to accomplish and why we are making the effort. Consider that b_1 and b_2 are our best point estimates of the corresponding population parameters. No test of statistical significance will change that fact. Each b is our current best estimate of the expected value of its sampling distribution. Since it is an unbiased estimate, if we were to replicate our estimation of the model, the chances are one in two that our new estimate for X, would be *less* than the initial estimate – in which case the coefficient would no longer meet the 0.05 level of significance. Likewise, the chances are one in two that our new estimate for X_2 would be larger than it was on initial trial, perhaps just enough larger to pass the 0.05 test.

Now let us return to the core issue of interpreting the results of a hypothesis test. What does it mean to say that a null hypothesis is (or is not) rejected at, say, the 0.05 level of significance in a two-tailed (or one-tailed) test? Bear in mind, first of all, that the value of α, and therefore the value of p, is a *conditional* probability, and the condition is an unknown state – namely, whether the null hypothesis is in fact true. Thus, in terms of the hypothesis test worked out above (where $Z = 13.16$), the conclusion would properly be:

> *If* the null hypothesis is in fact true, I should not expect to see a difference in means as large as 0.75; indeed, it would be an extremely unlikely observation. On the other hand, if the null is not true, then a difference of 0.75 *might* not be so unusual. Accordingly, since the value of Z corresponding to 0.75 is greater than the critical value, Z_c, my best guess is that the null is *probably not true*; I reject the null.

To that conclusion I could append a statement about 'level of significance'. If in advance of the calculations I had set Z_c in terms of the ordinate for $\alpha = 0.05$ in a two-tailed test, for example, I could add that 'the level of significance of the test is 0.05'. But this addition says only that the test allowed for a specified probability that the observed difference was due to sampling error. The value of α is set at some very low level at this stage of the research because, if I do reject the null hypothesis, I want to have confidence that the evidence on which I base that decision is not a result of Abelson's 'lumpy chance' (i.e., not a result of a good sampling procedure producing a 'bad' sample). Thus, it would *not* be correct to say, 'the probability that the null hypothesis is true is less than 5%'. This statement, as meaningless in the context of hypothesis testing as its counterpart was in the context of interval estimation,

stems from a confusion of two different conditional probabilities: the probability of the data, given a hypothesis, and the probability of a hypothesis, given the data (Abelson, 1995: 40–1). We can and do estimate the former – the likelihood of an observation, given some assumption/hypothesis about reality. If we must assign an empirical estimate to the probability of a hypothesis in light of our sample data, the best we can do is the maximum-variance estimation: the hypothesis either is or is not true ($p = 0.5$).

Decision-making on the basis of estimations from a single sampling is always a second-best approach, at least in principle. Replication gives a better base of information. It is replication that enables us to make good on the fact that 'statistical confidence' is in a *procedure*, not in any specific result of it; for replication starts us down that road of 'in the long run'. As Stigler (1999: 364) has remarked, and reinforced with illustrations, 'estimates of error based only upon within-sample variability tell but a part of the story, and often it is not the most important part'. It is far better to base an important decision on replicated estimations – that is, estimations from two or more independent probability samplings of the same population of observations – than it is to put all one's risk of a wrong decision in the basket of one sampling. But replication is easier said than done, in the context of random variables. There are so many sources of error; phenomena of interest are often the result of time-variant processes ('history matters'); replication is expensive.

CONCLUSION

The complex and still developing apparatus of statistical inference has limitations, to be sure. One of the hallmarks of the method of modern science is insistence on publicity, however, and that includes publicity of those limitations and their manifestations in any particular investigation. The apparatus of statistical inference does not create information out of nothing. Indeed, it does not really *create* information at all. Rather, it tries to make *explicitly available* to systematic use all of the information contained in sampled experiences. In doing that, it also urges – in a sense, forces – a person to explore all the assumptions that are involved both in the experiences and in potential uses (i.e., generalizations) of them. It offers a set of reasonably clear, openly replicable procedures for attempting to achieve an optimum in the inevitable trade-offs that must be made – for example, between the usefulness of some chunk of information and the chance that the information is wrong, or between the costs of acquiring newer, hopefully better information and the costs of being wrong in decisions based on information already at hand. Just as importantly, it offers these procedures and the standards they utilize as *public* goods, with the strong recommendation that all uses made of them should be publicly open and shared.

Stigler tells a story about the late seventeenth-century mathematician Jacob Bernoulli that, albeit partly conjectural, has a clear lesson still today. The conjectural part is that Bernoulli composed a masterpiece which was published only posthumously because he lacked a publicly accepted standard for the tolerance of uncertainty.

> Bernoulli had proved a marvelous approximation theorem, but when he tried an example, he guessed that certainty to one part in a thousand was needed to convince, and he found himself concluding that over 25,000 trials would be needed to make, for example, a statement about the chance of rain. That number was unacceptably large; inferences were made with confidence every day by ordinary people on the basis of far less evidence. (Stigler, 1999: 375)

Decisions under conditions of uncertainty, incorrigible uncertainty, are made ordinarily most days of an adult lifetime, often with hardly any deliberation over information and little or no effort to assess systematically the relative costs of being wrong in alternative decisions. Too often the temptation is to want certainty and, disappointed by its absence, to settle for the haphazard. Too often a person is lulled by egocentric bias into true belief: 'Why bother with sampling? The world is sufficiently as I see it to be, and I know it accordingly'. Rare is the society, moreover, lacking institutional features designed to encourage or even to enforce true belief (of specific nomenclature and bias). Those institutional features do include institutions of modern science (despite the latter's oft-manifested conceit of being larger than society). But the apparatus of statistical inference consists of techniques of gaining uses from information fraught with uncertainty, without either denying the uncertainty or losing touch with a basic attitude of scepticism.

That is a very difficult accomplishment. Inferential statistics is the single most powerful instrument human beings have yet invented for dealing with those difficulties of accomplishment. It is an instrument available for anyone to learn and to use.

NOTES

1 Actual practices of inference, in scientific research as elsewhere, often depart from these principles, sometimes widely (see Latour, 1987; Stich, 1990).

2 This regulative principle is much older than Kant or Newton, of course. The first poet whose name we know, Hesiod, warned against humankind's 'deepest illusion' – that we ever know beings as they are in themselves – and by the same token celebrated the significance of struggles to control definitions and understandings of the relations of being and meaning. Hesiod's warning recurs below – for example, as the category 'measurement error', which can be mistaken as a *derivative* category, as if we first spy the true value of a quantity and then assess the error of our estimate (Duncan, 1975: 101, 150–1).

3 By 'observation' I mean to include all of the sensory experiences – not only seeing (which, in the strong bias of European and Euro-American cultures, dominates the others) but also hearing, touching, smelling, and tasting.

4 This applies no less to the physical or natural sciences than to the social sciences. An illustration of the point can be appreciated in a claim by Hoyle, Burbidge, and Narlikar (2000: 320), all eminent physicists and cosmologists, that 'modern extragalactic observers very rarely describe their data without a great deal of interpretation, and literally all of this is done almost without exception by assuming a Friedmann [i.e., 'Big Bang'] model for the universe. ... [I]t is difficult to sort out what is actually observed from what is claimed to have been seen'.

5 Bear in mind that naming and classifying are not identical acts. The categories of a classification exist in determinate relation to each other, and assigning instances to those categories is governed accordingly. Assigning labels (proper names) to the categories can be done 'arbitrarily', although this assignment is nonetheless sensitive to at least some expectations within the limits of the language being used (see Bowker and Star, 1999; Foucault, 1970; Wittgenstein, 1968).

6 The fact of quantitative *relationship* should be emphasized; measurement is inherently comparative, just as is classification. Quantity need not be expressed numerically: comparatives and superlatives

(e.g., 'most', 'more', 'same', 'less', and 'least') are judgments of quantity and thus qualify as measurement. The advantages of numeration, when it is justifiable, are very substantial, however, for the enormous power of number theory and all of the technology derived from it can be applied to one's decisional problem.

7 As ambiguity of classification increases, the utility of fuzzy-set theory ('fuzzy logic') increases. For some general applications, see Montgomery (2000) and Ragin (2000); for applications to multivariate modeling and estimation techniques, see Manton et al. (1994).

8 The following account assumes measurement on a single dimension. Multidimensional scaling is more complicated, usually enough so that measurement at more than an ordinal level is very difficult to achieve.

9 This ignores the fact that, by quantum theory, specific properties of some entities do not have exact values until measured. Facile claims of parallel conditions notwithstanding, both substantive theory and mensural technologies in the social sciences are too weak to support the claim that specific states of social or cultural reality have similar properties. But there is reason to suspect that attitudinal and perhaps other cognitive states are often determined partly by the observational act (Duncan, 1984: 200–18).

10 Note that, as described here, the interval level preserves the categorical boundedness of kind. One can (as Stevens did) distinguish from this '*discrete* interval' level of measurement the '*continuous* interval' level by allowing in addition to constancy of interval length a repetitive divisibility of interval length.

11 Because of the lack of a fixed (or 'absolute') origin, multiplication and division cannot yield consistent results. Ratios are meaningless. For example, a net worth of $100 000 is *not* 10 times a net worth of $10 000, since it is possible to have negative net worth (total liability in excess of total assets); and because in principle the largest negative value is as undefined as the largest positive number, a fixed origin cannot be established – which means that we simply cannot estimate the factor by which $100 000 net worth exceeds $10 000 net worth.

12 That we have returned via cardinality, the most developed of the 'levels' of measurement, to (a now much enhanced appreciation of the complexity of) *counting* is testimony to the foolishness of 'debates' that either 'the quantitative' or 'the qualitative approach' to research is superior to the other. As should be clear by now, measurement without prior classification is impossible; and any classification scheme that strives even only for the ability to support comparative statements depends on measurement.

13 The concept of 'randomness' is complex and unsettled (see, e.g., Beltrami, 1999; Bennett, 1998). For practical purposes, approximations to randomness suffice; an example is the table of 'random numbers' that is generated by a computer algorithm.

14 These are important practical issues that should be addressed when designing elicitation techniques for the construction of observations – e.g., questions and question sequencing in an interview schedule, event sequences in an experiment, site sequencing in fieldwork, and so forth (see Fillmore, 1999; Shum and Rips, 1999; Tanur, 1992).

15 Accordingly, the remainder of this paragraph depends on some understandings that are not described until the section on 'Statistical Inference', and the novice reader can pass over this paragraph, without loss, until having read the subsection on 'Errors of Statistical Inference'.

16 This revised model is an example of what is sometimes called an 'error-in-variables' model. Note that if the model does include specification error (virtually always), it will be conflated with the measurement error in e_y (unless the two can somehow be separated). Measurement error is thus closely analogous to specification error or the 'missing variable' problem (Abelson, 1995: 8–9; Duncan, 1975: 117–18). Note also that whereas classical measurement theory assumes *independence* of measured observations, the study of process involves repeated (thus, non-independent) measurement. For some discussions of the tangle of problems therein, see Collins and Sayer (2001).

17 Matched data – that is, variables that are measured (presumably independently) by two or more different (but presumably equally neutral) mensural procedures (e.g., matched reports from employees and from the employees' firms, or from patients and the patients' physicians) – have used the 'instrumental variable' approach with some success. The results have generally not been encouraging with respect to either the volume and consequences of measurement error or the proposed solutions (see Ashenfelter and Krueger, 1994; Barron et al., 1997).

18 It parallels exactly a relationship known in language arts as 'synecdoche', a 'figure of speech' in which a part represents its whole. This parallel should be instructive in both directions. For a treatment of the circumstances and process by which different fields of social science developed their initial objects of statistical inference, see Stigler (1986, 1999).

19 The word 'stochastic' derives from a Greek verb that translates approximately as 'to guess'. This meaning is perfectly fitting, because statistical decision theory emphasizes that a decision made under conditions of uncertainty is indeed a 'best guess based on available information' *and* that our confidence in such a decision is confidence in the process by which we arrive at the decision, not in the specific decision itself. That is, the specific decision itself might be correct, or might be incorrect, and we can never know for sure which it is. But we can have confidence that the decisional process gives correct decisions 'in the long run' at some estimable rate of success.

20 At the simplest level, 'degrees of freedom' describes the relational constraints imposed by a specific classification of states of being. In the binomial case, for instance, there are two mutually exclusive states of being and thus only one degree of freedom. Two mutually independent binomial variables are constrained to one degree of freedom in their joint distribution $(1 \times 1 = 1)$. And so on. The statistical concept of degrees of freedom was developed by Ronald A. Fisher in work published in 1922 (see Stigler, 1986, 1999: Ch. 19).

21 For instance, statistical inference can be treated also as measurement theory (see, e.g., Bartholomew, 1996; Duncan, 1984). A single chapter, even a long one, cannot substitute for the coverage of a good textbook in statistical procedures (e.g., Freedman et al., 1978).

22 For instance, that a sample is always a sample of observations (i.e., observational events); that any observations are always a sample of some larger population of possible observations; that observations are always uncertain *both* because of the ever-present possibility of category error (wrongly classified observations) *and* because the representational property (i.e., part–whole relation) of any observation is inherently doubtful.

23 There are circumstances under which sufficient information *is* available to support directed selections. These circumstances occur, for instance, in exploratory stages of fieldwork, in some experimental designs that use 'cross-group matching', in techniques of 'effect sampling' in dynamical analysis, and in studies of organizations (see Carroll and Hannan, 2000: 85–98; Miller, 1989).

24 The insertion/reading of tendentious qualifiers (e.g., 'usually', as in the sentence just read, 'more or less', etc.) soon becomes tiresome and so has been minimized. The important point to bear in mind, here and throughout, is that scientific research is expensive (in skills, patience, money, and other scarce goods), and decisions about trade-offs have to be made accordingly. The weight of responsibility that must be borne by a set of research findings, and their author, may be little enough to justify the use of a particular technique (e.g., a non-neutral sampling technique) that would otherwise be inappropriate.

25 If, ignoring that we are sampling observations, we pretend that we are sampling the 'things' being observed, then with a sufficiently small population of those 'things' the identification is of course possible. This 'shortcut' is a common one. While it does prejudge issues about what is important in the observational act, it does not *necessarily* result in faulty inference (and faulty conclusions). But those prejudgments should be acknowledged at the very least – better yet, buttressed by empirical evidence.

26 Sampling frames are usually composed of 'things' (e.g., individual persons or households), not observations. A typical sampling frame for households in a particular community would be defined by the local telephone directory or by motor vehicle registrations or by some combination of these and other listings of the community's population of households.

27 In most applications of probability sampling the sampled population is defined as a spatial array, not a temporal (much less a perspectival) array, of possible observations. In the typical longitudinal-data or time-series design, for instance, the repeated observations are of properties of persons or households or some other organizational unit arrayed in the cross-section, sampled once with repetition of observation at specified intervals (a 'wave design') or sampled anew at each specified interval ('panel design') or a mixture of the two. However, insofar as interest is in understanding the dynamics of stationary and non-stationary stochastic processes, the sampled population of observations will be arrayed temporally as well as spatially. That is, the focus of sampling will be on temporal as well as spatial properties of the process. In a research problem from the theory of queuing, for example, sampled observations might be of 'waiting times' in specified states (see Tuma and Hannan, 1984: 45–8).

28 That is, the determination of each of the X_i is treated as probabilistic for the same reasons as the determination of Y. Note that 'gender' is here a crude proxy for 'prejudicial discrimination by gender', which is distributed probabilistically.

29 The interpretation of e as 'disturbance term' is slightly different, the difference signifying greater confidence in the completeness of one's motivating theory. If I believe that my theory (1) includes all determinants of Y, (2) prescribes the correct functional form of the model of strictly determinant relations, but (3) neglects all of the random-variable influences in that model, then I can treat these latter influences as 'disturbances' of the law-like process described by the strictly determinant part of the model (see Hausman, 1992).

30 A causal effect is considered asymmetrical when, for example, the effect on Y of a unit increase from some specified level of X does not equal the effect of a unit decrease from that same level of X (for illustration see Lieberson, 1985: 63–4). An effect is monotonic when the effect of X on Y is constant across all values of X. The term 'organizational scale' refers to the fact that human phenomena can exist at one or more levels of organization, ranging from the intra-individual to the inter-individual at various levels of aggregation (from dyad and triad to larger groups such as families, workplaces, commercial firms, whole societies, etc.). Causal relations specified at one level of scale need not be the same at a different level of scale. Moreover, causal relations can be specified as cross-level effects, such as the effect of a characteristic

of a family structure or a firm structure on specific individual members or groups of members (for illustrations see Achen and Shively, 1995; Bryk and Raudenbush, 1992).

31 Whereas 'internal validity' refers to the logical 'goodness' of descriptions/explanations pertaining to observations of variables and relationships at hand, 'external validity' refers to the logical 'goodness' of generalization from observations at hand to some larger population of observations. One might have high confidence in observations of how a specific process works under conditions of an experiment (a relatively abnormal set of conditions); one will likely have lower confidence that those observations are independent of the conditions of the experiment (Abelson, 1995: 132–55).

32 The random variable R (described in the missile example, above) is another, known as the Rayleigh distribution (after Lord Rayleigh, John William Strutt, in his 1877 work on the theory of sound). It is useful for wave propagation and analogous phenomena (Tuma and Hannan, 1984: 220–31).

33 Note that this last sentence illustrates the general rule that the mean of a sum is the sum of the weighted means of the elements of the summation, and the variance of the sum is the sum of the weighted variances of the elements, assuming independence of the elements.

34 The distribution is normalized by the degrees-of-freedom adjustment. The mean of the distribution becomes 0 and the variance 1, once the calculated value of χ_k^2 has been corrected by k (assuming independence).

35 Achieving independence among the missile events would be more difficult. All missiles would need to be constructed in advance, in order to avoid alteration in the construction of a later missile by information about the outcome of a prior test, and so on.

36 Some special cases of the problem of censored observation are treated below, in Chapter 18, as 'sample selection errors' and, relatedly, in Chapters 15 and 19, as 'case attritions' in designs that involve repeated observations over intervals of time.

37 The last two statistics confirm that, despite its lumpiness (the effect of credentialism), the distribution of observations is close to the standard normal distribution, for which skewness is zero and kurtosis is 3. But bear in mind that, under a wide range of circumstances, the normal distribution can be used even when the empirical distribution of observations diverges strongly from the normal. The critical condition is whether the *sampling distribution* of a particular statistic (e.g., a sample mean) is normal-like.

38 Recall the substitution of s for σ when calculating the standard error of the mean. The effect of this substitution tends to be conservative, as an inspection of the formula for the standard error of a sample

standard deviation or variance demonstrates (see the fourth and fifth panels of Table 4.1). In the present example the standard error of s is $2.44/(2 \times 8884)^{1/2} = 0.018$. The bounds of the 99.7% confidence interval for $s = 2.44$ are thus 2.386 and 2.494. Using each of these bounds (instead of $s = 2.44$) when calculating the standard error of the mean gives 0.0253 and 0.0265, respectively, instead of 0.0259 (i.e., a difference of less than 24 parts per thousand). These values imply 12.98 ± 0.050 and 12.98 ± 0.052, rather than 12.98 ± 0.051.

39 For a discussion of *ex post* manipulations of confidence intervals in order to obtain a probability value that seems more impressive, see Abelson (1995: 54–7).

40 The preceding two paragraphs touch on a debate that is not otherwise discussed in this chapter – namely, that between the so-called classical model of statistical inference and the Bayesian model (after Thomas Bayes, an eighteenth-century mathematician). The principal difference is that the classical model was presented as complete and self-sufficient: inferential decisions are strictly implied by proper application of the inference model. The Bayesian approach disputes that claim. Whether adopting all of the apparatus typically named 'Bayesian' or not, hardly any statistician or decision theorist today would agree that the classical model is complete and self-sufficient. No model or apparatus of inference relieves the researcher of the task of judgment. Nor can it remove the condition of uncertainty under which the judgment must be made (see Pratt et al., 1995; Gill, 2002).

41 This should be intuitively clear from a comparison of the improbability of seeing five consecutive heads to the (much greater) improbability of seeing 500 consecutive heads in fair tosses of a balanced coin. For another illustration, compare the 'critical values' in a set of t distributions to the corresponding critical value in a Z distribution. For instance, the Z value associated with an upper 5% bound is $+1.645$. The corresponding t value is 1.658 at $n = 120$, 1.671 at $n = 60$, 1.697 at $n = 30$, and 1.753 at $n = 15$.

42 The bias occurs because a sample containing few observations is less likely to include *unlikely* observations (i.e., those located in the tails of the population distribution of possible observations), and this neglect reduces the sample variance. For purposes of the sampling distribution of a standard deviation or variance, a sample is 'small' at $n < 100$. Recall that the standard error of $s = 2.44$ with $n = 8884$ is $\sigma_s = 0.018$. Had $s = 2.44$ been calculated on $n = 100$ instead, the standard error would have been 0.173. For any $n < 100$, calculation of s is by method of moments (see Table 4.1).

43 Indeed, recall from the earlier discussion of theoretical probability distributions that there is a different t distribution for each sample size (although as n

approaches and then exceeds 30, the t distributions increasingly approximate the Z distribution). Note, too, that because the degrees-of-freedom adjustment (using $n-1$ rather than n) in the calculation of s makes a noticeable difference in a small sample, for any given small sample the appropriate t distribution is for $n-1$, not n.

44 Notice that, if I *have* underestimated the variance, nothing from this correction will tell me the amount of underestimation, much less rectify it, nor even confirm that my estimate of the population variance *is* too low. Shifting to the t distribution means *only* that I use a more conservative representation of the sampling distribution of my statistic (here, the sample mean), in recognition of the greater likelihood that s is a poor approximation of σ.

45 When the metric is in proportions, the lower limit of 'large' is determined by whether the interval defined by three standard errors to each side of the sample proportion includes zero or one. If both values are excluded, the sample qualifies as 'large' and the normal distribution applies. In the present exercise the standard error of the sample proportion is 0.007, and $p \pm 3\sigma_p = 0.14 \pm 0.021$, which implies bounds well within the limits of zero and one.

46 Recall the earlier discussion of the magnified consequence of measurement error when constructing a difference term. Although separate and distinct from sampling error, measurement error certainly affects the goodness of a sample statistic as a point estimate of the corresponding parameter, and concern about measurement error applies when the statistic is a difference in sample means. However, bear in mind that a sample mean benefits from error compensation in a distribution of observations. For instance, as an estimate of the population mean weight of adults the mean body weight of 100 randomly selected adults is superior to 100 independent observations of any one of the 100 selected randomly; still better (since it involves only one error of measurement) is the aggregate weight of the 100 randomly selected adults, divided by 100. Thus, the effect of measurement error in the observed distribution of X in each of two independently sampled populations on the difference in sample means is mitigated by error compensation.

47 To follow the notation used earlier in this chapter, the degrees of freedom are, respectively, $k = n_1 - 1$ and $m = n_2 - 1$. The F ratio is highly sensitive to the assumption of normality in each population.

48 A perfectly rectangular distribution is one in which the relative frequencies of the categories (here, the social groupings) are equal. Increasing departure from a rectangular distribution means that the relative frequency of one (or more) of the categories is diminishing, as that of another (or others) is increasing.

49 Some limitations should be noted. First, my statement of substantive claim is deliberately ambiguous as to causal direction. Issues of causal inference, endogeneity, and the like, are considered in later chapters. Second, note from the table that I make no allowance for the fact that observations in 'age at first marriage' are truncated ('right censored') by that fact that 30% of the men and 22% of the women are 'not yet married'. Unless the social processes that resulted in 'completed schooling' operated the same for these adults as for those who did marry (at least once) before age 29, exclusion of the 'not yet married' from the analysis will produce non-random error in the analytic results. Issues of this source of error and how adjustments for it might be made are considered in Chapter 18. Third, in calculating means and standard deviations for the distributions in Table 4.2 I have been assuming that 'grade of school completed' is measured at an interval level. Obviously that assumption is not entirely sound. Notice has already been made of the presence of 'category effects' at grades 12 and 16 (correlated with school-leaving credentials). Now one must consider whether the assumption violation is uniform in effect across the comparisons. That is, can we assume that the relevant meaning(s) of 'grade 12 completion', relative to 'grade 11 completion' on the one side and 'grade 13 completion' on the other, are the same by gender and by marital status? Here agnosticism prevails, but in a careful analysis some evidence should be brought to bear. Issues of 'semantic' and 'functional equivalence' in mensural as well as classificatory distributions, briefly noted earlier in this chapter, are treated at greater length in other chapters.

50 Notice that in the latter phrasing I avoided saying 'barely overlapping'. This phrasing would be nonsensical; the intervals *either do or do not* overlap. See Abelson (1995: 74–5) on such tactics of 'word play'.

51 In the vocabulary of the next subsection of this chapter, the same statement reads 'results in a loss of power of the test'.

52 Here 'theoretical expectation' can be interpreted loosely to encompass hunches or simple assertions of fact, including the usual textbook examples such as 'Manufacturer M claims their product P lasts on average 14 years…'.

53 Note the locution: *not* confidence that such errors do not exist or have no effect; rather, confidence that such errors do not account for all of the observed effect. If we have reliable evidence of category errors, the information might enable some correction in the observations; if not, no correction is possible, and we have little means of estimating the effect on conclusions we draw from our observations, although sometimes 'fuzzy-set' techniques can be used. If we have reliable evidence of measurement errors but cannot use that evidence to make corrections without substantial risk of compounding errors, the evidence can be explicitly introduced into the

substantive models (theoretical expectations) that we use to analyze the observations and treated as specific determinants.

54 Expertise in a discipline does not inoculate against personal bias, deliberate or indeliberate. Studies of experts in various fields (e.g., physics, labor economics, demography, finance) demonstrate repeatedly a marked tendency to systematic overconfidence in their ability to make quantitative predictions or estimates of important parameters in their specialties. For a review with added evidence, see Fuchs et al. (1997: 20).

55 Remember, that statement is a *theoretical* expectation. It applies to empirical distributions only 'in the long run' – that is, in the very large aggregate.

56 We are assuming independent samplings; and the variances, while not equal (as estimated by the ratio of sample variances: $2.44^2/2.51^2 = 0.95$), are close enough to equality in view of the large sample sizes.

57 The same logic follows when using a different theoretical distribution (e.g., the *t* distribution).

58 The theorem proved by P.L. Chebyshev in 1867 (but already in 1853 by I.J. Bienaymé: see Stigler, 1999: 278, 283) implies that, for *any* distribution of measured observations, the observations that lie within ±1 standard deviation of the mean provide *no* useful information – the point being that knowledge of the distributional mean renders redundant the information from observations within the ± 1*s* interval. The utility of information increases as the observations diverge from the expected, – i.e., from the modal, the typical, the already known.

59 Bear in mind that all of this deliberation about minimizing error takes place when designing and executing the sample of observations. Once the observations have been made, errors of sampling as well as of measurement and classification, whatever their magnitude, are simply there, integral to the observations.

60 This terminological usage of β should not be confused with other uses of the same Greek letter, such as designation of a standardized regression coefficient.

61 If the second clause is puzzling, recall that the standard error of an estimate declines as sample size increases. With very large samples the chance of a statistically significant observed difference is no longer negligible. When sample sizes reach the tens of thousands or larger, virtually any observed difference will pass even the 'one in a thousand' test of statistical significance. Remember, the point of 'significance testing' is to assess sampling error; as *n* becomes very large, the effect of sampling error declines. So, one might ask, why not always use samples that are very large? Because they are very expensive and very difficult to manage (especially as they are samples of human beings).

62 An obvious cost of ritualized use of significance tests is lack of attention to power-of-test issues, which inhibits the development of explanatory models. This has been a concern especially among psychologists, who sometimes seek strong parallels between their research designs and those of physicists (see Widaman, 2000: 166).

63 Note that while the illustration uses notation that is typical of regression analysis, this convenience in no way alters the lesson – which applies without difference whether using regression techniques or analysis of covariance or an analysis directly of cross-tabulated observations as in a contingency table. For the novice reader, simply bear in mind that the terms b_i in the equation, known as 'regression coefficients' or 'slope coefficients', are sometimes interpretable as measures of the magnitude of effect of X on Y (see Chapter 8). More generally, a regression coefficient is a measure of sensitivity or a 'conversion factor' – as in, for example, the common formula for converting temperature on the Celsius scale to temperature on the Fahrenheit scale: $F = a + bC$, where $b = 5/9$ (i.e., $1°F = 5/9°C$), and $a = 32$ (a is known as 'the intercept', which is adjustment for the fact that the two scales have different zero points, i.e., $0°C = 32°F$).

REFERENCES

Abbott, Andrew and Barman, Emily (1997) 'Sequence comparison via alignment and Gibbs sampling', Adrian E. Raftery (ed.), *Sociological Methodology*, Vol. 27. Boston: Blackwell, pp. 47–87.

Abelson, Robert P. (1995) *Statistics as Principled Argument*. Hillsdale, NJ: Erlbaum.

Achen, Christopher H. and Shively, W. Phillips (1995) *Cross-Level Inference*. Chicago: University of Chicago Press.

Alston, William P. (1993) *The Reliability of Sense Perception*. Ithaca, NY: Cornell University Press.

Ashenfelter, Orley and Krueger, Alan B. (1994) 'Estimates of the economic return to schooling from a new sample of twins', *American Economic Review*, 84: 1157–73.

Barron, John M., Berger, Mark C. and Black, Dan A. (1997) 'How well do we measure training?', *Journal of Labor Economics*, 15: 507–28.

Bartholomew, David J. (1996) *The Statistical Approach to Social Measurement*. San Diego, CA: Academic Press.

Beltrami, Edward (1999) *What Is Random?* New York: Copernicus.

Bennett, Deborah J. (1998) *Randomness*. Cambridge, MA: Harvard University Press.

Berger, John (1972) *Ways of Seeing*. Harmondsworth: Penguin.

Bowker, Geoffrey C. and Star, Susan Leigh (1999) *Sorting Things Out*. Cambridge, MA: MIT Press.

Bryk, Anthony S. and Raudenbush, Stephen W. (1992) *Hierarchical Linear Models*. Newbury Park, CA: Sage.

Carroll, Glenn R. and Hannan, Michael T. (2000) *The Demography of Corporations and Industries*. Princeton, NJ: Princeton University Press.

Cliff, Norman (1989) 'Strong inferences and weak data', in J.A. Keats, R. Taft, R.A. Heath, and S.H. Lovibond (eds), *Mathematical and Theoretical Systems*. Amsterdam: Elsevier Science, pp. 69–77.

Cohen, Jacob (1988) *Statistical Power Analysis for the Behavioral Sciences* (2nd edition). Hillsdale, NJ: Erlbaum.

Cohen, Jacob (1994) 'The earth is round ($p < 0.05$)', *American Psychologist*, 49: 997–1003.

Cohen, Jacob and Cohen, Patricia (1983) *Applied Multiple Regression/Correlation Analysis for the Behavioral Sciences* (2nd edition). Hillsdale, NJ: Erlbaum.

Collins, Linda M. and Sayer, Aline G. (eds) (2001) *New Methods for the Analysis of Change*. Washington, DC: American Psychological Association.

Cover, Thomas and Thomas, Joy (1991) *Elements of Information Theory*. New York: Wiley.

Crary, Jonathan (1990) *Techniques of the Observer*. Cambridge, MA: MIT Press.

Duncan, Otis Dudley (1975) *Introduction to Structural Equation Models*. New York: Academic.

Duncan, Otis Dudley (1984) *Notes on Social Measurement*. New York: Russell Sage.

Ellis, Brian D. (1965) *Basic Concepts of Measurement*. Cambridge: Cambridge University Press.

Fillmore, Charles J. (1999) 'A linguistic look at survey research', in M.G. Sirken, D.J. Herrmann, S. Schechter, N. Schwarz, J.M. Tanur and R. Tourangeau (eds), *Cognition and Survey Research*. New York: Wiley, pp. 183–98.

Foucault, Michel (1970) *The Order of Things*. New York: Pantheon. First published in 1966.

Freedman, David A. (1991) 'Statistical models and shoe leather', in Peter V. Marsden (ed.), *Sociological Methodology, 1991*. Oxford: Basil Blackwell, pp. 291–313.

Freedman, David A., Pisani, Robert, and Purves, Robert (1978) *Statistics*. New York: Norton.

Fuchs, Victor R., Krueger, Alan B. and Poterba, James M. (1997) 'Why do economists disagree about policy?' NBER Working Paper No. 6151. Cambridge, MA: National Bureau of Economic Research.

Fuller, Wayne A. (1987) *Measurement Error Models*. New York: Wiley.

Geertz, Clifford (1973) *The Interpretation of Cultures*. New York: Basic Books.

Gill, Jeff (2002) *Bayesian Methods*. Boca Raton, FL: Chapman & Hall/CRC.

Goffman, Erving (1974) *Frame Analysis*. Cambridge, MA: Harvard University Press.

Greene, William H. (1993) *Econometric Analysis* (2nd edition). New York: Macmillan.

Groves, Robert M. (1999) 'Survey error models and cognitive theories of response behavior', in M.G. Sirken, D.J. Herrmann, S. Schechter, N. Schwarz, J.M. Tanur and R. Tourangeau (eds), *Cognition and Survey Research*. New York: Wiley, pp. 235–50.

Hausman, Daniel (1992) *The Inexact and Separate Science of Economics*. Cambridge: Cambridge University Press.

Hazelrigg, Lawrence (1995) *Cultures of Nature*. Gainesville: University Press of Florida.

Hazelrigg, Lawrence (2000) 'Reading Goffman's framing as provocation of a discipline', in G.A. Fine and G.W.H. Smith (eds), *Erving Goffman*, Vol. 3. Thousand Oaks, CA: Sage, pp. 137–60.

Horowitz, Joel (1997) 'Bootstrap methods in econometrics', in D.M. Kreps and K.F. Wallis (eds), *Advances in Economics and Econometrics*, Vol. 3. Cambridge: Cambridge University Press, pp. 189–222.

Hoyle, Fred, Burbidge, Geoffrey and Narlikar, Jayant V. (2000) *A Different Approach to Cosmology*. Cambridge: Cambridge University Press.

Kant, Immanuel (1952) *Critique of Pure Reason* (2nd edition). Chicago: Great Books. First published in 1787.

Kant, Immanuel (1974) *Anthropology from a Pragmatic Point of View*. The Hague: Martinus Nijhoff. First published in 1798.

Keister, Lisa A. (2000) *Wealth in America*. Cambridge: Cambridge University Press.

Kerszberg, Pierre (1989) *The Invented Universe: The Einstein–De Sitter Controversy (1916–17) and the Rise of Relativistic Cosmology*. Oxford: Clarendon.

Kim, Chang-Jin and Nelson, Charles R. (1999) *State-Space Models with Regime Switching*. Cambridge, MA: MIT Press.

Kish, Leslie (1965) *Survey Sampling*. New York: Wiley.

Latour, Bruno (1987) *Science in Action*. Cambridge, MA: Harvard University Press.

Lieberson, Stanley (1985) *Making It Count: The Improvement of Social Research and Theory*. Berkeley: University of California Press.

Lohr, Sharon L. (1999) *Sampling: Design and Analysis*. Pacific Grove, CA: Duxbury Press.

Manski, Charles F. (1995) *Identification Problems in the Social Sciences*. Cambridge, MA: Harvard University Press.

Manton, Kenneth G., Woodbury, Max A. and Tolley, H. Dennis (1994) *Statistical Applications Using Fuzzy Sets*. New York: Wiley.

Miller, Stephen H. (1989) *Experimental Design and Statistics* (2nd edition). New York: Methuen.

Mohr, John W. (1998) 'Measuring meaning structures', *Annual Review of Sociology*, 24: 345–70.

Montgomery, James D. (2000) 'The self as a fuzzy set of roles, role theory as a fuzzy system', in Michael E.

Sobel and Mark P. Becker (eds), *Sociological Methodology*, Vol. 30. Boston: Blackwell, pp. 261–314.

Pearson, Egon S. and Hartley, H.O. (1954) *Biometrika Tables for Statisticians*. Cambridge: Cambridge University Press.

Pratt, John W., Raiffa, Howard and Schlaifer, Robert (1995) *Introduction to Statistical Decision Theory*. Cambridge, MA: MIT Press.

Raftery, Adrian E. (2001) 'Statistics in sociology 1950–2000', in Michael E. Sobel and Mark P. Becker (eds), *Sociological Methodology*, Vol. 31. Boston: Blackwell, pp. 1–45.

Ragin, Charles (2000) *Fuzzy-Set Social Science*. Chicago: University of Chicago Press.

Rogosa, David (1995) 'Myth and methods', in J.M. Gottman (ed.), *The Analysis of Change*. Mahwah, NJ: Erlbaum, pp. 3–66.

Ryle, Gilbert (1971) 'The thinking of thoughts. What is "le Penseur" doing?', in *Collected Papers*, Vol. 2. London: Hutchison, pp. 480–96. First published in 1968.

Schaie, K. Warner (1996) *Intellectual Development in Childhood*. Cambridge: Cambridge University Press.

Schutz, Alfred (1967) *The Phenomenology of the Social World*. Evanston, IL: Northwestern University Press. First published in 1932.

Shum, Michael S. and Rips, Lance J. (1999) 'The respondent's confession', in M.G. Sirken, D.J. Herrmann, S. Schechter, N. Schwarz, J.M. Tanur and R. Tourangeau (eds), *Cognition and Survey Research*. New York: Wiley, pp. 95–109.

Snijders, Tom A.B. (2001) 'Sampling', in A.H. Leyland and H. Goldstein (eds), *Multilevel Modelling of Health Statistics*. Chichester: Wiley, pp. 159–74.

Sobel, Michael E. (1995) 'Causal inference in the social and behavioral sciences', in G. Arminger, C.C. Clogg and M.E. Sobel (eds), *Handbook for Statistical Modeling for the Social and Behavioral Sciences*. New York: Plenum, pp. 1–38.

Sobel, Michael E. (1998) 'Causal inference in statistical models of the process of socioeconomic achievement', *Sociological Methods and Research*, 27: 318–48.

Stevens, S.S. (1946) 'On the theory of scales of measurement', *Science*, 103: 677–80.

Stich, Stephen P. (1990) *The Fragmentation of Reason*. Cambridge, MA: MIT Press.

Stigler, Stephen M. (1986) *History of Statistics*. Cambridge, MA: Harvard University Press.

Stigler, Stephen M. (1999) *Statistics on the Table*. Cambridge, MA: Harvard University Press.

Tanur, Judith M. (ed.) (1992) *Questions about Questions*. New York: Russell Sage.

Tuma, Nancy Brandon and Hannan, Michael T. (1984) *Social Dynamics*. Orlando, FL: Academic Press.

Widaman, Keith F. (2000) 'Testing cross-group and cross-time constraints on parameters using the general linear model', in Todd D. Little, Kai Uwe Schnabel and Jürgen Baumert (eds), *Modeling Longitudinal and Multilevel Data*. Mahwah, NJ: Erlbaum, pp. 163–85.

Wilson, E.B. (1927) 'Probable inference, the law of succession, and statistical inference', *Journal of the American Statistical Association*, 22: 209–12.

Wittgenstein, Ludwig (1968) *Philosophical Investigations*. Oxford: Basil Blackwell. First published in 1953.

Yamane, Taro (1967) *Elementary Sampling Theory*. Englewood Cliffs, NJ: Prentice Hall.

5

Strategies for Analysis of Incomplete Data

MORTAZA JAMSHIDIAN

Missing data are a pervasive problem in almost all areas of empirical research. They arise, for example, during data recording (a datum is omitted), when responses are related to sensitive questions (e.g., age, income, drug use), when measurement of some of the variables is too expensive (e.g., measurement may require destroying expensive parts, an interviewer needs to travel a long distance), or when the experiment is run on a group of individuals over a period of time as in clinical studies (e.g., individuals may drop out of the study or not show up for certain visits). Efron (1994) defines *missing data* as a class of problems made difficult by the absence of some part of a familiar data structure. In the examples mentioned above, the missing structure is an observable covariate that is not recorded or observed. Efron's definition of missing data covers a broader class of problems. For example, the latent variables in factor analysis would be considered missing data by his definition. Viewing unobservable (latent) data as missing data can help us gain insight into models and develop computational methodology. For example, Rubin and Thayer (1982) developed an expectation–maximization (EM) algorithm to compute maximum likelihood (ML) estimates for the factor analysis model by treating the latent variables as missing data. I do not pursue the problem of unobservable data here, except to introduce the EM algorithm that is relevant to this topic;

the subject of missing data in the sense of Efron is too broad to be covered in one chapter. In this chapter I focus on describing and discussing a taxonomy of methods that can be used to analyze data sets with missing observable data (covariates).

The most commonly used techniques for treating missing data are *ad hoc* procedures that supply crude estimates for the missing values, allowing the researcher to analyze the newly completed data by using a complete data procedure. Such procedures often have no theoretical rationale and can lead to inefficient and biased inference. In practice, theoretically sound methods of handling incomplete data have been underutilized, mainly due to the paucity of missing-data subroutines in statistical software. Software to properly handle incomplete data is slowly emerging, however. Indeed, proper selection and apt use of state-of-the-art software requires understanding and familiarity with missing-data problems and methods. My aim in this chapter is to introduce and familiarize the reader with a few basic concepts that are essential in the analysis of incomplete data. Moreover, I will discuss a number of strategies to handle incomplete data and make comparisons among them.

I begin by describing three common missing-data mechanisms. Understanding these mechanisms is essential in choosing appropriate methodology to analyze incomplete data. I then turn to *ad hoc* methods, likelihood-based

Table 5.1   *The left-hand panel is an example of observation of three variables on six subjects, with question marks '?' indicating missing data. Each row in the right-hand panel gives a possible value of the random vector* R

y_1	y_2	y_3			
11	?	15	1	1	1
10	14	10	1	1	0
?	?	14	1	0	1
9	7	10	0	1	1
?	13	8	1	0	0
12	5	9	0	1	0
			0	0	1
			0	0	0

methods (including the EM algorithm), and simulation-based methods such as multiple imputation and the bootstrap. Finally, I use a small simulation study to compare the methods that I describe.

MISSING-DATA MECHANISMS

The term *missing-data mechanism* refers to the process by which the data become incomplete. Understanding this process is essential in the proper analysis of incomplete data. As we will see, a procedure may produce acceptable inferences under one missing-data mechanism, but lead to incorrect inferences under another missing-data mechanism. Two commonly used mechanisms are *missing completely at random* (MCAR) and *missing at random* (MAR). These terminologies were coined by Rubin (1976) and further described by Little and Rubin (1987). MCAR is a process in which missingness of the data is completely independent of both the observed and the missing values. MAR is a process in which missingness of the data is independent of the missing measurements, but depends on the observed measurements.

To give a more formal definition of these mechanisms, let the random variable (vector) Y correspond to the complete set of measurements on an individual or subject, and let R be the associated missing-value indicator. Let the pair of vectors (y, r) denote a particular realization of Y and R, with components of r taking values 1 or 0, respectively indicating whether the corresponding components of y are observed or not. As an example, consider the data in the left-hand panel of

Table 5.1. For these data, Y consists of three (random) variables. In this case there are eight possible missing-data patterns, therefore the random vector R has eight possible values, as shown in the right-hand panel of Table 5.1. The pair (y, r) for the first subject is y = (11,?,15) with r = (1,0,1), and that for the second subject is y = (10,14,10) with r = (1,1,1), and so on.

Under the MCAR mechanism, $P(R = r|y) = P(R = r)$ – that is, the conditional probability that R is equal to a specific value r given y is independent of y; or the value (or the knowledge) of y does not affect the probability distribution of the response R. For example, if the data are MCAR, then in the data of Table 5.1 the probability that R = (1,0,1) or R = (1,1,1) is completely independent of the values of the three covariates in y.

Under the MAR mechanism, $P(R = r|y) = P(R = r|y_{obs})$, where y_{obs} is the observed part of y. This means that the probability of observing a specific response pattern r depends on the values that are observed. For example, for the data of Table 5.1, if the data are MAR, then the probability that the response pattern is R = (1,0,1) could depend on the values of variables 1 or 3 and not 2, or the probability that R = (0,1,1) could depend on the values for the second and third variables, and not the first variable.

When the missing-data mechanism is neither MCAR nor MAR, and in particular the missingness depends on the missing values themselves, we call the process *missing not at random* (MNAR). The terms 'not missing at random (NMAR)' (e.g., Jamshidian and Bentler, 1999) and 'missing not at random (MNAR)' (e.g., Kenward and Molenberghs, 1998) have both been used. We, however, prefer MNAR and will use it throughout. For the data of Table 5.1, data would be MNAR if, for example, the probability that the response pattern is $\mathbf{R} = (1,0,1)$ depends on the missing value of the second variable. This probability may or may not depend on the values of the first and the third variable.

I use the following real example to further elucidate the three missing-data mechanisms. CESD is an index of depression used by the National Institute of Mental Health Center for Epidemiological Studies. CESD was measured at two time points in the Los Angeles Epidemiological Catchment Area study (Eaton and Kessler, 1995). There were 3047 individuals for whom CESD was measured at the first time point. In the second interview, 2240 of the 3047 cases had their CESD measured; thus 807 were missing for the second CESD measurement. For this example, the data would be MCAR if the missing CESDs at the second time point are completely independent of the depression level of individuals at both the first and the second time points. On the other hand, the data would be MAR if those individuals who did not show up for their second interview had high depression levels at the first time point, regardless of what their depression levels were at the time of the second interview. Finally, the data would be MNAR if the reason for those not showing up for the second interview had been that their depression levels at time 2 (not observed) were high (or low) and thus they did not submit to retesting. Note that in the latter case missingness depends on the missing values that would otherwise have been observed.

In general, to determine the *type* of missing-data mechanism, one must acquire information about the missing data. This information may be obtained by developing and relying on some reasonable theory about the missing data, or by collecting additional data, for example by follow-ups, to make the mechanism accessible (Graham and Donaldson, 1993; Little and Rubin, 1987: Section 12.6). Traditionally, follow-ups are used in situations where a case is completely missing. In our context, the follow-ups are used to obtain answers to previously skipped questions and/or to find the cause of missingness. An example of such a follow-up is given in a report by Huisman et al. (1998).

A few statistical tests have been developed to check MCAR. For example, MCAR can be checked by testing the equality of the distribution of observed variables across the missing patterns using a *t* test for location – see the program BMDP8D in Dixon (1988); see also Little (1988). In this procedure, for each variable with missing values, the sample is split into two groups consisting of cases with that variable observed and cases with that variable missing. Then for each of the other variables, we can compare the means of their observed values in the two groups with the two-sample *t* test. If any of the *t* tests show significant differences between the means, then there is evidence that the data are *not* MCAR. Little (1988) and, more recently, Krishnamoorthy and Pannala (1998) have proposed other procedures which are computationally more efficient than the procedure just described.

In some instances data are missing by design. For example, incomplete data may arise from merging multiple data sets that come from various sources. A specific example is in longitudinal studies when multiple data sets are merged and there is not a complete overlap on the timing of observations coming from various sources. An approach in modeling such data is to model the missing-data mechanism by incorporating the multiple data sources into the model. For example, if a factor analysis model is fitted to the data, one may use a multiple-group factor analysis model, where group membership is determined by the data source. In other instances where data are missing by design, the missing-data mechanism may be one of MCAR, MAR, or MNAR. To give an example, Murray and Findlay (1988) described data from a large multi-center trial of metopropol and ketanserin, two antihypertensive agents for patients with mild to moderate hypertension, with diastolic blood pressure an outcome measure of interest. Clinical visits were scheduled for weeks 0, 2, 4, 8, and 12. The protocol stated that patients with diastolic blood pressure exceeding 110 mmHg at either the 4- or 8-week visit should 'jump' to an open follow-up phase. In total, 39 of the 218 metapropol patients and 55 of the 211 ketanserin patients jumped to open follow-up. In this case the cause of missingness is observation of a high value for diastolic blood pressure; thus data are MAR.

In the section that follows I will discuss various methods for handling missing data. As we will see, there are several theoretically sound procedures available for the analysis of MCAR or MAR data. The MNAR case, however, is especially problematic since the missingness depends on the unobserved data. Consequently, it is difficult to assume a single model for the missing data. A reasonable approach is to model several missing-data mechanisms and examine the sensitivity of conclusions to the choice of one or another model. I will briefly discuss the MNAR case in the discussion of likelihood-based methods below; also, in my simulations I show that applying the wrong methodology to MNAR data can result in drastically biased inference.

METHODS OF HANDLING MISSING DATA

Ad hoc *methods*

Ad hoc methods are usually easy to use, which is their main advantage and likely the main reason for their frequent use. A serious disadvantage of these methods, however, is that they can lead to biased and inefficient estimates. In this subsection I will describe a few commonly used *ad hoc* methods.

Complete-case analysis method   One common approach to the analysis of incomplete data is to base the analysis on the completely observed cases and discard the incomplete cases. This method is known as *complete-case* (CC) *analysis* or *listwise deletion*. In fact, it is the default option in many statistical software packages. As an example, a CC analysis of the data of Table 5.1 will include only cases 2, 4, and 6. When data are MCAR, the complete cases are a random subsample of all the cases in the data set, thus CC leads to unbiased estimates. However, when the percentage of incomplete cases is large (say, over 20%), discarding these cases and using CC leads to significantly less efficient estimates compared to some other methods that use all of the observed data. Note that when 10 variables are independently measured and there is a 90% chance of observing a case of each single variable, then the probability that all 10 variables are observed for a specific case is only 35%.[1] In this situation there will be a significant loss of efficiency if CC is used.

Under the MAR or MNAR mechanisms the complete cases are no longer a random subsample of all the cases in the data set, and thus under these mechanisms CC can lead to biased estimates in addition to less efficient estimates.

Available-case analysis method   *Available-case* (AC) *analysis* uses the largest possible set of available cases to estimate parameters. For example, to conduct a regression analysis (e.g., Little, 1992) or a factor analysis (e.g., Brown, 1983), we require estimates of the mean and covariance matrix for the variables involved. To obtain these, when using AC, the mean and the variance for each variable are computed based on all the observed cases for the corresponding variable, and the covariance between a pair of variables is computed based on all the observed cases for that pair. For example, for the data of Table 5.1, the mean and variance for variable 1 are estimated by the sample mean and variance of the observed values 11, 10, 9, and 12; likewise those for variable 2 are computed based on the observed values 14, 7, 13, and 5. The covariance between variables 1 and 2 is estimated using the sample covariance for the observed pairs (10,14), (9,7), and (12,5).

Since AC uses more data than CC to estimate parameters, one might expect that estimates based on AC would be more efficient than similar estimates based on CC. If data are MCAR and the correlations between variables are modest, a simulation by Kim and Curry (1977) supports the expected conclusion that AC results in more efficient estimates than CC. Other simulations, however, indicate superiority of CC when these correlations are large (Azen and Van Guilder, 1981). It is not difficult to see that when data are MAR or MNAR, AC can lead to biased estimates. In addition, AC can result in nonpositive-definite covariance matrix estimates, which can produce correlation estimates that are out of the admissible range [−1, 1] (e.g., Bentler and Jamshidian, 1994).

Mean imputation method   Other *ad hoc* methods impute (fill in) the missing data. The *unconditional mean imputation* (UMI) is one of the simplest imputation methods in which the missing values of each variable are replaced by the mean of the observed values for that variable (for categorical variables one might consider imputing the mode). This imputation can also lead to biased estimates. For example, even when data are MCAR, UMI underestimates the variance of a variable.[2] More sophisticated versions of UMI impute the mean of variables for subjects that agree, or approximately agree, on some observed covariates, such as age or gender.

A method called hot-deck is an example of this type of imputation (e.g., Rubin, 1987).

It is appealing to take advantage of correlations that may exist between variables in a data set to fill in missing data. This is the basis of *conditional mean imputation* (CMI) methods. Buck's (1960) method is one of the most popular CMI procedures. In his method missing values are filled in by predictions from regression models that are fitted using the mean and covariance matrix estimated by CC. This method is more easily explained using the data of Table 5.1. To fill in the missing value in the first case (11,?, 5), variable 2 is regressed on variables 1 and 3 using the data provided by the three complete cases 2, 4, and 6. Say the resulting fitted model is $\hat{y}_2 = \hat{\alpha}_0 + \hat{\alpha}_1 y_1 + \hat{\alpha}_2 y_3$ for some least-squares estimates $\hat{\alpha}_0$, $\hat{\alpha}_1$, and $\hat{\alpha}_2$. Then the missing datum in case 1 is replaced by $\hat{\alpha}_0 + 11\hat{\alpha}_1 + 15\hat{\alpha}_2$. Similarly, to fill in the first and second missing data in case 3, variables 1 and 2 are respectively regressed on variable 3, using the three complete cases, and predictions from the resulting fitted models are used to fill in these data. This method often performs much better than UMI. The mean of the observed and imputed values from this procedure is a consistent estimate of the mean for MCAR data (Buck, 1960). This property also holds for MAR data under some mild regularity conditions. When data are multivariate normal, the variance and covariances are underestimated by Buck's method, but the extent of underestimation is often less than that in the UMI case.

There is a potential danger with single-imputation methods like those just described; the danger would be to treat the completed data set as if there had been no missing values. Indeed, we should distinguish between data that are actually observed and those that are imputed. There is an uncertainty associated with the filled-in values, which usually depends on the method of imputation. If we do not take this additional source of uncertainty into account in our final analysis, then our predictions are viewed as more precise than they really are. To address this problem, we must incorporate this additional source of uncertainty into the calculation of new standard errors. To give an example, suppose that an incomplete data set is imputed, and the resulting completed data are used to fit a factor analysis model. The output commonly includes standard errors

for the parameter estimates (e.g., factor loadings and unique variances). Under this circumstance the standard errors are underestimates of the true standard errors, because they have been computed in the absence of information that the data were imputed. In general, it is difficult to incorporate the uncertainty in imputed values in the final analysis. A method of multiple imputation that I will describe in a later section is a remedy for this problem.

Here I have described two basic UMI and CMI methods to impute missing values. There are various other imputation methods, and for those I refer the reader to Little and Rubin (1987), Nordholt (1998), Lakshminarayan et al. (1999) and references therein.

Likelihood-based methods

Maximum likelihood and the EM algorithm Inference based on maximum likelihood (ML) is popular since ML estimates are asymptotically (when the sample size is large) normal, unbiased, and efficient. In ML estimation, a distribution (model) for the data is assumed and the likelihood function based on this distribution is formulated and maximized with respect to model parameters. Then the maximizing parameter values and their standard errors are used to make inferences.

I will use the notation of the previous subsection to formally introduce ML estimation in the context of missing data. As before, let the random vector $\mathbf{Y}$ correspond to the complete set of measurements on a subject, $\mathbf{R}$ be the associated response indicator, and $(\mathbf{y}, \mathbf{r})$ denote a realization of $(\mathbf{Y}, \mathbf{R})$. In ML estimation, we assume a model for $(\mathbf{Y}, \mathbf{R})$ that specifies the joint distribution of $\mathbf{Y}$ and $\mathbf{R}$. Let $f(\mathbf{y}, \mathbf{r}; \boldsymbol{\theta}, \boldsymbol{\beta})$ denote the joint density of this distribution, where $\boldsymbol{\theta}$ and $\boldsymbol{\beta}$ are the unknown (model) parameter vectors that respectively depend on $\mathbf{Y}$ and $\mathbf{R}$. In many important applications $\boldsymbol{\theta}$ and $\boldsymbol{\beta}$ are disjoint, and we will assume this throughout. The joint density of $(\mathbf{Y}, \mathbf{R})$ can be written as

$$f(\mathbf{y}, \mathbf{r}; \boldsymbol{\theta}, \boldsymbol{\beta}) = f(\mathbf{y}; \boldsymbol{\theta}) \, f(\mathbf{r}|\mathbf{y}; \boldsymbol{\beta}),$$

where $f(\mathbf{y}; \boldsymbol{\theta})$ is the marginal density for the distribution of $\mathbf{Y}$, and $f(\mathbf{r}|\mathbf{y}; \boldsymbol{\beta})$ is the conditional density for the distribution of $\mathbf{R}$ given $\mathbf{Y}$; the latter is referred to as the density for the distribution of the missing-data mechanism.

To keep notation simple here and throughout, I denote densities generically by $f(\cdot)$ and distinguish them by their arguments.

Now, let $\mathbf{Y} = (\mathbf{Y}_{obs}, \mathbf{Y}_{mis})$, where $\mathbf{Y}_{obs}$ and $\mathbf{Y}_{mis}$ denote the observed and the missing parts of $\mathbf{Y}$, respectively, with realization $\mathbf{y} = (\mathbf{y}_{obs}, \mathbf{y}_{mis})$. The likelihood function is formulated based on the observed data. More specifically, we need the density $f(\mathbf{y}_{obs}, \mathbf{r}; \boldsymbol{\theta}, \boldsymbol{\beta})$ of the joint distribution of $(\mathbf{Y}_{obs}, \mathbf{R})$. This density can be obtained by integrating out $\mathbf{Y}_{mis}$ from $f(\mathbf{y}, \mathbf{r}; \boldsymbol{\theta}, \boldsymbol{\beta}) = f(\mathbf{y}_{obs}, \mathbf{y}_{mis}, \mathbf{r}; \boldsymbol{\theta}, \boldsymbol{\beta})$ as follows:

$$f(\mathbf{y}_{obs}, \mathbf{r}, \boldsymbol{\theta}, \boldsymbol{\beta}) = \int f(\mathbf{y}_{obs}, \mathbf{y}_{mis}; \boldsymbol{\theta})$$
$$\times f(\mathbf{r}|\mathbf{y}_{obs}, \mathbf{y}_{mis}; \boldsymbol{\beta}) \, d\mathbf{y}_{mis} \quad (5.1)$$

The likelihood of $\boldsymbol{\theta}$ and $\boldsymbol{\beta}$ is a function of $\boldsymbol{\theta}$ and $\boldsymbol{\beta}$, which is proportional to the density $f(\mathbf{y}_{obs}, \mathbf{r}, \boldsymbol{\theta}, \boldsymbol{\beta})$.

In most applications we are interested in estimating $\boldsymbol{\theta}$, whereas the estimate of $\boldsymbol{\beta}$ is not of interest. The question is, under what condition can we ignore $\boldsymbol{\beta}$ and $\mathbf{R}$? It is not difficult to see that the condition is related to the missing-data mechanism. As noted earlier, if data are MCAR, then the distribution of $\mathbf{R}$ will not depend on $\mathbf{Y}$, and thus we have $f(\mathbf{r}|\mathbf{y}_{obs}, \mathbf{y}_{mis}; \boldsymbol{\beta}) = f(\mathbf{r}; \boldsymbol{\beta})$. Using this in (5.1) implies that

$$f(\mathbf{y}_{obs}, \mathbf{r}; \boldsymbol{\theta}, \boldsymbol{\beta}) = f(\mathbf{y}_{obs}; \boldsymbol{\theta})f(\mathbf{r}; \boldsymbol{\beta}). \quad (5.2)$$

Thus, if data are MCAR, the log-likelihood function is given by

$$L(\boldsymbol{\theta}, \boldsymbol{\beta}; \mathbf{y}_{obs}, \mathbf{r}) = L_1(\boldsymbol{\theta}; \mathbf{y}_{obs}) + L_2(\boldsymbol{\beta}; \mathbf{r}), \quad (5.3)$$

where $L_1 = \log f(\mathbf{y}_{obs}; \boldsymbol{\theta})$ and $L_2 = \log f(\mathbf{r}; \boldsymbol{\beta})$. Similarly, if data are MAR, then the conditional distribution of $\mathbf{R}$ given $\mathbf{Y}$ will only depend on the $\mathbf{Y}_{obs}$ and $f(\mathbf{r}|\mathbf{y}_{obs}, \mathbf{y}_{mis}; \boldsymbol{\beta}) = f(\mathbf{r}|\mathbf{y}_{obs}; \boldsymbol{\beta})$. Again, using (5.1), we get

$$f(\mathbf{y}_{obs}, \mathbf{r}; \boldsymbol{\theta}, \boldsymbol{\beta}) = f(\mathbf{y}_{obs}; \boldsymbol{\theta}) f(\mathbf{r}|\mathbf{y}_{obs}; \boldsymbol{\beta}). \quad (5.4)$$

Thus, in this situation the log-likelihood function can be written as

$$L(\boldsymbol{\theta}, \boldsymbol{\beta}; \mathbf{y}_{obs}, \mathbf{r}) = L_1(\boldsymbol{\theta}; \mathbf{y}_{obs})$$
$$+ L_2(\boldsymbol{\beta}; \mathbf{r}|\mathbf{y}_{obs}), \quad (5.5)$$

where $L_1(\boldsymbol{\theta}; \mathbf{y}_{obs}) = \log f(\mathbf{y}_{obs}; \boldsymbol{\theta})$ and $L_2 = \log f(\mathbf{r}|\mathbf{y}_{obs}; \boldsymbol{\beta})$. From (5.3) and (5.5) we get the answer to the question of when we can ignore $\boldsymbol{\beta}$ and $\mathbf{R}$: if data are MCAR or MAR and we are only interested in estimating $\boldsymbol{\theta}$, then it suffices to maximize $L_1(\boldsymbol{\theta}; \mathbf{y}_{obs})$ and ignore the L_2 portion of the log-likelihood, which depends on the missing-data mechanism. Note that L_2 is independent of $\boldsymbol{\theta}$. This is why

the term *ignorable nonresponse* is used for the MAR and MCAR mechanisms. Analogously, the terminology *nonignorable nonresponse* or *informative nonresponse* is used for the MNAR mechanism.

In practice, if we have n independent observations, say $\mathbf{y} = (\mathbf{y}_1, \ldots, \mathbf{y}_n)$ with each $\mathbf{y}_i$ consisting of an observed part $\mathbf{y}_{obs,i}$ and a missing part $\mathbf{y}_{mis,i}$, and if the missing-data mechanism is ignorable, then we obtain the maximum likelihood estimate $\hat{\boldsymbol{\theta}}$ by maximizing, with respect to $\boldsymbol{\theta}$, the *observed log-likelihood*[3]

$$\ell(\boldsymbol{\theta}; \mathbf{y}_{obs}) = \sum_{i=1}^{n} \log f(\mathbf{y}_{obs,i}; \boldsymbol{\theta}).$$

This is what I denoted earlier, in the more general case, by $L_1(\boldsymbol{\theta}, \mathbf{y}_{obs})$. I use a simple example to clarify some of the ideas and notations. The example does not have much practical value in the sense of missing-data estimation, but its simplicity serves us to clarify ideas. Let $\mathbf{Y} \equiv (X, Z)$ have a bivariate normal distribution with the means of X and Y equal to zero, and their variances equal to 1. Suppose that we want to estimate ρ, the correlation between X and Y, based on the following type of data:

$$x \quad x_1 \, x_2 \, \ldots \, x_m \, x_{m+1} \, \ldots \, x_n$$
$$z \quad z_1 \, z_2 \, \ldots \, z_m \quad ? \quad \ldots \, ?$$

Here $\mathbf{y}_i = (x_i, z_i)$ consists of two variables, and for the first m cases both x and z are observed (i.e., $\mathbf{y}_{obs,i} = (x_i, z_i)$) and for the last $n - m$ cases x is observed (i.e., $\mathbf{y}_{obs,i} = x_i$) and z is missing (i.e., $\mathbf{y}_{mis,i} = z_i$). Now using the bivariate normal density and the fact that the marginal distribution of X is standard normal, the observed log-likelihood, up to an additive constant, is given by

$$\ell(\rho; \mathbf{y}_{obs}) = -\frac{1}{2}\left[m \log(1 - \rho^2) \right.$$
$$\left. + \frac{1}{1 - \rho^2}\sum_{i=1}^{m}(x_i^2 - 2\rho x_i z_i + z_i^2) - \sum_{i=m+1}^{n} x_i^2 \right].$$

The observed log-likelihood here is comprised of two parts: the first two terms in the brackets are contributions from the first m observed values of x_i and z_i, and the last term in the bracket is the contribution from the last $n - m$ partially observed cases. We maximize $\ell(\rho; \mathbf{y}_{obs})$ with respect to ρ to obtain the ML estimate of ρ. As is sensible, the last $n - m$ cases do not contribute to estimating the correlation ρ.

As in the example just shown, the log-likelihood function is often a nonlinear function of the parameters in $\boldsymbol{\theta}$, and its maximization requires iterative methods. When $\ell(\boldsymbol{\theta}; \mathbf{y}_{\text{obs}})$ is a smooth function of $\boldsymbol{\theta}$, in principle any smooth maximization algorithm can be applied to obtain the maximum likelihood estimate $\hat{\boldsymbol{\theta}}$. In the context of missing data, however, the EM algorithm of Dempster et al. (1977) is the most intuitive, and it often is the easiest algorithm to use.

To define an EM algorithm, one must designate what is referred to as the complete data. In our context it is natural to choose $\mathbf{y} = (\mathbf{y}_{\text{obs}}, \mathbf{y}_{\text{mis}})$ as the complete data. Let $f(\mathbf{y}; \boldsymbol{\theta})$ be the density for the distribution of the complete data, and let $\ell_c(\boldsymbol{\theta}; \mathbf{y}) = \log f(\mathbf{y}; \boldsymbol{\theta})$ be the corresponding *complete-data log-likelihood*. Then the EM algorithm starts with an initial guess for the parameter vector; called the initial guess $\boldsymbol{\theta}$. It then cycles, or iterates, through the following E- and M-steps until convergence:[4]

E-Step. Obtain

$$Q(\boldsymbol{\theta}', \boldsymbol{\theta}) \ \text{E} \ [\log(\ell_c(\boldsymbol{\theta}'; \mathbf{y}))|\mathbf{y}_{\text{obs}}, \boldsymbol{\theta}].$$

M-Step. Obtain: $\tilde{\boldsymbol{\theta}} = \arg[Q(\boldsymbol{\theta}', \boldsymbol{\theta})] \max_{\boldsymbol{\theta}'}$
Check convergence. If convergence is achieved stop. Otherwise, set $\boldsymbol{\theta} = \tilde{\boldsymbol{\theta}}$ and go to the E-step.

I will use the problem of estimation of the correlation ρ, described earlier, to illustrate the components of the EM algorithm. In that problem, if data were completely observed (i.e., we had observed $z_{m+1},\ldots,z_n$), then the complete-data log-likelihood evaluated at ρ would be given by

$$\ell_c(\rho'; \mathbf{x}, \mathbf{z}) = -\frac{1}{2}\left[n \log(1 - (\rho')^2) \right. $$
$$\left. + \frac{1}{1 - (\rho')^2} \ \sum_{i=1}^{n} (x_i^2 - 2\rho' x_i z_i + z_i^2) \right].$$

Obviously, this function is not computable, since the values of z_i for $i = m + 1,\ldots, n$ are not observed. The E-step of the EM algorithm computes the conditional expectation $\ell_c(\rho'; \mathbf{x}, \mathbf{z})$ given the observed values of x_i and z_i and a current parameter estimate ρ. The result is the function $Q(\rho', \rho)$. More specifically, let $A^* = \text{E}(A|x_1,\ldots, x_n, z_1,\ldots,z_m, \rho)$ for any A. Then

$$Q(\rho', \rho) = \ell_c^*(\rho'; \mathbf{x}, \mathbf{z})$$
$$= \text{E}\left[\ell_c(\rho', \mathbf{x}, \mathbf{z})\,|\,x_1,\ldots, x_n, z_1,\ldots, z_m, \rho\right]$$
$$= -\frac{1}{2}\left[n \log(1 - (\rho')^2 \right. $$
$$\left. + \frac{1}{1 - (\rho')^2} \sum_{i=1}^{n} (x_i^2 - 2\rho' x_i z_i^* + (z_i^2)^*) \right].$$

Note that since all the x_i are observed, then $x_i^* = x_i$ and $(x_i^2)^* = x_i^2$ for $i = 1,\ldots,n$. Similarly, $z_i^* = z_i$ and $(z_i^2)^* = z_i^2$ for the observed cases $i = 1,\ldots,m$. We use the conditional distribution of Z given X and ρ to obtain values of z_i^* and $(z_i^2)^*$ for the missing cases. This gives $z_i^* = \rho x_i$ and $(z_i^2)^* = (1-\rho^2) + \rho^2 x_i^2$ for $i = m + 1,\ldots,n$. Thus, for a given ρ, and using the observed values of x_i and z_i, we can compute the Q-function.

Essentially, $Q(\rho', \rho)$ approximates the observed log-likelihood $\ell(\rho'; \mathbf{y}_{\text{obs}})$ at the point $\rho' = \rho$. This is depicted in Figure 5.1, where I have plotted the observed log-likelihood $L = \ell(\rho'; \mathbf{y}_{\text{obs}})$, and $Q(\rho', 0.2)$ for a set of 200 observations from (X,Z) with correlation 0.5, and $m = 130 - \ell(\rho'; \mathbf{y}_{\text{obs}})$ is approximated by $Q(\rho', 0.2)$ at $\rho' = 0.2$. So if EM starts with the initial guess of $\rho' = 0.2$, this estimate will be updated to 0.4, the value that maximizes $Q(\rho', 0.2)$, as shown in the figure. So the next iteration of EM starts with $\rho = 0.4$, and subsequently $Q(\rho', 0.4)$ is maximized to update the estimate again. This process continues until the maximum of the observed log-likelihood $\ell(\boldsymbol{\theta}; \mathbf{y}_{\text{obs}})$ is reached.

The utility of the EM algorithm is that it replaces a typically difficult maximization problem, that of the observed log-likelihood, with a sequence of simple maximization problems, that of the Q-function. The example above, however, does not have this property; namely, maximization of the Q-function is as difficult as that of the log-likelihood $\ell(\boldsymbol{\theta}, \mathbf{y}_{\text{obs}})$. As we said, this example was not typical and we have only used it to demonstrate ideas.

Now we can turn to an application of EM and an example where the Q-function is much easier to maximize, as compared to the observed data log-likelihood. The application involves the estimation of the covariance matrix from incomplete data. Let $\mathbf{y} = (\mathbf{y}_1,\ldots,\mathbf{y}_n)$ be a set of n incomplete observations from a p-variate normal distribution with

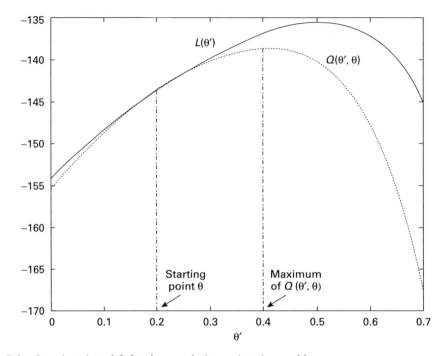

Figure 5.1   *Functions L and Q for the correlation estimation problem*

mean **0** and covariance Σ. I assume that each $\mathbf{y}_i$ is a row vector. The problem is to estimate the $p\,(p+1)/2$ parameters in Σ. Let $\mathbf{y}_{\text{obs},i}$ denote the observed data for the ith case. Then the observed data log-likelihood for this problem is given by

$$\ell(\textstyle\sum; \mathbf{y}_{\text{obs}}) = -\frac{1}{2}\sum_{i=1}^{n}\Big\{p_i\log(2\pi) + \log|\textstyle\sum_i|$$
$$+ \mathbf{y}_{\text{obs},i}\textstyle\sum_i^{-1}\mathbf{y}_{\text{obs},i}^{\mathrm{T}}\Big\},$$

where $p_i \le p$ is the number of variables observed for case i, and Σ_i is the appropriate submatrix of Σ depending on the observed components of $\mathbf{y}_{\text{obs},i}$. For example if $\mathbf{y}$ consists of four variables, and $\mathbf{y}_i = (3,?,1,?)$, with its first and third components observed, then $p_i = 2$ and Σ_i would be a 2×2 matrix with diagonal elements Σ_{11} and Σ_{33}, and off-diagonal element Σ_{13}.

The observed data log-likelihood given above is a complicated function in that each term in the summation varies from one missing-data pattern to another. This makes computation of $\ell(\Sigma; \mathbf{y}_{\text{obs}})$ as well as its maximization difficult. To maximize $\ell(\Sigma; \mathbf{y}_{\text{obs}})$ using the EM algorithm, we use the complete data $\mathbf{y}_i = (\mathbf{y}_{\text{obs},i}, \mathbf{y}_{\text{mis},i})$. Then the *complete-data log-likelihood* is given by

$$\ell_c(\textstyle\sum; \mathbf{S}) = -\frac{n}{2}\Big\{p\log(2\pi) + \log|\textstyle\sum|$$
$$+ \operatorname{trace}(\textstyle\sum^{-1}\mathbf{S})\Big\},$$

where $\mathbf{S} = (1/n)\sum_{i=1}^{n}\mathbf{y}_i^{\mathrm{T}}\mathbf{y}_i$, and the Q-function is

$$Q(\textstyle\sum', \textstyle\sum) = \mathrm{E}^*\{\ell_c(\textstyle\sum'; \mathbf{S})\}$$
$$= -\frac{n}{2}\Big\{p\log(2\pi)$$
$$+ \log|\textstyle\sum'| + \operatorname{trace}((\textstyle\sum')^{-1}\mathbf{S}^*)\Big\},$$

where $\mathrm{E}(\cdot) \equiv \mathrm{E}^*(\cdot|\mathbf{y}_{\text{obs},i}, i=1,\dots,n; \textstyle\sum)$ and

$$\mathbf{S}^* = \frac{1}{n}\sum_{i=1}^{n}\mathrm{E}^*\{\mathbf{y}_i^{\mathrm{T}}\mathbf{y}_i\}. \qquad (5.6)$$

Explicit formulas for computing $\mathbf{S}^*$ are given in the Appendix to this chapter. Note that in this case it is easy to obtain the maximum of Q, namely $\tilde{\Sigma} = \mathbf{S}^*$ is the maximizing value of $Q(\Sigma', \Sigma)$ with respect to Σ'. So for this problem the EM algorithm starts with an initial guess for the covariance matrix, say Σ, and proceeds as follows:

E-step. Compute $\mathbf{S}^*$ using equation (5.6).
M-step. Maximize $Q(\Sigma', \Sigma)$ with respect to Σ'. The maximizing value is $\tilde{\Sigma} = \mathbf{S}^*$.
Check convergence. If convergence is not achieved, replace Σ by $\tilde{\Sigma} = \mathbf{S}^*$ and go to the E-step.

It is well known that the EM algorithm converges slowly in some applications. A number of algorithms have been proposed to accelerate its convergence (see Jamshidian and Jennrich, 1997). An alternative to EM and its variants is to use other optimization algorithms such as quasi-Newton or the conjugate-gradient method to directly maximize $\ell(\theta; y_{obs})$ with respect to θ. The EM machinery can be used to make implementation of such algorithms simple. More specifically, the main ingredient required for implementation of these algorithms is the gradient of the observed data log-likelihood $\partial \ell(\theta; y_{obs})/\partial \theta$. This quantity can be computed by using the *Fisher identity*

$$\frac{\partial \ell(\theta; y_{obs})}{\partial \theta} = \frac{\partial Q(\theta', \theta)}{\partial \theta'} \Big|_{\theta' = \theta}.$$

To estimate the covariance matrix from incomplete data, the gradient is obtained by differentiating $Q(\Sigma', \Sigma)$ with respect to Σ' and evaluating the differential at $\Sigma' = \Sigma$ (e.g., Jamshidian and Jennrich, 1997).

Estimating standard errors An important advantage of maximum likelihood estimation, as compared to the *ad hoc* methods discussed earlier, is that asymptotic standard errors for ML estimates can be obtained. Under the MCAR mechanism we can assume that we have repeatedly sampled from the distribution $f(y_{obs}; \theta)$, and thus direct use of $\ell(\theta; y_{obs})$ for inference will be valid. For example, the observed information

$$I(\theta_j, \theta_k) = -\frac{\partial^2 \ell(\cdot)}{\partial \theta_j \partial \theta_k}$$

or the Fisher information

$$J(\theta_j, \theta_k) = E(I(\theta_j, \theta_k))$$

can be used to estimate standard errors of the parameters. More precisely, the negative of the inverse of the observed information or the inverse of the Fisher information matrix are estimates of the asymptotic covariance matrix of the ML estimates. On the other hand, when data are MAR, while maximization of $\ell(\theta; y_{obs})$ leads to 'correct' parameter estimates, we need to be cautious about making general inferences based on $\ell(\theta; y_{obs})$ alone (e.g., Kenward and Molenberghs, 1998). Considering equation (5.3), it is valid to obtain standard errors based on the observed

information by differentiating only $\ell(\theta; y_{obs})$, since the maximum likelihood of θ is functionally independent of β. However, when taking expectations to obtain the Fisher information, if data are MAR, then **R** cannot be ignored. Derivation of the Fisher information in this case is often not straightforward.[5] We agree with Kenward and Molenberghs (1998) that, '[g]iven the relative ease with which the observed information matrix can be calculated, using numerical differentiation if necessary, its use in missing data problems should be a rule rather than the exception'. A number of simple numerical differentiation methods are given by Jamshidian and Jennrich (2000) which can be used to produce very accurate estimates of standard errors in ML estimation. Finally, inferences made based on likelihood ratios, with common β, using $\ell(\theta; y_{obs})$ alone will be valid, again because the maximum likelihood of β is functionally independent of θ.

Likelihood-based analysis of MNAR data When data are MNAR, the missing data need to be modeled and incorporated in the likelihood estimation. Two approaches have mainly been used; the first, *the selection model* (see Chapter 18, this volume) is based on

$$f(y, r; \theta, \beta) = f(y; \theta) f(r|y; \beta).$$

For this case the missing-data mechanism is modeled through $f(r|y; \beta)$. This approach was first applied in economics for inferences based on samples subject to selectivity bias (Amemiya, 1984; Heckman, 1976). The second approach, called the *pattern-mixture model*, uses

$$f(y, r; \theta, \beta) = f(y|r; \theta) f(r; \beta).$$

This approach allows a different response model for each pattern of missing data. That is, it stratifies the population by the pattern of missing data, with a model for the whole population that is a mixture of the models for each pattern. In comparing selection models with pattern-mixture models, Little (1995) states:

> Selection models are more common and have conceptual advantages, but they require relatively detailed specification of the nature of the drop-out [missing] mechanism, at least within the framework of a likelihood analysis. Pattern-mixture models provide an interesting alternative approach, in that assumptions about the drop-out mechanism can be incorporated by restrictions on the parameters, thus

avoiding the need to specify the precise form of the drop-out model.

It is not possible to give specific methodologies that work in general for analysis of MNAR data. Modeling special cases can make for interesting research, and to my knowledge the literature in this area is limited. For further reading on the MNAR case I refer the interested reader to recent work by Cook (1997), Ibrahim and Lipsitz (1999), Kenward and Molenberghs (1998), Little (1995), Park (1998), Smith et al. (1999) and references therein.

Other approaches to likelihood estimation
As for other likelihood approaches, we can maximize the complete-data likelihood $f(\mathbf{y}; \boldsymbol{\theta}) = f(\mathbf{y}_{obs}, \mathbf{y}_{mis}; \boldsymbol{\theta})$ with respect to the missing values $\mathbf{y}_{mis}$ and the parameters $\boldsymbol{\theta}$ simultaneously. This method is useful in particular problems, but Little and Rubin (1983) show that it does not share the optimal properties of ML estimation, except under the trivial asymptotics in which the proportion of missing data goes to zero as the sample size increases. Interested readers can refer to Little and Rubin (1987, Section 5.4) for examples of this approach.

ML estimation is generally appropriate for large samples and mainly relies on asymptotic results; it generally performs well (for a simulation study, see Wang-Clow et al., 1995). One approach when dealing with small samples is to apply Bayesian inference[6] that adds a prior to the likelihood and bases inference on the posterior distribution. Little (1988) has shown that such an approach, when making inference about a mean from incomplete data, can yield inferences with good frequentist properties.[7] In general, Bayesian methods have been applied to multivariate problems with incomplete data. Little (1992) describes this approach in the context of regression and gives a number of references in Section 6 of his paper on the Bayesian literature for incomplete data.

Simulation-based methods

Simulation-based methods have surfaced in the context of incomplete-data analysis in the past twenty years or so. Methods such as multiple imputation (Rubin, 1987), data augmentation, and the Gibbs sampler offer Bayesian-based solutions to incomplete-data problems. The bootstrap is another type of simulation-based method in that it does not use the Bayesian framework, and it estimates $\boldsymbol{\theta}$ based on resampling from the observed data.

Many of the Bayesian-based methods are conceptually similar to the EM algorithm; they simply replace the E- and M-steps by draws from the current conditional distribution of missing data and $\boldsymbol{\theta}$. For example, data augmentation (Tanner and Wong, 1987) replaces the E-step by multiple imputation (see below), and the M-step by draws simulating the current estimate of the posterior distribution. The Gibbs sampler (Geman and Geman, 1984) or stochastic relaxation is another example that simulates data from the joint posterior of $\boldsymbol{\theta}$ and $\mathbf{y}_{mis}$ given $\mathbf{y}_{obs}$ to replace the E-step of the EM algorithm. We do not pursue these methods, because they are computationally intensive and involved, and they are often applicable in special cases where EM is computationally intractable. In this subsection, we will describe multiple imputation and the bootstrap in some detail. Multiple imputation is a Bayesian method that has recently become very popular in handling incomplete data; it does have something of an EM flavor to it. On the other hand, the bootstrap is of a different nature in that it is not Bayesian, as mentioned earlier, and it cannot be described as an extension of EM.

Multiple imputation Multiple imputation, proposed by Rubin (1987), is a simulation-based method whereby each missing value in a data set is replaced by $m(>1)$ simulated values creating m complete data sets. Then each of the m complete data sets is analyzed and the results are combined to make inferences.

Rubin's multiple imputation was originally intended for complex surveys to create multiple copies of (completed) public-use data sets that would be used and analyzed by different users (Rubin, 1996). In effect the data imputer would be distinct from the data analyzer. Over the years, however, because of increasing familiarity and software development – see, for example, SOLAS, distributed by Statistical Solution (http://www.statol.ie); J.L. Schafer's site (http://www.stat.psu.edu/~jls/mistoftwa.html); and T.E. Raghunathan's site (http://www.isr.umich.edu/src/smp/ive) – multiple imputation has come to be used to handle more general missing-data problems.

Multiple imputation is motivated by the Bayesian framework (see Rubin, 1987: Result 3.1). In this framework, it is assumed that θ is a random vector with density $f(\theta; \mathbf{y}_{obs}, \mathbf{y}_{mis})$. Then inference about θ is made via the posterior distribution of θ given the observed data $\mathbf{y}_{obs}$. This posterior can be written as

$$f(\theta|\mathbf{y}_{obs}) = \int f(\theta|\mathbf{y}_{obs}, \mathbf{y}_{mis}) \\ f(\mathbf{y}_{mis}|\mathbf{y}_{obs}) \, d\mathbf{y}_{mis}. \quad (5.7)$$

An interpretation of equation (5.7) is that the actual posterior of θ equals the average of the repeated imputations, which are draws from the *posterior predictive distribution* $f(\mathbf{y}_{mis}|\mathbf{y}_{obs})$ of missing data given the observed data. This suggests that the imputation values should be draws from $f(\mathbf{y}_{mis}|\mathbf{y}_{obs})$. I will discuss the imputation procedures shortly.

Result 3.2 of Rubin (1987) states

$$E(\theta|\mathbf{y}_{obs}) = E[E(\theta|\mathbf{y}_{obs}, \mathbf{y}_{mis})|\mathbf{y}_{obs}], \quad (5.8)$$

or the posterior mean of θ is the average of the repeated complete-data posterior means of θ. Furthermore,

$$\text{var}(\theta|\mathbf{y}_{obs}) = E[\text{var}(\theta|\mathbf{y}_{obs}, \mathbf{y}_{mis})|\mathbf{y}_{obs}] \\ + \text{var}[E(\theta|\mathbf{y}_{obs}, \mathbf{y}_{mis})|\mathbf{y}_{obs}], \quad (5.9)$$

or the posterior variance of θ is the sum of repeated complete-data variances of θ and the variance over repeated imputations of repeated complete-data posterior means of θ. Equations (5.8) and (5.9) suggest methods of combining complete-data estimates to obtain parameter estimates and their covariance estimates. More specifically, let $\hat{\theta}^{(1)}, \ldots, \hat{\theta}^{(m)}$ be m estimates of θ obtained from m completed data sets, and let $U_1, \ldots, U_m$ be the corresponding covariance matrices of the estimates. Then

$$\theta^* = \frac{1}{m} \sum_{i=1}^{m} \hat{\theta}^{(i)}$$

is a multiple imputation estimate of θ with the associated covariance of θ^*,

$$T = \bar{U} + \frac{m+1}{m} B,$$

where

$$\bar{U} = \frac{1}{m} \sum_{i=1}^{m} U^i$$

is the within-imputation variability, and

$$B = \frac{1}{m-1} \sum_{i=1}^{m} (\hat{\theta}^{(i)} - \theta^*)(\hat{\theta}^{(i)} - \theta^*)^{\mathrm{T}}$$

is the between-imputation variability.

When m is large, the quantity $\theta - \theta^*$ can be treated as normal with mean zero and covariance T (see Rubin, 1987), where θ is the true value. Rubin (1987, Chapter 3) gives specific small-m adjustments. Other related works on inference in multiple imputation are: Rubin and Schenker (1986) on interval estimation; Li et al. (1991a, 1991b) on combining p-values; and Meng and Rubin (1992) on performing likelihood ratio tests.

Now back to the problem of obtaining imputation values. As mentioned earlier, equation (5.7) suggests that imputations are based on the predictive density $f(\mathbf{y}_{mis}|\mathbf{y}_{obs})$. This task, however, is not straightforward. The most obvious problem is that $f(\mathbf{y}_{mis}|\mathbf{y}_{obs})$ depends on the unknown θ. A simple approach called 'poor man's data augmentation' by Wei and Tanner (1990) is to replace θ by $\hat{\theta}$, the maximum likelihood estimate of θ based on some model, and to draw the imputations from the density $f(\mathbf{y}_{mis}|\mathbf{y}_{obs}; \hat{\theta})$. Another method replaces θ by $\tilde{\theta}$, a single independent draw from the posterior density $f(\theta|\mathbf{y})$ of θ under a Bayesian model, and draws imputations from the density $f(\mathbf{y}_{mis}|\mathbf{y}_{obs}; \tilde{\theta})$. Rubin (1987) calls the imputation based on $\hat{\theta}$ *improper* and that based on $\tilde{\theta}$ *proper*.

Wang and Robins (1998) have studied the large-sample properties of proper and improper imputation methods. Theoretically, they have shown that for finite m, the 'improper' imputation is always to be preferred to the 'proper' imputation method, because of its strictly smaller asymptotic variance. Their result assumes large sample sizes and a moderate amount of missing data.

The number of imputations m is another important choice to be made. Often a value of m ranging from 2 to 5 is adequate. As the fraction of missing data gets large, a larger m will be required to obtain efficient estimates. The large-sample relative efficiency of estimation using a finite number versus an infinite number of multiple imputations is, in standard error units, $(1 + \gamma/m)^{-1/2}$, where γ is the fraction of missing information (see Rubin, 1987). For example, if $\gamma = 0.30$, then $m = 5$ imputations results in estimates that are only 3% less efficient than estimates based on an infinite number of imputations, i.e., $m = \infty$.

Although multiple imputation is most directly motivated from the Bayesian perspective, the resulting inferences can be shown to possess good sampling properties. For example, Rubin and Schenker (1986) show that in many cases interval estimates created using only $m = 2$ imputations provide randomization-based coverage to their nominal levels.[8] Rubin (2000) states that

> even doing multiple imputation relatively crudely, using simple methods, is very likely to be inferentially far superior to any other equally easy method to implement (e.g., complete-cases, available cases, single imputation, …) because the multiple copies of the dataset allow the uncertainty about the values of the missing data to be incorporated to the final inference; Heitjan and Rubin (1990) provides some evidence for this statement, as does Raghunathan and Paulin (1998).

Obviously, however, the quality of inference is directly related to the quality of imputed values.

As in ML analysis, multiple imputation can be used to analyze MCAR and MAR data. If the missing-data mechanism is informative and it is not modeled, then the results will most likely be biased.

Bootstrap methods Bootstrapping has received less attention in the context of incomplete-data analysis, as compared to multiple imputation and likelihood-based methods. This is most likely due to its inherent computational intensity. Efron (1994) describes three types of bootstrap methods for handling incomplete data: the *nonparametric bootstrap, full mechanism bootstrap*, and *multiple imputation bootstrap*.

Let $\mathbf{y} = \{\mathbf{y}_1,...,\mathbf{y}_n\}$ be n observations in a data set. As an example using the data in Table 5.1, $\mathbf{y}_1 = (11,?,15)$, $\mathbf{y}_2 = (10,14,10)$, etc. In the nonparametric bootstrap a bootstrap sample $\mathbf{y}^* = \{\mathbf{y}_1^*,...,\mathbf{y}_n^*\}$ is obtained by drawing the $\mathbf{y}_i^*$ randomly and with replacement from the set $\{\mathbf{y}_1,...,\mathbf{y}_n\}$. B such samples are drawn and a method M (e.g., maximum likelihood) is applied to each of the bootstrap samples $\mathbf{y}^*$ to obtain $(\boldsymbol{\theta}_1^*,...,\boldsymbol{\theta}_B^*)$. Parameter estimates and standard error estimates are obtained based on the empirical distribution of the B estimates $\boldsymbol{\theta}_i^*$. The nonparametric bootstrap is at best applicable to data that are MCAR or MAR. If the missing-data mechanism is nonignorable, then the results will not be valid. The nonparametric bootstrap has the advantage of applying in a simple way to any estimator $M(\mathbf{y})$. Of course, as Efron (1994) points out, this does not obviate the need to select the method M sensibly.

In the full mechanism bootstrap, first a method is used to fill in the missing data, and then the bootstrap samples are taken from the completed data. For example, to fill in the data, we can obtain the ML estimates of the mean and covariance under the assumption of normality from the observed incomplete data; call them $\hat{\boldsymbol{\mu}}$ and $\hat{\Sigma}$. Then we fill in a typical incomplete observation $\mathbf{y}_{\text{mis},i}$ based on the conditional distribution of missing data given the observed data by $E(\mathbf{y}_{\text{mis},i}|\mathbf{y}_{\text{obs},i},\hat{\boldsymbol{\mu}},\hat{\Sigma})$. Let $\{\tilde{\mathbf{y}}_1,...,\tilde{\mathbf{y}}_n\}$ denote the filled-in data set. A bootstrap sample $\mathbf{y}^* = (\mathbf{y}_1^*,...,\mathbf{y}_n^*)$ here consists of drawing the $\mathbf{y}_i^*$ randomly and with replacement from the set $\{\tilde{\mathbf{y}}_1,...,\tilde{\mathbf{y}}_n\}$. Say B bootstrap samples are drawn. Then according to the missing-data mechanism, which is assumed to be known here, holes are made in each of the complete-data bootstrap samples to obtain B sets of incomplete data. Then a missing-data method (e.g., maximum likelihood) is applied to each of the B incomplete data sets to obtain $(\boldsymbol{\theta}_1^*,...,\boldsymbol{\theta}_B^*)$, and, as before, the empirical distribution of these estimates is used to make inferences. If data are MCAR, the 'holes' can be made to duplicate the holes in the original data set. For example, suppose that, in the data in Table 5.1, $(9,7,10)$ is the first case drawn for a bootstrap sample. This case then will be replaced by $(9,?,10)$ since in the original data the second component of the first case is missing. When the data mechanism is either MAR or MNAR, then making the 'holes' should model the missing-data mechanism. This may be viewed as an advantage of the full-mechanism bootstrap in that it offers a simple method to model MAR or MNAR data. In practice, however, knowledge of the missing-data mechanism is often limited, especially in the case of MNAR, when the mechanism depends on the missing values.

For further discussion of bootstrap methods and a description of the multiple-imputation bootstrap we refer the reader to Efron (1994).

COMPARISON OF METHODS

In this section I use simulation to compare complete-case analysis, unconditional mean imputation, maximum likelihood, multiple imputation, the nonparametric bootstrap, and the full-mechanism bootstrap.[9] My aim is to illustrate how biasedness and unbiasedness of the parameter estimates depend on the missing-data mechanism, the method used to analyze the data, and the proportion of missing data.

I consider the problem of estimating a single parameter θ, namely the maximum eigenvalue of a covariance matrix Σ from incomplete data. I have chosen a single-parameter problem as opposed to a multiple-parameter problem mainly because it is simpler and demonstrates the main ideas effectively. At the same time, the single parameter that I estimate is a non-linear function of several parameters, namely the elements of the covariance matrix.

The data

For my simulations I generate 1000 cases from a trivariate normal distribution with mean zero, and covariance

$$\Sigma = \begin{pmatrix} 1 & 0.5 & 0.6 \\ 0.5 & 1 & 0.7 \\ 0.6 & 0.7 & 1 \end{pmatrix}.$$

The maximum eigenvalue of Σ is $\theta = 2.203$. It is θ that we wish to estimate.

For the data that I generated the sample covariance based on 1000 complete cases is

$$S = \begin{pmatrix} 0.9442 & 0.4839 & 0.5572 \\ 0.4839 & 1.0043 & 0.6680 \\ 0.5572 & 0.6686 & 0.9323 \end{pmatrix}.$$

The ML estimate of θ is the maximum eigenvalue of S, namely $\hat{\theta} = 2.104$.

To examine how incomplete data affects estimates, I delete some of the observations from the 1000 cases for variables 2 and 3. Variable 1 remains completely observed in every case. I use the following methods to induce missing data:

MCAR mechanism. Independently delete each single observation of variables 2 and 3 with probability p.

MAR mechanism. Standardize observed values of variable 1 to have mean 0 and variance 1. Denote the ith case of the standardized variable by v_{i1}. For $i = 1, \ldots, 1000$ and $j = 2,3$, calculate $u_{ij} = v_{i1} + z_{ij}$, where z_{ij} is a draw from the standard normal distribution. Delete the (i,j)th case if $u_{ij} > T$, where T is a fixed given tolerance value.

MNAR mechanism. Standardize observed values of variables 2 and 3 to have mean 0 and variance 1. Denote the standardized (i,j)th case by v_{ij}, $i = 1, \ldots, 1000$ and $j = 2,3$. For each i and j compute $u_{ij} = v_{ij} + z_{ij}$, where z_{ij} is an observation from the standard normal random variable. Delete the (i,j)th case if $u_{ij} > T$, where T is a fixed given tolerance value.

The values p and T are chosen to obtain the desired percentage of missingness in variables 2 and 3. Note that under MCAR, the missingness is independent of the observed or missing values, under MAR missingness in variables 2 and 3 depends on the observed values for variable 1, and under MNAR missingness in variables 2 and 3 depends on the deleted values themselves. In my simulations, for each of the three missing-data mechanisms, I generated 25 data sets with approximately 10% missing values in variables 2 and 3, and 25 data sets with approximately 30% missing values in variables 2 and 3. In total I analyze 150 data sets, all generated by inducing missing data in the 1000-case complete-data set with sample covariance matrix S given above.

Methods

To estimate θ, I estimate Σ from the relevant incomplete data (call the estimate $\hat{\Sigma}$). Then I use the maximum eigenvalue of $\hat{\Sigma}$ as the estimate of θ. I use the following methodologies to estimate Σ:

CC analysis. I remove any case with at least one incomplete observation, and estimate Σ by the sample covariance of the remaining completely observed cases.

UMI. For each variable, I impute the missing values by the mean of the observed cases for that variable. Then my estimate for Σ is the sample covariance matrix obtained from the completed data set.

ML. I use the EM algorithm to obtain the ML estimate of Σ.

Multiple imputation (MI). I use an 'improper' imputation method to multiply impute the missing data. I use improper imputation because, as mentioned, when the number of imputations m is small, estimates based on improper imputation can be significantly more efficient than those based on proper imputation. For my simulations I examine $m = 2$ imputations (MI2) and $m = 5$ (MI5) imputations. First, I obtain the ML estimate of Σ, call it $\hat{\Sigma}$. Then for each case, I draw from the conditional distribution of the missing data given the observed data and $\hat{\Sigma}$. More specifically, I fill in the missing data for a case by drawing from a (multivariate) normal distribution with mean $\hat{\Sigma}_{mo}\hat{\Sigma}_{oo}^{-1}\mathbf{y}_{obs}$ and covariance $\hat{\Sigma}_{mm} - \hat{\Sigma}_{mo}$ $\hat{\Sigma}_{oo}^{-1}\hat{\Sigma}_{mo}^{T}$, where $\mathbf{y}_{obs}$ is the observed part of the case, and $\hat{\Sigma}_{oo}$, $\hat{\Sigma}_{mo}$ and $\hat{\Sigma}_{mm}$ are appropriate submatrices of $\hat{\Sigma}$ corresponding to the observed and missing part of the case (for further explanation of this notation, refer to the Appendix to this chapter).

Nonparametric bootstrap (NPB). I draw, randomly and with replacement, $B = 50$ bootstrap samples of size 1000 each from the incomplete data. Then I apply EM on each of the 50 bootstrap samples to estimate Σ and subsequently its maximum eigenvalue θ. My nonparametric bootstrap estimate is then the mean of the 50 estimates of θ obtained from each bootstrap sample.

Full-mechanism bootstrap (FMB). I draw, randomly and with replacement, $B = 50$ bootstrap samples of size 1000 each from the incomplete data. Then for each bootstrap sample I apply the following procedure: I use multiple imputation, described above, with $m = 1$ to produce one set of complete data from the incomplete data. I then use the missing-data mechanism that I used to delete observations from my original complete data, to induce missing data in the newly completed data sets.[10] Finally, I apply EM to the resulting incomplete data set to obtain an estimate of Σ and subsequently θ. My full-mechanism bootstrap estimate is the mean of the 50 estimates of θ obtained from each bootstrap sample.

Results of simulation

The results of my simulations are shown in Figure 5.2, using boxplots. Each boxplot summarizes 25 estimates of θ obtained under various circumstances. The figure consists of six panels. The boxplots in each panel, from left to right, depict the estimates based on CC, UMI, ML, MI2, MI5, NPB, and FMB. The left and right column panels show the results of applying these methods to approximately 10% and 30% missing data, respectively. For the top two panels data are MCAR, for the middle two panels data are MAR, and for the bottom two panels data are MNAR. The dotted line in each plot shows the estimate $\hat{\theta} = 2.1041$ which is obtained when no datum is missing.

MCAR results. All the methods except UMI performed well under the MCAR mechanism. For UMI the results are significantly biased. While CC results in unbiased estimates, as expected, it is less efficient than ML, MI, and the bootstrap methods. Finally, again as expected, the variability of estimates for all methods increases as the proportion of missing data increases from 10% to 30%.

MAR results. Under MAR, both CC and UMI produce significantly biased estimates. That CC and UMI estimates are biased is not surprising, given that subsets of complete cases are not a random subsample of all the cases in the data set. Again as expected, ML, MI, and the bootstrap methods performed well under MAR. Note that in both MI and the bootstrap methods, I have used ML to estimate σ. Indeed, this has been a factor in producing sensible MI, NPB, and FMB estimates. As in the MCAR case, the variation in parameter estimates increases as the proportion of missing data increases. Curiously, however, when 30% of the data are missing, ML, MI, and the bootstrap estimates are centered slightly above the 2.1041 value and closer to the true value of $\theta = 2.2037$.

MNAR results. All the methods considered fail to produce unbiased estimates under the MNAR mechanism. When 10% of data were missing, NPB performed best, and when 30% of data were missing, FMB performed best. It is curious and noteworthy that the bootstrap estimates have less bias as the proportion of missing data increases, that is, they result in estimates that are closer to the true value of $\hat{\theta} = 2.2037$.

The following is a list of further observations on the performance of each method:

- CC produced reasonable estimates under MCAR, but its estimates were not statistically as efficient as ML, MI, or the bootstrap methods. CC produced biased estimates under MAR and MNAR.
- UMI underestimated the parameter θ under all missing-data mechanisms that I considered.
- ML performed well under MCAR and MAR mechanisms, but produced biased estimates for MNAR data.
- MI performed as well as ML for the MCAR and MAR data, and like ML produced biased estimates for MNAR data. It should be noted that MI entails a slightly higher computational cost than ML, since in each case the imputation values were

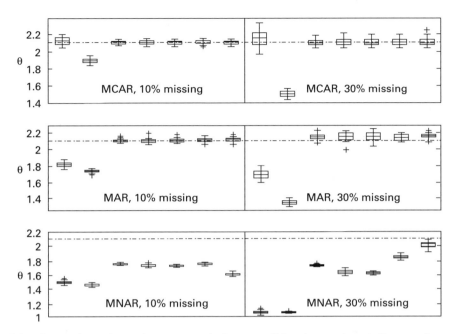

Figure 5.2 *Comparison of complete-case analysis, unconditional mean imputation, maximum likeli-hood, multiple imputation, nonparametric bootstrap, and full-mechanism bootstrap. The boxplots in each panel (from left to right) indicate performance of CC, UMI, ML, MI2, MI5, NPB, and FMB. The dashed line is the estimate of θ when no datum is missing.*

obtained based on the ML estimate of Σ. The number of imputations, 2 versus 5, seems to have had very little effect on the variability of estimates.

- The bootstrap methods considered performed well for both MCAR and MAR data. The bootstrap is the most computationally expensive method among the methods considered. While my bootstrap estimates were biased for MNAR data, they were best among all methods for this missing-data mechanism. The bias observed in NPB estimates for MNAR data is expected, since essentially each NPB estimate is the mean of 50 ML estimates. Note that ML estimates are biased for MNAR data. In FMB the bias for MNAR data may have resulted because in the first step of estimation we fill in the data by a single-imputation method. Obviously the quality of these imputations affects the final estimate. Note also that FMB estimates were obtained under the often unrealistic situation where we had full knowledge of the missing-data mechanisms.

We conclude this chapter by noting that the problem of incomplete data must be dealt with

seriously. Failure to do so can result in inferences that are virtually worthless. Steps should be taken to avoid missing values whenever possible by investing in the survey design and performing follow-ups. If the proportion of missing data is insignificant, then the biases from the missing-data mechanism and the choice of method to correct for missing data may also be insignificant. When missing data are inevitable and their proportion significant, then the missing-data process (mechanism) must be understood. Accordingly, an appropriate choice of methodology must be used for analysis. When the missing-data mechanism is not accessible or is not ignorable, then, as Little (1995) states, 'analyses should be conducted to assess sensitivity of results to plausible alternative specifications of mechanism'.

APPENDIX: FORMULA TO COMPUTE S*
IN (5.6)

To give an explicit formula for S^* we simplify our notation by dropping the i indices, and thus we denote a typical case by $\mathbf{y}$ instead of $\mathbf{y}_i$. Partition Σ according to the observed and missing values as

$$\Sigma = \begin{pmatrix} \sum_{oo} & \sum_{om} \\ \sum_{mo} & \sum_{mm} \end{pmatrix}',$$

where each of the submatrices Σ_{oo} etc. is an appropriate submatrix of Σ corresponding to the observed and missing values. For example, in a data set consisting of three variables, if in a particular case variables 1 and 3 are observed, Σ_{oo} is a 2×2 matrix consisting of elements $(1,1)$, $(1,3)$, $(3,1)$, and $(3,3)$ of Σ and Σ_{mo} is a 1×2 vector consisting of elements $(2,1)$ and $(2,3)$ of Σ. $\Sigma_{om} = \Sigma_{mo}^T$ and Σ_{mm} consists of element $(2,2)$ of Σ. Now

$$E^* (yy^T) = \begin{pmatrix} y_{obs} y_{obs}^T & y_{obs} y_{mis}^* \\ y_{mis}^* y_{obs}^T & E^* (y_{mis} y_{mis}^T) \end{pmatrix}$$

where $y_{mis}^* = \Sigma_{mo} \Sigma_{oo}^{-1} y_{obs}$ and $E^* (y_{mis} y_{mis}^T) = \Sigma_{mm} - \Sigma_{mo} \Sigma_{oo}^{-1} \Sigma_{om} + y_{mis}^* (y_{mis}^*)^T$.

ACKNOWLEDGMENT

The author would like to thank the anonymous referee and Melissa Hardy for valuable comments that led to a much improved presentation.

NOTES

1 Let O_i be the event that for a given case variable i is observed. The event that all 10 variables for this case are observed is $O_1 \cap O_2 \cap \ldots \cap O_{10}$. If the O_i are independent, then $P(O_1 \cap O_2 \cap \ldots \cap O_{10}) = P(O_1) P(O_2) \ldots P(O_{10}) = 0.9^{10} \approx 0.35$.

2 The variance estimates can be adjusted for bias (Little and Rubin, 1987, p. 44), but the adjustment is generally unsatisfactory (see Hegamin-Younger and Forsyth, 1998; Murray and Findlay, 1988).

3 In the context of missing data the log-likelihood function is often referred to as the *observed log-likelihood*. This is to be contrasted with *complete-data log-likelihood* which I will introduce in the context of the EM algorithm.

4 The EM iterates produce a sequence of points, say $\{\theta^{(k)}\} = \{\theta^{(1)}, \theta^{(2)}, \ldots\}$, starting from the initial guess θ. Under certain regularity conditions, this sequence converges to the ML estimate $\hat{\theta}$. Convergence to $\hat{\theta}$ means that $\lim_{k \to \infty} \|\theta^{(k)} - \hat{\theta}\| = 0$, or in words, the members of the sequence $\{\theta^{(k)}\}$ get arbitrarily close to $\hat{\theta}$ as the number of iterations k gets large. Various methods can be used to check convergence of a sequence. For example, one may declare that a sequence has converged if the norm of the difference between two consecutive members of the sequence is small, that is $\|\theta^{(k+1)} - \theta^{(k)}\| < \varepsilon$, where ε is a small positive number.

5 Kenward and Molenberghs (1998) give the Fisher information for two examples of bivariate binary data and bivariate Gaussian data for incomplete data.

6 Bayesian inference is an approach to inference based largely on Bayes' theorem and consisting of the following principles: (i) Obtain the likelihood, $f(x|\theta)$, describing the process giving rise to the data x in terms of the unknown parameter θ. (ii) Obtain the *prior distribution*, $f(\theta)$, expressing what is known about θ, prior to observing the data. (iii) Apply Bayes' theorem to derive the *posterior distribution* $f(x|\theta)$ expressing what is known about θ after observing the data. (iv) Derive appropriate inference statements from the posterior distribution. These may include specific inferences such as point estimates, interval estimates or probabilities of hypotheses.

7 In *frequentist inference* no prior distribution is assumed for θ, and θ is assumed to be nonrandom. *Frequentist properties* refers to the properties of estimators $\hat{\theta}$ obtained under this setting. ML estimation is an example of frequentist approach to inference. A property of an ML estimate $\hat{\theta}$, when the sample size is large, is that $\hat{\theta} - \theta \sim N(0, \Sigma)$, for some covariance matrix Σ. For other examples of frequentist properties see Little and Rubin (1987, pp. 84–8).

8 When constructing $100(1 - \alpha)\%$ confidence intervals, the probability $100(1 - \alpha)\%$ is called the nominal level. If a large number of confidence intervals are constructed using a large number of random samples, then provided that the intervals are 'constructed correctly', approximately $(1 - \alpha)$ of these intervals should contain the true parameter. Rubin and Schenker (1986) performed a simulation study, using nominal levels 90% and 95%, and showed that this property holds for intervals constructed using their method when $m = 2$.

9 The general procedure in this type of simulation is to manufacture a complete data set with known parameters. Then we delete information to create missing values in the data matrix. We use each of the missing-data methods, in turn, to compensate for the missing data and then estimate the parameter of interest. Since we know what the parameter value truly is, we can evaluate how well the methods perform by assessing how well they estimate their parameters.

10 Initially, the 50 samples of size 1000 in NPB and FMB are obtained as follows: (i) One thousand numbers are drawn, with replacement, from the set $\{1, 2, \ldots, 1000\}$. (ii) A bootstrap sample is formed by including the cases from the original data set with case number equal to those numbers drawn in (i). Note that a case may be included more than once in the bootstrap sample. From this point, the NPB and FMB part company in that in NPB each of the 50 bootstrap

samples are analyzed right away, while in FMB each of the samples is completed, then missing values are produced according to a missing-data mechanism in the newly completed data set and then the resulting data matrix is analyzed.

REFERENCES

Amemiya, T. (1984) 'Tobit models: a survey', *Journal of Econometrics*, 24: 3–61.

Azen, S. and Van Guilder, M. (1981) 'Conclusions regarding algorithms for handling incomplete data', in *Proceedings of the Statistical Computing Section, American Statistical Association 1981*, 53–6.

Bentler, P.M. and Jamshidian, M. (1994) 'Gramian matrices in covariance structure models', *Applied Psychological Measurement*, 18: 79–94.

Brown, C.H. (1983) 'Asymptotic comparison of missing data procedures for estimating factor loadings', *Psychometrika*, 48: 269–91.

Buck, S.F. (1960) 'A method for estimation of missing values in multivariate data suitable for use with an electronic computer', *Journal of the Royal Statistical Society B*, 22: 302–6.

Cook, N.R. (1997) 'An imputation method for non-ignorable missing data in studies of blood pressure', *Statistics in Medicine*, 16: 2713–28.

Dempster, A.P., Laird, N.M. and Rubin, D.B. (1977) 'Maximum likelihood from incomplete data via the EM algorithm (with discussion)', *Journal of the Royal Statistical Society B*, 39: 1–38.

Dixon, W.J. (ed.) (1988) *BMDP Statistical Software*, Berkeley: University of California Press.

Eaton, W.W. and Kessler, L.G. (1995) *Epidemiologic Field Methods in Psychiatry: The NIMH Epidemiologic Catchment Area Program*. New York: Academic Press.

Efron, B. (1994) 'Missing data, imputation, and the bootstrap (with discussion)', *Journal of the American Statistical Association*, 89: 463–79.

Geman, S. and Geman, D. (1984) 'Stochastic relaxation, Gibbs distributions and Bayesian restoration of images', *IEEE Transactions on Pattern Analysis and Machine Intelligence*, 6: 721–41.

Graham, J.W. and Donaldson, S.I. (1993) 'Evaluating interventions with differential attrition: The importance of non-response mechanism and use of follow-up data', *Journal of Applied Psychology*, 78: 119–28.

Heckman, J. (1976) 'The common structure of statistical models of truncation, sample selection and limited dependent variables, and a simple estimator for such models', *Annals of Economics and Social Measurement*, 5: 475–92.

Hegamin-Younger, C. and Forsyth, R. (1998) 'A comparison of four imputation procedures in a two-variable prediction system', *Educational and Psychological Measurement*, 58: 197–210.

Heitjan, D.F. and Rubin, D.B. (1990) 'Inference from coarse data via multiple imputation with application to age heaping', *Journal of the American Statistical Association*, 85: 304–14.

Huisman, M., Krol, B. and Van Sonderen, E. (1998) 'Handling missing data by re-approaching non-respondents', *Quality & Quantity*, 32: 77–91.

Ibrahim, J.G. and Lipsitz, S.R. (1999) 'Missing covariates in generalized linear models when the missing data mechanism is non-ignorable', *Journal of the Royal Statistical Society B*, 61: 173–90.

Jamshidian, M. and Bentler, P.M. (1999) 'ML estimation of mean and covariance structures with missing data using complete data routines', *Journal of Educational and Behavioral Statistics*, 24: 21–41.

Jamshidian, M. and Jennrich, R.I. (1997) 'Acceleration of the EM algorithm by using quasi-Newton methods', *Journal of the Royal Statistical Society B*, 59: 569–87.

Jamshidian, M. and Jennrich, R.I. (2000) 'Standard errors for EM estimation', *Journal of the Royal Statistical Society B*, 62: 257–70.

Kenward, M.G. and Molenberghs, G. (1998) 'Likelihood based frequentist inference when data are missing at random', *Statistical Science*, 13: 236–47.

Kim, J.O. and Curry, J. (1977) 'The treatment of missing data in multivariate analysis', *Sociol. Meth. Res.* 6: 215–40.

Krishnamoorthy, K. and Pannala, M.K. (1998) 'Some simple test procedures for normal mean vector with incomplete data', *Annals of the Institute of Statistical Mathematics*, 50: 531–42.

Lakshminarayan, K., Harp, S.A. and Samad, T. (1999) 'Imputation of missing data in industrial data bases', *Applied Intelligence*, 11: 259–75.

Li, K.H., Meng, X.L., Raghunathan, T.E. and Rubin, D.B. (1991a) 'Significance levels from repeated *p*-values with multiply-imputed data', *Statistica Sinica*, 1: 65–92.

Li, K.H., Raghunathan, T.E. and Rubin, D.B. (1991b) 'Large-sample significance levels from multiply imputed data using moment-based statistics and an *F* reference distribution', *Journal of the American Statistical Association*, 86: 1065–73.

Little, R.J.A. (1988) 'A test of missing completely at random for multivariate data with missing values', *Journal of the American Statistical Association*, 83: 1198–202.

Little, R.J.A. (1992) 'Regression with missing X's: A review', *Journal of the American Statistical Association* 87: 1227–37.

Little, R.J.A. (1995) 'Modeling the drop-out mechanism in repeated-measures studies', *Journal of the American Statistical Association*, 90: 1112–21.

Little, R.J.A. and Rubin, D.B. (1983) 'On jointly estimating parameters and missing data by maximizing the complete-data log-likelihood', *American Statistician*, 37: 218–20.

Little, R.J.A. and Rubin, D.B. (1987) *Statistical Analysis with Missing Data*. New York: Wiley.

Meng, X.L. and Rubin, D.B. (1992) 'Performing likelihood ratio tests with multiply-imputed data sets', *Biometrika*, 79: 103–11.

Murray, G.D. and Findlay, J.G. (1988) 'Correcting for the bias caused by drop-outs in hypertension trials', *Statistics in Medicine*, 7: 941–6.

Nordholt, E.S. (1998) 'Imputation: Methods, simulation experiments and practical examples', *International Statistical Review*, 66: 157–80.

Park, T. (1998) 'An approach to categorical data with non-ignorable nonresponse', *Biometrics*, 54: 1579–90.

Raghunathan, T.E. and Paulin, G.D. (1998) 'Multiple imputation in consumer expenditure survey: evaluation of statistical inference', in *Proceedings of the Business and Economic Section of the American Statistical Association*, 1–10.

Rubin, D.B. (1976) 'Inference and missing data', *Biometrika*, 63: 581–92.

Rubin, D.B. (1987) *Multiple Imputation for Non-response in Surveys*. New York: Wiley.

Rubin, D.B. (1996) 'Multiple imputation after 18+ years', *Journal of the American Statistical Association*, 91: 473–89.

Rubin, D.B. (2000) 'Software for multiple imputation'. http://www.statsolusa.com/so/as/rubin.html

Rubin, D.B. and Schenker, N. (1986) 'Multiple imputation for interval estimation from simple random samples with ignorable nonresponse', *Journal of the American Statistical Association*, 18: 366–74.

Rubin, D.B. and Thayer, D.T. (1982) 'EM algorithm for ML factor analysis', *Psychometrika*, 47: 60–76.

Smith, P.W.F., Skinner, C.J. and Clarke, P.S. (1999) 'Allowing for non-ignorable non-response in the analysis of voting intention data', *Applied Statistics*, 48: 563–77.

Tanner, M.A. and Wong, W. (1987) 'The calculation of posterior distributions by data augmentation', *Journal of the American Statistical Association*, 82: 528–58.

Wang, N. and Robins, J.M. (1998) 'Large-sample theory for parametric multiple imputation procedures', *Biometrika*, 85: 935–48.

Wang-Clow, F., Lange, M., Laird, N.M. and Ware, J.H. (1995) 'A simulation study of estimation for rates of change in longitudinal studies with attrition', *Statistics in Medicine*, 14: 283–97.

Wei, G.C.G. and Tanner, M.A. (1990) 'A Monte Carlo implementation of the EM algorithm and the poor man's data augmentation algorithms', *Journal of the American Statistical Association*, 82: 805–11.

6

Feminist Issues in Data Analysis

MARY MAYNARD

Given the extensive nature of their writing on research, together with current general interest in data analysis, it seems strange that feminists have not focused as explicitly on this issue as they have on others, although there are some notable exceptions (Acker et al., 1991; Bell, 1998; DeVault, 1999; Holland and Ramazanoğlu, 1994; Lather, 1993; Mauthner and Doucet, 1998; Skeggs, 1997). This may be because the emphasis in much of the recent social science literature on analysing data has been on providing strategies and tools to guide analysts in following more highly structured and systematic procedures. Concerns about the use of computers and of various software packages are indicative of this preoccupation. The advice, which tends to be about matters such as categorizing, coding, mapping, hyperlinks and retrieval, is mainly designed to improve the rigorousness and validity of the ways in which data are manipulated and presented. This, in turn, is linked to the desire of many qualitative researchers, in particular, to make a form of research which, in the past, has been criticized for being too subjective, unrepresentative and unscientific in its findings, become more reliable and, in its own terms, objective (Dey, 1993; Fielding and Lee, 1998). Yet, while this is an important and laudable aim, the standards employed in some research being distinctly opaque, there are also problems. For a start, there are many different kinds of data, with qualitative forms ranging from the more usual interview transcripts through to fieldnotes, observational and ethnographic material, photographs, diaries and other forms of documents and representational matter. There is no single best way of approaching such material, and some would argue that overstandardization unnecessarily constrains analysis and may impede efforts to obtain the most from data (Strauss, 1987). Another problem arises from the lack of consensus as to what 'analysis' actually means. It can, for instance, refer to how data are organized and manipulated, to the identification of key themes and relationships or to interpretation and the kinds and levels of understanding and explanation proffered (Coffey and Atkinson, 1996). While for some the meaning of the data comes from the patterns and regularities which emerge as a consequence of data sorting, for others it is a more creative and imaginative activity.

These two issues, standardization of technique and interpretation as data sorting, provide some insights into why feminist scholarship lacks specialized tomes on data analysis. First, early feminist work on research practice was highly critical of how an emphasis on technique and textbook recipes often fails to consider both the assumptions upon which they are based and the ways in which their operationalization may also introduce unrecognized preconceptions (Cook and Fonow, 1986; Graham, 1984; Oakley, 1981). This can lead to biased and contaminated outcomes and it is for this reason that the concept of 'reflexivity' has become a crucial component of many feminists' work. Secondly, many feminists, along with other researchers, do not regard analysis and interpretation as a separate stage or one of the final phases in the research process. Rather, it should be an ongoing aspect of research and not something reserved for the end. Skeggs (1994), for example, describes how she constantly analysed what she was hearing from the young women participating in her research and how her responses changed over time. This may itself become data requiring analysis. Thirdly, feminists tend to view research in holistic terms. The kind of information which is available for analysis and interpretation will very much depend on the design of the research project overall. The research issues to be addressed, how these are translated into questions for the field, and the data collection methods used will all influence the material which emerges and the possible latent meanings which lie within, together with the extent to which the latter are amenable to theoretical explanation. In short, then, feminists have tended to address issues about the analysis and interpretation of data as part of their wider methodological discussions about qualitative research (Finch and Mason, 1990). Interest in analysis has been there but is located within a wider context. Concerns about the extent to which people's accounts of their lives constitute experience, about how far interpretation should reflect participants' views or transcend them, about how to use respondents' words and whether it is ever possible to represent them accurately, issues to do with ethics and accountability, with how to produce plausible and reliable narratives, with who owns the interpretations and how to prevent participants being exploited – these, along with other matters, have been central to feminists' writing about research (Olesen, 1998, 2000). To a large extent, however, such discussions are embedded in more general methodological debates. Because of this it is not easy to produce a succinct critical overview of feminist views on data analysis.

In order to overcome such problems, this chapter will proceed in the following way. It begins by offering a general context within which to understand debates about feminist research. This focuses on early epistemological concerns and later key developments. The chapter then examines a range of ways in which feminists have explored data analysis and interpretation issues. This concentrates on language and meaning, the role of interpretation, taking a feminist standpoint, reflexivity, power and hierarchy, and ethics and empowerment. The chapter concludes with some general comments about feminists' work in this area.

FEMINIST SOCIAL RESEARCH: A CONTEXT

Second-wave feminist social research developed as a response to two related failings in Western social science and understanding. The first was the relative invisibility of women, together with a lack of focus on the gender-specific issues which influenced their lives. The second concerned the ways in which research and the construction of knowledge took place. It was suggested that the social world had been studied from the perspective of male interests and concerns and in ignorance of the different picture that emerged when focusing on women's lives or adopting their ways of seeing (Bernard, 1973; Callaway, 1981; Smith, 1988). Suggesting that the male perspective had been afforded a privileged epistemological position, Mackinnon (1982) referred to the 'male epistemological stance'. She argued that 'men create the world from their own point of view, which then becomes the truth to be described' (1982: 23). In other words, while purporting to be neutral and objective, the knowledge produced is partial and gendered. Mackinnon claimed that objectivity is the methodological stance of which objectification is the social practice. By this she means that claims to objectivity make the focus of research fraudulently appear as if it is independent of the social relations which both create and require it. In fact, the processes of knowledge construction and understanding are not immune from the exploitative and oppressive practices which characterize other social phenomena. It was the task of feminist social research to highlight the general inequalities and oppression experienced by women, as well as developing less biased and partial ways of researching and representing the social world.

Over the years, feminists have refined their ideas about epistemology, methods and methodology in relation to research, although there is no unified body of thought and healthy disputes abound (DeVault, 1999; Humphries, 1997; Lather, 1993; Maynard and Purvis, 1994; Oakley, 1998; Ribbens and Edwards, 1998). However, the nature of their contribution to critical reflection on the research process is sufficient to enable one commentator to conclude that 'the extensive and cogent criticisms which have been made by feminists of social science cannot be ignored' (May, 1993: 11). Indeed, they have contributed to the development of a critical awareness in the study of other oppressed and marginalized groups, for instance, ethnic minorities, gays and lesbians, people with disabilities and, more recently, children (Ali et al., 2000; Lewis and Lindsay, 2000; Plummer, 1995; Thomas, 1999).

Feminist discussions about research have, broadly speaking, been characterized by four major linked and overlapping phases (the debate over quantitative and qualitative methods, concerns about methodology, the impact of postmodernism and the reinstatement of realism), each having implications for the treatment and analysis of data. Initial focus was on which kinds of research methods and techniques were most appropriate for undertaking feminist work. Concerns were expressed about the greater legitimacy conventionally afforded to survey research and to approaches which emphasized the importance of scientific measurement and objectivity. Such research, it was argued, fractured people's lives in order to produce atomistic facts and measure the extent of social issues, the significance of which had been decided in advance of the research itself (Graham, 1984). Rather than emerging as a consequence of research, interpretation is limited by predetermined possibilities, and in this way meaning is imposed. Although some feminists continued to advocate the utility of surveys, questionnaires and other methods of research with the ability to generate numerical and statistical data about large-sample populations, many argued that qualitative methods of research were preferable. This was because they focused on the meanings and interpretations of those being researched, thereby enabling the researcher to see the social world through their participants' eyes. It was also felt that qualitative approaches were less likely to contradict feminist principles than quantitative ones, where respondents were treated in a detached and controlling manner as if their sole function was in the objectified role of providing data (Oakley, 1981). For this reason, adopting in-depth qualitative research techniques became something of a normative feminist convention, with quantitative work being

associated, somewhat simplistically, with positivism, and both being treated as 'a form of abuse' (Oakley, 2000). Currently, though, while still resolutely defended in some quarters, the old problematic orthodoxy about qualitative research is beginning to break down. A pragmatic approach towards mixing methods and even adopting quantitative ones has developed (Kelly, 1992). However, qualitative studies still remain the preferred research approach for many feminists, with the consequence that it is in this area that they have most to say about data analysis.

This debate about methods was related to a second issue concerning feminist methodology or research practice. Kelly (1988: 6) argued that what distinguishes feminist research from other forms is 'the questions we have asked, the way we locate ourselves within our questions, and the purposes of our work'. The emphasis was on research both as a form of social interaction and as an act of social construction, together with the implications of this for both practice and outcomes. For example, there are issues about how to make women's voices heard without distorting or exploiting them (Olesen, 2000). One particular concern here was to ensure that, throughout its process, feminist research is conducted in non-exploitative and ethically responsible ways. Criticism has been expressed about research which involves hierarchical power relationships, and strategies have been devised in response, such as treating interviewing as story-telling and participatory approaches (Dockery, 2000; Graham, 1984). Drawing from other sources, particularly ethnomethodology, the idea of reflexivity in research practice has been introduced in order to encourage continual reflection by researchers on their mode of involvement in the research process (Stanley, 1990). Such ideas have also influenced feminist ideas about analysing data and the processes through which it might be possible to reach authoritative conclusions (Holland and Ramazanoğlu, 1994).

A third influence on feminist thinking about research has been the debate about postmodernism. Feminism has not been immune from the 'turn to culture', with its emphasis on language, discourse and representation. This has involved a general move away from previous feminist preoccupations with inequality and the material world to a more epistemological concern with 'words' and the ways in which, through discourse and texts, things come to be 'known' (Barrett, 1992). This, in turn, has had profound implications for social research. 'Strong postmodernism', defined as 'a tendency towards nominalism – refusing the idea that there is a "reality", out in the real world, to which "concepts" actually refer', calls into question research involving anything other than textual analysis and deconstruction and treats all explications as inherently relative (Waugh, 1998). Although some feminists remained highly dismissive of such developments (Brodribb, 1992; Oakley, 1998), an associated decline in conducting and in the influence of feminist social research and analysis, from the late 1980s until the late 1990s, is discernible (Adkins and Lury, 1995; Jackson, 1998). This means that, when considering problems of handling data and interpretation, feminists have tended to focus, in particular, on issues of language, context and specificities.

More recently, however, a fourth phase in understanding feminist research has become apparent. This acknowledges that some elements of postmodern approaches are important to feminist research practice and the construction of knowledge, while also attempting to avoid what are now perceived by many as postmodernism's worst excesses. This rather middle-of-the-road approach involves retreating from the more extreme anti-materialist implications of postmodernism, which privileges culture and language while denying the existence of the 'social' (Adkins and Lury, 1995). It recognizes that language and discourse construct rather than reflect meanings and social reality and the need to understand the relationship between power and knowledge. However, it does not see this as being incompatible with a realist position that it is possible to understand how the social world is constructed, reproduced and transformed, or with the idea that it is possible to choose between accounts on the basis of rigorousness and reliability (Maynard, 1998). Such realism reinstates the axiom that there is 'knowledge' to be 'known', although this may be contested and modified. As a result, there is a move towards using research in more contingent ways. It is used to map aspects of the social world and develop empirically grounded concepts and theory. However, the latter are not regarded as definitive or as foreclosing meaning. From this perspective, analysis and interpretation are not about propounding universal truths but neither are they completely relativized.

Rather, the focus is upon continually opening up new fields of meaning and the generation of new understandings and possibilities (Maynard, 1998).

These four phases in feminist engagement with what it means to do research are not uncontentious, with disputes and disagreements being legion. However, they underpin the kinds of issues upon which feminists have focused when reflecting on data analysis and, therefore, form the basis of the rest of this chapter.

LANGUAGE AND MEANING

Much of the material which feminists are involved in analysing comprises talk from interviews. This may be the replies respondents have offered in response to specific questions or requests for views on particular topics. It might constitute narratives volunteered by participants in more unstructured research settings, for instance, when asked to reflect more generally on their lives and experiences. Sometimes the focus of the research will be on fairly immediate happenings or events. On other occasions, it may be some time since the issues the researcher is interested in occurred or they may involve a sequence of occurrences over a period of time, thereby involving questions about the role of memory and recall in the data which is available. Another factor here relates to the mode in which the material has been collected. While recording is relatively standard practice in most interviewing situations, this is not always possible or participants may object. In such cases researchers must either take surreptitious notes or resort to trying to remember salient points, recording them in note form as soon after the interview as possible. Overall, though, the analyst is likely to be faced with a huge amount of discourse. The status of this material in relation to its meaning is a problem for all researchers. However, there are some particularly pertinent issues for feminists.

One major area of importance for feminists is to do with the nature of experience in relation to language and accounts. It has generally been seen as an axiomatic feature of feminist social research that it should be grounded in women's experiences. Not only has it been regarded as a priority to have issues of significance to women included on the research agenda, but also it is crucial that these should be constructed from women's points of view. In this way women would be given a voice and previous silences and biases overcome. As Roseneil (1993: 178) has put it, 'the significance of women's consciousness and everyday life experiences … [were established] … as the material of research'.

However, although focusing on experience has provided a vantage point from which to construct new feminist understandings, the concept of experience itself is seldom defined in any systematic fashion. Rather, it tends to be taken as an unproblematic given, a self-explanatory concept that each feminist uses in her own way (Lazreg, 1994). This leads to a variety of usages and some difficulties when it comes to analysing material in terms of deciding what is actually being analysed. In the past, for instance, some writers appeared to assume that when women speak about their experiences they are providing direct access to lived reality or raw events. In other words, it was taken for granted that there is an unmediated and authentic correspondence between what has happened to women in the past (however recent) and how they refer to this in the present – that the latter is referential of the former. This ignores the ways in which events and feelings are redefined, reframed and reinterpreted, together with the role of memory and selective processes more generally in effecting this. As Haraway (1995: 113) counsels:

> 'women's experience' does not pre-exist as a kind of prior resource, ready simply to be appropriated into one or another description. What may count as 'women's experience' is structured within multiple and often inharmonious agendas. 'Experience', like 'consciousness', is an intentional construction, an artefact of the most importance.

The recounting of experience, then, must always be taken as an historical construction, one which involves the processes of remembering, reliving and recalling, often for the benefit of, and in collaboration with, others. The knowledge so revealed is necessarily partial, changing and cannot unquestioningly be taken as corresponding to some definitive truth.

In recent years debates about experience have been profoundly affected by the influence of postmodern thinking. Although writers collected under this nomenclature tend to be diverse, one common theme is that the self-contained, authentic and homogeneous subject, perceived by humanism and modernism to be discoverable below a veneer of cultural and ideological overlay, is, in reality, a construct of that very humanist and modernist discourse. In other words, there is no one 'true' and unified self and, therefore, no 'true' experience. That which is regarded as experience is always mediated through discourse. For Scott (1992: 34), for instance, experience is a 'linguistic' event that does not happen outside established meanings. Further, conflicts among and within discursive systems make multiple meanings and understandings possible. As Scott (1992: 26) explains,

> it is not individuals who have experiences, but subjects that are constituted through experience. Experience in this definition then becomes not the origin of our explanation, not the authoritative (because seen or felt) evidence that grounds what is known, but rather that which we seek to explain, that about which knowledge is produced.

In other words, the task for the social researcher is not to make experience visible, thereby assuming the prior existence of selves. Instead, rather than assuming that experience is something that people 'have', we should ask how conceptions of selves, of subjects and of identities are produced. On the one hand, then, there are feminists who accept people's recollection of experiences at face value and as the basis for interpretation. They are content to let the oral evidence, however collected, speak for itself. On the other, it is argued that, since data comprise only memories which are discursively constructed, they cannot provide knowledge of events or feelings. In this approach, no claims for the meaning of oral data would be made other than that it be treated as text. As Glucksman (1994: 159) explains, there is 'no possibility of critical assessment, by reference to material external to the discourse, of the relation between discursive and extra-discursive events'.

Clearly, the forms of analysis undertaken in these two cases, together with the nature of the knowledge formulated, are very different. However, drawing on the hermeneutic tradition, Glucksman (1994) has suggested an important alternative. This is to focus on the meaning that actions and experiences, or memories of them, have for respondents in research, with the aim of understanding the significance of these meanings, rather than the nature of some kind of social reality itself.

Experience, then, is something which we are actively engaged in constructing, rather than just the living through of events. However, that women's talk about their experiences is reconstruction does not make it invalid as a basis for shared understandings or social intervention. Instead of treating people's accounts either at face value or as text, there needs to be more discussion as to how to develop a critical appreciation and understanding of what people say. Two current options are to be found in Mauthner and Doucet's (1998) discussion of a 'voice-centred relational method' and Hollway and Jefferson's (2000) 'free-association and narrative interview'.

Another area of language and meaning significant to feminist analysis relates to the extent to which what is being said makes the same sense to interviewer and interviewee. Words, phrases or particular ways of speaking may mean different things to different people, depending on factors such as social class, ethnicity and culture, gender and age. Language usage is riddled with all sorts of unspoken and taken-for-granted assumptions which may change the meaning that it has for different speakers. Normative expectations and conventions as to who constitutes family and kin or the boundaries between public and private, for example, are very different between Afro-Caribbean, Asian, Muslim and white British culture. This leads to problems of the commensurability of concepts and terms across different groups. Good interviewers sensitively prepare for such social variation in the way they formulate questions, issues and topics and by paying assiduous attention to clarity during the interview itself. Sometimes, however, potential problems are not spotted until later, when the researcher is immersed in the analysis of the data. At that point, decisions have to be made about what a respondent means, usually in the context of what has been said in the interview more generally.

A third issue relates to researching potentially difficult or sensitive subjects and using particular kinds of language and terms. For example, Holland et al. (1998) have reflected on the difficulties experienced by the young women involved in their research on sexuality in talking about what were frequently sensitive issues. Often the young women did not have access to an appropriate language through which to discuss details of intimacy or bodily parts or were embarassed that the terms they did know would be considered coarse or inappropriate. This led to hesitations, silences and contradictions in their responses. During analysis, the researchers then had to decide whether these should be treated as a problem of communication between interviewer and participant, misunderstanding or lack of clarity on the part of the participant or, perhaps, as an indication of the complex and contradictory nature of the very experience or social situation being described. In this context, DeVault (1999) has pointed out that the terms 'silence' and 'silencing' can relate to a wide range of related but often different phenomena and the need to make known their assumptions and gaps. In the work on sexuality, this problem was dealt with by connecting what happened in the interviews to feminists' conceptualization of female sexuality. It was argued that young women have difficulty talking about sexuality because they are being asked to speak about what is usually silenced or unvoiced. Young women have difficulty speaking about sexual issues in an interview in the same way that they report having difficulties talking with young men about them in sexual situations. This is due to the contradictory nature of the social construction of female sexuality (Holland and Ramazanoğlu, 1994). The input of feminist theory into the data analysis process in this project supported such an interpretation of the accounts. This was rather than seeing them as due to defects in either the individuals concerned or in the interviewing process.

Understanding the meaning of accounts may also be informed by other kinds of material, in addition to cassette/disk recordings, transcripts and other forms of texts. For instance, body language, non-verbal exchanges, laughter and distress also provide a context from which to interpret what people have been saying. There are, therefore, three related levels of analysis through which interpretation may take place. These are the words and meanings offered by research participants, fieldnotes concerning the interviewees and the nature of the interview, and the use to be made of these data. It is to the latter issue that the chapter now turns.

THE ROLE OF INTERPRETATION

The issue of interpretation has been a vexed one for feminists. To begin with, there is a tension between the feminist emphasis on the legitimacy of women's own understanding of their experiences and the self-conscious stance that feminist work definitionally takes, whether this be based on theory, epistemology or politics. On the one hand, there are some kinds of feminist research which seem to see recounting what women say about their experiences as an end in itself. Reams of unmediated personal accounts are provided in the apparent belief that to do other than 'let women speak for themselves' constitutes a subordination and remedying of their views and, hence, the violation of their autonomy. On the other hand, this is at odds with the fact that *all* feminist work is theoretically grounded and that most feminists themselves argue that research cannot be apparently free of values in this way. For, of course, whatever particular kind is adopted, feminism provides a framework which is concerned to understand the social world in terms of gendered and other forms of social divisions. No feminist study can be completely inductive or solely based in grounded theory. This is a contradiction in terms in two senses. On the one hand, there is a possible conflict between viewing the world through a feminist lens and viewing it through that of the women being studied. On the other, there is a potential tension between the latter's views and experiences and what investigation shows to be the case about their situation. In particular, the question is raised of what feminists should do when faced with women's understandings of their experiences which are at odds with those suggested by taking a feminist position. In reviewing this issue, Olesen (2000: 236), for instance, cites Wasserfall's (1997) tension-ridden interaction between herself and research participants, Lawthom's (1997) problems as a feminist researcher working in non-feminist research and Davis and Gremmen's (1998) experience that feminist principles may sometimes impede the process of conducting feminist research.

Thus, the process of analysis is affected by a 'double subjectivity', that of the respondent and that of the researcher, and it is crucial for this matter to be acknowledged and the possibility of different interpretations from each confronted (Edwards, 1993). Addressing this issue in the context of their work on young women, AIDS and sexuality, Thomson and Scott (1990) acknowledge that although, as feminists, they were interested in exploring power in sexual relationships, they had to be mindful that not all the women were aware of any such power, even when they might appear to be clearly constrained. They write that 'we cannot then simply cull instances from our transcripts and treat them as reflections of reality ... Our interpretation has ... had to interact with the young women's accounts' (1990: 11–12).

A further difficulty is that the feminist political commitment to understanding gender and other forms of difference poses problems if it is not linked to an interpretive and synthesizing process which *connects* what is meant by experience to understanding. Simply to document what women say, without reflecting on it or providing a context, may produce interesting descriptive material but can be less than helpful about what the descriptions might mean. The issue here, then, is that although what women might say about their experiences may constitute a starting point for the production of feminist knowledge, this is not sufficient for understanding the practices and processes through which they are structured. Smith (1986: 6), for example, has written that it is important to be able to show women 'how their own social situation, their everyday world is organized and determined by social processes which are not knowable through the ordinary means through which we find our everyday world'. In other words, it is necessary to attempt to render intelligible those repetitions in social life which may be invisible or perceived in purely isolated and personal terms by the individual. It means going beyond what is said about experience, and this involves analysis and interpretation in order to connect what is said to a wider understanding.

Of course, such a process is fraught with difficulties. It necessarily involves selecting material from the large amount which is usually available. Whether working from transcripts, tapes or other forms of record and whether employing software packages or other methods of coding and sifting, analysing interviews entails searching for themes, analytic categories or emergent topics. It may involve summarizing what a respondent has said and placing it within a context of which they may be unaware. This is an act of objectification and one which feminists are supposed to avoid at all costs (Stanley and Wise, 1993). Yet, it is not clear how it might be possible to produce an analysis which goes beyond the experience of individuals at the same time as granting them full subjectivity. In fact, some writers have counselled that some kind of objectification may be an inescapable fact of doing research (Acker et al., 1991; Game, 1991; Lazreg, 1994). If there are to be quests for explanations, and questions are to be asked as to why things operate in a particular way, then some form of objectification may be unavoidable. Indeed, as Acker et al. (1991: 142) comment, 'we the researchers took the position that some process of objectification of the self is a necessary part of coming to an awareness of one's own existence; it is not less a part of coming to an understanding of others'. Finding out about others, then, may always involve a stance of methodological objectification. The very idea of 'giving women a voice' or 'letting them speak' is to constitute them as objects. This is not the same, however, as inscribing the researched as powerless, pathologized and without agency, as is sometimes implied in the literature. There is a difference between objectification and alienation, an oppressive process through which an individual's subjectivity is appropriated and denied. While the subject–object distinction may best be viewed as a continuum, with various degrees of relationship between researcher and researched available along it, rather than as a complete polarization, it cannot be completely abolished in research. To claim that 'they', that is women, are subjects in feminist analysis is to avert the issue of authorship and questions about power in the production of knowledge. It also raises problems about validity and objectivity. This is now considered via a discussion of the feminist standpoint approach.

TAKING A FEMINIST STANDPOINT

Feminists, along with other social scientists, have a history of being concerned about the plausibility and adequacy of the analyses and accounts which they produce. They have been critical of the unquestioning notion of objectivity which is the basis of scientific objectivism. This overlooks the extent to which the analyst is implicated in the generation of analysed material. It underplays the role of power relations throughout the research process.

From the start, it is necessary to disentangle two uses of the term 'objectivity' which tend to be used interchangeably (Skeggs, 1997). The first is to do with the plausibility, validity and adequacy of the analyses generated. The concern here would be with the extent to which the accounts given are reliable, responsible and satisfactory when evaluated in the context of the research undertaken. It implies that judgments can be made about the standards and rigorousness of the research and that, given this, some research is better than others. However, the emphasis for feminists would be on the ability of analyses to convince and persuade rather than on absolute validity. The second use of the notion 'objectivity' is better termed 'value neutrality' or 'value freedom' (Gouldner, 1973). This relates to the extent to which it is possible to eradicate our own personal beliefs, assumptions and biographies from research. Most feminists would argue that it is not possible to do the latter, although there is disagreement as to how researchers should respond to the situation. For some, it is a licence for an unbridled relativism, while for others it raises serious epistemological and practical issues as to how to proceed. However, it is important to recognize that the fact that the research process is informed by values does not mean that objective accounts, in the sense of being valid and rigorous, cannot be produced. Further, as Skeggs (1997) notes, researchers' values may enable them to recognize the importance of social factors that others overlook, for example gender, race and class.

Standpoint feminisms have been developed in order to tackle some of the above problems. Although there are a number of different standpoint positions, Sandra Harding's work is frequently adopted as the baseline approach. There are two major and related elements to standpoint feminisms. The first concerns the socially situated nature of knowledge. Drawing on the Marxist idea concerning the epistemic privilege of oppressed groups, Harding (1991) argues that understanding women's lives from a committed feminist position leads to more complete and less distorted knowledge than that produced through male science. Women and men lead lives that have significantly different contours and boundaries. The circumstances of women's daily existence give them a different standpoint on the world from that of men, and so access to different knowledge about their situation. Adopting a feminist standpoint can, therefore, indicate the existence of forms of human relationships which may not be visible from the position of the 'ruling gender'. It thus offers the possibility of more reliable understandings, along with the potential of extension to a range of other subordinate and underprivileged groups.

The second aspect of standpoint feminism is critical of science. Harding (1991, 1993) criticizes traditional formulations of objectivity for not being sufficiently rigorous, responsible and valid. She argues that objectivity is not some kind of complete state that can be ultimately and definitely achieved. Rather, it involves a process in which all the evidence marshalled in the creation of knowledge, including the hidden and unexplicated cultural agendas and assumptions of the knower/researcher, are called to account. Harding makes a distinction between 'strong' and 'weak' objectivity. Supposed scientific ways of ensuring objectivity are 'weak' because they deliberately suppress the ways in which the cultural and biographical aspects of 'knowing' help to create the knowledge which is produced, giving rise to a false sense of accuracy or truth. In contrast, 'strong' objectivity includes the systematic examination of such background and domain assumptions and influences, thereby transforming the 'reflexivity of research from a problem to a resource' (Harding, 1991: 164). While the act of researching involves the researcher and participant in the mutual creation of data, it is not usually possible to know what has been influential to the participant and her range of feelings. The researcher, however, can and must attempt to detail this. Strong objectivity, therefore, 'maximizes' the possibility of generating valid and plausible accounts by making what is usually hidden and unacknowledged visible and part of the equation in assessing knowledge claims.

Standpoint feminisms have been subjected to much critical feminist scrutiny and evaluation concerning, for instance, the silencing of Black feminist and lesbian standpoints, the potential existence of a multiplicity of incommensurable standpoints, and the dangers of essentialism (Gill, 1998). However, one major concern is how it might be operationalized, particularly in the context of analysis and interpretation. This requires consideration of the concept 'reflexivity'.

REFLEXIVITY

Feminists' concerns with reflexivity relate to anxieties about how 'strong' objectivity might be approximated, if not completely achieved. The idea of reflexivity, in the sense of continuous critical reflection on the research processes used to produce knowledge, offers one strategy. It is a response to the recognition that the cultural beliefs and behaviours of researchers shape the results of their analyses, the ignoring of which leads to weak objectivity. As Harding (1987: 9) explains, these behaviours are 'part of the empirical evidence for (or against) the claims advanced in the results of the research'. It is, therefore, necessary for the researcher to locate herself in relation to the research in four ways.

The first involves locating the researcher on the same critical plane as the researched. This does not mean that the researcher can put herself in their place. However, it does mean attending to the overall context of their lives and continually reflecting on its significance both for what they have to say and the sense the researcher wishes to make of this. Skeggs (1997) has written of how, at the beginning of her research, she saw a strong similarity between the women participants and the positions she had previously occupied herself. However, she recognized that she had now left this place. She poignantly reflects on the connections and disconnections which she felt and describes how deeply disturbing was the realization of her position as a privileged researcher. All of this affected her analysis and representation of the women, and it was important for this to be included in her account of it as part of the basis upon which readers' critical evaluation might be made.

A second form of reflexivity involves making explicit the grounds for conducting the research, clearly setting out the procedures used and explaining why things have been done in certain ways. While this might seem obvious, social scientists have traditionally been content to gloss this part of their work, giving more space to what tends to be regarded as the more important findings. However, many feminists see explication of analytic, as well as the practical, issues involved in research as a hallmark of its persuasiveness and credibility.

The third way of being reflexive in relation to research is for researchers to explore their 'intellectual autobiographies' by reflecting on the likely effect of their class, race, gender and other experiences and assumptions on research and its analysis. Reflexively acknowledging the role of one's own subjectivity in the construction and conduct of research challenges the idea of the researcher as an invisible and anonymous voice of authority (Stanley, 1990). For example, the contributors to the book *Research and Inequality* variously explore issues of social division and diversity within the research process (Truman et al., 2000). Their arguments make it clear that *their* position in relation to their experiences of, and assumptions about, such matters strongly influenced the accounts and analyses generated. They thus contribute towards making the relationship between researcher and researched more transparent and, thereby, to the feminist notion of strong objectivity.

A fourth kind of reflexivity involves reflecting on the role of emotions, particularly those of researchers. Traditionally, of course, the latter were neither expected nor encouraged to discuss feelings or states of mind, since it was thought that these would contaminate research findings. However, although problems of personal exposure in research have been part of feminist concerns for some time, relatively little attention to the issue has taken place outside of feminist scholarship (Carter and Delamont, 1996; but see also, for example, Lofland, 1971). This is despite the fact that many researchers will have found themselves in situations where they were angry, frightened or distressed. Others will have been involved with respondents who were themselves experiencing strong emotions of some kind.

Emotional reactions to the research situation can last long after the actual collection of the data has been completed and may be reactivated during the process of analysis. Researchers who have collected information about child sexual abuse or rape, for example, may be expecting to hear distressing stories, although this does not mean that they are necessarily prepared for the effects these might have on them. Others may stumble unexpectedly across accounts of horrific events. Reading the transcripts or listening to the tapes can be emotionally disturbing or shocking. Feminists have argued that, rather than denying such feelings, they should be harnessed for the purposes of analysis and interpretation. Kirkwood (1993), for example, describes her initial feelings of being overwhelmed as she tried to deal with respondents' accounts of domestic violence. It was necessary for her to untangle her

emotional responses and feed what she learnt from understanding them back to her analysis. This not only led to a better understanding of the women's experiences, but also freed up energy that she had previously been expending on dealing with feeling numb and ill. Mauthner and Doucet (1998) also make emotional response one element of their voice-centred relational method, which is rooted in reflexivity. This involves several strategies, such as reading transcripts for the main events and protagonists, recording their own responses to these, focusing on how respondents feel and speak about themselves, listening to how participants speak about interpersonal relationships and placing these within cultural contexts and social structures. This is followed by case studies and group work, before producing short portraits of remaining respondents and then breaking the transcripts into overlapping themes and sub-themes.

There are, however, some problems with treating reflexivity as a panacea for research. For instance, it can be a long and drawn-out practice, as Mauthner and Doucet (1998) describe. It is difficult to establish guidelines as to how far or for how long one should continue with the process. There are dangers that accounts of the process and of researchers' involvement come to dominate the analysis and findings of the research. As Skeggs (1997: 34) explained of her study, she did not want 'the complexities of the women's lives to be reduced to my history'. Further, feminists can *aim* at reflexivity but it is highly unlikely ever fully to be attained. Systematic self-knowledge is not transparently and readily available. Neither is it possible to break away from social constraints on ways of knowing or analysing on a whim. It is also too easy to identify the personal characteristics and circumstances of the researcher in a somewhat ritualistic manner, with little associated attempt to reflect on the significance of these for the research and its outcomes. While reflexivity is a laudable goal, therefore, it is not without inherent difficulties.

POWER AND HIERARCHY IN DATA ANALYSIS

Ideas about reflexivity also relate to concerns about power and hierarchy in research practices. Early on in the development of feminist debates about research, there was criticism of potentially exploitative practices where a researcher, powerful because of her position, invests nothing of herself in a project, while expecting other women to speak freely and frankly. Such power is also present in the analysing of data, when the respondents are absent and the researchers' decisions about interpretation are paramount. How might it be possible to guard against reading unwarranted meanings into texts or to ensure that appropriate connections are made between them? In addition to the strategies already discussed, there are other possibilities. One is to obtain respondents' feedback on the interpretation and analysis of research materials. Skeggs (1994) discusses, for example, how some of the young women in her study wanted to relisten to tapes of their interviews and how doing so turned into a regular social event. This afforded her the possibility of trying out some of her interpretive ideas with them and acted as a quasi-validation process. However, when she tried to make the research even more accountable to them by giving them material to read, the most common response was 'can't understand a bloody word it says' (1994: 86). In addition to the issue of why people who have already given time to someone else's research should be willing to invest further in it, this also draws attention to the impenetrability of academic writing, most of which has its own stylistic and narrative structure and house style. Involving participants in data analysis may also be beyond the resources and time-frame of a project. It also raises the issue of disagreement over interpretation and whose views would take precedence (Mauthner and Doucet, 1998).

Another way of attempting to reduce researcher power is by designing a project to be fully participatory. Here, the researched would be involved in the design and conduct of a whole research project and are not just drawn in for some kind of validation purpose during analysis (Truman et al., 2000). The idea is that the process is owned and shared by all participants, right through to interpretation and writing up, with the aim of generating positive changes among individuals and groups as a whole, rather than just involving them in the production of data (Dockery, 2000). This may well be an ideal way of proceeding. Research becomes an interactional and collaborative process. There are reciprocal inputs from researcher and researched in constructing meanings, and agreed conclusions on the interpretation of content are negotiated (Holland and Ramazanoğlu, 1994). However, it is one which, due to resource and other implications, is often beyond reach. Further, there are doubts as to whether fully collaborative research is ever possible, raising issues about synonymity of intention, understanding and outcome between participants and researchers (Lawthom, 1997; Wasserfall, 1997).

Although feminists may strive to eliminate power dynamics from data analysis and interpretation, then, many see this as an impossibility (Holland and Ramazanoğlu, 1994; Mauthner and Doucet, 1998). There is a conflict between the requirements made of feminist academic researchers and the needs and interests of the women they research, with each having an altogether different relationship to a project, despite what may be intended. Most of the time, researchers have the power (and associated responsibility) to reformulate the contents of interviews and the statements of respondents in their own terms. They write up the results and make decisions about dissemination and publication. As Roseneil (1993: 204) reflects on her attempt to involve her interviewees in the research process, 'in the final analysis, it has been *my* analysis which has triumphed; I have retained the power of authorship'. For Cotterill (1992: 604), 'the final shift of power between the researcher and respondent is balanced in favour of the researcher, for it is she who eventually walks away'.

There is, in addition, another way in which power may intrude on the data analysing process. This is in the context of team-working, where the goal is not necessarily participatory research. A number of feminist researchers have addressed this issue (Holland and Ramazanoğlu, 1994; Kelly et al., 1994; Ramazanoğlu, 1990). In many ways working as part of a feminist research team can be a supportive and empowering experience. Holland and Ramazanoğlu (1994) describe, for example, how analysis of material was shared in their research team. All members had to read all transcripts in order to understand the range and depth of the data and available interpretations. Coding was also a collective enterprise, with the categories used arising from discussions and debate in interacting with the data. The activity of analysis and interpretation was highly complex, involving moving backwards and forwards between fieldnotes, data summaries and theoretical propositions (Ramazanoğlu, 1990). Because the team was deliberately constructed so as to minimize hierarchy, the whole process had to be made as explicit as possible.

Working in a team meant that colleagues were available to discuss emotionally disturbing interviews, transcripts and tapes. However, it was also necessary to take account of feelings and emotions within the research team itself. This was particularly the case in any division of tasks or monitoring of procedures, leading inevitably to the negotiation of compromises and resolutions (Ramazanoğlu, 1990).

Difficulties, though, may arise in even the most self-consciously constructed feminist team. Members may be at different stages of their careeers, with associated different degrees of status. They may subjectively experience membership of the team differently. There may be subtle and hidden pressure (real or imagined) to adopt the ideas and perspectives of those whose knowledge and experience is thought to be superior. Thus, the social relationships within a team will influence how data are produced, analysed, interpreted and disseminated. As Ramazanoğlu (1990: 3) indicates, 'working as a research team cannot then be a process which can be taken for granted, nor can it be a set of relationships which is external to the conduct of the research'.

Finally, some feminists have questioned the emphasis which suggests that a researcher is necessarily all-powerful. The power dimension of the researched–researcher relationship may vacillate and change during the course of the research process. Further, participants may be reticent in the information and replies they give. They can embarrass, cut off, lie, humiliate, manipulate, and sometimes place the researcher in danger (Ribbens and Edwards, 1998; Wolf, 1996). Visweswaran, for example, writing from an anthropological perspective, is interested in how such a situation might contribute to understanding and knowledge. She asks what the implications are for research when 'the acts of subjects deflecting or refusing our inquiries form a part of the analysis' (1994: 13). Rather than omitting such material from the research process, where they can be recognized, she argues that moments of difficulty, attempts to mislead or to obfuscate should be seen as opportunities to enter these various systems of meaning and power. In this way, the power exercised by the research participant can become a component of data and, thereby, part of the analysis and interpretation being generated.

ETHICS AND EMPOWERMENT

There has been much discussion concerning whether feminist research could or should be empowering. Writers disagree as to what the term 'empowerment' means, although it is usually taken in some general sense to refer to a process through which individuals or groups gain access to knowledge, energy and authority in order that they might act or intervene on their own behalf (Opie, 1992; Rowlands, 1998; Truman et al., 2000). Analysis and interpretation of material on its own, of course, are unlikely to be empowering. However, the questions 'what is this for?' and 'to which uses will it be put and by whom?' are likely to influence decisions as to interpretation and the writing up of ideas. This may especially be the case if research is policy-based or is making policy recommendations.

The issues of empowerment and policy raise ethical matters about whether interpretations and analyses arising from research findings should always be placed in the public domain, without qualm, or whether there are occasions when it might be more prudent for them to be withheld. For there may be times when research outcomes are not positive. Research findings may report on, and thereby reproduce, racism and racist stereotypes. They may reveal illegal activities, such as under-age sex or drinking. They may highlight young single mothers' disinterest in young men and stable partnerships. Findings such as these may encourage harsh policy interventions, media backlash or other forms of attack. In some cases, feminists have felt unable to publish the results of their research for fear that it might be damaging to the women involved or to those in similar situations.

Some feminists have called for a set of specifically feminist ethics, arguing the need for clarity on these kinds of issues (Wolf, 1996). Others are more circumspect of the utility of being so prescriptive. Wheatley (1994) suggests that, given the diversity of feminist research and the intense debates which surround it, it is doubtful that a fully consensual feminist ethical statement is either desirable or attainable. Pointing to the difficulties which arise in resolving ethical issues generally, she suggests instead that what is required is sensitivity concerning the ethics and politics involved both in the research process and in the production of written accounts and analyses.

CONCLUSION

This chapter has sought to explore feminist views on data analysis. However, despite extensive writing on the nature of social research generally, this appears to be an area to which less specific attention has been given. In particular, there is little material discussing the actual processes through which analysis and interpretation occur and even less in the way of practical suggestions as to what procedures might be available and how they might be evaluated and used. Instead, as is reflected in the discussion here, when feminists discuss issues of analysis, they do so as part of more general methodological debates. These tend to be of a somewhat abstract and epistemological nature which, while important, offer little direct guidance to the researcher in the field. This neglect is somewhat surprising, given feminists' emphasis on the importance of the research process and the need for clarity as to how it is carried out. There is a need for feminists to articulate more fully the ways in which their analyses of data proceed. This will make an important contribution to discussions of reflexivity and strong objectivity. It will also be an important step in understanding how to actually 'do' feminist research.

REFERENCES

Acker, J., Barry, K. and Esseveld, J. (1991) 'Objectivity and truth. Problems in doing feminist research', in M.M. Fonow and J.A. Cook (eds), *Beyond Methodology*. Bloomington and Indianapolis: Indiana University Press.

Adkins, L. and Lury, C. (1995) 'Das "Soziale" in feministischen Theorien: Eine nützliche Analysekategorie?', in L.C. Armbruster, U. Müller and M. Stein-Hilbers (eds), *Neue Horizonte? Sozialwissenschaftliche Forschung über Geschlechter und Geschlechterverhältnisse*. Opladen: Leske + Budrich.

Ali, S., Coate, K. and wa Goro, W. (eds) (2000) *Global Feminist Politics*. London: Routledge.

Barrett, M. (1992) 'Words and things', in M. Barrett and A. Phillips (eds), *Destabilizing Theory*. Cambridge: Polity.

Bell, L. (1998) 'Public and private meanings in diaries', in J. Ribbens and R. Edwards (eds), *Feminist Dilemmas in Qualitative Research*. London: Sage.

Bernard, J. (1973) 'My four revolutions: an autobiographical history of the ASA', *American Journal of Sociology*, 78: 773–801.

Brodribb, S. (1992) *Nothing Mat(t)ers*. Melbourne: Spinifex Press.

Callaway, H. (1981) 'Women's perspectives: research as re-vision', in P. Reason and J. Rowan (eds), *Human Inquiry: A Sourcebook of New Paradigm Research*. Chichester: Wiley.

Carter, K. and Delamont, S. (1996) 'Introduction', in K. Carter and S. Delamont (eds), *Qualitative Research: The Emotional Dimension*. Aldershot: Avebury.

Coffey, A. and Atkinson, P. (1996) *Making Sense of Qualitative Data*. London: Sage.

Cook, J.A. and Fonow, M.M. (1986) 'Knowledge and women's interests: issues of epistemology and methodology in feminist sociological research', *Sociological Inquiry*, 56: 2–29.

Cotterill, P. (1992) Interviewing women: some issues of friendship, vulnerability and power, *Women's Studies International Forum*, 15(5/6): 593–606.

Davis, K. and Gremmen, I. (1998) 'In search of heroines: some reflections on normativity in feminist research', *Feminism and Psychology*, 8: 133–53.

DeVault, M. (1999) *Liberating Method. Feminism and Social Research*. Philadelphia: Temple University Press.

Dey, I. (1993) *Qualitative Data Analysis: A User-Friendly Guide for Social Scientists*. London: Routledge.

Dockery, G. (2000) 'Participatory research. Whose roles, whose responsibilities?', in C. Truman, D. Mertens and B. Humphries (eds), *Research and Inequality*. London: UCL Press.

Edwards, R. (1993) 'An education in interviewing. Placing the researcher and researched', in C.M. Renzetti and R.M. Lee (eds), *Researching Sensitive Topics*. London: Sage.

Fielding, N.G. and Lee, R. (1998) *Computer Analysis and Qualitative Research*. London: Sage.

Finch, J. and Mason, J. (1990) 'Decision taking in the fieldwork process: theoretical sampling and collaborative working', in R.G. Burgess (ed.), *Reflections on Field Experience, Studies in Qualitative Methodology*. Vol. 2. Greenwich, CT: JAI Press.

Game, A. (1991) *Undoing the Social*. Buckingham: Open University Press.

Gill, R. (1998) 'Dialogues and differences: writing, reflexivity and the crisis of representation', in K. Henwood, C. Griffin and A. Phoenix (eds), *Standpoints and Differences*. London: Sage.

Glucksman, M. (1994) 'The work of knowledge and the knowledge of women's work', in M. Maynard and J. Purvis (eds), *Researching Women's Lives from a Feminist Perspective*. London: Taylor and Francis.

Gouldner, A. (1973) 'The sociologist as partisan', in A. Gouldner, *For Sociology*. London: Allen Lane.

Graham, H. (1984) 'Surveying through stories', in C. Bell and H. Roberts (eds), *Social Researching*. London: Routledge & Kegan Paul.

Haraway, D. (1995) *Primate Visions*. New York: Routledge.

Harding, S. (1987) *Feminism and Methodology*. Milton Keynes: Open University Press.

Harding, S. (1991) *Whose Science? Whose Knowledge?* Buckingham: Open University Press.

Harding, S. (1993) 'Rethinking standpoint epistemology: what is "strong objectivity"', in L. Alcoff and E. Potter (eds), *Feminist Epistemologies*. London: Routledge.

Holland, J. and Ramazanoğlu, C. (1994) 'Coming to conclusions: power and interpretation in researching young women's sexuality', in M. Maynard and J. Purvis (eds), *Researching Women's Lives from a Feminist Perspective*. London: Taylor and Francis.

Holland, J., Ramazanoğlu, C., Sharpe, S. and Thomson, R. (1998) *The Male in the Head*. London: Tufnell Press.

Hollway, W. and Jefferson, T. (2000) *Doing Qualitative Research Differently*. London: Sage.

Humphries, B. (1997) 'From critical thought to emancipatory action: contradictory research goals?', *Sociological Research Online*, 2(1).

Jackson, S. (1998) 'Feminist social theory', in S. Jackson and J. Jones (eds), *Contemporary Feminist Theories*. Edinburgh: Edinburgh University Press.

Kelly, L. (1988) *Surviving Sexual Violence*. Cambridge: Polity.

Kelly, L. (1992) 'Journeying in reverse: possibilities and problems in feminist research on sexual violence', in L. Gelsthorpe and A. Morris (eds), *Feminist Perspectives in Criminology*. Buckingham: Open University Press.

Kelly, L., Burton, S. and Regan, L. (1994) 'Researching women's lives or studying women's oppression? Reflections on what constitutes feminist research', in M. Maynard and J. Purvis (eds), *Researching Women's Lives from a Feminist Perspective*. London: Taylor and Francis.

Kirkwood, C. (1993) 'Investing ourselves: use of researcher personal response in feminist methodology', in J. de Groot and M. Maynard (eds), *Doing Things Differently*. London: Macmillan.

Lather, P. (1993) 'Fertile obsession: validity after poststructuralism', *Sociological Quarterly*, 34(4): 673–93.

Lawthom, R. (1997) 'What can I do? A feminist researcher in non-feminist research', *Feminism and Psychology*, 7: 533–8.

Lazreg, M. (1994) 'Women's experience and feminist epistemology. A critical neo-rationalist approach', in K. Lennon and M. Whitford (eds), *Knowing the Difference: Feminist Perspectives in Epistemology*. London: Routledge.

Lewis, A. and Lindsay, G. (eds) (2000) *Researching Children's Perspectives*. Buckingham: Open University Press.

Lofland, J. (1971) *Analysing Social Settings: A Guide to Qualitative Observation and Analysis*. Belmont, CA: Wadsworth.

Mackinnon, C. (1982) 'Feminism, Marxism, method and the state: an agenda for theory', in N. Keohane, M. Rosaldo and B. Gelpi (eds), *Feminist Theory*. Brighton: Harvester.

Mauthner, N. and Doucet, A. (1998) 'Reflections on a voice-centred relational method: analysing maternal and domestic voices', in J. Ribbens and R. Edwards (eds), *Feminist Dilemmas in Qualitative Research*. London: Sage.

May, T. (1993) *Social Research*. Buckingham: Open University Press.

Maynard, M. (1998) 'Feminists' knowledge and the knowledge of feminisms', in T. May and M. Williams (eds), *Knowing the Social World*. Buckingham: Open University Press.

Maynard, M. and Purvis, J. (eds) (1994) *Researching Women's Lives from a Feminist Perspective*. London: Taylor and Francis.

Oakley, A. (1981) 'Interviewing women: a contradiction in terms', in H. Roberts (ed.), *Doing Feminist Research*. London: Routledge & Kegan Paul.

Oakley, A. (1998) 'Gender, methodology and people's ways of knowing: some problems with feminism and the paradigm debate in social science', *Sociology*, 32(4): 707–31.

Oakley, A. (2000) *Experiments in Knowing*. Cambridge: Polity.

Olesen, V. (1998) 'Feminisms and models of qualitative research', in N.K. Denzin and Y.S. Lincoln (eds), *The Landscape of Qualitative Research*. London: Sage.

Olesen, V. (2000) Feminisms and qualitative research at and into the millennium, in N.K. Denzin and Y.S. Lincoln (eds), *The Handbook of Qualitative Research* (2nd edition). Thousand Oaks, CA: Sage.

Opie, A. (1992) 'Qualitative research, appropriation of the "other" and empowerment', *Feminist Review*, 40 (Spring): 52–69.

Plummer, K. (1995) *Telling Sexual Stories: Power, Change and Social Worlds*. London: Routledge.

Ramazanoğlu, C. (1990) *Methods of Working as a Research Team*. London: Tufnell Press.

Ribbens, J. and Edwards, R. (eds) (1998) *Feminist Dilemmas in Qualitative Research*. London: Sage.

Roseneil, S. (1993) 'Greenham revisited: researching myself and my sisters', in D. Hobbs and T. May (eds), *Interpreting the Field*. Oxford: Oxford University Press.

Rowlands, J. (1998) 'A word of the times', in H. Afshar (ed.), *Women and Empowerment*. Basingstoke: Macmillan.

Scott, J. (1992) 'Experience', in J. Butler and J.W. Scott (eds), *Feminists Theorize the Political*. London: Routledge.

Skeggs, B. (1994) 'Situating the production of feminist ethnography', in M. Maynard and J. Purvis (eds), *Researching Women's Lives from a Feminist Perspective*. London: Taylor and Francis.

Skeggs, B. (1997) *Formations of Class and Gender*. London: Sage.

Smith, D. (1986) 'Institutional ethnography: a feminist method', *Resources for Feminist Research*, 15.

Smith, D. (1988) *The Everyday World as Problematic: A Feminist Sociology*. Milton Keynes: Open University Press.

Stanley, L. (1990) 'Feminist praxis and the academic mode of production', in L. Stanley (ed.), *Feminist Praxis*. London: Routledge.

Stanley, L. and Wise, S. (1993) *Breaking Out Again*. London: Routledge.

Strauss, A.L. (1987) *Qualitative Analysis for Social Scientists*. Cambridge: Cambridge University Press.

Thomas, C. (1999) *Female Forms*. Buckingham: Open University Press.

Thomson, R. and Scott, S. (1990) *Researching Sexuality in the Light of AIDS*. London: Tufnell Press.

Truman, C., Mertens, D. and Humphreys, B. (eds) (2000) *Research and Inequality*. London: UCL Press.

Visweswaran, K. (1994) *Fictions of Feminist Ethnography*. Minneapolis: University of Minnesota Press.

Wasserfall, R.R. (1997) 'Reflexivity, feminism and difference', in R. Hertz (ed.), *Reflexivity and Voice*. Thousand Oaks, CA: Sage.

Waugh, P. (1998) 'Postmodernism and feminism', in S. Jackson and J. Jones (eds), *Contemporary Feminist Theories*. Edinburgh: Edinburgh University Press.

Wheatley, E.E. (1994) 'How can we engender feminist ethnography with a feminist imagination?', *Women's Studies International Forum*, 17(4): 403–16.

Wolf, D.L. (ed.) (1996) *Feminist Dilemmas in Fieldwork*. Oxford: Westview Press.

7

Historical Analysis

DENNIS SMITH

This chapter places the process of data analysis in the broader context of historical inquiry. It examines the relationship between historical occurrences, historical evidence, historical analysis and some key feedback loops between them. It then goes on to consider specific issues and techniques in historical analysis, in each case paying particular attention to two specific attempts to formulate the issues involved and offer potential solutions. Drawing together a number of these issues, it goes on to look at the methodological strategies adopted by Barrington Moore, especially the way he combines the investigation of particular cases, the use of comparative analysis, counterfactual argument, the establishment of generalizations, and causal explanation.

WHAT IS HISTORY?

Strictly speaking, almost all data[1] are 'historical'. That is to say, by the time they arrive in the researcher's notes or on her computer they already refer to a world that has changed since yesterday and is continually changing. However, when the historical aspect of data is emphasized it is normally because they refer to a set of social arrangements that are so far removed in time from the present – and because so much change has occurred since 'then' – that important aspects of this 'other time' seem unfamiliar to us; they have to be discovered through historical research.[2]

Human beings shape and are shaped by history. The historical analyst is, unavoidably, 'within' history. The deepest source of the impulse to study history is the desire to understand ourselves. The previous three sentences use the term 'history' in two ways. The term 'history' sometimes refers to the process of change through time ('things happening'), and at other times it refers to the analysis of that process of change ('explaining, interpreting and understanding what has happened').[3] The complexity of the analyst's situation is suggested in Table 7.1. This table indicates certain relationships between historical occurrences, historical evidence and historical analysis, including two feedback loops.[4]

Each of these four aspects of history and/or historical analysis requires comment. Turning to the first aspect (A in Table 7.1), history as 'the occurrence through past time of events and processes within social relationships and social structures' encompasses two things. One of these is change within a *specific instance* of a type of relationship or structure – for example, change within a particular family as the children move through successive life-cycle stages. The other is change within a *particular kind* of relationship or structure – for example, change within the institution of the family as women acquire more rights and the balance of power becomes less favourable to males.

One example of a book that very successfully moves between histories of specific families and the history of kinship as an institution, particularly among the English middle

Table 7.1   *Four dimensions of history*

A. Historical occurrences	The *occurrence* through past time of events and processes within social relationships and social structures.
B. Historical evidence	*Recorded evidence* of the occurrence through past time of events and processes within social relationships and social structures. This may be, for example, written, oral or visual.
C. Historical analysis	The *analysis* of events and processes occurring through past time within social relationships and social structures.
D. Investigation of feedback loops	Investigation of *feedback loops* from historical analysis to (i) historical occurrences and (ii) historical evidence.

class in the late eighteenth and early ninteteenth centuries, is *Family Fortunes* (Davidoff and Hall, 1987). The book contains a series of richly detailed accounts of the fortunes of families such as the Cadburys, Quaker retailers and manufacturers, the Constables, Anglican corn factors,[5] the Courtaulds, Unitarian silk manufacturers, the Galtons, Quaker manufacturers and bankers, the Hills, Unitarian school proprietors, the Pattissons, Anglican lawyers, and the Ransomes, Quaker iron manufacturers. Interwoven with these highly specific accounts is a more general account of the way gender and class became articulated in the early phase of urban industrialization in English society. As the authors put it, 'the men and women of the provincial middle class adopted distinctively different class identities, … the language of class formation was gendered'. The richness of the individual case studies allows them to identify contradictions in the identities adopted, as expressed in the gendered language used. For example, some men grew to 'fear the latent power of domesticated women, yet there was also concern that domesticity was too important to be left in the hands of weak subordinates' (Davidoff and Hall, 1987: 451).

With respect to the second aspect (B in Table 7.1), that of historical evidence, this may be written down, for example in the form of letters, diaries, memoranda, reports, lists, guidebooks, advertising material and press reportage. It may be visual, including film, video and surviving art, arte-facts and architecture. It may also be oral, in the form of folksongs, an oral tradition, or interviews recorded either by a historian or someone else. One advantage of oral testimony taken directly by the researcher is that she can, so to speak, cross-question the witness. Another advantage is that many other clues, for example

tone of voice and body language, provide additional information that is not available from written testimony. A third advantage is that a witness may provide information in a conversation that would not otherwise be committed to permanent record, for example, about the character or behaviour of key officials within bureaucracies.[6]

However, in whatever form the evidence presents itself, the researcher needs to have as clear and accurate an idea as possible of the circumstances in which it was produced; a forced confession, for example, has a different significance from a memoir written as an act of choice. In every case, it is important to know who produced the material being treated as evidence, where they were located within the society concerned, who was their intended audience (e.g., friends, superiors within an organization, potential political supporters, posterity) and what their intentions were in producing the material. When using reports in a newspaper, for example, it is important to understand whether the proprietor has an identifiable political agenda and, if so, whether the topic being reported is relevant to that agenda.

With respect to the third aspect (C in Table 7.1), a distinction should be made between two analytical tasks. One is to provide an exegesis of the situational logic that explains the multiple intersecting chains of events that have occurred in a particular society during a particular time period. This involves not only assessing the subjective perceptions of the key actors involved – which affect the choices they make – but also identifying the objective constraints and possibilities inscribed in the specific conjunctures of structures and processes within which their lives were embedded. E.P. Thompson (1963) provides a good example of this approach in his classic work *The Making of the English Working Class.*

The second task, equally challenging, is to search for evidence that indicates the existence of social mechanisms that operate in more than one historical context (e.g., the putative tendency for oligopolies or monopolies to emerge within markets). More ambitious is the search for empirical generalizations with respect to similarities between social structures (such as cities and states) and social processes (such as urbanization and democratization) in a plurality of cases. In some cases, these empirical generalizations provide the basis for general statements that have a causal character. These general statements may take a strong form ('the existence or occurrence of X and Y causes Z to happen') or a weaker form ('when conditions X and Y are in existence, this strengthens the likelihood that Z will happen'). An example of an analysis concerned with the strong form is *States and Social Revolutions* (Skocpol, 1979b).

One way to sum up the difference between the two tasks for historical analysis just outlined is as follows. The first task is to discover 'what happened' in particular times and places; the second task is to discover 'what happens' under certain conditions, whenever they occur. An example of the first is *The Abolition of Feudalism* (Markoff, 1996). In this book, Markoff provides a plausible account of the process whereby – in a particular time and place – Parisian legislators and the peasantry throughout France turned their passion and their reforming zeal against the seigneurial system which sustained the privileged lifestyle of the nobility. He points out that there was nothing preordained or inevitable about the anti-seigneurialism of the French Revolution. It was a product of the revolutionary process as it worked itself out between 1788 and 1793 – in particular, an outcome of the way peasants and legislators reacted to each other.[7]

An example of the second approach is Barrington Moore's *Social Origins of Dictatorship and Democracy* (Moore, 1966). This is a comparative study of the violent forms taken by modernization between the seventeenth and twentieth centuries in Britain, France, the United States, India, China and Japan. Like Markoff, Moore is concerned with achieving an understanding of the causes of violent social change. However, Moore looks at several examples of societies undergoing such change and tries to find systematic differences between them as well as common threads running through the different cases.[8] He uses the information just identified in order to build empirical generalizations about typical patterns of social change. In other words, he begins with specific examples of *what happened* in particular places at particular times (e.g., France in the 1780s and 1790s) and works his way towards generalizations about *what happens* when particular kinds of social structure are subjected to particular kinds of pressure.[9]

So far, reference has been made to three aspects of history. At first sight, they appear to be related in a straightforward way, i.e., historical occurrences (A in Table 7.1) generate historical evidence (B) which is then subject to historical analysis (C). However, there is a fourth aspect, which is the existence of two feedback loops (D).

One feedback loop is from historical analysis to historical evidence. The investigative impulse that leads to a search for evidence is prompted by some form of 'puzzlement': by a curiosity that needs satisfying, a problem that needs 'solving' or a theory that needs 'testing'. It is easy to forget that the historical data collected for analysis are defined as 'relevant' by the form of puzzlement that exists in the researcher's head. In that sense data are always collected from a particular perspective. For example, a researcher with a specific interest in the supposed preconditions for democracy within societies (stemming, perhaps, from a desire to encourage its appearance) may be in danger of perceiving those supposed preconditions where they do not exist or of exaggerating their strength where they do exist.

An important source of the historian's puzzlement is the desire to have a plausible account of some aspect of the 'here and now' he or she occupies: how is that 'here and now' distinctive and why does it have the character it does? The historian looks to the past for answers to these questions.[10] To put it another way, we undertake historical analysis because of the desire to understand ourselves.[11] A problem arises in that our sense of identity is, potentially, at risk from findings that contradict our self-image. There is a very large danger of succumbing to wish-fulfilment, in other words, 'discovering' in history exactly the answer the researchers wanted and which was already in their minds when they started their inquiry. Because of this one of the main challenges facing historians is the need to preserve objectivity.[12]

The other feedback loop is less obvious. It stems from the fact that many participants in the events and processes historians study conduct their own historical analyses of the recent or distant past and try to feed conclusions drawn from these analyses into contemporary debate and action. To take some prominent examples, *The Communist Manifesto* (Marx and Engels, 2002) and *Mein Kampf* (Hitler, 1992) both contained analyses of recent European history and drew political conclusions that implied the need for violent action by the intended audiences of those works.

Continual dialogue is under way within the societies that historians study.[13] This dialogue concerns the direction that those societies, or particular aspects of them (e.g., a specific family, business, political party, ruling regime, or football team), have taken in the past and whether or how that direction should be altered in the future. Historians and historical sociologists are part of this dialogue.

Faced with the complexity that has just been set out, how do those who wish to analyse it react? One reaction is to focus upon achieving detailed accounts of complex, unique and contingent entities without attempting to make wider generalizations. This approach was criticized by Edgar Kiser and Michael Hechter (1991) who argued the need to reintroduce general theories into historical sociology. However, they have, in turn, been criticized for placing too great an emphasis upon a form of theory – rational choice – that is itself 'ahistorical' (Calhoun, 1998: 860). Critics such as Craig Calhoun prefer theory that is 'about the shape of history, its disjunctures as well as its continuities, and … self-conscious about its own historical specificity and that of the phenomena it studies' (1998: 868).[14] A similar approach is taken by the present author.[15]

However, the present scene is a highly disparate one, summarized as follows by the editors of a recent collection of essays on new methods in social history:

> Seemingly in reaction to the grandiose explanatory claims of some behaviorists and positivists, many historians increasingly turn to Geertzian-style[16] symbolic and interpretative anthropology for inspiration and, more recently, to postmodern and linguistic constructions of history's project. In the process, cultural explanation often has been cleaved from causal explanation, and indifference to formal social science has, in many important historical

circles at least, given way to profound skepticism about its power to elucidate. (Griffin and van der Linden, 1998: 6)

The present chapter is not written in any spirit of wishing to turn back this tide of interpretative and linguistic approach but rather with the desire to take stock of some other approaches which also make a contribution to the task of bringing order into the dense complexity confronted by historians and historical sociologists. These will be considered under four headings: time and periodization; spatiality and networks; analysing events; and making comparisons.

TIME AND PERIODIZATION

Isaac and Griffin (1989) have criticized many common practices in the use of time-series data in the field of US labour history.[17] They examined a large number of such studies and found three prevalent weaknesses. One was the separation of history from theory. In other words, according to this view, history is a storehouse of data with which to test theories that are developed before the encounter with historical data occurs: 'This practice begins with the abstract (the "theoretical") and then confronts time-ordered data on the past (the "historical") in order to validate or falsify theoretical statements' (Isaac and Griffin, 1989: 875). They give the example of population-ecology approaches to trade union organization (e.g., Hannan and Freeman, 1987) whose concepts are 'generally grounded in the general, ahistorical postulates of organizational demography rather than in the concrete history of trade unions' (Isaac and Griffin, 1989: 875).

A second weakness found by Isaac and Griffin is what they call 'ahistorical time' (1989: 875), in other words, a view of time as a linear organizing device for data. This results in a forced homogenization of time that suppresses crucial 'turning points' such as war, peace, depression and significant legislation. A third weakness was a preoccupation with technique and the demands of particular statistical practices at the expense of other requirements: for example, 'the theory of technique may limit or even preclude the examination and explanation of historical conditioning requiring analysis over much shorter periods of time' (1989: 877) which may be less convenient in statistical terms.

Isaac and Griffin present an alternative approach which they illustrate through an examination of the simple bivariate relationship between changes in strike frequency and three indicators of 'union viability' which are growth in membership, the number of unions founded or disbanded between 1882 and 1980. Their analysis is a correlational variant of moving regressions which they explain as follows:

> In 'moving regressions' a time-series regression model is fitted to a portion of the entire [data] series; the estimation is then 'moved' along the series, so that the next regression is based on another segment of data differing from the preceding one only by a few data points, often those immediately preceding and/or following the original data segment. (Isaac and Griffin, 1989: 879)

Issues relating to periodization are also explored by Jeffrey Haydu (1998), who is interested both in the logic of comparing time periods and the merits of narrative – and especially path dependency analysis – as a means of establishing and explaining connections between events in different periods. With respect to the first issue, Haydu adopts the distinction between generalizing and individualizing styles of comparative sociology. Generalizing comparisons which seek to establish causal arguments involves, he argues, a bias against taking into account a wide range of historical particulars relevant to each case. It also has to take into account the fact, pointed out by Sewell (1996), that the more independent two cases are with respect to each other, the less likely are they to be equivalent – and vice versa. This is a problem when one methodological desideratum in comparison is that any two cases should be both equivalent (so that the comparison is of like with like) and independent of each other (so as to eliminate mutual influence between them).

Individualizing accounts, which aim to highlight the distinctive features of each period, face the challenge of accounting for the differences they identify. The work of writers such as Bendix (1974) and Lamont (1992) illustrates the point that in order to construct such explanations the writers concerned have to introduce data and ideas from outside the case studies themselves. This chapter will return to issues of comparison later. However, the most interesting aspect of Haydu (1998) is his discussion of narratives, paths and problem-solving.

Haydu makes distinctions between three ways of analysing sequences of events within and across time periods.[18] The first way is the elaboration of a narrative that organizes events into a story with characters, a plot, a beginning, a middle and an end. This leaves still to be solved the problem of identifying the mechanisms through which earlier and later events are linked. This problem may be tackled through path dependency analysis. In other words, choices or conditions may be identified at particular points along a chain of events that foreclose options and 'steer' history in a particular direction. An example of this kind of analysis is the argument about the 'second industrial divide' made by Piore and Sabel (1984), who discuss the implications of the choice made by American business in the nineteenth century for mass production rather than flexible specialization.

Haydu proposes to move 'beyond' path dependency towards a 'problem-solving approach', in other words, one that pays attention to the ways in which outcomes at particular switch points (where individuals and groups make decisive choices) are themselves 'products of the past rather than historical accidents'. One implication of such a framework is that it is possible to see that 'solutions' adopted at one time may embody 'contradictions that generate later crises' and that they may also generate 'tools and understandings' (Haydu, 1998: 354) which subsequent actors may inherit and employ to cope with later crises. Haydu's approach does not assume that actors make 'rational' choices. He accepts that 'their definitions need not be accurate, their solutions calculated, or their actions instrumental' (1998: 355). What counts is their definitions of the situation, the ways these interact with those of other actors, and the objective pressures and opportunities that provide the context in which decisions are made.[19]

SPATIALITY AND NETWORKS

When we turn from time to space as a framing concept, there are some distinguished exemplars including the work of Ferdinand Braudel (1972) on the Mediterranean and D.W. Meinig (1988, 1993, 1999) on the shaping of America. However, Deane et al. (1998: 57) are broadly justified in their assertion that '"space" rarely enters historical discourse as an analytical construct'. They provide a useful guide to some of the payoffs that may come from the use of spatial-effects models.

Deane et al. are especially interested in patterns of geographical clustering where it can be shown that the occurrence of events such as crimes or religious activity in one locale is causally related to events in another location (and not simply an expression of shared social and economic characteristics).[20] The authors examine diffusion processes whereby spatial effects spread over time and space. This includes relatively modest local 'spillover' effects as well as more rapid and widespread processes which have some similarities to patterns of contagion or epidemics. Spatial effects of this kind may have positive effects, increasing the likelihood of like events occurring elsewhere, or negative effects, reducing that likelihood.

Analysis of such processes is based upon examination of a patterned distribution of a relevant variable 'or, better yet, the model errors (residuals) from a regression of this variable on a set of variables that are thought to be predictive of the outcome, or dependent, variable' (Deane et al., 1998: 60). The model of social diffusion used by the authors relies heavily, as they state, upon an analogy with the spread of contagious disease as discussed in the public health literature. In other words, the researcher is alert to the possibility of a 'contagion' spreading as a result of contact between 'infected' carriers and a population of 'susceptibles' who are open to influence (or 'infection') from carriers. The way a contagion spreads is affected by 'the density of infecteds, the density of susceptibles, the extent of contact between the two groups, and the virulence of the disease (the probability that a carrier will infect a susceptible when a contact is made)' (1998: 61).[21]

Contagion models, like other types of collective behaviour models, ideally require repeated observations at short time intervals. This is often difficult to achieve in practice, and it is often the case that the researcher has to be satisfied with a very small number of 'snapshots' of the relevant spatial clusters. In analysing these snapshots it is possible to identify departures from randomness which may be interpreted as the effects of diffusion processes whose magnitude and direction may be investigated using a spatial-effects regression model and suitable computer software.

Deane et al. illustrate their analytical technique[22] using two case studies. One relates to the expansion of church membership in the United States during the early twentieth century. They found a pattern of spatial diffusion that was consistent with the established history of revivalism. In other words, rates of diffusion were high both in counties with low rates of church membership (where there were many 'susceptibles') and in counties with high rates of church membership which were 'vulnerable to strong imitative/ conformity processes when surrounded by other counties with high adherence rates' (1998: 72). The other case study relates to patterns of lynching behaviour in the American South during the late nineteenth and early twentieth centuries. Here the application of spatial-effects regressions showed that if a lynching incident occurred in a particular county it actually lessened the likelihood of a similar incident occurring in nearby counties. They describe this as a 'negative spillover effect', suggesting that such incidents produced 'a "satisfied" white population, an intimidated black population, or both causal mechanisms' (1998: 73).

Spatiality is one dimension of the analysis of elite networks carried out by John F. Padgett and Christopher K. Ansell in their study of the rise of the Medici in early fifteenth-century Florence (Padgett and Ansell, 1993).[23] Their theme is the struggle for control of that city. Building on the work of Dale Kent,[24] they coded a core network data set with information on the following types of relation between Florentine elite families: intermarriage ties, trading or business ties, joint ownership or partnerships, bank employment, real estate ties, personal loans, patronage links, bonds of personal friendship, and surety ties. These network data were supplemented with attributional data from many sources relating to economic wealth, family social status,[25] level of tax assessment, and (not to forget the spatial element) neighbourhood residence within Florence. Using block-modelling methods, the authors identify clusters of correlations that identify a number of Medicean and non-Medicean blocks containing identifiable families, a few of which have split loyalties.[26]

Padgett and Ansell use their evidence to explain why Cosimo de' Medici found it effective to adopt a political style which they describe as 'robust action' (1993: 1263), a phrase which conveys the idea of speech and behaviour which are sphinx-like, multivocal, flexible and opportunistic. One interesting discovery they make is that the Medicean social network and those of the oligarchies that opposed them in Florentine society were broadly similar in social composition. This was a surprise since contemporaries and later historians had tended to label the Medici as leaders of the economically rising 'new men' in Florence. In fact, there was a slight bias towards economic linkages with rising trading families in the case of the Medici but they were, ironically, even more snobbish than their oligarchic opponents when it came to marriage ties. In sum, 'The Medici's distinctiveness within the elite ... was not that they represented new men [but] ... that they associated with them at all' (1993: 1284).

It is impossible to summarize all aspects of a complex and fascinating paper, but one other finding will be mentioned. Padgett and Ansell show that networks among the opponents of the Medici were densely interconnected. This produced complex crosspressures that inhibited united collective action. By contrast, the Medici party was 'an extraordinarily centralized, and simple, "star" or "spoke" network system, with very few relations among Medici followers' (1993: 1278). Since the Medici were the main factor holding the network together, this gave a high degree of strategic control. This was shown during the showdown between the Medici and their opponents in 1433 when the latter attempted to assemble their supporters in a particular piazza with a view to seizing control of the town hall. Only a proportion turned up and immediately began debating about the next move: 'a stochastic threshold equilibrium ensued, in which repeated efforts ... to assemble more troops ... were offset by other supporters' changing their mind and drifting away' (1993: 1279). Meanwhile, the Medici immediately and decisively mobilized their supporters, won the overwhelming support of the populace at large, and managed to secure the exile of their enemies.

ANALYSING EVENTS

The attempt by the Medici's opponents to seize power in Florence would be a prime candidate for analysis using yet another technique, event-structure analysis. This is expounded by Larry J. Griffin in a paper which focuses on a lynching that took place in Bolivar County, Mississippi, in 1930

(Griffin, 1993). Griffin's fundamental premise is that sociological explanation of such incidents 'requires that events and their contexts be openly theorized, factual material abstracted and generalized, and the causal connections between narrative sequences established in a way that can be explicitly replicated and criticized' (1993: 1100).[27]

Event-structure analysis requires the use of any relevant knowledge about general types of causal relationships of which the particular case being analysed provides a specific instance. For example, it is well established that during the 1930s in Mississippi, when a crowd of white men went in search of an African-American believed to be a murderer, they normally had the intention of lynching that person. That being so, there are grounds for asserting that – in the case analysed by Griffin – a police officer who did not intervene to stop such a crowd going about their business in that particular instance played a part in causing the death by lynching that subsequently occurred.

One way of seeking out or testing such general causal propositions is through the technique of counterfactual analysis. This involves asking how a change in specific antecedent conditions might or would have influenced subsequent events, producing a different outcome from the one that actually happened. Typically, counterfactual analysis involves drawing upon the researcher's stock of general causal knowledge and intermingling it with the particular facts of a specific case, also referring to other events similar in key respects but different in others.[28]

Griffin (1993: 1104) makes the crucial point that causal interpretations are 'built, brick by brick, by answering factual and counterfactual questions about historical sequences'.[29] Technology provides a potential adjunct to this process. Griffin pays particular attention to the event-structure analysis program (ETHNO) developed by David Heise (1988, 1989). By posing a series of questions about the narrative account offered by the researcher, this program encourages the analyst to replace 'temporal order' as an organizing principle with her 'expert judgement or knowledge' (Griffin, 1993: 1105) about the kind of causal connections involved. The revised account is then tested for its logical consistency. The programme does not provide 'answers' but asks systematic and rigorous questions whose object is to 'relentlessly probe the analyst's construction and comprehension of the event' and forcing her to be 'precise and meticulous' (1993: 1108).

Another computer-aided approach to analysing events is offered by Roberto Franzosi. In his account of the uses of 'narrative as data' (Franzosi, 1998), Franzosi offers an innovative strategy for studying conflict. He is particularly interested in the years between 1919 and 1922 which saw the rise of Italian Fascism. As a database he had some 15 000 newspaper articles (mainly from *Il Lavoro*, a socialist newspaper[30]) covering this period, which saw widespread labour mobilization, a factory occupation movement and, in 1922, Mussolini's takeover of power. He wants to know why the workers' movement grew strong and then fell away: 'Did workers' mobilization abate because they obtained what they were after? Or was such an impressive movement harshly repressed? … What was the movement all about? Who was involved? What were their actions?' (1998: 91).

Franzosi found that official strike statistics, while being readily available, provided little information about what employers, the state and other social groups were doing during periods of high mobilization. Instead, he turned to the narratives of the newspaper articles and police reports. Franzosi's contribution was to develop an approach to content analysis that used a coding scheme that was not dependent on the investigator's theoretical interests but '*on the inherent linguistic properties of the text itself*' (1998: 98; emphasis in original). This was based upon the application of a 'semantic grammar' expressed in terms of the basic pattern of subject–action–object and the relevant modifiers related to time, space, the demands of action, and the number, organization and type of subjects and objects.

This approach has many attractions. It focuses attention upon agency. Semantic grammar's mathematical underpinning lies in set theory, which is well adapted to relational database systems and therefore susceptible to computer-based storage and manipulation. The coded text retains much of the structure and texture of the original narrative. Finally, semantic grammar is suited to new tools of data analysis such as network models. In practical terms, it is possible to generate many network graphs indicating on the basis of very rich data which were the main actors in various spheres of action, who was initiating action and with respect to whom it was

oriented. Furthermore, it is possible to trace shifts in the patterns revealed by these graphs from one year to the next. In this way, as Franzosi (1998: 86) puts it, 'semantic grammars can achieve quality without sacrificing quantity'.

MAKING COMPARISONS

The final area explored is the methodology of comparison, and in this respect it is important to mention Charles Ragin's exploration of the logic of what he calls 'qualitative comparative analysis' or QCA (Ragin, 1998).[31] Ragin begins by noting the dilemma faced by sociologists who frequently find themselves having to choose between carrying out detailed studies of the complexities of a small number of cases and looking for general patterns that may be discerned within a large number of cases, none of which may be studied in any great depth.

Ragin (1998: 107) offers 'a middle path' based on the use of a 'configurational approach' involving the analysis of 'cross-case patterns'. The object of this exercise is to carry out holistic comparisons of cases as configurations and draw out their patterned similarities and differences. QCA is

> based on Boolean algebra, the algebra of logic and sets. [It] treats social scientific categories as sets and views cases in terms of their multiple memberships. … Each case is viewed as a member of multiple sets, and membership *combinations* are compared and contrasted to identify decisive patterns of similarity and difference, which in turn provides the basis for constructing causal arguments.

This permits analysis of 'multiple conjectural causation' (1998: 108), with no single cause being either sufficient or necessary.

This mode of analysis can be used to tackle an issue such as that expressed in the question as to what 'different configurations of conditions are relevant to ethnic mobilization among territorially-based linguistic minorities in Western Europe' (1998: 109–10). Faced with such a question, the 'researcher conducts an elaborate dialogue of ideas and evidence' and is likely to discover that 'perfect consistency in outcomes for the cases with the same combination of causal conditions is rare' (1998: 112). Such findings encourage the use of probabilistic modes of reasoning where appropriate (see Ragin, 1998: 115–21).

Charles Tilly (1984) provides a useful typology of approaches to comparative analysis. First, there are individualizing comparisons – as carried out by, for example, Max Weber (1988) and Otto Hintze (1973) – which attempt to isolate characteristics that are specific to particular instances. Reinhard Bendix adopts this approach. Tilly (1984: 96) comments: 'As a way of theorizing, and of illustrating theory, it works very well. As a way of testing a theory's validity, however, it leaves a great deal to be desired.' A second type consists of universalizing comparisons that attempt to identify common properties shared by all instances of a phenomenon. Tilly's chief example is the work of Theda Skocpol, who identifies a number of preconditions for social revolutions such as those that occurred in France (1789), Russia (1917) and China (1949).

Thirdly, there are encompassing comparisons which attempt to locate particular cases within larger structures and processes. Immanuel Wallerstein (1974, 1980, 1989) adopts this approach in his analyses of world systems (see also Smith, 1991: 95–104). Tilly points out that this is a difficult approach to implement and is vulnerable to functionalist oversimplification. However, he admires the attempts made by Stein Rokkan (1970) to practise this mode. Finally, there are variation-finding comparisons that seek a principle of variation within a specific phenomenon by systematically examining differences among instances. This very challenging mode requires very careful specification of the phenomena to be compared and clear methods of measurement. Barrington Moore is the author chosen by Tilly to illustrate this approach, although Tilly notes that Moore uses individualizing comparisons as well.[32]

As already noted, Barrington Moore's classic work is *Social Origins of Dictatorship and Democracy* (Moore, 1966)[33] which deals with six major cases (England, France, USA, India, China and Japan) and makes significant references to at least two more (Germany and Russia).[34] It is worth devoting some attention to this classic work since it shows how a particular author draws together a number of the issues raised in previous sections of this chapter. In particular, we may observe how he deals with the *interrelationships* between the investigation of particular cases, the use of comparative analysis, counterfactual argument, the establishment of generalizations, and causal explanation.

LEARNING FROM A CLASSIC

There are a number of factors that Moore treats as relevant to all of his case studies and so susceptible to comparative analysis. They include: the degree of strength possessed by commercializing tendencies favouring capitalist groups benefiting from the operation of the market in town and countryside; the degree to which the forms of commercialized agriculture adopted by the landowning upper classes depended on the backing of a repressive political apparatus; and the degree to which the structure of peasant society facilitated coordinated resistance from below to exploitation and repression.

As is well known, according to Moore, the democratic route (England, France, USA) is characterized by the predominance of strong commercializing tendencies, encompassing the emergence of powerful bourgeois interests. In the case of the route leading to Fascism (Japan, Germany), countervailing pressures from capitalist groups are insufficient to offset the political consequences of a labour-repressive form of agriculture backed by strong political controls, while peasant social structure is not conducive to effective resistance. In the case of the route leading to Communism (China, Russia), commercializing tendencies are very weak, while labour-repressive forms of agricultural exploitation are ineffective either to resist the impact of an existing rebellious peasant solidarity (Russia) or prevent its subsequent growth (China).

Moore was not attempting to identify a distinctive set of causes appropriate to each of the three routes to the modern world that he identifies. Instead, his causal analyses are directed to the explanation of concrete structural transformations within specific societies (particularly civil wars, revolutions, etc.). These analyses differ greatly among societies within the same route. This is very obvious when England, France, and the USA are compared. It is also evident when comparing the very different ways in which peasant revolution was brought about in Russia and China: in the case of Russia, rebellious peasant solidarity contributed greatly to the collapse of the Tsarist empire; and in the case of China, the empire disintegrated without much help from an atomistic and internally divided peasantry. The Chinese Communists had to forge a new solidarity among the rural labour force.

Moore does not attempt to iron out such differences in causal sequence. His routes are distinguished from one another not by sets of *causes* but by sets of *consequences* or outcomes. More specifically: a strong bourgeoisie that exercises the lion's share of political power is the outcome favourable to democracy; the Fascist form, whose values are an inversion of democratic ideology, is the expression of a dominant state, permeated with an agrarian upper-class tradition, engaged in incorporating the subordinate industrial classes within the polity; and the Communist form, made possible by the eradication of the aristocracy, incorporates peasants and workers within an authoritarian polity legitimated in terms of a freedom supposedly 'higher' than that offered by democracy.

Each route is characterized by a specific set of structural outcomes (and moral consequences) rather than by a specific set of causal antecedents, and the routes are located within a (largely implicit) dichotomous scheme distinguishing between democratic outcomes and non-democratic outcomes (dictatorship).

Comparative analysis, generalization, and causal explanation have a subtle and complex interrelationship in *Social Origins*, best expounded by means of illustration. For example, the third part of *Social Origins* contains a number of generalizations at which Moore arrives on the basis of comparisons drawn from the case studies in the first two parts of the book. Broadly speaking, these generalizations refer to two aspects of social structures (especially class relationships): the range of variation they manifest at a given stage of social development; and the propensity of each variant to foster specific kinds of political arrangement.

To give one instance of this argument, Moore identifies a range of variation in agrarian societies with respect to the relationship of the landed upper class to the monarchy, the form of commercial exploitation of agriculture by the aristocracy, and the relationship between the latter class and the urban bourgeoisie. For each variable he identifies conditions that are favourable or unfavourable to democratic outcomes. Moore sometimes uses comparisons to support generalizations within the particular case studies. Thus, for example, Moore argues that forms of feudalism with substantial bureaucratic elements were conducive to authoritarian modernization. This structural inheritance was common

to both Germany and Japan. In this respect they are unlike England, France and the USA, where feudalism was overcome or absent. In those societies, modernization took place early and under democratic auspices. Germany and Japan also differ from both Russia and China since those societies were agrarian bureaucracies with relatively few feudal elements.

Moore also uses comparison in another way. He may indicate that a specific society has unique characteristics that are significant because they exclude from it other characteristics about which he is able to generalize on a comparative basis. The logic of this is: the presence of characteristic X (unique to that society) means that characteristic Y (common to some other societies) is absent. For example: 'The special character of the Japanese feudal bond, with its much greater emphasis on status and military loyalty than on a freely chosen contractual relationship, meant that one source of the impetus behind the Western variety of free institutions was absent.'

Moore employs comparisons in at least two other ways in the case studies. A proposed generalization that appears at first sight to explain a specific case may be shown through comparative analysis to be inaccurate. For example, as he writes:

> One might start with a general notion to the effect that there is an inherent conflict between slavery and the capitalist system of formally free wage labor. Though this turns out to be a crucial part of the story [of the American Civil War], it will not do as a general proposition from which the Civil War can be derived as an instance. (1966: 114)

Moore brilliantly shows not only that capitalists in the Northern states and in England were quite prepared to cooperate with Southern slavery but also that in nineteenth-century Germany advanced industry had coexisted very well with a form of agriculture based on a highly repressive labour system. In other words, Moore shifts the terms of the question. Instead of applying a particular general proposition (crudely, 'slave' societies and 'free' societies must fight) to an exemplary instance (the United States) he sees his task as that of discovering the unique circumstances that made the United States an exception to the contrary general proposition ('slave' societies and 'free' societies can cooperate quite easily in many cases). As Moore (1966: 114) puts it: 'Special historical circumstances … had to be present in order to prevent agreement between an agrarian society based on unfree labor and a rising industrial capitalism'.

Comparative analysis is also used to produce evidence relevant to counterfactual argument. For example, would it have been possible in imperial China for one section of society to detach itself from the rest, take over government, and launch a conservative version of modernization? Moore (1966: 251–2) answers that:

If that had happened, historians might now be stressing the similarities between China and Japan rather than the differences … No flat answer is possible. Yet important factors were against it … [For example,] in China's premodern society and culture there was little or no basis out of which a militarist patriotism of the Japanese type could grow. In comparison with Japan, the reactionary nationalism of Chiang Kai-shek seems thin and watery. Only when China began to make over her institutions in the communist image did a strong sense of mission appear.

So far, we have seen how Moore deploys comparative analysis as a means of both sustaining and dismissing specific generalizations. However, Moore is also as interested in those characteristics of particular societies that are unique as he is in those that they share with other cases. For example, according to his analysis (conducted in the 1960s, it must be recalled), India's apparent failure to follow England, France and the United States in combining economic modernization with democracy provides a negative illustration of the tragic (or ironic) conclusion that the democratic route to modern society was a unique historical sequence that was probably already complete.

To summarize the argument and express it slightly differently, in *Social Origins* (and elsewhere) Moore uses comparative analysis mainly in two ways. First, he uses comparisons to test and, if necessary, reject causal explanations that depend on generalizations to explain specific cases. For example, at one point he considers the suggestion that within a polity the opposing interests of industrialists exploiting a formally free labour force and great landowners with a servile labour force will lead to violent conflict between them, as in the American Civil War. He responds to this by citing, as a contrary example, the peaceful accommodation between Junkers and the urban bourgeoisie that

occurred in nineteenth-century Germany (Moore, 1966: 114–15). In other words, he undermines the generalization being tested by showing that similar antecedents may be associated with different outcomes. Another way in which Moore uses comparative analysis is to arrive at generalizations with respect to (i) the range of variation possible within a given type of social structure or social process and (ii) the propensity for change in a particular direction associated with each variant. This is the core strategy of *Social Origins*.

These different uses of comparative method are explicitly acknowledged by Moore in the preface to *Social Origins* when he writes that 'Comparisons can serve as a rough negative check on accepted historical explanations. And a comparative approach may lead to new historical generalizations.' At the end of this paragraph, he adds: 'That comparative analysis is no substitute for detailed investigation of specific cases is obvious' (Moore, 1966: x–xi).

As far as Moore is concerned, comparative analysis and the detailed examination of specific cases are *equally* necessary. Explanation of specific social upheavals, such as a particular revolution, requires detailed examination of the actions and reactions of specific groups and strategically located individuals whose behaviour is intrinsic to the processes of structural change. It also allows close attention to be given to the way those actions and reactions are constrained by social structure. Human agency working through or tending to modify structure; the confining or facilitation of action by structure – this interplay requires careful narrative presentation. However, knowing a great deal about a specific civil war or revolution will not, by itself, tell you what might have happened as opposed to what did. Nor will it allow you to assess the relative significance of various antecedent structural tendencies.

Comparative analysis may help to identify a range of structural possibilities in a given type of society and work out the dilemmas and tendencies for change associated with each. It may also provide the researcher with a basis for discarding certain potential generalizations that would otherwise, if true, provide sufficient explanations of a series of specific instances. Comparative analysis might also suggest that, in combination, a certain set of structural tendencies, if found within a particular society, would strongly predispose it toward development in a certain direction and make other possibilities highly unlikely. Moore's (1966: 413ff.) discussion of tendencies favourable to the growth of parliamentary democracy at the end of *Social Origins* is an analysis of this kind.

CONCLUDING REMARKS

In this chapter it has been necessary to be highly selective in dealing with issues raised under the heading of historical analysis. The focus has been upon a number of techniques for collecting and manipulating historical data. Having placed that process in the broader context of historical inquiry – including the relationship between historical occurrences, historical evidence, historical analysis and some key feedback loops between them – the chapter went on to examine a number of specific issues and techniques, namely time and periodization, spatiality and networks, analyzing events, and making comparisons. Finally, attention was paid to the methodological strategies adopted by Barrington Moore, especially his approaches to the investigation of particular cases, the use of comparative analysis, counterfactual argument, the establishment of generalizations, and causal explanation.

The example of Moore is pertinent because he always ensured that issues relating to the selection of methodology were subordinated to the questions that inspired the process of historical inquiry in the first place. Methodology is, for some, a fascinating subject in itself. The very process of inquiry has its own allure. There is a temptation to begin with the thought 'I have a wonderful technique for measuring things. Let us go out and measure!' The particular potentialities and limitations of the researcher's methodology (especially the technologies and techniques upon which it is based) may begin to shape her definition of what is problematic about the world. Moore provides an example of a better approach, which is to begin with a problem about how the world works or has become the way it is – for example, 'what are the social origins of democracy?' or 'what part does violence play in social change?' – and then search for an appropriate methodology and relevant techniques with which to gather data which will be relevant to tackling those problems. Fortunately, that lesson has been well learned by the historians and historical sociologists whose work is cited in this chapter.[35]

NOTES

1 The word 'data' literally means 'that (or those) which is (are) given' although, as Joe Banks, my old colleague in the Leicester University Sociology Department, used to say, the proper word should be 'capta' since 'facts' or pieces of information are 'taken' from the world by the researcher (or somebody else) who made an active effort to produce them. Data are not lying around with a large label on them marked 'relevant information'. It is the researcher who defines what is relevant – or who accepts the definitions of relevance provided by others.

2 One of the strengths of a writer such as Foucault is that he is able to evoke in his readers a sense of 'unfamiliarity' about their own present, their here-and-now.

3 See, for example, Abrams (1982), Bloch (1954), Burke (1992), Pomper et al. (1998), Smith (1982b), Stern (1963) and Tosh (1984).

4 For discussions of the philosophy of historical analysis and social science in general, see Callinicos (1995), Collingwood (1946), Fisher (1970), Hollis (1994), Lloyd (1986, 1993), Runciman (1987) and Stanford (1986).

5 The artist John Constable came from this family.

6 See, for example, Seldon and Pappworth (1983) and Thompson (1978).

7 A closely-related text is *Revolutionary Demands. A Content Analysis of the Cahiers de Doléances of 1789* (Shapiro and Markoff, 1998) which analyses the complaints made against the French *ancien régime* in 1789.

8 Originally published in 1966, *Social Origins* went through several subsequent editions. This book continues to be enormously influential, as is shown by the volume of critical essays edited by Skocpol et al. (1998).

9 For previous discussions of Moore, upon which the present text partly draws, see Smith (1983, 1984a, 1984b, 1991).

10 For interesting discussions on the role of memory see, for example, Butler (1989), Kammen (1997) and Le Goff (1992).

11 However, this certainly does not imply that all history is concerned with national identity. There are many ways of saying 'we'. The tremendous vogue for genealogical research – tracing ancestors back through time – shows the great interest many people have in their identity as members of a family. There are associations in many countries studying the history and tradition of particular regions and localities. There are also histories of transnational religions (such as Christianity, Judaism and Islam), ethnicities and

empires, as well as continental histories (of Africa, Europe and so on) and global histories. In the past, emperors, kings and other potentates had dynastic histories written. See Diamond (1997), McNeil (1963), Ponting (1992), Roberts (1997) and Smith (1988).

12 See Elias (1987).

13 See, for example, John Markoff's (1996) discussion of the dialogue between legislators and peasants in the French Revolution.

14 See the debate in the *American Journal of Sociology* with contributions by Somers (1998), Kiser and Hechter (1998), Boudon (1998), Goldstone (1998) and Calhoun (1998).

15 See Smith (1983, 1991).

16 See Geertz (1971) and Walters (1980).

17 See also Griffin and Isaac (1992).

18 For interesting discussion, see Le Goff (1992).

19 Like Isaac and Griffin, Haydu draws upon American labour history to illustrate his case. See Haydu (1998: 359–67).

20 For example, if the patterns of crime on two adjacent areas (A and B) are similar it may reflect the fact that they both have the same demographic characteristics; it does not in itself show that what happens in area A is directly influencing what happens in area B, or vice versa.

21 An additional factor is the existence of a threshold value which is 'the rate at which new infections exceed removals'. The rate of diffusion is determined by 'the extent to which the threshold value is exceeded' (Deane et al., 1998: 61).

22 Technical details may be found in Deane et al. (1998: 63–7).

23 For another useful discussion, see Wellman and Wetherell (1996).

24 See Kent (1978). This is a detailed description of the network foundations and alliance systems of the Medici faction and their opponents in the early fifteenth century.

25 Measured by the date when the family was first represented on the Priorate or city council.

26 Padgett and Ansell (1993: 1311) write: 'our method is to correlate columns of "stacked" matrices (and transposes) across all strong tie networks, and then input the resulting correlation matrix into the standard Johnson's complete-link clustering algorithm. This produced the partition of families [shown].' Also 'blockmodel images of social bonds among clusters were generated by (a) aggregating each raw network matrix according to [the] . . . clustering of families and then (b) defining and drawing a social "bond" whenever the number of raw network ties between clusters equaled or exceeded two'.

27 For another approach to 'sequence analysis', see Abbott (1988, 1993).

28 For examples, see Moore (1978), Fearon (1991), Gould (1969) and Hawthorn (1991).

29 On counterfactual arguments, see also, for example, Fearon (1991), Gould (1969) and Hawthorn (1991).

30 Another source employed was *Avanti!*, also a socialist newspaper (Franzosi, 1998: 91).

31 See also Ragin (1987) and Ragin and Becker (1992).

32 For other approaches to comparative analysis, see Burawoy (1989), Crow (1997), McMichael (1990), Markoff (1990), Przeworski and Teune (1970), Ragin (1987), Ragin and Becker (1992), Skocpol (1979a, 1979b, 1984), Smith (1982a), Tilly (1984, 1997) and Wickham-Crowley (1991).

33 In this work, Moore defines his problem as being to 'explain the varied political roles played by the landed upper classes and the peasantry in the transformation from agrarian societies (defined simply as states where a large majority of the population lives off the land) to modern industrial ones. Somewhat more specifically, it is an attempt to discover the range of historical conditions under which either or both of these rural groups have become important forces behind the emergence of Western parliamentary versions of democracy, and dictatorships of the right and left, that is, fascist and communist regimes' (Moore, 1966: viii).

34 Moore's work is an exception to Ragin's dictum that comparativists tend to deal with either a very small number of cases (one or two) or a large number (say, 75) but not with a number in the middle range (say, 10). See Ragin (1998: 106).

35 For further reading on themes introduced in this chapter, see also Axtmann (1993), Bates et al. (1998), Collier and Mahoney (1996), Gotham and Staples (1996), Green and Shapiro (1994), Hall (1999), McDonald (1996) and Monkkonen (1994).

REFERENCES

Abbott, A. (1988) *The System of Professions*. Chicago: University of Chicago Press.

Abbott, A. (1993) 'Sequence analysis', *Annual Review of Sociology*, 21: 93–113.

Abrams, P. (1982) *Historical Sociology*. Shepton Mallet: Open Books.

Axtmann, R. (1993) 'Society, globalization and the comparative method', *History of the Human Sciences*, 6(2): 53–74.

Bates, R., Greif, A., Levi, M., Rosenthal, J.-L. and Weingast, B. (1998) *Analytic Narratives*. Princeton, NJ: Princeton University Press.

Bendix, R. (1974) *Work and Authority in Industry*. Berkeley: University of California Press.

Bloch, M. (1954) *The Historian's Craft*. Manchester: Manchester University Press.

Boudon, R. (1998) 'Limitations of rational choice theory', *American Journal of Sociology*, 104: 817–28.

Braudel, F. (1972) *The Mediterranean and the Mediterranean World in the Age of Philip II* (2 vols). London: Fontana.

Burawoy, M. (1989) 'Two methods in search of science. Skocpol versus Trotsky', *Theory & Society*, 18: 759–805.

Burke, P. (1992) *History and Social Theory*. Cambridge: Polity Press.

Butler, T. (ed.) (1989) *Memory: History, Culture and the Mind*. Oxford: Basil Blackwell.

Calhoun, C. (1998) 'Explanation in historical sociology: Narrative, general theory, and historically specific theory', *American Journal of Sociology*, 104: 846–71.

Callinicos, A. (1995) *Theories and Narratives. Reflections on the Philosophy of History*. Cambridge: Polity.

Collier, D. and Mahoney, J. (1996) 'Insights and pitfalls. Selection bias in qualitative research', *World Politics*, 49(1): 56–91.

Collingwood, R.G. (1946) *The Idea of History*. Oxford: Clarendon Press.

Crow, G. (1997) *Comparative Sociology and Social Theory. Beyond the Three Worlds*. London: Macmillan.

Davidoff, L. and Hall, C. (1987) *Family Fortunes. Men and Women of the English Middle Class 1780–1850*. London: Hutchinson.

Deane, G., Beck, E.M. and Tolnay, S.E. (1998) 'Incorporating space into social histories: How spatial processes operate and how we observe them', *International Review on Social History*, 43(Supplement): 57–80.

Diamond, J. (1997) *Guns, Germs and Steel: The Fates of Human Societies*. New York: Norton.

Elias, N. (1987) *Involvement and Detachment*. Oxford: Basil Blackwell.

Fearon, J.D. (1991) 'Counterfactuals and hypothesis testing in political science', *World Politics*, 43(2): 169–95.

Fisher, D.H. (1970) *Historians' Fallacies: Toward a Logic of Historical Thought*. New York: Harper & Row.

Franzosi, R. (1998) 'Narrative as data: Linguistic and statistical tools for the quantitative study of historical events', *International Review of Social History*, 43(Supplement): 81–104.

Geertz, C. (1971) *The Interpretation of Cultures*. New York: Basic Books.

Goldstone, J.A. (1998) 'Initial conditions, general laws, path dependence, and explanation in historical sociology', *American Journal of Sociology*, 104, 829–45.

Gotham, K.V. and Staples, W.G. (1996) 'Narrative analysis and the new historical sociology', *Sociological Quarterly*, 37: 481–501.

Gould, J.D. (1969) 'Hypothetical history', *Economic History Review*, 22(2): 195–207.

Green, D. and Shapiro, I. (1994) *The Pathologies of Rational Choice Theory*. New Haven, CT: Yale University Press.

Griffin, L.J. (1993) 'Narrative, event-structure analysis, and causal interpretation in historical sociology', *American Journal of Sociology*, 98: 1094–1133.

Griffin, L.J. and Isaac, L.W. (1992) 'Recursive regression and the historical use of 'time' in time-series analyses of historical process', *Historical Methods*, 25: 166–79.

Griffin, L.J. and van der Linden, M. (1998) 'Introduction', *International Review of Social History*, 43(Supplement): 3–8.

Hall, J.R. (1999) *Cultures of Inquiry*. Cambridge: Cambridge University Press.

Hannan, M. and Freeman, J. (1987) 'The ecology of organizational mortality: American labor unions, 1836–1985', *American Journal of Sociology* 92: 910–43.

Hawthorn, G. (1991) *Plausible Worlds: Possibility and Understanding in History and the Social Sciences*. New York: Cambridge University Press.

Haydu, J. (1998) 'Making use of the past: Time periods as cases to compare and as sequences of problem solving', *American Journal of Sociology*, 104: 339–71.

Heise, David (1988) 'Computer analysis of cultural structures', *Social Science Computer Review*, 6: 183–96.

Heise, David (1989) 'Modeling event structures', *Journal of Mathematical Sociology*, 14: 139–69.

Hintze, O. (1973) *The Historical Essays of Otto Hintze*, (ed.), Felix Gilbert. Oxford: Oxford University Press.

Hitler, A (1992) *Mein Kampf*. London: Pimlico. First published 1925–6.

Hollis, M. (1994) *The Philosophy of Social Science*. Cambridge: Cambridge University Press.

Isaac, L.W. and Griffin, L.J. (1989) 'Ahistoricism in time-series analyses of historical process: Critique, redirection, and illustrations from U.S. labor history', *American Sociological Review*, 54: 873–90.

Kammen, M. (1997) *In the Past Lane: Historical Perspectives on American Culture*. Oxford: Oxford University Press.

Kent, D. (1978) *The Rise of the Medici. Faction in Florence 1426–1434*. Oxford: Oxford University Press.

Kiser, E. and Hechter, M. (1991) 'The role of general theory in comparative-historical sociology', *American Journal of Sociology*, 97: 1–30.

Kiser, E. and Hechter, M. (1998) 'The debate on historical sociology: Rational choice theory and its critics', *American Journal of Sociology*, 104: 785–816.

Lamont, M. (1992) *Morals, Money and Manners: The Culture of the French and the American Upper-Middle Class*. Chicago:University of Chicago Press.

Le Goff, J. (1992) *History and Memory*. Cambridge: Cambridge University Press.

Lloyd, C. (1986) *Explanation in Social History.* Oxford: Basil Blackwell.

Lloyd, C. (1993) *The Structures of History.* Oxford: Basil Blackwell.

Markoff, J. (1990) 'A comparative method. Reflections on Charles Ragin's innovations in comparative analysis', *Historical Methods*, 23(4): 177–81.

Markoff, J. (1996) *The Abolition of Feudalism. Peasants, Lords and Legislators in the French Revolution.* University Park: Pennsylvania State University Press.

Marx, K. and Engels, F. (2002) *The Communist Manifesto*, (ed.), G. Stedman Jones. Harmondsworth: Penguin.

McDonald, T.J. (ed.) (1996) *The Historic Turn in the Human Sciences.* Ann Arbor: University of Michigan Press.

McMichael, P. (1990) 'Incorporating comparison within a world-perspective: An alternative comparative method', *American Sociological Review*, 55: 385–97.

McNeil, W.H. (1963) *The Rise of the West.* Chicago: University of Chicago Press.

Meinig, D.W. (1988) *The Shaping of America. A Geographical Perspective on 500 Years of History. Vol. 1: Atlantic America, 1492–1800.* New Haven, CT: Yale University Press.

Meinig, D.W. (1993) *The Shaping of America. A Geographical Perspective on 500 Years of History. Vol. 2: Continental America, 1800–1867.* New Haven, CT: Yale University Press.

Meinig, D.W. (1999) *The Shaping of America. A Geographical Perspective on 500 Years of History. Vol. 3: Transcontinental America, 1850–1915.* New Haven, CT: Yale University Press.

Monkkonen, E (1994) *Engaging the Past. The Uses of History across the Social Sciences.* Durham, NC: Duke University Press.

Moore, B. (1966) *Social Origins of Dictatorship and Democracy. Lord and Peasant in the Making of the Modern World.* Harmondsworth: Penguin.

Moore, B. (1978) *Injustice. The Social Bases of Obedience and Revolt.* London: Macmillan.

Padgett, J.F. and Ansell, C.K. (1993) 'Robust action and the rise of the Medici, 1400–1434', *American Journal of Sociology*, 98: 1259–1319.

Piore, M. and Sabel, C. (1984) *The Second Industrial Divide.* New York: Basic Books.

Pomper, P., Elphick, R.H. and Vann, R.T. (eds) (1998) *World History. Ideologies, Structures, and Identities*, Oxford: Blackwell.

Ponting, C. (1992) *A Green History of the World: The Environment and the Collapse of Great Civilizations.* New York: St Martin's Press.

Przeworski, A. and Teune, H. (1970) *The Logic of Comparative Social Inquiry.* New York: Wiley.

Ragin, C. (1987) *The Comparative Method. Moving beyond Qualitative and Quantitative Strategies.* Berkeley: University of California Press.

Ragin, C.R. (1998) 'The logic of qualitative comparative analysis', *International Review of Social History*, 43(Supplement): 105–24.

Ragin, C. and Becker, H.S. (eds) (1992) *What Is a Case? Exploring the Foundations of Social Inquiry.* Cambridge: Cambridge University Press.

Roberts, C.W. (ed.) (1997) *Text Analysis for the Social Sciences. Methods for Drawing Statistical Inferences from Texts and Transcripts.* Mahwah, NJ: Lawrence Erlbaum.

Rokkan, S. (1970) *Citizens, Elections, Parties: Approaches to the Comparative Study of the Process of Development.* Oslo: Universitetsforlaget.

Runciman, W.G. (1987) *A Treatise on Social Theory. Vol. I: The Methodology of Social Theory*, Cambridge: Cambridge University Press.

Seldon, A. and Pappworth, J. (1983) *By Word of Mouth. Elite Oral History.* London: Methuen.

Sewell, W.H. (1996) 'Three temporalities: Towards an eventful sociology', in T.J. McDonald (ed.), *The Historic Turn in the Human Sciences.* Ann Arbor: University of Michigan Press.

Shapiro, G. and Markoff, J. (1998) *Revolutionary Demands. A Content Analysis of the Cahiers de Doléances of 1789.* Stanford, CA: Stanford University Press.

Skocpol, T. (1979a) 'State and revolution: Old regimes and revolutionary crises in France, Russia and China', *Theory & Society*, 7(1–2): 7–95.

Skocpol, T. (1979b) *States and Social Revolutions.* Cambridge: Cambridge University Press.

Skocpol, T. (ed.) (1984) *Vision and Method in Historical Sociology.* Cambridge: Cambridge University Press.

Skocpol, T., with Ross, G., Smith, T. and Vichniac, J.E. (eds) (1998) *Democracy, Revolution, and History.* Ithaca, NY: Cornell University Press.

Smith, D. (1982a) *Conflict and Compromise. Class Formation in English Society, 1830–1914. A Comparative Study of Birmingham and Sheffield.* London: Routledge.

Smith, D. (1982b) 'Social history and sociology – more than just good friends', *Sociological Review*, 30: 286–308.

Smith, D. (1983) *Barrington Moore. Violence, Morality and Political Change.* London: Macmillan.

Smith, D. (1984a) 'Morality and method in the work of Barrington Moore', *Theory and Society*, 13: 151–76.

Smith, D. (1984b) 'Discovering facts and values', in T. Skocpol (ed.), *Vision and Method in Historical Sociology.* Cambridge: Cambridge University Press.

Smith, D. (1988) 'Lessons from the Annales school', *Theory, Culture and Society*, 5: 137–48.

Smith, D. (1991) *The Rise of Historical Sociology.* Cambridge: Polity.

Somers, M.R. (1998), '"We're No Angels": Realism, Rational Choice, and Rationality in Social Science', *American Journal of Sociology*, 104: 722–84.

Stanford, M. (1986) *The Nature of Historical Knowledge*. Oxford: Basil Blackwell.

Stern, F. (ed.) (1963) *The Varieties of History. From Voltaire to the Present*. Cleveland: Meridian Books.

Thompson, E.P. (1963) *The Making of the English Working Class*. Harmondsworth: Penguin.

Thompson, P. (1978) *The Voice of the Past*. London: Oxford University Press.

Tilly, C. (1984) *Big Structures, Large Processes, Huge Comparisons*. New York: Russell Sage Foundation.

Tilly, C. (1997) 'Means and ends of comparison in macrosociology', *Comparative Social Research*, 16: 43–53.

Tosh, J. (1984) *The Pursuit of History*. London: Longman.

Wallerstein, I. (1974) *The Modern World System. Capitalist Agriculture and the Origins of the World-Economy in the Sixteenth Century*. New York: Academic Press.

Wallerstein, I. (1980) *The Modern World System II. Mercantilism and the Consolidation of the European World-Economy 1600–1750*. New York: Academic Press.

Wallerstein, I. (1989) *The Modern World System III. The Second Era of Great Expansion of the Capitalist World-Economy 1730–1840s*. New York: Academic Press.

Walters, R.G. (1980) 'Signs of the times. Clifford Geertz and the historians', *Social Research*, 47: 537–56.

Weber, M. (1988) *The Agrarian Sociology of Ancient Civilizations*. London: Verso.

Wellman, B. and Wetherell, C. (1996) 'Social network analyses of historical communities: Some questions from the present to the past', *History of the Family*, 1(1): 97–121.

Wickham-Crowley, T.P. (1991) 'A qualitative comparative approach to Latin American revolutions', *International Journal of Comparative Sociology*. 32: 82–109.

PART II

---

*The General Linear Model
and Extensions*

8

Multiple Regression Analysis

ROSS M. STOLZENBERG

Regression is the commonplace of statistical analysis in the social sciences. The method is ubiquitous in research reports and journals. Convenient, low-cost computer programs are widely available for calculating regression analyses. Armed with these programs and inexpensive computers, students as well as journeyman researchers now calculate even complicated regression analyses easily, quickly, accurately, and inexpensively, without the drudgery and certainty of arithmetic error that were only recently the challenging hallmarks of the technique.

In the social sciences, regression analysis is often used to test hypotheses about the existence of causal effects, to estimate the strength of those effects, and to compare the strength of effects across groups. Regression also provides a powerful methodology for describing the distributions of variables, for estimating the distributions that these variables would have under hypothetical conditions, and for adjusting observed differences for the effects of confounding variables that would otherwise prohibit meaningful comparisons. Modest extensions of regression even provide powerful methods for analysis of cross-classified data.

To use regression analysis for answering social science questions, it is helpful to know the mathematics of how the method works. Without this knowledge, practitioners are likely to misuse, underuse or inefficiently use regression. Fortunately, introductions to regression and advanced treatments of the mathematics and statistics of regression analysis are abundant and available at every price, in every medium and probably in every modern written language, at every level of mathematical sophistication. Many of these texts and tracts are excellent, and many include examples from social science data.

Effective use of regression analysis for social science research also requires an understanding of how to manipulate regression results to answer social science questions. This effort tends to focus on creative but mathematically trivial algebraic manipulations that put regression results into a form that corresponds to the substantive questions that motivate the research. These manipulations sometimes translate regression estimates of several parameters of nonlinear and nonadditive functions into a single measure of how differences in independent variable values relate to differences in the value of a dependent variable. Similar manipulations are often used to indicate the combined effect of a set of independent variables on the mean of the dependent variable, or the combined effect of all the independent variables on the value of the dependent variable for a single interesting case. Although they are sometimes too simple to be noted in a mathematical treatment, these manipulations do much to put the results of a regression analysis into the language of the social science questions that motivate social science research. A researcher who is unaware of these manipulations will find it easy to illustrate regression concepts with social science data, but difficult to use regression to provide concise answers to interesting social science questions. Few texts on regression analysis provide much guidance on techniques that clarify the connection between regression results and the social science questions that motivate them.

In the limited space available, this chapter describes some key features of regression analysis. I focus on the uses to which regression can be put in social science research, rather than on the method as an object of intrinsic interest. In doing so, I seek balance between explication of the mathematical properties of regression and exposition of the manipulations that help transform regression results into answers to social science research questions. To the extent possible, I assume no prior knowledge of regression analysis and I work by example with a minimum of mathematical notation. Depending on their interests and previous experience, readers may find it useful to read sections of this chapter selectively. Several reference tables provide quick reference for those who already understand the method and wish to dispense with explanations altogether.

REGRESSION AS A METHOD FOR DESCRIBING POPULATION DATA

Simple regression: One independent variable

Among its other uses, regression analysis is a technique for describing the relationship between one variable (the dependent variable) and one or more other variables (the independent variables) in a specific body of data (a dataset). Independent variables are usually conceived as causes of the dependent variable, although notions of causality are sometimes only implicit, frequently speculative, and usually informal. *Simple regression* involves just one independent variable. *Multiple regression* involves more than one independent variable.

For an example of a regression problem, consider Table 8.1 and Figure 8.1. For each of the six New England states, Table 8.1 gives 1980 US Census data on the number of divorces (in hundreds) and the size of the urban population (in millions). Suppose that a policy analyst, perhaps working for a New England state government, has assembled these data to help understand why her own state has a higher than average number of divorces, compared to other states in the same geographic region. Assume that the data are measured without error, and that the analyst's interests do not extend beyond 1980 and the six New England states. (These assumptions are typical of case studies and focused policy studies, although not typical of

scientific research that seeks to establish general laws.)

The analyst's first task is to describe the variables in the dataset. This description helps to establish what constitutes a big or small difference between states in the variables under consideration. Without knowing what is a 'big' or 'small' difference in the values of variables, it is difficult or impossible to know if 'small' changes in one variable are associated with 'big' changes in another, or to define a 'big' effect of one variable on another. Descriptions can be arithmetic and graphic. Arithmetically, one could start by calculating variable means, to describe the central tendency of each variable; and by computing their standard deviations, to describe the extent to which data diverge from the mean. Means and standard deviations are shown in Table 8.1. The analyst might also describe the data graphically, by drawing a scatterplot as shown in Figure 8.1. Each point on the scatterplot represents a single data *case*. In this example, a case is a New England state. Because this particular dataset has few cases, and because they are all well known, it is possible and useful to label each data point with the United States Postal Service abbreviation for its name. Means are shown in Figure 8.1 as a horizontal line for Y, the number of divorces, and a vertical line for X_1, the urban population. Notice that the intersection of the means lies at the visual center of the distribution of data points.

Regression and related methods (such as the analysis of variance) focus attention on the means and standard deviations of variables. Regression can be described as a method that answers the question 'Why isn't the value of Y for every case equal to the mean of Y?'. So it is natural to express the values of variables for each of the six New England states as deviations from the variable means, and to measure those deviations in standard deviations of each variable. Table 8.2 accomplishes this restatement by subtracting the mean of each variable from each of its values and then dividing the difference by the variable's standard deviation. The resulting numbers are *standardized values*. (By convention, standardized values of variables are identified as such by the addition of an asterisk.) For example, Y^* for Vermont is $(26.23 - 81.7483)/55.7364 = -0.9961$. Notice that Y^* and X_1^* each have a mean of zero and a standard deviation of one.

Table 8.1   *Divorces and urban population of New England states, 1980*

State	Divorces (hundreds) Y	Urban population (millions) X_1
Vermont (VT)	26.23	0.173
Rhode Island (RI)	36.06	0.824
New Hampshire (NH)	52.54	0.480
Maine (ME)	62.05	0.534
Connecticut (CT)	134.88	2.450
Massachusetts (MA)	178.73	4.808
Mean (μ)	81.75	1.545
Standard deviation (σ) (population formula)	55.74	1.634

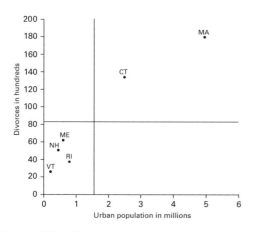

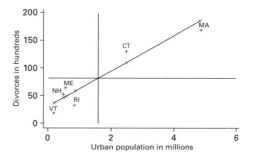

Figure 8.3   *Figure 8.1 with regression predictions and line*

Figure 8.1   *Divorces by urban population, New England states, 1980*

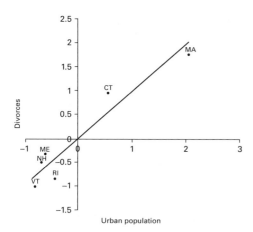

Figure 8.2   *Figure 8.1 in standardized metric*

Figure 8.2 is the scatterplot of the standardized data from Table 8.2. Geometrically, the pattern of points on this figure

constitutes the relationship or association between X_1 and Y. Notice that the pattern formed by the data points is identical in Figures 8.1 and 8.2. Because the patterns are the same, the relationship or association between X_1 and Y is unchanged by standardizing the variables, although the numbers that describe the *values* of X_1 and Y are changed. The axes in Figure 8.2 are in the locations occupied by the mean lines in Figure 8.1.

Replacing the plotted line with an equation
In both Figures 8.1 and 8.2, notice that the general pattern of the data points seems to describe an upwardly sloping, more or less straight line, starting at the lower left near the data point for Vermont, passing through the intersection of the two mean lines, and ending at the upper right near the point for Massachusetts. This verbal description is imprecise, lengthy and supplements rather than replaces the figures. This pattern can be

Table 8.2   Table 8.1 restated as standardized values, with regression calculations

State	Divorces (hundreds) Y^*	Urban population (millions) X_1^*	Product of X_1^* and Y^*	$\hat{Y}^*$	ε^*	$(\varepsilon^*)^2$
VT	−0.9961	−0.8396	0.8363	−0.8060	0.1901	0.0361
RI	−0.8197	−0.4411	0.3616	−0.4234	0.3963	0.1570
NH	−0.5240	−0.6514	0.3413	−0.6253	−0.1013	0.0103
ME	−0.3534	−0.6185	0.2186	−0.5937	−0.2403	0.0578
CT	0.9533	0.5537	0.5278	0.5315	−0.4217	0.1779
MA	1.7400	1.9968	3.4744	1.9169	0.1769	0.0313
Mean	0.0000	0.0000	0.9600	0.0000	0.0000	0.0784
Standard deviation (σ) (population formula)	1.0000	1.0000		0.9600	0.2800	0.0647

summarized more succinctly by drawing a straight line through the approximate center of these data points, starting at the lower left near the point for Vermont and ending near the point for Massachusetts, or by an equation of the form $\hat{Y} = \beta_0 + \beta_1 X_1$. The symbol ^ (circumflex, or 'hat') over the Y indicates that the values of $\hat{Y}$ are not the observed values of Y, but the estimates; these are values that *would* exist if all the data points were located exactly on the line. β_0 is called the intercept, or the value of Y when $X_1 = 0$ (i.e., where the line intercepts the Y axis). β_1 in this equation is called the slope of the line, expressed as changes in the value of $\hat{Y}$ per unit change in X. For example, if $\beta_1 = 1.5$, then $\hat{Y}$ changes 1.5 units for every one-unit change in X_1. β_1 is called the *metric regression coefficient,* the *unstandardized regression coefficient,* or simply the *regression coefficient.*

A line drawn on Figure 8.2 would be represented by the formula $\hat{Y}^* = \beta_0^* + \beta_1^* X_1^*$. Asterisks (*) again indicate standardized values of variables and coefficients of standardized variables. β_1^* is called the *standardized regression coefficient of X_1.* Consistent with our previous observation, that line passes through the means of both variables, which is the origin of Figure 8.2. So $\beta_0^* = 0$. β_0^* always equals zero, so it is omitted from the standardized regression equation. To calculate β_1^*, multiply the value of X_1^* by the value of Y^* for each of the six states and then compute the mean of these 'cross-products'. As shown in Table 8.2, the mean of the cross-products is 0.9600, so the equation for the line is

$$\hat{Y}^* = 0.9600 \, X_1^*. \qquad (8.1)$$

With β_1^* already computed, the metric regression coefficient β_1 can be obtained by multiplying β_1^* by the standard deviation of Y and dividing by the standard deviation of X_1: $\beta_1 = \beta_1^*(\sigma_y/\sigma_x) = 0.9600(55.74/1.634) = 32.74$. The constant term β_0 is also readily available as the mean of Y minus the product of β_1 times the mean of X_1: 81.75– $32.74 \times 1.545 = 31.17$. Figure 8.3 shows the line

$$\hat{Y} = 31.17 + 32.74X_1 \qquad (8.2)$$

added to Figure 8.1.

Several quantitative measures describe the 'goodness' of the fit of the regression line to the data:

- *Correlation of X_1 and Y.* The correlation (often called r or ρ) between X_1^* and Y^* is equal to β_1^*.
- *Correlation of predicted and observed values of Y.* For each of the six New England states in the standardized data, we can substitute the observed value of X_1^* into the equation $\hat{Y}^* = 0.9600 \, X_1^*$ to calculate the value of $\hat{Y}^*$. One measure of the goodness of fit between the predicted values $\hat{Y}^*$ and the observed values Y^* is the correlation between these predicted values of Y^* and the observed values of Y^*. In a regression with only one independent variable, that correlation equals β_1^*, the standardized regression coefficient. Thus, in the New England data used above, that correlation is 0.9600, which is a very high correlation indeed. The value of the correlation between predicted and observed values of Y is the same in the unstandardized regression as it is in the standardized regression.
- R^2 or r^2. A second measure of goodness of fit is the square of the correlation coefficient, r^2, which is $0.9600^2 = 0.9216$. The

value of R^2 is the same in standardized and unstandardized regressions. R^2 equals the variance (squared standard deviation) of $\hat{Y}^*$. R^2 also equals one minus the variance of ε^*.

- *Proportion of variance in Y^* explained by X_1^*.* A third measure of goodness of fit is the proportion of variance in Y^* explained by X_1^*, or the ratio of the variance of $\hat{Y}^*$ to the variance of Y^*; this quantity is equal to r^2, which equals the squared value of β_1^*. So X_1^* explains 92.16% of the variance in Y^*. The proportion of variance explained is the same in standardized and unstandardized regressions.

- *Prediction error for each case.* For any particular case in a dataset (e.g., Vermont), one can also measure the goodness of fit of a standardized regression equation by calculating the error, ε^*, or the difference between $\hat{Y}^*$ and Y^*. In the unstandardized equation, the error is ε. Notice that some of the values of ε^* (and ε) are positive and some are negative. As a property of regression, the sum of the values of ε^* is exactly zero, the sum of the values of ε is exactly zero, and so the means of both ε and ε^* are always exactly zero. Also as a property of regression, the correlation between ε^* and $\hat{Y}^*$ is always zero, as is the correlation between ε and $\hat{Y}$, and the correlations between ε and X_1 and ε^* and X_1^*. The correlation between ε^* and Y^*, and the correlation between ε and Y, are always precisely equal to the square root of $1-R^2$. The relationship between ε and ε^* is straightforward: $\varepsilon^* = \varepsilon/\sigma_Y$ and $\varepsilon = \varepsilon^*\sigma_Y$. In effect, regression permits one to divide the dependent variable into two uncorrelated components. The first component is $\hat{Y}$ (or $\hat{Y}^*$) and it is determined entirely by the independent variable. The second component is the prediction error for each case, and it is entirely independent of the independent variable. The variance of the dependent variable Y is equal to the sum of the variance of $\hat{Y}$ and the variance of ε. In the standardized regression, the variance of Y^* equals the sum of the variance of $\hat{Y}^*$ and the variance of ε^*. In this example, $0.9600^2 + 0.2800^2 = 1$.

- *Squared prediction error for each case.* Squaring the prediction errors converts all negative values to positive values. If the squared prediction error is used to assess the goodness of fit, errors from underprediction do not balance out errors from overprediction. In the standardized regression, the sum of squared errors lies between zero (which would obtain if every value of Y^* fell directly on the regression line), and N, the number of cases in the dataset. The mean of the squared errors lies between zero and one. The regression line calculated by the procedure described above is 'best' in that any other straight line would produce a higher sum of squared prediction errors. That is, no other value of β_1 (or β_1^*) would produce a smaller sum of squared errors. Because of this property, this line is called the *least-squares* or *ordinary least-squares* regression line.

- *Analysis of variance (ANOVA) for the regression.* Rarely reported in contemporary publications but still ubiquitous in regression analysis computer output, the analysis of variance for a regression of Y^* on X^* divides the total variation in Y^* into a component explained by the regression and a component left unexplained (Table 8.3). For a standardized regression analysis, necessary calculations (shown in Table 8.4) are greatly simplified by the fact that the means of Y^* and $\hat{Y}^*$ are both zero, and the sum of $(Y^*)^2$ is N, the number of cases. Thus, the bottom row of the ANOVA table can be completed without reference to the data. The regression sum of squares (RSS) can be calculated directly, or by multiplication of the total sum of squares (TSS) by the R^2 for the regression, and the error sum of squares can be calculated by subtraction of RSS from TSS, or by multiplying the TSS by $1-R^2$. If the sums of squares are calculated directly, then they can be used to calculate the R^2, since $R^2 = RSS/TSS$. Results for the unstandardized regression are obtained by multiplying the sums of squares in the ANOVA table by the variance of Y (population formula), 55.74^2 (Table 8.5).

Table 8.6 presents several measures for the New England data. For most purposes, the R^2 would be sufficient, as the R^2 (plus the sample size, and number of independent variables) summarizes all the information in Table 8.5. In short, a small number of calculations produce a large amount of information about the relationship between Y and X_1, and that information has many convenient properties.

Table 8.3 *Regression ANOVA table for complete population data on N cases*

Source of variation	Sum of squares	Degrees of freedom	Mean square
Regression	RSS = Sum of squared values of $(\hat{Y} - \mu_Y)$ = $TSS - ESS$	DF_R = Number of independent variables = k	RSS/DF_R
Error	ESS = Sum of squared values of ε = $TSS - RSS$	DF_ε = N minus number of independent variables minus 1 = $N-k-1$	ESS/DF_ε
Total	TSS = Sum of squared values of $(Y - \mu_Y)$ = $RSS + ESS$	$DF_T = N-1$	TSS/DF_T

Table 8.4 *ANOVA table for standardized regression of Y^* on X_1^*, population data formulas*

Source of variation		Sum of squares	Degrees of freedom	Mean square
Regression	$\Sigma\hat{Y}^{*2}$	5.5296	1	5.5296
Error	$\Sigma\varepsilon^{*2}$	0.4704	4	0.1176
Total	ΣY^{*2}	6.0000	5	1.2000

Table 8.5 *ANOVA table for metric regression of Y on X_1, population data formulas*

Source of variation		Sum of squares	Degrees of freedom	Mean square
Regression	$\Sigma(\hat{Y} - \mu_Y)^2$	17 177.98	1	17 177.98
Error	$\Sigma \varepsilon^2$	1 461.32	4	365.33
Total	$\Sigma(Y - \mu_Y)^2$	18 639.28	5	3 727.86

Table 8.6 *Several goodness-of-fit measures for New England data regressions*

Goodness-of-fit measure	Standardized regression	Unstandardized regression
Correlation of X and Y	0.9600	0.9600
Correlation of predicted and observed values of Y ($r_{Y,\hat{Y}}$)	0.9600	0.9600
R^2	0.9600^2 = 0.9216	0.9600^2 = 0.9216
Proportion of variance explained	0.9216	0.9216

Interpreting the results Results should be described in terms that relate to the question that motivates the research, and should give a sense of the size of observed effects relative to observed levels of dependent variables. For example:

For the six New England states in 1980, the mean number of divorces is 8175 and the mean size of the urban population is 1.545 million persons. On average, the number of divorces increases by 3274 for each

Table 8.7 *Means and standard deviations of divorce analysis variables, 1980, 50 states*

Variable	Symbol	Mean	Standard deviation (population formula)
Number of divorces (hundreds)	Y	236.8	253.4878
Urban population (millions)	X_1	3.328	4.131704
Nonurban population (millions)	X_2	1.190	0.903216

additional million persons in the state's urban population. Stated in standardized units, each change of one standard deviation in the size of the urban population is associated with a change of 0.96 standard deviations in the number of divorces. The size of the urban population explains 92.16% of the variance in the number of divorces per state. In short, the size of the urban population largely explains interstate variation in the number of divorces in the New England region.

Multiple regression: Several independent variables

Although the regression of number of divorces on urban population tells something important about the relationship between the number of divorces and the size of the urban population in states, it does not tell much. For example, it tells nothing about the effect of the nonurban population size on the number of divorces. One might expect that states with more nonurban people produce more divorces too, and one might wish to compare the effects of urban and nonurban population size on the number of divorces. Further, one might wish to extend the analysis to data for the entire United States.

Let us begin by extending the analysis to the United States as a whole. First, we calculate the means and standard deviations of our variables (Table 8.7). As before, the unit of analysis is the state.

Next, we regress Y on X_1, and, separately, regress Y on X_2. To avoid confusion, we will dispense with symbols for coefficients in these analyses. Table 8.8 shows the regression of Y on X_1. Urban population size seems to

Table 8.8 *Simple regression of hundreds of divorces (Y) on urban population in millions (X_1)*

Independent variable	Metric coefficient	Standardized coefficient
Constant	45.75	*
Urban population (millions), X_1	57.40	0.94
Proportion of variance explained	0.8753	

Note: *In standardized regression, constant is zero

have a stronger effect on the number of divorces in the United States as a whole than in the New England states alone. In the US as a whole, the metric coefficient for X_1 is 57.40, compared to 32.74 in the New England states. The standardized coefficient is 0.94, which is nearly identical to the value of 0.96 found in New England. In the US as a whole, X_1 explains 88% of the variance in Y, compared to 92% in New England. The similarity of the standardized regression coefficients and percentages of variance explained in the US as a whole and in New England indicates that the association between X_1 and Y is about the same in both analyses. Thus, the larger metric coefficient in the US as a whole is due to the larger ratio of the standard deviation of Y to the standard deviation of X_1 in the US as a whole.

Table 8.9 shows the regression of Y on X_2, the size of the nonurban population in each state. The standardized regression coefficient of X_2 is 0.67 and the proportion of variance explained is 45%. Adding the percentages of variance in Y explained by X_1 and X_2 (0.88 + 0.45) suggests the impossible conclusion that X_1 and X_2 together explain 133% of the variance in Y. The problem is that X_1 and X_2 are highly correlated. Table 8.10 shows that this correlation is 0.6681. Unless the

Table 8.9 *Simple regression of hundreds of divorces (Y) on nonurban population in millions (X_2)*

Independent variable	Metric coefficient	Standardized coefficient
Constant	13.70	
Nonurban population (millions), X_2	187.5	0.67
Proportion of variance explained		0.45

Table 8.11 *Multiple regression of Y on X_1 and X_2*

Independent variable	Metric coefficient	Standardized coefficient
Constant	22.76	
Urban population (millions), X_1	52.92	0.8626
Nonurban population (millions), X_2	31.83	0.1134
R^2	0.8829	

Table 8.10 *Correlations among Y, X_1 and X_2 in 50 states, 1980*

	Y	X_1	X_2
Number of divorces (hundreds), Y	1.0000		
Urban population (millions), X_1	0.9356	1.0000	
Nonurban population (millions), X_2	0.6681	0.6429	1.0000

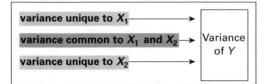

Figure 8.4 *Relationship between variance of Y and variances of X_1 and X_2*

correlation between these variables is taken into account, their combined association with Y is overestimated.

Pictorially, the situation can be represented by Figure 8.4. If we estimate the effects of X_1^* and X_2^* on Y^* with two separate regression analyses, then we double-count the contribution of the variance that is common to X_1^* and X_2^*, first in the regression of Y^* on X_1^* and second in the regression of Y^* on X_2^*. (Mathematically, we violate the inclusion–exclusion principle.) One solution to this problem is to estimate a single standardized regression equation in which X_1^* and X_2^* are both independent variables and Y^* is the dependent variable, and adjustment is made for their common variance, or *covariance* or correlation. The necessary calculations can be obtained by solving the following simultaneous equations in which the correlations among the observed variables (*r*) are known from the data and the β_1^* and β_2^* are unknown:

$$r_{YX_1} = \beta_1^* r_{X_1X_1} + \beta_2^* r_{X_1X_2}$$
$$r_{YX_2} = \beta_1^* r_{X_2X_1} + \beta_2^* r_{X_2X_2}$$

Substituting the correlations from Table 8.10 as appropriate, we get:

$$0.9356 = \beta_1^* + 0.6429\beta_2^*$$
$$0.6681 = 0.6429\beta_1^* + \beta_2^*$$

Solving the equations, we get $\beta_1^* = 0.8626$ and $\beta_2^* = 0.1134$, as reported in Table 8.11.

The R^2 for the analysis can be obtained by multiplying the standardized coefficient for each independent variable by the correlation of that independent variable with the dependent variable, and then summing the products. Alternatively, it can be obtained by computing the variance of $\hat{Y}^*$. The metric coefficients are obtained by multiplying the standardized coefficient for each independent variable by the standard deviation of the dependent variable and then dividing by the standard deviation of that independent variable. The constant term for the metric regression is obtained by multiplying the mean of each independent variable by the metric coefficient for that variable, summing the results and subtracting that from the mean of the dependent variable.

Goodness-of-fit measures are readily obtained as well, as shown in Table 8.12.

Once again the largest remaining task appears to be to describe the results in sufficient detail to give the reader a sense of the size of these effects. The following paragraph might be used:

In the 50 American states in 1980, the mean number of divorces is 23 680, the mean size of the urban population is 3.328 million and the mean size of the nonurban population

Table 8.12 *Several goodness-of-fit measures for multiple regression analysis of 50-state data*

Goodness-of-fit measure	Standardized regression	Unstandardized regression
Multiple correlation of independent variables with Y	0.9396	0.9396
Correlation of predicted and observed values of Y ($r_{Y, \hat{Y}}$)	0.9396	0.9396
R^2	0.8829	0.8829
Proportion of variance explained	0.8829	0.8829

is 1.190 million. On average, the number of divorces increases about 1.6 times as much for each additional urban resident as for each additional nonurban resident. In particular, the number of divorces increases by 5292 for each additional million urban residents, and by 3183 for each additional million nonurban residents. In standardized terms, the number of divorces is about eight times as sensitive to the urban population size as to the nonurban population size: The number of divorces increases by 0.8626 standard deviations for every standard deviation of increase in the urban population, and by 0.1134 standard deviations for every standard deviation of increase in the nonurban population. Together, urban and nonurban population size explain 88.29% of the variance in the number of divorces per state.

Estimating Y under hypothetical circumstances

It is sometimes informative to select interesting or illustrative values of independent variables and then to ask what value the dependent variable would assume, on average, if the independent variables took on those particular values. Calculations of this sort are natural in regression analysis because $\hat{Y}$ is the *expected value* of *Y, given the hypothetical values of the independent variables* (sometimes called the conditional expectation of Y give the values of X_1 and X_2). For example, in a multiple regression with two independent variables, and when the independent variables assume some particular values

of interest (say x_1 and x_2), those values can be inserted into the regression equation to estimate the mean of Y that would be expected, on average, for data cases in which $X_1 = x_1$ and $X_2 = x_2$. This property of regression can be written as follows:

$$E(Y \mid X_1 = x_1, X_2 = x_2)$$
$$= \beta_0 + \beta_1 x_1 + \beta_2 x_2. \quad (8.3)$$

In words, the expectation of Y, given that X_1 equals x_1 and X_2 equals x_2, is β_0 plus the product of β_1 and x_1 plus the product of β_2 and x_2. This feature of regression is useful when researchers wish to imagine the consequences of hypothetical circumstances. For example, Stolzenberg (1990) used this method to compare the expected occupational status of Hispanic men to the expected occupational status of non-Hispanic men who had different *sets* of attributes characteristic of prototypical immigrants and native-born persons, including educational attainment, English language fluency and age.

In the 50-state divorce analysis, one could use the regression results to compare divorce frequency in two hypothetical states with populations of 2 million persons each. In the first state, the population is divided evenly between urban and nonurban locations, with a million urban residents and a million nonurban residents. In the second state, three times as many residents live in urban areas (1.5 million) as live in nonurban areas (0.5 million). Inserting the population figures for the first state into the regression equation, we get

$$E(Y) = 22.76 + 52.92 \times 1.0$$
$$+ 31.83 \times 1.0 = 107.51. \quad (8.4)$$

For the second state we get

$$E(Y) = 22.76 + 52.92 \times 1.5$$
$$+ 31.83 \times 0.5 = 118.06. \quad (8.5)$$

Table 8.13   *Regression decomposition of number of divorces, Missouri and New Jersey, 1980*

State	X_1 Urban population size (millions) (A)	X_2 Nonurban population size (millions) (B)	Y Divorces (hundreds) (C)	$\hat{Y}$ (Divorces expected given X_1 and X_2) (D)	ε (Observed minus expected) (E)
Missouri	3.349 588	1.567 098	275.95	249.93	26.02
New Jersey	6.557 377	0.807 446	277.96	395.52	−117.56
Difference (MO − NJ)	−3.207 789	0.759 652	−2.01	−145.59	143.58

Thus, for states of 2 million residents, the change from an equal urban–nonurban population split to a three-to-one preponderance of urban residents over nonurban residence is associated with an increase of about 10% in the number of divorces (118.06/107.51 = 1.098).

Hypothetical calculations are credible only if the hypothetical values of independent variables fall within the range of values observed in the dataset used to estimate the regression coefficients. For example, with about 24 million residents in 1980, California is the largest state in the data used in the state divorce frequency regression analysis above. So it would be a risky business to use those regression results to estimate the expected number of divorces in a hypothetical state with 200 million urban and 200 million nonurban residents. Significance tests and confidence intervals for these estimates are discussed later in this chapter.

Comparing two specific data cases

The 50-state regression results can be used to compare the values of pairs of states that have such different population distributions that they may seem to be impossible to compare meaningfully. For example, we might wish to compare the number of divorces in Missouri to the number in New Jersey. But a simple comparison seems unreasonable because New Jersey has about twice as many urban residents as Missouri, and Missouri has about twice as many nonurban residents as New Jersey. However, it would be reasonable to wish to compare the numbers of divorces after holding constant the sizes of the urban and nonurban populations of these two states. To do so, we can make use of the fact that our regression analysis decomposes the number of divorces in each state into a component that is expected on the basis of the state's urban and nonurban population sizes ($\hat{Y}$), and a component that is due to other

unspecified factors (ε). Looking at Table 8.13, notice that Missouri has 201 fewer divorces than New Jersey (column C). Column D compares the numbers of divorces that would be expected on the basis of urban and nonurban population differences: Column D shows that on the basis of population alone, one would expect Missouri to have 14 559 fewer divorces than New Jersey. Column E compares the numbers of divorces after removing the contribution of the sizes of the urban and nonurban population. Column E shows that after adjusting for differences between Missouri and New Jersey in the sizes of the urban and nonurban populations, Missouri has 14 358 more divorces than New Jersey. In short, if urban–nonurban residential location is a cause of divorce, then the near-equality of the numbers of divorces in these states appears to be an artifact of their very different numbers of urban and nonurban residents.

Dummy variables and adjusted differences in subgroup means

A *dummy variable* is a variable that equals one if a condition exists and zero if it does not exist. In the 50-state data, one might divide the states into mutually exclusive regions representing the West, South, Northeast and Northcentral areas of the country. Variables X_w, X_s, X_n, and X_c then could be defined, with $X_w = 1$ if a state is in the West region and $X_w = 0$ otherwise; $X_s = 1$ if a state is in the South region and $X_s = 0$ otherwise; $X_n = 1$ if a state is in the Northeast region and $X_n = 0$ otherwise, and $X_c = 1$ if a state is in the Northcentral region and $X_c = 0$ otherwise. One way to calculate the mean of Y, the number of divorces per state (in hundreds of divorces), would be to calculate the mean of Y separately for states in each of these regions. Results would be as shown in Table 8.14.

Table 8.14 *Mean number of divorces per state, by region, 1980*

Region	Divorces per state (hundreds)
Northeast	193.04
Northcentral	243.36
South	277.63
West	210.76
Total	236.79

Another way to calculate these means would be to regress Y on any three of the four regional dummy variables. For example, regressing Y on X_n, X_c and X_s yields the following regression:

$$\hat{Y} = 210.76 - 17.72X_n + 32.60X_c + 66.87\,X_s,\ R^2 = 0.0173. \quad (8.6)$$

For states in the the Northeast region, X_n equals one and X_c and X_s both equal 0, so $\hat{Y} = 210.76 - 172.72 + 0 + 0 = 193.04$, which is precisely the same number obtained by calculating the mean of Y for states in the Northeast region. For states in the West, X_n, X_c, and X_s all equal 0, so $\hat{Y} = 210.76$, which is exactly the same number obtained by calculating the mean of Y for states in the West. The regression constant term provides the mean in the region for which there is no dummy variable (the West), and the coefficients of the dummy variables indicate the *difference* between the mean of Y in the region that they represent (in this case the Northeast, Northcentral or South regions) and the mean of Y in the region that is not represented by any dummy variable (in this case, the West). It does not matter which of the regional variables is omitted from the analysis, so long as one and only one of the regional dummy variables is omitted. For example, X_w could have been included and X_n omitted:

$$\hat{Y} = 193.04 + 50.32\,X_c + 17.72\,X_w + 84.59\,X_s,\ R^2 = 0.0173. \quad (8.7)$$

In equation (8.7), with X_w included and X_n excluded, states in the Northeast region would have X_c, X_w, and X_s all equal to zero, so the mean would equal just the constant term, 193.04, which is precisely the same number obtained by the previous regression and by the direct computation of means by region. In passing it is worth noting that these two regressions of Y on three dummy variables for region amount to a one-way analysis of variance of Y on region. The R^2 obtained in these equations is the square of the intraclass correlation coefficient of the one-way ANOVA.

Suppose we wished to compare differences between the mean of Y in regions, but to do so without the influence of differences in states' urban and nonurban population sizes (X_1 and X_2). To hold constant X_1 and X_2, simply add them to the equation. The regression coefficients for X_n, X_c, and X_s remain as estimates of the difference between the mean of Y in these regions and the mean in the region for which the dummy variable has been omitted (the West), with the added stipulation that these coefficients are differences after holding constant the effects of urban and nonurban population size in states. Results are as follows:

$$\hat{Y} = 44.44 + 56.42X_1 + 17.14X_2 - 114.75X_n - 21.05X_c + 30.96X_s,\ R^2 = 0.9218. \quad (8.8)$$

So, after adjusting for the effects of X_1 and X_2, the mean of Y is 114.75 lower in the Northeast than in the West, 21.05 lower in the Northcentral region than in the West, and 30.96 higher in the South than in the West. Notice the considerable change in regional mean differences when the effects of X_1 and X_2 are held constant.

Regression standardization

Regression standardization provides another method for comparing the mean of Y in different subgroups of a dataset. Regression standardization draws its name from demographic standardization, a technique it sometimes replaces. Nomenclature can be confusing: regression standardization has nothing whatsoever to do with *standardized regression coefficients*. Regression standardization comes in several varieties.

Variety 1: Standard means, variable coefficients In one variant of regression standardization, the same regression model is estimated separately in two or more subgroups of the dataset. The means of independent variables are calculated in one of those subgroups, which serves as the *standard subgroup*. Means from the standard subgroup are then substituted into the regression equation for each subgroup, producing an expected value of Y given independent variable means of the standard subgroup. Calculations below illustrate this procedure with a comparison of the mean number of divorces per state in the South and West regions of the US, using the 50-state data used above. Table 8.15 gives means of X_1, X_2 and Y for states in the South and West. Notice that the mean number of divorces per state (in hundreds) is 277.6 in the South and 210.8 in the West. So the *unadjusted data* show about 6700 more divorces per state in the South than in the West (277.6 – 210.8).

Table 8.16 shows the results of regressing Y on X_1 and X_2 for states in the South and, separately, for states in the West. The constant term and independent variable coefficients for states in the South are different from those obtained for states in the West, so it appears that the *relationship* of the number of divorces with urban and nonurban population size is not the same in the South as in the West. Next, these coefficients and the means from the South are used to calculate the expectation of Y given each region's regression coefficients and the South means. For the South,

$$E(Y \mid \text{South coefficients and South means})$$
$$= -14.45 + 77.97 \times 3.11$$
$$+ 31.75 \times 1.56 = 277.6; \qquad (8.9)$$

and for the West,

$$E(Y \mid \text{West coefficients and South means})$$
$$= 18.59 + 53.31 \times 3.11$$
$$+ 81.59 \times 1.56 = 311.7. \qquad (8.10)$$

These findings might be written up as follows:

> If the relationship of Y with X_1 and X_2 is allowed to vary across regions, but the means of X_1 and X_2 are standardized to values observed in the South, then the South shifts from an average of 6700 *more* divorces per state than the West to an average of 3400 *fewer* divorces per state. These findings suggest that the apparent greater average number of divorces in the South than in the West is an artifact of the differences between these regions in the numbers of urban and nonurban residents per state.

Variety 2: Standard coefficients, variable means   A second variety of regression

Table 8.15   Means of selected state characteristics, by South and West region

Variable	Variable mean	
	South	West
Urban population (millions), X_1	3.11	2.79
Nonurban population (millions), X_2	1.56	0.54
Number of divorces (hundreds), Y	277.63	210.76
Number of states, N	16	13

Table 8.16   Regression of Y and X_1 and X_2 for the South and West

Variable	Regression coefficient	
	South	West
Constant	–14.45	18.59
Urban population (millions), X_1	77.97	53.31
Nonurban population (millions), X_2	31.75	81.59
R^2	0.96	0.99

standardization estimates a regression in one subgroup only, and then combines those regression coefficients with the means in each other subgroup to calculate an expected mean of Y given the coefficients from the standard subgroup and the means of the other subgroup. For example, if the regression coefficients from the South are used as the standard, and the means for the South and the West are applied, the following results are obtained. For the South,

$$E(Y \mid \text{South coefficients and South means})$$
$$= -14.45 + 77.97 \times 3.11$$
$$+ 31.75 \times 1.56 = 277.6; \qquad (8.11)$$

and for the West,

$$E(Y \mid \text{South coefficients and West means})$$
$$= -14.45 + 77.97 \times 2.79$$
$$+ 31.75 \times 0.54 = 220.2. \qquad (8.12)$$

These results and the previous standardization results might be written up together as follows:

> If the relationship of Y with X_1 and X_2 is standardized to the regression equation fitted in the South only, but the means of X_1 and X_2 are set to their observed values in each region, then the South falls from an average of 6700 more divorces per state than

the West, to an average of 5700 more divorces per state than the West. This result suggests that regional differences in the relationship of Y with X_1 and X_2 contribute modestly to the difference between the mean of Y in the South and in the West. However, standardizing on the means of X_1 and X_2 suggests that it is differences in average sizes of the urban and nonurban populations of these states that accounts for the higher mean number of divorces in Southern states compared to Western states.

An early but still exemplary application of regression standardization is O.D. Duncan's (1968) paper 'Inheritance of Poverty or Inheritance of Race'. Duncan asks if black men earn less money than white men because black and white men have different work-related characteristics, or because their characteristics are treated differently in the labor market. In one analysis, Duncan performs a regression analysis of the earnings of black men and calculates the means of all variables for white men and for black men. The regression coefficients for blacks represent the labor market processes by which their educational attainment and other characteristics generate dollars of income. Duncan applies to this regression equation the observed means of variables for whites, thereby simulating a situation in which differences between white and black workers are eliminated, while differences in their labor market treatment are unchanged. He concludes that the source of black–white earnings differences is the black–white difference in labor market treatment, which is reflected in his analysis by differences in regression coefficients. Of course, Duncan's analysis standardizes only for variables that are included in his regression equation. Analyses with different independent variables might produce different conclusions.

Interpretation of the multiple regression R^2

The R^2 is often interpreted as a measure of the *quality* of a multiple regression analysis or the theory that motivates it. This interpretation is appropriate when the purpose of the model is solely to forecast values of the dependent variable. For example, engineers sometimes construct regression models

of complicated manufacturing processes. Independent variables in these analyses are measures of raw material inputs, and the dependent variable is a measure of the output from that process. Once estimated, a model of this sort might be used to make quick estimates of factory output at one time from measurements of raw materials consumed at an earlier time. An analysis like this is a convenient alternative to full-scale simulation of manufacturing processes, but its usefulness entirely depends upon its ability to produce values of $\hat{Y}$ that correspond closely to Y. R^2 is one measure of that correspondence.

Unlike factory input–output analysis, most social science research focuses on measuring the *effects* of independent variables rather than on forecasting or predicting the values of dependent variables (Holland, 1986). Further, many social processes are believed to have a large random (and therefore unexplainable) component. For example, social mobility analysts often estimate regression models in which the occupational status of adult men (sons) is regressed upon the occupational and educational characteristics of their fathers when the sons were adolescents. Naïve critics sometimes complain that these regressions have low R^2 statistics. These critics seldom consider that political battles and bloody wars have been fought to create a society less oppressive than one in which a father's occupation, years of schooling, and dollar income completely determine the occupational status of his son 20 or 30 years later. In such analyses, the R^2 can be interpreted as a characteristic of social process under analysis; a low R^2 indicates large amounts of a certain type of mobility, rather than a deficiency in the analysis.

When a statistical analysis is designed to untangle the effects of correlated causes of some dependent variable, R^2 can provide an especially myopic view of the quality of a regression analysis. For example, the multiple regression analysis of divorces in 50 states found substantially different coefficients for urban and nonurban population size. The difference between these coefficients informs thinking about how differences between urban and nonurban environments, or differences between the kinds of people who choose to live in urban and nonurban environments, affect divorce prevalence. However, the R^2 for this multiple regression analysis is 0.8829, which is hardly any larger than 0.8753, which is the R^2 for the simple regression of divorce frequency on urban population alone. Here, as in most situations in which the purpose of research is to understand the effects of suspected causes on a dependent variable, the independent variable coefficients are much more informative than the R^2.

R^2 corrected for degrees of freedom

A final word of caution about R^2 concerns its tendency to become large when regression analyses are estimated with small datasets. As the number of independent variables in a regression approaches the number of cases in the dataset used to estimate the regression, the value of R^2 tends to rise. A researcher who wishes to remove the effect of the number of cases can compute the R^2 corrected for degrees of freedom, which is more often called the *corrected* R^2, $\bar{R}^2$ or 'R-bar-squared.' Where N is the number of cases in the dataset, and k is the number of independent variables in the regression,

$$\bar{R}^2 = 1-(1 - R^2)\frac{N - 1}{N - k}. \qquad (8.13)$$

For example, if a regression analysis with 15 independent variables was fitted to a dataset with 25 cases and an R^2 of 0.8 were obtained, $\bar{R}^2$ would equal $1 - (1-0.8)(25-1)/(25-15) = 0.52$. Of course, $\bar{R}^2$ informs substantive questions only in situations in which the proportion of variance explained by a regression is itself informative. Those situations are rare in social science research.

Assumptions and computational requirements

Three commonly encountered conditions, usually the result of computer programming errors, make the numerical calculations of regression analysis impossible to compute:

More independent variables than data cases

Strictly speaking, the number of data cases must be at least one more than the number of independent variables in the regression. In practice, the number of data cases should exceed the number of independent variables by a substantial number. Technically and more accurately, the data cases must be sufficiently different from each other to permit solution of the simultaneous equations used to calculate the regression coefficients. This issue is considered in the next section.

Invariant variables

Computer programming errors sometimes reduce to zero the variation in variables. If a variable does not vary, then it has no variance to be explained by regression or any other method. Similarly, a variable that does not vary cannot explain the variance in another variable. For example, in a sample of sixth-grade students, a variable indicating grade in school cannot serve as an independent variable. In a sample of living persons, year of death cannot serve as a dependent variable. Programming errors are commonplace and all computer manipulations of data should be checked in several different ways.

Collinearity and multicollinearity among independent variables

Two variables are *collinear* if one explains all the variance in the other. For example, if X_1 is the urban population of states in *millions* of persons and X_4 is urban population in *thousands* of persons, X_1 and X_4 cannot both serve as independent variables in the same regression analysis. For another example, one might construct a variable equal to one if a survey respondent is male and zero otherwise, and another variable equal to one if a survey respondent is female and zero otherwise. It would not be possible to compute a single regression equation in which both of these variables are independent variables.

Collinearity is a special case of *multicollinearity*. An independent variable is *multicollinear* with other independent variables if all of the variance in the first variable is explained by the others. Regression coefficients for multicollinear variables cannot be computed. In the 50-state data, one might divide the states into mutually exclusive regions representing the West, South, Northeast and Northcentral areas of the country. Variables X_w, X_s, X_n, and X_c could then be defined, with $X_w = 1$ if a state is in the West region and $X_w = 0$ otherwise; $X_s = 1$ if a state is in the South region and $X_s = 0$ otherwise, $X_n = 1$ if a state is in the Northeast region and $X_n = 0$ otherwise, and $X_c = 1$ if a state is in the Northcentral region and $X_c = 0$ otherwise. These variables are multicollinear with each other. However, any three of these four state variables will not be multicollinear with each other. Perhaps the easiest way to identify the source of multicollinearity among the independent variables in a regression is to regress each independent variable on all of the others. If a variable is multicollinear with others, then the regression of that variable on the others will have an R^2 of 1 or nearly so. If a regression includes independent variables $X_1, X_2, ..., X_k$, this method will require k separate regressions. Some useful diagnostic signs of multicollinearity include large, statistically insignificant standardized coefficients and pairs of large, statistically insignificant coefficients with opposite signs. However, these diagnostic signs are not infallible.

Collinearity problems have four general solutions. First, variables that are theoretically as well as empirically similar can be summed or otherwise combined into a new variable. Simple additive functions of variables are sometimes useful for this purpose. Factor analysis, canonical correlations analysis and structural equations modeling with latent factors provide more powerful and elegant solutions. Second, some of the highly correlated variables can be dropped from the analysis. For example, if the first-year graduate school grade point average of MBA students is regressed on their IQ test scores, Scholastic Aptitude Test (SAT) scores, Graduate Record Examination scores and Graduate Management Admission Test scores, then multicollinearity is almost sure to occur. The analyst might solve this collinearity problem by forgoing the use of one or more of these test scores in her analysis or by first standardizing each of these scales to a mean of zero and a standard deviation of one, and then constructing a new ability measure by summing each respondent's rescaled score on all four tests. Third, the analyst can sometimes solve collinearity and multicollinearity problems by making use of computational algorithms that tolerate near-collinearity. However, as the cost of computing declines, most widely-used regression programs use very precise, computationally intensive algorithms in all regression calculations. If collinearity problems occur, it is increasingly likely that they have occurred with collinearity-resistant software. Fourth, and finally, an empirical Bayes technique called ridge regression can sometimes provide relief from collinearity and multicollinearity problems. Ridge regression estimates are biased, but they tend to produce lower estimation error than unbiased ordinary least-squares estimates when high levels of multicollinearity are present. Although there may be successful illustrations of ridge regression with sociological data, I am unaware of any successful use of ridge regression to provide estimates that answer substantive questions in sociology.

REGRESSION IN MATRIX NOTATION, AND STANDARD ASSUMPTIONS

Many useful results in regression are more easily explained in matrix notation than in scalar (nonmatrix) notation. This section presents the ordinary least-squares regression model in matrix notation. A working knowledge of matrix notation is necessary to understand most statistical reference works on regression and related methods.

Definitions

Define the following terms:

n	The number of observed cases in the sample data.
N	The number of elements in the population from which the sample data are drawn.
K	The number of independent variables, $X_1, X_2, ... , X_K$.
J	$K+1$.
X_{ij}	The value of X_j for the ith data case.
$X_{i, K+1}$	1 (the variable $X_J = X_{K+1} = 1$ for all cases; the regression coefficient for X_{k+1} is the regression constant term).
Y_i	The value of the dependent variable of the regression for the ith data case.
ε_i	The random disturbance for the ith case.
$\mathbf{X}$	A matrix with n rows (one for each data case) and $k+1$ columns, giving the values of the independent variables for all cases.
$\mathbf{Y}$	A matrix (vector) with n rows (one for each data case) and one column, giving the values of the dependent variable for all cases
ε	A matrix (vector) with n rows (one for each data case) and one column, giving the values of the disturbances for all cases.

Assumptions

Make the following assumptions.

1. **Linearity.** For the ith case, the value Y_i is produced by a process described as

$$Y_i = \sum_{j=1}^{K+1} \beta_j X_{ij} + \varepsilon_i. \qquad (8.14)$$

For the entire dataset, the processes that produce all the Y_i can be written as

$$Y = X\beta + \varepsilon. \qquad (8.15)$$

2. **Identification.** X has rank K (i.e., the X_js are not collinear or multicollinear).
3. **Disturbances.** $\text{var}[\varepsilon] = \sigma^2 I$; $E[\varepsilon \,|\, X] = 0$. Conditional on X, the expectations of the disturbances are all zero; all disturbances have population variance equal to the constant σ^2 (*homoscedasticity*); the disturbances are uncorrelated with each other (*independence*); and the disturbances are uncorrelated with X (that is, $X'\varepsilon = 0$ and $\varepsilon'\varepsilon = \sigma^2$).
4. **Constant X.** X is a matrix of constants. In experiments, this means that values of X are determined by the experimenter before the experiment. In nonexperimental research, this is an assumption that the values of X (but not the values of Y or ε) would be fixed in repeated samples. The assumption of constant X implies that errors in the sample data are uncorrelated with X.
5. **Normal ε.** $\varepsilon \,|\, X \sim N[0, \sigma^2 I]$. This assumption is helpful in deriving in small-sample results, and is largely unnecessary for large samples.

Calculation of regression coefficients and standard errors

The linearity assumption indicates that $Y = X\beta + \varepsilon$. Pre-multiplying both sides of this equation by X' and then again pre-multiplying both sides by $[X'X]^{-1}$ yields $[X'X]^{-1}[X'Y] - [X'X]^{-1}[X'e] = \beta$. But $X'\varepsilon = 0$ (by assumptions) so

$$\beta = [X'X]^{-1}[X'Y]. \qquad (8.16)$$

$\hat{\beta}$ is the sample estimate of β and is estimated from X and Y. Standard errors, significance tests and confidence intervals are available from the result $\hat{\beta} \,|\, X \sim N[\beta, \sigma^2(X'X)^{-1}]$. In practice σ^2 is almost never known, but is estimated as $s^2 = (e'e)/(n-K)$, where $e = Y - X\hat{\beta}$. So the variance–covariance matrix of $\hat{\beta}$ is given by $s^2(X'X)^{-1}$, distributed as t with $n-K-1$ degrees of freedom.

REGRESSION INFERENCE OF POPULATION PARAMETERS

The sampling variation and covariation of sample estimates

Regardless of the analyst's philosophical perspective on significance tests, they are generally expected for sample estimates of population characteristics, including regression coefficients. However, as the cost of computing plummets and the availability of huge datafiles grows, it has become common for analysts to examine datasets with thousands or tens of thousands of observations. When sample sizes become very large, even trivial results are statistically significant. It is useful to remember that a significant coefficient is merely a nonzero estimated coefficient that is *distinguishable* from zero. *Statistical significance is not a measure of strength or importance.* If a regression coefficient is distinguishable from zero (i.e., statistically significant), analysts are well advised to focus attention on the size of effects they find.

All significance tests are based on the notion that a researcher with limitless resources could draw many samples from the population under study. If each sample consists of n data cases, and if the same statistical analyses are performed in each sample, then the set of all possible samples of size n from the population provides a distribution of the estimates. For example, the distribution of estimates of the mean of variable Y is called the *sampling distribution* of the sample mean. The distribution of estimates of some regression coefficient β_i in the regression of Y on independent variables $X_1, X_2, ..., X_k$ is called the *sampling distribution of the sample estimate of β_i*. The circumflex designates an estimate, including sample estimates of regression parameters. For example, $\hat{\beta}_i$ denotes the sample estimate of regression coefficient β_i; $\hat{Y}$ denotes the sample estimate of $\hat{Y}$, the regression prediction of Y. In practice, circumflexes are cumbersome, so sample estimates are often distinguished from actual parameter values by context and accompanying verbiage rather than by symbols.

Sampling considerations lead to some important regression concepts, including the following:

- *The error of an estimate.* The difference between the estimate and the quantity that it estimates. For example, the error of $\hat{\beta}_i$ is $\hat{\beta}_i - \beta_i$.
- *The bias of an estimator.* The bias of estimator $\hat{\beta}_i$ of a coefficient β_i is the difference between the expectation of the estimator and the value of the coefficient, $E[\hat{\beta}_i] - \beta_i$. The estimator is said to be *biased* if the mean of the sampling distribution of $\hat{\beta}_i$ is not equal to β_i. Unbiased estimators are

common, but no single estimate of β_i is likely to have an error of zero. Biased estimators are commonly disparaged, but some biased estimators produce estimates with smaller errors, on average, than some unbiased estimators.

- *The standard error* of $\hat{\beta}_i$, S.E.$\hat{\beta}_i$. This is the standard deviation of the *sampling distribution* of $\hat{\beta}_i$. Recall that the standard error of the mean of a variable is the standard deviation of the sampling distribution of the sample estimate of the population mean. Under simple random sampling, S.E.$\hat{\beta}_i$ is proportional to $\sqrt{n-K-1}$, the square root of the sample size minus the number of regressors minus 1. Thus, all else equal, one must approximately quadruple the sample size to reduce standard errors by about half.

- *Consistent estimator.* A method for calculating an estimate is *consistent* if larger samples produce estimates with smaller errors.

- *Best.* A method for producing sample estimates of population parameters is *best* if the sampling distribution of those estimates has the smallest variance. That is, the best estimator produces estimates with the smallest standard errors.

- *BLUE.* As a mathematical property, regression estimates of β_i are linear. As a statistical property, they can be shown to be unbiased. Among linear, unbiased estimators, regression estimates of β_i can be shown to be best. Thus, the sophomorically amusing jargon, BLUE, 'best linear unbiased estimator'.

- *The variance–covariance matrix of regression coefficient estimates.* If one drew an infinite number of samples of size n from a population and estimated the same multiple regression in each sample, one would have a new dataset in which each sample was a data case, and the estimated regression coefficients for that sample were the variables. The standard deviation of each regression coefficient would be its standard error. The covariances between those estimates would be the error covariances of the estimates. When arranged in a matrix these variances and covariances are called the variance–covariance matrix of estimates.

Once the variance–covariance matrix of estimates is available, many tests are available. The variance–covariance matrix of regression coefficient estimates can be calculated in two straightforward ways. The first method (and the most common) is based on the central limit theorem and requires some modest assumptions about the data under analysis. The second method is to simulate the distribution of samples by resampling ('bootstrapping') the dataset, calculating the regression analysis in each of the resampled datasets, and then using the observed distribution of regression coefficient estimates to calculate the variance–covariance matrix of the estimates. In practice, with large samples, both techniques produce identical test outcomes nearly all of the time. With small samples, surprising results appear frequently in all aspects of data analysis.

Some useful significance tests

There are three main varieties of tests of hypotheses: likelihood tests, Wald tests, and Lagrange multiplier tests. In large samples, all three tests are asymptotically equivalent, so the choice among them tends to be made on the basis of convenience (for discussion, see Greene 2000: 149–60). If least-squares methods are used for regression calculations, as is usually the case, then likelihood tests are based on the t, F, and Pearson χ^2 (often abbreviated G^2) distributions. If maximum likelihood estimation methods are used to calculate regression coefficients (rather than the usual least-squares methods of regression), then those calculations produce the log-likelihood statistic λ as a natural byproduct. If λ is calculated, then the quantity -2λ, (often called L^2), is distributed as χ^2 and is used for tests. L^2 has convenient additivity properties that G^2 lacks.

Depending on the test used, the critical region for a test statistic may be determined according to the t, χ^2, F or another distribution. Depending on the hypothesis, a reliable test sometimes can be accomplished by various methods, allowing the analyst to choose among two or even three of these distributions. It can be demonstrated that if a test statistic is distributed as t with df degrees of freedom, then, with some modification, its square will also be distributed as χ^2 with df degrees of freedom, and it will also be distributed as F with 1 (in the numerator) and df (in the denominator) degrees of freedom, where df is the same numerical value.[1]

Modern computer programs have made it easy to compute significance tests on most regression parameter estimates. These programs obviate the need for manual calculations of significance tests. These programs have also reduced to historical curiosities the clever tricks and libraries of personal computer programs that earlier generations of regression analysts used to test hypotheses about functions of several coefficients, or to make simultaneous tests of several hypotheses. For the analyst with mathematical training and inclination, it is still extremely useful to learn the theory behind these tests. Artful data analysts frequently invent new statistics for which new tests are required, and some computer programs include more of the standard significance tests than others. For those who lack interest or facility with mathematics, statistical experts and diligent computer programmers must suffice. Table 8.17 gives the formulas for some useful regression significance tests for analyses involving one regression equation estimated on one sample.

Covariance analysis: Tests for group differences in regression coefficients   A regression equation is a mathematical representation of the structure by which various characteristics of data cases are related. Much research is undertaken to examine group differences in structure. So it is often useful to ask if and how the parameters of a regression equation differ across several groups. For example, one might examine the structure of wage determination by estimating the effects of educational attainment and age on earnings of employed persons. One might then ask if these effects are different for men and women. For another example, one might estimate the effects of family income and parental educational attainment on survey respondents' years of school completed; after performing this analysis for the population as a whole, one might also ask if effects are different for members of different race ethnicity groups.

Sampling error alone could produce group differences in regression parameter estimates, so significance tests are required. The set of appropriate tests and procedures is called the analysis of covariance (ANCOVA). ANCOVA tests three major null hypotheses:

(a) *Equal constants*: Is it possible to reject the null hypothesis that the regression constant term is the same for all the groups considered?

(b) *Equal coefficients*: After allowing for group differences in intercepts, is it possible to reject the null hypothesis that the coefficients of all independent variables in the analysis are identical in all groups considered?

(c) *Overall homogeneity*: Is it possible to reject the null hypothesis that the regression constants and the independent variable coefficients are the same for all groups considered?

The test of equal constants is accomplished by creating a dummy variable for membership in each of the groups except one (hereafter called the *reference group*). The regression is computed first without these dummy variables, and then with them. The 'multiple partial *F* test' tests the null hypothesis that the dummy variables (and therefore differences among the intercepts for the groups) are all zero. The choice of which group dummy to omit is arbitrary and inconsequential for the test. (Intercept differences between specific pairs of groups can be tested by testing the hypothesis that their dummy variables have equal coefficients.)

There are two basic approaches to the tests of equal coefficients and overall homogeneity. The first approach is to divide one's data into cases belonging to each of the groups under investigation, and then to estimate the regression analysis separately in each group. Significance tests for important group differences are available by comparing coefficients and R^2 statistics. A second approach uses dummy variables to represent groups. With modern computer programs, the second approach usually simplifies significance testing and calculation of differences between groups. The first approach usually simplifies calculation of regression coefficients in each group.

The second approach has three basic steps:

1. Construct a dummy variable for membership in each of the groups except one (the *reference group*).
2. Construct new variables equal to the product of each of the dummy variables and each of the regression independent variables.
3. Estimate three separate regression equations: the regression of the dependent variable on only the independent variables; the regression of the dependent variable on the independent variables and

Table 8.17 *Common regression significance tests*

	Null hypothesis	Description of test	Alternative hypothesis	A test statistic (TS) for this test	TS distribution, degrees of freedom, α (significance level)	Notes on use
1a	$H_0 : \beta_i = 0$	'Two-tailed significance test' for one coefficient	$H_a : \beta_i \neq 0$	$\hat{\beta_i}/\text{S.E.}\hat{\beta_i}$	Reject null if TS> $t_{n-K-1}\,(1-\alpha/2)$	Usually use two-tailed test for control variables; use one-tailed tests for theoretically developed hypotheses.
1b	$H_0 : \beta_i = 0$	'One-tailed significance test' for one coefficient	$H_a : \beta_i > 0$	$\hat{\beta_i}/\text{S.E.}\hat{\beta_i}$	Reject null if TS> $t_{n-K-1}\,(1-\alpha)$	
1c	$H_0 : \beta_i = 0$	'One-tailed significance test' for a coefficient	$H_a : \beta_i < 0$	$-\hat{\beta_i}/\text{S.E.}\hat{\beta_i}$	Reject null if TS> $t_{n-K-1}\,(1-\alpha)$	
2	$H_0 : \beta_1 = \beta_2 = \ldots = \beta_{k-1} = \beta_k = 0$	All coefficients in an equation equal to zero	$H_a : \beta_1, \beta_2, \beta_{k-1}, \beta_k$ not all zero	$\dfrac{R^2/K}{(1-R^2)/(n-K-1)}$	Reject null if TS> $F_{k,\,n-K-1}\,(1-\alpha)$	This is the test for 'overall significance' of regression.
3	$H_0 : \beta_{l+1} = \beta_{l+2} = \ldots = \beta_{l+M} = 0$	Several coefficients in same equation all equal to zero	$H_a : \beta_{l+1}, \beta_{l+2}, \ldots, \beta_{l+M}$ not all 0	$\dfrac{(R_2^2 - R_1^2)/M}{(1-R_2^2)/(n-M-l-1)}$	Reject null if TS> $F_{M,\,n-M-l-1}\,(1-\alpha)$	Called *multiple partial F test*; useful (a) when several regression dummy variables, interaction terms or polynomial terms correspond to a single theoretical variable, or (b) when testing for subgroup differences represented by dummy variables and interaction terms. Regress Y on $X_1, \ldots, X_l$ to obtain R_1^2. Regress Y on $X_1, \ldots, X_l, X_{l+1}, \ldots, X_M$ to obtain R_2^2.

Table 8.17 (Continued)

	Null hypothesis	Description of test	Alternative hypothesis	A test statistic (TS) for this test	TS distribution, degrees of freedom, α (significance level)	Notes on use
4a	$H_0: \beta_1 = c$, where c is a constant	One coefficient equals a specified constant	$H_a: \beta_1 \neq c$	$(\hat{\beta}_1 - c)/S.E.\beta_i$	Reject null if TS> $t_{n-k-1}(1-\alpha/2)$	
4b	$H_0: \beta_i = c$, where c is a constant	One coefficient equals zero	$H_a: \beta_1 > c$	$(\hat{\beta}_1 - c)/S.E.\beta_i$	Reject null if TS> $t_{n-k-1}(1-\alpha)$	
4c	$H_0: \beta_i = c$, where c is a constant	One coefficient equals zero	$H_a: \beta_1 < c$	$-(\hat{\beta}_1 - c)/S.E.\beta_i$	Reject null if TS> $t_{n-k-1}(1-\alpha)$	
5a	$H_0: \beta_i = \beta_j$	Two coefficients in same equation equal to each other ('two-tailed')	$H_a: \beta_i \neq \beta_j$	$\dfrac{\hat{\beta}_i - \hat{\beta}_j}{\sqrt{(S.E.\hat{\beta}_i)^2 + (S.E.\hat{\beta}_j)^2 - 2cov(\hat{\beta}_i,\hat{\beta}_j)}}$	Reject null if TS> $t_{n-k-1}(1-\alpha/2)$	$cov(\hat{\beta}_i,\hat{\beta}_j)$ is the covariance of the sample estimates of the coefficients. Obtain $cov(\hat{\beta}_i,\hat{\beta}_j)$ from variance–covariance matrix of the coefficient estimates.
5b	$H_0: \beta_i = \beta_j$	Two coefficients in same equation equal to each other ('one-tailed')	$H_a: \beta_i > \beta_j$	$\dfrac{\hat{\beta}_i - \hat{\beta}_j}{\sqrt{(S.E.\hat{\beta}_i)^2 + (S.E.\hat{\beta}_j)^2 - 2cov(\hat{\beta}_i,\hat{\beta}_j)}}$	Reject null if TS> $t_{n-k-1}(1-\alpha)$	
6	$H_0: Y_i = \hat{Y}_i \mid X_1 = x_{1i}, X_2 = x_{2i},..., X_k = x_{ik} = c$, where c is a constant	Regression prediction for a case in the data used to estimate the regression equals a constant c, with specific independent variable values	$H_a: (\hat{Y} \mid X_1 = x_{1i}, X_2 = x_{2i},...,X_k = x_{ik}) \neq c$	$\dfrac{(\hat{Y}_i \mid X_1 = x_{1i}, X_2 = x_{2i},...,X_k = x_{ik}) - }{s\sqrt{h_i}}$	Reject null if TS> $t_{n-k-1}(1-\alpha/2)$	$h_i = \mathbf{x}_i(\mathbf{X'X})^{-1}\mathbf{x}_i'$, where $\mathbf{x}_i$ is the vector of values of the Xs for the case in which $X_1 = x_{1i}, X_2 = x_{2i},..., X_k = x_{ik}$, and s is the mean square error for the regression ($s^2 = [\mathbf{e'e}]/[n-K]$).

(Continued)

Table 8.17 *(Continued)*

	Null hypothesis	Description of test	Alternative hypothesis	A test statistic (TS) for this test	TS distribution, degrees of freedom, α (significance level)	Notes on use
7	$\hat{Y}_i \mid X_1 = x_{j1},\ X_2 = x_{j2},\dots,$ $X_k = x_{jk} = c$, where c is a constant	Regression forecast for a new case not in the data used to estimate the regression equals a constant c, with specified independent variable values	$H_a : (\hat{Y}_i \mid X_1 = x_{j1},$ $X_2 = x_{j2},\dots,\ X_k = x_{jk}) \neq c$	$\dfrac{(\hat{Y}_i \mid X_1 = x_{j1},\ X_2 = x_{j2},\dots,X_k = x_{jk}) - c}{s\sqrt{1 + h_j}}$	Reject null if TS > $t_{n-K-1}\ (1-\alpha/2)$	Use in forecasting (predicting) the value of the dependent variable for a hypothetical case with specified values of independent variables.
8	$H_0 : E(\hat{Y}_i \mid X_1 = x_{j1},\ X_2 = x_{j2},\dots,$ $X_k = x_{jk} = c) = c$, where c is a constant and number of cases $= n'$	Prediction for expected value of new case not in data used to estimate the regression equals constant c, with specified independent variable values	$H_a : (\hat{Y}_i \mid X_1 = x_{j1},$ $X_2 = x_{j2},\dots,\ X_k = x_{jk}) \neq c$	$\dfrac{(\hat{Y}_i \mid X_1 = x_{j1},\ X_2 = x_{j2},\dots,X_k = x_{jk}) - c}{s\sqrt{1/n' + h_j}}$	Reject null if TS > $t_{n-K-1}\ (1-\alpha/2)$	Use in predicting the value of the expectation of $\hat{Y}$ in a sample of n' cases. Useful in regression standardizations, in which the means of independent variables from one subgroup are multiplied by the coefficients of those variables obtained from regression analysis of another dataset to obtain an expected value of the dependent variable under hypothetical conditions.

the dummy variables; and the regression of the dependent variable on the independent variables, the dummy variables, and the products of the dummy variables and the independent variables.

For an example of the second approach, suppose an analyst wishes to investigate the extent to which persons' educational attainment is affected by the educational attainment of their parents. For a stark, but still useful analysis, this analyst might use survey data to estimate the regression of respondent's educational attainment Y on the educational attainment of the respondent's father (X_1) and the educational attainment of the respondent's mother (X_2). The analyst would also define three dummy variables for race: D_1, which equals 1 for respondents who report themselves to be white, and zero for all others; D_2, which equals 1 for respondents who report themselves to be black, and zero for all others; and D_3, which equals 1 for respondents who report themselves to be neither black nor white, and zero for all others. Suppose that the analyst wishes to compare blacks and nonblack–nonwhites to whites: D_1 would be dropped from consideration. The variables D_2X_1, D_2X_2, D_3X_1, and D_3X_2 would be constructed by multiplying various combinations of dummy and independent variables. Then the analyst would estimate the following regression equations (I use α and γ to distinguish the coefficients obtained from each regression analysis):

$$\hat{Y} = \beta_0 + \beta_1 X_1 + \beta_2 X_2, \tag{8.17}$$

$$\hat{Y} = \alpha_0 + \alpha_1 X_1 + \alpha_2 X_2$$
$$+ \alpha_3 D_2 + \alpha_4 D_3, \tag{8.18}$$

$$\hat{Y} = \gamma_0 + \gamma_1 X_1 + \gamma_2 X_2 + \gamma_3 D_2$$
$$+ \gamma_4 D_3 + \gamma_5 (D_2 X_1) + \gamma_6 (D_2 X_2)$$
$$+ \gamma_7 (D_3 X_1) + \gamma_8 (D_3 X_2). \tag{8.19}$$

Equation (8.17) includes no measures or mechanisms that could allow the intercept term or any coefficients to vary across subgroups of the dataset. Equation (8.18) includes dummy variables that allow the intercept to vary across the three racial subgroups, but it contains no mechanism that could allow the independent variable coefficients to vary across subgroups.[2] The hypothesis that all groups have the same intercept can be tested by using the R^2 statistics for equations (8.17) and (8.18) to compute the multiple

partial F test (Table 8.17, row 3) of the null hypothesis that all the group dummy variables have coefficients of zero (i.e., $H_0 : \alpha_3 = \alpha_4 = 0$).

By very similar arithmetic, equation (8.19) permits the intercept to vary across race groups and it allows coefficients of X_1 and X_2 to vary across groups. For example, for a white, D_2 and D_3 are both zero, so all terms of equation (8.19) that include D_2 or D_3 are also zero, and the regression is given by $\hat{Y} = \gamma_0 + \gamma_1 X_1 + \gamma_2 X_2$. For a person in the black race category, $D_3 = 0$ and $D_2 = 1$, so all terms involving D_3 are zero. For a respondent in the black race category, the constant term is $\gamma_0 + \gamma_3$, the coefficient of X_1 is $\gamma_1 + \gamma_5$ and the coefficient of X_2 is $\gamma_2 + \gamma_6$. The coefficient γ_5 is the difference between the coefficient of X_1 for whites and for blacks, and the standard error of γ_5 is the standard error for that difference.

Table 8.18 gives coefficient estimates for equations (8.17)–(8.19) based on data from the 1994 General Social Survey, a personal interview survey of a national sample of the adult population of the United States. Table 8.19 gives results of tests of ANCOVA significance tests based on the R^2 statistics in Table 8.18. The test reported in the first row of Table 8.19 rejects the null hypothesis that the neither independent variable coefficients nor intercepts are different for whites, blacks and others ($p < 0.02$). This test does not indicate if the intercepts, coefficients, or both differ across race categories. The test reported in the second row of Table 8.19 rejects the null hypothesis that intercepts are equal in all groups ($p < 0.01$). But the test reported in the third row fails to reject ($p \geq 0.05$) the null hypothesis that all four of the race–parental schooling interactions have zero coefficients. More precisely, we cannot reject the hypothesis that sampling error alone accounts for the race differences in effects of parental schooling shown in equation (8.19). Lacking evidence of race differences in the coefficients of parental schooling, we would conclude that equation (8.19) adds needless complication to the model provided by equation (8.18).

It is important to emphasize that the significance test in line 3 of Table 8.19 *does not reject* the hypothesis that race differences in parental schooling effects exist. Those differences might exist, but these tests indicate that our estimates of them cannot be distinguished from differences due to random sampling error, at a 5% significance level.

Table 8.18 *Regression of schooling on parents' schooling and race dummies, with standard errors (in parentheses) and t-statistics (in brackets) 1994 General Social Survey*

Independent variable	Overall homogeneity model (8.17)	Different intercepts but equal variable coefficients model (8.18)	Different intercepts and different coefficients model (8.19)
Father's schooling, X_1	β_1 0.216 (0.017) [12.57]	α_1 0.211 (0.017) [12.21]	γ_1 0.340 (0.081) [4.22]
Mother's schooling, X_2	β_2 0.145 (0.021) [6.90]	α_2 0.150 (0.021) [7.10]	γ_2 −0.010 (0.086) [−0.12]
White dummy, D_1		α_3 −0.618 (0.284) [−2.17]	γ_3 −0.861 (0.703) [−1.22]
Black dummy, D_2		α_4 −0.985 (0.330) [−2.99]	γ_4 −0.882 (0.845) [−1.04]
White father's schooling, D_1X_1			γ_5 −0.130 (0.083) [−1.57]
White mother's schooling, D_1X_2			γ_6 0.169 (0.089) [1.91]
Black father's schooling, D_2X_1			γ_7 −0.178 (0.096) [−1.86]
Black mother's schooling, D_2X_2			γ_8 0.181 (0.104) [1.75]
Constant	β_0 9.704 −0.194 [50.08]	α_0 10.335 −0.321 [32.20]	γ_0 10.488 (0.668) [15.70]
n	2015	2015	2015
R^2	0.211	0.215	0.217

Further, the tests reported in Table 8.19 are two-tailed tests, based on the absence of a substantive hypothesis about the signs of the race-parental schooling variable coefficients. If one hypothesized negative values for γ_5 and γ_7, and positive values for γ_6 and γ_8, then the γ_6, γ_7, and γ_8 would each be statistically significant (one-tailed tests, $p \leq 0.05$). Informative significance testing always requires guidance by a substantive theory.

It is also important to emphasize that the race–parental schooling interactions in model (8.19) can be interpreted as race differences in the effects of parental schooling, *and* as

Table 8.19 ANCOVA tests for Table 8.18 regressions

Test	F	Degrees of freedom	Significance level
1. Test of model C vs model A (overall homogeneity)	2.561 94	6, 2006	0.018
2. Test of model B vs model A (unequal coefficients but equal intercepts)	5.121 01	2, 2010	0.006
3. Test of model C vs model B (unequal coefficients)	1.280 97	4, 2006	0.275

schooling differences in the effects of race. For example, the positive value of γ_6 (0.169; statistically significant, $p \leq 0.05$, one-tailed test) indicates that the effect of mother's schooling is larger for whites than for persons in the 'other' race category. But that same coefficient indicates that the effect of white race is larger at higher levels of mother's educational attainment than at lower levels of mother's educational attainment. This last point is discussed further in the section on nonlinear and nonadditive models.

NONLINEAR AND NONADDITIVE MODELS

In spite of its name, linear regression analysis is a powerful tool for examining *nonlinear* and *nonadditive* relationships among variables. Although the regression method estimates the parameters of a linear combination of independent variables, the dependent variable and each of the independent variables can be a nonlinear function of a variable, and the independent variables can be nonlinear and nonadditive functions of other variables. This property of regression permits it to be used to examine a wide range of nonlinear and nonadditive models. This section considers the estimation and interpretation of some useful and common nonlinear and nonadditive models.

Effect measures

Philosophical arguments about the nature of causation notwithstanding (see Holland, 1986), in most social science uses of regression, the *effect* of an independent variable on a dependent variable is the *rate* at which differences in the independent variable are associated with (or cause) differences or changes in the dependent variable. This definition is usually operationalized with measures that state the rate of change in the dependent variable per unit change in the causal (or independent) variable. For example, path coefficients, regression coefficients, and beta weights are all rate-of-change measures. Rate-of-change measures are usually contrasted with variance-explained measures. The Pearsonian correlation (r), the R^2 statistic, $\bar{R}^2$, and the coefficient of alienation ($\sqrt{1-R^2}$) are all variance-explained measures. Variance-explained effect measures are cumbersome because they lack direct correspondence to theoretical statements of the form, 'X causes Y', and because they do not indicate how much change in a dependent variable is produced, on average, by a given change in an independent variable.

Mathematically, rate-of-change measures are *derivatives* (when there is only one independent variable) or *partial derivatives* (when there is more than one independent variable): The derivative dY/dX is the *rate* at which a dependent variable Y changes per unit change in independent variable X. The partial derivative $\partial Y/\partial X_i$ is the *rate* at which dependent variable Y changes per unit change in independent variable X_i, net of the effects of other independent variables in the model that influence Y. Pictorially, the derivative is the slope of the graph relating values of Y to values of X_i, and the partial derivative is the slope of the multidimensional surface relating values of Y to values of the independent variables that cause Y in the model. Thus when

$$Y = \beta_0 + \sum_{i=1}^{i} \beta_i X_i + \varepsilon, \qquad (8.20)$$

then the graph relating Y to X_1 is a straight line, and $\partial Y/\partial X_1$ is merely the coefficient for X_1.

The effect of X_i on Y is said to be *linear* if $\partial Y/\partial X_i$ equals a constant. Equivalently, linearity

Table 8.20 *Some common measures of effect of X_i on Y evaluated at X = x*

Scale for measuring changes in X_i (independent variable)	Scale for measuring changes in Y (dependent variable)	Common name for effect measure	Common formulas for effect measure (partial derivative) when $X_i = x_i$ and $Y = y$
Natural	Natural	Unstandardized effect, metric effect, raw effect	$\dfrac{\partial Y}{\partial X_i}$
Natural	Proportional change	Rate of return to X_i	$\dfrac{\partial Y/y}{\partial X_i} = \dfrac{\partial Y}{\partial X_i}\dfrac{1}{y}$
Proportional change	Proportional change	Point elasticity of Y with respect to X_i	$\dfrac{\partial Y/y}{\partial X_i/x_i} = \dfrac{\partial Y}{\partial X_i}\dfrac{x_i}{y}$
Standardized ($\mu = 0,\ \sigma = 1$)	Standardized ($\mu = 0,\ \sigma = 1$)	Standardized effect, beta, β_i	$\dfrac{\partial Y^*}{\partial X_i^*} = \dfrac{\partial Y/\sigma_Y}{\partial X_i/\sigma_{X_i}} = \dfrac{\partial Y}{\partial X_i}\dfrac{\sigma_{X_i}}{\sigma_Y}$
Natural	Standardized ($\mu = 0,\ \sigma = 1$)	Semi-standardized[a]	$\dfrac{\partial Y^*}{\partial X_i} = \dfrac{\partial Y/\sigma_Y}{\partial X_i} = \dfrac{\partial Y}{\partial X_i}\dfrac{1}{\sigma_Y}$

[a]This effect measure is not commonly used, but it is particularly applicable to situations in which Y is a continuous variable that lacks an intuitively meaningful metric, and X_i is a dummy variable or other variable that assumes only integer values.

is the property that an additional unit of X_i is always associated with the same number of additional units of Y (i.e. $\partial^2 Y/\partial X_i^2 = 0$). A statement that the effect of X_i on Y is *nonlinear* is a statement that $\partial Y/\partial X_i$ varies according to the value of X_i (i.e., $\partial^2 Y/\partial X_i^2 \neq 0$).

The effect of X_i on Y is said to be *additive* with respect to some other independent variable X_j if the rate of change in Y per unit change in X_i does not vary according to the value of X_j (i.e., $\partial^2 Y/\partial X_j X_i = 0$). Effects of independent variables on a dependent variable are said to be *nonadditive* if these effects do vary according to the value of other independent variables. Nonlinear and nonadditive effects are common in social science research and theory:

- Education and labor market researchers often find that the effects of schooling increase as the total amount of schooling increases: for example, an additional year of schooling has a greater effect on political liberalism and earnings for persons who have already completed 11 years of school than for people who have already completed only 6 years of school.
- At very early ages, the mental ability of individuals increases with each additional year of age. At later ages, the association between age and 'intelligence' vanishes, and then, at even higher ages, the effect of age on intelligence becomes negative.
- Educational attainment appears to modify the effect of increasing age on individuals'

adult intelligence and health. The rate of change increases with each additional year of schooling completed by the individual.
- Observing that neighborhoods tend to have either very high or very low proportions of minority residents, analysts have hypothesized that residential race discrimination declines drastically, or 'tips' as the proportion of minority group members in the neighborhood approaches some threshold value, perhaps 5%, 10%, or 20%.
- Economists talk of 'increasing returns to scale', as the unit cost of producing a good drops at ever-increasing rates as the volume of production increases.

In computing rates of change, analysts can choose the scales on which changes in variable values are measured. The most common choices are the natural metric of the variable, the standardized metric (mean of zero and standard deviation of one), and the proportional metric. Table 8.20 lists various combinations of some commonly used scales and the usual name for the (partial) derivative of Y with respect to X_i. The 'semi-standardized' metric is not widely used, although it is well suited to situations in which an independent variable X_i is a dummy variable. The semi-standardized effect is the number of standard deviations of change in Y associated with a change from 0 to 1 in the dummy variable X_i.

Economists tend to use elasticities and rates of return more than sociologists.

Sociologists tend to use standardized effects more than economists. But, aside from the obvious connection between investment theory and rates of return, disciplinary differences in these practices may be more the result of custom than anything else. Unless motivated by a particular theoretical concern, researchers in both disciplines use the standardized or percentage metric primarily to skirt problems of interpretation when one or both variables are measured according to a scale that has no intuitively meaningful unit, as in the case of many attitude scales used in survey research, or when scales of different independent variables are not directly comparable, as when work is measured in hours and income is measured in dollars. Standardized effects avoid interpretational problems when variables are measured on scales that lack a meaningful zero point and/or comparable units of measurement.

The relationships among unstandardized effects, standardized effects, elasticities, and rates of return are straightforward. In the notation of partial derivatives, the rate of change in Y per unit change in X can be written as $\partial Y / \partial X_1$, where ∂Y is the change in Y and ∂X_1 is the change in X_1. (This is a gross simplification of the mathematical concepts, but not a distortion of them.) Thus the unstandardized effect is $\partial Y / \partial X_1$. To measure changes in one of these variables in standardized units, divide it by the variable's standard deviation. Thus the standardized effect of X_i on Y is

$$\frac{\partial Y / \sigma_Y}{\partial X_1 / \sigma_{X_1}} = \frac{\partial Y}{\partial X_1} \frac{\sigma_{X_1}}{\sigma_Y}.$$

Similarly, to measure change in one of these variables in proportional terms, divide the change in the variable by the initial value of the variable. Thus the elasticity of Y with respect to X is

$$\frac{\partial Y / Y}{\partial X_1 / X_1} = \frac{\partial Y}{\partial X_1} \frac{X_1}{Y}$$

And the rate of return to Y is

$$\frac{\partial Y / Y}{\partial X_1} = \frac{\partial Y / \partial X_1}{Y}.$$

To give an empirical example, consider the model $Y = 4 + 3X_1 + 2X_2 + \varepsilon$, where Y, X_1, and X_2 are variables and ε is an error term with an expectation of zero such that X and Z are uncorrelated with ε. Suppose also that the standard deviation of X_1 is 2 and the standard

deviation of Y is 12. The unstandardized effect of X_1 on Y is 3. To get the standardized effect, we multiply 3 by 2 (the standard deviation of X_1) and divide by 12 (the standard deviation of Y), obtaining a value of 0.5. To calculate the point elasticity, we must choose values of X_1 and Y at which to calculate the point elasticity. When $X = 7$ and $Y = 4$, the elasticity equals the unstandardized effect multiplied by 7/4, or $3 \times 7/4 = 5.25$, indicating a *rate of change* (not an actual change) of 5.25% in Y per 1% change in X_1. Similarly, calculation of the rate of return requires choice of a value of Y. When $Y = 6$, the rate of return is $3 \times 1/6 = 0.5$, indicating a rate of change of 50% in Y per unit change in X_1. When $Y = 15$, the rate of return is $3 \times 1/15 = 0.2$, indicating a 20% change in Y per unit change in X_1. Note that the elasticity varies with the values of X_1 and Y in this example, that the rate of return varies with the value of Y, and that the standardized and unstandardized effects are constant over the range of X_1 and Y. Below, I discuss models in which the point elasticity or the rate of return is constant and the standardized and unstandardized effects vary with the values of X_1 and/or Y.

Some useful nonlinear and nonadditive specifications

Multiplicative interactions Independent variables X_1 and X_2 are said to interact if their effects on the dependent variable Y are nonadditive. When the independent variable X_1 is hypothesized to interact with independent variable X_2, but not other independent variables, then the following function may prove to be useful:

$$Y = \beta_0 + \beta_1 X_1 + \beta_2 X_2 + \beta_3 X_1 X_2$$
$$+ \sum_{i=1}^{I} \alpha_i Z_i + \varepsilon, \qquad (8.21)$$

where X_1, X_2 and the Z_i are independent variables, Y is the dependent variable, the β_i are regression coefficients, the α_i are regression coefficients, and ε is the error. In practice, this equation is estimated by creating a variable X_3 equal to the product of X_1 and X_2 and then regressing Y on X_1, X_2, X_3 and the Z_i. $X_1 X_2$ (or X_3) is called a *multiplicative interaction term*. The null hypothesis that $\beta_3 = 0$ may be tested by the usual t-test, for the significance of a regression coefficient. If the coefficient for the product $X_1 X_2$ is significantly different from zero, then the researcher has evidence that the effects of X_1 and X_2 on Y are nonadditive. With evidence that nonadditivity is present, neither the coefficient for X_1 nor the coefficient for X_2 can be interpreted meaningfully without simultaneously considering the coefficient for the product term.

In equation (8.21) the effect of X_1 on Y is $\partial Y/\partial X_1 = \beta_1 + \beta_3 X_2$. The effect of X_2 on Y is $\partial Y/\partial X_2 = \beta_2 + \beta_3 X_1$. Thus, the effect of X_1 on Y changes linearly with X_2, and the effect of X_2 on Y changes linearly with X_1. Notice that the Z_i do not enter into the formulas for the effects of X_1 and X_2 on Y; this is the mathematical equivalent of saying that the Z_i do not interact with X_1 or X_2 in causing Y. Effects of X_1 and X_2 on Y can also be expressed in standardized form by multiplying the metric, or unstandardized, effect of X_1 by the ratio of the standard deviations, σ_{X_1}/σ_Y. Notice that the standardized effect of X_1, like its unstandardized effect, varies according to the value of X_2.

Researchers sometimes subtract a constant from X_1 and/or X_2 before calculating the product of these variables. This procedure alters the correlation of $X_1 X_2$ with X_1 and X_2, thereby seeming to offer a remedy for the near-collinearity among independent variables in regression equations that include X_1, X_2 and $X_1 X_2$. However, any nonadditive *effects* of X_1 and X_2 on Y are unchanged by adding or subtracting constants to either or both of these variables before calculating their product.[3] In addition, this procedure does not at all change the *joint* statistical significance of the coefficients of X_1, X_2 and $X_1 X_2$. Finally, subtracting constants from X_1 and X_2 before calculating their product provides opportunities for mischief by permitting the analyst to pick subtraction constants that reduce to zero the coefficients for X_1 and/or X_2. To do so, first calculate the regression $Y = \beta_0 + \beta_1 X_1 + \beta_2 X_2 + \beta_3 X_1 X_2$ to obtain values of β_1, β_2, and β_3, then define new variables $X_1' = (X_1 - (-\beta_2/\beta_3))$ and $X_2' = (X_2 - (-\beta_1/\beta_3))$. Next, estimate the regression equation, $Y = \alpha_0 + \alpha_1 X_1 + \alpha_2 X_2 + \alpha_3 X_1' X_2'$. The new regression will explain exactly the same variance in Y as the original, but the effects of X_1 and X_2 (not the effects of X_1' and X_2') will be 'moved' to the product term, where they will be hidden from view. However, effect measures for X_1 and X_2 will be identical to effect measures obtained from the old regression results.

Parabolas, higher-order polynomials and fractional polynomials   The parabola is one of the most useful mathematical functions in regression analysis of social data. The general functional form of the parabola is $Y = \beta_0 + \beta_1 X + \beta_2 X^2 + \varepsilon$. Because social science models generally involve several independent variables, it is useful to generalize the function to

$$Y = \beta_0 + \beta_1 X_1 + \beta_2 X_1^2 + \sum_{i=1}^{I} \alpha_i Z_i + \varepsilon, \quad (8.22)$$

where the βs and the αs are parameters; where X_1, Y, and the Z_i are variables; and where ε is the error. The usefulness of the parabola grows out of the many shapes it can assume, dependent only on the values of β_1 and β_2. Figure 8.5 shows some of those shapes.

Part of the tremendous appeal of the parabolic function for social science research stems from the fact that its parameters can be estimated with ordinary least-squares regression. Thus to fit equation (8.22) one would merely create a new variable equal to X_1^2 and then regress Y on X_1, X_1^2, and the Z_i. The t-statistic for β_2 would be used to test the null hypothesis that the coefficient for X_1^2 is zero. If that coefficient is zero, then one cannot reject the hypothesis that the relationship between Y and X is either linear or else of a nonparabolic, nonlinear form. Because scientific aesthetics prefer simplicity and because a model with one coefficient for X generally is considered simpler than a model with coefficients for X_1 and X_1^2, then we act as if X_1 has only linear effects if the coefficient for X_1^2 is not statistically significant. But if the coefficient for X_1^2 is significantly different from zero, then the researcher has evidence that the relationship between Y and X is nonlinear and that this relationship is fitted more accurately by a parabola than by a straight line. For both mathematical and statistical reasons, once one has drawn this conclusion, then the coefficients of X_1 and X_1^2 no longer have separate interpretations – they must be considered simultaneously.[4] The *mathematical* reason is that both β_1 and β_2 are integral components of $\partial Y/\partial X_1$, the effect of X on Y. More precisely, in equation (8.22), according to the rules of calculus, $\partial Y/\partial X_1 = \beta_1 + 2\beta_2 X$. The *statistical* reason is that, if the regression is estimated with sample data of fixed size, then X_1 and X_1^2 are substantially correlated or, more likely, highly correlated. This correlation causes the sampling errors of the estimates of β_1 and β_2 to be substantially confounded. That is, the error correlation between estimates of

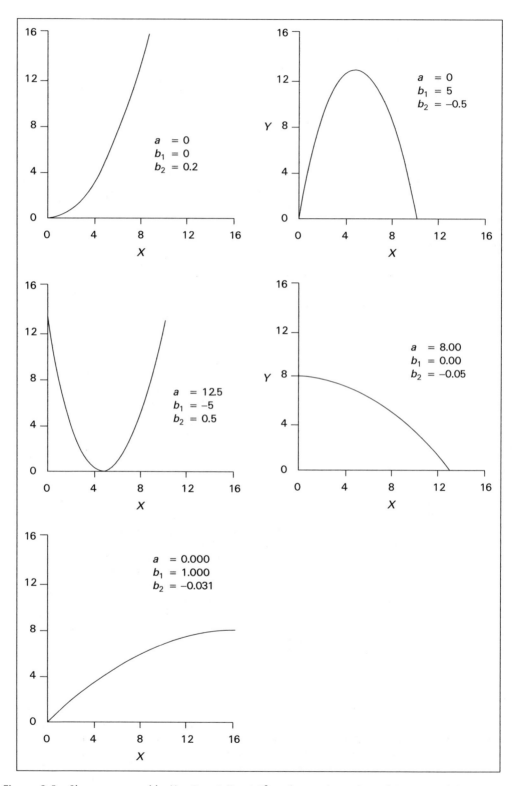

Figure 8.5   *Shapes assumed by* $Y = \beta_0 + \beta_1 X + \beta_2 X^2$ *under varying values of* β_0, β_1, *and* β_2

β_1 and β_2 is high, making it difficult to fully distinguish the estimate of β_1 from the estimate of β_2.[5] This error correlation is not a problem if one wishes to estimate $\partial Y/\partial X_1$, since the attribution of error to one coefficient rather than another is irrelevant to the error of the estimate of $\partial Y/\partial X_1$. Finally, notice that the effect of X_1 on Y in the parabolic case is a linear function of X: $\partial Y/\partial X_1 = \beta_1 + 2\beta_2 X_1$. Thus the *effect* of X_1 on Y changes by $2\beta_2$ units per unit change in X_1.

For an empirical example of parabolas, I turn to Rees and Schultz's (1970: 136) analysis of hourly earnings. Rees and Schultz were interested in finding the effect of worker's age on earnings, but they hypothesized that several factors other than age affect earnings, that earnings increase with age during the first part of men's careers but decrease with age in the second part, and that the processes affecting earnings vary from one occupation to another. To allow for occupational differences in the earnings process, Rees and Schultz constructed separate earnings models for incumbents of each occupation they examined. To allow for effects of variables besides age that they hypothesized to affect earnings, they also included in the model seniority, years of schooling, a measure of job-related experience and training, and distance from the employee's home to his job. And to allow for the nonlinear effects of age on earnings, they included age and age squared. They did not suspect interactions among any variables, so they used an additive model and estimated parameters by regressing earnings on age, age squared, and the other variables just mentioned. Applying their model to the earnings of maintenance electricians, they obtained a coefficient for age (in years) of 0.031 and a coefficient of −0.0032 for age squared. By applying the formula for the partial derivative, we can use these results to find the unstandardized effect of age on earnings at different ages: At an age of X years, the effect of age on earnings is 0.031 + 2(−0.0032)X. The effect of age on earnings at various ages is shown in Table 8.21. Notice in Table 8.21 how the effect of age on earnings declines and ultimately becomes negative as age increases.

This discussion of effects in parabolic models has assumed that all variables were measured in their natural (unstandardized) metrics and that β_1 and β_2 are unstandardized regression coefficients. However, it is sometimes useful to measure causal effects

Table 8.21 Results from Rees and Schultz's parabolic model of hourly earnings

Age (years)	Metric effect of age (change in hourly earnings, in dollars, per additional year of age)
20	0.0182
30	0.0118
40	0.0054
50	−0.0010
60	−0.0074
70	−0.0138

according to a standardized metric. For a linear function, standardized effects are just the standardized regression coefficients of the regression equation that are calculated as an intermediate step in most linear regression algorithms. To find the standardized effect when dealing with a parabolic function, we adjust the numerator and denominator of the partial derivative to measure Y and X_1 in standardized units. Applying the usual arithmetic, we get

$$\frac{\partial Y^*}{\partial X_1^*} = \frac{\partial Y/\sigma_Y}{\partial X_1/\sigma_{X_1}} = \frac{\partial Y}{\partial X_1}\frac{\sigma_{X_1}}{\sigma_Y}.$$

Thus, at a given value of X, the standardized effect of X_1 on Y is obtained by first calculating $\partial Y/\partial X$ from the formula $\partial Y/\partial X_1 = \beta_1 + 2\beta_2 X_1$ and then multiplying the result by the ratio of the standard deviation of X_1 divided by the standard deviation of Y. Notice that the standardized effect varies according to the value of X_1.

In presenting findings from a parabolic model, the researcher probably will wish to evaluate the metric and standardized effects of X_1 on Y at several different values of X_1. These values may be chosen for their substantive significance or because they have some intuitive appeal. For example, in the analysis of effects of schooling on earnings, one may wish to calculate the effect of schooling on earnings at the sample mean of the schooling distribution and at 6, 9, and 12 years of schooling. Or, in another analysis, one may wish to calculate the effect of X_1 on Y at the sample mean of X and at one standard deviation above and one standard deviation below the mean.

Parabolic models are a special case of higher-order polynomials, and higher-order polynomials are themselves a special case of fractional polynomials. The presentation here follows the separate treatment given these very similar topics in the literature.

An Ith-order polynomial of X_1 (with error term ε and additional independent variables $Z_1, Z_2, ..., Z_J$) is an equation of the form

$$Y = \beta_0 + \sum_{i=1}^{I} \beta_i X_1^i + \sum_{j=1}^{J} \alpha_j Z_j + \varepsilon, \quad (8.23)$$

where Y is the dependent variable, X_1 and the Z_j are independent variables, ε is the error term, and β_0 is a constant. For example, a fourth-order polynomial of X_1 is

$$Y = \beta_0 + \beta_1 X_1 + \beta_2 X_1^2 + \beta_3 X_1^3 + \beta_4 X_1^4$$
$$+ \sum_{j=1}^{J} \alpha_j Z_j + \varepsilon, \quad (8.24)$$

A mathematical property of higher-order polynomials is their ability to change from positive to negative slope and vice versa. Over a fixed range, an Ith-order polynomial can change direction of slope as many as $I - 1$ times, depending on the values of coefficients. Each change of direction is called a point of inflection. For example, a parabola (second-order polynomial) can reverse the direction of its slope once, although it need not do so, as shown in Figure 8.5. A fourth-order polynomial can have as many as three inflection points over a fixed range, depending on coefficient values, although it need not have any inflection points at all.

The effect of X_1 on Y in a higher-order polynomial is the partial derivative $\partial Y/\partial X_1$, which is given by the formula

$$\partial Y/\partial X_1 = \sum_{i=1}^{I} \beta_i X_1^{i-1}. \quad (8.25)$$

For example, in a fourth-order polynomial,

$$Y = \beta_0 + \beta_1 X_1 + \beta_2 X_1^2 + \beta_3 X_1^3 + \beta_4 X_1^4$$
$$+ \sum_{j=1}^{J} \alpha_j Z_j + \varepsilon, \quad (8.26)$$

$$\partial Y/\partial X_1 = \beta_1 + 2\beta_2 X_1 + 3\beta_3 X_1^2 + 4\beta_4 X_1^3. \quad (8.27)$$

Once $\partial Y/\partial X_1$ is calculated for a given value of X_1, standardized effects, point elasticities, and rates of return can be calculated easily by multiplying $\partial Y/\partial X_1$ by σ_{X_1}/σ_Y, by X_1/Y, or by $1/Y$, respectively.

Fractional polynomials are higher-order polynomials that include negative as well as positive powers of the independent variable of interest, for example,

$$Y = \beta_0 + \alpha_1 X_1^{-1} + \alpha_2 X_1^{-2} + \beta_3 X_1 + \beta_4 X_1^2$$
$$+ \sum_{j=1}^{J} \gamma_j Z_j + \varepsilon. \quad (8.28)$$

By the laws of exponents, this function is equivalent to

$$Y = \beta_0 + \alpha_1(1/X_1) + \beta_2(1/X_1^2) + \beta_3 X_1$$
$$+ \beta_4 X_1^2 + \sum_{j=1}^{J} \gamma_j Z_j + \varepsilon. \quad (8.29)$$

More parsimoniously, fractional polynomials are functions of the form

$$Y = \beta_0 + \sum_{m=1}^{M} \alpha_m X_1^{-m} + \sum_{i=1}^{I} \beta_i X_1^i$$
$$+ \sum_{j=1}^{J} \gamma_j Z_j + \varepsilon, \quad (8.30)$$

and the partial derivative $\partial Y/\partial X_1$ is

$$\partial Y/\partial X_1 = \sum_{m=1}^{M} (-m) \alpha_m X_1^{-m-1}$$
$$+ \sum_{i=1}^{I} i\beta_i X_1^{i-1}. \quad (8.31)$$

In addition to the full range of functional forms that can be represented by linear and higher-order polynomial functions, the fractional polynomials include rapid as well as gradual changes in direction of slope, as well as asymptotic behavior near extreme values.

Log transformation of independent variables Another common method in the analysis of nonlinear effects is the logarithmic function. The general form of the logarithmic function commonly used in additive models is

$$Y = \beta_0 + \beta_1 \ln(X_1) + \sum_{i=2}^{I} \beta_i X_i + \varepsilon, \quad (8.32)$$

where Y is the dependent variable, X_1 is the independent variable that is logged, other independent variables are $X_2, X_3, ..., X_I$, ε is the error term, and β_0 is a constant; $\ln$ is the natural logarithm function. Two examples of the sorts of relationships that can be fitted with the logarithm function are shown in Figure 8.6. Looking at the solid line in that figure, notice that the logarithmic function can be used when the effect of X_1 on Y is always positive (that is, increases in X_1 are associated with increases in Y) but is stronger (i.e., steeper) for low values of X_1 than for high values of X_1. Looking at the dashed line, notice that the logarithmic function can also

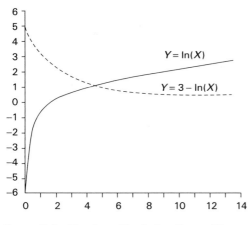

Figure 8.6 *Two logarithmic functions of X*

be used to fit situations in which the effect of X_1 is negative but is stronger at low values of X_1 than at high values of X_1. These situations correspond to the notion of decreasing marginal effects of X_1 on Y.

An advantage of the logarithm specification is that it is simple to use. So long as X_1 assumes only positive values (logarithms are defined only for numbers greater than zero), application of the logarithmic function requires only that one take the log of X_1 and then treat $\ln(X_1)$ (rather than X_1) as an independent variable in ordinary least-squares analysis. The unstandardized coefficient of $\ln(X_1)$ can be interpreted as the rate of change of Y per unit change in the *logarithm* of X_1. Clearly, the standardized coefficient for $\ln(X_1)$ can be interpreted as the number of standard deviations of change in Y that occur per standard deviation of change in the *logarithm of X_1*, but such interpretations are clumsy and obscure – few variables in real life are measured on logarithmic scales, so people have little intuitive sense of how big units of $\ln(X_1)$ are, even if they are quite familiar with the units of X_1. (Consider, for example, how many *log* years of schooling one must complete in order to obtain a high-school diploma.) However, the effect of X_1 on Y in a logarithmic specification can be meaningfully interpreted by turning again to partial derivatives. In the function

$$Y = \beta_0 + \beta_1 \ln(X_1) + \sum_{i=2}^{I} \beta_i X_i + \varepsilon, \quad (8.33)$$

$\partial Y/\partial X_1 = \beta_1/X_1$. Using this formula, one can calculate easily the unstandardized effect of

X_1 on Y at any given value of X_1. And, as in the case of the parabola, one can calculate the standardized effect of X_1 on Y at any value of X_1 by first calculating the unstandardized effect at that value and then multiplying it by σ_{X_1}/σ_Y. But perhaps even more useful is the fact that since $\partial Y/\partial X_1 = \beta_1/X_1$, then

$$\frac{\partial Y}{\partial X_1/X_1} = \beta_1.$$

And, because $\partial X_1/X_1$ is just the mathematical expression for the proportional change in X_1, the rate of change in Y with respect to proportional change in X_1 is constant and equal to the unstandardized regression coefficient for $\ln(X_1)$. That is, Y changes with respect to X_1 at a rate of β_1 units of Y per 100% increase in X_1.

For an example of the use of the logarithmic specification, I turn to Blau and Schoenherr's (1971: 63–4) analysis of the effects of agency size (i.e., number of employees) on the number of hierarchical levels in agency organization. Blau and Schoenherr regress the number of hierarchical levels on the log of organizational size and measures of automation and the division of labor in the agency. They find a standardized coefficient of 0.75 for the log of agency size and find coefficients of −0.11 and 0.16 for division of labor and automation, respectively. No doubt because the log of size has so little intuitive meaning, they conclude only that size has the 'dominant' effect on the number of hierarchical levels (1971: 73). However, we can be considerably more precise by calculating the partial derivative of Y (number of levels) with respect to X_1 (size).

The unstandardized coefficient of $\ln(\text{size})$ is 4.36. Applying the formula for the partial derivative of Y with respect to X_1, we find that the unstandardized effect of size (not the logarithm of size) is 4.36 divided by the size of the organization. Blau and Schoenherr report that the mean of size is 1195 persons. Thus at the mean of size, the unstandardized effect of size on levels is 0.0036 (= 4.36/1195) levels per additional person. But perhaps the most intuitively appealing measure of the effect of size on number of levels is the rate of change in levels per proportional change in Y. The coefficient of 4.36 for $\ln(\text{size})$ indicates a *rate of change* of 0.0436 (= 4.36/100) levels per change of 1% in organization size at *any* value of size. In passing, I reconstructed the metric coefficient for

$\log_{10}$(size) from the standardized coefficient for $\log_{10}$(size) reported by Blau and Schoenherr (1971) and then I calculated the coefficient for ln(size) by multiplying the coefficient for $\log_{10}$(size) by $\log_{10}(e)$, where e is the base of the natural logarithm. Note that a change in size of 100% will not necessarily produce a change of 4.36 levels, since the base of the percentage increases as size increases. Rather, $\partial Y/(\partial X_1/X_1)$ is the *rate* of change in Y per proportional change in X_1, expressed as units of change in Y per 100% increase in X_1. It is usually helpful to divide the value of $\partial Y/(\partial X_1/X_1)$ by 100, to express the rate of change as units of Y per percentage point of change in X_1.

COMBINED TYPE LOG-MULTIPLICATIVE MODELS   It is possible to combine various nonadditive and nonlinear models to fit situations in which nonadditivities and nonlinearities are present. Thus, for example, the following function is useful when X_1 and X_2 are believed to interact *and* X_2 is hypothesized to have nonlinear effects on Y:

$$Y = \beta_0 + \beta_1 X_1 + \beta_2 \ln X_2 + \beta_3 (X_1 \ln X_2)$$
$$+ \sum_{i=1}^{I} + \alpha_i Z_i + \varepsilon. \qquad (8.34)$$

The effect of X_1 on Y is $\partial Y/\partial X_1 = \beta_1 + \beta_3 \ln X_2$. The effect of X_2 on Y in this specification is $\partial Y/\partial X_2 = (\beta_2 + \beta_3 X_1)(1/X_2)$. However, the effect of X_2 can be written more simply if it is stated as a rate of change in Y per proportional change in X_2:

$$\frac{\partial Y}{\partial X_2/X_2} = \beta_2 + \beta_3 X_1.$$

That is, the rate of change in Y per doubling of the value of X_2 is $\beta_2 + \beta_3 X_1$, and the rate of change in Y per percentage point of increase in X_2 is $(\beta_2 + \beta_3 X_1)/100$. Note that this rate of *proportional* change in X_2 is a *linear* function of X_1.

Investment models and log transformation of the dependent variable   Some situations in social and economic life may be usefully conceptualized as investments. For example, human capital theory treats time spent in school as an investment; one hears parents speak of the onerous aspects of childrearing as investments; the phrase 'emotional investment' is commonplace; one makes political

investments; and so on. Because investment models are so often useful in conceptualizing social phenomena, I now give some attention to the measurement of effects in investment processes.

As always in causal analysis, the first question about investment models concerns the choice of a mathematical function to represent the process. To find such a function, consider the effect of time on money invested in a savings account. Where R is the interest rate, P is the initial deposit, X is the amount of time during which the money is on deposit, and P' is the amount of money in the account at the end of the deposit period, the effect of X on the deposit is given by the usual interest formula: $P' = P(1 + R)X$. This formula is the standard model for all investment processes.

To write the interest formula in a more general form, let $\beta_0 = \ln P$, let $\beta_1 = \ln(1 + R)$, and let $Y = P'$. Then, where e is the base of natural logarithms,

$$Y = P' = P(1 + R)^X$$
$$= e^{\beta_0} + e^{\beta_1 X} = e^{\beta_0 + \beta_1 X}. \qquad (8.35)$$

Taking logarithms of both sides gives

$$\ln(Y) = \beta_0 + \beta_1 X, \qquad (8.36)$$

which is a function that can be estimated by ordinary linear regression.

In most social science applications, several different investment processes are assumed to be operating and the researcher wishes to separate out the effects of each. Accordingly, the logarithmic form of the model can be generalized to

$$\ln(Y) = \beta_0 + \sum_{i=1}^{I} \beta_i X_i + \varepsilon, \qquad (8.37)$$

where the X_i are the amounts of different types of investments and where Y is a variable (not necessarily dollars) representing the quantity in which the return is 'paid'. As a practical matter, this means that the parameters of an investment model can be calculated simply by replacing the dependent variable in a regression with its logarithm.

The nonlogarithmic form of the investment model is $Y = e^{\beta_0 + \Sigma \beta_i X_i + \varepsilon}$. For this functional form, the effect of one of the Xs on Y (say, X_1) is $\partial Y/\partial X_1 = \beta_1 e^{\beta_0 + \Sigma \beta_i X_i + \varepsilon} = \beta_1 Y$. So the rate of change in Y with respect to X_1 varies with the value of Y or, alternatively, with the values of the X_i. At specific values of Y or specific values of the X_i the standardized effect of X_1 can be calculated by first calculating $\partial Y/\partial X_1$ and then multiplying by σ_{X_1}/σ_Y. Note that the standardized effect varies according to the value of Y or the values of the X_i at which it is calculated. More conveniently, one can state the effect of X_1 on Y as a constant rate of proportional change in Y per unit change in X_1: if $\partial Y/\partial X_1 = \beta_1 Y$, then

$$\frac{\partial Y/Y}{\partial X_1} = \beta_1.$$

The use of the investment model usually focuses attention on rates of return. We now consider the relationship between rates of return and other measures of causal effect. First some definitions are required. Rates of return (for example, R in equation (8.35)) are normally stated as proportional changes in the dependent variable per *elemental time period* (see Debreu, 1987: 34). The *effective rate of return* to a causal variable X_1 is used here to mean the proportional change in the dependent variable that is caused by X_1, over the course of one elemental time period. In equation (8.35), the effective rate of return is R or its algebraic equivalent $e^{\beta}-1$. In equation (8.37), the effective rate of return to X_1 (one of the X_i) is $e^{\beta_1}-1$. Elemental time periods frequently are divided into subintervals, with returns computed and compounded in each subinterval – for example, mortgage notes often involve monthly interest computations. Whether calculated for an elemental time period or for a subinterval of an elemental period, rates of return are always expressed as proportional changes in the dependent variable per elemental period. However, when returns are calculated in subintervals, the effective rate of return over the elemental time period will exceed the rate of return in the subinterval, due to compounding. The smaller the subinterval, the smaller the rate of return over the elemental interval. As subintervals grow smaller, however, the rate of return in the subintervals approaches a limit. When the investment process is written as equation (8.37), this limit is

$$\frac{\partial Y/Y}{\partial X_1} = \frac{\partial Y}{\partial X_1}\frac{1}{Y}.$$

Thus when subintervals are only an instant long, the rate of return to X_1 in the interval is $(\partial Y/\partial X_1)(1/Y)$. I therefore call this limit the *instantaneous rate of return* to X_1 and I have already shown that

$$\frac{\partial Y/Y}{\partial X_1} = \beta_1.$$

To a certain extent, it makes no difference whether one uses the effective or the instantaneous rate of return in interpretation of investment models. Since the instantaneous rate equals β_1, and the effective rate equals $e^{\beta_1}-1$, the effective rate can be calculated from the instantaneous rate. And in most cases the effective and instantaneous rates are approximately equal. In particular, when β_1 is between -0.1 and $+0.1$, then $e^{\beta_1}-1$ is approximately equal to β_1. However, it is worth noting that the instantaneous rate of return seems particularly well suited to investment models of social processes. In business, the elemental time period of an investment is always explicit and fixed by custom, convenience, or, probably most often, the frequency with which profits are counted, taxed, or distributed. In many social processes, the elemental time period is not so easy to determine, since accounts are not formally balanced. And if a process is hypothesized or observed to operate continuously, as is probably the case in most social processes, it may make more sense to think in terms of instantaneous rates of return than to select some arbitrary elemental time period.

Further, there are certain methodological advantages to using instantaneous rather than effective rates of return in causal analysis. In investment models – that is, in equations like (8.37) – the instantaneous rate of return is clearly and simply related to partial derivatives and can be obtained directly from a multiple regression analysis. And, as we have just seen, simple manipulations of instantaneous rates of return allow them to be compared with other partial derivative-based measures of causal effect generated from other functional forms.

Constant elasticity of substitution: The Cobb–Douglas model The following function occurs with some regularity in sociological and economic analysis:

$$Y = \beta_0 X_1^{\beta_1} X_2^{\beta_2} \ldots X_I^{\beta_I}\varepsilon, \qquad (8.38)$$

or, in a simpler notation,

$$Y = \beta_0 \left(\prod_{i=1}^{I} X_i^{\beta_i}\right)\varepsilon. \qquad (8.39)$$

In economics, equation (8.38) is known as the Cobb–Douglas production function. In sociology, it seems to have no established name, though it is often called a multiplicative model. Since there are numerous other models that are also multiplicative, I refer to this equation as the Cobb–Douglas function.

One of the appeals of the Cobb–Douglas function is that its parameters can be estimated by ordinary least-squares regression. To see this, take logarithms of both sides of the equation and then apply the laws of logarithms to obtain the following:

$$\ln(Y) = \ln \beta_0 + \sum_{i=1}^{I} \beta_i \ln X_i + \ln \varepsilon. \qquad (8.40)$$

Thus the parameters of the Cobb–Douglas function can be estimated by regressing the log of Y on the logs of the X_i.

Sociologists and economists tend to apply the Cobb–Douglas function for different reasons. In economics, a major appeal of the Cobb–Douglas function is that it produces constant, easily calculated elasticities of substitution. In sociology, the function is usually applied when the researcher expects interactions among *all* the variables in the models. In thinking about performance in school, for example, one might hypothesize that certain characteristics of individuals not only reduce performance but also reduce the effects of other variables on performance. If all causal variables in the model either enhanced or reduced the effects of all the other causal variables, then there would be some basis for using the Cobb–Douglas specification. Mathematically, the interdependence of effects in the Cobb–Douglas function can be seen by examining the formula for the metric effect of any causal variable on Y:

$$\left(\beta_1 \beta_0 \prod_{i=2}^{I} X_i^{\beta_i} \right) X_1^{\beta_i - 1} \varepsilon. \qquad (8.41)$$

Note that every independent variable in the model appears in the formula for the metric effect of every single other variable in the model. And since the standardized effect is equal to the product of the metric effect with σ_{X_1}/σ_Y, every causal variable in the model also appears in the formula for the standardized effect.

While the formula for $\partial Y/\partial X_1$ clearly communicates the existence of interactions among variables in the Cobb–Douglas function, it has two problems. First, the error term ε appears in equation (8.41). Since ε is unobservable, its appearance in (8.41) calls for some strong assumptions in order to make

this formula useful. Second, equation (8.41) is so complicated that it sheds little light on causal effects in the Cobb–Douglas specification, regardless of one's willingness to make strong assumptions. Both these problems are readily solved, however. By measuring effects as instantaneous rates of return rather than as metric and standardized effects, the Cobb–Douglas function yields effect measures that are simple in form and exclude ε. To see this, recall that the instantaneous rate of return to X_1 is the proportional change in Y per unit change in X_1. Mathematically, then, the instantaneous rate of return is

$$R_1 = \frac{\partial Y/Y}{\partial X_1} = (1/Y) \left(\beta_1 \beta_0 \prod_{i=2}^{I} X_i^{\beta_i} \right) X_1^{\beta_i - 1} \varepsilon. \qquad (8.42)$$

Substituting $\beta_0 \prod_{i=1}^{I} X_i^{\beta_i} \varepsilon$ in place of Y and canceling terms gives $R_1 = \beta_1/X_1$.

When effects are measured as elasticities, the Cobb–Douglas function offers a quite simple formula for the effect of X_1 on Y. Recall that the elasticity is the proportional change in Y per proportional change in X. If E_1 denotes the elasticity of Y with respect to X_1, we can write

$$E_1 = \frac{\partial Y/Y}{\partial X_1/X_1} = \frac{\partial Y/Y}{\partial X_1} X_1 = R_1 X_1$$

$$= (\beta_1/X_1) X_1 = \beta_1.$$

In short, in the Cobb–Douglas function, the point elasticity of Y with respect to X_1 is β_1. More simply, Y changes with respect to X_1 at a rate of β_1 percentage points of change in Y per 1% change in X_1. While the point elasticity of Y with respect to X_1 is constant in the Cobb–Douglas specification, metric and standardized effects vary with the values of Y and X_1.

Proportions, probabilities and other range-delimited dependent variables When the dependent variable Y in a regression analysis is conceptually limited to a specified range, it is desirable that the regression analysis should always predict values of $\hat{Y}$ that are within that range. For example, survey respondents are sometimes asked to estimate the probability that an event will occur in the future; a regression analysis of the determinants of those probabilities should predict only probabilities between 0 and 1. Similarly, education studies sometimes seek to predict the proportion of a school's student population that drops out before graduation. One would be suspicious of a regression analysis that predicts probabilities smaller than zero or larger than one. And it would be difficult indeed to interpret a regression prediction that more than 100% (or less than 0%) of a school population drops out. Similarly, SAT scores for college admissions are constrained to values between 200 and 800. It would be difficult to interpret a regression prediction of scores outside this interval. These problems can be avoided by using certain nonlinear functions. The most common of these are the probit and logit transformations of the dependent variable.

PROBIT TRANSFORMATION   Suppose that values of Y are constrained to the interval from 0 to 1. Let Φ indicate the standard normal cumulative distribution function (i.e., the area under the standard normal curve), let $\Phi^{-1}(Y)$ indicate the inverse normal cumulative distribution function evaluated at Y, and let ϕ indicate the standard normal density function (the height of the normal curve evaluated at Y). Three properties of the normal distribution are useful here. First, although Y is constrained to the interval $(0,1)$, $\Phi^{-1}(Y)$ can take on values between $-\infty$ and $+\infty$. Second, Φ takes on values only in the range $(0,1)$. Third, $\Phi[\Phi^{-1}(Y)] = Y$. These characteristics make the following an appropriate model for estimating the effects of independent variables $X_1, X_2, \ldots, X_I$ on Y:

$$\Phi^{-1}(Y) = \beta_0 + \sum_{i=1}^{I} \beta_i X_i + \varepsilon. \qquad (8.43)$$

That is, we define a new variable $\Psi = \Phi^{-1}(Y)$ and regress Ψ on the independent variables. Once the regression is fitted, $\hat{\Psi}$ can be calculated for any particular data case, and the corresponding predicted value of Y can be obtained by calculating $\Phi(\hat{\Psi})$. To obtain the effect of X_1 on Y, apply Φ to both sides of equation (8.43) to obtain

$$Y = \Phi\left(\beta_0 + \sum_{i=1}^{I} \beta_i X_i + \varepsilon\right). \qquad (8.44)$$

Ignoring ε and taking the partial derivative gives the result

$$\partial Y/\partial X_1 = \beta_1 \phi\left(\beta_0 + \sum_{i=1}^{I} \beta_i X_i\right). \qquad (8.45)$$

So the effect of X_1 on Y can be obtained by picking values of X_1 at which to evaluate that

effect, and then applying those values and β_1 to equation (8.45). Alternatively, one can pick a value of Y at which to evaluate the effect of X_1: because $\Phi^{-1}(Y) = \beta_0 + \sum_{i=1}^{I} \beta_i X_i + \varepsilon$, the formula for $\partial Y/\partial X_1$ can be rewritten

$$\partial Y/\partial X_1 = \beta_1 \phi[\Phi^{-1}(Y)], \qquad (8.46)$$

permitting one to choose a value of Y at which to evaluate the effect of X_1 on Y.

More generally, when Y is bounded in the interval $[a,b]$, define $\Psi = (Y' - a)/(b - a)$. Ψ is bounded in the interval $(0,1)$. Regress $\Phi^{-1}(\Psi)$ on independent variables $X_1, \ldots, X_k$. The partial derivative of Y with respect to X_i is

$$\partial Y/\partial X_1 = (b - a)\, \beta_1\, \phi\left(\beta_0 + \sum_{i=1}^{I} \beta_i X_i\right).$$

For example, if Y were SAT scores, a would be the lower limit for these scores (200) and b would be the upper limit (800).

LOGIT TRANSFORMATION   Alternatively, the logit transformation can be used to accommodate a dependent variable that is constrained to the interval $(0,1)$. An appropriate regression model is

$$\ln [Y/(1-Y)] = \beta_0 + \sum_{i=1}^{I} \beta_i X_i + \varepsilon.$$

To estimate this model, define $\Upsilon = \ln [Y/(1-Y)]$ and estimate the regression model $\Upsilon = \beta_0 + \sum_{i=1}^{I} \beta_i X_i + \varepsilon$. Then the effect of X_1 on Y can be evaluated at specific values of Y from the following result:

$$\partial Y/\partial X_1 = \beta_1 Y(1-Y). \qquad (8.47)$$

Or one can choose values of the X_i at which to evaluate the effect of X_1, using the formula

$$\partial Y/\partial X_1 = \beta_1\, \frac{e^{\beta_0 + \Sigma \beta_i x_i}}{(e^{\beta_0 + \Sigma \beta_i x_i})^2}. \qquad (8.48)$$

More generally, when Y is bounded in the interval (a,b), define $\Upsilon = (Y - a)/(b - a)$. Υ is bounded in the interval $(0,1)$. Regress $\ln (\Upsilon/(1-\Upsilon))$ on independent variables $X_1, \ldots, X_k$. The partial derivative of Y with respect to X_i is

$$\partial Y/\partial X_1 = \frac{1}{b-a}\, \beta_1\, \frac{e^{\beta_0 + \Sigma \beta_i x_i}}{(e^{\beta_0 + \Sigma \beta_i x_i})^2}. \qquad (8.49)$$

$\sqrt{Y}$ transformation It is sometimes possible to reduce heteroscedasticity or to improve model fit in a regression analysis by taking the square root of the dependent variable. Doing so gives the regression model,

$$\sqrt{Y} = \beta_0 + \sum_{i=1}^{I} \beta_i X_i + \varepsilon. \tag{8.49}$$

To obtain $\partial Y/\partial X_1$, first square both sides of the equation to get an equation that predicts Y:

$$Y = \left(\beta_0 + \sum_{i=1}^{I} \beta_i X_i + \varepsilon\right)^2. \tag{8.50}$$

Applying the chain rule for partial derivatives to this model gives

$$\partial Y/\partial X_1 = 2\beta_1\left(\beta_0 + \sum_{i=1}^{I} \beta_i X_i + \varepsilon\right), \tag{8.51}$$

which can be used to calculate $\partial Y/\partial X_1$ at specific values of the independent variables. Since $\beta_0 + \sum_{i=1}^{I} \beta_i X_i + \varepsilon = \sqrt{Y}$, we can substitute that expression into (8.51) to get

$$\partial Y/\partial X_1 = 2\beta_1\sqrt{Y}, \tag{8.52}$$

which can be used to calculate the effect of X_1 on Y at a specified value of Y. In either case, the effect is the rate of change in Y with respect to X_j.

Exponential transformation of Y It is sometimes useful to exponentiate Y, and to estimate the model

$$e^Y = \beta_0 + \sum_{i=1}^{I} \beta_i X_i + \varepsilon. \tag{8.53}$$

Equivalently, one can write

$$Y = \ln\left(\beta_0 + \sum_{i=1}^{I} \beta_i X_i + \varepsilon\right). \tag{8.54}$$

Partial derivatives can be computed at specific values of the independent variables, or at a specific value of Y, as follows:

$$\frac{\partial Y}{\partial X_1} = \frac{\beta_i}{\beta_0 + \sum_{i=1}^{I} \beta_i x_i} \tag{8.55}$$

and

$$\frac{\partial Y}{\partial X_1} = \beta_i/Y. \tag{8.56}$$

Table 8.22 summarizes commonly used non-linear and nonadditive models, their functional forms, and interpretable effect measures for the reader's convenience.

WEIGHTED DATA

It is common for social science datasets to include a variable called a *weight*. In the most general terms, the weight for a data case is a measure of the emphasis given to it in computing regression coefficients and other statistics. A dataset in which all cases have the same weight is equivalent to a dataset in which there are no weights at all. Weights are almost always positive real numbers; a weight of zero is equivalent to deleting a case from the dataset; negative weights serve unusual computational purposes that are not relevant to any topic discussed in this chapter.

There are several varieties of weights. *Frequency weights* are weights that are constructed to permit a single case to represent the data for several identical cases. *Sampling weights* are weights that are used to obtain unbiased estimates of population parameters when cases are selected from the population with unequal (but known) probabilities of selection. *Weighted least-squares* (WLS) weights are weights used to remedy heteroscedasticity. *Generalized least-squares* (GLS) weights are used to remedy both heteroscedasticity and correlations among regression errors. Other weights are available for a variety of other purposes. Ingenious computer programmers often construct special weights as a convenient way to do unusual calculations. Authorities often disagree, sometimes severely, about the appropriateness of different weighting procedures.

Virtually all contemporary, widely used computer programs for regression computations permit the use of weights. Programs differ in their computational procedures for using weights, and analysts are well advised to learn the details of procedures followed by the program that they use. I now discuss briefly three different types of weights and then discuss computational formulas for using them.

Frequency weights

When several data cases in a sample have identical values on all variables, it is computationally efficient to include in the dataset only one of those identical cases, plus an additional variable indicating the total number of cases with those values. That additional variable, denoted w_i, is the *frequency weight*. Frequency-weighted data are a convenient way to construct a dataset from published

Table 8.22 *Some nonlinear and nonadditive models estimable by regression, with convenient effect measures*

Common names	Common use	Function	Convenient effect measure	Formula for convenient effect measure
Multiplicative interaction model; linear additive model with multiplicative interaction term	When combined effects of two independent variables are different from sum of their separate effects	$Y = \beta_0 + \beta_1 X_1 + \beta_2 X_2 + \beta_3 X_1 X_2 + \sum_{i=1}^{I} \alpha_i Z_i + \varepsilon$	Metric effect (units of change in Y per unit of change in X_1)	$\partial Y / \partial X_1 = \beta_1 + \beta_3 X_2$
Fractional polynomial (including quadratic, higher-order polynomial, and fractional polynomial as special cases)	When there are nonlinear effects of X_1	$Y = \beta_0 + \sum_{m=1}^{M} \alpha_m X_1^{-m} + \sum_{i=1}^{I} \beta_i X_1^{i} + \sum_{j=1}^{J} \gamma_j Z_j + \varepsilon$	Metric effect (units of change in Y per unit of change in X_1)	$\partial Y / \partial X_1 = \sum_{m=1}^{M} (-m)\, \alpha_m X_1^{-m-1} + \sum_{i=1}^{I} i \beta_i X_1^{i-1}$
Log transform of independent variable	When there are decreasing marginal effects of X_1	$Y = \beta_0 + \beta_1 \ln(X_1) + \sum_{i=2}^{I} \beta_i X_i + \varepsilon$	Units of change in Y per proportional change in X_1	$\dfrac{\partial Y}{\partial X_1 / X_1} = \beta_1$
Combined type log-multiplicative interaction models	Nonadditive effects of X_1 and X_2 plus decreasing effects of X_2	$Y = \beta_0 + \beta_1 X_1 + \beta_2 \ln X_2 + \beta_3 (X_1 \ln X_2) + \sum_{i=1}^{I} \alpha_i Z_i + \varepsilon$	Metric effect (units of change in Y per unit of change in X_1)	$\partial Y / \partial X_1 = \beta_1 + \beta_3 \ln X_2$ $\partial Y / \partial X_2 = \beta_2 / X_2 + \beta_3 X_1 / X_2$
Investment model; semi-logged model	When theory indicates an investment process; when all independent variables have increasing marginal effects; to improve model fit; to reduce heteroscedasticity	$\ln(Y) = \beta_0 + \sum_{i=1}^{I} \beta_i X_i + \varepsilon$	Rate of return per elemental time period	Return per elemental period $= e^{\beta_1} - 1$
			Instantaneous rate of return	Instantaneous rate of return $= \dfrac{\partial Y / Y}{\partial X_1} = \beta_1$

(Continued)

Table 8.22 (Continued)

Common names	Common use	Function	Convenient effect measure	Formula for convenient effect measure
Constant elasticity of substitution (CES) model; Cobb–Douglas production function; fully logged model	When indicated by theory; to improve model fit	$\ln Y = \ln \beta_0 + \sum_{i=1}^{I} \beta_i \ln X_i + \ln \varepsilon$	Point elasticity	$\dfrac{\partial Y/Y}{\partial X_1/X_1} = \beta_1$
Probit transformation	When Y is logically limited to values in the interval [a,b]; for predicting percentage of total, probability, or other constrained quantities	$\Phi^{-1}[(Y-a)/(b-a)] = \beta_0 + \sum_{i=1}^{I} \beta_i X_i + \varepsilon$	Metric effect at specific values of independent variables, or at specified value of dependent variable (units of change in Y per unit of change in X_1)	$\partial Y/\partial X_1 = (b-a)\beta_1\phi\left(\beta_0 + \sum_{i=1}^{I}\beta_i X_i\right)$ $\partial Y/\partial X_1 = (b-a)\beta_1 \phi[(Y-a)/(b-a)]$
Logit transformation	When Y is logically limited to values in the interval [a,b]; for predicting percentage of total, probability, or other constrained quantities	$\ln[\Upsilon/(1-\Upsilon)] = \beta_0 + \sum_{i=1}^{I}\beta_i X_i + \varepsilon,$ where $\Upsilon = (Y-a)/(b-a)$	Metric effect at specific values of independent variables, or at specified value of dependent variable (units of change in Y per unit of change in X_1)	$\partial Y/\partial X_1 = \beta_1 \Upsilon(1-\Upsilon)/(b-a)$ $\partial Y/\partial X_1 = [\beta_1/(b-a)][e^{\beta_0 + \Sigma\beta_i X_i}/(e^{\beta_0 + \Sigma\beta_i X_i})^2]$

(Continued)

Table 8.22 (*Continued*)

Common names	Common use	Function	Convenient effect measure	Formula for convenient effect measure
Square-root transformation of Y	When all independent variables have increasing marginal effects; to improve model fit; to reduce heteroscedasticity	$\sqrt{Y} = \beta_0 + \displaystyle\sum_{i=1}^{I} \beta_i X_i + \varepsilon$	Metric effect at specific values of independent variables, or at specified value of dependent variable (units of change in Y per unit of change in X_1)	$\partial Y/\partial X_1 = 2\beta_1 \left(\beta_0 + \displaystyle\sum_{i=1}^{I} \beta_i X_i + \varepsilon \right)$ $\partial Y/\partial X_1 = 2\beta_1 \sqrt{Y}$
Exponential transformation of Y	When all independent variables have decreasing marginal effects; to improve model fit; to reduce heteroscedasticity	$e^Y = \beta_0 + \displaystyle\sum_{i=1}^{I} \beta_i X_i + \varepsilon$	Metric effect at specific values of independent variables, or at specified value of dependent variable (units of change in Y per unit of change in X_1)	$\partial Y/\partial X_1 = \beta_1 / \left(\beta_0 + \displaystyle\sum_{i=1}^{I} \beta_i X_i \right)$ $\partial Y/\partial X_1 = \beta_1 / Y$

frequency tabulations. In a dataset of this type, each cell in the tabulation corresponds to a case in the dataset; the variable values that define the row and column headings of the table are the values of those same variables in the corresponding case in the dataset. The entry in each cell of the tabulation is the frequency weight, w_i, for the corresponding case in the dataset.

Sampling weights

If a sample is drawn from a population that includes several subgroups of interest, it is sometimes useful to use different sampling probabilities to select members of each subgroup. If data cases are sampled with unequal sampling probabilities, then *sampling weights* can be applied so that these unequal sampling probabilities do not bias the sample estimates of population parameters. The sampling weight for a data case is a positive real number that is proportional to the reciprocal of the probability with which the case was selected. As a computational convenience, all weights in a sample are usually multiplied by a constant that makes their sum equal to the sample size, although weights are often renormed to sum to n in the course of subsequent computation too. More precisely, if p_i represents the probability with which the ith case is selected, and n is the number of cases in the entire sample, then the sampling weight for the ith case is

$$w_i = \frac{1}{p_i} \left[\frac{n}{\sum_{i=1}^{n} 1/p_i} \right]. \qquad (8.57)$$

Variance–covariance weights (weighted and generalized least squares)

WLS weights   If it is discovered that the heteroscedasticity assumption of regression is violated, then weights based on the variances of errors (variance weights) can be used to help correct the problem. Consider the generic regression equation described earlier in equation (8.14):

$$Y_i = \sum_{j=1}^{K+1} \beta_j X_{ij} + \varepsilon_i.$$

Let σ_i^2 represent the variance of the error for the ith data case. Recall that one of the usual assumptions of regression asserts that all of the ε_i have the same variance (i.e. $\sigma_i^2 = \sigma^2$, for all

i, where σ^2 is a constant), and that the ε_i are uncorrelated with each other. If it is discovered that this assumption of homoscedasticity is not true, then WLS weights can be used to resolve problems caused by heteroscedasticity. If the values of σ_i^2 are known, then the appropriate weight to correct for heteroscedasticity is $w_i = 1/\sigma_i^2$. For computational convenience, it is usual to multiply these weights by a constant (shown in brackets below) to make their sum equal to the sample size:

$$w_i = \frac{1}{\sigma_i^2} \left[\frac{n}{\sum_{i=1}^{n} 1/\sigma_i^2} \right]. \qquad (8.58)$$

Weights described by equation (8.58) are *WLS weights*. Note that the σ_i^2 are particular to the calculation of a specific regression analysis based on a specific dataset. Different regressions would require different variance weights in each analysis. Further, it is virtually always true that σ_i^2 is neither known nor knowable.

Depending on circumstances, it may be possible to estimate σ_i^2. For example, if values of σ_i^2 are assumed to be equal within subsets of the sample data, then σ_i^2 can be estimated by (a) calculating the regression by the usual means, (b) calculating ε_i for each case, (c) calculating the sample estimate of the population variance of ε (that is, s^2 as an estimate of σ^2) within each data subset for which the ε_i are assumed to be invariant, (d) using those variance estimates within each subset to calculate weights defined in equation (8.58). The regression is then recalculated using the estimated weights. However, an analyst might also decide that if subgroups have different error variances, then regressions should be estimated separately in each subgroup, rather than adjusting for heteroscedasticity in a single analysis.

GLS weights   If it is discovered that errors for different cases are correlated, or both correlated and heteroscedastic, then an $n \times n$ matrix of weights can be applied to the data to correct for correlated errors and/or heteroscedasticity. There is no reasonable alternative to matrix notation in this case, so make the following definitions: Σ_u is the $n \times n$ variance–covariance matrix of the error terms, σ^2 is a scalar (equal to the mean of the variances of the ε_i), and Ω is the $n \times n$ matrix that summarizes the inequality of variances of the ε_i and the covariances among them, such that $\Sigma_u = \sigma^2 \Omega$. The GLS weight matrix is the matrix inverse of Ω, denoted Ω^{-1}. Depending on circumstances, it may or may not be possible to estimate σ^2 and $\mathbf{\Omega}$.

Weighted regression calculations

Formulas for means and standard deviations   If data are weighted, then the formulas for the sample mean and sample estimate of the population standard deviation of variable X in a sample of size n are as follows.

To simplify subsequent formulas and to be sure that the sum of weights equals the number of cases in the dataset, let

$$w_i' = w_i \frac{n}{\sum_{i=1}^{n} w_i} .$$

then the weighted sample mean is

$$\overline{X} = \frac{\sum_{i=1}^{n} w_i' X_i}{n} ,$$

and the sample estimate of the population standard deviation is

$$s_x = \sqrt{\frac{1}{n-1} \sum_{i=1}^{n} w_i' (X_i - \overline{X})^2}$$

Formulas for regressions   For more complicated calculations, matrix notation is necessary. For frequency weights, sampling weights and weighted least-squares weights, define the weight matrix as $\mathbf{W}$, an $n \times n$ matrix with diagonal elements w_i' as defined above and off-diagonal elements all zero. For GLS weights, define $\mathbf{W} = \mathbf{\Omega}^{-1}$. The estimated regression coefficients are obtained as follows:

$$\boldsymbol{\beta} = (\mathbf{X'WX})^{-1}\mathbf{X'WY},$$

with sampling variance–covariance matrix

$$\sigma^2(\mathbf{X'WX})^{-1}.$$

As in the unweighted case, σ^2 is not observed, but is estimated by s^2, the sample estimate of the population variance of ε. The first step to calculating s^2 is to calculate the squared regression residual for each data case. The second step is to calculate the sum of these squared residuals and to divide by $n-k$.

When weights are sampling weights, some authorities note that sampling weights are not proper WLS or GLS weights and so should not be treated as such. Based on that assertion, these authorities argue that if the regression model is correctly specified, and there is no association of sample weight with the size of the squared error, then it does not matter if s^2 is calculated without weighting. This reasoning suggests the formula:

$$s^2 = \sqrt{\frac{1}{n-k} \sum_{i=1}^{n} (Y_i - \hat{Y}_i)^2}. \qquad (8.59)$$

Other authorities note that regression specifications are inevitably found to be incorrect, if only because theories and knowledge both evolve, and datasets inevitably lack some important variables. These authorities assert that results can be misleading if s^2 is calculated without weights in a sample for which the mean squared residuals are substantially different for oversampled population segments (with small weights) than for undersampled population segments (with large weights). This reasoning suggests the formula

$$s^2 = \sqrt{\frac{1}{n-k} \sum_{i=1}^{n} w_i' (Y_i - \hat{Y}_i)^2}. \qquad (8.60)$$

Formula (8.59) appears to be more often favored by authorities with backgrounds in econometrics. Formula (8.60) appears to be more often favored by authorities with backgrounds in sampling and other social science disciplines.

Combining weights

A dataset may be weighted in several ways at once. For example, a number of identical cases, each having the same sampling weight, may be represented by a single case with (1) a frequency weight to indicate the number of identical cases and (2) a sampling weight based on the probability with which they were each sampled. The appropriate weight would be the product of the sampling weight and the frequency weight. When GLS weights and sampling weights both exist, they could be combined multiplicatively or not, depending on one's view of the controversy surrounding equations (8.59) and (8.60).

GENERAL SOURCES FOR THIS CHAPTER

There are many outstanding texts that explicate regression and related statistical methods. Many of them bear such astonishing similarity to each other that it is neither possible nor desirable to draw sharp distinctions among them. To the very sociological author of this chapter, the reason for this similarity appears to be that regression has grown from a single technique into a language for thinking about data and theory testing. Like all languages, the notational structure of regression has simplified and standardized over time, and a core vocabulary has developed. I have drawn on so many of these texts so often for so long that I cannot accurately identify all the sources from which this chapter is drawn. However, I can identify and recommend the following: Fox (1997), Greene (2000), Hanushek and Jackson (1977), Hayashi (2000), Kennedy (1998) and Meyers (1990).

NOTES

1 For example, in a bivariate regression model, one can perform a t test of the regression coefficient $\hat{\beta}$ with df degrees of freedom, or perform an F test of the model with 1 and df degrees of freedom, where the numerical value of t^2 will equal the value of F. These two approaches are equally good tests of the null hypothesis that $\beta = 0$. The reader should refer to Chapter 4 for a description of the relationship among these three distributions.

2 For example, in equation (8.18) if respondents are white, then D_2 and D_3 are both zero, causing the values of $\alpha_3 D_2$ and $\alpha_4 D_3$ to be zero and therefore without any effect on anything; the intercept is α_0. If respondents are black, then D_3 is zero, causing the values of $\alpha_4 D_3$ to be zero and therefore ineffectual; but D_2 equals one, so that $\alpha_3 D_2$ equals α_3 and the intercept equals the sum of α_0 and α_3. Thus, α_3 is the estimated difference between the intercept for blacks and the intercept for whites and the standard error for α_3 is the standard error of that difference. Similar results obtain for nonblack–nonwhites: For nonblack–nonwhites, $D_2 = 0$, $D_3 = 1$, and the intercept is $\alpha_0 + \alpha_4$.

3 To see this, consider the model

$$\hat{Y} = b_0 + b_1 X_1 + b_2 X_2 + b_3 X_1 X_2.$$

Now let a and b be constants, and let β_0, β_1, β_2, and β_3 be coefficients. Define two new variables, $X_1 = X_1 - a$ and $X_2 = X_2 - b$ and consider the model

$$\hat{Y} = \beta_0 + \beta_1 X_1 + \beta_2 X_2 + \beta_3 X_1 X_2.$$

The effects of X_1 and X_2 on Y are $\partial Y/\partial X_1 = \beta_1 + \beta_3 X_2$ and $\partial Y/\partial X_2 = \beta_2 + \beta_3 X_1$. Making use of the definitions of X_1 and X_2, we can write

$$\hat{Y} = \beta_0 + \beta_1 X_1 + \beta_2 X_2 + \beta_3 X_1 X_2$$
$$= \beta_0 + \beta_1 (X_1 - a) + \beta_2 (X_2 - b)$$
$$\quad + \beta_3 (X_1 - a)(X_2 - b)$$
$$= (\beta_0 - \beta_1 a - \beta_2 b + \beta_3 ab) + (\beta_1 - \beta_3 b) X_1$$
$$\quad + (\beta_2 - \beta_3 a) X_2 + \beta_3 X_1 X_2.$$

The last expression is just the regression of Y on X_1, X_2 and $X_1 X_2$, with coefficients equal to the terms in parentheses. But the coefficients of that regression have been defined already as b_0, b_1, b_2, and b_3. So we can write $(\beta_0 - \beta_1 a - \beta_2 b + \beta_3 ab) = b_0$, $(\beta_1 - \beta_3 b) = b_1$, $(\beta_2 - \beta_3 a) = b_2$, and $\beta_3 = b_3$. Solving these equations for β_1, β_2, and β_3 yields $\beta_3 = b_3$, $\beta_2 = b_2 + b_3 a$, and $\beta_1 = b_1 + b_3 b$. Substituting $\beta_3 = b_3$, $\beta_2 = b_2 - b_3 a$, and $\beta_1 = b_1 + b_3 b$ for β_1, β_2 and β_3 in the expressions for $\partial Y/\partial X_1$ and $\partial Y/\partial X_2$ and collecting terms, we get $\partial Y/\partial X_1 = b_1 + b_3 X_2$, which is precisely the formula for $\partial Y/\partial X_1$, and $\partial Y/\partial X_2 = b_2 + b_3 X_1$, which is precisely the formula for $\partial Y/\partial X_2$. In short, in the multiplicative interaction model, subtracting constants from X_1 and X_2 before calculating their product does not alter their effects on Y, and does not change the coefficient of the multiplicative interaction term.

4 It has been suggested that the coefficient for X_2 in the parabolic function can be interpreted as a measure of convexity or concavity. Such an interpretation is possible, but I find it more straightforward to calculate the partial derivative in the usual way and investigate its changes over the range of X.

5 In a sample of infinite size, the correlation of a normally distributed X with X^2 is zero, and there is no confounding of sampling errors in measurement of β_1 with sampling errors in measurement of β_2. Infinite samples of normally distributed variables are extremely rare if not actually unknown in social science data.

REFERENCES

Blau, Peter Michael and Schoenherr, Richard A. (1971) *The Structure of Organizations.* New York: Basic Books.

Debreu, Gerard (1987) *Theory of Value: An Axiomatic Analysis of Economic Equilibrium.* New Haven, CT: Yale University Press.

Duncan, Otis Dudley (1968) 'Inheritance of poverty or inheritance of race', in Daniel P. Moynihan (ed.), *On Understanding Poverty.* New York: Basic Books, pp. 85–110.

Fox, John (1997) *Applied Regression Analysis, Linear Models and Related Methods.* Thousand Oaks, CA: Sage.

Greene, William H. (2000) *Econometric Analysis.* (4th edition). Englewood Cliffs, NJ: Prentice Hall.

Hanushek, Eric and Jackson, John (1977) *Statistical Methods for Social Scientists.* New York: Academic Press.

Hayashi, Fumio (2000) *Econometrics.* Princeton, NJ: Princeton University Press.

Holland, Paul W. (1986) 'Statistics and causal inference', *Journal of the American Statistical Association,* 81: 945–60.

Kennedy, Peter (1998) *A Guide to Econometrics* (4th edition). Cambridge, MA: MIT Press.

Myers, Raymond (1990) *Classical and Modern Regression with Applications* (2nd edition). Boston: PWS-Kent.

Rees, Albert and Schultz, George (1970) *Workers and Wages in an Urban Labour Market.* Chicago: University of Chicago Press.

Stolzenberg, Ross M. (1990) 'Ethnicity, geography and occupational achievement of Hispanic men in the United States', *American Sociological Review,* 55: 34–45.

9

Incorporating Categorical Information into Regression Models:

The Utility of Dummy Variables

MELISSA HARDY AND JOHN REYNOLDS

In this chapter we explain various methods for specifying qualitative indicators as explanatory variables in routine regression analyses. As discussed in Chapter 3, measures of central tendency and variability for nominal classifications rely on frequency information, since counts represent the single numerical dimension of nominal schemes. The newcomer to statistics is therefore often surprised to learn that analytic techniques, such as regression and its extensions, do not require interval measurement of information for that information to be represented in the analysis.

Within this context, the term 'represented' is key, since to perform statistical analyses we clearly need 'numbers'. It is what the numbers represent that can provide us with flexibility. In the case of a measure of age, 31 may represent 31 years, 31 months, 31 weeks or 31 days, hours, or minutes, depending on the study question and the population being sampled. As Chapter 2 explained, to represent the information contained in a classification scheme with numerically coded variables, we must link a category 'name' to a number. We can define this linkage in a variety of ways, depending on how we wish to capture the information. In the case of binary-coded dummy variables, we may link a category name, say, woman, to a value of 1 for a variable we may call gender, with those

who are 'not woman' coded 0. The numerical values used to represent the set of categories are determined by the hypotheses of group differences the researcher wants to test (Hardy, 1993). The number of dummy variables used to represent the classification scheme is determined by how many categories the researcher wants to keep distinct. If the original classification contains too much detail, researchers can combine categories, so long as they are careful to ensure that these combinations are theoretically and empirically similar.

Later chapters address techniques for analyzing qualitative dependent variables in single-equation and multiple-equation models. In this chapter, we will concentrate on ways to maximize information by using dummy variables as exogenous variables in standard regression analysis. We will assume that the reader is familiar with the coding techniques discussed in Chapter 2. Our purpose here is to describe issues of statistical analysis and interpretation when dummy variables are specified. In the first section of the chapter, we will move from the simplest specification of a model with one binary classification variable to models with one multinomial classification variable, then multiple classification variables, ending with a model that includes both dummy variables and interval variables.

Once we have elaborated the basic interpretations of these partial effects, we will expand the specification to include interaction terms so that we can test whether relationships are uniform across subgroups. We compare the interaction models to separate subgroup regression models and demonstrate the similarities and differences between the two approaches. We conclude this section of the chapter with an illustration of the decomposition of group differences. This technique proves useful in policy analyses, for example, by allowing researchers to demonstrate the relative magnitude of two of the components of group differences – differences in the demographic composition of the groups versus differences in how characteristics are translated into outcomes.

The middle section of the chapter demonstrates how dummy variables can be used to manage missing data and censored observations. Using dummy variables in this manner allows the researcher to analyze data of a heterogeneous group of observations, rather than dividing the observations into more homogeneous subgroups. For example, if a sample of individuals includes both married and unmarried persons, one would often like to include some information on spouses as predictors without sacrificing the comparison across marital statuses.

Dummy variables also allow the researcher to assess the randomness of missing data. By specifying a dummy variable as a flag for missing information, one can control in the equation for the possibility that unwillingness or inability to report certain types of information may not be independent of the outcome measure under study. For example, imagine that a researcher is interested in how occupational knowledge affects workers' intentions of changing jobs or rates of job turnover (Waite and Berryman, 1986). Using survey data, the researcher wants to determine whether workers with relatively extensive knowledge about different occupations are more likely to voice intentions to change jobs or more likely to have changed jobs. Accurate knowledge of occupations is assumed to lead to better occupational choices and thus lower rates of turnover. However, refusal to answer the 'occupational knowledge' questions may also be an indicator of lack of knowledge. In other words, rather than answer incorrectly, the worker simply refused. Instead of excluding those observations as missing data or assigning them an arbitrary value on the measure of occupational knowledge, the researcher can use dummy variables to test the hypothesis that those with missing data more closely resemble respondents providing incorrect responses.

We will discuss three types of coding schemes – binary coding, effects coding, and contrast coding – and apply them to the study of differences among race/ethnic groups. The most common coding approach is binary coding, which includes choice of a 'reference group'. All other categories of the original qualitative variable (e.g., race and ethnic identity) are included in the equation as dummy variables and are compared to the 'excluded' category, that is, the 'reference group' or the category not explicitly specified as a dummy variable. Effects coding, in contrast, compares each category's mean value on the outcome to the mean of all category means. Researchers familiar with analysis of variance (ANOVA) techniques will recognize the connections to effects-coded dummy variables. Contrast-coded dummy variables are most useful when the researcher is interested in making 'nested' group comparisons. For example, if we were coding distinct occupational categories, we might want to compare 'white-collar' to 'blue-collar' occupations; then within 'white-collar' occupations, we might want to compare 'upper white-collar' with 'lower white-collar' occupational subgroups. Eventually we would have defined enough contrasts to exhaust the information, but we would be capturing group differences relative to differences between (or among) the broadest groups, then between (among) subgroups, until the information is fully incorporated into the specification. All coding techniques share one basic rule: any classification with j categories requires only $j - 1$ dummy variables to exhaust the category information. Inclusion of j dummy variables results in perfect multicollinearity, a singular matrix, and an inestimable model (see Stolzenberg, Chapter 8, for a more general discussion of multicollinearity). Finally, we will point to other techniques (and therefore other chapters) in which dummy variables have an important role to play.

Our analysis examples are based on data from the base year of the National Education Longitudinal Study (NELS), which is a nationally representative study of eighth graders in 1988. The NELS study was designed and administered by the National Opinion Research Center and the Educational Testing Service. The NELS used a two-stage stratified probability design to select a nationally representative sample of students and schools. From a universe of 40 000 schools, 815 public and 237 private schools agreed to participate. Within each of these schools, 24 students were randomly selected from the entire roster of eighth-grade students, and an additional two or three Hispanic or Asian students were selected as well. Overall, 24 599 students completed the self-administered base-year questionnaire.

REGRESSION MODELS WITH DUMMY VARIABLE PREDICTORS

We chose a limited number of variables to illustrate various features of regression models with dummy variables. Our dependent variable is the students' science test scores.[1] Independent variables include race/ethnicity (African Americans, Asians, Hispanics, Whites);[2] gender; number of siblings; education of mother; education of father; and family income. Table 9.1 reports the three alternative coding schemes for the race/ethnicity variable. The first column includes binary coding, with Whites as the reference group. The second column contains effects coding, with the same set of contrasts as the first column. The third column includes contrast coding, which compares Whites to non-Whites; Asians to Hispanics and Blacks; and Hispanics to Blacks. Keep in mind that fitting the model is unaffected by how the information on the classification is captured, so long as the rules of each coding scheme are met. The major reason for choosing one coding scheme over another is the analyst's preference for the manner in which the information is reported.

Begin by assuming that our primary interest is in gender and race/ethnic differences in students' understanding of science. For a baseline we could generate a mean science score (and standard deviation) for the entire sample. Then we could estimate a mean for female students and a mean for male students. Similarly, we could estimate different means for Asians, Hispanics, African Americans, and Whites. Finally, we could use gender and race/ethnicity to jointly classify students and calculate means and standard deviations for

Table 9.1 *Coding schemes to model race/ethnic differences in science scores*

	Binary coding	Effects coding	Contrast coding
First dummy variable			
Asian	1	1	$-\frac{1}{3}$
Black	0	0	$-\frac{1}{3}$
Hispanic	0	0	$-\frac{1}{3}$
White	0	−1	1
Second dummy variable			
Asian	0	0	1
Black	1	1	$-\frac{1}{2}$
Hispanic	0	0	$-\frac{1}{2}$
White	0	−1	0
Third dummy variable			
Asian	0	0	0
Black	0	0	1
Hispanic	1	1	−1
White	0	−1	0

Note: The text refers to the three dummy variables as Asian, Black, and Hispanic under binary coding; Effect$_1$, Effect$_2$, and Effect$_3$ under effects coding; and Contrast$_1$, Contrast$_2$, and Contrast$_3$ under contrast coding.

the eight possible subgroups. We have done just this in Table 9.2, which reports means, standard deviations, and the number of cases in the overall sample and subsamples.[3] However, this approach becomes unwieldy when we want to assess subgroup differences while, at the same time, controlling for other characteristics that are likely to influence test scores.[4] The alternative is to move to a standard ordinary least-squares (OLS) regression approach, which requires that we are able to meet the underlying assumptions of this model. In Chapter 8, Stolzenberg lists these assumptions, and they apply in this context as well as any other.

Models with qualitative predictors

The simplest model addresses gender differences in expected science test scores and can be specified as follows:

$$y = \beta_0 + \beta_1 \text{ Female} + \varepsilon, \qquad (9.1)$$

Table 9.2   *Science scores by gender and race/ethnicity*

	Mean	Std dev.	N
Total sample	50.77	10.17	20 342
Boys	51.73	10.72	10 087
Girls	49.82	9.50	10 255
Asians	52.90	10.64	1 260
Blacks	44.24	7.71	2 435
Hispanics	46.19	8.46	2 473
Whites	52.50	10.06	14 174
Asian boys	54.43	11.10	643
Black boys	44.55	8.10	1 174
Hispanic boys	47.13	9.26	1 182
White boys	53.44	10.57	7 088
Asian girls	51.30	9.89	617
Black girls	43.95	7.33	1 261
Hispanic girls	45.32	7.56	1 291
White girls	51.56	9.44	7 086

where the intercept, β_0, reports the expected science score for an eighth-grade boy and β_1, which is often called the 'slope' in a bivariate regression model, is the difference between the expected science score for eighth-grade girls and eighth-grade boys, girls being the included category. In other words, the gender dummy variable named 'Female' is coded 1 for girls, 0 for boys. If β_1 is negative, then girls (on average) have lower science scores; if positive, girls average higher scores.

Let us pause to make several points. First, although the parameters of the standard bivariate OLS model are the intercept and slope, in this case we are estimating two distinct values rather than a straight line joining two points. We cannot define a regression 'line' because the explanatory variable is not continuous; rather, it is discrete and binary. We can estimate the expected value for boys by substituting into the equation. Boys have a value of 0 on the explanatory variable Female, therefore their expected value is simply β_0. We can estimate the expected value for girls by substituting into the same equation. Girls have a value of 1 for Female, therefore their expected value is $\beta_0 + \beta_1$. Given that the mean is the OLS estimate of central tendency,[5] our expected values from the regression estimation are nothing more than the subgroup means for boys and girls. The reader can confirm this point by comparing the results from equation (9.1) in Table 9.3 with the subgroup means reported in Table 9.2.[6] From the results of equation (9.1), we

see that girls are expected to score 1.91 points lower than boys on the science test and, although this difference is statistically significant, gender explains less than 1% of the variance in science scores.

One assumption we may want to check at this point is the assumption of homogeneity of variance. For our inference tests to be valid, we must assume that the variability around our expected values is the same, within the bounds of sampling error. Since in this model our expected values are subgroup means, we are necessarily assuming an equivalence of subgroup variances. We can test whether the variances are the same by forming a ratio of one group variance to the other, placing the larger variance on top, and adjusting for degrees of freedom. Since an *F*-ratio is the ratio of two chi-squared distributed random variables, and variance estimates are chi-squared distributed, we can use an *F*-test to try to confirm that we have met this assumption (see Chapter 4). To estimate the variance of the mean score for boys, we can square the standard deviation for boys from Table 9.2. To perform the *F*-test, we must then divide the variance by the appropriate degrees of freedom, which is the number of cases involved in the calculation of the variance minus 1, or $N_{boys} - 1$.[7] Using the same procedure to estimate the variance of the mean score for girls, we can then take the ratio of the two variances:

$$F_{10\,086,\,10\,254} = \frac{10.72^2/10\,086}{9.50^2/10\,254}$$

$$= \frac{0.011\,39}{0.0088} = 1.29,[8]$$

which is sufficiently close to 1.0 for us to proceed.[9]

If the classification variable has more than two categories, then additional dummy variables are needed to fully capture the information. Equation (9.2) defines race/ethnic differences in science scores. Using Whites as the reference category, we include three dummy variables to distinguish expected scores for Asians, Blacks, and Hispanics, respectively:

$$y = \beta_0 + \beta_1 \text{Asian} + \beta_2 \text{Black} + \beta_3 \text{Hispanic} + \varepsilon. \tag{9.2}$$

The results reported in the second column of Table 9.3 provide us with the information we need to calculate subgroup means. The

Table 9.3 *Science scores regressed on gender and race/ethnicity*

	(9.1) b/s.e.(b)	(9.2) b/s.e.(b)	(9.3) b/s.e.(b)	(9.4) b/s.e.(b)
Female	−1.905*** (0.142)		−1.795*** (0.135)	−1.878*** (0.162)
Asian		0.395 (0.284)	0.376 (0.283)	0.991* (0.396)
Black		−8.263*** (0.212)	−8.231*** (0.211)	−8.891*** (0.303)
Hispanic		−6.315*** (0.211)	−6.275*** (0.210)	−6.307*** (0.302)
Female × Asian				−1.258* (0.566)
Female × Black				1.276** (0.422)
Female × Hispanic				0.065 (0.420)
Intercept	51.730*** (0.101)	52.502*** (0.081)	53.399*** (0.105)	53.441*** (0.114)
R^2	0.0088	0.0970	0.1048	0.1055
F	180.047***	728.147***	595.055***	342.492***
Std error	10.125	9.664	9.623	9.620
N	20 342	20 342	20 342	20 342

*$p < 0.05$, **$p < 0.01$, ***$p < 0.001$; two-tailed tests.

estimate of β_0 reports the expected score for Whites, 52.50. Both Blacks and Hispanics score lower, on average, than Whites. Blacks' average score is 8.26 points lower; Hispanics average 6.32 points lower. The estimate of β_1 for the dummy variable indicating Asians, on the other hand, is +0.40, suggesting that Asian eighth-graders score 0.40 points higher than Whites, on average. However, when compared to its standard error, the coefficient measuring the difference between Asians and Whites is not statistically significant at conventional levels. Therefore, our conclusion is that Whites and Asians score higher than Blacks and Hispanics, on average.[10]

In both equations (9.1) and (9.2), we are estimating the expected value of the dependent variable as a function of a single explanatory variable. That fact is clearer, perhaps, in equation (9.1), because only one variable was named on the right-hand side of the equation. In the second equation, we 'named' three dummy variables; however, those three variables comprise one set of information. The inclusion of any combination of three race/ethnic categories as each of the three dummy variables would have accomplished the same task. And regardless of which category was used as the reference category, the fit of the model would have been the same. Approximately 10% of the variance in

science scores is explained by race/ethnic group differences.

This caution is important for several reasons. First, some researchers decide to choose a reference category such that the number of significant dummy variable coefficients is maximized. Although reporting results in this manner may appear more impressive, it remains an arbitrary distinction. The number of significant subgroup differences is the same, regardless of how they are specified. Whether inclusion of the classification is sensible in terms of model specification is better tested through an F-test for a significant change in R^2.

The third model in this section specifies both gender and race/ethnic group differences, but rather than looking at gross differences by subgroup, the researcher wants to assess race/ethnic differences while controlling for gender and assess gender differences while controlling for race/ethnicity. By including both explanatory concepts in one model, we test for compositional differences that might account for the subgroup differences:

$$y = \beta_0 + \beta_1 \text{Female} + \beta_2 \text{Asian} + \beta_3 \text{Black} + \beta_4 \text{Hispanic} + \varepsilon. \quad (9.3)$$

For example, if Hispanic students were primarily female students, then one reason why Hispanic students might be registering lower average scores is that eighth-grade girls average lower scores and Hispanic students are disproportionately female. Given the sampling design, we have no reason to expect this outcome. In fact, the subgroup differences between boys and girls as well as those among race/ethnic subgroups should change very little. The results reported in column 3 of Table 9.3 confirm our expectation. We find the same pattern of subgroup results, although we must adjust our interpretation of coefficients. β_0 is the expected score for White eighth-grade boys; β_1 estimates the expected difference between eighth-grade boys and girls, controlling for race/ethnicity. And β_2 estimates the expected difference in average scores for Asians compared to Whites, β_3 for Blacks compared to Whites, and β_4 for Hispanics relative to White students, controlling for gender. The fact that these coefficients change little from equations (9.1) and (9.2) to equation (9.3) indicates that gender composition is not a function of race/ethnicity. (A Pearson chi-squared test of independence between race/ethnicity and gender equals 7.06 with 3 degrees of freedom, which is not significant at $p < 0.05$.)

The final equation in this sequence not only includes all possible information on subgroups (both gender and race/ethnic), but also includes all possible interactions among subgroups. The coefficients β_5 to β_7 estimate these interaction effects, each of which tests the hypothesis that the effect of gender is different for Asians versus Whites, for Blacks versus Whites, and for Hispanics versus Whites:

$$y = \beta_0 + \beta_1 \text{Female} + \beta_2 \text{Asian} + \beta_3 \text{Black} + \beta_4 \text{Hispanic} + \beta_5 (\text{Female} \times \text{Asian}) + \beta_6 (\text{Female} \times \text{Black}) + \beta_7 (\text{Female} \times \text{Hispanic}) + \varepsilon. \quad (9.4)$$

The interpretation of β_0 does not change; however, the interpretations of the coefficients for Asian, Black, and Hispanic do change. For example, β_2 tests whether Asian boys score differently, on average, than White boys; β_3 tests whether Black boys score differently than White boys; and β_4 tests whether Hispanic boys score differently than White boys. Coefficients β_5 to β_7, that is, the coefficients for the interaction terms, estimate the relative race/ethnic differences for girls compared to boys.

The results reported in the fourth column of Table 9.3 demonstrate how gender differences vary by race/ethnicity, and conversely how the differences between Whites and other race/ethnic groups vary by gender. For example, β_5 (−1.26) tells us that Asian girls (compared to White girls) do not score as high as Asian boys (compared to White boys). In fact, the difference between Asian girls and White girls is (+0.99 − 1.26 = −0.27), which suggests a small average decrement for Asian girls compared to White girls. The positive coefficient for Female × Black indicates that the decrement which characterizes Black girls when compared to White girls ($\beta_3 + \beta_6$) is not as large as the difference between Black boys and White boys (β_3).

Since the coefficient for Hispanic does not noticeably change from equation (9.3) to equation (9.4), we know that the difference between Hispanics and Whites is roughly the same for boys and girls. The coefficient for Asian increases almost threefold, which suggests that, whereas Asian boys may score better than White boys, Asian girls score no better than White girls, that is, the 'Asian–White' difference is primarily among boys, not among girls. The shift in the coefficient for Blacks is in the opposite direction: the negative coefficient for Black indicates a larger negative difference. In other words, although African Americans average lower scores than Whites, the difference is larger between groups of boys than between groups of girls.

The information carried by each coefficient has therefore been reframed as the specification has been modified. The coefficients for the gender or race/ethnic dummy variables now capture a group comparison that is specific to gender (or race/ethnicity): the coefficient for female compares only Whites by gender; the coefficients for race/ethnic groups compare only boys by race/ethnicity. The coefficients for the interaction terms estimate the 'difference in the difference'. The question addressed by β_5, 'Is the difference between Asian and White girls the same as the difference between Asian and White boys?', is answered 'No, it must be adjusted by −1.26; the difference between Asian and White girls is smaller by 1.26 points on average'.

We can reaffirm these conclusions by calculating the expected values for the eight subgroups under the assumption of equivalent race/ethnic differences across gender in equation (9.3) and relaxing that assumption in equation (9.4). Table 9.4 presents these

Table 9.4   *Expected science scores by gender and race/ethnicity, based on results from Table 9.3*

Using equation (9.3); assumes no gender by race/ethnicity interactions

Asian boys	53.40 + 0.38	=	53.780
Black boys	53.40 − 8.23	=	45.170
Hispanic boys	53.40 − 6.28	=	47.120
White boys	53.40 + 0	=	53.400
Asian girls	53.40 + 0.38 − 1.80	=	51.980
Black girls	53.40 − 8.23 − 1.80	=	43.370
Hispanic girls	53.40 − 6.28 − 1.80	=	45.320
White girls	53.40 + 0 − 1.80	=	51.600

Using equation (9.4); models all gender by race/ethnicity interactions

Asian boys	53.44 + 0.99	=	54.432
Black boys	53.44 − 8.89	=	44.550
Hispanic boys	53.44 − 6.31	=	47.133
White boys	53.44 + 0	=	53.441
Asian girls	53.44 + 0.99 − 1.88 − 1.26	=	51.297
Black girls	53.44 − 8.89 − 1.88 + 1.28	=	43.949
Hispanic girls	53.44 − 6.31 − 1.88 + 0.07	=	45.321
White girls	53.44 + 0 − 1.88 + 0	=	51.563

calculations. Given that the explanatory information included on the right-hand side of the equation is limited to two nominal classifications, the number of expected values for the dependent variable is limited to the number of logical combinations of these two sets of categories: two gender categories by four race/ethnic categories, for a total of eight expected values.

Although the differences between the first panel (derived from equation (9.3)) and the second panel (derived from equation (9.4)) are not large, the rank ordering of Asian and White girls switches when we introduce the interaction terms. Assuming equivalent effects, Asian girls are expected to outperform White girls in this sample. Allowing for differential effects, Asian girls, on average, underperform with respect to White girls in this sample. By comparing the mean values for the race/ethnic by gender subgroups in Table 9.2 with those reported in the lower panel of Table 9.4, we find the results are identical.

Tests of model fit

Comparing equations (9.3) and (9.4) poses a number of possible inference questions. The question of whether knowing the gender of the student leads to significantly different predicted science scores is answered by testing model fit in equation (9.1). The standard R^2 test assesses the increment in R^2 attributable to the inclusion of explanatory information relative to what is left unexplained. The formula is

$$F_{k,N-k-1} = \frac{R^2/k}{(1-R^2)/(N-k-1)}, \quad (9.5)$$

where N denotes the sample size and k equals the number of explanatory variables in the model, excluding the constant. Both the numerator and the denominator of this F-test are adjusted for degrees of freedom. The F-test for equation (9.1) in Table 9.3 is simply

$$F_{1,20\,340} = \frac{0.0088/1}{(1-0.0088)/20\,340}$$

$$= \frac{0.0088}{0.9912/20\,340} = 180.58.$$

Even with such a low level of explanatory power, the F-test indicates a significant improvement in model fit. Keep in mind that statistical 'significance' is an indicator of the reliability of the estimates rather than the degree of conceptual insight gained from the model. Similarly, the test for the race/ethnic differences captured in equation (9.2) in Table 9.3 depends on the same type of F-test; however, in this case, the degrees of freedom in the numerator and denominator are equal to 3 and $N - 4$, respectively:[11]

$$F_{3, 20\,338} = \frac{0.0970/3}{(1 - 0.0970)/20\,338}$$

$$= \frac{0.032\,333}{0.9030/20\,338} = 728.23$$

What the standard R^2 test actually evaluates is whether a model including the explanatory variables explains significantly more variation in the outcome (y) than a model that assumes the variation in y is random (i.e., a model including only one parameter, the intercept β_0).[12] The F-test for a significant increase in R^2 can be extended to successive comparisons of equations in Table 9.3. For example, equation (9.4) asks whether gender differences vary significantly by race/ethnicity, and whether race/ethnic differences are conditioned by gender, by including interaction terms between the gender and race/ethnicity dummy variables. The test of this hypothesis is given by the F-test for a significant increase in R^2 from equation (9.3) (that assumes no interactions) to equation (9.4). The formula for this F-test is a more generic form of the standard R^2 test and equals

$$F_{df\,1\,=\,k_{eq.4}\,-\,k_{eq.3},\,df\,2\,=\,N\,-\,k_{eq.4}\,-\,1}$$

$$= \frac{(R^2_{eq.4} - R^2_{eq.3})/(k_{eq.4} - k_{eq.3})}{(1 - R^2_{eq.4})/(N - k_{eq.4} - 1)} \quad (9.6)$$

where $k_{eq.3}$ refers to the number of explanatory variables in equation (9.3) and $k_{eq.4}$ refers to the number of explanatory variables in equation (9.4). The result for the F-test of change in R^2 from equation (9.3) to equation (9.4) in Table 9.3 is as follows:

$$F_{3, 20\,334} = \frac{(0.1055 - 0.1048)/(7 - 4)}{(1 - 0.1055)/20\,334}$$

$$= \frac{0.0007/3}{0.8945/20\,334} = 5.30.$$

The comparison of equations (9.3) and (9.4) provides a good example of what is gained by investigating interaction terms. Clearly, the improvement in model fit is very small, as is often the case. Looking for differential effects generally does not lead to large increases in explained variance, an outcome that should not be surprising since we are simply repartitioning the variance. The distinction between the specification of equations (9.3) and (9.4) lies in the constraints imposed on the coefficient estimates. In equation (9.3), the gender difference (the average difference in science scores between boys and girls) is constrained to be equal across the four race/ethnic groups; the coefficient for gender is averaged across all respondents, regardless of race/ethnicity. Similarly, the race/ethnic difference (the average differences in science scores among Whites and non-White race/ethnic groups) is constrained to be the same for boys and for girls; the coefficient for Asian compares all Asians to all Whites, regardless of gender.[13] In equation (9.4), those constraints are relaxed. Rather than averaging these differences and providing the information in a single coefficient, the information is partitioned by gender and contained in two coefficients per race/ethnic group comparison.

Tests of subgroup differences

Performing t-tests on the coefficients for each of the dummy variables establishes whether the group indicated by the dummy variable is significantly different from the reference group. The researcher's choice of reference group should therefore reflect the subgroup differences of primary interest. Nevertheless, additional questions of group differences may be of interest. In model (9.2), for example, the researcher may want to know whether science scores differ between Asians and Hispanics, or between African Americans and Hispanics. These t-tests can be performed after the fact by using a t-test for the difference between two coefficients. But the analyst also can often get a rough estimate of whether such t-tests will indicate significant differences by applying some simple logic to the situation. For example, if Asians do not score differently from Whites, but Hispanics and African Americans do score differently from Whites, it is likely that Asians score differently from African Americans and Hispanics. Further, since the sign of the coefficient for Asian students is positive, any t-test of the difference between two coefficients involving Asian students generally will yield a larger *t*-value than such tests involving Whites.

For model (9.2), Table 9.3 shows that Blacks' and Hispanics' average science scores are significantly different from Whites' scores, while the average science scores of Asians are not (ignoring for the moment the influence of gender). The *t*-test comparing Whites and Hispanics is equal to the coefficient for Hispanics, −6.32, divided by its standard error, 0.21, yielding a *t*-test value of −30.10. In other words, the difference between Whites' and Hispanics' average science scores in the NELS is just over 30 times the amount you would expect from random sampling error *if* there was in fact no difference between Whites' and Hispanics' average science scores in the population.

What about the difference between Asians and Hispanics? Given the coding scheme for the three group dummy variables, model (9.2) does not provide a coefficient and standard error that immediately yields the test of the hypothesis that there is a group difference. However, given information on how far each group's mean score is from the mean score of Whites, we can combine this information to yield a single *t*-test of the difference in means between Asians and Hispanics. The formula for the *t*-test is

$$t = \frac{b_1 - b_3}{\sqrt{\mathrm{var}(b_1) + \mathrm{var}(b_3) - 2\mathrm{cov}(b_1, b_3)}} \quad (9.7)$$

where var(*b*) refers to the variance of the coefficient, which is also equal to the squared standard error of *b*, and cov(b_1, b_3) equals the covariance between the coefficients.[14] The covariance between the group dummy variable for Asians and Hispanics is equal to 0.0066, and the variances can be calculated by squaring the estimates of their standard errors from model (9.2) (the numbers below are slightly different from those obtained by squaring the values in Table 9.3 due to rounding; e.g., the standard error for the Asian–White difference is actually 0.2841; also, for space considerations we do not present the entire variance–covariance matrix of the slopes). Plugging these values into formula (9.7) gives

$$t = \frac{0.40 - (-6.32)}{\sqrt{0.0807 + 0.0444 - 2 \times 0.0066}}$$

$$= \frac{6.72}{\sqrt{0.0807 + 0.0444 - 2 \times 0.0066}} = 20.09,$$

indicating there is a significant difference between Asians' and Hispanics' mean science scores as well.

Although the tests described above rely on taking the difference between two coefficients associated with one or another subgroup, in other circumstances inferentially assessing subgroup differences relies on summing two coefficients. For example, earlier we reported that the inclusion of the gender-by-race/ethnic interaction terms was important because it allowed us to accurately reproduce the rank ordering of the subgroups. Without the interaction term, Asian girls were predicted to outperform White girls, and that difference was presented as significant because the coefficient for Asian was statistically significant and, given the specification of the equation, it applied equally to girls and boys. When we allowed the Asian–White difference to be gender-specific, that is, for the difference between Asian and White boys as distinct from the difference between Asian and White girls, that rank ordering switched. What does that change in ordering mean? Can we assume, now, that White girls in the population are expected to outperform Asian girls?

This type of inferential question requires an inferential test of the White–Asian difference among girls. The coefficient for Asian in equation (9.4) relative to its standard error provides an inferential test of the statistical significance of the Asian–White difference in science scores among boys. Before we can test the Asian–White difference among girls, we have to figure out what it is. Because of the way gender is coded, the 'effect' of being Asian, rather than White, for girls is the sum of the coefficient for Asian (0.99) and the coefficient for the interaction term between Asian and gender (−1.26). When we sum those two coefficients, we have a negative 'effect' of −0.27. In other words, Asian girls are predicted to score 0.27 points worse than White girls in this sample. But what can we say about the population? Is −0.27 statistically different from 0?

To conduct this inference test, we need the following formula:

$$t = \frac{b_1 + b_2}{\sqrt{\mathrm{var}(b_1) + \mathrm{var}(b_2) + 2\mathrm{cov}(b_1, b_2)}}. \quad (9.8)$$

Similar to the one we used previously, we are again combining the information contained in two coefficient estimates with their standard errors and the covariance of the estimates.

To continue with this example, we have:

$$t = \frac{0.99 - 1.26}{\sqrt{0.1570 + 0.3200 + 2 \times (-0.1570)}}$$

$$= \frac{-0.27}{\sqrt{0.1630}} = -0.67.$$

We conclude, then, that correcting the error in ranking Asian and White girls using information from equation (9.4) was not to suggest that White girls in the population would outperform Asian girls, but to show that we should expect no difference. Although Asian boys outperform White boys, Asian and White girls would be expected to average about the same score.

Adding continuous variable predictors to the model

The geometry of the regression model applies only when at least one explanatory variable is measured in a continuous metric. It is the continuity of measurement that provides an infinite number of predicted values of Y, each value contingent on a particular value of the explanatory variable and the parameter estimates in the model. We now introduce several variations on the theme of introducing an interval independent variable: family income. Table 9.5 reports estimates from four approaches to scaling the metric of income: income measured in thousands of dollars, dollar income (in thousands) centered around the mean, the natural log of family income, and the natural log centered around the mean log income. Each pair of model results tests two specifications: a model that adds family income as an explanatory variable and a second model that also includes an interaction term between gender and family income:

$$y = \beta_0 + \beta_1\text{Female} + \beta_2\text{Asian} + \beta_3\text{Black}$$
$$+ \beta_4\text{Hispanic} + \beta_5(\text{Female} \times \text{Asian})$$
$$+ \beta_6(\text{Female} \times \text{Black}) + \beta_7(\text{Female}$$
$$\times \text{Hispanic}) + \beta_8\text{Income} + \varepsilon, \qquad (9.9)$$

$$y = \beta_0 + \beta_1\text{Female} + \beta_2\text{Asian} + \beta_3\text{Black}$$
$$+ \beta_4\text{Hispanic} + \beta_5(\text{Female} \times \text{Asian})$$
$$+ \beta_6(\text{Female} \times \text{Black}) + \beta_7(\text{Female}$$
$$\times \text{Hispanic}) + \beta_8\text{Income} + \beta_9(\text{Female}$$
$$\times \text{Income}) + \varepsilon. \qquad (9.10)$$

A comparison of models (9.9a) and (9.9b) in Table 9.5 illustrates that recentering the

distribution of family income around its mean value changes only the estimate of the constant. All other coefficient estimates, standard errors, and model fit statistics are the same. Rescaling family income around the mean value of the income distribution simply shifts the number line below the distribution such that a value of zero in the recentered distribution now denotes 'average family income'. Since the constant in any regression model reports the predicted value of Y (science score) when all independent variables are set to zero, the constant in model (9.9a) tells us the expected science score for a White male student from a family with 'zero' income. In contrast, the constant in model (9.9b) gives us the expected science score for a White male student from a family with 'average' income. A comparison of models (9.10a) and (9.10b) also demonstrates the shift in the value of the constant. In addition, the value of the coefficient for Female (the included category on gender) changes once the interaction term is added. The −1.6 in model (9.10a) tells us the expected difference in science scores between White boys and girls when family income equals zero. The −0.005 coefficient for the interaction terms indicates that this gender gap in scores widens by 0.005 for every thousand dollars of family income. Hence, in model (9.10b), the coefficient for Female is −1.8, which estimates the expected gender gap in science scores at 'average' family income ($43 693). The interaction term is not significantly different from zero, which suggests that, although a small gender difference in the effect of family income is measured in the sample, this measurement is not sufficiently reliable to conclude that such a difference exists in the population. Nevertheless, other coefficient estimates are adjusted for this respecification – a respecification of scale rather than of functional form.

The reader can confirm that using the log transformation of family income rather than the original metric again changes coefficient estimates, since the specification of logged family income does change the functional form of the relationship. Comparing the constants from models (9.9c) and (9.9d) demonstrates the same type of shift as we observed for (9.9a) and (9.9b). The reader must keep in mind, however, that the recentering incorporated into models (9.9d) and (9.10d) is based on the mean value of the logged family income, 10.24, which translates into

Table 9.5 Science scores regressed on gender, race/ethnicity, and income

	Income in $1000s		Income in $1000s, centered		Logged income		Logged income, centered	
	(9.9a) b/s.e.(b)	(9.10a) b/s.e.(b)	(9.9b) b/s.e.(b)	(9.10b) b/s.e.(b)	(9.9c) b/s.e.(b)	(9.10c) b/s.e.(b)	(9.9d) b/s.e.(b)	(9.10d) b/s.e.(b)
Female	-1.823*** (0.158)	-1.596*** (0.212)	-1.823*** (0.158)	-1.798*** (0.158)	-1.761*** (0.157)	1.695 (1.246)	-1.761*** (0.157)	-1.690*** (0.159)
Asian	0.997** (0.386)	0.998** (0.386)	0.997** (0.386)	0.998** (0.386)	1.255** (0.385)	1.279*** (0.385)	1.255** (0.385)	1.279*** (0.385)
Black	-7.732*** (0.298)	-7.673*** (0.300)	-7.732*** (0.298)	-7.673*** (0.300)	-7.013*** (0.300)	-6.844*** (0.306)	-7.013*** (0.300)	-6.844*** (0.306)
Hispanic	-5.319*** (0.296)	-5.269*** (0.298)	-5.319*** (0.296)	-5.269*** (0.298)	-4.945*** (0.296)	-4.823*** (0.300)	-4.945*** (0.296)	-4.823*** (0.300)
Female × Asian		-1.519** (0.552)		-1.519** (0.552)		-1.334* (0.550)		-1.334* (0.550)
Female × Black		1.345** (0.418)		1.227** (0.418)		1.021* (0.425)		1.021* (0.425)
Female × Hispanic		0.025 (0.414)		0.025 (0.414)		0.100 (0.417)		0.100 (0.417)
Family Income (see note)	0.047*** (0.001)	0.049*** (0.002)	0.047*** (0.001)	0.049*** (0.002)	2.033*** (0.059)	2.215*** (0.088)	2.033*** (0.059)	2.215*** (0.088)
Female × Family income		-0.005 (0.003)		-0.005 (0.002)		-0.330** (0.118)		-0.330** (0.118)
Intercept	51.112*** (0.133)	50.994*** (0.152)	53.154*** (0.110)	53.140*** (0.112)	32.135*** (0.626)	30.226*** (0.926)	52.948*** (0.112)	52.904*** (0.113)
R^2	0.1492	0.1493	0.1492	0.1493	0.1551	0.1554	0.1551	0.1554
F	445.795***	396.576***	445.795***	396.576***	466.612***	415.774***	466.612***	415.774***
Std error	9.382	9.382	9.382	9.382	9.349	9.348	9.349	9.348
N	20342	20342	20342	20342	20342	20342	20342	20342

*$p < 0.05$, **$p < 0.01$, ***$p < 0.001$; two-tailed tests.

Note: In models (9.9a) and (9.10a), income is measured in thousands of dollars; in models (9.9b) and (9.10b), income is measured in thousands of dollars and centered around $43 693. In models (9.9c) and (9.10c), income is transformed by the natural log; in models (9.9d) and (9.10d) income is logged and centered around 10.24.

Table 9.6 *Science scores regressed on race/ethnicity and income by gender*

	Females b/s.e.(b)	Males b/s.e.(b)
Asian	−0.055	1.279**
	(0.367)	(0.409)
Black	−5.823***	−6.844***
	(0.276)	(0.324)
Hispanic	−4.723***	−4.823***
	(0.271)	(0.318)
Family income	1.884***	2.215***
(see note)	(0.074)	(0.093)
Intercept	51.215***	52.904***
	(0.105)	(0.120)
R^2	0.1436	0.1534
F	464.199***	422.791***
Std error	8.743	9.925
N	10 255	10 087

$*p < 0.05$, $**p < 0.01$, $***p < 0.001$; two-tailed tests.

Note: Family income transformed by the natural log and centered around 10.24.

approximately $28 000.[15] The constant in model (9.9d) therefore estimates the expected science score of a student whose family income is about $28 000. Since the science test score of the student is a positive function of family income, basing the constant on a family income of $28 000 versus a family income of $0 raises the expected value of the test score.

A comparison of models (9.10c) and (9.10d) indicates the same shift in the constant as noted above. In addition, the coefficient for the dummy variable coded 1 if the student was female is also reduced a bit in size when we test to see if the relationship between family income and test score differs for boys versus girls. In models (9.10c) and (9.10d), we see that the gender gap between the scores of boy and girl students widens as family income increases. The coefficient for Female estimates the science disadvantage of girls at 1.69 points, on average, at average log income ($28 000); as income increases, the weighting factor for boys is 2.22 (the coefficient for log family income) and 1.89 for girls (2.22 − 0.33). So, although average science score increases as family income increases, the rate of increase is greater for boys than for girls. Hence, the gender gap widens as given:

White, female student, $28 000	51.21
White, male student, $28 000	52.90
White, female student, $56 000	52.52
White, male student, $56 000	54.44
White, female student, $84 000	53.29
White, male student, $84 000	55.34

Comparing a single model with interactions to within-group regressions

One of the most common errors made in analyzing subgroup differences occurs when researchers who hypothesize the existence of subgroup differences in the outcome and/or in the process, perform regression within the subgroups. Performing subgroup regressions is in itself not necessarily an error. The error lies in drawing inferences about subgroup differences in the determinants of the dependent variable based on whether or not coefficients across all subgroups produce the same 'pattern of significance'.[16]

Table 9.6 provides us with the results from estimating our basic regression model within gender subgroups. Because all respondents in one model are female, and all respondents in the other are male, the dummy variable for gender is omitted. Further, the interaction terms denoting gender differences in race/ethnic comparisons and gender differences in the assessments across family income become unnecessary. Given that we are estimating our model only on girls or only on boys, we are controlling for gender by sample definition.

Compare the results of these gender-specific models to the results from model (9.10d) in Table 9.5. If the reader can keep in mind the meaning of the coefficient estimates in model (9.10d), the comparison to the models in Table 9.6 is straightforward. For example, the constant in model (9.10d) is 52.90, which is the expected score for White boys at average income; it is reproduced as the constant in the males model in Table 9.6. Combining 52.9 with the coefficient for Female, we reproduce 51.21, the constant in the model for girls in Table 9.6. The coefficient for log family income reappears in the model for girls in Table 9.6; that coefficient minus 0.33 (the coefficient for the gender/income interaction) is the marginal effect of family income for girls. The reader can confirm that the coefficients for race/ethnicity follow the same pattern.

What about the inferential tests? Are they consistent as well? They are, assuming you know what the default inference tests for the various coefficients mean. From model

(9.10d) we learned that at average log income, girls score lower than boys, on average; Asian boys score higher than White boys; White boys score higher than Black or Hispanic boys; and average scores for boys are higher at higher family income levels. We also learn that the comparison of Asian girls to White girls is much smaller than for their male counterparts; that the comparison of Black and White girls is somewhat smaller than for their male counterparts; that the comparison of Hispanic and White girls cannot be said to differ from what was estimated for their male counterparts; and that as family income increases, so do the girls' scores, on average – but not by as much as the boys' scores increase.

What we know from the models in Table 9.6 is that among girls we find no difference between Whites and Asians, but we do find reliable differences between Whites and both Blacks and Hispanics. Among boys, Asians score better than Whites, who score better than Blacks and Hispanics. Among both boys and girls, higher family incomes are associated with higher average scores.

Results from the two approaches are therefore consistent. But the statistical information and the inferential tests are presented with a different emphasis. The subgroup regressions provide information on the gender-specific effects and the statistical significance of each of the explanatory variables, conditional on gender. Questions about subgroup *differences* can only be answered by performing additional *t*-tests for the *difference in coefficient estimates* relative to the standard error of that difference, which is inefficiently estimated by this approach. In the pooled regression, however, the information on group differences is provided by the specification, since the inferential tests of interaction terms are themselves tests of group differences in the effects of explanatory variables. If we want to know about the size and statistical significance of gender-specific effects for girls (since they are coded 1 on gender), we must perform additional *t*-tests of the sum of coefficients (see formula (9.8)), since the gender-specific effects for the included category require the combination of two pieces of information: the effect for boys and the gender difference in the effect for girls versus boys.

Decomposing group differences

One of the more common uses of dummy variables in social science research relates to

our interest in inequality and the process of discrimination. Typically, we include dummy variables for gender and/or race/ethnicity, for example, so we can assess subgroup differences in outcomes once individual characteristics legitimately linked to the outcomes have been controlled. Therefore, the set of regression equations often begins with a preliminary assessment of subgroup differences, the inclusion of additional factors theoretically linked to the distribution of outcomes, and then the specification of interaction terms to determine whether these theoretically relevant factors differentially translate into outcomes for the separate subgroups. At this point, a common question is to ask how much of the initial difference that was observed can be attributed to endowments versus discrimination. Perhaps a more value-neutral or generic terminology is to ask how much of an observed subgroup difference is attributable to differences in composition versus differences in process. Deriving answers to these questions requires that we decompose regression results into the two components, a procedure introduced by Oaxaca (1973).

The information required for the decomposition consists of group-specific means and group-specific coefficients for all variables in the equation. One way to proceed is therefore to estimate within-group regression, since the point is to obtain group-specific weights for the variables rather than to inferentially test whether the coefficients are significantly different. To develop this example with our data, we return to a relatively simple model that expresses science scores as a function of race/ethnicity and household income. We assume that there are K sets of variables such that each X vector superscripted with k represents a vector of regressors that comprise the kth variables set. Writing the equations separately, we are interested in the following:

$$\bar{Y}_m = \hat{\beta}_{m0} + \sum_{k=1}^{K} \bar{X}_m^{(k)\prime} \hat{\beta}_m^{(k)} \qquad (9.11)$$

$$\bar{Y}_f = \hat{\beta}_{f0} + \sum_{k=1}^{K} \bar{X}_f^{(k)\prime} \hat{\beta}_f^{(k)} \qquad (9.12)$$

where $\bar{Y}_i$ is the mean science score, $\hat{\beta}_{i0}$ is the estimated constant, $\hat{\beta}_i^{(k)}$ is the column vector of estimated regression coefficients for the set of k variables, and $\bar{X}_i^{(k)\prime}$ is a row vector of variable means for the k regressors. Following

Table 9.7   Estimated regression coefficients and mean values for men and women

Variable	Men				Women			
	Model 1	Model 2	Model 3	Means	Model 1	Model 2	Model 3	Means
Constant	52.90	46.06	–	–	51.21	45.39	–	–
Income	2.22	2.22	2.22	0.0479	1.89	1.88	1.88	–0.0402
Asian	1.28	8.12	54.18	0.0637	–0.05	5.77	51.16	0.0602
Black	–6.84	–	46.06	0.1164	–5.82	–	45.39	0.1230
Hispanic	–4.82	2.02	48.08	0.1172	–4.82	1.10	46.49	0.1259
White	–	6.84	52.90	0.7027	–	5.82	51.22	0.6909

Oaxaca's notation, the gender gap in science scores can be decomposed as follows:

$$\bar{Y}_m - \bar{Y}_f = (\hat{\beta}_{m0} - \hat{\beta}_{f0}) + \sum_{k=1}^{K} \bar{X}_f^{(k)\prime} \Delta\hat{\beta}^{(k)}$$

$$+ \sum_{k=1}^{K} \Delta\bar{X}^{(k)\prime} \hat{\beta}_m^{(k)} \qquad (9.13)$$

where $\Delta\hat{\beta}^{(k)} = \hat{\beta}_m^k - \hat{\beta}_f^k$ and $\Delta\bar{X}^{(k)\prime} = \bar{X}_m^{(k)} - \bar{X}_f^{(k)}$. We can determine each variable's contribution to the endowment (composition) component as $\Delta\bar{X}^{(k)\prime}\hat{\beta}_m^{(k)}$ and to the discrimination (process) component as $\bar{X}_f^{(k)}\Delta\hat{\beta}^{(k)}$. Because the contribution of the intercept, or constant, term is not invariant to scaling differences in the regressors, using this type of decomposition procedure when dummy variables are specified must be examined more closely.

We include race/ethnicity as a set of dummy variables, which are added to the prediction equation. The means of the dummy variables can be written as $\overline{DV}_{ij}, j = 1,\ldots, j$, where $\sum_{j=1}^{J} \overline{DV}_{ij} = 1$ and $i = $ m,f. In the following set of calculations, we examine three variants of the same model. Model 1 sets the reference category to 'White'. Model 2 designates African Americans as the reference category. And model 3 is a 'no intercept' model, which allows us to include all four race/ethnic groups, with no excluded category.[17] Here, for the sake of improved clarity, we will distinguish between the estimated coefficients for interval explanatory variables ($\hat{\beta}$) and the estimated coefficients for dummy variables ($\hat{\delta}$) in models that include an intercept.

Results for the three regression models as well as the gender-specific mean values of the explanatory variables are reported in Table 9.7. We then use this information to substitute into the expanded formula for decomposing the gender gap in science scores, using a regression that incorporates dummy variables as follows:

$$\bar{Y}_m - \bar{Y}_f = (\hat{\beta}_{m0} - \hat{\beta}_{f0}) + \sum_{k=1}^{K} \bar{X}_f^{(k)} \Delta\hat{\beta}^{(k)}$$

$$+ \sum_{j=2}^{J} \overline{DV}_f (\hat{\delta}_m - \hat{\delta}_f) + \sum_{k=1}^{K} \Delta\bar{X}^{(k)} \hat{\beta}_m^{(k)}$$

$$+ \sum_{j=2}^{J} (\bar{V}_m - \bar{V}_f)\hat{\delta}_m. \qquad (9.14)$$

Table 9.8 reports the results of this decomposition procedure. The unadjusted difference between the mean science score for boys and the mean science score for girls is $51.73 - 49.82 = 1.91$ points. Results for each model are disaggregated into the portion of that difference due to process differences (what Oaxaca refers to as discrimination) and compositional differences (or endowments). Each model yields the same overall attribution: 1.619 points (or 84.8% of the difference) is due to differences in regression coefficients; 0.287 points (or 15.2% of the difference) is due to compositional differences, or differences in mean values. For example, if students from lower-income households scored worse on the exam, and the average household income for girls was less than that for boys, this *compositional* difference in household income would likely be reflected in somewhat lower scores for girls. In contrast, if each $1000 increase in average household income produces a two-point gain, on average, for boys, but only a one-point gain, on average, for girls, then this *process* difference will also be reflected in lower scores for girls, compared to boys, at any given level of household income. The decomposition of our results suggests that a much higher proportion of the difference in science scores is attributable to differences in the gender-specific weights assigned to the various characteristics than to the between-group differences in the characteristics themselves.

Table 9.8 *Calculating decomposition of gender gap in science score from three regression models*

	Model 1		Model 2		Model 3	
Variable	Process	Composition	Process	Composition	Process	Composition
Formula	$\hat{\beta}_{0m} - \hat{\beta}_{0f}$	0.000	$\hat{\beta}_{0m} - \hat{\beta}_{0f}$	0.00	$\hat{\beta}_{0m} - \hat{\beta}_{0f}$	
Constant	52.9–51.21=1.690		46.06 – 45.39 = 0.67			
Formula	$\bar{X}_t(\hat{\beta}_m - \hat{\beta}_f)$	$(\bar{X}_m - \bar{X}_f)\hat{\beta}_m$	$\bar{X}_t(\hat{\beta}_m - \hat{\beta}_f)$	$(\bar{X}_m - \bar{X}_f)\hat{\beta}_m$	$\bar{X}_t(\hat{\beta}_m - \hat{\beta}_f)$	$(\bar{X}_m - \bar{X}_f)\hat{\beta}_m$
Income	-0.0402 × 0.33 = -0.013	0.0881 × 2.22 = 0.196	-0.0402 × 0.33 = -0.013	0.0881 × 2.22 = 0.196	-0.0402 × 0.33 = -0.013	0.0881 × 2.22 = 0.196
Asian	0.0602 × 1.33 = 0.080	0.0035 × 1.28 = 0.004	0.0602 × 2.35 = 0.1415	0.0035 × 8.12 = 0.028	0.0602 × 3.02 = 0.1818	0.0035 × 54.18 = 0.1896
Black	0.1230 × (-1.02) = -0.125	-0.0066 × (-6.84) = 0.045			0.1230 × 0.67 = 0.0824	-0.0066 × 46.06 = -0.3040
Hispanic	0.1259 × (-0.10) = -0.013	-0.0087 × (-4.82) = 0.042	0.1259 × 0.92 = 0.1158	-0.0087 × 2.02 = -0.0176	0.1259 × 0.159 = 0.2002	-0.0087 × 48.08 = -0.4183
White			0.6909 × 1.02 = 0.7047	0.0118 × 6.84 = 0.0807	0.6909 × 1.69 = 1.1676	0.0118 × 52.90 = 0.6242
Total	1.619	0.287	1.619	0.287	1.619	0.287

Notice that all three models provide the same decompositions, and that the contribution of income is invariant across the models. In comparing models 1 and 2, which use different reference groups, the partial contribution of the constant and the partial contributions of the individual race/ethnic groups differ. However, if we consider that the contribution of the constant reflects the contribution of gender differences among Whites, then the race/ethnic contribution to both process and compositional differences is the same across the two models: 1.632 and 0.091. We can derive the correct partial contributions of each race/ethnic group only in the third model (the no-intercept model). Here the results indicate that the gender difference among Whites is 72% of the process-related difference: to the extent that being White translates into higher science test scores, it does so more effectively for boys than for girls.

Our success in attributing partial contributions to race/ethnic categories in other than an arbitrary manner (a manner which was contingent on the group selected as the reference group) was possible in this instance because we specified only one qualitative construct – race/ethnicity. Had we included a second construct, for example a set of dummy variables for household composition, we would have faced the same situation as we faced in models 1 and 2. We would be able to correctly attribute some portion of the difference to differences in household composition, but we would be unable to assign partial contributions to 'living with both parents' versus 'living with mother only' versus 'living with father only' and so on (Oaxaca and Ransom, 1999).

ALTERNATIVE CODING SCHEMES

Binary coding of dummy independent variables is often the default approach taken by researchers; however, other coding options have a variety of features to recommend them. Use of binary coding is particularly useful when the comparison of successive groups to a single reference category captures the sample statistics (and associated inferential tests) in which the researcher is interested.[18] If the researcher seeks to construct the comparisons to test other forms of alternative hypotheses, it is a relatively straightforward

practice to structure the coding accordingly. In the remainder of this section, we discuss two alternative coding schemes: effects coding and contrast coding.

Effects coding

As mentioned earlier, two of the major requirements of coding schemes are that they exhaust the information of the classification and that they facilitate hypothesis testing consistent with the theory. Table 9.1 provides examples of how we would utilize effects coding and contrast coding of dummy variables to capture the information of race/ethnicity. The middle column describes three dummy variables generated by effects coding. We retain Whites as the reference group; however, whereas the reference group in binary-coded dummy variables is uniformly coded 0, the reference group in effects-coded dummy variables is always coded –1. The group-coded contrast defined by each dummy variable is between the reference group and the group coded 1. In this example, $Effect_1$ contrasts Whites with Asians, $Effect_2$ contrasts Whites with Hispanics, and $Effect_3$ contrasts Whites with African Americans. On the surface, these comparisons appear to be the same ones we assessed in the previous section, but it is in the construction of the comparisons and the interpretation of the coefficients that the two approaches differ.

When the sizes of the groups being contrasted are equal, the zero-coded categories do not influence the comparison. However, when subgroup sizes are unequal (as is frequently the case), the influence of zero-coded groups is present, though minimal; the influence of the zero-coded groups increases as the expected value for all zero-coded observations departs from the expected value for all respondents, ignoring group membership (Cohen and Cohen, 1983).

Table 9.9 reports zero-order correlations, means, and standard deviations for the effects-coded dummy variables and test score. Whereas the mean values for binary-coded dummy variables are equivalent to the proportion of cases in the designated group (i.e., the category coded 1), the mean value for effects-coded dummy variables indicates the discrepancy in category ns between the reference group (coded –1) and the group coded 1. The mean value is simply $(n_j - n_{ref})/N$. A negative sign indicates that the reference

Table 9.9   Zero-order correlations and descriptive statistics for science scores, gender, and race/ethnicity using effects coding

	Science	Effect$_1$	Effect$_2$	Effect$_3$
Effect$_1$	−0.177			
Effect$_2$	−0.249	0.796		
Effect$_3$	−0.281	0.797	0.752	
Mean	50.77	−0.635	−0.575	−0.577
Std dev.	10.17	0.596	0.698	0.695

Table 9.10   Science scores regressed on gender and race/ethnicity using effects coding

	b/s.e.(b)
Effect$_1$	3.941***
	(0.216)
Effect$_2$	−2.769***
	(0.169)
Effect$_3$	−4.718***
	(0.170)
Intercept	48.956***
	(0.099)
R^2	0.0970
F	9.664
Std error	728.147***
N	20 342

*$p < 0.05$, **$p < 0.01$, ***$p < 0.001$; two-tailed tests.

Note: Effect$_1$ is coded +1 for Asians, 0 for Blacks, 0 for Hispanics, and −1 for Whites. Effect$_2$ is coded 0 for Asians, +1 for Blacks, 0 for Hispanics, and −1 for Whites. Effect$_3$ is coded 0 for Asians, 0 for Blacks, +1 for Hispanics, and −1 for Whites.

group contains more observations than the group coded 1, and the numerical value indicates the magnitude of this discrepancy relative to total sample size. In our example, since the number of non-Hispanic Whites exceeds the number in other race/ethnic categories, all means are negative.

Zero-order correlations of the effects-coded variables with test score increase in absolute value as the expected values for test score by group diverge. However, because the sample is not evenly divided across race/ethnic categories, interpretation of zero-order correlations remains ambiguous. Zero-order correlations among the dummy variables themselves continue to indicate relative group size. A correlation of 0.5 among effects-coded dummy variables will occur only when all groups are the same size.

Table 9.10 includes estimates of the regression coefficients. Although the difference in coding schemes produces different coefficient estimates, the overall fit of the model (indicated here by R^2) and the significance of the relationship between race/ethnicity and test score (indicated by the F-test for R^2) empirically reproduce earlier results. Shifting from binary coding to effects coding changes the way the information is represented, but it does not change the underlying sets of relationships. We are simply viewing it from a somewhat different perspective.

As before, the subgroup contrast exists only as a partial effect – assuming the information is fully captured and specified in the equation. Here, the regression constant (B_0) is the unweighted mean of all race/ethnic group means, and it serves as the reference point against which all subgroup differences are assessed,[19] an approach which makes the unstandardized regression coefficients independent of relative group size. Since the effects-coded dummy variables for race/ethnicity are the only independent variables specified in the equation, the partial regression

coefficient for Effect$_1$ (controlling for Effect$_2$ and Effect$_3$) contrasts Asian students with the unweighted mean of the groups' mean test score for all race/ethnic groups.

To calculate expected test scores for students in each of the race/ethnic subgroups, we substitute into the equations, multiplying the correct value of the independent variable for each of the subgroups by the regression coefficient and adding the sum of those products to the constant. To calculate the expected test score for Asians, we have

$$48.956 + 3.941 \times 1 - 2.769 \times 0 - 4.718 \times 0 = 52.897;$$

for Blacks we have

$$48.956 + 3.941 \times 0 - 2.769 \times 0 - 4.718 \times 1 = 44.238;$$

and for Hispanics we have

$$48.956 + 3.941 \times 0 - 2.769 \times 1 - 4.718 \times 0 = 46.187.$$

An important difference between calculating expected values using effects coding and using binary coding is apparent when we consider Caucasian students. Rather than looking to the constant for the appropriate predicted value, we have

$$48.956 + 3.941 \times (-1) - 2.769 \times (-1) - 4.718 \times (-1) = 52.502.$$

Notice that we have reproduced the subgroup means reported in the third panel of Table 9.2. Notice also that if you add the four subgroup means and divide by 4, you reproduce the intercept – the unweighted mean of group means.

To conclude, the interpretation of the regression coefficients for effects-coded dummy variables differs from the interpretation of binary-coded variables. Rather than capturing the difference between an included group and the reference group, the coefficients of effects-coded variables capture each subgroup's departure from an average test score. A coefficient near zero would suggest that the subgroup was 'typical'. A positive coefficient indicates that the subgroup was better than average, whereas a negative coefficient signifies that the subgroup's performance was worse than average. Therefore, if the researcher is interested in illustrating the distinctiveness of each subgroup, use of effects coding will estimate that 'uniqueness' and provide an inferential test of its reliability (Cohen and Cohen, 1983).

Contrast-coded variables

The final coding scheme we will discuss is that of contrast codes, which are illustrated in the right-hand column of Table 9.1. By using contrast coding, researchers can organize comparisons to test their specific hypotheses as long as three conditions are met: the information in the classification scheme must be fully represented;[20] the set of codes for any single dummy variable must sum to zero; and the codes for any two dummy variables must be orthogonal. A common way to approach contrast coding is to identify a meaningful way in which some of the subgroups can be combined. Using race/ethnicity as an example, we could invoke a majority versus minority distinction and initially hypothesize that Caucasian children will score higher, on average, than non-Caucasian children. The first contrast-coded variable reflects that grouping by coding Caucasian children +1 and Asian, Hispanic and African American children $-\frac{1}{3}$. The second and third dummy variables must now disaggregate the non-Caucasian category. The second variable compares test scores for Asian children (coded +1) to scores for Hispanic and African American children (coded $-\frac{1}{2}$), and the third

Table 9.11 *Zero-order correlations and descriptive statistics for science scores, gender, and race/ethnicity using contrast coding*

	Science	Contrast$_1$	Contrast$_2$	Contrast$_3$
Contrast$_1$	0.258			
Contrast$_2$	0.229	0.258		
Contrast$_3$	–0.045	0.006	0.005	
Mean	50.77	0.596	–0.059	–0.002
Std dev.	10.17	0.613	0.345	0.491

dummy variable compares Hispanic children (coded –1) to African American children (coded +1). We have created the necessary number of dummy variables, $j - 1 = 3$. The sum of the codes for each of the three dummy variables is zero. And we can check the orthogonality of this set of contrasts coded by summing the products of successive pairs of codes. For example, summing the products of codes for the first and second variables, we have $1 \times 0 + (-\frac{1}{3}) \times 1 + (-\frac{1}{3}) \times (-\frac{1}{2}) + (-\frac{1}{3}) \times (-\frac{1}{2}) = 0$.[21]

Table 9.11 reports zero-order correlations, means, and standard deviations for the contrast-coded dummy variables defined in Table 9.1. The means and standard deviations of contrast-coded variables are also a function of the relative sizes of the subgroups. Because the coding scheme uses fractional quantities between 0 and 1, the relationship between the subgroups' frequencies and the mean values is less straightforward. The correlations among dummy variables in the same set are non-zero, as before, even though the codes of contrast-coded dummy variables must be orthogonal. Requiring that the coding scheme be orthogonal is not the same thing as requiring that the variables themselves be orthogonal or independent (in other words, display a correlation of zero). In testing the orthogonality of the codes, we are concerned that the products of codes within subgroups sum to zero. If we imagine a cross-tabulation of one dummy variable by another, the cell percentages based on column totals would have to be the same as the marginal percentages on the rows to produce a zero correlation. That outcome is not a function of the coding scheme as such. Rather, it is a function of relative subgroup size. Only if observations are equally divided across all groups will the correlation be zero.[22]

The regression estimates are reported in Table 9.12. Once again, the values for R^2 and

Table 9.12 *Science scores regressed on gender and race/ethnicity using contrast coding*

	b/s.e.(b)
Contrast$_1$	3.546***
	(0.114)
Contrast$_2$	5.122***
	(0.203)
Contrast$_3$	–0.974***
	(0.138)
Intercept	48.956***
	(0.099)
R^2	0.0970
F	9.664
Std error	728.147***
N	20 342

*$p < 0.05$, **$p < 0.01$, ***$p < 0.001$; two-tailed tests.

Note: Contrast$_1$ is coded $-\frac{1}{3}$ for Asians, $-\frac{1}{3}$ for Blacks, $-\frac{1}{3}$ for Hispanics, and +1 for Whites. Contrast$_2$ is coded +1 for Asians, $-\frac{1}{2}$ for Blacks, $-\frac{1}{2}$ for Hispanics, and 0 for Whites. Contrast$_3$ is coded 0 for Asians, –1 for Blacks, +1 for Hispanics, and 0 for Whites.

its *F*-test are the same as those reported earlier, underscoring the explanatory equivalence of the three approaches. In considering the regression results, we must again emphasize that the interpretation is contingent on considering partial regression coefficients. Specifying the full set of dummy variables for a given construct (the $j - 1$ dummy variables) is an essential component of the interpretation. The interpretation of the intercept in this model is the same as in the model with effects-coded dummy variables. The intercept reports the unweighted mean of all subgroup means, and it again provides the reference point for assessing group effects. Each dummy specifies a contrast between two subgroups or two sets of aggregated subgroups. Net of the influence of other contrasts, the partial regression coefficient for a contrast-coded dummy variable reflects the difference between the unweighted mean of means for the groups with non-zero codes on that variable. For example, the first contrast-coded dummy variable assigns the same code ($-\frac{1}{3}$) to Asians, Hispanics, and African Americans, and a code of 1 to Caucasians. All the subgroups have non-zero codes, so all groups are implied in this contrast. The regression coefficient (3.532) reflects the contrast between White and non-White students. To calculate the group contrast, we use the following:

$$\text{Contrast}_j = \beta \times \left(\frac{NG1 + NG2}{NG1 \times NG2}\right) \quad (9.15)$$

where $NG1$ is the number of groups sharing a given code and $NG2$ is the number of subgroups sharing the second numerical code, and β is the regression coefficient. In the contrast between White and non-White students we have

$$\text{Contrast}_1 = 3.546 \times \left(\frac{1 + 3}{1 \times 3}\right) = 3.536 \times \frac{4}{3} = 4.728.$$

The remaining contrasts are:

$$\text{Contrast}_2 = 5.122 \times \left(\frac{1 + 2}{1 \times 2}\right) = 5.122 \times \frac{3}{2} = 7.683,$$

$$\text{Contrast}_3 = -0.974 \times \left(\frac{1 + 1}{1 \times 1}\right)$$
$$= -0.974 \times \frac{2}{1} = -1.948.$$

Comparing these values to the group means reported in Table 9.2 verifies that each contrast does reproduce the differences in group means. For example, the difference between the mean for White students and unweighted mean of the means for non-White students is

$$52.50 - [(52.90 + 44.24 + 46.19)/3]$$
$$= 52.50 - 47.78 = 4.72.[23]$$

The standard error for each contrast is produced by multiplying the standard error for the regression coefficient by the same factor used to weight the coefficient itself. For example, the standard error for the contrast of White to non-White students (Contrast$_1$) is $0.114 \times 1.333 = 0.152$. The *t*-tests associated with these coefficients allow us to determine generalizability to the population.

SPECIFICATION FLEXIBILITY USING DUMMY VARIABLES

To this point, we have demonstrated how dummy variables can be used to specify categorical variables in regression equations, how they can be used to estimate differences in within-group regression coefficients, how group differences can be decomposed into separate components, and how alternative coding schemes can facilitate the testing of various types of hypotheses regarding group differences. In this final section we will describe three uses of dummy variables that provide the researcher with additional flexibility in model specification: the use of dummy variables to form 'embedded' variables, to adjust for missing data (a special case of embedded variables), and to specify discontinuities in relationships. We end with brief descriptions of how dummy variables can be used in other types of models.

Embedded variables

A limitation that researchers routinely face involves the availability of information across sample members for variables included in a given data set. A variety of circumstances can limit availability. Data can be missing for cases because of refusals to answer a question, because a skip pattern was inadvertently missed, or because an interview had to be terminated before completion. These circumstances of missing data, the problems it can introduce, and some techniques for addressing these problems are considered in Chapter 5. Another condition that produces uneven arrays of information is when the measures or classifications apply to a subset of sample members because of a status they occupy or a behavior they perform. Information on marital satisfaction can be assessed only among those who are currently married. Hourly wages, fringe benefits, job tenure, or type of work can be assessed only among the currently employed. Type of pension plan, whether an employer makes contributions, or the minimum age at which benefits can be received is applicable only to those who participate in employer-sponsored pension plans. And so on.

If a researcher is interested in population differences in income satisfaction or income adequacy, for example, information about marital status and employment will likely be considered relevant. One approach that has been taken by researchers is to estimate different models on different subsamples. For example, limit the analysis sample to people who are married and employed and include information about the marriage and the job. Then sort respondents into remaining categories – married but not employed, employed but not married, and neither married nor employed – and specify the variables associated with marriage and/or employment only

where they apply. However, this approach is not efficient, and it creates the same difficulties in judging subgroup differences in the effects of other predictor variables that we encountered in the earlier discussion of subgroup regressions. If we can assume these classification variables are exogenous, then we can use embedded variables, a special case of interaction terms, to analyze the full sample.[24]

The use of embedded variables requires the construction of a binary-coded dummy variable to indicate whether the information is present (versus absent) and an interaction term between this dummy variable and the variable referencing the information of interest (which may be captured by another dummy variable or by an interval measure; it makes no difference). The goal is to calculate the partial effect of the variable of interest for the appropriate subsample. So, for example, once a dummy variable that indicates 'married' is included, additional information about the marital relationship (e.g., satisfaction, duration of marriage, whether it is a first marriage, etc.) can be included. Those who are married will have the appropriate values included in the data matrix (e.g., '5' for very satisfied, '1' for first marriage, and '14' for the duration of the marriage). Those who are not currently married will have zeros in these places in the data matrix.

In our example, we use embedded variables to address a problem of missing data on mother's education and father's education. In this data set, about 12% of respondents provide no information on mother's education, and about 16% provide no information on father's education. If we could assume that data on these measures were missing at random and that the reasons for non-response (which remain unmeasured) were uncorrelated with the characteristics of interest to us, we could proceed with an analysis of the subsample of cases that have valid data on both measures. But as the chapters in this *Handbook* routinely caution, proceeding on the basis of a well-founded (and tested) assumption is one thing; simply assuming is quite another.

We therefore create two dummy variables: VALMOMED, which is coded 1 for valid information on mother's education and 0 for missing data; and VALDADED, which is coded 1 for valid information on father's education and 0 when these data are missing.[25] The data arrays for Mother's_Educ. and Father's_Educ. also contain zeroes for missing data.[26] The specification for this model is as follows:

$$
\begin{aligned}
y = {} & \beta_0 + \beta_1 \text{Female} + \beta_2 \text{Asian} + \beta_3 \text{Black} \\
& + \beta_4 \text{Hispanic} + \beta_5 (\text{Female} \times \text{Asian}) \\
& + \beta_6 (\text{Female} \times \text{Black}) + \beta_7 (\text{Female} \\
& \times \text{Hispanic}) + \beta_8 \text{Income} \qquad (9.16) \\
& + \beta_9 \text{Mother's\_Educ.} \\
& + \beta_{10} \text{VALMOMED} \\
& + \beta_{11} \text{Father's\_Educ.} \\
& + \beta_{12} \text{VALDADED} + \varepsilon.
\end{aligned}
$$

Results are reported in Table 9.13. Among children who report valid information on parental education, children with more highly educated mothers are expected to score higher than those with less educated mothers. A similar conclusion holds for children of more highly educated fathers, although the coefficient of father's education is larger than the effect for mother's education. These are the effects of the embedded variables, and they apply only to the subsample who issued valid reports. What of those whose information on parental education was missing? Apparently, not knowing parents' education is also linked to test performance. Here the effects are negative, indicating that children who could not offer this information tended to score lower than children who could provide it. Again, the effect of father's education – or, in this case, failure to report father's education – was a stronger predictor. Results for other predictors remain largely unchanged, with the exception of the coefficient for Asian, which is smaller and less precisely measured in this elaborated model.

Embedded variables allow us to capture important subgroup differences in science scores by retaining cases missing on parent's education, and they prevent an unnecessary loss of statistical power.[27] The lower average science scores for girls and boys whose parents have lower levels of education (e.g., less than 12 years) may be due to living in non-traditional family structures, or they may reflect a home environment with less parental involvement or less emphasis placed on education, all of which are associated with lower educational attainment (Amato, 2000; Astone and McLanahan, 1991; Biblarz and Raftery, 1999; Downey, 1995; McLanahan and Sandefur, 1994; Sandefur and Wells, 1999). Significant differences between those who report versus those who do not report parents' education may even continue into adult life (see Reynolds and Ross, 1998, for a comparable analysis of adult physical and

Table 9.13 *Science scores regressed on gender, race/ethnicity, income, and parent's education (example of embedded dummy variable specification)*

	b/s.e.(b)
Female	−1.599***
	(0.151)
Asian	0.702
	(0.372)
Black	−6.945***
	(0.289)
Hispanic	−3.786***
	(0.287)
Female × Asian	−1.473**
	(0.529)
Female × Black	1.420***
	(0.395)
Female × Hispanic	0.483
	(0.392)
Family income (see note)	1.025***
	(0.062)
Mother's educ.	0.383***
	(0.028)
Valid data, mother's education	−3.757***
	(0.432)
Father's educ.	0.628***
	(0.026)
Valid data, father's education	−7.103***
	(0.396)
Intercept	50.417***
	(0.219)
R^2	0.2180
F	473.418***
Std error	8.993
N	20 342

*$p < 0.05$, **$p < 0.01$, ***$p < 0.001$; two-tailed tests.

Note: Family income transformed by the natural log and centered around 10.24.

psychological well-being), underscoring the importance of making well-founded decisions about how to handle missing information.

Piecewise linear regression

In addition to providing a method for including the information contained in classifications as independent variables, dummy variables can also be used to model kinks in the regression line. Methods for modeling curvilinear relationships are described in Stolzenberg (Chapter 8). In contrast, the approach described below models kinks or breaks in the line rather than curves. The previous section on embedded variables provides

Table 9.14   *Science scores regressed on gender, race/ethnicity, income, and parents' education (example of piecewise dummy variable specification)*

	b/s.e.(b)
Female	−1.599***
	(0.151)
Asian	0.643
	(0.373)
Black	−6.927***
	(0.289)
Hispanic	−3.877***
	(0.288)
Female × Asian	−1.471**
	(0.529)
Female × Black	1.395***
	(0.395)
Female × Hispanic	0.468
	(0.393)
Family income (see note)	1.021***
	(0.062)
Mother's education	0.378***
	(0.055)
# Yrs mother's education exceeds 12	−0.001
	(0.074)
Valid data, mother's education	−3.670***
	(0.651)
Father's education	0.454***
	(0.055)
# Yrs father's education exceeds 12	0.256***
	(0.073)
Valid data, father's education	−5.316***
	(0.637)
Intercept	50.429***
	(0.219)
R^2	0.219
F	407.055***
Std error	8.990
N	20 342

*$p < 0.05$, **$p < 0.01$, ***$p < 0.001$; two-tailed tests.

Note: Family income transformed by the natural log and centered around 10.24.

a description of the general framework of this procedure, but we will discuss this application as a special case.

Suppose we suspect that the level of father's education is only a factor in predicting differences in students' test performances if his education extends beyond receipt of a high-school diploma. In other words, for the regression line predicting test performance (Y_i) as a function of father's education (X_i), we would draw a line horizontal to the X-axis that extended from the Y-axis to the point corresponding to 12 years of schooling. At that point, we would angle the line upward, giving

it a positive slope thereafter. Conceptually, we are saying that children of fathers who have a high-school diploma or less share the same average test score, but among children whose fathers went to school beyond high school, the predicted level of performance increases as the amount of post-high-school education increases. To generalize from this example, we can use this approach when we expect the relationship between an outcome variable and a predictor variable to be sensitive to some threshold value on the independent variable. Whether an issue of duration or intensity or amount, we may believe that the existence of this threshold structures the relationship. We therefore model the relationship to take this structural threshold into account.

To return to our empirical example, the value of 12 represents our threshold value of a high-school diploma. To estimate the shift in slope that occurs at this point, we must first construct a second education variable that rescales years of schooling relative to the threshold of 12. We accomplish this by subtracting the threshold value of 12 from each observed value. Then we define an implicit dummy variable equal to 1 if education exceeds the threshold of 12 and 0 otherwise. Similar to the use of embedded variables, the new education variable is the product of the implicit dummy and the second education variable: it equals 0 when schooling is 12 or fewer years; it equals the number of years beyond 12 for those exceeding the threshold. The value of the conditional variable reports how much additional education, after high school, the respondent has.[28] The model is specified as:

$$y = \beta_0 + \beta_1 \text{Female} + \beta_2 \text{Asian} + \beta_3 \text{Black}$$
$$+ \beta_4 \text{Hispanic} + \beta_5 (\text{Female} \times \text{Asian})$$
$$+ \beta_6 (\text{Female} \times \text{Black}) + \beta_7 (\text{Female}$$
$$\times \text{Hispanic}) + \beta_8 \text{Income} \qquad (9.17)$$
$$+ \beta_9 \text{Mother's\_Educ.} + \beta_{10} \text{MomPiece}$$
$$+ \beta_{11} \text{VALMOMED}$$
$$+ \beta_{12} \text{Father's\_Educ.} + \beta_{13} \text{DadPiece}$$
$$+ \beta_{14} \text{VALDADED} + \varepsilon,$$

where β_{12} estimates the slope for father's years of schooling less than or equal to 12 and $\beta_{12} + \beta_{13}$ estimates the slope beyond 12 years of schooling. In other words, β_{13} represents the average increment in test scores recorded by children of fathers with more education. Results for this equation are reported in Table 9.14. First, the reader should note that the size of the coefficient for mother's education has changed little, whereas the coefficient for father's education is noticeably smaller. When we turn our attention to the two additional variables we have specified – DadPiece and MomPiece (or the number of years of schooling the parent completed beyond 12) – we see that only the former has a significant estimated effect, and the effect is positive. For children whose fathers had a high-school diploma or less, the partial slope of education is 0.454; for children whose father had additional schooling after high school, the partial slope is 0.454 + 0.256 = 0.710, an increase of more than 50%. The results suggest no such shift in the influence of mothers' education, that is to say, there is evidence of a simple linear effect. As noted earlier, the researcher can use equation (9.12) to test the significance of post-threshold values. In this case, since the increment makes the effect larger, the expectation is that this combined effect is statistically significant. In other circumstances, however, the post-threshold effect may be weaker than the pre-threshold effect, in which case it is useful to test whether the post-threshold effect is statistically significant.

Dummy variables in logit models

In any number of quantitative applications, the dependent variable is a log transformation. Dependent variables with skewed distributions are routinely logged in statistical analyses, and logit models, log-linear analyses, and hazard models all are based on logarithmic transformations. If both the dependent and the independent variables are logarithms, the coefficient is known as an elasticity, reporting percentage increment or decrement in the dependent variable for each 1% increment in the independent variable. Models in which the independent variable is a logarithm and the dependent variable is not allow an interpretation of proportional effects in terms of a b-unit change in the dependent variable for each 1% increase in the independent variable. Finally, when the dependent variable is logarithmic and the independent variable is a standard binary-coded dummy variable, the interpretation is greatly facilitated by taking advantage of the inverse logarithmic function, also called the exponential function.[29]

As an example, we estimate a standard logit regression model (see Long and Cheng, Chapter 11) predicting whether a respondent expects to complete at least a college degree versus whether she or he does not. We use the same core set of predictor variables – gender, race/ethnicity, interactions between gender and race/ethnicity, income – and add the student's science score, in this case, as a predictor as well. The model we estimate is

$$y^* = \beta_0 + \beta_1 \text{Female} + \beta_2 \text{Asian} + \beta_3 \text{Black} + \beta_4 \text{Hispanic} + \beta_5 (\text{Female} \times \text{Asian}) + \beta_6 (\text{Female} \times \text{Black}) + \beta_7 (\text{Female} \times \text{Hispanic}) + \beta_8 \text{Income} \quad (9.18) + \beta_9 \text{Science} + \varepsilon,$$

where

$$y^* = \ln \left[\frac{\Pr(y = 1 | X_k)}{1 - \Pr(y = 1 | X_k)} \right].$$

The results can be found in Table 9.15. We refer the reader to Long and Cheng (Chapter 11) for a full explanation of these models, the appropriate inference tests, and more. Here we wish merely to illustrate an easy approach to interpretation.

The standard regression coefficients are reported in the middle column. The right-hand column, headed e^b, in Table 9.15, contains the exponentiated value of the estimated regression coefficients. As the reader can confirm, when the regression coefficient is positive, its exponentiated value is greater than 1. When it is negative, the exponentiated value is less than 1 but greater than 0. The interpretation of the exponentiated slopes is quite straightforward when the independent variables are measured with dummy variables. We see, for example, that White girls are 1.527 times as likely as White boys to expect to complete a college degree, controlling for income and science score. Asian, Black and Hispanic boys (at constant income and test score) are more likely than White boys to hold this expectation. In fact, Asian and Black boys are more than twice as likely as White boys (2.120 and 2.349, respectively) to expect to complete their degrees.

The reader should be careful, however, in interpreting the exponentiation of the estimated coefficients for the interaction terms. For example, the interaction between gender and Black (−0.210) is significant at conventional levels, indicating that the difference in expectations between Black girls and White girls is not as large as what we noted among the boys. But recall that the estimated difference between Black and White girls is captured by two coefficients: 0.854 and −0.210,

Table 9.15 *Logit regression of college expectations on gender, race/ethnicity, income, and science scores*

	b/s.e.(b)	e^b
Female	0.423***	1.527
	(0.040)	
Asian	0.752***	2.120
	(0.111)	
Black	0.854***	2.349
	(0.074)	
Hispanic	0.155*	1.167
	(0.071)	
Female × Asian	0.101	1.106
	(0.164)	
Female × Black	−0.210*	0.810
	(0.100)	
Female × Hispanic	−0.154	0.858
	(0.097)	
Family income (see note)	0.390***	1.477
	(0.018)	
Science score	0.079***	1.082
	(0.002)	
Intercept	−3.422***	
	(0.105)	
Sample proportion expects college degree	0.687	
Chi-square	3267.74***	
−2 × Log-likelihood	21 898.59	
N	20 252	

*$p < 0.05$, **$p < 0.01$, ***$p < 0.001$; two-tailed tests.

Note: Family income transformed by the natural log and centered around 10.24.

which, when combined, equals 0.644. When we exponentiate 0.644 we get 1.904, which tells us that Black girls are 1.904 times as likely as White girls to expect to complete their college degrees. If that is the case, what does the 0.810 (the exponentiated value of −0.210) mean? It tells us that the odds of expecting a degree for Black girls relative to White girls is only four-fifths as large (81%) as the odds of Black boys, relative to White boys, expecting a college degree.

Dummy variables and latent variables

In our examples to this point, we have used dummy variables to indicate membership in a group or category of demographic description, as in gender (indicated by Female) or race/ethnicity (indicated by Black and Hispanic), all of which are observed characteristics of the respondents. Now we extend our notion of dummy variables to the arena of latent, or unobserved, variables. In these cases, we imagine some underlying disposition or propensity that drives behavior. For example, imagine you offer a tray filled with chocolate candies to a roomful of guests. You observe that 40% of your guests select a piece from the tray, 30% politely decline the chocolate, and 30% look longingly at the plate, begin to reach for a piece of chocolate, then sigh, return their hands to their laps, and say 'Oh, I guess not'. What has happened? You have an observed behavior – whether they took a chocolate or did not. But why did some take the chocolate, some quickly decline, and others reluctantly decline the treat?

One way to conceptualize the behaviors you just observed is to imagine that each guest is characterized by some underlying affinity for chocolate candy. Some guests like chocolate very much, others like it not at all, while still others like chocolate but believe (for whatever reason) that they shouldn't indulge that desire. Within the framework of an offering to guests, the question is twofold: what are the underlying propensities of your guests, and how do those (unobserved) propensities fit the (observed) behavior? Within the framework of latent variables, we imagine that each guest has a threshold level of desire. If the appearance of the chocolate pushes them past their threshold, they select a piece; if it does not, they decline. What we observe in the behavior is whether the threshold has been surpassed. For 40% of the guests, the threshold was surpassed; for 60% it was not, perhaps because they do not like chocolate very much or at all or because other considerations (e.g., calories, satiation) override their affinity for chocolate. Therefore the binary variable that indicates whether a chocolate was taken or not is an observed measure, which is suggestive of some underlying variable that is both continuous and normally distributed.[30]

This conceptualization forms the basis of binary probit analysis and ordered probit analysis (see Long and Cheng, Chapter 11). It also supports the calculation of various types of correlation coefficients. For example, the biserial correlation coefficient measures the strength of relationship between a continuous variable and a binary variable where the binary variable is a crude indicator of an underlying continuous and normally distributed variable. The point biserial correlation coefficient is a measure of association between a continuous variable and a binary variable (taking the values of 0 and 1), where the binary variable represents a true dichotomy, as in gender (male versus female) or marital status (married versus not married). A tetrachoric correlation coefficient is a measure of the relationship between two dichotomous variables, as in a 2×2 table. In contrast to phi, which is the measure of association for two binary nominal variables, the tetrachoric correlation assumes that the two dichotomies are indicators of two underlying continuous variables, both of which are normally distributed. This is another way of saying that the tetrachoric correlation assumes bivariate normality.

Using dummy variables as indicators of continuous latent variables is the basis for the endogenous switching model. For example, we may be interested in an analysis of children, some of whose parents are separated (Winship and Mare, 1983). Following the procedures we described earlier in the chapter, we could simply define a dummy variable coded 1 if the child's parents are separated and 0 if they are not. We can then use this dummy variable as an independent variable in a model predicting school performance. But note that, by assumption, we define parental separation as exogenous. In other words, it is determined outside the system being studied – in this example, the system of individual and family characteristics that influence a child's school performance. Is that a reasonable assumption?

Perhaps we can conceptualize this binary measure of 'parental separation' as a crude indicator of marital conflict: when the parents' threshold for conflict is exceeded, they separate. In this case, we focus on the predictability of the outcome D (separated or not), which sorts children into homes with broken versus intact marriages. We then assign to each child a value on a 'new' variable (Z^*) that captures the likelihood that his or her parents are separated. Then we examine what predicts school performance for these children, each of whom is now characterized by an imputed value on this latent variable – marital conflict. The specification of the model is therefore

$$y = \beta_0 + \beta_1 X_1 + \beta_2 Z^* + e, \qquad (9.19)$$

where the probability that the child's parents are separated (that the value of the dummy variable is 1) is equal to the cumulative density function of Z^* ($\text{cdf}(Z^*)$), and the probability that the parents are together (that the value of the dummy variable is 0) is equal to $1 - \text{cdf}(Z^*)$.

The distinction between dummy variables as direct indicators of group membership versus observed indicators of latent variables is especially important for structural equation modeling and path analysis. The central issue involves the use of a dummy variable as an intervening variable between exogenous predictors (the X variables) and endogenous outcomes (the Y variables). When specified as independent variables, dummy variables are assumed to be discrete measures of group membership. However, when dummy variables are analyzed as dependent (endogenous) variables, they are often assumed to be logit or probit functions of underlying probabilities. Issues of identification vary depending on the assumptions made about D and Z^*.

CONCLUSIONS

In this chapter, we have developed the use and interpretation of dummy variables in a variety of contexts. In addition, we have pointed the reader to later chapters in which dummy variables will resurface in both new and familiar ways. Our concentration has been on the use of dummy variables as exogenous predictors. In that context, the framework we developed can be applied to the variety of regression techniques, including regression with limited dependent variables, Poisson regression, generalized least squares, structural equation models and hierarchical linear models. The use of dummy variables as dependent variables, as variables endogenous to the system of relationships being studied, we leave to the later chapters.

ACKNOWLEDGMENTS

The authors wish to thank Ronald Oaxaca for his comments on the chapter.

NOTES

1 Scores were based on student responses to multiple-choice tests in the subject area of science, which included 25 questions taken from the fields of life sciences, earth sciences, physical sciences, and chemistry. Our analyses use a standardized form of

the original scores, scaled to have a weighted mean of 50 and a standard deviation of 10.

2 We excluded students who reported other race/ethnic memberships.

3 The second and third panels could be reproduced in one-way ANOVAs; the bottom panel by a two-way ANOVA.

4 Again, we could manage this extension by moving to analysis of covariance designs, but as the number of controls and other variables of interest grows, the regression approach becomes increasingly attractive.

5 The method of OLS estimates measures of central tendency under the constraint that the errors (the difference between predicted and observed values) sum to zero. That estimation constraint is in force for calculating mean values of a single distribution as well as estimating the series of conditional means that define regression models.

6 The reader can also confirm that, had we coded boys 1 and girls 0 on the gender variable, the estimate of β_0 would have been 49.82 and the estimate for β_1 would have been +1.91, indicating that, on average, boys scored 1.91 points higher than girls. The findings reported in the text demonstrate that, on average, girls scored 1.91 points lower than boys. The same results are simply reported in different form.

7 We subtract 1 from N because the calculation of the variance requires us to use the sample estimate of the mean. Because we must rely on a sample statistic, we 'lose' one degree of freedom. 'Losing' one degree of freedom means that we have linearly constrained one observation out of the N observations with which we started. We can see that it is just one observation by noting that, if we have a specific value for the sample mean and we have specific observations for $N-1$ cases, then the equality $\sum X_i/N = \bar{X}$ will be true if we assign a value to the Nth case that makes it true, hence the 'constraint'.

8 In these examples we report more decimal places for some calculations and fewer for others. In general, the rule is not to round until the final step of the calculation. A careful reading by Richard Leigh, our copyeditor, ensured that we reported intermediate calculations in sufficient detail for the results to be consistent.

9 The value of 1.0 occurs when the subgroup variances are the same, which confirms the homogeneity-of-variance assumption. So long as the F value is within sampling error of 1.0 ('sufficiently close'), we can fail to reject the hypothesis that the variances are equal. If we reject the null hypothesis on the basis of the F test, then we must adjust our approach to take into account heteroscedasticity (see Stolzenberg, Chapter 8).

10 The reader may note that the phrase 'on average' is frequently included in the discussion of our results. The reason for that qualifying phrase is that our analyses do not suggest that all students who are White scored better than all students who are Black or Hispanic. Indeed, we could easily identify particular Black or Hispanic students who scored better than particular White students. It is also possible that the highest science score was recorded by a Black or Hispanic student. But our research questions are not about one-to-one pairings of particular students. Instead, we inquire about 'typical' performance by group membership. To say that the sampling distributions of subgroup means have little overlap is to establish the likelihood of group differences in the population. It does not, however, preclude overlap of the observed distributions (see Chapter 2).

11 The difference in explained variance is accomplished by the addition of three independent variables, hence we constrain three additional observations in accomplishing the estimation of their coefficients. The 3 degrees of freedom in the numerator reflect their addition. The degrees of freedom in the denominator link the amount of still unexplained variance to the number of still unconstrained observations, hence $N-4$, where 4 is the number of coefficients estimated, including the constant.

12 In a model which specifies only the constant, the value of the constant is the mean of the dependent variable. In other words, in the absence of additional information from independent variables, the OLS estimate of Y is the mean of Y.

13 To be entirely accurate, we should note that the coefficient is based on the average gender difference, once differences due to race/ethnicity are held to the side, i.e., controlled. The reader should refer to Chapter 8 for an explanation of the partialling procedure used in multiple regression.

14 Note that these do not refer to the *sample* variance and covariance of the variables, but to the *sampling* variance and covariance of the OLS regression coefficients. See Chapter 4.

15 One can move back and forth between natural logarithmic values and the original metric by means of the inverse log function, which is the same as the exponential function. Since the natural logarithm has base e, which is equal to 2.71828 ..., if one calculates e to the power 10.24, the result is 28 001.03, which we approximated as $28 000.00. Also note that the logarithmic transformation is not a linear transformation; therefore, specifying ln(income) rather than income as the independent variable tests whether the relationship between family income and test score is better specified in proportional rather than absolute terms (see Stolzenberg, Chapter 8).

16 One approach used to compare two or more regressions is the Chow test (Chow, 1960). The Chow test assumes that the error terms for the separate regressions are independently and normally distributed with zero mean and constant variance. Let RSS$_p$

denote the residual sum of squares from the pooled regression, RSS_k the residual sum of squares from each of the k subgroup regressions, and RSS_s the sum of all RSS_k from the first to the kth subgroup regression. The Chow test evaluates the ratio of RSS_p (in the numerator), to RSS_s (in the denominator), with both numerator and denominator adjusted for appropriate degress of freedom. A test value that exceeds the critical value allows the researcher to reject the null hypothesis that the within-group regressions are the same. Two caveats apply: the assumption of homoscedasticity must be met and there must be sufficient degrees of freedom to support within-group regressions. This approach is analogous to an increment in R^2 test that compares R^2 values from regressions with and without a full set of interaction terms.

17 In our earlier discussion, we assumed that we would be working with an intercept model, which requires that one of the categories on the qualitative variable be omitted. If we attempt to enter all categories and calculate an intercept, we define a model with perfect multicollinearity. However, if we exclude the intercept, then we again have an identified system and can calculate unique coefficients for each of the categories. Rather than express the difference between the expected value of the included group and the reference group, the coefficient now simply reports the expected value. Of course, if one chooses to add a second set of dummy variables to exploit the information of a second qualitative construct, the situation reverts to that which we originally described: one of the categories must be chosen as a reference group and excluded from the specification.

18 The reader is reminded that use of binary coding produces an estimate of difference in the expected value of the dependent variable for the included group relative to the reference group, for example, $\hat{Y}$ for the included group minus $\hat{Y}$ for the reference group, with the appropriate standard error of the difference.

19 The unweighted mean of subgroup means and the grand mean, or sample mean, are different measures. Whether they differ in numerical value depends on the relative size of subgroups. The grand mean is a weighted mean of subgroup means, since each observation is equally weighted. Therefore if we have 14 173 non-Hispanic Whites in the sample and 1260 Asians, the mean for Asians is weighted by 1260 and the mean for non-Hispanic whites is weighted by 14 173. In contrast, the *unweighted* mean of group means weights each group mean *equally*, ignoring the number of respondents on which the mean is based. As a consequence, group means based on a small number of cases and group means based on many more cases are not adjusted to reflect these differences in the number of cases; instead, the difference in reliability is reflected in the standard errors.

20 We still require $j - 1$ dummy variables to fully capture j subgroup differences.

21 As is the case with the other coding schemes, researchers have various options from which to choose.

22 ANOVA designs, for example, require equal cell frequencies for the design to be orthogonal, a situation that is similar to the one described here.

23 The slight difference is due to rounding error.

24 Estimating regression equations within subgroups also potentially confounds the processes that produce the distribution of role incumbents (e.g., the process that predicts who is likely to be married) and, within the specified role combinations, the outcome distribution of interest (the process underlying financial satisfaction). Therefore, one important limitation of analyzing subsamples in this way is the potential endogeneity problem (which is discussed in Chapter 8) and the negative consequences of unspecified sample selection bias. Endogenous switching models (discussed in Chapter 18) provide a better approach when endogeneity is present. For our purposes, we assume that neither employment nor marital status is endogenous to the determination of financial satisfaction, although these are assumptions that we would need to test and verify as reasonable before proceeding.

25 The actual coding scheme used for these dummy variables will not influence the estimation of the conditional effect, so long as the group distinction is signaled. The coding does, however, influence the interpretation of the coefficient for the dummy variable.

26 Clearly, the inclusion of the dummy variable to signal whether data are missing or valid is crucial to this specification. Without the inclusion of these dummy variables, the zero value on mother's and father's education would be 'read' by the computer as 'no' formal education, which is not what we want.

27 The negative sign on the knowledge variables effectively counters the positive effects of years of schooling at levels less than the completion of high school (12 years). In general, *knowing* that parents had low levels of education predicted lower average test scores; *knowing* that parents had high levels of education predicted higher average test scores; and *knowing* that parents completed about 12 years of schooling is associated with no significant differences in average test scores.

28 As both Stolzenberg and Jaccard and Dodge discuss in this volume, regression analysis can be used to capture different forms of relationships. All that is required is that the researcher be clear as to the form she or he anticipates. If we believed that the effect of education varied across the full range of educational values, we might try specifying the relationship as a quadratic (see Stolzenberg, Chapter 8). In this case, however, we are suggesting that the effect of additional

parental education on children's scores is linear, both above and below the threshold, but that the strength of this effect is not the same. We suspect that the slope above the high-school threshold is steeper than the slope below it.

29 Mathematical functions can often be coupled as 'function and inverse function', since such a coupling allows one to 'do' and 'undo' the calculation almost as easily as word processors allow us to 'undo' a change we just made in our text. Addition and subtraction, multiplication and division, logarithmic and exponential functions are three examples of such couplings.

30 One of the dilemmas in assuming underlying latent variables that drive behaviors is that the researcher often has more than one possible candidate.

REFERENCES

Amato, Paul R. (2000) 'The consequences of divorce for adults and children', *Journal of Marriage and the Family*, 62(4): 1269–87.

Astone, Nan M. and McLanahan, Sara S. (1991) 'Family-structure, parental practices and high-school completion', *American Sociological Review*, 56(3): 309–20.

Biblarz, Timothy J. and Raftery, Adrian E. (1999) 'Family structure, educational attainment, and socioeconomic success: Rethinking the "pathology of matriarchy"', *American Journal of Sociology*, 105(2): 321–65.

Chow, Gregory C. (1960) 'Tests of equality between sets of coefficients in two linear regressions', *Econometrica*, 28(3): 591–605.

Cohen, Jacob and Cohen, Patricia (1983) *Applied Multiple Regression/Correlation Analysis for the Behavioral Sciences*. Hillsdale, NJ: Lawrence Erlbaum Associates.

Downey, Douglas B. (1995) 'Understanding academic achievement among children in stephouseholds – the role of parental resources, sex of stepparent, and sex of child', *Social Forces*, 73(3): 875–94.

Hardy, Melissa A. (1993). *Regression with Dummy Variables*. Newbury Park, CA: Sage.

McLanahan, Sara and Sandefur, Gary (1994) *Growing Up with a Single Parent: What Hurts, What Helps*. Cambridge, MA: Harvard University Press.

Oaxaca, Roland (1973) 'Male–female wage differentials in urban labor markets', *International Economic Review*, 14: 693–709.

Oaxaca, Roland and Ransom, Michael R. (1999) 'Identification in detailed wage decompositions', *Review of Economics and Statistics*, 81(1): 154–7.

Reynolds, John and Ross, Catherine (1998) 'Social stratification and health: Education's benefit beyond economic status and social origins', *Social Problems*, 45: 221–47.

Sandefur, Gary, D. and Wells, T. (1999) 'Does family structure really influence educational attainment?' *Social Science Research*, 28(4): 331–57.

Waite, Linda J. and Berryman, Sue E. (1986) 'Job stability among young women: A comparison of traditional and nontraditional occupations', *American Journal of Sociology*, 92(3): 568–95.

Winship, Christopher, and Mare, Robert D. (1983) 'Structural equations and path analysis for discrete data', *American Journal of Sociology*, 89: 54–110.

10

Analyzing Contingent Effects in Regression Models

JAMES JACCARD AND TONYA DODGE

Interaction analysis in the context of the general linear model is an important enterprise. An increasing number of theories hypothesize the presence of contingent relationships or interaction effects. The issues in formally testing and evaluating such effects can be complex. The present chapter considers such issues. We begin by discussing the concept of interaction and elaborate two approaches to parameterizing interaction effects. We then consider the analysis of contingent relationships for the case of nominal variables, a mixture of nominal and continuous variables, and all continuous variables. Both two-way and three-way interactions are considered in the context of the general linear model as implemented through ordinary least-squares regression analysis. We conclude by discussing a range of topics relevant to interaction analysis.

BASIC CONCEPTS

The concept of interaction

There are many ways in which interaction effects have been conceptualized in the social sciences and there has been controversy about the best way to think about the concept of interaction. One school of thought conceptualizes interaction effects in terms of contingent relationships. This perspective can

be illustrated using a three-variable system in which one of the variables is construed as a dependent or outcome variable, a second variable is viewed as an independent or predictor variable, and a third variable is viewed as a moderator variable. Conceptually, the dependent variable is thought to be influenced by the independent variable. An interaction effect is said to exist when the effect of an independent variable on a dependent variable differs depending on the value of the moderator variable. For example, the effect of number of years of education on income potential may differ depending on one's ethnicity. Education may have a larger impact on income potential for some ethnic groups than other ethnic groups. As another example, the effect of social class on how often someone uses a health clinic may vary depending on gender. In this case, how often someone uses a health clinic is the outcome or dependent variable, social class is the independent variable, and gender is the moderator variable.

The 'moderator approach' to interaction analysis requires that the theorist specify a moderator variable and what we call a focal independent variable, namely the independent variable whose effect on the dependent variable is said to be moderated by the moderator variable. Most formal research questions lend themselves to the specification of one of the predictors as having 'moderator' status, and the designation of which variable takes on moderator status is often conceptually straightforward. For example, suppose one wants to determine if the effectiveness of a clinical treatment for depression is more effective for males than females. It is evident in this case that gender is the moderator variable, and the presence versus absence of the treatment is the focal independent variable. On the other hand, there are situations where one theorist's moderator variable might be another theorist's focal independent variable and vice versa. For example, a consumer psychologist who studies product quality and product choice might be interested in the effect of product quality on product purchase decisions and how this is moderated by the pricing of products. In contrast, a marketing researcher using the same experimental paradigm as the consumer psychologist might be interested in the effect of product pricing on product purchase decisions and how this is moderated by product quality. In both cases, the designation of the moderator variable follows from the theoretical orientation of the researcher. Neither specification is better than the other and statistically the results of an interaction analysis will be the same. The two designations simply represent different perspectives on the same phenomena.

The moderator approach to interaction analysis emphasizes the notion of contingent effects or contingent relationships. Some social scientists choose to define interaction effects differently, using instead the conceptual scheme suggested by the classic analysis of variance model. This approach does not make distinctions between moderator variables and independent variables but instead emphasizes additive and non-additive effects of two or more independent variables. The different approaches are best illustrated using a 2 × 2 factorial design focused on the analysis of means of a continuous outcome variable. Consider an experiment where caseworkers read a report about potential child abuse in which a perpetrator physically harms a child victim. The report that the caseworkers read was identical in all respects except that for half of the caseworkers the perpetrator was male, whereas for the other half the perpetrator was female. Also, for half of the caseworkers the victim was male, while for the other half the victim was female. The design is a 2 × 2 factorial manipulating the gender of the perpetrator and the gender of the victim. The outcome variable was how serious the

Table 10.1   *Mean seriousness judgments*

	Male victim	Female victim	Marginal mean
Male perpetrator	70	90	80
Female perpetrator	50	60	55
Marginal mean	60	75	67.5

act of physical aggression was judged to be, as rated on a scale ranging from 0 to 100, with higher scores indicating greater levels of judged seriousness. Table 10.1 presents the sample means for the data. Using sample notation and assuming equal sample sizes N per cell, let the grand mean across all observations be M and the sample means for the four different groups comprising the factorial design be M_{jk}, where the first subscript refers to the level of the perpetrator factor (1 = male, 2 = female) and the second subscript refers to the level of the victim factor (1 = male, 2 = female). Let the marginal means be represented by $M_{1.}$, $M_{2.}$, $M_{.1}$, and $M_{.2}$, where the dot subscript indicates that the mean is computed collapsing across the factor signified by the dot.

To apply the moderator approach, the theorist specifies a focal independent variable and a moderator variable. In this case, we will use the gender of the perpetrator as the focal independent variable and the gender of the victim as the moderator variable. Of interest is whether the effect of gender of the perpetrator on judged seriousness is different for female victims than for male victims. The effect of gender of the perpetrator on judged seriousness when the victim is male can be expressed in terms of population means as $\mu_{11} - \mu_{21}$. For the sample data in Table 10.1, it is $70 - 50 = 20$ such that when the violent act is directed at a male victim, the actions of a male perpetrator are rated, on average, 20 units higher than those of a female perpetrator. The effect of gender of the perpetrator on judged seriousness when the victim is female is $\mu_{12} - \mu_{22}$, which in Table 10.1 is estimated to be $90 - 60 = 30$. If the effects are identical for both male and female victims, then $(\mu_{11} - \mu_{21}) - (\mu_{12} - \mu_{22})$ will be zero. The relevant interaction parameter is $\delta = (\mu_{11} - \mu_{21}) - (\mu_{12} - \mu_{22})$ and researchers are typically interested in making inferences about this parameter. For the data in Table 10.1, the sample estimate of this parameter is $(70 - 50) - (90 - 60) = -10$.

In the classic analysis of variance model the focus is not on contingent relationships in the spirit of the moderator approach, instead concern is with estimating 'additive effects' and 'interaction effects'. Each level of each factor has an additive effect associated with it. For a given level of the first factor, the additive effect is defined as $\tau(a)_j = \mu_j - \mu_{..}$. For example, the additive effect of the perpetrator being a male is estimated from the data in Table 10.1 as being $80 - 67.5 = 12.5$. This indicates that the estimated effect of the perpetrator being male is to raise scores, on average, 12.5 units above the grand mean. The additive effect for a given level of the second factor is $\tau(b)_k = \mu_{.k} - \mu_{..}$. For example, the estimated effect of the victim being female is to raise scores, on average, $75 - 67.5 = 7.5$ units above the grand mean. One model characterizing scores on the outcome variable does so in terms of these additive effects:

$$Y_{ijk} = \mu_{..} + \tau(a)_j + \tau(b)_k + \varepsilon_{ijk},$$

where Y_{ijk} is the score of individual i in group j for the first factor and group k for the second factor, $\mu_{..}$ is the population grand mean, $\tau(a)_j$ and $\tau(b)_k$ are the population additive effects as defined above, and ε_{ijk} is an error term. An alternative model includes interaction effects in addition to these additive effects. The interaction effects are defined by subtracting the additive effects from each of the group means and then subtracting the grand mean from these 'residualized' group means,

$$\tau(ab)_{jk} = \mu_{jk} - \tau(a)_j - \tau(b)_k - \mu_G,$$

and the model is

$$Y_{ijk} = \mu_G + \tau(a)_j + \tau(b)_k + \tau(ab)_{jk} + \varepsilon_{ijk}.$$

The parameter $\tau(ab)$ represents a definition of interaction focused on the joint influence of the two factors independent of additive effects. In the analysis of variance model, the focus is on estimating $\tau(a)_j$, $\tau(b)_k$ and $\tau(ab)_{jk}$ and making inferences about their significance and magnitude.

The moderator approach and analysis of variance approach are closely related statistically but the parameters in the two frameworks are conceptually distinct. In practice, most researchers adopt a moderator framework either implicitly or explicitly (Jaccard,

1998) and we will do so in this chapter. This is not to say that the moderator approach is better or worse than other methods for parameterizing interaction effects. Rather it represents a framework that maps onto the way that researchers often frame their theoretical questions. For discussions of the classic analysis of variance approach, see Jaccard (1998) and Kirk (1995).

The regression model, dummy variables and product terms

We develop methods for interaction analysis using the linear model in the context of ordinary least-squares (OLS) regression. In the two-predictor case, the model has the general form

$$Y_i = \alpha + \beta_1 X_i + \beta_2 Z_i + \varepsilon_i,$$

where α is the intercept, β_1 and β_2 are unstandardized regression coefficients, and ε_i is an error term. When a predictor variable is nominal, we represent it in the equation using dummy variables with dummy coding. A nominal variable consisting of k levels is represented by $k - 1$ dummy variables and each dummy variable consists of scores of ones and zeros (see Chapter 2). We refer to the group that is assigned zeros across all dummy variables as the *reference group*. All of the standard assumptions of OLS regression are made (see Chapter 8). Our discussion is limited to cases where the predictor variables are fixed and between-subjects in character, although we consider other scenarios in the concluding section of this chapter.

The most common approach to modeling interactions in regression analysis is to use product terms. Consider the following (non-interactive) model with two continuous predictors:[1]

$$Y = \alpha + \beta_1 X + \beta_2 Z + \varepsilon.$$

To illustrate an interaction model, we conceptualize Z as the moderator variable and consider the possibility that the effect of X (the focal independent variable) on the outcome variable differs depending on the value of Z. One way of expressing this is to model β_1 (which reflects the effect of X on the outcome variable) as a linear function of Z:

$$\beta_1 = \alpha' + \beta_3 Z. \tag{10.1}$$

According to this formulation, for every one unit by which Z changes, the value of β_1 is predicted to change by β_3 units. We now substitute the above expression for β_1 in the original equation, yielding:

$$Y = \alpha + (\alpha' + \beta_3 Z)X + \beta_2 Z + \varepsilon.$$

Multiplying this out yields

$$Y = \alpha + \alpha' X + \beta_3 XZ + \beta_2 Z + \varepsilon,$$

and after assigning new labels to the coefficients and rearranging terms, we obtain an interaction model with a product term:

$$Y = \alpha + \beta_1 X + \beta_2 Z + \beta_3 XZ + \varepsilon.$$

Other conceptual specifications of interaction models lead to the same equation, and other forms of interaction lead to different equations. Our point is to show that including a product term in a model serves to define one type of interaction model (i.e., where the effect of the focal independent variable on the outcome variable is said to be a linear function of the moderator variable) and to draw attention to this frequently encountered equation.

Hierarchically well-formulated models

A hierarchically well-formulated (HWF) model is one in which all lower-order components of the highest-order product term are included in the model. For example, if interest is in a two-way interaction between X and Z, then an HWF model includes X, Z, and XZ as predictors. If interest is in a three-way interaction between X, Z and Q, then an HWF model includes X, Z, Q, XZ, XQ, QZ, and XZQ as predictors, that is, the three-way term, all possible two-way terms and all 'main effect' terms. For a qualitative predictor with dummy variables D_1 and D_2 and a continuous predictor Z, an HWF interaction model includes D_1, D_2, Z, D_1Z, and D_2Z. Most (but not all) applications of interaction analysis involve HWF models, and this is the structure that we attend to in this chapter.

Given an HWF model, the typical strategy used to evaluate interactions is hierarchical analysis. Consider the three-way interaction model for continuous predictors Q, X, and Z. The HWF model is

$$Y = \alpha + \beta_1 X + \beta_2 Z + \beta_3 Q + \beta_4 XZ + \beta_5 XQ + \beta_6 QZ + \beta_7 XZQ + \varepsilon.$$

To test if the highest-order interaction term(s), in this case QXZ, is non-trivial, one compares the fit of a model that includes the term(s) representing the interaction with a model that eliminates the term(s), that is, it compares the above equation with

$$Y = \alpha + \beta_1 X + \beta_2 Z + \beta_3 Q + \beta_4 XZ + \beta_5 XQ + \beta_6 QZ + \varepsilon.$$

If the difference in model fit is non-trivial, then this suggests that the interaction term is important and the equation is then interpreted using methods discussed later. However, if the difference in the model fits is trivial, then the conclusion is that the interaction term(s) is unnecessary and can be ignored or eliminated. A typical strategy is to perform a test of statistical significance of the change in squared multiple correlations between the two equations in accord with the following formula:

$$F = [(R_2^2 - R_1^2)/(k_2 - k_1)]/[(1 - R_2^2)/(N - k_2 - 1)], \qquad (10.2)$$

where R_2 is the multiple correlation for the equation that includes the higher-order product terms, R_1 is the multiple correlation for the equation that excludes the higher-order product terms, k_2 is the total number of predictors in the equation that includes the higher-order product terms, k_1 is the total number of predictors in the equation that excludes the higher-order product terms, and N is the sample size. The resulting F statistic is distributed as F with $k_2 - k_1$ and $N - k_2 - 1$ degrees of freedom.

In the above example, the three-way interaction was represented by a single product term, that is, it was a single-degree-of-freedom interaction. In such cases, the statistical significance of the interaction can be determined either by conducting a hierarchical test of changes in R^2 as per equation (10.2) or by examining the significance test of the regression coefficient associated with the single product term. If the regression coefficient for the product term is not statistically significant, then this implies that the interaction effect is not statistically significant. In traditional OLS regression, the F test of the regression coefficient associated with a single-degree-of-freedom interaction will be identical to the hierarchical F test that compares the fit of models with and without the interaction term.

Sometimes omnibus interaction effects cannot be captured in a single product term. This is the case for interactions involving a nominal variable with more than two levels.

For example, the interaction between a nominal variable represented by two dummy variables, D_1 and D_2, and a continuous variable, Z, is captured by the presence of two product terms in an HWF model: $D_1 Z$ and $D_2 Z$. This is because one must multiply all the variables representing one variable by all the variables representing the other variable in order to examine the interaction effect between the two. In such cases, the test of the omnibus interaction must rely on the hierarchical procedure because it is possible for an omnibus effect to be statistically significant but for the regression coefficients associated with each product term to be statistically non-significant. The reason for this will be apparent in later sections.

Simple main effects and interaction contrasts

In addition to an omnibus test of an interaction, two additional types of contrasts are often associated with interaction analysis. The first type of contrast is a simple main effect analysis and refers to whether the focal independent variable has an effect on the outcome variable at a given level of the moderator variable. For example, for the data in Table 10.1, we could ask if the gender of the perpetrator affects the perceived seriousness of the action depicted in the case study when the victim is a male. This focuses on a test of the null hypothesis $H_0 : \mu_{11} - \mu_{21} = 0$. Or one could ask if the gender of the perpetrator affects the perceived seriousness of the action depicted when the victim is a female. This simple main effect contrast focuses on a test of the null hypothesis $H_0 : \mu_{12} - \mu_{22} = 0$. Simple main effect contrasts are informative because they provide perspectives on whether the focal independent variable has an effect on the outcome variable at each level or at theoretically important levels of the moderator variable.

The second type of contrast is a single-degree-of-freedom interaction contrast and it focuses on how the effect of the focal independent variable on the outcome variable changes as one moves from one level of the moderator variable to another level. For a factorial design, the focus of interaction contrasts is on a 2×2 table or sub-table that compares the difference between two mean differences. In the child abuse example, the parameter $\delta = (\mu_{11} - \mu_{21}) - (\mu_{12} - \mu_{22})$ reflects a single-degree-of-freedom interaction contrast, as it specifies how the effect of the gender of the perpetrator differs for male victims as compared to female victims. In factorial designs where one of the factors has more than two levels, there are multiple 2×2 sub-tables, hence there are multiple single-degree-of-freedom interaction contrasts. For example, consider a study that uses gender as the focal independent variable and religion (Catholic, Protestant or Jewish) as the moderator variable in a 2×3 factorial design. There are three 2×2 sub-tables that might be of interest: (1) male versus female by Catholic versus Protestant; (2) male versus female by Catholic versus Jewish; and (3) male versus female by Protestant versus Jewish. In each sub-table, we can calculate if the gender difference for one of the religious groups is equal to the gender difference for the other religious group, for example, $(\mu_{\text{Male,Catholic}} - \mu_{\text{Female,Catholic}}) - (\mu_{\text{Male,Protestant}} - \mu_{\text{Female,Protestant}})$. The difference between the mean differences is reflected in a single number (e.g., a value of 2.5 indicates that the gender difference for Catholics is 2.5 units higher than the gender difference for Protestants) and therefore represents a single-degree-of-freedom interaction contrast that contributes to the omnibus interaction effect. In most interaction analyses, investigators are interested in pursuing some subset of single-degree-of-freedom interaction contrasts for purposes of elucidating the nature of the interaction between two variables.

Conditioned coefficients

In the sections that follow, we describe a variety of forms of interaction analysis. A central feature of the analyses is the interpretation of the regression coefficients associated with a given predictor in the context of a traditional OLS regression analysis. An important principle that applies in HWF models is the conditional nature of coefficients for predictors that are involved in product terms. When a predictor variable is included in a product term in an HWF model, then the coefficient for that predictor is conditioned on the other predictor involved in the product term being zero. For example, in the equation $Y = a + b_1 X + b_2 Z + b_3 XZ + e$, the coefficient b_1 is a conditioned coefficient reflecting the slope of Y on X when $Z = 0$. Similarly, the coefficient b_2 is a conditioned coefficient reflecting the slope of Y on Z when $X = 0$. Some researchers mistakenly interpret b_1 and b_2 as reflecting main effects when they are part of an HWF model with product terms, but this is not the case, at least as the term 'main effect' is traditionally used. The conditional nature of the coefficients associated with the component parts of a product term must be kept in mind when interpreting them, and we make use of this property continually in the following sections.

As will be seen, the omnibus test of an interaction effect involves a straightforward application of equation (10.2). Somewhat more involved is the interpretation of the regression coefficients contained within an HWF model. Each coefficient refers to a single-degree-of-freedom contrast, either of a simple main effect type or an interaction contrast type. Researchers must decide what sets of single-degree-of-freedom contrasts they are interested in and then locate these in the model for purposes of formal evaluation. In the sections that follow, we describe strategies that permit analysts to isolate single-degree-of-freedom contrasts that will often be of interest, recognizing that the specific contrasts one pursues will be dictated by theoretical and substantive considerations.

CONTINGENT RELATIONSHIPS AMONG CONTINUOUS VARIABLES

Two-way interactions

We illustrate the analysis of interactions between two continuous variables using a case where Y is the outcome variable, X is the focal independent variable and Z is the moderator variable. For reasons that will become apparent, we adopt the common practice of centering the two predictors, that is, subtracting the sample mean of the variable from its raw score. The centered variables are denoted X_c and Z_c.

We begin by forming a 'main effect' model consisting of the two predictors without a product term. The sample equation is

$$Y = a + b_1 X_c + b_2 Z_c + e.$$

The interaction model is formed by multiplying the X_c and Z_c variables and then adding this product term to the equation:

$$Y = a + b_1 X_c + b_2 Z_c + b_3 X_c Z_c + e. \quad (10.3)$$

The test of significance of the fit of the interaction model versus the main effect model is

performed using equation (10.2). The F ratio for this test is equivalent in value to the F ratio associated with b_3 because the omnibus interaction has a single degree of freedom. Other indices of differential fit include the magnitude of the difference in squared multiple correlations between the two equations and differences in the standard error of estimates, though care must be taken in the interpretation of such standardized effect sizes (McClelland and Judd, 1993; Jaccard, 1998).

The b_3 coefficient reflects an interaction contrast as applied to two continuous variables. b_3 provides information about how the slope of Y on X is predicted to change as a function of Z (per equation 10.1). It indicates for every one unit by which Z changes, the number of units by which the *slope* of Y on X is predicted to change. It reflects an interaction because it indicates how the relationship between Y and X changes as one moves from one level or value of the moderator to another value.

The coefficient b_1 reflects a simple main effect. It is the slope of Y on X (or X_c) when Z_c equals zero. Because Z_c is the centered Z variable, a score of zero on Z_c corresponds to the mean value on Z. Given this, b_1 is the slope of Y on X when Z is at its sample mean. The significance test, estimated standard error and confidence intervals for b_1 provide perspectives on the magnitude and stability of the parameter estimate associated with this simple main effect.

It is possible to calculate the simple main effect of Y on X at any value of Z. This can be done algebraically from equation (10.3), as described later, but calculation of the estimated standard error and confidence intervals associated with the parameter estimate requires additional information. Probably the simplest way to obtain the relevant estimates is to transform Z to isolate the simple main effect of interest and then rerun equation (10.3) on a computer using the transformed variable. For example, suppose the original Z variable was scored from 1 to 20 and we wanted to isolate the simple main effect corresponding to the slope of Y on X when Z is 13. If we subtract a constant of 13 from each person's score on Z, the range of Z shifts from 1 to 20 to -12 to $+7$. We refer to this new variable as Z_{13}. A score of 0 on Z_{13} corresponds to a score of 13 on the original Z measure. We then use Z_{13} to form the product term and analyze the data as before using the equation:

$$Y = a + b_1 X_c + b_2 Z_{13} + b_3 X_c Z_{13} + e.$$

In this new equation, the b_1 coefficient for X_c is the slope of Y on X when Z_{13} equals zero. This corresponds to the slope of Y on X when Z is 13 on the original metric. The significance test, estimated standard error and confidence intervals provide perspectives on the magnitude and stability of the parameter estimate associated with this simple main effect. The value of b_3 and its estimated standard error and significance test are unaffected by this transformation.

In interaction models involving continuous variables, the single-degree-of-freedom contrasts typically of interest are those associated with b_3 (which is an interaction contrast) and also selected simple main effects at theoretically interesting values of the moderator variable. The transformation strategy allows one to isolate any single-degree-of-freedom simple main effect of probable interest. Typically, researchers will report a simple main effect at a low, a medium and a high value of Z to provide perspectives on the slope of Y on X across a wide range of Z values.

Three-way interactions

In the case of a three-way interaction, it is useful to make distinctions between the focal independent variable, a first-order moderator variable and a second-order moderator variable. As with a two-way interaction, the first-order moderator variable 'qualifies' the effect of the focal independent variable on the outcome variable. The second-order moderator variable influences the way the first-order moderator variable qualifies the impact of the focal independent variable on the outcome variable. As one moves across the values or levels of the second-order moderator variable, the qualifying effects of the second-order moderator variable change. The traditional model for a three-way interaction among continuous variables is an HWF model that includes product terms for all pairs of variables involved in the three-way interaction as well as a product term across the three terms:

$$Y = a + b_1X + b_2Z + b_3Q$$
$$+ b_4XZ + b_5XQ + b_6ZQ$$
$$+ b_7XZQ + e. \qquad (10.4)$$

Because the three-way interaction is captured in a single predictor (i.e., it is represented by

a single degree of freedom), the significance test for b_7 yields the same conclusion of statistical significance as the hierarchical omnibus test using equation (10.2).

If X is conceptualized as the focal independent variable, Z as the first-order moderator variable, and Q as the second-order moderator variable, then the coefficient b_1 is a simple main effect. It is conditioned on zero because it is part of the product terms and estimates the slope of Y on X when both Q and Z equal zero. For example, suppose that Y is a measure of job performance, X is a measure of job difficulty, Z is a measure of work experience and Q is a measure of work motivation. Each is measured on a 1 to 100 scale and mean-centered prior to the analysis and the formation of product terms. In this scenario, b_1 is the estimated effect of job difficulty on job performance when both work experience and work motivation equal their sample mean. One can calculate the simple main effect of Y on X at any combination of values for X and Q using the transformation strategy described earlier. For example, if we want to estimate the slope of Y on X (and its standard error and confidence intervals) for the case where $Z = 75$ and $Q = 50$, we subtract 75 from Z and 50 from Q. This shifts the scale for Z from 1 to 100 to -74 to 25 and the scale for Q from 1 to 100 to -49 to 50. A score of zero on Z_{75} corresponds to a value of 75 on the original scale of Z and a score of zero on Q_{50} corresponds to a value of 50 on the original scale of Q. We submit the three-way regression model to computer analysis:

$$Y = a + b_1X + b_2Z_{75} + b_3Q_{50}$$
$$+ b_4XZ_{75} + b_5XQ_{50} + b_6Z_{75}Q_{50}$$
$$+ b_7XZ_{75}Q_{50} + e. \qquad (10.5)$$

b_1 now reflects the slope of Y on X when $Q = 50$ and $Z = 75$. The b_7 coefficient is unaffected by this transformation.

The coefficient b_4 in equation (10.4) is also a conditioned coefficient because it is part of a higher-order product term. It is the estimate of the slope for the XZ term (i.e., the two-way interaction) when Q equals zero. If all the predictor variables are centered prior to analysis and the centered variables are used to calculate the product terms, b_4 is the coefficient for the XZ product term when Q equals its sample mean. To calculate the XZ product term coefficient and its estimated standard error at any desired value of Q, one can use the transformation strategy described above. For example, in equation (10.5), b_4 reflects the two-way interaction parameter for the XZ product term when $Q_{50} = 0$ or when $Q = 50$.

The coefficient b_7 estimates how the qualifying effect of Z on the XY relationship changes as a function of Q. Specifically, the coefficient for the XZ product term is assumed to be a linear function of Q and b_7 reflects the number of units by which this slope is predicted to change given a one-unit change in Q. For example, if $b_7 = 5$, then this means that for every one unit increase in Q, the coefficient for the XZ term is predicted to change by 5 units. b_7 is thus an interaction contrast for the three-way interaction.

The essence of the three-way interaction is captured in b_7. By mapping out simple main effects at selected values of Q and Z and two-way interaction parameters at selected values of Q, an intuitive feel for the nature of the three-way interaction can usually be gained. For example, if one calculates the two-way interaction coefficient for XZ at a low, a medium and a high value of Q, then this provides a sense of how the two-way interaction varies across a wide range of Q values. Similarly, reporting simple main effects on Y of X at a low, a medium and a high value of Z crossed with a low, a medium and a high value of Q can provide a more intuitive sense of the interaction than relying just on the interpretation of the b_7 coefficient alone.

CONTINGENT RELATIONSHIPS BETWEEN CONTINUOUS AND NOMINAL VARIABLES

Two-way interactions

We consider interaction analysis between a continuous predictor and a nominal predictor first for the case where the continuous predictor is conceptualized as the focal independent variable and the nominal variable is the moderator variable. We then reverse the roles of the two predictors and reconceptualize the analysis where the nominal variable is given focal independent variable status and the continuous predictor is given moderator status.

As discussed in Chapter 9, a nominal variable is represented by dummy variables in the regression equation and we employ dummy coding for the coding scheme. As general notation, we say that a dummy variable 'represents' a given group on a variable if that group is assigned scores of 1 on the variable and all other groups are assigned zeros. For

example, the dummy variables D_{Z1} and D_{Z2} represent groups 1 and 2 on Z respectively, with group 3 being the reference group or the group assigned zeros on all dummy variables in the equation that represents the nominal variable of interest. In the example developed here, X is a continuous variable and Z is a nominal variable with three levels.

The main effect model is

$$Y = a + b_1X + b_2D_{Z1} + b_3D_{Z2} + e,$$

and the HWF interaction model multiplies the X variable by each of the dummy variables representing Z:

$$Y = a + b_1X + b_2D_{Z1} + b_3D_{Z2} \\ + b_4XD_{Z1} + b_5XD_{Z2} + e. \quad (10.6)$$

The omnibus test of the interaction effect between X and Z relies on the comparison of these two equations using equation (10.2). In this case, the hierarchical test is required to evaluate the omnibus effect because the interaction is represented by two terms, i.e., it has two degrees of freedom. It is possible for both b_4 and b_5 in equation (10.6) to be statistically non-significant but still observe a statistically significant omnibus effect.

The coefficient b_1 in the interaction model is a simple main effect. Because it occurs in the product terms, it is conditioned on D_{Z1} being zero and D_{Z2} being zero. A score of zero on both D_{Z1} and D_{Z2} characterizes the reference group of Z, so b_1 is the estimate of the slope of Y on X for the reference group of Z, in this case the third group of Z. The estimated standard error, confidence intervals, and significance test for the coefficient give a sense of the magnitude and stability of this parameter estimate. Researchers will probably be interested in describing the slope and estimated standard error of Y on X for each group of Z. A straightforward but somewhat inelegant way of accomplishing this is to re-define the dummy variables so that a different group becomes the reference group and then re-estimate the model. For example, for the equation

$$Y = a + b_1X + b_2D_{Z1} + b_3D_{Z3} \\ + b_4XD_{Z1} + b_5XD_{Z3} + e, \quad (10.7)$$

b_1 is the slope of Y on X when D_{Z1} and D_{Z3} equal zero, which corresponds to the estimated slope for the second group on X. In the equation

$$Y = a + b_1X + b_2D_{Z2} + b_3D_{Z3} \\ + b_4XD_{Z2} + b_5XD_{Z3} + e,$$

b_1 is the slope of Y on X when D_{Z2} and D_{Z3} equal zero, which corresponds to the estimated slope for the first group on X.

The coefficients for b_4 and b_5 in equation (10.6) each represent single-degree-of-freedom interaction contrasts. b_4 is the difference in the slope of Y on X for the group scored 1 on the dummy variable in the product term (D_{Z1}) minus the reference group of Z. In this case b_4 is the difference in the slope of Y on X for the first and third groups on Z. b_5 is the difference in slopes for the second group of Z and the reference group of Z. Equation (10.6) does not contain information on the difference in slopes between group 1 of Z and group 3 of Z. However, this can be obtained from one of the 'auxiliary' equations that was evaluated for purposes of isolating the various simple main effects. For example, in equation (10.7), b_4 represents the difference in the slope of Y on X for the first and second groups of Z. Each interaction contrast provides information about whether the effect of X on Y changes as a function of Z, that is, whether the slope of Y on X is different for a given pair of groups defined by Z.

Researchers performing an interaction analysis for a continuous focal independent variable and a nominal moderator variable typically report simple main effects for each group defined by the nominal moderator variable and also report the results of all possible pairwise comparisons of slope differences between the groups defined by the moderator variable.

When the roles of the focal independent variable and the moderator variable are reversed, the same equations can be used for analysis, but the interpretational emphasis changes. For consistency, we respecify the equations using X notation to indicate a focal independent variable and Z notation to indicate a moderator variable. This yields an example where the X variable is nominal and the Z variable is continuous, resulting in the following HWF interaction equation:

$$Y = a + b_1 D_{X1} + b_2 D_{X2} + b_3 Z_c$$
$$+ b_4 D_{X1} Z_c + b_5 D_{X2} Z_c + e \qquad (10.8)$$

For reasons that will become apparent, we center the Z variable prior to analysis and use the centered Z variable during the formation of product terms.

With a nominal focal independent variable, primary interest is in documenting mean differences on the outcome variable as a function of the groups characterizing the nominal variable. For example, if Y is a measure of blood pressure and X is ethnicity (African Americans, Mexican Americans, and European Americans), then our primary interest is in exploring mean differences in blood pressure as a function of these groups. Suppose the moderator variable is social class (measured on a 0 to 100 scale, with larger numbers indicating higher social class). Of interest is whether the patterning of mean differences among the ethnic groups changes as a function of social class. In the equations that follow, let the dummy variable D_{X1} represent African Americans, D_{X2} represent Mexican Americans, and D_{X3} represent European Americans.

The omnibus test of the interaction is identical to before, comparing the equation with product terms in it to the equation that omits the product terms vis-à-vis equation (10.2). The isolation of simple main effects focuses on b_1 and b_2 in equation (10.8). The coefficient b_1 represents the predicted mean difference on Y between the group scored 1 on D_{X1} and the reference group on X, in this case African Americans minus European Americans. However, because D_{X1} appears in the product terms, this coefficient is conditioned on Z_c being zero. b_1 is therefore the predicted mean difference between the two groups when Z equals its sample mean. The coefficient b_2 represents the predicted mean difference on Y between the group scored 1 on D_{X2} and the reference group on X, in this case Mexican Americans minus European Americans when Z equals its sample mean. The simple main effect comparing African Americans and European Americans is not formally represented in equation (10.8). It can be estimated by redefining the reference group through the use of different dummy variables for ethnicity and then recomputing the analysis. For example, in the equation

$$Y = a + b_1 D_{X1} + b_2 D_{X3} + b_3 Z_c$$
$$+ b_4 D_{X1} Z_c + b_5 D_{X3} Z_c + e, \qquad (10.9)$$

the reference group is Mexican Americans and b_1 reflects the simple main effect comparing the predicted mean Y values for African Americans and Mexican Americans when Z equals its sample mean. A simple main effect at any value of Z can be isolated using the transformation strategy discussed above. For example, instead of the centered Z value, Z_c, equation (10.8) could be subjected to analysis using Z minus 25 (i.e., Z_{25}) in place of Z_c. The coefficients for the simple main effects now represent the mean differences on blood pressure as a function of ethnicity when $Z = 25$.

Returning to the original equation (10.8), the coefficients b_4 and b_5 reflect single-degree-of-freedom interaction contrasts. The b_4 coefficient indicates how much the mean difference between the group scored 1 on the dummy variable in the product term and the reference group is predicted to change given a one-unit increase in Z. In the present example, b_4 is how much the mean difference between African Americans and European Americans is predicted to change given a one-unit increase in social class. Using the same principle, b_5 is how much the mean difference between Mexican Americans and European Americans is predicted to change given a one-unit increase in social class. Finally, in equation (10.9), b_4 is how much the mean difference between African Americans and Mexican Americans is predicted to change given a one-unit increase in social class. The significance tests, estimated standard errors and confidence intervals of these coefficients provide perspectives on their magnitude and stability.

Researchers performing an interaction analysis for a nominal focal independent variable and a continuous moderator variable typically report simple main effects corresponding to all possible pairwise comparisons of means for the groups defined by the focal independent variable at a low, a medium and a high value of Z. This provides perspectives on how the predicted mean differences vary across a wide range of values of Z and often yields a more intuitive feel for the interaction than relying exclusively on the values of b_4 and b_5.

Three-way interactions

To illustrate the analysis of a three-way interaction, we consider a case where the focal independent variable is continuous and the moderator variables are each nominal with two levels. Let D_{Z1} be the dummy variable for the first-order moderator variable and D_{Q1} be the dummy variable for the second-order moderator variable. Group 2 of Z is the reference group for Z and group 2 of Q is the reference group for Q. Each of the moderator variables can be represented by a single predictor because each has two levels. Let the outcome variable be a measure of the severity of headaches that people with migraine

headaches get and the focal independent variable be a measure of how much stress they perceive themselves as having in their life. The first-order moderator variable was a clinical treatment devised by a psychologist to reduce the effect of stress on headache severity. Individuals in the study either received the treatment (group 1) or were in a wait-listed control group (group 2). The prediction was that the impact of stress on headache severity would be less for those in the treatment group than those in the control group. The clinician felt that the treatment would be more effective for females than males, implying that the qualifying effect of the treatment versus control variable differs as a function of gender. Gender is the second-order moderator, with females representing group 1 and males representing group 2.

The main effect model is

$$Y = a + b_1X + b_2D_{Z1} + b_3D_{Q1} + e.$$

The traditional three-way interaction model is formed by multiplying the three variables by one another and then adding this product term to an HWF model, which yields

$$\begin{aligned} Y = a &+ b_1X + b_2D_{Z1} + b_3D_{Q1} \\ &+ b_4XD_{Z1} + b_5XD_{Q1} + b_6D_{Z1}D_{Q1} \\ &+ b_7XD_{Z1}D_{Q1} + e. \end{aligned}$$

The significance test of the omnibus interaction effect is captured in b_7 because the three-way interaction has a single degree of freedom. The coefficient b_1 is a simple main effect and reflects the slope of Y on X when the other variables in the product terms that include X are zero. In this case, b_1 is the slope of Y on X when $D_{Z1} = 0$ and $D_{Q1} = 0$. A predictor profile of $D_{Z1} = 0$ and $D_{Q1} = 0$ refers to males in the control group, so b_1 is the estimated slope of headache severity on stress for control group males. The analogous simple main effects and associated estimated standard errors can be estimated for any of the four groups by redefining the reference groups on Z and Q through the use of dummy variables that are scored differently. For example, to estimate the simple main effect for experimental group males, we would analyze the equation

$$\begin{aligned} Y = a &+ b_1X + b_2D_{Z2} + b_3D_{Q1} \\ &+ b_4XD_{Z2} + b_5XD_{Q1} + b_6D_{Z2}D_{Q1} \\ &+ b_7XD_{Z2}D_{Q1} + e. \end{aligned}$$

b_1 is the desired simple main effect, and its associated significance test, estimated standard error and confidence intervals provide perspectives on its stability and magnitude.

In the original equation for this analysis, b_4 is a single-degree-of-freedom interaction contrast associated with the two-way interaction between X and D_{Z1}. Invoking principles from the previous sections of this chapter, b_4 reflects the difference in the slope of Y on X for the group scored 1 on D_{Z1} and the reference group on Z when $D_{Q1} = 0$. In this case, it is the difference in the slope of Y on X for experimental participants minus control participants focusing just on males. To isolate the corresponding effect for females, we could re-estimate the model using:

$$Y = a + b_1X + b_2D_{Z1} + b_3D_{Q2}$$
$$+ b_4XD_{Z1} + b_5XD_{Q2} + b_6D_{Z1}D_{Q2}$$
$$+ b_7XD_{Z1}D_{Q2} + e.$$

b_4 is the desired interaction contrast for females.

b_7 is a single-degree-of-freedom interaction contrast associated with the three-way interaction. It reflects the estimated difference between the two-way interaction parameters for the focal independent variable and the first-order moderator variable as a function of the second-order moderator variable. In this case, it is b_4 for just males minus b_4 for just females and directly tests the hypothesized three-way interaction posited by the investigator.

For three-way interactions of this nature, researchers typically will report the simple main effects for each of the groups defined by the factorial combination of Z and Q as well as the results of all possible pairwise contrasts of slopes of Y on X for the groups defined by Z at each level of Q. In addition, the values of the single-degree-of-freedom three-way interaction contrasts (in this case b_7) are also reported.

CONTINGENT RELATIONSHIPS AMONG NOMINAL VARIABLES

Two-way interactions

We illustrate the analysis of interactions between two nominal variables using a 2×3 factorial design. The first factor, X, is conceptualized as the focal independent variable and the second factor, Z, is the moderator variable. Dummy variables with dummy coding are used to represent each variable. To make the description concrete, let Y be a measure of attitudes towards abortion, X be the gender of the respondent, and Z be the respondent's religion. For gender, group 1 refers to females and group 2 refers to males. For religion, group 1 is Catholics, group 2 is Protestants, and group 3 is Jews. The researcher hypothesized that the effect of gender on attitudes toward abortion would differ depending on the religious background of the individual, with Catholics showing a smaller gender difference than either of the other two religious groups.

To test the omnibus interaction effect, we first form a 'main effect' model:

$$Y = a + b_1D_{X1} + b_2D_{Z1} + b_3D_{Z2} + e.$$

The interaction model is formed by multiplying all the dummy variables for X by all the dummy variables for Z and adding these product terms to the equation:

$$Y = a + b_1D_{X1} + b_2D_{Z1}$$
$$+ b_3D_{Z2} + b_4D_{X1}D_{Z1}$$
$$+ b_5D_{X1}D_{Z2} + e. \qquad (10.10)$$

The significance of the omnibus interaction is evaluated by comparing the fit of the two models using equation (10.2).

b_1 represents a single-degree-of-freedom simple main effect. It is the predicted mean difference between males and females when $D_{Z1} = 0$ and $D_{Z2} = 0$. A predictor profile of $D_{Z1} = 0$ and $D_{Z2} = 0$ corresponds to Jews, so b_1 is the estimated gender difference in attitudes toward abortion for Jews. The simple main effect of gender for the other two religious groups can be isolated by redefining the dummy variables of Z so that the reference group is not Jews. For example, in the equation

$$Y = a + b_1D_{X1} + b_2D_{Z1}$$
$$+ b_3D_{Z3} + b_4D_{X1}D_{Z1}$$
$$+ b_5D_{X1}D_{Z3} + e, \qquad (10.11)$$

b_1 is the estimated gender difference in attitudes for Protestants.

b_4 in equation (10.10) is a single-degree-of-freedom interaction contrast. It, and the coefficient for all the other product terms, focuses on a 2×2 sub-table of the overall 2×3 design. The sub-table focuses on the groups scored 1 on each of the dummy variables in the product term and the reference groups on each of the dummy variables in the product term. In the case of b_4, the relevant 2×2 sub-table is males versus females by Catholics versus Jews. In the case of b_5, the relevant 2×2 sub-table is males versus females by Protestants versus Jews. The coefficient itself is a two-way interaction parameter of the predicted difference between two mean differences, as described in earlier sections of this chapter (see the example in Table 10.1). In equation (10.10), b_4 is the predicted mean difference between males and females for Catholics minus the predicted mean difference between males and females for Jews. It reflects whether the predicted effect of X (gender) on Y (attitudes toward abortion) for group 1 of Z (Catholics) differs from that of group 3 of Z (Jews). b_5 is the predicted mean difference between males and females for Protestants minus the predicted mean difference between males and females for Jews. It reflects whether the predicted effect of X (gender) on Y (attitudes) for group 2 of Z (Protestants) differs from that of group 3 of Z (Jews). The interaction contrast comparing gender differences for Catholics versus Protestants can be found in equation (10.11) – see b_4. As before, the estimated standard error, confidence intervals and significance tests associated with any of these coefficients provide perspectives on the magnitude and stability of the parameter estimates.

For two-way interactions among nominal variables, researchers typically will report the simple main effects corresponding to all possible pairwise comparisons among means for the groups defined by X at each level of Z. In addition, the single-degree-of-freedom interaction contrasts for theoretically interesting 2×2 sub-tables are reported.

Three-way interactions

To illustrate a three-way interaction with nominal variables, we will add a second-order moderator variable to our earlier example. The second-order moderator has two levels and represents whether the research participant lives in a rural (group 1) or urban (group 2) environment. The researcher hypothesizes that the qualifying effects of religion on gender differences in attitudes towards abortion will be more pronounced for those living in rural settings than for those living in urban settings. Place of residence is represented in the analysis by a dummy variable with dummy coding (D_{Q1}). The HWF model that defines the three-way interaction model is

$$
\begin{aligned}
Y = {} & a + b_1 D_{X1} + b_2 D_{Z1} + b_3 D_{Z2} \\
& + b_4 D_{Q1} + b_5 D_{X1} D_{Z1} + b_6 D_{X1} D_{Z2} \\
& + b_7 D_{X1} D_{Q1} + b_8 D_{Z1} D_{Q1} \\
& + b_9 D_{Z2} D_{Q1} + b_{10} D_{X1} D_{Z1} D_{Q1} \\
& + b_{11} D_{X1} D_{Z2} D_{Q1} + e.
\end{aligned} \tag{10.12}
$$

To test the omnibus three-way interaction, this model is contrasted with a model that omits the two three-way interaction terms (those associated with b_{10} and b_{11}), using equation (10.12).

b_1 reflects a single-degree-of-freedom simple main effect contrast, namely the predicted mean difference in attitudes towards abortion as a function of gender when $D_{Z1} = 0$, $D_{Z2} = 0$ and $D_{Q1} = 0$. The predictor profile $D_{Z1} = 0$, $D_{Z2} = 0$ and $D_{Q1} = 0$ corresponds to Jews who live in urban settings, hence b_1 reflects the effect of gender for this particular group (i.e., it is the predicted mean difference between males and females for urban Jews). The simple main effect for any other group defined by a combination of Z and Q can be obtained by redefining the reference group through the inclusion of different dummy variables and then re-estimating the equation. For example, to isolate the simple main effect of gender for Jews who live in rural settings, one would estimate the equation

$$
\begin{aligned}
Y = {} & a + b_1 D_{X1} + b_2 D_{Z1} + b_3 D_{Z2} \\
& + b_4 D_{Q2} + b_5 D_{X1} D_{Z1} + b_6 D_{X1} D_{Z2} \\
& + b_7 D_{X1} D_{Q2} + b_8 D_{Z1} D_{Q2} \\
& + b_9 D_{Z2} D_{Q2} + b_{10} D_{X1} D_{Z1} D_{Q2} \\
& + b_{11} D_{X1} D_{Z2} D_{Q2} + e.
\end{aligned} \tag{10.13}
$$

b_1 in this equation represents the simple main effect of gender for rural Jews.

Each of the coefficients in equation (10.12) associated with a product term reflects an interaction contrast. Coefficients b_5 and b_6 reflect two-way interaction contrasts, as described in the previous section. However, because these product terms are also part of the three-way product terms, they are conditioned on D_{Q1} being zero. Thus, b_5 refers to the 2×2 sub-table for males versus females by Catholics versus Jews for people who live in urban settings. b_6 refers to the 2×2 sub-table for males versus females by Protestants versus Jews for people who live in urban settings. The coefficients are differences between mean differences, as defined in earlier sections of this chapter. For example, b_5 is the predicted difference in mean attitudes for males versus females for urban Catholics minus the corresponding gender difference for urban Jews. Again, any 2×2 sub-table of interest can be isolated by redefining the reference groups on selected variables. For example, in equation (10.13), b_5 refers to the 2×2 sub-table for males versus females by rural Catholics versus rural Jews.

The b_{10} and b_{11} coefficients in equation (10.12) reflect single-degree-of-freedom interaction contrasts associated with the three-way interaction. Each reflects the predicted difference in the two-way interaction parameters for a 2×2 sub-table defined by X and Z at any two levels of Q. The predicted difference is between the two-way interaction parameter for the group scored 1 on D_{Q1} and the two-way interaction parameter for the reference group on Q. In our example, b_{10} is the difference in the two-way interaction parameter between those in rural and urban settings when attention is focused on the 2×2 sub-table for males versus females by Catholics versus Jews. b_{11} is the difference in the two-way interaction parameter between those in rural versus urban settings when attention is focused on the 2×2 sub-table for males versus females by Protestants versus Jews. Any single-degree-of-freedom interaction contrast can be isolated by redefining the reference groups on selected variables. For example, in the equation

$$
\begin{aligned}
Y = a &+ b_1 D_{X1} + b_2 D_{Z1} + b_3 D_{Z3} + b_4 D_{Q1} \\
&+ b_5 D_{X1} D_{Z1} + b_6 D_{X1} D_{Z3} \\
&+ b_7 D_{X1} D_{Q1} + b_8 D_{Z1} D_{Q1} \\
&+ b_9 D_{Z3} D_{Q1} + b_{10} D_{X1} D_{Z1} D_{Q1} \\
&+ b_{11} D_{X1} D_{Z3} D_{Q1} + e,
\end{aligned}
$$

b_{10} is the difference in the two-way interaction parameter between those in rural versus urban settings when attention is focused on the 2×2 sub-table for males versus females by Catholics versus Protestants. For a more detailed discussion of the interpretation and specification of three-way interaction parameters among nominal variables, see Jaccard (1998).

ADDITIONAL CONSIDERATIONS

The preceding sections have described methods for testing omnibus interaction effects for a wide range of interaction models and elucidated the nature of the single-degree-of-freedom contrasts that the regression coefficients reflect in a model. The general strategy for

interaction analysis is to characterize an interaction effect by first assigning the predictors the conceptual status of being either a focal independent variable or a moderator variable (either a first-order moderator variable or a second-order moderator variable). An HWF model is specified by the formation of product terms and the omnibus test for the interaction effect is performed by comparing this model against a model that excludes the relevant product terms. Interaction analysis is usually accompanied by a set of single-degree-of-freedom contrasts that reflect either simple main effects or interaction contrasts. The analyst must specify those single-degree-of-freedom contrasts that are of conceptual interest and then pursue the evaluation of those contrasts by interpreting the relevant regression coefficients that reflect them. The isolation of such contrasts will sometimes require transformations of the predictor variables or the redefinition of dummy variables and the estimation of several different equations that are statistically redundant. The present section places these issues into a broader analytical context and also discusses more specific considerations in interaction analysis.

Control for experimentwise error

In any given interaction analysis, multiple single-degree-of-freedom simple main effect contrasts and interaction contrasts usually are performed. When this is the case, the per-comparison alpha level remains at the specified alpha for a given contrast (usually 0.05), but the probability of at least one Type I error occurring across the set of contrasts exceeds the per-comparison alpha. In such instances, some researchers will invoke statistical adjustments that maintain the experimentwise alpha level (i.e., the probability of obtaining at least one Type I error across a set of contrasts) at a specified level across the contrasts. The most popular method for doing so is the traditional Bonferroni procedure, although more powerful methods exist and should be used instead. For a discussion of these methods and issues in their use, see Jaccard (1998) and Westfall et al. (1999).

Omnibus tests and interaction effects

A common strategy used in interaction analysis is to first perform an omnibus test of an interaction effect and then to pursue single-degree-of-freedom interaction contrasts only if the omnibus effect is statistically significant. The omnibus test is used as a basis for protecting the analysts against inflated Type I errors across the single-degree-of-freedom interaction contrasts underlying the omnibus interaction. In general, these two-step approaches have been discredited as an effective means of controlling experiment-wise error rates (Jaccard, 1998; Wilkinson, 1999). An alternative strategy is to move directly to the single-degree-of-freedom contrasts that are of theoretical interest and to invoke controls for experiment-wise error at that level independent of the results of an omnibus test (using modified Bonferroni methods or other approaches discussed in Jaccard, 1998; Kirk, 1995; and Westfall et al., 1999). This does not mean that omnibus tests of interactions will never be meaningful. Such tests may be of interest if one wants to document the effect size of an overall interaction between two or more variables. In addition, if the omnibus interaction is not close to attaining statistical significance, then it is highly unlikely that any of the interaction contrasts will be non-trivial. The omnibus test can be an effort-saving device, though one must be cautious in such uses.

Alternative single-degree-of-freedom contrasts

In previous sections, we elucidated a wide range of single-degree-of-freedom contrasts that researchers might be interested in pursuing in the context of interaction analysis. Though prevalent, these contrasts are not exhaustive and researchers may be interested in other forms of single-degree-of-freedom contrasts. Consider, for example, a 2×3 factorial design focusing on gender (male versus female) by religion (Catholic versus Protestant versus Jewish). A single-degree-of-freedom interaction contrast focuses on a 2×2 sub-table of the design. An example of an interaction contrast that differs from those discussed would be a 2×2 sub-table that collapses Catholics and Protestants into a single group, yielding a 2×2 sub-table of gender (male versus female) by religion (Christian versus non-Christian). Such an interaction contrast may be of theoretical interest and can be pursued in the context of the linear model. For a discussion of such contrasts and

how to implement them, see Cohen and Cohen (1983), Boik (1993) and Jaccard (1998). The crux of the matter is that theorists must specify those interaction contrasts that are theoretically compelling and then pursue an analytic strategy that permits effective analysis of such contrasts.

Calculating coefficients of focal independent variables at different moderator values

In previous sections, coefficients for the focal independent variable were calculated at different values of the moderator variable by either transforming the continuous predictor or redefining the reference group of a nominal predictor and then rerunning the regression analysis on the computer. This approach, though cumbersome, has the advantage of producing the estimated standard errors and confidence intervals for all of the parameters of interest. Such confidence intervals are not readily calculated by hand (for relevant formulas, see Aiken and West, 1991). Occasions may arise where one wishes to calculate the coefficients from the initial equation without generating confidence intervals and without redoing the analyses with transformed variables. This section describes how to do so.

Consider the case where X is the focal independent variable and Z is the moderator variable in the equation

$$Y = \alpha + \beta_1 X + \beta_2 Z + \beta_3 XZ + \varepsilon. \quad (10.14)$$

We want to determine the coefficient for X at some value of Z. We first isolate all terms on the right-hand side of the equation that contain X,

$$\beta_1 X + \beta_3 XZ,$$

and then factor out the X,

$$X(\beta_1 + \beta_3 Z),$$

which yields the coefficient for X at any value of Z, namely

$$\beta \text{ for } X \text{ at } Z = \beta_1 + \beta_3 Z \quad (10.15)$$

For example, in equation (10.14), if $\beta_1 = 1.2$ and $\beta_3 = 0.05$, then the coefficient for X when $Z = 2$ is $1.2 + 0.05 \times 2 = 1.3$. Note that when $Z = 0$, the value of the coefficient in equation (10.15) is β_1, which underscores the point that β_1 is conditioned on Z being zero If X and Z are dummy variables, the logic of equation (10.15) holds but is focused only on the relevant dummy variables. For example, suppose X has two dummy variables and Z has two dummy variables, yielding the equation

$$Y = \alpha + \beta_1 D_{X1} + \beta_2 D_{X2} + \beta_3 D_{Z1}$$
$$+ \beta_4 D_{Z2} + \beta_5 D_{X1} D_{Z1} + \beta_6 D_{X1} D_{Z2}$$
$$+ \beta_7 D_{X2} D_{Z1} + \beta_8 D_{X2} D_{Z2} + \varepsilon.$$

Suppose we want to isolate the coefficient for the group scored 1 on D_{X1} versus the reference group on X for the case where $D_{Z1} = 1$ and $D_{Z2} = 1$. We first isolate only the terms and coefficients that directly involve D_{X1},

$$\beta_1 D_{X1} + \beta_5 D_{X1} D_{Z1} + \beta_6 D_{X1} D_{Z2},$$

and factor out D_{X1} to yield

$$D_{X1}(\beta_1 + \beta_5 D_{Z1} + \beta_6 D_{Z2})$$

so that

$$\beta \text{ for } X \text{ at } D_{Z1} \text{ and } D_{Z2} = \beta_1$$
$$+ \beta_5 D_{Z1} + \beta_6 D_{Z2}.$$

In the case where $\beta_1 = 0.2$, $\beta_5 = 0.3$, $\beta_6 = 0.4$, $D_{Z1} = 1$ and $D_{Z2} = 1$, the coefficient for D_{X1} is $0.2 + 0.3 \times 1 + 0.4 \times 1 = 0.9$.

Equations for three-way interactions use the same logic. In the case of three continuous predictors X, Q, and Z, the traditional interaction equation is

$$Y = \alpha + \beta_1 X + \beta_2 Q + \beta_3 Z$$
$$+ \beta_4 XQ + \beta_5 XZ + \beta_6 QZ$$
$$+ \beta_7 XQZ + \varepsilon.$$

The coefficient for X at a given combination of scores on Q and Z is

$$\beta \text{ for } X \text{ at } Q \text{ and } Z = \beta_1$$
$$+ \beta_4 Q + \beta_5 Z + \beta_7 QZ,$$

and the coefficient for XQ at a given value of Z is

$$\beta \text{ for } XQ \text{ at } Z = \beta_4 + \beta_7 Z.$$

The bilinear nature of interactions for continuous variables

When a continuous variable is part of an interaction, it is important to keep in mind that the use of product terms as described in this chapter tests only for an interaction that has a specific form, namely a bilinear interaction. Other forms of interaction may be operating, and exploratory analyses should routinely be performed to ensure that the correct type of interaction is being modeled. For example, consider a case where the moderator variable is nominal with two groups, and the X and Y variables are both continuous. If the relationship between Y and X is roughly linear in one group but curvilinear in another group, then the product-term approach described in the present chapter represents a mis-specified model. The interactive model we formulated assumes that for both groups, Y changes as a linear function of X and that the nature of the interaction is characterized by non-parallel lines. However, this is not the case for these data. Alternative modeling strategies are required.

In the case of two continuous predictor variables, the classic product-term approach reflects a narrowly defined but probably widely applicable interaction form. As noted earlier, if X is the focal independent variable and Z is the moderator variable, the product-term approach models the coefficient for X as a linear function of Z. It is possible that the coefficient for X changes as a non-linear function of Z, and if this is the case the traditional product-term approach represents a mis-specified model. A crude but sometimes informative way to explore this issue is to use a variant of bandwidth regression (Hamilton, 1992). In this approach, the moderator variable is grouped into 5–10 equal sized, ordered categories. The mean or median Z is calculated for each group. A regression analysis is then performed, regressing the outcome onto X for each group, separately. Examination of the coefficients for X across the 5–10 groups should reveal a trend whereby the coefficient increases or decreases as a roughly linear function of the mean or median Z for each group. Stated another way, if one plots from such an analysis the coefficients against the mean (or median) Z values, a linear trend should be evident. If this is not the case, then a more complex interaction form may be needed.

Such complex interactions often can be modeled using product terms in conjunction with polynomial terms. For an introduction to polynomial analysis with interaction terms in multiple regression, see Jaccard et al. (1990). The steps for applying a model that assumes that the coefficient for X is a quadratic function of Z, where both X and Z are continuous, are as follows:

1. Identify the focal independent variable, X, and the moderator variable, Z.

2. Make any desired transformations on X and Z (e.g., mean-center).
3. Calculate the square of the moderator variable, Z^2.
4. Calculate product terms between X and Z and X and Z^2.
5. Fit the equation $Y = \alpha + \beta_1 X + \beta_2 Z + \beta_3 Z^2 + \beta_4 XZ + \beta_5 XZ^2 + \varepsilon$.

A hierarchical test for improvement in model fit by adding the XZ^2 term indicates if the quadratic interaction effect is non-trivial (or one can simply examine the significance of β_5). The coefficient for X at a given value of Z is defined by $\beta_1 + \beta_4 Z + \beta_5 Z^2$. The coefficient β_1 is the coefficient for X when $Z = 0$. One can transform Z (in step 2 above) so that a score of zero on the transformed variable takes on a theoretically meaningful value to isolate the relevant coefficient and confidence interval for the coefficient for X at a given value of Z.

For the case involving a nominal and a continuous variable, assume Z is a dummy variable scored with 1s and 0s to represent group membership. In this case, Y is a non-linear function of X for at least one of the groups, possibly both of them. Fit the model $Y = \alpha + \beta_1 X + \beta_2 Z + \beta_3 X^2 + \beta_4 XZ + \beta_5 X^2 Z + \varepsilon$. The effect of X on Y when $Z = 0$ is reflected by the quadratic model $\alpha + \beta_1 X + \beta_3 X^2$ within this equation. To find the effect of X when $Z = 1$, recode Z by reverse-coding it, recalculate the product terms, and re-run the computer program, again focusing on the resulting $\alpha + \beta_1 X + \beta_3 X^2$ terms in the equation.

Partialling the component terms

It is sometimes stated that the product terms in regression equations represent interaction effects. By and of themselves, the product terms reflect an amalgamation of main effects and interactions. In general, it is only when the component parts of the product term are included in the equation along with the product term that the orderly relationships described in this chapter emerge (coupled with an unconstrained intercept term). It is possible to model interactions in ways that lead one to exclude one or more of the component parts of the product term, but this typically represents interactions of a different form than those considered here. If an HWF model is not used, then the coefficients associated with product terms will be affected by

the scaling of the variables involved and the coefficients will change depending on the means of the variables involved.

Multiple interaction effects

Consider a case where an investigator desires to model an outcome, Y, as a function of three continuous predictors, X, Q, and Z. The researcher does not expect a three-way interaction between the predictors but wants to evaluate all possible two-way interactions. There are multiple strategies that might be used. Some analysts perform a 'chunk' test in which the fit of a model with all (two-way) interaction terms included is contrasted with the fit of a model with none of the interaction terms, that is to say, the interactions are tested as a 'chunk' (Kleinbaum, 1994). If the difference in fit of the two models is trivial, then this suggests that none of the interaction terms is necessary and they are dropped from the model. If application of the 'chunk' test reveals a non-trivial difference in model fit, then this suggests that at least one interaction term is important to retain. At this point a hierarchical backward elimination strategy is used, comparing the fit of a model that includes all of the interaction terms with the fit of a model that drops a particular term(s) of interest (vis-à-vis equation (10.2)). For example, if one is interested in evaluating the XZ interaction, one would compare the fit of the model

$$Y = \alpha + \beta_1 Q + \beta_2 X + \beta_3 Z + \beta_4 QX + \beta_5 QZ + \beta_6 XZ + \varepsilon$$

with the fit of the model

$$Y = \alpha + \beta_1 Q + \beta_2 X + \beta_3 Z + \beta_4 QX + \beta_5 QZ + \varepsilon.$$

If the difference in fit between the models is trivial, then this suggests that the XZ term can be eliminated. However, if the difference in the fit of the model is non-trivial, then the term should be retained.

Some analysts systematically evaluate each interaction term in this fashion. Other analysts choose one term to focus on first, and if that term is eliminated, evaluate the remaining interaction terms with the previously eliminated term(s) expunged from the model. For example, if we tested XZ first for possible elimination and ultimately decided to drop it from the model, then the evaluation of QZ would focus on a backward elimination test where XZ was not present in the model, that is, we would evaluate

$$Y = \alpha + \beta_1 Q + \beta_2 X + \beta_3 Z + \beta_4 QX + \beta_5 QZ + \varepsilon$$

versus

$$Y = \alpha + \beta_1 Q + \beta_2 X + \beta_3 Z + \beta_4 QX + \varepsilon.$$

The choice of which term to evaluate first for possible elimination is based sometimes on theoretical criteria, sometimes on whichever term has the largest p value associated with its logistic coefficient in the full equation, and sometimes on both.

In multiple-interaction scenarios there are many model-fitting criteria that can be invoked for the trimming of terms, and controversy exists about the advisability of each. Consideration of the relevant issues is beyond the scope of this chapter. Interested readers are referred to Bishop et al. (1975), Hosmer and Lemeshow (1989), and Jaccard (1998) for a discussion of germane issues. The reader should be forewarned that seeming 'anomalies' can occur as multiple-interaction terms of the same order are considered. For example, the 'chunk' test might indicate that at least one of the product terms should be retained in the model, but the evaluation of each individual term may suggest that each term can be eliminated from the model. Or the 'chunk' test may suggest that all of the terms be eliminated, whereas evaluation of the individual terms may suggest otherwise. Or the results of the individual tests of one term may suggest that the term be retained and that all others be eliminated, but when the others are eliminated, the candidate for retention becomes non-significant and of trivial predictive value. How one deals with these scenarios depends on the theoretical questions being addressed, one's overarching statistical framework (e.g., null hypothesis testing, magnitude estimation, interval estimation) and the patterning of the data. In most analytic situations, the choice of terms to trim will be straightforward and non-controversial, but this is not always the case.

When two separate interaction terms are included in the regression equation (e.g., for three continuous predictors, Q, X, and Z and both XZ and QZ are retained in the equation but no other interaction terms are), then the coefficient for a given interaction term is interpreted as described in previous sections, but with the proviso that the other two-way interaction (as well as all other covariates) are statistically held constant. The coefficient for any lower-order term is conditioned on the other variables in *all* product terms that it is involved with being zero.

Multicollinearity

Some researchers are wary of interaction analysis with product terms because the product term often is highly correlated with the component parts used to define the product term. If XZ is highly correlated with either X, Z or both, the fear is that the evaluation of the interaction effect will be undermined due to classic problems of multicollinearity. This generally will not be the case unless the multicollinearity with the product term is so high (e.g., 0.98 or greater) that it disrupts the computer algorithm designed to isolate the relevant standard errors. A sense that collinearity with XZ is non-problematic is indicated by the fact that the wide range of transformations for continuous predictors discussed in earlier sections will usually alter the correlation between XZ and its component parts, but will have no effect on the value of the regression coefficient for the product term, its estimated standard error, or the critical ratio testing its statistical significance. If collinearity was crucial, then the coefficient and its estimated standard error would not remain invariant as the correlation between XZ and its component parts changes. For a discussion of the rationale of this phenomenon, see Jaccard et al. (1990). High collinearity between X and Z (i.e., the component parts of a product term), on the other hand, can lead to serious problems.

Standardized coefficients, unstandardized coefficients and psychometric issues

The regularities for the regression coefficients discussed in this chapter apply to the unstandardized coefficients associated with the predictor variables. Although it is possible to use standardized coefficients in the analysis of interactions, such coefficients have the potential to lead theorists astray and we recommend against their use. As one illustration, consider a simple bivariate regression where we regress a measure of income onto the number of years of education in order to determine the 'value' of a year of education.

The analysis is conducted among two different ethnic groups, African Americans and European Americans. Suppose that the analysis yielded identical standardized regression coefficients in the two groups, indicating that for every one standard deviation by which education changes, income is predicted to change 0.50 standard deviations. One might conclude from this that the 'value' of education is the same in the two groups. Suppose that the standard deviation for education is 3.0 in both groups but that for income it is 15 000 for European Americans and 6000 for African Americans. Such a state of affairs yields unstandardized coefficients of 2500 for European Americans and 1000 for African Americans. Whereas for European Americans an additional year of education is predicted to be worth $2500, for African Americans it is only worth $1000. There is a clear disparity between the groups.

The problem with the standardized analysis is that it creates different metrics for the two groups. The metric is in units of $15 000 for the European Americans but is in units of $6000 for African Americans. Comparing groups on these different metrics is somewhat like measuring income in units of dollars for one group but units of British pounds for another group and then comparing groups without acknowledging the difference between the dollar and the pound. For a discussion of other limitations of standardized coefficients, see Jaccard et al. (1990).

Metric assumptions are important for effective interaction analysis. Some of the underlying issues are best understood by conceptualizing measurement in terms of classic latent variable modeling. An observed measure of a construct is viewed as an indicator of a latent variable that represents the true construct in question. In practice, we do not know a person's true score on this construct, but use the observed measure to estimate it. The observed measure can be influenced not only by the person's true standing on the latent variable, but also by measurement error. A path diagram of the model is presented in Figure 10.1. If we assume a linear relationship between the observed measure and the latent variable, Figure 10.1 implies a regression equation in which the observed measure is regressed onto the latent variable:

$$Y = \alpha + \beta LY + \varepsilon.$$

Groups may differ on either the intercept, slope, or error variance of this measurement

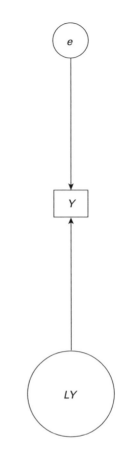

Figure 10.1 *Path diagram of a measurement model*

model and such differences can affect inferences about the true state of affairs regarding group differences on the latent variables (which are of primary theoretical interest). For example, two groups may have identical mean scores on the latent variable but if they differ on their intercepts for the measurement model, the mean scores of the observed measures will be different. If two groups differ in the regression coefficient of the measurement model, then they can exhibit unequal variances on the observed measures even when they have equal variances on the latent variable. If two groups differ in their error variances, then the measures are differentially reliable for the groups. The cleanest scenario analytically is where groups have identical intercepts and slopes in the measurement model and the error variances are equal and zero (or near zero). Deviations from this may introduce problems for interaction analysis. For a discussion of metric implications, methods for testing metric equivalence, and methods for metric adjustments, see Vandenberg and Lance (2000) and Busemeyer and Jones (1983).

Confounded interactions

Some analysts have noted that interaction effects are sometimes confounded with curvilinear effects of X on Y (e.g., Lubinski and Humphries, 1990). Data may be the result of a generating process that results from a curvilinear relationship between X and Y, but when an interaction model is fitted to the data using X, Y, and a third variable Z, a significant interaction effect is observed. Some analysts suggest routinely testing for curvilinear effects between Y and X before pursuing interaction analysis, and others suggest routinely adding curvilinear terms (e.g., polynomials) as covariates when conducting interaction analysis. In our opinion, analysts need to carefully think about the possible models that can account for data and then explore these models accordingly. If a curvilinear effect model is not theoretically plausible and makes no conceptual sense, then it should not be pursued. If such a model is theoretically viable, then it should be considered. It may be the case that an interaction term becomes statistically non-significant when covariates for curvilinear effects are introduced. This does not necessarily invalidate the interaction model. It only suggests that an alternative model can also account for the data. The bottom line is that common sense and theory need to frame the type of models explored and that researchers must recognize that multiple models may need to be considered and contrasted before settling upon an interaction model. The studies of Lubinski and Humphries as well as others suggest that researchers should consider the viability of curvilinear models as competing alternative models when contemplating interaction models.

Optimal experimental designs and statistical power

Several analysts have lamented the difficulty of detecting interaction effects in linear models because of low statistical power. McClelland and Judd (1993) explore a host of reasons that may underlie low statistical power in field settings. These researchers note that the statistical power to detect an interaction effect is heavily dependent on the nature of the distributions of the component variables of the product term (i.e., X and Z for the product term XZ). McClelland and Judd (1993) suggest design strategies based on the oversampling of extreme cases of X and Z that can be used when practical constraints dictate a small sample size and statistical power for detecting an interaction is expected to be low.

Some common misapplications

Instances exist in the literature of poor practices with respect to interaction analysis, and we wish to call attention to two such cases. The first involves the interpretation of regression equations computed in multiple groups. Suppose one wanted to compare the effects of a continuous variable X on an outcome variable, Y, for two different groups, males and females. It is not uncommon for researchers to do so by calculating separate regression equations for males and females and then examining whether the coefficient for X is 'statistically significant' (i.e., has an associated p value less than 0.05) in both analyses. If the coefficient is statistically significant in one group but not the other, then the conclusion is that X is more important for the one group than the other. This logic is flawed because the researcher never performs a formal statistical test of the *difference* between the coefficients for the two groups. For example, it is possible for the coefficient for one group to have a p value of 0.051 and the coefficient for the other group to have a p value of 0.049. Even though one is 'statistically significant' and the other is not, the coefficients are almost certain to be comparable in magnitude. Formal interaction analysis through product terms in a single equation is preferable because it provides a means of formally testing the difference between coefficients.

Another practice that we observe too often is interaction analysis by means of reducing a continuous variable to a two-valued indicator through the use of a median split. This strategy is often invoked so that interactions can be explored using the traditional analysis of variance model. Such practices are undesirable because they throw away useful information, they result in less statistical power, and they can introduce false interaction effects (Maxwell and Delaney, 1993). Interactions between continuous and nominal predictors can be effectively analyzed in the context of the general linear model without recourse to reducing the continuous predictor to a crude, bi-level indicator.

Extensions of regression models for interaction analysis

The present chapter has considered the case of interaction analysis using traditional OLS regression. There are important extensions of this framework using other analytic schemes. It is well known that measurement error causes bias in regression coefficients, and this also is true in the case of interaction analysis. Effective methods that adjust for measurement error in large-sample situations are available from the literature on latent variable modeling (see Jaccard and Wan, 1996; Bollen and Paxton, 1998; Arminger and Muthén, 1998). Traditional assumptions of OLS may be violated and specialized methods have evolved for interaction analysis in such cases (e.g., DeShon and Alexander, 1996). Extensions of slope comparisons to longitudinal designs and repeated-measure situations are discussed in James and Tetrick (1984). Random-coefficient models are a form of interaction analysis that permits coefficients to randomly vary across units of analysis and which offers methods for testing explanatory theories of such variation (see Bryk and Raudenbush, 1992). Finally, OLS regression is a special case of a more general class of models based on the generalized linear model (McCullagh and Nelder, 1989). The principles discussed in this chapter can be extended to such models, permitting the effective analysis of interactions for a wide range of data. For an example of an extension of interaction analysis to the generalized linear model characterizing logistic regression, see Jaccard (2000).

NOTE

1. For the sake of pedagogy, we omit the *i* subscripts indicating the individual scores for each variable.

REFERENCES

Aiken, L. and West, S. (1991) *Multiple Regression*. Newbury Park, CA: Sage.

Arminger, G. and Muthén, B. (1998) 'A Bayesian approach to nonlinear latent variable models using the Gibbs sampler and the Metropolis–Hastings algorithm', *Psychometrika*, 63: 271–300.

Bishop, Y.M., Fienberg, G. and Holland, P. (1975) *Discrete Multivariate Analysis: Theory and Practice*. Cambridge, MA: MIT Press.

Boik, R.J. (1993) 'The analysis of two factor interactions in fixed effects linear models', *Journal of Educational Statistics*, 18: 1–40.

Bollen, K.A. and Paxton, P. (1998) 'Interactions of latent variables in structural equation models', *Structural Equation Modeling*, 5: 267–93.

Bryk, A. and Raudenbush, S. (1992) *Hierarchical Linear Models: Applications and Data Analysis Methods*. Newbury Park, CA: Sage.

Busemeyer, J. and Jones, L. (1983) 'Analysis of multiplicative combination rules when the causal variables are measured with error', *Psychological Bulletin*, 93: 549–62.

Cohen, J. and Cohen, P. (1983) *Applied Multiple Regression/Correlation Analysis for the Behavioral Sciences*. Hillsdale, NJ: Erlbaum.

DeShon, R. and Alexander, R. (1996) 'Alternative procedures for testing regression slope homogeneity when group error variances are unequal', *Psychological Methods*, 1: 261–77.

Hamilton, L.C. (1992) *Regression with Graphics: A Second Course in Applied Statistics*. Belmont, CA: Duxbury.

Hosmer, D.W. and Lemeshow, S. (1989) *Applied Logistic Regression*. New York: Wiley.

Jaccard, J. (1998) *Interaction Effects in Factorial Analysis of Variance*. Newbury Park, CA: Sage.

Jaccard, J. (2000) *Interaction Effects in Logistic Regression*. Newbury Park, CA: Sage.

Jaccard, J. and Wan, C. (1996) *LISREL Approaches to Interaction Effects in Multiple Regression*. Newbury Park, CA: Sage.

Jaccard, J., Turrisi, R. and Wan, C. (1990) *Interaction Effects in Multiple Regression*. Newbury Park, CA: Sage.

James, L. and Tetrick, L. (1984) 'A multivariate test of homogeneity of regression weights for correlated data', *Educational and Psychological Measurement*, 44: 769–80.

Kirk, R. (1995) *Experimental Design: Procedures for the Behavioral Sciences*. Pacific Grove, CA: Brooks/Cole.

Kleinbaum, D.G. (1994) *Logistic Regression: A Self-Learning Text*. New York: Springer-Verlag.

Lubinski, D. and Humphries, L. (1990) 'Assessing spurious 'moderator effects': Illustrated substantively with the hypothesized ("synergistic") relation between spatial and mathematical ability', *Psychological Bulletin*, 107: 385–93.

Maxwell, S. and Delaney, H. (1993) 'Bivariate median splits and spurious statistical significance', *Psychological Bulletin*, 113: 181–90.

McClelland, G.H. and Judd, C.M. (1993) 'Statistical difficulties of detecting interactions and moderator effects', *Psychological Bulletin*, 114: 376–90.

McCullagh, P. and Nelder, J.A. (1989) *Generalized Linear Models*. London: Chapman & Hall.

Vandenberg, R.J. and Lance, C. (2000) 'A review and synthesis of the measurement invariance literature: Suggestions, practices, and recommendations for organizational research', *Organizational Research Methods*, 3: 4–69.

Westfall, P.H., Tobias, R., Rom, D., Wolfinger, R. and Hochberg, R.D. (1999) *Multiple Comparisons and Multiple Tests Using the SAS System*. Cary, NC: SAS Institute.

Wilkinson, L. (1999) 'Statistical methods in psychology journals: Guidelines and explanations', *American Psychologist*, 54: 594–604.

11

Regression Models for Categorical Outcomes

J. SCOTT LONG AND SIMON CHENG

The linear regression model (LRM) is the most commonly used statistical method in the social sciences. A key advantage of the LRM is that the results have a simple interpretation: for a unit change in a given independent variable, the expected value of the outcome changes by a fixed amount, holding all other variables constant. Unfortunately, the application of the LRM is limited to cases in which the dependent variable is continuous and uncensored.[1] If the LRM is used when the dependent variable is categorical, censored, or truncated, the estimates are likely to be inconsistent, inefficient, or simply nonsensical. When the dependent variable is continuous and censored or truncated, models for limited dependent variables such as tobit need to be used. These are discussed in Chapter 18 of this *Handbook*. Of particular concern for our chapter are models for binary, ordinal, or nominal outcomes.

There is a wide and increasing variety of models that can be used for categorical outcomes. These include binary logit and probit, ordinal logit and probit, multinomial and conditional logit, and multinomial probit. Within the last 15 years, computational problems for estimating these models by maximum likelihood have been solved and the models can be easily estimated with readily available software. But, since these models are non-linear, interpretation is much more difficult than for the LRM. Proper interpretation involves *post-estimation analysis* that transforms the estimated parameters into more substantively useful information.

The focus of our chapter is on the most basic models for categorical outcomes. These models are extremely useful in and of themselves and also serve as the foundation for a vast and increasing number of alternative models that are available for categorical outcomes. Our review emphasizes the similarities among the models, noting that models for ordinal and nominal outcomes can be developed as generalizations of models for binary outcomes. Methods of interpretation are also shared by these models. Accordingly, we begin with a general discussion of issues of interpretation for nonlinear models. This is followed by a review of general issues related to estimating, testing and assessing fit of these models. The remaining sections consider models for binary, ordinal, and nominal outcomes.

NONLINEARITY AND INTERPRETATION

Models for categorical outcomes are non-linear, and understanding the implications of nonlinearity is fundamental to the proper interpretation of these models. Unfortunately, data analysts have often limited their interpretation to a table of coefficients

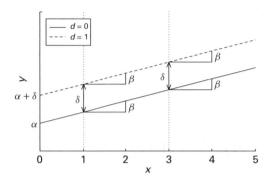

Figure 11.1   *A simple linear model*

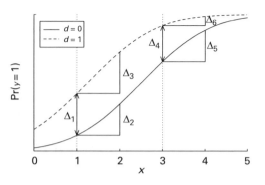

Figure 11.2   *A simple nonlinear model*

accompanied by a brief description of the signs and significance levels of the coefficients. This unnecessary limitation can be avoided if the implications of nonlinearity are fully understood. Accordingly, in this section we focus heuristically on the idea of nonlinearity and its implications for the proper interpretation of these models. Specific details as they apply to particular models are given later in the chapter.

Figure 11.1 shows a simple linear regression model, where y is the dependent variable, x is a continuous independent variable, and d is a binary independent variable. The model being estimated is

$$y = \alpha + \beta x + \delta d,$$

where for simplicity we have assumed that there is no error term. The solid line plots y as x changes for $d = 0$: that is, $y = \alpha + \beta x$. The dashed line plots y as x changes when $d = 1$, which simply changes the intercept: $y = \alpha + \beta x + \delta 1 = (\alpha + \delta) + \beta x$.

The effect of x on y can be computed as the partial derivative or slope of the line relating x to y, often called the *marginal change*:

$$\frac{\partial y}{\partial x} = \frac{\partial(\alpha + \beta x + \delta d)}{\partial x} = \beta.$$

This equation is the ratio of the change in y to the change in x, where the change in x is infinitely small, holding d constant. In a linear model, the marginal change is the same at *all* values of x and d. Consequently, when x increases by one unit, y increases by β units regardless of the current values for x and d. This is shown by the four small triangles with bases of length 1 and heights of β.

The effect of d cannot be computed with a partial derivative since d is discrete. Instead,

we measure the *discrete change* in y as d changes from 0 to 1, holding x constant:

$$\frac{\Delta y}{\Delta d} = (\alpha + \beta x + \delta 1) - (\alpha + \beta x + \delta 0) = \delta.$$

When d changes from 0 to 1, y changes by δ units regardless of the level of x. This is shown by the two arrows marking the distance between the solid and dashed lines.

The distinguishing feature of interpretation in the LRM is that the effect of a given change in an independent variable is the same regardless of the value of that variable at the start of its change and regardless of the level of the other variables in the model. Accordingly, interpretation only needs to specify which variable is changing, by how much, and that all other variables are being held constant. Another simplification due to the linearity of the model is that a discrete change of one unit equals the marginal change. This will not be true, however, for nonlinear models, as we now show.

Figure 11.2 plots a logit model where $y = 1$ if some event occurs, say if a person is in the labor force, else $y = 0$. The curves are from the logit equation[2]

$$\Pr(y = 1) = \frac{\exp(\alpha + \beta x + \delta d)}{1 + \exp(\alpha + \beta x + \delta d)}. \quad (11.1)$$

Once again, x is continuous and d is binary.

The nonlinearity of the model makes it more difficult to interpret the effects of x and d on the probability of an event occurring, since neither the marginal nor the discrete change with respect to x or d is constant. This is illustrated by the triangles. Since the solid curve for $d = 0$ and the dashed curve for

$d = 1$ are not parallel, $\Delta_1 \neq \Delta_4$. And the effect of a unit change in x differs according to the level of both d and x: $\Delta_2 \neq \Delta_3 \neq \Delta_5 \neq \Delta_6$. *In nonlinear models the effect of a change in a variable depends on the values of all variables in the model and is no longer simply equal to a parameter in the model.*

There are several general approaches for interpreting nonlinear models:

1. Marginal and discrete change coefficients can be computed at a representative value of the independent variables, such as when all variables equal their means. Alternatively, the discrete and marginal changes can be computed for all values in the sample and then averaged.
2. Predicted values can be computed at values of interest and presented in tables or plots.
3. The nonlinear model can be transformed to a model that is linear or multiplicative in some other outcome. For example, the logit model in equation (11.1) can be written as

$$\ln\left(\frac{\Pr(y=1)}{1-\Pr(y=1)}\right) = \alpha + \beta x + \delta d,$$

which can then be interpreted with methods for the linear model. The model can also be expressed as a multiplicative model in terms of odds:

$$\frac{\Pr(y=1)}{1-\Pr(y=1)} = \exp(\alpha + \beta x + \delta d).$$

Note, however, that here the difficulty is in the meaning of the transformed dependent variable.

Each of these approaches is discussed later in this chapter.

ESTIMATION, TESTING, AND FIT

While the focus of our review is on the form and interpretation of models for categorical outcomes, it is important to begin with general comments on estimation, testing, and measuring fit.

Estimation

Each of the models that we consider can be estimated by maximum likelihood (ML).[3]

Under the usual assumptions, the ML estimator is consistent, efficient, and asymptotically normal. These desirable properties hold as the sample size approaches infinity. While ML estimators are not necessarily bad estimators in small samples, the small-sample behavior of ML estimators for the models we consider is largely unknown. With the exception of the binary logit model, which can be estimated with exact permutation methods using LogXact (Cytel Software Corporation, 2000), alternative estimators with known small-sample properties are not available. Based on both his experience with these methods and discussion with other researchers, Long (1997: 53–4) proposed the following guidelines for the use of ML in small samples:

> It is risky to use ML with samples smaller than 100, while samples over 500 seem adequate. These values should be raised depending on characteristics of the model and the data. First, if there are many parameters, more observations are needed. A rule of at least ten observations per parameter seems reasonable (which does not imply that less than 100 is not needed if you have only two parameters). Second, if the data are ill-conditioned (e.g., independent variables are highly collinear) or if there is little variation in the dependent variable (e.g., nearly all of the outcomes are 1), a larger sample is required. Third, some models seem to require more observations, such as the ordinal regression model.

Numerical methods are used to compute ML estimates. These methods work extremely well when the data are clean, variables are properly constructed, and the model is correctly specified. In some cases, problems with convergence occur if the ratio of the largest standard deviation to the smallest standard deviation among independent variables is large. For example, if income is measured in units of $1, recoding income to units of $1000 may resolve problems with convergence. Overall, numerical methods for ML estimation work well when your model is appropriate for your data. In using these models, Cramer's (1986: 10) advice should be taken very seriously: 'Check the data, check their transfer into the computer, check the actual computations (preferably by repeating at least a sample by a rival program), and always remain suspicious of the results, regardless of the appeal.'

Statistical tests

Coefficients estimated by ML can be easily tested with standard Wald and likelihood ratio (LR) tests. Even though the LR and Wald tests are asymptotically equivalent, in finite samples they give different answers, particularly for small samples. In general, it is unclear which test is to be preferred. In practice, the choice of which test to use is often determined by convenience, although many statisticians (including us) prefer the LR test. While the LR test requires the estimation of two models, the computation of the test only involves subtraction. The Wald test only requires estimation of a single model, but the computation of the test involves matrix manipulations. Which test is more convenient depends on the software being used. Regarding significance levels for tests based on small samples, Allison (1995: 80) suggests that, contrary to standard advice of using larger p-values in small samples, given that the degree to which ML estimates are normally distributed is unknown in small samples, it is reasonable to require smaller p-values in small samples.

Measures of fit

Residuals and outliers When assessing a model it is useful to consider how well the model fits each case and how much influence each case has on the estimates of the parameters. Pregibon (1981) extended methods of residual and outlier analysis from the LRM to the case of binary logit and probit; see also Cook and Weisberg (1999: Part IV). Similar methods for ordinal and nominal outcomes are not available. However, models for ordinal and nominal outcomes can often be expressed as a series of binary models (as shown below). Methods developed for binary models can be applied to each of these models, providing potentially useful information about the fit of the model.

Scalar measures of fit In addition to assessing the fit of each observation, a single number to summarize the overall goodness of fit of a model would be useful in comparing competing models and ultimately in selecting a final model. While the desirability of a scalar measure of fit is clear, in practice their use is problematic. Selecting a model that maximizes the value of a given measure of fit does not necessarily lead to a model that is optimal in any sense other than the model having a larger value of that measure. While measures of fit provide some information, it

is partial information that must be assessed within the context of the theory motivating the analysis, past research, and the estimated parameters of the model being considered. For details of the many measures that have been proposed, see Long (1997: Chapter 4).

MODELS FOR BINARY OUTCOMES

The binary logit and probit models, referred to jointly as the binary regression model (BRM), can be derived in three ways. First, an unobserved or latent variable can be hypothesized, along with a measurement model relating the latent variable to the observed binary outcome. Second, the model can be constructed as a probability model. Finally, the model can be generated as a random utility or discrete choice model. While we focus on the first two approaches, the third approach is used to explain the multinomial probit model.

A latent variable model

Assume a *latent* variable y^* ranging from $-\infty$ to ∞ that is related to the observed independent variables by the structural equation

$$y_i^* = x_i\beta + \varepsilon_i,$$

where i indicates the observation and ε is a random error. The form of this equation is identical to that of the LRM, with the important difference that the dependent variable is unobserved.

The observed binary variable y is related to y^* by a simple measurement equation:

$$y_i = \begin{cases} 1 & \text{if } y_i^* > 0, \\ 0 & \text{if } y_i^* \leq 0. \end{cases}$$

Cases with positive values of y^* are observed as $y = 1$, while cases with negative or zero values of y^* are observed as $y = 0$. For example, let $y = 1$ if a woman is in the labor force and $y = 0$ if she is not. The independent variables might include number of children, education, and expected wages. Not all women in the labor force are there with the same certainty. One woman might be close to leaving the labor force, while another woman could be firm in her decision to work. In both cases, we observe $y = 1$. The idea of a latent y^* is that an underlying *propensity to work* generates the observed state. While we cannot

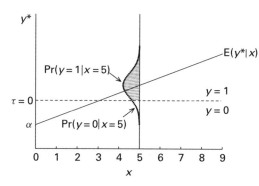

Figure 11.3   *Relationship between latent variables y^* and $Pr(y = 1)$ for BRM*

directly observe the propensity, at some point a change in y^* results in a change in what we observe, namely, whether a woman is in the labor force.

The latent variable model for binary outcomes is illustrated in Figure 11.3 for a single independent variable, where we use the simpler notation $y^* = \alpha + \beta x + \varepsilon$. For a given value of x, illustrated in the figure for $x = 5$,

$$Pr(y = 1|x) = Pr(y^* > 0|x).$$

Substituting the structural model and re-arranging terms:

$$\begin{aligned} Pr(y = 1|x) &= Pr(\alpha + \beta x + \varepsilon > 0|x) \\ &= Pr(\varepsilon > -[\alpha + \beta x]|x) \\ &= Pr(\varepsilon \le \alpha + \beta x|x). \end{aligned} \quad (11.2)$$

This equation shows that the probability depends on the distribution of the error. Two distributions are commonly assumed. First, ε is distributed normally with $E(\varepsilon) = 0$ and $var(\varepsilon) = 1$, which leads to the binary probit model. Specifically, equation (11.2) becomes

$$Pr(y = 1 \mid x) = \int_{-\infty}^{\alpha + \beta x} \frac{1}{\sqrt{2\pi}} \exp\left(-\frac{t^2}{2}\right) dt.$$

Alternatively, ε is assumed to have a logistic distribution with $E(\varepsilon) = 0$ and $var(\varepsilon) = \pi^2/3$, leading to the binary logit model:

$$Pr(y = 1 \mid x) = \frac{\exp(\alpha + \beta x)}{1 + \exp(\alpha + \beta x)}. \quad (11.3)$$

The peculiar value assumed for $var(\varepsilon)$ in the logit model illustrates a basic point regarding the identification of models with latent outcomes. In the LRM, $var(\varepsilon)$ can be estimated since y is observed. For the BRM, $var(\varepsilon)$ must be assumed since the dependent variable is unobserved. The model is unidentified unless an assumption is made about the variance of the errors. For probit, we assume $var(\varepsilon) = 1$ since this leads to a simple equation for the model. In the logit model, the variance is set to $\pi^2/3$ since this leads to the simple form of equation (11.3). While the value assumed for $var(\varepsilon)$ is arbitrary, the value does *not* affect the computed value of the probability (see Long, 1997: 49–50, for a simple proof). In effect, changing the assumed variance affects the spread of the distribution, but not the proportion of the distribution above or below the threshold. If a different value is assumed, the values of the structural coefficients are changed in a uniform way. This is illustrated in Figure 11.4.

Overall, the probability of the event occurring is the cumulative density function (cdf) of the error term evaluated at given values of the independent variables:

$$Pr(y = 1|\mathbf{x}) = F(\mathbf{x}\boldsymbol{\beta}), \quad (11.4)$$

where

$$\mathbf{x}\boldsymbol{\beta} = \beta_0 + \beta_1 x_1 + \cdots + \beta_K x_K$$

and F is the normal cdf Φ for the probit model and the logistic cdf Λ for the logit model. The relationship between the linear latent variable model and the resulting S-shaped probability model is shown in Figure 11.5 for a model with a single independent variable. Figure 11.5(a) shows the error distribution for nine values of x. The area where $y^* > 0$ corresponds to $Pr(y = 1|x)$ and has been shaded. Figure 11.5(b) plots $Pr(y = 1|x)$ corresponding to the shaded regions in Figure 11.5(a). As we move from $x = 1$ to 2 only a portion of the thin tail crosses the threshold in Figure 11.5(a), resulting in a small change in $Pr(y = 1|x)$ in Figure 11.5(b). As we move from $x = 2$ to 3 to 4, thicker regions of the error distribution slide over the threshold and the increase in $Pr(y = 1|x)$ becomes larger. The resulting curve is the well-known S-curve associated with the BRM.

A nonlinear probability model

The BRM can also be derived without appealing to a latent variable. This is done by specifying a nonlinear model relating the xs to the probability of an event. Following Theil (1970), the logit model can be derived by constructing a model in which $Pr(y = 1|\mathbf{x})$ is forced to be within the range 0 to 1. For

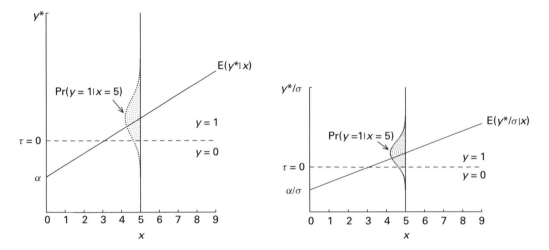

Figure 11.4   *Effect of variance of error on Pr ($y = 1|x$) in the binary regression model*

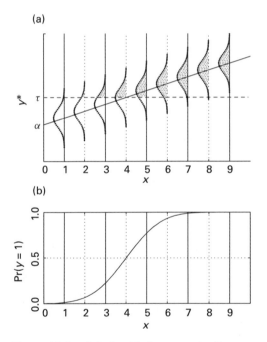

(a)

(b)

Figure 11.5   *Relationship between the linear model for y^* and the nonlinear model for Pr($y = 1$) for binary outcomes: (a) plot of y^*; (b) plot of Pr($y = 1|x$)*

example, in the linear probability model Pr($y = 1|x$) = $x\beta + \varepsilon$, the probabilities can be greater than 1 and less than 0. To constrain the range of possible values, first transform the probability into *odds*:

$$\Omega(x) = \frac{\Pr(y=1 \mid x)}{\Pr(y=0 \mid x)} = \frac{\Pr(y=1 \mid x)}{1 - \Pr(y=1 \mid x)}.$$

The odds indicate how often something happens (e.g., $y = 1$) relative to how often it does not happen (e.g., $y = 0$). The odds vary from 0 when Pr($y = 1|x$) = 0 to ∞ when Pr($y = 1|x$) = 1. The log of the odds, or *logit*, ranges from $-\infty$ to ∞. This suggests a model that is linear in the logit:

$$\ln \Omega(x) = x\beta.$$

This equation is equivalent to our earlier definition of the logit model in equation (11.3).

Other binary regression models are created by choosing functions of $x\beta$ that range from 0 to 1. Cumulative distribution functions have this property and readily provide a number of examples. For example, the cdf of the standard normal distribution results in the probit model.

Interpretation

To make our discussion concrete, we use an example from Mroz (1987) on the labor force participation of women using data from the 1976 Panel Study of Income Dynamics.[4] The sample consists of 753 white, married women between the ages of 30 and 60. The dependent variable LFP = 1 if a woman is employed (57%) or else 0. The independent variables are listed in Table 11.1.

Table 11.1   *Descriptive statistics for the labor force participation example*

Name	Mean	Std dev.	Min	Max	Description
K5	0.24	0.52	0.00	3.00	No. of children aged 5 and younger
K618	1.35	1.32	0.00	8.00	No. of children aged 6–18
Age	42.54	8.07	30.00	60.00	Wife's age in years
WC	0.28	0.45	0.00	1.00	1 if wife attended college; else 0
HC	0.39	0.49	0.00	1.00	1 if husband attended college; else 0
Lwg	1.10	0.59	−2.05	3.22	Log of wife's estimated wage rate
Income	20.13	11.63	0.00	96.00	Family income excluding wife's wages

Note: $N = 753$.

Table 11.2   *Logit and probit analyses of labor force participation*

	Logit		Probit		Ratio	
Variable	β	z	β	z	β	z
Constant	3.182	4.94	1.918	5.04	1.66	0.98
K5	−1.463	−7.43	−0.875	−7.70	1.67	0.96
K618	−0.065	−0.95	−0.039	−0.95	1.67	1.00
Age	−0.063	−4.92	−0.038	−4.97	1.66	0.99
WC	0.807	3.51	0.488	3.60	1.65	0.98
HC	0.112	0.54	0.057	0.46	1.95	1.17
Lwg	0.605	4.01	0.366	4.17	1.65	0.96
Income	−0.034	−4.20	−0.021	−4.30	1.68	0.98
$-2 \ln L$	905.27		905.39			1.00

Note: $N = 753$. β is an unstandardized coefficient; z is the z-test for β. 'Ratio' is the ratio of a logit to a probit coefficient.

Based on the specification

$$\Pr(LFP = 1) = F(\beta_0 + \beta_1 K5$$
$$+ \beta_2 K618 + \beta_3 Age$$
$$+ \beta_4 WC + \beta_5 HC$$
$$+ \beta_6 Lwg + \beta_7 Income),$$

a binary logit and probit were estimated, with results given in Table 11.2. The 'Ratio' columns show that the logit coefficients are about 1.7 times as large as those for probit, with the exception of the coefficient for HC which is the least statistically significant parameter. This illustrates how the magnitudes of the coefficients are affected by the assumed var(ε). The significance tests are quite similar since they are not affected by var(ε).

Predicted probabilities   In general, the estimated parameters from the BRM provide only information about the sign and statistical significance of the relationship between an independent variable and the outcome. More substantively meaningful interpretations are based on the predicted probabilities and

functions of those probabilities (e.g., ratios, differences). For example, Figure 11.6 plots the probit model with two independent variables,

$$\Pr(y = 1 \mid x, z)$$
$$= \Phi(1 + 1x + 0.75z), \qquad (11.5)$$

and illustrates the basic issues involved in interpretation. Each point on the surface corresponds to the predicted probability for given values of x and z. For example, the point in the northwest corner corresponds to $\Pr(y = 1 \mid x = -4, z = 8)$. Interpretation can proceed by presenting a table of predicted probabilities at substantively interesting values of the independent variables, by plotting the predicted probability while holding all but one variable constant, or by computing how much the predicted probability changes when one independent variable changes while holding the others constant.

While Figure 11.6 is for two independent variables, the idea extends to more variables. For example, consider the effects of age and income from our example of labor force participation. First, set all variables but Age

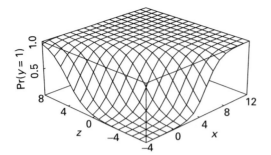

Figure 11.6   Plot of the binary probit model
$Pr(y = 1 \mid x, z) = \Phi(1.0 + 1.0x + 0.75z)$

Table 11.3   The probability of employment by college attendance and the number of young children

Number of young children	Predicted probability		
	Did not attend	Attended college	Difference
0	0.61	0.78	0.17
1	0.27	0.45	0.18
2	0.07	0.16	0.09
3	0.01	0.03	0.02

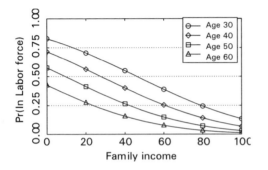

Figure 11.7   The probability of labor force participation by age and family income for women without some college education

and Income to their means. Holding Age at 30, compute the predicted probability of labor force participation as Income ranges from 0 to 100 using the equation

$$\widehat{\Pr}(\text{LFP} = 1 \mid \mathbf{x}^*) = \Phi(\mathbf{x}^* \hat{\boldsymbol{\beta}}),$$

where $\mathbf{x}^*$ contains the assumed values of each variable. These predictions are plotted with the line marked with circles in Figure 11.7. This process is repeated holding Age at 40, 50, and 60. The nonlinearities in the effects are apparent, with the effect of Income decreasing with Age. When relationships are nonlinear, plots are often useful for uncovering relationships.

In other cases, a table is a more useful way to summarize results. For example, holding all variables at their means except for the wife's education and the number of young children, Table 11.3 clearly shows the effects of education and family on labor force participation.

Marginal and discrete change   Another useful method of interpretation is to compute

the change in the probability of the outcome event as one variable changes, holding all other variables constant. In economics, the most commonly used measure of change is the marginal change, shown by the tangent to the probability curve in Figure 11.8:

$$\text{Marginal change} = \frac{\partial \Pr(y = 1 \mid \mathbf{x})}{\partial x_k}.$$

This value is often computed with all variables held at their means or by computing the marginal change for each observation in the sample and then averaging across all observations.

Alternatively, the discrete change in the predicted probabilities for a given change in an independent variable can be used. Let $\Pr(y = 1 \mid \mathbf{x}, x_k)$ be the probability of an event given $\mathbf{x}$, noting in particular the value of x_k. Thus, $\Pr(y = 1 \mid \mathbf{x}, x_k + \delta)$ is the probability with x_k increased by δ, all other variables held constant at specified values. The *discrete change* for a change of δ in x_k is

$$\frac{\Delta \Pr(y = 1 \mid \mathbf{x})}{\Delta x_k} = \Pr(y = 1 \mid \mathbf{x}, x_k + \delta)$$
$$- \Pr(y = 1 \mid \mathbf{x}, x_k),$$

which can be interpreted as saying that, for a change in variable x_k from x_k to $x_k + \delta$, the predicted probability of an event changes by $\Delta \Pr(y = 1 \mid \mathbf{x}) / \Delta x_k$, holding all other variables constant.

As shown in Figure 11.8, in general the marginal change and discrete change will not be equal:

$$\frac{\partial \Pr(y = 1 \mid \mathbf{x})}{\partial x_k} \neq \frac{\Delta \Pr(y = 1 \mid \mathbf{x})}{\Delta x_k}.$$

The two measures of change differ since the model is nonlinear and the rate of change is

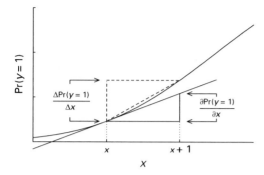

Figure 11.8 *Marginal change compared to discrete change in the BRM*

constantly changing. The discrete change measures the actual amount of change over a finite change in an independent variable, while the marginal measures the instantaneous rate of change. The two measures will be similar when the discrete change occurs over a region of the probability curve that is roughly linear. In practice, we prefer the discrete change since it measures the actual change occurring, regardless of the approximate linearity of the model in that area of the curve.

While measures of change are straightforward in the LRM, there is an important problem in nonlinear models: *the magnitude of the change in the probability for a given change in an independent variable depends both on the level of the independent variables and on the start value of the variable that is changing.* This is illustrated in Figure 11.6. Consider the effect of a unit change in *x*, which corresponds to a change along a line running southwest to northeast. For example, consider the change in probability when *x* changes from −4 to −3, with *z* = 8. This change is quite small since the predicted probability is already near 1 at *x* = −4 and *z* = 8. Now, consider the same change in *x* when *z* = 4. The change is now much larger. Clearly, the amount of change caused by a unit change in *x* depends on the level of *z* and also on the start value for *x*. The key problem in using measures of change in nonlinear models is to decide on the level of each control variable and the value at which you want to start the change for a given variable.

Figure 11.8 also illustrates a subtle but important point about computing discrete change that was raised by Kaufman (1996). Consider the point on the curve at $\Pr(y = 1 \mid x)$. When *x* increases by 1, $\Pr(y = 1)$ increases by

some amount. When *x* decreases by 1, $\Pr(y = 1)$ decreases by an amount that is smaller than the change caused by the one-unit increase. Because of this asymmetry around a given point on the curve, it is useful to center the change around a given value of *x*. For example, rather than examining the quantity

$$\frac{\Delta\Pr(y=1\mid \mathbf{x})}{\Delta x_k} = \Pr(y=1\mid \mathbf{x}, x_k + 1)$$
$$- \Pr(y=1\mid \mathbf{x}, x_k),$$

the *centered discrete change* can be used:

$$\frac{\Delta\Pr(y=1\mid \mathbf{x})}{\Delta x_k} = \Pr\left(y=1\mid \mathbf{x}, x_k + \frac{1}{2}\right)$$
$$- \Pr\left(y=1\mid \mathbf{x}, x_k - \frac{1}{2}\right).$$

This is the measure that we report in our examples.

Table 11.4 contains measures of discrete change for the probit model of women's labor force participation. For example, the effects can be interpreted as follows: For a woman who is average on all characteristics, an additional young child decreases the probability of employment by 0.33. A standard deviation change in age centered around the mean will decrease the probability of employment by 0.12, holding other variables constant. If a woman attends college, her probability of being in the labor force is 0.18 greater than that of a woman who does not attend college, holding other variables at their means.

Odds ratios   Recall that the logit model, but not the probit model, can be written as linear in the log of the odds of the event occurring:

$$\ln \Omega(\mathbf{x}) = \mathbf{x}\boldsymbol{\beta}.$$

Taking the exponential,

$$\Omega(\mathbf{x}, x_k) = \exp(\mathbf{x}\boldsymbol{\beta})$$
$$= e^{\beta_0}e^{\beta_1 x_1}\dots e^{\beta_k x_k}\dots e^{\beta_K x_K},$$

where $\Omega(\mathbf{x}, x_k)$ makes explicit the value of variable x_k. To assess the effect of x_k, we want to see how the odds change when x_k changes by some quantity δ, which is often set to 1 or the standard deviation of x_k. If we change x_k by δ, the odds become

$$\Omega(\mathbf{x}, x_k + \delta)$$
$$= e^{\beta_0}e^{\beta_1 x_1}\dots e^{\beta_k x_k}e^{\beta_k \delta}\dots e^{\beta_K x_K}.$$

Table 11.4 *Discrete change in the probability of employment*

Variable	Centered unit change	Centered standard deviation change	Change from 0 to 1
K5	−0.33	−0.18	–
K618	−0.02	−0.02	–
Age	−0.01	−0.12	–
WC	–	–	0.18
HC	–	–	0.02
Lwg	0.14	0.08	–
Income	−0.01	−0.09	–

Note: Changes are computed with other variables held at their means.

The *odds ratio* is simply

$$\frac{\Omega(\mathbf{x}, x_k + \delta)}{\Omega(\mathbf{x}, x_k)} = e^{\beta_k \delta},$$

which can be interpreted as saying that, for a change of δ in x_k, the odds are expected to change by a factor of $\exp(\beta_k \delta)$, holding all other variables constant. Importantly, the effect of a change in x_k does *not* depend on the level of x_k or on the level of any other variable.

The factor change and standardized factor change coefficients for the logit model analyzing labor force participation are presented in Table 11.5. Here is how some of the coefficients can be interpreted: For each additional young child, the odds of being employed are decreased by a factor of 0.23, holding all other variables constant. For a standard deviation increase in wages, the odds of being employed are 1.43 times greater, holding all other variables constant. Being ten years older decreases the odds by a factor of $e^{-0.063 \times 10} = 0.52$, holding all other variables constant.

Since the odds ratio is a multiplicative coefficient, 'positive' effects are greater than one, while 'negative' effects are between zero and one. Therefore, positive and negative effects should be compared by taking the inverse of the negative effect (or vice versa). For example, a positive factor change of 2 has the same magnitude as a negative factor change of 0.5. Second, a constant factor change in the odds does not correspond to a constant change or constant factor change in the probability. For example, if the odds are 2:1 and are doubled to 4:1, the probability changes from 0.667 to 0.800, a change of 0.133. If the odds are 10:1 and double to 20:1, the change in the probability is only $0.952 - 0.909 = 0.043$. While the odds in each case change by a constant factor

Table 11.5 *Factor change coefficients for labor force participation*

Variable	Logit coefficient	Factor change	Std factor change	z-value
Constant	3.182	–	–	4.94
K5	−1.463	0.232	0.465	−7.43
K618	−0.065	0.937	0.918	−0.95
Age	−0.063	0.939	0.602	−4.92
WC	0.807	2.242	–	3.51
HC	0.112	1.118	–	0.54
Lwg	0.605	1.831	1.427	4.01
Income	−0.035	0.966	0.670	−4.20

of 2, the probabilities do not change by a constant amount. Consequently, when interpreting a factor change in the odds, it is *essential* to know what the current level of the odds or probability is.

Summary For nonlinear models, no single approach to interpretation can fully describe the relationship between a variable and the outcome probability. The data analyst should search for an elegant and concise way to summarize the results that does justice to the complexities of the nonlinear model. To do this, it is often necessary to try each method of interpretation before a final approach is determined.

MODELS FOR ORDINAL OUTCOMES

While there are several models for ordinal outcomes, we focus on the ordered logit and ordered probit models, which are the most commonly used models for ordinal outcomes in the social sciences. These models, referred to jointly as the ordered regression model (ORM), were introduced by McKelvey and Zavoina (1975) in terms of an underlying latent variable. At about the same time, the model was developed in biostatistics (McCullagh, 1980), where it is referred to as the *proportional odds model*, the *parallel regression model*, or the *grouped continuous model*. After presenting the ORM, we consider several less common models for ordinal outcomes.

A latent variable model

The close relationship between the BRM and the ORM is easily shown in the latent variable formulation of the model. Using the same structural model

$$y_i^* = \mathbf{x}_i\boldsymbol{\beta} + \varepsilon_i,$$

we simply expand the measurement model to divide y^* into J ordinal categories:

$$y_i = m \text{ if } \tau_{m-1,} \le y_i^* < \tau_m, \, m = 1,\ldots,J.$$

The *cutpoints* or *thresholds* $\tau_1,\ldots,\tau_{J-1}$ are estimated and, for reasons that are explained below, we assume $\tau_0 = -\infty$ and $\tau_J = \infty$. For example, people respond to the statement 'A working mother can establish just as warm and secure a relationship with her child as a mother who does not work' with the ordinal categories: 'Strongly disagree' (SD), 'Disagree' (D), 'Agree' (A), and 'Strongly agree' (SA). The latent variable is the propensity to agree that working mothers can be good mothers, leading to the measurement model:

$$y_i = \begin{cases} 1 \Rightarrow \text{SD} & \text{if } \tau_0 = -\infty \le y_i^* < \tau_1, \\ 2 \Rightarrow \text{D} & \text{if } \tau_1 \le y_i^* < \tau_2, \\ 3 \Rightarrow \text{A} & \text{if } \tau_2 \le y_i^* < \tau_3, \\ 4 \Rightarrow \text{SA} & \text{if } \tau_3 \le y_i^* < \tau_4 = \infty. \end{cases}$$

For a single independent variable, this ORM is shown in Figure 11.9. The predicted probability of an outcome is the area under the curve between a pair of cutpoints at a given level of the independent variables. For example, we observe $y = 2$ when y^* falls between τ_1 and τ_2:

$$\Pr(y = 2 \mid \mathbf{x}) = \Pr(\tau_1 \le y^* < \tau_2 \mid \mathbf{x}).$$

Substituting $y^* = \mathbf{x}\boldsymbol{\beta} + \varepsilon$ and using some algebra, the predicated probability is the difference

$$\Pr(y = 2 \mid \mathbf{x}) = F(\tau_2 - \mathbf{x}\boldsymbol{\beta}) - F(\tau_1 - \mathbf{x}\boldsymbol{\beta}),$$

where F is the cdf for the assumed distribution of the errors. As with the BRM, if F is normal with $\text{var}(\varepsilon) = 1$, we have the ordinal probit model; if F is logistic with $\text{var}(\varepsilon) = \pi^2/3$, we have the ordinal *logit* model. In general, for each outcome m,

$$\begin{aligned} &\Pr(y = m \mid \mathbf{x}) \\ &= F(\tau_m - \mathbf{x}\boldsymbol{\beta}) - F(\tau_{m-1} - \mathbf{x}\boldsymbol{\beta}). \end{aligned} \quad (11.6)$$

For $y = 1$, the second term drops out since $F(-\infty - \mathbf{x}\boldsymbol{\beta}) = 0$; for $y = J$, the first term equals $F(\infty - \mathbf{x}\boldsymbol{\beta}) = 1$. Thus, with two outcome categories, the model is identical to the binary regression model (see equation (11.4)).

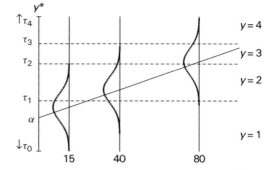

Figure 11.9 *Relationship between observed y and latent y* in ordinal regression model with a single independent variable*

Parameterization In the BRM, we assumed that $\tau = 0$ in order to identify the model. The ORM is commonly identified in either of two ways. First, some software assumes that $\tau_1 = 0$ and estimates the intercept β_0, while other programs assume that $\beta_0 = 0$ and estimate the threshold τ_1. The choice of parameterization does not affect estimates of the slopes, but does affect the estimates of β_0 and the τs. Importantly, the parameterization does not affect the predicted probabilities.

The parallel regression assumption

To understand and interpret the ORM, it is helpful to reformulate the model in terms of the *cumulative probability* that an outcome is less than or equal to m:

$$\Pr(y \le m \mid \mathbf{x}) = \sum_{j=1}^{m} \Pr(y = j \mid \mathbf{x}).$$

Expanding $\Pr(y = j \mid \mathbf{x})$ with equation (11.6) and canceling terms leads to the simple expression

$$\Pr(y \le m \mid \mathbf{x}) = F(\tau_m - \mathbf{x}\boldsymbol{\beta}). \quad (11.7)$$

This equation both shows the link between the BRM and the ORM and makes explicit a fundamental assumption of the ORM.

Consider the case with a single independent variable:

$$\begin{aligned} \Pr(y \le m|x) &= F(\tau_m - [\alpha + \beta x]) \\ &= F([\tau_m - \alpha] + \beta x) \quad (11.8) \\ &= F(\alpha_m^* + \beta x). \end{aligned}$$

The new notation makes it clear that the cumulative probability equation is identical to a binary regression. That is, the ORM is equivalent to simultaneously estimating $J-1$ binary regressions. For example, with four outcomes we would simultaneously estimate three equations:

$$\Pr(y \le 1 \,|\, x) = F(\alpha_1^* + \beta x),$$
$$\Pr(y \le 2 \,|\, x) = F(\alpha_2^* + \beta x), \qquad (11.9)$$
$$\Pr(y \le 3 \,|\, x) = F(\alpha_3^* + \beta x).$$

While the α_m^*s differ across equations, the βs do not. This is reflected by the lack of subscripts for β. The $J-1$ binary regressions are assumed to have *exactly* the same value across all equations. This assumption is referred to either as the *parallel regression assumption* (since plotting equation (11.8) for $m=1$ to $J-1$ results in parallel curves) or, for the ordinal logit model, as the *proportional odds assumption*.

   While the constraint of parallel regressions or proportional odds is implicit in the ordinal regression model, in our experience the assumption is violated in many applications. This is illustrated with an example.

Attitudes toward working mothers   The 1977 and 1989 General Social Survey asked respondents to evaluate the statement 'A working mother can establish just as warm and secure a relationship with her child as a mother who does not work'. Responses were coded as: 1 = Strongly disagree (SD); 2 = Disagree (D); 3 = Agree (A); and 4 = Strongly agree (SA). The variables used in our analysis are described in Table 11.6. Estimates from ordered logit are given in the first column of Table 11.7, with estimates from three binary logits on cumulative probabilities in the last three columns. The parallel regression assumption requires that the βs in the last three equations are equal. While some of the estimates are similar across equations (e.g., White), others are quite different (e.g., Male).

   Formal tests are also available. A score test is included in SAS's LOGISTIC procedure (SAS Institute 1990: 1090). An approximate LR test is in Stata's *omodel* command (Wolf and Gould, 1998). These are omnibus tests that do not allow you to tell if the problem only exists for some of the independent variables. Brant's (1990) Wald test allows both an overall test that all β_m are equal, and tests of the equality of coefficients for individual variables. This test is available in Stata through the *brant* command (Long and Freese, 2001). In our example, the value of the Brant test for

Table 11.6   *Descriptive statistics for the attitudes toward working mothers example*

Name	Mean	Std dev.	Min	Max	Description
Yr89	0.40	0.49	0.00	1.00	Survey year: 1 = 1989; 0 = 1977
Male	0.47	0.50	0.00	1.00	1 = male; 0 = female
White	0.88	0.33	0.00	1.00	1 = white; 0 = non-white
Age	44.94	16.78	18.00	89.00	Age in years
Ed	12.22	3.16	0.00	29.00	Years of education
Prst	39.59	14.49	12.00	82.00	Occupational prestige

Note: $N = 2293$.

Table 11.7   *Ordered logit and cumulative logit regressions*

Variable		Ordered logit	Cumulative Logits $m \le 1$	$m \le 2$	$m \le 3$
Yr89	β	0.524	0.965	0.565	0.319
	z	6.33	6.26	6.09	2.80
Male	β	−0.733	−0.305	−0.691	−1.084
	z	−9.23	−2.36	−7.68	−8.88
White	β	−0.391	−0.553	−0.314	−0.393
	z	−3.27	−2.40	−2.24	−2.49
Age	β	−0.022	−0.017	−0.025	−0.019
	z	−8.52	−4.06	−8.84	−4.94
Ed	β	0.067	0.105	0.053	0.058
	z	4.20	4.14	2.86	2.27
Prst	β	0.006	−0.001	0.010	0.006
	z	1.84	−0.25	2.50	1.14

Note: β is an unstandardized coefficient; z is a z-test of β.

the hypothesis that all coefficients are parallel is 49.18 with 12 degrees of freedom, providing strong evidence that the assumption of parallel regressions is violated. Looking at the tests for individual variables, we find that the evidence against parallel regressions is strongest for the variables Yr89 ($\chi^2 = 13.01$, df = 2, $p < 0.01$) and Male ($\chi^2 = 22.24$, df = 2, $p < 0.01$).

Interpretation

If the idea of a latent variable makes substantive sense (and supposing that the assumption of parallel regressions is not violated), simple interpretations are possible by rescaling y^* and computing standardized coefficients. When concern is with the observed categories, the methods illustrated for the BRM can be extended to multiple outcomes. Since the ORM is nonlinear in the outcome probabilities, no single approach can fully describe the relationship between a variable and the outcome probabilities. Consequently, you should consider each of these methods before deciding which approach is most effective in a given application.

*Partial change in y** In the ORM, $y^* = \mathbf{x}\boldsymbol{\beta} + \varepsilon$ and the marginal change in y^* with respect to x_k is

$$\frac{\partial y^*}{\partial x_k} = \beta_k.$$

Since y^* is latent, the marginal cannot be interpreted without standardizing y^*. The variance of y^* can be estimated by the quadratic form

$$\hat{\sigma}_{y^*}^2 = \hat{\boldsymbol{\beta}}' \, \widehat{\text{var}}(\mathbf{x}) \, \hat{\boldsymbol{\beta}} + \text{var}(\varepsilon), \qquad (11.10)$$

where $\widehat{\text{var}}(\mathbf{x})$ is the covariance matrix for the observed $\mathbf{x}$; $\hat{\boldsymbol{\beta}}$ contains ML estimates; and $\text{var}(\varepsilon) = 1$ for the probit model and $\pi^2/3$ for the logit model. Then, the y^*-*standardized* coefficient for x_k is

$$\beta_k^{Sy^*} = \frac{\beta_k}{\sigma_{y^*}},$$

which says that, for a unit increase in x_k, y^* is expected to increase by $\beta_k^{Sy^*}$ standard deviations, holding all other variables constant. With σ_k equal to the standard deviation for x_k, the *fully standardized coefficient* is

$$\beta_k^S = \frac{\sigma_k \beta_k}{\sigma_{y^*}} = \sigma_k \beta_k^{Sy^*},$$

which can be interpreted as saying that, for a standard deviation increase in x_k, y^* is expected to increase by β_k^S standard deviations, holding all other variables constant.

For our example using the ordinal logit model, $\hat{\sigma}_{y^*}^2 = 3.77$ and the standardized coefficients can be interpreted as follows: In 1989, support was 0.27 standard deviations higher than in 1977, holding all other variables constant. Each standard deviation increase in education increases support by 0.11 standard deviations, holding all other variables constant.

Predicted probabilities The predicted probabilities and cumulative probabilities can be estimated as

$$\begin{aligned} \widehat{\Pr}(y = m \mid \mathbf{x}) &= F(\hat{\tau}_m - \mathbf{x}\hat{\boldsymbol{\beta}}) \\ &\quad - F(\hat{\tau}_{m-1} - \mathbf{x}\hat{\boldsymbol{\beta}}), \\ \widehat{\Pr}(y \leq m \mid \mathbf{x}) &= F(\tau_m - \mathbf{x}\hat{\boldsymbol{\beta}}). \end{aligned} \qquad (11.11)$$

Either set of probabilities can be plotted. For example, in Figure 11.10(a) the predicted probabilities for each outcome are plotted. The probability of strongly agreeing, indicated with circles, at age 20 is 0.39. As age increases the probability decreases to 0.25 at age 50 and 0.15 at age 80. The probability of disagreeing, indicated by triangles, is nearly the mirror image. It begins at 0.16 at age 20 and ends at 0.34 at age 80. There is a smaller change in the probability of strongly disagreeing, indicated by diamonds, that starts at 0.04 and ends at 0.12. The probability of agreeing, shown by squares, illustrates an unusual characteristic of the ORM, which also occurs with nominal models. The effect of age on agreeing is initially positive and then negative. As age increases from 20, more cases from category SA move into category A than move from A into D, which increase the probability of A. With increasing age, more cases leave A for D than enter A from SA, resulting in a smaller probability.

Cumulative probabilities can be plotted as shown in Figure 11.10(b). The cumulative probabilities 'stack' the corresponding probabilities from Figure 11.10(a) and show the overall increase with age in negative attitudes toward the statement that working women can have a warm relationship with their children. The information in the graph can be viewed in two ways. First, height within a category (e.g., the height of the trapezoid labeled 'Strongly Agree') corresponds to the predicted probability for that category. Second, the height from the x-axis to the top of a category is the probability for all categories at or below that level.

Tables can also be used to present probabilities. Table 11.8 contains the predicted probabilities for men and women by the year of the survey, along with differences by gender in the probabilities within year and across years. The first thing to notice is that men are more likely than women to disagree and strongly disagree that working women can have as warm of relationships with their children. Second, between 1977 and 1989 there was a movement for both men and women toward more positive attitudes.

Both partial and discrete change can also be used. The partial derivative of equation (11.6),

(a)

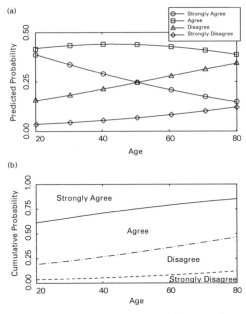

(b)

Figure 11.10   (a) Predicted and (b) cumulative predicted probabilities for women in 1989

Table 11.8   *Predicted probabilities by gender and year*

1977	SD	D	A	SA
Men	0.19	0.40	0.32	0.10
Women	0.10	0.31	0.41	0.18
Men – Women	0.09	0.09	–0.09	–0.08
1989	SD	D	A	SA
Men	0.12	0.34	0.39	0.15
Women	0.06	0.23	0.44	0.27
Men – Women	0.06	0.11	–0.05	–0.12
Change from 1977 to 1989	SD	D	A	SA
Men	–0.07	–0.06	0.07	0.05
Women	–0.04	–0.08	0.03	0.09

$$\frac{\partial \Pr(y = m|\mathbf{x})}{\partial x_k} = \frac{\partial F(\tau_m - \mathbf{x}\boldsymbol{\beta})}{\partial x_k} - \frac{\partial F(\tau_{m-1} - \mathbf{x}\boldsymbol{\beta})}{\partial x_k}$$

$$= \beta_k [f(\tau_{m-1} - \mathbf{x}\boldsymbol{\beta}) - f(\tau_m - \mathbf{x}\boldsymbol{\beta})],$$

is the slope of the curve relating x_k to $\Pr(y=m|\mathbf{x})$, holding all other variables constant. The sign of the marginal is not necessarily the same as the sign of β_k, since $f(\tau_{m-1} - \mathbf{x}\boldsymbol{\beta}) - f(\tau_m - \mathbf{x}\boldsymbol{\beta})$ can be negative. Accordingly, the sign of the estimated βs in the ORM should not be used as a quick indication of the direction of a variable's effect on any of the outcome categories (as illustrated by the curve for agreeing in Figure 11.10(a)).[5] Since the marginal effect depends on the levels of all variables, we must decide on which values of the variables to use when computing the effect. As with the BRM, the marginal can be averaged over all observations or computed at the mean of all variables. Keep in mind that the marginal change does *not* indicate the change in the probability that would be observed for a unit change in x_k, unless an independent variable is varying over a region of the probability curve that is nearly linear. When the curve is approximately linear, the marginal effect can be used to summarize the effect of a unit change in the variable on the probability of an outcome.

Since interpretation using marginal effects can be misleading when the probability curve

is changing rapidly or when an independent variable is a dummy variable, we prefer using discrete change. The discrete change in the predicted probability for a change in x_k from the start value x_S to the end value x_E (e.g., a change from $x_k = 0$ to $x_k = 1$) is

$$\frac{\Delta \Pr(y = m|\mathbf{x})}{\Delta x_k} = \Pr(y = m|\mathbf{x}, x_k = x_E)$$
$$- \Pr(y = m|\mathbf{x}, x_k = x_S),$$

where $\Pr(y = m|\mathbf{x}, x_k)$ is the probability that $y = m$ given $\mathbf{x}$, noting a specific value for x_k. This equation says that when x_k changes from x_S to x_E, the predicted probability of outcome m changes by $\Delta \Pr(y = m|\mathbf{x})/\Delta x_k$, holding all other variables at $\mathbf{x}$.

As with the BRM, the value of the discrete change depends on: (1) the value at which x_k starts; (2) the amount of change in x_k; and (3) the values of all other variables. Most frequently each continuous variable except x_k is held at its mean. For dummy independent variables, the change might be computed for both values of the variable. For example, we could compute the discrete change for age separately for men and women.

Table 11.9 contains measures of discrete change for our example using the ordered logit model. We see, for example, that the probability of strongly disagreeing is 0.08 higher for men than women, holding all other variables at their means. For variables that are not binary, the discrete change can be interpreted for a unit change centered around the mean, for a standard deviation change centered around the mean, and when the variable goes from its minimum to its maximum value. For example, for each additional year of education, the probability of strongly

Table 11.9 *Discrete change in the probability of attitudes about working mothers for the ordered logit model*

Variable	Change	$\bar{\Delta}$	SD	D	A	SA
Overall probability			0.11	0.33	0.40	0.16
Yr89	$0 \to 1$	0.06	−0.05	−0.08	0.05	0.07
Male	$0 \to 1$	0.09	0.08	0.11	−0.08	−0.10
White	$0 \to 1$	0.05	0.04	0.06	−0.04	−0.06
Age	$\Delta 1$	0.00	0.00	0.00	−0.00	−0.00
	$\Delta\sigma$	0.04	0.04	0.05	−0.04	−0.05
	ΔRange	0.18	0.18	0.19	−0.18	−0.19
Ed	$\Delta 1$	0.01	−0.01	−0.01	0.01	0.01
	$\Delta\sigma$	0.03	−0.02	−0.03	0.02	0.03
	ΔRange	0.16	−0.15	−0.17	0.16	0.17
Prst	$\Delta 1$	0.00	−0.00	−0.00	0.00	0.00
	$\Delta\sigma$	0.01	−0.01	−0.01	0.01	0.01
	ΔRange	0.05	−0.04	−0.06	0.04	0.06

Note: $0 \to 1$ is change from 0 to 1; $\Delta 1$ is centered change of one around the mean; $\Delta\sigma$ is centered change of one standard deviation around the mean; ΔRange is change from the minimum to the maximum; $\bar{\Delta}$ is the average absolute discrete change.

agreeing increases by 0.01, holding other variables constant at their means. For a standard deviation increase in age, the probability of disagreeing increases by 0.05, holding other variables at their means. Moving from the minimum prestige to the maximum prestige changes the predicted probability of strongly agreeing by 0.06, holding all other variables at their means.

The J discrete change coefficients for a variable can be summarized by computing the average of the absolute values of the changes across all of the outcome categories:

$$\bar{\Delta} = \frac{1}{J} \sum_{j=1}^{J} \left| \frac{\Delta \Pr(y = j | \mathbf{x})}{\Delta x_k} \right|.$$

The absolute value is taken since the sum of the changes without taking the absolute value is necessarily zero. The average absolute discrete change in the table clearly shows that the respondent's gender, education, and age have the strongest effects on attitudes about working mothers.

Odds ratios To illustrate the use of odds ratios, consider the coefficient for gender from Table 11.7: $\beta_{\text{Male}} = -0.733$, so that $\exp(-\beta_{\text{Male}}) = 2.1$. This tells us that the odds of SD versus the combined outcomes D, A, and

SA are 2.1 times greater for men than women, holding other variables constant. Similarly, the odds of SD and D versus A and SA are 2.1 times greater for men than women; and the odds of SD, D, and A versus SA are 2.1 times greater.

The coefficient for age is $\beta_{\text{Age}} = -0.022$ with standard deviation $s_{\text{Age}} = 16.8$. Thus, $100[\exp(-s_{\text{Age}} \beta_{\text{Age}}) - 1] = 44$, which means that, for a standard deviation increase in age, the odds of SD versus D, A, and SA are increased by 44%, holding other variables constant. Similarly, the odds of SD and D versus A and SA are 44% greater for every standard deviation increase in age; and the odds of SD, D, and A versus SA are 44% greater.

Summary The ordered regression model is the most frequently used model for ordinal outcomes. However, as our discussion has shown, this model imposes the strong assumption of parallel regressions or proportional odds. We recommend that you always test this assumption, ideally in a way that allows you to assess which variables are violating the assumption (which can suggest problems in the specification of the model). In our experience, outcomes that are considered ordinal often contain complexities that are 'assumed away' by the ORM. For example, a variable could be ordered differently with respect to different independent variables. Alternatively, it might be ordered on more than one dimension or be only partially ordered. Accordingly, we suggest that if your outcome is ordinal, you also consider the ordinal models discussed in the next section as well as models for nominal outcomes.

LESS COMMON MODELS FOR

ORDINAL OUTCOMES

In this section we consider briefly several less commonly used models for ordinal outcomes. While we do not consider methods of interpretation, the same approaches as discussed above can be used after making the appropriate change to the formula for computing predicted probabilities. The first two models that we consider, the generalized ordered logit model and the stereotype model, relax the assumption of equal βs over outcome categories that is found in the ORM. The last two models, the adjacent categories model and the continuation ratio model, propose alternative comparisons for the ordinal categories.

Generalized ordered logit model

The parallel regression assumption results from assuming the same coefficient vector β for all comparisons in the $J - 1$ equations:

$$\ln \Omega_{y \leq m}(\mathbf{x}) = \tau_m - \mathbf{x}\beta,$$

where

$$\Omega_{y \leq m}(\mathbf{x}) = \frac{\Pr(y \leq m|\mathbf{x})}{\Pr(y > m|\mathbf{x})}.$$

The generalized ordered logit model (GOLM) removes the restriction of parallel regressions by allowing β to differ for each of the $J-1$ comparisons. That is,

$$\ln \Omega_{y \leq m}(\mathbf{x}) = \tau_m - \mathbf{x}\beta_m$$
$$\text{for } m = 1, ..., J-1.$$

Or, in terms of odds,

$$\Omega_{y \leq m}(\mathbf{x}) = \exp(\tau_m - \mathbf{x}\beta_m)$$
$$\text{for } m = 1, ..., J-1.$$

Predicted probabilities are computed by solving these equations, resulting in:

$$\Pr(y = 1|\mathbf{x}) = \frac{\exp(\tau_1 - \mathbf{x}\beta_1)}{1 + \exp(\tau_1 - \mathbf{x}\beta_1)},$$

$$\Pr(y - j|\mathbf{x}) = \frac{\exp(\tau_j - \mathbf{x}\beta_j)}{1 + \exp(\tau_j - \mathbf{x}\beta_j)}$$
$$- \frac{\exp(\tau_{j-1} - \mathbf{x}\beta_{j-1})}{1 + \exp(\tau_{j-1} - \mathbf{x}\beta_{j-1})} \quad \text{for } j = 2,..., J-1,$$

$$\Pr(y = J|\mathbf{x}) = 1 - \frac{\exp(\tau_{J-1} - \mathbf{x}\beta_{J-1})}{1 + \exp(\tau_{J-1} - \mathbf{x}\beta_{J-1})}.$$

To insure that $\Pr(y = j|\mathbf{x})$ is between 0 and 1, it must be the case that $\tau_j - \mathbf{x}\beta_j \geq \tau_{j-1} - \mathbf{x}\beta_{j-1}$. If this constraint is not imposed during estimation, it is possible that predicted probabilities can be negative or greater than 1. Once predicted probabilities are computed, all of the approaches used to interpret the ORM results can be readily applied.

While we have not seen social science applications of this model, it has been discussed by Clogg and Shihadeh (1994: 146–7), Fahrmeir and Tutz (1994: 91), and McCullagh and Nelder (1989: 155). Applications may become more common since this model has recently been programmed for Stata by Fu (1998).

The stereotype model[6]

The *stereotype ordered regression model* (SORM) was proposed by Anderson (1984) in response to the restrictive assumption of parallel regressions in the ordered regression model. The SORM is a compromise between allowing the coefficients for each independent variable to vary by outcome category and restricting them to be identical across all outcomes. The SORM is defined as[7]

$$\ln \frac{\Pr(y = q)}{\Pr(y = r)} = (\alpha_q - \alpha_r)\beta_0 + (\phi_q - \phi_r)\mathbf{x}\beta,$$
$$\tag{11.12}$$

where β_0 is the intercept and β is a vector of coefficients associated with the independent variables; since β_0 is included in the equation, it is not included in β. The αs and ϕs are scale factors associated with the outcome categories. To see how these work, consider a model with two independent variables and three outcomes:

$$\ln \frac{\Pr(y=1)}{\Pr(y=2)} = (\alpha_1 - \alpha_2)\beta_0 + (\phi_1 - \phi_2)\beta_1 x_1$$
$$+ (\phi_1 - \phi_2)\beta_2 x_2,$$

$$\ln \frac{\Pr(y=1)}{\Pr(y=3)} = (\alpha_1 - \alpha_3)\beta_0 + (\phi_1 - \phi_3)\beta_1 x_1$$
$$+ (\phi_1 - \phi_3)\beta_2 x_2,$$

$$\ln \frac{\Pr(y=2)}{\Pr(y=3)} = (\alpha_2 - \alpha_3)\beta_0 + (\phi_2 - \phi_3)\beta_1 x_1$$
$$+ (\phi_2 - \phi_3)\beta_2 x_2.$$

The model allows the coefficients associated with each independent variable to differ by a scalar factor that depends on the pair of outcomes on the left-hand side of the equation. For example, in the equation comparing outcomes 1 and 2, the coefficient β_1 for x_1 is rescaled by the factor $\phi_1 - \phi_2$; for outcomes 1 and 3, by the factor $\phi_1 - \phi_3$; and for 2 and 3, by the factor $\phi_2 - \phi_3$. The same factors are also used for the coefficient for x_2. Similarly, the αs allow different intercepts for each pair of outcomes.

As the model stands, it is overparameterized (i.e., there are too many unconstrained αs and ϕs to allow the parameters to be uniquely determined) and constraints must be imposed to identify the model. The model can be identified in a variety of ways. For example, we can assume $\phi_1 = 1$, $\phi_J = 0$, $\alpha_1 = 1$, and $\alpha_J = 0$. Or, using the approach from log-linear models for ordinal outcomes, the model is identified by the constraints $\sum_{j=1}^{J} \phi_j = 0$ and $\sum_{j=1}^{J} \phi_j^2 = 1$. See DiPrete (1990) for further discussion.

The model we have presented above, which does *not* include any order restrictions, is commonly referred to as the stereotype model. However, Anderson (1984) referred to the model without ordering constraints as the 'ordered regression model'. The stereotype model includes additional constraints that insure the ordinality of the outcomes: $\phi_1 = 1 > \phi_2 > \ldots > \phi_{J-1} > \phi_J = 0$.

Equation (11.12) can be used to compute the predicted probabilities:

$$\Pr(y=m|\mathbf{x}) = \frac{\exp(\alpha_m \beta_0 + \phi_m \mathbf{x}\boldsymbol{\beta})}{\sum_{j=1}^{J} \exp(\alpha_j \beta_0 + \phi_j \mathbf{x}\boldsymbol{\beta})}.$$

This formula can be used for interpreting the model using methods discussed above. The model can also be interpreted in terms of the effect of a change in x_k on the odds of outcome q versus r. After rewriting equation (11.12) in terms of odds,

$$\Omega_{q|r}(\mathbf{x}, x_k) = \frac{\Pr(y=q)}{\Pr(y=r)} = \exp[(\alpha_q - \alpha_r)\beta_0$$
$$+ (\phi_q - \phi_r)\mathbf{x}\boldsymbol{\beta}],$$

it is easy to show that

$$\frac{\Omega_{q|r}(\mathbf{x}, x_k + 1)}{\Omega_{q|r}(\mathbf{x}, x_k)} = e^{(\phi_q - \phi_r)\beta_k} = \left(\frac{e^{\phi_q}}{e^{\phi_r}}\right)^{\beta_k}.$$

Thus the effect of x_k on the odds of q versus r differs across outcome comparisons according to the scaling coefficients ϕ.

DiPrete (1990) used a general ML program in GAUSS to estimate this model. Recently, Hendrickx's (2000) *mclest* command in Stata can also be used to estimate the model. Note that these programs do not impose the ordinality constraint $\phi_1 = 1 > \phi_2 > \ldots > \phi_{J-1} > \phi_J = 0$. Since the SORM is closely related to the multinomial logit model (MNLM), discussed below, the model can be informally assessed by examining the parameters from the MNLM to see if the structure of the stereotype model is approximated. This approach was taken by Greenwood and Farewell (1988).

Adjacent categories model

The adjacent categories model (Agresti, 1990: 318; Clogg and Shihadeh, 1994: 149–54) is a special case of the multinomial logit model considered in the next section. The model is specified as

$$\ln \left[\frac{\Pr(y=m \mid \mathbf{x})}{\Pr(y=m+1 \mid \mathbf{x})}\right] = \tau_m - \mathbf{x}\boldsymbol{\beta},$$

where the outcome is the log of the odds of category m versus category $m+1$. Note that the vector $\boldsymbol{\beta}$ is the same for all values of m. Taking exponentials,

$$\Omega_{m|m+1}(\mathbf{x}) = \frac{\Pr(y=m|\mathbf{x})}{\Pr(y=m+1|\mathbf{x})} = \exp(\tau_m - \mathbf{x}\boldsymbol{\beta}).$$

From this it follows readily that for a unit increase in x_k, $\Omega_{m|m+1}$ changes by a factor of $\exp(-\beta_k)$, holding all other variables constant.

Using simple but tedious algebra, these equations can be solved for the predicted probabilities:

$$\Pr(y = m \mid \mathbf{x}) = \frac{\exp\left(\sum_{r=m}^{J-1}[\tau_r - \mathbf{x}\boldsymbol{\beta}]\right)}{1 + \sum_{q=1}^{J-1}\left[\exp\left(\sum_{r=q}^{J-1}[\tau_r - \mathbf{x}\boldsymbol{\beta}]\right)\right]}$$

for $m = 1,\dots, J-1$

$$\Pr(y = J \mid \mathbf{x}) = 1 - \sum_{q=1}^{J-1}\Pr(y = q \mid \mathbf{x})$$

These probabilities can be used in the methods of interpretation that were discussed for the ORM.

The continuation ratio model

The *continuation ratio model* was proposed by Fienberg (1980: 110) and designed for ordinal outcomes in which the categories represent the progression of events or stages in some process through which an individual can advance.[8] For example, the outcome could be faculty rank, where the stages are assistant professor, associate professor, and full professor. A key characteristic of the process is that an individual must pass through each stage. For example, to become an associate professor you must be an assistant professor; to be a full professor, an associate professor. While there are versions of this model based on other binary models (e.g., probit), here we consider the logit version.

If $\Pr(y = m \mid \mathbf{x})$ is the probability of being in stage m given x, then the probability of being in stage m or later is

$$\Pr(y \geq m \mid \mathbf{x}) = \sum_{j=m}^{J}\Pr(y = j \mid \mathbf{x}).$$

The *conditional* probability of being in stage m given that you are in stage m or later (e.g., the probability of being an associate professor given that you have progressed from the rank of assistant professor) is

$$\Pr(y = m \mid y \geq m, \mathbf{x}) = \frac{\Pr(y = m \mid \mathbf{x})}{\Pr(y \geq m \mid \mathbf{x})}.$$

Accordingly, the probability of being beyond stage m is

$$\Pr(y > m \mid y \geq m, \mathbf{x}) = 1 - \Pr(y = m \mid y \geq m, \mathbf{x})$$

$$= \frac{\Pr(y > m \mid \mathbf{x})}{\Pr(y \geq m \mid \mathbf{x})}.$$

Using these probabilities, we can compute the odds of being in stage m compared to being past stage m, given that a respondent is in stage m or later:

$$\frac{\Pr(y = m \mid y \geq m, \mathbf{x})}{\Pr(y > m \mid y \geq m, \mathbf{x})} = \frac{\Pr(y = m \mid \mathbf{x})}{\Pr(y > m \mid \mathbf{x})}.$$

We can then construct a model for the log odds:

$$\ln\left[\frac{\Pr(y = m \mid \mathbf{x})}{\Pr(y > m \mid \mathbf{x})}\right] = \tau_m - \mathbf{x}\boldsymbol{\beta} \text{ for } m = 1,\dots, J-1,$$

where the $\boldsymbol{\beta}$s are constrained to be equal across outcome categories, while the constant term τ_m differs by stage. As with other logit models, we can also express the model in terms of the odds:

$$\frac{\Pr(y = m \mid \mathbf{x})}{\Pr(y > m \mid \mathbf{x})} = \exp(\tau_m - \mathbf{x}\boldsymbol{\beta}).$$

Accordingly, $\exp(-\beta_k)$ can be interpreted as the effect of a unit increase in x_k on the odds of being in m compared to being in a higher category, given that an individual is in category m or higher, holding all other variables constant.

The formula for the predicted probabilities highlights the structure of the model. The probability of $y = 1$ is computed from $\Pr(y = 1 \mid \mathbf{x})/\Pr(y > 1 \mid \mathbf{x}) = \exp(\tau_1 - \mathbf{x}\boldsymbol{\beta})$ just as in the model binary logit:

$$\Pr(y = 1 \mid \mathbf{x}) = \frac{\exp(\tau_1 - \mathbf{x}\boldsymbol{\beta})}{1 + \exp(\tau_1 - \mathbf{x}\boldsymbol{\beta})}.$$

The probability that $y = 2$ equals:

$$\Pr(y = 2 \mid \mathbf{x})$$
$$= \frac{\exp(\tau_2 - \mathbf{x}\boldsymbol{\beta})}{[1 + \exp(\tau_2 - \mathbf{x}\boldsymbol{\beta})][1 + \exp(\tau_1 - \mathbf{x}\boldsymbol{\beta})]}.$$

In general,

$$\Pr(y = m \mid \mathbf{x}) = \frac{\exp(\tau_m - \mathbf{x}\boldsymbol{\beta})}{\prod_{j=1}^{m}[1 + \exp(\tau_j - \mathbf{x}\boldsymbol{\beta})]}$$

for $m = 1,\dots, J-1,$

$$\Pr(y = J \mid \mathbf{x}) = 1 - \sum_{j=1}^{J-1}\Pr(y = j \mid \mathbf{x}).$$

These predicted probabilities can be used for interpreting the model.

For ordinal outcomes, we also recommend using models for nominal outcomes, which are now discussed. If a dependent variable is ordinal and a nominal model is used, there is a loss of efficiency since information is being ignored. On the other hand, when an ordinal model is applied to a nominal dependent variable, the resulting estimates are biased or nonsensical. Overall, if there are concerns about the ordinality of the dependent variable, the potential loss of efficiency in using models for nominal outcomes is outweighed by avoiding potential bias. Of course, these models must also be used when the dependent variable is nominal. We consider three closely related models: the multinomial logit model, the conditional logit model, and the multinomial probit model.

Multinomial logit

The MNLM can be thought of as simultaneously estimating binary logits for all comparisons among the outcome categories. Indeed, Begg and Gray (1984) show that estimates from binary logits are consistent estimates of the parameters of the MNLM. For example, let y be a nominal outcome with categories A, B, and C and suppose we have a single independent variable x. We can estimate the effect of x on y by running three binary logits:

$$\ln\left[\frac{\Pr(A|\mathbf{x})}{\Pr(B|\mathbf{x})}\right] = \beta_{0,A|B} + \beta_{1,A|B}x,$$

$$\ln\left[\frac{\Pr(B|\mathbf{x})}{\Pr(C|\mathbf{x})}\right] = \beta_{0,B|C} + \beta_{1,B|C}x,$$

$$\ln\left[\frac{\Pr(A|\mathbf{x})}{\Pr(C|\mathbf{x})}\right] = \beta_{0,A|C} + \beta_{1,A|C}x,$$

where the subscripts on the βs indicate which comparison is being made. The three binary logits include redundant information in the sense that the following equality must hold:

$$\ln\left[\frac{\Pr(A|x)}{\Pr(B|x)}\right] + \ln\left[\frac{\Pr(B|x)}{\Pr(C|x)}\right] = \ln\left[\frac{\Pr(A|x)}{\Pr(C|x)}\right].$$

This implies that

$$\beta_{0,A|B} + \beta_{0,B|C} = \beta_{0,A|C}$$
$$\beta_{1,A|B} + \beta_{1,B|C} = \beta_{1,A|C} \qquad (11.13)$$

Accordingly, if there are three outcomes, only two binary logits are needed since the remaining comparison can be derived. In general, with J outcomes, only $J-1$ binary logits are needed.

The problem with estimating the MNLM by a series of binary logits is that each binary logit is based on a different sample since only cases from two outcomes are used. Consequently, the equalities in equation (11.13) will not hold exactly. Programs for the MNLM *simultaneously* estimate the $J-1$ binary logits, thus insuring that the implied equalities hold. Specific packages differ in which comparisons are estimated. For example, one program might estimate $A|C$ and $B|C$, while another might estimate $A|B$ and $C|B$.

Formally, the MNLM can be written as

$$\Pr(y_i = m \mid \mathbf{x}_i) = \frac{\exp(\mathbf{x}_i\boldsymbol{\beta}_{m|r})}{\sum_{j=1}^{J} \exp(\mathbf{x}_i\boldsymbol{\beta}_{j|r})}, \qquad (11.14)$$

where r is the reference category used by the software estimating the model. Regardless of the reference category used, the predicted probability for a given outcome is identical. Alternatively, the model can be written in terms of logits,

$$\ln \Omega_{m|r}(\mathbf{x}_i) = \mathbf{x}_i\boldsymbol{\beta}_{m|r} \qquad (11.15)$$

or in terms of odds,

$$\Omega_{m|r}(\mathbf{x}_i) = \exp(\mathbf{x}_i\boldsymbol{\beta}_{m|r}). \qquad (11.16)$$

Note that with J dependent categories, there are $J-1$ non-redundant coefficients associated with each independent variable x_k. In our simple example, the coefficients $\beta_{1,A|C}$ and $\beta_{1,B|C}$ completely describe the effects of x on the three outcome categories. Accordingly, to test that a variable has no effect, you need to test that $J-1$ coefficients are simultaneously equal to zero. In our example, to test the effect of x the hypothesis is

$$H_0: \beta_{1,A|C} = \beta_{1,B|C} = 0.$$

Or, more generally, the hypothesis that x_k does not affect the dependent variable can be written as

$$H_0: \beta_{k,1|b} = \cdots = \beta_{k,J|b} = 0$$

Table 11.10   *Descriptive statistics for the occupational attainment example*

Name	Mean	Std dev.	Min	Max	Description
White	0.92	0.28	0.0	1.0	Race: 1= white; 0 = non-white.
Ed	13.10	2.95	3.0	20.0	Education: Number of years of formal education.
Exp	20.50	13.96	2.0	66.0	Possible years of work experience: Age minus years of education minus 5.

Note: N = 337.

where b is the base category. Since $\beta_{k,b|b}$ is necessarily 0, the hypothesis imposes constraints on $J-1$ parameters. This hypothesis can be tested with either a Wald or an LR test using standard procedures available with most packages that estimate the MNLM. Both types of test are distributed as chi-square with $J-1$ degrees of freedom.

Interpretation of the MNLM   While the MNLM is mathematically a simple extension of the binary model, interpretation is difficult due to the large number of possible comparisons. For example, with three outcomes you can compare 1|2, 1|3, and 2|3. With four outcomes, 1|2, 1|3, 1|4, 2|3, 2|4, and 3|4. And so on. To illustrate how to interpret the model, we consider the effects of race, education, and work experience on occupation.

The 1982 General Social Survey asked respondents their occupation. These occupations were recoded into five broad categories: menial jobs (M), blue-collar jobs (B), craft jobs (C), white-collar jobs (W), and professional jobs (P). This outcome is one that many would argue is ordered. However, as illustrated by Miller and Volker (1985), different orderings lead to different outcomes. Accordingly, a nominal model is appropriate. Three independent variables are considered, which are described in Table 11.10. The estimated coefficients in Table 11.11 are the standard output from a program that estimates the MNLM and correspond to the equations:

$$\ln \Omega_{B|M}(\mathbf{x}_i) = \beta_{0,B|M} + \beta_{1,B|M}\,\text{White}$$
$$+ \beta_{2,B|M}\text{Ed} + \beta_{3,B|M}\text{Exp},$$

$$\ln \Omega_{C|M}(\mathbf{x}_i) = \beta_{0,C|M} + \beta_{1,C|M}\,\text{White}$$
$$+ \beta_{2,C|M}\text{Ed} + \beta_{3,C|M}\text{Exp},$$

$$\ln \Omega_{W|M}(\mathbf{x}_i) = \beta_{0,W|M} + \beta_{1,W|M}\,\text{White}$$
$$+ \beta_{2,W|M}\text{Ed} + \beta_{3,W|M}\text{Exp},$$

$$\ln \Omega_{P|M}(\mathbf{x}_i) = \beta_{0,P|M} + \beta_{1,P|M}\,\text{White}$$
$$+ \beta_{2,P|M}\text{Ed} + \beta_{3,P|M}\text{Exp}.$$

The estimated coefficients can be plugged into equation (11.14) to compute predicted probabilities that can be used in the same way as shown for ordinal outcomes.

Marginal and discrete change can be used in the same way as in models for ordinal outcomes. Marginal change is defined as

$$\frac{\partial \Pr(y = m \mid \mathbf{x})}{\partial x_k} = \Pr(y = m \mid \mathbf{x})$$

$$\left[\beta_{k,m \mid J} - \sum_{j=1}^{J} \beta_{k,j \mid J} \Pr(y = j \mid \mathbf{x}) \right].$$

Since this equation combines all of the $\beta_{k,j|J}$s, the marginal effect of x_k on $\Pr(y = m|\mathbf{x})$ need not have the same sign as the corresponding coefficient $\beta_{k,m|J}$ (keep in mind that the $\beta_{k,j|J}$s are from equations for the odds of outcomes, not probabilities of being in various outcomes). Discrete change is defined as

$$\frac{\Delta \Pr(y = m \mid \mathbf{x})}{\Delta x_k} = \Pr(y = m \mid \mathbf{x}, x_k = x_E)$$
$$- \Pr(y = m \mid \mathbf{x}, x_k = x_S).$$

One difficulty with nominal outcomes is the large number of coefficients that need to be considered: one for each variable times the number of outcome categories. A plot, such as Figure 11.11, can help you see the pattern in the effects. In this case it is easy to see that the effects of education are largest and those of experience are smallest. Alternatively, each coefficient can be interpreted individually, for example, the effects of a standard deviation change in education are largest, with an increase in the probability of over 0.35 for professional occupations. The effects of race are also substantial, with average blacks being less likely to enter blue-collar, white-collar, or professional jobs. The expected changes due to a standard deviation change in experience are much smaller and show that experience increases the probabilities of more highly skilled occupations.

Table 11.11 *Logit coefficients for an MNLM model of occupational attainment*

Comparison		Constant	White	Ed	Exp
			Logit coefficient for		
B|M	β	0.741	1.237	−0.099	0.0047
	z	0.49	1.71	−0.97	0.27
C|M	β	−1.091	0.472	0.094	0.0277
	z	−0.75	0.78	0.96	1.66
W|M	β	−6.239	1.571	0.353	0.0346
	z	−3.29	1.74	3.01	1.84
P|M	β	−11.518	1.774	0.779	0.0357
	z	−6.23	2.35	6.79	1.98

Note: N = 337. β is a logit coefficient for the indicated comparison; z is a z-value. Job types: M = menial; B = blue-collar; C = craft; W = white-collar; P = professional.

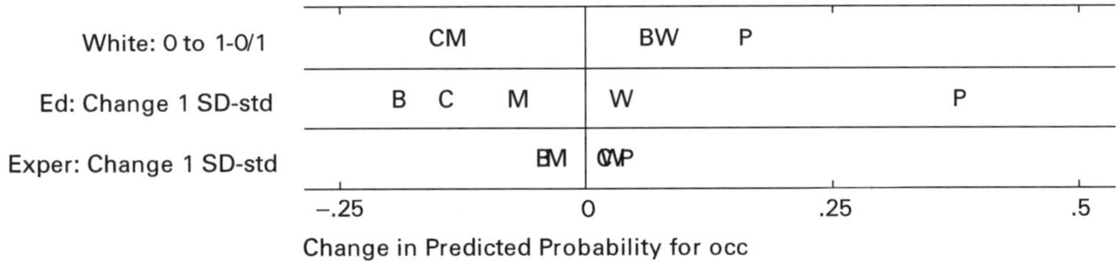

Figure 11.11 *A discrete change plot for the MNLM of occupations. Control variables are held at their means. Jobs are classified as: M = menial; C = craft; B = blue-collar; W = white-collar; and P = professional. 0 → 1 is a change from 0 to 1; Δσ is a change of one standard deviation centered around the mean.*

While discrete change is useful, it is essential to remember that different values are obtained at different levels of the variables. Further, discrete change does not indicate the dynamics among the dependent outcomes. For example, a decrease in education increases the probability of both blue-collar and craft jobs, but how does it affect the odds of a person choosing a craft job relative to a blue-collar job? To deal with these issues, the odds ratios can be used.

As with the binary model, the factor change in the odds of one outcome compared to another is a simple transformation of the estimated coefficients:

$$\frac{\Omega_{m|n}(\mathbf{x}, x_k + \delta)}{\Omega_{m|n}(\mathbf{x}, x_k)} = e^{\beta_{k, m|n}\delta}.$$

This odds ratio says that, for a unit change in x_k, the odds are expected to change by a factor of $\exp(\beta_{k,m|n})$, holding all other variables constant, and that for a standard deviation change in x_k, the odds are expected to change by a factor of $\exp(\beta_{k,m|n}s_k)$, holding all other variables constant.

To illustrate how to interpret the odds ratios for the MNLM, consider the coefficients for the effect of race on occupational attainment. These are shown in Table 11.12. The odds ratio for the effect of race on having a professional versus a menial job is 5.90, which means that the odds of having a professional occupation relative to a menial occupation are 5.9 times as great for whites as for blacks, holding education and experience constant.

To fully understand the effects of race, the coefficients for comparisons among all pairs of outcomes should be considered, even though they provide redundant information. However, to consider all of the coefficients for even a single variable with only five dependent categories is complicated. Consequently, we recommend that these coefficients be plotted (see Long, 1997: Chapter 6

Table 11.12 *Odds ratios for the effects of race on occupational attainment*

Factor change in the odds of *m* vs *n*			Outcome *n*				
			M	B	C	W	P
Outcome	M	Menial	–	0.29	0.62	0.21	0.17
m	B	Blue-collar	3.44	–	2.15	0.72	0.58
	C	Craft	1.60	0.47	–	0.33	0.27
	W	White-collar	4.81	1.40	3.00	–	0.82
	P	Professional	5.90	1.71	3.68	1.23	–

Note: The coefficients in the table are exp $(\hat{\beta}_{1,m|n})$.

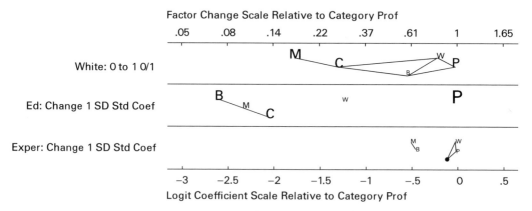

Figure 11.12 *Odds ratio plot with the size of letters corresponding to the magnitude of the discrete change in the probability (computed with all variables held at their means). Jobs are classified as: M = menial; C = craft; B = blue-collar; W = white-collar; and P = professional. The superscript S indicates that the odds ratios are being plotted for a standard deviation change of the variable.*

for full details), as illustrated in Figure 11.12. In this plot, the outcome categories are indicated by letters. Distances between letters for a given variable indicate the magnitude of the corresponding $\beta_{k,m|n}$ (i.e., the coefficient for independent variable x_k for outcome *m* versus *n*) when measured using the logit coefficient scale at the bottom. The scale at the top indicates the factor change $\exp(\beta_{k,m|n})$. The size of the letters is proportional to the square of the discrete change that was plotted in Figure 11.11. The square is used so that the area of the letter corresponds to the size of the discrete change. The graph shows that race orders occupations from menial to craft to blue-collar to white-collar to professional. The dotted lines show that none of the adjacent categories is significantly differentiated by race. Being white increases the odds of being a craft worker relative to having a menial job, but the effect is not significant. However, being white significantly increases the odds of being a blue-collar

worker, a white-collar worker, or a professional relative to having a menial job. The effects of Ed and Exp can be interpreted similarly.

The conditional logit model

The conditional logit model (CLM) is closely related to the MNLM.[9] The key difference is that in the CLM each independent variable is measured for each outcome category. For example, in modeling which mode of transportation people use for commuting, we might consider three modes of travel: train, car, and bus. The amount of time it takes to get to work depends on the mode of transportation and specific characteristics of an individual. For example, if you live next to a bus stop, your time by bus will be less than that of someone who has a 30-minute walk to the bus stop. Thus, each independent variable is defined for each outcome category. This information is entered into the CLM as follows:

$$\Pr(y_i = m | \mathbf{z}_i) = \frac{\exp(\mathbf{z}_{im}\boldsymbol{\gamma})}{\sum_{j=1}^{J} \exp(\mathbf{z}_{ij}\boldsymbol{\gamma})} . \qquad (11.17)$$

This equation can be compared to the MNLM:

$$\Pr(y_i = m | \mathbf{x}_i) = \frac{\exp(\mathbf{x}_i \boldsymbol{\beta}_{m|J})}{\sum_{j=1}^{J} \exp(\mathbf{x}_i \boldsymbol{\beta}_{j|J})} . \qquad (11.18)$$

In equation (11.18) there are $J-1$ parameters $\beta_{k,m|r}$ for each x_k, but only a single value of x_k for each individual. In equation (11.17) there is a single γ_k for each variable z_k, but there are J values of the variable for each individual.

Applications of the CLM are relatively rare outside the area of travel demand analysis (where the method was initially developed) since appropriate data are not readily available. Hoffman and Duncan (1988), however, provide a useful comparison of multinomial and conditional logit models applied to outcomes of marriage and welfare status. They also consider a mixed model that includes elements of both models.

Independence of irrelevant alternatives

In both the MNLM and the CLM, there is an implicit assumption referred to as the *independence of irrelevant alternatives* (IIA). To understand this assumption, note that the odds in these models do not depend on other outcomes that might be available:

$$\frac{\Pr(y = m | \mathbf{x})}{\Pr(y = n | \mathbf{x})} = \exp(\mathbf{x}[\boldsymbol{\beta}_{m|J} - \boldsymbol{\beta}_{n|J}]),$$

$$\frac{\Pr(y = m | \mathbf{z})}{\Pr(y = n | \mathbf{z})} = \exp([\mathbf{z}_m - \mathbf{z}_n]\boldsymbol{\gamma}).$$

This implies that adding or deleting outcomes does not affect the odds among the remaining outcomes. This point is often made with the red bus/blue bus example attributed to McFadden. Suppose that you have the choice of a red bus or a car to get to work and that the odds of taking a red bus compared to a car are 1:1. IIA implies that the odds will remain 1:1 between these two alternatives if a new bus company comes to town that is identical to the red bus company except for the color of the bus. Thus, the probability of driving a car can be made arbitrarily small by adding enough different colors of buses! More reasonably, we would expect that the odds of

a red bus compared to a car would be reduced to 1:2 since half of those riding the red bus would be expected to ride the blue bus.

There are two tests of the IIA assumption. Hausman and McFadden (1984) proposed a Hausman-type test and McFadden et al. (1976) proposed an approximate LR test that was improved by Small and Hsiao (1985). Details on computing these tests can be found in Zhang and Hoffman (1993) or Long (1997: Chapter 6). Our experience with these tests is that they often give inconsistent results and in practice provide little guidance as to violations of the IIA assumption. Unfortunately, there do not appear to be simulation studies that examine their small-sample properties. Perhaps as a result of the practical limitations of these tests, McFadden (1973) suggested that IIA implies that the multinomial and conditional logit models should only be used in cases where the outcome categories 'can plausibly be assumed to be distinct and weighed independently in the eyes of each decision maker'. Similarly, Amemiya (1981: 1517) suggests that the MNLM works well when the alternatives are dissimilar. Care in specifying the model to involve distinct outcomes that are not substitutes for one another seems to be reasonable, even if unfortunately ambiguous, advice.

Multinomial probit

While logit and probit models for binary and ordinal outcomes are essentially equivalent, the multinomial probit model (MNPM), initially proposed by Aitchison and Bennett (1970), has important features that are not found in the MNLM. In particular, the MNPM does not require the IIA assumption. However, until recently, the computations necessary for estimating the MNPM made the model impractical for all but the simplest applications. Recent work by McFadden (1989) has made progress in solving the computational problems and there are at least two programs that can estimate the MNPM: Limdep (Greene, 1995) and GAUSSX (Breslaw, 2002). Now that estimation is computationally feasible for modestly sized models, the focus has turned to issues of identification (Keane, 1992), which are discussed below.

The MNPM is generally developed as a discrete choice model, which we will do using three outcome categories. See Pudney (1989) for a detailed discussion or Long (1997:

Chapter 6) for an introduction. Let u_j be the utility associated with choice j. Then,

$$u_1 = \mathbf{x}\boldsymbol{\beta}_1 + \varepsilon_1,$$
$$u_2 = \mathbf{x}\boldsymbol{\beta}_2 + \varepsilon_2,$$
$$u_3 = \mathbf{x}\boldsymbol{\beta}_3 + \varepsilon_3,$$

where $\mathbf{x}$ is a vector of independent variables and ε_j is the error for outcome j. In the MNPM, the εs are assumed to have a multivariate normal distribution with mean zero and

$$\text{cov}\begin{pmatrix}\varepsilon_1 \\ \varepsilon_2 \\ \varepsilon_3\end{pmatrix} = \begin{pmatrix}\sigma_1^2 & \sigma_{12} & \sigma_{13} \\ \sigma_{21} & \sigma_2^2 & \sigma_{23} \\ \sigma_{31} & \sigma_{32} & \sigma_3^2\end{pmatrix}.$$

The correlated errors avoid the restriction of IIA. For example, in the red bus/blue bus example we would expect the errors to be negatively correlated to reflect that these options are close substitutes. If the εs have an extreme value distribution, the resulting model is the MNLM, where the IIA assumption is necessary since $\text{cov}(\varepsilon)$ must be diagonal for the extreme value distribution.

The outcome chosen by an individual is based on a comparison of the utilities associated with the choices. An individual chooses outcome j over outcome k if $u_j > u_k$. For example,

$$\Pr(1 \text{ over } 2|\mathbf{x}) = \Pr([\mathbf{x}\boldsymbol{\beta}_1 + \varepsilon_1] > [\mathbf{x}\boldsymbol{\beta}_2 + \varepsilon_2])$$
$$= \Pr([\varepsilon_1 - \varepsilon_2] > [\mathbf{x}\boldsymbol{\beta}_2 - \mathbf{x}\boldsymbol{\beta}_1]),$$

$$\Pr(1 \text{ over } 3|\mathbf{x}) = \Pr([\mathbf{x}\boldsymbol{\beta}_1 + \varepsilon_1] > [\mathbf{x}\boldsymbol{\beta}_3 + \varepsilon_3])$$
$$= \Pr([\varepsilon_1 - \varepsilon_3] > [\mathbf{x}\boldsymbol{\beta}_3 - \mathbf{x}\boldsymbol{\beta}_1]).$$

Accordingly, the probability of choosing outcome 1 would be

$$\Pr(1|\mathbf{x}) = \Pr([1 \text{ over } 2]$$
$$\text{and } [1 \text{ over } 3]|\mathbf{x}).$$

The last quantity involves multiple integrals, which leads to computational difficulties in estimating the MNPM. In our experience, for a multinomial logit model that can be estimated in a minute, the corresponding probit model might take hours to estimate.

The model is not identified unless restrictions are placed on $\text{cov}(\varepsilon)$, an issue that is discussed by Keane (1992). Without restrictions, a proportional change in all elements of $\text{cov}(\varepsilon)$ and the βs does not affect the probabilities. And adding a constant to each β_0 leaves the probabilities unchanged since it is only the difference in utilities that determines the choice. Standard identification conditions involve normalizing the variance of

one alternative and restricting the utility function to 0. Formally, the model can be identified by setting $u_3 = 0$ and $\sigma_1 = 1$, as follows:

$$u_1 = \mathbf{x}\boldsymbol{\beta}_1 + \varepsilon_1,$$
$$u_2 = \mathbf{x}\boldsymbol{\beta}_2 + \varepsilon_2,$$
$$u_3 = 0,$$

with covariance matrix

$$\text{cov}\begin{pmatrix}\varepsilon_1 \\ \varepsilon_2\end{pmatrix} = \begin{pmatrix}1 & \sigma_{12} \\ \sigma_{21} & \sigma_2^2\end{pmatrix}.$$

While these conditions *formally identify* the model, Keane finds that this identification is fragile. That is, additional restrictions beyond those required for formal identification are necessary in order to avoid the substantial risk of obtaining unreliable results. Our experience in experiment with the MNPM leads us to fully endorse Keane's (1992) statement: 'Given the lack of practical experience with [multinomial probit] models, however, there is a need to develop a "folklore" concerning the conditions under which the model performs well.' Thus, while the MNPM appears to offer substantial advantages over the MNLM in avoiding the IIA assumption, in practice this model remains difficult to use.

CONCLUSIONS

In this chapter we have considered what we believe are the most basic and useful models for the analysis of categorical dependent variables. However, in the limited space available, it is impossible to consider all of the important issues related to these models. Topics that have not been discussed include: robust, exact, and nonparametric methods of estimation, specification tests (Davidson and MacKinnon, 1993: 522–8; Greene, 2000: 827–31), complex sampling, multiple equation systems (see Browne and Arminger, 1995, for a review), and hierarchical models (Longford, 1995: 551–6).

There are several sources that we recommend for obtaining further information. Maddala (1983) considers dozens of models for categorical and limited dependent variables. McCullagh and Nelder (1989) discuss some of the same models from the standpoint of the generalized linear model. King (1989) presents many of these models with particular application to political science. Agresti (1990) is particularly useful if all of your variables are nominal or ordinal. Powers and Xie (2000) consider both regression models and log-linear models. Greene's (1995) Limdep will estimate many of the models discussed here as well as many others; the manual provides a wealth of information. Finally, our review has not considered the many useful models for count outcomes (e.g., how many times a person went to a doctor, how many patents a company received). Fortunately, Cameron and Trivedi (1998) provide an extensive review of these models; Long (1997: Chapter 8) provides a more elementary introduction.

Until recently, the models considered in this chapter required specialized software. Now, however, each of these models can easily be estimated on typical desktop computer (with the exception of the MNPM). A detailed discussion of the use of SAS for these models is found in Allison (1999). Long and Freese (2001) provide information on estimating these models in Stata and give a series of commands that facilitate the types of interpretation that we recommend. Since many packages do not make it simple to compute many of the quantities that we find useful for interpretation, Cheng and Long have written a series of Excel files that facilitate post-estimation interpretation (see http://www.indiana.edu/~jslsoc/xpost.htm).

ACKNOWLEDGMENTS

This chapter draws on the more detailed presentation in Long (1997). Examples of software to estimate the models considered in this paper can be found at www.indiana.edu/~jslsoc/rm4cldv.htm. We would like to thank Melissa Hardy and an anonymous reviewer for their valuable comments.

NOTES

1 The use of the LRM with a binary dependent variable leads to the linear probability model. However, nonlinear models for binary outcomes, discussed in this chapter, have key advantages over the linear probability model, as discussed below.

2 The α, β, and δ parameters in this equation are unrelated to those in Figure 11.1.

3 A full discussion of ML estimation is beyond the scope of this chapter; see Long (1997) for a general overview, Eliason (1993) for a more detailed introduction, and Cramer (1986) for a more advanced discussion.

4 These data were generously made available by Thomas Mroz.

5 Note, however, that since equation (11.7) is a binary logit for any given m, the sign of an estimated β indicates the direction of the effect of a variable on the probability of being less than or equal to some category.

6 The name of this model appears to come from a line in Anderson (1984) in which he discusses how cases might be allocated to ordinal outcomes: 'One possibility is that the judge has loose stereotypes for each category and that a new case for categorization is fitted into the most appropriate category.'

7 The stereotype model can be set up in several different ways. For example, in some presentations, it is assumed that $\beta_0 = 0$ and fewer constraints are imposed on the αs. Here we parameterize the model to highlight its links to other models that we consider.

8 For a discussion of the links between this model and survival analysis, see Allison (1995).

9 Indeed, the CLM can be used to estimate the MNLM. This is often useful since programs for CLM allow constraints to be added that are not easy to impose in programs for the MNLM.

REFERENCES

Agresti, A. (1990) *Categorical Data Analysis*. New York: Wiley.

Aitchison, J. and Bennett, J. (1970) 'Polychotomous quantal response by maximum indicant', *Biometrika*, 57: 253–62.

Allison, P.D. (1995) *Survival Analysis Using the SAS System*. Cary, NC: SAS Institute, Inc.

Allison, P.D. (1999) *Logistic Regression Using the SAS System: Theory and Application*. Cary, NC: SAS Institute, Inc.

Amemiya, T. (1981) 'Qualitative response models: A survey', *Journal of Economic Literature*, 19: 1483–1536.

Anderson, J.A. (1984) 'Regression and ordered categorical variables (with discussion)', *Journal of the Royal Statistical Society Series B*, 46: 1–30.

Begg, C.B. and Gray, R. (1984) 'Calculation of polychotomous logistic regression parameters using individualized regressions', *Biometrika*, 71: 11–8.

Brant, R. (1990) 'Assessing proportionality in the proportional odds model for ordinal logistic regression', *Biometrics*, 46: 1171–8.

Breslaw, J. (2002). *GAUSSX Version 5.0*. Westmount, PQ: Econotron Software (http://www.econotron.com/gaussx/download/gaussx.pdf).

Browne, M.W. and Arminger, G. (1995) 'Specification and estimation of mean- and covariance-structures models', in G. Arminger, C.C. Clogg, and M.E. Sobel (eds), *Handbook of Statistical Modeling for the Social and Behavioral Sciences*. New York: Plenum Press, pp. 185–249.

Cameron, A.C. and Trivedi, P.K. (1998) *Regression Analysis of Count Data*. New York: Cambridge University Press.

Clogg, C.C. and Shihadeh, E.S. (1994) *Statistical Models for Ordinal Variables*. Thousand Oaks, CA: Sage.

Cook, R.D. and Weisberg, S. (1999) *Applied Regression Including Computing and Graphics*. New York: Wiley.

Cramer, J.S. (1986) *Econometric Applications of Maximum Likelihood Methods*. Cambridge: Cambridge University Press.

Cytel Software Corporation (2000) *LogXact Version 4*. Cambridge, MA: Cytel Software Corporation.

Davidson, R. and MacKinnon, J.G. (1993) *Estimation and Inference in Econometrics*. New York: Oxford University Press.

DiPrete, T.A. (1990) 'Adding covariates to loglinear models for the study of social mobility', *American Sociological Review*, 55: 757–73.

Eliason, S. (1993) *Maximum Likelihood Estimation*. Newbury Park, CA: Sage.

Fahrmeir, L. and Tutz, G. (1994) *Multivariate Statistical Modeling Based on Generalized Linear Models*. Springer Series in Statistics. New York: Springer-Verlag.

Fienberg, S.E. (1980) *The Analysis of Cross-Classified Categorical Data* (2nd edition). Cambridge, MA: MIT Press.

Fu, V.K. (1998) 'sg88: Estimating generalized ordered logit models', *Stata Technical Bulletin*, 44: 27–30.

Greene, W.H. (1995) *LIMDEP Version 7.0*. Bellport, NY: Econometric Software.

Greene, W.H. (2000). *Econometric Analysis* (4th edition). Upper Saddle River, NJ: Prentice Hall.

Greenwood, C. and Farewell, V. (1988) 'A comparison of regression models for ordinal data in an analysis of transplanted-kidney Function', *Canadian Journal of Statistics*, 16: 325–35.

Hausman, J.A. and McFadden, D. (1984) 'Specification tests for the multinomial logit model', *Econometrica*, 52: 1219–40.

Hendrickx, J. (2000) 'sbe37: Special restrictions in multinomial logistic regression', *Stata Technical Bulletin*, 56: 18–26.

Hoffman, S.D. and Duncan, G.J. (1988). 'Multinomial and conditional logit discrete-choice models in demography', *Demography*, 25: 415–27.

Kaufman, R.L. (1996) 'Comparing effects in dichotomous logistic regression: A variety of standardized coefficients', *Social Science Quarterly*, 77: 90–109.

Keane, M.P. (1992). 'A note on identification in the multinomial probit model', *Journal of Business and Economic Statistics*, 10: 193–200.

King, G. (1989) *Unifying Political Methodology: The Likelihood Theory of Statistical Inference*. Cambridge: Cambridge University Press.

Long, J.S. (1997) *Regression Models for Categorical and Limited Dependent Variables*. Thousand Oaks, CA: Sage.

Long, J.S. and Freese, J. (2001) *Regression Models for Categorical Dependent Variables Using Stata*. College Station, TX: Stata Press.

Longford, N.T. (1995) 'Random coefficient models', in G. Arminger, C.C. Clogg and M.E. Sobel (eds) *Handbook of Statistical Modeling for the Social and Behavioral Sciences*. New York: Plenum Press, pp. 519–77.

Maddala, G.S. (1983) *Limited-Dependent and Qualitative Variables in Econometrics*. Cambridge: Cambridge University Press.

McCullagh, P. (1980) 'Regression models for ordinal data (with discussion)', *Journal of Royal Statistical Society Series B*, 42: 109–42.

McCullagh, P. and Nelder, J.A. (1989) *Generalized Linear Models* (2nd edition). New York: Chapman & Hall.

McFadden, D. (1973) 'Conditional logit analysis of qualitative choice behavior', in P. Zarembka (ed.), *Frontiers of Econometrics*. New York: Academic Press, pp. 105–42.

McFadden, D. (1989) 'A method of simulated moments for estimation of discrete response models without numerical integration', *Econometrica*, 57: 995–1026.

McFadden, D., Tye, W. and Train, K. (1976) 'An application of diagnostic tests for the independence from irrelevant alternatives property of the multinomial logit model', *Transportation Research Board Record*, 637: 39–45.

McKelvey, R.D. and Zavoina, W. (1975) 'A statistical model for the analysis of ordinal level dependent variables', *Journal of Mathematical Sociology*, 4: 103–20.

Miller, P.W. and Volker, P.A. (1985) 'On the determination of occupational attainment and mobility', *Journal of Human Resources*, 20: 197–213.

Mroz, T.A. (1987) 'The sensitivity of an empirical model of married women's hours of work to economic and statistical assumptions', *Econometrica*, 55: 765–99.

Powers, D.A. and Xie, Y. (2000) *Statistical Methods for Categorical Data Analysis*. San Diego, CA: Academic Press.

Pregibon, D. (1981) 'Logistic regression diagnostics', *Annals of Statistics*, 9: 705–24.

Pudney, S. (1989) *Modelling Individual Choice: The Econometrics of Corners, Kinks and Holes*. Oxford: Basil Blackwell.

SAS Institute (1990) *SAS/STAT User's Guide. Version 6* (4th edition). Cary, NC: SAS Institute, Inc.

Small, K.A. and Hsiao, C. (1985) 'Multinomial logit specification tests', *International Economic Review*, 26: 619–27.

Theil, H. (1970) 'On the estimation of relationships involving qualitative variables', *American Journal of Sociology*, 76: 103–54.

Wolfe, R. and Gould, W. (1998) 'sg76: An approximate likelihood ratio test for ordinal regression models', *Stata Technical Bulletin*, 42: 24–7.

Zhang, J. and Hoffman, S.D. (1993) 'Discrete-choice logit models: Testing the IIA property', *Sociological Methods and Research*, 22: 193–213.

12

Log-Linear Analysis

DOUGLAS L. ANDERTON AND ERIC CHENEY

Outcomes of interest to social scientists are most frequently measured as categories. So it is not surprising that methods for the analysis of categorical outcomes, such as those in Chapter 11, are among the most widely used and published statistical methods in the social sciences. This chapter also discusses methods for the analysis of categorical data, but with a somewhat different emphasis. The log-linear model discussed in this chapter can be viewed as a special case of both the regression models for categorical data of Chapter 11 and of event-history models in Chapter 16. What distinguishes the model and examples of this chapter are largely their emphasis on explaining the frequency of categorical outcomes and a historical emphasis in log-linear modeling on the patterns of interrelationships among categorical variables.

Many different substantive fields have contributed to the development of log-linear models. Agresti (1990) provides a historical overview of these diverse developments, and Powers and Xie (2000) discuss resulting differences in the philosophies of categorical data analysis. Given the history of log-linear models, many readers will associate such models with the analysis of cross-classified data or contingency tables (e.g., Fienberg, 1977; Goodman, 1978), and the sometimes unique notation or algorithms associated with this special case. In this chapter, however, we follow the more unifying approach of recent texts (e.g., Long, 1997; Powers and Xie, 2000), presenting these models as a special case of the general linear model. Nonetheless, most of the

chapter is devoted to the application of this general model to the analysis of cross-classified data before concluding with some more general applications of the model.

THE LOG-LINEAR MODEL

A major attraction of log-linear models is that they provide the researcher with the statistical methods to model categorical variables and their interrelationships through a set of estimation and modeling strategies similar to conventional regression. The log-linear model predicts the frequency or count of category outcomes as a linear combination of a matrix of independent variables and a vector of coefficients. As such, log-linear models are a special case of the general linear model. The general log-linear model is specified as

$$\ln\left(\frac{\mathbf{m}}{\mathbf{z}}\right) = \mathbf{X}'\hat{\boldsymbol{\beta}} + \boldsymbol{\varepsilon}, \qquad (12.1)$$

where $\mathbf{m}$ is a vector of n dependent values or frequencies, $\mathbf{z}$ is a vector of n fixed denominators or exposures to risk, $\hat{\boldsymbol{\beta}}$ is a vector of k estimated coefficients, $\mathbf{X}$ is an $n \times k$ matrix of independent variable values, and $\boldsymbol{\varepsilon}$ is a vector of n error terms. Alternatively, we may write

$$\ln\left(\frac{m_i}{z_i}\right) = \hat{\beta}_1 x_{i1} + \hat{\beta}_2 x_{i2} + \dots + \hat{\beta}_k x_{ik} + \varepsilon_i. \quad (12.2)$$

When faced with categorical data, the researcher typically analyzes the counts of outcomes or events and the statistics derived from such counts, including proportions, percentages, odds, probabilities, and so forth. Counts of events are typically presented in frequency or contingency tables. Such tables show the distribution of outcomes for each variable conditional on the distribution of the other variables. Log-linear frequency models allow for a regression approach to model the interrelationships in such data.

We will refer to the model in which z in equation (12.1) is fixed to a vector of ones as the log-linear *frequency* model, since the dependent variable of equation (12.1) is then simply a vector of the log of frequencies. When the vector z is fixed to a number of trials, a population at risk, or a population duration exposed to risk, from which m is a vector of the number of successes or events, we will refer to the model as the *log-rate* model. In this case the left-hand side of equation (12.1) is the log of rates comprised of a variable frequency of outcomes m among a fixed exposure to risk z.

It is helpful to think of this as analogous to ordinary least-squares regression with a quantitative dependent variable. That is, while ordinary least-squares regression models $E(Y|X)$, or the mean value of Y given X, log-linear analysis models the *expected counts* of Y given X. Since counts within sets and subsets are the building blocks of probability, log-linear analysis ultimately allows the researcher to study the effects of independent variables on the probability, odds, and relative risks of events. The following example illustrates the basic regression approach.

Illustration of regression approach to a frequency model

In this example, we will use data from the 1996 Survey of Income and Program Participation (SIPP: US Bureau of the Census, 1996).[1] The data file is conditioned to contain only those people aged 18 years or older who are currently married and whose spouse is present. We are interested in whether there is a relationship between husband's status of first marriage (i.e., not previously married) and wife's status of first marriage. Table 12.1 is produced from these data.

For this example, we will use a frequency model, that is, z_i is a constant equal to one. To

Table 12.1 *First marriage among married couples*

	First marriage	Husband Yes	No	Total
Wife	Yes	13 045	1 663	14 708
	No	1 441	2 438	3 879
	Total	14 486	4 101	18 587

obtain some desirable statistical properties to be discussed later, we want to model the log of counts in each of the cells in Table 12.1 as our dependent variable. In matrix terms, the parameterization of our model is

$$\ln \begin{bmatrix} 13\,045 \\ 1\,663 \\ 1\,441 \\ 2\,438 \end{bmatrix} = \begin{bmatrix} 9.477 \\ 7.416 \\ 7.273 \\ 7.799 \end{bmatrix} = \begin{pmatrix} 1 & 1 & 1 & 1 \\ 1 & 1 & 0 & 0 \\ 1 & 0 & 1 & 0 \\ 1 & 0 & 0 & 0 \end{pmatrix} \times \begin{bmatrix} \hat{\beta}_0 \\ \hat{\beta}_1 \\ \hat{\beta}_2 \\ \hat{\beta}_3 \end{bmatrix} + \begin{bmatrix} \varepsilon_1 \\ \varepsilon_2 \\ \varepsilon_3 \\ \varepsilon_4 \end{bmatrix}.$$

(12.3)

Alternatively,

$$\ln(m_i) = \hat{\beta}_0 + \hat{\beta}_1 w_i + \hat{\beta}_2 h_i + \hat{\beta}_3 wh_i + \varepsilon_i. \quad (12.4)$$

The interpretation of this equation is straightforward. $\hat{\beta}_0$ and the first column in the X matrix model a constant effect on the cells of the table. This constant applies to all cells of the table and x_{i1} is coded 1 for all cases. $\hat{\beta}_1$ and the second column of X model the effect on frequency of couples where the wife is in her first marriage. This effect applies only to the two cells where the wife is first married, as specified by these cases being coded 1 in the second column of the design matrix X. $\hat{\beta}_2$ and the third column of X represent couples where the husband is in his first marriage, and x_{i3} is coded 1 only for the appropriate cells of cases. The final column of X and $\hat{\beta}_3$ model the interaction effect of first marriage, or the intersection of both husband and wife being in their first marriage, which applies to only one cell of the table.[2]

With the model parameterized as above, we may use maximum likelihood estimation to obtain solutions to the unknown coefficients. Let us assume we carry out such a procedure and obtain the vector of $\hat{\beta}$ estimates.[3] Estimating $\hat{\beta}$ yields the following linear equation:[4]

$$\ln \begin{bmatrix} 13\,045 \\ 1\,663 \\ 1\,441 \\ 2\,438 \end{bmatrix} = \begin{bmatrix} 9.477 \\ 7.416 \\ 7.273 \\ 7.799 \end{bmatrix} = \begin{pmatrix} 1 & 1 & 1 & 1 \\ 1 & 1 & 0 & 0 \\ 1 & 0 & 1 & 0 \\ 1 & 0 & 0 & 0 \end{pmatrix} \times \begin{bmatrix} 7.799 \\ -0.383 \\ -0.526 \\ 2.586 \end{bmatrix} + \begin{bmatrix} 0 \\ 0 \\ 0 \\ 0 \end{bmatrix}.$$

(12.5)

Table 12.2   *Predicting log frequencies*

		Husband	
	First marriage	Yes	No
Wife	Yes	$\hat{\beta}_0 + \hat{\beta}_1 + \hat{\beta}_2 + \hat{\beta}_3 = 9.477$	$\hat{\beta}_0 + \hat{\beta}_1 = 7.416$
	No	$\hat{\beta}_0 + \hat{\beta}_2 = 7.273$	$\hat{\beta}_0 = 7.799$

Like all regression models, a non-zero and significant coefficient implies an effect on the dependent variables. In this model the main effects – the marginal effects of each variable by itself – are given by $\hat{\beta}_1$ and $\hat{\beta}_2$. If these effects are significant then the distribution of individuals varies by wife, or husband, being first married, respectively. Frequently we expect main effects to be significant and to mirror what we already know about the distribution of cases across marginal outcomes. So, in log-linear analysis we are often more interested in interaction terms which reveal relationships among the categorical variables. The coefficient for the interaction term $\hat{\beta}_3$ is a significantly positive value, $\hat{\beta}_3 = 2.586$. This implies a positive relationship between males with first-marriage status and females with first-marriage status, since this combination of traits will increase the predicted frequencies.

Table 12.2 presents the coefficients used to predict the log of **Y**. When looking at Table 12.2 one sees how the effects replicate certain cells of the table after canceling out coefficient terms for corresponding dummy variables with zero values in the design matrix for equation (12.4). Table 12.2 thus helps visualize the effects of variables conditioning on the different levels of the variables and the interaction term.

The predicted log frequency for couples where wives and husbands are both not in first marriages (i.e., are previously married) is simply given by the coefficient $\hat{\beta}_0 = 7.799$. These are the individuals coded zero (i.e., the excluded category) in each column of **X** other than the first. In other cells of the table predicted frequencies are higher or lower than these excluded category cases, depending upon the value of estimated co-efficients which apply to the cell. A positive coefficient indicates cases are more likely than the excluded category, while a negative value indicates they are less likely. In the presence of significant interaction terms it is necessary to condition the interpretation of the estimated coefficients at certain values of the other independent variables. For example, in the vector $\hat{\boldsymbol{\beta}}$ of coefficients above we see

that the effect of a wife being in her first marriage is $\hat{\beta}_1 = -0.383$ when the husband is not in his first marriage, that is, $x_{i3} = 0$. We may interpret this to mean that a unit change in the status of first marriage – meaning wives in their first marriage versus wives who have been through a divorce – results in a -0.383 change in the logged frequencies when their husbands are not in their first marriage. However, since the effect of having only one marriage among women depends on the status of first-time marriage among husbands, we must carry the interpretation further. Thus, for women with only one marriage with husbands of only one marriage, the total effect is $\hat{\beta}_1 + \hat{\beta}_2 + \hat{\beta}_3 = 0.383 + (-0.526) + 2.586 = 1.678$. The total effect of 1.678 on the log frequencies suggests that women in their first marriage with first-time marriage husbands are more common, increasing the predicted log frequency to $7.799 + 1.678 = 9.477$. In contrast, for first-married women having a husband with prior divorce, the effect is simply $\hat{\beta}_1 = -0.383$. This suggests that when the husband has a prior divorce, there is a negative relationship between women's first marriage and the log frequencies. The effect on the log frequencies for men in their first marriage whose wives have had a prior marriage is simply $\hat{\beta}_2 = -0.526$. This suggests a negative relationship between the first-marriage status of husbands and previous divorce status of wives. In the end, the example tells us that opposites do not attract; people marrying for the first time tend to marry others marrying for the first time. Also, to a lesser extent, people with a spouse with a prior divorce tend to be divorced themselves.

The substantive sampling models

The conceptual flexibility of the log-linear frequency model is reflected in the fact that there are three different sampling models, or sets of sampling assumptions, under which the model can be readily estimated with the same results (Fienberg, 1977: 131–3; Powers and Xie, 2000: 102–3). In all three cases the dependent variable m_i is a set of counts or frequencies. The most obvious model to consider in such a case is to assume that these counts are the result of a simple Poisson process and are thus observations from conditional independent Poisson distributions. Alternatively, we can consider observed frequencies as arising from some number of independent multinomial distributions such that the overall model is that of product-multinomial sampling. A final, perhaps less obvious, model is that of a special case, when the sample size N is fixed, of observations arising from a single multinomial sampling distribution. The formulation of the Poisson model, for example the likelihood kernel, is extremely simple and is the sampling model used in most programs which use maximum likelihood methods of estimation (Powers and Xie, 2000).

For the case of the log-rate model, z_i is a population or population-duration exposure to risk. And the sampling model can be regarded as a product of a Poisson-distributed frequency of events occurring to this risk set, that is, an exponential hazard rate model with fixed exposures to risk. The likelihood function for a rate model is, under very general conditions, proportional to the Poisson likelihood by a factor not dependent upon parameters (Powers and Xie, 2000: 155). Thus, the rate model can be estimated using the Poisson regression model for the counts of events. The log of frequencies in the rate model is simply offset by the log of the exposure to risk. Specific software to estimate log-linear rate models may require specification of the exposure variable or of the log exposure (i.e., offset). In either case, the offset is incorporated through a fixed coefficient and is thus a constraint upon the estimation rather than a random variable expressed as a weighting of the likelihood function.

Estimation

Most current implementations of log-linear modeling software rely upon maximum likelihood estimation using the sampling models above. Historically, however, three different estimation methods have found common use: iterative proportional fitting (IPF) algorithms; general linear models through iteratively reweighted least squares (GLM-IRLS); and standard maximum likelihood estimation (MLE). A number of other solutions, such as minimum χ^2 models, have been less widespread in use (for a discussion of several such estimators, see Powers and Xie: 2000: Appendix B).

Iterative proportional fitting Iterative proportional fitting is a general method that is readily adaptable to a wide variety of log-linear models. In each iteration, model coefficients are adjusted to produce a change in estimated model frequencies generally proportionate to the deviation of these estimates from observed frequencies (see Goodman, 1978: 102–7, for an illustration). For standard log-linear models, including adaptations to non-hierarchical and ordinal data, etc., these algorithms converge to MLE solutions (Goodman, 1978; Fienberg, 1977). IPF algorithms were common in early single-purpose log-linear analysis software packages, in part because simple MLE algorithms, such as unmodified Newton–Raphson, are not always appropriate for complex log-linear models. However, adaptations of the IPF method to accommodate variations in the log-linear model are considerably slower than their use for standard hierarchical frequency table models or the more recent and robust MLE algorithms suitable for log-linear modeling. And, as a matter of practicality, since multi-purpose software packages generally already have both GLM and MLE algorithms with appropriate modifications to handle log-linear models, it is increasingly rare to find software relying upon IPF methods.

Iteratively reweighted least squares Iteratively reweighted least-squares methods can also be used to estimate log-linear models as a special case of the generalized linear model.[5] In IRLS the model parameter estimates of the log-linear model, for example, are iteratively updated as

$$\hat{\boldsymbol{\beta}}_{+1} = \hat{\boldsymbol{\beta}} + (\mathbf{X}'\mathbf{W}\mathbf{X})^{-1}\mathbf{X}'(\mathbf{y} - \hat{\mathbf{y}}), \qquad (12.6)$$

where $\mathbf{y}$ is the conditional mean response variable

$$\hat{\mathbf{y}} = \exp{(\mathbf{X}'\boldsymbol{\beta})} \qquad (12.7)$$

and $\mathbf{W}$ is the weights matrix

$$\mathbf{W} = \mathbf{X}'\hat{\boldsymbol{\beta}}. \qquad (12.8)$$

IRLS solutions are straightforward for several variants of the log-linear model (see Powers and Xie, 2000: Appendix B).

Maximum likelihood estimation Flexible MLE methods are now the most common algorithms used for estimating log-linear models. In maximum likelihood methods parameters are again iteratively updated as, for example, in the Newton–Raphson iteration,

$$\hat{\beta}_{+1} = \hat{\beta} - \mathbf{H}^{-1}\mathbf{J}, \qquad (12.9)$$

where $\mathbf{H}$ and $\mathbf{J}$ are the matrices of respectively second- and first-order partial derivatives of the log-likelihood function with respect to the model parameters β.

The log-likelihood function for the Poisson sampling frequency model is simply

$$\ln L(\beta) = \sum_{i=1}^{n} (y_i \ln \hat{y}_i + \hat{y}_i). \qquad (12.10)$$

Increasingly, with capable software implementations, the details of estimation are hidden from users and of concern only with complicated design matrices or special estimation requirements beyond standard frequency or log-rate models. These are most often straightforward MLE algorithms. However, there are exceptions which cannot be estimated through the three methods above. Ordinal models discussed later in this chapter, for example, require special algorithms specific to their purpose.

Properties of model estimates For all three estimation methods model coefficients are unbiased, that is, the expected value $E(\hat{\beta})$ equals β. In IRLS estimation $\hat{\beta}$ has an exact normal distribution, $N(\beta, \mathbf{S}^{-1})$. In MLE estimation it has an approximate normal distribution, $N(\beta, \mathbf{S}^{-1})$ where β is the asymptotic mean of $\hat{\beta}$ and the matrix $\mathbf{S}^{-1}$ is the asymptotic covariance matrix of $\hat{\beta}$ (see Haberman, 1978, for a fuller treatment). The asymptotic covariance matrix $\mathbf{S}^{-1}$ may be derived from the inverse information matrix $(-\mathbf{H}^{-1})$ at the completion of the MLE iterations. The square roots of the diagonal elements of this matrix then provide asymptotically unbiased estimates of the standard errors of coefficients for the construction of standardized coefficients, tests of coefficient significance and confidence interval estimates.

INTERPRETATION OF COEFFICIENTS

Additive

A conventional regression approach to the interpretation of estimates is appropriate in log-linear frequency models. That is, as a special form of the general linear model, the additive coefficient (i.e., from equation (12.2)) can be interpreted as a change in the natural logarithm of the dependent variable for a unit change in the independent variable.

The illustration of previous divorce patterns among married couples serves as an example of how interpreting the additive effects may uncover relationships among variables. Let us extend that illustration now to demonstrate the use of significance tests in log-linear analysis. A natural starting point is to model the main effects, or in this case the parameters measuring the first-marriage status among husbands and wives. Our model for this example is now parameterized as follows:

$$\ln \begin{bmatrix} 13\,045 \\ 1\,663 \\ 1\,441 \\ 2\,438 \end{bmatrix} = \begin{bmatrix} 9.477 \\ 7.416 \\ 7.273 \\ 7.799 \end{bmatrix} = \begin{pmatrix} 1 & 1 & 1 \\ 1 & 1 & 0 \\ 1 & 0 & 1 \\ 1 & 0 & 0 \end{pmatrix} \times \begin{bmatrix} \hat{\beta}_0 \\ \hat{\beta}_1 \\ \hat{\beta}_2 \end{bmatrix} + \begin{bmatrix} \varepsilon_1 \\ \varepsilon_2 \\ \varepsilon_3 \\ \varepsilon_4 \end{bmatrix},$$

$$(12.11)$$

or alternatively as

$$\ln(m_i) = \hat{\beta}_0 + \hat{\beta}_1 w_i + \hat{\beta}_2 h_i + \varepsilon_i. \qquad (12.12)$$

Table 12.3 presents the coefficients, standardized errors, and the probability of $E(\hat{\beta}_i) = 0$, that is, the significance level of $\hat{\beta}_i$. From these coefficients we see that the effects of both wives and husbands being first married are positive and significant. Again, although significant, this finding comes as no surprise. It is apparent in Table 12.1 that first marriages are more frequent than remarriages for currently married wives and husbands. Coefficients simply estimate the magnitude of these effects, confirm their direction and establish their statistical significance.

The main effect $\hat{\beta}_1$ simply tells us that first-married wives are more frequent in the marginal distribution of wives' marital status and $\hat{\beta}_2$ tells us that the same is true for husbands. Clearly, since the marginal frequency of first marriage is greater among both husbands and wives, the expected frequency of couples where both partners are first married will also be greater. However, in this model we have not included an interaction effect to test whether the frequency of couples where both husbands and wives are first married is greater, or less, than the frequency we would expect given the higher marginal frequencies expected from effects $\hat{\beta}_1$ and $\hat{\beta}_2$.

Table 12.3   *Coefficients and standard errors*

Parameter	Estimated coefficient	Standard error	Probability of $E(\hat{\beta}_i) = 0$
$\hat{\beta}_0$	6.752	0.021	$p < 0.0001$
$\hat{\beta}_1$	1.333	0.018	$p < 0.0001$
$\hat{\beta}_2$	1.262	0.018	$p < 0.0001$

Multiplicative

Taking the anti-log, the log-linear model can be rewritten as

$$\frac{\mathbf{m}}{\mathbf{z}} = \exp(\mathbf{X}'\hat{\boldsymbol{\beta}} + \varepsilon). \qquad (12.13)$$

With the model expressed in this multiplicative form, the exponentiated coefficients can be interpreted as the relative odds of a particular outcome. Let us continue with the example of previous divorce status among married couples. First we will analyze the marginal odds, conditional odds, and the odds ratio through standard cross-tabular analysis of Table 12.1. Then we will show how the log-linear analysis replicates the odds ratio analysis through a regression-based approach.

The cross-tabular approach   The odds of an event happening are defined as $p/(1 - p)$, where p is the probability that the event will occur. Examining Table 12.1, we see that the probability that a wife is in her first marriage is $14\,708/18\,587 \approx 0.791$; the probability of a wife's prior divorce is $3879/18\,587 \approx 0.209$. The odds that a married woman is in her first marriage are thus $14\,708/3879 \approx 3.792$ to 1. What we have calculated is often called the marginal odds. Similarly, the marginal odds that a married husband is in his first marriage are $14\,486/4101 = 3.532$. If we wished to calculate separate odds of first marriage for husbands with divorced wives and then again for husbands with first-married wives, we would calculate the conditional odds. For example, the conditional odds of first marriage for men with first-married wives is $13\,045/1663 \approx 7.844$. The conditional odds of first marriage status for men with previously divorced wives is $1441/2438 \approx 0.591$. Continuing, the conditional odds of first marriage for women with a first-married husband is $13\,045/1441 \approx 9.053$. The conditional odds that a woman is in her first marriage given that her husband has been previously divorced is $1663/2438 \approx 0.682$. Perhaps the most interesting odds entity to

analyze is the joint odds ratio comparing the odds of first marriage for women with first-married husbands to the odds of first marriage for women with divorced husbands. For Table 12.1, such an odds ratio is $9.053/0.682 \approx 13.27$.[6] We may say that the odds are roughly 13 to 1, or thirteen times as great, that first-married women have a first-married husband rather than a previously divorced husband. This odds ratio reflects the association between husband's and wife's previous marital experiences and is symmetric in this example (i.e., a 2×2 table). If, for example, we compare the odds that a first-married husband has a first-married wife to the odds he has a previously divorced wife, we would obtain the same odds ratio (i.e., $7.844/0.591 \approx 13.27$). Again, the analysis suggests a relationship between the prior divorce status of husbands and wives.

The log-linear approach   Let us start with the coefficients from the model of Table 12.3, which included only main effects, and hypothesized there was no interaction between husband's and wife's previous marital status. Exponentiating these coefficients yields the marginal odds found in our cross-tabular analysis above. For example, recall that $\hat{\beta}_1$ models the effect of a wife being in her first marriage on the log frequencies. If we exponentiate $\hat{\beta}_1 = 1.333$ we obtain $e^{\hat{\beta}_1} = 3.792$, which is the marginal odds of a woman being in her first marriage. Similarly, if we exponentiate $\hat{\beta}_2 = 1.262$ we obtain $e^{\hat{\beta}_2} = 3.532$, the marginal odds of a husband being in his first marriage.

What if we consider the interaction between variables? Recall the estimates for such a model in equation (12.5) produced $\hat{\beta}_0 = 7.799$, $\hat{\beta}_1 = -0.383$, $\hat{\beta}_2 = -0.526$, $\hat{\beta}_3 = 2.586$. Exponentiating these coefficients yields the conditional odds and odds ratio found in our cross-tabular analysis above. For example, recall that $\hat{\beta}_1$ models the effect of a wife being in her first marriage on the log frequencies. If we exponentiate $\hat{\beta}_1 = -0.383$ we obtain the conditional odds that a woman is in her first marriage given that her husband has been previously divorced: $e^{\hat{\beta}_1} = e^{-0.382} \approx 0.682$. Similarly, recall that $\hat{\beta}_2$ parameterizes couples where the husband has no prior divorce. Accordingly, the conditional odds that a husband is in his first marriage are $e^{\hat{\beta}_2} = e^{-0.526} \approx 0.591$ given that his wife has had a prior marriage. Finally, recall that $\hat{\beta}_3$ parameterized the interaction effect of the intersection of both husband's and wife's first-marriage status. If we exponentiate this term we obtain the joint odds ratio $e^{\hat{\beta}_3} = e^{2.586} \approx 13.27$. If one compares the log-linear results to the cross-tabular approach, we see that we have replicated the analysis of odds using a powerful regression approach.

It is important to note that any quantitative variable is acceptable in the matrix $\mathbf{X}$; that is, the columns or variables in the design matrix $\mathbf{X}$ are not limited to 0–1 category indicator variables. For all cases, we may use a standard slope interpretation of the effects of a unit change in X_j on odds or the odds ratio for a particular outcome. That is, exponentiating coefficients yields either the marginal odds, conditional odds, or an odds ratio for the effect of a unit change in X on the predicted frequencies. If, for example, X were the number of pre-school children in an area and the dependent frequency were that of working age adults in the area, the exponentiated coefficient or odds ratio would give the change in marginal odds of working age adults for each additional pre-school child in the area.

Using predicted probabilities

Since the odds of an event are defined as $p/(1 - p)$, it is easy to unwind the odds of an event into the original probability π. If the odds are a to 1 that an event will occur, then the probability that the event will occur is $p = a/(1 + a)$. The change in odds for a change in an independent variable of Δx_{ij} is $e^{\hat{\beta}_j \Delta x_{ij}}$, and where x_{ij} is a dummy variable the change in odds for being in the category indicated by x_{ij} is simply $e^{\hat{\beta}_j}$. As a result, for dummy variables the effect a particular coefficient has on the probability π of an event or outcome is

$$\Delta \pi = \frac{e^{\hat{\beta}_j}}{1 + e^{\hat{\beta}_j}}, \qquad (12.14)$$

and the probability π of an event or outcome for a given covariate pattern (i.e., set of values for $\mathbf{X}_i$) is

$$\pi_i = \frac{\exp(\mathbf{X}_i'\hat{\boldsymbol{\beta}})}{1 + \exp(\mathbf{X}_i'\hat{\boldsymbol{\beta}})}. \qquad (12.15)$$

Since the log-linear model is fully generalizable to interval-level covariates, the underlying probability equation (12.15) is a curvilinear one. This means that the effect of a particular covariate on the probability of an outcome may be quite different across a range of values. As such, the effect of a quantitative independent variable on the probability of an outcome is meaningful only if evaluated at a stated value of x_{ij} and understood to be the instantaneous rate of change in the probability of the modeled outcome at that value of x_{ij}.

In our example there are no continuous or interval-level covariates. Again, for example, if x_{ij} were the number of pre-school children in an area and the dependent frequency was that of working-age adults in the area, the change in the probability of additional adults for a change from 1 to 101 children in the area might be considerably different from that for a change from 1000 to 1100 children. The proportional impact of such a change is quite different, even though the numerical change in x_{ij} is identical in each case. Simple probability statements could be made only about changes in specific values of the covariate. Or alternatively, the overall non-linear functional relationship between the covariate and outcome probabilities could be presented such as in a graph of outcome probabilities for changing values of x_{ij}.

Let us illustrate the cross-tablular approach to finding the conditional probability of divorce using Table 12.1, and then follow through with the log-linear approach to modeling probabilities with this same frequency table.

The cross-tabular approach Examining a cross-tabulation can reveal change in conditional probabilities. Table 12.1 shows that the probability that a woman is in her first marriage, given that her husband is not in his first marriage, is $1663/4101 \approx 0.406$. Similarly, the probability that a husband is in his first marriage, given that his wife is divorced, is $1441/3879 \approx 0.371$. Notice that we could have found these probabilities with the method $p = a/(1 + a)$. For example, recall that the odds of a woman being in her first marriage given that her husband was not was 0.682; as such, the corresponding probability is $p = 0.682/(1 + 0.682) \approx 0.406$. Similarly, the probability that a husband is in his first marriage given that his wife is not is $p = 0.591/(1 + 0.591) \approx 0.371$.

The log-linear approach Log-linear analysis yields the same results as the standard cross-tabular analysis. Recall that $\hat{\beta}_1 = -0.383$. By the method $e^{\hat{\beta}_1}/(1 + e^{\hat{\beta}_1})$ we obtain $e^{-0.382}/(1 + e^{-0.382}) \approx 0.406$, which is the probability that a woman is in her first marriage given that her husband is previously divorced. Similarly, recall that $\hat{\beta}_2 = -0.526$. By the method $e^{\hat{\beta}_1}/(1 + e^{\hat{\beta}_1})$ we obtain $e^{-0.526}/(1 + e^{-0.526}) \approx 0.371$, which is the probability that a husband is in his first marriage given that his wife is previously divorced.

Enhancing substantive interpretations

Traditional cautions regarding the interpretation of significance probabilities (see Raftery, 1995) are only amplified by the fact that log-linear models often include a large number of parameters. These problems are especially acute in frequency-table models which include all marginal effects (i.e., coefficients for all categories regardless of statistical or substantive significance) and hierarchical representation of effects requiring coefficients for all lower-order interactions in the model. In analyzing a $4 \times 4 \times 4$ frequency table, for example, a model including all main order effects results in ten coefficients (i.e., a constant and three main effects each represented by three dummy variables and one excluded category). A model including all two-way interactions results in 37 coefficients and, including the three-way interaction, yields a model with 64 coefficients. Random appearances of statistical significance become a not uncommon event in such models.

Substantively grounded coefficients and interpretation of effects contribute to a more meaningful analysis than an overreliance on statistical significance. Odds ratios which give the proportional deviation in risk corresponding to a nominal membership category readily provide a clear interpretation of substantive effects. When variables such as very finely graded nominal taxonomies or even continuous covariates are entered into log-linear models, the substantive interpretation afforded by odds ratios may suffer. Using, for example, a real-valued percentage of minority residents or a single-dollar income amount as covariates in a log-linear model would then estimate the odds ratio for a one-unit change in the percentage or dollar amount. However, we seldom see situations in which a 1% or $1 change is substantively meaningful. To achieve a more meaningful interpretation of such effects one can present the change in odds corresponding to a substantively significant change in the independent variable. One can, for example, present the odds ratio corresponding to a change of one interquartile range in the covariate:

$$\text{Odds effect of } \Delta_{\text{IQR}} x_{ij}$$
$$= \exp(Q_3 - Q_1)\hat{\beta}_{ij}, \qquad (12.16)$$

where Q_1 and Q_3 indicate the lower and upper quartile values of x_{ij}, respectively.

ASSESSING GOODNESS-OF-FIT

Standard cross-tabular analysis makes use of the Pearson chi-square test of independence among the conditional distributions found in the frequency table. In using the Pearson chi-square to test goodness-of-fit for any model, the general form is a comparison of observed and expected values (i.e., the predicted frequencies for a given hypothesis or model)

$$\chi^2 = \sum_{i=1}^{n} \frac{(\widehat{m}_i - m_i)^2}{\widehat{m}_i}, \qquad (12.17)$$

where m_i are the observed frequencies and $\widehat{m}_i$ are the expected frequencies. The degrees of freedom for the goodness-of-fit test are n minus the number of parameters used to generate expected values. Significance of the difference between the observed values and expected values from a hypothesized model is determined in standard fashion.

A common hypothesis tested in log-linear models is that of independence between the covariates in the model. Expectations under independence are simply the predictions from a model including only the main effects, or marginal distributions, of each covariate. For a simple two-way frequency table this reduces to the familiar Pearson chi-square (i.e., with expected values equal to the product of row and column probabilities multiplied by the total table frequency). The traditional chi-square test is a test of the goodness-of-fit of the null hypothesis of independence or main effects only. This same inferential strategy carries over to assessing the goodness-of-fit for any number of competing log-linear models the researcher is interested in evaluating.

Likelihood ratio chi-squares

Because log-linear analysis makes use of maximum-likelihood theory, an alternative to equation (12.17) based on such estimation may be used. The likelihood ratio chi-square test statistic is given by:

$$G^2 = 2\sum_{i=1}^{n} m_i \ln\left(\frac{m_i}{\hat{m}_i}\right) = 2(L_h^2 - L_s^2) \quad (12.18)$$

In the alternative form of computation, directly from log-likelihoods, L_h^2 is the log-likelihood of the hypothesized independence model with main effects only and L_s^2 is the log-likelihood of the observed data replicated by a saturated model with all effects. G^2 is asymptotically distributed as χ^2 if the hypothesized model is consistent with the data. The degrees of freedom for G^2 can be found by the difference between the number of cells in the table and the number of parameters fitted.

Comparing χ^2 to G^2 for Table 12.1 under the independence model, we have

$$\chi^2 = \frac{(13\,045 - 11\,462.86)^2}{11\,462.86}$$

$$+ \frac{(1663 - 3245.14)^2}{3245.14}$$

$$+ \frac{(1441 - 3023.14)^2}{3023.14} + \frac{(2438 - 855.86)^2}{855.86}$$

$$= 4742.52$$

and

$$G^2 = 2\left[13\,045 \ln\left(\frac{13\,045}{11\,462.86}\right)\right.$$

$$+ 1663 \ln\left(\frac{1663}{3245.14}\right)$$

$$+ 1441 \ln\left(\frac{1441}{3023.14}\right)$$

$$\left. + 2438 \ln\left(\frac{2438}{855.86}\right)\right]$$

$$= 4118.61,$$

or, using the alternative computation, $G^2 = 2(2078.963 - 19.658) = 4118.61$. In practice, the values of L_h^2 and L_s^2 used with the alternative computation may easily be obtained from statistical software.

In theory, equations (12.17) and (12.18) are asymptotically equivalent. For this illustration we see some sampling variability between χ^2 and G^2. However, with either statistic we reach the same statistical inference. Again, the degrees of freedom are equal to $n - k$. The large values of χ^2 and G^2 both imply that the independence model does not fit these data at any reasonable significance level.

Partitioning likelihood ratio chi-squares

Similar to ANOVA, in log-linear analysis we may conceive of the total amount of variance in the frequency table as due to a different number of effects. The modeling goal is to account for this variance in a parsimonious manner. But there are many equations to choose from. For example, to model our first example, we may choose between the following models:

$$\ln(m_i) = \hat{\beta}_0 + \hat{\beta}_1 w_i + \hat{\beta}_2 h_i + \varepsilon_i, \quad (12.19)$$

$$\ln(m_i) = \hat{\beta}_0 + \hat{\beta}_1 w_i + \hat{\beta}_2 h_i + \hat{\beta}_3 w h_i + \varepsilon_i. \quad (12.20)$$

Equation (12.19) is said to be included in equation (12.20) in a hierarchy of equations. Equation (12.19) is often called a reduced model. The statistical question is whether equation (12.20) explains a significant additional amount of variance in the table compared to equation (12.19). One strategy would be to fit both models and calculate G_r^2 for the reduced model and G_f^2 for the model which includes it, and find the difference. In practice, the following formula also yields the desired quantity:

$$G^2 = G_r^2 - G_f^2 = 2(L_r^2 - L_f^2), \quad (12.21)$$

where L_r^2 and L_f^2 are the log-likelihoods of the respective models. G^2 from equation (12.21) is distributed as χ^2 with degrees of freedom equal to $df_r - df_f$. It provides a test for the significance of the difference in the fitted model frequencies. In this particular example, the test is equivalent to that above for the independence hypothesis.

Bayesian information criterion

Raftery (1995) recommends a Bayesian approach to offset some of the limitations of χ^2-based test statistics. With large samples, χ^2 statistics can become overly sensitive to departures from the null hypothesis, sometimes to the point where very small and perhaps substantively meaningless departures are statistically significant. This situation may yield a false impression of the explanatory importance of additional variables introduced into a log-linear model. Thus, the researcher may add variables that are not meaningfully related to the outcome under study. In addition, when faced with many variables and hypotheses, G^2 may not be helpful in choosing between competing models since with large samples G^2 is overly sensitive and inadequate for discriminating among variables and models. Raftery (1995) recommends the Bayesian information criterion,

$$\text{BIC} = G^2 - df \ln n. \qquad (12.22)$$

Equation (12.22) shows that the larger the sample, the greater the test statistic G^2 is penalized for each estimate added to the log-linear model. Using equation (12.21), G^2 is found and substituted into equation (12.22). If the BIC is negative, then the model with L_r is preferred to that with L_f. If it is positive, then the model with L_f is preferred to that with L_r.

TABULAR ANALYSIS

General versus tabular model formats

The saturated model for the two-way table of first marriage of husband and wife above (i.e., Table 12.1 and equation (12.2)) is an example of tabular log-linear analysis. The dependent variable values, m_{ij}, in the modeling are the aggregated, or tabulated, frequency counts for marginal categories of cases specified by the design variables **X**. The primary interest in most tabular log-linear analyses is in what interaction terms in the model reveal about the relationships or independence between marginal variables. In the case of our example, the fact that the coefficient for the interaction of wife's and husband's first marriage is substantial and significant reveals the association of this trait in marriage partners. The frequency, in this case, is a means to an end. The distribution of cases reveals the association of interest. The substantive meaning of the frequency for any unique covariate pattern is of less interest than the fact that the distribution reveals a relationship between independent variables.

Hierarchical modeling and exceptions

To test a simple associational (or independence) hypothesis, the coefficient for the interaction must be estimated as an effect conditioned on marginal frequencies. Presenting the tabular model format, prevalent notation for the model effects is typically to use alphabetical designations for main effects and combinations of these for higher-order interactions. The effects of wife's marriage, husband's marriage, and the interaction of wife's and husband's first marriage (i.e., β_1, β_2, and β_3 in the examples above) are then written as W, H, and WH. Similarly, for a three-way interaction term to be a simple test of more complex associational effects, the relevant marginal effects must be conditioned upon. If we extended our model to include age (A), for example, then the three-way interaction (AWH) is a straightforward test of the joint association of all three variables only if the main effects (A, H, W) and all lower-order marginal effects (AW, AH, WH) are conditioned upon (i.e., included) in the same equation. Such models are generically referred to as hierarchical log-linear models.

Although the circumstances are relatively rare, and should not be approached without caution, there are times when we wish to employ non-hierarchical models. One of the most common examples is that of a nested effect. In a nested model one or more of the covariates is allowed to vary only within marginal categories of another. To analyze, for example, frequency of recidivism among individuals convicted of different types of crimes (T), we might impose a model which put a causal primacy on the facility in which the individual was incarcerated and rehabilitated (F). That is, we might make a strong assumption that recidivism among different types of offenders has no inherent marginal effect but that the marginal effect depends entirely upon the facility and the programs it offers. If such a strong assumption were warranted, we might then fit the nested model (including only the effects F and TF) without conditioning upon the marginal type of offender. The assumptions of non-hierarchical models are generally strong hypotheses which should be founded upon either solid theoretical expectations or a priori evidence. The same data, for example, could be fitted as a hierarchical model (including T, F and TF). If there were indeed no marginal effect on recidivism of type of offender the coefficients would reveal this fact and the need to condition upon this marginal effect in the model could be reassessed.

Table 12.4   *First marriage among married couples by wife's age and gender*

			Husband		
		First marriage	Yes	No	Total
Age ≤ 34	Wife	Yes	3 844	485	4 329
		No	312	258	570
		Total	4 156	743	4,899

			Husband		
		First marriage	Yes	No	Total
34 < Age < 68	Wife	Yes	7 795	1 080	8 875
		No	1 016	1 924	2 940
		Total	8 811	3 004	11 815

			Husband		
		First marriage	Yes	No	Total
Age ≥ 68	Wife	Yes	1 406	98	1 504
		No	113	256	369
		Total	1 519	354	1 873

Table 12.5   *Association models applied to Table 12.4*

Association models	Goodness-of-fit likelihood ratio Chi-square	df	Incremental likelihood ratio Chi-square	df
Constant only	26 001.46	11	–	
H,W,A	4 660.88	7	–	
H,W,A,WH	548.86	6	4112.02[a]	1
H,W,A,HA	4 449.96	4	210.93[a]	2
H,W,A,WA	4 229.68	4	431.20[a]	2
H,W,A,HA,WH	337.94	3	4322.95[a]	3
H,W,A,WA,WH	117.66	3	4543.23[a]	3
H,W,A,WA,HA	4 018.75	3	642.13[a]	4
H,W,A,WA,HA,WH	88.98	2	4571.90[a]	5
H,W,A,WA,HA,WH,HWA	0.00	0	89.00[b]	2

[a]Comparing with *H,W,A*.
[b]Comparing with *H,W,A,WA,HA,WH*.

Example: Three-way table

As suggested, tabular log-linear analysis most often involves more complex tabulations than our example of a two-way table above. We will illustrate the model fitting and interpretation issues through an analysis of a three-way table. Again, we use wife's first marriage (*W*) and husband's first marriage (*H*) as two marginal effects. However, recognizing that age is closely linked to prior marriage prospects, we introduce wife's age (*A*) as a third marginal effect in the analysis (see Table 12.4).

Table 12.5 presents hypothesis tests for all the hierarchical models. The goodness-of-fit chi-square according to equation (12.18) compares each model to the saturated model. The incremental likelihood ratio chi-square from equation (12.21) compares added two-way effects to the model of all main effects (i.e., independence) and three-way effects to the model with all two-way effects. The BIC from equation (12.22) is not presented in Table 12.5 because it was very similar to the incremental likelihood ratio chi-square in each case. Since G^2 and the BIC were statistically significant for the saturated model, there is evidence of a three-way interaction term in our model.

We chose the full hierarchical model parameterized as

$$
\begin{aligned}
\ln(m_i) = {} & \hat{\beta}_0 + \hat{\beta}_1 w_i + \hat{\beta}_2 h_i + \hat{\beta}_3 a_{2i} + \hat{\beta}_4 a_{3i} \\
& + \hat{\beta}_5 w h_i + \hat{\beta}_6 w a_{2i} + \hat{\beta}_7 w a_{3i} + \hat{\beta}_8 h a_{2i} \\
& + \hat{\beta}_9 h a_{3i} + \hat{\beta}_{10} h w a_{2i} + \hat{\beta}_{11} h w a_{3i} + \varepsilon_i.
\end{aligned}
$$

Table 12.6 presents the estimated coefficients and odds ratios for the three-way table.

Table 12.6 *Coefficients and odds ratios estimated from Table 12.4*

Variable	Parameter	Estimated coefficient	Odds ratio
Constant	β_0	5.553*	–
w	β_1	0.631*	1.880
h	β_2	0.190	1.209
a_2	β_3	2.009*	7.457
a_3	β_4	−0.008	0.992
wh	β_5	1.880*	6.554
wa_2	β_6	−1.209*	0.299
wa_3	β_7	−1.591*	0.204
ha_2	β_8	−0.829*	0.437
ha_3	β_9	−1.008*	0.365
hwa_2	β_{10}	0.735*	2.085
hwa_3	β_{11}	1.601	4.959

*$p < 0.0001$

Except for β_4 and β_2, all coefficients are statistically significant at $\alpha = 0.0001$. Interpreting the coefficients is straightforward.

The odds ratios for $\hat{\beta}_{10}$ and $\hat{\beta}_{11}$, for example, indicate that couples where both spouses are first married and where wife's age is between 34 and 68 are roughly twice as frequent, and where wife's age is over 68 are five times more common, respectively, than we would expect after conditioning upon all other effects in the model. The significance of these effects suggests that the joint occurrence of first marriage for both spouses is associated with wife's age in a manner not explained by main effects ($\hat{\beta}_0$ through $\hat{\beta}_4$), the association of first marriage among both spouses ($\hat{\beta}_5$) or the association of wife's first marriage status with her age ($\hat{\beta}_6$ and $\hat{\beta}_7$).

Fixed margins and the logit model

As Goodman (1978) and Haberman (1978) note, the logit model from Chapter 11 is closely related to the log-linear model discussed above. The logit model may be considered a special case of log-linear models arising from fixed marginal distributions (i.e., fitting a non-saturated model appropriate to the logit regression to be fitted). Suppose, for example, that we have the three variables from Table 12.4 above – wife's first marriage (*W*), husband's first marriage (*H*) and wife's age (*A*). A typical logit regression might ask how the odds the wife will be first married are influenced by the husband being first married, the wife's age, and the interaction of these two model terms.

Table 12.7 *Equivalent logistic and log-linear models*

Logistic independent variables	Log-linear marginals
None	W,A,H,AH
A	W,A,H,AH,WA
H	W,A,H,AH,WH
A,H	W,A,H,AH,WA,WH
A,H,AH	W,A,H,AH,WA,WH,WAH

Various log-linear models equivalent to logit regressions can be specified through determining the appropriate model with fitted and fixed marginal distributions (see Table 12.7). The third of these models, for example, states that first marriage of the wife is dependent only upon the husband's first marriage. Or, equivalently, that first marriage of the wife is independent of age given husband's first marriage. The logit regression model to estimate these conditional effects would be

$$\text{logit}(w_i) = \hat{\beta}_0 + \hat{\beta}_1 h_i + \varepsilon_i, \quad (12.23)$$

where $e^{\hat{\beta}_1}$ yields the conditional odds of a wife being in a first marriage given her husband is also in a first marriage. Although the approach is considerably less parsimonious, the same coefficient could be obtained from the log-linear regression

$$\begin{aligned}\ln(m_i) = &\hat{\beta}_0 + \hat{\beta}_1 a_{2i} + \hat{\beta}_2 a_{3i} + \hat{\beta}_4 w_i \\ &+ \hat{\beta}_5 h_i + \hat{\beta}_6 a_{2i} h_i + \hat{\beta}_7 a_{3i} h_i \\ &+ \hat{\beta}_8 w_i h_i + \varepsilon_i.\end{aligned} \quad (12.24)$$

as $e^{\hat{\beta}_8}$. Coefficients from fitting this particular example are given in Table 12.8.

The coefficient from the log-linear model for the interaction of wife's first marriage and husband's first marriage (i.e., 2.586) is identical to the logistic regression coefficient for the effect of husband's first marriage on the probability the wife is in a first marriage. In both cases first marriage of the husband increases the odds of a wife also being first married by a factor in excess of 13 ($e^{2.586} = 13.27$). Standard errors for both coefficients are, of course, also identical. And note that the constant from the logistic regression for the mean probability the wife will be in a first marriage is given by the main effect for that term in the log-linear model (i.e., −0.383). This example demonstrates the fact that the logistic regression model can be considered as a special case of the log-linear model, as

Table 12.8 *Comparing logistic regression and log-linear models*

Independent variable	Log-linear model	Logistic regression
Constant	6.091	**–0.383**
a_2	1.397	
a_3	–0.741	
w	**–0.383**	
h	–0.066	**2.586**
a_2h	–0.646	
a_3h	–0.265	
wh	**2.586**	

Haberman (1978) and others have suggested. However, as a practical matter, when hypotheses correspond to those of the logistic regression model parsimony, more appropriate tests of model fit and the availability of specific classification diagnostics would all suggest that appropriate logistic regression software and statistics should be utilized.

COVARIATE SCALE AND DIMENSIONALITY

Interval-level variables

Working with frequency-table models, the elements of X are most often dichotomous variables indicating membership in a qualitative category (e.g., a row or column of a frequency table). However, the log-linear model of equation (12.1) readily incorporates interval-level data. No assumption is made about the data matrix X which prohibits a variable from being an interval-level measurement. In the same log-linear model we may have dummy variable representations of nominal-level characteristics (e.g., sex, ethnicity, religion) and interval ones (e.g., income, scores, age) or interactions across these measurement types. In fact, as a general design matrix X can also incorporate any contrast or effect coding necessary to represent testable hypotheses. The only substantial impact of including interval-level variables in the model is on substantive interpretation of the coefficients, and hence the odds ratio, describing the effect of a unit change in the now interval-level, independent variable.

Interval proxies for ordinal variables Use of interval-level measurements also allows the log-linear model to address some cases in which variables are ordinal. In the simplest case, any ordinal variable in the model might be characterized not only by categories of membership, but also by additional measurements on the category that captures the ordinal nature of the variable and satisfy interval-level measurement assumptions. We may, for example, wish to model social classes as ordinal categories. Yet we might also have interval-level measurements of mean socioeconomic status in each class. The interval-level measure, it could be argued, captures or reflects much of the ordinal information in the social class categories. The interval measurement by itself might be substituted in the analysis for its measurement properties. Or, if we doubt the adequacy of the interval scale for capturing group differences, we may simply use a nominal-level log-linear model. However, another option for incorporating the ordinal information from interval-level measurements on categories is to specify a hybrid model which makes less rigorous assumptions about the adequacy of interval measurements yet uses these measures as proxies to capture ordinal aspects of association.

Since ordinal models are sensible only for three or more categories, we will consider a simple 3×3 frequency table to illustrate the use of interval proxies. The most common strategy is (1) to model main effects (or even basic interactions) using the nominal categorizations while (2) using interval-level measurements on categories to capture the ordinal aspects in specific interaction terms. Such hybrid ordinal models are also parsimonious. For example, in the case of a 3×3 table this model would be written with only one coefficient for the interaction term:

$$\ln(m_i) = \hat{\beta}_0 + \hat{\beta}_1 r_{2i} + \hat{\beta}_2 r_{3i} + \hat{\beta}_3 c_{2i} + \hat{\beta}_4 c_{3i} + \hat{\beta}_5 \mu_i v_i + \varepsilon_i. \quad (12.25)$$

This model is called the linear-by-linear association model (Haberman, 1978; Goodman, 1984) since it assumes that the association between variables is captured by a linear association between interval measurements μ_i and v_i on the respective ordinal categories of the variables. The strength of this association is given by the coefficient β_5. Expected frequencies from the main effects are not subject to interval-level assumptions. As a result, the location, or central tendency, of the interval measurements is irrelevant. Only the intervals between the μ_i and v_i are relevant to the test of association in coefficient β_5.

Integer rank scoring   Where the order of categories is known and interval measurements on the categories are either not available or inadequate, one alternative is to substitute the ordinal ranking of categories for μ and ν (in equation (12.25)),

$$\ln(m_i) = \hat{\beta}_0 + \hat{\beta}_1 r_{2i} + \hat{\beta}_2 r_{3i} + \hat{\beta}_3 c_{2i} \\ + \hat{\beta}_4 c_{3i} + \hat{\beta}_5 j_i k_i + \varepsilon_i, \qquad (12.26)$$

where $j = 1,...,3$ and $k = 1,...,3$ are the row and column ranks, respectively. The resulting uniform association model depends upon the assumption that real differences in adjacent ranks are uniformly spaced and, as a result of this assumption, odds ratios across any two adjacent (e.g., row or column) categories are invariant (Powers and Xie, 2000).[7]

A slightly more conservative approach might also assume that some, but not all, of the ordinal variables can be represented by ranks in testing interactions. Conventionally, using terminology drawn from two-way frequency tables, if the row variable may be represented in tests of association through rank scoring the model is called a column-effect model. The model is called a row-effect model when the column variable is represented by ranks in tests of association (Goodman, 1984; Powers and Xie, 2000). The effect which is not specified as a rank score is then estimated from the model fitting. For example, in the row-effect model the column is specified as a simple rank while the row-specific rank effect φ_{ji} or scores are estimated from the data,

$$\ln(m_i) = \hat{\beta} + \hat{\beta}_1 r_{2i} + \hat{\beta}_2 r_{3i} + \hat{\beta}_3 c_{2i} \\ + \hat{\beta}_4 c_{3i} + \phi_i j_i k_i + \varepsilon_{ij}. \qquad (12.27)$$

This terminology – row and column effect – loses meaning in more complex multivariate models, and it is more useful to simply identify variables for which integer scoring (and hence an assumption of uniform differences in adjacent categories) is used and those for which latent scores are estimated.

Latent category scores   Either of the solutions above – interval or rank proxies – requires prior knowledge that the categories are correctly ordered and that differences in odds-ratio effects between categories are invariant. Alternative approaches allow the researcher to assume that the scores and ordering of categories are unknown and must be estimated as latent structures from the observed data. The most widely known, and general, of these alternatives is Goodman's

(1979, 1984) Model II. The form of the model, again using our example of a 3×3 table with row and column effects, is

$$\ln(m_i) = \hat{\beta}_0 + \hat{\beta}_1 r_2 + \hat{\beta}_2 r_3 + \hat{\beta}_3 c_2 \\ + \hat{\beta}_4 c_3 + \hat{\phi}_{ji} \hat{\varphi}_{ki} + \varepsilon_i, \qquad (12.28)$$

where ϕ_i and φ_k are ordinal latent row and column scores to be estimated from the data, with $j, k = 1,...,3$ indexing respective nominal categories of each score. Indeed, this model looks very much like the linear-by-linear association model except that category scores are estimated from the data and no coefficient is needed to scale the effect of the interaction on the outcome variable. Normalization constraints are needed to identify the location and scale the latent scores. Common normalization constraints (e.g. Powers and Xie, 2000) are to fix

$$\sum_{i=1}^{j} \phi_i = 0, \quad \sum_{i=1}^{k} \varphi_i = 0, \quad \sum_{i=1}^{j} \phi_i^2 = 1, \qquad (12.29)$$

with the first two of these constraints fixing location of the scores and the third setting the relative scale of either one of the scores, leaving scale effects to be estimated for the other score. With these constraints the estimation of the scores then reveals the underlying ordinal nature of both row and column effects for the model of equation (12.28). The extension of the model to larger numbers of categories is straightforward, as is the extension to multiple dimensions (Becker and Clogg, 1989). Equation (12.28), however, is not technically a log-linear model and requires a specific iterative method other than IPF, IRLS or MLE, discussed earlier, because of the multiplicative interaction of two unknowns in the model. Where only one score is ordinal and tests of association are asymmetric, the ordinal logit models of Chapter 11 are again preferable. However, Goodman's Model II is a very useful extension of log-linear models in the case of association between ordinal variables (e.g., Clogg, 1992).

Example: Ordinal data and complex hypotheses

Goodman (1984) illustrates his Model II for ordinal categories using, in part, the data of Table 12.9. These data show the father to son mobility in ranked (i.e., ordinal) occupational status categories for a sample of British subjects. In modeling a mobility table such as

Table 12.9   *Cross-classification of British male sample according to each subject's occupational status category and his father's occupational status category using seven status categories*

Father's status	Subject's status						
	1	2	3	4	5	6	7
1	50	19	26	8	18	6	2
2	16	40	34	18	31	8	3
3	12	35	65	66	123	23	21
4	11	20	58	110	223	64	32
5	14	36	114	185	715	258	189
6	0	6	19	40	179	143	71
7	0	3	14	32	141	91	106

Source: Goodman (1984).

Table 12.10   *Association models applied to Table 12.9 with main diagonal deleted*

Association models	Goodness-of-fit likelihood ratio	d.f.
Null association	408.37	29
Uniform association	30.39	28
Row effect	26.29	23
Column effect	25.43	23
Latent category scores (II)	21.49	18

status categories. The last model uses latent category scores (i.e., Model II). The degrees of freedom are adjusted for the deletion of diagonal terms.

From these models it is apparent that only the quasi-independence model fails to adequately fit the data. Any of the models specifying an ordinal association adequately captures that association between the off-diagonal elements of the mobility matrix. Thus, there is evidence that equally spaced scores represent the association.

Collapsibility and expansion of incomplete tables

The dimensionality of nominal scales A persistent issue in the analysis of categorical data is that of determining the underlying dimensionality of observed categorizations and cross-classifications. Unfortunately, with finite and frequently limited sample sizes, changes in the nominal classification of a population can obscure real relationships or, less frequently, create the false appearance of a relationship where none exists. An occupational classification of the population without sufficient detail might, for example, confound an analysis linking specific causes of death to the individual's most recent occupational employment. Conversely, an overly detailed classification might dilute the sample size for each occupation to the point that a major relationship between, for example, manufacturing employment and deaths due to injury is not apparent in detailed occupational categories. Analytical results are inherently linked to the nominal classifications underlying them.

There is a significant literature underlying the tortuous issues involved in the subjective

this, we might simply use frequency models discussed earlier in this chapter and ignore the unique nature of the data. However, the nature of the data admits to several more complex hypotheses and potentially more informative analyses.

To begin with, Goodman and others suggest that if we are truly interested in mobility, rather than intergenerational stability, we might ignore the diagonal frequencies of this table and adjust our degrees of freedom accordingly. These cases are simply excluded from modeling so that hypotheses apply only to the off-diagonal elements reflecting mobility from father to son.

Table 12.10 shows the results of several ordinal models of this section fitted to the data by Goodman (1984). As usual, the null association model refers to the independence model, called the quasi-independence model to distinguish it, in which off-diagonal frequencies are determined only by the main effects or marginal distribution of father's and son's statuses. The uniform association, row- and column-effect models use integer rank scoring to capture ordinal aspects of the construction of nominal classifications (for reviews, see Bowker and Star, 1999; Lakoff, 1987). Even where an initial nominal scale is provided, log-linear analysis raises the question of whether the scale is appropriate or necessary for a given model of association. For example, Goodman (1981) suggests we might test the homogeneity of subtables within a $j \times k$ cross-classification using ordinary chi-square tests for quasi-independence to consider the wisdom of collapsing row or column categories. A chi-square test for the $2 \times k$ subtable containing the third and fourth rows of the original table might then be useful in considering whether these two rows should be combined as not significantly different within the overall model of association. Since row classifications may not be independent of column classifications (e.g., symmetric mobility tables) the situation may be slightly more complicated and involve a joint test of quasi-independence for corresponding rows and columns. Such a test is easily constructed as a chi-square test of quasi-independence in a $j \times k$ subtable deleting all entries not in the corresponding row and columns being tested for homogeneity (Goodman, 1981).

Examining the homogeneity of sequential subtables could progressively collapse detailed classifications into those which are necessary to portray a given association. However, there are difficulties with this method. First, where more than one reclassification is to be considered, the order of testing and reclassification can affect subsequent results. Like all stepwise methods, the results can depend heavily upon the criteria used to determine the order of model adjustments. Second, a casual use of the criteria tends toward data dredging in that potentially significant negative findings may be devalued and discarded while collapsed classifications might give rise to sample-dependent statistical significance. And, finally, the examination of homogeneity in subtables is increasingly cumbersome as the number of variables included in the model increases.

Collapsibility of association hypotheses

Log-linear modeling can provide insight into the overall dimensionality of an association hypothesis through identifying the significant interactions among any set of variables. Consider a model in which the dependent variable consists of the counts from a three-way frequency table – for example,

Table 12.4 above with wife's divorce status (W), husband's divorce status (H), and age of wife (A) as marginal, or independent, variables. If the association between wife and husband's prior divorce status is unaffected when partialling by the wife's age, then a parsimonious model of the association would not require age to be examined. More formally, if the partial association of WH in a three-way table of W by H by A is equivalent to the marginal association WH in a two-way table of W by H, then the three-way table is collapsible across A without loss of information regarding the association of W and H. If a saturated model is fitted to the three-way frequency table, conditions of collapsibility are simply that the three-way interaction term AWH and at least one of the two-way interactions AH or AW are non-significant.

Collapsibility is useful to achieve parsimony in models of frequency tables. For the more general form of equation (12.1) the conditions of collapsibility are analogous to those of omitted variable bias in ordinary least squares (Powers and Xie, 2000). In ordinary regression we are usually concerned with the effect of omitting a variable on the relationship between an independent and dependent variable. In log-linear models, we are more often concerned about the effect of collapsing, or omitted, variables on the estimates of interactions between independent variables. Any variable can be omitted without bias to an estimated interaction between two other independent variables unless the variable to be omitted is unconditionally related to one of two variables whose association is of primary interest and affects the other of the two variables directly or indirectly.

Expansion of incomplete tables   Willikens (1982) offers a practical approach to data-deficient settings which is nearly the opposite of the notion of collapsing frequency tables. In the analysis of limited secondary data, such as that from historically limited sources often found in less-developed countries, published marginal tables are often available without corresponding multidimensional detail. Suppose, for example, that we wish to have historical tabulations involving occupation (O), age (A) and wealth (W). Unfortunately, we find that we can secure only two-way tabulations corresponding to occupation by age (OA) and by wealth (OW) but not age by wealth (AW) or a three-way tabulation (OAW). What if we were willing to assume age and wealth were independent of each other once the effects of occupation were taken into account (i.e., that terms corresponding to *AW* and *OAW* would be insignificant if we had fitted a saturated model to the missing three-way tabulation)? Although this is a bold assumption, Willikens (1982) demonstrates that the IPF algorithm can be used to provide MLE estimates of the cell frequencies (without actually fitting parameters to the partially observed data under such a hypothesis). Estimated tabulations of *AW* and *OAW* are thus obtained which are equivalent to the predictions of a log-linear modeling of the observed marginal effects of occupation, age, wealth, and interactions of occupation by age and occupation by wealth, presuming true effects of *AW* and *OAW* are nil. The method Willikens suggests is only appropriate, of course, for cases where data exist in principle but are not observed. The estimation should not be extended to frequencies which represent impossible cases or are null by construction (i.e., structural zeros).

EXPOSURE AND OFFSET MODELS

Poisson regression

In the previous sections of this chapter we have largely focused upon tabular log-linear modeling. However, the general log-linear model in equation (12.1) is, with the Poisson sampling model, simply a case of Poisson regression. And tabular log-linear modeling can be viewed as a special case of Poisson regression. Since either application involves a similar solution to equation (12.1), the distinction between tabular log-linear models and more general uses of Poisson regression is largely a matter of emphasis and the nature of the data analyzed.

In most tabular analyses m_i is an aggregate frequency of cases with a unique covariate pattern of marginal traits, x_{ij}, $i = 1, \ldots, k$, in a multidimensional tabulation. The emphasis of modeling is then on what effects reveal about the distribution of cases across traits, and on what interaction terms reveal about relationships among the independent variables. Prediction of the dependent counts and a causal modeling that provides a substantive understanding of processes resulting in the dependent variable are not usually emphasized. In contrast, the aims of Poisson regression are more traditionally those of regression in general – to model influences on the dependent variable with the aims of prediction and explanation. Many counts, or Poisson-distributed variables, are substantively important dependent variables. Criminal recidivism, deaths, frequency of strikes and organizational promotions, for example, are among frequencies which have been analyzed using Poisson regression. In such cases, the substantive emphasis is on the explanation of events measured by the dependent frequencies.

Tabular analysis tends also, by its nature, to be aggregated. In the simple case, each row in the design matrix **X** represents a group of cases with a unique combination of covariates and the corresponding element of **m** gives the frequency of such cases. Where interval-level data are incorporated into such models (see the previous section), these data are usually in the form of an aggregated measurement across the cases with a unique covariate pattern. In contrast, Poisson regression is often used with individual-level data. Individual cases – the frequency of automobile accidents, sick days or number of sexual partners, for example – could be modeled as a dependent frequency m_i with individual covariate values of any permissible nature incorporated in the **X** matrix to provide a meaningful explanation or prediction. Of course, Poisson regression can also be readily applied to aggregated data including tabulations.

Constant hazards and exponential regression

If the vector of constants **z** is specified as a population-duration exposure to risk, rather than a simple population at risk, the dependent ratio m_i/z_i can be interpreted as a hazard, or rate of risk, to members of the population per time duration. Suppose, for example, that the dependent frequency m_i is a count of individuals of different gender (*G*) being first promoted in two different divisions (*D*) of an organization over the past five years since the organization was founded. Not all individuals in the organization were subject to the risk for the entire five years. Once promoted, individuals were no longer at risk of first promotion. New hires may have entered within the past five years and been subject to risk for only a fraction of this time.[8] And some individuals may have been subjected to the risk for a period of time but then left the organization and been censored from further risk. If we were to compute the person-months of exposure to risk of promotion among the employees of different divisions and gender, we could enter this into the model as a constant of exposure z_i. Using this specification we could then model the constant monthly hazard of promotion over the past five years and the proportional effect of covariates such as gender or division on these otherwise constant risks of promotion:

$$\ln \left(\frac{\text{promotions}}{\text{person-months at risk}} \right)$$

$$= \ln \left(\frac{m_i}{z_i} \right) = \hat{\beta}_0 + \hat{\beta}_1 g_i + \hat{\beta}_2 d_i + \varepsilon_i. \quad (12.30)$$

This constant hazard model is simply a case of ordinary grouped exponential regression. Women, for example, might have been proportionately less likely to be promoted over the entire five years than men, or those in a certain division, such as information technology, may be more likely than others to be promoted.

Piecewise proportional hazards

Most often, hazard models (such as those in Chapter 13) do not assume that the risk of an event is constant over the entire duration of exposure to risk. Instead, we might assume that hazards change across this time and attempt to model the changing level, or shape, of hazards as well as estimating coefficients for other effects upon risk. For example, suppose that in this organization the hazards of promotion increase, or decrease, over the time exposed to risk (T) or employment tenure. Looking at current employees, we hypothesize that the hazards of promotion are very low over the first two years of employment, then fairly high for the next two years, and then drop back down to a lower level if promotion has not occurred in that time. Accordingly, we have three categories of time (T) over which the hazard varies, as well as varying by gender (G) and across two divisions (D). Without interactions, this model could be written as

$$\ln \left(\frac{m_i}{z_i} \right) = \hat{\beta}_0 + \hat{\beta}_1 g_i + \hat{\beta}_2 d_i + \hat{\beta}_3 t_{2i}$$

$$+ \hat{\beta}_4 t_{3i} + \varepsilon_i. \quad (12.31)$$

where β_1 and β_2 give the proportional increase or decrease in hazards due to gender and division, while β_3 and β_4 give the proportional increase or decrease in hazards during the third to fourth years of employment and after four years of employment. The effects of gender and division raise or lower hazards proportionally across the entire time of exposure to risk. However, the time variables affect hazards across all groups for only a specific segment of the exposure to risk. These time effects can then be thought of as specifying the shape of a baseline piecewise hazard function over time which other covariates then raise or lower proportionately.

In our example gender and division are fixed covariates and do not change over the exposure to risk. It may be, however, that employees change division over time and the value of that covariate is actually time-varying or time-dependent. This case can be modeled through equation (12.1) by changing the notion of what constitutes a case or observation. Suppose we were to represent the data so that each case is not a person but a person-month, or more generally a person-spell, exposed to risk of the event. The value of covariates could then change with each spell or observation, allowing covariate values to change over time (see Allison, 1982, for a discussion of estimation concerns for discrete-time event histories with time-varying covariates, as well as extensions to the model presented here). As complexities such as time-dependent variables are introduced into the log-linear modeling framework, however, the model becomes cumbersome and such data may be best addressed by the related hazard models discussed in Chapter 13.

Interpretation of incidence rate ratios

Coefficient interpretations in the ordinary case of the frequency model were discussed earlier. The differences in interpretation for the log-rate or hazards-model cases are relatively straightforward. In log-rate regression, for example, exponentiated coefficients are often referred to as incidence rate ratios (IRRs) rather than odds ratios. This terminology simply refers to the fact that in models with a population exposed to risk specified as z_i, e^{β_j} gives the relative increase in the rate of incidence (e.g., per person) for a one-unit increase in the corresponding independent variable. If, for example, e^{β_1} for gender (G) in

Table 12.11   *Gastrointestinal deaths and exposure to risk by age and per-capita family income, Northampton and Holyoke, Massachusetts, 1850–1912*

Age group	Above median income	Gastrointestinal deaths	Person-years of exposure to risk
< 1	N	40	955
	Y	6	317
1–4	N	24	3422
	Y	5	1056.5
5–14	N	14	6869
	Y	3	2539.5
15–34	N	23	8901.5
	Y	10	12833
35–54	N	12	4952
	Y	7	4737.5
55–69	N	4	1093
	Y	6	1486
70+	N	4	478
	Y	4	294

Source: Anderton's data, see Hautaniemi et al. (2000)

the example above were 0.5, we would conclude that the relative rate of promotion among women, conditioning on other independent variables, was half that of men. Terminology for coefficients of the piecewise hazards regression varies somewhat among authors. Even if the exposure variable is specified as a person-duration exposed to risk, exponentiated coefficients can still be considered IRRs for the increase in the rate of incidence (now per person-duration hazards). However, if the shape of the underlying hazard function (i.e., the specified piecewise time pattern of risks) is correctly specified, or, alternatively, piecewise increments in time become smaller and smaller, coefficients approach those of ordinary proportional hazards regression (see Chapter 13). As a result, exponentiated coefficients are sometimes referred to as hazards ratios, which give the relative increase in the instantaneous hazard of an event for a one-unit increase in the corresponding independent variable.

Examples: Rate or piecewise hazard regression

Table 12.11 provides an illustration of data which might be used for a log-rate regression, or for a piecewise hazards modeling over a synthetic cohort. The dependent frequency m_i is a count of deaths due to gastrointestinal illnesses at each age in a historical sample. The offset z_i is set equal to the observed population-years of exposure to risk for all sample individuals and which produced the observed deaths. In addition to age group, a dichotomous variable indicating that the individual lived in a family with above median per-capita income at the onset of their exposure to risk is included as a covariate. The data come from a panel sample of two mill towns in Massachusetts during a period of unexpectedly high mortality (from 1850 through 1912), and attempt to address the long-standing question of whether income affected mortality in emerging mill towns during this period (see Hautaniemi et al., 2000).

A log-rate regression was fitted to these data with covariates of age and income. Since this is a pooled panel sample of individuals across this period and no individuals are followed throughout their life course, the underlying hazard function to be estimated by age is only a synthetic one. Table 12.12 gives the incidence rate ratios from this regression. From these results we can see that the relative rate of death from gastrointestinal diseases in the nineteenth century was more than three times as high for infants as for those over 70 (the excluded category with an IRR of 1.0). The hazards for age groups from 5 to 54 are considerably lower, up to a fifth of the rate for those over 70. Again

Table 12.12 *Poisson rate regression for gastrointestinal deaths*

Variable	IRR
<1	3.250*
1–4	0.578
5–14	0.164*
15–34	0.166*
35–54	0.201*
55–69	0.420
Income	0.538*

*Model and all noted coefficients significant at $p < 0.001$

(accepting the synthetic cohort for discussion purposes), this age pattern might be thought of as a piecewise hazard function for gastrointestinal deaths in this sample population over this period. Meanwhile, the coefficient for having a greater than median per-capita income (computed within decade) shows that the relative rate of such deaths for higher-income families was about half that of those with less than median per-capita income. From this limited modeling, income clearly lowered the risks substantially for this common nineteenth-century cause of death.

CONCLUSIONS

This chapter surveys a wide range of log-linear models and methods, beginning with the general log-linear model and then focusing on the logic of log-linear tabular analysis and the relationship of such models to the logistic regression model. It then presents basic extensions to these models in the form of methods which can be used to incorporate interval or ordinal-level information for marginal categorical variables and issues of dimensionality in tabular analyses. Finally, it returns to the more general form of the model and extensions to Poisson regression and exposure or log-rate models. The breadth of the treatment necessarily compromises the ability to provide a thoroughly comprehensive treatment of all issues involved in any one application. Many of the topics we have covered are approached in greater detail in comprehensive texts such as Agresti (1990), Cameron and Trivedi (1998), Long (1997) and Powers and Xie (2000). Fortunately,

there is also substantial overlap to be found in the relationship between log-linear models and those of Chapters 11 and 13. Many of the specific topics we felt obliged to omit from our treatment may be found in the surrounding material.

As the relationship of log-linear models to the general linear model and Poisson regression has become more apparent, the specialized notation and language developed for tabular applications have become less pronounced. Classic texts of the relatively recent decades past can confront the reader with a focus divorced from general linear models and a variety of unique tabular analysis notations. Nonetheless, some texts remain irreplaceable, including, for example, Fienberg (1977), Haberman (1978), Goodman (1978) and Goodman (1984). Some of the recent texts noted above also provide a valuable link between the findings of these earlier volumes and a more contemporary regression-oriented notation. We have found Powers and Xie (2000) of particular pedagogical use in this regard.

Special-purpose software packages with mnemonic names such as ECTA (Everyman's Contingency Table Analysis) were a mainstay of log-linear modeling in the 1970s. Virtually all major software packages adopted log-linear modeling routines soon thereafter. BMDP's 4F (Dixon, 1990) is an example of such table-oriented log-linear analysis routines. GLIM (see Lindsey, 1989), LIMDEP (see Greene, 1995) and other matrix- and regression-oriented packages were the most flexible early software implementations. Since the 1990s regression-oriented software with tremendous flexibility to specify complex models has become common within major multi-purpose software programs. The Poisson regression routine in STATA (Stata Corp., 2001), for example, incorporates exposures or offsets, uses general MLE routines for solution, can accommodate aggregated or individual-level frequency data, and provides complete control over construction of cases and design matrices. With such software virtually all of the models discussed in this chapter can be readily estimated. A number of models which involve scaling and latent structures (e.g., some of the ordinal models discussed in the section on covariate scale and dimensionality) and others beyond our exposition require more specialized software or user-written routines. Software for such models is, however, quickly becoming more widespread within modular software programs such as STATA and SAS (SAS Institute, 1990).

NOTES

1 The data for this example come from the second Topical Module data file.

2 We have chosen to use {0,1} dummy variable coding in the design matrix **X**. Other methods for coding model effects are perfectly acceptable, such as contrast coding or an effect-coded vector constraining the sum of parameters. Effect coding of this sort is, in fact, common in early presentations of log-linear models (e.g., Fienberg, 1977). These alternative design matrix strategies yield equivalent models, although the interpretation of the coefficients will be relative to the coding design.

3 Such estimation methods are discussed in detail at a later point.

4 The vector of error terms contains only zeros in this model because we are estimating four linear equations using four parameters. Such models are called 'saturated models' and yield no stochastic error. We include the zero vector of error terms at this point for consistency in presentation.

5 In the case of the logit and log-linear models the results are equivalent to maximum likelihood regression.

6 Decimal values are rounded to three places unless the reported value is a ratio of two component fractions, in which case we will round to two decimal places.

7 These assumptions can also be related to those of Chapter 11 for the special case of ordered logit regression and, as in that case, should not be accepted without critical examination and confirmation.

8 Individuals enter exposure to risk at the start of the observation or at first hire after the beginning of the study. This is not a case of less tractable 'left censoring' where individuals enter observation midway in their exposure to risk.

REFERENCES

Agresti, A. (1990) *Categorical Data Analysis.* New York: Wiley.

Allison, Paul (1982) 'Discrete-time methods for the analysis of event histories', in S. Leinhardt (ed.), *Sociological Methodology 1982.* San Francisco: Jossey-Bass, pp. 61–98.

Becker, M.P. and Clogg, C.C. (1989) 'Analysis of sets of two-way contingency tables using association

models', *Journal of the American Statistical Association*, 84: 142–51.

Bowker, Geoffrey C. and Star, Susan Leigh (1999) *Sorting Things Out: Classification and its Consequences.* Cambridge, MA: MIT Press.

Cameron, A.C. and Trivedi, P.K. (1998) *Regression Analysis of Count Data.* New York: Cambridge University Press.

Clogg, C.C. (1992) 'The impact of sociological methodology on statistical methodology', *Statistical Science*, 7: 183–207.

Dixon, W.J. (ed.) (1990) *BMDP Statistical Software Manual, Vol. 1.* Berkeley: University of California Press.

Fienberg, S.E. (1977) *The Analysis of Cross-classified Categorical Data.* Cambridge, MA: MIT Press.

Goodman, L.A. (1978) *Analyzing Qualitative/ Categorical Data: Log-linear Models and Latent-Structure Analysis.* Cambridge, MA: Abt Books.

Goodman, L.A. (1979) 'Simple models for the analysis of association in cross-classifications having ordered categories', *Journal of the American Statistical Association*, 47: 537–52.

Goodman, Leo A. (1981) 'Criteria for determining whether certain categories in a cross-classification table should be combined, with special reference to occupational categories in an occupational mobility table', *American Journal of Sociology*, 87: 612–50.

Goodman, L.A. (1984) *The Analysis of Cross-classified Data Having Ordered Categories.* Cambridge, MA: Harvard University Press.

Greene, W.H. (1995) *LIMDEP Version 7.0.* Bellport, NY: Econometric Software.

Haberman, S.J. (1978) *Analysis of Qualitative Data, Vol. 1: Introductory Topics.* Orlando, FL: Academic Press.

Hautaniemi, Susan I., Anderton, Douglas L. and Swedlund, Alan (2000) 'Matching 1850–1912 death records to a geographic census sample in two Massachusetts towns', *Historical Methods*, 33(1): 16–29.

Lakoff, George (1987) *Women, Fire, and Dangerous Things: What Categories Reveal about the Mind.* Chicago: University of Chicago Press.

Lindsey, J.K. (1989) *The Analysis of Categorical Data Using GLIM.* New York: Springer-Verlag.

Long, J.S. (1997) *Regression Models for Categorical and Limited Dependent Variables.* Thousand Oaks, CA: Sage.

Powers, D.A. and Xie, Y (2000) *Statistical Methods for Categorical Data Analysis.* San Diego, CA: Academic Press.

Raftery, A.E. (1995) 'Bayesian model selection in social research, in P.V. Marsden (ed.), *Sociological Methodology 1995.* Cambridge, MA and Oxford, UK: Blackwell, pp. 111–63.

SAS Institute, Inc. (1990) *SAS/STAT User's Guide, Version 6* (4th edition). Cary, NC: SAS Institute.

Stata Corporation. (2001) *Stata Reference Manual, Release 7, Vol. 2*. College Station, TX: Stata Press.

US Bureau of the Census (1996) *SIPP Users Guide*. Washington, DC: Governement Printing Office.

Willikens, F. (1982) 'Multidimensional population analysis with incomplete data, in Kenneth C. Land and Andrei Rogers (eds), *Multidimensional Mathematical Demography*. New York: Academic Press, pp. 43–111.

PART III

Longitudinal Models

13

Modeling Change

NANCY BRANDON TUMA

Although much social scientific research focuses on relationships at some point in time, change has been a topic of deep and abiding interest. Studies of change seek to comprehend not only the nature of variation but also how variation comes about. That is, they attempt to *understand* change.

When researchers refer to modeling change, they usually mean change in something over *time*, where the units of time may be decades, years, months, weeks, days, or even minutes and seconds, depending on the phenomenon being studied. There are also models of change over other dimensions, such as space – for example, how political preferences vary from one region of a country to another. The present chapter provides an introduction to issues arising in modeling and analyzing change over time. It only occasionally mentions models of change over space.

Several following chapters (Chapters 14–17) are concerned with specific models of change, and sections of a few other chapters (in particular, Chapters 12, 19, 20, and 21) also touch on models of change. In addition to discussing general issues in modeling and analyzing change, the present chapter supplements the other chapters by pointing to some noteworthy approaches to modeling change over time that are not discussed elsewhere in this volume.

There exist two decidedly different approaches to modeling change, and the chapter opens by explaining these two approaches. Three main sections follow. The first discusses some key dimensions on which models of change vary and can usefully be classified (e.g., the type of outcome, and whether time is discrete or continuous). Such classifications are helpful for researchers trying to identify the type of model of change for their particular scientific problem. The second section describes several examples of one approach to modeling change, called a theory-dominant approach below – an approach not covered elsewhere in this volume. The chapter concludes with a review of a variety of research and data-collection design issues relevant to studying change empirically.

TWO APPROACHES: MODELS OF CHANGE VERSUS MODELING CHANGE

Social scientific approaches to change over time in some phenomenon of interest fall mainly on a continuum between two ideal types. Occasionally they combine elements of different approaches on this continuum.

One end of the continuum may be termed the *data-dominant* approach. In this type of approach, researchers have empirical data on change in some phenomenon of interest to them, and they wish to analyze these data in order to draw some general conclusions about social life. For example, they may have measures of countries' attributes annually, of firms' characteristics monthly, of people's employment statuses weekly, or of experimental subjects' agreement with a group every minute. The phenomenon being studied may steadily increase, consistently decrease, slowly or rapidly fluctuate, or be stable over time.

The purposes of research based on a data-dominant approach vary widely. Since the nature of the research objectives often influences how change over time is modeled, it is helpful to distinguish the main types of goals.

Firstly, researchers may wish to *describe* patterns of change – that is, to form empirical generalizations on the basis of the available data. In this instance, the usual aim is to obtain a relatively accurate but parsimonious summary of large quantities of information in the available data. For example, they may wish to summarize change over time in patterns of economic growth in a country or a set of countries.

Secondly, they may wish to *associate* patterns of change in some phenomenon with other patterns that are regarded as *correlates* of the change, but that are not necessarily thought to be *causes* of the change. They may believe that particular changes in the phenomenon of interest tend to be associated with certain other patterns but be indifferent or agnostic concerning what is a cause and what is an effect. For instance, they may wish to associate patterns of economic growth in a country with having a certain type of social and political structure, but they may not care whether a particular type of social or political structure actually promotes economic growth.

Thirdly, they may wish to *explain* patterns of change in some phenomenon in terms of other patterns that are hypothesized to be causes of the change, and that are not seen simply as correlates of change. As an example, they may want to learn whether the introduction of certain governmental policies fosters or promotes economic growth.

Lastly, they may wish to *predict* change in the phenomenon in the future, or in a social context other than the source of the data being analyzed. To illustrate, they may wish to predict economic growth in the near future in the country from which the available data came, or in another country with similar characteristics. Usually forecasts are improved by knowledge of causes, but information on the correlates of change is sometimes nearly as helpful.

A data-dominant approach is very common in the social sciences. When adopting this approach, researchers frequently consider *existing models of change* and select one that seems to fit key characteristics of the available data. Often the model that the researcher chooses is *informed* by theory but *not derived* directly from a specific theory of change. Because a data-dominant approach is so common in the social sciences, most chapters in this volume focus on the set of existing models of change from which researchers usually choose.

At the other end of the continuum is what may be called a *theory-dominant* approach. In this approach, researchers start with a theory of change in some phenomenon and then translate the theory into a model of change. The model is derived directly from the theory, as far as possible, and includes a bare minimum of supplementary assumptions (e.g., about initial conditions). Researchers then use the model to draw out various implications pertaining to the phenomenon. Next, they may assess the theory and the model informally by deciding whether those implications are broadly consistent with available information about the phenomenon. Alternatively or additionally, they may use the implications of the model to decide what empirical data are needed to perform a critical test of the theory and the model. They may then collect such data and use them to estimate and formally test the model. The results of these tests permit them to assess the model and the theory from which the model was derived.

The theory-dominant approach is widespread in the physical and some natural sciences. For example, physicists have deduced implications of Einstein's theory of relativity for various observable phenomena and then designed ways to collect empirical data that test various aspects of the theory. Most of the empirical data sets used to test the theory would never have been collected if physicists had not first deduced that certain data would allow it to be tested.

The models of change that result from a theory-dominant approach are often very specific to a particular phenomenon. Consequently, a model of change developed using the theory-dominant approach may have little impact on the development of models of change in other, unrelated phenomena, even if it is an excellent model of the phenomenon for which it was originally developed. The theory-dominant approach is still relatively rare in the social sciences. A few examples of models of change developed by social scientists who have adopted a theory-dominant approach are described in the section after next.

CLASSIFYING MODELS OF CHANGE

Whether someone takes a data-dominant or a theory-dominant approach to modeling change, it is useful to classify the resulting models on various dimensions. Such a classification can help researchers who want to choose a suitable model for analyzing available empirical data or to build an appropriate, theory-based model of change in the phenomenon of interest to them.

Variable-based versus agent-based models

Most existing models of change are *variable-based*. There are units of analysis (e.g., people, households, organizations, countries, social networks, social events, cultural artifacts), and each unit of analysis has attributes that are measured by variables (e.g., age, size). With this type of model, the objective is to study change in one or more variables describing the units of analysis. For example, a researcher may wish to describe, explain, or predict change over time in the size of a household or firm in terms of other time-invariant or time-varying variables that describe characteristics of the household or firm.

Other models of change are *agent-based* (cf. Macy and Willer, 2002). Like the units of analysis in most variable-based models, agents may be people, organizations, countries – any kind of social actor.[1] With agent-based models, the objective is to study the sequence of actions and interactions of the agents over time and perhaps the consequences of the agents' actions for higher-level structures. For example, the goal may be to study a sequence of exchanges among actors in order to study the emergence of various properties of groups (e.g., norms of exchange, or the structure of a group's social hierarchy). Most game-theoretic models are agent-based, and so are many computer simulation models; for some examples, see the next section.

The distinction between variable-based and agent-based models is useful but should not be overdrawn. In agent-based models, one can regard whether a particular agent acts at some point in time as a variable. Further, if an agent does act at a certain time, the nature of the action can usually be classified in some way (e.g., as hostile, neutral, or supportive of another actor; as information-seeking versus information-giving). Actions that are classifiable can be coded as variables.

Nonetheless, even though actions of agents and the consequences of agents' actions can be treated as variables, modeling such variables is rarely the *primary* objective of the researchers who develop agent-based models.

Time: discrete or continuous

Changes in a phenomenon may occur at discrete points in time or continuously in time. For example, the majority political party in the US Senate changes at discrete points in time, usually only following biennial elections.[2] In contrast, many phenomena can change at any continuous moment in time. There is, for instance, no set time when people marry, have children, change jobs, move geographically, and die; or when firms introduce new products, change their chief officers, adopt new strategies, merge with other firms, and file for bankruptcy.

In modeling change over time, researchers need to consider *both* when changes can occur in principle (i.e., at discrete time points or continuously) *and* when changes are observed and measured. Observations of change in a phenomenon may range from as few as two points in time, to several points in time, to many discrete points in time, to essentially continuously in time. Continuous (or essentially continuous) observations and measurements are invaluable when changes can occur at any moment in time as they mean that the data can record more changes (and skip fewer changes). Greater frequency of measurements in time is extremely helpful when studying change in some phenomenon over time because additional measurements facilitate the selection of one explanation of change rather than another. Designs for observing the phenomenon of interest and their consequences are discussed in more detail in the final section of this chapter.

Models of difference versus dynamic models

A related distinction that arises when modeling change concerns whether a model is intended to be a *model of difference* or a *dynamic model*, that is, a model of the evolution of a social process over time.

Variable-based models are sometimes models of difference and sometimes dynamic models. The choice of one type rather than the other depends on the researcher's objectives and possibly also on the characteristics of the available data. A model of difference, for instance, is conventional when an experimenter is interested only in whether a particular treatment influences the outcome of interest. If the goal is to discover whether a treatment has some effect, then there is no inherent scientific reason to choose a dynamic model. On the other hand, researchers who are interested in the fundamental nature of social processes and their consequences will ordinarily prefer dynamic models.

Agent-based models are almost always dynamic models because the goal is to imitate interactions and behaviors of agents over time. Each agent responds to the prior action(s) of one or more other agents in the system, leading to an extended sequence of behaviors over time.

At first glance it may appear that a model of difference is the more natural choice when the times of changes are discrete, and that a dynamic model is the more natural choice when the times of changes are continuous. Such an association may exist in previous social scientific research, but it is by no means inevitable. Change in the majority party in the Senate tends to occur at discrete time points (at biennial elections), as noted above; however, a researcher may be interested in the *process* of change in political control during some historical period, in which case a discrete-time dynamic model would be highly suitable. Contrarily, a person's earnings are subject to change at any continuous moment in time, but a researcher might want to learn only if participation in an experimental job training program boosts earnings. Then a model of the difference in earnings before and after participation in the job training program would be appropriate.

Types of outcomes

In variable-based models, the outcome of interest is typically called the dependent variable. Usually it is a single variable, but it may also be two or more interdependent variables (e.g., a husband's and wife's weekly hours of work). Models of change in a single variable tend to be easier to manipulate than models of change in several interdependent variables.

Researchers who wish to understand associations among variables may choose to model change in tabular arrays, that is, in cross-classifications of variables (see Chapter 12). In most instances, time is one of the several cross-classified variables comprising the tabular array.

Still more complex are models of change in social networks. In these models, the nodes in the social network are usually taken as fixed, though in principle nodes could be added or removed over time. More often models of change in a social network focus on changes in the linkages between a fixed set of nodes. That is, the linkages between the nodes in the network may be created or broken, strengthened or weakened. Changes in the linkages between the nodes may result in change in various higher-level network properties, for example, the connectedness of the network. Models of change in social networks are not covered in this volume. See Snijders (2003) or Wasserman and Faust (1994) for an introduction to this topic.[3]

The outcome of interest in an agent-based model may also be a single variable or a set of several interdependent variables. However, it may also be an emergent property of a group or set of agents, such as certain structural properties of the group.

Types of variables

Researchers working with variable-based models of change routinely distinguish their *dependent variables* (outcomes of interest) from the *independent variables* (other variables believed to be correlates, predictors, or causes of the dependent variables). Independent variables may be further categorized as *explanatory variables* or *control variables*.

The distinction between an explanatory and a control variable reflects the way a researcher views the role of an independent variable in the analysis rather than its actual impact. Explanatory variables are ones regarded as potentially causing the outcome; they are typically ones about which the researcher has formulated hypotheses that are to be tested in the analysis. In contrast, control variables are ancillary variables that the researcher believes to be associated with both the dependent variable and one or more explanatory variables. Such ancillary variables need to be measured and *controlled* in order to distinguish the genuine effects of the explanatory variables on the dependent variable from spurious effects resulting from associations between the explanatory variables and other predictor variables of no particular theoretical interest.

Although independent variables are often regarded as potential causes of dependent variables, causation is notoriously difficult to establish. Chapter 21 in this volume contains a lengthy discussion of the complex issues associated with establishing causation rather than just association. Temporal ordering is conventionally assumed to be an important feature of causal relationships because it is almost always assumed that what happened in the past may have a causal effect on the future, but that what happens in the future cannot have a causal impact on the past.[4] Consequently, as Chapter 21 points out, analysis of longitudinal data can be very helpful in evaluating whether an association between two variables reflects a causal relationship between them.

Measurement scale of variables

Both dependent and independent variables are further categorized by their scale of measurement. Both types of variables may be either discrete (i.e., their measurement scale can be mapped onto a set of points or numerals) or continuous (i.e., their measurement scale can be mapped onto a segment of what mathematicians call a 'real line' or continuum of numbers).

Discrete variables can be further divided into those whose scales are nominal (i.e., values are arbitrary and cannot be ordered), ordinal (i.e., values can be ordered but distances between values are arbitrary), interval (i.e., both values and the distances between values can be ordered), and cardinal (i.e., there is a meaningful, nonarbitrary zero point such that a particular value can be said to be a certain multiple of some other specific value). Binary-valued discrete variables (also known as indicator, dummy, or 0–1 variables) are the most common type of discrete variable. Discrete variables may also be polytomous (i.e., have more than two distinct values). A polytomous discrete variable is often recoded as a series of binary-valued discrete variables, especially when the polytomous variable is an independent variable. Though there are some exceptions, it is generally not advisable to recode a polytomous discrete dependent variable as a set of binary-valued variables and then to model each of the resulting binary-valued variables. This is because the resulting set of binary-valued variables have an intrinsic negative covariance. It turns out to be easier to model a polytomous discrete dependent variable directly; see the discussion of modeling polytomous discrete variables in Chapter 11.

Since continuous variables can be mapped onto a real line, and since points on a real line are ordered, the values of continuous variables are always ordered. Moreover, the distances between two points on a real line can be ordered; consequently, numerical differences between various values of a continuous variable can be compared. Hence, continuous variables have measurement scales that are either interval or cardinal.

Whether a continuous variable has an interval or cardinal scale depends on whether its scale has a meaningful, nonarbitrary zero point. Various scales for measuring temperature illustrate this distinction. On the Fahrenheit (F) scale of temperature, the zero point is arbitrary. Consequently, one cannot legitimately claim that 100°F is twice 50°F. In contrast, on the kelvin (K) scale of temperature, zero is the point at which molecular movement is a minimum. The pressure of an ideal gas in a container with a fixed volume is zero at 0 K, and it is twice as great at 100 K as at 50 K. Consequently, the zero point on the kelvin scale is not arbitrary but has a real physical meaning.

Occasionally the scale used to measure a variable may have a mixture of continuous and discrete values. In these instances, it is ordinarily assumed that the true values of the variable are continuous and that the discrete values are the result of using a measurement procedure that records only discrete values for certain ranges of the variable (i.e., the variable is censored). For example, respondents to a survey may be asked to report their annual income to the nearest dollar if it is a typical, middling value (e.g., between $10 000 and $100 000) but only whether it falls in certain ranges if it is very low (e.g., below $10 000) or very high (e.g., above $100 000).

Deterministic versus probabilistic models

Some models of change are fundamentally deterministic. Such models posit specific relationships among variables or specific rules that govern actions of agents. Although it may appear that a deterministic model of change must be simple, since by definition everything is determined, in actuality deterministic models can be very complicated. The relationships and rules built into a deterministic model may be so numerous and complex that the model's implications are far from obvious.

Although deterministic models are not probabilistic by definition, a random disturbance is sometimes added after the implications of the deterministic model have been deduced. Even though a model is fundamentally deterministic, the addition of a random disturbance implies that the outcome of interest occurs with some probability distribution – namely, the probability distribution of the random disturbance that is added to the solution of the deterministic model. For example, Coleman (1968) proposed several differential equation models of change in continuous variables (see also Chapters 14 and 15). These models can be solved using integral calculus or other standard techniques for solving differential equations. The addition of a standard normal (i.e., Gaussian) disturbance to the solution for the continuous dependent variable is a common way of converting the differential equation model into a statistical model that can be estimated from longitudinal data. Adding a normally distributed disturbance to the solution is equivalent to assuming that the outcome has a normal distribution, conditional on other variables in the model. This model is fundamentally deterministic, however, because the stochastic component is added to the solution in a post hoc fashion and is not intrinsic to the model: a random disturbance with a different probability distribution could be added instead.

Other models of change are intrinsically probabilistic or stochastic. Variable-based stochastic models posit that particular variables have a certain probabilistic relationship to one another. Agent-based probabilistic models assume that agents' actions are governed by certain rules that apply with specific probabilities.

Probabilistic models are usually more realistic than deterministic models because few real-world outcomes occur with certainty at a specific time and with a definite value. The certainty of death and taxes is a widely accepted maxim. But, it is not certain *when* death will occur or why; it is also uncertain *whether* taxpayers will file a tax return, report their income accurately, or pay the tax they owe. Consequently, it is more realistic to develop probabilistic than deterministic models of the time of death and of taxpayers' payment of their taxes.

Social versus asocial models

Although social scientists' models of change deal with certain aspects of social life, relatively few of them are intrinsically social. In a model that is *intrinsically social*, the actions and/or characteristics of one actor, agent, or unit of analysis depend explicitly (although not necessarily directly) on the actions and/or characteristics of other actors and agents in the social system.[5]

Agent-based models are almost always intrinsically social. These kinds of models postulate that the actions and characteristics of agents are influenced by the actions and characteristics of the other agents in a given social system.

In contrast, most variable-based models of change are not intrinsically social, and in that sense they are *asocial*. In most variable-based models, the outcome for one unit of analysis is ordinarily assumed to be statistically independent of the actions and characteristics of other units of analysis. Such models are social only in the sense that the variables in them are socially meaningful.

Consider, for example, a status attainment model in which a person's occupational status at one time (e.g., adulthood) depends on predetermined conditions (e.g., the person's situation in childhood and adolescence). Each adult's occupational attainment (a socially meaningful outcome) is assumed to depend on various other socially meaningful independent variables that are determined beforehand (e.g., the person's gender, race, family background, completed education), plus a random disturbance. Coefficients of the independent variables are assumed to link an adult's occupational status to the values of the independent variables in the model. However, in most status attainment models, an adult's status is assumed *not* to depend on the characteristics of the other people in the same social system, and thus these models are not intrinsically social in the sense defined above.

Variable-based models that are intrinsically social are fairly rare, probably because such models tend to be quite complex and therefore present many mathematical, methodological, and statistical challenges. For example, a status attainment model may be modified to allow the random disturbances for two siblings to co-vary because of unspecified unobserved variables that are assumed to influence each sibling's attainment in the same way (e.g., the unobserved variables may be attributes of the home environment). These shared unobserved variables are typically represented by a component of the random disturbance that has a nonzero covariance for siblings. But, net of this component of the random disturbance shared by siblings, one sibling's attainment is usually assumed to be independent of every other sibling's attainment, as well as independent of every other person's attainment. Thus, these variance-components models, as they are typically called, are social, but in an indirect and fairly limited way (see Chapter 19).

Multi-level variable-based models of change (see Chapter 20) provide a somewhat similar way of making variable-based models more social. These models postulate that socially meaningful variables measured on a higher level (e.g., the level of a school or classroom) affect the values of variables measured for a lower-level unit of analysis (e.g., a pupil in a school or classroom).

To give yet another and rather different example, some variable-based models informed by queuing theory have assumed that a change in the characteristics of one unit of analysis depends on the characteristics of the other units (see Boylan, 1992, 1993). The interdependence of the units occurs because they are in the same queue. Consequently, the relative position of every unit in the queue depends on the positions of all other units in the same queue.

Another example is furnished by diffusion models. In these models, the likelihood that one unit of analysis has an event depends on the previous events experienced by other units in the system (cf. Marsden and Podolny, 1990; Strang and Tuma, 1993). Diffusion models postulate that past outcomes for certain units have causal effects on future outcomes for other units.[6]

Drawing implications of models: deduction versus computation

In order for a model of change to be useful, researchers need to know its implications for phenomena that are observable. The implications of the model can then be compared with what is observed. Similarities between the model's implications and empirical observations can offer support for the model and for the theory associated with the model, or they can cast the model and theory into doubt.

The implications of most common models of change are deduced mathematically. The particular mathematical tools used to deduce a model's implications depend, of course, on the mathematical properties of the model. For example, if researchers choose a differential equation model of change in one or more variables (Chapter 14, this volume; Coleman, 1968; Tuma and Hannan, 1984: Chapters 11–15), they typically deduce the model's implications using standard techniques for solving differential equations. On the other hand, if researchers select a Markov or another similar probabilistic model of change in a categorical variable, they might deduce its implications using Laplace transforms (see Tuma and Hannan, 1984: Chapter 4).

Differences in the mathematical tools used to draw implications of models are rarely consequential for social scientists' purposes. The primary exception occurs when a model of change is so complex that its implications cannot be deduced formally or mathematically, at least without undue difficulty. In such instances, researchers may examine the implications of the model through computation. That is, they may compute results for the model over time under various hypothetical conditions (i.e., scenarios). They may then try to reach generalizations about the model's implications by searching for patterns among the results that are computed for numerous and widely varying scenarios.

More specifically, researchers using variable-based models may choose hypothetical values of parameters and select values of the independent variables for a sample of cases in a pseudo-random way, and then calculate how the value of the outcome varies over time, whether it reaches an equilibrium value, and, if so, what the equilibrium value of the outcome is. Very complex linear programming models of the American economy illustrate this point. Such models may have so many equations, and so many variables in each equation, that a computational approach to learning the implications of any particular model often turns out to be more tractable than pure mathematical deduction.

To give another example, researchers may have estimated parameters in a variable-based model from sample data using standard methods of statistical estimation and inference and then wish to use the parameter estimates to predict the implications of the model for the entire US population. Often the best way of forecasting the model's implications is first to compute the implications of the model for each individual surveyed in a previous census or in a large sample of the US population and next to aggregate the results predicted for these individuals.

In contrast, researchers using agent-based models may develop a simulation model (usually a computer simulation) in which agents behave according to certain rules, perhaps with some degree of randomness, and then compute how the agents behave in response to one another's actions over time and in the long run.

Computational approaches to drawing the implications of a model can be particularly useful when researchers are interested in the *time path of change* and not simply in an equilibrium or final result. Although the time path of change, and in particular the *average* time path of change, can be deduced mathematically for a great many models, computing realizations of the time path can be highly instructive. A computational approach is especially valuable for probabilistic models when few cases are involved, or when there is some probability (often a small probability) of a certain kind of change that thereafter leads to a drastically different time path and long-run result than would otherwise have occurred.

For example, deterministic models of diffusion of information, a social practice, or a disease in a population may have a certain smooth time path that eventually reaches some long-run equilibrium value. If one of these deterministic diffusion models is converted into an analogous stochastic diffusion model, the time path of the stochastic version may jump around considerably. Further, sometimes the implications of the deterministic model for the time path and long-run equilibrium value are numerically quite different from the average time path and long-run value of the corresponding stochastic model. More surprisingly yet, the values predicted by the stochastic version of the diffusion model may not be concentrated around its average. There can be fairly high probabilities of markedly different values and low probabilities of intermediary values; for some concrete examples, see Bartholomew (1982). A computational approach can reveal these anomalies.

MODELS OF CHANGE: SOME EXAMPLES

As noted at the beginning of this chapter, there is an important division between social scientists who adopt a data-dominant approach to modeling change and those who take a theory-dominant approach. For the former group, various features of the research and data-collection designs typically have big impacts on the model of change used to study the phenomenon of interest. Some of the key features of research and data-collection designs that are relevant to modeling change are outlined in the next section. For the latter group of researchers who have a theory-dominant approach, features of the research and data-collection design are more often consequences of the model that is developed.

As noted early in this chapter, social scientists taking a theory-dominant approach may develop an excellent model of change in a certain phenomenon, but their model may not be directly or easily translated into a model of change in any other phenomenon. Such models can, nevertheless, be regarded as exemplars of modeling change using this approach. It is worthwhile describing a few of these models before turning to a discussion of research and data-collection designs that are of such great importance to researchers using a data-dominant approach.

Evolution of cooperation

Work on the impact of various strategies on cooperation among actors over time provides a famous example of a theory-dominant approach to modeling change. This research mainly uses agent-based models of strategies governing actors' interactions, with each strategy (i.e., each set of rules of behavior) translated into a computer routine or program. That is, a computer routine simulates or models an agent's behavior at a given time when the agent has adopted a certain strategy for responding to another agent's past actions. Such models are intrinsically social because each agent's action at a given time depends on the previous (usually recent) actions of another agent, as well as on environmental characteristics that provide a structure of incentives for various possible actions. These models are dynamic because they specify the process of interaction, which unfolds step by step over time.

The basic environment is usually referred to as an iterated prisoners' dilemma game between two agents. It is structured to offer moderate rewards to both agents when they cooperate with one another in a given game (i.e., in a single round of interactions).

However, it also puts the two agents in direct competition with one another. Competition arises because in any given trial, each agent obtains the highest reward by *not* cooperating (i.e., by *defecting*) when the other agent acts in a cooperative way. More specifically, in any single trial of the game, each agent *gains the most* if he does not cooperate (i.e., defects) and the other agent cooperates, *gains the least* if he cooperates and the other agent defects, and *gains an intermediary amount* if both agents cooperate or if both defect. The two agents gain more when they both cooperate than when they both defect.

A major objective of this line of research is to identify a strategy that maximizes an agent's gains over a long series of trials, independently of the strategy adopted by the other agent. The environment is designed so that the long-run gains of both agents are maximized by the adoption of strategies that foster high levels of cooperation between the two agents over time, even though the *potential* gain in any given round is greatest if the agent does not cooperate. Each agent's dilemma is that defection maximizes the potential gain in a given trial but does not tend to maximize joint gains, or even the agent's own gains, in a lengthy series of repeated trials.

To study this problem, Axelrod (1984) invited other people to propose a variety of strategies and to embed each strategy in a computer routine that simulated the actions of an agent who adopted a particular strategy. He then paired the computer routines performing the various proposed strategies and had them iterate over an extended series of games. A particular strategy might do well (i.e., lead to a high overall gain) against certain strategies but do poorly against certain other strategies. The goal was to find strategies that would do relatively well no matter what strategy was adopted by the other agent.

Axelrod discovered that a simple tit-for-tat strategy yielded the highest overall gain among the various strategies that were proposed. This strategy, which was suggested and then expressed as a four-line(!) computer program by Anatol Rapoport, starts by cooperating on the first trial (i.e., starts *nice*). On each trial thereafter, the agent imitates whatever the other agent did on the previous trial. Thus, the agent behaves cooperatively if the other agent cooperated on the previous trial and behaves competitively (i.e., defects) if the other agent defected on the previous trial. Pitting tit-for-tat against tit-for-tat leads both agents to cooperate for ever. But if the original, nice tit-for-tat strategy is modified slightly so that each begins by defecting (i.e., starts *mean*), then both agents will always defect. Finally, if the original tit-for-tat strategy with a nice start is matched against a tit-for-tat with a mean start, the two agents will cycle endlessly between cooperating and defecting. With a purely imitative strategy, actions on the initial round are critical.

While the original, nice tit-for-tat strategy was the best of those proposed, some other strategies were nearly as successful. Axelrod attempted to identify general characteristics of strategies that led to comparatively high scores on total gain in a lengthy series of interactions. He found that the higher-scoring strategies tended not only to be nice (i.e., start cooperatively) but also to be *forgiving* (i.e., more likely to cooperate, even if the other agent had recently defected). In sum, higher-scoring strategies did tend to have some broadly similar characteristics.

Although Axelrod measured a strategy's success in a lengthy series of interactions by a dependent variable (each agent's total gain), his main method of evaluating the various agent-based models differed from the methods typically used to evaluate variable-based models. He did not try to model total gain as a dependent variable; he did not collect empirical data on real agents' behaviors; and he did not select a 'best' model through statistical inference and hypothesis testing. Rather, he considered many different behavioral models of agents' actions and reactions. The data were generated by computer routines that simulated a sequence of interactions resulting from adoption of a particular strategy. Each strategy was then evaluated by computing the variable measuring success (the total gain in a lengthy series of interactions) and simply determining whether it yielded a higher score than the other proposed strategies. The whole approach was different from what is typical with a data-dominant approach because the goal was different: to evaluate a model grounded in a theory of successful behavior in a sequence of repeated interactions.

Artificial societies

Another example of a theory-dominant approach to modeling change is provided by work on computer simulation models of artificial societies.[7] Key elements in these models are ordinarily an environment (e.g., a distribution of one or more resources arrayed spatially in a 'landscape'), a set of agents who are also arrayed spatially and who may be heterogeneous, and a variety of rules. The rules specify such things as how resources are created and depleted over time, how agents are born and die, and how agents behave in general and in response to various changing conditions. More specifically, there may be rules for how agents search for resources, move spatially, consume resources, and stockpile resources. There may also be rules for how agents interact with other agents whom they encounter over time. For instance, an agent may cooperate with another agent to achieve some goal (e.g., trade or share resources, or 'marry' to create a 'child' or new agent). Contrarily, one agent may seek to dominate or even to 'kill' (i.e., eliminate) another agent. Often the rules are probabilistic. For example, probabilistic rules usually govern where in the spatial array an agent looks for resources, where the agent moves, and how the agent acts toward other agents whom the agent encounters over time.

After developing such a computer simulation model, researchers prescribe certain initial conditions (e.g., how agents and resources are initially arrayed over the landscape) and then allow the changes to occur step by step. In most instances, there is not a single dependent variable but a multiplicity of variables that change over time and often over space, too. By monitoring a variety of attributes over a long series of time points, the researchers learn how a hypothetical society evolves over time. They study how both variations in rules and various random events can lead the hypothetical society to evolve differently.

A number of models of artificial societies like those sketched above have been developed; for numerous references, see Epstein and Axtell (1996). Researchers have learned that many well-known features of real-world societies (e.g., population growth and decline, migration and spatial differentiation, formation of social hierarchies, transmission of culture) can result from basic principles and rules that are comparatively simple. As in the case of research on the evolution of cooperation, the entire approach in this line of research has differed from that typically taken by scholars adopting a data-dominant approach.

Social mobility

Although most efforts at modeling social mobility have utilized a data-dominant approach, a theory-dominant approach has occasionally been adopted. Two examples deserve mention here because they are distinctly different from the agent-based models described above.

One worth noting is Harrison White's (1970) classic proposal to model chains of vacancies. White made this proposal as part of an empirical study of the mobility of clergy in several Protestant churches in the US. He first theorized about the process of mobility of clergy and then collected empirical data.

Before White, social scientists studying social mobility invariably took the individual (or occasionally a family) as the unit of analysis and generally concentrated on the attributes of individuals (or families) that foster particular patterns of social mobility (e.g., upward rather than downward mobility). That is, before White, most models of social mobility were variable-based, probabilistic models of people's moves.

White's efforts at modeling social mobility were not novel from a mathematical viewpoint. In fact, he relied on standard and rather simple probabilistic models. His main innovation was a shift in theoretical perspective; it consisted of switching the basic unit of analysis from an individual person to a vacant social position.[8] In his empirical application, the set of social positions consisted of the roster of ministerial positions in a particular Protestant denomination in the US. The relevant individuals were the people who had been ordained as ministers in that denomination.

In White's conceptualization, the mobility of the Protestant clergy is a consequence of social processes that create vacant positions.[9] As he saw it, a vacant position in a given church could arise either because a new ministerial position is created (e.g., because a local parish church is growing) or because someone in a ministerial position leaves it (e.g., dies, retires, moves to a nonministerial position, or departs to fill another position that is vacant).

When a position becomes vacant, it is occasionally eliminated (e.g., because a local parish church is downsizing), but more often prompts a search for a new clergyman to fill the vacancy. If the vacant position is to be filled rather than eliminated, it represents a career opportunity for an ordained clergyman.

This opportunity might be secured either by someone holding an existing ministerial position or by someone in the pool of eligible clergy (e.g., a newly ordained minister, an unemployed clergyman, or someone temporarily in a nonministerial position). If a vacancy is filled by someone holding an existing ministerial position, it creates a new vacancy. In this way vacancies cascade through the organization (i.e., the roster of ministerial positions in the church), creating a chain of vacancies. Eventually the chain of vacancies terminates, either because a vacant position is eliminated, or because a vacancy is filled by someone who is not in a ministerial position (e.g., a newly ordained or unemployed clergyman).

White believed that a vacant ministerial position would usually be filled relatively quickly, unless it was to be eliminated entirely. Consequently, he did not consider the duration of vacancies, or the timing of filling them, to be scientifically interesting issues.[10] In contrast, he did regard the length of vacancy chains as a topic that merited scientific study. Hence, he collected empirical data on the length of vacancy chains and then examined the relationship of chain length to various attributes of ministerial positions and their occupants. Thus, his reasoning pointed him in the direction of modeling event sequences of vacancies (see Chapter 17) rather than modeling event histories of vacancies (see Chapter 16; Tuma and Hannan, 1984: Chapters 3–10).[11] It is important to stress, however, that in White's case, his approach to modeling social mobility resulted from his theoretical perspective. He did not decide that he had a certain kind of data (e.g., event sequences) and then look for an existing model of event sequences.

White's vacancy-chain model illustrates one type of dynamic, match-making model. A vacancy-chain model can sensibly be applied to other systems, as White recognized. The basic requirements are a system of social positions that exist independently of those who occupy positions, and a relatively bounded pool of individuals (or other agents) who tend to circulate among those positions.

Sørensen (1977, 1979) developed other models of social mobility that incorporated White's idea that job vacancies are the driving force underlying the social mobility of individuals. For example, in a 1977 article in the *American Sociological Review*, he postulated that there is a system of jobs offering rewards and that the rewards offered by jobs in this system have a certain probability distribution (namely, an exponential distribution). He assumed that people are heterogeneous in their resources but that each person's resources are fixed over time (i.e., over a career). Each person's fixed resources determine the maximum attainable level in the job-reward hierarchy. When people first enter the labor force (i.e., at the start of a career), they take jobs offering rewards that are at, or usually below, the maximum appropriate to their fixed resources. The distribution of people across the job-reward hierarchy at their career start is an initial condition specified by the researcher.

He assumed that job vacancies are created at a constant proportion that is independent of the rewards offered by a job. Sørensen focused on downward moves of vacancies and contrarily on the counterflowing upward moves of people. Although he acknowledged that real people also move laterally and downward, his model ignored these possibilities, which he considered to be scientifically less interesting than people's upward moves. Most people move upward in the job-reward hierarchy over time because they start below the maximum appropriate for their level of resources. Concomitantly, vacancies move downward in the job-reward hierarchy because of Sørensen's assumption that job vacancies are never filled by people who are underqualified in terms of their resources, only by people who are either appropriately or overqualified. Note that his assumptions imply that people are more overqualified for their job at the start of their career than at any later point. Sørensen was well aware of human capital theorists' arguments about work experience (e.g., Becker, 1975) and did not deny that the acquisition of work experience over a career leads job rewards to increase. One of his main goals, however, was to contrast the human capital theory of career advancement with a theory that ignored work experience in order to discover what insights could be gained from making assumptions that were different and admittedly oversimplified.

From a shortlist of rather simple assumptions, Sørensen then proceeded to derive such things as the promotion rate, the number of job shifts that a person would make during a career, and the time path of a person's job rewards over his or her career. In his 1977 article, Sørensen did not seek to estimate or test the expressions that he derived for various quantities. Rather, his intention was to demonstrate that a theory-based model could generate equations for the attainment of job rewards and the rate of upward moves over time that resembled the equations that had previously been estimated by himself and several other scholars who had adopted a data-dominant approach in the past.

RESEARCH DESIGN ISSUES

When modeling change over time in order to analyze *empirical* data, researchers tend to choose one of the set of existing models of change. Often various features of the research design used to make measurements over time are key factors affecting both what one can learn about change and how one can sensibly model it. As in any empirical study, one must consider the *sampling scheme*: how entities are selected for observation. In addition, one needs to consider features pertaining to both when data are *collected* and when the outcome and the independent variables in the study are *measured*. This section discusses how characteristics of the sampling scheme, data-collection design, and observation plan for temporal measurements affect a researcher's ability to model and empirically study change.

Sampling scheme

Sometimes the sample coincides with the population of interest. For instance, the sample in cross-national studies is often comprised of all, or virtually all, countries in the world. Or the sample may consist of a single country, with data for some lengthy series of time points,[12] because research goals are directed at understanding social processes in that country. When the sample corresponds to the population of interest for all practical purposes, sampling issues arise only indirectly (e.g., due to missing information on some sample members for certain time points or time periods).

In much social scientific research, however, the sample does not coincide with the population of interest. Then the main issues are whether the sample is *representative* of the population and whether the sample size is *large enough* to yield reliable conclusions about the population. The overall research design may be experimental or nonexperimental, and considerations pertaining to sampling are not exactly the same for these two types of designs.

In an experiment, investigators randomly assign subjects (i.e., the units of analysis, such as people) to various conditions, in particular, to various treatment and placebo groups.[13] When subjects are randomly assigned to treatment and placebo groups (i.e., to different values of the key independent variables), other variables are distributed independently of the theoretically interesting variables (e.g., a treatment group versus the placebo group). Consequently, there is little (if any) need to include supplementary control variables in the models used to analyze experimental data. For this reason, experimenters are often concerned primarily that the scope conditions of the study are satisfied and do not try to choose subjects randomly from the population. Additionally, statistical tests can have adequate statistical power, even when based on comparatively small samples, if experimental treatments are assigned randomly, because ancillary control variables are then statistically independent of the treatments. For example, sample sizes in social psychological experiments with a few treatment groups often range between 50 and 100.

In contrast, in analyses of nonexperimental data, the independent variables of greatest interest (namely, the hypothesized explanatory variables) tend to be correlated not only with each other but also with additional variables that are of no theoretical interest but that are strongly associated with the outcome of interest. These other variables are introduced as control variables so that the effects on change of the hypothesized explanatory variables can be distinguished from the effects of the control variables (see above, p. 312). Consequently, it is often advisable to include far more independent variables (many of which may be correlated with each other) and to have considerably larger sample sizes when analyzing nonexperimental data rather than experimental data. It also becomes much more important to select a sample randomly from the population.

A sample must be chosen probabilistically from the population if a researcher would like to use methods of statistical estimation and inference to generalize from nonexperimental data to the population. Studies of nonprobabilistic samples provide many insights into social life but have irremediable shortcomings if a researcher wants to generalize to a population larger than the sample studied.[14]

There are various types of probabilistic samples, and the particular type affects what can be learned. Nonetheless, types of probability sampling schemes are not reviewed here because their impacts on estimation and inference are similar in principle whether or not one is modeling change. Useful references on sampling, of differing technicality and practicality, include both older classics, such as Cochran (1977), Deming (1950), and Kish (1965), and recent texts, such as Lohr (1999) and Thompson (1997). For a general introduction to basic ideas and issues pertaining to sampling, see Stuart (1984).

When modeling change and then estimating that model, a few sampling issues do arise that are rarely discussed by researchers analyzing data pertaining to a single point in time. One such issue is whether there is a sample of 'newborns' or 'survivors', where these terms may refer to any entities of social scientific interest that persist long enough to have a distinct identity and history over time (e.g., people, firms, social movements).[15] By definition, a newborn has no previous history; therefore, a sample of newborns is usually followed *forward in time* (i.e., studied *prospectively*).[16] In contrast, by definition, survivors have lived or existed for a while and already have some history. Consequently, a sample of survivors may be studied *retrospectively* (i.e., followed *backward in time*), prospectively, or both.

From a sampling perspective, it is important that survivors tend to differ from newborns in nonrandom ways that may be relevant to the outcome of interest. In particular, the propensity to have a certain outcome is often different for the types of people, groups, and entities that tend to survive than for those types that tend not to survive. If newborns are studied prospectively, researchers are able to observe death and/or loss of sample members as well as the particular outcome of interest. Hence, they can then try to investigate whether there is a relationship between the outcome and the tendency to survive. When one has a sample of survivors, it is very difficult to determine if there is such a relationship, and whether it might bias conclusions about the outcome. Consequently, caution is needed in interpreting results based on estimating models of change from data on

a sample of survivors rather than from a sample of newborns.

A second distinctive sampling issue when modeling and analyzing change concerns fluctuations in the effective sample size over time. In analyzing relationships at a point in time from data collected at that time, the size of the sample analyzed equals the size of the target sample, decremented by the number of nonparticipants (i.e., those for whom there are no data at all) and the number of participants with missing information on variables included in the analysis. Although reductions in the sample size for these two reasons create problems for any empirical analysis, a great deal is known about ways of dealing with them. These topics are not discussed here because they are not unique to modeling and studying change (see Chapter 5).

Another issue concerns the fact that the analyzable sample tends to become smaller and smaller for times either further backward or further forward from the time when the sample is selected. In a prospective study of either newborns or survivors, the sample tends to decrease over time because of *sample attrition*: the situation that, as time elapses, some members of the original sample cannot be located, cannot be contacted, refuse to provide information, and so on. In a retrospective study of survivors, the sample members often vary in age and the length of their relevant histories. As a result, the effective sample size in a retrospective study of survivors tends to shrink going backward in time as well as going forward in time. In sum, even if one draws a seemingly large sample at time t, its effective size at times $t \pm u$ may be much smaller than necessary to draw reliable conclusions about *change*.

A related but separate issue concerns the fact that a sample chosen to be representative of the population at time t may become increasingly less representative of the population going either backwards or forwards in time. This problem occurs primarily when there are multiple data collections, a topic discussed further below.

Times of data collection and measurements

Other important issues concern when data are collected and when variables are measured. To clarify the distinction between the data-collection times and the times of measurements, consider a *cross-sectional survey*, which collects data from people or firms at a single point in time. Even though data are collected at only one time, by asking questions about the past and by examining existing written and electronic records, outcomes and independent variables may be measured continuously for some window of time, or at N time points, where N may range from one to a sizable number.

In contrast, there may be W times or waves of data collection – for example, W surveys of people. One prototype of this data-collection design consists of a *repeated cross-sectional survey* in which different individuals are surveyed at each of the W data collections. Although there are W separate data collections, each one is a cross-sectional survey: no individual is intentionally surveyed more than once. Each of the W data collections may, however, gather very detailed information about the past, yielding measurements of variables at N different time points, or even continuously for some window of time.

Examples of a repeated cross-sectional survey design include the General Social Survey (GSS) and the National Election Study (NES), both of which collect data from fresh samples of noninstitutionalized adults in the US every year or so. The GSS and the NES mainly measure variables at the survey time or at one time point in the past (e.g., at age 16). But, for example, they also ask about respondents' voting behavior at several discrete points in time, namely, the times of selected previous elections. With data of this kind, researchers can, for example, compare changes in political-party preferences from one election to another and also examine to what extent changes in reported preferences depend on when the data are collected. For instance, analysis of the data may reveal not only which individual characteristics are associated with preferring a particular political party but also whether there is a 'bandwagon' effect in which respondents over-report voting in the distant past for candidates of the political party that won in the most recent election before the survey.

A *W-wave panel survey*, in which essentially the same individuals are surveyed repeatedly, is another standard design with W data collections. Each wave may measure the same variables as in previous waves, different variables, or a combination of the same and different variables. As above, variables may be measured at the time of the survey, at previous times, or at both.

If the same variable is measured at each of the W waves, then there are *W-wave panel data* (i.e., W *repeated measures*) on this variable.[17] Naturally, there may again be more than W measurements of variables if some of the data collections seek to measure variables before the first survey or to fill in the values of variables between successive surveys.[18]

If different variables are measured at each of the W waves, it is possible to study how variables measured at later time points are related to variables measured at earlier time points. For example, a researcher could investigate how a person's income at a later wave is related to childhood and adolescent experiences that were measured at the first wave. However, it is not possible to study *change* in any variable if different variables are measured at every wave.

There are still other and more complex designs in which data are collected at W points in time, far more than can be enumerated here. One more complex design that deserves to be mentioned is a *rotating or rolling panel survey*, exemplified by the Current Population Survey (CPS). In this type of design, the full sample at a given data collection consists of Q subsamples, each of which is retained in the sample for Q (or more) successive data collections; each subsample is surveyed at Q of the data collections when it is in the sample.[19] Thereafter, a subsample is replaced by a newly drawn subsample that is followed over time in a similar way. The process of drawing a subsample, following it for some number of data collections, and then replacing it with a newly drawn subsample is repeated over and over again.

The Q repeated surveys on each sample member provide measurements on variables at the times of the surveys (and at other past time points chosen by the researchers). Keeping Q relatively small helps to reduce sample losses due to migration of sample members. It also helps to prevent respondents from feeling overburdened with too many surveys and therefore from refusing to continue to answer questions.

Most importantly, this design allows the full sample to be continually refreshed. Drawing a new subsample every few waves helps to ensure that the full sample is representative of the larger population over time. This is a crucial advantage when there are multiple major objectives. For example, for the CPS, these objectives are: to generalize to a specific population at a particular time (e.g., the US population in March 2000); to monitor trends in this population over a long time period (i.e., when W is much larger than Q); and to gather information about individuals' changes over shorter time periods. The main potential shortcoming of this type of design (other than cost and complexity) is that members of a subsample may not undergo much change if the length of time that they are followed is too short.

In sum, there is no intrinsic connection between the times when data are collected and the times when outcomes and variables are measured, except that measurement times cannot be after the time of the last data collection.[20] For estimating and evaluating a model of change, the critical factor is the N times when variables are measured. The Q times when data are collected from a *particular* subsample and the W times when data are collected from *any* subsample are of secondary importance.

Times of measurements As explained above, when modeling and analyzing change over time, the times when variables are *measured* (especially the outcome) matter most. Various statistical techniques may be effectively used to *impute* (i.e., fill in) the values of independent variables at times other than when they were actually measured (see Chapter 5, this volume; Little and Rubin, 2002). But using such techniques to impute the values of *outcomes* at times other than when they were actually measured can easily lead to biased results and erroneous conclusions. Hence, the models of change in an outcome that can be utilized in empirical analyses are *fundamentally* constrained by the times when the outcome is measured.

Most obviously, if the dependent variable is measured at only one time point, one cannot study how it changes, as was noted previously. If the dependent variable is measured at only two time points (e.g., before and after an experimental treatment; at the time of an interview and at labor force entry), the opportunities to study the change *process* and to evaluate a *dynamic model* of change are negligible. One can tell *if* a change has occurred and sometimes *how much* change has occurred, but not much else. In this situation, it is wise to consider only models of difference in the dependent variable. To give an analogy, a straight line can be drawn through any two points, but to determine whether a relationship is linear or nonlinear, at least

three points are needed. Similarly, given measurements on an outcome at two time points, one can detect whether the outcome changed, but not how it evolved (e.g., linearly or nonlinearly).

Often the dependent variable is measured at N time points, where N is greater than 2 but still a relatively small number. There is then some information about the time path of change, so that one can begin to study the process of change. In this situation, one can estimate not only a model of difference, but even a model of 'difference in differences'. For example, if $N = 3$ (and the times between measurements are equal), one can study if the difference between the first two time points is the same as the difference between the last two time points. As N increases, the data provide increasingly more information about how changes unfold over time, and whether patterns of change (and of difference in changes) are constant over time, vary with a certain trend, fluctuate up and down, or shift in an even more complex way.

For an in-depth study of change, one needs measures of the outcome at more than a few time points. Measurements for an entire and essentially continuous window of time are ideal. Such data are sometimes termed *sample path data*.

Sample path data on continuous variables are rare because such variables tend to undergo frequent but small changes. It is hard to collect complete information on all changes when a continuous variable exhibits this pattern of change. However, sample path data on a continuous variable can be collected if it occasionally *jumps* to a new level (rather than continually changes a little). For example, salaried employees in large organizations are typically given salary increases only at intermittent intervals (e.g., annually and when they change jobs). Consequently, sample path data on people's salaries in large organizations can be collected by recording both when they receive each salary increase and how big each salary increase is. Models for continuous dependent variables that change in jumps have been discussed by Petersen (1988, 1990).

More often data on a continuous dependent variable are collected only at N discrete time points chosen by the researcher, such as the times of a panel survey. When such data are all that is available, researchers often adopt discrete-time models of change in a continuous dependent variable. However, a continuous-time dynamic model, usually framed in terms of some kind of differential-equation model, can also be estimated, as discussed at length by Petersen in Chapter 14. (See also Tuma and Hannan, 1984: Chapters 11–15.)

Sample path data on a discrete outcome were named *event histories* by Tuma et al. (1979) (see also Hannan and Tuma, 1979), where an *event* refers to a change in the value of the outcome. Because event histories provide complete information on the outcome, there are enormous opportunities to analyze both the timing of changes and the impacts of population heterogeneity on that timing. Some possibilities are outlined in Chapter 16; for more comprehensive treatments, see Cox and Oakes (1984), Tuma and Hannan (1984) and Kalbfleisch and Prentice (1980).[21]

Times of data collections Although the times when variables are measured matter most in modeling and analyzing change, the times when data are *collected* matter, too. Particularly pertinent features of the data-collection plan are the *number of data collections*, the *spacing between data collections*, and the *total width of the data-collection window* (i.e., the length of time from the first to the last data collection). For a single data collection, the spacing of data collections and the total width of the data-collection window are immaterial. For multiple data collections, the total width of the data-collection window depends on the number and spacing of data collections; consequently, the subsequent discussion of these three features below is intermingled.

NUMBER OF DATA COLLECTIONS   The most obvious advantage of a *single* data collection is that, for any given sample size, it almost always costs markedly less than multiple data collections. A methodological benefit is that a researcher draws a single sample and then gathers data on essentially the same sample members over time. Further, comparability of measurement instruments over time is easier to achieve with a single data collection.

A single data collection has, however, some notable drawbacks for studying change. One basic disadvantage concerns the fact that information on many phenomena of interest needs to be collected contemporaneously. People's feelings and beliefs clearly fall in this category, but so do many 'objective' (i.e., factual)

variables. For example, most adults are barely able to report their earnings and hours of work last month with reasonable accuracy. Only a smattering can furnish comparable information for the more distant past. Hence, multiple data collections are required to gather data suitable for analyzing change in variables that cannot be accurately recalled – unless someone else previously recorded the values of these variables over time.

Second, ordinarily a single data collection means that researchers can collect data only on a sample of survivors (i.e., those who survived until the time of the data collection). As mentioned in the section on sampling schemes, survivors typically differ systematically from nonsurvivors, often in ways related to the outcome of interest. Consequently, conclusions about change based on analyzing data on a sample of survivors are subject to certain kinds of biases that can be avoided only by analyzing prospective data on a sample of newborns.

A single data collection need not be limited to a sample of survivors if some person or entity (e.g., the United Nations) previously collected and stored the desired information. Under this circumstance, a single data collection simply requires finding the information in potentially disparate sources, establishing comparability of the information across sources and over time, and putting the information in a form suitable for analyzing change. For example, there exist written and electronic records on many attributes of countries covering long periods of time. Such archival information permits social scientists to study not only surviving countries but also ones that have ceased to exist.

In contrast, it is rare to find existing records over time that contain suitable information for studying changes in people's behaviors, let alone their beliefs and moods. Hence, to study these kinds of topics, social scientists are constrained either to gather whatever data they can from a sample of survivors in a single data collection, or else to utilize multiple data collections.

By collecting data on *multiple* occasions, researchers gain great flexibility in terms of possible sampling schemes. It becomes possible to sample newborns and study them prospectively, or to sample survivors and study them retrospectively, prospectively, or both. Researchers can draw fresh samples at each wave (i.e., conduct repeated cross-sectional surveys), collect data from the same sample at each wave (i.e., conduct a *W*-wave panel survey), or gather data on both previously drawn samples and newly drawn supplementary or replacement samples at successive waves (i.e., conduct a rotating panel survey like the CPS).

In order to model and analyze the changes for individuals in a sample, multiple data collections almost always involve surveying some sample members repeatedly over time. When collecting such data, there occur two main kinds of problems that affect empirical studies of change, both of which were mentioned above. One is sample attrition over time (i.e., loss of sample members); the other concerns degradation of sample representativeness over time. The latter refers to the fact that a sample may be representative of the population at time *t* but often becomes increasingly less representative of that population at times before and after time *t*.

Cumulative attrition from a sample over time becomes substantial eventually, even if the follow-up rate of sample members from one wave to the next is high. To make matters worse, the validity of conclusions is compromised if the outcome is related to sample loss across successive data collections, especially if the same factors affect both the outcome and sample losses.

With regard to the cumulative impact of sample attrition, consider a *W*-wave panel survey in which the follow-up rate of sample members from one survey to the next is *r*, with sample losses strictly random (i.e., not systematically associated with anything). If *r* is 0.95 (in practice, a very high level), there will be complete data on 63% of the original sample after 10 waves and on only 38% after 20 waves.[22] If *r* is 0.90 (also a high level), there will be complete data on 39% of the original sample after 10 waves but on only 14% after 20 waves. Thus, even very high rates of sample retention (i.e., very low rates of attrition) from one wave to the next have huge cumulative impacts on the size of the sample with complete data as the number of data collections grows. In many instances, there may be *partial* longitudinal information about many sample members (i.e., data on them for many waves, but not all). However, many modeling and methodological challenges arise in using temporally incomplete information on sample members – too many to discuss in this chapter.

The above examples of the cumulative impacts of attrition assume that sample retention and its converse, sample attrition, are strictly random. But this rarely happens. If sample retention is associated only with exogenous variables, bias is unaffected; however, efficiency declines for the estimated effects related to the exogenous variables associated with sample loss.

For example, attrition from surveys of adults in the US tends to be higher for men than women, for nonwhites than whites, and for less-educated people than for more-educated people. As the number of waves of a panel survey of a random sample of US adults grows, the number of nonwhite males with little education for whom there are complete data over time can easily become a small fraction of the original number. As a consequence of differential rates of sample attrition, the confidence intervals for the estimated effects for a subsample with characteristics associated with unusually high rates of attrition can become unacceptably wide as the number of data collections increases.

Moreover, in many instances, sample attrition is associated with the outcome. That is, there may be unforeseen 'sampling on the dependent variable' (see Chapter 18) because sample losses are associated with the values of the outcome.

To give an extreme example, suppose data on geographical or residential mobility are collected using a *W*-wave panel design. Respondents who move between successive waves are much more likely to be lost in subsequent surveys than those who do not move. Hence, sample members who participate in all *W* waves of the survey will almost surely report less geographical mobility than occurred in the population. That is, one value of the dependent variable (namely, moving) is underreported by sample members who continue to be surveyed because they almost certainly include a disproportionate number of nonmovers.

Further, some independent variables that affect the outcome may also affect the ability to continue to survey people who move. The association between the factors influencing the outcome and the factors related to sample attrition has still more damaging consequences for analyses of change that are based on the temporally complete data on sample members who remain throughout the study.

For instance, education and occupation are known to be associated with the propensity to move from one place to another. These same variables are also associated with survey researchers' ability to locate and survey people who have moved (e.g., highly educated professionals are easier to track over time than unskilled laborers with little education). Consequently, the estimated effects on geographical mobility of these two independent variables (and other variables correlated with them) will be biased if the effects are estimated from data on the subsample that is surveyed at all, or almost all, *W* waves.

In sum, researchers who model and analyze change using data collected from the same sample members on multiple occasions need to be sensitive to the potential difficulties arising due to sample attrition, and they need to be cautious in their interpretations of conclusions based on analyzing temporally complete data for the sample members who are followed throughout the study. While sample weighting and model-based adjustments, of the sort described in Chapters 5 and 18, can be useful if sample losses are purely random (i.e., noninformative), such adjustments are problematic if sample attrition is associated with both the outcome and independent variables affecting the outcome (i.e., informative).

Another common problem with multiple data collections is that an original sample becomes increasingly less *representative* of the larger population that is of fundamental interest as the number of data collections grows, and, in particular, as the length of the window from the first to last data collection increases. Over time, the original sample and the population often diverge because each changes, but in different ways.

For one thing, as time passes, the original members of a sample get older or die. Naturally, members of the population also get older and die over time; however, most populations of interest to social scientists are continually regenerated by various 'birth' and other social processes through which populations acquire new members. Consequently, the age distribution in a sample can eventually become markedly older than the age distribution in the population. This happens because a sample does not normally acquire new members, except as the result of a carefully planned sampling and data-collection design.

The problem of sample aging is especially acute in panel surveys that are long relative to the length of the lives of the entities studied. For example, in the Panel Study of Income Dynamics (PSID), a sample of households was chosen in 1968 and has been surveyed almost annually (recently biennially) since then. By 1998, the individuals in the original sample households were 30 years older than in 1968, assuming they had not died. Thus, the age distribution of the PSID sample of individuals interviewed in 1998, as well as in 1968, was much older than the age distribution of adults in the US in 1998.

The age distributions of the US population and the PSID sample have not actually become drastically different over time only because of a fortunate early decision of the PSID researchers to follow everyone in the original households, including children, as well as everyone who later joined new households formed by anyone in any of these households. As a result, the PSID is among the few long-running panel surveys whose follow-up procedures have allowed the sample to expand over time and, in particular, to add new younger members.

Quite aside from differences in the age distribution, the population and a sample may experience other dissimilar compositional changes over time. Again, much forethought about the sampling scheme and data-collection design is needed to avoid problems resulting from the divergence in the compositions of the population and a sample drawn from it in the past.

As an example, again consider the PSID sample chosen in 1968. Over time this sample has increasingly diverged from the US population because of high levels of immigration to the US. Further, immigrants to the US have come from very different parts of the world over time. As a result, as the years have passed, the original 1968 PSID sample members and their progeny have become less and less representative of the US population in terms of both length of residence in the US and national origins. Given the PSID's focus on income and household dynamics, the absence of post-1968 immigrants reduces the usefulness of the data on the original PSID sample for generalizing about the US population with the passage of time.

To have samples that continue to be representative of a larger population, it is best to draw supplementary samples in later data collections.[23] Nevertheless, for a variety of reasons, it is not only difficult and costly to draw such supplementary samples[24] but also hard to merge the data on supplementary samples with the data on earlier samples in ways that permit useful analyses of change. To give one simple example, much information about supplementary samples in the earlier years of a panel study is inevitably missing because members of the supplementary samples cannot recall their actions or situation in the distant past. Consequently, the ongoing addition of supplementary samples does not always yield information on the variables necessary to study certain kinds of changes.

Despite this caveat, drawing supplementary samples to refresh previously drawn samples and/or drawing entirely fresh samples are important ways to help ensure that the sample analyzed is representative of the population of interest over an extended period of time. Additionally, sample refreshment helps to avoid problems arising from overburdening respondents and from respondents learning to answer questions in ways that are atypical for 'green' respondents.[25]

SPACING OF DATA COLLECTIONS Closely spaced data collections are invaluable for measuring ephemeral information with some degree of accuracy. One can almost always measure values of variables at the time of a data collection (i.e., obtain contemporaneous or at least fairly recent measurements). Contemporaneous measurements are ordinarily believed to be the most complete and the most accurate; they are especially critical when variables can shift rapidly or refer to things of little enduring importance to the individual surveyed. For example, people's psychological moods and attitudes need to be measured contemporaneously, whereas dates of events that people regard as highly salient to their lives can often be measured retrospectively with a fair degree of accuracy.

On the other hand, data collections can be spaced too closely, especially when human agents are responsible for furnishing the information. If the data collections are spaced very closely, attrition can rise because those supplying the information may become annoyed by frequent surveys and become unwilling to participate. The burden of responding frequently can also lower the quality of the information given by those who do continue to participate.

WIDTH OF DATA-COLLECTION WINDOW Another feature of the observation plan that should be noted are the *widths* of the windows of time over which data are collected and over which variables are measured. These two widths are not the same since the data-collection window may be as short as a single point in time. The width of the window for temporal measurements usually exceeds the width of the data-collection window because researchers tend to collect some information about the past.

Other things being equal, wider time windows raise the chances of observing more change and different patterns of change, both of which are desirable when trying to investigate change by analyzing empirical data. On the other hand, wider time windows frequently aggravate various methodological problems, including ones discussed earlier in this section. For example, a wider window of time increases the likelihood of changes in the measurement instruments (e.g., the meanings of variables may change over time and be misinterpreted as changes in the variable's values), alterations in the sample of units studied (e.g., due to sample losses for random and possibly also nonrandom reasons), differences between the sample and the population from which it was drawn (because there are additions to as well as losses from the population), unanticipated changes in the relationships between variables, and fluctuations in the extent of random noise. In sum, wider time windows increase the risk of instability in the social environment being studied.

The advantages and disadvantages of wider versus narrower time windows depend on the phenomenon being studied and the methods available for collecting data. When designing a particular study, researchers should carefully weigh the benefits of wider rather than narrower windows of time for both the data collection and the measurements of variables. It must be recognized, however, that the opportunity to choose the width of the time window is often limited. Indeed, for researchers who analyze data collected by other scholars, the opportunities to choose may be almost nonexistent.

NOTES

1 The units of analysis in variable-based models are not always social actors.

2 A senator's death, resignation, or defection from a political party occasionally leads to a change in the majority party at an unexpected time point. Events such as these occur so rarely that their irregular timing can be ignored in most instances.

3 These references were suggested by Stanley Wasserman (personal communication).

4 Economists (cf. Lucas, 1981; Lucas and Sargent, 1981) have proposed and studied models in which agents' rational expectations for the future influence short-run changes in various outcomes. Rational-expectation models may seem to postulate that the future affects the past. In actuality, agents' expectations for the future are inevitably based on what has already happened. Consequently, expectations are formed before future outcomes occur.

5 Models in which influence is explicit but indirect are exemplified by models in which a focal actor is influenced by structurally equivalent actors who are not directly linked to the focal actor (Burt, 1987).

6 Diffusion models are often elaborated in order to model change over space, as well as change over time.

7 Scholars affiliated with the Santa Fe Institute have played a leading role in this line of research.

8 A similar focus on the moves of vacancies rather than of people was suggested around the same time in an unpublished report by Lansing et al. (1969).

9 One might argue that the processes involved in the recruitment of people to the ministry, their preparation for ordination as ministers, and the departure of some existing clergy from the active ministry should also be considered. These other social processes were, however, not central to White's agenda.

10 Further, he found that the available data on timing were not very accurate (White, personal communication).

11 At the time of White's study, methods for analyzing event sequences and event histories had not yet been developed in any systematic way. Indeed, the term 'event history' was not coined until 1979 (see Tuma et al., 1979), although a form of event history analysis was first proposed and applied in sociology in Tuma (1976).

12 In this situation, time-series analysis (see Brockwell and Davis, 2002) is customary if the outcome is continuous and measured at discrete points in time, or event-history analysis (see Chapter 15; Tuma and Hannan, 1984) if the outcome is discrete and measured continuously.

13 Placebo groups – groups that do not receive any treatment – are often called 'control groups'. The term 'control group' is avoided in this chapter to minimize potential confusion with 'control variables'.

14 Popular nonprobabilistic methods include convenience sampling (choosing sample members by whatever method seems most convenient) and quota sampling (choosing sample members so that they have some a priori distribution of particular attributes). Although similar to the population on certain attributes, a quota sample does not satisfy statistical criteria for representativeness.

15 When there are good archival records about the population of interest, it is occasionally possible to sample entities that are deceased or that no longer exist. For example, data are plentiful on countries and political organizations that no longer exist. Further, ancient but very thorough records of parish churches and population registries on members of households sometimes let demographers study fertility, nuptiality, and mortality using samples in which everyone died centuries ago (e.g., Laslett, 1973).

16 A newborn may have social origins (e.g., parental characteristics) that affect its future.

17 Even variables that do not vary over time in principle may be measured repeatedly. Repeated measures of supposedly time-invariant variables (e.g., a person's date of birth or father's completed education) are routinely used to study the reliability of measurements. This is an important topic, but it is not discussed further in this volume.

18 Sometimes each data collection attempts to replicate measurements over time collected at an earlier survey. For example, the birth dates of children may be collected at multiple surveys. This design yields repeated measurements on the dates in fertility histories for overlapping periods of time. Such data allow researchers both to study the reliability of the reporting of birth dates and to analyze factors affecting the temporal spacing of children's births.

19 The CPS has eight subsamples. Each one is surveyed for four months in a row, then not interviewed for the next eight months, and then again surveyed for the next four months before being dropped.

20 Occasionally respondents are asked to report what they will do in the future; however, such questions cover what respondents *expect* to happen, which is not necessarily what actually *will* happen.

21 In Chapter 17, Abbott and MacIndoe describe models for analyzing *event sequences*, which give information on the series of values of the discrete outcome over time, but not the times when there is a change from one value to another. Another subset of event histories are event counts, which report the number of events within given intervals, but neither the exact order nor the exact times of the events. For an introduction to models for analyzing event counts, see King (1989) and Winkelmann (2000).

22 The fraction with complete information on W waves is r^{W-1}.

23 For this reason, new samples of immigrants were added to the PSID in 1990 and again in 1997. The 1990 sample did not represent all immigrants well and was dropped after 1995.

24 For instance, in the case of the PSID, it is hard to develop lists of post-1968 immigrants from which new supplementary samples of immigrants can be chosen.

25 When respondents are surveyed repeatedly, especially when they are asked certain similar questions over and over again, some respondents learn to give answers that will not trigger extra questions. For

example, they may learn that, if they report buying a major item last month, they will then be asked a series of questions about how they chose it, what it cost, and how they are financing it. In the future, respondents may decide to say they have not made any new purchases lately.

REFERENCES

Axelrod, Robert (1984) *The Evolution of Cooperation*. New York: Basic Books.

Bartholomew, D.J. (1982) *Stochastic Models for Social Processes* (3rd edition). London: Wiley.

Becker, Gary S. (1975) *Human Capital* (2nd edition). New York: Columbia University Press.

Boylan, Ross D. (1992) 'A queuing model of the macro–micro connection: With special attention to stratification', *Journal of Mathematical Sociology*, 16(4): 267–84.

Boylan, Ross D. (1993) 'The effect of the number of diplomas on their value', *Sociology of Education*, 66(3): 206–21.

Brockwell, Peter J. and Davis, Richard A. (2002) *Introduction to Time Series and Forecasting* (2nd edition). Berlin: Springer-Verlag.

Burt, Ronald S. (1987) 'Social contagion and innovation: Cohesion versus structural equivalence', *American Journal of Sociology*, 92: 1287–335.

Cochran, William G. (1977) *Sampling Techniques* (3rd edition). New York: Wiley.

Coleman, James S. (1968) 'The mathematical study of change', in Hubert M. Blalock Jr. and Ann B. Blalock (eds), *Methodology in Social Research*. New York: McGraw-Hill, pp. 428–78.

Cox, D.R. and Oakes, D. (1984) *Analysis of Survival Data*. London: Chapman & Hall.

Deming, William E. (1950) *Some Theory of Sampling*. New York: Dover.

Epstein, Joshua M. and Axtell, Robert (1996) *Growing Artificial Societies: Social Science from the Bottom Up*. Washington, DC: Brookings Institution Press.

Hannan, Michael T. and Tuma, Nancy Brandon (1979) 'Methods for temporal analysis', *Annual Review of Sociology*, 5: 303–28.

Kalbfleisch, J.D. and Prentice, R.L. (1980) *The Statistical Analysis of Failure Time Data*. New York: Wiley.

King, Gary (1989) *Unifying Political Methodology: The Likelihood Theory of Statistical Inference*. New York: Cambridge University Press.

Kish, Leslie (1965) *Survey Sampling*. New York: Wiley.

Lansing, John B., Clifton, Charles Wade and Morgan, James N. (1969) *New Homes and Poor People*. Ann Arbor, MI: Survey Research Center, Institute for Social Research, University of Michigan.

Laslett, Peter, (1973) *The World We Have Lost* (2nd edition). New York: MacMillan.

Little, Roderick J.A. and Rubin, Donald B. (2002) *Statistical Analysis with Missing Data*. New York: Wiley.

Lohr, Sharon L. (1999) *Sampling: Design and Analysis*. Pacific Grove, CA: Duxbury Press.

Lucas, Robert E., Jr. (1981) *Studies in Business-Cycle Theory*. Cambridge, MA: MIT Press.

Lucas, Robert E., Jr. and Sargent, Thomas J. (eds) (1981) *Rational Expectations and Econometric Practice*. Minneapolis: University of Minnesota Press.

Macy, Michael W. and Robert Willer (2002) 'From factors to actors: Computational sociology and agent-based modeling', *Annual Review of Sociology*, 28: 143–66.

Marsden, Peter V. and Podolny, Joel (1990) 'Dynamic analysis of network diffusion processes', in H. Flap and J. Weesie (eds), *Social Networks through Time*. Utrecht: ISOR, University of Utrecht.

Petersen, Trond (1988) 'Studying change over time in a continuous dependent variable: Specification and estimation of continuous state space hazard rate models', in Clifford Clogg (ed.), *Sociological Methodology 1988*, Vol. 18. San Francisco: Jossey-Bass, pp. 137–64.

Petersen, Trond (1990) 'Analyzing continuous state space failure time processes: Two further results', *Journal of Mathematical Sociology*, 15(3–4): 247–57.

Snijders, T.A.B. (2003) 'Models for longitudinal network data', in P. Carrington, J. Scott and S. Wasserman (eds), *Models and Methods in Social Network Analysis*. New York: Cambridge University Press.

Sørensen, Aage B. (1977) 'The structure of inequality and the process of attainment', *American Sociological Review*, 42: 965–78.

Sørensen, Aage B. (1979) 'A model and a metric for the analysis of the intragenerational status attainment process', *American Journal of Sociology*, 85(2): 361–84.

Strang, David, and Tuma, Nancy Brandon (1993) 'Spatial and temporal heterogeneity in diffusion', *American Journal of Sociology*, 99: 614–39.

Stuart, Alan (1984) *The Ideas of Sampling*. London: Griffin.

Thompson, M.E. (1997) *Theory of Sample Surveys*. London: Chapman & Hall.

Tuma, Nancy Brandon (1976) 'Rewards, resources and the rate of mobility: A nonstationary multivariate stochastic model', *American Sociological Review*, 41: 338–60.

Tuma, Nancy Brandon and Hannan, Michael T. (1984) *Social Dynamics: Models and Methods*. Orlando, FL: Academic Press.

Tuma, Nancy Brandon, Hannan, Michael T. and Groeneveld, Lyle P. (1979) 'Dynamic analysis of event histories', *American Journal of Sociology*, 84: 820–54.

Wasserman, Stanley, and Faust, K. (1994) *Social Network Analysis: Methods and Applications*. New York: Cambridge University Press.

White, Harrison C. (1970) *Chains of Opportunity: System Models of Mobility in Organizations*. Cambridge, MA: Harvard University Press.

Winkelmann, Rainer (2000) *Econometric Analysis of Count Data* (3rd edition). Berlin: Springer-Verlag.

14

Analyzing Panel Data: Fixed- and Random-Effects Models

TROND PETERSEN

Panel data arise from a variety of processes, including quarterly data on economic results, biennial election data, and marital life histories. Their central feature is that one records at regular intervals the state each individual in the panel occupies, with some units observed at two or more points in time. Usually the observation intervals are equi-spaced, so that one knows the states occupied during say the first week of January each year, for example, the marital status, occupation, and wage. One typically knows only whether a change in states occurred between two panel dates, but not the exact date within the period.

Panel data are used in two important ways. The first is to control for unobserved explanatory variables. The dependent variable can be continuous or categorical. The estimated equations are static, the same as one would specify with cross-sectional data. But with repeated observations on each individual one is in a better position to account for unmeasured variables. The second is to analyze change over time, for example, how individuals move between statuses, such as marital states or wage changes between panel dates.

We review techniques used for dealing with unobserved explanatory variables in static models for panel data. This is where panel data analysis has made its most impressive advances, through the use of fixed-effects and random-effects models.

The procedures developed for dealing with unobserved variables have relevance beyond the panel data setting. They can be used for all data having a so-called group or multi-level structure. Examples are data on several firms and multiple workers within each firm, on several schools and multiple students within each school, and so forth. The group is the firm or the school, the so-called higher level. The individual observations, the lower level, give multiple data points on workers or students from each firm or school. In panel data the group is the individual, the higher level. The observations at each point in time would be the lower level, with multiple observations on the individual.

Dynamic models for panel data have been less compelling and more complex (see Tuma and Hannan, 1984: Part III). Some models relate the value of the dependent variable in a given period to its value in the prior period and to other variables, using so-called difference equation models. Other models are derived from an underlying diffusion process, where the dependent variable changes all the time and only in small amounts (Coleman, 1968). However, many processes studied with these models are failure-time or event-history processes, as in individual-level histories of wages and socio-economic status. Such variables stay constant for finite periods of time but then often change by large amounts (e.g., Rosenfeld, 1980; Petersen, 1988). These should

Table 14.1 *Example of panel data for nine individuals and five time periods*

Individual	Period	Dependent variable		Independent variables			
				Time-varying		Time-constant	
		Wages	Position	Educational level	Marital status	Socio-economic background	Sex
(1)	(2)	(3)	(4)	(5)	(6)	(7)	(8)
1	1	10	1	14	0	20	0
2	3	15	0	16	1	40	1
3	5	24	1	18	0	75	0
4	1	15	0	18	1	50	0
4	2	20	0	18	1	50	0
4	3	25	1	18	1	50	0
5	2	20	0	16	1	75	1
5	3	25	1	17	1	75	1
5	4	30	0	18	1	75	1
6	3	25	1	16	0	60	0
6	4	30	0	16	1	60	0
6	5	35	0	16	0	60	0
7	1	25	0	16	0	90	0
7	2	25	0	17	1	90	0
7	3	25	0	18	0	90	0
8	1	10	0	16	0	30	0
8	2	20	1	17	1	30	0
8	3	30	1	18	0	30	0
9	1	32	0	16	0	80	1
9	2	32	0	16	1	80	1
9	3	25	1	16	0	80	1
9	4	41	0	17	0	80	1
9	5	41	0	18	1	80	1

Note: Column 1 indexes individuals 1–9. Column 2 indexes the time period (1–5) for each observation on each individual. Columns 3–4 give the values for two dependent variables. These may vary over time for an individual and may vary between individuals. Columns 5–8 give values for independent variables. Columns 5–6 give values for variables that may vary over time for an individual, such as their educational level and marital status. Columns 7–8 give values for variables that cannot vary over time for an individual, such as socio-economic background at time of birth and their sex.

preferably be analyzed using hazard-rate models, which may have to be adjusted to deal with the nature of panel data (e.g., Petersen, 1991), but not with models developed for diffusion processes. But lacking complete event histories, various dynamic panel-data models may provide the best solution.

We outline the structure of panel data, before going on to discuss linear regression models for continuous outcomes for analyzing such data. Toward the end of the chapter we introduce nonlinear models for categorical dependent variables, and then multi-level models.

PANEL DATA: DATA WITH A GROUP OR MULTI-LEVEL STRUCTURE

An example of panel data is given in Table 14.1. Column 1 lists the individuals. Column 2 lists

the periods or the times at which measurements were obtained. Individuals may be observed in up to five periods. Columns 3 and 4 list values on a continuous dependent variable (wages) and a categorical dependent variable (the job or position held), respectively. Columns 5 and 6 list values for two independent variables that both can change over time, referred to as time-varying: one continuous (educational level) and one categorical (marital status). Columns 7 and 8 list values for two independent variables that cannot change over time, referred to as time-constant: one continuous (socio-economic background) and one categorical (sex). Each of the eight columns corresponds to a distinct variable in the data set. In analyzing panel data, the identity of individuals is essential. For example, for individual 4 we need to know that the observations in periods 1–3 pertain to her rather than individual 7.

Individuals 1–3 are observed in only one period each, hence there is only one line or data record per individual. They do not provide panel data information. Individual 1 entered the panel in period 1 and then dropped out before period 2. Individual 2 entered in period 3 and dropped out before period 4. These dropouts can be due to a death, due to failure to satisfy conditions for inclusion in the panel such as being employed, or because the data collectors lost track of the individual. Individual 3 entered in the last period of observation.

Individuals 4–8 are each observed for three periods. Individual 9 is observed for all five periods. These six individuals all provide panel data information. The more time points an individual is observed, the more information that individual provides. A panel data set where each individual has been observed at each of the possible time points is called *balanced*. Otherwise it is *unbalanced*, which is the common situation.

CONTINUOUS DEPENDENT VARIABLES: THE SPECIFICATIONS

The models

Let y_{it} denote the continuous dependent variable for individual i in period t. For the independent variables it is instructive to distinguish two kinds: those that for an individual may vary over time, such as wages and marital status; and those that are time-constant, such as sex and race. The former are collected in the vector x_{it}, the latter in z_i, of dimensions $K_1 \times 1$ and $K_2 \times 1$. As panel data allow careful control for unobservables, for the time-constant variables it is also useful to introduce a vector of unobserved variables z_i^u. These distinctions – between time-varying and time-constant and, for the latter, between observed and unobserved – are important. We use them to clarify what can be estimated and which interpretations can be given to estimates. There is also a dummy variable D_i for each individual, equal to 1 if individual i and 0 otherwise.

Let $\bar{y}_i$ and $\bar{x}_i$ be the averages of y_{it} and of x_{it} across time for individual i. The corresponding average of z_i is just z_i. In Table 14.1, for the variables in columns 3, 5, and 7, the averages are 20, 18, and 50 for individual 4, while 25, 17, and 75 for individual 5. The

variables in columns 5–6 correspond to x_{it}, those in columns 7–8 to z_i, while z_i^u is not observed, hence no columns.

There are four separate models with four corresponding estimators that are often specified for such data. Each illustrates a different aspect of the data, reflecting different modeling assumptions. We state them here for reference and then discuss each separately below:

$$y_{it} = \beta_{0T} + \beta_{1T}x_{it} + \beta_{2T}z_i + \varepsilon_{it}, \qquad (14.1)$$

$$\bar{y}_i = \beta_{0B} + \beta_{1B}\bar{x}_i + \beta_{2B}z_i + \xi_i, \qquad (14.2)$$

$$y_{it} = \beta_{0W} + \beta_{1W}x_{it} + \beta_{2W}z_i$$
$$\qquad + \beta_{3W}z_i^u + \epsilon_{it} \qquad (14.3a)$$
$$= \beta_{0W} + \beta_{1W}x_{it} + \alpha_i D_i + \epsilon_{it}, \qquad (14.3b)$$

$$y_{it} = \beta_{0R} + \beta_{1R}x_{it} + \beta_{2R}z_i + v_i + e_{it}. \qquad (14.4)$$

In (14.1), we use the notation

$$\beta_{1T}x_{it} = \beta_{11T}x_{1it} + \cdots + \beta_{1kT}x_{kit},$$

where x_{1it} is the value of the first variable in x_{it}, β_{11T} its effect, and so on. β_{0T} denotes the constant term. Similar notation holds for β_{2T} and for the β-vectors in (14.2)–(14.4). ε_{it}, ξ_i, ϵ_{it}, and e_{it} are error terms. α_i is explained below.

The specifications in (14.1)–(14.4) are referred to as the *total, between, within*, and *random-effects* equations; hence the four separate subscripts to the β-vectors. The estimates will differ between the specifications, as will the error terms.

In (14.1), each observation on an individual is treated as a separate observation without reflecting that it comes from the same individual, thus ignoring the grouped nature of the data. It corresponds to what would be specified and estimated with cross-sectional data.

In (14.2), one regresses the individual-level average value of the dependent variable on the individual-level average values of the independent. If a person were single for five years and married for five, the average value of the corresponding dummy variable would be 0.50. The average value of the dummy variable for sex would be 0 or 1, as sex is constant over time.

In (14.3), one includes a dummy variable D_i for each individual i and estimates its effect α_i, thus accounting for the grouped nature of the data. This variable D_i captures all the time-constant variables, measured and unmeasured, z_i and z_i^u. The single number α_i gives their combined effect $\beta_{2W}z_i + \beta_{3W}z_i^u$, which also could be nonlinear.

In (14.4), one has two error terms for each individual, thus also accounting for the grouped nature of the data. The first, v_i, is individual-specific and constant over time: constant for each individual but differing between. The second, e_{it}, varies within and between individuals.[1]

The random-effects model makes one crucial assumption: The individual-specific and idiosyncratic error terms v_i and e_{it} are independent of each other and of the measured variables x_{it} and z_i. Once made, this assumption carries over to the error terms in the total and between models.

Relationships between the models

It is sometimes argued that there is one underlying model here, given by the random-effects specification. Then the parameters in (14.1)–(14.4) refer to the same quantities. If so, especially the total and between models should be viewed as simplifications, even special cases. This holds also for the within model, provided the assumption of the random-effects model is correct. We then have several relationships between each of the models (14.1)–(14.3) and (14.4). These are summed up in (14.5)–(14.8), where the relevant quantities from (14.1)–(14.3) are on the left-hand side and those from (14.4) on the right-hand side:

$$\varepsilon_{it} = v_i + e_{it} \ (total), \qquad (14.5)$$

$$\xi_i = v_i + \bar{e}_i \ (between), \qquad (14.6)$$

$$\epsilon_{it} = e_{it} \ (within), \qquad (14.7)$$

$$\alpha_i = \beta_{2R}z_i + v_i \ (within). \qquad (14.8)$$

In (14.6), $\bar{e}_i$ is the average over time t of individual i's idiosyncratic error e_{it}.

Rearranging (14.8), we also get

$$v_i = \alpha_i - \beta_{2R}z_i = \beta_{3W}z_i^u, \qquad (14.9)$$

which shows that the person-specific error term captures the effects of all the unmeasured time-constant variables, $\beta_{3W}z_i^u$.

The error term ε_{it} in the total model equals the sum of the two errors in the random-effects model, from (14.5). The error term ξ_i in the between model is the average value for individual i of those two errors, from (14.6). When the assumption of the random-effects model holds, its idiosyncratic error term is identical to that in the within model,

$e_{it} = \epsilon_{it}$, from (14.7). Then the fixed effect α_i equals the effect of the measured time-constant variables z_i plus the individual-specific error term v_i in the random-effects model, from (14.8). Equivalently, the individual-specific error term in the random-effects model equals the effect $\beta_{3W}z_i^u$ of the unmeasured time-constant variables, from (14.9).

The assumption made in the random-effects model, that v_i is independent of the measured x_{it} and z_i, is identical to the assumption that the unmeasured time-constant variables z_i^u are independent of all the measured variables.

In the fixed-effects model no such assumption is needed. The dummy variable D_i for individual i can be correlated with all the measured time-varying variables x_{it}.

For the estimates from the within model to be unbiased in the conventional sense, the idiosyncratic error term ϵ_{it} still needs to be independent of the measured variables x_{it} and D_i. As a practical matter, it often appears easier to measure all relevant time-constant variables than all relevant time-varying ones. So also in the fixed-effects model there may be so-called omitted-variable bias, arising from failure to measure all relevant time-varying variables.

If the assumption of the random-effects model is correct, that z_i^u is independent of the measured variables, then regressing y_{it} on x_{it} and z_i will give the same estimates as regressing it on the same variables plus z_i^u. This follows from a general result in linear regression analysis: When excluded variables are independent of included variables, estimates will be the same as if they were included. In that case, random-effects estimates coincide with those in the within model.

These kinds of considerations are important in panel-data analysis. One assumes correctness of the random-effects model. The other models are then seen as variations upon it.

But there is an alternative and often equally valid way to view this: The estimators corresponding to the four models are not necessarily variations on the same model, but rather different ways of describing the data, each yielding relevant insight in its own right. Such a view becomes fruitful when there is reason to suspect mis-specification of the models, violation of assumptions, and more. There are usually solid grounds for such suspicion.

Table 14.2 *Estimates of the effects of marital status and years of education on the logarithm of the hourly wage among male Norwegian white-collar employees in 1991–97, also controlling for age and year (effects not reported). Estimated standard errors are given in parentheses*

	β_T	β_B	β_W	β_R
	1	2	3	4
Constant	4.250 (0.002)	4.191 (0.004)	2.994 (0.003)	4.302 (0.003)
Marital status[a]				
Married	0.134 (0.001)	0.157 (0.002)	0.063 (0.001)	0.080 (0.001)
Separated	0.138 (0.002)	0.153 (0.006)	0.069 (0.001)	0.086 (0.001)
Divorced	0.118 (0.001)	0.137 (0.003)	0.061 (0.002)	0.077 (0.001)
Widower	0.067 (0.004)	0.079 (0.008)	0.041 (0.003)	0.052 (0.003)
Education (years)	0.055 (0.000)	0.053 (0.000)	0.014 (0.000)	0.042 (0.000)
Residual variances[b]				
$\hat{\sigma}_\varepsilon^2$	0.0525			
$\hat{\sigma}_\xi^2$		0.0482		
$\hat{\sigma}_\alpha^2$			0.2471	
$\hat{\sigma}_{v(1)}^2$				0.0535
$\hat{\sigma}_{v(2)}^2 = \hat{\sigma}_\varepsilon^2 - \hat{\sigma}_e^2$				0.0473
$\hat{\sigma}_\varepsilon^2 = \hat{\sigma}_e^2$			0.0052	0.0052

Note: In addition to the variables reported in the table, there are controls for age (one continuous variable) and calendar year (six dummy variables). Some additional dummy variables for marital status were included (see note a below).

[a]The reference category is single. Three additional categories were controlled as dummy variables, but their effects are not reported in the table: registered partner, separated partner, and divorced partner. These correspond to a legal category in Norway, registered partner.

[b]The residual variances were obtained as follows. Column 1, for $\hat{\sigma}_\varepsilon^2 = 0.0525$, corresponds to (14.10) computed from (14.23). Column 2, for $\hat{\sigma}_\xi^2 = 0.0482$, corresponds to (14.11). Column 3, for $\hat{\sigma}_\alpha^2 = 0.2471$, comes from a formula similar to (14.16), while $\hat{\sigma}_e^2 = 0.0052$, corresponding to (14.12), was computed from (14.26). Column 4, for $\hat{\sigma}_{v(1)}^2 = 0.0535$, comes from a standard formula used in random-effects analysis (here given by the program STATA), while $\hat{\sigma}_{v(2)}^2 = 0.0473$ comes from (14.27), as the difference between $\hat{\sigma}_\varepsilon^2 = 0.0525$ (in column 1) and $\hat{\sigma}_e^2 = 0.0052$ (in column 3 or 4). In column 4, $\hat{\sigma}_e^2 = 0.0052$ comes from the same estimator as $\hat{\sigma}_\varepsilon^2 = 0.0052$ in column 3.

Residual variances: The variance components

The random-effects specification is often referred to as the variance-component model. The reason is that the variance of the error term σ_ε^2 in the total equation equals the sum of the variances σ_v^2 and σ_e^2 of the individual-specific and idiosyncratic error terms in the random-effects model. We have:

$$\sigma_\varepsilon^2 = \sigma_v^2 + \sigma_e^2 \tag{14.10}$$

$$\sigma_{\xi_i}^2 = \sigma_v^2 + \frac{1}{T_i}\sigma_e^2 \tag{14.11}$$

$$\sigma_e^2 = \sigma_\varepsilon^2 \tag{14.12}$$

where T_i is the number of periods for which individual i was observed. Again, equality (14.12) holds when the individual-specific error term v_i is independent of the measured variables x_{it} and z_i.

In regression analysis of cross-sectional data one rarely pays attention to the residual variance σ_ε^2. For panel data this may be different. There it can be decomposed into two parts. The first, σ_v^2, measures the amount of variability between individuals in the impact of the unmeasured time-constant variables.

When big, there are major differences between individuals in the unmeasured variables net of the measured ones. The second part, σ_e^2, measures the amount of variability within an individual across time periods in the impact of the unmeasured time-varying variables. From the two components one gets a sense of the main sources in the residual variation. Does it come from unmeasured time-constant variables that vary between individuals and induce between-individual variation in the dependent variable? Or is it due to unmeasured time-varying variables that induce within-individual variation over time in the dependent variable? It is relatively straightforward to estimate the two components of the residual variation, as explained briefly in a later section.

Example

An example of all four estimators is given in Table 14.2. The data are on white-collar employees in Norway in the period 1991–97, with observations on 188 376 persons and 517 960 person-years. Not every person is present in every year. The dependent variable is the natural logarithm of the hourly wage. The independent variables are marital status (five values), years of education, and age, plus dummy variables for the years. All the independent variables are time-varying. The analysis pertains to men.

At first glance, the total and between estimates are similar. So are the within and random-effects estimates. But the latter pair differs substantially from the former. Further discussion follows below.

THE TOTAL ESTIMATOR

The first specification is the so-called *total* equation (14.1). The least-squares estimator of (14.1) is referred to as the *total estimator* or often the pooled or ordinary least squares estimator, denoted $\hat{\beta}_T$, which encompasses $\hat{\beta}_{0T}$, $\hat{\beta}_{1T}$, and $\hat{\beta}_{2T}$. It ignores the grouped nature of the data with repeated observations on each individual. For example, in Table 14.1, the estimator treats observations 1–3 on individual 4 as if they came from three separate people, in the same manner and without distinguishing them from observations 1–3 on individual 5. Under the assumption usually made in cross-sectional analysis, that the error term is independent of the measured independent variables, least squares yields correct estimates of the β_T coefficients: consistent and unbiased. It will, however, generally be less efficient than the random-effects estimator discussed below.

The total estimator corresponds roughly to the one obtained in standard cross-sectional analysis, except that each individual may contribute with more than one observation. The estimates describe the data 'correctly'.

One may use the total estimator $\hat{\beta}_T$ to compute estimates of one or both of the variance components in (14.10). A later section explains one way of estimating these, by combining results from the total and within equations.

Column 1 in Table 14.2 shows results from the total estimator. Hourly wages are roughly 12–14% higher for married, separated, or divorced than single men.

THE BETWEEN ESTIMATOR

We also have use for the so-called *between* or *average* equation (14.2). Here one regresses the average value $\bar{y}_i$ for individual i of y_{it} across time on the average value $\bar{x}_i$ of x_{it} across time and on the time-constant variables z_i. These averages are computed separately for each

individual i. The least squares estimator of (14.2) is usually referred to as the *between* estimator $\hat{\beta}_B$, hence the subscript B, which encompasses $\hat{\beta}_{0B}$, $\hat{\beta}_{1B}$, and $\hat{\beta}_{2B}$.

This estimator makes comparisons between individuals in their average outcomes. Assuming the correctness of the model, $\hat{\beta}_B$ from (14.2) estimates the same parameters as $\hat{\beta}_T$ from (14.1). It just uses the data less efficiently, with only one observation per individual. This is so since (14.2) obtains by aggregating (14.1) up to the individual-level average, for each individual, first by summing over time periods and next by dividing by the number of periods, yielding a so-called *ecological regression equation*. The error term ξ_i is then the average of the error term in (14.1). With no mis-specification, the numerical values of $\hat{\beta}_T$ and $\hat{\beta}_B$ should be the same or close. In practice there is always mis-specification. The two may then easily diverge. Even so, each is of interest in its own right.

For some variables the between estimator does not compute coefficients. This is the case, in balanced panels, for macro-economic conditions such as the unemployment rate. In each period its value is the same for all individuals. Across periods it varies, from year to year, but in the same way for all individuals. When one computes the average $\bar{x}_i$ of such a variable over time for individual i, then this average becomes the same for all individuals. In the between regression it takes a constant value $\bar{x}$. Hence its effect cannot be estimated.

As with the total estimator, one may use the between estimator to compute estimates of some of the variance components.

Column 2 in Table 14.2 shows the results from the between estimator. These are similar to those from the total estimator in column 1, as one would expect. The standard errors are larger in column 2, reflecting the lower efficiency of the between estimator. The estimated residual variance in the between equation is smaller than in the total, as it should be according to (14.11).

THE WITHIN ESTIMATOR:
FIXED-EFFECTS PROCEDURES

The specifications and estimators

With repeated observations on each individual, one is in a position to elaborate the specification of the regression equation. The standard procedure is to include an additional person-specific variable that is time-invariant. There are two approaches. The first specifies a so-called *within* or *fixed-effects* equation (14.3); note that it is usual to suppress the dummy variable D_i in (14.3b) to give

$$y_{it} = \beta_{0W} + \beta_{1W}x_{it} + \alpha_i + \epsilon_{it}, \qquad (14.13)$$

and observe also from (14.3b) that

$$\alpha_i = \beta_{2W}z_i + \beta_{3W}z_i^u.$$

Equation (14.13) captures the effects of the measured and unmeasured time-constant variables z_i and z_i^u. The error term ϵ_{it} is different from ε_{it} in (14.1), since here we also control for the person-specific variable D_i.

In (14.3b) one thus includes a dummy variable D_i for each person i and then estimates its effect α_i, one per person. Each person is treated as a group in the data, in the same way one would treat a set of occupations as separate groups each with its own dummy variable in a cross-sectional data set.

The least-squares estimator of (14.3) is interchangeably referred to as the within, fixed-effects, or sometimes the least-squares dummy-variables estimator. In computing the estimates, one must either set the constant term β_{0W} equal to zero or one must constrain the α_i to sum to zero, to avoid the so-called dummy-variable trap.

One can estimate this equation because there are multiple observations per individual, allowing identification of the α_i. The question is: how?

Before elaborating, it is instructive to state the estimators for β_{1W}, β_{0W} and the α_i from (14.13), for the moment ignoring β_{2W} in (14.3a):

$$\hat{\beta}_{1W} = \left[\sum_{i=1}^{N} \sum_{t}^{T_i} (x_{it} - \bar{x}_i)(x_{it} - \bar{x}_i)' \right]^{-1}$$

$$\times \left[\sum_{i=1}^{N} \sum_{t}^{T_i} (y_{it} - \bar{y}_i)(x_{it} - \bar{x}_i) \right], \qquad (14.14a)$$

$$\hat{\beta}_{0W} = \bar{y} - \hat{\beta}_{1W}\bar{x}, \qquad (14.14b)$$

$$\hat{\alpha}_i = \bar{y}_i - \hat{\beta}_{0W} - \hat{\beta}_{1W}\bar{x}_i$$
$$= (\bar{y}_i - \bar{y}) - \hat{\beta}_{1W}(\bar{x}_i - \bar{x}), \qquad (14.14c)$$

where T_i is the number of periods for which individual i is observed. The prime and –1 in (14.14a) denote matrix transpose and inverse, respectively. Neither is important for understanding the point to be made here. $\bar{y}$ and $\bar{x}$ are the overall averages across individuals and time periods of dependent and independent variables.

The expression in (14.14a) shows the following: The estimator $\hat{\beta}_{1W}$ uses the within individual-level deviation of each variable from its mean across time, hence the name *within estimator*. From each variable, y_{it} or x_{it}, one subtracts its mean value over time for the individual. For example, from a person's employment status (0 or 1) in year t, one subtracts her average employment status across the years she was observed. Or from a person's age in year t one subtracts her average age across years.

The central point here is that one can estimate β_{1W} without estimating the individual-specific effects α_i. Only effects of time-varying variables x_{it} can be estimated.

It is instructive to inspect the within estimator $\hat{\beta}_{1W}$ in the case of one independent variable, say, x_{1it}. It then becomes a single number from

$$\hat{\beta}_{1W} = \left[\sum_{i=1}^{N} \sum_{t}^{T_i} \frac{1}{(x_{1it} - \bar{x}_{1i})^2} \right]$$

$$\times \left[\sum_{i=1}^{N} \sum_{t}^{T_i} (y_{it} - \bar{y}_i)(x_{1it} - \bar{x}_{1i}) \right]. \qquad (14.15)$$

For each individual, one looks at the deviation between the value x_{1it} in year t and its average value $\bar{x}_{1i}$ across years.

The interpretation of the coefficients in the within estimator is important. Consider a dummy variable for being married. Its coefficient reports how much the mean value of the dependent variable changes when individuals change from being single to being married, controlling for the other variables. The comparison is not between single and married people, as in cross-sectional analyses. It is between people who first were single and then married, and how the mean value on the dependent variable changed when they changed marital status.

The estimator $\hat{\beta}_{0W}$ for the constant term is the standard formula in regression analysis. The estimator for each α_i gives the individual's deviation from the overall intercept $\hat{\beta}_{0W}$: one 'intercept' per individual. Note here that the $\hat{\alpha}_i$ sum to zero, which can be checked from (14.14b) and (14.14c). One of several measures of how much variability there is between individuals in the individual-specific effects may be obtained from

$$\hat{\sigma}_\alpha^2 = \frac{1}{N - (K_1 + 1)} \sum_{i=1}^{N} (\bar{y}_i - \hat{\beta}_{0W} - \hat{\beta}_{1W}\bar{x}_i)^2$$

$$= \frac{1}{N - (K_1 + 1)} \sum_{i=1}^{N} \hat{\alpha}_i^2, \qquad (14.16)$$

where K_1 is the number of explanatory variables in x_{it}, and N is the number of individuals. This gives the variance of the $\hat{\alpha}_i$, where $\sum \hat{\alpha}_i = 0$.

Elaboration

But what about the effects on β_{2W} of the time-constant variables z_i? To assess this, specify an equation that includes z_i in addition to D_i, an elaboration of (14.13):

$$y_{it} = \beta_{0W} + \beta_{1W}x_{it} + \beta_{2W}z_i \\ + \alpha_i D_i + \epsilon_{it}. \qquad (14.17)$$

To see what happens once one includes both z_i and D_i requires two steps. These show how one gets to the least-squares estimator in (14.14a) that controls for all the individual-specific dummy variables.

For the first step, as in (14.2), where the average equation was derived, we can compute the individual-level average of the fixed-effects equation (14.17) that includes z_i:

$$\bar{y}_i = \beta_{0W} + \beta_{1W}\bar{x}_i + \beta_{2W}z_i + \alpha_i + \bar{\epsilon}_i. \qquad (14.18)$$

In this form, when aggregated up to one observation per individual, the equation, unlike (14.2), cannot be estimated. With only one observation per individual i we cannot estimate the individual-level effects α_i. One could, however, treat the sum $\alpha_i + \bar{\epsilon}_i$ as an error term and then estimate (14.18), yielding the same results as in (14.2), ignoring the specification with the α_i as fixed effects.

The second step is to subtract, for each individual, this aggregate equation from the fixed-effects equation in (14.17), yielding

$$y_{it} - \bar{y}_i = (\beta_{0W} - \beta_{0W}) + \beta_{1W}(x_{it} - \bar{x}_i) \\ + \beta_{2W}(z_i - z_i) \\ + (\alpha_i - \alpha_i) + (\epsilon_{it} - \bar{\epsilon}_i) \qquad (14.19a)$$

$$= \beta_{1W}(x_{it} - \bar{x}_i) + (\epsilon_{it} - \bar{\epsilon}_i). \qquad (14.19b)$$

This is the resulting least-squares estimating equation for the effects of the measured variables x_{it} and z_i when one controls for D_i through its effects α_i. It shows that, when the effects α_i are included, we cannot estimate the β_{2W} of the measured time-constant variables z_i, that is, of variables such as sex and race. The latter disappears because $z_i - z_i = 0$.

The intuition is simple. Once D_i is controlled, there is for individual i no variation across time in the time-constant variables z_i: D_i and z_i are totally collinear. The effects of all

time-invariant variables in z_i will be picked up by the person-specific effects α_i, ruling out estimation of the effects of z_i. One may thus estimate the effects α_i of D_i, or the effects β_{2W} of z_i, but not both. As mentioned, α_i also picks up the effects of the unmeasured time-constant variables z_i^u. So when one estimates the effects of α_i one controls for both z_i and z_i^u, whereas when one estimates the effects of z_i no control is made for z_i^u.

The within estimates obtain, then, first by subtracting from the dependent variable y_{it} its average $\bar{y}_i$ over time, and second by subtracting from each of the independent variables in x_{it} their averages $\bar{x}_i$ over time, where the averages are computed for each individual i. For a variable that stays constant over time, the value in the year is the same as the average value across years. Hence, it cancels in the regression equation. After having subtracted the means, one computes the ordinary least-squares estimator. This yields the same results as computing least squares on (14.3b) with inclusion of all the person-specific dummy variables.[2]

Advantages and drawbacks

The fixed-effects procedure has wonderful advantages but also drawbacks.

Its enormous strength is that one can control for *all* unmeasured variables z_i and z_i^u and get consistent estimates of β_{1W} for variables that vary over time. The unmeasured variables need not be independent of the measured. Going from cross-sectional to panel data in a linear regression model allows one to estimate the effects of measured time-varying variables and at the same time to control for all measured and unmeasured time-constant variables.

The principal drawback of this procedure is that one can only estimate the effects of variables x_{it} that vary over time. This is a major problem, because in most applications the researcher's interest rarely is only in the subset of variables that vary over time. But for those, the fixed-effects procedure is unparalleled: it reports how much the dependent variable on average changes when individuals change values on independent variables.

Table 14.1 illustrates the issues. The effects of socio-economic background and sex (columns 7 and 8) cannot be estimated in the fixed-effects analysis. For both variables, the mean value across periods for an individual equals its value in each period. For example, for individual 4, socio-economic background has value 50 in each period, hence a mean of 50, and 50 minus 50 gives 0. The same is the case for the individual's sex. In (14.19a) all that enters into the expression is zero.

A related but less serious drawback is that individuals with no across-time variation in some of the variables do not contribute to the analysis as far as those variables are concerned; the values cancel in (14.19a). Individuals with no across-time variation in any of the variables do not contribute at all in the estimation. This may reduce the sample size considerably relative to the total estimator in (14.1).

Again, Table 14.1 illustrates the relevant situations. Consider first individuals 4–6, each with variation on the dependent variable in column 3. Individual 4 has no variation in any of the independent variables, and will not contribute at all to the within estimator. Individual 5 has variation in one independent variable, education, but not in the other, marital status. The individual's value 1 on marital status will not contribute toward estimating the parameters. It cancels in (14.19a). The symmetrical case is individual 6, with no variation in education but in marital status. Consider next individual 7, with no variation on the dependent variable, but variation on both independent variables. The value on the dependent variable will not contribute to the estimation, only the values on the two independent variables. This can be seen from the left-hand side of (14.19a); it equals zero. Consider, finally, individuals 8 and 9, with variation on the dependent and both independent variables. They contribute toward the estimation with all the variables.

In summary, the fixed-effects procedure uses the data less efficiently (Hsiao, 1986: 47). Partly it does so because observations with no within-individual variation over time are not used for estimating β_{1W}; the data on such individuals are ignored. Partly it does so because it uses up a large number of degrees of freedom in estimating the effects of the person-specific dummy variables.

But the within estimator provides something no other estimator does: it allows one to answer very precisely what happens to the dependent variable when individuals change values on independent variables.

Example

Column 3 in Table 14.2 shows the results from the within estimator. These are rather different from the total and between estimators in columns 1 and 2: parameter estimates are 40–75% lower. This means that differences between individuals are larger than those that occur within an individual over time.

The contrasts between the estimators allow substantive comparisons. According to the total and between estimators in columns 1 and 2, married or previously married men do better than single, earning about 12–14% more per hour. However, these estimates do not show that getting married increases one's wages with that amount. Instead, according to the within estimator in column 3, as men move from being single to married and then to various previously married states, the impact on their wages is on average 4–7%, much smaller than the average difference between single and married or previously married men. One way to interpret this is that men who marry are different from those who do not. There are large differences between single and married or previously married men. But only about half of this difference comes about as a result of getting married. The other half is there as a permanent trait of men who eventually get married.

The effect of education is much bigger in the total and between than the within estimator, a return of about 5.5% per year of education versus 1.4% in the within estimator. Making comparisons between individuals, men with one more year of education on average earn about 5.5% more. But making within-individual comparisons, acquiring one additional year of education increases the individual's wages by only 1.5%. This can be interpreted as follows. Men who undertake education are on average more productive or can command higher wages than those who do not; they would receive a wage differential of about 4.1% (= 5.5 − 1.4), even with no additional education. But it could also be the case that it takes time for the return to education to manifest itself at the individual level. To see its impact would require a longer time frame, where one assessed the return, say, ten years later. This is not addressed by the present analysis.

The estimated residual variance in the within equation is small, about a tenth of the total residual variance from the total equation in column 1. Once account has been taken of all time-constant variables plus measured time-varying ones there is minimal idiosyncratic residual variance left at the individual level. However, the variance of the individual-specific fixed effects is large. This means that the time-constant variables account for a large proportion of the variance in the dependent variable.

RANDOM-EFFECTS PROCEDURES

The second specification that takes into account the grouped nature of the data is the so-called *random-effects* equation (14.4). There, v_i is treated as a random variable, as an individual-specific error term. It is assumed to be independent of the observed variables x_{it} and z_i and of e_{it}.

One then estimates β_R and the variances of v_i and e_{it}, denoted σ_v^2 and σ_e^2, where $\hat{\beta}_R$ encompasses $\hat{\beta}_{0R}$, $\hat{\beta}_{1R}$, and $\hat{\beta}_{2R}$. The individual-specific error term v_i is perfectly correlated across periods for the same individual. For the total error term, $v_i + e_{it}$, the serial correlation across periods then equals σ_v^2. If no distribution is assumed for v_i and e_{it}, generalized least squares estimation is used. It accounts for the serial correlation in the error structure. The random-effects estimator $\hat{\beta}_R$ becomes a matrix-weighted average of the within and between estimators $\hat{\beta}_{1W}$ and $\hat{\beta}_B$. If a normal or other distribution is assumed for the two error terms, maximum likelihood estimation is used. There is rarely much justification for assuming a distribution for the error terms.

This random-effects estimator uses information also on individuals who were observed for only one time period. They will contribute their data to the part of the estimator that comes from the between estimator $\hat{\beta}_B$. It also allows estimation of coefficients for variables that do not change over time.

As in the case of the within estimator, one can derive a specification that shows which aspects of the data are used. To see this, first define

$$\theta_i \equiv 1 - \sqrt{\frac{\sigma_e^2}{\sigma_e^2 + T_i \sigma_v^2}} = 1 - \frac{1}{\sqrt{1 + T_i \sigma_v^2/\sigma_e^2}}, \quad (14.20)$$

a weighting factor used below. There are many ways to estimate σ_e^2 and especially σ_v^2. Some expressions are given in the next section. These usually involve the residuals from the total, within, and between regressions. The estimates get inserted into (14.20), yielding an estimate of θ_i, which then is used. In the example in Table 14.2, the estimates

are $\hat{\sigma}_{v(1)}^2 = 0.0535$ and $\hat{\sigma}_e^2 = 0.0052$, discussed in the next section. The subscript $v(1)$ indicates that this is one of several alternative estimators.

With the quantity θ_i in hand – derived from the residual variances from one or more of the total, within, and between estimators – the random-effects estimator obtains by doing linear least squares on the data transformed as follows:

$$\begin{aligned}
y_{it} - \theta_i \bar{y}_i = &(1 - \theta_i)\,\beta_{0,R} + \beta_{1,R}\,(x_{it} - \theta_i \bar{x}_i) \\
&+ \beta_{2,R}(z_i - \theta_i z_i) + (1 - \theta_i)v_i \\
&+ (e_{it} - \theta_i \bar{e}_i).
\end{aligned} \quad (14.21)$$

From each variable one subtracts its mean weighted with the estimate of θ_i. For the two error terms, no such weighting is made since both are unobservable. The within estimator obtains when $\theta_i = 1$, the total when $\theta_i = 0$.

There are some instructive special cases of the random-effects estimator. First, when the estimate of σ_v^2 equals zero, in which case $\theta_i = 0$, then the random-effects estimator $\hat{\beta}_R$ coincides with the total estimator $\hat{\beta}_T$. There are no person-specific effects, that is, no unmeasured time-constant variables, with $v_i = 0$ for all i. The within and between variation are given equal weight.

Second, when the ratio σ_v^2/σ_e^2 grows large, in which case θ_i approaches 1, the random-effects estimator $\hat{\beta}_{1R}$ reduces to the within estimator $\hat{\beta}_{1W}$, with no effects estimated for z_i, as can be seen from (14.21). The intra-person variance dominates in estimating β_R. This makes sense. When the within-individual variation around the regression line for each individual, as measured by σ_e^2, given x_{it}, z_i, and v_i, is small compared to the between-individual variation in the regression line, as measured by σ_v^2, then the within estimator dominates the estimate of β_R. The most precise regression line is the within-individual line. There is little residual variation within individuals but relatively large residual variation between individuals. The between variation gets ignored in estimating the parameters.

Third, when the number of periods T_i grows large, the random-effects estimator converges to the within estimator: the within-individual variation dominates in estimating β_R, as in the second case, where θ_i approaches 1. In my experience the convergence is rapid; in some applications a T_i of 50 or so gives a random-effects estimator almost identical to the fixed-effects estimator. Now, 50 is a large number of periods in most panel data sets, but in other settings where these models can be used – all settings with data with a group structure, such as samples of schools and students within each school – 50 or more observations within each group is common.

There is a fourth case which cannot be derived directly from θ_i. When there is no within variation in any of the independent variables, where at the individual level all variables are time-constant, the random-effects estimator converges to the between (or total) estimator (Baltagi, 2001: 18).

The random-effects procedure has drawbacks as well as advantages. Its main drawback is that one must assume that the unmeasured time-constant variables captured by v_i are independent of the measured variables (Baltagi, 2001: 20). This is a strong assumption. Its violation leads to inconsistent estimates of β_R.

Its main advantages, compared to the fixed-effects procedure are, first, that one can estimate the effects of both time-constant and time-varying variables and, second, that it uses information on all individuals and all variables on each individual, even those that are constant over time.

Column 4 in Table 14.2 shows the results from the random-effects estimator. Each coefficient lies between the within and between (or total) estimates, larger than the within but smaller than the between. Except for the education coefficient, they are closer to the within than to the total and between estimates. The closeness to the within estimates is not surprising. The estimated ratio $\hat{\sigma}^2_{v(1)}/\hat{\sigma}^2_e$ is 10.3 (= 0.0535/0.0052), in which case, for $T_i = 5$, $\hat{\theta}_i = 0.86$. This is close to the second special case above, where θ_i approaches 1. Then the random-effects converges to the within estimator.

The estimated residual variance is much larger for the person-specific than the idiosyncratic error, in both estimates of $\hat{\sigma}^2_v$; that is, $\hat{\sigma}^2_{v(1)} = 0.0535$ and $\hat{\sigma}^2_{v(2)} = 0.0473$, to which we return below. As in the within equation, this means that, net of measured variables, differences between individuals are more important than differences within individuals over time.

ESTIMATING THE VARIANCE COMPONENTS

There are many ways to obtain estimates of the variance components. The technical literature is not helpful in sorting these out or in

assessing their relative strengths. Typically they involve the residual variances from the total, within, and between estimators (Hsiao, 1986: 38).

The central idea is that one first can estimate the total residual variance σ^2_ε from the total regression, which gives the sum of the person-specific σ^2_v and idiosyncratic σ^2_e residual variances, from (14.10). If one next can estimate the idiosyncratic component σ^2_e, one can finally retrieve an estimate of person-specific component σ^2_v as the difference between σ^2_ε and σ^2_e using (14.10).

The estimator for the total residual ε_{it} from the total equation is given by

$$\hat{\varepsilon}_{it} = \widehat{v_i + e_{it}} = y_{it} - \hat{\beta}_{0T} - \hat{\beta}_{1T}x_{it} - \hat{\beta}_{2T}z_i \quad (14.22)$$

from which we get the estimator for the total residual variance as

$$\hat{\sigma}^2_\varepsilon = \widehat{\sigma^2_v + \sigma^2_e} = \frac{1}{N\bar{T} - K_1 - K_2 - 1}$$

$$\times \sum_{i=1}^{N} \sum_{t}^{T_i} (y_{it} - \hat{\beta}_{0T} - \hat{\beta}_{1T}x_{it} - \hat{\beta}_{2T}z_i)^2 \quad (14.23)$$

where $\bar{T}$ is the average number of periods for which indviduals are observed. We correct for the number of degrees of freedom by subtracting K_1 and K_2 from the number of observed person-years $N\bar{T}$. This is a common estimator for σ^2_ε.

But how can one extract an estimator for σ^2_e? A common and simple way is to use the residuals ϵ_{it} from the within estimator. Note that when the assumption of the random-effects model holds, that v_i is independent of the measured variables, then from (14.7)

$$\epsilon_{it} = e_{it}. \quad (14.24)$$

As an estimator of e_{it} one can thus use the estimator of ϵ_{it} from the within regression, namely

$$\hat{e}_{it} = \hat{\epsilon}_{it}$$

$$\equiv y_{it} - \hat{\beta}_{0W} - \hat{\beta}_{1W}x_{it} - \hat{\alpha}_i,$$

$$= (y_{it} - \bar{y}_i) - \hat{\beta}_{1W}(x_{it} - \bar{x}_i), \quad (14.25)$$

where the expression for $\hat{\alpha}_i$ from (14.14c) was inserted to get the third equality. One estimator of σ^2_e is then the estimator of σ^2_ϵ from the within regression

$$\hat{\sigma}^2_e = \hat{\sigma}^2_\epsilon \equiv \frac{1}{N\bar{T} - N - K_1 - 1}$$

$$\times \sum_{i=1}^{N} \sum_{t}^{T_i} [(y_{it} - \bar{y}_i) - \hat{\beta}_{1W}(x_{it} - \bar{x}_i)]^2. \quad (14.26)$$

Finally, with estimators of the total and idiosyncratic residual variances we can extract an estimator of the individual-specific residual variance:

$$\hat{\sigma}_v^2 = \hat{\sigma}_\varepsilon^2 - \hat{\sigma}_e^2. \qquad (14.27)$$

The numerical values of σ_v^2 and σ_e^2 are informative. The first gives the amount of variation *between* individuals in the impact of the unmeasured variables v_i. When large, the unmeasured variables account for large differences between individuals, given x_{it}, z_i. The second, σ_e^2, gives the average variation within an individual over time, given the measured x_{it}, z_i and unmeasured v_i variables. Comparing σ_v^2 and σ_e^2, one can discuss whether differences caused by unmeasured variables tend to be larger between individuals than within individuals over time, again, given x_{it}, z_i.

As already discussed, Table 14.2 shows that the variance of the individual-specific error term is much larger than of the idiosyncratic error term. It reports two different estimators of σ_v^2, one based on (14.27) (i.e., $\hat{\sigma}_{v(2)}^2$), one on a different formula often used (e.g., STATA). Given the logarithmic scale, the two are similar, $\hat{\sigma}_{v(1)}^2 = 0.0535$ versus $\hat{\sigma}_{v(2)}^2 = 0.0473$. But of potential concern is that $\hat{\sigma}_{v(1)}^2 = 0.0535$ is larger than the total residual variance $\hat{\sigma}_\varepsilon^2 = 0.0525$ from the total equation. The sum of $\hat{\sigma}_{v(2)}^2 = 0.0473$ and $\hat{\sigma}_e^2 = 0.0052$ equals the total residual variance in the total equation $\hat{\sigma}_\varepsilon^2 = 0.0525$. As this illustrates, there are many ways to estimate the variances of the error terms. These can give different answers.

FIXED- VERSUS RANDOM-EFFECTS PROCEDURES

Researchers sometimes argue that one estimator is better than another, that one corresponds to a correct model while others do not. If so, the model assumed correct should be emphasized. Econometricians have given considerable thought to these issues (e.g., Hsiao, 1986: 41–8; Wooldridge 2002: Chapter 10). But often it may be more fruitful to think of the estimators as reporting on different aspects of the data. No estimator is then necessarily better, they just answer different questions.

Accepting this reasoning, it may in most applications make sense to report several estimators. The total estimator is clearly of interest. It reports roughly what one would get with cross-sectional data. The between estimator is of less interest, though it can be useful to report for descriptive purposes. The random-effects estimator is of the same quantity as the total estimator. It is just more efficient. The within estimator is always of considerable interest, since it controls for all time- invariant measured and unmeasured variables.

In practice one may first report the total and possibly the between estimator. Thereafter some discussion of the comparative advantages of the within- and random-effects estimators is usually warranted. When the number of periods T_i is large, the two estimators more or less coincide. For small T_i the situation is different: they may give diverging answers. The trade-off then is that the random-effect estimator uses the data more effectively, but it relies on the assumption that the unmeasured time-constant variables captured by v_i are independent of the measured x_{it} and z_i. Some procedures are available for testing this assumption (see Hsiao, 1986: 48–9; Chamberlain, 1982). It is of course no different from the assumption always made in analyzing data from cross-sectional samples.

If one wants to estimate the effects of time-invariant variables, the fixed-effect estimator is useless. Reporting both estimators may then be the preferred solution. When the two differ significantly, there may be cause for further speculation and investigation, perhaps by testing for independence of v_i and x_{it}, z_i.

It is sometimes claimed that fixed-effects estimates are superior. This seems plausible, since in these one has controlled for all time-invariant variables that matter for the dependent variable. The danger of omitted-variable bias is reduced. The fixed-effects procedure is then appealing.

But nothing is this simple. The fact is that the regression with fixed effects is not better than the one without. It just answers a different question. The fixed-effects analysis addresses within-individual changes or differences. For example, as individuals change from being single to being married, what are the changes in wages earned? This can be estimated once one knows the wages of each individual before and after marriage. The regression equation without fixed effects answers a question tilted more toward differences between individuals: what are the wages of single versus married persons? It does not directly make intra-individual comparisons, of the impact of moving from one state to another. Both questions are relevant to answer. And each answer correctly addresses the corresponding question.

Rather than focusing all attention on omitted-variable bias, the researcher may reflect on which questions would be most relevant to answer. These will then decide the corresponding specification of the regression equation. If the interest is in the effect of marriage, comparing single to married persons, while controlling for age and education, a regression including those variables provides the correct answer, as in columns 1 and 2 in Table 14.2. There is no omitted-variable bias relative to the question posed. Clearly, the estimated effect of marriage may partially reflect the operation of excluded variables. But the interest was not in the effect of marriage net of those additional variables. If the interest is in the effect of marriage net of the same variables plus all individual-level variables that are constant over time, that is, assessing the impact of marital changes within an individual's life, then the fixed-effects estimates provide the correct answer.

STATIC MODELS FOR BINARY DEPENDENT VARIABLES

Nonlinear models for panel data are more complex. Binary logit and probit models are well understood. The dependent variable for individual i in period t is C_{it}, equal to 0 or 1, as in the example in column 4 of Table 14.1. As in the linear case, panel data allow better control for unobserved variables that affect C_{it}, whether someone is in category 0 or 1 on the dependent variable. In the logit model one may estimate both fixed- and random-effects specifications. In the probit model only the latter is available.

To fix ideas, consider the binary dependent C_{it} variable and the corresponding logit equation

$$P(C_{it} = 1 | x_{it}, z_i)$$
$$= \frac{\exp(\delta_0 + \delta_1 x_{it} + \delta_2 z_i)}{1 + \exp(\delta_0 + \delta_1 x_{it} + \delta_2 z_i)}, \quad (14.28)$$

where δ_1 and δ_2 are the effect parameters for x_{it} and z_i and δ_0 is a constant term. This is equivalent to the total equation in the linear case.

If there are unobserved variables in (14.28), maximum likelihood estimation

yields inconsistent estimates of δ ($= \delta_0, \delta_1, \delta_2$), even when the unobservables are independent of the observables, unlike the linear case, a general result in nonlinear models. The unobserved time-constant variables are again captured by a dummy variable D_i, one per individual. Specify

$$P(C_{it} = 1 | x_{it}, z_i, D_i)$$
$$= \frac{\exp(\delta_0 + \delta_1 x_{it} + \delta_2 z_i + \mu_i D_i)}{1 + \exp(\delta_0 + \delta_1 x_{it} + \delta_2 z_i + \mu_i D_i)}$$
$$= \frac{\exp(\delta_0 + \delta_1 x_{it} + \delta_2 z_i + \mu_i)}{1 + \exp(\delta_0 + \delta_1 x_{it} + \delta_2 z_i + \mu_i)}. \quad (14.29)$$

As in the linear case, it turns out that there are two approaches for estimating δ ($= \delta_0, \delta_1, \delta_2$), the fixed- and random-effects procedures. In the former one controls for the unobserved variables by a dummy variable D_i, with fixed effect μ_i, one per person. In the latter one treats μ_i as a random variable.

In the logit model, the fixed-effects procedure raises new issues. Unlike the linear case on page 337, one does not proceed by estimating the effects of dummy variables specified for each individual. Doing so would yield inconsistent estimates of δ when T_i is finite, a result that generally holds when one goes from a linear to a nonlinear model with individual-level specific effects (e.g., Chamberlain, 1980). There is, however, a solution allowing consistent estimation of δ while not estimating the μ_i.

Rather than estimating the effects of one dummy variable per person, one can, from (14.29), compute a so-called sufficient statistic in which δ_1 but not $\mu_i D_i$ occurs, but where D_i is still controlled. This allows one to consistently estimate δ_1 (Chamberlain, 1980). No estimates can be obtained for the constant term δ_0 or the effects δ_2 of time-invariant variables z_i; their effects are absorbed into the μ_i, as in the linear model. The sufficient statistic is computed for each individual by conditioning on the sum of C_{it} across t. The estimator is more complicated than in the linear case, but some software has implemented it, such as STATA. Its advantages and drawbacks are the same as those of the fixed-effects estimator in the linear case: one need not assume that μ_i is independent of x_{it}, z_i, but one cannot estimate the effects of time-constant variables z_i, and the estimator uses the data less efficiently. Individuals with no variation on either dependent or independent variables do not contribute in the estimation.

In the random-effects procedure μ_i is treated as a random variable. One then estimates δ $(= \delta_0, \delta_1, \delta_2)$ and the distribution of μ_i. One may impose a specific distribution on μ_i, such as a normal, and then estimate its variance, or one may use a nonparametric estimator (e.g., Dempster et al., 1977). The random-effects procedure has the same drawbacks and advantages as in the linear case. Its main drawback is that one must assume that the unmeasured variables are independent of the measured. This is a strong assumption, the same as always made in cross-sectional analysis. Its main advantages are first that one can estimate the effects of both time-constant and time-varying variables, and second that information on all individuals and all variables on each individual, even those that are constant over time, is used.

If instead of a logit one considers a probit model, a fixed-effects estimator is no longer available, only the random-effects estimator is (Chamberlain, 1980). The sufficient statistic required in order to compute the fixed-effects estimator is available only for a limited class of models.

MULTI-LEVEL ANALYSIS

Panel data have a so-called multi-level structure, as already discussed. The higher level is the individual. The lower level consists of the observations for the individual at each point in time. In the models considered on pages 337–42 above, this was accounted for in the following way. In the fixed-effects model, there was a separate dummy variable for each individual in the data, for the higher level. This amounts to the modeling assumption that each individual has a separate intercept. They start at different levels on the y-axis once the xs are set to zero. But thereafter the slope parameters are the same. The changes in the dependent variable resulting from increases in independent variables are the same across individuals. In the random-effects model each individual has an individual-specific error term but otherwise identical slope parameters.

A multi-level model takes this one step further. Not only may intercepts vary between individuals, so also may the effect coefficients for the independent variables. Often the coefficients themselves are specified as functions of exogenous variables. Such procedures have become common in social scientific analysis (Mason et al., 1983; Hsiao, 1986: Section 6.5; Kreft and de Leeuw, 1998).

Also in these models one distinguishes between fixed- and random-effects procedures. In the fixed-effects procedure one estimates separate effect coefficients for each group in the data (see Kreft and de Leeuw, 1998: 36–9). In panel data, that would be for each individual. In data on firms and workers within firms, it would be for each firm, with firm-specific effects of sex and other variables. One may report how the effects vary between individuals or firms. One may, for example, report the variance and the various percentiles of the effects. In the random-effects procedure one specifies a distribution for the effect parameters. One would typically estimate the mean and variance of this distribution and would especially investigate how this mean varies with characteristics of the group. The mean would give the average size of the effect parameters across groups. The variance would indicate the variability in these effect parameters (see Kreft and de Leeuw, 1998: 39–44).

CONCLUDING REMARKS

The analysis of linear static equations for continuous dependent variables using panel data has been thoroughly investigated. The results are impressive. Moreover, they apply in all situations where the data have a group structure: such as schools and students within schools, and firms and workers within firms (e.g., Petersen and Morgan, 1995). They allow accounting for unobserved variables in a rigorous manner. This involves distinguishing processes that occur within a unit – individual or firm – from those that occur between. The analysis of logit and probit models for panel data is also well established. One can still expect advances in analyzing nonlinear models for panel data for continuous and categorical dependent variables (e.g., Pinheiro and Bates, 2000; McCulloch and Searle, 2001). These developments draw on analysis of covariance methodology, as has been well established for the linear case with continuous outcomes. The results are not likely to be as accessible as in linear models. The tool of decomposing the variability into within and between components is less straightforward to implement. For many nonlinear models fixed-effects procedures yielding consistent estimators are not available.

NOTES

1 Sometimes researchers also introduce fixed or random effects for the time period. In the analysis below, period effects are introduced by a set of dummy variables. Their effects are estimated along with the effects of the observed variables.

2 The standard errors of coefficients obtained from (14.19b) will, however, be incorrect since they use the incorrect degrees of freedom, in balanced data $N - K_1$ rather than $N(T - 1) - K_1$. In balanced data, multiplying the reported standard errors with the ratio $(N - K_1)/[N(T - 1) - K_1]$ yields the correct standard errors. Regression programs for panel data that use the estimator in (14.14a) provide the correct standard errors.

REFERENCES

Baltagi, Badi H. (2001) *Econometric Analysis of Panel Data* (2nd edition). New York: Wiley.

Chamberlain, G. (1980) 'Analysis of covariance with qualitative data', *Review of Economic Studies*, 47: 225–38.

Chamberlain, G. (1982) 'Multivariate regression models for panel data', *Journal of Econometrics*, 18: 5–46.

Coleman, J.S. (1968) 'The mathematical study of change', in H.M. Blalock and A. Blalock (eds), *Methodology in Social Research*. New York: McGraw-Hill, pp. 428–78.

Dempster, A.P., Laird, N. and Rubin, D.B. (1977) 'Maximum likelihood from incomplete data via the EM algorithm', *Journal of the Royal Statistical Society Series B*, 39: 1–38.

Hsiao, C. (1986) *Analysis of Panel Data*. New York: Cambridge University Press.

Kreft, Ita and de Leeuw, Jan (1998) *Introducing Multilevel Modeling*. Thousand Oaks, CA: Sage.

Mason, W.M., Wong, George Y. and Entwisle, B. (1983) 'Contextual analysis through the multilevel linear model', in S. Leinhardt (ed.), *Sociological Methodology 1983–1984*. San Francisco: Jossey-Bass, pp. 72–103.

McCulloch, Charles E. and Searle, Shayle R. (2001) *Generalized, Linear, and Mixed Models*. New York: Wiley.

Petersen, T. (1988) 'Analyzing change over time in a continuous dependent variable: Specification and estimation of continuous state space hazard rate models', in C.C. Clogg (ed.), *Sociological Methodology 1988*. Washington, DC: American Sociological Association, pp. 137–64.

Petersen, T. (1991) 'Time-aggregation bias in continuous-time hazard-rate models', in P.V. Marsden (ed.), *Sociological Methodology 1991*. Cambridge, MA: Basil Blackwell, pp. 263–90.

Petersen, Trond and Morgan, Laurie (1995) 'Separate and unequal: occupation-establishment segregation and the gender wage gap', *American Journal of Sociology*, 101(2): 329–65.

Pinheiro, José C. and Bates, Douglas M. (2000) *Mixed-Effects Models in S and S-Plus*. New York: Springer-Verlag.

Rosenfeld, R.A. (1980) 'Race and sex differences in career dynamics', *American Sociological Review*, 45: 583–609.

Tuma, N.B. and Hannan, M. T. (1984). *Social Dynamics. Models and Methods*. Orlando, FL: Academic Press.

Wooldridge, Jeffrey M. (2002) *Econometric Analysis of Cross Section and Panel Data*. Cambridge, MA: MIT Press.

15

Longitudinal Analysis for Continuous Outcomes:

Random Effects Models and Latent Trajectory Models

GUANG GUO AND JOHN HIPP

In this chapter, we discuss longitudinal analysis for linear data and their social science applications. We describe the basic statistical models and substantive motivations behind the statistical models, drawing applications from sociological, demographic, psychological, economic, and health-related research. We emphasize the practical usage of longitudinal analysis.

Longitudinal linear data are a sample of units of analysis, in which at least some of the units are measured twice or more. Examples include individuals and organizations measured repeatedly over time. Longitudinal linear data can be generated from panel studies, in which each unit of analysis is followed up at equal or unequal intervals. Panel data are sometimes referred to as pooled time-series and cross-sectional data. Longitudinal linear data may be viewed as a sample of short time series, with the number of units equal to the number of time series. In contrast, the data, for example, generated by the daily Dow Jones index represent a single long time series. This chapter does not deal with data based on one single long time series. Longitudinal linear data should be distinguished from longitudinal binary data and longitudinal

event history data (Cox and Oakes, 1984; Kalbfleisch and Prentice, 1980; Allison, 1995). Like their linear counterpart, longitudinal binary data are also measured at multiple time points, but they only take on values of one or zero. Statistical models for longitudinal binary data require distinct estimation techniques. The basic event history data differ from longitudinal linear data in at least two ways. First, the dependent variable in event history data analysis is the occurrence of an event over time. Second, the dependent variable in basic event history data is measured only once, even though the independent variables may be measured repeatedly over time. More complex event history data may consist of repeated measures of the occurrence of an event over time. This chapter focuses on techniques for longitudinal linear data.

Most longitudinal analyses may be considered as growth curve modeling that investigates the changes in the dependent variable over time as a function of time and the independent variables, which may or may not be time-varying. Growth curve models may be used to examine the factors that influence the growth of quantitative variables such as height and weight among growing children.

This chapter discusses two classes of growth curve models: the *random effects growth curve models* and the *latent trajectory models* (LTMs), beginning with the former. The random-intercept-only model and the compound symmetry model (the most basic random effects model for longitudinal data) may be described in the tradition of the mixed models (Searle, 1971; Searle et al., 1992), multilevel models (Mason et al., 1983; Goldstein, 1987, 1995; Bryk and Raudenbush, 1992), or econometric random effects models (Greene, 1997), all of which are closely related. Other types of random effects growth curve models, such as the AR(1) model, the unstructured model, and the spatial power model, will also be discussed. We will refer to all of these models for longitudinal analysis as random effects models. We then move on to another group of random effects growth curve models: random coefficient models. We discuss these because they are practically identical to some of the most important LTMs. To clarify the terms to be used in the chapter, both the random effects model and LTM include random-intercept-only and random coefficient models.

Recent years have seen the popularization of structural equation growth curve models or LTMs (McArdle, 1988; McArdle and Epstein, 1987; Meredith and Tisak, 1990; Muthén, 1991; Bollen and Curran, 2004). Many structural equation growth curve models and the random effects growth curve models are based on the same conceptualization. We will describe the structural equation growth curve models, compare them with their random-effects counterparts, and point out that some of the most important growth models are essentially identical across the two statistical traditions.

Sometimes, longitudinal data are used to estimate fixed effects models. The phrase 'fixed effects' can mean quite different things in different fields. Statisticians and biostatisticians refer to fixed effects as effects of observed variables. They view the random effects model as the mixed model in which the effects of unobserved variables (random effects) are estimated side by side with the effects of observed variables (fixed effects). On the other hand, in much of the social science and especially the economics literature, the fixed effects represent the unobserved effects that are constant across all measures of a cluster. In such a case, longitudinal data are used as a methodological tool to provide

an additional handle for the substantive question of the analyst.

The fixed effects model based on longitudinal data allows us to control for unmeasured effects that are constant across repeated measures over time. These unmeasured effects cannot otherwise be easily controlled for. The fixed effects model based on longitudinal linear data is straightforward conceptually and statistically. The estimation of such models can be accomplished by widely available software for ordinary least squares (OLS) linear regression. Space considerations prevent us from treating this fully. Interested readers may wish to refer to Liker et al. (1985) for an introduction. They may also wish to refer to applications that apply the techniques. Guo and VanWey (1999) used repeated measures of individuals over time to control for unmeasured family intellectual climate, family value system, and family genetic heritage model in an analysis of family size and intellectual development. England et al. (1996) studied the effect of gender composition on starting wages in an organization, pooled across all job spells for each worker to control for such unmeasured and unchanging personal characteristics as intelligence, preferences resulting from early socialization, life cycle plans, and unmeasured human capital. Firebaugh and Beck (1994), in a re-examination of the benefit of the economic growth for the masses, used data from 62 countries spanning two decades. The longitudinal data enabled them to take into account constant and unmeasured national characteristics including nation's location, topography, climate, history, culture, economic system, political system, religious composition, and so on.

RANDOM EFFECTS GROWTH CURVE MODELS

Examples

To motivate this approach, we briefly describe four published longitudinal analyses. Some of the descriptions may be clearer after the technical description that follows these examples.

Assessing the effects of school-based education Rosenbaum and Hanson (1998) estimated the short- and long-term effects of the Drug Abuse Resistance Education (DARE) program on students' attitudes, beliefs, social skills, and drug use behaviors. The Illinois DARE evaluation was designed with one pretest and multiple post-tests. Pretest data were collected in 1989 shortly after a portion of the participating schools received the DARE program in the spring of 1990. Two types of surveys were administered each year over the six years of data collection: one for students and one for teachers. The student survey collected data on drug-related beliefs, attitudes, and behaviors. The teacher survey provided additional information on students' exposure to post-DARE drug prevention programs during each current academic year. DARE, the independent variable of primary interest, is time-fixed, though some time-varying independent variables measuring drug prevention programs may be constructed using the yearly teacher survey. The analysis showed that DARE had no long-term effects on a wide range of drug use measures.

The role of stress and mood in sickle cell disease pain Porter et al. (2000) give another example of longitudinal analysis, in which a relatively small number of individuals (15) were measured a large number of times (an average of 94). The 15 individuals with sickle cell disease completed daily diaries about their pain, stress, mood, and health care and medication use for an average of 94 days on a daily basis. Multilevel random effects models indicated that stress was significantly and positively related to same-day pain ratings. Mood also showed significant association with same-day pain. A first-order autoregressive error structure was assumed for the random effects models to correct for the autocorrelation between successive measurements of each individual. The autoregression refers to the observation that measures closer in time are more similar than measures more distant in time.

Factors predicting rate of cognitive decline in probable Alzheimer's disease Rasmusson et al. (1996) present an example of negative growth for the dependent variable. A total of 132 probable Alzheimer's disease patients were tested for cognitive performances every 6 months for up to 7½ years. Random effects regression models with a random intercept accounting for individual-specific effect were estimated. The analysis showed that patients with left-handedness, family history of dementia, and more years of education are related to more rapid cognitive decline.

The timing of the influences of cumulative poverty on children's cognitive ability and achievement Guo (1998) used only two measures of cognitive development per child, one from childhood and the other from adolescence. Hypothesizing that childhood and adolescence are two qualitatively different developmental stages, Guo asked if cumulative poverty during childhood exerts maximum effect on children's cognitive outcomes, or if cognitive outcomes are more a function of the length of exposure to poverty regardless of the life stage in which the child is exposed to poverty. The study distinguished between ability and achievement. Ability is a more stable trait than achievement and tends to be determined by both environmental and genetic factors early in life. Achievement, on the other hand, is more acquired. Data from the National Longitudinal Survey of Youth (NLSY) were employed. Random effects models with a random intercept at the child level showed that long-term poverty has substantial influences on both ability and achievement, but the time patterns of these influences are distinctly different. Childhood appears to be a much more crucial period for the development of cognitive ability than early adolescence. In contrast, poverty experienced in adolescence appears to be more influential on adolescent achievement than poverty experienced earlier in life.

Random effects growth curve models

The data and the basic growth curve model through an example The random effects growth curve models for longitudinal data are closely related to the mixed model (Searle, 1971; Searle et al., 1992), multilevel models (Mason et al., 1983; Goldstein, 1987, 1995; and Bryk and Raudenbush, 1992), and econometric random effects models (Greene, 1997). We present various aspects of the models through an example of sibship size and intellectual development.

Our example is concerned with modeling effects of sibship size on intellectual development over time, taking into consideration the change in sibship size during a child's growth. Most of the evidence for the relationship between intellectual development and family size has been gathered from cross-sectional analysis in which intellectual development measured at one point in time is regressed on family size measured at the same point in

Table 15.1   *Data for first three children*

Cid	Mid	PIATR	age	year	female	momedu	income	sibship
803	1	23	6	88	1	12	11 752	3
803	2	43	8	90	1	12	24 200	3
803	3	49	10	92	1	12	22 500	3
803	4	81	12	94	1	12	21 248	2
803	5	76	14	96	1	12	24 500	2
4901	1	20	6	88	0	14	49 500	2
4901	2	38	8	90	0	14	52 518	2
4901	3	48	10	92	0	14	55 334	2
4901	4	60	12	94	0	14	57 823	2
4901	5	63	14	96	0	14	72 443	2
9201	1	19	6	88	0	12	27 570	1
9201	2	56	8	90	0	12	31 500	1
9201	3	50	10	92	0	12	25 790	2
9201	4	60	12	94	0	12	18 605	2
9201	5	71	14	96	0	12	25 060	2

time, adjusting for socioeconomic variables. The resource dilution theory is usually invoked to interpret the regression results (Blake, 1981, 1989). This theory suggests that a child's intellectual development depends on family resources. The more children in a family, the more the resources are divided, the fewer resources each child will enjoy, and therefore the poorer each child's development will be.

However, if sibship size does dilute family resources and affect intellectual growth, the sibship size that dilutes resources is not necessarily the sibship size measured in cross-sectional data. For instance, since a family acquires children gradually over a number of years, not all siblings would influence a given child's intellectual development at all times. The number of siblings that may influence the child's intellectual development changes over time. Moreover, children undergo intellectual development continually and intellectual development may be more sensitive to environmental influences such as family size at some ages than others. Fortunately, all of these concerns can be dealt with in the framework of the random effects growth curve model with appropriate longitudinal data.

We use data from the children of the NLSY to motivate and illustrate the various models. The dependent variable in the illustration is the raw score of the reading recognition assessment of the Peabody Individual Achievement Test (PIATR). The test was given to all children aged 5 or older at two-year intervals. We first limit our analysis to a sample of children who were measured at all

five time points in 1988, 1990, 1992, 1994, and 1996. Later in this illustration, we will randomly delete (1) 15% of the measures (not children) and (2) one year of data, to demonstrate the modeling techniques when the longitudinal data are not balanced or not of equal intervals.

Table 15.1 displays the data for the first three children in the dataset. The first and second columns are child ID and measurement ID, respectively. The repeated measures of the children are stacked in a long string. The third column gives PIATR, the raw score of the test. The raw score has a tendency to increase, which makes the interpretation easier. Alternatively, we may choose to model the standardized score. In such a case, the trajectory would be a flat line, but the child-specific trajectories could still be differentiated and analyzed. The additional columns give the child's age at the test, year of the test, gender of the child, mother's education, family income for the year when the test was given, and sibship size, which does change over time for children 1 and 3.

When each unit of analysis is measured four times or more, a quadratic growth curve model may be used to describe the basic growth pattern in the data:

$$Y_{ij} = \beta_0 + \beta_1 age_{ij} + \beta_2 age_{ij}^2 + u_j + e_{ij}, \quad (15.1)$$

where Y_{ij} is the observed PIATR score for child j at age i, β_0 is the intercept, u_j is the child-specific random effect or the random intercept, and e_{ij} is the measure-specific random effect or the OLS-like error term. The standard assumptions are that u_j and e_{ij}

Table 15.2   Coefficients and their t statistics from random effects growth curve models of cognitive developmental data measured five times at two-year intervals from the NLSY, with the growth curve modeled quadratically

Variance structure	CS	AR(1)	UN	OLS
Intercept	10.5 (20.0)	10.2 (19.2)	10.35 (43.0)	10.63 (18.3)
age	8.86 (50.9)	8.99 (48.9)	8.59 (51.0)	8.83 (30.1)
age^2	−0.37 (−20.4)	−0.38 (−20.8)	−0.35 (−22.9)	−0.37 (−12.1)
σ_u^2	81.1 (14.3)			
σ_e^2	43.8 (31.9)			124.8 (35.7)
σ^2		120.3		
$\rho_{AR(1)}$		0.766		
ρ (correlation)	0.64			0.0
−2logL	18 070.5	17 650.5	16 992.5	19 552.9
AIC	18 074.5	17 654.5	17 022.5	19 554.9
BIC	18 083.0	17 663.0	17 086.0	19 559.2
Children/measures	510/2550	510/2550	510/2550	510/2550

are mutually independent $N(0, \sigma_u^2)$ and $N(0, \sigma_e^2)$ random variables, where σ_u^2 and σ_e^2 are between-child variance and within-child variance, respectively. In addition to what is captured by the observed variables, this model assumes that each measure is subject to two effects. One (e_{ij}) is unique to each measure and the other (u_j) is the same for all measures of a child, but differs by child. The quantities σ_e^2 and σ_u^2 are these two effects' variances, respectively. A large between-child variance indicates large differences in PIATR across children. A large within-child variance indicates large differences across the measures of a child in the data.

The within-child or intraclass correlation can be obtained from $\rho = \sigma_u^2/(\sigma_u^2 + \sigma_e^2)$. Thus, the correlation is the between variance divided by the total variance. Given the within variance, larger between variances lead to larger correlations, indicating that there are larger differences across individuals relative to the differences across measures of the same individual. In the extreme case, when the within variance is negligible, the correlation would approach one. In such a case, the measures of the same individual would be nearly identical.

Model (1) is a two-level multilevel model and can be written as such

$$Y_{ij} = \beta_{0j} + \beta_1 age_{ij} + \beta_2 age_{ij}^2$$
$$+ e_{ij} \quad \text{(level 1 model)} \quad (15.2)$$

$$\beta_{0j} = \beta_0 + u_j \text{ (level 2 model)} \quad (15.3)$$

The combination of models (2) and (3) is equivalent to model (1), which may be viewed as the so-called combined model. The

addition of the child-specific random effect u_j is the only difference between this model and a corresponding conventional OLS regression model. The assumption is that, controlling for the child-specific random effect u_j, the multiple measures of the child will be independent.

The first column in Table 15.2 presents the parameter estimates from equation (15.1). Our analysis file consists of 510 children and 2550 measures of PIATR. The between variance of 81.1 is large relative to the within variance of 43.8, indicating that the main source of variation is child-specific and that the measures of the same child are highly correlated (0.64). The coefficients of age and of age squared can be used to construct the model-implied growth curve. CS stands for 'compound symmetry' and describes the covariance structure for the model. We will discuss the compound symmetry model more below. The last column in the same table presents parameter estimates from a corresponding OLS regression model, which assumes that the measures of the same child are independent. In this case, ignoring the dependence does not seem to bias the point estimate of the growth curve. The values of −2logL, AIC, and BIC can be used to compare across the models with different error structure. Program 1 in the Appendix to this chapter provides SAS codes for the compound symmetry model.

Modeling covariance structure   In a multilevel analysis such as students embedded in schools, a random intercept model like (15.1) is the standard model and often sufficient. Such a model assumes that all students in a

Table 15.3   *Correlation matrix for PIATR across different test years*

	PIATR88	PIATR90	PIATR92	PIATR94	PIATR96
PIATR88	1.00				
PIATR90	0.63	1.00			
PIATR92	0.52	0.79	1.00		
PIATR94	0.50	0.74	0.84	1.00	
PIATR96	0.42	0.68	0.82	0.84	1.00

school are subject to the same school-specific random effect, that is, any two students in a school would be correlated to the same degree. In longitudinal analysis, this assumption is typically inappropriate. When multiple measures of a unit of analysis are obtained sequentially, measures close to each other tend to be more similar than measures far apart. In other words, longitudinal data tend to follow autoregressive structure over time. This characteristic feature of longitudinal data is shown in the correlation matrix for PIATR across different test years (Table 15.3). Another feature of this correlation matrix may be particular to our dataset: the correlations among older children tend to be higher than those among younger children. Here, we will describe two solutions: a covariance structure that accounts for the first-order autoregressive process; and the unstructured covariance structure that allows all the parameters in the covariance structure to be freely estimated. In the next section, on the LTM, we will describe random coefficient models as an alternative for modeling longitudinal data and compare them with LTMs. These random coefficient models are also the random effects models.

A standard solution to autocorrelation in longitudinal data is to allow the covariance structure to be autoregressive of order 1 or AR(1). Since equations that are written in scalars cannot readily describe AR(1) covariance structure, we employ matrix notation. The general form of random effects models can be written as the general form of the mixed model (Searle, 1971; Searle et al., 1992),

$$Y = X\beta + Zu + e, \qquad (15.4)$$

where $\mathbf{Y}$ is the vector of observations $\mathbf{Y}_i$, $\mathbf{X}$ is the matrix of observed predictors, $\boldsymbol{\beta}$ is the vector of parameters for the observed predictors, $\mathbf{Z}$ is the known design matrix for the vector of unknown random effects $\mathbf{u}$, and $\mathbf{e}$ is the vector of random errors e_i. The mixed model assumes

that $\mathbf{u}$ and $\mathbf{e}$ are mutually independent and each normally distributed with $E[\mathbf{u}] = \mathbf{0}$, $E[\mathbf{e}] = \mathbf{0}$, $\mathrm{var}[\mathbf{u}] = \mathbf{G}$, and $\mathrm{var}[\mathbf{e}] = \mathbf{R}$. Then the covariance matrix of $\mathbf{Y}$ is $\mathrm{var}[\mathbf{Y}] = \mathbf{ZGZ}' + \mathbf{R} = \boldsymbol{\Sigma}$. The parameters in $\boldsymbol{\Sigma}$ can be estimated by the method of maximum likelihood (ML) or restricted maximum likelihood (REML). With $\boldsymbol{\Sigma}$, $\boldsymbol{\beta}$ can be estimated via generalized least squares. All the random effects growth curve models can be described by (15.4).

The random effects model (15.4) obtains various growth curve models by varying the covariance structure $\boldsymbol{\Sigma}$. For OLS regression with the assumptions of independent observations and homoscedasticity,

$$\boldsymbol{\Sigma} = \begin{pmatrix} \sigma^2 & & & \\ & \sigma^2 & & \\ & & \ddots & \\ & & & \sigma^2 \end{pmatrix}, \qquad (15.5)$$

where all the elements on the main diagonal are equal to a single value, σ^2, and all the elements off the main diagonal are zero. For a random intercept (compound symmetry) model like (15.1) (column 1 in Table 15.2), the covariance matrix for cluster j, or child j in our current example, is

$$\boldsymbol{\Sigma}_j = \begin{pmatrix} \sigma_u^2 + \sigma_e^2 & & & \\ \sigma_u^2 & \sigma_u^2 + \sigma_e^2 & & \\ \vdots & \vdots & \ddots & \\ \sigma_u^2 & \sigma_u^2 & \cdots & \sigma_u^2 + \sigma_e^2 \end{pmatrix}, \quad (15.6)$$

and the covariance matrix for all N clusters (or children) is

$$\boldsymbol{\Sigma} = \begin{pmatrix} \boldsymbol{\Sigma}_1 & & & \\ & \boldsymbol{\Sigma}_2 & & \\ & & \ddots & \\ & & & \boldsymbol{\Sigma}_N \end{pmatrix}, \qquad (15.7)$$

where $\boldsymbol{\Sigma}_1, \boldsymbol{\Sigma}_2, \ldots, \boldsymbol{\Sigma}_N$ are the diagonal blocks. Within each block of the covariance matrix for cluster j, all the main diagonal elements are the total variance of Y_{ij} consisting of both the within variance σ_e^2 and the between variance σ_u^2, and all the off-diagonal elements are the between variance σ_u^2. It is now easy to see why this covariance structure is called compound symmetry. This model assumes that all measures of a child are correlated in the same way, and this assumption is implied by the same off-main diagonal elements in a block. This model also assumes that the measures across different children are not correlated, as indicated by the zero elements off the diagonal blocks.

The AR(1) covariance structure can also be described in this framework. The covariance matrix for cluster j (or child j) with measures can be written as

$$\Sigma_j = \sigma^2 \begin{pmatrix} 1 & \rho & \rho^2 & \cdots & \rho^{l_j-1} \\ \rho & 1 & \rho & \rho^2 & \cdots & \rho^{l_j-2} \\ \cdots & & & & \cdots \\ \rho^{l_j-1} & \cdots & & & \rho & 1 \end{pmatrix}, \quad (15.8)$$

where ρ is the correlation between any two measures of a cluster (or child) that are measured in two adjacent time periods. The correlation between any two measures measured two time periods apart is assumed to be ρ^2. In general, the correlation between any two measures k time periods apart is assumed to be ρ^k. The further apart the two measures in time, the weaker the correlation between them. However, the rate of weakening is assumed to be constant. The correlation parameter in the AR(1) model in Table 15.2 is estimated to be 0.76. Program 2 in the Appendix provides SAS codes for the basic AR(1) model.

With the correlation parameter, the AR(1) model accomplishes the task of allowing measures closer to each other in time to be more similar. However, the assumption that any two measures adjacent in time are correlated at a constant value can be too restrictive for certain applications. This assumption can be relaxed completely by allowing an unstructured covariance matrix,

$$\Sigma_j = \begin{pmatrix} \sigma_{11}^2 & & & \\ \sigma_{21}^2 & \sigma_{22}^2 & & \\ \vdots & \vdots & \ddots & \\ \sigma_{l_j1}^2 & \sigma_{l_j2}^2 & \cdots & \sigma_{l_jl_j}^2 \end{pmatrix}. \quad (15.9)$$

The parameter estimates for the unstructured covariance matrix (UN) in Table 15.2 are

$$\Sigma_j = \begin{pmatrix} 24 & & & & \\ 28 & 128 & & & \\ 31 & 137 & 203 & & \\ 34 & 135 & 186 & 224 & \\ 30 & 111 & 162 & 180 & 209 \end{pmatrix}. \quad (15.10)$$

These parameter estimates are not presented in the column of UN in Table 15.2 because of the limited space. The estimates in (15.10) show that both variances and covariances grow dramatically as children get older and score higher on the PIATR. Program 3 in the Appendix shows SAS codes for the unstructured model.

Table 15.2 presents four sets of growth curve estimates under the assumption of four covariance structures. Choosing among the four can be aided by the values of two model-fitting criteria produced in the output of PROC MIXED in SAS: Akaike's information criterion (AIC) and Schwarz's Bayesian criterion (BIC). Since some of the models are not nested, the conventional log-likelihood ratio test may not be used. The AIC and BIC are basically log-likelihood values adjusted for the number of parameters estimated in the model. The smaller the value, the more preferred the model. The model of compound symmetry is preferred over the OLS model. The autoregressive AR(1) covariance structure in turn shows significant improvement over the model of compound symmetry. However, the values of AIC and BIC are both the smallest for the unstructured covariance, which appears to be the preferred model for this application.

In other applications where the number of time periods is large relative to the number of units of analysis, the number of parameters that need to be estimated can grow sharply for the unstructured model. In the earlier example of stress and sickle cell disease pain, with $r = 94$ time periods and 15 individuals, an unstructured covariance model would need to estimate $\frac{1}{2}(r+1)r = 4465$ parameters for the covariances alone. In such cases, the AR(1) model is probably more practical than the unstructured.

Most analysts are primarily interested in the estimate of the fixed effects, the parameters of age and age squared in this example, rather than the covariance structure. In this particular example, the estimate of growth curve appears to be largely unaffected by the covariance structure chosen. As we shall see

Table 15.4   *Coefficients and their t statistics from random effects growth curve models of cognitive developmental data measured five times at two-year intervals from the NLSY, with the growth curve modeled by a categorical variable*

Variance structure	CS	AR(1)	UN	OLS
Intercept (age 14)	59.1 (117)	59.1 (119)	59.1 (94.7)	59.1 (117)
age 6	−43.6 (−105)	−43.6 (−78.1)	−43.6 (−76.9)	−43.6 (−61.0)
age 8	−27.7 (−66.7)	−27.7 (−54.2)	−27.7 (−60.6)	−27.7 (−38.7)
age 10	−15.4 (−37.2)	−15.4 (−34.9)	−15.4 (−43.6)	−15.4 (21.5)
age 12	−6.41 (−15.4)	−6.4 (−19.3)	−6.4 (−18.9)	−6.4 (−8.9)
σ_u^2	86.5 (14.5)			
σ_e^2	43.9 (31.9)			130.4 (35.6)
σ^2		124.5		
$\rho_{AR(1)}$		0.775		
ρ (correlation)	0.66			0.0
−2logL	18 093.6	17 661.5	17 051.6	19 649.8
AIC	18 097.6	17 665.5	17 081.6	19 651.8
BIC	18 106.1	17 673.9	17 145.1	19 656.0
Children/measures	510/2550	510/2550	510/2550	510/2550

in later examples, however, incorporating the appropriate covariance structure is essential for sound parameter estimates and inferences of fixed effects.

Social scientists often restrict their focus to a linear, quadratic, or cubic growth curve. The four models in Table 15.4 show that the growth curve can be modeled by a categorical variable quite easily. The categorical variable approach should probably be considered before the parametric approach because not all trajectories follow a linear, quadratic, or cubic pattern. Modeling the covariance as unstructured again appears to be the preferred model by the values of AIC and BIC. The four growth curves based on the fixed parameter estimates under the four models seem comparable.

We have added covariates to the random effects growth curve models of cognitive development (Table 15.5). About 30% of our measures of cognitive development have a missing value on one or more of the covariates included in the model. In order to render the results across different tables comparable for the purpose of illustration, we have imputed the missing values using all the available variables.[1] As before, the values of AIC and BIC point to the unstructured model as the desired model. The predictor of primary interest is sibship size, which is measured as a time-varying covariate of number of children in the family at the time of the cognitive test. The sibship size has a small and significant negative effect on PIATR. This sibship size was measured as the number of children in the family at the year of PIATR test,

so can vary over time for a particular child. Unlike the previous models without covariates, most of the fixed effects vary substantially across models of different covariance structures. For example, the effect of sibship size is reduced from −0.926 in the OLS model to −0.343 in the unstructured model, and the effect of income is reduced from 0.065 in the compound symmetry model to 0.035 in the unstructured model. This points to the importance of modeling the covariance structure properly.

Unbalanced and unequally spaced data
Social science longitudinal data are almost always unbalanced, unequally spaced, or both. These data need special treatment. Unbalanced data occur when units of analysis have varying numbers of measures. An unbalanced sample in our current example would occur when children have varying numbers of cognitive measures. The NLSY data are naturally unbalanced because while the children of the NLSY are of different ages, testing begins at a particular age. Our sample of 550 children are balanced only because we have deleted those children who were tested fewer than five times. Unbalanced data are frequently generated by missing values. When using listwise deletion, a measure is missing if the value of any variable is missing. In our example of 510 children and 510 × 5 = 2550 measures, without imputation, about 30% of the measures of cognitive development would not have be used in the analysis with covariates because of missing values on one or more

Table 15.5   *Coefficients and their t statistics from random effects growth curve models of cognitive developmental data measured five times at two-year intervals from the NLSY with covariates*

Variance structure	CS		AR(1)		UN		OLS	
Intercept	0.31	(0.13)	−0.21	(−0.09)	1.645	(1.08)	−0.55	(−0.33)
age	8.85	(50.1)	8.99	(48.4)	8.56	(50.5)	8.81	(31.5)
age^2	−0.37	(−20.4)	−0.39	(−20.8)	−0.35	(−22.9)	−0.37	(−12.8)
Income ($10 000)	0.065	(2.0)	0.038	(1.41)	0.035	(1.32)	0.22	(5.50)
Momedu	0.73	(4.0)	0.81	(4.5)	0.66	(5.7)	0.89	(7.58)
White	3.18	(3.0)	2.63	(2.65)	1.54	(2.69)	2.75	(4.85)
Black	−1.17	(−1.0)	−1.39	(−1.36)	0.957	(1.61)	−1.24	(−2.12)
Female	2.65	(3.34)	2.23	(2.99)	1.07	(2.50)	2.75	(6.50)
Sibship size	−0.476	(−1.89)	−0.509	(−2.06)	−0.343	(−2.01)	−0.926	(−4.93)
σ_u^2	70.0	(13.9)						
σ_e^2	44.0	(31.8)					112.4	(35.6)
σ^2			110.8					
$\rho_{AR(1)}$			0.745					
ρ (correlation)	0.61						0.0	
−2logL	18 028.7		17 611.2		16 960.6		19 306.0	
AIC	18 032.7		17 615.2		16 990.6		19 308.0	
BIC	18 041.5		17 623.7		17 054.1		19 312.3	
Children/measures	510/2550		510/2550		510/2550		510/2550	

of these covariates. The basic theory of the random effects models applies to unbalanced longitudinal data so long as the measures that are missing are missing at random.

However, when the longitudinal data are unbalanced, additional efforts are needed to make sure that the available measures are placed at locations along the time scale that correspond to the times the measures are taken. In SAS, this is accomplished by declaring a categorical variable indexing the time periods. With this modification, all techniques for longitudinal data discussed in the chapter can be applied directly to unbalanced data. The first two columns of Table 15.6 show the estimates of the AR(1) and unstructured models, respectively. These estimates are from an unbalanced dataset created from the 510 children with 15% of the measures deleted randomly. The substantive results are broadly similar to those in Table 15.5. See Program 4 in the Appendix for an SAS example program for unbalanced data.

Some studies are longitudinal, but the follow-up interviews are not implemented at equal intervals. The 20-year longitudinal study in Baltimore (Furstenberg et al., 1987) started between 1965 and 1967 with 403 pregnant adolescents who came to a large community-based hospital in western Baltimore. Furstenberg et al. interviewed the adolescent mothers and their firstborn children five more times during the 20-year

period following the first birth, recording a wealth of information on topics including the children's educational experience and the family's changing social and economic status. However, these five follow-ups were not spaced equally, with most occurring during the first few years after the initial study.

For unequally spaced data, several of the covariance structures are still applicable. Since the compound symmetry covariance does not attempt to account for the time trend it is applicable even when the data are unequally spaced. The unstructured model is also applicable because this general model can account for all time trends and idiosyncrasies in the data. While these two models are still appropriate, the compound symmetry model is seldom adequate for longitudinal data when each unit of analysis has three or more measures and the unstructured model is sometimes too general, containing too many parameters.

The intermediate AR(1) model is not appropriate for unequally spaced data because the model assumes that all time periods are equal in length and that the correlation ρ is constant for any two time periods. Therefore, the spatial power covariance structure preserves the Markovian spirit of the AR(1) and generalizes directly for unequally spaced data. In the spatial power model,

Table 15.6 *Coefficients and their t statistics from random effects models of cognitive developmental data measured five times at two-year intervals from the NLSY: unbalanced and unequally spaced data*

Variance structure	Unbalanced: 15% measures deleted		Unequally spaced: PIATR90 deleted	
	AR(1)	UN	Spatial power	UN
Intercept	−1.0 (−0.41)	1.36 (0.85)	−0.766 (−0.31)	1.26 (0.81)
age	9.03 (44.4)	8.60 (47.2)	8.92 (46.2)	8.48 (49.6)
age^2	−0.39 (−19.5)	−0.36 (−21.0)	−0.37 (−19.5)	−0.34 (−21.7)
Income ($10 000)	0.037 (1.36)	0.027 (0.99)	0.041 (1.46)	0.038 (1.35)
Momedu	0.89 (4.77)	0.69 (5.71)	0.91 (4.87)	0.71 (6.01)
White	2.60 (2.57)	1.41 (2.34)	2.43 (2.45)	1.45 (2.53)
Black	−1.41 (−1.34)	0.76 (1.22)	−1.49 (−1.45)	0.87 (1.46)
Female	2.26 (2.98)	1.39 (3.09)	2.25 (3.02)	1.08 (2.52)
Sibship size	−0.605 (−2.28)	−0.378 (−2.03)	−0.697 (−2.60)	−0.387 (−2.18)
σ^2	111.0 (58.0)		109.7 (23.3)	
$\rho_{AR(1)}$	0.742 (22.8)		0.86 (116)	
−2logL	15 211.9	14 625.8	14 380.5	13 772.2
AIC	15 215.9	14 655.8	14 384.5	13 792.2
BIC	15 224.3	14 719.4	14 393.0	13 834.6
Children/measures	510/2180	510/2180	510/2040	510/2040

$$\Sigma_j = (\sigma'_{ii}), \ \sigma'_{ii} = \text{cov}(y_{ij}, y'_{i'j}) = \sigma^2 \rho^{|t'_i - t_i|} \quad (15.11)$$

where the covariance between two measures at t'_i and t_i is directly related to the distance between the two time points. In SAS, this is done by specifying SP(POW) and a continuous variable that indexes time. The last two columns of Table 15.6 are estimates of the AR(1) and unstructured models, respectively, of our NLSY children dataset with the measure of PIATR in year 1990 deleted for all children. The unequally spaced data consist of 510 children and $510 \times 4 = 2040$ measures. The substantive results remain similar to those in Table 15.5. See Program 5 in the Appendix for an SAS example program for unequally spaced data.

In this particular dataset, all children are unequally spaced in the same manner, with all children measured at the same but unequal intervals. In a more complicated situation, children may be measured at child-specific unequal intervals. For instance, child 1 could be measured at years 0, 1.5, 4, 7, and 10, child 2 could be measured at years 0.5, 2, 3, 5, and 11, and so on. In such cases, the spatial power model would still be applicable because it keeps accurate track of the elapsed time between any two measures. The unstructured model, however, may not be applicable because the number of time points at which the measure is taken could be too many to construct a reasonably sized covariance matrix.

LATENT TRAJECTORY MODELS AND RANDOM EFFECTS MODELS

Latent trajectory, or latent growth curve, models are a relatively new technique that is gaining in popularity (McArdle, 1988; McArdle and Epstein, 1987; Meredith and Tisak, 1990; Muthén, 1991). Like the random effects models described in the previous section, this technique explicitly models the trajectory of a dependent variable over time and is a useful descriptive strategy for modeling change over time. While these models are sometimes referred to as latent growth models (McArdle, 1988; Mehta and West, 2000), the more general term 'latent trajectory' captures the notion that these models can also estimate functions that decrease over time (Nagin and Tremblay, 1999).

This section describes the latent trajectory models and shows the equivalence between the basic LTMs and random coefficient models, which are a special class of random effects models. There is a direct correspondence between many LTMs and random effects models. While a complete comparison of the two classes of the models is outside the

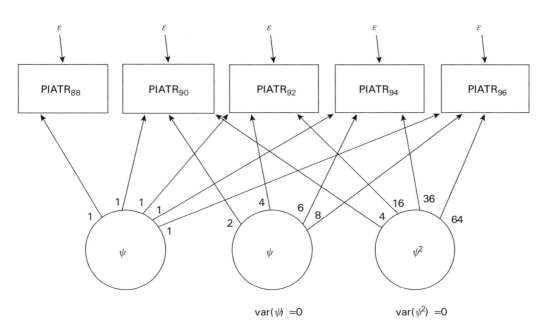

Figure 15.1 *Four-wave random intercept latent trajectory model*

scope of this paper, we will briefly compare a number of key models here.

The random-intercept-only model

Figure 15.1 shows a path diagram for a four-wave random intercept LTM of the same cognitive development data we used earlier for the random effects models. We use common structural equation model (SEM) notation, denoting latent variables as circles and observed variables as rectangles. Paths with arrows show directed relations, while straight lines without arrows represent covariances. Because the children could be either 5 or 6 years old when they were first tested, it is more convenient in this context of LTMs to model the growth curve through time periods rather than age. We will discuss the strategies of accounting for age at a later point.

The time-changing outcome variables have residuals denoted by ε. These residuals are assumed to be uncorrelated and have the same variance. In this model, the cognitive development trajectory is assumed to be influenced by three latent variables (α, β, β^2). The latent variable α is modeled with a mean effect and the variance of the mean effect. This mean effect is assumed to be the same for the PIATR scores across time periods and

the variance allows the children within the sample to have individual-specific trajectories, which differ only by intercept. The latent variables β and β^2 each are modeled with only a mean effect. Their variances are fixed at zero.

While a familiar strategy in SEM scales a path from the latent variable to one of the indicators while freely estimating the other paths, a latent trajectory model as specified in Figure 15.1 fixes the values of all of the paths. Fixing all the paths from α to the developmental measures at one makes α act like an intercept. By allowing the fixed paths from β to increase linearly (0,2,4,6), β acts like a slope. Since the fixed paths from β^2 grow quadratically (0,4,16,36), β^2 acts like a quadratic term. In general, the paths from the latent intercept are always scaled to one, the paths from the linear latent variable are scaled to the linear time trend, and the paths from the quadratic latent variable are simply the square of the path loadings for the slope latent variable. It is through these paths that we specify the trajectory of the dependent variable.

The first column in Table 15.7 presents the estimates of this LTM. The coefficients of t (time period) and t^2 are estimated instead of the coefficients of *age* and *age²*. With $\chi^2 = 1043.3$ on 15 degrees of freedom (df), the

Table 15.7 *Coefficients and their t statistics from latent trajectory models and random effects growth curve models of cognitive developmental data measured five times at two-year intervals from the NLSY: random intercept models and random coefficient quadratic models*

Models	Random intercept model		Random coefficient model	
Methods	LTM	Random	LTM	Random
Intercept	15.598 (31.48)	15.598 (31.45)	15.598 (61.22)	15.598 (61.22)
t	8.623 (52.74)	8.623 (52.62)	8.623 (53.18)	8.623 (53.23)
t^2	−0.399 (−20.35)	−0.399 (−20.33)	−0.399 (23.96)	−0.399 (−23.98)
σ_u^2	86.319 (14.47)	86.319 (14.47)	12.599 (5.56)	12.599 (5.57)
σ_t^2			6.190 (6.90)	6.188 (6.90)
$\sigma_{t^2}^2$			0.038 (3.78)	0.038 (3.79)
$\sigma_{u,t}$			11.401 (11.19)	11.401 (11.20)
σ_{u,t^2}			−1.109 (−10.73)	−1.109 (−10.74)
σ_{t,t^2}			−0.421 (−4.68)	−0.421 (−4.68)
σ_e^2	43.873 (31.94)	43.873 (31.94)	23.149 (22.56)	23.149 (22.58)
−2logL		18 094.2	17 113.59	17 113.6
AIC		18 104.2		17 133.6
BIC		18 125.4		17 175.9
χ^2	1043.329		64.755	
df	15		10	
RMSEA	0.367		0.104	
Children/measures	510/2550	510/2550	510/2550	510/2550

model shows a poor fit to the observed covariance matrix. See Program 6 in the Appendix for an Mplus example program for the LTM compound symmetry model.

This random intercept LTM turns out to be exactly equivalent to the random effects random intercept model (or random effects compound symmetry model); the estimates of the latter were in the second column in Table 15.7. The two sets of estimates are identical within rounding errors.[2] The LTM and the random effects compound symmetry model share exactly the same interpretation. The intercept, slope, and quadratic terms in the random effects model are represented by the mean effects of the three latent variables (α, β, β^2) in the LTM and the variance of the random effect in the random effects model is equivalent to the variance of α in the LTM. Both models may be thought of as a random-intercept-only model. This same LTM can be obtained by fixing the variance of α at zero and allowing the residuals of the developmental measures to be correlated at the same level (see Figure 15.1).

The random coefficient model

The raw cognitive score has a tendency to grow as the children get older. So does the variance of the scores. To capture the time

trends and to improve the fit of the model, we estimate a random quadratic LTM (unshaded portion of Figure 15.2). In addition to allowing the intercept to vary as in the random intercept LTM (Figure 15.1), we now allow both the slope β and the quadratic term β^2 to vary across children. The covariances among the intercept, the slope, and the quadratic terms are also freely estimated. The residual terms of the dependent variables (the reading scores) are constrained to be equal over time and their covariances are constrained to zero. We will relax this assumption of equal residual terms in a later model. With a $\chi^2 = 64.7$ on 10 df, the model shows a much better fit to the data (column 3 in Table 15.7). Program 7(a) in the Appendix provides an Mplus example program for the LTM random coefficient model.[3]

The estimates of an equivalent random effects model are presented in column 4 in Table 15.7. Again, the two sets of estimates are identical (see program 7(b) in the Appendix for the SAS codes). The random effects model can be described by the equation

$$Y_{ij} = \beta_0 + \beta_1 t_{ij} + \beta_2 t_{ij}^2 + u_{0j}$$
$$+ u_{ij} t_{ij} + u_{2j} t_{ij}^2 + e_{ij}, \qquad (15.12)$$

where t is time period indexing the time PIATR is taken, u_{0j} is the random intercept, u_{1j} is the random coefficient for t_{ij}, and u_{2j} is

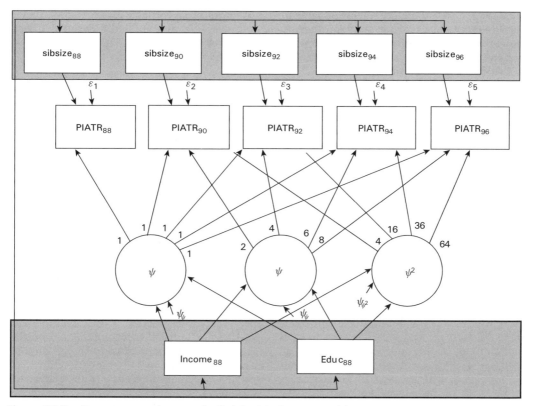

Figure 15.2 *Four-wave random quadratic latent trajectory model*

Note: Shaded section at the bottom adds time-invariant predictors; shaded section at the top adds time-varying predictors. The error terms on the latent variables (the ζs) are allowed to covary with each other.

the random coefficient for t_{ij}^2. The random coefficients in this model and the equivalent LTM model share a clear substantive interpretation. The random coefficient u_{1j}, for instance, represents an effect of t, specific to child j and in addition to the mean effect (β_1) of t. In other words, u_{1j} represents a correction from the mean slope effect for child j.

The random effects random coefficient model can be considered as an alternative to the AR(1) and unstructured models within the framework of the random effects model. In other words, the random coefficient model can be considered an alternative approach to longitudinal analysis. In our example, the average raw reading scores of the children as well as the variances of these raw scores increase sharply over the eight years under study. The increased variance over time is accounted for by the two added random parameters for the slope and the quadratic term. In the corresponding covariance structure for the random-effects random coefficient model (not shown), the size of the

variance and covariance is a function of time or age, and therefore allowed to be positively related to the time period, thus accommodating the heteroskedasticity over time (increasing variance over time).

A random quadratic LTM (Figure 15.2) may be written as

$$y_{it} = \Lambda_{1t}\alpha_i + \Lambda_{2t}\beta_i + \Lambda_{3t}\beta_i^2 + e_{it}, \quad (15.13)$$

where Λ_{1t} is one for all t, Λ_{2t} is related to time t linearly with $\Lambda_{20} = 0$, $\Lambda_{21} = 1$, $\Lambda_{22} = 2$, $\Lambda_{23} = 3$, and Λ_{3t} is related to time t quadratically with $\Lambda_{30} = 0$, $\Lambda_{31} = 1$, $\Lambda_{32} = 4$, $\Lambda_{33} = 9$. The model has three latent variables; α_i is the latent intercept for cluster (or child) i, β_i is the latent slope, and β_i^2 is the latent quadratic term. Each of the three latent variables has both a fixed component u and a random component ζ,

$$\alpha_i = u_\alpha + \zeta_{\alpha_i}$$
$$\beta_i = u_\beta + \zeta_{\beta_i}$$
$$\beta_i^2 = u_{\beta^2} + \zeta_{\beta_i^2} \quad (15.14)$$

where $u_\alpha, u_\beta, u_{\beta^2}$ are the means for the intercept, slope, and quadratic terms, respectively, and ζ_{α_i}, ζ_{β_i}, $\zeta_{\beta_i^2}$ are the random components of the intercept, slope, and quadratic terms, respectively. The z terms have zero means and are assumed to be uncorrelated with e_{it}. In this framework, as in the random effects model, the LTM allows each cluster (or child) i to have its own distinct trajectory because the random component z is child-specific.

The children in our sample were aged 5 or 6 in 1988. Modeling the trajectory through time periods as a single sample implicitly assumes that the parameter estimates are the same for both age groups. However, there are a number of strategies that allow taking into account the age effect. We could model the trajectory through age as we did through time periods; model the LTM as usual while adding age as a covariate predicting the latent variables; or model by age group. The first approach would have ten outcome variables (one for each age) rather than five as previously (one for each time period). In Figures 15.1 and 15.2, this would involve drawing one rectangle for each age and ten rectangles in total (not shown). In this approach, an individual aged 6 in 1988 would have reading score values for ages 6, 8, 10, 12, and 14. For ages 5, 7, 9, 11, and 13, this individual would have missing values, as they were not assessed at these ages. In Figure 15.2, the second approach would amount to adding an exogenous dummy variable (coded 1 for those aged 6 in 1988) predicting the latent intercept, slope, and quadratic variables. In our example, the age coefficient for the latent intercept indicates that children aged 6 score about 5.5 points higher on PIATR at the first time point than do the children aged 5 (Table 15.8). The third approach splits the sample by age and estimates the same model for each age group. Doing so, we find that the predicted trajectories for the two groups lie nearly on top of those from the model including a dummy variable for age (not shown). This suggests that allowing full interactions for the two groups shows no improvement in model fit. However, this need not be the case in all empirical applications.

LTMs allow considerable flexibility in estimating change over time. In addition to a linear change over time and a quadratic term to show the bend in the curve over time, various nonlinear trajectories are straightforward to model (Browne, 1993; Browne and du Toit, 1991; Cudeck, 1996). Distributions such as gamma and exponential have been attempted (du Toit and Cudeck, 2001). One recent application applied a cosine function to model the seasonal variation in crime rates for cities over time (Hipp et al., in press).

The random coefficient model with predictors

The LTM approach described so far can be extended by including predictors of the latent trajectories. We illustrate this by going back to our quadratic model of 510 children. We include predictors measured at the beginning of the study period to test what effect they have on both initial status of the reading scores and their growth over the 8-year period. Thus, in addition to our dummy variables for age, we also include dummy variables for gender, race (white, black, and others), family income in 1988, mother's education in 1988, and sibship size in 1988 (Table 15.8). In Figure 15.2, this model would include the shaded portion at the bottom. For simplicity, Figure 15.2 shows just two of the predictors. These time-invariant variables are allowed to predict the latent intercept, slope, and quadratic term.

The LTM in Figure 15.2 also demonstrates another way of modeling the error structure in the longitudinal data. To accommodate the much wider range of scores in 1996, when the children were 13 or 14 years old, than in 1988, when the children were 5 or 6, the LTM allows the residual terms of the dependent variables to be freely estimated. This is in addition to the random slope and quadratic term in the LTM. As mentioned earlier, both these random terms are added originally to model the increasing variations in the PIATR scores as the children grow older. Allowing these residual terms to vary over time shows a chi-square improvement of 32.9 on 4 df in the quadratic model as compared to a model that constrains the residual terms for the reading scores to be equal. This significant result suggests that it is more appropriate to allow these residual terms to vary over time.

There are interesting results from this model (column 1 in Table 15.8). While mother's education has a positive effect on the latent intercept, it has no effect on the growth of the reading score over time. This suggests that the advantages of a mother's education are transmitted to children early in life (placing children at a higher starting

Table 15.8 *Coefficients and their t statistics from latent trajectory models and random effects growth curve models of cognitive developmental data measured five times at two-year intervals from the NLSY: random coefficient quadratic models with covariates*

Models	Sibship size, time-invariant		Sibship size, time-varying	
Methods	LTM	Random	LTM	Random
Latent intercepts				
Intercept	3.10 (1.94)	3.10 (1.94)	2.80 (1.80)	2.80 (1.80)
t (slope)	14.42 (5.78)	14.42 (5.79)	12.82 (5.77)	12.82 (5.77)
t^2 (quadratic)	−1.14 (−2.21)	−1.14 (−2.21)	−0.959 (−2.09)	−0.959 (−2.09)
Predicting intercept				
Age	5.23 (12.47)	5.23 (12.48)	5.24 (12.51)	5.24 (12.51)
Income ($10 000)	0.123 (0.87)	0.123 (0.87)	0.119 (0.85)	0.119 (0.85)
Momedu	0.693 (5.57)	0.693 (5.58)	0.702 (5.68)	0.702 (5.68)
White	1.67 (3.04)	1.67 (3.04)	1.69 (3.07)	1.69 (3.07)
Black	1.14 (1.99)	1.14 (1.99)	1.137 (1.99)	1.137 (1.99)
Female	1.065 (2.60)	1.065 (2.60)	1.058 (2.59)	1.058 (2.59)
Sibship size	−0.451 (−2.40)	−0.451 (−2.40)		
Predicting slope				
Age	0.737 (1.13)	0.737 (1.13)	0.785 (1.20)	0.785 (1.20)
Income ($10 000)	0.550 (2.51)	0.550 (2.51)	0.528 (2.41)	0.528 (2.41)
Momedu	0.055 (0.28)	0.055 (0.28)	0.112 (0.59)	0.112 (0.59)
White	1.519 (1.77)	1.519 (1.77)	1.591 (1.86)	1.592 (1.86)
Black	−0.616 (0.69)	−0.616 (0.69)	−0.649 (−0.73)	−0.649 (−0.73)
Female	2.083 (3.26)	2.083 (3.26)	2.031 (3.18)	2.031 (3.18)
Sibship size	−0.430 (−1.46)	−0.430 (−1.47)		
Predicting quadratic				
Age	−0.380 (−2.82)	−0.381 (−2.82)	−0.388 (−2.88)	−0.388 (−2.88)
Income ($10 000)	−0.048 (−1.05)	−0.048 (−1.05)	−0.046 (−1.01)	−0.046 (−1.01)
Momedu	0.017 (0.41)	0.017 (0.41)	0.011 (0.27)	0.011 (0.27)
White	−0.382 (−2.16)	−0.382 (−2.16)	−0.391 (−2.21)	−0.391 (−2.21)
Black	−0.165 (−0.89)	−0.165 (−0.89)	−0.158 (−0.86)	−0.158 (−0.86)
Female	−0.397 (−3.01)	−0.397 (−3.01)	−0.389 (−2.95)	−0.389 (−2.95)
Sibship size	0.051 (0.84)	0.051 (0.84)		
Sibship size (t)			−0.374 (−2.28)	−0.374 (−2.28)
Variances				
σ^2_u	13.483 (5.02)	13.483 (5.05)	13.351 (4.97)	13.352 (4.98)
σ^2_t	32.967 (8.75)	32.967 (8.33)	32.942 (8.73)	32.942 (8.29)
$\sigma^2_{t^2}$	0.957 (5.14)	0.957 (5.09)	0.944 (5.07)	0.944 (5.01)
$\sigma^2_{e,88}$	7.631 (3.01)	7.631 (2.89)	7.776 (3.06)	7.776 (2.94)
$\sigma^2_{e,90}$	25.101 (12.75)	25.101 (12.63)	25.194 (12.78)	25.194 (12.64)
$\sigma^2_{e,92}$	19.016 (9.54)	19.016 (9.13)	19.057 (9.57)	19.057 (9.14)
σ^2_{e94}	27.593 (10.72)	27.593 (10.47)	27.394 (10.69)	27.394 (10.41)
$\sigma^2_{e,96}$	20.530 (3.97)	20.530 (3.94)	20.766 (4.02)	20.766 (3.98)
Covariances				
$\sigma_{u,t}$	8.098 (3.26)	8.098 (3.05)	8.206 (3.30)	8.206 (3.09)
σ_{u,t^2}	−1.423 (−2.99)	−1.423 (−2.81)	−1.439 (−3.02)	−1.439 (−2.84)
σ_{t,t^2}	−5.159 (−6.65)	−5.159 (−6.42)	−5.120 (−6.60)	−5.120 (−6.36)
Model-fit				
−2logL		16 787.3		16 791
AIC		16 857.3		16 857
BIC		17 005.5		16 997
χ^2	52.12		82.5	
df	20		42	
CFI	0.987		0.983	
TLI	0.970		0.974	
RMSEA	0.056		0.044	
Children/measures	510/2550	510/2550	510/2550	510/2550

point), but that the reading trajectories of such children run parallel to those of other children once schooling starts. In contrast, while having no effect on the starting point, higher household income appears to translate into steeper reading score gains for this sample of children. Of particular interest for the dilution theory, children from households with larger numbers of siblings have lower reading scores initially. Each additional child reduces the score almost half a point. However, larger family size in 1988 does not show significant effects on the later reading trajectories. Program 8(a) in the Appendix describes an Mplus program for this model. The equivalent random effects model estimated by PROC MIXED in SAS (Program 8(b)) produces identical results.

Our earlier theoretical discussion of the family size effect requires treating sibship size as a time-varying covariate. This is straightforward to accomplish with an LTM. Rather than including a single variable for sibship size in 1988 that predicts the three latent variables, such an LTM includes a sibship size variable in each of the five study years and allows them to directly predict the reading score in the appropriate year. This conforms to the full model shown in Figure 15.2 with the shaded portion at the top. The sibship size variables are all allowed to covary with the other exogenous predictors. If we had theoretical reasons to expect sibship size to show different effects on reading scores across years, we could estimate different values for these parameters at each time point. Alternatively, we can constrain these paths to have equal values. Since these two approaches are nested, a likelihood ratio test can be performed on them; indeed, such a test shows chi-square improvement of just 2.2 on 4 df, suggesting that there is no significant change in the sibship size effect over time. In this model, an increase of one sibling in the family reduces the reading score by about 0.37 points in that year (column 3 in Table 15.8). The Mplus program for the time-varying covariate model is given in Program 9 in the Appendix. The SAS code for the time-varying model is the same as that for the time-invariant one.

One appealing feature of LTM within the SEM framework is that it provides a stable of well-studied measures for assessing overall model fit (Bollen and Stine, 1993). While no single measure can establish the 'truthfulness' of a model, SEM allows one to test how well the model-implied covariance matrix is able to replicate the sample covariance matrix. This provides a chi-square test as well as other heuristic measures for assessing how closely the covariance matrix is replicated. In our final model (column 3 in Table 15.8), the comparative fit index (CFI) of 0.98, the Tucker–Lewis index (TLI) of 0.97, and the root mean square error of approximation (RMSEA) of 0.044 show satisfactory fit. The chi-square of 82.5 on 42 df is still significant (the critical value at the 0.05 level of significance is 58.1), but since this is a sample of 2550 measures on 510 children, we have considerable power to detect misspecification in the covariance matrix (Bollen, 1989; Matsueda and Bielby, 1986; Saris and Satorra, 1993).

In contrast, the random effects model is usually not concerned with the overall model fit. The common practice in the random effects model is to compare with the null model (the model without covariates) and among a number of working models. The lack of concern for the overall model fit does not necessarily imply that random effects models fit worse than the LTM. As we have shown, they are, after all, frequently identical models. Nevertheless, the conscious efforts of comparing the working model with the saturated model (the perfect model or the observed data) by the LTM or SEM analysts do seem to set a higher bar for model fitting.

NOTES

1 The current example is mainly for the purpose of illustration of the growth curve techniques. A more conclusive analysis would need to analyze the entire NLSY sample and to impute the missing values properly by such means as multiple imputation.

2 For accurate comparison, the models run in PROC MIXED must be run using maximum likelihood, rather than restricted maximum likelihood.

3 LTMs can also be estimated in SAS using PROC CALIS. While this would yield similar results, we use Mplus and AMOS since they both allow the modeling of missing data using maximum likelihood.

APPENDIX. EXAMPLE PROGRAMS FOR LONGITUDINAL ANALYSIS IN SAS AND MPLUS

1. SAS programs for compound symmetry models

```
proc mixed data = a noclprint covtest;
class id;
model piatr = age agesq/solution ddfm = bw notest;
random intercept/sub = id;
run;

proc mixed data = a noclprint covtest;
class id;
model piatr = age agesq/solution ddfm = bw notest;
repeated/sub = id type = cs;
run;
```

The two programs are equivalent. The first program appears more natural for multi-level analysis. 'noclprint' is a print control command. 'covtest' specifies significance tests for covariance estimates. The 'solution' in the model line request for the print of the fixed effects. 'sub = id' informs the program of the clustering in the data (the measures having the same id belong to the same child).

2. SAS program for AR(1) models

```
proc mixed data = a noclprint covtest;
class id;
model piatr = age agesq/solution ddfm = bw notest;
repeated/sub = id type = ar(1);
run;
```

3. SAS program for unstructured models

```
proc mixed data = a noclprint covtest;
class id;
model piatr = age agesq/solution ddfm = bw notest;
repeated/sub = id type = un;
run;
```

4. SAS program for unbalanced data

```
proc mixed data = a noclprint covtest;
class id year;
model piatr = age agesq income momedu white black female sibship/solution
ddfm = bw notest;
repeated year/sub = id type = ar(1);
run;
```

The variable 'year' is declared categorical and placed behind 'repeated' to align the available measures.

5. SAS program for unequally spaced data

```
proc mixed data = a noclprint covtest;
class id year;
model piatr = age agesq/solution ddfm = bw notest;
```

```
repeated year/sub = id type = sp(pow) (yearcon);
run;
```

In addition to specifying 'sp(pow)', the program creates a continuous variable 'yearcon', which has the same value as 'year' but which is continuous. The program needs (yearcon) to know the distance between any two time points.

6. Mplus LTM compound symmetry model

```
title:
Mimicking the Compound Symmetry model with a LTM of reading data;
data:
    file = b2imp1w.raw;
!First list the variables in the data set;
variable:
    names =
        age88 age90 age92 age94 age96
        hhchld88 hhchld90 hhchld92 hhchld94 hhchld96
        ageold momed88 white black female hhchld88 finc88;
!Now select the variables used in the analysis;
    usevariables =
    read88 read90 read92 read94 read96;
!Must use 'meanstructure' analysis for LTM;
    analysis:
analysis:
    type = meanstructure;
!First scale each time point measure to have a lambda value of 1 from the intercept;
model:
    readint by read88@1 read90@1 read92@1 read94@1 read96@1;
!Scale each time point measure to have a linearly increasing lambda value from the
slope latent variable;
    readslp by read88@0 read90@2 read92@4 read94@6 read96@8;
!Scale each time point measure to have a quadratically increasing lambda value from
the quadratic latent variable;
    readquad by read88@0 read90@4 read92@16 read94@36 read96@64;
!Fix the means of the observed measures to zero;
    [read88-read96@0];
!Freely estimate the means of the latent variables
    [readint readslp readquad];
!Fix the variances of the slope and quadratic latent variables to zero;
    readint readslp@0 readquad@0;
!Fix the covariances of the latent variables to zero;
    readint with readslp@0;
    readint with readquad@0;
    readslp with readquad@0;
!Constrain the variances of the residuals to be equal;
    read88-read96 (1);
output:
    sampstat standardized tech1;
```

7(a). Mplus LTM random coefficient model

```
title:
unconditional,quadratic growth model of reading data;
data:
    file = z:\b2imp1w.raw;
```

```
variable:
  names =
  age88 age90 age92 age94 age96
  hhchld88 hhchld90 hhchld92 hhchld94 hhchld96
  ageold momed88 white black
    female hhchld88 finc88;
  usevariables =
  read88 read90 read92 read94 read96;
analysis:
  type = meanstructure;
model:
  readint by read88@1 read90@1 read92@1 read94@1 read96@1;
  readslp by read88@0 read90@2 read92@4 read94@6 read96@8;
  readquad by read88@0 read90@4 read92@16 read94@36 read96@64;
  [read88-read96@0];
  [readint readslp readquad];
!The default in M-Plus is to freely estimate the variances of the latent variables;
!Freely estimate the covariances of the latent variables (this is also a default);
  readint with readslp readquad;
  readslp with readquad;
  read88-read96 (1);
output:
  sampstat standardized tech1;
```

7(b). SAS codes for random coefficient model

```
proc mixed data = a1 noclprint covtest method = ml; class id; where (year = 88 |
year = 90 | year = 92 | year = 94 | year = 96);
model read = time timesq/solution ddfm = bw notest;
random intercept time timesq/sub = id type = un;
repeated/sub = id type = vc r rcorr;
run;
```

8a. Mplus LTM random
coefficient model with time-invariant variables

```
title:
conditional,quadratic growth model of reading data;
data:
  file = z:\b2imp1w.raw;
Define:
  finc88 = faminc88/10000;
variable:
  names =
  age88 age90 age92 age94 age96
  hhchld88 hhchld90 hhchld92 hhchld94 hhchld96
  ageold momed88 white black female hhchld88 finc88;
  usevariables =
  read88 read90 read92 read94 read96
  ageold momed88 white black female hhchld88 finc88;
analysis:
  type = meanstructure;
model:
  readint by read88@1 read90@1 read92@1 read94@1 read96@1;
!Note that we can rescale time to units of one- the parameter values will be
    half those scaling it to two;
```

```
readslp by read88@0 read90@1 read92@2 read94@3 read96@4;
readquad by read88@0 read90@1 read92@4 read94@9 read96@16;
[read88-read96@0];
[readint readslp readquad];
readint with readslp readquad;
readslp with readquad;
```
!Note: commenting out this line allows estimating the residuals at each time point;
```
! read88-read96 (1);
```
!The following regress each latent variable on the time-invariant predictors;
```
readint on ageold finc88 momed88 white black female hhchld88;
readslp on ageold finc88 momed88 white black female hhchld88;
readquad on ageold finc88 momed88 white black female hhchld88;
output:
sampstat standardized tech1;
```

8(b). SAS codes for the random coefficient model with covariates: time-invariant or time-varying

proc mixed data = a1 noclprint covtest method = ml; class id; where (year = 88 |
year = 90 | year = 92 | year = 94 | year = 96);
model read = time timesq agedum invfinc invmomed white black female invhhchd
time*agedum time*invfinc time*invmomed time*white
time*black time*female time*invhhchd
timesq*agedum timesq*invfinc timesq*invmomed timesq*white
timesq*black timesq*female timesq*invhhchd
/ solution ddfm = bw notest;
random intercept time timesq / sub = id type = un;
repeated / sub = id type = un(1) r rcorr;
run;

The un(1) covariance structure allows the elements on the diagonal to be freely estimated, but constrains the off-diagonal elements to be the same. It is an intermediate form of covariance between the AR(1) and the UN.

9. Mplus LTM random coefficient model with time-vavrying variables

```
title:
conditional,quadratic growth model of reading data (time-varying HH size);
data:
file = z:\b2imp1w.raw;
Define:
finc88 = faminc88 / 10000;
variable:
names =
age88 age90 age92 age94 age96
hhchld88 hhchld90 hhchld92 hhchld94 hhchld96
ageold momed88 white black female hhchld88 finc88;
usevariables =
read88 read90 read92 read94 read96
momed88 white black female
hhchld88 hhchld90 hhchld92 hhchld94 hhchld96 ageold finc88;
analysis:
type = meanstructure;
model:
readint by read88@1 read90@1 read92@1 read94@1 read96@1;
```

```
readslp by read88@0 read90@1 read92@2 read94@3 read96@4;
readquad by read88@0 read90@1 read92@4 read94@9 read96@16;
[read88-read96@0];
[readint readslp readquad];
readint with readslp readquad;
readslp with readquad;
! read88-read96 (1);
readint on ageold finc88 momed88 white black female;
readslp on ageold finc88 momed88 white black female;
readquad on ageold finc88 momed88 white black female;
```
!For time-varying variable: regress each reading score on the sibship size variable at the same time point;
!Note that the number in parentheses constrains these parameters to be equal;
```
    read88 on hhchld88(2);
    read90 on hhchld90(2);
    read92 on hhchld92(2);
    read94 on hhchld94(2);
    read96 on hhchld96(2);
output:
    sampstat standardized tech1;
```

REFERENCES

Allison, Paul D. (1995) *Survival Analysis Using the SAS System: A Practical Guide*. Cary, NC: SAS Institute Inc.

Blake, Judith (1981) 'Family size and the quality of children', *Demography*, 18: 421–42.

Blake, Judith (1989) *Family Size and Achievement*, Studies in Demography 3. Berkeley: University of California Press.

Bollen, Kenneth A. (1989) *Structural Equations with Latent Variables*. New York: Wiley.

Bollen, Kenneth A. and Curran, Patrick J. (2004) *Latent Trajectory Models: A Structural Equation Approach*. New York: Wiley.

Bollen, Kenneth A. and Stine, Robert A. (1993) *Testing Structural Equation Models*. Newbury Park, CA: Sage.

Browne, Michael W. (1993) 'Structured latent curve models', in C.M. Cuadras and C.R. Rao (eds), *Multivariate Analysis: Future Directions 2*. New York: Elsevier Science, pp. 171–97.

Browne, Michael W. and du Toit, S.H.C. (1991) 'Models for learning data', in L.M. Collins and J.L. Horn (eds), *Best Methods for the Analysis of Change*. Washington, DC: American Psychological Association, pp. 47–68.

Bryk, Anthony S. and Raudenbush, Stephen W. (1992) *Hierarchical Linear Models: Applications and Data Analysis Methods*. Newbury Park, CA: Sage.

Cox, David R. and Oakes, D. (1984) *Analysis of Survival Data*. New York: Chapman & Hall.

Cudeck, Robert (1996) 'Mixed-effects models in the study of individual differences with repeated measures data', *Multivariate Behavioral Research*, 31: 371–403.

du Toit, Stephen H.C. and Cudeck, Robert (2001) 'The analysis of nonlinear random coefficient regression models with LISREL using constraints', in R. Cudeck, S. du Toit and D. Sörbom (eds), *Structural Equation Modeling: Present and Future*. Lincolnwood, IL: Scientific Software International.

England, Paula, Reid, Lori L. and Kilbourne, Barbara Stanek (1996) 'The effect of the sex composition of jobs on starting wages in an organization: Findings from the NLSY', *Demography*, 33: 511–21.

Firebaugh, Glenn and Beck, Frank D. (1994) 'Does economic growth benefit the masses? Growth, dependence, and welfare in the Third World', *American Sociological Review*, 59: 631–53.

Furstenberg, Frank F. Jr, Brooks-Gunn, J. and Morgan, S. Philip (1987) *Adolescent Mothers in Later Life*. New York: Cambridge University Press.

Goldstein, Harvey (1987) *Multilevel Models in Educational and Social Research*. London: Griffin.

Goldstein, Harvey (1995) *Multilevel Statistical Models* (2nd edition). London: Arnold.

Greene, William H. (1997) *Econometric Analysis*. New York: Macmillan.

Guo, Guang (1998) 'The timing of the influences of cumulative poverty on children's cognitive outcomes in childhood and early adolescence', *Social Forces*, 77: 257–87.

Guo, Guang and VanWey, Leah (1999) 'Family size and children's intellectual development: Is the relationship causal?', *American Sociological Review*, 64: 169–87.

Hipp, John R., Bauer, Daniel J., Curran, Patrick J. and Bollen, Kenneth A. (in press) 'Crimes of opportunity or crimes of emotion: Testing two explanations of social change in crime', *Social Forces*.

Kalbfleisch, J.D. and Prentice, R.L. (1980) *The Statistical Analysis of Failure Time Data.* New York: Wiley.

Liker, Jeffrey K., Augustyniak, Sue and Duncan, Greg J. (1985) 'Panel data and models of change: A comparison of first difference and conventional two-wave models', *Social Science Research*, 14: 80–101.

Mason, William M., Wong, G.M. and Entwisle, Barbara (1983) 'Contextual analysis through the multilevel linear model', *Sociological Methodology*, 15: 72–103.

Matsueda, Ross L. and Bielby, William T. (1986) 'Statistical power in covariance structure models', in N.B. Tuma (ed.), *Sociological Methodology*, Vol. 16. Washington, DC: American Sociological Association, pp. 120–58.

McArdle, J.J. (1988) 'Dynamic but structural equation modeling of repeated measures data', in John R. Nesselroade and Raymond B. Cattell (eds), *Handbook of Multivariate Experimental Psychology* (2nd edition). New York: Plenum, pp. 561–614.

McArdle, J.J. and Epstein, David (1987) 'Latent growth curves within developmental structural equation models', *Child Development*, 58: 110–33.

Mehta, Paras D. and West, Stephen G. (2000) 'Putting the individual back into individual growth curves', *Psychological Methods*, 5: 23–43.

Meredith, William and Tisak, John (1990) 'Latent curve analysis', *Psychometrika*, 55: 107–22.

Muthén, Bengt O. (1991) 'Analysis of longitudinal data using latent variable models with varying parameters' in L.M. Collins and J.L. Horn (eds), *Best Methods for the Analysis of Change: Recent Advances, Unanswered Questions, Future Directions*. Washington, DC: American Psychological Association.

Nagin, Daniel and Tremblay, Richard E. (1999) 'Trajectories of boys' physical aggression, opposition, and hyperactivity on the path to physically violent and nonviolent juvenile delinquency', *Child Development*, 70: 1181–96.

Porter, Laura S., Gil, Karen M., Carson, James W., Anthony, Kelly K. and Ready, Jawana (2000) 'The role of stress and mood in sickle cell disease pain: An analysis of daily diary data', *Journal of Health Psychology*, 5: 53–63.

Rasmusson, D. Xeno, Carson, Kathryn A., Brookmeyer, Ronald, Kawas, Claudia and Brandt, J. (1996) 'Predicting rate of cognitive decline in probable Alzheimer's disease', *Brain and Cognition*, 31: 133–47.

Rosenbaum, Dennis P. and Hanson, Gordon S. (1998) 'Assessing the effects of school-based drug education: A six-year multilevel analysis of project D.A.R.E.', *Journal of Research in Crime and Delinquency*, 35: 381–412.

Saris, Willem E. and Satorra, Albert (1993) 'Power evaluations in structural equation models', in K.A. Bollen and J.S. Long (eds), *Testing Structural Equation Models*. Newbury Park, CA: Sage, pp. 181–204.

Searle, S.R. (1971) *Linear Models*. New York: Wiley.

Searle, S.R., Casella, George and McCulloch, Charles E. (1992) *Variance Components*. New York: Wiley.

16

Event History Analysis

PAUL ALLISON

Event history analysis is a term commonly used to describe a variety of statistical methods that are designed to describe, explain or predict the occurrence of events. Outside the social sciences, these methods are often called *survival analysis*, owing to the fact that they were originally developed by biostatisticians to analyze the occurrence of deaths. But despite their biomedical origin, these same methods are perfectly suitable for studying a vast array of social phenomena such as births, marriages, divorces, job terminations, promotions, arrests, migrations, and revolutions. There also many other names for event history methods, including failure time analysis, hazard analysis, transition analysis, and duration analysis.

In general, an event may be defined as a *qualitative* change that occurs at some particular point in time. To apply event history methods you need event history data – a longitudinal record of when events occurred to some individual or sample of individuals. For example, if you ask a sample of women to report the birth dates of all their children, you will get a set of event history data that will allow you to analyze the occurrence of births. Of course, if you want to do a causal or predictive analysis, you would also want to measure possible explanatory variables, such as the woman's date of birth, race, education, family income, marital status, and so on. Some of these may be constant over time (like race or region of origin) while others (like marital status and income) may vary

with time. As we shall see, the distinction between time-constant and time-varying explanatory variables can be very important in selecting a method of analysis.

Some kinds of event history analysis allow for repeated events and different kinds of events. But it is helpful to postpone these complications until we have dealt with the simpler situation in which each individual experiences no more than one event, and all events are assumed to be of the same type. The classic example is where the event of interest is a death and we do not distinguish different kinds of deaths.

PROBLEMS WITH CONVENTIONAL METHODS: RECIDIVISM EXAMPLE

To appreciate the virtues of event history analysis, it is helpful to consider the problems that arise in attempting to apply conventional methods (like linear regression) to the analysis of event history data. Here is an example. In the early 1970s, researchers conducted a field experiment on 432 inmates who were released from Maryland state penitentiaries (Rossi et al., 1980). Half of them were randomly assigned to receive financial aid (roughly equivalent to unemployment compensation) for the first three months after their release. The other half got no money. The goal was to determine whether financial aid would reduce the likelihood of arrest. At the time of their release, the subjects completed an extensive interview about their past history. They were then followed for one year after their release, and the event of interest was the first arrest, the date of which was obtained from police records. Only about 25% of the inmates were arrested. During the one-year follow-up, they were also interviewed at regular intervals to ascertain changes in employment status, marital status, and so on.

Now, how should one analyze such data? An obvious approach would be to do a logistic regression in which the dependent variable is whether or not a person was arrested. The independent variables could include such things as receipt of financial aid, years of schooling, age at release, and number of prior convictions. This would not be a bad method, but neither is it ideal. For one thing, the method does not make use of the timing of the arrests. It is reasonable to suppose that, on average, people who were arrested in the first week after being released had a higher propensity toward crime than those who were arrested near the end of the one-year period. But the logistic regression treats them as identical.

A potential solution to this problem is to use the length of time from release to first arrest as the dependent variable, and do an ordinary linear regression instead of a logistic regression. That might work well if all the released inmates were arrested but, as already noted, only 25% were arrested during the one-year follow-up. What should be done with the other 75% who were not arrested? In the parlance of event history analysis, cases that do not experience the event during the period of observation are called 'censored'. Virtually all event history data contain some censored observations, and all methods that claim the title of event history methods are designed to deal with censoring in one way or another.

If the number of censored cases is small, it is tempting to exclude them from the analysis. But few researchers would want to lose 75% of the cases. Alternatively, one could assign the maximum time observed – one year in this example – as the value of the dependent variable for censored cases. But clearly this is an underestimate. It has been shown that both of these *ad hoc* methods can lead to substantial biases (Sørensen, 1977; Tuma and Hannan, 1978).

Regardless of whether you do logistic regression of arrest status or linear regression of time to arrest, there is another problem that is even more serious than censoring: How do you include variables that vary over the one-year follow-up period? Take employment status, for instance. In each of the 52 weeks of observation, we know whether the person was employed full-time or not. One possibility would be to include 52 dummy variables for employment status in the regression model. Aside from being unwieldy, however, this would raise the possibility of reverse causation. If someone is arrested in the 10th week and incarcerated as a result, that could have a big impact on whether he is employed in the 12th week. The result would potentially be a large bias in estimating the effect of employment status on arrest. To my knowledge, there is no *ad hoc* solution to this problem that even comes close to the event history methods we will consider shortly.

To sum up, event history data typically have two characteristics that make conventional methods unsuitable: censoring and time-varying explanatory variables (also known as time-dependent covariates). All event history methods deal with censoring in some way. Some also deal with time-varying explanatory variables. Before examining these methods in more detail, we need to take a closer look at various kinds of censoring.

CENSORING

Censoring can take several different forms. In the recidivism example we have just considered, all the censored cases were *right censored*. Or more accurately, their *event times* were right censored. An event time is said to be right censored if all we know is that it is greater than some number c, called the censoring time. For the recidivism example, if arrest times are measured in weeks from release, then $c = 52$. In this case, the censoring time is the same for everyone, so the data are described as *singly right censored*. In many other data sets, however, the censoring times (or potential censoring times) vary across observations. This could happen, for example, if prisoners are released at different points in calendar time, but everyone is followed up until some particular date in calendar time. Those released earlier have longer potential censoring times than those released later.

This variation in censoring times is relatively unproblematic if censoring occurs simply because the researcher stops the follow-up according to some prespecified rule. On the other hand, we also treat observations as right censored if the follow-up stops for reasons that are not under control of the researcher. For example, people may die, move away, or refuse to continue participating in the study. Censoring of this sort is called *random censoring*, but it is important to understand that in this context random does not mean that the censoring is unrelated to anything else. Rather, it means that the censoring is part of the phenomenon under investigation, not a part of the research design.

Random censoring *is* potentially problematic. Conventional event history methods implicitly assume that random censoring is *noninformative*. This means that the fact that an individual is censored at a certain point in time does not provide any information about that individual's risk of experiencing the event. In the recidivism example, suppose that some of the released prisoners died during the one-year follow-up period (in fact, none did). The usual approach would be to treat their arrest times as censored at the time of death. This censoring would be noninformative if those who were censored by death had the same risk of arrest as those who did not die.

Unfortunately, there are many situations in which it is not plausible to assume that censoring is noninformative. More unfortunate is the fact that there is no way to test this assumption. Worse still, even if one is certain that the assumption is violated, there is no generally acceptable way to correct for such violations. So we are stuck with using the conventional methods despite the fact that they may produce somewhat biased estimates. The lesson here is that, in designing and executing the collection of event history data, one should do everything possible to minimize random censoring.

Although right censoring is by far the most common kind of censoring, some event history data may also have left censoring. An event time is said to be left censored if all we know about it is that it is less than some number *c*. For example, suppose we do a prospective study of intravenous drug users with the aim of determining when and if they contract HIV. At the onset of the study, however, some users are found to have already contracted the disease, and we have no way of knowing when that happened. These cases are left censored. Most event history methods,

like Cox regression, are not designed to handle left censoring.

Finally, an observation is called *interval censored* if we know that an event occurred between time *a* and time *b*, but we do not know exactly when it happened within the interval. This kind of censoring is also quite common. For the intravenous drug user example, the study might administer blood tests at six-month intervals. If a particular person is HIV-negative at one screening but HIV-positive at the next, the time of the event is interval censored. If the intervals are regularly spaced for all observations, the data can often be analyzed by the discrete-time methods described later.

NONPARAMETRIC ESTIMATION OF SURVIVAL DISTRIBUTIONS

Without a doubt, the oldest method of event history analysis is the life table, with the first known example appearing in the seventeenth century. The life table can be regarded as a nonparametric method for estimating the probability distribution of event times even when some of the observed event times are right censored. More specifically, the goal is to estimate the *survivor function*, denoted by $S(t)$. This is the probability that an event has not yet occurred by time *t*. (If the event is death, we say that the individual has *survived* to time *t*). We would like to be able to estimate this probability for any value of *t*.

When there are no censored cases, this is an easy task. To estimate the probability of surviving to a specified time *t*, we simply calculate the proportion of cases that are still alive at time *t*. There is also little difficulty if all censoring occurs at the end of the study. Again, we calculate the proportion of cases surviving to each specified time *t*, except that we have to stop at the earliest censoring time. In the recidivism study, for example, all the censoring occurred at 52 weeks. So we can easily estimate the survivor function for weeks 1 to 52, but cannot go any further.

This simple approach does not work, however, if some censoring times are smaller than some event times. That is when a life table is necessary. Here is an example. The sample consisted of 1296 nursing home patients who were followed from the date of entry to the date of discharge or the date of censoring (Morris et al., 1994). (These data are available

Table 16.1 *Life table for discharge of nursing home patients*

Interval		Number	Number	Effective sample	Conditional probability	Survival
(Lower	Upper)	failed	censored	size	of failure	
0	150	719	0	1296.0	0.5548	1.0000
150	300	172	0	577.0	0.2981	0.4452
300	450	78	40	385.0	0.2026	0.3125
450	600	40	56	259.0	0.1544	0.2492
600	750	17	72	155.0	0.1097	0.2107
750	900	7	42	81.0	0.0864	0.1876
900	1050	4	37	34.5	0.1159	0.1714
1050		0	12	6.0	0	0.1515

on the web at http://lib.stat.cmu.edu/datasets/csb/). About 20% of the discharge times were censored because patients were still in the nursing home when the study terminated. Our goal is to estimate the survivor distribution for length of stay, that is, the number of days between entry and discharge. For the uncensored patients, the length of stay varied between 0 and 942. For the censored patients, the censoring times varied between 365 and 1092 (by design, everyone was followed for at least one year).

Table 16.1 displays a typical life table for these data. The time scale has been divided into seven intervals, each 150 days long, plus a final open-ended interval. In practice, the number of intervals and their upper and lower boundaries are somewhat arbitrary. The last column, labeled 'Survival', is the goal of the calculations. It is the estimated probability of surviving (still being in the nursing home), at the start of each interval. Thus, we see that the estimated probability of still being in the nursing home at 300 days is 0.3125.

The preceding columns give the intermediate calculations. 'Number failed' is the number of people who experience the event during each interval. 'Number censored' is the number of people whose censoring time falls within the interval. For example, among those people who had not yet been discharged when the study terminated, 40 had been in the nursing home between 350 and 450 days. The next column, 'Effective sample size', is an estimate of the number of people 'at risk' of discharge during that interval. The presumption is that people who were censored within the interval were only at risk for half the interval. Therefore, the effective sample size is the number who had not yet been discharged at the start of the interval, minus half

the number who were censored within the interval. For the third interval, 405 patients had not yet been discharged at 300 days. But 40 of those patients were censored between time 300 and 450. So the effective sample size is 405 – 40/2 = 385. The 'Conditional probability of failure' is an estimate of the probability that someone who survived to the start of the interval (had not yet been discharged) was discharged during the interval. It is simply the number who failed divided by the effective sample size. In the first interval, the estimated conditional probability of failure is 719/1296 = 0.5548.

Once we have the conditional probabilities of failure, it is easy to calculate the survivor probabilities. The probability of surviving to time 150 is just 1 minus the probability of failing in the first interval: $1 - 0.5548 = 0.4452$. What is the probability of surviving to time 300? To get to 300, you have to survive the first interval and then survive the second interval. The probability of doing that is the probability of surviving the first interval times the conditional probability of surviving the second interval, given that you have survived the first: $(1 - 0.5548)(1 - 0.2981) = 0.3125$. Similarly, the estimated probability of surviving to time 450 is $(1 - 0.5548)(1 - 0.2981) \times (1 - 0.2026) = 0.2492$. Continuing in this fashion, we get the survival probabilities for the starting times for each interval. These probabilities are graphed as a function of time in Figure 16.1. Graphs of this sort are often referred to as *survival curves*.

One problem with the life table method is that the division of time into intervals is arbitrary. We can avoid this by using the Kaplan–Meier method (Kaplan and Meier, 1958), which modifies the life table in two ways. First, the time intervals are defined by the smallest time units observed in the data

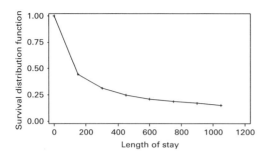

Figure 16.1 *Estimated survivor function using life table method*

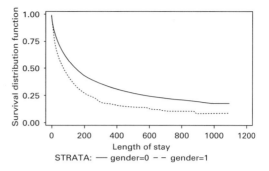

STRATA: — gender=0 – – gender=1

Figure 16.3 *Survival curves for men and women using Kaplan–Meier method*

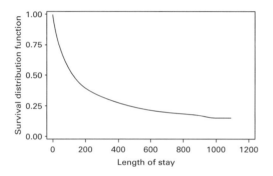

Figure 16.2 *Estimated survivor function using Kaplan–Meier method*

set. For the nursing home data, time is measured in days, so each day is a separate interval in the life table. (That can produce a very long table, but attention is usually focused on graphs). Second, the effective sample size for each interval is just the number of cases who have not yet had the event at the beginning of the interval. Thus, we do not subtract half the censored cases within the interval. Since the intervals are small, this usually makes little difference.

Figure 16.2 shows the Kaplan–Meier graph for the nursing home discharge data. The shape is essentially the same as the graph in Figure 1, but the curve is considerably smoother because many more points are plotted. For those time points that are plotted in Figure 16.1, the estimated survivor probabilities are, in fact, very close to the corresponding probabilities in Figure 16.2.

Survival curves get more interesting when you compare them for different groups. For the nursing home data, Figure 16.3 shows separate curves for men and women (with

men coded 1 and women coded 0). The curve for women is always higher than that for men, which tells us that at every point in time women have a higher probability of still being in the nursing home. Equivalently, for whatever reason, men are being discharged more rapidly than women.

There are many different statistical tests for the null hypothesis that two groups have the same survivor function, the most common of which is the log-rank test. For these data, the log-rank statistic is 37.2 which (under the null hypothesis) has a chi-square distribution with 1 degree of freedom. This is highly significant, so we reject the null hypothesis and conclude that the survivor functions are different for males and females.

PARAMETRIC REGRESSION MODELS

Simple comparison of survival curves may be informative but it is usually not sufficient. Typically, researchers will want to adjust for other variables via some kind of regression model. A fairly simple regression model for event history data is the accelerated failure time (AFT) model, one member of the more general class of parametric regression models. Assume, for the moment, that there is no censoring, and let T_i be the event time for the ith individual in the sample. Let $x_{i1},...,x_{ik}$ be a set of explanatory variables for individual i. (These are not allowed to vary with time.) The AFT model is

$$\log T_i = \beta_0 + \beta_1 x_{i1} + \cdots + \beta_k x_{ik} + \sigma \varepsilon_i, \quad (16.1)$$

where log is the natural logarithm, ε_i is a random disturbance with a fixed variance, and σ is a scale parameter that controls the variance

Table 16.2   *Estimates of a lognormal regression model for nursing home stays*

Variable	Estimate	Standard error	Chi-square	p
Intercept	4.689	0.637	54.16	<0.0001
Age	0.015	0.007	4.03	0.0446
Male	−0.602	0.134	20.09	<0.0001
Married	−0.153	0.160	0.91	0.3395
Treatment	0.190	0.111	2.92	0.0875
Health status	−0.312	0.060	26.73	<0.0001
Scale (σ)	1.940	0.045		

of the random component in the equation. We further assume that ε_i is independent of the x variables and of any other ε_j. These assumptions imply the usual assumptions of the linear regression model. So, if there are no censored data, we can get best linear unbiased estimates of the β coefficients by ordinary least squares (OLS), using log T as the dependent variable.

Of course, most event history data have at least some censoring and OLS just will not work in that situation. Censoring is easily handled by the method of maximum likelihood (ML) which, under fairly broad conditions, produces coefficient estimates that are consistent, asymptotically efficient, and asymptotically normal. Many software packages (e.g., SAS, Stata, SYSTAT, BMDP, S-PLUS) have ML procedures for at least some versions of the AFT model.

To implement ML, it is necessary to specify the probability distribution of the random disturbance term ε. A standard normal distribution would be the most familiar choice. But there are three other distributions that are also commonly used for this kind of modeling: extreme value, logistic, and log-gamma. Each of these distributions has an implied distribution for the event time T, as shown in the following table:

Distribution of ε	Distribution of T
Normal	Lognormal
Logistic	Log-logistic
Extreme value	Weibull
	(or exponential)
Log-gamma	Gamma

Typically, we refer to the different submodels by the distribution of T. The gamma model is the most general model because it has both the lognormal and Weibull models as special cases.

What is the point of considering different distributions for ε? Each of these distributions

has somewhat different implications for *hazard functions*, an important concept in event history analysis that we shall discuss in the next section.

Table 16.2 shows the results from fitting a lognormal regression model to the length-of-stay data for a nursing home. In addition to the gender variable, the model includes variables for age, marital status, health status and 'treatment'. Health status was coded as integer values from 2 through 5, with higher scores indicating worse health. The treatment variable was a dummy variable for whether or not the patient was admitted to one of 18 nursing homes (out of a total of 36) that received special treatment: higher *per-diem* payments for accepting more disabled Medicaid patients, and bonuses for improving patient's health status and discharging patients within 90 days.

In Table 16.2, we see a highly significant effect of gender, with males having shorter lengths of stay. This is consistent with the survival curve comparison, but now we are controlling for several other variables. The coefficient of −0.602 is the effect of gender on the logarithm of length of stay, which is not readily interpretable. We can get an interpretable number by exponentiating the coefficient: exp(−0.602) = 0.55. This tells us that the expected length of stay for men is only 55% of the expected length of stay for women.

Older patients have somewhat longer lengths of stay, an effect that is just barely statistically significant (at the 0.05 level). More specifically, if we calculate 100[exp(0.015)−1] = 1.5, we can conclude that each additional year of age (at admission) is associated with a 1.5% increase in expected length of stay (controlling for other variables in the model). Contrary to expectation, patients in the treatment nursing homes had longer lengths of stay (not statistically significant) and patients with poorer health status had *shorter* lengths of stay (highly significant).

Although AFT models can be very useful, there are a few limitations with this approach. First, results can vary depending on the distribution chosen for ε, and it may be difficult to determine which is the more appropriate distribution. For example, if a Weibull model is fitted to the nursing home data, the *p*-value for treatment goes down to 0.04, which many would judge to be statistically significant. A second problem is that most software for fitting these models does not allow for time-varying explanatory variables (although some software for the Weibull model can do this).

These problems do not occur with the method of Cox regression, which will be discussed in the next section. Nevertheless, AFT models (along with other parametric regression models) have some advantages over Cox regression: they are much better at handling left censoring and irregular interval censoring; and they make it much easier to generate predicted times to events.

COX REGRESSION

By far the most popular method for analyzing event history data is Cox regression. First proposed by the British statistician, Sir David Cox, in 1972, this method has many attractive features: minimal assumptions about the distribution of event times; ease of incorporating time-varying explanatory variables; ability to handle both continuous- and discrete-time data; capacity for semiparametric stratification; and allowance for left truncation. Cox (1972) actually did two things: he proposed a new model called the *proportional hazards* (PH) model, and he devised a new estimation method now known as *partial likelihood*.

In the PH model, the dependent variable is $h(t)$, the hazard of an event at time t. Specifically, if there are no time-varying explanatory variables, the PH model may be written as

$$\log h_i(t) = \alpha(t) + \beta_1 x_{i1} + \cdots + \beta_k x_{ik}. \quad (16.2)$$

Obviously, to understand this model, it is essential to have a clear understanding of what $h(t)$ is. Roughly speaking, $h(t)$ can be interpreted as the instantaneous probability that an event will occur at time t. That is not quite accurate, however, because unlike a probability, the hazard can be greater than one (although it can never be less than zero).

Here is a formal definition. Let $P(t, t + \Delta t)$ be the conditional probability that an event occurs in the time interval $(t, t + \Delta t)$, given that it has not already occurred prior to t. To get the hazard function, we divide this probability by the length of the interval Δt, and take the limit as Δt goes to 0:

$$h(t) = \lim_{\Delta t \to 0} \frac{P(t, t + \Delta t)}{\Delta t} \quad (16.3)$$

The hazard is allowed to be different at every point in time t, which is why we call it a hazard *function*. In equation (16.2) the hazard has an i subscript to indicate that it can vary across individuals. If $h(t)$ has a constant value r, it can be interpreted as the expected number of events in a one-unit interval of time. Alternatively, $1/r$ is the expected length of time until the next event. Suppose, for example, that the events are residence changes, time is measured in years, and the estimated hazard of a residence change is 0.20. That would imply that, for a given individual, the expected number of changes in a year is 0.20 and the expected length of time between changes is $1/0.20 = 5$ years.

Like a probability (from which it is derived), the hazard is never directly observed. Nevertheless, it governs both the occurrence and timing of events, and models formulated in terms of the hazard may be estimated from observed data. Going back to (16.2) for the PH model, notice that on the right-hand side there is an unspecified function of time $\alpha(t)$. We could make this more specific by assuming, for example, that $\alpha(t) = \alpha_0 + \alpha_1 t$, where α_0 and α_1 are constants to be estimated. This would give us a parametric PH model known as the Gompertz model. Alternatively, if we specified $\alpha(t) = \alpha_0 + \alpha_1 \log t$, we would get a Weibull model (which also happens to be an AFT model, although expressed in different form). But the beauty of Cox's PH model is that it is not necessary to decide what $\alpha(t)$ is. We can estimate the β coefficients for any function $\alpha(t)$ without restriction. The partial likelihood method is what makes this possible.

Why is (16.2) called the proportional hazards model? Because if we take the ratio of the hazards for any two individuals at the same time $h_i(t)/h_j(t)$, where $i \neq j$, that ratio is a constant that does not depend on time. One

Table 16.3   *Estimates of a proportional hazards regression model for nursing home stays*

Variable	Estimate	Standard error	Chi-square	p
Age	−0.006	0.004	1.79	0.1806
Male	0.362	0.075	23.52	<0.0001
Married	0.115	0.088	1.71	0.1905
Treatment	−0.081	0.064	1.64	0.2005
Health status	0.166	0.035	22.62	<0.0001

implication of this property is that the 'effect' of any explanatory variable is invariant over time. While this may seem restrictive, the PH model is much more flexible than the parametric models we have already considered. Furthermore, as we shall see, the model can easily be extended to allow for nonproportional hazards.

Now let us consider the partial likelihood estimation method, which is what makes it possible to estimate the βs without specifying $\alpha(t)$. The method is very much like maximum likelihood but instead of maximizing the full likelihood function, one works with a portion of the likelihood function that depends on the βs but not on $\alpha(t)$. This part of the likelihood depends only on the order in which events occur, not on the exact times of the events. Some information is lost in the process, but what is gained is a great deal of robustness. In practice, the partial likelihood is treated almost exactly the same as if it were an ordinary likelihood function. Nearly all full-featured statistical packages (SAS, SPSS, Stata, S-PLUS, SYSTAT, BMDP) include a procedure for doing partial likelihood estimation of the PH model.

Let us apply the method to our nursing home discharge data. Table 16.3 shows results of a Cox regression with the same explanatory variables as in Table 16.2 for the lognormal model. To specify the model, virtually all Cox regression software requires that the dependent variable be listed in two parts: a variable containing the time of the event or censoring, and a variable indicating whether or not that time was a censoring time or an event time. A list of independent variables is the only other information that is required.

Comparing Table 16.3 with Table 16.2, there are a couple of noteworthy differences. First, unlike most regression methods, there is no intercept reported in the computer output. That is because the intercept (if there really is one) is part of the $\alpha(t)$ function in (16.2), which drops out of the estimation

process. The other big difference is that the signs of the coefficients are all the opposite of what they were in Table 16.2. Again, that is no accident, and it stems from the fact that the dependent variable in the AFT model is the event time, while the dependent variable in the PH model is the hazard for the event. If the hazard for some event is low, then the event is unlikely to occur and the expected time until an event occurs will be large. On the other hand, if the hazard is high, the event is very likely to occur and the expected time to the event will be small. So hazards and event times are inversely related.

Despite these apparent differences, the results in Tables 16.2 and 16.3 are reasonably consistent. Both tables show highly significant effects of gender and health status. For the other variables, the p-values from the Cox regression are a bit higher than those for the AFT regression. One consequence is that 'Age', which was marginally significant in the AFT regression, is no longer significant in the Cox regression.

To interpret the magnitudes of the coefficients, it is helpful to first transform them using the same formula as for the AFT models: $100[\exp(\beta)-1]$. This gives the percent change in the *hazard* of an event for each one-unit increase in a particular explanatory variable (holding other variables constant). For 'Male', we have $100[\exp(0.362) - 1] = 44\%$. This says that males have a hazard of discharge that is 44% higher than the hazard for females (after adjusting for the other variables in the model). For 'Health status', we have $100[\exp(0.166) - 1] = 18\%$. This says that for each one-unit increase in the health status scale, the hazard for discharge goes up by 18%.

TIME-DEPENDENT COVARIATES

There are no time-dependent covariates in the nursing home discharge data – all the independent variables were measured at the time of admission. In principle, however, some of these variables, like health status, could change during the nursing home stay. If we had measurements on these changing variables, how could we incorporate them into the analysis? It is easy to build them into the PH model. For example, suppose that $x_{i1}(t)$ denotes a patient's health status at time t, where t is the length of time since admission to the nursing home. Then we could write the model:

$$\log h_i(t) = \alpha(t) + \beta_1 x_{i1}(t) \\ + \beta_2 x_{i2} + \cdots + \beta_k x_{ik}. \qquad (16.4)$$

This equation says that the hazard of discharge at time t depends on the patient's health status at the same time t. According to this model, any change in health status produces an immediate change in the hazard of discharge.

While it is simple to modify the model to allow for time-dependent covariates, it may not be so easy to estimate that model. One of the attractions of the partial likelihood method is that it is relatively straightforward to incorporate time-dependent covariates into the estimation process. To do that, however, you need appropriate data. Ideally, one should know the values of the time-dependent covariates at every point during the observation period. That may not be difficult for some variables, like marital status. If we know the dates of any changes in marital status and we know the status before and after the change, then we can assign a marital status for every day of observation.

On the other hand, it may be difficult to get daily measurements of health status. Instead, we may only know health status at weekly or monthly intervals. In such cases, it is necessary to devise some plausible rule for assigning values to the days in between. One possible rule would be to presume that each measured value remains in effect until the next measurement. Another possibility is to do some kind of linear interpolation. Such choices must be made by the investigator, often on the basis of substantive considerations.

Once these issues have been resolved, the next question is how to implement the estimation process. It turns out that there are two rather different computational roads that lead to the same result. In the first approach – let us call it the programming method – there is a single record for each individual. The changing values of the time-dependent covariate are coded in multiple variables on that record. For example, if health status is measured monthly and patients are observed for a maximum of three years, one would need 36 variables to describe the health status measurements.

To specify the model, it is necessary to write a small program that assigns the appropriate value of health status to each time at which a discharge occurs. This program must be executed as part of the estimation process, not before. The reason is subtle but extremely important. If someone is discharged on day 125, that person is compared to all the other persons who were still in the nursing home 125 days after admission – the 'risk set' for day 125. In doing that comparison, it is necessary to retrieve the values of health status on day 125 for all the people at risk of discharge. But many of those people might also be in other risk sets. If a discharge occurred on day 100, for example, the program must retrieve the values of health status on day 100 for all the people in that risk set. But all the people in the nursing home on day 125 will also have been there on day 100. So, for a given individual, different values of the time-dependent covariates are retrieved at different points in time.

The other computational approach to time-dependent covariates is known as *episode splitting* (also called the counting process method). In this method, each individual may be represented in the data set by more than one record. Each record corresponds to an interval of time during which *all the covariates are constant*. The records must contain the following variables: the starting time of the interval (measured as time since admission), the stopping time (also measured as time since admission), the values of all independent variables (both time-constant and time-dependent), and a censoring indicator. Any record that does not end in an event is treated as censored. Time-constant variables are replicated across the multiple records for each individual. In doing the analysis, one simply specifies the variables for starting time, stopping time, censoring, and the covariates. At the analysis stage, there is no distinction between time-varying and time-constant explanatory variables. That is because, within each record, both are constant.

The choice between these two computational approaches depends greatly on the

Table 16.4   *Estimates of a proportional hazards regression model for nursing home stays, with treatment by time interaction*

Variable	Estimate	Standard error	Chi-square	p
Age	−0.005	0.004	1.59	0.2066
Male	0.361	0.075	23.36	<0.0001
Married	0.109	0.088	1.52	0.2173
Treatment	−0.240	0.085	7.94	0.0048
Health status	0.165	0.035	22.34	<0.0001
Treat. × Time	0.0013	0.0004	7.70	0.0055

software being used. Some programs (like SPSS and BMDP) use only the programming method. Other programs (like Stata) use only the episode splitting method. And some (like SAS) allow for both methods, either separately or in combination. If correctly implemented, both approaches should produce exactly the same numerical output. I tend to favor the episode splitting approach because it makes it easier to avoid mistakes. After you have created the multiple records, you can examine them carefully to see if they conform to your intentions. And once you have constructed the data set, you can specify the models in a very simple form.

On the other hand, there are certain situations where the programming method is much simpler. Here is one example. For the model displayed in Table 16.3, an implicit assumption is that each independent variable has the same effect at all points in time. This is a crucial implication of the proportional hazards assumption. But what if that assumption is not true? Perhaps there is a large effect of the treatment on the hazard of discharge when people are first admitted to the nursing home, but the effect becomes progressively smaller as time goes on. The Cox model can be modified to express this idea by including an interaction between treatment and time. Specifically, if x_k is the treatment variable, we can include the product of x_k and t:

$$\log h_i(t) = \alpha(t) + \beta_1 x_{i1} + \dots + \beta_k x_{ik} + \beta_{k+1} x_{ik} t.$$

This model says that the 'effect' of x_k is a linear function of t. Alternatively, letting $z_i(t) = x_{ik} t$, we can write this model as

$$\log h_i(t) = \alpha(t) + \beta_1 x_{i1} + \dots + \beta_k x_{ik} + \beta_{k+1} z_i(t).$$

In short, we now have a model with a time-dependent covariate z. But the episode splitting method will not work for this model because there are no intervals during which $z(t)$ is constant. Hence, we must use the programming method. We will skip the details

because the implementation varies greatly across software packages.

Table 16.4 shows the results of estimating the interaction model using the programming method. We see that the interaction term is statistically significant beyond the 0.01 level, indicating that the effect of treatment does vary with time since admission. More specifically, the 'main effect' of treatment represents the effect of treatment at time 0, the date of admission. It is negative (−0.240) and highly significant. Applying the $100[\exp(\beta) - 1]$ transformation, we may say that at the time of admission, the treated group has a 21% lower hazard of discharge than the control group. However, for each additional day since admission, the effect of treatment goes up by 0.0013, implying that the effect is zero at 185 days. After that, the treatment effect becomes steadily more positive. At one year, it is equal to the coefficient at admission, only in the opposite direction. This explains why, overall, we do not see much effect of treatment in Table 16.3. The early negative effect is balanced by the later positive effect.

This example illustrates one way to test the proportional hazards assumption in the Cox regression model: check to see if variables have significant interactions with time. In this case, the method of diagnosis is also the cure. By including interactions with time, we extend the Cox model to allow for nonproportional hazards.

STRATIFICATION

Another useful feature of Cox regression is the ability to control for one or more variables in a completely nonparametric manner. This is called *stratification*, although the meaning of this term is somewhat different than in other contexts. For example, in the nursing home study, suppose that we want to

Table 16.5 *Estimates of a proportional hazards regression model for nursing home stays, with stratification by health status*

Variable	Estimate	Standard error	Chi-square	p
Age	−0.006	0.004	2.11	0.1457
Male	0.356	0.075	22.64	<0.0001
Married	0.119	0.088	1.82	0.1768
Treatment	−0.251	0.086	8.62	0.0033
Treat. × Time	0.0014	0.0005	8.91	0.0028

estimate the effect of the treatment controlling for health status, but we do not want to assume that the effect of health status satisfies the proportional hazards assumption. We specify the following model:

$$\log h_i(t) = \alpha_{\mathrm{H}}(t) + \beta_1 x_{i1}$$
$$+ \ldots + \beta_k x_{ik} + \beta_{k+1} z_i(t). \quad (16.5)$$

The only difference between this equation and the one in the preceding section is that the unspecified function of time $\alpha_{\mathrm{H}}(t)$ is now subscripted with an H. This indicates that there may be a different unspecified function of time for each value of the health status variable. Consequently, the model allows for differences in the discharge rate across the four possible values of health status, but these differences may vary with time. On the other hand, the coefficients of the other variables are assumed to be the same within each health stratum.

Models with stratification can be easily estimated using the partial likelihood method. Table 16.5 shows the results of stratifying by health status for the nursing home data. Although health status does not show up in the table, it *is* being controlled, and in a way that is less restrictive than in Table 16.4. Nevertheless, the results for the other variables are only slightly different in Table 16.5 than in Table 16.4.

LEFT TRUNCATION AND LATE ENTRY

Conventional Cox regression programs presume that there is some common origin time (time 0) at which everyone begins to be at risk of an event. For the nursing home study, the origin time was the day on which each person was admitted to the nursing home. The event time was then the number of days between admission and discharge. The implication is that if a person was discharged on, say, day 279, that person was *at risk* of a discharge every day between 0 and 279.

That is not always a plausible assumption. Suppose the nursing home study was conducted in the following way. On a certain date, all patients currently residing in the nursing home were recruited into the study and then followed forward until discharge or censoring. One could set the origin time to be the date of recruitment, and then the event time would be the difference between recruitment date and discharge date. But the recruitment date is a purely arbitrary point in time, and there is no reason to think the hazard for discharge would depend on time since that arbitrary point. Instead, one could, as before, record discharge times as time since admission. But that raises a new problem. By design, it is not really possible for a person to be discharged between the date of admission and the date of recruitment. If the person had been discharged during that interval, he or she would not be available for recruitment and would not have been in the study.

This problem is known as left truncation or late entry to the risk set. The solution is to continue to measure discharge times from the date of admission, but remove individuals from the risk set during the interval from admission to recruitment. Most Cox regression programs cannot do this, but many now have this capability. To implement these procedures, all that is necessary is to specify an entry time and an event time for each individual.

COMPETING RISKS

All the techniques we have discussed so far presume that events are indistinguishable: all deaths are the same, all arrests are the same, all nursing home discharges are the same. For many applications, however, events can be

Table 16.6   *Estimates of a Cox regression model for exits from power*

Variable	Estimate	Standard error	Chi-square	p
Manner	0.250	0.124	4.07	0.0437
Year	−0.018	0.008	4.83	0.0280
Age	0.023	0.005	18.33	<0.0001
Conflict	0.094	0.128	0.54	0.4608
Income	−0.177	0.082	4.64	0.0312
Literacy	0.0007	0.003	0.05	0.8212

separated into different types, and the different types may have potentially different causes. For example, if the event is a job termination, we might expect that job performance would have very different effects on the hazard of quitting and the hazard of being fired.

Here is a more detailed example. The data consist of information on 438 principal leaders of developing countries during the past 60 years (Bienen and van de Walle, 1991). (This data set is available on the web at www.ssc.upenn.edu/~allison under the name leaders.dat) For each leader, we have information on the number of years in power, and the manner in which he was removed from power: constitutional means (146 cases), nonconstitutional means (*coup d'etat*, assassination, etc.; 154 cases), or death from natural causes (27 cases). Another 111 of the leaders were still in power (censored) when the study terminated in 1987. These three modes of exit from office are appropriately regarded as *competing risks* because the occurrence of any one of them removes the individual from risk of the other two.

The goal is to estimate the effects of several explanatory variables on the hazard of leaving office. The covariates we shall examine are:

Manner   1 = nonconstitutional entry to power, 0 = constitutional).
Year   Year of entry into power.
Age   Age on assuming power.
Conflict 1 = medium or high ethnic conflict, otherwise 0.
Income   Natural logarithm of GNP per capita, 1973.
Literacy Literacy rate.
Region   0 = Middle East, 1 = Africa, 2 = Asia, 3 = Latin America.

Table 16.6 presents results from a Cox regression predicting the hazard of leaving office, without distinguishing the manner of departure. (For a more detailed analysis of these data, see Allison, 1995.) Age at entry has a strong and unsurprising effect: leaders who are older when they assumed power are more likely to leave quickly. There is also some evidence that higher rates of departure are associated with lower country income, earlier starting years, and the seizure of power by nonconstitutional means.

But this analysis lumps together three different kinds of events that may, in fact, be quite different. To disaggregate these event types, we first specify a separate hazard function for each event type. Specifically, $h_{ij}(t)$ is the hazard for person i experiencing an event of type j at time t. Then we write a separate proportional hazards equation for each event type:

$$\log h_{ij}(t) = \alpha_j(t) + \beta_{1j}x_{i1} + \dots + \beta_{kj}x_{ik}, \quad j = 1,\dots,3. \quad (16.6)$$

Estimating these three equations is a simple task that can be done with conventional software for Cox regression. The basic rule is this: estimate each equation separately by estimating a Cox model for that specific event type, treating all other events as though the individual was censored at the time of event occurrence. In practice, this is easily accomplished by repeatedly estimating the same model, each time specifying different sets of events to be treated as censored.

Table 16.7 displays results from doing this for the three modes of departure from office. What is of interest here is that many variables have quite different effects on the different modes. Age, for example, is the only variable that has a significant effect on the hazard of a natural death. Age also affects exits by constitutional means, but has no apparent effect on nonconstitutional exits. On the other hand, the hazard of a nonconstitutional exit decreases with calendar time (year), but the hazards for the other two modes are unaffected. Increases in income appear to reduce the hazard of nonconstitutional exit, but do

Table 16.7 Estimates of Cox regression models for three types of exit

Variable	Estimate	Standard error	Chi-square	p
Constitutional exits				
Manner	−0.336	0.217	2.39	0.1223
Year	0.003	0.012	0.06	0.8123
Age	0.025	0.008	8.66	0.0032
Conflict	−0.023	0.194	0.01	0.9067
Income	−0.119	0.116	1.06	0.3038
Literacy	0.014	0.005	6.21	0.0127
Nonconstitutional exits				
Manner	0.686	0.175	15.45	<0.0001
Year	−0.036	0.012	8.85	0.0029
Age	0.009	0.008	1.19	0.2745
Conflict	0.437	0.201	4.73	0.0296
Income	−0.435	0.144	9.17	0.0025
Literacy	−0.006	0.005	1.49	0.2214
Death from natural causes				
Manner	0.089	0.536	0.03	0.8679
Year	−0.055	0.035	2.53	0.1117
Age	0.084	0.019	19.32	<0.0001
Conflict	−0.474	0.494	0.92	0.3380
Income	0.141	0.271	0.27	0.6014
Literacy	−0.010	0.013	0.66	0.4156

not affect constitutional exits. If a leader gained power by nonconstitutional means, he is far more likely to be ousted by nonconstitutional means. In short, the factors affecting an exit from power seem to depend rather heavily on the type of exit.

UNOBSERVED HETEROGENEITY

If you look closely at equation (16.2) for Cox's PH model, you will notice that there is no random disturbance term. That does not mean that the model is deterministic because the dependent variable – the hazard – represents only the *propensity* for events to occur. Two people with the same hazard can end up with very different event times. Nevertheless, the model does say that all variations in the hazard are completely explained by the covariates that are included in the model, an unlikely assumption for virtually any real application.

Suppose we expand the model to include a random disturbance term ε which represents unobserved heterogeneity:

$$\log h_i(t) = \alpha(t) + \beta_1 x_{i1} + \ldots + \beta_k x_{ik} + \varepsilon_i.$$

As in conventional linear models, we might further assume that ε_i has normal distribution with mean 0 and constant variance, and is uncorrelated with any of the xs. What would such a model imply? There are two major implications of unobserved heterogeneity:

1. There will be an artifactual tendency for the observed hazard function to decrease with time. Thus, it will appear that the longer people survive, the lower their risk of death.

2. Estimates of the β coefficients using conventional methods will be biased toward zero, a phenomenon known as heterogeneity shrinkage (Gail et al., 1984). Fortunately, standard error estimates will still be valid, as will tests of hypotheses that coefficients are 0. Note that heterogeneity shrinkage is a potential problem for many other nonlinear models, including logistic regression (Allison, 1987).

Although there have been extensive efforts to devise methods to overcome these problems

Table 16.8 *Cox regression for 395 jobs, with and without standard error corrections*

Variable	Estimate	Standard error	Chi-square	Robust standard error	Robust chi-square
Schooling	0.187	0.029	41.80	0.046	16.43
Prestige	−0.079	0.006	154.30	0.006	163.40
Salary (logged)	−0.597	0.114	27.21	0.142	17.55
Time	0.269	0.029	83.45	0.031	77.50

(Heckman and Singer, 1984; Elbers and Ridder, 1982; Hougaard 1986), I believe that the attempt is futile when no more than one event is observed for each individual, as in the case of death. There simply is not enough information in the data to effectively distinguish between heterogeneity and time dependence. On the other hand, when multiple events are observed for each individual, models with unobserved heterogeneity can be reliably estimated (Yamaguchi, 1986).

REPEATED EVENTS

All the methods discussed so far presume that each individual experiences no more than one event. Yet most events that are interesting to social scientists are repeatable: births, marriages, divorces, arrests, job terminations, residential moves, etc. Here is a simple example. For 100 persons, we have data on the lengths of 395 jobs they held over a ten-year period (data set jobmult.dat, available at www.ssc.upenn.edu/~allison). The number of jobs held by each person ranged from 1 to 10. The goal is to estimate a model in which the hazard of job termination (which may be voluntary or involuntary) depends on four explanatory variables: years of schooling, occupational prestige, salary (logged) at the beginning of each job, and time at the start of each job (in years since the beginning of the first job).

One simple approach is to treat each job as a separate observation, and estimate a Cox regression model for length of the job. The first three columns of Table 16.8 report results from such an analysis. All four variables have highly significant coefficients. More schooling increases the hazard of termination, higher prestige and higher salary reduce the hazard of termination, and the rate of termination increases with time.

A major problem with this analysis, however, is that it ignores the potential dependence among the several jobs for the same person. If a person's first job is very short, we might expect that later jobs would be short as well. If job lengths are positively correlated, treating them as if they were independent observations will result in standard errors that are underestimated and test statistics that are too high. There are several methods available to deal with the problem of dependence. We will consider two that are readily available: robust standard errors and fixed effects models.

The method of robust standard errors does not involve any changes in the coefficient estimates, but modifies the standard errors to correct for dependence. Based on work of Huber (1967) and White (1980), the calculation of robust standard errors is sometimes called the 'sandwich' method because of the structure of the matrix formula. For Cox regression, several major software packages (SAS, Stata, S-PLUS) now provide robust standard errors as an option. The last two columns of Table 16.8 give robust standard errors and the associated chi-squares (the squared ratio of the coefficient to its standard errors). The chi-squares for education and salary are substantially smaller after the correction, although still highly significant.

The fixed effects method is a rather different approach to repeated events. First, it is based on a model that explicitly allows for unobserved heterogeneity across individuals,

$$log\, h_{ij}(t) = \alpha(t) + \beta_1 x_{ij1}$$
$$+ \ldots + \beta_k x_{ijk} + \varepsilon_i, \qquad (16.7)$$

where $h_{ij}(t)$ is the hazard for event j for individual i. The term ε_i represents unobserved heterogeneity that is specific to individual i but constant across events j. Rather than assuming that ε_i is a random variable, we assume that it is just some constant value that differs across individuals (hence the term 'fixed effects'). To estimate this model with conventional software, we must combine the ε_i with $\alpha(t)$ to get

$$log\, h_{ij}(t) = \alpha_i(t) + \beta_1 x_{ij1} + \ldots + \beta_k x_{ijk},$$

Table 16.9 Fixed effects Cox regression for 395 jobs

Variable	Estimate	Standard error	Chi-square	p
Schooling	0			
Prestige	−0.056	0.010	32.64	< 0.0001
Salary (logged)	−0.866	0.174	24.66	< 0.0001
Time	0.021	0.039	0.28	0.5988

which says that each individual has a distinct baseline hazard function. In this form, the model is easily estimated using the method of stratification described earlier (Allison, 1996). Each individual constitutes a distinct stratum.

Results for a fixed effects analysis of the job termination data are shown in Table 16.9. The most obvious feature of these results is the null estimate for schooling, which illustrates a peculiar disadvantage of fixed effects methods – you cannot estimate the effects of any variables that are constant over time for the individual. That is because the method only uses information about within-individual variation. In effect, we are asking the question, 'For each person, why are some jobs longer and others shorter?'. Variables that do not vary within persons cannot provide any answers to this question.

That does not mean, however, that schooling is not controlled in this analysis. In fact, fixed effects methods control for *all* variables that are constant within individuals, whether they can be measured or not. Hence, the analysis reported in Table 16.9 controls for race, sex, region of birth, family background, stable personality characteristics, and so on. For nonexperimental designs, where the control of such factors is a major issue, this is a very attractive feature.

Because of the controls for unmeasured factors, the fixed effects method often produces results that are markedly different from a conventional analysis, even with robust standard errors. That is not the case in this example, where the coefficients for prestige and salary are similar in Tables 16.8 and 16.9. On other hand, the coefficient for time is markedly lower in Table 16.9 than in Table 16.8, and is no longer statistically significant. The other thing to keep in mind about the fixed effects method is that, when unobserved factors are uncorrelated with the measured variables, there may be a substantial loss of power, that is the standard errors may be appreciably higher than in a conventional analysis. That is because the between-individual variation contributes nothing to the analysis.

Two other approaches to repeated events are generalized estimating equations (GEE) and random effects (mixed) models. The GEE method uses the robust standard errors method, but also produces more efficient estimates of the coefficients. Random effects models may be based on equation (16.7), but ε_i is treated as a random variable with a specified probability distribution. Random effects estimates are potentially more efficient than those produced by the fixed effects method, but they do not control for unobserved factors that are correlated with the variables in the model. These two methods are currently only available in specialized packages, but may see more widespread implementation in the near future.

DISCRETE-TIME AND TIED DATA

So far we have assumed that events can occur at any point in time and event times are measured with perfect precision. Under that assumption, it is impossible for two events to occur at *exactly* the same time. In practice, however, event times are often measured quite coarsely. We may only know the week, month, or year in which an event occurred. In such situations, many individuals may have 'tied' event times. That is, two or more individuals may have events at the same measured times.

The Cox regression method, in its classic form, is not appropriate when the data contain tied event times. When such data occur, most Cox regression programs invoke an approximate partial likelihood method proposed by Peto (1972) and Breslow (1974). However, this approximation may be poor when there are lots of tied event times. A much better approximation (Efron, 1977) is available in some programs. Better still are two exact methods, one that assumes that event times are truly continuous (a reasonable assumption for most applications) and another that assumes that event times are truly discrete (which may be appropriate for some special applications). Both of these exact methods are computationally intensive, however, and may be impractical for larger data sets with many ties.

There is another approach to coarse event times that is quite different in implementation but actually estimates the same underlying models as the exact Cox regression methods (Allison, 1982, 1984, 1995). The basic idea is very simple. For each unit of time that an individual is observed, create one observational record. For each record, create a dependent variable that is coded 1 if an event occurred during this unit of time, otherwise 0. Independent variables take on whatever values were measured at the beginning of that time unit. After pooling all the records, do a logistic regression predicting the dependent variable from the independent variables. This will produce maximum likelihood estimates of the 'truly discrete' model that can also be estimated by some Cox regression programs. Alternatively, to estimate the 'truly continuous' model, one may specify a complementary log-log link for the binary regression model. Unlike the exact partial likelihood methods, this maximum likelihood approach can readily handle large data sets with large numbers of tied event times.

BIBLIOGRAPHIC NOTE

There are many textbooks on event history (survival analysis) but the best tend to have a biomedical orientation. Of these, my favorites are Collett (1994) and Hosmer and Lemeshow (1999). Other useful texts from this perspective include Klein and Moeschberger (1997) and Kleinbaum (1996), the latter focusing exclusively on Cox regression. For texts by social scientists, see Blossfeld et al. (1989) and Yamaguchi (1991).

REFERENCES

Allison, Paul D. (1982) 'Discrete-time methods for the analysis of event histories', in Samuel Leinhardt (ed.), *Sociological Methodology 1982*. San Francisco: Jossey-Bass, pp. 61–98.

Allison, Paul D. (1984) *Event History Analysis*. Thousand Oaks, CA: Sage.

Allison, Paul D. (1987) 'Introducing a disturbance into logit and probit regression models', *Sociological Methods and Research*, 15: 355–74.

Allison, Paul D. (1995) *Survival Analysis Using the SAS System: A Practical Guide*. Cary, NC: SAS Institute.

Allison, Paul D. (1996) 'Fixed effects partial likelihood for repeated events', *Sociological Methods and Research*, 25: 207–22.

Bienen, Henry S. and van de Walle, Nicholas (1991) *Of Time and Power*. Stanford, CA: Stanford University Press.

Blossfeld, Hans-Peter, Hamerle, Alfred and Mayer, Karl Ulrich (1989) *Event History Analysis*. Hillsdale, NJ: Lawrence Erlbaum.

Breslow, Norman (1974) 'Covariance analysis of censored survival data', *Biometrics*, 30: 89–99.

Collett, David (1994) *Modelling Survival Data in Medical Research*. London: Chapman & Hall.

Cox, David R. (1972) 'Regression models and life tables', *Journal of the Royal Statistical Society, Series B*, 34: 187–202.

Efron, Bradley (1977) 'The efficiency of Cox's likelihood function for censored data', *Journal of the American Statistical Association*, 76: 312–19.

Elbers, C. and Ridder, G. (1982) 'True and spurious duration dependence: The identifiability of the proportional hazard model', *Review of Economic Studies*, 49: 403–10.

Gail, Mitchell H., Wieand, S. and Piantadosi, S. (1984) 'Biased estimates of treatment effect in randomized experiments with nonlinear regression and omitted covariates', *Biometrika*, 71: 431–44.

Heckman, James J. and Singer, Burton (1984) 'A method for minimizing the impact of distributional assumptions in econometric models for duration data', *Econometrica*, 52: 63–132, 271–320.

Hosmer, David W. and Lemeshow, Stanley (1999) *Applied Survival Analysis*. New York: Wiley.

Hougaard, P. (1986) 'Survival models for heterogeneous populations derived from stable distributions', *Biometrika*, 73: 387–96.

Huber, P.J. (1967) 'The behavior of maximum likelihood estimates under nonstandard conditions', in L. Le Cam and J. Neyman (eds), *Proceedings of the Fifth Berkeley Symposium on Mathematical Statistics and Probability*. Berkeley: University of California Press, pp. 221–33.

Kaplan, E.L. and Meier, P. (1958) 'Nonparametric estimation from incomplete observations', *Journal of the American Statistical Association*, 53: 457–81.

Klein, John P. and Moeschberger, Melvin L. (1997) *Survival Analysis: Techniques for Censored and Truncated Data*. New York: Springer-Verlag.

Kleinbaum, David G. (1996) *Survival Analysis: A Self-Learning Text*. New York: Springer-Verlag.

Morris, Carl N., Norton, Edward C. and Zhou, Xiao H. (1994) 'Parametric duration analysis of nursing home usage', in N. Lange, L. Ryan, L. Billard, D. Brillinger, L. Conquest and J. Greenhouse (eds), *Case Studies in Biometry*. New York: Wiley, pp. 231–48.

Peto, R. (1972) Contribution to the discussion of Cox (1972), *Journal of the Royal Statistical Society Series B*, 34: 205–7.

Rossi, Peter H., Berk, Richard A. and Lenihan, Kenneth J. (1980) *Money, Work and Crime*. New York: Academic Press.

Sørensen, Aage B. (1977) 'Estimating rates from retrospective questions', in D.R. Heise (ed.), *Sociological Methodology 1977*. San Francisco: Jossey-Bass, pp. 209–23.

Tuma, Nancy B. and Hannan, Michael T. (1978) 'Approaches to the censoring problem in analysis of event histories', in Karl F. Schuessler (ed.), *Sociological Methodology 1979*. San Francisco: Jossey-Bass, pp. 209–40.

White, Halbert A. (1980) 'A heteroskedasticity-consistent covariance matrix estimator and a direct test for heteroskedasticity', *Econometrica*, 48: 817–38.

Yamaguchi, Kazuo (1986) 'Alternative approaches to unobserved heterogeneity in the analysis of repeatable events', in Nancy B. Tuma (ed.), *Sociological Methodology 1986*. Washington, DC: American Sociological Association, pp. 213–49.

Yamaguchi, Kazuo (1991) *Event History Analysis*. Thousand Oaks, CA: Sage Publications.

17

Sequence Analysis and Optimal Matching Techniques for Social Science Data

HEATHER MACINDOE AND ANDREW ABBOTT

A wide variety of work in social science is concerned with sequences of events or phenomena. This includes studies of careers (sequences of jobs), events in the life course (education, work, family formation), sequences of actions (processes of innovation, or the adoption of policy initiatives), and cultural symbols (the order of steps in traditional dances).[1] Sequence data are simply an ordered listing of items, which may be events, numbers or anything else. The term *sequence analysis* (SA) refers to a body of questions about social processes and a collection of analytical techniques designed to address them. Researchers are typically interested in three questions concerning sequence data (Abbott, 1990):

1. Are there patterns among a set of sequences?
2. If such patterns exist, how are they produced?
3. What are the consequences of such patterns?

There are numerous ways to investigate sequence data. SA is characterized by the fact that it takes whole sequences of data as its units of analysis, rather than individual data points. The input data for such analyses are ordered arrays.[2] The more familiar way to approach such data is as time series. Such data are the object of well-known methods, which treat series data as generated by an underlying stochastic process, using individual data points as units of analysis. These methods do not concern us here.[3] The common characteristic of the SA methods is that they treat each data sequence as a whole, rather than as stochastically generated from point to point as in time series or event history analysis. It is as if one were comparing many time series to one another as whole units. Since they make no stochastic assumptions, SA methods are also appropriate for sequences that are not generated step by step, such as sequences of steps in the labor process or stages of a ritual, although they have more commonly been used for temporal sequences.[4]

There are various types of SA methods (see Abbott, 1995), but here we are concerned with optimal matching (OM) or alignment methods. We begin with an overview of OM, addressing issues such as data, coding, temporality, and cost assignment. We then illustrate the usual OM algorithm using a set of hypothetical sequences and conclude with an application of OM to a sample of career sequences.[5]

OPTIMAL MATCHING

OM methods were developed by molecular biologists for the rapid analysis of protein and DNA sequences. In biology, the characteristic task was to search a large database for close matches to a particular sequence of interest, typically a recently discovered protein. Algorithms performing this task first appeared in the early 1970s. By 1980, there was a substantial body of research, reviewed in Sankoff and Kruskal (1983), which remains the classic text in the field. OM algorithms were first used in social science by Abbott and Forrest (1986). The authors applied OM to sequences of figures in various ritual dances in order to investigate patterns of solidarity in rural England during the nineteenth century. The stability of patterns in the performance of such dances was used as an indicator of the stability of the village dance tradition generally and, by implication, of the way of life which sustained it.

OM is essentially the first step in an SA analysis. OM algorithms are used to calculate a distance measure for each pair of sequences in a data set. For a given number of sequences, N, the total number of pairwise distances calculated by the OM algorithm will be equal to $(N(N-1))/2$. These distances are a measure of the degree of similarity between any given pair of sequences in the data. The pairwise distances output from the OM algorithm subsequently become the input for the second step in SA. In this second step a separate analytic technique – typically clustering or scaling – is applied to the distance matrix to determine if there are meaningful groupings in the data. These groupings answer the first basic question about sequence data – whether patterns exist among the sequences. The resulting typology can be used as a dependent or independent variable in further analyses, which take up the other two sequence questions: what determines the sequences and what they in turn determine. These further analyses, then, are the third step in SA.[6]

It should be emphasized that OM, like many other sequence methodologies, is basically descriptive as opposed to causal in its orientation. Unlike other forms of quantitative analysis, OM is not concerned with hypothesis testing. Instead it is a means to 'preprocess' sequence data for further analyses oriented toward classification or typology

building. But OM alone cannot answer questions about the presence of patterns in sequence data. Rather, it produces input for further exploratory analysis. Separate literatures address the use of clustering, scaling and other forms of downstream analysis.[7] These techniques will not be addressed here. The remainder of this chapter concerns the first step in OM-based SA: how OM algorithms calculate distances between pairs of sequences. Once this is clearly understood, the reader can elaborate the further analyses with ease.

OM algorithms define simple algebras that create a metric for distances between whole sequences of events. The general approach is to measure those distances in terms of various elementary operations that turn one sequence into another. In the simplest version of OM, sequences can be changed in two basic ways. First, one can replace (or substitute) an element of a sequence with a different element. Second, one can insert or delete an element from the sequence. These elementary operations are called replacement, insertion, and deletion, the latter two collectively known as *indel*.[8] In some sense, the 'distance' between two sequences should be a function of the number of these elementary operations – replacements and indels – required to transform one sequence into another. There are many ways to make this transformation, however, so the distance should be a function of the *minimum* number of these elementary operations required to accomplish the transformation. This minimum distance in terms of elementary operations is referred to as the Levenshtein distance after its Russian inventor.[9]

Consider two simple sequences of letters: 'PSYCHOLOGY' and 'SOCIOLOGY'. There are numerous ways to transform the first sequence into the second (and vice versa). The operations used in the transformation can most easily be seen in an alignment of the two sequences, one on top of the other. We use the letter 'ϕ' (indicating a null element) to hold a place in one sequence when an insertion is made in the other sequence. Exact matches in an alignment are underlined in both sequences. One possible alignment of these two sequences would be to delete P, pick up the S match, replace O for Y, pick up the C match, replace I for H, and pick up the remaining exact matches (OLOGY). A second possibility would be to

P S Y C H <u>O</u> L <u>O</u> G Y   P S Y C H <u>O</u> L <u>O</u> G Y
φ <u>S</u> O <u>C</u> I <u>O</u> L <u>O</u> G Y   S O C I φ <u>O</u> L <u>O</u> G Y

Figure 17.1   *Two possible alignments of the sequences 'PSYCHOLOGY' and 'SOCIOLOGY'*

P S Y C H <u>O</u> L <u>O</u> G Y
φ φ φ B I <u>O</u> L <u>O</u> G Y

P S Y C H <u>O</u> L <u>O</u> G Y   P S Y C H <u>O</u> L <u>O</u> G Y
B φ φ φ I <u>O</u> L <u>O</u> G Y   φ B I φ φ <u>O</u> L <u>O</u> G Y

Figure 17.2   *Three possible alignments of the sequences 'PSYCHOLOGY' and 'BIOLOGY'*

replace S for P, O for S, C for Y, I for C, delete H, and pick up the remaining exact matches (OLOGY). Figure 17.1 depicts these two alignments. Three operations are used in the first alignment (one deletion and two replacements), and five operations are used in the second alignment (four replacements and one deletion). In the most basic sense, we can say that the first alignment requiring three operations is 'less costly' than the second alignment which uses five.[10]

Alternatively, we might consider two other sequences, PSYCHOLOGY and BIOLOGY. As shown in Figure 17.2, the minimum number of elementary operations required to turn the first sequence into the second is five (three deletions and two replacements). There are numerous ways this can be done.

These are very simple sequence comparisons, but they serve to illustrate how the elementary operations of replacements and indels can be used to determine a minimum 'distance' between two pairs of sequences. We can say that the sequences PSYCHOLOGY and SOCIOLOGY which require a minimum of three operations to transform one sequence into the other are in some sense 'closer' to each other than PSYCHOLOGY and BIOLOGY which require a minimum of five operations.

If the analyst determines that the replacement and indel operations are of equal importance, the distance between two sequences is simply the sum of the minimum number of operations required to transform one sequence into the other. (This is the case in the illustrations in the preceding paragraphs.) In this instance an identical weight or 'cost' has been assigned to all elementary operations. However, an analyst may have

theoretical reasons to treat some elementary operations as 'more costly' than others. Different replacements can be weighted differently in accordance with this theoretically driven scheme. Consider, for example, a set of career sequences consisting of five hierarchically ordered jobs 1 to 5 within an organization. In this simple code, job 1 is an entry-level position, jobs 2 through 4 are intermediate positions, and job 5 is a senior vice president position. Instead of assigning one standard replacement cost, the analyst may elect to define a replacement cost matrix in which the replacement of sequence element 1 for element 2 is less costly than the replacement of element 1 by element 5.

The cost of indel operations can also be adjusted for the given empirical problem. Indels can be weighted linearly, or, as is more common in the biological literature, they can be assigned a single 'gap cost' that may or may not be augmented by a smaller cost linear in the length of the inserted (or deleted) material.[11] The indel weight can also vary with respect to the replacement costs. One important variation in applications of OM algorithms in social science, then, is the setting of these various costs (see the discussion on cost assignment below). However, there are some algorithms, generally those directed at much fainter types of regularities, that do not involve cost setting, but simply define weighted objective functions on the data that can be maximized in order to find shared patterns (see the discussion on alternate algorithms below; see also Gusfield, 1997).

For sequences and accompanying cost assignments of any complexity, finding the minimum distance between any two sequences, subject to given costs, is a non-obvious task. It is solved by dynamic programming, programming that handles a large computing problem by solving a set of smaller ones whose results depend 'dynamically' on one another. In OM, that dependence takes the form of ordering the smaller problems recursively. The exact nature of the recursion depends on the elementary operations chosen for the underlying sequence algebra. (We give an example below.) Thus, for any pair of sequences and fixed set of substitution costs, dynamic programming will calculate a minimum cost for transforming one sequence into another. This cost is a distance measure that can be used in further analysis to classify the sequences.[12]

Creation of the OM distances proceeds in several stages. The data must first be coded into a set of sequences using a finite set of states. A replacement cost matrix must then be defined on these states and an indel cost (gap cost) scheme must be chosen. The algorithm is then applied, resulting in a matrix of distances between all pairs of sequences. Finally, the distance matrix itself must then be analyzed, typically with some form of dual-data reduction scheme like cluster analysis or multidimensional scaling. We now turn to a more detailed discussion of the various steps of OM, including data and coding, temporality, cost assignment, sequence lengths, and alternate algorithms.

Data and coding

As previously mentioned, sequence data consist of ordered listings of items. These items – the elements of the sequence – are a finite set of meaningful codes determined by the researcher. They may be events, letters, numbers, or anything else. OM methods generally apply to ordered sequences of potentially repeating events; see Abbott (1990, 1995) for a more extensive discussion of sequence properties. Coding schemes for sequence data are as various as the types of data themselves.[13] Some researchers use official classifications (Carpenter, 1996, codes official job titles at the US Department of Agriculture), official statistics (Modell, 1997, codes number of communions per year by individuals in a Swedish town), or variants of official classifications (Stovel, 2001, uses number of lynchings per year in US southern counties to calculate and code lynching rates). Others create 'complex events' for their sequences by cross-classifying a number of separate

events (Blair-Loy, 1997, uses both occupation and organization codes, incorporating nine job categories with four firm size categories). Finally, some researchers use coding schemes that are standard within a literature, such as the Goldthorpe class scheme employed by Chan (1995) and Halpin and Chan (1998). In the only study of the impact of coding on OM results, Forrest and Abbott (1990) found that divergent coding schemes had surprisingly weak impact on the final analysis.[14]

Temporality

Related to issues of coding are those of temporality.[15] Some sequence data, such as career sequences, exist in 'real time'. These sequences consist of jobs held over some period of time coded at regular intervals (e.g., one job per year). The implicit assumption here is that causal processes work at constant rates in all times and in all cases. OM allows ways to relax this assumption. One alternative is to use 'time-warping' algorithms (see Kruskal and Liberman, 1983). A simpler method is to transform the data. Abbott and Hrycak (1990) propose several different temporal structurings in addition to the 'raw' data structuring with its assumption of constant rates. One approach is to reduce all careers to the same length and then align the proportions of careers spent in different jobs. Another approach is to recode the sequences using a logarithmic transformation of the elapsed period in each job. This logarithmic method assumes that causal processes operate at equal rates across careers in the short run (small differences are emphasized) but at varying rates in the long run. See Abbott and Hryack (1990) for further detail. Stovel (2001) developed another approach to temporality in her historical study of lynchings in the southern US. Although county lynching sequences showed no patterns under standard temporality, Stovel hypothesized that lynchings might have important legacy effects through their retention in local memory. So she allowed each lynching to enjoy a finite, decaying presence for a few time periods after the one in which it occurred. Under this new temporality, strong patterns appeared. For some OM applications, sequence patterns do not exist in 'real time', but in purely abstract order. These applications typically investigate the formal order of cultural artifacts such as figure sequences in dances (Abbott and

Forrest, 1986), chapter sequences in physics and sociology texts (Levitt and Nass, 1989), patterns in folktales (Forrest and Abbott, 1990), or rhetorical structures in sociology articles (Abbott and Barman, 1997). Here temporal transformation is irrelevant.[16]

Cost assignment

The assignment of costs to the elementary operations involved in the transformation of sequences is a critical element of OM analysis. After coding their data, analysts must set replacement and indel costs for use by the OM algorithm. A number of different approaches to cost assignment are present in the literature on OM applications to social science data. A few writers (Dijkstra and Taris, 1995; Pentland et al., 1998) have simply set all replacements and indels to a single figure on the grounds that they lacked any theoretical reason for doing otherwise. In this instance, the distance between two sequences is equal to the minimum number of operations (replacement and indels) required to transform one sequence into another.

Most researchers, however, have specified replacement or substitution costs with a simple matrix. All possible sequence elements are arrayed across the columns and down the rows of this matrix. Consider, for example, a set of sequences of varying lengths with six possible elements: A, B, C, X, Y, Z. Figure 17.3 is a possible replacement cost matrix. The rows and columns represent the sequence elements in numeric or alphabetic order. The zeros in the main diagonal of the matrix indicate that there is no cost associated with perfect matches in a sequence alignment. The elements of this matrix are the cost for replacing the row element with column element or vice versa. For example, the 1 in cell (A, B) indicates that the cost for replacing A with B is 1. Likewise, the 1 in cell (B, A) indicates that the cost for replacing B with A is 1.[17]

The elements of the replacement cost matrix can be derived in a number of ways. In the simple example in Figure 17.3 the replacement cost associated with any two (non-identical) sequence elements is the number of letters of the alphabet between the two elements plus 1. While the formula behind this sample replacement cost matrix has no intrinsic meaning, an analyst working

	A	B	C	X	Y	Z
A	0	1	2	23	24	25
B	1	0	1	22	23	24
C	2	1	0	21	22	23
X	23	22	21	0	1	2
Y	24	23	22	1	0	1
Z	25	24	23	2	1	0

Figure 17.3   Sample replacement cost matrix

with real sequence data is challenged to assign replacement (and indel) costs in a meaningful manner. One common strategy is to compute the replacement cost matrix from the element-to-element transition rates in the data sequences when taken in the traditional way, one step at a time. This assumes that less frequent transitions are more 'costly' than more frequent ones. Some researchers assign substitution costs on the basis of some known linear property of the categories (Carpenter, 1996, uses job salary). Others have used theoretically generated costs. Still others have derived costs from rater rankings (Abbott and Forrest, 1986; Forrest and Abbott, 1990), usually organized into hierarchies.

A number of researchers have used hierarchical cost structures in which there are major costs between large branches and minor ones between small ones. (The Beldings software used for some of these studies actually takes its cost input in this fashion; see Abbott and Hrycak, 1990. A similar cost structure is used in the OM section of Abbott and Barman, 1997, although with different software.) Those who have used cross-classification of simple events to develop more complex 'sequence events' have had to derive highly differentiated cost schemes (e.g., Abbott and Hrycak, 1990; Abbott and DeViney, 1992; Stovel et al., 1996). Often these have combined several types of information. For example, Abbott and Hrycak's (1990) study of the careers of eighteenth-century German musicians combined information on job positions (e.g., instrumentalist, composer, cantor, etc.) with 'sphere-of-activity' (court, church, school, etc.) differences. Stovel et al. (1996) combined information on bank branch differences with information on job differences, using transition information as a measure of distance for both kinds of differences. The determination of replacement costs is a vital step in OM analysis.

Indel costs are another important matter. The original applications of OM in social science were done with what, in hindsight, were relatively high indel costs (see discussion on the relationship between indel and replacement costs below). For example, Abbott's early applications all set the indel cost at a value equal to the largest substitution cost plus the difference between the largest and the next largest (as in the original Beldings programs; see Appendix A at the end of this chapter). A number of other researchers followed Abbott in using this high indel value, usually setting indels equal to at least the largest substitution cost (e.g., Stovel et al., 1996; Pentland et al., 1998). Some analysts have tried several different insertion costs (e.g., Levitt and Nass, 1989; Poole and Holmes, 1995; Chan, 1995) without seeing serious variation in results. Setting replacement and indel costs for a given set of sequence data requires sensitivity to the relationship between the replacement and indel costs, which is constrained by the operation of the OM algorithms.

The relationship between indel and replacement cost is important. Since the OM algorithm searches for the minimum cost to transform one sequence into another, a particularly high indel cost relative to the replacement cost can coerce the alignment algorithms in important ways (Gauvreau, personal communication, 1994). In particular, if sequences are of equal length, and indels are set to any cost greater than half the largest substitution cost, indels will never be used by the algorithm in calculating the pairwise distances between the sequences. Where sequences are unequal in length, indel costs greater than one half the largest replacement cost would prevent the algorithm from using any more indels than exactly enough to offset that difference in sequence lengths. Thus, for most applications in which alignment of similar but separated portions of sequences is desired, indels should be set much lower than their values in the original social science applications of OM. To figure out appropriate costs, it is helpful to watch the effect of changing the indel level on a number of alignment pairs. Some software packages have such a facility. For example, the EXPLORE module of Abbott's OPTIMIZE program allows visual inspection of the alignment of any pair of sequences, allowing the user to shift the indel cost and watch the effect on the alignment. Using this module, Abbott and

his students (see Blair-Loy, 1997; Carpenter, 1996) ascertained that indel costs in the vicinity of 0.1 times the largest substitution cost tend to pick up the sequence regularities that seemed substantively interesting.

Sequence lengths

The length of a sequence may influence the calculation of pairwise costs across the sequence data set. For example, compare the sequences 'ABC' and 'ABD' to the pairing 'ABC' and 'ABDXYZ'. In the first pair of sequences we know that the minimum number of operations to transform one sequence into the other is 1 (replace 'C' with 'D'). For the second pairing, the extra length of the second sequence (ABDXYZ) requires three additional operations to transform the sequences, for a total of four operations (replacing 'C' with 'D' then inserting 'XYZ' or replacing 'D' with 'C' and deleting 'XYZ'). Since we may not want disparity in sequence length to unduly influence the calculation of pairwise distances, it is common to standardize the pairwise distances with respect to length.

Researchers have used several corrections to address the fact that variation in sequence length means that some pairs of sequences have a greater potential distance between them than do others. Abbott and many others have dealt with this by dividing the final pairwise distance by the length of the longer sequence of the pair. For the sequences discussed in the preceding paragraph, we would divide the distance between the first set of sequences ('ABC' and 'ABD') by 3 and the distance between the second pair of sequences ('ABC' and 'ABDXYZ') by 6. The unstandardized distances, 1 and 4 respectively, become 0.333 and 0.667.[18] Other researchers (Dijkstra and Taris, 1995) have standardized their sequence data by arbitrarily 'reducing' all sequences to equal length. This seems a less desirable approach to standardization as it unnecessarily discards some of the sequence content.

Alternate algorithms

One of the advantages of OM as a sequence technique is that different alignment algorithms can be used to investigate different aspects of sequence resemblance. Often in sequence analysis we are not interested in the resemblance of whole sequences, but instead want to investigate common subsequences. The researcher is faced with the problem of determining if some short pattern is common to most sequences. Until recently the detection of subsequence regularities was hindered by computational difficulty. However, an algorithm due to Lawrence et al. (1993) gives a solution, finding for any group of sequences the optimal common subsequence across the group. This optimal common subsequence need not appear in all sequences and need not appear in total in any single sequence. Also, it can start at points that vary widely across the sequences. Abbott and Barman (1997) utilize this algorithm to detect subsequence regularities in rhetorical structures of sociology articles. This flexible aspect of OM merits further attention in social science applications.[19] We now turn to a more detailed discussion and illustration of the basic OM algorithm, known after its originators as the Needleman–Wunsch algorithm.

THE OPTIMAL MATCHING ALGORITHM

In this section, we review the operation of the basic OM algorithm using a simple set of sequences. While the discussion of alignments and solution arrays may seem daunting, we believe that the payoff to the reader in increased understanding of the operation of the OM algorithm is substantial. It is too easy, particularly with the range of available software, for SA techniques to become a 'black box' which spits out a distance matrix whose origin is not very clearly understood by the analyst. While portions of the following may be tedious, we hope that the illustration furthers understanding of how the basic OM algorithm works.

Suppose that we have up to eight years of data for five people working in an organization that has five hierarchical job levels. We use a very simple code, 1 to 5, beginning with 1 to indicate an entry-level position and ending with 5 to indicate the most senior position. It is important to note that the numbers 1 to 5 have no intrinsic meaning, they are simply codes representing five jobs in increasing hierarchy. The jobs could easily have been coded A, B, C, D, E or j1, j2, j3, j4, j5. The sample sequences are shown in Figure 17.4.[20]

In general, the sequences exhibit upward mobility through the five job levels. One exception is sequence C, which starts at a

Sequence	Years							
	1	*2*	*3*	*4*	*5*	*6*	*7*	*8*
A	1	1	1	1	2	2	2	2
B	1	1	2	2	3			
C	3	3	4	5				
D	1	1	2	2	3	3		
E	1	2	2	3	3	4	5	5

Figure 17.4 *Sample career sequences*

mid-level job, as opposed to the other sequences which begin with an entry-level position. Sequence E indicates steady progress through the job ranks, as compared to sequence A which is equally divided between the first two job levels, with no promotion past level 2. Sequences B, C, and D are all shorter than the other sequences, perhaps indicating that these workers left the organization or that data on these workers were missing for certain years.[21]

As discussed earlier in the chapter, the OM algorithm measures a distance between all pairs of sequences in a data set in terms of elementary operations: replacements and insertions or deletions (indels). If we assume a uniform cost of 1 for all operations, the pairwise distance measure is equal to the minimum number of operations (replacements or indels) required to transform one sequence into another. The one exception is a 'perfect match', the replacement of a sequence element for itself (e.g., 2 for 2). This replacement has a cost of zero. In the common sense we are not 'replacing' anything with these exact matches, but rather adding equivalent items to an alignment of two sequences.

There are two ways to depict the operation of the OM algorithm. One method is to view the elements of two sequences in alignment with one sequence on top of the other. We did this earlier in the chapter with the sequences 'PSYCHOLOGY' and 'SOCIOLOGY'. If sequences are short and the costs assigned to replacements and indels are simple, the minimum distance between two sequences can easily be determined by visual inspection of these alignments. However, when sequences or costs (of replacements or indels) become more complex, the progression of the OM algorithm can be illustrated with a matrix that we will call the solution array. We consider alignments and solution arrays in turn with respect to the sample career sequences in Figure 17.4.

| Sequence D | 1 <u>1</u> <u>2</u> <u>2</u> <u>3</u> <u>3</u> φ φ φ | <u>1</u> 1 <u>2</u> <u>2</u> <u>3</u> <u>3</u> φ φ φ | <u>1</u> 1 <u>2</u> <u>2</u> 3 <u>3</u> φ φ |
| Sequence E | φ <u>1</u> <u>2</u> <u>2</u> <u>3</u> <u>3</u> 4 5 5 | <u>1</u> φ <u>2</u> <u>2</u> <u>3</u> <u>3</u> 4 5 5 | <u>1</u> 2 <u>2</u> <u>2</u> 3 <u>3</u> 4 5 5 |

Figure 17.5   *Three possible alignments of sequences D and E from Figure 17.4*

| Sequence A | 1 1 1 <u>1</u> <u>2</u> <u>2</u> 2 2 φ φ φ | <u>1</u> 1 1 <u>1</u> <u>2</u> 2 2 2 |
| Sequence E | φ φ φ <u>1</u> <u>2</u> <u>2</u> 3 3 4 5 5 | <u>1</u> 2 <u>2</u> 3 3 4 5 5 |

Figure 17.6   *Two possible alignments of sequences A and E from Figure 17.4*

Alignments

If the sequences and associated cost structure determined by the researcher are not too complex, the simplest way to determine the minimum distance between two sequences is through visual inspection of sequence alignments. An alignment is a row of vertical pairs of sequence elements: the upper member of each pair is in one sequence; the lower member is in the other. As we stated earlier, there may be numerous ways to align two sequences. Figure 17.5 shows three alignments of sequences D and E from Figure 17.4.

Recall that the letter 'ϕ' (indicating a null element) is used to hold a place in one sequence when an insertion or deletion is made in the other sequence. Exact matches in an alignment are underlined in both sequences. The first alignment picks up the exact match of the first five elements of sequence E with the second through sixth elements of sequence D and uses four indels (indicated by ϕ). The second alignment is nearly identical and also uses four indels. The third alignment picks up the exact matches of the first, third, and fifth elements in the two sequences. Replacements are used to align the second, fourth, and sixth elements and two indels are used to align the seventh and eighth elements. In total, five operations are used in the third alignment. We record the minimum distance between these two sequences as 4. Either set of operations depicted in the first and second alignments of Figure 17.5 can be used.

Consider one more example, the alignment of sequences A and E (again from Figure 17.4) shown in Figure 17.6. The first alignment matches the first three elements of sequence E with the fourth through sixth elements of sequence A. The alignment uses six indels and two replacements, for a total of eight operations. The only matched elements in the

Table 17.1   *Pairwise distances for sequences in Figure 17.4*

	A	B	C	D
B	4			
C	8	5		
D	4	1	6	
E	7	5	4	4

second alignment are the first items in the two sequences. This alignment uses 7 replacements. Again, since we are searching for the least costly way to align the sequences, we select the operations shown in the second alignment and record the minimum pairwise distance as 7.

With a simple set of distances and cost assumptions, it is relatively easy to determine the alignment and corresponding distance between two sequences by visual inspection. Table 17.1 displays the complete distance table for the illustrative sequences in Figure 17.4 (indel and replacement costs equal 1). These distances can be easily obtained through visual inspection of the sequences. Appendix B at the end of this chapter provides a sample TDA (Transition Data Analysis) syntax file which uses OM to calculate the minimum pairwise distances for the sequences in Figure 17.4. TDA is a software package with an OM module that is available over the internet.[22]

As previously discussed, sequence length can influence the calculation of the pairwise distances. While our sample sequences are reasonably close in length, we choose to standardize the pairwise distances by dividing by the length of the longer sequence in a pair. Table 17.2 contains these standardized distances. By referring back to Figure 17.4, the reader will see that sequences B and D are indeed similar and that A and C on the one hand and A and E on the other are – for

Table 17.2 *Standardized pairwise distances for sequences in Figure 17.4*

	A	B	C	D
B	0.50			
C	1.00	0.63		
D	0.50	0.17	0.75	
E	0.88	0.63	0.50	0.50

differing reasons in the two cases – quite dissimilar. However, note that one might think that B is more like E than like C, despite the equal distances in the table. The reason is that B and C share only one element, while B looks like E with the end chopped off and the beginning expanded. But if we want to capture that sense that B and E are really closer than B and C because one looks like an expanded part of the other, we need to allow for differing indel and replacement costs. To do that, we need to use a more complex display for alignment. This more complex display is called a *solution array*.

Solution array

As sequences and cost structures become more complex, visual inspection is no longer adequate to determine the minimum distance between pairs of sequences. A formal algorithm is necessary to guarantee minimization. The operation of that algorithm can be illustrated by a solution array, an $(N + 1) \times (M + 1)$ matrix (where N and M are the lengths of two sequences). One sequence spans the columns while the other sequence spans the rows. These are the 'column sequence' and 'row sequence' respectively, although it should be noted that we are using the solution array to create an over/under alignment just like those earlier in the chapter in Figures 17.1, 17.2, 17.5 and 17.6 (so one can also think of the column sequence as the 'top sequence' and the row sequence as the 'bottom sequence' in an over/under alignment). Tracing a path through the matrix (from the upper left-hand cell to the lower right-hand cell) indicates one way of over/under aligning the two sequences using indels and substitutions. The solution array allows us to keep track of the costs of the alignment as we go along, and allows us to figure out not only the minimum distance between the sequences, but also the actual alignment that produces it.

The algorithm starts at the upper left corner and works to the lower right corner, building the alignment from left to right. (It would get the same solution in the other direction – lower right cell to upper left cell – so this is arbitrary.) Moving to the right in the solution array is equivalent to appending an element (say, X) to the column (upper) sequence and appending a null to the row (lower) sequence in the alignment. (Remember the sequences are being built from the left – 'appending' here does not mean adding something on the end of the already complete data sequences, but adding something onto the end of what has so far been built up.) Moving down in the solution array is equivalent to appending an element (say, Y) to the row (bottom) sequence and appending a null to the column (top) sequence. Moving right and down diagonally means appending (say) X to the column (top) sequence and (say) Y to the row (bottom) sequence. For simplicity, we call these 'moving right', 'moving down', and 'moving right-down'. Note that the first two are what we have called indels and the last is what we have called a replacement.

It is necessary to keep track of costs as we go along. To see how this works, it is useful to consider an example. Consider the solution array for sequences B (1 1 2 2 3) and D (1 1 2 2 3 3) in Figure 17.7. The sequences themselves are in bold face: B (the 'column sequence') spans the columns, D (the 'row sequence') spans the rows. We will for the present assume a single cost (of 1) for indels and replacements, so the solution array is in this case simply replicating an alignment shown already. The 0 in the upper left-hand cell is the starting cost, when nothing is aligned. Consider moving right (remember the formal sense of this) from this cell. This means appending 1 in the column sequence and null (ϕ) in the row sequence. In the cell to the right of the 0, the left-hand number (1) refers to the cost of this move (an indel, costing 1). The right-hand number refers to the total cost to this point, which is also 1. If we move right again, we append another 1 to the column sequence and another null (ϕ) to the row sequence (we have now aligned 11 with null null ($\phi\phi$)). The cost of moving right is again 1, but now the total cost (the right-hand number) is 2. And so on all the way to the end, where five moves to the right have cost us a total of 5.

A precisely similar argument takes us down the column immediately below the 0. In this

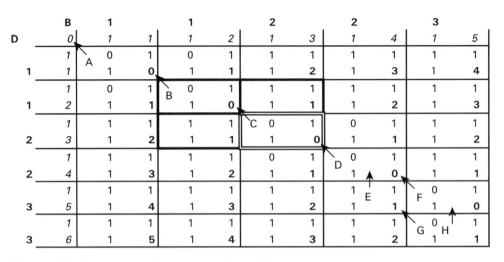

Figure 17.7 *Solution array for sequences B and D*

case it is the upper number that is the cost of the individual move (in this case moving down) and the lower number that is the total cost so far. By the end of the column we have six nulls (ϕ) in the column (top) sequence aligned with the row (bottom) sequence, at a total cost of 6. The first row and column in the solution array are called the 'boundaries'.

Consider now the interior cells of the solution array. Each cell has four elements. Three we have already encountered. The lower left element is the cost of entering the current cell by moving right, just as it was in the boundary row at the top of the solution array. The upper right element is the cost of entering the cell by moving down, just as it was in the boundary row on the left-hand side of the array. These upper right and lower left elements are both indels (at a cost of 1 in this example). The lower right element is the cost of arriving in the current cell, just as it was in the boundary cells. But there are now several ways to do that, and so this number will be the *minimum* cost of arriving in the current cell. It is not yet obvious how to find that minimum.

The only unfamiliar number in the interior cells is the upper left number which is, as the reader probably suspects, the cost of entering the cell by moving right-down diagonally, that is, by appending the column sequence element to the column sequence and the row sequence element to the row sequence. This is a replacement, using our earlier terminology, and has a cost (for the present) of 1 if there is a mismatch and 0 if there is a match.

For the first interior cell – the one diagonally right and down from the 0 – this move aligns 1 in the column sequence with 1 in the row sequence, a perfect match, with a cost of 0.

To figure out the proper value for the lower right-hand element of an interior cell – the minimum cost of arriving in that cell – we must consider the three ways of getting there: moving right, moving down, and moving right-down. Consider the double-outlined cell in Figure 17.7 and its three predecessor cells (the left, above and left-above cells). First, we move right into the double-outlined cell from the 'left-hand predecessor'. The total cost of this way of aligning will be the cost of getting to that left-hand predecessor (which is contained in its lower right element) plus the moving right cost itself, the lower left element of the current cell. For the double-outlined cell (or 'current cell') in the middle of Figure 17.7, this is 1 + 1 = 2. (The 2 does not appear anywhere because it is not the minimum.) Second, we move down into the current cell from the 'above predecessor'. The total cost of this way of aligning will be the cost of getting to that above predecessor (which is contained in its lower right element) plus the moving down cost itself, the upper right element of the current cell. For the current cell, this cost too is 1 + 1 = 2. Third, we move right-down into the current cell from the 'left-above predecessor', and again the total cost of this move is the cost of arriving in that predecessor (found in its lower right corner) plus the moving right-down (replacement) cost. In the current cell,

Arrow	A	B	C	D	F	H
Sequence B	1	1	2	2	3	φ
Sequence D	1	1	2	2	3	3
Cost	0	0	0	0	0	1

Arrow	A	B	C	D	E	G
Sequence B	1	1	2	2	φ	3
Sequence D	1	1	2	2	3	3
Cost	0	0	0	0	1	0

Figure 17.8   *Optimal (minimum-cost) alignments of sequences B and D*

this total cost is $0 + 0 = 0$. Obviously this last is the minimum cost of the three ways to move into the current cell. Thus, 0 becomes the lower right-hand element of the double-outlined cell.

The whole algorithm consists of filling in all the cells. Note that we must always have calculated all the predecessors of a current cell to calculate that cell. There are many possible orders of calculation that meet this condition. All give the same answer. The operation of the OM algorithm is illustrated in the solution array for sequences B and D in Figure 17.7.

Although the algorithm seeks the minimal cost alignment of two sequences, we must retrace our steps in order to identify that alignment. There may be more than one such alignment. The backwards-pointing arrows in Figure 17.7 indicate the actual alignment: the series of operations that produces the lowest cost alignment of the two sequences. This minimum cost path is found by moving backwards in the array from the lower right-hand cell towards the upper left-hand cell. We begin at the lower right-hand cell, which is by definition on the minimum cost alignment. We then must figure out which routes into that cell produced the minimum that appears in it. For the lower right-hand cell in Figure 17.7, it is clear that we could have entered by moving right-down $(1 + 0 = 1)$ or by moving down $(0 + 1 = 1)$. So we place backwards-flowing arrows leading into those cells. Each backwards arrow labels a move that produced the minimum value in the current cell. For each cell that a backwards arrow takes us to, we then examine how we got into *those* cells, and so on until we arrive at the upper left cell of the solution array. In contrast to the forward solution phase, there is no need to examine all the cells, only those that turn out to be 'on the track' of the arrows. The arrows in Figure 17.7 in fact identify the two actual minimal alignments. They are both exactly the same up to the end, where one of them matches the lone column 3 with the first of the two 3s in the

Sequence elements	1	2	3	4
1	0	1	2	3
2	1	0	1	2
3	2	1	0	1
4	3	2	1	0

Figure 17.9   *Replacement cost matrix for solution array in Figure 17.10*

row sequence, and the other matches it with the second. These two alignments are shown in the over/under format in Figure 17.8. For sequences B and D, there are two optimal alignments, each with a total cost of 1. The solution array has, with great elaboration, replicated what is quite obvious by inspection. We have labeled the actual steps of the alignments with capital letters to make the correspondence between the over/under and solution array formats clear.

The solution array quickly becomes more complex, however, when sequences are longer and replacement costs are not all uniform and differ from the indel cost. In order to demonstrate how complicated this problem can be, imagine that our sequence elements are not hierarchical job levels, but rather types of work assignments. These can repeat in a bewildering number of orders. Assume that the work assignments differ on some simple scale, such that it makes sense to think of the cost of substituting one work assignment for another as being equal to the absolute value of the difference between the numbers used to index them. This is the cost scheme shown in Figure 17.9.

Two possible examples of these work assignment sequences might be 4 3 2 4 2 2 4 3 4 and 3 1 3 4 3 1 1 2 4 (labeled F and G, respectively). Let indels be worth 1 apiece, following the remarks above (in discussion on cost assignment) about allowing room for serious search for resemblance off the diagonal. Figure 17.10 gives the solution array for this pair of sequences. Note that the indel costs all remain 1, but that the replacement costs vary with the pairings involved. As the

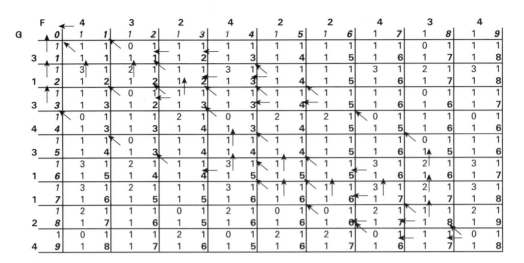

Figure 17.10   *Solution array for work assignment sequences F and G*

backwards arrows indicate, the minimum cost of 8 can be obtained in dozens of ways. None of these, however, is obvious by inspection. Nor is the straight diagonal (pure replacements from one end to the other) a minimal alignment (it costs 10 – the 3/1 mismatch in the second position and the 4/1 mismatch in the eighth position kill it.)

AN EMPIRICAL EXAMPLE: PATHS TO SOLO PRACTICE

We now turn to an empirical example of sequence analysis using career histories of lawyers. Previous research indicates that solo practitioners are, on average, among the lowest-ranked members of the legal profession with regard to various measures of occupational prestige and income (Carlin, 1962; Heinz and Laumann, 1982; Sandefur, 2001). Nevertheless, solo practitioners constitute the largest single segment of the legal profession in the United States, constituting approximately 46% of private practitioners and 33% of the total lawyer population (Curran and Carson, 1994). There is considerable variation in income among solo practitioners. For example, there are highly compensated personal injury defense lawyers and meagerly compensated divorce lawyers (and vice versa). We might want to investigate whether a solo practitioner's previous legal jobs impact his success in solo practice.

Sequence analysis can be used to address this question. More specifically, we might wish to know whether there are typical patterns that lead to a career as a solo practitioner and, if such patterns exist, whether they can explain any variation within solo practice ranks with respect to variables of interest such as income.

To investigate questions about career paths among solo practitioners we use data from the 1995 Chicago Lawyers Survey. We examine a set of retrospective career histories reported by a sample of practicing lawyers who had offices in the city of Chicago in 1995. This random sample included professionals from a variety of legal practice settings including private law firms, local, state and federal government, corporate house counsels, law professors, military lawyers and solo practitioners. Thirteen percent (103 lawyers) of the sample were engaged in solo practice at the time of the survey. The data we examine consist of 103 job sequences coded at yearly intervals. Each sequence begins with the respondent's first legal job after graduation from law school and ends with his current position at the time of the survey in 1995 (in all cases solo practice). The elements in the sequences are jobs within practice settings, so multiple jobs within a practice setting are counted.[23] The data were coded using a simplified code for five possible positions: solo practice (S), firm (F), government (G), house counsel (H), and non-legal positions (N). Three sample sequences are displayed in

Respondent 1	F	F	F	F	F	F	F	F	H	H	H	H	S	S	S	S
Respondent 2	G	G	G	G	G	G	G	F	F	F.2	F.2	F.2	F.2	S	S	S	S
Respondent 3	S	S	S	S												

Figure 17.11   *Sample career sequences*

Table 17.3   *Description of career clusters*

Cluster	N	% of solos	Description	Sample sequence
1	36	35.0	Firm	F F F F F S S S S
2	19	18.4	Prodigal Solos	F F N N N N S S S
3	17	16.5	Solos Only	S S S S S S
4	10	9.7	Government	F F G G G G G S S
5	8	7.8	Shifters	F F F.2 F.2 F.3 F.3 F.3 F.4 S S S S
6	6	5.8	House Counsel	F H H H H S S S S
7	7	6.8	Residual	H N N G G F F F F S S

Figure 17.11. Respondent 1 worked in one law firm for 8 years, then as a house counsel for a corporation for 4 years, and has been in solo practice for 4 years. Respondent 2 began his career in government (7 years), then worked in one law firm (coded as 'F') for 2 years, then moved to a different law firm (coded as 'F.2') for 4 years before moving to solo practice. Respondent 3 has been in solo practice since graduation from law school.

As previously discussed, an important step in SA is the assignment of replacement and indel costs. We consider mean income across practice settings to be a relatively good indicator of the ease or difficulty of moving from one practice setting to another. For example, since the mean income for solo practitioners in the sample is closer to the mean income for government lawyers than it is to the mean income for firm lawyers, we argue that moving between solo practice and government practice settings is in some sense 'easier' than moving between law firms and private practice. Thus, we use information on mean income in a legal practice setting to determine the replacement cost matrix.[24] Following conventions established in the SA literature, we set indel costs equal to 0.1 multiplied by the largest replacement cost. (See preceding discussion of indel costs for more detail.) Using this cost scheme, we performed OM analysis on the 103 career sequences. The output from this analysis is a pairwise distance matrix for the sample of career sequences. We standardized the distance matrix by dividing each pairwise distance by

the length of the longer sequence in the pair. We then analyzed this standardized distance matrix using hierarchical cluster analysis to determine if any substantively meaningful groups emerged from the data.

Cluster analysis of the distances from the OM analysis indicates that there are several distinct paths to solo practice. Table 17.3 reports the seven-cluster solution.[25] Six substantively interesting clusters emerge:

1. Firm: Solo practitioners who typically began their practices after employment at up to three law firms.
2. Prodigal solos: Solo practitioners who returned to the practice of law in solo practice after having one or more non-legal jobs.
3. Solos only: Respondents who were solo practitioners for their entire careers.
4. Government: Respondents who typically came to the practice of law through government employment.
5. Shifters: Solo practitioners who moved from firm to firm (typically four to eight firms) before entering solo practice.
6. House counsel: Respondents who worked in house counsel positions before entering solo practice.

There are some career patterns that may appear in the sample, but do not occur with sufficient frequency to characterize a career cluster. An example of one such pattern is lawyers who began their professional life as solo practitioners, left solo practice to spend

Table 17.4 *Distribution of career clusters across cohorts*

	Cohort		
Cluster	21+ years (1941–1973)	11–20 years (1974–1983)	10 or fewer years (1984–1995)
Firm	22.7	42.9	45.8
Prodigal Solos	20.5	22.9	8.3
Solos Only	15.9	11.4	25.0
Government	9.1	8.6	12.5
Shifters	11.4	5.7	4.2
House Counsel	9.1	2.9	4.2
Residual	11.4	5.7	0.0

Table 17.5 *Features of career clusters*

Cluster	# Practice settings	# Jobs	Years in solo practice	Total years in practice	% Career spent in 1st job	% Cluster female
Firm	2.3	2.8	10.1	17.8	23	20
Prodigal Solos	3.2	3.8	10.6	21.0	18	16
Solos Only	1.0	1.0	19.4	19.4	100	18
Government	2.3	2.4	12.4	19.9	23	30
Shifters	2.5	7.1	6.1	25.0	12	0
House Counsel	2.3	2.7	10.5	21.2	27	17
Residual	4.5	6.3	5.6	22.7	1	29

the majority of their career in another (more lucrative) practice setting, then returned to solo practice near the end of their career.

If we examine the distribution of career clusters across cohorts (Table 17.4) within the 1995 sample of solo practitioners, we find that the firm cluster is most dominant, particularly in the youngest cohort. For example, 46% of the respondents in the youngest cohort in 1995 belonged to the firm cluster. The increasing dominance of the firm cluster speaks to the expansion of the legal profession, notably the growth in scale and number of law firms and the related increased opportunity for lawyers from local and regional law schools to be employed in law firms.

Some interesting patterns emerge when we examine some descriptive statistics for the career clusters (Table 17.5). We see that the solos only cluster has the highest mean years in solo practice. The shifters have an average of 7.1 jobs over 2.5 practice settings, while their closest peers in the firm cluster have an average of 2.8 jobs over 2.3 practice settings. Thirty-three percent of the sample of solo practitioners reported engaging in 'other non-legal work' simultaneously with their solo practice. Generally the other work reported is real estate, arbitration, other business and (for a small number)

contract work for other law firms. It is notable that prodigal solos report the highest mean number of hours per week spent in other work (28.8); see Table 17.6. This makes sense, considering that they were previously in non-legal jobs some of which might lend themselves to part-time work.

An examination of mean income across career clusters produces some surprising results. The shifters have the second highest mean income on average (after respondents in the house counsel cluster). The job histories exhibited by shifters had the potential to mark them as the losers of the sample: these respondents moved from law firm to law firm without partnership or promotion. However, the mean income of this group tells another story. It would seem that the human capital acquired by moving through numerous different firms benefits this group of respondents, who, far from being the 'losers' among solo practitioners, report on average $21 000 more income per year than their peers in the firm cluster. An examination of the descriptives for these two groups (see Table 17.5) confirms this interpretation: while the shifters spend on average 7 *more* years practicing law than the firm cluster, they spend 4 years *less* in solo practice.

Table 17.6   *Legal work, non-legal work and mean income by career cluster*

Cluster	% Report other non-legal work	Hours/week other work	Hours/week legal work	Mean legal income
Firm	33	24.6	43.8	69 450
Prodigal Solos	47	28.8	34.8	62 342
Solos Only	29	10.8	44.0	48 148
Government	30	11.3	53.9	71 842
Shifters	0	0.0	45.8	90 975
House Counsel	17	4.0	60.0	131 918
Residual	57	20.2	44.4	28 535

Table 17.7   *Distribution of legal effort within career clusters*

% Legal effort in fields of law	All Solos	Cluster 1 Solos Only	Cluster 2 Prodigals	Cluster 3 Firms	Cluster 4 Shifters	Cluster 5 House Counsel	Cluster 6 Govt.
Corporate	20.5	8.8	0.0	7.9	47.3	21.6	21.3
Regulatory	2.5	1.8	0.0	0.5	0.0	16.7	2.4
General corporate	10.0	8.6	9.6	16.6	16.9	12.1	2.6
Political	0.6	0.6	1.0	0.0	0.0	0.0	1.3
Personal/small business	27.0	33.1	37.6	33.4	13.3	14.1	26.5
Personal plight	34.0	40.5	41.1	34.0	22.4	35.4	45.9
Residual fields	7.5	6.6	10.7	7.6	0.0	0.0	0.0

Finally, we examine the career clusters according to the distribution of legal effort reported by solo practitioners across various fields of law. Using the categories of legal effort in Heinz and Laumann (1982), we examine the distribution of legal effort within career clusters.[26] Not surprisingly, the most legal effort across all career clusters is expended in the personal plight area (Table 17.7). But there is some interesting variation within the fields of law that lends further credence to the career clusters identified via OM and cluster analysis. While all solo practitioners report a significant amount of personal plight work, the government cluster reports the highest level of personal plight work, notably criminal defense work. In addition, while very little political legal work is reported by solo practitioners, members of the government cluster report the highest amount. Members of the firm and shifters clusters report the highest amount of general corporate legal work. Shifters report the highest proportion of corporate work. This distribution of corporate legal work among firm and shifters is consistent with business referrals from the previous places of employment.

In summary, SA aids in the identification of typical paths to solo practice. There is a shift across the cohorts in the 1995 sample toward the firm career cluster. This speaks to the expansion in the scale of law and the increased opportunities for local and regional law school graduates to be employed in firms. Finally, an examination of the distribution of legal effort in the various career clusters suggests that career paths to solo practice impact the type of law that solo practitioners practice once they start practicing on their own. The descriptive analyses on lawyers career clusters is presented here as a simple illustration of SA. It is only the beginning of a rigorous analysis of this data. A final analysis would make use of more formal models using the career clusters as independent variables to predict outcomes of interest (such as income).[27]

CONCLUSION

This chapter has discussed various issues important to OM analysis and has described the operation of its most basic algorithm. It should be apparent that, like all types of analysis, OM relies heavily on the analyst's previous decisions about coding, indel and replacement costs. Representing sequence data in a clear manner and determining a substantively meaningful cost scheme are central to the OM exercise, which is itself simply the beginning of an analysis of sequence data. Clustering or scaling techniques are necessary to analyze the output from the OM algorithm. Finally, further interpretation is required to understand the clusters (if any) that emerge from the analysis of the distance data. But with careful attention OM reveals patterns in the data undiscoverable by any other method.

APPENDIX A. SOFTWARE FOR OPTIMAL MATCHING

A variety of software packages have been used in social science applications of OM. Most of the early work (Abbott and Forrest, 1986; Abbott and Hrycak, 1990; Forrest and Abbott, 1990; Abbott and DeViney, 1992; Poole and Holmes, 1995) utilized the 'Beldings Program Series', a set of VMS FORTRAN programs originally written for CDC computers by David Bradley of Long Beach State University in the mid-1970s. In the early 1990s, Abbott developed OPTIMIZE (written in C and available on the Internet), a package for multiple alignment of small data sets (Carpenter, 1996; Blair-Loy, 1997). Although OPTIMIZE is not supported or maintained, the program includes a unique module (the Explore module) for visually inspecting the change in pairwise alignments as costs are adjusted. Katherine Stovel's SAS/IML program DISTANCE has been used by some working with larger data sets (Stovel, 2001; Stovel et al., 1996). Others have used standard biological packages, which include a larger variety of algorithms (e.g., algorithms with affine gap costs) such as PILEUP (Chan, 1995; Halpin and Chan, 1998) and CLUSTALG (Wilson et al., 1999). The example used in the 'OM Algorithm' section in this chapter (see Appendix B) was computed using TDA, a package originally developed for event history models by Goetz Rohwer. TDA is freeware, distributed under the terms of the GNU General Public License. It is available for download – along with a user's manual and an archive of sample files – from http://steinhaus.stat.ruhr-uni-bochum.de/. At this point, then, the would-be user has several software options.

APPENDIX B. TDA SAMPLE DATA AND COMMAND FILES

```
# FOR MORE INFORMATION ABOUT THE SYNTAX COMMANDS USED IN THIS
# FILE SEE TDA USER'S MANUAL SECTION 3.4, 'Sequence Data Concepts'

# example.cf – this is a sample TDA command file for optimal matching using sequences in
# Figure 17.4 syntax begins here, explanatory notes (denoted by #) follow the syntax

mdef(SCOST,5,5) =
0, 1, 1, 1, 1,
1, 0, 1, 1, 1,
1, 1, 0, 1, 1,
1, 1, 1, 0, 1,
1, 1, 1, 1, 0;

# the mdef command defines a 5x5 replacement cost matrix named SCOST

nvar(
 dfile = example.dat,
 Y{1,8} = c1,
);
seqdef = Y1,,Y8;
```

```
# the nvar command reads in new variables from the data file example.dat
# seqdef defines sequences specifying 8 columns of data
# see below for example.dat

seqm(
 icost = 1,
 scost = SCOST,
 df = example.tst,
 tst = 1, 2, 3,
 dtda = example.tda,
) = example.d1;

# seqm is the optimal matching command
# icost = 1 sets indel cost at 1
# scost = SCOST sets substitution cost equal to the previously defined matrix

# example.d1 is an output file which includes the final pairwise distances
# in this file, the first two columns indicate the sequences being compared, columns 3-4
# indicate the lengths of the respective sequences, and column 5 contains the final pairwise
# distances calculated by the OM algorithm. This corresponds to a lower triangular matrix
# of pairwise distances. It can be
# read into a clustering or scaling program for further analysis.
```

```
# example.dat – sample sequence data from Figure 17.4 formatted for TDA

1 1 1 1 2 2 2 2
1 1 2 2 3 –1 –1 –1
3 3 4 5 –1 –1 –1 –1
1 1 2 2 3 3 –1 –1
1 2 2 3 3 4 5 5
```

ACKNOWLEDGMENTS

The authors thank Ed Laumann and Jack Heinz for the use of the 1995 Chicago Lawyers data, and Phaedra Daipha and Julia Gwynne for reading and commenting on previous drafts.

NOTES

1 See Abbott and Tsay (2000) for a recent review of the literature applying optimal matching techniques to social science data. For an earlier review of the sequence literatures in psychology, economics, archaeology, linguistics, political science, and sociology, see Abbott (1995).

2 SA concerns arrays with one ordered dimension. In principle, there exist 'spatial' analytic systems that apply the equivalent approaches to ordered arrays in two-dimensional space.

3 This chapter does not debate the merits of various analytic strategies for the analysis of time series data (e.g., event history analysis). For a discussion of the merits of SA relative to other analytical strategies for time series data, see Abbott and Tsay (2000) or Abbott and Hrycak (1990).

4 For a more extended discussion of these differences, see Abbott and DeViney (1992) and Abbott and Tsay (2000).

5 A variety of other methods are mentioned in Abbott and DeViney (1992), particularly those of Heise (1991) and Abell (1993).

6 In what follows, we use OM to refer interchangeably to the first step (OM proper) and to that type of SA that uses OM as its first step. The difference should be clear from the context.

7 See Aldenderfer and Blashfield (1984) or Arabie et al. (1987).

8 In some accounts the 'replacement' operation is termed 'substitution'. Both terms refer to the exchange of one sequence element for another. This chapter discusses only the simplest form of OM algorithm, the so-called Needleman–Wunsch algorithm. For a much larger variety of OM algorithms, see Gusfield (1997). Ideally, the analyst can design an algorithm to seek particular kinds of regularities of theoretical interest. Here we consider only the simplest form of pattern search, one that is agnostic about the regularities that it expects.

9 See Sankoff and Kruskal (1983).

10 The reader should not be distracted by the fact that these sequences of letters form familiar words. The sequences MXZKPCTYLZ and XYKNCTYLZ produce the same results.

11 That is, the indel cost may simply be a fixed value x or the indel cost may be designated as $x + by$, where x represents the fixed cost portion of the indel operation and by represents an additional indel cost y which is multiplied by the length of the indel b. With this method of indel cost assignment, the analyst is able to make the indel cost a function of the length of the insertions (or deletions). In applications where we are mostly interested in what *matches* between sequences, we would use a fixed gap cost and make it small. When the duration of insertions is important, we would weight indels linearly.

12 For an introduction to dynamic programming, see Nemhouser (1966).

13 See Abbott and Tsay (2000) for a more complete discussion of coding techniques that have been used in social science applications of OM.

14 The authors had five coders code the dance sequences they had analyzed in 1986 and looked at variation in the results. Even though the coders varied both in their particular codings and, especially, in the level of detail, the results were remarkably stable, both in the comparative results (using scaling and clustering) and in Monte Carlo significance testing of resemblance of the actual distances produced.

15 See Abbott (2001) – particularly Chapter 7 – for a theoretical discussion of temporality.

16 Transformations of temporality are of course possible in other methodological approaches that operationalize time as a variable. But the flexibility of OM in this regard has encouraged analysts to confront our standard assumptions about temporality, as, for example, the idea (absolutely assumed in event history methods as customarily used) that causality moves at the same pace in all cases.

17 Replacement costs must be symmetric in order to guarantee that the distances derived have the metric properties of null self-distance, symmetry and the triangle inequality.

18 Abbott's OPTIMIZE program performs this standardization automatically, as do the Beldings programs, Stovel's SAS programs. TDA does not produce standardized output.

19 The Lawrence et al. algorithm is merely one of the literally dozens of different algorithms available to analyze sequence resemblance. As it happens, the Lawrence et al. algorithm does not use replacement algebras like the Needleman–Wunsch algorithm discussed at length below. Rather, it uses a Markov chain Monte Carlo method – Gibbs sampling. Note that the question solved by the Lawrence et al. algorithm – 'what is the best common subsequence of a certain length?' – is not the same as the 'what are the sequence types?' question that gets most of our attention here.

20 For example, the following table presents the same sequences shown in Figure 17.4, coded with letters:

1   A A A A B B B B
2   A A B B C
3   C C D E
4   A A B B C C
5   A B B C C D E E

21 In general, missing data are a problem for OM analysis, as they are for standard methods for sequence or time series data. But the kind of problem they present varies with the kind of (and location in the sequence of) missing data. It can be possible to search for regularities in ways that are not bothered by a type of missing data.

22 TDA is available for download from http://steinhaus.stat.ruhr-uni-bochum.de/. Appendix B contains the syntax file 'example.cf', a TDA command file using the data in Figure 17.4, and 'example.dat', containing the formatted data. This example produces an output file 'example.dl' that contains the final pairwise distances for the sequences contained in Figure 17.4. See the TDA manual (available at the given web address), notably the section on 'Sequence Data Concepts', for thorough instructions and additional examples. See Appendix A for other software options.

23 Consider, for example, respondent 2 in Figure 17.11. This respondent had three jobs in two practice settings prior to entering solo practice.

24 More specifically, we calculated the elements of our replacement cost matrix as follows: R_{LS} (Replacement cost law firm/solo practice) $= |I_L - I_S| / [(I_L + I_S)/2]$, the absolute value of the difference between the mean income of law firm practitioners and the mean income of solo practitioners divided by the average income across the two practice settings.

25 Clusters calculated using Ward's method.

26 These six general categories of legal effort are as follows:

1. Corporate: antitrust (defendants), business litigation, business real estate, business tax, labor/management, securities.
2. General corporate: antitrust (plaintiff), banking, commercial law, general corporate matters, personal injury (defense).
3. Personal/small business: personal business, (general) civil litigation, (personal) real estate, (personal) tax matters, probate.
4. Regulatory: labor/unions, patents, public utilities.

5. Political: criminal prosecution, municipal law.

6. Personal plight: civil rights, criminal defense, divorce law, general family, personal injury (plaintiff).

27 Abbott and DeViney (1992) employed regression using optimal matched data as dependent variables. They were seeking to predict the sequences and timing of the adoption of five basic welfare state policies common in advanced countries ($N = 18$). The data were policy sequences (defined as sequences of a 32-state variable describing which of the five policies a given country possessed in a given quinquennium). These were analyzed with OM, and the results were then scaled, using a standard multidimensional scaling program. The resulting two-dimensional solution proving satisfactory, Abbott and DeViney tried to predict each dimension using a variety of variables indicating modernization, state strength, and left politics. There are a variety of detailed results, both positive and negative – for example, a larger service sector makes health insurance come later, a larger aged population does *not* make pensions come earlier, etc. See also Stovel (2001) and Halpin and Chan (1998) for more complex examples of SA than those offered here.

REFERENCES

Abbott, Andrew (1990) 'A primer on sequence methods', *Organization Science*, 1(4): 375–92.

Abbott, Andrew (1995) 'Sequence analysis: new methods for old ideas', *Annual Review of Sociology*, 21: 93–113.

Abbott, Andrew and Barman, Emily (1997) 'Sequence comparison via alignment and Gibbs sampling', *Sociological Methodology*, 27: 47–87.

Abbott, Andrew and DeViney, S. (1992) 'The welfare state as transnational event', *Social Science History*, 16: 245–74.

Abbott, Andrew and Forrest, John (1986) 'Optimal matching method for historical sequences', *Journal of Interdisciplinary History*, 16: 471–94.

Abbott, Andrew and Hrycak, Alexandra (1990) 'Measuring resemblance in sequence data: An optimal matching analysis of musicians' careers', *American Journal of Sociology*, 96: 144–85.

Abbott, Andrew and Tsay, Angela (2000) 'Sequence analysis and optimal matching methods in sociology: Review and prospect', *Sociological Methods and Research*, 29: 3–76.

Abell, Peter (1993) 'Some aspects of narrative method', *Journal of Mathematical Sociology*, 18: 93–134.

Aldenderfer, Mark S. and Blashfield, R. (1984) *Cluster Analysis*. Newbury Park, CA: Sage Publications.

Arabie, Phipps, Carroll, J. and DeSarbo, W. (1987) *Three-Way Scaling and Clustering*. Sage University Paper series on Quantitative Applications in the Social Sciences, series no. 07-065. Newbury Park, CA: Sage Publications.

Blair-Loy, Mary (1997) 'Career patterns of executive women in finance: An optimal matching analysis', *American Journal of Sociology*, 104(5): 1346–97.

Carlin, Jerome E. (1962) *Lawyers On Their Own: A Study of Individual Practitioners in Chicago*. New Brunswick, NJ: Rutgers University Press.

Carpenter, D. (1996) 'Corporate identity and administrative capacity in executive departments'. PhD dissertation, University of Chicago.

Chan, T-W. (1995) 'Optimal matching analysis: A methodological note on studying career mobility', *Work and Occupations*, 22(4): 467–90.

Curran, Barbara A. and Carson, Clara N. (1994) *The Lawyer Statistical Report: The US Legal Profession in the 1990s*. Chicago: American Bar Foundation.

Dijkstra, W. and Taris, T. (1995) 'Measuring the agreement between sequences', *Sociological Methods and Research*, 24: 214–31.

Forrest, John and Abbott, Andrew (1990) 'The optimal matching method for studying anthropological sequence data', *Journal of Quantitative Anthropology*, 2: 151–70.

Gusfield, D. (1997) *Algorithms on Strings, Trees, and Sequences: Computer Science and Computational Biology*. New York: Cambridge University Press.

Halpin, B. and Chan, T.W. (1998) 'Class careers as sequences: An optimal matching analysis of work-life histories', *European Sociological Review*, 14(2): 111–30.

Heinz, John P. and Laumann, E.O. (1982) *Chicago Lawyers*. Evanston, IL: Northwestern University Press.

Heise, D. (1991) 'Event structure analysis', in N. Fielding and R. Lee (eds), *Using Computers in Qualitative Research*. Newbury Park, CA: Sage, pp. 136–63.

Kruskal, J.B. and Liberman, M. (1983) 'The symmetric time-warping problem', in D. Sankoff and J.B. Kruskal (eds), *Time Warps, String Edits, and Macromolecules*. Reading, MA: Addison-Wesley, pp. 125–61.

Lawrence, C.E., Altschul, S.F., Boguski, M.S., Liu, J.S., Neuwald, A.F. and Wooton, J.C. (1993) 'Detecting subtle sequence signals', *Science*, 262: 208–14.

Levitt, B. and Nass, C. (1989) 'The lid on the garbage can', *Administrative Science Quarterly*, 34: 190–207.

Modell, J. (1997) 'The representation of human lives in social science and social history'. Unpublished MS, Carnegie-Mellon University.

Nemhouser, George L. (1966) *Introduction to Dynamic Programming*. New York: Wiley.

Pentland, B.T., Roldan, M., Shabana, A.A., Soe, L.L. and Ward, S.G. (1998) 'Lexical and sequential variety in organizational processes'. Unpublished MS, Michigan State University.

Poole, M.S. and Holmes, M.E. (1995) 'Decision development in computer assisted group decision-making', *Human Communication Research*, 22: 90–127.

Rohwer, Goetz and Potter, Ulrich (2002) *TDA Users Manual*, Ruhr University, Bochum, Germany.

Sandefur, Rebecca (2001) 'Work and honor in the law: Prestige and the division of lawyers' labor', *American Sociological Review*, 66: 361–82.

Sankoff, D. and Kruskal, J.B. (eds) (1983) *Time Warps, String Edits, and Macromolecules*. Reading, MA: Addison Wesley.

Stovel, K. (2001) 'Local sequential patterns', *Social Forces*, 79: 843–80.

Stovel, K., Savage, M. and Bearman, Peter (1996) 'Ascription into achievement: Models of career systems at Lioyds Bank, 1890–1970', *American Journal of Sociology*, 102: 358–99.

Wilson, Clarke, Harvey, Andrew and Thompson, Julie (1999) 'Clustal G: Software for analysis of activities and sequential events'. Paper presented at the Workshop on Longitudinal Research in Social Science, Ontario, Canada.

PART IV

New Developments in Modeling

18

Sample Selection Bias Models

VINCENT KANG FU, CHRISTOPHER WINSHIP
AND ROBERT D. MARE

This chapter provides an overview of models for sample selection bias and practical guidance on the use of these models. Samples that are not representative of the population of interest are common in social research. These samples may arise as an inherent part of the social process or may result from the sampling procedure. Models for sample selection bias provide a means to produce valid inferences from these nonrepresentative samples.

We outline the standard estimation techniques for selection models, which rely on strong parametric assumptions. We will discuss research on the conditions under which standard estimators are most useful and demonstrate the application of several estimators through an empirical example. We then discuss some of the recent research on semiparametric estimators that relax the statistical assumptions of standard estimators. We discuss empirical applications of these new estimators and present results from Monte Carlo simulations undertaken by us to examine the sensitivity of standard parametric estimators to departures from normality.

This chapter draws heavily on Winship and Mare (1992), updating that paper with citations to more recent literature and supplementing it with an empirical example and Monte Carlo simulations. Berk (1983) provides an introductory discussion of selection bias, while Vella (1998) discusses the available estimators in greater detail than we do. Pagan and Ullah (1999) provide a more detailed review of semiparametric estimators.

We emphasize the literature that in our judgment is most useful to sociologists seeking to understand how to apply selection models in empirical research. We do not discuss models for treatment effects, nor do we discuss models for panel data. Models for treatment effects compare individuals selected into two or more groups, whereas selection models usually describe selection into a single group. For discussions of these topics, see Winship and Morgan (1999), Winship and Sobel (this volume), and Vella (1998).

THE STRUCTURE OF SELECTION

Sample selection bias occurs when observations are selected into a sample based on the values of the dependent variable. This leads to biased inferences when the observed data are not a representative sample of the population in which the researcher is interested. One solution to this problem might be to draw a sample that is indeed representative, but this is impossible for many important social processes. The classic example is modeling women's wages. If the aim is to estimate a typical woman's returns on schooling, then estimating regression coefficients from a sample of employed women will not do because the only women appearing in the sample are employed women. These women are not representative of all women if, as seems reasonable, women with higher

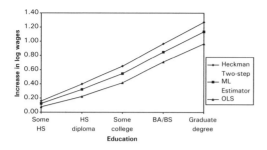

Figure 18.1 *Increase in log hourly wages relative to respondents with no high school.*

expected wages are more likely to be employed. Thus, conventional methods for estimating a model for women's wages require unobservable data – the wages of women who are not working. Models for sample selection bias provide a way around this problem. With well-specified models for the outcome of interest and for selection into the sample, selection models enable researchers to produce valid estimates from nonrepresentative data.

To illustrate the bias that appears when conventional estimates are calculated from a biased sample, let us consider an empirical illustration of a model showing the effect of education on women's wages. The data describe married, spouse-present women from the 1990 US Census 5% Public Use Microdata Sample (United States Department of Commerce, 1993). We model the natural logarithm of women's hourly wages, using dummy variables for the various levels of education. Figure 18.1 shows the increase in log wages for different levels of education relative to those who completed no years of high school. The flattest line shows the pattern of increases based on ordinary least-squares (OLS) regression estimates. The two steeper lines show the pattern of increases produced by models for sample selection bias that correct for the non-representativeness of the data. The three sets of estimates all show an increase in wages with education. However, the magnitude of the increases depend on the estimator. In this instance, sample selection bias produces a downward bias in the OLS regression estimates. In general, however, selection may bias estimated effects in either direction.

Selection takes a variety of forms. *Incidental selection* (Goldberger, 1981) occurs when the likelihood that an observation appears in the sample is a stochastic function of the dependent variable. This occurs when, in a situation like the example above, women with higher expected wages are more likely to appear in the sample. In a model that includes schooling as the only regressor, women with more schooling are more likely to appear in the sample because they have higher expected wages. The selection process is systematic but still stochastic. There is no expected wage cut-off point below which no women appear in the sample. Such a sample can also be *truncated* (Heckman, 1987), meaning that no information at all is available about women who are excluded from the sample. This selection process leads to violations of the OLS regression assumption that (1) the expected value of the error conditional on X is zero and the weaker assumption that (2) the errors and X are uncorrelated. Women with less schooling will tend to have more positive errors if they are actually employed and thus have observed wages.

The same OLS regression assumptions are also violated when incidental selection occurs with a *censored* (as opposed to truncated) sample. In this case, respondents who were excluded from the truncated sample actually do appear in the sample. Their values on the regressors are known, but information is missing about their values on the dependent variable. Either nothing is known about the dependent variable value, or all that is known is that the dependent variable is outside of a particular bound but the exact value is unknown. If the dependent variable is completely unobserved in a censored sample, OLS regression using only women with observed values on the dependent variable is equivalent to the case of a truncated sample. If instead a bound is available, coding a respondent's hourly wages at the known bound will not produce consistent estimates because the error term will be biased. In our example, suppose some women with wages below the minimum wage were censored and their wages were coded at the minimum wage. Then the expected value of the errors at any level of schooling will be positive because the negative errors that were extreme enough to bring the wage below the minimum wage are no longer so extreme. The expected values of the errors will become increasingly positive at lower levels of schooling. Once again we have violations of OLS regression assumptions that will lead to biased and inconsistent estimates.

Explicit selection occurs when selection is a deterministic process (Goldberger, 1981).

When the selection process is explicit (as opposed to incidental), a sample is truncated when observations with values of the dependent variable beyond a given bound are completely excluded. An example of explicit selection with a truncated sample is estimating the relationship between wages and education from a sample that discards respondents with wages higher than a certain threshold, such as $30 per hour. This biases the errors downward. As education increases, the only respondents who remain in the sample are those with sufficiently negative error terms to bring their hourly wages below $30. This induces a negative correlation in the sample between the error and education. The result is biased and inconsistent coefficient estimates. Censoring can also occur with explicit selection. Observations with values of the dependent variable beyond a given bound are included in the sample, but the only information available about these observations is their values on the regressors and that their values on the dependent variable are beyond the bound. This also leads to biased inferences if OLS regression is used.

Another type of selection occurs when the sample is selected based on values of the measured independent variables. Respondents with more than a high school diploma might be excluded from the sample. In this situation, OLS regression estimates are unbiased and consistent if the functional form of the relationship between schooling and hourly wages is properly specified (DuMouchel and Duncan, 1983; Little and Rubin, 1987; Winship and Radbill, 1994).

SOCIAL SCIENCE EXAMPLES OF SELECTION BIAS

To make the issues that selection models address more concrete, we briefly present several empirical applications of these models in the sociology literature. Most recent applications in sociology employ standard parametric estimators for selection models with continuous outcomes, although estimators that relax parametric assumptions and models for categorical outcomes have been available for quite some time. The examples below demonstrate the wide applicability of selection models, which reflects the pervasiveness of selection bias.

An important consideration in understanding changes over time in employment patterns is changes over time in the characteristics of individuals who are defined to be at risk of employment. Mare and Winship (1984) consider this issue in an investigation of employment trends from the 1960s to the 1980s of young black and white men who are out of school. Increases in school enrollment during the period (especially among black youths) induced changes over time in the composition of the out-of-school population. Because people who stay in school longer have better average employment characteristics than those who drop out, the out-of-school population became increasingly composed of young men with poor employment prospects. Thus, without changes in any other conditions, increases in school enrollment led to decreases in the employment rates of the out-of-school population. Selection models allow examinations of changes over time in employment rates to account for the bias induced by changes in school enrollment patterns. This relationship between school enrollment and employment explains, in part, why the gap in the employment rates of young blacks and whites grew during the 1960s and 1970s while other indicators showed gains in the relative socio-economic status of blacks.

Another area in which selection models have proved fruitful is the analysis of the criminal justice system's treatment of suspected criminals. The stages through which a suspected criminal might pass and the gate-keeping mechanisms at each stage result in the imprisonment of a highly selected population. The progression from arrest to prosecution, conviction, and finally imprisonment provides a number of institutionalized mechanisms through which some suspects obtain their release while others move deeper into the system. Unmeasured characteristics may affect continuation from one stage to the next, necessitating models that account for selection bias. For example, researchers studying imprisonment outcomes use selection models to account for the process through which persons are convicted because they recognize that those who are ultimately imprisoned are not a representative sample of those who commit crimes (Steffensmeier and Demuth, 2000; Peterson and Hagan, 1984; Zatz and Hagan, 1985).

A concern of life-course research is the institutionalization and deinstitutionalization of life-course transitions. Han and Moen (1999) observed that as the retirement age has fallen in recent years, retirement age has also become more variable. They develop a model explaining several indicators of retirement age, but only retirees have observed retirement ages. Consequently, they use a selection model to simultaneously model age at retirement and retirement itself. Unobserved factors such as retirement benefits and wealth could affect both the retirement decision and retirement age. The selection model accounts for the bias induced by omitting these unobserved factors.

The situations described above reflect rich substantive connections between the selection process and the outcome of interest. Selection models are also useful in more mundane situations where the selection condition is more of a methodological issue. These situations may occur, for example, when a researcher encounters a censored variable in the course of estimating an earnings regression. In order to protect the anonymity of survey respondents, incomes are often top-coded. That is, earnings exceeding a given threshold are coded at the threshold. This form of selection bias can be addressed in a straightforward way. Morgan (1998), for example, uses a model that accounts for top-coded earnings in a study of the gender gap in earnings for engineers. Selection models can also be useful in correcting biases that arise from attrition in panel studies and non-response in cross-sectional samples.

MODELS OF SELECTION

We now provide a brief overview of two selection models. We start by discussing the censored regression or tobit model. Due to limited space we forgo discussion of the very closely related truncated regression model (Hausman and Wise, 1976, 1977). For more detailed classifications, see Amemiya (1985) and Heckman (1987).

Tobit model

The censored regression or tobit model is appropriate when the dependent variable is censored at some upper or lower bound as an artifact of how the data are collected or measured (Tobin, 1958; Maddala, 1983). For censoring at a lower bound, the model is:

$$Y_{1i}^* = X_i\beta + \varepsilon_i, \qquad (18.1)$$

$$Y_{1i} = \begin{cases} Y_{1i}^* & \text{if } Y_{1i}^* > 0, \\ 0 & \text{if } Y_{1i}^* \leq 0, \end{cases} \qquad (18.2)$$

where, for the ith observation, Y_{1i}^* is an unobserved continuous latent variable, Y_{1i} is the observed variable, X_i is a vector of values on the independent variables, ε_i is the error, and β is a vector of coefficients to be estimated, typically including an intercept. We assume that ε_i is uncorrelated with X_i and is independently and identically distributed. The model can be generalized by replacing the zero threshold in equations (18.2) with a known nonzero constant. The censoring point may also vary across observations, leading to a model that is formally equivalent to models for survival analysis (Kalbfleisch and Prentice, 1980; Lancaster, 1990).

OLS estimates of equation (18.1) are subject to selection bias. For observations with $Y_{1i} > 0$, the model implies:

$$Y_{1i} = X_i\beta + E[\varepsilon_i \mid Y_{1i}^* > 0] + \eta_i$$
$$= X_i\beta + E[\varepsilon_i \mid \varepsilon_i > -X_i\beta] + \eta_i, \qquad (18.3)$$

where η_i is the difference between ε_i and $E[\varepsilon_i \mid Y_{1i}^* > 0]$ and is uncorrelated with both terms. Selection bias results because $E[\varepsilon_i \mid \varepsilon_i > -X_i\beta]$ in equation (18.3) is a function of $-X_i\beta$. The smaller the $-X_i\beta$, that is, the smaller the rate of censoring, the greater is the conditional expected value of ε_i. The negative correlation between $-X_i\beta$ and ε_i implies that OLS estimates of the regression of Y_{1i} on X_i are biased and inconsistent. It can be shown that inclusion of observations for which $Y_{1i} = 0$ also leads to biased estimates of the regression. Equation (18.3) also shows how selectivity bias may be interpreted as an omitted variable bias (Heckman, 1979). The term $E[\varepsilon_i \mid Y_{1i}^* > 0]$ can be thought of as an omitted variable that is correlated with X_i and affects Y_{1i}. Its omission leads to biased and inconsistent OLS estimates of β.

Mare and Chen (1986) use the tobit model to examine the effect of parents' socioeconomic characteristics on years of graded schooling completed by their offspring, a variable that is censored for persons with more than 12 years of school. Seltzer and Garfinkel (1990) and Seltzer (1991) use tobit models to analyze the determinants of property and child support awards to mothers and amounts paid by noncustodial fathers after divorce, which are zero for substantial proportions of mothers. In studying how families finance college educations, Steelman and Powell (1989) construct tobit models of the sources of college funding, including parents' contributions, loans, savings, and scholarships, each of which has a logical floor of zero. Hoffman (1984) uses a tobit model to examine the determinants of pious bequests in rural Lyonnais and Beaujolais between 1521 and 1737. Jacobs and O'Brien (1998) use a tobit model to analyze differences across cities in the rate of killings committed by the police, which was zero in many cities. Iannaccone (1994) estimates a tobit model of church attendance measured by the annual number of weeks attending services, which is censored from below at zero and from above by 52.

Standard sample selection model

A generalization of the tobit model is to specify that a second variable Y_{2i}^* affects whether Y_{1i} is observed or not. That is, retain the basic model equation (18.1), but replace (18.2) with:

$$Y_{1i} = \begin{cases} Y_{1i}^* & \text{if } Y_{2i}^* > 0, \\ 0 & \text{if } Y_{2i}^* \leq 0. \end{cases} \quad (18.4)$$

Variants of this model depend on how Y_{2i} is specified. Commonly Y_{2i}^* is determined by a binary regression model:

$$Y_{2i}^* = \mathbf{Z}_i\boldsymbol{\alpha} + v_i \quad (18.5)$$

$$Y_{2i} = \begin{cases} 1 & \text{if } Y_{2i}^* > 0, \\ 0 & \text{if } Y_{2i}^* \leq 0, \end{cases} \quad (18.6)$$

where Y_{2i}^* is a latent continuous variable. In a model for the wages and employment of women, Y_{1i} is the observed wage, Y_{2i} is a dummy variable indicating whether a woman works, and Y_{2i}^* indexes a woman's propensity to work (Gronau, 1974). In a variant of this model, Y_{2i} is hours of work and equations (18.5) and (18.6) are a tobit model (Heckman, 1974). In both variants, Y_{1i}^* is only observed for women with positive hours of work. One can modify the model by assuming, for example, that Y_{1i} is dichotomous. If ε_i and v_i follow a bivariate normal distribution, this leads to a bivariate probit selection model. Maddala (1983), Lee (1983), and Dubin and Rivers (1989) discuss these and other variants of the model.

The bias in an OLS regression of Y_{1i} on $\mathbf{X}_i$ in the general selection case is similar to that in the tobit model. When $Y_{2i}^* > 0$,

$$Y_{1i} = \mathbf{X}_i\boldsymbol{\beta} + \mathrm{E}[\varepsilon_i | Y_{2i}^* > 0] + \eta_i$$
$$= \mathbf{X}_i\boldsymbol{\beta} + \mathrm{E}[\varepsilon_i | \mathbf{Z}_i\boldsymbol{\alpha} + v_i > 0] + \eta_i. \quad (18.7)$$

The OLS regression of Y_{1i} on $\mathbf{X}_i$ is biased and inconsistent if ε_i is correlated with either v_i or the $\mathbf{Z}_i$. If the variables in $\mathbf{Z}_i$ are included in $\mathbf{X}_i$, ε_i and $\mathbf{Z}_i$ are uncorrelated by assumption. If, however, $\mathbf{Z}_i$ contains additional variables, then ε_i and $\mathbf{Z}_i$ may be correlated. ε_i and v_i are correlated when unobserved variables affect both selection and the outcome. When ε_i and v_i are not correlated $(\sigma_{\varepsilon v} = 0)$, selection depends only on the observed variables in $\mathbf{Z}_i$ not in $\mathbf{X}_i$. In this case propensity score methods (Rosenbaum and Rubin, 1983) are appropriate for correcting for selectivity bias (Heckman and Robb, 1985, 1986a, 1986b).

Selection models are closely related to models for treatment effects in the presence of nonrandom assignment. Treatment effects models concern nonrandom selection into two or more conditions or samples, whereas sample selection usually refers to selection into a single condition. One sort of treatment effects model is the endogenous switching regression model. This model is a generalization of the standard treatment effects model that allows the effects of the independent variables to vary across treatments. For more details of this model see Mare and Winship (1988), and for more details about models for treatment effects see Winship and Morgan (1999) and Chapter 21 (this volume).

ESTIMATORS

A large number of estimators have been proposed for selection models. These estimators vary in the strength of the assumptions they make. Standard estimators for selection models rely on strong assumptions about the distributions of error terms to produce coefficient estimates. Two general classes of methods, maximum likelihood (ML) and nonlinear least squares, typically assume bivariate normality of ε_i and v_i. The most popular method is that of Heckman (1976, 1979), which only assumes that v_i in equation (18.5) is normally distributed and $\mathrm{E}[\varepsilon_i | v_i]$ is linear (Olsen, 1980). Computer software packages such as Stata (Stata Corp, 2001) can be used to estimate basic sample selection models. SAS currently provides no ready-made routines for any selection models, but a user-contributed routine for Heckman's estimator is available. LIMDEP (Greene, 1998) implements a number of estimation strategies and selection models, including cases where the selection equation is a tobit model, a multinomial logit, or multiple-criteria model, and the outcome equation is a linear, probit, or tobit model.

Much of the recent research on selection models has focused on developing estimation techniques that relax the strong assumptions of earlier estimators. Recently researchers have been concerned with the sensitivity of the Heckman estimator to the normality and linearity assumptions. Because ML and nonlinear least squares make even stronger assumptions, they are typically more efficient (Nelson, 1984) but even less robust to violations of distributional assumptions. This potential lack of robustness is also a property of Olsen's (1980) linear probability estimator which assumes that errors are uniformly as opposed to normally distributed. The main concern of the recent literature is the search for alternatives to the Heckman estimator that do not depend on normality and linearity assumptions.

We begin by discussing the bivariate normal ML estimator and the Heckman two-step estimator. We also present coefficients produced by these estimators for our empirical example of a model for women's wages. Then we discuss concerns with the precision of these estimators and their sensitivity to distributional assumptions, and review alternatives that have been proposed. Finally, we present evidence from Monte Carlo simulations evaluating various estimators to understand better the robustness of estimators to departures from bivariate normality.

Maximum likelihood estimator

The ML estimator imposes the strongest statistical assumptions on the selection model. The typical assumption is that the error terms (ε_i, ν_i) follow a bivariate normal distribution, $N(0, \Sigma)$, where

$$\Sigma = \begin{pmatrix} \sigma_\varepsilon^2 & \sigma_{\varepsilon\nu} \\ \sigma_{\varepsilon\nu} & \sigma_\nu^2 \end{pmatrix}. \tag{18.8}$$

These distributional assumptions give the following log-likelihood function:

$$L = \sum_i \left\{ Y_{2i}^* \ln \left[\int_{-\infty}^{z_i\alpha} \phi(Y_{1i} - X_i\beta, \nu)d\nu \right] + (1-Y_{2i})^* \ln \left[\int_{z_i\alpha}^{\infty} \int_{-\infty}^{\infty} \phi(\varepsilon,\nu)d\varepsilon d\nu \right] \right\} \tag{18.9}$$

where ϕ is the bivariate normal probability density function. The first portion of the function is the likelihood of the observed values of Y_{1i} for the respondents. The second portion is the likelihood for respondents with missing Y_{1i}. This log-likelihood function can be maximized in the usual manner to produce coefficient estimates for both the selection equation and the outcome equation. Statistical packages such as Stata (Stata Corp, 2001) and LIMDEP (Greene, 1998) provide software for estimating this model. Like other ML estimates, these estimates are consistent and efficient if the model is specified correctly. However, if the distributional assumptions are not met, there is no guarantee that the estimated coefficients are consistent. In most applications of selection models, researchers do not have enough knowledge about the social process of interest to specify the correct error distribution.

The bivariate normal distribution is one of many possible specifications for the error terms. See Lee (1983) and Vella (1998) for a discussion of other parametric assumptions. Other work includes ML estimators of Gallant and Nychka (1987) and van der Klaauw and Koning (2003) that approximate the error distribution with a flexible parametric distribution that has the bivariate normal as a special case.

To illustrate the ML estimator for the standard sample selection model, we present an empirical example using a model for women's employment and wages. We use data on married, spouse-present women aged 25–59 from the 1990 US Census 5% Public Use Microdata Sample. Of the 1 984 591 women in the sample, 1 463 942 (74%) were employed. Employment is defined as having positive hours worked in 1989. The dependent variable is the natural logarithm of hourly wages in 1989. The first column of Table 18.1 presents the coefficients from an OLS regression of log hourly wages for the biased sample of employed women.

Estimates like these may arise in practice from the application of so-called 'two-part models' which model selection into the sample and the outcome separately (Duan et al., 1983; Leung and Yu, 1996). The age coefficients from our estimates show the familiar parabolic relationship between wages and age. Black, Hispanic, and Asian women have higher wage rates than white women controlling for age and education. And as expected, wages increase with education.

In the second column are ML estimates of coefficients from a standard selection model. The regressors in the employment (selection) equation are dummy variables for race and education, other household income in thousands of dollars (household income less respondent's earnings), number of persons in the household, respondent's school enrollment status, and presence of own children aged 0–5 in the household. The table only lists the coefficients for the wage equation. The age coefficients change by a negligible amount compared to the OLS estimates. However, the education coefficients change substantially, as shown graphically in Figure 18.1. The differences in the coefficients suggest that the sample of employed women is indeed a biased sample for the purpose of estimating the effects of education on wage rates for women. Further evidence for this is the large and highly significant estimate for ρ, the correlation between the error terms in the employment and wage equations. That the relationship between education and wages is steeper in the corrected estimates is consistent with the argument that women who earn higher wages are more likely to participate in the labor market. The biased sample contains an excess of less educated women with high earning power, artificially inflating expected wages at lower levels of schooling, resulting in a flatter relationship between education and wages in the OLS estimates. The coefficients corrected for sample selection bias account for the overrepresentation of these women in the sample and describe a steeper relationship between wages and education. The race coefficients also change once the correction for sample selection bias is applied.

Because we do not know if the true error distribution is bivariate normal, we cannot know for certain that these ML estimates are closer to the true population values than the OLS estimates. However, the changes in these estimates illustrate the effect that selection corrections can have.

Heckman's estimator

An estimator that does not depend so crucially on the assumption of bivariate normality is Heckman's two-step estimator. This estimator involves (a) estimation of the selection model (equations (18.5)–(18.6)); (b) calculating the expected error, $E[\varepsilon_i | v_i > -Z_i\alpha]$, for each observation using the estimated α; and (c) using the expected error as a regressor in equation (18.1). We can rewrite equation (18.7) as

$$Y_{1i} = X_i\beta + E(\varepsilon_i | v_i > -Z_i\alpha) + \eta_i. \quad (18.10)$$

If v_i is normally distributed with variance $\sigma_v^2 = 1$ and $E(\varepsilon_i | v_i)$ is linear in v_i then $E(\varepsilon_i | v_i) = \sigma_{\varepsilon v} v_i$ and

$$E(\varepsilon_i | v_i > -Z_i\alpha) = \frac{\sigma_{\varepsilon v} \, \phi(-Z_i\alpha)}{1 - \Phi(-Z_i\alpha)}$$
$$= \sigma_{\varepsilon v} \lambda(-Z_i\alpha), \quad (18.11)$$

where ϕ and Φ are the standard normal density and cumulative distribution functions, respectively, and $\sigma_{\varepsilon v}$ is the covariance between ε_i and v_i. The ratio $\lambda(-Z_i\alpha) = \phi(-Z_i\alpha)/[1 - \Phi(-Z_i\alpha)]$ is the inverse Mills ratio and is actually the hazard of not having an observed value for Y_{1i}. The inverse Mills ratio is a nonlinear transformation of the probit index and a decreasing function of the probability of selection. Substituting equation (18.11) into (18.10), we get

$$Y_{1i} = X_i\beta + \sigma_{\varepsilon v}\lambda(-Z_i\alpha) + \eta_i, \quad (18.12)$$

where η_i is uncorrelated with both X_i and $\lambda(-Z_i\alpha)$.

The assumption that ε_i and v_i follow a bivariate normal distribution is sufficient but not necessary to establish the conditions needed for this specification. Bivariate normality implies (a) a linear relationship between $E(\varepsilon_i | v_i)$ and v_i, and (b) a marginally normal error v_i which produces the inverse Mills ratio formula. However, other properties of the bivariate normal distribution are not used in arriving at equation (18.12). In particular, no assumptions are needed about the marginal distribution of ε_i or its higher moments. This contrasts with the ML method, which makes stronger assumptions.

Estimation of equation (18.12) by OLS gives consistent parameter estimates, but special formulas are needed to calculate correct standard errors because the errors, η_i, are heteroskedastic and not independent. More efficient estimates can also be obtained by generalized least squares (GLS) (Heckman, 1979; Maddala, 1983).

Table 18.1 *Coefficient estimates for determinants of women's wages*

Variable		OLS	MLE	Two-step	FE100	FE200	FE500	FE50	FE5
Age		0.0218	0.0226	0.0223	0.0207	0.0206	0.0216	0.0240	0.0269
		(0.0005)	(0.0005)	(0.0005)	(0.0005)	(0.0005)	(0.0005)	(0.0006)	(0.0006)
Age^2		-0.0002	-0.0002	-0.0002	-0.0002	-0.0002	-0.0002	-0.0002	-0.0003
		(0.0000)	(0.0000)	(0.0000)	(0.0000)	(0.0000)	(0.0000)	(0.0000)	(0.0000)
Race:	White (omitted)								
	Black	0.0643	0.0869	0.1046	0.1033	0.1036	0.1102	0.1185	0.1206
		(0.0022)	(0.0023)	(0.0024)	(0.0022)	(0.0022)	(0.0024)	(0.0027)	(0.0034)
	Hispanic	0.0269	0.0209	0.0171	0.0171	0.0170	0.0167	0.0213	0.0229
		(0.0024)	(0.0024)	(0.0025)	(0.0024)	(0.0024)	(0.0025)	(0.0028)	(0.0035)
	Asian	0.0661	0.0494	0.0365	0.0347	0.0348	0.0399	0.0461	0.0552
		(0.0032)	(0.0032)	(0.0034)	(0.0033)	(0.0033)	(0.0034)	(0.0036)	(0.0043)
	Other	-0.0612	-0.0676	-0.0718	-0.0743	-0.0742	-0.0686	-0.0596	-0.0526
		(0.0065)	(0.0066)	(0.0069)	(0.0067)	(0.0067)	(0.0068)	(0.0070)	(0.0083)
Education:	No HS (omitted)								
	Some HS	0.0785	0.1242	0.1601	0.1614	0.1614	0.1613	0.1697	0.1696
		(0.0037)	(0.0037)	(0.0039)	(0.0045)	(0.0045)	(0.0046)	(0.0052)	(0.0063)
	HS diploma	0.2236	0.3218	0.3987	0.3997	0.3996	0.4000	0.3987	0.3959
		(0.0034)	(0.0035)	(0.0040)	(0.0050)	(0.0050)	(0.0053)	(0.0058)	(0.0069)
	Some college	0.4130	0.5450	0.6490	0.6425	0.6424	0.6471	0.6464	0.6295
		(0.0034)	(0.0037)	(0.0045)	(0.0054)	(0.0054)	(0.0056)	(0.0062)	(0.0073)
	BA	0.7079	0.8518	0.9655	0.9582	0.9582	0.9575	0.9545	0.9300
		(0.0035)	(0.0039)	(0.0048)	(0.0056)	(0.0056)	(0.0059)	(0.0065)	(0.0076)
	Graduate degree	0.9674	1.1368	1.2698	1.2739	1.2744	1.2800	1.2786	1.2563
		(0.0038)	(0.0042)	(0.0053)	(0.0063)	(0.0063)	(0.0066)	(0.0073)	(0.0085)
Constant		1.1760	0.9273	0.7438					
		(0.0110)	(0.0113)	(0.0122)					
ρ			0.4037	0.6690					
			(0.0038)						
λ				0.4834					
				(0.0057)					
r^2		0.134							

Standard errors are in parentheses. Standard errors for the FE100, FE200, FE500, FE50, and FE5 estimates are Huber–White heteroskedasticity-consistent standard errors. All estimates are significant at the $p < 0.0001$ level. A total of 1 984 591 women are in the sample, of which 1 463 942 were employed.

The third column in Table 18.1 presents the wage equation coefficients produced by the Heckman two-step estimator for the model of women's wages and employment. Inserting the correction term into the wage equation has a sizable effect on the coefficients. The differences between these estimates and the OLS estimates are even more extreme than the differences between the ML and OLS estimates. As Figure 18.1 shows, the effect of education on wages is stronger for these estimates than for the ML estimates. Compared to the OLS estimates, the differences in the race effects are in the same directions and larger than the differences between the OLS estimates and the ML estimates. The coefficients for age are basically identical across the three estimators. The estimated standard errors tend to be larger for these estimates than for the OLS and ML estimates. The differences between these estimates and the ML estimates arise because of the differences in the assumptions underlying the two estimation techniques. We do not have a strong basis for preferring one selection model estimator over the other because it is not known if the data are consistent with either of the sets of assumptions underlying the two estimators.

According to equation (18.12), the coefficient for the inverse Mills ratio λ is $\sigma_{\varepsilon v}$, the covariance between the error terms for the selection and outcome equations. With the standard assumption for probit models that var$(v_i) = 1$, we have $\hat{\sigma}_{\varepsilon v} = \rho\sigma_{\varepsilon}$. Thus, under the assumption of bivariate normality the estimated coefficient for λ is the product of the correlation between ε and v, and the standard deviation of the error term for the outcome equation. The estimate for ρ is substantially larger for the two-step estimator than for the ML estimator. However, like the ML estimates, the two-step estimates provide strong evidence for the existence of selection bias. This is established by the test of the null hypothesis that the coefficient for λ is 0.

Robustness of Heckman's estimator

There has been substantial concern about the robustness of these parametric estimators for the sample selection model. These concerns have focused on the precision of the estimated coefficients in equation (18.12), and on violations of the assumptions about the error distributions.

The precision of the estimates in equation (18.12) is sensitive to collinearity between X and λ. Stolzenberg and Relles (1997) and Puhani (2000) observe that the inverse Mills ratio is an approximately linear function over a wide range of its argument. This can lead to a high degree of collinearity between X and $\lambda(-Z\alpha)$ because variables that affect the outcome often also affect selection. If X and Z are identical then the model is only identified because λ is nonlinear. Since it is seldom possible to justify the form of λ on substantive grounds, successful use of the method usually requires that at least one variable in Z be excluded from X. Even with this exclusion restriction, X and $\lambda(-Z\alpha)$ may still be highly collinear, leading to imprecise estimates. One consequence of this is that the two-step estimator may perform worse than OLS and the ML estimator when the regressors in the outcome and selection equations are highly correlated (Nawata, 1993, 1994). Furthermore, the exclusion restrictions impose a specific set of assumptions on predicted values (Little, 1985).

Collinearity between X and λ also depends on the effectiveness with which the probit equation at the first stage predicts which observations are selected into the sample. The probit model produces predicted probabilities close to 1 or 0 when it has extreme values for $-Z\alpha$. These extreme values for the argument of $\lambda(-Z\alpha)$ reduce the linearity of the relationship between λ and Z and allow for more precise estimates of the coefficients in equation (18.12). Leung and Yu (1996) present evidence from Monte Carlo studies demonstrating that a wide range of values for $-Z\alpha$ leads to more precise estimates of the coefficients in equation (18.12) even when Z and X are highly correlated. Leung and Yu explain that this accounts for the poor performance of Heckman's estimator compared to OLS documented in earlier simulation studies (Hay et al., 1987; Manning et al., 1987).

Researchers have also focused on the robustness of selection model estimators to violations of assumptions about the error distribution. The assumed bivariate normality of v_i and ε_i in the selection model establishes the two conditions necessary for Heckman's estimator. First, normality and homoskedasticity of v_i is needed for consistent and efficient estimation of α in the probit model. Second, the normality assumption implies a particular nonlinear relationship for the effect of $Z_i\alpha$ on Y_{1i} through λ. If the expectation of ε_i conditional on v_i is not linear and/or v_i is not normal, λ misspecifies the relationship between $\mathbf{Z}_i\alpha$ and Y_{1i} and the model may yield biased results.

Several studies have used simulations to investigate the bias in the single-equation tobit model when the error is not normally distributed. In a model with only an intercept – that is, a model for the mean of a censored distribution – when errors are not normally distributed, the normality assumption leads to substantial bias. This result holds even when the true distribution is close to the normal – for example, the logistic (Goldberger, 1983). When the normality assumption is wrong, moreover, ML estimates may be worse than simply using the observed sample mean. For samples that are 75% complete, bias from the normality assumption is minimal; in samples that are 50% complete, the bias is substantial in the truncated case, but not the censored; and in samples that are less than 50% complete, it is substantial in almost all cases (Arabmazar and Schmidt, 1982). Paarsch (1984) also finds that ML estimates and two-step estimates perform poorly when the errors follow a Cauchy distribution, although they do perform well when the errors follow a Laplace distribution.

Surprisingly little research has investigated the effect of nonbivariate normal errors on the behavior of parametric estimators for the standard selection model that assume bivariate normality. Zuehlke and Zeman (1991) find no consistent mean-square-error (MSE) advantage for the two-step estimates over OLS when the errors follow t or χ^2 distributions. Cosslett (1991) reports that the ML estimator produces biased estimates when the error distribution is a bivariate normal mixture distribution created from two pairs of bivariate normal random variables where one pair has much larger variances than the other.

Other research has shown that the Heckman estimator is not better than OLS in small samples. Stolzenberg and Relles (1990) find that the average absolute error for Heckman's estimator is the same as that for OLS with samples of size 500 and 90% censoring. Zuehlke and Zeman (1991) use samples of size 100 before selection and find that on average OLS estimates have smaller MSEs than Heckman estimates. Recent work has also focused on the theoretical properties of two-step estimators. Newey (1999a) identifies conditions under which a two-step estimator is consistent even when the error distribution is misspecified. Newey establishes this proof for a two-step estimator that uses

$\mathbf{Z}\alpha$ instead of the inverse Mills ratio, $\lambda(-\mathbf{Z}\alpha)$, as the correction term. However, little guidance is available regarding how often the conditions required for consistency hold.

Research on the behavior of Heckman's estimator has not produced a comprehensive understanding of its properties. Existing Monte Carlo studies are still unrealistic simulations of actual empirical models because they include only one or two regressors in each of the selection and outcome equations. Few models of interest contain so few regressors. However, existing Monte Carlo evidence and theoretical knowledge of the behavior of OLS regression estimates support the use of selection models when the sample is at least moderately large (500–1000), when exclusion restrictions can be imposed, and when the selection equation (18.5) effectively models selection into the sample. However, the lack of robustness to nonnormality of estimators for tobit models and the sensitivity of standard estimators to model specification have led to a substantial amount of research on estimators that relax statistical assumptions of the standard estimators.

Semiparametric extensions of Heckman's estimator

There are two main issues in estimating equation (18.12). First, is the equation that predicts selection into the sample consistently estimated? That is, are estimates of α, which derive from the selection equation, consistent? This depends on the assumptions that (a) the independent variables in that equation ($\mathbf{Z}_i$) have linear effects, and (b) the errors in the selection equation are normally distributed. Assumption (a) depends on the same considerations as any linear model as to whether interactions or other nonlinear transformations of the regressors should be included. Unfortunately, a strong substantive rationale for the regressors included in the selection equation is often unavailable. Likewise, assumption (b) in practice seldom rests on a firm substantive basis.

Second, what function should be chosen for λ, which dictates how the predicted probabilities of sample selection affect the dependent variable in equation (18.12)? When bivariate normality of the errors holds, λ is the inverse Mills ratio. When this assumption does not hold, inconsistent estimates may result. Moreover, since the regressors in the main and sample selection equation ($\mathbf{X}_i$ and $\mathbf{Z}_i$) are often highly collinear, estimates of β in (18.12) may be highly sensitive to misspecification of λ.

Much of the recent research on models for selection has focused on developing estimators that do not rely on these distributional and functional form assumptions. Many of the new estimators relax the assumptions of Heckman's two-step approach. At one extreme are nonparametric estimators that make assumptions about neither the error distribution nor the functional form of the relationship between the regressors and the outcome (Das et al., 2003). However, most of the new estimators are semiparametric estimators that make stronger assumptions than the nonparametric estimators. The approach of most of the new models is as follows.

First step: Estimation of the selection equation
The selection model, equations (18.5)–(18.6), is estimated using a semiparametric or nonparametric method for binary regression models. These methods include Manski's (1975, 1985) maximum score method, nonparametric ML estimation (Cosslett, 1983), weighted average derivatives (Stoker, 1986; Powell et al., 1989), kernel estimation (Bierens, 1987; Powell, 1987; Robinson, 1988; Ahn and Powell, 1993; Ichimura, 1993; Klein and Spady, 1993; Chen and Lee, 1998), spline methods and series approximations (Härdle, 1990; Andrews, 1991; Donald, 1995; Newey, 1999b). Two bases for evaluating these methods are: the trade-off that they make between efficiency and the strength of their prior assumptions; and their asymptotic distribution. Chamberlain (1986), Newey (1990), and Newey and Powell (1993) establish theoretical upper bounds for the efficiency of nonparametric methods under different sets of assumptions. Kernel methods (Ichimura, 1993; Klein and Spady, 1993) and variants of the weighted average derivatives (Stoker, 1991) reach these bounds, but other methods that make weaker assumptions, such as the method of scoring (Manski, 1975), do not. For still others, the efficiency is unknown (Cosslett, 1983). We discuss some of the assumptions made in alternative semiparametric and nonparametric approaches below. Asymptotic normality has been established for all these estimators except those of Manski and Cosslett. Unfortunately, procedures that implement these estimators are not available in statistical packages such as Stata (Stata Corp, 2001) or LIMDEP (Greene, 1998). The only exception is the procedure that implements Manski's maximum score estimator in LIMDEP.

Kernel estimation is one approach that has been frequently used for the first stage of selection models in empirical applications. This approach is as follows. Assume that we have multiple observations of Y_2 for each possible value of the vector Z_i. Let $g(Z)$ be the function for the conditional mean of Y_2 given Z. Then a nonparametric estimator of the conditional mean function is

$$\hat{g}(Z) = (1/n) \sum_i Y_{2i}, \quad \text{for all } Z_i = Z,$$

where n is the number of observations for which $Z_i = Z$. For example, if we were predicting whether individuals were employed or not (Y_{2i}) from their level of educational attainment (Z_i), our nonparametric estimate would simply be the proportion of persons who are employed at each level of educational attainment. This estimator makes no assumption about how Z enters g (e.g., that it is linear, making the model semiparametric), or about the distribution of the error v (which would make the model parametric). If data are grouped so that multiple values of Y_{2i} are known for each value of Z_i, this procedure is straightforward. If, however, Z_i varies continuously, so that there is at most one observation of Y_{2i} at each value of Z_i, kernel estimation is required.

The kernel method uses observations (Y_{2j}, Z_j) where Z_j is close to Z_i, to estimate the mean of Y_{2i}. We assume that g_i is continuous and calculate a weighted average of the Y_{2i} to estimate g_i, where observations that are close to Z_i are weighted more heavily than observations that are further away; that is, $\hat{g}_i = \sum_j K_{ij} Y_{2j} / \sum_j K_{ij}$, where $K_{ij} = K[(Z_i - Z_j)/h]$. Although many functions are possible for K, the choice of function does not usually affect the estimates. K is assumed to have a maximum at zero and to decrease as the absolute size of $Z_i - Z_j$ increases. The researcher selects h, known as the bandwidth of K, to control the smoothness of the estimator (Härdle, 1990). As the sample increases, h should gradually approach zero, which guarantees a consistent estimate of g_i.

Second step: Estimation of the outcome equation As in Heckman's method, the second stage is to estimate equation (18.12), using the estimates of α or g_i from the first stage. Several approaches are available to estimate (18.12) without parametrically specifying λ. One approach is to approximate λ through splines (Newey, 1999b), a series expansion (Newey, 1999b) based on a particular functional form, such as Edgeworth series (Lee, 1982), or Fourier series (Heckman and

Robb, 1985), or by step functions (Cosslett, 1991), with the number of terms gradually increasing with sample size. A second possibility is to use kernel methods and difference out λ (Robinson, 1988; Powell, 1987; Ahn and Powell, 1993). In this approach one differences out the nuisance function $\lambda(g_i)$ by estimating equation (18.12) across differences between pairs of observations:

$$Y_{1i} - Y_{1j} = (\mathbf{X}_i - \mathbf{X}_j)\,\boldsymbol{\beta} + [\lambda(g_i) - \lambda(g_j)]$$
$$+ \,\varepsilon_i - \varepsilon_j. \qquad (18.13)$$

If one only uses pairs for which the probability of selection is equal ($g_i = g_j$), then the terms in λ simply drop out of equation (18.13) and OLS can be used. If λ is continuous, for pairs i, j for which $g_i \approx g_j$, $\lambda(g_i) \approx \lambda(g_j)$, and $\lambda(g_i) - \lambda(g_j)$ will be near zero. Powell's procedure uses all pairs and weights more heavily pairs for which the difference $g_i - g_j$ is smaller. As the sample increases, more weight is placed on pairs for which $g_i \approx g_j$, thus guaranteeing consistency of the estimator. Powell's approach will only identify the effects of variables in $\mathbf{X}$ that vary across individuals with similar g. As a result, it is not possible to identify the intercept using his approach. Estimates of intercepts may be important, for example, when using selection models to evaluate social programs. Heckman (1990) and Andrews and Schafgans (1998) provide methods for estimating the intercept using observations that have a high probability of selection into the sample.

APPLICATIONS OF SEMIPARAMETRIC ESTIMATORS

Although many semiparametric estimators for selection models have been developed, these estimators are not commonly used in empirical applications. However, existing applications do provide some information about the effect of the assumptions of parametric estimators. Comparisons of parametric estimates with semiparametric estimates have typically shown that results can vary across estimators. Newey et al. (1990) and Ahn and Powell's (1993) results permit a comparison of estimates of a model for women's wages using (a) Heckman's two-step estimator, (b) weighted kernel estimates of the hours equation and probit estimates of the selection equation, (c) series expansion estimates of λ with probit estimates of the selection equation, and (d) weighted kernel estimates of both the hours and the selection equations. Newey et al. (1990) note that the weighted kernel and series expansion

results are generally similar to those from Heckman's method, although one can see that their standard errors are also typically slightly larger. Ahn and Powell (1993) report that several of their method (d) point estimates differ markedly from those of other methods and have much larger standard errors as well.

Schafgans' (1998, 2000) work on ethnic and gender differences in wages in Malaysia also provides an opportunity to compare semiparametric and parametric estimates. Schafgans estimates a model for wages and labor force participation and uses Ichimura's (1993) semiparametric kernel estimator to estimate coefficients for the selection equation. The second step, for the wage equation, is also a semiparametric kernel estimator (Robinson, 1988; Powell, 1987). Additionally, Schafgans uses the method of Andrews and Schafgans (1998) to estimate the intercept of the wage equation to carry out an Oaxaca (1973) wage decomposition. Schafgans compares the semiparametric estimates with ML and Heckman two-step estimates. The different estimation techniques produce different estimates for both the selection equation and the outcome equation. The differences are substantial enough to have important policy consequences. For example, the parametric estimators suggest that ethnic Malay men and women both suffer discrimination, whereas the semiparametric estimators provide only modest evidence that ethnic Malay men suffer discrimination and no evidence at all that ethnic Malay women suffer wage discrimination.

Martins (2001) uses parametric and semiparametric selection model estimators to investigate the wages and labor force participation of Portuguese women. She uses Klein and Spady's (1993) kernel estimator for the selection equation and Newey's (1999b) series estimator for the wage equation. She compares results from these estimators with OLS and ML estimates. The semiparametric estimators increase the magnitudes of the estimated coefficients and the coefficients reach levels of statistical significance attained by neither the ML nor the OLS estimates.

Grasdal (2001) analyzes data from a randomized experiment to determine how well selection model estimators correct the biases induced by sample attrition. The substantive aim is to determine the effectiveness of a rehabilitation program designed to bring long-term sick workers back to work. Data from surveys conducted before and after the randomly assigned treatment is applied to the treatment group are supplemented with administrative data for respondents lost in the second wave due to attrition. Grasdal uses a probit model and Manski's (1975) maximum score estimator to estimate coefficients for the selection equation for the probability that respondents present in the survey's first wave will appear in the survey's second wave. In the outcome model for post-treatment earnings, Grasdal uses three pairs of selection terms to produce semiparametric estimates of the coefficients in the outcome equation: the inverse Mills ratio and the linear probit index; the linear probit index and its square; and the index from the maximum score estimator and its square. Grasdal compares these estimates with Heckman two-step estimates, ML estimates, and the 'true' experimental estimate of the treatment effect. The experimental benchmark estimate of the treatment effect is not significantly different from zero and none of the selection estimators produces estimated treatment effects significantly different from zero. All of the selection model estimates except for the two-step estimate are within the 95% confidence interval of the experimental estimate.

We also produced our own set of semiparametric estimates for the model of women's wages and employment. The fourth through eighth columns of coefficients in Table 18.1 come from a selection model estimator that relies on a semiparametric 'fixed-effects' (FE) estimator for the outcome equation. For these estimates we used a probit model for the selection equation. For the outcome equation we grouped together observations with similar predicted probabilities of selection and used indicator variables for each group to approximate the selection correction term. This is equivalent to the method that Cosslett (1991) used in the second step of the estimator that he proposed. Instead of imposing a functional form such as the inverse Mills ratio on the selection correction term, this approach imposes no restrictions.

We used five procedures to define the groups for this estimator. The first two procedures used fixed-width probability intervals to define groups. The first procedure (FE100) used intervals of width 0.01 starting from 0 to create up to 100 groups. The second procedure (FE200) used intervals of width 0.005 starting from 0 to create up to 200 groups. The final three procedures defined groups based on the number of observations in each group. These procedures started with the list of observations sorted by their predicted probability of selection. The first of these methods (FE500) drew a group boundary after every 500th observation. This

gave groups of size 500, except for the final group, since the number of observations was not a multiple of 500. Similarly, we defined groups of size 50 (FE50) and 5 (FE5). Because of the heteroskedasticity in the error terms of these models, we report the Huber–White heteroskedasticity-consistent standard errors (Huber, 1967; White, 1980) for these models in Table 18.1.

Rosenbaum (1995), in writing about estimators for treatment effects, suggests that creating groups of fixed size is undesirable because doing so may group together observations with a wide range of probabilities of selection, especially for observations which have a low probability of being selected. However, consistency for Cosslett's two-step estimator requires that the number of groups increases with the number of observations.

The education coefficient estimates are very close to those of the two-step model. There are negligible differences among the FE estimates and all are very close to the two-step estimates. For the age effects, the coefficient for the linear term (0.0207 to 0.0269) becomes larger, whereas the coefficient for the squared term becomes more negative (−0.000 19 to −0.000 28) as the number of groups increases (FE100, FE200, FE500, FE50, FE5). The OLS, two-step, and ML estimates fall in the middle of the FE estimates. There is also variability among the different FE estimates of the race coefficients, with the effects generally becoming more positive as the number of groups increases. The FE estimates of the race coefficients are roughly in the same range as the other estimates.

The standard errors for the FE estimates increase as the number of groups increases. The standard errors of these estimates are also generally larger than those of the ML and two-step estimates. The differences are especially pronounced for the coefficients of the education variables. However, any differences in the standard errors are minor compared to the scale of the estimated coefficients.

For this example, the results from the Heckman two-step estimator are quite robust to the relaxation of assumptions about λ, although these results come from an exceptionally large sample. However, the other empirical applications discussed above suggest that coefficient estimates are often sensitive to the estimation techniques employed. The advantage of evaluating semiparametric estimators with empirical applications like these is that the estimators are applied to situations encountered in actual empirical research.

However, the drawback is that analysts do not know the true nature of the underlying error distribution, nor do they know the true values of the population parameters they are estimating. Thus, in order to provide evidence of a different sort, we carried out Monte Carlo simulations using a variety of error distributions to evaluate the sensitivity of estimators to departures from bivariate normality.

EVALUATING ESTIMATORS WITH
MONTE CARLO STUDIES

Much of the evidence for the sensitivity of selection model estimators to distributional assumptions comes from simulations and analyses of the single-equation tobit model (Arabmazar and Schmidt, 1981, 1982; Goldberger, 1983; Paarsch, 1984). The theoretical work proposing and discussing new estimators typically presents only brief comparisons of results from the new and old estimators (e.g., Cosslett, 1991). We briefly present here a more elaborate set of simulations using a variety of error distributions and a number of different estimators. The Appendix to this chapter provides a fuller description of how the simulations were carried out.

We simulated datasets for the following model of wages and labor force participation:

$$Y_{1i}^* = \beta_0 + X_{1i}\beta_1 + X_{2i}\beta_2 + \varepsilon_i, \quad (18.14)$$

$$Y_{2i}^* = \alpha_0 + Z_{1i}\alpha_1 + X_{2i}\alpha_2 + v_i, \quad (18.15)$$

where Y_{1i}^* is log hourly wages, X_{1i} is years of work experience, X_{2i} is years of schooling, Y_{2i}^* is hours worked, and Z_{1i} is a dummy variable for the presence of young children at home. Following equation (18.4), women's wages are observed if their hours worked are positive. The selection equation is estimated as a binary outcome, following equation (18.6). Each simulated dataset had 1000 observations. One hundred sets of regressors were generated and were used for each error distribution at each level of censoring. Datasets were subjected to three approximate levels of censoring (20%, 50%, and 80%). Eight different error terms were produced for the simulations: a distribution with beta-distributed marginals; a bivariate normal distribution; a distribution using normal random variables with a cubic relationship between the two error terms; a mixture distribution with each error term equal to the sum of two normal random variables with drastically different variances; a distribution based

on gamma random variables with a linear relationship between the two error terms; a distribution based on gamma random variables with a cubic relationship between the two error terms; a distribution with uniform marginals; and a distribution that substitutes t-distributed random variables into the formulas used to generate bivariate normal random variables. The correlations between pairs of errors ranged from 0.44 to 0.85.

To produce coefficient estimates from these simulated datasets we used OLS, ML, and Heckman two-step estimators, as well as most of the FE estimators used in the empirical example. For the FE estimators, we did not use groups of size 500 because our preselection sample size was only 1000.

Space considerations preclude a detailed description of the findings. We focus this discussion on the coefficient for education in the wage equation. Education is present in both the wage and the selection equations and thus its estimates are most sensitive to model specification. Table 18.2 presents the education coefficient's mean estimate and root mean square error (RMSE) for each error distribution and estimator. The true value of the coefficient is 0.100.

In these simulations both the parametric ML and two-step estimators are relatively robust to distributional misspecification, with the ML estimator having a slight advantage. We focus first on the RMSE because it reflects both bias and variability. These two parametric estimators consistently perform better than the FE estimators by the RMSE criterion. The parametric estimators usually have smaller RMSEs than the FE estimators which impose weaker statistical assumptions. Of the 96 (4 estimators × 8 error distributions × 3 censoring levels) FE RMSEs, only 9 are smaller than the RMSEs for either the ML or two-step estimator. The RMSEs for the ML estimator are smaller than the RMSEs for the two-step estimator in all but four instances, although the differences are usually small.

It is useful to compare the performance of these two parametric estimators under bivariate normality to their performance when the error distribution is not bivariate normal. The RMSEs for the two estimators at 20% censoring range from 0.004 to 0.013 for the eight error distributions, with the RMSEs for bivariate normal errors falling in the bottom third of this range. At 50% censoring, the RMSEs for these two estimators range from 0.010 to 0.030, with the RMSEs for bivariate normal errors falling in the bottom quarter of this range. At 80% censoring,

Table 18.2 Estimates of education effect on wages

Error distribution	Mean estimate							RMSE						
	OLS	2-step	MLE	FE100	FE200	FE50	FES	OLS	2-step	MLE	FE100	FE200	FE50	FES
Approximately 20% censoring														
Beta	0.089	0.098	0.100	0.100	0.101	0.100	0.101	0.012	0.006	0.006	0.012	0.013	0.014	0.016
Bivariate normal	0.080	0.100	0.100	0.100	0.101	0.098	0.101	0.020	0.007	0.005	0.012	0.013	0.018	0.022
Cubic bivar. normal	0.076	0.103	0.100	0.100	0.101	0.092	0.100	0.024	0.007	0.005	0.013	0.014	0.019	0.021
Bivar. norm. var. mix.	0.065	0.099	0.099	0.098	0.098	0.093	0.101	0.036	0.011	0.009	0.017	0.020	0.029	0.039
Gamma	0.097	0.099	0.098	0.099	0.099	0.099	0.099	0.006	0.006	0.006	0.006	0.006	0.006	0.007
Cubic gamma	0.086	0.104	0.101	0.101	0.101	0.096	0.100	0.015	0.007	0.006	0.009	0.009	0.010	0.010
t distribution	0.063	0.100	0.101	0.100	0.099	0.088	0.098	0.038	0.013	0.009	0.019	0.021	0.034	0.038
Uniform	0.088	0.099	0.099	0.101	0.101	0.099	0.100	0.013	0.005	0.004	0.009	0.009	0.010	0.011
Approximately 50% censoring														
Beta	0.075	0.095	0.100	0.103	0.104	0.101	0.106	0.027	0.015	0.014	0.020	0.022	0.022	0.025
Bivariate normal	0.055	0.101	0.100	0.100	0.102	0.082	0.098	0.046	0.014	0.012	0.022	0.026	0.028	0.025
Cubic bivar. normal	0.037	0.106	0.098	0.101	0.102	0.062	0.101	0.064	0.016	0.010	0.026	0.028	0.043	0.028
Bivar. norm. var. mix.	0.027	0.099	0.099	0.098	0.100	0.069	0.100	0.073	0.026	0.017	0.044	0.047	0.044	0.047
Gamma	0.094	0.101	0.098	0.100	0.100	0.099	0.099	0.013	0.013	0.012	0.012	0.012	0.012	0.015
Cubic gamma	0.028	0.121	0.098	0.105	0.105	0.015	0.106	0.073	0.026	0.014	0.021	0.023	0.090	0.033
t distribution	0.022	0.103	0.100	0.098	0.101	0.066	0.099	0.079	0.030	0.021	0.046	0.048	0.052	0.047
Uniform	0.073	0.099	0.100	0.100	0.101	0.093	0.099	0.028	0.010	0.009	0.019	0.021	0.023	0.024
Approximately 80% censoring														
Beta	0.046	0.096	0.098	0.102	0.100	0.093	0.099	0.061	0.044	0.054	0.067	0.079	0.043	0.052
Bivariate normal	0.005	0.103	0.101	0.106	0.108	0.058	0.099	0.098	0.043	0.034	0.058	0.073	0.058	0.048
Cubic bivar. normal	-0.041	0.086	0.079	0.091	0.089	0.014	0.084	0.142	0.041	0.031	0.050	0.062	0.090	0.042
Bivar. norm. var. mix.	-0.022	0.108	0.099	0.106	0.110	0.038	0.099	0.124	0.066	0.047	0.080	0.097	0.078	0.069
Gamma	0.079	0.102	0.094	0.105	0.105	0.095	0.106	0.042	0.038	0.039	0.045	0.047	0.043	0.050
Cubic gamma	-0.113	0.067	0.100	0.090	0.096	-0.050	0.086	0.213	0.058	0.048	0.053	0.058	0.153	0.053
t distribution	-0.037	0.103	0.102	0.102	0.110	0.015	0.089	0.140	0.066	0.056	0.087	0.112	0.101	0.081
Uniform	0.025	0.096	0.097	0.102	0.109	0.075	0.095	0.079	0.039	0.032	0.049	0.063	0.045	0.043

The true value of the coefficient is 0.100.

the RMSEs range from 0.031 to 0.066, with the RMSEs for bivariate normal errors falling in the bottom third of this range. By the RMSE criterion, distributional misspecification hurts the performance of these two parametric estimators. However, these two parametric estimators still perform better than the FE estimators we considered here.

One might expect the FE estimators to have larger RMSEs but be less biased than the parametric estimators because the FE models involve more parameters but impose weaker assumptions. However, the parametric estimators actually perform better than the FE estimators with respect to bias. The mean of the estimates for these two estimators is never more than 0.05 from the true value at 20% censoring. At 50% censoring, there are two instances where the bias is greater than 0.05. At 80% censoring there are five such instances. The FE estimators also show a pattern of increasing bias at higher levels of censoring. At 20% censoring, the FE estimators have three instances where the bias is greater than 0.05. At 50% censoring there are eight such instances. At 80% censoring, each FE estimator has a bias greater than 0.05 for at least half of the error distributions. The FE50 estimator performs particularly poorly with respect to bias – in 16 of the 24 cells (3 censoring levels × 8 error distributions) the bias is greater than 0.05. The bias of the other three FE estimators is similar, with the total number of cells across the different levels of censoring where the bias is greater than 0.05 ranging from four to six for each estimator.

These simulations can also be used to compare the performance of models that account for selection bias with OLS estimates using only the selected sample. In these simulations all six selection estimators clearly are an improvement over OLS. The two parametric estimators have RMSEs that are always smaller than or equal to those for OLS. Most of the time, the RMSEs of the parametric estimators are less than half of the RMSE for the corresponding OLS estimates. The FE estimators also perform better than OLS, having smaller RMSEs in 77 of the 96 cells. With respect to bias, the OLS estimates perform poorly compared to the selection estimators at all levels of censoring. In only one cell was the mean of the estimates within 0.05 of the true value. In the 23 remaining cells, the mean of the estimates ranged from –0.113 to 0.094, or 6% to 213% less than the true value.

The strong performance of the two parametric estimators is quite surprising given concerns about the performance of these

estimators when the error distribution is not bivariate normal. The ML estimator, which has the strongest parametric assumptions, actually performs best by both the RMSE and bias criteria. These patterns are largely consistent at the different levels of censoring and for the different error distributions. However, it is important to note that all of the regression equations we estimated were correctly specified. Thus, these simulations do not reveal how misspecification of the regression equations affects coefficient estimates. It is also possible that the parametric estimators would perform worse with smaller samples or with proportions censored greater than 0.8. In any case, these results are consistent with Vella's (1998: 144) observation that there is 'a growing feeling that the parametric procedures perform well if the conditional mean of the model is correctly specified'. These findings are also consistent in tenor with Newey's (1999a) finding that under some conditions, coefficient estimates from a two-step model with a linear correction term are consistent even when the error distribution is misspecified.

MANSKI'S BOUND APPROACH

Although semi- and nonparametric methods are conservative, they are not free of assumptions. For example, λ is usually assumed to enter equation (18.12) additively. Without such assumptions it is often impossible even to put a bound on the conditional mean of Y_1 given $\mathbf{X}$, the usual quantity estimated in regression analysis, much less obtain a consistent point estimate. In an important set of papers Manski (1989, 1990, 1994, 1995; Horowitz and Manski, 1998, 2000) shows the overwhelming role that assumptions play in producing estimates from selection models. Without prior assumptions about the selection process, it is impossible to obtain point estimates of the true regression model when selection occurs. Under some conditions, however, it is possible to place bounds on the expected value of the dependent variable in the absence of assumptions about the selection process. A regression model can be written as

$$E(Y_1|\mathbf{X}) = E(Y_1|\mathbf{X}, Y_2 = 1)\,P(Y_2 = 1)$$
$$+ E(Y_1|\mathbf{X}, Y_2 = 0)\,P(Y_2 = 0), \quad (18.16)$$

where all of the notation is defined as above. All of the components in equation (18.16) can be estimated from observed data except

$E(Y_1|X, Y_2 = 0)$, the expected value of Y_1 given X for cases that are not in the selected sample. Unless one can put bounds on this value, sample data provide no information about the true regression of Y_1 on X. Manski derives bounds for $E(Y_1|X)$ when Y_1 is dichotomous and for conditional *medians* when Y_1 is continuous (Manski 1989, 1990, 1994, 1995). All else being equal, the tightness of the bound varies inversely with the proportion of cases in the sample with unobserved outcomes. Beresteanu and Manski (2000a, 2000b) provide computer programs for doing this type of analysis. Horowitz and Manski (1998) discuss how estimates based on weights and imputation relate to bounds. Although narrow bounds can be informative, wide bounds suggest that point estimates are largely a consequence of untestable identifying assumptions (Horowitz and Manski, 2000).

CONCLUSION

Despite the significant recent advances in research on selection models, our general recommendation about the use of selection models is little changed from Winship and Mare's (1992) recommendations. Infallible models for sample selection bias do not exist. Holes still exist in our knowledge of the empirical behavior of the maximum likelihood and Heckman two-step estimators for the standard selection model. There is room for improvement in our theoretical knowledge about the behavior of these models as well. Available empirical applications of semiparametric selection model estimators have shown that results are sensitive to the estimation method used, whereas our Monte Carlo simulations emphasize the robustness of the traditional ML and two-step estimators. When selection is an issue, therefore, empirical results are likely to remain ambiguous (Manski, 1989). What should the researcher do? Because one's results may depend on the method used, researchers should be explicit about the assumptions behind their methods and explore the robustness of their substantive conclusions across a variety of methods used to correct for selection bias. Manski et al. (1992) exemplify this approach in their analysis of the effects of family structure on the likelihood of dropping out of high school, which includes parametric and nonparametric models, and an analysis of bounds. Unfortunately, analyses of this type are difficult to undertake because of the lack of readily available software to compute estimates using many of the new semiparametric estimators.

APPENDIX

This Appendix provides a more complete description of how the datasets used in the Monte Carlo simulations were created. We simulated datasets for the following model of women's wages and labor force participation:

$$Y_{1i}^* = 0.2 + 0.02X_{1i} + 0.1X_{2i} + \varepsilon_i,$$

$$Y_{2i}^* = \alpha_0 - 10Z_{1i} + 4X_{2i} + v_i,$$

where Y_1^* is log hourly wages and Y_2^* is hours worked. Y_1^* depends on years of work experience X_1 and years of schooling X_2. Y_2^* depends on the presence of young children in the home (measured by the dummy variable Z_1) and years of schooling X_2. Women's wages are unobserved if hours worked is negative. The constant in the hours equation, α_0, varies depending on the desired level of censoring. The selection equation is estimated as a binary outcome using a probit model. ε and v are the error terms for the log wage and hours equations, respectively.

Each simulated dataset contained 1000 observations. Stata 7.0's random number generator (Stata Corp, 2001), using a seed of 2818, produced values for the regressors. Values for years of work experience were uniformly distributed between 0 and 35. Values for years of schooling were uniformly distributed between 0 and 20. Presence of young children at home was an indicator variable with half the values randomly chosen to be 1 and the other half 0.

One hundred datasets of explanatory variables were produced. These hundred datasets were used for each combination of the three levels of censoring and eight types of error terms. Datasets were subjected to three approximate levels of censoring (20%, 50%, and 80%). Eight different types of error terms were produced for the simulations using Stata's random number generator. Table 18.3 describes the error terms.

Table 18.3   *Error terms for simulations*

Error distribution	Description
Beta	$\varepsilon = 2\beta_1 - 1$ $v = 20\beta_2 - 10$ $\beta_1 \sim$ Beta(0.5, 0.4) $= \eta_1/(\eta_1 + \eta_2)$ $\beta_2 \sim$ Beta(0.5, 0.6) $= \eta_1/(\eta_1 + \eta_3)$ $\eta_1 \sim \chi_1^2$ $\eta_2 \sim \chi_{0.8}^2$ $\eta_3 \sim \chi_{1.2}^2$ The beta-distributed error terms simulated here both have U-shaped distributions. A beta random variable can be generated from pairs of independent chi-square random variables (Johnson and Kotz, 1970: 38). To induce correlation between two beta random variables, we generated two beta random variables from *three* chi-square random variables. The beta random variables were then rescaled. The observed correlation was 0.45.
Bivariate normal	$(\varepsilon, v) \sim N(0,0;\ \sigma_\varepsilon = 0.7,\ \sigma_v = 9,\ \rho = 0.7)$ The observed correlation was 0.70.
Cubic bivariate normal	$\varepsilon \sim N(0, \sigma_1 = 0.7)$ $v = 9\varepsilon + 3.5\varepsilon^2 + 2.5\varepsilon^3 + 0.51N(0, 81) - 3.5\sigma_1^2$ An assumption of Heckman's estimator is that there is a linear relationship between the two error terms. In order to investigate the possible consequences of violating this assumption, the error term for the wage equation is a normal random variable, whereas the error term for the hours equation is a cubic function of the first error term plus an additional normal random component. The observed correlation was 0.85.
Bivariate normal variance mixture	$\varepsilon = 0.75\eta_{11} + 0.25\eta_{12}$ $v = 0.75\eta_{21} + 0.25\eta_{22}$ $(\eta_{11}, \eta_{21}) \sim N(0,0;\ \sigma_{11} = 0.7,\ \sigma_{12} = 9,\ \rho_1 = 0.7)$ $(\eta_{12}, \eta_{22}) \sim N(0,0;\ \sigma_{21} = 3.5,\ \sigma_{22} = 45,\ \rho_2 = 0.7)$ Each error term is the sum of two normal random variables with drastically different variances. The observed correlation was 0.70. Results from this pair of error terms demonstrate consequences of one form of a violation of the homoskedasticity assumption.
Gamma	$\varepsilon \sim$ Gamma(1,0.5) $v \sim$ Gamma(1,1) $+ 0.7\varepsilon$ Both of these error terms have severely skewed distributions. The observed correlation was 0.44.
Cubic gamma	$\varepsilon =$ Gamma(1,0.5) $v =$ Gamma(1,1) $+ 0.7\varepsilon + 2.5\varepsilon^2 + 1.5\varepsilon^3$ The observed correlation was 0.77. Results from these error terms demonstrate consequences of one form of violation of the assumption that the error terms are linearly related.
Uniform	$\varepsilon \sim$ Uniform(−1,1) $v \sim$ Uniform(−10,10) The observed correlation was 0.68. The two random variables were constructed from the univariate cumulative distribution functions of a pair of bivariate normal random variables with correlation 0.70.
t distribution	$\varepsilon \sim t_{10}$ $v = 8.4\varepsilon + 8.57t_{10}$ The formulas for generating bivariate normal random variables were used to generate pairs of random variables based on the t distribution. The observed correlation was 0.70.

REFERENCES

Ahn, H. and Powell, J. (1993) 'Semiparametric estimation of censored selection models with a nonparametric selection mechanism', *Journal of Econometrics*, 58: 3–29.

Amemiya, T. (1985) *Advanced Econometrics*. Cambridge, MA: Harvard University Press.

Andrews, D. (1991) 'Asymptotic normality of series estimators for nonparametric and semiparametric regression models', *Econometrica*, 59: 307–45.

Andrews, D. and Schafgans, M. (1998) 'Semiparametric estimation of the intercept of a sample selection model', *Review of Economic Studies*, 65: 497–517.

Arabmazar, A. and Schmidt, P. (1981) 'Further evidence on the robustness of the tobit estimator to heteroskedasticity', *Journal of Econometrics*, 17: 253–8.

Arabmazar, A. and Schmidt, P. (1982) 'An investigation of the robustness of the tobit estimator to non-normality', *Econometrica*, 50: 1055–63.

Beresteanu, A. and Manski, C. (2000a) *Bounds for Matlab*. Department of Economics, Northwestern University, Evanston, IL (http://www.faculty.econ.northwestern.edu/faculty/manski/bounds_matlab.pdf).

Beresteanu, A. and Manski, C. (2000b) *Bounds for Stata*. Department of Economics, Northwestern University, Evanston, IL (http://www.faculty.econ.northwestern.edu/faculty/manski/bounds_stata.pdf).

Berk, R. (1983) 'An introduction to sample selection bias in sociological data', *American Sociological Review*, 48: 386–98.

Bierens, H. (1987) 'Kernel estimators of regression functions', in T. Bewley (ed.), *Advances in Econometrics Fifth World Congress 1985, Volume 1*. New York: Cambridge University Press, pp. 99–144.

Chamberlain, G. (1986) 'Asymptotic efficiency in semi-parametric models with censoring', *Journal of Econometrics*, 32: 189–218.

Chen, S. and Lee, L. (1998) 'Efficient semiparametric scoring estimation of sample selection models', *Econometric Theory*, 14: 423–62.

Cosslett, S. (1983) 'Distribution-free maximum likelihood estimator of the binary choice model', *Econometrica*, 51: 765–82.

Cosslett, S. (1991) 'Semiparametric estimation of a regression model with sample selectivity', in W. Barnett, J. Powell and G. Tauchen (eds), *Nonparametric and Semiparametric Methods in Econometrics and Statistics: Proceedings of the Fifth International Symposium in Economic Theory and Econometrics*. New York: Cambridge University Press, pp. 175–97.

Das, M., Newey, W. and Vella, F. (2003) 'Nonparametric estimation of sample selection models', *Review of Economic Studies*, 70: 33–58.

Donald, S. (1995) 'Two-step estimation of heteroskedastic sample selection models', *Journal of Econometrics*, 65: 347–80.

Duan, N., Manning, W., Morris, C. and Newhouse, J. (1983) 'A comparison of alternative models for the demand for health care', *Journal of Business and Economic Statistics*, 1: 115–26.

Dubin, J. and Rivers, D. (1989) 'Selection bias in linear regression, logit and probit models', *Sociological Methods and Research*, 18: 360–90.

DuMouchel, W. and Duncan, G. (1983) 'Using sample survey weights in multiple regression analyses of stratified samples', *Journal of the American Statistical Association*, 78: 535–43.

Gallant, A.R. and Nychka, D.W. (1987) 'Semi-nonparametric maximum likelihood estimation', *Econometrica*, 55: 363–90.

Goldberger, A. (1981) 'Linear regression after selection', *Journal of Econometrics*, 15: 357–66.

Goldberger, A. (1983) 'Abnormal selection bias' in S. Karlin, T. Amemiya, and L. Goodman (eds), *Studies in Econometrics, Time Series, and Multivariate Statistics*. New York: Academic Press, pp. 67–84.

Grasdal, A. (2001) 'The performance of sample selection estimators to control for attrition bias', *Health Economics*, 10: 385–98.

Greene, W. (1998) *LIMDEP Version 7.00 User's Manual* (revised edition). Plainview, NY: Econometric Software.

Gronau, R. (1974) 'Wage comparisons – selectivity bias', *Journal of Political Economy*, 82: 1119–43.

Han, S. and Moen, P. (1999) 'Clocking out: Temporal patterning of retirement', *American Journal of Sociology*, 105: 191–236.

Härdle, W. (1990) *Applied Nonparametric Regression*. New York: Cambridge University Press.

Hausman, J. and Wise, D. (1976) 'The evaluation of results from truncated samples: The New Jersey income maintenance experiment', *Annals of Economic and Social Measurement*, 5(4): 421–45.

Hausman, J. and Wise, D. (1977) 'Social experimentation, truncated distributions, and efficient estimation', *Econometrica*, 45: 919–38.

Hay, J., Leu, R. and Rohrer, P. (1987) 'Ordinary least squares and sample-selection models of health-care demand', *Journal of Business and Economic Statistics*, 5: 499–506.

Heckman, J. (1974) 'Shadow prices, market wages and labor supply', *Econometrica*, 42: 679–94.

Heckman, J. (1976) 'The common structure of statistical models of truncation, sample selection and limited dependent variables and a simple estimator for such models', *Annals of Economic and Social Measurement*, 5: 475–92.

Heckman, J. (1979) 'Sample selection bias as specification error', *Econometrica*, 47: 153–61.

Heckman, J. (1987) 'Selection bias and self-selection', in J. Eatwell, M. Milgate and P. Newmann (eds), *The New Palgrave*. New York: Stockton, pp. 287–97.

Heckman, J. (1990) 'Varieties of selection bias', *American Economic Review*, 80(2): 313–18.

Heckman, J. and Robb, R. (1985) 'Alternative methods for evaluating the impact of interventions', in J. Heckman and B. Singer (eds), *Longitudinal Analysis of Labor Market Data*. New York: Cambridge University Press, pp. 156–245.

Heckman, J. and Robb, R. (1986a) 'Alternative methods for solving the problem of selection bias in evaluating the impact of treatments on outcomes', in H. Wainer (ed.), *Drawing Inferences from Self-Selected Samples*. New York: Springer-Verlag, pp. 63–107.

Heckman, J. and Robb, R. (1986b) 'Alternative identifying assumptions in econometric models of selection bias', *Advances in Econometrics*, 5: 243–87.

Hoffman, P. (1984) 'Wills and statistics: Tobit analysis and the counter reformation in Lyon', *Journal of Interdisciplinary History*, 14: 813–34.

Horowitz, J. and Manski, C. (1998) 'Censoring of outcomes and regressors due to survey nonresponse: Identification and estimation using weights and imputations', *Journal of Econometrics*, 84: 37–58.

Horowitz, J. and Manski, C. (2000) 'Nonparametric analysis of randomized experiments with missing covariate and outcome data' (with discussion) *Journal of the American Statistical Association*, 95: 77–88.

Huber, P. (1967) 'The behavior of maximum likelihood estimates under non-standard conditions', in L. LeCam and J. Nyman (eds), *Proceedings of the Fifth Berkeley Symposium on Mathematical Statistics and Probability*. Berkeley: University of California Press, pp. 221–33.

Iannaccone, X. (1994) 'Why strict churches are strong', *American Journal of Sociology*, 99: 1180–211.

Ichimura, H. (1993) 'Semiparametric least squares estimation of single index models', *Journal of Econometrics*, 58: 71–120.

Jacobs, D. and O'Brien, R. (1998) 'The determinants of deadly force: A structural analysis of police violence', *American Journal of Sociology*, 103: 837–62.

Johnson, N. and Kotz, S. (1970) *Distributions in Statistics: Continuous Univariate Statistics – 2*. New York: Wiley.

Kalbfleisch, J. and Prentice, R. (1980) *The Statistical Analysis of Failure Time Data*. New York: Wiley.

Klein, R. and Spady, R. (1993) 'An efficient semiparametric estimator for binary response models', *Econometrica*, 61:387–421.

Lancaster, T. (1990) *The Econometric Analysis of Transition Data*. New York: Cambridge University Press.

Lee, L. (1982) 'Some approaches to the correction of selectivity bias', *Review of Economic Studies*, 49: 355–72.

Lee, L. (1983) 'Generalized econometric models with selectivity', *Econometrica*, 51: 507–12.

Lee, M. and Melenberg, B. (1998) 'Bounding quantiles in sample selection models', *Economics Letters*, 61: 29–35.

Leung, S. and Yu, S. (1996) 'On the choice between sample selection and two-part models', *Journal of Econometrics*, 72: 192–229.

Little, R. (1985) 'A note about models for selectivity bias', *Econometrica*, 53: 1469–74.

Little, R. and Rubin, D. (1987) *Statistical Analysis with Missing Data*. New York: Wiley.

Maddala, G. (1983) *Limited-Dependent and Qualitative Variables in Econometrics*. New York: Cambridge University Press.

Manning, W., Duan, N. and Rogers, W. (1987) 'Monte Carlo evidence on the choice between sample selection and two-part models', *Journal of Econometrics*, 35: 59–82.

Manski, C. (1975) 'Maximum score estimation of the stochastic utility model of choice', *Journal of Econometrics*, 3: 205–28.

Manski, C. (1985) 'Semiparametric analysis of discrete response: Asymptotic properties of the maximum score estimator', *Journal of Econometrics*, 27: 313–33.

Manski, C. (1989) 'Anatomy of the selection problem', *Journal of Human Resources*, 24: 343–60.

Manski, C. (1990) 'Nonparametric bounds on treatment effects', *American Economic Review*, 80: 319–23.

Manski, C. (1994) 'The selection problem', in C. Sims (ed.), *Advances in Econometrics, Sixth World Congress*. New York: Cambridge University Press, pp. 143–70.

Manski, C. (1995) *Identification Problems in the Social Sciences*. Cambridge, MA: Harvard University Press.

Manski, C., McLanahan, S., Powers, D. and Sandefeur, G. (1992) 'Alternative estimates of the effects of family structure during adolescence on high school graduation', *Journal of the American Statistical Association*, 87: 25–37.

Mare, R. and Chen, M. (1986) 'Further evidence on number of siblings and educational stratification', *American Sociological Review*, 51: 403–12.

Mare, R. and Winship, C. (1984) 'The paradox of lessening racial inequality and joblessness among black youth: Enrollment, enlistment, and employment, 1964–1981', *American Sociological Review*, 49: 39–55.

Mare, R. and Winship, C. (1988) 'Endogenous switching regression models for the causes and effects of discrete variables', in J.S. Long (ed.), *Common Problems/ Proper Solutions: Avoiding Error in Quantitative Research*. Newbury Park, CA: Sage, pp. 132–60.

Martins, M. (2001) 'Parametric and semiparametric estimation of sample selection models: An empirical application to the female labour force in Portugal', *Journal of Applied Econometrics*, 16: 23–39.

Morgan, L. (1998) 'Glass-ceiling effect or cohort effect? A longitudinal study of the gender earnings gap for engineers, 1982 to 1989', *American Sociological Review*, 63: 479–93.

Nawata, K. (1993) 'A note on the estimation of models with sample-selection biases', *Economics Letters*, 42: 15–24.

Nawata, K. (1994) 'Estimation of sample selection bias models by the maximum likelihood estimator and Heckman's two-step estimator', *Economics Letters*, 45: 33–40.

Nelson, F. (1984) 'Efficiency of the two-step estimator for models with endogenous sample selection', *Journal of Econometrics*, 24: 181–96.

Newey, W. (1990) 'Efficient estimation of semiparametric models via moment restrictions', Department of Economics, Massachusetts Institute of Technology, Cambridge, MA.

Newey, W. (1999a) 'Consistency of two-step sample selection estimators despite misspecification of distribution', *Economics Letters*, 63: 129–32.

Newey, W. (1999b) 'Two-step series estimation of sample selection models'. Working Paper 99–04, Department of Economics. Massachusetts Institute of Technology, Cambridge, MA.

Newey, W. and Powell, J. (1993) 'Efficiency bounds for some semiparametric selection models', *Journal of Econometrics*, 58: 169–84.

Newey, W., Powell, J. and Walker, J. (1990) 'Semiparametric estimation of selection models: Some empirical results', *American Economic Review*, 80: 324–8.

Oaxaca, R. (1973) 'Male–female wage differentials in urban labor markets', *International Economic Review*, 14: 693–709.

Olsen, R. (1980) 'A least squares correction for selectivity bias', *Econometrica*, 48: 1815–20.

Paarsch, H. (1984) 'A Monte Carlo comparison of estimators for censored regression models', *Journal of Econometrics*, 24: 197–213.

Pagan, A. and Ullah, A. (1999) *Nonparametric Econometrics*. New York: Cambridge University Press.

Peterson, E. and Hagan, J. (1984) 'Changing conceptions of race: Towards an account of anomalous findings of sentencing research', *American Sociological Review*, 49: 56–70.

Powell, J. (1987) 'Semiparametric estimation of bivariate latent variable models'. Working Paper no. 8704, University of Wisconsin Social Systems Research Institute, Madison.

Powell, J., Stock, J. and Stoker, T. (1989) 'Semiparametric estimation of index coefficients', *Econometrica*, 57: 1403–30.

Puhani, P. (2000) 'The Heckman correction for sample selection and its critique', *Journal of Economic Surveys*, 14: 53–68.

Robinson, P. (1988) 'Root-N-consistent semiparametric regression', *Econometrica*, 56: 931–54.

Rosenbaum, P. (1995) *Observational Studies*. New York: Springer-Verlag.

Rosenbaum, P. and Rubin, D. (1983) 'The central role of the propensity score in observational studies for causal effects', *Biometrika*, 70: 41–55.

Schafgans, M. (1998) 'Ethnic wage differentials in Malaysia: Parametric and semiparametric estimation of the Chinese–Malay wage gap', *Journal of Applied Econometrics*, 13: 481–504.

Schafgans, M. (2000) 'Gender wage differences in Malaysia: Parametric and semiparametric estimation', *Journal of Development Economics*, 63: 351–78.

Seltzer, J. (1991) 'Legal custody arrangements and children's economic welfare', *American Journal of Sociology*, 96: 895–929.

Seltzer, J. and Garfinkel, I. (1990) 'Inequality in divorce settlements: An investigation of property settlements and child support awards', *Social Science Research*, 19: 82–111.

Stata Corp. (2001) *Stata Statistical Software: Release 7.0*. College Station, TX: Stata Corporation.

Steelman, L. and Powell, B. (1989) 'Acquiring capital for college: The constraints of family configuration', *American Sociological Review*, 54: 844–55.

Steffensmeier, D. and Demuth, S. (2000) 'Ethnicity and sentencing outcomes in U.S. federal courts: Who is punished more harshly?' *American Sociological Review*, 65: 705–29.

Stoker, T. (1986) 'Consistent estimates of scaled coefficients', *Econometrica*, 54: 1461–81.

Stoker, T. (1991) 'Equivalence of direct, indirect, and slope estimators of average derivatives', in W. Barnett, J. Powell, and G. Tauchen (eds), *Nonparametric and Semiparametric Methods in Econometrics and Statistics: Proceedings of the Fifth International Symposium in Economic Theory and Econometrics*. New York: Cambridge University Press, pp. 99-118.

Stolzenberg, R. and Relles, D. (1990) 'Theory testing in a world of constrained research design: The significance of Heckman's censored sampling bias correction for nonexperimental research', *Sociological Methods and Research*, 18: 395–415.

Stolzenberg, R. and Relles, D. (1997) 'Tools for intuition about sample selection bias and its correction', *American Sociological Review*, 62: 494–507.

Tobin, J. (1958) 'Estimation of relationships for limited dependent variables', *Econometrica*, 26: 24–36.

United States Department of Commerce, Bureau of the Census (1993) *Census of Population and*

Housing, 1990 United States: Public Use Microdata Sample: 5% Sample [MRDF]. Second release. Washington, DC: US Department of Commerce, Bureau of the Census [producer]. Ann Arbor, MI: Inter-University Consortium for Political and Social Research [distributor].

van der Klaauw, B. and Koning, R. (2003) 'Testing the normality assumption in the sample selection model with an application to travel demand', *Journal of Business and Economic Statistics*, 21: 31–42.

Vella, F. (1998) 'Estimating models with sample selection bias: A survey', *Journal of Human Resources*, 33: 127–69.

White, H. (1980) 'A heteroskedasticity-consistent covariance matrix estimator and a direct test for heteroskedasticity', *Econometrica*, 48: 817–30.

Winship, C. and Mare, R. (1992) 'Models for sample selection bias', *Annual Review of Sociology*, 18: 327–50.

Winship, C. and Morgan, S. (1999) 'The estimation of causal effects from observational data', *Annual Review of Sociology*, 25: 659–706.

Winship, C. and Radbill, L. (1994) 'Sampling weights and regression analysis', *Sociological Methods and Research*, 23: 230–57.

Zatz, M. and Hagan, J. (1985) 'Crime, time, and punishment: An exploration of selection bias in sentencing research', *Journal of Quantitative Criminology*, 1: 103–26.

Zuehlke, T. and Zeman, A. (1991) 'A comparison of two-stage estimators of censored regression models', *Review of Economics and Statistics*, 73: 185–8.

19

Structural Equation Modeling

JODIE B. ULLMAN AND PETER M. BENTLER

In previous chapters special cases of the general linear model have been discussed and illustrated. This chapter builds on these prior chapters through the introduction of a set of advanced statistical modeling techniques also based on the general linear model called structural equation modeling (SEM). An important advantage of SEM over the basic general linear model is that dependent variables can also play the role of predictor variables within the same model. A second advantage of SEM relative to analyses based on the general linear model is the ability to estimate nonlinear models for categorical and censored data.

In this chapter we will begin at a very basic level by defining SEM and illustrating some of the reasons why it may be a potentially useful tool for researchers. In this introduction we will place SEM on a continuum of the basic and advanced statistical approaches presented in this book. We will examine the types of research questions that are addressed through SEM and also examine statistical issues that are unique to SEM. Following this introduction we will present a general procedure for specifying and testing a structural equation model with an example from an evaluation of the Drug Abuse Resistance Education (DARE) program. In this section we also present statistical issues, perhaps previously addressed in other chapters, but nonetheless particularly relevant to SEM. This section also includes the fundamental

equations and matrices for the Bentler–Weeks specification of structural equation models (Bentler and Weeks, 1980). After presentation of a basic SEM analysis we discuss two advanced SEM techniques: multiple-group models and structural equation models of means and covariances. We conclude the chapter with a real data example of another advanced SEM application: latent growth modeling.

OVERVIEW OF STRUCTURAL EQUATION MODELS

Conceptually, structural equation modeling is a collection of statistical techniques that allow a set of relationships between one or more independent variables (IVs), either continuous or discrete, and one or more dependent variables (DVs), either continuous or discrete, to be examined. Both IVs and DVs can be either measured variables (directly observed) or latent variables. A latent variable is a variable that is not directly measured but is assessed indirectly through two or more measured (observed) variables.

On a continuum of complexity of the general linear model, with a simple bivariate correlation or *t* test as the most basic form and with multiple regression in the middle of continuum, a full structural equation model would be at the complex end. That said, it

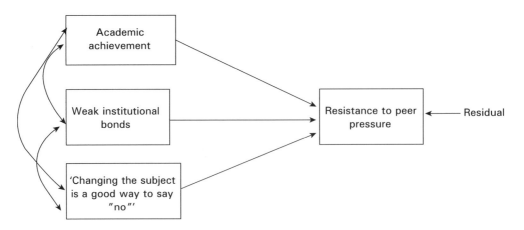

Figure 19.1   *Path diagram of a multiple regression model*

should be restated that SEM is a set of techniques and, as in the general linear model, can be specialized into specific types of models and analysis. Structural equation modeling is also referred to as causal modeling, causal analysis, simultaneous equation modeling, analysis of covariance structures, path analysis, or confirmatory factor analysis.

Because SEM is a set of techniques, SEM models can be estimated that are similar to other standard statistical analyses. It is helpful to look at these familiar techniques analyzed through SEM to lay the groundwork for advanced specialized applications of SEM. Viewing a well-known statistical technique through 'SEM eyes' allows basic SEM principles to be illustrated using a familiar example. Therefore we begin at a basic level with a multiple regression model. A researcher might be interested in children's substance use behavior and hypothesize a relationship between a single measured variable (perhaps resistance to peer pressure) and three measured predictor variables (perhaps responses to a DARE curriculum variable such as 'Changing the subject is a good way to say "no"', students' academic achievement and degree of weak institutional bonds). This multiple regression model is presented in diagram form in Figure 19.1.

Models in diagram form

Figure 19.1 is an example of a path diagram. Path diagrams are fundamental to SEM because they allow researchers to diagram the hypothesized set of relationships – the model. The diagrams are helpful in clarifying a researcher's ideas about the relationships among variables, and they can be directly translated into the equations needed for the analysis.

Several conventions used in developing SEM diagrams are illustrated in Figure 19.2. Measured variables, also called *observed variables*, *indicators*, or *manifest variables*, are represented by squares or rectangles. In Figure 19.2, they have verbal labels as well as V designations. Relationships between variables are indicated by lines; lack of a line connecting variables implies that no direct relationship has been hypothesized. Lines have either one or two arrows. A line with one arrow represents a hypothesized direct relationship between two variables. The variable with the arrow pointing to it is the DV. A line with an arrow at both ends indicates a covariance between the two variables with no implied direction of effect.

Returning to Figure 19.1, all four of the measured variables appear in boxes connected by lines with arrows indicating that responses to 'Changing the subject is a good way to say "no"', academic achievement and weak institutional bonds (the IVs) predict resistance to peer pressure (the DV) in adolescents. As in multiple regression we hypothesize that resistance to peer pressure could be predicted by academic achievement, degree of institutional bonds, and student's response to 'Changing the subject is a good way to say "no"'. The presence of a residual indicates imperfect prediction.

Although SEM can be used to estimate multiple regression models, one of the major

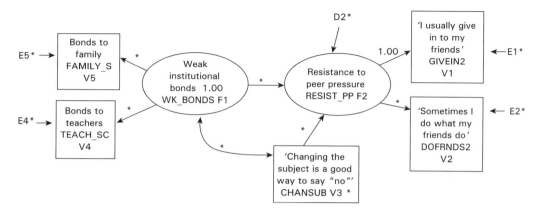

Figure 19.2 *Example of a structural equation model of resistance to peer pressure*

advantages of SEM versus multiple regression is the ability to analyze models that are more complex than a simple multiple regression model. One type of complexity that researchers using SEM are uniquely able to incorporate in their analyses is the use of latent variables, hypothetical constructs. Figure 19.2 shows a more complicated latent variable model of resistance to peer pressure. Here constructs are represented by circles or ovals. Constructs are shown with verbal labels as well as F designations. Constructs have two or more indicators, and are also called *latent variables*, *factors*, or *unobserved variables*.

In the model of Figure 19.2, there are two latent variables (constructs): Resistance to peer pressure (RESIST_PP) and Weak institutional bonds (WK_BONDS). Notice the direction of the arrows connecting the Resistance to peer pressure construct (factor) to its indicators: the construct *predicts* the measured variables. The implication is that the underlying construct, RESIST_PP, drives the degree of agreement with the statements 'I usually give in to my friends when they pressure me' (GIVEIN2) and 'Sometimes I do what my friends do even though I know it isn't right' (DOFRNDS2). It is impossible to measure a construct directly, so we do the next best thing and measure indicators of resistance to peer pressure. We hope that we are able to tap into adolescents' resistance to peer pressure by measuring several observable indicators. In this example we use just two indicators. Similarly, the latent variable representing Weak institutional bonds predicts strength of

bonds to family (FAMILY_S) and bonds to teachers (TEACH_SC).

RESIST_PP is a latent variable (factor) that is predicted by responses to 'Changing the subject is a good way to say "no"' (CHANSUB, a measured variable), and WK_BONDS (a factor). Notice the line with the arrow at both ends connecting WK_BONDS and CHANSUB. This line with an arrow at both ends implies that there is a relationship between the variables but makes no prediction regarding the direction of the effect.

In Figure 19.2, bonds to family, bonds to teachers, degree of endorsement of the two peer pressure measured variables, and the latent variable, RESIST_PP, all have one-way arrows pointing to them. These variables are DVs in the model. CHANSUB and WK_BONDS are IVs in the model; as such they have no one-way arrows pointing to them. Notice that all the DVs, both observed and unobserved, have arrows labeled 'E' or 'D' pointing toward them. Es (errors) point to measured variables; Ds (disturbances) point to latent variables (factors). As in multiple regression, nothing is predicted perfectly; there is always residual or error. In SEM, the residual, the variability not accounted for by the predictor(s), is included in the diagram with these paths.

The part of the model that relates the measured variables to the factors is sometimes called the *measurement model*. In this example, the two constructs (factors), WK_BONDS and RESIST_PP, and the indicators of these constructs (factors), form the *measurement model*. The hypothesized relationships among the constructs, in this example just the one path between WK_BONDS and RESIST_PP, are called the *structural model*. Predictive relationships are examined in SEM. For example, in this model we are interested in whether each latent variable (RESIST_PP and WK_BONDS) predicts the measured variables associated with it. Additionally, it is hypothesized that RESIST_PP is predicted by WK_BONDS. Note that both of these models include hypotheses about relationships among variables (covariances) but not about means or mean differences. Mean differences associated with group membership can also be tested within the SEM framework but are not demonstrated in this chapter.

Advantages of SEM

There are a number of advantages to the use of SEM rather than traditional 'measured variable only' techniques such as regression or multivariate analyses of variance. When relationships among factors are examined, the relationships are free of measurement error because the error has been estimated and removed, leaving only common variance. Reliability of measurement can be accounted for explicitly within the analysis by estimating and removing the measurement error. Additionally, as was seen in Figure 19.2, complex relationships can be examined. When the phenomena of interest are complex and multidimensional, SEM is the only analysis that allows complete and simultaneous tests of all the relationships. Researchers often pose hypotheses at the level of the construct. With other statistical methods these construct-level hypotheses are tested at the level of a measured variable (an observed variable with measurement error). Mismatching the level of hypothesis and level of analysis, although problematic and often overlooked, may lead to faulty conclusions. A distinct advantage of SEM is the ability to test construct-level hypotheses at the appropriate level. As previously stated, in SEM, in contrast to the basic general linear model, DVs can also play the role of predictor variables in the model as a whole. So, in Figure 19.2, RESIST_PP is a DV with respect to WK_BONDS and CHANSUB. Yet it is also a predictor of GIVEIN2 and DOFRNDS2. This feature allows SEM to model mediation effects. Here, RESIST_PP is a mediator of the effect of WK_BONDS and CHANSUB on GIVEIN2 and DOFRNDS2.

THREE GENERAL TYPES OF RESEARCH QUESTIONS THAT CAN BE ADDRESSED WITH SEM

SEM allows a broad range of questions to be addressed. Some of these questions are similar to those answered with other statistical techniques already outlined in previous chapters. In this section we will discuss three general types of research questions (model adequacy, parameter estimation, and comparison of nested models) that are particularly well addressed through the use of SEM techniques.

Adequacy of model

The fundamental question that is addressed through the use of SEM techniques involves a comparison between a data set, an empirical covariance matrix, and an estimated population covariance matrix that is produced as a function of the model parameter estimates. The major question asked by SEM is: Is the covariance matrix that is estimated from the model equal to the true population covariance matrix? Of course, we do not have the true population covariance matrix, so in practice the question is modified to: 'Does the model produce an estimated population covariance matrix that is consistent with the sample (observed) covariance matrix?' If the model is good the parameter estimates will produce an estimated matrix that is close to the sample covariance matrix. In turn, the sample covariance matrix is assumed to be representative of the population covariance matrix, so it can be assumed that the model describes the population. 'Closeness' is evaluated primarily with the chi-square test statistic and fit indices.

It is possible to estimate a model, with a factor structure, at one time point and then test if the *factor structure* remains the same across time points. For example, we could assess the strength of the indicators of children's resistance to peer pressures (endorsement of the two peer pressure variables) and weak institutional bonds (bonds to family and bonds to teachers) when children are 12 and then assess the same factor structure when the children are 14, 16, and 18. Using this longitudinal approach we could assess if the factor structure, the construct itself, remains the same across this time period or whether the relative weights of the indicators change as children develop.

In addition to examining the factor structure longitudinally, it is possible to examine the rate of individual change in a construct over time. Using latent growth curve modeling, we can test the hypothesis that children's degree of resistance to peer pressure changes at different rates. We can also test hypotheses about the shape of change, that is, whether the change over time is linear or quadratic. Other questions that might be addressed with this approach could be: Do children have the same rate of change of resistance to peer pressure? Or are children's initial levels of resistance to peer pressure associated with their rate of change in the construct?

Another exciting new development in SEM techniques is multilevel modeling. Now, hypotheses about data with a hierarchical, or nested, structure can be tested. For example, DARE is a program given to classrooms of children. Therefore children are nested within classrooms. Resistance to peer pressure is one of the DARE core constructs. Imagine that we would like to test the hypothesis that participation in DARE predicts more resistance to peer pressure. Traditional analyses of this type of data might look only at the level of the child and ignore the fact that DARE is given to classrooms of children, not to children individually – participation is a group-level, not individual, variable. (An example of an individual variable might be gender or age.) If only the children's data are analyzed and there is a sizable intraclass correlation, the standard errors may be too small and erroneous conclusions drawn. On the other hand, if the individual children's data are ignored and only the classroom data are analyzed, then the small size shrinks and power may suffer. Use of a multilevel analysis approach can address the problem of statistical assumption violation and low power and also allow analysis of data with predictors at different levels of measurement, such as classroom-level variables of DARE participation and number of students in the class. Using this technique, models are developed for both the children's data and the classroom-level data, and predictors are allowed at both levels and across levels. A complete discussion of multilevel models is outside the scope of this chapter; however, the interested reader should refer to Bryk and Raudenbush (1992), Kreft and de Leeuw (1998), and Snijders and Bosker (1999) for detailed general discussions of hierarchical

modeling. For detailed discussion of hierarchical modeling within the SEM, the reader is referred to Bentler and Liang (2003), Chou et al. (1998), Heck and Thomas (2000), and Muthén (1994).

Significance of parameter estimates

Significance of parameter estimates is routinely evaluated in many statistical analyses. In SEM we are interested in a system of relationships, and hence we are interested in evaluating a complex set of parameter estimates. Model estimation for parameters (path coefficients, variances and covariances) and their standard errors is generated under the implicit assumption that the model fit is very good and the standard errors are appropriately calculated. If model fit is very close, then the estimates and standard errors may be taken seriously, and individual significance tests on parameters may be performed. In SEM we can simultaneously test the significance of a set of path coefficients, factor loadings, variances and covariances.

Using the example illustrated in Figure 19.2 we could test the hypothesis that WK_BONDS predicts RESIST_PP. This would be a test of the path coefficient between the two latent variables (the null hypothesis for this test would be $H_0: \gamma = 0$, where γ is the symbol for the path coefficient between an IV and a DV). This parameter estimate is then evaluated with a z test (the parameter estimate divided by the estimated standard error).

Comparison of nested models

The ability to test competing theories is one of the greatest strengths of SEM. Nested models (models that are subsets of one another) representing different theories may be compared statistically, thus providing a strong theoretical test of the models. From the example in Figure 19.2, we could pose a nested model that could be compared to the fuller model that is illustrated. A possible nested model could remove the path from WK_BONDS to RESIST_PP. This nested model would hypothesize that CHANSUB is the only predictor of RESIST_PP. To test this hypothesis, the chi-square from the fuller model depicted in Figure 19.2 would be subtracted from the chi-square for the nested model that removed the path from WK_BONDS to RESIST_PP. The corresponding degrees of freedom for these two models would also be subtracted. The difference in chi-squares, based on the difference in degrees of freedom, would be evaluated for significance using a chi-square table of significance. If the difference is significant, the fuller model that includes the removed path is needed to explain the data. If the difference were not significant, the nested model, which is more parsimonious than the fuller model, would be accepted as the preferred model. This would imply that WK_BONDS is not needed when predicting RESIST_PP.

A FOUR-STAGE GENERAL PROCESS OF MODELING

The process of modeling could be thought of as a four-stage process: model specification, model estimation, model evaluation, and model modification. In this section each of these stages will be discussed and illustrated with an example based on data collected as part of an ongoing DARE evaluation (see Dukes et al., 1995, for a full description of the study). This example uses data from students' responses immediately following completion of the DARE program (see Dukes et al., 1995).

Model specification/hypotheses

The first step in the process of estimating a structural equation model is model specification. This stage consists of: stating the hypotheses to be tested in both diagram and equation form; statistically identifying the model; and evaluating the statistical assumptions that underlie the model. We discuss each of these components using the model for resistance to peer pressure (Figure 19.2) as an example, and then discuss and illustrate the computer process of model specification using the EQS 6.0 SEM software program.

Model hypotheses and diagrams In this phase of the process, the model is specified, that is, the specific set of hypotheses to be tested is given. This is done most frequently through a diagram. Figure 19.2 is an example of hypothesis specification. This example has five measured variables: FAMILY_S, the average of three responses to statements about bonds to family; TEACH_SC, the average of three responses to statements that query

bonds to teachers; GIVEIN2, a five-point Likert scale measure of degree of endorsement of the statement 'I usually give in to my friends when they pressure me'; DOFRNDS2, a five-point Likert scale measure of degree of agreement with the statement 'Sometimes I do what my friends do even though I know it isn't right'; and CHANSUB, the degree of endorsement of the statement 'Changing the subject is a good way to say "no"'. These Likert scale responses are treated, as is common in the social sciences, as continuous measures. It would, however, be possible to estimate these models treating these variables as ordinal variables.

The example of Figure 19.2 contains some asterisks and a 1. The asterisks indicate parameters (variances and covariances of IVs and regression coefficients) to be estimated. The variances of IVs are parameters of the model and are estimated or fixed to a particular value. The number 1 indicates that a parameter, either a path coefficient or a variance, has been set (fixed) to the value of 1. (The rationale behind 'fixing' paths will be discussed in the section on identification).

Our example contains two hypothesized latent variables (factors): WK_BONDS and RESIST_PP. The WK_BONDS factor is hypothesized to have two indicators, FAMILY_S and TEACH_SC. The existence of weaker institutional bonds predicts weaker bonds to both family and teacher. Note that the direction of the prediction matches the direction of the arrows. RESIST_PP also has two indicators: GIVEIN2 and DOFRNDS2. Greater resistance to peer pressure predicts higher scores on both the peer pressure measured variables. This model also hypothesizes that both WK_BONDS and CHANSUB are predictive of RESIST_PP. Also notice the line with the doubled-headed arrow that directly connects WK_BONDS and CHANSUB. This path indicates a hypothesized covariance between these variables.

Bentler–Weeks model specification The relationships in the diagram are directly translated into equations, and the model is then estimated. The analysis proceeds by specifying a model as in the diagram and then translating the model into a series of equations or matrices. One method of model specification is the Bentler–Weeks method (Bentler and Weeks, 1980). In this method every variable in the model, latent or measured, is either an IV or a DV. The parameters

Table 19.1   *Equivalence of matrices of Bentler–Weeks and LISREL model specifications*

Bentler–Weeks model			LISREL model			
Symbol	Name	Contents	Symbol	Name	LISREL two-letter specification	Contents
β	Beta	Matrix of regression coefficients of DVs predicting other DVs	1. β	1. Beta	1. BE	Matrix of regression coefficients of latent DVs predicting other latent DVs
			2. Λ_y	2. Lambda y	2. LY	Matrix of regression coefficients of measured DVs predicting other latent DVs
γ	Gamma	Matrix of regression coefficients of DVs predicting IVs	1. Γ	1. Gamma	1. GA	Matrix of regression coefficients of latent DVs predicting other latent IVs
			2. Λ_x	2. Lambda x	2. LX	Matrix of regression coefficients of measured DVs predicting other latent IVs
Φ	Phi	Matrix of covariances among the IVs	1. Φ	1. Phi	1. PI	Matrix of covariances among the latent IVs
			2. Ψ	2. Psi	2. PS	Matrix of covariances of errors associated with latent DVs
			3. Θ_δ	3. Theta-delta	3. TD	Matrix of covariances among errors associated with measured DVs predicted from latent IVs
			4. Θ_ε	4. Theta-epsilon	4. TE	Matrix of covariances among errors associated with measured DVs predicted from latent DVs

to be estimated are the regression coefficients and the variances and covariances of the IVs in the model (Bentler, 2001). Another common model estimation method is the LISREL model (Jöreskog, 1971). The equivalence of the matrices of the Bentler–Weeks model and the LISREL model is given in Table 19.1. In Figure 19.2 the regression coefficients and covariances to be estimated are indicated with an asterisk (*).

In the example, RESIST_PP, DOFRNDS2, GIVEIN2, FAMILY_S, and TEACH_SC are all DVs because they all have at least one line with a single-headed arrow pointing to them. Notice that RESIST_PP is a latent variable and also a DV. Whether or not a variable is observed makes no difference to its status as a DV or IV. Although RESIST_PP is a factor, it is also a DV because it has arrows from both WK_BONDS and CHANSUB. The

seven IVs in this example are CHANSUB, WK_BONDS, D2, E1, E2, E4, E5.

Residual variables (errors) of measured variables are labeled E and errors of latent variables (called disturbances) are labeled D. It may seem odd that a residual variable is considered an IV, but remember the familiar regression equation:

$$Y = X\beta + e, \qquad (19.1)$$

where Y is the DV and X and e are both IVs.

In fact the Bentler–Weeks model *is* a regression model, expressed in matrix algebra as

$$\eta = B\eta + \gamma\xi \qquad (19.2)$$

where, if q is the number of DVs and r is the number of IVs, then η (eta) is a $q \times 1$ vector of DVs, $\mathbf{B}$ (beta) is a $q \times q$ matrix of regression coefficients between DVs, γ (gamma) is a $q \times r$ matrix of regression coefficients between DVs and IVs, and ξ (xi) is an $r \times 1$ vector of IVs.

In the Bentler–Weeks model only independent variables have variances and covariances as parameters of the model. These variances and covariances are in Φ (phi), an $r \times r$ matrix. Therefore, the parameter matrices of the model are $\mathbf{B}$, γ, and Φ. Unknown parameters in these matrices need to be estimated. The vectors of dependent variables, η, and independent variables, ξ, are not estimated.

The diagram for the example is translated into the Bentler–Weeks model, with $r = 7$ and $q = 5$, as follows:

$$
\begin{array}{ccc}
\eta & = & \mathbf{B} \qquad\qquad\qquad \eta
\end{array}
$$

$$
\begin{bmatrix} V1 \text{ or } \eta_1 \\ V2 \text{ or } \eta_2 \\ V4 \text{ or } \eta_3 \\ V5 \text{ or } \eta_4 \\ F2 \text{ or } \eta_5 \end{bmatrix} = \begin{bmatrix} 0 & 0 & 0 & 0 & 1 \\ 0 & 0 & 0 & 0 & * \\ 0 & 0 & 0 & 0 & 0 \\ 0 & 0 & 0 & 0 & 0 \\ 0 & 0 & 0 & 0 & 0 \end{bmatrix} \begin{bmatrix} V1 \text{ or } \eta_1 \\ V2 \text{ or } \eta_2 \\ V4 \text{ or } \eta_3 \\ V5 \text{ or } \eta_4 \\ F2 \text{ or } \eta_5 \end{bmatrix}
$$

$$
\begin{array}{ccc}
+ & \gamma & \xi
\end{array}
$$

$$
+ \begin{bmatrix} 0 & 0 & 1 & 0 & 0 & 0 & 0 \\ 0 & 0 & 0 & 1 & 0 & 0 & 0 \\ 0 & * & 0 & 0 & 1 & 0 & 0 \\ 0 & * & 0 & 0 & 0 & 1 & 0 \\ * & * & 0 & 0 & 0 & 0 & 1 \end{bmatrix} \begin{bmatrix} V3 \text{ or } \xi_1 \\ F1 \text{ or } \xi_2 \\ E1 \text{ or } \xi_3 \\ E2 \text{ or } \xi_4 \\ E4 \text{ or } \xi_5 \\ E5 \text{ or } \xi_6 \\ D2 \text{ or } \xi_7 \end{bmatrix}
$$

Notice that η is on both sides of the equation. This is because DVs can predict one another in SEM. The diagram and matrix equations are identical. Notice that the asterisks in Figure 19.2 directly correspond to the asterisks in the matrices, and that these matrix equations directly correspond to simple regression equations. In the matrix equations the number 1 indicates that we have 'fixed' the parameter, either a variance or a path coefficient, to the specific value of 1. Parameters are generally fixed for identification purposes. Parameters can be fixed to any number; most often, however, parameters are fixed to 1 or 0. The parameters that are fixed to 0 are also included in the path diagram but are easily overlooked because the zero parameters are represented by the *absence* of a line in the diagram.

As stated above, what makes this model different from ordinary regression is the possibility of having latent variables as DVs and predictors, as well as the possibility of DVs predicting other DVs. The latter occurs with nonzero elements in $\mathbf{B}$. When all elements in $\mathbf{B}$ are zero, no DVs are predicted by other DVs, and the only coefficients needed are in γ; these give weights for the IVs in predicting the DVs. In such a case the model is a set of regression equations, albeit possibly with latent variables. But when $\mathbf{B}$ has nonzero elements, certain DVs are predicted by other DVs, and the model is no longer just regression-like. In the example, there are two nonzero elements in $\mathbf{B}$ (a fixed 1 and a free parameter, *), so this is not just a regression model. In more complex models, so-called nonrecursive models, free parameters exist in some symmetric elements of $\mathbf{B}$, such as the (1, 2)th and the (2, 1)th elements (which here would indicate V1 predicting V2 while also V2 predicts V1).

Carefully compare the diagram in Figure 19.2 with this matrix equation. The 5×1 vector of values to the left of the equal sign, the eta (η) vector, is a vector of DVs listed in the order GIVEIN2 (V1), DOFRNDS2 (V2), TEACH_SC (V4), FAMILY_S (V5), and RESIST_PP (F2). The beta matrix ($\mathbf{B}$), is a 5×5 matrix of regression coefficients among the DVs.

The 5×7 gamma matrix (γ) contains the regression coefficients that are used to predict the DVs from the IVs. The five DVs that are associated with the rows of this matrix are in the same order as above. The seven IVs that identify the columns are, in the order indicated, CHANSUB (V3), WK_BONDS (F1), the four E(rror)s for V1, V2, V4, V5 and the D(isturbance) of F2. The 7×1 vector of IVs is in the same order.

The matrix equation summarizes compactly all the equations in the model. Each row of the matrix equation gives one regression-like equation; with five rows there are five equations. To illustrate, the third row gives

$$
\begin{aligned}
V4 = {} & 0V1 + 0V2 + 0V4 + 0V5 + 1F2 \\
& + 0V3 + 0F1 + 0E1 + 0E2 \\
& + 1E4 + 0E5 + 0D2,
\end{aligned}
$$

where the numbers in front of the variable names are coefficients taken from the third rows of $\mathbf{B}$ and γ in turn and the variables are the dependent and then the independent variables in the sequence we have listed them. Therefore this equation simplifies to V4 = 1F2 + 1E4, where 1 is a fixed path from F2 to V4, and from E4 to V4, in the model. In Figure 19.3 you will see this equation as one of the five equations in the EQS model file setup. The 7×7 symmetric Φ matrix contains the variances and covariances that are to be estimated for the IVs:

$$
\Phi =
\begin{array}{c}
\text{V3 or } \xi_1 \\
\text{F1 or } \xi_2 \\
\text{E1 or } \xi_3 \\
\text{E2 or } \xi_4 \\
\text{E4 or } \xi_5 \\
\text{E5 or } \xi_6 \\
\text{D2 or } \xi_7
\end{array}
\begin{bmatrix}
* & 0 & 0 & 0 & 0 & 0 & 0 \\
* & 1 & 0 & 0 & 0 & 0 & 0 \\
0 & 0 & * & 0 & 0 & 0 & 0 \\
0 & 0 & 0 & * & 0 & 0 & 0 \\
0 & 0 & 0 & 0 & * & 0 & 0 \\
0 & 0 & 0 & 0 & 0 & * & 0 \\
0 & 0 & 0 & 0 & 0 & 0 & *
\end{bmatrix}.
$$

These equations form the basis of an EQS (a popular SEM computer package) syntax file used to estimate the model. The syntax for this model is presented in Figure 19.3. The model is specified in EQS using a series of regression equations. In the /EQUATIONS section, as in ordinary regression, the DV appears on the left-hand side of the equation, and its predictors are on the right-hand side. But unlike regression, the predictors may be IVs or other DVs. Measured variables are referred to by the letter V and the number corresponding to the variable given in the /LABELS section. Errors associated with measured variables are indicated by the letter E and the number of the variable. Factors are referred to with the letter F and a number given in the /LABELS section. The errors, or disturbances, associated with factors are referred to by the letter D and the number corresponding to the factor. An asterisk indicates a parameter to be estimated. Variables included in the equation without asterisks are considered parameters fixed to the value 1. The variances of IVs are parameters of the model and are indicated in the /VARIANCES paragraph. In the /PRINT paragraph, FIT=ALL requests all goodness-of-fit indices available. Take a moment to confirm that the diagram relationships exactly match the regression equations given in the syntax file.

Identification In SEM a model is specified, parameters for the model are estimated using sample data, and the parameters are used to produce the estimated population covariance matrix. But only models that are identified can be estimated. A model is said to be identified if there is a unique numerical solution for each of the parameters in the model. For example, suppose both that the variance of $y = 10$ and that the variance of $y = \alpha + \beta$. Any

```
/TITLE
  Basic SEM model
/SPECIFICATIONS
  DATA = 'D:\EQS6\DARE data.ESS';
  VARIABLES = 5; CASES = 4578; GROUPS = 1;
  METHODS = ML, ROBUST;
  MATRIX = RAW;
  ANALYSIS = COVARIANCE;
/LABELS
  V1 = GIVEIN2; V2 = DOFRNDS2;
  V3 = CHANSUB; V4 = TEACH_SC;
  V5 = FAMILY_S;
  F1 = WK_BONDS; F2 = RESIST_PP;
/EQUATIONS
  ! Resistance to Peer Pressure
    V1 = + 1F2 + 1E1;
    V2 = + *F2 + 1E2;
  ! Weak Institutional Bonds
    V4 = + *F1 + 1E4;
    V5 = + *F1 + 1E5;
    F2 = + *F1 + *V3 + 1D2;
/VARIANCES
  V3 = *;
  F1 = 1.00;
  E1 = *;
  E2 = *;
  E4 = *;
  E5 = *;
  D2 = *;
/COVARIANCES
  F1, V3 = *;
/PRINT
  FIT = ALL;
  TABLE = EQUATION;
/LMTEST
/WTEST
/END
```

Figure 19.3 *EQS syntax for modeling resistance to peer pressure*

two values can be substituted for α and β as long as they sum to 10. There is no unique numerical solution for either α or β, that is, there are an infinite number of combinations of two numbers that would sum to 10. Therefore this single equation model is not identified. However, if we fix α to 0 then there is a unique solution for β, 10, and the equation is identified. It is possible to use covariance algebra to calculate equations and assess identification in very simple models; however, in large models this procedure quickly becomes unwieldy. For detailed, technical discussion of identification, see Bollen (1989). The following guidelines are rough, but may suffice for many models.

The first step is to count the number of data points and the number of parameters that are to be estimated. The data in SEM are the variances and covariances in the sample covariance matrix. The number of data points is the number of nonredundant sample variances and covariances,

$$\text{Number of data points} = \frac{p(p+1)}{2}, \qquad (19.3)$$

where p equals the number of measured variables. The number of parameters is found by adding together the number of regression coefficients, variances, and covariances that are to be estimated (i.e., the number of asterisks in a diagram).

If there are more data points than parameters to be estimated, the model is said to be overidentified, a necessary condition for proceeding with the analysis. If there are the same number of data points as parameters to be estimated, the model is said to be just identified. In this case, the estimated parameters perfectly reproduce the sample covariance matrix, and the chi-square test statistic and degrees of freedom are equal to zero, and the analysis is uninteresting because hypotheses about adequacy of the model cannot be tested. However, hypotheses about specific paths in the model can be tested. If there are fewer data points than parameters to be estimated, the model is said to be underidentified and parameters cannot be estimated. The number of parameters needs to be reduced by fixing, constraining, or deleting some of them. A parameter may be fixed by setting it to a specific value or constrained by setting the parameter equal to another parameter.

In the example of Figure 19.2, there are five measured variables so there are $5(5 + 1)/2 = 15$ data points (5 variances and 10 covariances). There are 12 parameters to be estimated in the hypothesized model: five regression coefficients, six variances and one covariance. The hypothesized model has three fewer parameters than data points, so the model may be identified.

The second step in determining model identifiability is to examine the measurement portion of the model. This deals with the relationship between the measured indicators and the factors. It is necessary both to establish the scale of each factor and to assess the identifiability of this portion of the model.

To establish the scale of a factor, the variance for the factor is fixed to 1, or the regression coefficient of the factor on one of the measured variables is fixed to 1. Fixing the

regression coefficient to 1 gives the factor the same variance as the measured variable. If the factor is an IV, either alternative is acceptable. If the factor is a DV, most researchers fix the regression coefficient to 1. In the example, the variance of WK_BONDS was set to 1 (normalized) while the scale of RESIST_PP was set equal to the scale of GIVEIN2.

To establish the identifiability of the measurement portion of the model, look at the number of factors and the number of measured variables (indicators) loading on each factor. If there is only one factor, the model may be identified if the factor has at least three indicators with nonzero loading and the errors (residuals) are uncorrelated with one another. If there are two or more factors, again consider the number of indicators for each factor. If each factor has three or more indicators, the model may be identified if errors associated with the indicators are not correlated, each indicator loads on only one factor, and the factors are allowed to covary. If there are only two indicators for a factor, the model may be identified if there are no correlated errors, each indicator loads on only one factor, and none of the covariances among factors is equal to zero.

In the example, there are two indicators for each factor. The errors are uncorrelated and each indicator loads on only one factor. Additionally, the covariance between the factors is not zero. Therefore, this part of the model may be identified. Note that identification may still be possible if errors are correlated or variables load on more than one factor, but it is more complicated.

The third step in establishing model identifiability is to examine the structural portion of the model, looking only at the relationships among the latent variables (factors). Ignore the measured variables for a moment; consider only the structural portion of the model that deals with the regression coefficients relating latent variables to one another. If none of the latent DVs predict each other (the beta matrix is all zeros) the structural part of the model may be identified. The peer pressure example has only one latent DV, so this part of the model may be identified. If the latent DVs do predict one another, look at the latent DVs in the model and ask if they are recursive or nonrecursive. If the latent DVs are recursive there are no feedback loops among them, and there are no correlated disturbances (errors) among them. (In a feedback loop, DV1 predicts DV2 and DV2 predicts DV1. That is, there are two lines linking the factors, one with an arrow in one direction and the other line with an arrow in the other direction. Correlated disturbances are linked by single curved lines with double-headed arrows.) If the structural part of the model is recursive, it may be identifiable. These rules also apply to path analysis models with only measured variables. The peer pressure example is a recursive model and therefore may be identified.

If a model is nonrecursive either there are feedback loops among the DVs or there are correlated disturbances among the DVs, or both. Two additional conditions are necessary for identification of nonrecursive models, each applying to each equation in the model separately. Looking at each equation separately, for identification it is necessary that each equation has at least one less than the number of latent DVs excluded from it. The second condition is that the *information matrix* (a matrix necessary for calculating standard errors) is of full rank and can be inverted. The inverted information matrix can be examined in the output from most SEM programs. If, after examining the model, the number of data points exceeds the number of parameters estimated and both the measurement and structural parts of the model are identified, there is good evidence that the whole model is identified.

Sample size and power Covariances are less stable when estimated from small samples. SEM is based on covariances. Parameter estimates and chi-square tests of fit are also very sensitive to sample size. Therefore SEM is a large-sample technique. MacCallum et al. (1996) present tables of minimum sample size needed for tests of goodness of fit based on model degrees of freedom and effect size.

Missing data Problems of missing data are often magnified in SEM due to the large number of measured variables employed. The researcher who relies on using complete cases only is often left with an inadequate number of complete cases to estimate a model. Therefore adequate missing-data computation is particularly important in many SEM models. When there is evidence that the data are missing at random (MAR – missingness may depend on the IVs but not DVs) or missing completely at random (MCAR – missingness is unrelated to the IVs or the DVs), a preferred method of imputation is to use the expectation–maximization (EM) algorithm to obtain maximum likelihood (ML) estimates (Little and Rubin, 1987; see also Chapter 5, this volume). Some software packages now include procedures for optimally utilizing available estimating missing data, including the EM algorithm. EQS 6 (Bentler, 2001) produces the EM-based ML solution automatically, based on computations due to Jamshidian and Bentler (1999). It should be noted that if the data are not normally distributed, maximum likelihood test statistics – including those based on the EM algorithm – may be quite inaccurate.

Additionally, a missing-data mechanism can be explicitly modeled within the SEM framework. Treatment of missing-data patterns through SEM is not demonstrated in this chapter; the interested reader is referred to Allison (1987) or Muthén et al. (1987). All of these authors assume that the data are multivariate normally distributed, a very restrictive assumption in practice, as will be discussed next. The more general case, when the parent distribution is possibly nonnormal, is discussed in Yuan and Bentler (2000). They provide a means for accepting the EM-based estimates of parameters, but correcting standard errors and test statistics for nonnormality in an approach reminiscent of Satorra and Bentler (1994). Their approach has been uniquely incorporated into the EQS 6 program (Bentler, 2001).

Multivariate normality and outliers Most of the estimation techniques used in SEM assume multivariate normality. To determine the extent and shape of nonnormally distributed data, examine the data for evidence of outliers, both univariate and multivariate, and evaluate the skewness and kurtosis of the distributions for the measured variables. If significant skewness is found, transformations can be attempted; however, often variables are still highly skewed or highly kurtotic even after transformation. Additionally, multivariate normality can also be examined through the use of Mardia's coefficients of multivariate skew and kurtosis. Some variables, such as drug use variables, are not expected to be normally distributed in the population anyway. If transformations do not restore normality, or a variable is not expected to be normally distributed in the population, an estimation method can be selected that addresses the nonnormality.

Residuals After model estimation, the residuals should be small and centered around zero. The frequency distribution of the residual covariances should be symmetric. Residuals in the context of SEM are residual *covariances,* not residual *scores.* Non-symmetrically distributed residuals in the frequency distribution may signal a poorly fitting model; the model is estimating some of the covariances well and others poorly. It sometimes happens that one or two residuals remain quite large, although the model fits reasonably well and the residuals appear to be symmetrically distributed and centered around zero. Typically, more informative than the ordinary residuals are the residuals obtained after standardizing the sample covariance matrix to a correlation matrix and similarly transforming the model matrix. In this metric, it is correlations that are being reproduced, and it is easy to see whether a residual is small and meaningless or too large for comfort. For example, if a sample correlation is 0.75 and the corresponding residual is 0.05, the correlation is largely explained by the model. In fact, an average of these standardized root mean square residuals (SRMS) has been shown to provide one of the most informative guides to model adequacy (Hu and Bentler, 1998, 1999).

The computer process So far we have outlined the components (specification of hypotheses, identification, and evaluation of assumptions underlying the model) of the model specification stage of the SEM process. Now we provide a brief tutorial on the software (EQS) implementation of this stage.

The first step of the model fitting process, model specification, is nicely summarized in the EQS syntax shown in Figure 19.3. The data file is specified after the keyword DATA=. The number of measured variables is given after VARIABLES=, the sample size is indicated after CASES=, and the number of samples is given after GROUPS=. The estimation method, type of data matrix and type of analysis are also indicated. Labels are provided for each measured (V) and latent (F) variable. As we stated previously, the /EQUA-TIONS section specifies each predictive relationship in the model. Notice that there are as many equations as DVs. The asterisks indicate parameters to be estimated. Notice that in the equation for V1 the parameter estimating the relationship between V1 and F2 has been fixed to one for identification.

The scale of the F2 latent variable has been set equal to the variance of GIVEIN2. In the next paragraph /VARIANCES specifies the variances to be estimated. Notice that the variance of F1 has been fixed to 1 for identification purposes.

Model estimation techniques and test statistics

After the model specification component is completed, the population parameters are estimated and evaluated. We now discuss several popular estimation techniques and provide guidelines for selection of estimation technique and test statistic. We conclude with a computer procedure discussion that provides implementation guidelines using EQS.

The goal of estimation is to minimize the difference between the observed and estimated population covariance matrices. To accomplish this goal a function, *F*, is minimized, where

$$F = (s - \sigma(\Theta))'W(s - \sigma(\Theta)). \quad (19.4)$$

Here **s** is the data (the observed sample covariance matrix stacked into a vector); **σ** is the estimated population covariance matrix (again, stacked into a vector) and (**Θ**) indicates that **σ** is derived from the parameters (the regression coefficients, variances and covariances) of the model. **W** is the matrix that weights the squared differences between the sample and estimated population covariance matrix.

In factor analysis the observed and reproduced correlation matrices are compared. This idea is extended in SEM to include a statistical test of the differences between the observed covariance matrix and the estimated population covariance matrix that is produced as a function of the model. If the weight matrix, **W**, is chosen correctly, at the minimum with the optimal **Θ̂**, *F* multiplied by $N - 1$ yields a chi-square test statistic.

The trick is to select **W** so that the sum of weighted squared differences between observed and estimated population covariance matrices has a statistical interpretation. In an ordinary chi-square, the weights are the set of expected frequencies in the denominator of the chi-square test statistic. If we use some other numbers instead of the expected frequencies, the result might be some sort of test statistic, but it would not be a χ^2 statistic, i.e., the weight matrix would be wrong.

In SEM, estimation techniques vary by the choice of **W**. Unweighted least-squares estimation (ULS) does not standardly yield a χ^2 statistic or standard errors, though these are provided in EQS. ULS estimation does not usually provide the best estimates, in the sense of having the smallest possible standard errors, and hence is not discussed further (see Bollen, 1989, for further discussion of ULS).

Maximum likelihood is usually the default method in most programs because it yields the most precise (smallest variance) estimates when the data are normal. Generalized least squares (GLS) has the same optimal properties as ML under normality. When the data are symmetrically but not normally distributed, elliptical distribution theory (EDT) is an option (Shapiro and Browne, 1987). Another option in EQS is heterogeneous kurtosis (HK) theory (Kano et al., 1990), which allows different variables to be nonnormal but symmetric in different ways. The asymptotically distribution-free (ADF) method has no distributional assumptions and hence is most general (Browne, 1984), but it is impractical with many variables and inaccurate without very large sample sizes. Satorra and Bentler (1988, 1994, 2001) and Satorra (2000) have also developed an adjustment for nonnormality that can be applied to the ML, GLS, EDT, or HK chi-square test statistics. Briefly, the Satorra–Bentler scaled χ^2 is a Bartlett-type correction to the χ^2 test statistic. EQS also corrects the standard errors for parameter estimates to adjust for the extent of nonnormality (Bentler and Dijkstra, 1985).

The performance of the χ^2 test statistic derived from these different estimation procedures is affected by several factors, among them (1) sample size, (2) nonnormality of the distribution of errors, of factors, and of errors and factors, and (3) violation of the assumption of independence of factors and errors. The goal is to select an estimation procedure that, in Monte Carlo studies, produces a test statistic that neither rejects nor accepts the true model too many times. Several studies provide guidelines for selection of appropriate estimation methods and test statistics. The following sections summarize the performance of estimation procedures examined in Monte Carlo studies by Hu et al. (1992) and Bentler and Yuan (1999).

Hu et al. varied sample size from 150 to 5000 and Bentler and Yuan (1999) examined sample sizes ranging from 60 to 120. Both studies examined the performance of test statistics derived from several estimation methods when the assumptions of normality and independence of factors were violated.

Estimation methods/test statistics and sample size Hu et al. found that when the normality assumption was reasonable, both the ML and the scaled ML performed well with sample sizes over 500. When the sample size was less than 500 GLS performed slightly better. Interestingly, the EDT test statistic performed a little better than ML at small sample sizes. It should be noted that the EDT estimator assumes that all variables have the same kurtosis, although the variables need not be normally distributed. (If the distribution is normal there is no excess kurtosis.) The HK method, which allows varying kurtosis, performed similarly. Finally, the ADF estimator was poor with sample sizes under 2500.

In small samples in the range of 60 to 120, when the number of subjects was greater than the number (p^*) of nonredundant variances and covariances in the sample covariance matrix, that is, $p^* = [p(p + 1)]/2$ where p is the number of variables, Bentler and Yuan found that a test statistic based on an adjustment of the ADF estimator and evaluated as an F statistic was best. This test statistic (Yuan and Bentler, 1999) adjusts the chi-square test statistic derived from the ADF estimator as

$$T_\ell = \frac{[N - (p^* - q)]T_{\mathrm{ADF}}}{(N - 1)\,(p^* - q)} \qquad (19.5)$$

where N is the number of subjects, q is the number of parameters to be estimated, and T_{ADF} is the test statistic based on the ADF estimator.

Estimation methods and nonnormality When the normality assumption was violated, Hu et al. found that the ML and GLS estimators worked well with sample sizes of 2500 and greater. The GLS estimator was a little better with smaller sample sizes, but led to acceptance of too many models. The EDT and HK estimators accepted far too many models. The ADF estimator was poor with sample sizes under 2500. Finally, the scaled ML performed about the same as the ML and GLS estimators and better than the ADF estimator at all but the largest sample sizes. (This is interesting in that the ADF estimator has no distributional assumptions and, theoretically,

```
GOODNESS OF FIT SUMMARY FOR METHOD = ROBUST

  INDEPENDENCE MODEL CHI-SQUARE = 1019.603 ON 10 DEGREES OF FREEDOM

  INDEPENDENCE AIC = 999.60267 INDEPENDENCE CAIC = 925.84407
      MODEL AIC   = 19.72606        MODEL CAIC = -2.40152

  SATORRA-BENTLER SCALED CHI-SQUARE = 25.7261 ON  3 DEGREES OF FREEDOM
  PROBABILITY VALUE FOR THE CHI-SQUARE STATISTIC IS   .00001

  FIT INDICES
  -----------
  BENTLER-BONETT      NORMED FIT INDEX = .975
  BENTLER-BONETT   NON-NORMED FIT INDEX = .925
  COMPARATIVE FIT INDEX (CFI)       = .977
  BOLLEN   (IFI) FIT INDEX          = .978
  MCDONALD (MFI) FIT INDEX          = .997
  ROOT MEAN-SQUARE ERROR OF APPROXIMATION (RMSEA) = .042
  90% CONFIDENCE INTERVAL OF RMSEA (.028, .057)
```

Figure 19.4   *Test statistic and fit indices for peer pressure model*

should perform quite well under conditions of nonnormality.) With small sample sizes the Yuan–Bentler test statistic performed best.

Estimation methods and dependence   The assumption that errors are independent underlies SEM and other multivariate techniques. Hu et al. also investigated estimation methods and test-statistic performance when the errors and factors were made dependent but uncorrelated. Factors were made dependent but uncorrelated by creating a curvilinear relationship between the factors and the errors. Correlation coefficients examine only linear relationships; therefore, although the correlation is zero between factors and errors, they are dependent.

ML and GLS performed poorly, always rejecting the true model. ADF was poor unless the sample size was greater than 2500. EDT was better than ML, GLS, and ADF, but still rejected too many true models. The scaled ML was better than the ADF estimator at all but the largest sample sizes. The scaled ML performed best overall with medium to larger samples sizes and the Yuan–Bentler test statistic performed best with small samples.

Some recommendations for choice of estimation method/test statistic   Sample size and plausibility of the normality and independence assumptions need to be considered in selection of the appropriate estimation technique. The ML, scaled ML, and GLS estimator may be good choices with medium to large samples and evidence of the

plausibility of the normality assumptions. The independence assumption cannot be routinely evaluated. The scaled ML is fairly computer-intensive. Therefore, if time or cost are an issue, ML and GLS are better choices when the assumptions seem plausible. ML estimation is currently the most frequently used estimation method in SEM. In medium to large samples the scaled ML test statistic is a good choice with nonnormality or suspected dependence among factors and errors. In small samples the Yuan–Bentler test statistic seems best. The test statistic based on the ADF estimator (without adjustment) seems like a poor choice under all conditions unless the sample size is very large (in excess of 2500). Similar conclusions were found in studies by Fouladi (2000), Hoogland (1999), and Satorra (1992).

Computer procedure and interpretation   The model in Figure 19.2 is estimated using ML estimation and the Satorra–Bentler scaled chi-square test statistic because the data are not normally distributed, thus violating multivariate normality. In this model Mardia's normalized multivariate kurtosis is 26.49. This can be interpreted like a z-score. Therefore the probability level associated with a normalized estimate of 26.49 is less than 0.001. In Figure 19.3 the estimation method is indicated after METHODS=. Output for the model estimation and chi-square test statistic is given in Figure 19.4.

Several chi-square test statistics are given in the full output. In the severely edited output reproduced here only the chi-square associated with the Satorra–Bentler scaled chi-square are given. 'INDEPENDENCE MODEL CHI-SQUARE = 1019.603', with 10 degrees of freedom, tests the hypothesis that the measured variables are orthogonal. Therefore, the probability associated with this chi-square should be small, typically less than 0.05. The model chi-square test statistic is labeled 'SATORRA–BENTLER SCALED CHI-SQUARE = 25.7261', based on 3 degrees of freedom; this tests the hypothesis that the difference between the estimated population covariance matrix and unstructured population covariance matrix (as represented by the sample covariance matrix) is not significant. Ideally, the probability associated with this chi-square should be large, greater than 0.05. In Figure 19.4 the probability associated with the model chi-square equals $p = 0.000\ 01$. Strictly interpreted, this indicates that the estimated model-based population covariance matrix and the unstructured population covariance matrix, viewed through the sample covariance matrix, do differ significantly, that is, the model does not fit the data. However, the chi-square test statistic is strongly affected by sample size. The function minimum multiplied by $N - 1$ equals the chi-square. Therefore we will examine additional measures of fit before we draw any conclusions about the adequacy of the model.

Model evaluation

In this section we examine three aspects of model evaluation. First, we discuss the problem of assessing fit in an SEM model. We then present several popular fit indices. We conclude with a discussion of evaluating direct and indirect parameter estimates.

Evaluating the overall fit of the model The model chi-square test statistic is highly dependent on sample size – it is given by $(N - 1)F_{min}$, where N is the sample size and F_{min} is the value of F from (19.4) at the function minimum. Therefore the fit of models estimated with large samples, as seen in the peer pressure model, is often difficult to assess. Fit indices have been developed to address this problem. There are five general classes of fit indices: comparative fit; absolute fit; proportion of variance accounted for; parsimony-adjusted proportion of variance accounted for; and residual-based fit indices.

A complete discussion of model fit is outside the scope of this chapter, therefore we will focus on two of the most popular fit indices: the comparative fit index (CFI: Bentler, 1990); and a residual-based fit index, the root mean square error of approximation (RMSEA: Browne and Cudeck, 1993; Steiger, 2000; Steiger and Lind, 1980). Ullman (2001) and Hu and Bentler (1999) offer more detailed discussions of fit indices.

One type of model fit index is based on a comparison of nested models. Nested models are models that are subsets of one another. At one end of the continuum is the uncorrelated variables or independence model: the model that corresponds to completely unrelated variables. This model would have degrees of freedom equal to the number of data points minus the number of variances that are estimated. At the other end of the continuum is the saturated (full or perfect) model with zero degrees of freedom. Fit indices that employ a comparative fit approach place the estimated model somewhere along this continuum, with 0.00 indicating an awful fit, equivalent to that of the independence model where no covariances are being explained, and 1.00 indicating perfect fit.

The normed fit index is the easiest index to understand. It summarizes the improvement in chi-square in going from the independence model to the model of interest, relative to the starting point. In our example NFI = $(1019.603 - 25.7261)/1019.603 = 0.975$, indicating excellent fit. This index underestimates fit in small samples. The CFI assesses fit relative to other models, and uses an approach based on the noncentral χ^2 distribution with noncentrality parameter τ_i. If the estimated model is perfect $\tau_i = 0$; therefore, the larger the value of τ_i, the greater the model misspecification.

$$\text{CFI} = 1 - \frac{\tau_{\text{est. model}}}{\tau_{\text{indep. model}}} \qquad (19.6)$$

So, clearly, the smaller the noncentrality parameter, τ_i, for the estimated model relative to the τ_i for the independence model, the larger the CFI and the better the fit. The τ value for a model can be estimated by

$$\hat{\tau}_{\text{indep. model}} = \chi^2_{\text{indep. model}} - df_{\text{indep. model}}$$

$$\hat{\tau}_{\text{est. model}} = \chi^2_{\text{est. model}} - df_{\text{est. model}} \qquad (19.7)$$

where $\hat{\tau}_{\text{est.model}}$ is set to zero if negative.

For our example,

$$\hat{\tau}_{\text{indep. model}} = 1019.603 - 10 = 1009.603$$

$$\hat{\tau}_{\text{est. model}} = 25.7261 - 3 = 22.7261$$

so that

$$\text{CFI} = 1 - \frac{22.7261}{1009.603} = 0.977.$$

CFI values greater than 0.95 are often indicative of good fitting models (Hu and Bentler, 1999). The CFI is normed to the 0–1 range, and does a good job of estimating model fit even in small samples (Hu and Bentler, 1998, 1999).

The RMSEA (Steiger and Lind, 1980; Steiger, 2000) estimates the lack of fit in a model compared to a perfect or saturated model by

$$\text{estimated RMSEA} = \sqrt{\frac{\hat{\tau}}{Ndf_{\text{model}}}} \qquad (19.8)$$

where $\hat{\tau} = \hat{\tau}_{\text{est.model}}$ as defined in equation (19.7). As noted above, when the model is perfect, $\hat{\tau} = 0$, and the greater the model misspecification, the larger $\hat{\tau}$. Hence RMSEA is a measure of noncentraility relative to sample size and degrees of freedom. For a given noncentrality, large N and df imply a better-fitting model, that is, a smaller RMSEA. Values of 0.06 or less indicate a close-fitting model (Hu and Bentler, 1999). Values larger than 0.10 are indicative of poor-fitting models (Browne and Cudeck, 1993). Hu and Bentler (1999) found that in small samples the RMSEA overrejected the true model, that is, its value was too large. Because of this problem, this index may be less preferable with small samples. As with the CFI, the choice of estimation method affects the size of the RMSEA.

For our example, $\hat{\tau} = 11.3775$, therefore

$$\text{RMSEA} = \sqrt{\frac{22.7261}{4241 \times 3}} = 0.04.$$

Both the CFI and RMSEA values of 0.98 and 0.04, respectively, well exceed guideline cutoff values for evidence of good fit. Thus we can conclude that we have adequate evidence that the model fits the data despite the significant chi-square.

Interpreting parameter estimates: Direct effects The model fits, but what does it mean? The hypothesis is that the observed covariances among the measured variables arose because of the linkages between variables specified in the model. We conclude that we should retain our hypothesized model because the fit indices provide evidence of good fit.

Next, researchers usually examine the statistically significant relationships within the model. Figure 19.5 contains edited EQS output for evaluation of the regression coefficients for the example. If the unstandardized parameter estimates are divided by their respective standard errors, a z-score is obtained for each estimated parameter that is evaluated in the usual manner,

$$z = \frac{\text{parameter estimate}}{\text{std error for estimate}} \qquad (19.8)$$

Because of differences in scales, it is sometimes difficult to interpret unstandardized regression coefficients; therefore, researchers often examine standardized coefficients. Both the standardized and unstandardized regression coefficients for the final model are in Figures 19.5 and 19.6. In Figure 19.6 the standardized coefficients are in parentheses. Looking at Figure 19.5 in the section labeled 'MEASUREMENT EQUATIONS WITH STANDARD ERRORS AND TEST STATISTICS', for each dependent variable there are five pieces of information: the unstandardized coefficient is given on the first line; the standard error of the coefficient, given the assumption of normality, is given on the second line; and the test statistic for the coefficient, given normality, is given on the third line. The fourth line contains the standard error after adjustment for nonnormality (Bentler and Dijkstra, 1985), and the fifth line gives the test statistic after adjustment for the nonnormality. For example for FAMILY_S (V5) predicted from WK_BONDS (F1), if normal theory methods are used,

$$\frac{0.444}{0.021} = 20.732, \, p < 0.05$$

with an adjustment to the standard error for the nonnormality,

$$\frac{0.444}{0.026} = 17.408, \, p < 0.05$$

It could be concluded that FAMILY_S is a significant indicator of WK_BONDS; the

```
MEASUREMENT EQUATIONS WITH STANDARD ERRORS AND TEST STATISTICS
STATISTICS SIGNIFICANT AT THE 5% LEVEL ARE MARKED WITH @.
(ROBUST STATISTICS IN PARENTHESES)

GIVEIN2      = V1 = 1.000 F2 +   1.000 E1

DOFRNDS2     = V2 = 1.292*F2 +   1.000 E2
                    .111
                  11.641@
                 (   .123)
                 ( 10.535@

TEACH_SC     = V4 = .446*F1  +   1.000 E4
                    .022
                  20.159@
                 (   .026)
                 ( 17.408@

FAMILY_S     = V5 = .444*F1  +   1.000 E5
                    .021
                  20.732@
                 (   .025)
                 ( 17.621@

CONSTRUCT EQUATIONS WITH STANDARD ERRORS AND TEST STATISTICS
STATISTICS SIGNIFICANT AT THE 5% LEVEL ARE MARKED WITH @.
(ROBUST STATISTICS IN PARENTHESES)

RESIST_P = F2 =      .020*V3 +      .317*F1  +1.000 D2
                     .011              .026
                    1.898           12.200@
                 (   .011)         (   .029)
                 (  1.807)         ( 11.104@
```

```
MAXIMUM LIKELIHOOD SOLUTION (NORMAL DISTRIBUTION THEORY)
STANDARDIZED SOLUTION:                                            R-SQUARED

GIVEIN2 = V1      = .520 F2 +     .854 E1                           .270
DOFRNDS2 = V2     = .645*F2 +     .764 E2                           .416
TEACH_SC = V4     = .517*F1 +     .856 E4                           .267
FAMILY_S = V5     = .562*F1 +     .827 E5                           .316
RESIST_P = F2     = .043*V3 +     .539*F1  +.846 D2                 .285
```

Figure 19.5 *Parameter estimates and standardized solution for peer pressure example*

weaker the weak institutional bonds the weaker the bonds to family. TEACH_SC is a significant indicator of WK_BONDS. DOFRNDS2 is a significant indicator of RESIST_PP. Because the path from RESIST_PP to GIVEIN2 is fixed to 1 for identification, a standard error is not calculated. If this standard error is desired, a second run is performed with the DOFRNDS2 path fixed to 1 instead.

As seen in Figure 19.5, the relationships between the constructs appear in the EQS section labeled 'CONSTRUCT EQUATIONS WITH STANDARD ERRORS AND TEST STATIS- TICS'. WK_BONDS significantly predicts RESIST_PP (RESIST_PP is reverse-coded, so high scores on resistance to peer pressure imply *low* resistance to peer pressure). CHAN- SUB does not predict RESIST_PP.

Interpreting parameter estimates: Indirect effects A particularly strong feature of SEM is the ability to test not only direct effects between variables but also indirect effects.

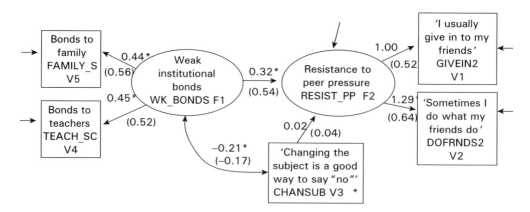

Figure 19.6 *Example with unstandardized and standarized coefficients*

Mediational hypotheses are not well illustrated in the peer pressure example so a better example is shown in Figure 19.7. Imagine that students are assigned to one of two teaching methods for a statistics class (coded 0 and 1). Final exam scores are recorded at the end of the quarter. The direct effect of teaching method on exam score is path *a*. But is it reasonable to suggest that mere assignment to a teaching method creates the change? Perhaps not. Maybe, instead, the teaching method increases a student's motivational level and higher motivation leads to a higher grade. The relationship between the treatment and the exam score is *mediated* by motivation level. Note that this is a different question than is posed with a direct effect: 'Is there a difference between the treatment and control group on exam score?' The indirect effect can be tested by testing the product of paths *b* and *c*. This example uses only measured variables and is called *path analysis*; however, mediational hypotheses can be tested using both latent and observed variables and can involve quite long chains of mediation across many variables. A more detailed discussion of indirect effects can be found in Baron and Kenny (1986), Collins et al. (1998), MacKinnon et al. (2000), and Sobel (1987).

Model modification

There are at least two reasons for modifying an SEM model: to test hypotheses (in theoretical work) and to improve fit (especially in

exploratory work). SEM is a confirmatory technique, therefore when model modification is done to improve fit the analysis changes from confirmatory to exploratory. Any conclusions drawn from a model that has undergone substantial modification should be viewed extremely cautiously. Cross-validation should be performed on modified models whenever possible.

The three basic methods of model modification are the chi-square difference, Lagrange multiplier (LM), and Wald tests. All are asymptotically equivalent under the null hypothesis, but they approach model modification differently. Currently there is no adjustment for violation of multivariate normality for the LM test or the Wald test. Care is needed if these tests are employed when there is evidence of nonnormality. However, Satorra and Bentler (2001) present procedures for Satorra–Bentler scaled chi-square difference tests. Therefore when there is non-normality the chi-square difference test may be preferable for *post hoc* model modifications. Here each of these approaches will be discussed with reference to the peer pressure example.

Chi-square difference test If models are nested, the χ^2 value for the larger model is subtracted from the χ^2 value for the smaller, nested model and the difference, also a χ^2, is evaluated with degrees of freedom equal to the difference between the degrees of freedom in the two models. In the peer pressure model we could test whether or not CHANSUB predicted RESIST_PP using the

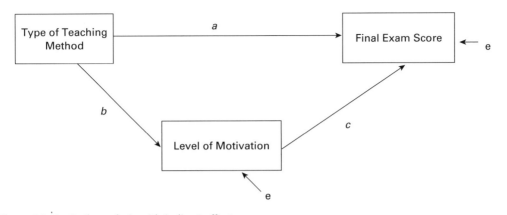

Figure 19.7 *Path analysis with indirect effect*

chi-square difference test. The model chi-square from the full model would be subtracted from the chi-square from a model estimated without the path from CHANSUB to RESIST_PP. This smaller model has one more degree of freedom and is nested within the larger model. If the chi-square difference test is significant we could conclude that CHANSUB does predict RESIST_PP. Notice that we did not delete the 'changing the subject' *variable* from the model, just the path. Had we deleted the variable the *data* would be different and the models would not be nested.

At least two potentially problematic issues arise that are specific to the use of chi-square difference tests. Because of the relationship between sample size and χ^2, it is hard to detect a difference between models when sample sizes are small. Additionally, and perhaps somewhat less important given current computer capabilities, two models must be estimated to use the chi-square difference test.

Lagrange multiplier test The LM test also compares nested models but requires estimation of only one model. The LM test asks whether the model would be improved if one or more of the parameters in the model that are currently fixed were estimated – or, equivalently, what parameters should be added to the model to improve the fit of the model.

The LM test applied to the peer pressure example indicates that if a path were added predicting TEACH_SC from CHANSUB the expected drop in χ^2 value would be 25.204. This is one path, so the χ^2 value of 25.204 is evaluated with 1 degree of freedom. The *p*

level for this difference is $p < 0.001$, implying that over and above the relationship between CHANSUB and WK_BONDS, there is a unique, significantly nonzero, relationship between CHANSUB and TEACH_SC. If the decision is made to add the path, the model is re-estimated. In this example the decision is made not to add this path.

The LM test can be examined either univariately or multivariately. There is a danger in examining only the results of univariate LM tests because overlapping variance between parameter estimates may make several parameters appear as if their addition would significantly improve the model. All significant parameters are candidates for inclusion by the results of univariate LM tests, but the multivariate LM test identifies the single parameter that would lead to the largest drop in model χ^2 and calculates the expected change in χ^2. After this variance is removed, the next parameter that accounts for the largest drop in model χ^2 is assessed similarly. After a few candidates for parameter additions are identified, it is best to add these parameters to the model and repeat the process with a new LM test, if necessary. Ideally, with this set of procedures a new sample should be used each time to avoid capitalizing on chance variation in the data and to replicate the findings.

Wald test While the LM test asks which parameters, if any, should be added to a model, the Wald test asks which, if any, could be deleted. Are there any parameters that are currently being estimated that could, instead, be fixed to zero? Or, equivalently, which parameters are not necessary in the model? The Wald test is analogous to backward deletion of variables in stepwise regression, where one seeks a nonsignificant change in R^2 when variables are left out.

When the Wald test is applied to the example, the only candidate for deletion is the regression coefficient predicting RESIST_PP from CHANSUB. If this parameter is dropped, the χ^2 value increases by 3.265, a nonsignificant change ($p = 0.071$). The model is not significantly degraded by deletion of this parameter. The decision is made to keep the path because this path was central to the hypothesis. However, if the goal is development of a parsimonious model, it might also be reasonable to drop the path. Notice that unlike the LM test, *nonsignificance* is desired when using the Wald test. When only a single parameter is evaluated, the Wald test is just the square of the z test we previously gave ($1.134 = 1.065^2$).

Some caveats and hints on model modification Because both the LM test and Wald test are stepwise procedures, Type I error rates are inflated. Hancock (1999) presents procedures for adjusting for Type I error inflation with a Scheffé-type procedure. A very simple approach is to use a conservative probability value (say, $p < 0.01$) for adding parameters with the LM test. Cross-validation with another sample is also highly recommended if modifications are made. If numerous modifications are made and new data are not available for cross-validation, compute the correlation between the estimated parameters from the original, hypothesized model and the estimated parameters from the final model using only parameters common to both models. If this correlation is high (greater than 0.90), relationships within the model have been retained despite the modifications.

Unfortunately, the order in which parameters are freed or estimated can affect the significance of the remaining parameters. MacCallum (1986) suggests adding all necessary parameters before deleting unnecessary parameters. In other words, do the LM test before the Wald test.

A more subtle limitation is that tests leading to model modification examine overall changes in χ^2, not changes in individual parameter estimates. Large changes in χ^2 are sometimes associated with very small changes in parameter estimates. A missing parameter may be statistically needed but the estimated coefficient may have an uninterpretable sign. If this happens it may be best not to add the parameter, although the unexpected result may help to pinpoint problems with one's theory. Finally, if the hypothesized model is wrong, tests of model modification, by themselves, may be insufficient to reveal the true model. In fact, the 'trueness' of any model is never tested directly, although cross-validation does add evidence that the model is correct. Like other statistics, these tests must be used thoughtfully.

If model modifications are done in hopes of developing a well-fitting model, the fewer modifications the better, especially if a cross-validation sample is not available. If the LM test and Wald tests are used to test specific hypotheses, the hypotheses will dictate the number of necessary tests.

MULTIPLE-GROUP MODELS

The example shown in this chapter uses data from a single sample. It is also possible to estimate and compare models that come from two or more samples, called multiple-group models (Jöreskog, 1971; Sörbom, 1974). The basic null hypothesis tested in multiple-group models is that the data from each group are from the same population with the same hypothesized model structure. For example, if data are drawn from a sample of boys and a sample of girls for the peer pressure model, the general null hypothesis tested is that the two groups are drawn from the same population. If such a restrictive model was acceptable, a single model and model-reproduced covariance matrix would approximate the two sample covariance matrices for girls and boys. Typically, identical models do not quite fit, and some differences between models must be allowed.

The analysis begins by developing well-fitting models in separate analyses for each group. The models are then tested in one overall analysis with none of the parameters across models constrained to be equal. This unconstrained multiple-group model serves as the baseline against which to judge more restricted models. Following baseline model estimation, progressively more stringent constraints are specified by constraining various parameters across all groups. When parameters are constrained they are forced to be equal to one another. In EQS, an LM test is available to evaluate whether the constraint is acceptable or needs to be rejected. The same result can be obtained by a chi-square difference test. The goal is to not degrade the models by constraining parameters across the groups; therefore, a *nonsignificant* χ^2 is required. If a significant difference in χ^2 is found between the models at any stage, the LM test can be examined to locate the specific parameters that are different in the groups. Such parameters should remain estimated separately in each group, that is, the specific *across-group* parameter constraints are released.

Hypotheses are generally tested in a specific order. The first step is usually to constrain the factor loadings (regression coefficients) between factors and their indices to equality across groups. In our hypothetical two-group model of resistance to peer pressure this would be equivalent to testing if the factor structure (the measurement model) of Weak institutional bonds and Resistance to peer pressure is the same for girls and boys. If these constraints are reasonable, the χ^2 difference test between the restricted model and the baseline model will be nonsignificant for both groups. If the difference between the restricted and nonrestricted models is significant, we need not throw in the towel immediately; rather, results of the LM test can be examined and some equality constraints across the groups can be released. Naturally, the more parameters that differ across groups, the less alike the groups are. See Byrne et al. (1989) for a technical discussion of these issues.

If the equality of the factor structure is established, there are options in terms of the order in which to test the equality of the samples. Often a reasonable second step is to ask if the factor variances and covariances are equal. If these constraints are feasible, the third step examines equality of the factor regression coefficients. Again, in our hypothetical two-group model this is equivalent to testing if the coefficient predicting Resistance to peer pressure from Weak institutional bonds is the same for girls and boys. If all of these constraints are reasonable, the last step is to examine the equality of residual variances across groups, an extremely stringent hypothesis not often tested. If all of the regression coefficients, variances, and covariances are the same across groups, it is concluded that these two samples arise from the

same population. An example of multiple-group modeling of program evaluation that utilizes a Solomon four-group design can found in Dukes et al. (1995).

Hitherto we have discussed modeling only variances and covariances. Means and intercepts can also be modeled using SEM techniques. Mean structures can be employed in single-group models; however, modeling means and intercepts is perhaps most commonly done in the context of a multiple-group model. In the next section we discuss incorporating a mean structure within a SEM model. Following this brief discussion we present a second example that incorporates a completely different type of model using a mean and covariance structure.

INCORPORATING A MEAN AND COVARIANCE STRUCTURE

Modeling means in addition to variances and covariances requires no modification of the Bentler–Weeks model. Instead a constant, a vector of 1s (labeled V999 in EQS), is included in the model as an independent variable. As a constant, this independent 'variable' has no variance and no covariances with other variables in the model. Regressing a variable (either latent or measured) on this constant yields an intercept parameter. The model-reproduced mean of a variable is equal to the sum of the direct and indirect effects for that variable. Therefore if a variable is predicted only from the constant, the intercept is equal to the mean; otherwise the mean is a function of path coefficients. In the hypothetical two-group resistance to peer pressure model, using a mean structure we could test the hypothesis that boys and girls have different average levels of resistance to peer pressure.

Another type of model that incorporates a mean structure is a latent growth curve model. Using intercept parameters, growth curve models allow questions to be examined about individual rate of change and average level of construct. A very simple example of a latent growth model will be illustrated next.

An extension of the basic model: Latent growth model example

Latent growth curve modeling is a type of single-group SEM model that employs intercept parameters to examine hypotheses

```
/TITLE
  Latent growth model
/SPECIFICATIONS
  DATA = 'D:\EQS6\lgm ny56789.ESS';
  VARIABLES = 8; CASES = 350; GROUPS = 1;
  METHODS = ML,ROBUST;
  MATRIX = RAW;
  ANALYSIS = MOMENT;
/LABELS
  V1 = GPA5; V2 = RELFAM45; V3 = DEV5; V4 = DEV6; V5 = DEV7;
  V6 = DEV8; V7 = DEV9; V8 = SEX9; F1 = INTERCEPT; F2 = LSLOPE;
/EQUATIONS
    V3 = + 1F1 + 0F2 + 1E3;
    V4 = + 1F1 + 1F2 + 1E4;
    V5 = + 1F1 + 2F2 + 1E5;
    V6 = + 1F1 + 3F2 + 1E6;
    V7 = + 1F1 + 4F2 + 1E7;

    F1 = *V999 + D1;
    F2 = *V999 + D2;
/VARIANCES
    D1,D2 = *;
    E3 TO E7    = *;
/COVARIANCES
    D1,D2 = *;
/LMTEST
/WTEST
/PRINT
    FIT = ALL;
    TABLE = EQUATION;
/END
```

Figure 19.8   *EQS syntax for latent growth model of general deviance*

about change. Specifically, questions about individual growth across multiple time points can be answered. The ability to look at individual change in both latent and observed variables across multiple time periods is one of the primary advantages of using this SEM application. Inter- and intra-participant variability in both rate of change and level of variable can also be tested, as can hypotheses about the relationship between the intercept and the slope. For example, we can ask whether the initial level of a variable relates to the rate of change in that variable. Finally, these models allow for statistical testing of the predictors for both (1) rate and shape of change in variables across time points and (2) levels of variables.

Data from this example are from part of a longitudinal study of 350 participants (254 women and 96 men). Details about the data collection and measures employed can be found in Ullman and Newcomb (1999). In this example we will look at change in the construct of general deviance (McGee and Newcomb, 1992) across a 16-year span. General deviance is a composite variable composed of measures of licit drug use (cigarettes and alcohol), illicit drug use (marijuana, heroin, cocaine), degree of social conformity (degree of law abidance, liberalism, and religiosity) and deviance (fighting, stealing, shoplifting). This very simple example models change in one measured variable (general deviance composite) across time. It is also completely feasible to model change in latent variables across time and also model change in more than one latent or measured variable across time.

Latent growth models can be employed with longitudinal data collected at three or more time points. In this example we use data collected at five time points (1980, 1984, 1988, 1992, and 1996). Participants were aged 15–16 in 1980. Although any type of trend can be hypothesized and tested, typically a linear trend is examined first. After

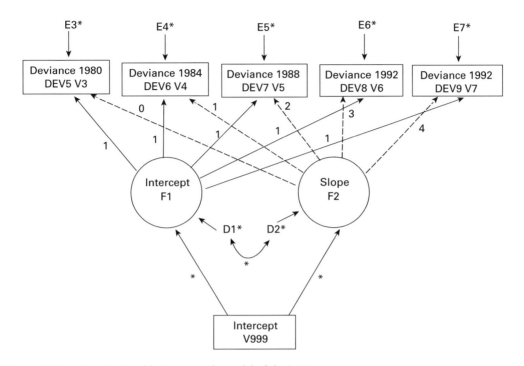

Figure 19.9 *Hypothesized latent growth model of deviance*

determining that the hypothesis of 'no change' can be rejected, we begin the modeling process by testing for a linear trend across the 16-year time frame. EQS syntax for this model is given in Figure 19.8 and the diagram for this model is given in Figure 19.9.

Notice the differences in Figure 19.8 between the syntax in the latent growth model and the syntax for the standard SEM model presented in Figure 19.3. First notice ANALYSIS=MOMENT; this indicates that intercepts in addition to variances and covariances will be modeled. Also, notice in Figures 19.8 and 19.9 that both the intercept and the slope are considered to be latent variables.

The intercepts are estimated by regressing both latent variables on a 'variable' that really is just a vector of 1s. In EQS this constant is labeled V999. In the /EQUATIONS section notice that all of the factor loadings are fixed – no paths are estimated. Although it is possible to estimate parameters for the intercept and slope, typically all, or most, of the paths are fixed. Generally, the paths from the latent variable for the intercept to the indicators are fixed to 1. The paths from the slope latent variable to its predictors are fixed to coefficients

that represent the shape of the function being tested. In this case we hypothesize a linear change and our time points are equally spaced so we simply use 0, 1, 2, 3, and 4.

After the general deviance model is specified, we generate a set of ML estimates. We also tested the model for compliance with the multivariate normality assumption and found Mardia's normalized coefficient to be 105.33, $p < 0.001$. Based on these results, we must assume multivariate *non*normality; therefore, we used the Satorra–Bentler scaled chi-square to evaluate the model. Severely edited output with test statistic and fit index information is given in Figure 19.10.

Given the output presented in Figure 19.8, we have evidence that the model of linear change fits the data: $\chi^2(N = 350, 10) = 20.61$, $p = 0.02$, CFI = 1.00, RMSEA = 0.055. Given evidence of fit, parameter estimates are examined. Truncated output for the parameter estimates is given in Figure 19.11.

As seen in the section labeled 'CONSTRUCT EQUATIONS WITH STANDARD ERRORS AND TEST STATISTICS' the unstandardized intercept (INTERCEPT) is 1.138, $z = 10.37$, $p < 0.001$. This tests the hypothesis that the

```
GOODNESS OF FIT SUMMARY FOR METHOD = ROBUST

  INDEPENDENCE MODEL CHI-SQUARE =  68.724 ON  10 DEGREES OF FREEDOM

  INDEPENDENCE AIC=  48.72422     INDEPENDENCE CAIC =      .14489
  MODEL AIC       =   .61637             MODEL CAIC = -47.96296


  SATORRA-BENTLER SCALED CHI-SQUARE = 20.6164 ON  10 DEGREES OF FREEDOM
  PROBABILITY VALUE FOR THE CHI-SQUARE STATISTIC IS  .02393


  FIT INDICES (BASED ON COVARIANCE MATRIX ONLY, NOT THE MEANS)
  ------------
  BENTLER-BONETT  NORMED FIT INDEX    = .930
  BENTLER-BONETT NON-NORMED FIT INDEX= 1.053
  COMPARATIVE FIT INDEX (CFI)         = 1.000
  BOLLEN    (IFI) FIT INDEX           = 1.036
  MCDONALD (MFI) FIT INDEX            = 1.003
  ROOT MEAN-SQUARE ERROR OF APPROXIMATION (RMSEA) = .055
  90% CONFIDENCE INTERVAL OF RMSEA        (       .019,       .089)
```

Figure 19.10 *Test statistic and fit indices for latent growth model*

intercept at the initial level (the level with the slope fixed to zero) is zero, i.e., children have different starting levels of general deviance. This hypothesis is easily rejected given the results of the z test. In our model this hypothesis is not particularly interesting because we would expect nonzero values for general deviance at the first time point. The slope parameter is examined next and certainly is of interest. The unstandardized slope of general deviance (LSLOPE) is –0.161, $z = 5.46$, $p < 0.001$. From this we can conclude that over the 16-year span of this study general deviance declined significantly.

Other hypotheses are also of interest in this analysis. Do participants have the same starting level for general deviance? Do participants change their levels of general deviance at different rates? Finally, is participants' starting level of general deviance associated with their rate of change in general deviance? These questions are answered in Figure 19.11 in the sections labeled 'VARIANCES OF INDEPENDENT VARIABLES'. Indeed, participants have significantly different starting levels of general deviance; the variance of D1 INTERCEP is 2.219, $z = 3.024$, $p < 0.001$. After adjusting the standard error for the variance of the slope of general deviance for nonnormality, we conclude that participants' rate of change in general deviance remains unchanged: D2 LSLOPE = 0.085, $z = 1.67$, $p > 0.05$. Finally, the

initial level of participants' general deviance is associated with participants' rate of change, the covariance between D1 and D2 being -0.352, $z = -2.169$, $p < 0.05$. The higher participants' level of general deviance in 1980, the slower their rate of change in deviance.

At this point it would be reasonable to estimate a new model that adds predictors of the linear change or initial level, or adds a quadratic component to describe change in general deviance. Unfortunately, these further analyses are outside the scope of this chapter. The reader interested in an in-depth discussion of latent growth models may want to refer to Curran (2000), Duncan et al. (1999), Khoo and Muthén (2000), McArdle (1986), McArdle and Epstein (1987), and Mehta and West (2000).

CONCLUSIONS

In this chapter we have attempted to introduce the reader to a powerful statistical technique, structural equation modeling. This technique allows examination of complex systems of variables that are both observed and unobserved. The use of latent variables allows relationships between theoretically error-free constructs to be examined. SEM also allows researchers to test hypotheses at the level of the construct rather then needing

```
CONSTRUCT EQUATIONS WITH STANDARD ERRORS AND TEST STATISTICS
  STATISTICS SIGNIFICANT AT THE 5% LEVEL ARE MARKED WITH @.
  (ROBUST STATISTICS IN PARENTHESES)

 INTERCEP = F1 =    1.138*V999 + 1.000 D1
                     .110
                   10.372@
                 (   .110)
                 ( 10.372@

 LSLOPE = F2   =   -.161*V999 + 1.000 D2
                     .030
                   -5.460@
                 (   .030)
                 ( -5.460@
```

VARIANCES OF INDEPENDENT VARIABLES

STATISTICS SIGNIFICANT AT THE 95% LEVEL ARE MARKED WITH @.

```
              E                           D
            ----                        ---
 E3   - DEV5   15.379*I   D1   - INTERCEP    2.219*I
               1.233 I                        .352 I
              12.472@I                       6.305@I
             (  3.156)I                    (   .734)I
             (  4.873@I                    (  3.024@I
                     I                            I
 E4   - DEV6    1.672*I   D2   - LSLOPE       .085*I
                .202 I                        .031 I
               8.279@I                       2.765@I
             (   .467)I                    (   .051)I
             (  3.584@I                    (  1.674)I
                     I                            I
 E5   - DEV7    1.700*I                            I
                .159 I                            I
              10.686@I                            I
             (   .475)I                           I
             (  3.578@I                           I
                     I                            I
 E6   - DEV8    2.085*I                            I
                .179 I                            I
              11.665@I                            I
             (   .508)I                           I
             (  4.106@I                           I
                     I                            I
 E7   - DEV9     .832*I                            I
                .144 I                            I
               5.777@I                            I
             (   .252)I                           I
             (  3.298@I                           I
                     I                            I
```

VARIANCES OF INDEPENDENT VARIABLES

STATISTICS SIGNIFICANT AT THE 95% LEVEL ARE MARKED WITH @.

```
              E                           D
            ----                        ---
                     I   D2   - LSLOPE      -.352*I
                     I   D1   - INTERCEP     .093 I
                     I                     -3.788@I
                     I                    (   .162)I
                     I                    ( -2.169@I
                     I                            I
```

Figure 19.11   *Parameter estimates for latent growth model*

to default to testing a construct-level hypothesis with a variable measured with error.

Our goal was to provide a general overview of SEM using applied examples. Therefore, we began the chapter with a brief introduction to the method. We used a real data example from the DARE literature to demonstrate basic modeling techniques and issues. After introducing the fundamental theoretical underpinnings and basic modeling techniques we presented a very simple example of an exciting new extension of basic SEM models, latent growth curve modeling, using data from a 16-year longitudinal study. SEM is a rapidly growing statistical area with much research into basic statistical topics such as model fit, model estimation with nonnormal data, estimating missing data/sample size. Research also abounds in new application areas such as latent growth curve modeling and multilevel models. This chapter has presented a general overview of the field but hopefully enticed readers to continue studying SEM, following the exciting growth in this area, and most importantly modeling their own data!

ACKNOWLEDGMENTS

This chapter was supported in part by NIDA grant DA 01070–28. Portions of the chapter appear in John A. Schinka and Wayne F. Velicer (eds), *Handbook of Psychology*, Vol. 2: *Research Methods in Psychology*, published in 2002 by John Wiley & Sons, Inc.

REFERENCES

Allison, P.D. (1987) 'Estimation of linear models with incomplete data', in C. Clogg (ed.), *Sociological Methodology 1987* San Francisco: Jossey Bass, pp. 71–103.

Baron, R.M. and Kenny, D.A. (1986) 'The moderator–mediator variable distinction in social psychological research: Conceptual, strategic, and statistical considerations', *Journal of Personality and Social Psychology*, 51: 1173–82.

Bentler, P.M. (1990) 'Comparative fit indexes in structural models', *Psychology Bulletin*, 107: 256–9.

Bentler, P.M. (2001) *EQS 6 Structural Equations Program Manual*. Encino, CA: Multivariate Software.

Bentler, P.M. and Dijkstra, T. (1985) 'Efficient estimation via linearization in structural models', in P.R. Krishnaiah (ed.), *Multivariate analysis VI*. Amsterdam: North-Holland, pp. 9–42.

Bentler, P.M. and Liang, J. (2003) 'Two-level mean and covariance structures: Maximum likelihood via an EM algorithm', in N. Duan and S. Reise (eds), *Multilevel Modeling: Methodological Advances, Issues and Applications*. Mahwah, NJ: Erlbaum, pp. 53–70.

Bentler, P.M. and Weeks, D.G. (1980) 'Linear structural equation with latent variables', *Psychometrika*, 45: 289–308.

Bentler, P.M. and Yuan, K-H. (1999) 'Structural equation modeling with small samples: Test statistics', *Multivariate Behavioral Research*, 34(2): 181–97.

Bollen, K.A. (1989) *Structural Equations with Latent Variables*. New York: Wiley.

Browne M.W. (1984) 'Asymptotically distribution-free methods for the analysis of covariance structures', *British Journal of Mathematical and Statistical Psychology*, 37: 62–83.

Browne, M.W. and Cudeck, R. (1993) 'Alternative ways of assessing model fit', in K.A. Bollen and J.S. Long (eds), *Testing Structural Models*. Newbury Park, CA: Sage.

Bryk, A.S. and Raudenbush, S.W. (1992) *Hierarchical Linear Models*. Newbury Park, CA: Sage.

Byrne, B.M., Shavelson, R.J. and Muthén, B. (1989) 'Testing for the equivalence of factor covariance and mean structures: The issue of partial measurement invariance', *Psychological Bulletin*, 105: 456–66.

Chou, C.-P., Bentler, P.M., and Pentz, M.A. (1998) 'Comparisons of two statistical approaches to study growth curves: The multilevel model and the latent curve analysis', *Structural Equation Modeling*, 5: 247–66.

Collins, L.M., Graham, J.W. and Flaherty, B.P. (1998) 'An alternative framework for defining mediation', *Multivariate Behavioral Research*, 33: 295–312.

Curran, P.J. (2000) 'A latent curve framework for the study of developmental trajectories in adolescent substance use', in J.R. Rose, L. Chassin, C.C. Presson and S.J. Sherman (eds), *Multivariate Applications in Substance Use Research: New Methods for New Questions*. Mahwah, NJ: Erlbaum, pp. 1–42.

Dukes, R.L., Ullman, J.B. and Stein, J.A. (1995) 'An evaluation of D.A.R.E. (Drug Abuse Resistance Education) using a Solomon four-group design with latent variables', *Evaluation Review*, 19: 409–33.

Duncan, T.E., Duncan, S.C., Strycker, L.A., Li, F. and Alpert, A. (1999) *An Introduction to Latent Variable Growth Curve Modeling: Concepts, Issues, and Applications*. Mahwah, NJ: Lawrence Erlbaum Associates.

Fouladi, R.T. (2000) 'Performance of modified test statistics in covariance and correlation structure analysis under conditions of multivariate nonnormality', *Structural Equation Modeling*, 7: 356–410.

Hancock, G.R. (1999) 'A sequential Scheffé-type respecification procedure for controlling Type I error in exploratory structural equation model modification', *Structural Equation Modeling*, 6: 158–68.

Heck, R.H. and Thomas, S.L. (2000) *An Introduction to Multilevel Modeling Techniques*. Mahwah, NJ: Lawrence Erlbaum Associates.

Hoogland, J.J. (1999) 'The robustness of estimation methods for covariance structure analysis'. Unpublished doctoral dissertation, Rijksuniversiteit Groningen, Netherlands.

Hu, L. and Bentler, P.M. (1998) 'Fit indices in covariance structural equation modeling: Sensitivity to underparameterized model misspecification', *Psychological Methods*, 3: 424–53.

Hu, L. and Bentler, P.M. (1999) 'Cutoff criteria for fit indexes in covariance structure analysis: Conventional criteria versus new alternatives', *Structural Equation Modeling*, 6: 1–55.

Hu, L.-T., Bentler, P.M. and Kano Y. (1992) 'Can test statistics in covariance structure analysis be trusted?', *Psychological Bulletin*, 112: 351–62.

Jamshidian, M. and Bentler, P.M. (1999) 'ML estimation of mean and covariance structures with missing data using complete data routines', *Journal of Educational and Behavioral Statistics*, 24: 21–41.

Jöreskog, K.G. (1971) 'Simultaneous factor analysis in several populations', *Psychometrika*, 57: 409–42.

Kano, Y., Berkane, M. and Bentler, P.M. (1990) 'Covariance structure analysis with heterogeneous kurtosis parameters', *Biometrika*, 77: 575–85.

Khoo, S.-T. and Muthén, B. (2000) 'Longitudinal data on families: Growth modeling alternatives', in J.S. Rose, L. Chassin, C.C. Preston and S.J. Sherman (eds), *Multivariate Applications in Substance Use Research: New Methods for New Questions*. Mahwah, NJ: Lawrence Erlbaum Associate, pp. 43–78.

Kreft, I. and de Leeuw, J. (1998) *Introducing Multilevel Modeling*. London: Sage.

Little, R.J.A. and Rubin, D.B. (1987) *Statistical Analysis with Missing Data*. New York: Wiley.

MacCallum, R. (1986) 'Specification searches in covariance structure modeling', *Psychological Bulletin*, 100: 107–20.

MacCallum, R.C., Browne, M.W. and Sugawara, H.M. (1996) 'Power analysis and determination of sample size for covariance structure modelling', *Psychological Methods*, 1: 130–49.

McArdle, J.J. (1986) 'Latent variable growth within behavior genetic models', *Behavior Genetics*, 16: 163–200.

McArdle, J.J. and Epstein, D. (1987) 'Latent growth curves within developmental structural equation models', *Child Development*, 58: 110–33.

McGee, L. and Newcomb, M.D. (1992) 'General deviance syndrome: Expanded hierarchical evaluations at four ages from early adolescence to adulthood', *Journal of Consulting and Clinical Psychology*, 60: 766–76.

MacKinnon, D.P., Krull, J.L. and Lockwood, C.M. (2000) 'Equivalence of mediation, confounding and suppression effect', *Prevention Science*, 1: 173–81.

Mehta, P.D. and West, S.G. (2000) 'Putting the individual back into individual growth curves', *Psychological Methods*, 5: 23–43.

Muthén, B.O. (1994) 'Multilevel covariance structure analysis', *Sociological Methods and Research*, 22: 376–98.

Muthén, B., Kaplan, D. and Hollis, M. (1987) 'On structural equation modeling with data that are not missing completely at random', *Psychometrika*, 52: 431–62.

Satorra, A. (1992) 'Asymptotic robust inferences in the analysis of mean and covariance structures', *Sociological Methodology*, 22: 249–78.

Satorra, A. (2000) 'Scaled and adjusted restricted tests in multi-sample analysis of moment structures', in D.D.H. Heijmans, D.S.G. Pollock and A. Satorra (eds) *Innovations in Multivariate Statistical Analysis: A Festschrift for Heinz Neudecker* Dordrecht: Kluwer Academic, pp. 233–47.

Satorra, A. and Bentler, P.M. (1988) 'Scaling corrections for chi-square statistics in covariance structure analysis', *Proceedings of the American Statistical Association*, 308–13.

Satorra, A. and Bentler, P.M. (1994) 'Corrections to test statistics and standard errors in covariance structure analysis', in A. von Eye and C.C. Clogg (eds), *Latent Variables Analysis: Applications for Developmental Research*. Thousand Oaks, CA: Sage, pp. 399–419.

Satorra, A. and Bentler, P.M. (2001) 'A scaled difference chi-square test statistic for moment structure analysis', *Psychometrika*, 66: 507–14.

Shapiro, A. and Browne, M.W. (1987) 'Analysis of covariance structures under elliptical distributions', *Journal of the American Statistical Association*, 82: 1092–7.

Snijders, T.A.B. and Bosker, R.J. (1999) *Multilevel Analysis: An Introduction to Basic and Advanced Multilevel Modeling*. London: Sage.

Sobel, M.E. (1987) 'Direct and indirect effects in linear structural equation models', *Sociological Methods and Research*, 16: 155–76.

Sörbom, D. (1974) 'A general method for studying differences in factor means and factor structures between groups', *British Journal of Mathematical and Statistical Psychology*, 27: 229–39.

Steiger, J. (2000) 'Point estimation, hypothesis testing and interval estimation using the RMSEA: Some comments and a reply to Hayduck and Glaser', *Structural Equation Modeling*, 7(2): 149–62.

Steiger, J.H. and Lind, J. (1980) 'Statistically based tests for the number of common factors'. Paper presented at the meeting of the Psychometric Society, Iowa City.

Ullman, J.B. (2001) 'Structural Equation Modeling', in B.G. Tabachnick and L.S. Fidell, *Using Multivariate Statistics* (4th edition). Boston: Allyn & Bacon, pp. 653–771.

Ullman, J.B. and Newcomb, M.D. (1999) 'The transition from adolescent to adult: A time of change in general and specific deviance', *Criminal Behavior and Mental Health*, 9: 101–17.

Yuan, K.-H. and Bentler, P.M. (1999) '*F* tests for mean and covariance structure analysis', *Journal of Educational and Behavioral Statistics*, 24: 225–43.

Yuan, K.-H. and Bentler, P.M. (2000). 'Three likelihood-based methods for mean and covariance structure analysis with nonnormal missing data', in Michael E. Sobel and Mark P. Becker (eds), *Sociological Methodology 2000*. Boston: Blackwell, pp. 165–200.

20

Multilevel Modelling

WILLIAM BROWNE AND JON RASBASH

In the social, medical and biological sciences multilevel or hierarchically structured populations are the norm. For example, school education provides a clear case of a system in which individuals are subject to the influences of grouping. Pupils or students learn in classes; classes are taught within schools; and schools may be administered within local authorities or school boards. The *units* in such a system lie at four different levels of a hierarchy. Pupils are assigned to level 1, classes to level 2, schools to level 3 and authorities or boards to level 4. Units at one level are recognized as being grouped or nested within units at the higher level. Other examples of hierarchical populations are people within households, within areas; patients in wards within hospitals; or animals within herds within farms. Such hierarchies are often described in terms of *clusters* of level 1 units within each level 2 unit, etc., and the term *clustered population* is used.

A common criticism of using statistical models to analyse quantitative data in the social sciences is that the standard methods place too much attention on the individual, and too little on the social and institutional contexts in which the individuals are located. Multilevel modelling redresses this imbalance by simultaneously modelling processes at all levels of the population hierarchy. By focusing attention on the levels of the hierarchy in the population, multilevel modelling enables the researcher to understand where and how effects are occurring.

Fitting a model which does not recognize the existence of clustering creates serious technical problems. For example, ignoring clustering will generally cause standard errors of regression coefficients to be underestimated. Consider a population where voters are clustered into wards and wards into constituencies. If the data are analysed ignoring the hierarchical structure of the population then the resulting underestimated standard errors might lead to the inference that there was a preference for one party when in fact the difference could be ascribed to chance. Correct standard errors would only be estimated if variation at the ward and constituency level was allowed for in the analysis. Multilevel modelling provides an efficient way of doing this. It also makes it possible to model and investigate the relative sizes and effects of ward and constituency characteristics on electoral behaviour, as well as that of individual characteristics such as gender and age.

We begin by developing the basic two-level model. Then we describe the use of contextual variables. Having done so, we describe how repeated measures or growth curve models can be fitted in a multilevel framework. We then proceed to describe multilevel multivariate response models, and multilevel models with discrete responses. Next we examine how multilevel models can be fitted in situations where the population structure is complex but not necessarily purely hierarchical. This is followed by a brief description

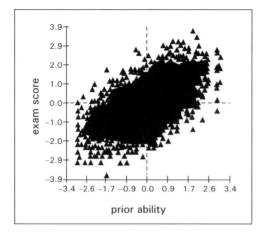

Figure 20.1 *Plot of exam score against prior ability for an educational data set*

RANDOM INTERCEPT AND RANDOM SLOPE MODELS

In this section we develop the basic two-level random intercept and random slope models. We locate the discussion in the context of an educational example where we have exam scores on pupils nested within schools. However, the ideas apply to any two-level structure – patients in hospitals, people in households, people in geographical areas, and so on. These basic models for two-level structures readily extend to structures with three or more levels – pupils within classes within schools, or people within families within geographical areas.

In our educational example we have data on 4059 students. The response is the exam score at age 16, and one of the main explanatory variables is a measure of prior ability of the students when they entered secondary school. Both these variables are standardized normal variables and their plot is shown in Figure 20.1.

We can write the standard regression model relating exam score to prior ability as

$$y_i = \beta_0 + \beta_1 x_i + e_i, \tag{20.1}$$

which gives us a single prediction line. Once we make this a multilevel model we can have a different prediction line for each school. Two possible models are: the *random intercept model*, where schools differ in terms of their intercept only, which gives rise to a set of parallel lines; and the *random slopes model*, where schools vary in terms of both their slopes and their intercepts, which gives rise to a set of (potentially) crossing lines. In the rest of this section we deal with these two models in turn.

Random intercept model

We can extend equation (20.1) to represent the random intercept model:

$$y_{ij} = \beta_{0j} + \beta_1 x_{ij} + e_{0ij}. \tag{20.2}$$

Here y_{ij} is the exam score for the ith child in the jth school, β_{0j} is the intercept for the jth school, β_1 is the slope coefficient for the prior ability variable, x_{ij} is the prior ability value for the ith child in the jth school, and e_{0ij} is the departure of the ith child in the jth school from its school's predicted line. The intercept for the jth school is expressed as

$$\beta_{0j} = \beta_0 + u_{0j} \tag{20.3}$$

where β_0 is the average intercept for all the schools in the sample, and u_{0j} is a random departure for the jth school. Substituting (20.3) into (20.1), we have

$$y_{ij} = \beta_0 + \beta_1 x_{ij} + u_{0j} + e_{0ij} \tag{20.4}$$

In the basic multilevel model we assume that

$$u_{0j} \sim N(0, \sigma_{u0}^2),$$
$$e_{0ij} \sim N(0, \sigma_{e0}^2).$$

Here we have hit one of the key differences between multilevel models and standard multiple regression. This model has two random variables for modelling the unexplained variance: a pupil-level random variable, e_{0ij}; and a school-level random variable, u_{0j}. Standard multiple regression only ever has one random variable for modelling the unexplained variance, often called the error term. As multilevel models become more complex, the unexplained variance is often structured by many random variables.

We estimate four parameters in this model. Two of them, β_0 and β_1, are like standard multiple regression coefficients: they give the average prediction line from which the jth school's line is offset by a random departure u_{0j}. These regression coefficients are called *fixed parameters*. In all the models described in this chapter fixed parameters are denoted by β; level 2 random departures (or 'random effects') are denoted by u and level 1 random effects by e. We also estimate the variance of the school-level intercept departures (σ_{u0}^2) and the variance of pupils' exam scores around their school's summary line (σ_{e0}^2).

In this model we have two levels. Pupils are the lowest-level units; generically the lowest level is called level 1. Pupils are nested within the higher-level units, schools; generically the higher level is called level 2. If we had a three-level nested population structure, for example pupils within classes within schools, then pupils would be level 1, classes would be level 2 and schools would be level 3.

The correlation between two students in the same school, which is referred to as the 'intra-level-2-unit correlation' is given by

$$\rho = \frac{\sigma_{u0}^2}{\sigma_{u0}^2 + \sigma_{e0}^2},$$

that is, the between-school variance over the total variance. The higher the value of this correlation, the more similar two students from the same school are, compared to two students picked at random from the population. That is, the 'clustering' effect of the higher-level units, in this case schools, is stronger. As the effect of clustering increases it becomes more important from both technical and substantive considerations to use multilevel techniques.

The technical issue is that standard multiple regression assumes that the observations are independent. Clearly, in the presence of clustering, this assumption is false. This results in the standard errors of the regression coefficients produced by multiple regression being underestimated, which can lead to incorrect inferences. You will be inferring that relationships are more significant than they actually are.

The substantive issue is that in the presence of high amounts of clustering much of the total variability is between higher-level units, and therefore it becomes important to explore the nature of this variability. Multilevel models provide an excellent framework for exploring differences between higher-level units.

The results for a random intercept model on our example educational data set with

Table 20.1 *Estimates for a random intercepts model*

Parameter	Estimate (s.e.)
Fixed	
β_0 (intercept)	0.002 (0.040)
β_1 (prior ability)	0.563 (0.013)
Random	
σ_{u0}^2 (between schools)	0.092 (0.018)
σ_{e0}^2 (between students)	0.057 (0.013)

4059 pupils from a sample of 65 schools are shown in Table 20.1. We see that the overall intercept, β_0, is close to zero, which we would expect since both the exam score and prior ability variables have been normalized. There is a strong positive association between prior ability and exam score, β_1. We also see significant between-school and between-student variability. The intra-school correlation is $0.092/(0.092 + 0.057) = 0.14$.

Residuals in a random intercepts model We may wish to explore the school and student random departures, known as *residuals*. In ordinary multiple regression, we can estimate the residuals simply by subtracting the predictions for each individual from the observed values. In multilevel models with residuals at each of several levels, a more complex procedure is needed. The true values of the level 2 residuals are unknown, but we will often require to obtain estimates of them. The iterated generalized least-squares algorithm (see below) directly estimates the fixed parameters and the covariance matrix of the multilevel residuals (random effects). We can in fact predict the actual values of the residuals given the observed data and the estimated parameters of the model.

The prediction procedure for residuals in a random intercepts model is as follows. Suppose that y_{ij} is the observed value for the ith student in the jth school and that $\hat{y}_{ij}$ is the predicted value from the average regression line. Then the *raw residual* for this subject is $r_{ij} = y_{ij} - \hat{y}_{ij}$. The raw residual for the jth school is the mean of these over the students in the school. Write this as r_{+j}. Then the predicted level 2 residual for this school is given by

$$\hat{u}_{0j} = \frac{\sigma_{u0}^2}{\sigma_{u0}^2 + \sigma_{e0}^2/n_j} \, r_{+j},$$

where n_j is the number of students in this school.

The multiplier in the above formula is always less than or equal to 1, so that the estimated residual is usually smaller in magnitude than the raw residual. We say that the raw residual has been multiplied by a *shrinkage factor* and the estimated residual is sometimes called a shrunken residual. The shrinkage factor will be noticeably less than 1 when σ^2_{e0} is large compared to σ^2_{u0} or when n_j is small (or both). In either case we have relatively little information about the school (its students are very variable or few in number) and the raw residual is pulled in towards the population average line. For more details on the derivation of the formula for $\hat{u}_{0j}$ see Goldstein (1995: Appendix 2.2). Henceforth in this chapter 'residual' will mean shrunken residual. Note that we can now estimate the level 1 residuals simply by the formula

$$\hat{e}_{0ij} = r_{ij} - \hat{u}_{0j}.$$

Residuals are typically used for two purposes. The first is diagnostic, for example to check that they are normally distributed, typically by constructing normal plots of standardized residuals against their normal scores or finding outlying units.

The second is to compare units. Figure 20.2 shows a plot of the estimated school-level residuals $(\hat{u}_{0j})$ from the model in Table 20.1, with their associated confidence intervals for the 65 schools in the example data set. The residuals are ranked on the plot. Recall that the school-level residuals $(\hat{u}_{0j})$ are the intercept departures of the *j*th school from the average line for all schools defined by $\hat{\beta}_0 + \hat{\beta}_1 x_{ij}$. Figure 20.2 shows that there are a group of 15 or so schools that are significantly above the average line (confidence intervals do not descend through the line $y = 0$), another group of 15 or so schools that are significantly below the average line (confidence intervals do not ascend through the line $y = 0$), and a middle group of 30 or so schools that show no significant difference from the average line. The estimated school-level intercept residuals can be used to form 65 separate prediction equations, one for each school:

$$\hat{y}_{ij} = \hat{\beta}_{0j} + \hat{\beta}_1 x_{ij}.$$

This prediction equation, when applied to each school's data, produces the 65 parallel lines shown in Figure 20.3.

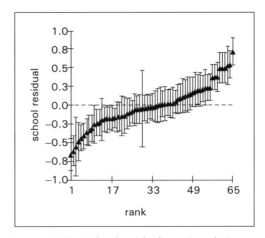

Figure 20.2 *School residuals against their rank, with associated 95% confidence intervals*

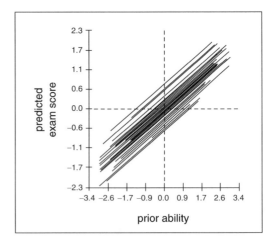

Figure 20.3 *Sixty-five predicted school lines from the random intercept model*

Random versus fixed effects models In this chapter we are describing random effects models for multilevel data structures. However, it is useful at this point to discuss the differences between random and fixed effects models, since often multilevel data are analysed using fixed effect models. The basic random intercept model described above is

$$y_{ij} = \beta_0 + \beta_1 x_{ij} + u_{0j} + e_{0ij},$$
$$u_{0j} \sim N(0, \sigma^2_{u0}),$$
$$e_{0ij} \sim N(0, \sigma^2_{e0}).$$

An alternative model for these data is to fit a dummy variable or fixed effect for each school's intercept term. That is,

$$y_{ij} = \sum_{j}^{J} \alpha_j Z_{ij} + \beta_1 x_{ij} + e_{0ij},$$

$$e_{0ij} \sim N(0, \sigma_{e0}^2),$$

where J is the total number of schools, α_j is the intercept for the jth school, and Z_{ij} is a dummy variable which takes value 1 if individual i attends school j, 0 otherwise. The random effects model regards the sampled schools as being randomly sampled from a larger population of schools; this population can be described by a statistical distribution. In the above model the population distribution for school effects is assumed to be $N(0, \sigma_{u0}^2)$. The multilevel model estimates σ_{u0}^2 directly. This allows us to make inferences to the population of schools from which we have drawn our sample. By contrast, the fixed effects model makes no distributional assumptions about the school effects.

The school effects (or school-level residuals) derived from a random effects model exploit the fact that school effects come from a distribution for which we have estimates of the distributional parameters, that is $N(0, \hat{\sigma}_{u0}^2)$. Therefore, a school effect estimated for a school for which we have very little data will be 'shrunk' towards the mean of the school effects distribution according to the formula for $\hat{u}_{0j}$ given earlier. If we believe that the schools in our data set come from a larger population of schools that can be characterized by a statistical distribution, then this shrinkage is a desirable property, since we are using information on all schools in our sample to position the school effect for any one school. The fixed effects model makes no distributional assumptions and each school effect is estimated without reference to the other schools in the sample.

In addition to allowing a greater generality of inference, the random effects model has an important practical advantage in that the number of parameters estimated does not increase as the number of units (in this case schools) increases. In our example data set we have 65 schools and we estimate four parameters (β_0, β_1, σ_{u0}^2, σ_{e0}^2); if we had 1000 schools we still have the same four parameters (they would of course be more precisely estimated by virtue of being derived from a larger data set). In a fixed effects model we have to fit 1000 dummy variables. Probably not many studies have 1000 schools; however, other multilevel data structures, for example repeated measures on individuals or

individuals within families, commonly have several thousand higher-level units. These practical problems for fixed effects models are further compounded when we want to fit random slope models (as described later): here, in addition to a set of J dummy variables for the intercept, another set of J variables are required to represent the interaction of the intercept dummies by the x variable whose slope we want to allow to vary across schools. As shown below, the random effects model only requires two further parameters to specify this model.

One disadvantage of random effects models is that the higher-level residuals are assumed to be uncorrelated with predictor variables. Such correlations can arise when important predictor variable(s) are missing from the model which determine both the predictor variables in the model and the higher-level residuals. In this case the higher-level residuals and the correlated predictor variable(s) are said to be endogenous and the random effects model is misspecified. The fixed effects model incorporates terms for the correlation between the coefficients of the predictor variables and the fixed effects representing the higher-level units (e.g., schools). In the presence of this kind of endogeneity the fixed effects model may be preferred because the coefficients of the correlated predictor variable(s) are unbiased, which is not the case in the random effects model.

One easy test for the endogeneity of higher-level residuals and fixed part predictor variables is to fit both the fixed and random effects model. If the standard errors of the predictor variables are consistent in both models, then you can safely use the random effects model. This is the basis of the so-called Hausman test (Hausman, 1978) for endogeneity. If there is some change across the two models then you have to make a judgement as to whether the generality of the random effects model warrants sacrificing accuracy of the point estimates. Often this judgement will depend on your focus. If you are very interested in making statements about variation between higher-level units, you will incline towards the random effects model. However, if you are concerned with precisely estimating average relationships and not interested in the structure and causes of higher-level variation, you will incline towards the fixed effects model.

In the case of the random effects model for our example data set, the fixed coefficient of the prior ability variable, which is potentially endogenous with the school effects, changes from 0.563 (0.013) to 0.559 (0.013) when moving from a random to a fixed effects model; this indicates there is no problem of endogeneity.

As in single-level models, the level 1 residuals and fixed part predictor can also be endogenous. In this case the technique of instrumental variables (see Verbeek, 2000, for details) can be used to obtain unbiased estimates of the fixed effects.

Random slopes model

We can extend the random intercept model to allow for the possibility of schools having different slopes by allowing the slope coefficient, β_1, to vary randomly at the school level. That is,

$$y_{ij} = \beta_{0j} + \beta_{1j}x_{1ij} + e_{ij},$$
$$\beta_{0j} = \beta_0 + u_{0j},$$
$$\beta_{1j} = \beta_1 + u_{1j}, \qquad (20.5)$$
$$\begin{bmatrix} u_{0j} \\ u_{1j} \end{bmatrix} \sim N(0, \Omega_u), \qquad \Omega_u = \begin{bmatrix} \sigma_{u0}^2 & \\ \sigma_{u01} & \sigma_{u1}^2 \end{bmatrix},$$
$$e_{0ij} \sim N(0, \sigma_{e0}^2).$$

u_{0j} and u_{1j} are random departures at the school level from β_0 and β_1. They allow the jth school's summary line to differ from the average line in both its slope and intercept. u_{0j} and u_{1j} follow a multivariate normal distribution with mean 0 and covariance matrix Ω_u. In this model we have two random variables at level 2, so Ω_u is a 2×2 covariance matrix. The elements of Ω_u are $\mathrm{var}(u_{0j}) = \sigma_{u0}^2$ (the variation across the school summary lines in their intercepts), $\mathrm{var}(u_{1j}) = \sigma_{u1}^2$ (the variation across the school summary lines in their slopes) and $\mathrm{cov}(u_{0j}, u_{1j}) = \sigma_{u01}$ (the school-level intercept/slope covariance). Students' scores depart from their schools summary line by an amount e_{0ij}.

The results from this model are shown in Table 20.2. The significant value for σ_{u1}^2 is evidence that the slope coefficient of prior ability varies across schools. In addition, there is a significant positive covariance between intercepts and slopes, estimated as 0.018, suggesting that schools with higher intercepts tend to have steeper slopes. This will lead to a fanning-out pattern when we plot the schools' predicted lines.

Figure 20.4 shows the 65 predicted school lines from the random slope model. We see

Table 20.2   Estimates for a random slopes model

Parameter	Estimate (s.e.)
Fixed	
β_0 (intercept)	−0.012 (0.040)
β_1 (prior ability)	0.566 (0.020)
Random	
Level 2	
σ_{u0}^2 (intercept)	0.090 (0.018)
σ_{u01} (covariance)	0.018 (0.006)
σ_{u1}^2 (prior ability)	0.015 (0.004)
Level 1	
σ_{e0}^2	0.55 (0.012)

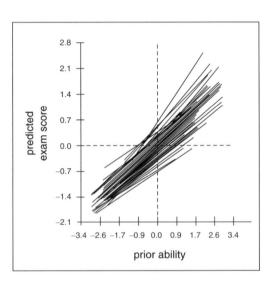

Figure 20.4   School prediction lines from a random slopes model

that schools' lines cross. So questions such as 'which school is better?' now have to be qualified: 'which school is better, for students of a given prior ability score?'.

We can go on and add further pupil-level explanatory variables to our model such as gender, socio-economic status or ethnicity, just as we would in multiple regression. As well as estimating an average effect, we can make the coefficients of these variables random at the school level to see if these average effects vary across schools. All the examples of explanatory variables listed are student or level 1 explanatory variables. In the next section we look at adding level 2 explanatory variables.

Table 20.3 *Effect of adding contextual variables modelling average school ability*

Parameter	Estimate (s.e.) A	Estimate (s.e.) B	Estimate (s.e.) C
Fixed:			
β_0 (intercept)	−0.012 (0.040)	−0.117 (0.08)	−0.184 (0.084)
β_1 (prior ability)	0.566 (0.020)	0.554 (0.020)	0.460 (0.042)
β_2 (mid)		0.084 (0.092)	0.149 (0.098)
β_3 (high)		0.231 (0.105)	0.324 (0.101)
β_4 (prior ability.mid)			0.089 (0.049)
β_5 (prior ability.high)			0.177 (0.055)
Random:			
Level 2			
σ_{u0}^2 (intercept)	0.090 (0.018)	0.078 (0.016)	0.078 (0.016)
σ_{u01} (covariance)	0.018 (0.006)	0.013 (0.006)	0.011 (0.005)
σ_{u1}^2 (prior ability)	0.015 (0.004)	0.015 (0.004)	0.011 (0.004)
Level 1			
σ_{e0}^2	0.553 (0.012)	0.553 (0.012)	0.55 (0.012)
Deviance	9316.9	9312.6	9303.76

CONTEXTUAL EFFECTS

Many interesting questions in social science are concerned with how individuals are affected by their social contexts. For example, do girls learn more effectively in a girls' school or a mixed-sex school? Do low-ability pupils fare better when they are educated alongside higher-ability pupils, or are they discouraged and fare worse? In this section we extend the random slopes model of equation (20.5) to address the second question. For each school we calculate the average prior ability of its pupils. Based on these averages, the bottom 25% of schools are coded 1 (low), the middle 50% coded 2 (mid) and the top 25% coded 3 (high). Note that when contextual variables are formed from a function of lower-level variables in this way, the resulting variables are referred to as compositional variables by some writers.

This categorical school-level contextual variable can be included in the model by adding explanatory variables for the mid and high groups which are contrasted with the reference group, low. The results are shown in model B of Table 20.3. Children attending mid and high ability schools score 0.084 and 0.231 points more than children attending low ability schools. The effects are of borderline statistical significance. This model assumes that the contextual effects of school ability are the same across the intake ability spectrum because these contextual effects are modifying the intercept term. For example, the effect of being in a high ability school is

the same for low ability and high ability pupils. To relax this assumption we need to include the interaction between prior ability and the school ability contextual variables.

This is done in model C, where the slope coefficient for prior ability for pupils from low intake ability schools is 0.460. For pupils from mid ability schools the slope is steeper, $0.460 + 0.089$, and for pupils from high ability schools the slope is steeper still, $0.460 + 0.177$. These two interaction terms have explained variability in the slope of prior ability in terms of a school-level variable, therefore the between-school variability of the prior ability slope (σ_{u1}^2) has been substantially reduced (from 0.015 to 0.011). We now have three different linear relationships between exam score and prior ability for pupils from low, mid and high ability schools. The prediction line for low ability schools is

$$\hat{\beta}_0 + \hat{\beta}_1 \text{ prior\_ability}_{ij},$$

and the prediction line for the high ability schools is

$$\hat{\beta}_0 + \hat{\beta}_1 \text{ prior\_ability}_{ij} + \hat{\beta}_3 \text{ high}_j + \hat{\beta}_5 \text{ prior\_ability.high}_{ij}.$$

The difference between these two lines, that is, the effect of being in a high ability school, is

$$\hat{\beta}_3 \text{ high}_j + \hat{\beta}_5 \text{ prior\_ability.high}_{ij}.$$

The graph of this last function, along with its confidence envelope, is shown in Figure 20.5. This graph shows how the effect of pupils

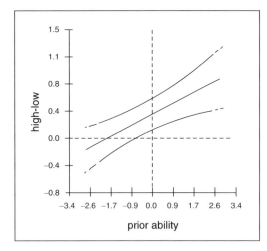

Figure 20.5 *High-low school ability difference as a function of pupil-level prior ability*

being in a high ability school as compared to a low ability school changes across the spectrum of pupil prior ability.

MULTILEVEL REPEATED MEASURES MODELS

Repeated measures data occur in many application areas, in particular in growth studies, where child or animal growth is measured over time. Repeated measurements also occur in medical applications and clinical trials where health outcomes, for example blood pressure or cell counts, are measured at different occasions, often before and after treatment with a particular drug. The important idea is that the measurements are nested within a subject and measure the same quantity but at different times. Note that repeated measurements can occur at a higher level of the hierarchy; for example in education at the school level, different cohorts of children may be measured over time and so the repeated measures are made on the higher-level units, schools.

There are two possible types of timing patterns for the measurements. Firstly, the timings may be systematic, which often happens in clinical trials and other designed experiments. Here each individual is measured at designated time intervals or ages. Secondly, the timings may be random, which occurs in observational studies. Here, for example, a growth study of wild animals may rely on the

animals being trapped and measured, which will happen at random times. As we generally fit the age/time of observation as a predictor variable, both these types of measurements will be fitted by exactly the same method. Note that if the observations occur at designated time points the data could be alternatively fitted as a multivariate response model, as described later.

Fitting repeated measures using a multilevel model

To fit repeated measures data using a multilevel model we consider the individual measurements as the level 1 units and the individuals as level 2 units. Measurements are regarded as independent and identically distributed observations within an individual. This means that in growth studies it would be as acceptable to observe individuals who shrink over time as individuals who grow and even individuals whose measurement fluctuates. Even though this assumption may not make sense in certain scenarios, we would generally fit the age or time of measurement as a predictor that now means that, instead of the measurements being independent and identically distributed observations, the fluctuations (residuals) from a growth versus age regression line are independent. Even this assumption may not be valid, and so models that implicitly model correlation between measurements are required and these are discussed in a later section. We will now illustrate repeated measures modelling in the following example.

An example

Our example concerns a longitudinal study of a cohort of 407 students from 33 infant schools who entered school in 1982. Each student's reading attainment was tested on up to six occasions between 1982 and 1989. For a student we have both their reading score and age at each occasion they were tested. More details of the study are available in Tizard et al. (1988).

The reading score is based on a different test, depending on the age of the children. These tests have then been scaled so that the scores are comparable. The test scores have been adjusted so that the mean score for the tests at a given age group is equal to the average age at that age group, and the variance

Table 20.4 *Results for variance components models (20.6) and (20.7)*

Parameter	Model (20.6) estimate (s.e.)	Model (20.7) estimate (s.e.)
Fixed:		
β_0 (intercept)	7.115 (0.053)	7.117 (0.041)
β_1 (age)	–	0.997 (0.007)
Random:		
σ_{u0}^2 (between individuals)	0.078 (0.083)	0.603 (0.048)
σ_{e0}^2 (within individuals)	4.562 (0.172)	0.307 (0.012)
Likelihood	7685.736	3795.588

has also been adjusted. The age variable has then been centred.

So we have a data set that has three levels. As the data are repeated measures we have individual reading test scores as the lowest level, with up to six level 1 units in each level 2 unit, the individual. Then the individuals are nested within level 3 units, schools, although in our analysis for simplicity this level will be ignored.

Typically we will be interested in how reading attainment changes as students get older, and how this pattern varies from student to student. The most basic model we could fit would be a simple variance components model with response y_{ij} being reading score:

$$y_{ij} = \beta_0 + u_{0j} + e_{0ij},$$
$$u_{0j} \sim N(0, \sigma_{u0}^2), \qquad (20.6)$$
$$e_{0ij} \sim N(0, \sigma_{e0}^2).$$

The estimates for this model are given in the middle column of Table 20.4. In this model we have not adjusted for age of the individuals and so the variance at level 1 is much greater than the variance at level 2. We can now add the age variable as a fixed effect:

$$y_{ij} = \beta_0 + \beta_1 x_{1ij} + u_{0j} + e_{0ij},$$
$$u_{0j} \sim N(0, \sigma_{u0}^2), \qquad (20.7)$$
$$e_{0ij} \sim N(0, \sigma_{e0}^2).$$

Here x_{1ij} is the age of individual j at time i. The estimates for model (20.7) are given in the right-hand column of Table 20.4. Here we see that the level 1 variance has shrunk dramatically with the addition of the age parameter. The age parameter estimate is approximately 1, which is an artefact of how the reading variable was created. The likelihood has been dramatically reduced and so this is a significantly better model for the data. We can also see that now the level 2 variance (between individuals) is double the level 1 variance. It is often the case in repeated

measures models that the majority of the variation is at level 2 rather than level 1, which is different from most multilevel models. The current model is fitting a simple common regression line for the relationship between reading and age with residuals to allow parallel regression lines for each individual.

We will now increase the complexity of the model by allowing regression lines with different slopes for each individual. The model is a standard random slopes regression model.

$$y_{ij} = \beta_{0j} + \beta_{1j} x_{1ij} + e_{ij},$$
$$\beta_{0j} = \beta_0 + u_{0j},$$
$$\beta_{1j} = \beta_1 + u_{1j}, \qquad (20.8)$$
$$\begin{bmatrix} u_{0sj} \\ u_{1j} \end{bmatrix} \sim N(0, \Omega_u), \qquad \Omega_u = \begin{bmatrix} \sigma_{u0}^2 & \\ \sigma_{u01} & \sigma_{u1}^2 \end{bmatrix},$$
$$e_{0ij} \sim N(0, \sigma_{e0}^2).$$

The estimates for model (20.8) are given in the middle column of Table 20.5. Here we see that allowing the slopes of the individual regression lines to vary has again reduced the level 1 variance. There is significant variation between the slopes of the lines and the likelihood has again been reduced by a large amount, suggesting this is a significantly better model than model (20.7).

We can elaborate this model further by allowing each regression between reading and age to be a quadratic curve rather than a straight line. The equation for this model is given by

$$y_{ij} = \beta_{0j} + \beta_{1j} x_{1ij} + \beta_{2j} x_{1ij}^2 + e_{ij},$$
$$\beta_{0j} = \beta_0 + u_{0j},$$
$$\beta_{1j} = \beta_1 + u_{1j}, \qquad (20.9)$$
$$\beta_{2j} = \beta_2 + u_{2j},$$
$$\begin{bmatrix} u_{0j} \\ u_{1j} \\ u_{2j} \end{bmatrix} \sim N(0, \Omega_u), \qquad \Omega_u = \begin{bmatrix} \sigma_{u0}^2 & & \\ \sigma_{u01} & \sigma_{u1}^2 & \\ \sigma_{u02} & \sigma_{u12} & \sigma_{u2}^2 \end{bmatrix},$$
$$e_{0ij} \sim N(0, \sigma_{e0}^2).$$

Table 20.5   *Results for random slopes models (20.8) and (20.9)*

Parameter	Model (20.8) estimate (s.e.)	Model (20.9) estimate (s.e.)
Fixed:		
β_0 (intercept)	7.117 (0.043)	7.115 (0.046)
β_1 (age)	0.995 (0.012)	0.995 (0.007)
β_2 (age squared)	–	0.001 (0.003)
Random:		
Level 2		
σ^2_{u0} (intercept)	0.683 (0.053)	0.765 (0.060)
σ_{u01}	0.123 (0.012)	0.139 (0.014)
σ^2_{u1} (age)	0.037 (0.004)	0.039 (0.004)
σ_{u02}	–	–0.014 (0.003)
σ_{u12}	–	–0.002 (0.001)
σ^2_{u2} (age squared)	–	0.001 (0.000)
Level 1		
σ^2_{e0}	0.161 (0.007)	0.134 (0.007)
Likelihood	3209.392	3137.620

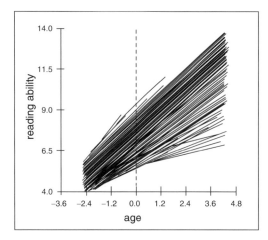

Figure 20.6   *Plot of individual reading versus age regression curves for model (20.9)*

The resulting estimates are given in the right-hand column of Table 20.5. Here we again see a decrease in likelihood and a reduction of level 1 variance. The age-squared fixed effect estimate is very small, but there is some variability around this estimate. We can plot the resulting curves for the individuals as shown in Figure 20.6. Often in growth studies it is common to fit a polynomial relationship between height or weight and age as we have done here for reading ability.

MULTIVARIATE MODELS

In previous sections we have considered only a single response variable. In this section we look at models where we wish simultaneously to model several responses as functions of explanatory variables. The ability to do this provides us with tools for tackling a wide range of problems. These problems include missing data and rotation or matrix designs for surveys.

We shall be using data consisting of scores on two components of a science examination taken in 1989 by 1905 students in 73 schools in England to illustrate the multilevel multivariate response model. The examination is the General Certificate of Secondary Education (GCSE) taken at the end of compulsory schooling, normally when students are 16 years of age. The first component is a traditional written question paper (marked out of a total score of 160), and the second consists of coursework (marked out of a total score of 108). This coursework includes projects undertaken during the course and marked by each student's own teacher, but also 'moderated' (i.e., a sample checked) by external examiners. Interest in these data centres on the relationship between the component marks at both the school and student level, whether there are gender differences in this relationship and whether the variability differs for the two components.

Table 20.6 *Data matrix for the examination data*

Student	Response y_{ij}	Intercepts		Gender	
		Written z_{1ij}	Coursework z_{2ij}	Written $z_{1ij} x_j$	Coursework $z_{2ij} x_j$
1 (female)	y_{11}	1	0	1	0
1	y_{12}	0	1	0	1
2 (male)	y_{21}	1	0	0	0
2	y_{22}	0	1	0	0
3 (female)	y_{31}	1	0	1	0

Specifying a multivariate model

To define a multivariate (in the case of our example a bivariate) model we treat the individual student as a level 2 unit and the 'within-student' measurements (in our case written and coursework responses) as level 1 units. Each level 1 measurement 'record' has a response, which is either the written paper score or the coursework score. The basic explanatory variables are a set of dummy variables that indicate which response variable is present. Further explanatory variables are defined by multiplying these dummy variables by individual-level explanatory variables, for example gender. Omitting school identification, the data matrix for three students, two of whom have both measurements and the third who has only the written paper score, is displayed in Table 20.6. The first and third students are female (1) and the second is male (0).

The statistical model for the two-level model, ignoring the school level, is written as follows:

$$y_{ij} = \beta_0 z_{1ij} + \beta_1 z_{2ij} + \beta_2 z_{1ij} x_j + \beta_3 z_{2ij} x_j + u_{0j} z_{1ij} + u_{1j} z_{2ij},$$

$$z_{1ij} = \begin{cases} 1 & \text{if written,} \\ 0 & \text{if coursework,} \end{cases} \quad z_{2ij} = 1 - z_{1ij},$$

$$x_j = \begin{cases} 1 & \text{if girl,} \\ 0 & \text{if boy,} \end{cases}$$

$$\text{var}(u_{0j}) = \sigma_{u0}^2, \quad \text{var}(u_{1j}) = \sigma_{u1}^2,$$

$$\text{cov}(u_{0j}, u_{1j}) = \sigma_{u01}$$

(20.10)

There are several interesting features of this model. There is no level 1 variation specified, because level 1 exists solely to define the multivariate structure. The level 2 variances and covariance are the (residual) between-student variances. In the case where only the intercept dummy variables are fitted, and in the case where every student has both scores, the model estimates of these parameters become the usual between-student estimates

of the variances and covariance. The multilevel estimates are statistically efficient, even where some responses are missing.

Thus, the formulation as a two-level model allows for the efficient estimation of a covariance matrix with missing responses, where the missingness is at random. This means, in particular, that studies can be designed in such a way that not every individual has every measurement, with measurements randomly allocated to individuals. Such 'rotation' or 'matrix' designs are common in many areas and may be efficiently modelled in this way (for a more detailed discussion, see Goldstein, 1995: Chapter 4). The ability to provide estimates of covariance matrices at each higher level of a data hierarchy enables further models such as multilevel factor analyses to be fitted (see Rowe and Hill, 1997).

A third level, school, can be incorporated, and this is specified by inserting a third subscript, k, and two associated random intercept terms:

$$y_{ijk} = \beta_0 z_{1ijk} + \beta_1 z_{2ijk} + \beta_2 z_{1ijk} x_{jk} + \beta_3 z_{2ijk} x_{jk} + v_{0k} z_{1ijk} + v_{1k} z_{2ijk} + u_{0jk} z_{1ijk} + u_{1jk} z_{2ijk},$$

$$z_{1ijk} = \begin{cases} 1 & \text{if written,} \\ 0 & \text{if coursework,} \end{cases} \quad z_{2ijk} = 1 - z_{1ijk},$$

$$x_{jk} = \begin{cases} 1 & \text{if girl,} \\ 0 & \text{if boy,} \end{cases}$$

(20.11)

$$\begin{bmatrix} v_{0k} \\ v_{1k} \end{bmatrix} \sim N(0, \Omega_v), \quad \Omega_v = \begin{bmatrix} \sigma_{v0}^2 & \\ \sigma_{v01} & \sigma_{v1}^2 \end{bmatrix},$$

$$\begin{bmatrix} u_{0jk} \\ u_{1jk} \end{bmatrix} \sim N(0, \Omega_u), \quad \Omega_u = \begin{bmatrix} \sigma_{u0}^2 & \\ \sigma_{u01} & \sigma_{u1}^2 \end{bmatrix},$$

The 2×2 covariance matrix between written and coursework responses is partitioned into a between-student component Ω_u and a between-school component Ω_v. The mean of the written paper responses for boys is estimated by β_0, the mean of coursework

Table 20.7 *Results from a multivariate response model of the GCSE data*

Parameter	Estimate (s.e.)
Fixed:	
β_0 (written)	49.5 (0.90)
β_1 (coursework)	69.7 (1.2)
β_2 (written.girl)	−2.5 (0.6)
β_3 (coursework.girl)	6.8 (0.7)
Random:	
Level 3 (school)	
σ_{v0}^2 (written)	46.8 (9.2)
σ_{v01} (covariance)	24.9 (8.9), $\rho = 0.42$
σ_{v1}^2 (coursework)	75.2 (14.6)
Level 2 (student)	
σ_{u0}^2 (written)	124.6 (4.3)
σ_{u01} (covariance)	73.0 (4.2), $\rho = 0.49$
σ_{u1}^2 (coursework)	180.1 (6.2)

responses for boys is estimated by β_1, the girl–boy difference for the written paper responses is estimated by β_2, and the girl–boy difference for the coursework responses is estimated by β_3. The results are shown in Table 20.7. The girls do somewhat worse on the written paper (−2.5) but considerably better than the boys on the coursework component of the examination (6.8). The coursework component also has a larger variance at both student and school level, with correlations between coursework and written 0.42 and 0.49 at school and student level, respectively. The intra-school correlation is 0.27 for the written paper and 0.29 for the coursework.

This model could be extended further, by allowing the girl–boy differences for each response to vary across schools. Further explanatory variables can be added and their coefficients can vary randomly at either level.

Another interesting example of multilevel multivariate modelling is given in Duncan et al. (1999). Here individuals have two responses. The first is a binary response indicating whether or not an individual smokes. The second is only present for those individuals who smoke, and is the number of cigarettes smoked. This model has two interesting features. Firstly, if we were to model the number smoked as a continuous univariate response, there would be a large spike at zero, which would violate any simple normal theory and is tricky to model correctly. However, in the multivariate framework, these individuals are properly included by the first binary response. Secondly, the covariance between the two responses at higher levels

can be very informative. In Duncan et al. the individuals were nested within neighbourhoods. A positive covariance at the neighbourhood level means that smokers who are in an area where the probability of smoking is high will tend to smoke more cigarettes than smokers in an area where the probability of smoking is low. In other words, if you are a smoker and a lot people around you are smoking you will smoke more cigarettes than if you are not surrounded by smokers.

MULTILEVEL MODELS FOR DISCRETE RESPONSE DATA

So far we have assumed that the response variable of interest was a continuous variable. In the previous section we showed how to combine several continuous variables via a multivariate model. We also mentioned an example that involved a smoking response that was not regarded as continuous but took values that were either 0 or 1. In this section we will look at multilevel models where the response variable is discrete.

There are two main types of discrete data variables. The first type are proportional data, where the response can take values 0, $1/N$, $2/N,\ldots,1$ (with the special case of binary 0,1 data), N being the size of the population, for example the proportion of people who pass a maths test, are in favour of abortion, or own red cars. The second type are count data where the response can take any positive integer value, for example the number of instances of a particular disease, the number of children born on a particular day, or the number of cars that travel through a road junction in a 10-minute period.

It is common practice to use the binomial distribution to fit models to proportional data and the Poisson distribution to fit models to count data. In the rest of this section we will concentrate mainly on binomial models, and mention Poisson models only briefly at the end of the section. Other more complex models with discrete responses, such as multi-category data (ordered and unordered) and event history data, will be discussed briefly with further references later in this chapter.

Binomial data

When we consider proportional data we have a response saying that x out of y observations

Table 20.8 *Common link functions for the binomial distribution*

Function name	Formula
Logit	$\log_e [\pi/(1-\pi)]$
Probit	$\Phi^{-1}(\pi)$
Complementary log-log	$\log_e [-\log_e(1-\pi)]$

have a particular property, for example 8 out of 10 people questioned eat meat. Here our response is whether people eat meat and any individual person either eats meat or does not. So we assume that in the population in general there is an underlying probability π, such that $0 \leq \pi \leq 1$ that a person eats meat. We have taken 10 people at random and found that 8 of them eat meat, so an estimate of π based on our 10 people is $8/10 = 0.8$.

Of course we may expect the probability that people eat meat to be different depending on characteristics of the individual. For example, if an individual's parents are vegetarian we might expect them to be more likely to be vegetarian; gender and religion may also influence whether a person eats meat.

We could of course fit a model to this data set assuming the variable to be normally distributed, but this may give us problems. For example, suppose we fitted a model for the probability of eating meat with predictors *age* and *gender* and got the following fixed effects estimates:

$$\pi_i = 0.8 + 0.05 \; gender_i + 0.003 \; age_i,$$

where $gender_i = 1$ for male, 0 for female. Then for a male aged 52 the estimated probability of eating meat is $1.006 > 1.0$. A probability that does not lie between 0 and 1 is clearly a problem, so we generally model the probabilities with a binomial distribution rather than a normal distribution.

Since the prediction equation can theoretically generate values in the range $(-\infty, \infty)$, we need to transform via a function the probability π to a value that lies on the whole real line. These functions are known as link functions and there are three common link functions for the binomial distribution as shown in Table 20.8. We will use the logit function in the examples that follow, but the other two functions can be used in an analogous way. Generally, modelling binomial data with a logit function is known as logistic regression and is not in itself a multilevel technique. To translate logistic regression to multilevel logistic regression is analogous to moving

from linear modelling to normal response multilevel modelling. As we will see in the example that follows, we have a higher-level classification of the data across which we believe the probability response varies.

Example: a data set on political voting intentions

This example comes from the longitudinal component of the British Election Study (see Heath et al., 1996). It consists of a sub-sample of 800 voters grouped within 110 voting constituencies who were asked how they voted in the 1983 British general election. For our purposes the responses are classified simply as to whether or not the individual voted Conservative. We are interested in establishing what factors influence whether a voter votes Conservative while accounting for different underlying probabilities due to the constituencies. We have as predictor variables four attitudinal variables that describe the individual voters' attitude (on a 21-point scale) to important issues of the day, namely defence, unemployment, taxes and privatization.

To start our analysis we will fit a simple variance components model as follows:

$$y_{ij}|u_{0j} \sim \text{Binomial } (1, \pi_{ij}),$$
$$\text{logit } (\pi_{ij}) = \beta_0 + u_{0j}, \qquad (20.12)$$
$$u_{0j} \sim N(0, \sigma_{u0}^2).$$

Unlike the normal models that we have fitted so far, the variance at level 1 is constrained by the binomial assumption and is not estimated. In fact, when we use the logistic link function the level 1 variance is approximately $\pi^2/3 = 3.29$. When we fit the above model to the voting data set we get the estimates given in the middle column of Table 20.9. Here we see that the variance between constituencies is a lot smaller than the variance within constituencies (3.29).

To interpret the fixed effect intercept value, β_0, we need to use the anti-logit function to transform the value back to the probability scale. Here we have $[1 + \exp (0.248)]^{-1} = 0.438$, which is an estimate of the median proportion of people voting Conservative.

To answer our questions on the effects of the attitudinal variables we need to expand our model as follows:

Table 20.9   *Estimates for two variance component models fitted to the voting data set*

Parameter	Model (20.12) estimate (s.e.)	Model (20.13) estimate (s.e.)
Fixed:		
β_0 (intercept)	−0.248 (0.081)	−0.367 (0.095)
β_1 (defence)	–	0.093 (0.018)
β_2 (unemployment)	–	0.069 (0.014)
β_3 (taxes)	–	0.046 (0.019)
β_4 (privatisation)	–	0.143 (0.018)
Random:		
σ^2_{u0} (between constituencies)	0.134 (0.091)	0.167 (0.119)

$$y_{ij}|u_{0j} \sim \text{Binomial}\,(1, \pi_{ij}),$$
$$\text{logit}(\pi_{ij}) = \beta_0 + \beta_1 x_{1ij} + \beta_2 x_{2ij}$$
$$+ \beta_3 x_{3ij} + \beta_4 x_{4ij} + u_{0j},$$
$$u_{0j} \sim N(0, \sigma^2_{u0}). \qquad (20.13)$$

Here x_{1ij} is opinion on defence, x_{2ij} is opinion on unemployment, x_{3ij} is opinion on taxes and x_{4ij} is opinion on privatization. The results of fitting model (20.13) can be seen in the right-hand column of Table 20.9. Here we see that all attitudinal variables have positive predictors, and this is due to the way the scales were created. We can conclude that a person is more likely to vote Conservative if they have the following views:

- They are in favour of Britain possessing nuclear weapons.
- They prefer more unemployment if it in turn leads to low inflation.
- They are against paying more taxes to pay for more government spending.
- They are in favour of privatization of public services.

All the predictors were centred, so we can now interpret the person with 0 for all attitudinal variables as a person with average views. Such a person has an estimated $[1 + \exp(0.367)]^{-1} = 0.409$ probability of voting Conservative.

To interpret the effect of the predictor variables due to the non-linear relationship between the response and the predictor variables it is best to consider specific cases in isolation. For example, a person whose view on possessing nuclear weapons is 5 points above average (assuming all other variables are 0) will have an estimated $[1 + \exp(0.367 - 5 \times 0.093)]^{-1} = 0.524$ probability of voting Conservative. As all the predictors are on the

same scale we can compare their parameter estimates, and this shows that a person's view on privatization has the greatest effect on their underlying probability of voting Conservative.

Count data

As with the proportional data that we studied earlier in this section, count data have restrictions on the values they take. Count data must take positive integer values (or zero), and so if we were to fit the count response as a normal response we could get predicted counts that were negative. This is clearly a problem, and so instead the Poisson distribution is used. The Poisson distribution has a parameter that represents the rate at which events occur in the underlying population. A log link function is used for the Poisson distribution, since we need to convert our prediction equation values, which can lie in the range $(-\infty, \infty)$, so that they lie in the range $(0, \infty)$.

The fitting of Poisson models is essentially similar to binomial models. A health-based example of a multilevel Poisson model involving counts of deaths due to malignant melanoma in the European Community is given in Langford et al. (1998).

NON-HIERARCHICAL MULTILEVEL MODELS

In the models discussed in this chapter so far we have assumed the populations from which data have been drawn are hierarchical. This assumption is not always justified. Two main types of non-hierarchical model will be considered in this section, cross-classified models and multiple-membership models.

Table 20.10 *Patients cross-classified by hospital and neighbourhood*

	Neighbourhood 1	Neighbourhood 2	Neighbourhood 3
Hospital 1	×	××	
Hospital 2	××	××	×
Hospital 3	×××		××
Hospital 4	×	××	××
Hospital 5	××		

Two-way cross-classifications – a basic model

Suppose we have data on a large number of patients, attending many hospitals, and we also know the neighbourhood in which each patient lives. Suppose that we regard patient, neighbourhood and hospital as important sources of variation for the patient-level outcome measure we wish to study. Now, typically hospitals will draw patients from many different neighbourhoods and the inhabitants of a neighbourhood will go to many hospitals. No pure hierarchy can be found, and patients are said to be contained within a cross-classification of hospitals by neighbourhoods. This is represented diagrammatically in Table 20.10 for the case of 20 patients contained within a cross-classification of three neighbourhoods by five hospitals.

There are many other examples of two-way cross-classifications: pupils grouped within a cross-classification of primary school by secondary school (see Goldstein and Sammons, 1997); patients grouped within a cross-classification of primary by secondary health care units; in survey analysis we can have individuals grouped within a cross-classification of interviewers by areas (see O'Muircheartigh and Campanelli, 1999).

The basic two-way, normal response, cross-classified variance components model can be written as

$$y_{i(j_1, j_2)} = (X\beta)_{i(j_1, j_2)} + u_{j1}$$
$$+ u_{j_2} + e_{i(j_1, j_2)},$$
$$u_{j_1} \sim N(0, \sigma_{u1}^2), \quad (20.14)$$
$$u_{j_2} \sim N(0, \sigma_{u2}^2),$$
$$e_{i(j_1, j_2)} \sim N(0, \sigma_e^2),$$

where $(X\beta)_{i(j_1, j_2)}$ is the linear predictor. Using the example of students within a cross-classification of primary by secondary schools, $y_{i(j_1, j_2)}$ is the exam score at age 16 of the ith student, contained in the cell defined by primary school j_1 and secondary

school j_2; u_{j_1} is the random effect for primary school j_1, u_{j_2} is the random effect for secondary school j_2, and $e_{i(j_1, j_2)}$ is a level 1 residual for the ith student contained in the cell defined by primary school j_1 and secondary school j_2.

The results for this model fitted to an educational data set with 3435 students who attended 148 primary schools and 19 secondary schools in Fife, Scotland, are shown in Table 20.11. Model A fits students within primary schools and ignores secondary school, model B fits students within secondary schools and ignores primary school, and model C fits the cross-classification. The response is an attainment score at age 16, and the explanatory variable, vrq, is a verbal reasoning measure taken at age 11. Notice that in all three models the sum of the variance components is 4.53. When one side of the cross-classification is ignored, the released variance is split between the classification left in the model and the pupil-level variance, inflating both estimates. This has the most drastic effect when the primary school hierarchy is ignored; in this case (model B) the inflated estimate of the between secondary school variance is 2.5 times its standard error, as opposed to 0.5 times its standard error in the full model.

A variety of more complex patterns of cross-classification are possible. A fuller account is given in Rasbash and Browne (2000).

Multiple-membership models

Where lower-level units are influenced by more than one higher-level unit from the same classification we have a multiple-membership model. For example, if patients are treated by several nurses, then patients are 'multiple members of' nurses. Each of the nurses treating a patient contributes to the treatment outcome.

A two-level multiple-membership model can be written as

Table 20.11 *Comparison of results from incomplete nested model versus full cross-classified model for the Fife educational data*

	Pupils within primary school model A	Pupils within secondary school model B	Crossed model C
Fixed:			
β_0 (intercept)	5.97 (0.07)	6.023 (0.06)	5.98 (0.07)
β_1 (vrq)	0.16 (0.003)	0.16 (0.003)	0.16 (0.003)
Random:			
σ_{u1}^2 (primary school variance)	0.28 (0.06)		0.27 (0.06)
σ_{u2}^2 (secondary school variance)		0.05 (0.02)	0.01 (0.02)
σ_e^2 (pupil variance)	4.25 (0.10)	4.48 (0.11)	4.25 (0.10)
Deviance	14 845.9	14 918.16	14 845.6

$$y_{i\{j\}} = (XB)_{i\{j\}} + \sum_{h \in \{j\}} u_h \pi_{ih} + e_{i\{j\}},$$

$$u_h \sim N(0, \sigma_u^2),$$

$$e_{i\{j\}} \sim N(0, \sigma_e^2), \qquad (20.15)$$

$$\sum_h \pi_{ih} = 1,$$

where $\{j\}$ is the full set of level 2 units, in this case nurses. The level 1 units, patients, are indexed uniquely by i and may be a 'member of' more than one nurse. The index h uniquely indexes nurses, and π_{ih} is a predetermined weight declaring the proportion of membership of patient i to nurse h. For example, if we knew that a quarter of patient i's treatment was administered by nurse h then a weight of 0.25 might be reasonable. Often we will not have information at this level of detail, in which case we assume equal weights.

To clarify this, consider a simple example. Suppose we have four patients (P1,...,P4) treated by up to two of three nurses (n1, n2, n3). The weighted membership matrix, π, might look like that shown in Table 20.12. Here patient 1 was seen by nurses 1 and 3 but not nurse 2, and so on. If we substitute the values of π_{ih}, i and h from Table 20.12 into model (20.15) we get the following series of equations:

$$y_{1\{j\}} = (XB) + 0.5u_1 + 0.5u_3 + e_{1\{j\}},$$

$$y_{2\{j\}} = (XB) + 1u_1 + e_{2\{j\}},$$

$$y_{3\{j\}} = (XB) + 0.5u_2 + 0.5u_3 + e_{3\{j\}},$$

$$y_{4\{j\}} = (XB) + 0.5u_1 + 0.5u_2 + e_{4\{j\}}.$$

A fuller account of multiple membership models, along with an example analysis, is given in Rasbash and Browne (2000).

Table 20.12 *Weighted membership matrix for patients and nurses*

	n1 ($h = 1$)	n2 ($h = 2$)	n3 ($h = 3$)
P1 ($i = 1$)	0.5	0	0.5
P2 ($i = 2$)	1	0	0
P3 ($i = 3$)	0	0.5	0.5
P4 ($i = 4$)	0.5	0.5	0

ESTIMATION ALGORITHMS FOR MULTILEVEL MODELS

In this chapter so far we have given estimates for parameters in many multilevel models without giving any formulae for calculating these estimates. Unlike standard regression models, in multilevel modelling there is no simple formula that can be used to directly calculate parameter estimates. Instead there are two possible types of approach that are used, iterative procedures and simulation-based procedures.

Iterative (deterministic) methods

In iterative approaches we start with initial estimates of the parameters of interest. We split the parameters into groups and proceed by estimating a group of parameters conditional on the estimates of the other parameters being true. Through estimating the groups of parameters in turn, iterative procedures converge to a point estimate for each parameter and a standard error. With modern computer speeds iterative procedures are generally very quick and give good estimates for most problems. There are many possible iterative-based procedures. Iterated generalized least squares (IGLS) was introduced by Goldstein (1986) and is based on iterating between two weighted least-squares regressions for the fixed and random parts of the model, respectively. It produces maximum likelihood (ML) estimates but can be modified to the restricted IGLS method to produce REML estimates (see Goldstein, 1989). The technique of 'Fisher scoring' can also be used to generate ML estimates for multilevel models (see Longford, 1987). The EM algorithm (Dempster et al., 1977) is another iterative procedure that can be adapted to fit multilevel models, producing empirical Bayes estimates (see Bryk and Raudenbush, 1992, for details).

For some problems, including multilevel discrete response models, the above methods cannot be used in their standard form; instead approximations are introduced into the algorithms based on Taylor series linearization, and the estimates produced are no longer ML but are quasilikelihood estimates. There are two forms of linearization, and these result in marginal quasilikelihood (Goldstein, 1991) and penalized quasilikelihood (Laird, 1978) estimates. See Goldstein (1995: Chapter 5) for more details.

Adaptive quadrature has recently been used to fit a wide range of multilevel models for continuous and discrete responses (see Rabe-Hesketh et al., 2002).

Simulation-based methods

In simulation-based procedures the aim is not to converge to a point estimate for each parameter. Instead, the aim is to generate a sample of estimates from the distribution of each parameter of interest. Given this sample of values from the distribution of the parameter, we can construct many different summary statistics, including plots of its distribution function and accurate confidence intervals. Simulation methods often involve generating many thousands of simulated draws and so are consequently often much slower than iterative procedures and require more computer storage. They do, however, give better estimates for some problems and can be applied to more complicated models where there are at present no equivalent deterministic iterative procedures. The methods can be split into two areas, bootstrap methods and Markov chain Monte Carlo (MCMC) methods.

Bootstrapping (Efron and Tibshirani, 1993) involves generating many simulated data sets based on the current data set and then fitting the same model (usually through an iterative procedure as detailed above) to each of these simulated data sets to give a set of parameter estimates for each data set. The method used to generate the simulated data sets can be based either on the distributional assumptions of the model (parametric bootstrapping) or on resampling from the values of the (unshrunken) residuals (non-parametric bootstrapping). Bootstrapping can also be used to correct the bias in the quasilikelihood methods used to fit discrete response multilevel models.

MCMC methods (see Gilks et al., 1996) are commonly used to fit Bayesian multilevel models. Bayesian statistics has a different philosophy from the classical (frequentist) methods. In a Bayesian framework all unknown parameters have prior distributions (that represent our knowledge about the parameters prior to data collection), and the aim is to estimate the joint posterior distribution of the unknown parameters (which is constructed by combining these prior distributions with the data likelihood function). Although this means that Bayesian multilevel models are different from the models described in this chapter, by including so-called 'diffuse' prior distributions the Bayesian posterior distribution can resemble the likelihood function. Then point estimates produced by the MCMC procedures will be approximately the same as the REML estimates from the equivalent model. However in Bayesian statistics interval estimates and the form of the posterior distribution are generally more important than point estimates.

MCMC algorithms involve simulating values for the unknown parameters in turn from their conditional posterior distributions and thus producing for each parameter an autocorrelated sample (chain) of estimates. This sample can then be used to produce point and interval estimates and even an estimate of the whole distribution. Figure 20.7 contains many of the summary statistics that can be produced. It should be noted that as the chain of values produced is autocorrelated, MCMC methods often have to be run for many iterations.

OTHER TOPICS IN MULTILEVEL MODELLING

In this section we will explain briefly (with references) other areas of multilevel modelling which we have not covered in the earlier sections. Most of these areas are at the edge of current research.

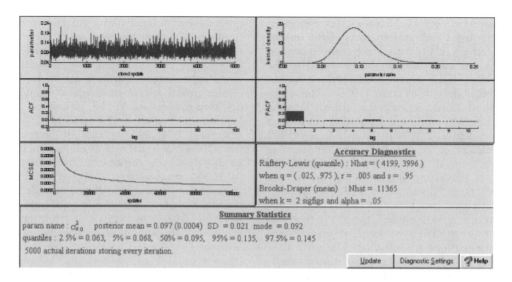

Figure 20.7   *Summary information for an MCMC chain for a variance parameter, as given in the software package MLwiN*

Outliers and diagnostics in multilevel modelling

The detection of outliers and other diagnostics, such as the identification of data points with a large influence or leverage, are as important in multilevel modelling as in any other statistical modelling. Often significant fixed effects or significant higher-level variance may be due to a data point or points that are outlying. However, in complex data structures such as multilevel modelling the concept of an outlier is not so easily defined. This is particularly true as an observation could be an outlier, but a higher-level unit could also be an outlier. The statistical techniques used for exploring outliers in complex data structures are discussed in Langford and Lewis (1998).

Weighting in multilevel modelling

Individual units may have differential weights attached to them, for example as a result of varying sample selection probabilities from a survey. Thus in a two-level model we may have differential weights attached to both the level 2 and level 1 units. Weighting for differential selection probabilities in multilevel models is discussed in Pfefferman et al. (1998).

Multilevel survival models

This class of models, also known as event duration models, have as their response variable the length of time between 'events'. Such events may be, for example, birth and death, or the beginning and end of a period of employment, with corresponding times being length of life or duration of employment.

The multilevel structure of such models arises in two general ways. The first is where we have repeated durations within individuals. Thus, individuals may have repeated spells of various kinds of employment of which unemployment is one, or women may have repeated spells of pregnancy. In this case we have a two-level model with individuals at level 2, often referred to as a renewal process. We can include explanatory dummy variables to distinguish different kinds or 'states' of employment or pregnancy, such as the sequence number. The second kind of model is where we have a single duration for each individual, but the individuals are grouped into level 2 units. In the case of employment duration the level 2 units would be firms or employers. If we had repeated measures on individuals within firms, then this would give rise to a three-level structure.

A characteristic of duration data is that for some observations we may not know the exact duration but only that it occurred within a certain interval. This is known as interval censored data – if less than a known value, left censored data, if greater than a known value, right censored data. For example, if we know at the time of a study that someone began her pregnancy before a certain date then the information available is only that the duration is longer than a known value. In another case we may know that someone entered and then left employment between two measurement occasions, in which case we know only that the duration lies in a known interval. For a description of multilevel survival models, see Goldstein (1995: Chapter 12).

Multilevel time series or auto-correlation models

The standard assumption in multilevel models is that the level 1 residuals are independent. In some situations this assumption is false. For growth measurements the specification of level 2 variation serves to model a separate curve for each individual. If measurements on an individual are obtained very close together in time, they will tend to have similar departures from an individual's underlying growth curve. That is, there is an 'autocorrelation' between the level 1 residuals. A detailed discussion of multilevel autocorrelation models is given in Goldstein et al. (1994).

Multilevel categorical response models

In an earlier section we dealt with discrete response models where the response is a proportion, for example the voting example or a count. In fact the response in the voting example could have been altered from the binary response 'whether people voted Conservative or not' to a categorical response as to which party they voted for. This response would then have a fixed number of categories, one for each party, and each voter i would have a probability of voting for each party c, where the probabilities for a single voter will sum to 1: $\sum_c p_{ic} = 1$. This type of response is fitted with a multinomial model.

Another type of categorical response, common in market research data, is the ordered categorical response. For example, people are often asked to choose one of {very good, good, OK, poor, very poor} to describe their opinion of an item. Again each individual will have probabilities of choosing each category that sum to 1, but the categories have a definite order so the probabilities of being in particular categories are correlated. This type of response is fitted using an ordered multinomial model. As with the binomial and Poisson

models, multinomial models can be extended to multilevel multinomial models, where individuals in a particular higher-level unit share the same underlying category probabilities. See Goldstein (1995: Section 7.4) for more details.

Complex level 1 variation

In the models discussed in this chapter we have fitted a single constant term for the level 1 variation. Often the level 1 variation will be non-constant; this situation is often referred to as heteroscedasticity. In multilevel models it is straightforward to directly model level 1 variation as a function of explanatory variables.

Meta-analysis

The purpose of meta-analysis is to provide an overall summary of results when information from several studies on the same topic is available. These 'studies' may be centres in a single clinical trial, distinct experimental studies, distinct (or possibly overlapping) observational surveys, or mixtures of these. Meta-analysis can therefore be regarded as a special case of the general hierarchical data model, where individual observations are nested within studies or centres.

In applied work, it is often assumed that the effect of interest is constant across the component studies (Thompson and Pocock, 1991), yielding the so-called 'fixed effects' model. The assumption of homogeneity can, however, be relaxed to allow for random variation between studies of the effects, yielding the so-called 'random effects' model (DerSimonian and Laird, 1986). Statistical models for this case can be fitted using a variance components multilevel model formulation. A general multilevel formulation (Goldstein, 1995), however, allows more general random coefficient models to be studied, and we describe this in more detail below. A straightforward extension is to include covariates in such a model and to observe the extent to which they account for between-study variation. An additional problem is when some studies provide individual level data, while for others only summary results (such as means) are available; it is now possible to use methods of meta-analysis to combine such results efficiently (Goldstein et al., 2000).

SOFTWARE AND OTHER RESOURCES FOR MULTILEVEL MODELLING

Multilevel modelling is a fairly new technique and so the software available can be broadly split into three categories: general-purpose statistics packages, special-purpose multilevel modelling packages, and other special-purpose software with some multilevel modelling facilities. The following are general-purpose statistics packages:

BMDP – http://www.statsol.ie/prbm.htm
GENSTAT – http://www.nag.co.uk/stats/tt-soff.asp
SAS (PROC MIXED) – http://www.sas.com
STATA – http://www.stata.com
S-PLUS – http://www.splus.mathsoft.com

Among the multilevel modelling packages are:

HLM – http://www.ssicentral.com/hlm/hlm.htm
MIXOR/MIXREG – http://www.uic.edu/~hedecker/mix.html
MLwiN – http://www.ioe.ac.uk/mlwin/
VARCL – http://www.gamma.rug.nl/

The following other special-purpose packages can be used:

BUGS (WinBUGS) – http://www.mrc.bsu.cam.ac.uk/bugs/
EGRET – http://www.cytel.com/products/egret/egret1.html
LISREL – http://www.ssicentral.com/lisrel/mainlis.htm
Mplus – http://www.statmodel.com
SABRE – http://www.cas.lancs.ac.uk/software/sabre3.1/sabre.html

These packages vary in terms of estimation methods used, size and type of models allowed and speed of computation. Several papers have compared the performance of packages on particular multilevel problems (e.g., Kreft et al., 1994; Zhou et al., 1999).

This chapter has been written with no emphasis on any particular software package. The authors, however, are both members of the team that produce the software package MLwiN, and a lot of the material in this chapter is covered in greater detail in the package user manual (Rasbash et al., 2000). This can be downloaded for free from the MLwiN website http://www.ioe.ac.uk/ mlwin, which also contains more information on the package.

The TRaMSS (Teaching Resources and Materials for Social Scientists) website at www.tramss.data-archive.ac.uk includes a free training version of the MLwiN software, along with a set of downloadable tutorials. These tutorials take the user through a series of worked examples that cover the basic concepts of multilevel modelling.

Many books have been written on multi-level modelling at both an introductory and more advanced levels. The beginner might consult Hox (1994), Kreft and de Leeuw (1998) and Snijders and Bosker (1999). More technical texts worth looking at are Bryk and Raudenbush (1992), Goldstein (1995) and Longford (1993).

REFERENCES

Bryk, A.S. and Raudenbush, S.W. (1992) *Hierarchical Linear Models*. Newbury Park, CA: Sage.

Dempster, A.P., Laird, N.M. and Rubin, D.B. (1977) 'Maximum likelihood from incomplete data via the EM algorithm (with discussion)', *Journal of the Royal Statistical Society, Series B*, 39: 1–38.

DerSimonian, R. and Laird, N. (1986) 'Meta-analysis in clinical trials', *Journal of Controlled Clinical Trials*, 7: 177–88.

Duncan, C., Jones, K. and Moon, G. (1999) 'Smoking and deprivation: are there neighbourhood effects?', *Social Science and Medicine*, 48: 497–506.

Efron, B. and Tibshirani, R. (1993) *An Introduction to the Bootstrap*. New York: Chapman & Hall.

Gilks, W.R., Richardson, S. and Spiegelhalter, D.J. (1996) *Markov Chain Monte Carlo in Practice*. London: Chapman & Hall.

Goldstein, H. (1986) 'Multilevel mixed linear model analysis using iterative generalised least squares', *Biometrika*, 73: 43–56.

Goldstein, H. (1989) 'Restricted unbiased iterative generalised least squares estimation', *Biometrika*, 76: 622–3.

Goldstein, H. (1991) 'Nonlinear multilevel models with an application to discrete response data', *Biometrika*, 78: 45–51.

Goldstein, H. (1995). *Multilevel Statistical Models*. London: Edward Arnold.

Goldstein, H. and Sammons, P. (1997) 'The influence of secondary and junior schools on sixteen year examination performance: A cross-classified multi-level analysis', *School Effectiveness and School Improvement*, 8: 219–30.

Goldstein, H., Healy, M.J.R. and Rasbash, J. (1994) 'Multilevel time series models with applications to repeated measures data', *Statistics in Medicine*, 13: 1643–55.

Goldstein, H., Yang, M., Omar, R., Turner, R. and Thompson, S. (2000) 'Meta-analysis using multilevel models with an application to the study of class size effects', *Applied Statistics*, 49: 1–14.

Hausman, J.A. (1978) 'Specification tests in econometrics', *Econometrica*, 46: 1251–71.

Heath, A., Yang, M. and Goldstein, H. (1996) 'Multilevel analysis of the changing relationship between class and party in Britain 1964–1992', *Quality and Quantity*, 30: 389–404.

Hox, J.J. (1994) *Applied Multilevel Analysis*. Amsterdam: TT-Publikaties.

Kreft, I. and de Leeuw, J. (1998) *Introducing Multilevel Modeling*. London: Sage.

Kreft, I.G.G., de Leeuw, J. and van der Leeden, R. (1994) 'Review of five multilevel analysis programs: BMDP-5V, GENMOD, HLM, ML2, and VARCL', *American Statistician*, 48: 324–35.

Laird, N.M. (1978) 'Empirical Bayes methods for two-way contingency tables', *Biometrika*, 65: 581–90.

Langford, I.H. and Lewis, T. (1998) 'Outliers in multilevel models (with discussion)', *Journal of the Royal Statistical Society, Series A*, 161: 121–60.

Langford, I.H., Bentham, G. and McDonald, A. (1998) 'Multilevel modelling of geographically aggregated health data: A case study on malignant melanoma mortality and UV exposure in the European Community', *Statistics in Medicine*, 17: 41–58.

Longford, N.T. (1987) 'A fast scoring algorithm for maximum likelihood estimation in unbalanced mixed models with nested random effects', *Biometrika*, 74: 817–27.

Longford, N. (1993) *Random Coefficient Models*. Oxford: Oxford University Press.

O'Muircheartaigh, C. and Campanelli, P. (1999) 'A multilevel exploration of the role of interviewers in survey non-response', *Journal of the Royal Statistical Society, Series A*, 162: 437–46.

Pfeffermann, D., Skinner, C.J., Holmes, D.J., Goldstein, H. and Rasbash, J. (1998) 'Weighting for unequal selection probabilities in multilevel models', *Journal of the Royal Statistical Society, Series B*, 60: 23–40.

Rabe-Hesketh, S., Skrondal, A. and Pickles, A. (2002) 'Reliable estimation of generalised linear mixed models using adaptive quadrature', *The Stata Journal*, 2: 1–21.

Rasbash, J. and Browne, W.J. (2000) 'Non-hierarchical multilevel models', in A. Leyland and H. Goldstein (eds), *Multilevel Modelling of Health Statistics*. Chichester: Wiley.

Rasbash, J., Browne, W., Goldstein, H., Yang, M., Plewis, I., Draper, D., Woodhouse, G., Langford, I., Lewis, T. and Healy, M. (2000) *A User's Guide to MLwiN* (2nd edn). London: Institute of Education.

Rowe, K.J. and Hill, P.W. (1997) 'Simultaneous estimation of multilevel structural equations to model students' educational progress'. Paper presented to the Tenth International Congress for School Effectiveness and Improvement, Memphis, Tennessee.

Snijders, T.A.B. and Bosker, R.J. (1999) *Multilevel Analysis: An Introduction to Basic and Advanced Multilevel Modeling*. London: Sage.

Thompson, S.G. and Pocock, S.J. (1991) 'Can meta-analyses be trusted?', *Lancet*, 338(8775): 1127–30.

Tizard, B., Blatchford, P., Burke, J., Farquhar, C. and Plewis, I. (1988) *Young Children at School in the Inner City*. Hove: Lawrence Erlbaum.

Verbeek, M. (2000) *A Guide to Modern Econometrics*. New York: Wiley.

Zhou, X, Perkins, A.J. and Hui, S.L. (1999) 'Comparisons of software packages for generalized linear multilevel models', *American Statistician*, 53: 282–90.

## 21

Causal Inference in Sociological Studies

CHRISTOPHER WINSHIP AND MICHAEL SOBEL

Throughout human history, causal knowledge has been highly valued by laymen and scientists alike. To be sure, both the nature of the causal relation and the conditions under which a relationship can be deemed causal have been vigorously disputed. A number of influential thinkers have even argued that the idea of causation is not scientifically useful (e.g., Russell, 1913). Others have argued that forms of determination other than causation often figure more prominently in scientific explanations (Bunge, 1979). Nevertheless, many modern scientists seek to make causal inferences, arguing either that the fundamental job of science is to discover the causal mechanisms that govern the behavior of the world and/or that causal knowledge enables human beings to control and hence construct a better world.

The latest round of interest in causation in the social and behavioral sciences is recent: functional explanations dominated sociological writing before path analysis (Duncan, 1966; Stinchcombe, 1968) stole center stage in the late 1960s. These developments, in conjunction with the newly emerging literature on the decomposition of effects in structural equation (causal) models, encouraged sociologists to think about and empirically examine chains of causes and effects, with the net result that virtually all regression coefficients came to be interpreted as effects, and causal modeling became a major industry dominating the empirical literature. Further

methodological developments in the 1970s and the dissemination of easy-to-use computer programs for causal modeling in the 1980s solidified the new base. This resulted in the merger of structural equation models with factor analysis (Jöreskog, 1977), allowing sociologists to purportedly model the effects of latent causes on both observed and latent variables.

Although the use of structural equation models *per se* in sociology has attenuated, a quick perusal of the journals indicates that most quantitative empirical research is still devoted to the task of causal inference, with regression coefficients (or coefficients in logistic regression models, generalized linear models, etc.) routinely being understood as estimates of causal effects. Sociologists now study everything from the effects of job complexity on substance abuse (Oldham and Gordon, 1999) to the joint effects of variables ranging from per capita gross domestic product to the female labor force participation rate on cross-national and intertemporal income inequality (Gustafsson and Johansson, 1999), to cite but two recent examples.

While the causal revolution in sociology encouraged sociologists to think more seriously about the way things work and fostered a more scientific approach to the evaluation of evidence than was possible using functionalist types of arguments, there have also been negative side effects. First, even though knowledge of causes and consequences is clearly of great importance, many social scientists now seem to think that explanation is synonymous with causal explanation. Of course, to the contrary, we may know that manipulating a certain factor 'causes' an outcome to occur without having any understanding of the mechanism involved. Second, researchers also sometimes act as if the only type of knowledge worth seeking is knowledge about causes. Such 'causalism' is misdirected, and although this chapter focuses on the topic of causal inference, it is important to note that a number of important concerns that social scientists address do not require recourse to causal language and/or concepts. Consider two types of examples.

Demographers are often interested in predicting the size and composition of future populations, and there is a large literature on how to make such projections. These predictions may then be used to aid policy-makers to plan for the future, for example, to assess how much revenue is needed to support Social Security and Medicare. In making these projections, demographers make various assumptions about future rates of fertility, migration, and mortality. While these rates are certainly affected by causes (such as a major war), when making projections, interest only resides in using a given set of rates to extrapolate to the future. (Similarly, economists perform cost-benefit analyses and predict firms' future profits; as above, causal processes may be involved here, but the economist is not directly interested in this. In the foregoing cases, prediction *per se* is the objective and causal inference is only potentially indirectly relevant.)

Second, a researcher might be interested in rendering an accurate depiction of a structure or process. For example, an ethnographer might wish to describe a tribal ceremony, a psychologist might wish to describe the process of development of children of a certain age, or a sociologist might wish to describe the economic structures that have emerged in Eastern Europe following the collapse of communism (Stark and Bruszt, 1998). To be sure, some scholars believe that description is only a first step on the road to causal explanation, but this view is not held universally. Many historians have argued that their job is solely to accurately chronicle the past, rather than attempting to locate causes of historical events or delineate some grand plan by which history is presumed to unfold (see Ferguson, 1997, for a brief review).

Although the meaning of the term 'causal effect' when used in regression models is not explicated in most articles, econometricians and sociological methodologists (e.g., Alwin and Hauser, 1975) who use this language typically interpret the coefficients as indicating how much the dependent variable would increase or decrease (either for each case or on average) under a hypothetical intervention in which the value of a particular independent variable is changed by one unit while the values of the other independent variables are held constant. Sobel (1990) provides additional discussion of this issue. While researchers acknowledge that the foregoing interpretation is not always valid, it is often held that such an interpretation is warranted when the variables in the model are correctly ordered and combined with a properly specified model derived from a valid substantive theory. Thus, a regression coefficient is dubbed an effect when the researcher believes that various extra-statistical and typically unexplained considerations are satisfied.

During the 1970s and 1980s, while sociologists and psychometricians were busy refining structural equation models and econometricians were actively extending the usual notions of spuriousness to the temporal domain (Granger, 1969; Geweke, 1984), statisticians working on the estimation of effects developed an explicit model of causal inference, sometimes called the Rubin causal model, based on a *counterfactual account* of the causal relation (Holland, 1986, 1988; Holland and Rubin, 1983; Rosenbaum, 1984a, 1984b, 1986, 1987, 1992; Rosenbaum and Rubin, 1983; Rubin, 1974, 1977, 1978, 1980, 1990). Influential work has also been done by several econometricians (e.g., Heckman, 1978; Heckman and Hotz, 1989; Heckman et al., 1998; Manski 1995, 1997; Manski and Nagin, 1998). Fundamental to this work has been the metaphor of an experiment and the goal of estimating the effect of a particular 'treatment'. In important respects this work can be thought of as involving a careful and precise extension of the conceptual apparatus of randomized experiments to the analysis of nonexperimental data. This line of research yields a precise definition of a (treatment) effect and allows for the development of mathematical conditions under which estimates can or cannot be interpreted as causal effects; see Pratt and Schlaifer (1988) for the case of regression coefficients, Holland (1988) and Sobel (1998) on the case of recursive structural equation models with observed variables, and Sobel (1994) on the case of structural equation models with observed and latent variables.

Using the conditions discussed in the literature cited above, it is clear that many of the 'effects' reported in the social sciences should not be interpreted as anything more than sophisticated partial associations. However, the encouraging news is that these conditions can also be used to inform the design of new studies and/or develop strategies to more plausibly estimate selected causal effects of interest. In this chapter, our primary purposes are to introduce sociologists to the literature that uses a counterfactual notion of causality and to illustrate some strategies for obtaining more credible estimates of causal effects. In addition (and perhaps more importantly), we believe that widespread understanding of this literature should result in important changes in the way that virtually all empirical work in sociology is conducted.

We proceed as follows: In the next section we briefly introduce different notions of the causal relation found primarily in the philosophical literature. We then present a model for causal inference based on the premise that a causal relation should sustain a counterfactual conditional. After introducing this model, we carefully define the estimands of interest and give conditions under which the parameters estimated in sociological studies with nonexperimental data are identical to these estimands. From there we turn to a discussion of the problem of estimating effects from nonexperimental data. We start by examining the conditions under which what we call the standard estimator – the difference in the mean outcome between the treatment and control group – is a consistent estimate of what is defined as the average causal effect. We then discuss the sources of bias in this estimator. Following this, we briefly examine randomized experiments. We then focus on situations where assignment to the 'treatment' is nonrandom: we discuss the concept of ignorability in the context of the counterfactual causal model; and we examine the assignment equation and define what is known as a propensity score. We then provide a brief examination of different methods for estimating causal effects. Specifically, we examine matching, regression, instrumental variables, and methods using longitudinal data. We conclude by suggesting that the literature on counterfactual causal analysis

provides important insights as to when it is valid to interpret estimates as causal effects and directs our attention to the likely threats to the validity of such an interpretation in specific cases.

PHILOSOPHICAL THEORIES OF CAUSALITY

Hume and regularity theories

Philosophical thinking about causality goes back to Aristotle and before. It is, however, generally agreed that modern thinking on the subject starts with Hume. Hume equated causation with temporal priority (a cause must precede an effect), spatiotemporal contiguity, and constant conjunction (the cause is sufficient for the effect or 'same cause, same effect'). Subsequent writers have argued for simultaneity of cause and effect. Those who take such a position are compelled to argue either that the causal priority of the cause relative to the effect is nontemporal or allow that it is meaningful to speak of some form of 'reciprocal' causation (Mackie, 1974). In that vein, to the best of our knowledge, every serious philosopher of causation maintains that an asymmetry between cause and effect is an essential ingredient of the causal relationship. That is, no one has seriously argued for the notion of 'reciprocal' causality, sometimes found in empirical articles in the social sciences, that uses simultaneous equation models and cross-sectional data. The contiguity criterion has also been criticized by those who advocate action at a distance.

Most of the criticism of Hume, however, has focused on the criterion of constant conjunction. Mill (1973) pointed out there might be a plurality of causes and that, as such, an effect might occur in the absence of any particular cause. He also pointed out that a cause could be a conjunction of events. Neither of these observations vitiates Hume's analysis, however, since Hume was arguing for a concept of causality based on the idea of sufficiency. Mill, though, clearly wants to argue that the cause (or what has come to be known as the full cause or philosophical cause) is a disjunction of conjunctions constituting necessary and sufficient conditions for the effect. See also Mackie (1974) on the idea of a cause as a necessary condition for the effect.

It is also worth noting that the constant conjunction criterion applies to a class of cases deemed sufficiently similar (to produce the same effect). The problem here is that if the effect does not occur in some instance, one can always argue after the fact that this case does not belong in the class. This can create problems at the epistemological level.

A different sort of criticism (primarily) of the constant conjunction criterion has also been made. Hume argued not only that the causal relation consisted of the three ingredients identified above, but also that these alone constituted the causal relation (as it exists in the real world as opposed to our minds). By denying that there could be something more to the causal relation, Hume essentially equated causation with universal predictability. Many subsequent writers have found this argument to be the most objectionable aspect of Hume's analysis since sequences satisfying the foregoing criteria – for example, waking up then going to sleep – would be deemed causal. However, no one seems to have succeeded in specifying the ingredient that would unambiguously allow us to distinguish those predictable sequences that are causal from those that are not (Mackie, 1974).

An important line of inquiry with ancient roots (e.g., Aristotle's efficient cause) that attempts to supply the missing link argues that the causal relationship is generative, that is, instead of the effect being merely that which inevitably follows the cause, the cause actually has the power to bring about the effect (Bunge, 1979; Harré, 1972; Harré and Madden, 1975). This occurs because properties of the objects and/or events constituting the cause and the effect are linked by one or more causal mechanisms. Such a way of thinking is commonplace in modern sociology, with many arguing that the central task of the discipline is to discover the causal mechanisms accounting for the phenomenon under investigation. However, neither sociologists nor philosophers seem to have successfully explicated such notions as yet. It is not enough to say, as Harré does, that a mechanism is a description of the way in which an object or event brings into being another, for this is obviously circular. For other attempts, see Simon (1952) and Mackie (1974).

Although Mill replaced the constant conjunction criterion with the notion that the full (or philosophical) cause should be necessary and sufficient for the effect, he also recognized that such an analysis did not address the objection that the causal relationship could not be reduced to a form of universal predictability. In that regard, he also argued that the cause should also be the invariable antecedent of the effect; in modern parlance, he is arguing the view, now widely espoused, that causal relationships sustain counterfactual conditional statements. This idea is developed more fully below.

Manipulability theories

Mill was also perhaps the first writer to distinguish between the causes of effects (what are known as regularity theories, i.e., the necessary and sufficient conditions for an effect to occur) and the effects of causes. In manipulability theories (Collingwood, 1998), the cause is a state that an agent induces that is followed by an effect (the effect of a cause). In this account, there is no attempt to ascertain the full cause, as in regularity theories. Manipulability theories are not at odds with regularity theories, but the goal is less ambitious, and whether or not the putative cause is deemed causal can depend on other events that are not under current consideration as causes; these events constitute the causal field (Anderson, 1938) or background in which the particular cause of interest is operating. By way of contrast, in a regularity theory, these events would be considered part of the full cause – the set of necessary and/or sufficient conditions. For example, suppose that the putative cause is driving 20 or more miles per hour over the speed limit on a deserted curvy road, and the effect is driving off the side of the road. Suppose also that the effect occurs if either the driver exceeds the speed limit by more than 30 mph, or the driver exceeds the speed limit by between 20 and 30 mph, the road surface is wet, and the tires have less than some prespecified amount of tread. Then driving in excess of the speed limit causes driving off the road, but in the second case the effect occurs only under the two additional standing conditions. In some other context, the excess speed and the road surface might be regarded as standing conditions and the condition of the tire tread the cause.

Manipulability theories have been criticized by philosophers who find the notion of an agent anthropomorphic. They would argue, for example, that it is meaningful to talk about the gravitational pull of the moon causing tides, though the moon's gravitational pull is not manipulable. Others, however, have questioned whether it is meaningful to speak of causation when the manipulation under consideration cannot actually be induced – for example, raising the world's temperature by 10 degrees Fahrenheit (Holland, 1986).

Singular theories

Regularity theories of the causal relationship are deterministic, holding in all relevant instances. Notwithstanding the theoretical merits of such notions, our own knowledge of the world does not allow us to apply such stringent conditions. Consequently, a large literature on probabilistic causation has emerged (see Sobel, 1995, for a review), the majority of which is concerned with the problem (now formulated probabilistically) of distinguishing between causal and noncausal (or spurious) relationships. Unlike the deterministic literature on this subject, which attempts to explicate what it is that differentiates universal predictability from causation, most of this literature jumps directly to the problem of inference, offering operational, and seemingly appealing, criteria for deciding whether or not probabilistic relationships are genuine or spurious. In our opinion, the failure in much of this work to first define what is meant by causality has been a major problem. Pearl (2000) represents the most recent and sophisticated work stemming from this tradition.

With minor variants, most of the literature states that a variable X does not cause a variable Y if the association between these two variables vanishes after introducing a third variable Z, which is temporally prior to both X and Y; that is, X and Y are conditionally independent given Z. It bears noting that the literature on path analysis and the more general literature on structural equation models use essentially the same type of criteria to infer the presence of a causal relationship. For example, in a three-variable path model with response Y, if X and Y are conditionally independent given Z, then, in the regression of Y on X and Z, the coefficient on X (X's direct effect) is 0.

In singular theories of the causal relation, it is meaningful to speak of causation in specific instances without needing to fit these instances into a broader class, as in regularity theories (Ducasse, 1975). Thus, in some population of interest it would be possible for the effect to occur in half the cases where the cause is present and it would still be meaningful to speak of causation. Notice how

probability emerges here, but without arguing that the causal relationship is probabilistic. Singular theories also dovetail well with accounts of causation that require the causal relationship to sustain a counterfactual conditional. Thus, using such accounts, one might say that taking the drug caused John to get well, meaning that John took the drug and got better – and that had John not taken the drug, he would not have gotten better. However, taking the drug did not cause Jill to get better means either that Jill took the drug and did not get better or that Jill took the drug and got better, but she would have gotten better even if she had not taken the drug. Of course, it is not possible to verify that taking the drug caused John to get better or if Jill takes the drug and gets better that it in fact either did or did not cause Jill to get better. But (as we shall see below), it is possible to make a statement about whether or not the drug helps on average in some group of interest. In experimental studies, we are typically interested in questions of this form. However, as noted previously, social scientists who do not use experimental data and who speak of 'effects' in statistical models also make (explicitly or implicitly) statements of this type.

We now turn to the subject of causal inference, that is, making inferences about the causal relation. As noted earlier, the appropriateness of a particular inferential procedure will depend on the notion of causation espoused if it is espoused, explicitly or implicitly, at all. For example, under Hume's account, a relationship between a putative cause and an effect is not causal if there is even a single instance in which the effect does not occur in the presence of the cause. Thus, statistical methods, which estimate the relative frequency of cases in which the outcome follows in the presence of the purported cause, should not be used to make an inference about the causal relationship as understood by Hume. Similar remarks typically apply to the use of statistical methods to make causal inferences under other regularity theories of causation.

A SINGULAR, MANIPULABLE, COUNTERFACTUAL ACCOUNT OF CAUSALITY

The model for causal inference introduced in this section is based upon a counterfactual notion of the causal relation in which singular causal statements are meaningful. We shall refer to this model as the counterfactual model. This model provides a precise way of defining causal effects and understanding the conditions under which it is appropriate to interpret parameter estimates as estimates of causal effects. For simplicity, we shall focus on the case where the cause is binary, referring to the two states as the treatment and control conditions; the model is easily generalized to the case where the cause takes on multiple values. Under the model, each unit (individual) has two responses, a response to the treatment and a response in the absence of treatment. Of course, in practice, a unit cannot be subjected to both conditions, which implies that only one of the two responses can actually be observed. For a unit, the response that is not observed is the counterfactual response.

Factual and counterfactual outcomes

For concreteness, consider again whether or not taking a drug causes (or would cause) John to get better. Suppose that it is possible for John to be exposed to either condition. Then there are four possible states:

1. John would get better if he took the drug, and he would get better if he did not take the drug.
2. John would not get better if he took the drug, and he would not get better if he did not take the drug.
3. John would get better if he took the drug, but he would not get better if he did not take the drug.
4. John would not get better if he took the drug, but he would get better if he did not take the drug.

Consider, for example, case 3. Here it is natural to conclude that the drug causes John to get better (assuming he took the drug). For if John took the drug, he would get better, but if he did not take the drug, he would not get better. Similarly, in case 4 one would conclude that taking the drug causes John to get worse. In cases 1 and 2 one would conclude that the drug does not cause John to get better.

In the 1920s, Neyman (1990) first proposed a notation for representing the types of possibilities above that has proven indispensable; this notation is one of the two or three most important contributions to the modern literature on causal inference and without it (or something comparable) it would not be possible for this literature to have developed.

To represent the four possible states above, we denote a particular unit (John) from a population P of size N using the subscript i. Let lower case x be an indicator of a (potentially) hypothetical treatment state indicator with $x = t$ when the individual receives the treatment and $x = c$ when they are in the control condition. Let Y_{xi} denote the outcome for case i under condition x, with $Y_{xi} = 1$ if i gets better and $Y_{xi} = 0$ if i does not get better. Thus the four states above can represented respectively, as:

1. $Y_{ti} = Y_{ci} = 1$: John would get better if he took the drug, and he would get better if he did not take the drug.
2. $Y_{ti} = Y_{ci} = 0$: John would not get better if he took the drug, and he would not get better if he did not take the drug.
3. $Y_{ti} = 1, Y_{ci} = 0$: John would get better if he took the drug, but he would not get better if he did not take the drug.
4. $Y_{ti} = 0$, $Y_{ci} = 1$: John would not get better if he took the drug, but he would get better if he did not take the drug.

Let $\mathbf{Y}_t$ and $\mathbf{Y}_c$ represent the column vectors containing the values of Y_{ti} and Y_{ci}, respectively, for all i. Any particular unit can only be observed in one particular state. Either $x = t$ or $x = c$, where the state that does hold defines the factual condition. As a result, either Y_{ti} or Y_{ci}, but not both, is observed. As emphasized in a seminal paper by Rubin (1978), counterfactual causal analysis is at its core a missing-data problem. We can only observe the outcome for a particular unit under the treatment or the control condition, but not both. In order to carry out a counterfactual analysis it is necessary to make assumptions about these 'missing' counterfactual values. As we discuss below, different assumptions with regard to the counterfactual values will typically lead to different estimates of the causal effect.

The data we actually see are the pairs (Y_i, X_i), where $X_i = t$ if the unit actually receives the treatment, $X_i = c$ otherwise, and Y_i is the actual observed response for unit i. Thus, when $X_i = t$, $Y_i = Y_{ti}$ since $x = t$ is the factual condition, and Y_{ci} is unobserved since $x = c$ is the counterfactual condition. Similarly, when

$X_i = c$, $Y_i = Y_{ci}$ since $x = c$ is the factual condition and Y_{ti} is unobserved since $x = t$ is the counterfactual condition.

Unit effects

We define the effect of the drug on John, or what is known as the *unit effect*, as:

$$\delta_i = Y_{ti} - Y_{ci}, \qquad (21.1)$$

which equals 1 if the drug is beneficial, −1 if it is harmful, and 0 otherwise. The unit effect is what is meant by the causal effect of a treatment for a particular individual in the counterfactual model. The unit effects are not averages or probabilities.

Clearly the unit effects are not observable since only Y_{ti} or Y_{ci} is actually observed. Inferences about these effects will only be as valid as our assumptions about the value of the response under the counterfactual condition. For example, most of us would accept the statement 'Turning the key in the ignition caused the car to start' (presuming we put the key in the ignition and the car started), because we believe that had the key not been placed in the ignition and turned, the car would not have started. We might also be inclined to believe that a person's pretest score on a reading comprehension test would closely approximate the score they would have obtained three months later in the absence of a reading course, thereby allowing us to equate the unit effect with the difference between the before and after scores. However, we might not be as ready to believe that a volunteer's pretest weight is a good proxy for what their weight would have been six months later in the absence of some particular diet.

Unfortunately, many of the most important questions in human affairs concern the values of unit effects. A typical cancer patient wants to know whether or not chemotherapy will be effective in his or her case, not that chemotherapy is followed by remission in some specified percentage of cases. In the social and behavioral sciences, knowledge is often crude and attempts to speculate about precise values or narrow ranges of the unit effects would not be credible. But if interest centers on well-defined aggregates of cases (populations), rather than specific cases, values of the unit effects are not of special interest. Nevertheless – and this is critical – the unit effects are the conceptual building blocks used to define so-called 'average causal effects' (to be defined shortly), and it is these averages of unit effects about which inferences typically are desired.

It is important to recognize that values of the unit effects (and hence their average) depend on the way in which the exposure status of units is manipulated (either actually or hypothetically). While this may seem obvious, the substantive implications are worth further discussion. To take a concrete and sociologically important example, suppose interest centers on estimating the effect of gender on earnings in the population of American adults. Holland (1986: 955) argued that gender is an inherent attribute of units: 'The only way for an attribute to change its value is for the unit to change in some way and no longer be the same unit.' Hence gender cannot be viewed as a potential cause. By way of contrast, Sobel (1998) argued that we can readily imagine the case where Jack was born Jill or Jill was born Jack, hence gender can be treated as a cause. Thus (as certain technical conditions discussed later would be satisfied in this case), the average effect of gender can be consistently estimated, using sample data, as the mean difference in male and female earnings. One might object, however, that this is not the effect of interest, for it combines a number of cumulative choices and processes that lead to sex differences in earnings, not all of which are of interest.

To be more concrete, suppose interest centers on earnings differences within a particular employment position. The issue is the earnings Jill would have were she male, net of those processes that are not deemed of interest. For example, suppose that Jill went to a university and studied English literature, but that had she been born as Jack, she would have studied engineering. In all likelihood, Jill, had she been Jack, would be working at a different job, and the earnings in this counterfactual job would be different from the earnings of the counterfactual Jack, who holds the same job as the real Jill. But if the latter comparison is the one of interest, the first counterfactual Jill (i.e., the engineer) is not of interest since he differs in key ways from Jill due to differences in gender that are prior to the employment situation being considered.

As for this second counterfactual Jill, i.e., Jack, who has the same job as the real Jill, one might want to argue that he must at least share all Jill's features and history (at least all that which is relevant to the earnings determination in the current arrangement) prior to some designated time at which the process of interest begins (e.g., the first day of work for the current employer). There seems to be no general procedure for creating such a counterpart. In specific cases, however, reasonable procedures may exist. A situation that has recently received attention is the contrast between orchestras that do and do not use a blind auditions process (Goldin, 1999). By having the individual audition behind a screen, knowledge of a candidate's gender as well as other physical characteristics is withheld from the evaluation committee. Here the manipulable treatment is not gender *per se*, but knowledge of an individual's gender and its possible effects on the evaluation of performers.[1] The development of 'internet' or what are sometimes called remote organizations, where all communication between employees is through email, may provide similar possibilities for disguise (Davis, 2000).

The foregoing discussion forces attention on the assumption that each unit could be potentially exposed to the values of the cause other than the value the unit actually takes. In particular, the way in which a unit is exposed to these other counterfactual states may be critical for defining and understanding the magnitude of an effect of interest. For example, the efficacy of a drug may depend on whether the drug is administered intravenously or orally. Similarly, the (contemplated) effect of gender on earnings may depend on the manner in which gender is hypothetically manipulated. This may be of great importance for estimating the effect of gender; for example, the difference between the sample means in earnings of men and women above estimates the effect of gender under one counterfactual, but not necessarily others. This suggests that sociologists who want to use observational studies to estimate effects (that are supposed to stand up to a counterfactual conditional) need to carefully consider the hypothetical manipulations under which units are exposed to alternative values of the cause. In some instances, such reflection may suggest that the issue of causation is misdirected. In this case, questions about the association (as opposed to the causal effect) between one or more other variables and a response are often easily answered using standard statistical methods.

An additional critical point is that the counterfactual model as presented above is appropriate only if there is no interference or interaction between units (Cox, 1958); using the current example, John's value on the response under either condition does not depend on whether or not any other unit receives the drug. Rubin (1980) calls the assumption of no interference the stable unit treatment value assumption. There are clearly many situations of interest where such an assumption will not be reasonable. For example, the effect of a job training program on participants' earnings may well depend on how large the program is relative to the local labor market. To date, little work has been done on such problems.

Average effects

As noted above, the unit effect, although unobservable, is the basic building block of the counterfactual model. Typically social scientists are interested in the average effect in some population or group of individuals. Throughout the paper we will use the expectation operator, E[ ], to represent the mean of a quantity in the population. The average effect is then

$$\delta = E[\mathbf{Y}_t - \mathbf{Y}_c] = \sum_{i \in P} (Y_{ti} - Y_{ci})/N, \quad (21.2)$$

where (as shown) the expectation operator is taken with respect to the population P. This is known as the *average causal effect* (Rubin 1974, 1977, 1978, 1980) within the population P.

The average effect of an intervention may depend on covariates, $\mathbf{Z}$. An investigator may wish to know this either because such information is of inherent interest or because it is possible to implement different treatment policies within different covariate classes. Thus, we define the average effect of X within the subpopulation where $\mathbf{Z} = \mathbf{z}$ as

$$\delta_z = E[\mathbf{Y}_t - \mathbf{Y}_c | \mathbf{Z} = \mathbf{z}]$$
$$= \sum_{i \in P | \mathbf{Z} = \mathbf{z}} (Y_{ti} - Y_{ci})/N_z, \quad (21.3)$$

where N_z is the number of individuals in the population for whom $\mathbf{Z} = \mathbf{z}$. Note that (21.3) involves a comparison of distinct levels of the cause for different values of $\mathbf{Z}$. Comparisons of the difference in the size of the causal effect in different subpopulations may also be of interest:

$$\delta_z - \delta_{z^*} = E[Y_t - Y_c | Z = z]$$
$$- E[Y_t - Y_c | Z = z^*]. \qquad (21.4)$$

It is important to note that in the counterfactual framework comparisons of this type are descriptive, not causal. It is possible that such comparisons might suggest a causal role for one or more covariates, but in the context of the question under consideration (the effect of X), the subpopulations defined by Z only constitute different strata of the population.

INFERENCES ABOUT AVERAGE CAUSAL EFFECTS

Inferences about population parameters are usually made using sample data. In this section, we assume that a simple random sample of size n has been taken from the population of interest. We begin by considering the case where interest centers on estimation of the average causal effect within a population.

The standard estimator

Let $E[Y_t]$ be the average value of Y_{ti} for all individuals in the population when they are exposed to the treatment, and let $E[Y_c]$ be the average value of Y_{ci} for all individuals when they are exposed to the control. Because of the linearity of the expectation operator, the average treatment effect in the population is equal to

$$\delta = E[Y_t - Y_c] = E[Y_t] - E[Y_c]. \quad (21.5)$$

Because Y_{ti} and Y_{ci} are only partially observable (or missing on mutually exclusive subsets of the population,' δ cannot be calculated. However, it can be estimated consistently in some circumstances.

Consider the most common estimator, often called the standard estimator, which we denote as S^*. Note that the averages or expected values $E[Y_t | X = t]$ and $E[Y_c | X = c]$ differ, respectively, from $E[Y_t]$ and $E[Y_c]$. The former two terms are averages with respect to the disjoint subgroups of the population for which Y_{ti} and Y_{ci} are observed, whereas $E[Y_t]$ and $E[Y_c]$ are each averages over the whole population, and, as noted earlier, are not calculable. $E[Y_t | X = t]$ and $E[Y_c | X = c]$ can be estimated, respectively, by their sample analogs, the mean of Y_i for those actually in the treatment group, $\bar{Y}_t$, and the mean of Y_i for those actually in the control group, $\bar{Y}_c$. The standard estimator for the average treatment

effect is the difference between these two estimated sample means:

$$S^* = \bar{Y}_t - \bar{Y}_c. \qquad (21.6)$$

Note that there are two differences between equations (21.5) and (21.6). Equation (21.5) is defined for the population as a whole, whereas equation (21.6) represents an estimator that can be applied to a sample drawn from the population. Second, all individuals in the population contribute to both terms in equation (21.5). However, each sampled individual is only used once either in estimating $\bar{Y}_t$ or $\bar{Y}_c$ in equation (21.6). As a result, the way in which individuals are assigned (or assign themselves) to the treatment and control groups will determine how well the standard estimator, S^*, estimates the true average treatment effect, δ.

To understand when the standard estimator consistently estimates the average treatment effect for the population, let π equal the proportion of the population in the treatment group. Decompose the average treatment effect in the population into a weighted average of the average treatment effect for those in the treatment group and the average treatment effect for those in the control group and then decompose the resulting terms into differences in average potential outcomes:

$$\delta = \pi \, \delta_{i \in T} + (1 - \pi) \, \delta_{i \in C}$$
$$= \pi \, (E[Y_t | X = t] - E[Y_c | X = t])$$
$$+ (1 - \pi) \, (E[Y_t | X = c] - E[Y_c | X = c])$$
$$= (\pi \, E[Y_t | X = t] + (1 - \pi) \, E[Y_t | X = c])$$
$$- (\pi \, E[Y_c | X = t] + (1 - \pi) E[Y_c | X = c])$$
$$= E[Y_t] - E[Y_c]. \qquad (21.7)$$

This is the same result we obtained in equation (21.5). The quantities $E[Y_t | X = c]$ and $E[Y_c | X = t]$ that appear explicitly in the second and third lines of equation (21.7) cannot be directly estimated because they are based on unobservable values of Y_t and Y_c. If we assume that $E[Y_t | X = t] = E[Y_t | X = c]$ and $E[Y_c | X = t] = E[Y_c | X = c]$, substitution into (21.7) gives:

$$\delta = (\pi \, E[Y_t | X = t] + (1 - \pi) \, E[Y_t | X = c])$$
$$- (\pi \, E[Y_c | X = t] + (1 - \pi) E[Y_c | X = c])$$
$$= (\pi \, E[Y_t | X = t] + (1 - \pi) \, E[Y_t | X = t])$$
$$- (\pi \, E[Y_c | X = c] + (1 - \pi) E[Y_c | X = c])$$
$$= E[Y_t | X = t] - E[Y_c | X = c]. \qquad (21.8)$$

Thus, a sufficient condition for the standard estimator to consistently estimate the true average treatment effect in the population is that $E[Y_t | X = t] = E[Y_t | X = c]$ and $E[Y_c | X = t] = E[Y_c | X = c]$. (Note that a sufficient condition for this to hold is that treatment assignment be random.) In this case, since $E[Y_t | X = t]$ can be consistently estimated by its sample analog, $\bar{Y}_t$, and $E[Y_c | X = c]$ can be consistently estimated by its sample analog, $\bar{Y}_c$, the average treatment effect can be consistently estimated by the difference in these two sample averages.

Sources of bias

Why might the standard estimator be a poor (biased and inconsistent) estimate of the true average causal effect? There are two possible sources of bias in the standard estimator. Define the 'baseline difference' between the treatment and control groups as $E[Y_c | X = t] - E[Y_c | X = c]$. This quantity can be thought of as the difference in outcomes between the treatment and control groups in the absence of treatment. With a little algebra, it can be shown that the expected value of the standard estimator is equal to:

$E[S^*]$ = Average treatment effect
　　　　+ (Difference in baseline Y)
　　　　+ $(1 - \pi)$ (Difference in average
　　　　treatment effect for the
　　　　treatment and control groups),

or, in mathematical notation,

$$E[S^*] = E[Y_t | X = t] - E[Y_c | X = c]$$
$$= \delta + (E[Y_c | X = t] - E[Y_c | X = c])$$
$$+ (1 - \pi)(\delta_t - \delta_c), \qquad (21.9)$$

where $\delta_t = E[Y_t | X = t] - E[Y_c | X = t]$ is the average treatment effect among those in the treatment group and $\delta_c = E[Y_t | X = c] - E[Y_c | X = c]$ is the average treatment effect among those in the control group. Equation (21.9) shows the two possible sources of bias in the standard estimator. The first source of bias is the baseline difference, defined above. The second source of bias, $\delta_t - \delta_c$, is the difference in the treatment effect for those in the treatment and control groups. Often this is not considered, even though it is likely to be present when there are recognized incentives for individuals (or their agents) to select into the treatment group. Instead, many researchers (or more accurately, the methods that they use) simply assume that the treatment effect is constant in the population, even when common sense dictates that the assumption is clearly implausible (Heckman, 1997a, 1997b;

Heckman et al., 1997; Heckman and Robb, 1985, 1986, 1988).

To clarify these issues consider a specific example – the effects of a job training program on individuals' later earnings. Assume that potential trainees consist of both unskilled and skilled workers. Further assume that the training program is aimed at upgrading the skills of unskilled workers who are in fact the individuals who take the program. Plausibly, in the absence of the training program, the earnings of unskilled workers would be lower on average than those of the skilled workers. Thus a simple comparison of the post-training earnings of the unskilled workers to those of the skilled workers would understate the effect of the program because it fails to adjust for these preprogram differences. However, it might well be the case that the training program raises the earnings of unskilled workers, but would have no effect on the earnings of skilled workers. In this case, net of the preprogram differences in earnings, the difference in the post-training earnings of unskilled workers and those of skilled workers would overstate the average effect of training for the two groups as a whole.

Note, however, that in this example the average treatment effect over the two groups combined, δ, is unlikely to be the quantity of interest. In particular, what is likely to be of interest is whether the unskilled workers have benefitted from the program. Heckman (1992, 1996, 1997a) and Heckman et al. (1997) have argued that in a variety of policy contexts, it is the average treatment effect for the treated that is of substantive interest. The essence of their argument is that in deciding whether a policy is beneficial, our interest is not whether on average the program is beneficial for all individuals, but rather whether it is beneficial for those individuals who would either be assigned or assign themselves to the treatment. This is fortunate from a statistical perspective since most methods of adjustment only attempt elimination of the baseline difference. Few techniques are available to adjust for the differential treatment effects component of the bias. Often with nonexperimental data the best that we can do is to estimate the effect of treatment on the treated.

Randomized experiments

Since Fisher invented the concept of randomization, experimenters in many disciplines have argued that in a randomized experiment inferences about the effect of X could be made using the standard estimator. It is important to note that although statisticians had used Neyman's notation to make this argument, outside of statistics, where this notation was not well known, the argument was sustained largely by intuition, without explicit consideration of the estimand (21.6).

To intuitively understand how randomization works, note that in a randomized experiment, the units for whom $X = t$ and the units for whom $X = c$ are each random samples from the population of interest. Hence, $\bar{Y}_t$ is an unbiased and consistent estimate of $E(Y_t)$ and $\bar{Y}_c$ is an unbiased and consistent estimate of $E(Y_c)$. As a result,

$$E[\bar{Y}_t - \bar{Y}_c] = E[\bar{Y}_t] - E[\bar{Y}_c] = E[Y_t] - E[Y_c]$$
$$= E[Y_t - Y_c] = \delta. \qquad (21.10)$$

Of course in practice, randomized studies have their difficulties as well. Not all subjects will comply with their treatment protocol. Treatment effects may be different for compliers and noncompliers. Some statisticians argue that the effect of interest in this case is δ, while others argue that the estimate of interest is the average causal effect in the subpopulation of compliers. (We discuss the technical aspects of this issue further in the section below on instrumental variables; see also Angrist et al. (1996).) Experimental mortality is another well-known threat to inference (Campbell and Stanley, 1966). The usual approach to this problem is to assume that the only impact of experimental mortality is to reduce the size of the experimental groups, thereby increasing the standard errors of estimates. This is tantamount to assuming that experimental mortality is independent of the potential responses Y_t and Y_c.

Ignorability

Sociologists do not typically conduct randomized studies. It might appear that the foregoing results suggest that it is not possible to make well-supported causal inferences from observational studies. This is incorrect. Random assignment is sufficient (but not necessary) for $E(Y_t) = E(Y_t | X = t)$ and $E(Y_c) = E(Y_c | X = c)$, (which is necessary for the difference between the sample means to be an unbiased and consistent estimator of (21.1), the average causal effect).

A more general sufficient condition for the standard estimator to be unbiased and consistent is what is known as ignorability. Ignorability holds if

$$(Y_t, Y_c) \perp X, \qquad (21.11)$$

where '$\perp$' indicates that Y_x and X are independent, that is, Y_t and Y_c are independent of X.[2] Note that ignorability does not imply that X and the observed Y are independent. In fact, in many situations they will be related because there is a treatment effect and/or because of systematic differences in who is assigned to the treatment and control group. Ignorability is a more general condition than random assignment, since random assignment insures that treatment assignment, X_i, is independent of all variables whereas ignorability only requires that the potential outcomes, Y_x, be independent of X_i.

To understand why ignorability is sufficient for consistency of the standard estimator, consider the well-known theorem from probability theory that if two random vectors, Z and W, are independent ($Z \perp W$), then the mean of Z conditional on W is equal to the conditional mean of Z, that is, $E(Z | W) = E(Z)$. Thus a sufficient condition that $E(Y_x) = E(Y_x | X = x)$ is for $Y_x \perp X$ for $x = t, c$. In other words, the potential responses Y_t and Y_c are independent of X, the treatment assignment.

Now consider the case where interest focuses on causal analysis within subgroups. The sample data can be used to estimate $E(Y_t | X = 0, Z = z)$ and $E(Y_c | X = 1, Z = z)$, respectively. In the case where Z takes on a small number of values, the sample means within subgroups (provided there are cases in the data) can be used to estimate these quantities. Here Y_t and Y_c need to be independent of X within the strata defined by the different levels of Z. Arguing as before, when $X = x$, the response Y that is observed is Y_x; thus $E[Y | X = x, Z = z] = E[Y_x | X = x, Z = z]$. In order that $E[Y_x | X = x, Z = z] = E[Y_x | Z = z]$, it is sufficient that

$$(Y_t, Y_c) \perp X | Z = z; \qquad (21.12)$$

that is, treatment assignment must be ignorable within the strata defined by Z. When this holds, it implies that

$$E[Y_t | X = t, Z = z] - E[Y_c | X = c, Z = z]$$
$$= E[Y_t | Z = z] - E(Y_c | Z = z) = \delta_z, (21.13)$$

the average causal effect of X on Y at level $Z = z$ as defined by equation (21.2). Equation (21.13) indicates that a key strategy for estimating a causal effect is to find covariates Z

such that, within the strata of Z ignorability holds. This strategy is one manifestation of the more general strategy of using some method to control for Z so that, conditional on Z, ignorability holds.

How might it be the case that $E(Y_t \mid X = t) = E(Y_t)$ and $E(Y_c \mid X = c) = E(Y_c)$ in either a sample as a whole or within strata defined by different values of Z? The analysis above indicates that in a controlled but nonrandomized experiment, the assignment method will not lead to bias in the standard estimator if assignment (X) is independent of both Y_t and Y_c. For example, if students in a large section of an introductory sociology course are divided into two groups on the basis of which side of the room they sit on and the two groups are then taught using two competing texts, it might be reasonable (unless one suspects that there was a systematic seating pattern, as would be the case if tardy students always sat on the left) to proceed as if (21.4) holds.

While a great deal of causal knowledge has been obtained without conducting randomized experiments, it has also been well documented that analyzing data from nonrandomized experiments and observational studies as if they were from randomized experiments can yield misleading results. Examples include many medical studies where physicians assigned patients to treatment and overstated the efficiency of treatment (Freedman et al., 1998); similar results have occurred in the analysis of various social programs where program administrators assign subjects to treatment groups (LaLonde, 1986) or subjects select their own treatments. Here, even sophisticated attempts to adjust for the absence of randomization may yield misleading and/or inconclusive results. For example, Nye et al. (1999) suggest that the many econometric studies of the effect of small classroom size on academic achievement based on observational studies and nonrandomized experiments have not yielded a set of consistent conclusions, much less good estimates of the true effects. By way of contrast, these authors demonstrate that there are long-term beneficial effects of small classroom size using data from a large randomized experiment – Project Star.

Propensity scores and the assignment equation

If we have a large sample and there is good reason to believe that the Y_x and X are independent within the strata that are defined by some set of variables Z, then our analysis task is conceptually straightforward. We can simply use the standard estimator to estimate average causal effects within strata. If an estimate of the average effect for the population as a whole is desired, stratum-level average effects can be combined by using a weighted average, where the weights are proportionate to the population proportions within each stratum.

With small samples it can be either impossible or undesirable to carry out analysis within strata. What, then, are we to do? Suppose that treatment assignment is not random but that the probabilities of assignment to the treatment groups (X) are a known function of measured variables Z (e.g. age, sex, education), that is,

$$\Pr(X = t \mid Z = z) = P(Z). \qquad (21.14)$$

Equation (21.14) is what is known as the *assignment equation* and $P(Z)$ is what is known at the *propensity score*. The propensity score is simply the probability that a unit with characteristics Z is assigned to the treatment condition. In practice $P(Z)$ might have the form of a logit equation. If ignorability conditional on Z holds, then

$$\Pr(X = t \mid Z = z, Y_t, Y_c)$$
$$= \Pr(X = t \mid Z = z). \qquad (21.15)$$

The condition expressed by equation (21.15) is sometimes known as 'selection on the observables' (Heckman and Robb, 1985). Here the probability of being assigned to the treatment condition is a function of the observable variables Z and is conditionally independent of the (only partially observable) variables Y_t and Y_c. Rosenbaum and Rubin (1983) show that under these conditions

$$(Y_t, Y_c) \perp X \mid P(Z), \qquad (21.16)$$

that is, ignorability holds conditional on the propensity score.

Equations (21.15) and (21.16) provide a critical insight. They show that what is critical in estimating the causal effect of X is that we condition on those variables that determine assignment, that is, X_i. This is quite different from the standard view in sociology, where it is typically thought that what is important is to take into account all the variables that are causes of Y. What the counterfactual approach demonstrates is that what is critical is to condition on those **Z**s that result in ignorability holding, that is Y_t and Y_c being independent of X.

Rosenbaum and Rubin (1983) show that over repeated samples there is nothing to be gained by stratifying in a more refined way on the variables in **Z** beyond the strata defined by propensity score. The propensity score contains all the information that is needed to create what is known as a balanced design – that is, a design where the treatment and control groups have identical distributions on the covariates.

If our sample is sufficiently large that it is possible to stratify on the propensity score, $P(\mathbf{Z})$, then as before we can use the standard estimator within strata defined by $P(\mathbf{Z})$. If this is not the case, the propensity score can still be a key ingredient in an analysis. We discuss this in the next section, where we examine matching estimators.

In general the propensity score is not known. Typically, it is estimated using a logit model. One, however, cannot actually know that a particular **Z** includes all the relevant variables; thus, biases arising from unmeasured variables may be present. Detecting such biases and assessing the uncertainty due to potential biases is important; such issues have received a great deal of attention in the work of Rosenbaum (for a summary, see Rosenbaum, 1995: Chapters 4–6).

ESTIMATION OF CAUSAL EFFECTS

For many readers the discussion to this point may bear little relation to what they learned in statistics courses as graduate students. As noted at the beginning of this chapter, a principal virtue of the counterfactual model is that it provides a framework within which to assess whether estimators from various statistical models can appropriately be interpreted as estimating causal effects.

In this final section of the chapter, we wish to briefly examine the properties of a few statistical methods when they are considered from the perspective of the counterfactual model. In particular, we will examine matching, regression, instrumental variables, and methods for longitudinal data. Space limitations prevent us from considering these methods in any depth. However, other chapters in this handbook provide comprehensive introductions to many of these methods.

Matching

Matching is commonly used in biomedical research. It is closely related to stratification. In essence matching is equivalent to stratification where each stratum has only two elements, with one element assigned to the control condition and the other to the treatment. Smith (1997) provides an excellent introduction for sociologists. To match, one identifies individuals in the treatment and control groups with equivalent or at least similar values of the covariates **Z** and matches them, creating a new sample of matched cases. The standard estimator is then applied to the matched sample. By construction, the treatment and control cases in the matched sample have identical values of **Z** (or nearly so). Thus, matching eliminates the effect of any potential differences in the distribution of **Z** between the treatment and control groups by equating the distribution of **Z** across the two groups.

Matching has several advantages. First, it makes no assumption about the functional form of the dependence between the outcome of interest and **Z**s. As such, it is a type of nonparametric estimator. Second, matching insures that the **Z**s in the treatment group are similar (matched) to those in the control group.[3] Thus, matching prevents us from comparing units in the treatment and control groups that are dissimilar. We do not compare 'apples' and 'oranges'. Third, since fewer parameters are estimated than in a regression model, matching may be more efficient. Efficiency can be important with small samples.

A major problem with the traditional matching approach, however, is that if there are more than a few covariates in **Z**, it may be difficult to find both treatment and control cases that match unless an enormous sample of data is available. Matching on the propensity score is an attractive alternative to attempting to match across all covariates in **Z** since it involves matching on only a single dimension. *Nearest available matching on the estimated propensity score* is the most common and one of the simplest methods (see Rosenbaum and Rubin, 1985). First, the propensity scores for all individuals are estimated with a standard logit or probit model. Individuals in the treatment group are then listed in random order.[4] The first treatment case is selected, and its propensity score is noted. The case is then matched to the control case with the closest propensity score.

Both cases are then removed from their respective lists, and the second treatment case is matched to the remaining control case with the closest propensity score. This procedure is repeated until all the treatment cases are matched. Other matching techniques that use propensity scores are implemented by: using different methods and different sets of covariates to estimate propensity scores; matching on key covariates in Z that one wants to guarantee balance on first, and then matching on propensity scores; defining the closeness of propensity scores and Zs in different ways; and/or matching multiple control cases to each treatment case (see Rosenbaum, 1995; Rubin and Thomas, 1996; Smith 1997).

Matching works because it amounts to conditioning on the propensity score. Thus if ignorability holds conditional on the propensity score, the standard estimator on the matched sample will be unbiased and consistent. A couple of caveats, however, are in order about matching. First, if there are treatment cases where there are no matches, the estimated average causal effect only applies to cases of the sample of treated cases for which there are matches. Second, the consistency of the standard estimator on the matched sample under ignorability holds only if cases are truly matched on a random basis. Often for a particular treatment case there may be only one or two control cases that are an appropriate match. In this case, the matching process is clearly not random. As a result, although the original sample may be balanced conditional on the propensity score, this may not be true of the matched sample that has been derived from the overall sample. Because of this, it is good practice to examine the means and variances of the covariates in Zs in the treatment and control groups in the matched samples to insure that they are comparable. If one believes that one's outcomes are likely to be a function of higher-order nonlinear terms or interactions of the covariates, then the two groups must be similar on these moments of Z also.[5]

An alternative approach that avoids the latter problem with matching is to use the original sample of treatment and control cases, but to weight cases by the inverse of their propensity scores. As with matching, this creates a balanced sample. One then computes the standard estimator on the weighted sample. As is the case with matching, this is a form of nonparametric estimation. Thus, if ignorability holds, the standard estimator will provide an unbiased and consistent estimate of the average causal effect. In general, however, one should probably exclude treatment and control cases that do not have counterparts with similar propensity scores (Robins, personal communication). One wants to avoid the problem of comparing 'apples' to 'oranges'. This means that one should first omit from the sample those treatment and control cases that do not have similar counterparts in the other group and then re-estimate the remaining cases' propensity scores. These re-estimated propensity scores can then be used in an analysis of the inverse-weighted sample. A second advantage of this estimator is that it will generally use most of the sample, whereas matching can involve throwing out a considerable number of cases. As far as we are aware, little work has been done that investigates this estimator.[6]

Regression

Regression models (and various extensions thereof, such as logistic regression) are frequently used by quantitative social scientists. Typically, such models are parametric, specifying the functional form of the relationship between independent variables and the response. If the model is correctly specified, matching, which provides a nonparametric estimator, is inefficient relative to modeling, as observations are discarded. However, if this is not the case, inconsistent estimates of effects will result when such models are used.

As noted above, it is standard to interpret the coefficient for a particular variable in a regression model as representing the causal effect of that variable on the outcome 'holding all other variables in the model constant'. We hope by this point that we have convinced the reader that this interpretation is almost always unreasonable. The inferential task is difficult enough when there is only a single variable X whose causal effect is of interest. We view the all too common attempt when one has nonexperimental data to make causal inferences about a series of Xs within a single model as hazardous. The threats to the validity of such claims are simply too great in most circumstances to make such inferences plausible. The relevant question, then, is under what conditions in the context of the counterfactual model a regression estimate for a single variable can be interpreted as a causal effect.

Above we have treated X_i as a dichotomous variable taking on values t and c. More generally, we may let X_i be a numerical-valued variable taking on many values; as before, X_i is the observed (or factual) level of the treatment. Consider the following standard regression equation:

$$Y_i = \beta_0 + X_i\beta + \varepsilon_i, \qquad (21.17)$$

where $\varepsilon_i = Y_i - (\beta_0 + X_i\beta)$, $\beta = \text{cov}(Y,X)/\text{var}(X)$, and $\beta_0 = \bar{Y} - \bar{X}_i\beta$, the standard ordinary least-squares estimators. Note that this equation only pertains to the one value of Y_i and X_i that is observed for each individual in the data. This equation could be augmented to include a matrix of control variables $\mathbf{Z}$. If ε_i is assumed to be independent of X_i, (21.17) implies[7] that

$$E[Y|X] = \beta_0 + X_i\beta. \qquad (21.18)$$

Now consider the following equation as part of a counterfactual model:

$$Y_{xi} = \gamma + X_i\delta + e_{xi}, \qquad (21.19)$$

where Y_{xi} has a distinct value for every value of X_i, factual and counterfactual, and e_{xi} is an error with mean 0. In equation (21.19), δ represents the average causal effect of X_i on Y_{xi}. The critical question is under what conditions $\beta = \delta$, that is, estimation of β provides an estimate of the average causal effect of X_i, δ.

As in the case of the standard estimator, a sufficient condition is that the Y_{xi} and X_i (the realized X_i) be independent of each other, that is, ignorability holds. This condition is equivalent to each of the e_{xi} and X_i being independent. Note, however, that this is not equivalent to the condition that ε_i and X_i be independent, a condition that is sufficient for ordinary least squares to consistently estimate the conditional expectation equation (21.18). The error, ε_i, is associated with the realized values of Y_{xi}, Y_i, and consists of a single value for each individual, i, whereas e_{xi} is defined for each potential value of X_i and its value Y_{xi}. In general, the independence of X_i and ε_i does not imply ignorability. This is critical. Equation (21.18) provides a description of the data – how the expected value of Y varies with X. Equation (21.19) defines a causal relation between Y and X. In general these will be different.

Adopting a counterfactual perspective has important implications for how one does regression analysis. The standard approach in regression analysis is to determine the set of variables needed to predict a dependent variable Y. Typically, the researcher enters variables into a regression equation and uses t tests and F tests to determine whether the inclusion of a variable or set of variables significantly increases R^2.

From a counterfactual perspective, the ability to predict Y and thus the standard t and F tests are irrelevant. Rather the focus, at least in the simplest cases, is on the estimation of the causal effect of a single variable (what we have called the treatment effect). The key question is whether the regression equation includes the appropriate set of covariates such that ignorability holds (Pratt and Schlaifer, 1988). To attempt to achieve this, the researcher needs to stratify on, or enter as controls, variables that determine the treatment variable, X_i. These variables may or may not be significantly related to the dependent variable Y_i. The criteria for deciding whether a variable should be included in the equation is not whether it is significant or not, but rather whether our estimate of the treatment effect and the confidence interval surrounding it is changed by the variable's inclusion. In particular, we need to include variables that are likely to be highly correlated with X_i since their inclusion is likely to change the inferences we make about the likely size of X's effect even though these variables may well not significantly increase R^2 precisely because they are highly correlated with X. Strong candidates for controls in the regression equation are variables that the researcher believes are likely to determine X. In the particular case where X is dichotomous, we can borrow the strategy used in matching and condition on the propensity score by entering it as a control variable. This approach may be particularly attractive when there are few degrees of freedom associated with the regression model.

Instrumental variables

The counterfactual framework has provided important insight into instrumental variable estimators (Winship and Morgan, 1999). The typical assumption in instrumental variables is that the effect of treatment is constant across the populations. In many situations, however, this is unreasonable. What does an instrumental variable estimator estimate when the treatment effects vary? Recent work by Imbens and Angrist (1994), Angrist and Imbens (1995), Angrist et al. (1996), and Imbens and Rubin (1997) investigates this issue by extending the potential outcome framework discussed at the beginning of this chapter. This extension is accomplished by assuming that treatment received is a function of an exogenous instrument R_i. R_i might be the treatment individuals are assigned to (Angrist et al., 1996), an incentive to be in either the treatment or control group, or any variable that directly affects the treatment received, but not the treatment outcome.

For simplicity, assume that both the treatment and the instrument are binary. Treatment is determined nonrandomly. However, an incentive to enroll in the treatment program (e.g., a cash subsidy), R_i, is assigned randomly. R_i is an instrument for X_i in that R_i affects X_i, but has no direct effect on Y_i. When both the treatment and incentive are binary, individuals eligible to receive the treatment can be divided into four mutually exclusive groups termed 'compliers', 'defiers', 'always takers' and 'never takers'. Individuals who would enroll in the program if offered the incentive and who would not enroll in the program if not offered the incentive are labeled 'compliers' (i.e., when $R_i = 1$, $X_i = t$ and when $R_i = 0$, $X_i = c$). Likewise, individuals who would only enroll in the program if *not* offered the incentive are 'defiers' (i.e.,when $R_i = 1$, $X_i = c$ and when $R_i = 0$, $X_i = t$). Individuals who would always enroll in the program, regardless of the incentive, are 'always takers' (i.e., when $R_i = 1$, $X_i = t$ and when $R_i = 0$, $X_i = t$). Finally, individuals who would never enroll in the program, regardless of the incentive, are 'never takers' (i.e., when $R_i = 1$, $X_i = c$ and when $R_i = 0$, $X_i = c$). Note that the usage here is nonstandard in that the terms 'compliers' and 'defiers' refer to how an individual responds to the incentive, not simply whether they comply or not with their treatment assignment in a traditional experiment, the standard denotation of these terms.

Based on the potential treatment assignment function, Imbens and Angrist (1994) define a monotonicity condition. For all individuals, an increase in the incentive, R_i, must either leave their treatment status the same, or, among individuals who change, cause them to switch in the same direction. For example, the typical case would be that an increase in the incentive would cause more individuals to adopt the treatment condition,

but would not result in anyone refusing the treatment condition who had previously accepted it. The general assumption is that there be either defiers or compliers but not both in the population.[8]

When the treatment assignment process satisfies the monotonicity condition, the conventional instrumental variable estimate is an estimate of what is defined as the local average treatment effect (LATE), the average treatment effect for either compliers alone or for defiers alone, depending on which group exists in the population.[9] LATE is the average effect for that subset of the population whose treatment status is changed by the instrument, that is, that set of individuals whose treatment status can be potentially manipulated by the instrument. The individual-level treatment effects of always takers and never takers are not included in LATE.

Because of LATE's nature, it has three problems: first, LATE is determined by the instrument and thus different instruments will give different average treatment effects; secondly, LATE is the average treatment effect for a subset of individuals that is unobservable; and thirdly, LATE can sometimes be hard to interpret when the instrument measures something other than an incentive to which individuals respond.

Longitudinal data

Longitudinal data are often described as a panacea for problems of causal inference. Nothing could be farther from the truth. As in any causal analysis, the critical issue is what assumptions the analysis makes about the counterfactual values. As discussed below, different methods of analysis make quite different assumptions. Unfortunately, these are often not even examined, much less tested. Here we briefly discuss these issues (see Winship and Morgan, 1999, who provide a more extensive discussion).

Let Y_i^s equal the value of the observed Y for person i at time s. Let Y_{ti}^s equal the value of Y for individual i under either the factual or counterfactual condition of receiving the treatment. Let Y_{ci}^s equal the value of Y for individual i under either the factual or counterfactual condition of not receiving the treatment. Let the treatment occur at a single point in time, s'. We assume that for $s < s'$, $Y_{ti}^s = Y_{ci}^s$, that is, the treatment has no effect on an individual's response prior to the treatment.

Below we discuss how a test of this assumption provides an important method for detecting model misspecification.

A variety of methods are often used to analyze data of the above type. We discuss the two most commonly used in sociology with the aim of demonstrating the different assumptions each makes about the value of Y^s under the counterfactual condition. After this, we briefly discuss the implications of the counterfactual perspective for the analysis of longitudinal data.

The simplest case uses individuals as their own control cases. Specifically, if we have both test and pretest values on Y, Y^s_i and $Y^{s^*}_i$ where $s < s' < s^*$, then $Y^{s^*}_i - Y^s_i$ is an estimate of the treatment effect for individual i. The problem with this approach is that it assumes that Y would be constant between s and s^* in the absence of treatment. Changes may occur because of aging or changes in the environment. If one's data contains longitudinal information for a control group, however, the assumption of no systematic increase and decrease with time in Y in the absence of treatment can be tested. Preferably, the control group will consist of individuals who are similar to those in the treatment group both in terms of covariates $\mathbf{Z}$ and their initial observations on Y. This might be accomplished, for example, using matching. The simplest approach then would be to test whether the mean or median of Y of the control group shifts between times s and s^*. This test, of course, is only useful if we are correct in assuming that in the absence of treatment, the responses of individuals in the treatment and control group would change with time in similar ways.

If Y does systematically change over time in the absence of treatment, what is the researcher to do? Two very different choices are available. One could analyze the post-test observations using cross-sectional methods such as matching or regression. Here the presence of pretest data is a considerable advantage. Specifically, we can also analyze the pretest observations on the treatment and control groups as if they were post-test observations, using the same cross-sectional methods (Heckman and Hotz, 1989; Rosenbaum, 1995). Since the treatment group has yet to receive the treatment, a finding of a treatment effect in the pretest data is evidence that one's method inadequately adjusts for differences between the treatment and control groups. A considerable advantage of having

pretest and post-test data when one is either using individuals as their own controls or using cross-sectional methods to estimate a treatment effect is that the availability of pretest data allows the researcher to test whether the particular cross-sectional model under consideration is consistent with the data.

The other approach when one has longitudinal data is to use the fact that one has observations over time to adjust for possible differences between the treatment and control groups. The two most common methods used in sociology are *change score analysis* and the *analysis of covariance* (Allison, 1990; Winship and Morgan, 1999). Change score analysis amounts to estimating the following regression equation:

$$Y^{s^*}_i - Y^s_i = X_i \beta + u_i, \qquad (21.20)$$

where additional covariates $\mathbf{Z}$ could be potentially added as controls. Alternatively, analysis of covariance amounts to estimating the equation

$$Y^{s^*}_i = Y^s_i \alpha + X_i \beta + u_i \qquad (21.21)$$

or, equivalently,

$$Y^{s^*}_i - \alpha Y^s_i = X_i \beta + u_i, \qquad (21.22)$$

where, as before, covariates $\mathbf{Z}$ could be added to the equation as controls. As we discuss below, α will always be between zero and one. Comparing equations (21.20) and (21.21) we see that both methods involve adjusting the post-test outcome $Y^{s^*}_i$ by subtracting out some portion of the pretest outcome Y^s_i. Change score analysis amounts to setting the adjustment factor, α, to one.

A large literature has debated the relative merits of these two approaches (see Allison, 1990, for a discussion). From the counterfactual perspective, the key observation is that both methods make different assumptions about how Y^s_i will change over time in the absence of treatment. Change score analysis assumes that in the absence of treatment, differences, on average, between individuals over time will remain constant. Returning to our old convention that $X = t$ or c, change score analysis implies that

$$E[Y^s_{ci} \mid X = t] - E[Y^s_{ci} \mid X = c]$$
$$= E[Y^{s^*}_{ci} \mid X = t] - E[Y^{s^*}_{ci} \mid X = c], \qquad (21.23)$$

that is, the difference in the mean of Y_c for individuals in the treatment group and individuals in the control group will remain constant between times s and s^*. Alternatively, the analysis of covariance model assumes that

$$E[Y_{ci}^s \mid X = t] - E[Y_{ci}^s \mid X = c]$$
$$= \alpha(E[Y_{ci}^{s^*} \mid X = t]$$
$$- E[Y_{ci}^{s^*} \mid X = c]), \qquad (21.24)$$

that is, the difference between the mean of Y_c for individuals in the treatment group and those in the control group will shrink by a factor α.

It is often argued that a distinct advantage of the analysis of covariance model over the change score model is that the adjustment factor, α, is estimated. This is incorrect if equation (21.20) is estimated by OLS, which is the standard procedure.[10] In this case α, by construction, will be equal to the intragroup correlation between $Y_i^{s^*}$ and Y_i^s. As a result, α will be between zero and one, except in rare cases where it is negative.

Comparing equations (21.22) and (21.23) shows that change score analysis and analysis of covariance models make different assumptions about how the difference between $E[Y_{ci}^s]$ for the treatment and control groups changes with time. Change score analysis assumes that this difference will remain constant, whereas the analysis of covariance assumes that it will shrink by a fixed factor α, the within-group correlation between the responses between time s and s^*. Whether β in equation (21.20) or equation (21.21) consistently estimates δ will depend on which, if either, of these assumptions is correct (Holland and Rubin, 1983).

As Heckman and Hotz (1989) have argued, with only a single pretest and post-test, it is impossible to determine which assumption is correct since there are not observations at a sufficient number of time points to determine how the difference in average outcome for the treatment and control groups changes over time in the absence of treatment. In fact, the assumptions in the change score and analysis of covariance model may be simultaneously incorrect. The difference between the outcomes for the treatment and control groups may shrink by a factor other than α, or the difference might potentially increase, which would be inconsistent with both models. A possible example of the latter would be in the examination of the effects of educational attainment on mental

ability of children (Winship and Korenman, 1997). A plausible assumption in this case is that in the absence of additional education, the difference in mental ability between higher- and lower-ability children would grow with age.

Other more sophisticated methods for analyzing longitudinal data are available. Economists are particularly interested in what is known as the difference-in-difference model (e.g., Card and Krueger, 1995; Ashenfelter and Card, 1985). This model is similar to the change score model except that, instead of assuming that in the absence of treatment the difference between individuals' outcomes remains constant, it assumes that this difference changes at a fixed linear rate. The change score model allows the intercept to vary across individuals. The difference-in-difference model, in addition, allows the coefficient on time/age to vary across individuals. Heckman and Robb (1986, 1988) provide an extensive review of different methods.

Different methods make different assumptions about what will occur in the absence of treatment – that is, they make different assumptions about what will be true in the counterfactual condition. As a result, different methods are likely to provide different estimates of the treatment effect (LaLonde, 1986). Which method should a researcher use? In some cases, theoretical considerations may suggest that one method is more appropriate than another (Allison, 1990). In sociology, however, our theories are often sufficiently weak or there may be competing theories such that it is impossible with any confidence to assume that one particular model is the appropriate one for analysis.

Heckman and Hotz (1989) argue that it is critical that one have sufficient pretest (or post-test) observations so that it is possible to test one's model against the data. As discussed earlier, one can treat one's pretest data as if they, or some portion of them, are post-test data and then estimate whether there is evidence of a 'treatment' effect on the data. One can also perform a similar analysis when one has multiple post-test values dividing them into a 'pretest' and 'post-test' group. Lack of evidence for a treatment effect is evidence that the model being used has appropriately adjusted for differences between the treatment and control groups. Of course, more than one model may be consistent with the data and these different models may produce different estimates of the treatment effect. Unless there is a compelling reason to choose one model over another, one should pool one's estimates of the effect across models. Raftery (1995) discusses how this can be done within a Bayesian framework.

CONCLUSION

The purpose of this chapter has been to provide an introduction to the counterfactual model of causal inference and to briefly examine its implications for the statistical analysis of causal effects. In the introduction we argued that the counterfactual model of causal inference had the potential to change the way that sociologists carried out empirical analyses. We summarize the chapter by providing a list of what we believe are the most important contributions and insights of CMCI for empirical research:

1. Estimating the effect of a single variable (treatment) on an outcome is quite difficult. Attempts to estimate the effects of multiple variables simultaneously are generally ill advised.
2. CMCI provides a general framework for evaluating the conditions under which specific estimators can be interpreted as estimating a causal effect.
3. A particular strength of CMCI is its ability to make explicit the possibility that the size of a treatment effect may vary across individuals.
4. Often it is only possible to estimate the size of the treatment effect for the treated. However, under some circumstances this is precisely what is of interest.
5. Causal analysis is at core a missing-data problem. The key question is what the values of the outcome would have been under the counterfactual condition.
6. Different assumptions about the counterfactual values will typically result in different estimates of the causal effect.
7. CMCI asks the researcher to fully specify the implicit manipulation or 'experiment' associated with the estimation of a causal effect. In some cases, such as when estimating the effect of gender, what the manipulation of interest is may be unclear.
8. An effect may be inconsistently estimated for two different reasons: failure to control for differences between the treatment and control group in the absence of treatment; and failure to take account of the fact that the size of the treatment effect differs for individuals in the treatment and control groups.
9. In order to consistently estimate a causal effect, ignorability (or ignorability given covariates) must hold, that is, treatment received (X) must be independent of the partially observed outcome variables Y_x.
10. The key to consistently estimating a causal effect is to control for those variables, either by matching, stratification, or regression, that determine (or are associated with) treatment status.
11. Matching provides a powerful nonparametric alternative to regression for the estimation of a causal effect that should be more frequently used by sociologists.
12. The traditional logic in which one or more variables are included in a regression model because they significantly increase R^2 as judged by a t test or F test is irrelevant to the assessment of the causal effect of a particular variable (the treatment).
13. Variables should be included as controls if they substantially change the estimate of the treatment effect. Often these will be variables that are highly correlated with the treatment variable and as such may have insignificant coefficients.
14. Instrumental variable estimators only estimate the effect of the treatment for those individuals whose treatment status is changed by varying the value of the instrument. In general, it is impossible to identify who belongs to this group.
15. Longitudinal data are not a panacea for causal analysis. As with any causal analysis, assumptions need to be made about the values of the outcome under the counterfactual condition. Different models involve different assumptions and as a result will generally give different estimates.
16. With longitudinal data, as with any analysis, it is important to test whether the assumptions implicit in the model hold by testing the model against the data.

The length of this list indicates that the implications for empirical research of the CMCI are considerable. We believe that as sociologists come to better understand and appreciate the counterfactual model, the CMCI will change the way they do research. Hopefully, the consequence of this will be much clearer thinking about causality and the problems in estimating specific causal effects, resulting in better estimates of the size of actual effects.

ACKNOWLEDGMENT

The authors would like to thank Melissa Hardy, David Harding, and Felix Elwert for comments on an earlier draft of this paper.

NOTES

1 We are grateful to Felix Elwert for bringing this example to our attention.

2 More precisely, this is the definition of *strong* ignorability. *Weak* ignorability requires that Y_t and Y_c be individually independent of X, whereas strong ignorability requires that they be jointly independent. In general, the distinction between strong and weak ignorability is of no substantive consequence.

3 In two empirical papers, Heckman et al. (1997, 1998) show that the bias due to selection on the unobservables, although significant and large relative to the size of the treatment effect, is small relative to the bias that results from having different ranges of Zs for the treatment and control groups and different distributions of the Zs across their common range. Matching solves both of the latter problems, although the average effect is not for the total population, but only that portion of the population where the treatment and control groups have common Z values.

4 In most empirical applications of matching techniques, the treatment group is considerably smaller than the control group. This need not be the case in all applications, and if the reverse is true, then the nearest available matching scheme described here runs in the opposite direction. Treatment cases would be matched to the smaller subset of control cases.

5 There is an important intellectual tension here. An attraction of the matching estimator is that in theory it is nonparametric. This means that we do not need to know how our two outcome variables, Y_t and Y_c are functionally related to our Zs. For this to actually be the case, our matched data set needs to be balanced on all the moments of Z. This, however, will only occur if the distribution of Z is exactly the same for the treatment and control group. But then we are back to the problem of traditional matching where one is trying to equate groups across a potentially large number of variables.

6 In principle, the propensity score can also be entered as a control variable in a regression model. Rubin and Rosenbaum have advocated matching since it implicitly deals with the problem of nonlinearity and uses fewer degrees of freedom, making it more efficient.

7 It is only necessary that the ε_i and X_i be mean-independent, that is, $E[\varepsilon_i \mid X] = 0$. In general, independence is a more desirable property since it means that mean independence will hold under any transformation of Y.

8 Note that when an instrument is valid, there must be at least some compliers or some defiers, otherwise the sample would be composed of only always takers and never takers. In this case, R_i would not be a valid instrument because it would have no effect on the treatment received, and thus R_i and treatment received would be uncorrelated.

9 The exclusion restriction that defines LATE is stronger than the conventional exclusion restriction that the instrument must be mean-independent of the error term. Instead, Imbens and Angrist (1994) require that the instrument be fully independent of the error term. Imbens and Rubin (1997) argue that the strong independence restriction is more realistic because it continues to hold under transformations of the outcome variable. An assumption about the distribution of the outcome is thereby avoided.

10 Equation (21.20) could be estimated by instrumental variables. Then, however, the issues with instrumental variable estimators discussed in the previous section arise.

REFERENCES

Allison, P.D. (1990) 'Change scores as dependent variables in regression analysis', in C.C. Clogg (ed.), *Sociological Methodology 1990*. Oxford: Blackwell, pp. 93–114.

Alwin, Duane F. and Hauser, Robert M. (1975) 'The decomposition of effects in path analysis', *American Sociological Review*, 40: 37–47.

Anderson, John (1938) 'The problem of causality', *Australasian Journal of Psychology and Philosophy*, 16: 127–42.

Angrist, J.D. and Imbens, G.W. (1995) 'Two-stage least squares estimation of average causal effects in models with variable treatment intensity', *Journal of the American Statistical Association*, 90: 431–42.

Angrist, J.D., Imbens, G.W. and Rubin, D.B. (1996) 'Identification of causal effects using instrumental variables', *Journal of the American Statistical Association*, 91: 444–72.

Ashenfelter, O. and Card, D. (1985) 'Using the longitudinal structure of earnings to estimate the effect of training programs', *Review of Economics and Statistics*, 67: 648–60.

Bunge, Mario A. (1979) *Causality and Modern Science* (3rd edition). New York: Dover.

Campbell, Donald T. and Stanley, J.C. (1966) *Experimental and Quasi-experimental Designs for Research*. Chicago: Rand McNally.

Card, David and Krueger, Allan (1995) *Myth and Measurement: The New Economics of the Minimum Wage*. Princeton, NJ: Princeton University Press.

Collingwood, Robin G. (1998) *An Essay on Metaphysics*. Oxford: Oxford University Press. First published in 1940.

Cox, David R. (1958) *The Planning of Experiments*. New York: Wiley.

Davis, Joyce (2000) 'PubNet: A case study of race, gender, and nationality in a virtual organization'. Unpublished. Department of Sociology, Harvard University.

Ducasse, Curt J. (1975) 'On the nature and observability of the causal relation', in E. Sosa (ed.), *Causation and Conditionals*. London: Oxford University Press, pp. 114–25. First published in 1926.

Duncan, Otis D. (1966) 'Path analysis: Sociological examples', *American Journal of Sociology*, 72: 1–16.

Ferguson, Niall (1997) 'Virtual history: Towards a "chaotic" theory of the past', in Niall Ferguson (ed.), *Virtual History: Alternatives and Counterfactuals*. London: Picador, pp. 1–90.

Freedman, David, Pisani, Robert and Purves, Roger (1998) *Statistics* (3rd edition). New York: W.W. Norton.

Geweke, John (1984) 'Inference and causality in economic time series models', in Zvi Griliches and Michael E. Intriligator (eds), *Handbook of Econometrics* Vol. 2. Amsterdam: North-Holland, pp. 1101–44.

Goldin, Claudia (1999) 'Orchestrating impartiality: The impact of "blind" auditions on female musicians'. Unpublished. Department of Economics, Harvard University.

Granger, Clive W. (1969) 'Investigating causal relationships by econometric models and cross-spectral methods', *Econometrica*, 37: 424–38.

Gustafsson, Björn and Johansson, Mats (1999) 'What makes income inequality vary across countries?', *American Sociological Review*, 64: 585–685.

Harré, Rom (1972) *The Philosophies of Science*. Oxford: Oxford University Press.

Harré, Rom and Madden, Edward H. (1975) *Causal Powers: A Theory of Natural Necessity*. Oxford: Basil Blackwell.

Heckman, J.J. (1978) 'Dummy endogenous variables in a simultaneous equation system', *Econometrica*, 46: 931–61.

Heckman, J.J. (1992) 'Randomization and social policy evaluation', in C.F. Manski and I. Garfinkel (eds), *Evaluating Welfare and Training Programs*. Cambridge, MA: Harvard University Press, pp. 201–30.

Heckman, J.J. (1996) 'Randomization as an instrumental variable', *Review of Economics and Statistics*, 77: 336–41.

Heckman, J.J. (1997a) 'Instrumental variables: A study of implicit behavioral assumptions used in making program evaluations', *Journal of Human Resources*, 32: 441–62.

Heckman, J.J. (1997b) 'Identifying and estimating counterfactuals in the social sciences: The role of rational choice theory'. Unpublished. University of Chicago.

Heckman, J.J. and Hotz, V.J. (1989) 'Choosing among alternative nonexperimental methods for estimating the impact of social programs: The case of manpower training', *Journal of the American Statistical Association*, 84: 862–80.

Heckman, J.J. and Robb, R. (1985) 'Alternative methods for evaluating the impact of interventions', in J.J. Heckman and B. Singer (eds), *Longitudinal Analysis of Labor Market Data*. Cambridge: Cambridge University Press, pp. 156–245.

Heckman, J.J. and Robb, R. (1986) 'Alternative methods for solving the problem of selection bias in evaluating the impact of treatments on outcomes', in H. Wainer (ed.), *Drawing Inferences from Self-selected Samples*, New York: Springer-Verlag, pp. 63–113.

Heckman, J.J. and Robb, R. (1988) 'The value of longitudinal data for solving the problem of selection bias in evaluating the impact of treatment on outcomes', in G. Duncan and G. Kalton (eds), *Panel Surveys*. New York: Wiley, pp. 512–38.

Heckman, J.J., Smith, J. and Clements, N. (1997) 'Making the most out of programme evaluations and social experiments: Accounting for heterogeneity in programme impacts', *Review of Economic Studies*, 64: 487–535.

Heckman, J.J., Ichimura, H., Smith, J. and Todd, P. (1998) 'Characterizing selection bias using experimental data', *Econometrica*, 66: 1017–99.

Holland, Paul W. (1986) 'Statistics and causal inference' (with discussion), *Journal of the American Statistical Association*, 81: 945–70.

Holland, Paul W. (1988) 'Causal inference, path analysis, and recursive structural equation models' (with discussion), in C.C. Clogg (ed.), *Sociological Methodology 1988*. Washington, DC: American Sociological Association, pp. 449–93.

Holland, Paul W. and Rubin, Donald B. (1983) 'On Lord's paradox', in Howard Wainer and Samuel Messick (eds), *Principals of Modern Psychological Measurement*. Hillsdale, NJ: Lawrence Erlbaum, pp. 3–35.

Imbens, G.W. and Angrist, J.D. (1994) 'Identification and estimation of local average treatment effects', *Econometrica*, 62: 467–75.

Imbens, G.W. and Rubin, D.B. (1997) 'Estimating outcome distributions for compliers in instrumental variables models', *Review of Economic Studies*, 64: 555–74.

Jöreskog, Karl G. (1977) 'Structural equation models in the social sciences: Specification, estimation and testing', in Paruchuri R. Krishnaiah (ed.), *Applications of Statistics*. Amsterdam: North-Holland, pp. 265–87.

LaLonde, R. (1986) 'Evaluating the econometric evaluations of training programs with experimental data', *American Economic Review*, 76: 604–20.

Mackie, John L. (1974) *The Cement of the Universe*. Oxford: Oxford University Press.

Manski, C.F. (1995) *Identification Problems in the Social Sciences*. Cambridge, MA: Harvard University Press.

Manski, C.F. (1997) 'Monotone treatment response', *Econometrica*, 65: 1311–34.

Manski, C.F. and Nagin, D.S. (1998) 'Bounding disagreements about treatment effects: A case study of sentencing and recidivism', *Sociological Methodology*, 28: 99–137.

Mill, John S. (1973) A *System of Logic, Ratiocinative and Inductive*, in John M. Robson (ed.), *The Collected Works of John Stuart Mill*, Vol. 7. Toronto: University of Toronto Press. First published in 1843.

Neyman, Jerzy (1990) 'On the application of probability theory to agricultural experiments. Essays on principles, Section 9' (with discussion). *Statistical Science*, 4: 465–80. First published in 1923.

Nye, Barbara, Hedges, Larry V. and Konstantopoulos, Spyros (1999) 'The long-term effects of small classes: A five-year follow-up of the Tennessee Class Size Experiment', *Educational Evaluation and Policy Analysis*, 21: 127–42.

Oldham, Greg R. and Gordon, Benjamin I. (1999) 'Job complexity and employee substance use: The moderating effects of cognitive ability', *Journal of Health and Social Behavior*, 40: 290–306.

Pearl, Judea (2000) *Causality: Models, Reasoning, and Inference*. Cambridge: Cambridge University Press.

Pratt, John W. and Schlaifer, Robert (1988) 'On the interpretation and observation of laws', *Journal of Econometrics*, 39: 23–52.

Raftery, Adrian E. (1995) 'Bayesian model selection in social research', in Peter V. Marsden (ed.), *Sociological Methodology 1995*. Cambridge, MA: Blackwell Publishers, pp. 111–63.

Robins, James M. (1989) 'The analysis of randomized and nonrandomized AIDS treatment trials using a new approach to causal inference in longitudinal studies', in Lee Sechrest, Howard Fredman and A. Mulley (eds), *Health Services Research Methodology: A Focus on AIDS*. Rockville, MD: US Department of Health and Human Services, pp. 113–59.

Rosenbaum, Paul R. (1984a) 'From association to causation in observational studies: The role of tests of strongly ignorable treatment assignment', *Journal of the American Statistical Association*, 79: 41–8.

Rosenbaum, Paul R. (1984b) 'The consequences of adjustment for a concomitant variable that has been affected by the treatment', *Journal of the Royal Statistical Society, Series A*, 147: 656–66.

Rosenbaum, Paul R. (1986) 'Dropping out of high school in the United States: An observational study', *Journal of Educational Statistics*, 11: 207–24.

Rosenbaum, Paul R. (1987) 'The role of a second control group in an observational study' (with discussion)', *Statistical Science*, 2: 292–316.

Rosenbaum, Paul R. (1992) 'Detecting bias with confidence in observational studies', *Biometrika*, 79: 367–74.

Rosenbaum, Paul R. (1995) *Observational Studies*. New York: Springer-Verlag.

Rosenbaum, Paul R. and Rubin, Donald B. (1983) 'The central role of the propensity score in observational studies for causal effects', *Biometrika*, 70: 41–55.

Rosenbaum, Paul R. and Rubin, Donald B. (1985) 'Constructing a control group using multivariate matched sampling methods that incorporate the propensity score', *American Statistician*, 39: 33–8.

Rubin, Donald B. (1974) 'Estimating causal effects of treatments in randomized and nonrandomized studies', *Journal of Educational Psychology*, 66: 688–701.

Rubin, Donald B. (1977) 'Assignment to treatment groups on the basis of a covariate', *Journal of Educational Statistics*, 2: 1–26.

Rubin, Donald B. (1978) 'Bayesian inference for causal effects: The role of randomization', *Annals of Statistics*, 6: 34–58.

Rubin, Donald B. (1980) Comment on 'Randomization analysis of experimental data: The Fisher randomization test', by D. Basu, *Journal of the American Statistical Association*, 75: 591–3.

Rubin, Donald B. (1990) 'Formal modes of statistical inference for causal effects', *Journal of Statistical Planning and Inference*, 25: 279–92.

Rubin, Donald B. and Thomas, N. (1996) 'Matching using estimated propensity scores: Relating theory to practice', *Biometrics*, 52: 249–64.

Russell, Bertrand (1913) 'On the notion of cause', *Proceedings of the Aristotelian Society (New Series)*, 13: 1–26.

Simon, Herbert A. (1952) 'On the definition of the causal relation', *Journal of Philosophy*, 49: 517–28.

Smith, H.L. (1997) 'Matching with multiple controls to estimate treatment effects in observational studies', *Sociological Methodology*, 27: 325–53.

Sobel, Michael E. (1990) 'Effect analysis and causation in linear structural equation models', *Psychometrika*, 55: 495–515.

Sobel, Michael E. (1994) 'Causal inference in latent variable models', in Alexander von Eye and Clifford

C. Clogg (eds), *Latent Variables Analysis: Applications for Developmental Research*. Thousand Oaks, CA: Sage, pp. 3–35.

Sobel, Michael E. (1995) 'Causal inference in the social and behavioral sciences', in Gerhard Arminger, Clifford C. Clogg and Michael E. Sobel (eds), *Handbook of Statistical Modeling for the Social and Behavioral Sciences*. New York: Plenum, pp. 1–38.

Sobel, Michael E. (1998) 'Causal inference in statistical models of the process of socioeconomic achievement: A case study', *Sociological Methods and Research*, 27: 318–48.

Stark, David C. and Bruszt, Laszio (1998) *Postsocialist Pathways: Transforming Politics and Property in East Central Europe*. Cambridge: Cambridge University Press.

Stinchcombe, Arthur L. (1968) *Constructing Social Theories*. New York: Harcourt, Brace and World.

Winship, Christopher and Korenman, Sanders (1997) 'Does staying in school make you smarter? The effects of education on IQ in *The Bell Curve*', in Stephen Fienberg, Daniel Resnick, Bernie Devlin, and Kathryn Roeder (eds), *Intelligence, Genes, and Success: Scientists Respond to* The Bell Curve. New York: Springer-Verlag, pp. 215–34.

Winship, Christopher and Morgan, Stephen L. (1999) 'The estimation of causal effects from observational data', *Annual Review of Sociology*, 25: 650–707.

22

The Analysis of Social Networks

RONALD L. BREIGER

The study of social relationships among actors – whether individual human beings or animals of other species, small groups or economic organizations, occupations or social classes, nations or world military alliances – is fundamental to the social sciences. Social network analysis may be defined as the disciplined inquiry into the patterning of relations among social actors, as well as the patterning of relationships among actors at different levels of analysis (such as persons and groups).

Following an introduction to data analysis issues in social networks research and to the basic forms of network representation, three broad topics are treated under this chapter's main headings: types of equivalence, statistical models (emphasizing a new class of logistic regression models for networks), and culture and cognition. Each section emphasizes data-analytic strategies used in exemplary research studies of social networks. Computer programs and related issues are briefly treated at the end of the chapter.

FROM METAPHOR TO DATA ANALYSIS

Network metaphors have long had great intuitive appeal for social thinkers and social scientists. Writing in 1857, Marx (1956: 96) said that 'society is not merely an aggregate of individuals; it is the sum of the relations in which these individuals stand to one another'. Thirty-five years later, Durkheim, in his Latin thesis, traced his interest in social

morphology to that of the eighteenth-century thinker Montesquieu, who had identified various types of society, such as monarchy, aristocracy, and republic, 'not on the basis of division of labor or the nature of their social ties, but solely according to the nature of their sovereign authority', and Durkheim went on to criticize this strategy as a failure to see 'that the essential is not the number of persons subject to the same authority, but the number bound by some form of relationship' (Durkheim, 1965: 32, 38). Leopold von Wiese, a writer within the German 'formal school' centered around Georg Simmel, asked his reader to imagine what would be seen if 'the constantly flowing stream of interhuman activity' were halted in its course for just one moment, and suggested that 'we will then see that it is an apparently impenetrable network of lines between men'; furthermore, 'a static analysis of the sphere of the interhuman will ... consist in the dismemberment and reconstruction of this system of relations' (von Wiese, 1941: 29–30). In America, Charles Horton Cooley proclaimed the necessity of a 'social' or 'sociological' pragmatism (Joas, 1993: 23), a tradition within which not only consciousness of social relations, but self-consciousness, was theorized explicitly, and within which 'a man may be regarded as the point of intersection of an indefinite number of lines representing social groups, having as many arcs passing through him as there are groups' (Cooley, 1964: 148). The English social anthropologist A.R. Radcliffe-Brown (1940) wrote that 'direct observation does reveal to us that … human beings are connected by a complex network of social relations. I use the term "social structure" to denote this network'.

One prominent commentator on the history of social scientific thought and on contemporary development writes that 'network sociology is doing the very thing that early sociologists and anthropologists saw as crucial – the mapping of the relations that create social structures' (Turner, 1991: 571). Much contemporary research over the past decades can be seen as a move from network thinking as vague metaphors to the elaboration of the network concept to the point where it can be used as an exact representation of at least some central elements of social structure (Freeman, 1989; Smith-Lovin and McPherson, 1993; Wellman, 1988). A particularly notable move from metaphor to analytical method is the relatively recent development of highly sophisticated computer programs for producing pictorial representations of social networks. Freeman (2000) illustrates some of the newest procedures for producing web-based pictures that allow viewers to interact with the network data and thus to use visual input in exploring a variety of analytical models of their structural properties.

Qualitative or quantitative?

Many of the quantitative techniques of data analysis taken up in other chapters of this *Handbook* may be considered to study networks of statistical relationships among variables. In contrast, because social network actors are in most studies concrete and observable (such as individual persons, groups, nations, and alliances) or collectivities of observable agents (such as occupations or classes), the relationships of interest to an analyst of social networks are usually in the first instance social or cultural, binding together and differentiating concrete entities, rather than statistical encodings. Indeed, some social network theorists and data analysts emphasize the extent to which the inductive modeling strategies of network analyses are subversive of the usual canons of statistical methods (Levine, 1999) or they portray network analysts as 'eschewing … interactional approaches such as statistical (variable) analyses … [in order to] pursue transactional studies of patterned social relationships' (Emirbayer, 1997: 298).

Much progress has in fact been made in recent decades in the statistical analysis of social networks. A number of important extensions of the general linear model have been developed in recent decades specifically to model (for example) the likelihood of a relationship existing from one actor to another, taking into account the *lack* of independence among social relationships and the presence of specifiable patterns of dependence. These statistical models will be reviewed in this chapter. Nonetheless, it is useful to keep in mind the very considerable extent to which social network analysis as a strategy of empirical research is indeed difficult to contain within the conventionally established headings of statistical data analysis, to the point of suggesting a highly distinctive research orientation within the social sciences. Even the effort to maintain distinctions between quantitative and qualitative forms of data analysis is challenged by the progress that has been made in the analysis of social networks.

Despite the development of important statistical models for social networks, therefore, as one strand of recent research deserving exposition, it will be useful to emphasize other strands that portray network analysis as a form of data analysis moving in directions quite different from statistical modeling. Even with respect to mathematical models, some of the most important progress in network analysis is more likely to be treated in texts on applied abstract algebra (Kim and Roush, 1983; Lidl and Pilz, 1998) than in statistics texts, owing to progress that has been made in visualizing and modeling complex structures as distinct from estimating relevant quantities. A related point is that samples of independent actors or relationships are only rarely the focus of network analysis. It has been famously suggested (Barton, 1968) that, just as a physiologist would be misled by sampling every hundredth cell of a dissected laboratory animal in an effort to understand its bodily structure and functioning, so a scientist interested in social structure and behavior would be misled by reliance on random samples wrenched out of their embedded interactional context; at a minimum, highly innovative sampling theory and methods need to be developed afresh (as they are, for example, in McPherson, 1982). In contrast to random samples, full data on the presence or absence of social relations among all the members of a bounded population are often required, and network analysts have formulated the problem of boundary specification (Laumann et al., 1983; Marsden, 1990) in an effort to gain analytical leverage on this requirement. Furthermore, whether in laboratory experiments furthering exchange theory (Molm and Cook, 1995) or in broad observations on new forms of 'recombinant property' taking shape in post-Communist eastern Europe (Stark, 1996), the innovations in data analysis of social networks are very often substantive rather than statistical in nature.

Finally, the very distinction between 'quantitative' and 'qualitative' approaches to data analysis is called into question by network analysis, in ways that go beyond the distinction between (quantitative) statistics and (qualitative) algebra. Typically a network analysis is a case study (Ragin and Becker, 1992) situated with explicit temporal and spatial reference (Abbott, 1999: 193–226), and important contributions to data analysis have combined ethnographic work and field observation with application of network algorithms, as in Faulkner's (1983) study of the patterning of business relations between movie directors and music composers in the Hollywood film industry. From a more avowedly subversive stance, theorists within contemporary science studies have coined the 'intentionally oxymoronic' term 'actor-network' as a word that '[performs] both an elision and a difference between what Anglophones distinguish by calling "agency" and "structure"' (Law, 1999: 5), and Latour (1988) has rewritten the history of Louis Pasteur as the interpenetration of networks of strong microbes with networks of weak hygienists, viewing the microbes as 'a means of locomotion for moving through the networks that they wish to set up and command' (p. 45). In the work of analysts such as these there has arisen a form of 'post-modern' network analysis emphasizing the difficulty of establishing clear boundaries between network actors and connections, between agency and structure.

Networks data often arise from actors who are engaged (often directly, often metaphorically) in conversation with one another, and an increasingly prominent strand of network analysis emphasizes the discursive framing and cultural embedding of social networks (Bearman and Stovel, 2000; McLean, 1998; Mische, 2003; Mische and White, 1998; Mohr, 2003; Snow and Benford, 1988; Steinberg, 1999), in effect continuing the pragmatist strand of network research introduced above. My goal in this chapter will be to present the most important issues in data analysis pertaining to social networks, while seeking to relate the specifics of data analysis to the swirl of strategies (statistical, algebraic, substantive, discursive, and cultural) that are motivating much of the contemporary work.

NETWORK BASICS

A social network orientation conceptualizes social phenomena as patterned arrays of relationships that join social actors. Basic representations of network structure include the who-to-whom matrix (and multimatrix formulations), the affiliation network, and the egocentric network. I will briefly introduce each of these representations, while at the same time pointing interested readers to the more extended and comprehensive, book-length treatments of Degenne and Forsé (1999), Knoke and Kuklinski (1982), Scott (1991), and Wasserman and Faust (1994). Methods of collecting network data are treated in these sources. Elementary properties of single networks (such as density) and their actors (such as the various measures of actor centrality) are likewise reviewed comprehensively in each of the above-cited works, but these concepts are not essential to the topics covered in this chapter.

Who-to-whom networks (one-mode format)

Most often in practice, a network is defined on a single set of social actors. (Practical research problems of boundary specification of these sets are treated in Laumann et al., 1983). To consider a small, made-up example for illustrative purposes, we might have four individual persons named A, B, C, and D. A *type of relation* is a set of social ties of a given type (such as 'dislikes', 'trades with', or 'borrows money from') connecting some pairs of the actors in this set. (More formally, a *tie* is an ordered pair of actors, of the form [A, B], indicating that actor A initiates an instance of the given type of relation to actor B, and we say, for example, 'A likes B'.) With respect to the relation 'who likes whom', which we will call relation R, we might observe that persons A and B like each other mutually, but that no other ties of liking (whether mutual or one-way) appear among our actors. Look ahead to Figures 22.1(b)–(d), which represent, in their left-hand column, a graphical representation of this structure. The mathematics of graphs of network ties such as these provides a basis for analyzing a great variety of systems of connections and exchange, including, for example, communication and kinship structures in Oceania (Hage and Harary, 1996).

The tie of liking from actor A to actor B in Figure 22.1 is matched by a tie from B to A, and this defines a *symmetric* (or *mutual*, or *reciprocated*) tie. Ties may, on the other hand, not have this property. Consider panel (d) of Figure 22.1, and suppose that, in addition to the liking relation, we have also collected data on the relation of dislike (which we will call relation T). Panel (d) reports that, whereas person A likes person B (see the graph of relation R), person A dislikes person C (reported in the graph of relation T) and person C does not dislike A. The tie of dislike from A to C is therefore an example of an *asymmetric* tie.

Is it the case in general that 'liking' is a social relation that emphasizes reciprocity, whereas 'disliking' is a relation that consists predominantly of asymmetric connections? Posing this question and many others like it brings out the power of a *multiple-network* formulation. This formulation consists of several distinct kinds of social relations (a separate network for each type) defined on the same set of actors, for example relations R and T as reported in panel (d) of Figure 22.1. The cultural signification of different types of tie (such as liking and its opposite) may be associated with distinctive structural features (such as reciprocity and asymmetry, or with the patterning of indirect connections – such as 'enemy of a friend' – implied by the graphs of network relations). A multiple-network formulation allows study of 'relational contrast' and of systematic representation of relations among types of tie. Harrison White and associates have pioneered multiple-network analyses (see the discussion in White, 1992: 78–102).

Graphs of network connections among a set of people have an equivalent representation that is much more convenient for computers and even for some forms of analysis done without mechanical assistance. These graphs may be represented as matrices. For example, the matrix representations of relations R and T in Figure 22.1(d) are:

	Relation R					Relation T			
	A	B	C	D		A	B	C	D
A	0	1	0	0	A	0	0	1	1
B	1	0	0	0	B	0	0	0	1
C	0	0	0	0	C	0	0	0	0
D	0	0	0	0	D	0	0	0	0

Construction of a graph's matrix representation is straightforward. Each of our social actors is given a unique row number and the corresponding column number. Rows represent senders of ties and columns represent recipients. The graph of relation R shows a tie from person A to person B and a tie from B to A; these are the only ties of liking reported among the four people. Therefore, the matrix representation of relation R (shown above) reports a 1 in cell $[A, B]$, a 1 in cell $[B, A]$, and a 0 in all other cells. The cells along the principal diagonal of the matrix, reporting ties from a person to herself (termed *reflexive* ties) – such as $[A, A]$ and $[B, B]$ – are often not defined (and omitted from analysis) in studies of interpersonal relations. However, reflexive relations (see for example relation R in Figure 22.1(a)) are often of substantive importance in studies of actors larger than individual persons. For example, suppose A, B, C, and D are four organizations, and we study the relation of whether there is intermarriage among and between organizations' members. Now the existence of a reflexive tie is an empirical question.

The examples considered so far involve ties measured only as 'present' or 'absent' (1 or 0 in the matrix representation). However, network studies may include ties measured at the ordinal, interval, or ratio levels as well, with the appropriate numerical *value* of each tie entered above its 'arrow' in the graph or in the corresponding cell of the matrix representation. For example, Han and Breiger (1999) combine network and statistical (log-linear) methods in a study of the *number* of times each major Wall Street investment firm (among the 19 studied) served as a lead manager in a capital-raising syndicate involving each other bank.

A particular advantage of the matrix formulation is that it allows computation of compound relations. Consider again Figure 22.1(d). Notice that person A has a tie of type R to person B, and that person B has a tie of type T to person D. A *compound relational tie* is the logical imputation of joining these relations together. In this example, person *A* has a compound tie of type *RT* to person *D*. Computation of compound relations is facilitated by the fact that matrix multiplication (or Boolean multiplication in the case of 0–1 data), for example the product of the matrix representations *R* and *T* shown above, yields the entire set of compound ties among the actors in our set. Many analytic methods for the study of compound ties and multiple networks are provided in Pattison (1993), and several are reviewed in subsequent sections of this chapter.

Affiliation networks (two-mode format)

Whereas most network studies pertain to who-to-whom data such as the representations discussed until now, there has also been a great deal of development of studies of networks among different types of entities: for example, among persons and groups, or members and committees, or organizations and agendas. Sociologist Erving Goffman, in his discussion of 'tie signs', wrote that

> the individual is linked to society through two principal social bonds: to collectivities through membership, and to other individuals through social relationships. He in turn helps make a network of society by linking through himself the social units linked to him. (Goffman, 1971: 188)

In elaborating 'membership network analysis' as distinct from who-to-whom studies, Breiger (1974, 1990) worked with a rectangular data matrix with persons arrayed as the rows and groups as the columns. (Because rows and columns represent different types of entity, this representation is often called *two-mode*, in contrast to the *one-mode* who-to-whom relations considered above.) In this 'membership matrix' a 1 appears in a given cell to indicate that a particular person belongs to a particular group. Again using matrix multiplication, it is straightforward to construct two networks from this one: a network of pairs of groups connected by the number of members they share, and a separate network of persons connected by the number of groups to which each pair of people jointly belong.

McPherson (1982, 2001) develops an innovative procedure for drawing inferences about interorganizational networks from a random sample of persons. Bearman (1991) employs this formalism in a theoretical investigation of Durkheim's theory of forms of suicide. Mische and Pattison (2000) investigate

two- and three-mode relations among persons, organizations, and agendas within a social movement. Skvoretz and Faust (1999) present probabilistic models for assessing degrees of overlap.

Ego-centered networks

A third major type of network representation (in addition to who-to-whom networks and affiliation or membership networks) is the *ego-centered network*. This consists of looking at relations from the orientation of a particular person (or a sample of unconnected individuals). The anthropologist A.L. Epstein (1969) intensively studied, on the basis of what was essentially a diary study, the meetings and greetings of one individual in an African town over a period of several days (e.g., 'James' wife was standing in the doorway when Chanda arrived at the house'). Epstein used this ego-centered study of relationships to illustrate the 'haphazard character of much of urban social life', and to study 'a complex system of organizing relationships' that this community's residents had developed (Epstein, 1969: 80). Lonkila (1997) reports comparative research on Russian and Finnish ego-centered networks of daily contact, based on diary studies.

Sociologists have combined ego-centered networks with the powerful ability to generate statistical inferences that arises from random sampling of individuals. For example, Nan Lin and associates (see Lin, 1982) studied hundreds of individuals, asking each person about network contacts who may have helped in getting a job. The investigators were able to study how the occupational prestige of the respondent's network contact mediated the effects of occupational origin on the prestige of the job obtained. A national-level study along similar lines is the 1985 social networks module of the General Social Survey conducted by the National Opinion Research Center (see Burt, 1984), which asked respondents: 'Looking back over the last six months – who are the people with whom you discussed matters important to you?' Among the many ego-centered network studies conducted on the basis of these representative data are studies of the effects of age and socioeconomic status on kinds of relations (e.g., kin versus coworker) used in Americans' networks (Burt, 1990), and research into homogeneity (e.g., the extent to which Protestants tended to name other Protestants as their network discussion partners) in discussion of important matters (Marsden, 1988). In France, various forms of sociability (such as sports, evenings on the town, dinner parties, card games) and mutual help between households have been studied in a number of samples each of which exceed 4000 respondents (reviewed in Degenne and Forsé, 1999: 35–54).

Ego-centered formulations have led to important studies of personal communities cross-nationally and globally, as in the studies collected in Wellman (1999). Data on personal networks and ego-centered formulations can often be analyzed by qualitative (ethnographic) or quantitative (statistical techniques for random samples) methods covered in other chapters of this *Handbook*, and so they will not be further considered here.

TYPES OF EQUIVALENCE

A fundamental problem of network analysis on which much progress has been made is that of representing a complex network by a simpler structure. A large web of social relations might be organized around *cliques* of individuals, all of whom have mutual relations with one another. Early efforts at network analysis focused on locating cliques (Festinger, 1949; Forsyth and Katz, 1946; Luce and Perry, 1949), a concept that has been substantially generalized in more recent work (see the extensive review in Wasserman and Faust, 1994: 249–90). Cliques were usually studied in a single network of relations (e.g., friendship ties) and taken to reflect integrative bonds among members.

A signal advance was the formulation by Lorrain and White (1971) of a multiple-network and algebraic approach to the definition of equivalence among sets of network actors, based on the authors' recognition (p. 78) that 'a network in fact consists of holes, decouplings, dissociations; ties can reflect conflict as well as solidarity, they reflect interdependence, [but] not necessarily integration'. Lorrain and White were extending a tradition of modeling multiple networks of kinship relations (such as marriage and descent) that extends back to Lévi-Strauss's collaborator André Weil (1969) and that has relied on the algebra of groups and semigroups for representing the cumulation (such as 'cousin') of multiple relations (such as 'father's sister's

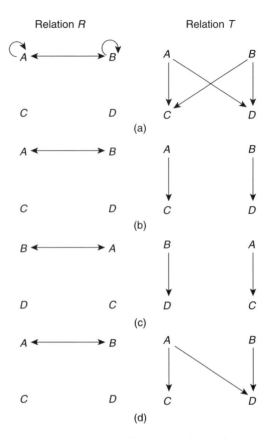

Figure 22.1 *Structural, automorphic and regular equivalence. (a) Partition (AB) (CD) is a structural equivalence. (b) Partition (AB) (CD) is an automorphic equivalence. (c) Relabeling nodes in (b) establishes an automorphism (A→B, B→A, C→D, D→C). (d) Partition (AB) (CD) is a regular equivalence.*

Source: Pattison (1993: 26).

son'; White, 1963; Boyd, 1969). Lorrain and White (1971) sought to reduce networks consisting of multiple types of social relations (such as friendship and enmity) down to simpler network structures. They sought (p. 80) to locate 'sets of individuals … who are placed similarly with respect to all other sets of individuals, to the extent that total relations and flows are captured by the aggregation of detailed relations consonant with those equivalence sets of individuals'. Specifically, two individuals A and B are *structurally equivalent* if they have exactly the same network links to and from other network members. Two individuals who are structurally equivalent need not be in the same clique, and indeed they need have no connections with one another.

An illustration of structural equivalence is given in Figure 22.1(a) (taken from Pattison, 1993: 24–36, whose excellent treatment I am condensing). The figure shows a multiple network consisting of two types of relation (R and T) on four individuals (A through D). In Figure 22.1(a) individuals A and B are structurally equivalent, as are C and D. Notice, for example, that the relations of individual A (sending and receiving ties of type R from A and B; sending ties of type T to C and D) are identical to those of individual B. By the same definition, C and D are structurally equivalent even though they send no ties to each other or to the same third parties.

A significantly expanded repertoire of equivalence types for social networks followed Lorrain and White's formulation of structural equivalence. In common parlance, two opposing football quarterbacks occupy equivalent roles, as do fathers in France and China. Structural equivalence, however, is too 'concrete' a concept to relate people such as these who do not have the same relations with the same others. More 'abstract' or 'general' forms of role equivalence were formulated, having structural equivalence as a special case. *Automorphic equivalence* (Borgatti et al., 1989; Pattison, 1980; Winship, 1988) equates two individuals if they are linked to the same 'kinds' of others. An automorphism is a relabeling of the actors in a network that preserves structure. Consider Figures 22.1(b)–(c) (again following Pattison, 1993: 26). The vertices A, B, C, D of Figure 22.1(b) may be relabeled B, A, D, C, respectively (see Figure 22.1(c)). The networks in Figures 22.1(b)–(c) are identical except for the exchange of labels between actors A and B and between actors C and D. Thus, A and B are automorphically equivalent, as are C and D. The concept of power as studied in experimental exchange networks (Cook et al., 1983; Markovsky et al., 1988) rests on the idea that two actors who are automorphically equivalent have the same power relative to others (see Borgatti and Everett, 1992).

The most important generalization of automorphic equivalence is *regular equivalence* (White and Reitz, 1983, 1989). We say in common parlance that the father of two children plays an equivalent role to the father of three. Regular equivalence extends automorphic equivalence, so to speak, to situations such as this one. More formally (again following Pattison, 1993: 25), two individuals

A and B are regularly equivalent if (a) whenever A has a link of type R to an individual C, then B has a link of type R to some individual who is regularly equivalent to C, and similarly for the links of type R from B to D; and if (b) whenever an individual C is linked to A by R, then some individual D who is regularly equivalent to C is linked by R to B. In Figure 22.1(d), A and B are regularly equivalent, and so are C and D. (Notice that Figure 22.1(d) differs from Figure 22.1(b) only in that A now has a tie to two others instead of one. Regular equivalence loosens automorphic equivalence to cases such as this one.)

Blockmodels

Research on real-world social networks rarely uncovers substantial equivalence by any of the above definitions. Following up Lorrain and White's (1971) algebraic modeling of social networks, in the mid-1970s Harrison White and collaborators (Arabie et al., 1978; Breiger et al., 1975; White et al., 1976) proposed blockmodel analysis as a loosening of the concept of structural equivalence so as to allow more wide-ranging applicability in research studies.

A *blockmodel* of a multirelational network consists simultaneously of (a) a partition of actors in the network into discrete subgroups or positions, and (b) for each pair of positions, a statement of the presence or absence of a relational tie within or between the positions in each of the relations (White et al., 1976). As Faust and Wasserman (1992) point out in their review and synthesis of blockmodeling procedures, a blockmodel is thus a *model*, or a *hypothesis* about a multirelational network. It presents general features of the network – relations among positions – rather than information pertaining to individual actors.

Structural equivalence (the pure definition introduced above) induces a blockmodel, as illustrated by the five-actor multiple network U in Table 22.1. (Once again, I follow aspects of the more detailed presentation of Pattison, 1993: 30). Networks in Table 22.1 are represented as matrices, with a 1 in cell (i, j) of matrix R_k indicating that actor i directs a relationship of type k to actor j. If we partition rows and columns of U into two positions (the first-listed three actors, and the last two, respectively), we can represent network U by blockmodel B (see Table 22.1), in which rows

Table 22.1 *A blockmodel and multiple networks for which it is a fat fit, a lean fit, and an α-blockmodel (α = 0.5)*

Blockmodel B		Network U for which B is a fat fit		Network V for which B is a lean fit		Network W for which B is an α-blockmodel (α = 0.5)	
R_1	R_2	R_1	R_2	R_1	R_2	R_1	R_2
10	01	111|00	000|11	011|00	000|10	011|00	000|10
01	00	111|00	000|11	000|00	000|11	100|10	001|01
		111|00	000|11	110|00	000|00	110|00	100|11
		000|11	000|00	000|11	000|00	100|01	000|00
		000|11	000|00	000|00	000|00	001|10	100|00

Corresponding density matrices

U				V				W			
R_1		R_2		R_1		R_2		R_1		R_2	
1.00	0.00	0.00	1.00	0.44	0.00	0.00	0.50	0.56	0.17	0.22	0.67
0.00	1.00	0.00	0.00	0.00	0.50	0.00	0.00	0.33	0.50	0.17	0.00

Source: Pattison (1993: 30).

and columns index not actors but aggregates of actors or positions. Breiger et al. (1975) term the fit of the blockmodel to network U a 'fat fit' in that a 1 in the blockmodel corresponds to a full submatrix of relations, and a 0 in the model corresponds to a submatrix in which relations are entirely absent. Pure structural equivalence always induces a 'fat fit' blockmodel.

The early papers on blockmodel analysis loosened structural equivalence in two ways. In a 'lean fit' blockmodel a 0 is defined as above (to correspond to a submatrix in which relations are entirely absent), whereas a 1 corresponds to a submatrix in which only *some* ties are present. An α-blockmodel (Arabie et al., 1978) specifies that the density of ties needed such that a submatrix is coded 1 in a blockmodel be at least α. For example, network W in Table 22.1 is represented by blockmodel B for α = 0.50. Blockmodels can be derived inductively by the use of hierarchical clustering algorithms such as STRUCTURE (Burt, 1976) and CONCOR (Breiger et al., 1975), important features of which are implemented in the UCINET package of programs (Borgatti et al., 1999) along with a wide variety of other blocking procedures, and new procedures continue to enter the research literature (see Anheier et al., 1995). The above-mentioned loosening of the structural equivalence concept, and the advent of practical search methods for inducing a blockmodel, led to a veritable explosion of social network research, much of which is reviewed in Wellman (1988) and in Wasserman and Faust (1994).

Although initially developed as reduced-form representations of networks exhibiting a loosened form of *structural* equivalence (as described above), blockmodel concepts have also been developed for more *abstract* forms of equivalence such as regular equivalence. Batagelj et al. (1992) prove, for example, that a network characterized by regular equivalence may be partitioned into blocks such that each block is either null or has the property that there is at least one 1 in each of its rows and in each of its columns, and they have developed a local optimization procedure to locate regular or 'near regular' partitions of network actors into blocks. These authors have proposed to combine structural and regular forms of equivalence within the same analysis, a 'generalized blockmodeling' (Doreian, 1999).

Strategies for data analysis

Certain kinds of theory in sociology and related social sciences take the form of assertions that complex social structures may be represented in 'reduced form' as elementary structures. Analysts have restated hypotheses drawn from theories such as these as claims about the macro-structure of relations and absences of relation (i.e., as blockmodel images), and then investigated the fit of the hypothesized structures to actual networks of relations and flows. Several examples will be mentioned.

World-system theory postulates a world stratification system among three tiers of states (core, periphery, and semi-periphery), but theorists such as Andre Gunder Frank and Daniel Chirot disagree about the composition of the tiers. Steiber (1979) began with a three-block image of world-system trade flows and two different partitions of nations into strata: one based on identifying socialist states with the semi-periphery, and one based on 'purely economic' criteria. Steiber applied both of these a priori partitions to multiple-network data on world trade flows (separate networks for crude materials, machinery, and so on), finding that one partition fit the postulated blockmodel image much more consistently than the other.

A distinction between 'segmentary social structure' and 'hierarchy' was formulated as two different reduced-form blockmodel images by Anheier et al. (1995: 868) and proved central in elaborating a relational representation for 'cultural fields' and the differing forms of social capital of 139 writers in a major German city. Here again, blockmodel images posed on theoretical criteria were used in the interpretation of observed data on multiple networks (such as awareness, friendship, assistance, and dinner invitations among the writers).

Gerlach's (1992) blockmodel analysis of the Japanese corporate network rests on hypotheses that are formulated with reference to the blocks. For example, analysis of relationships among the blocks is hypothesized to show that blocks dominated by financial firms are disproportionately linked to the rest of the network. 'In particular, these blocks should be heavily involved in the sending of ties of coordination and control through directorship and ownership interlocks' (p. 113). Gerlach studied relationships among 60 of the largest financial and industrial firms in Japan with reference to relationships among the firms, including bank borrowing, equity in one firm held by another, and director interlocks.

In addition to the research strategy that moves from general theory to the formulation of hypothetical blockmodel images and only then to the question of whether the blockmodel characterizes the data, an alternative strategy which is more common is purely inductive. Search algorithms such as STRUCTURE or CONCOR or more recently formulated search procedures are typically applied to data first, and the reduced-form blockmodel images that are uncovered are subsequently interpreted. Many studies combine inductive and deductive features, as is the case with the German writers study (Anheier et al., 1995) and the study of the Japanese corporate structure (Gerlach, 1992) discussed above.

A third type of research strategy has been to emphasize relations among types of relations (rather than among specific social actors), asking, for example, how ties of friendship combine with ties of enmity. (Are friends of enemies taken to be enemies? Are enemies of enemies taken to be friends?) This strategy rests on the algebra of relations that was at the heart of Lorrain and White's (1971) original paper on structural equivalence and specified by Boorman and White (1976) with respect to blockmodel images. This strategy has been most thoroughly elaborated in two volumes, those of Boyd (1991) and Pattison (1993). A particular research example was Breiger and Pattison's (1978) recasting of Granovetter's (1973) 'strength of weak ties' argument as the postulation of a particular semigroup multiplication table, and an application identifying the relative strength of business, community affairs, and informal social relations in two different communities (reviewed in Pattison, 1993: 256–8).

A fourth type of research strategy has been to generalize beyond structural equivalence to network analyses based on more abstract forms of equivalence. Smith and White (1992) study international commodity trade flows over a 15-year period on the basis of regular-equivalence measures among pairs of states. The researchers' dissatisfaction with structural-equivalence approaches is motivated, in part, by the tendency of these approaches to 'conflate' spatial proximity of nations with global role structure. Using a form of regular equivalence, Smith and White (1992: 860) search for equivalence between countries 'based on similarity in their volumes of trade on each commodity for recursively equivalent trade partners (that is, "substitutable" trade partners which in turn have similar volumes of trade on each commodity with *their* recursively equivalent trade partners)'. Gulati and Gargiulo (1999: Fig. 2) identify positions in interorganizational alliance structures on the basis of a form of abstract equivalence (related to the 'triad census' referenced in the following section of this chapter). Generalizing beyond structural equivalence in a different way, Doreian (1999) compares regular-equivalence and structural-equivalence blockmodels for several different networks, emphasizing also the optimization algorithm of Batagelj et al. (1992).

STATISTICAL MODELS FOR
NETWORK STRUCTURE

The major problem encountered in efforts to make statistical inferences from network data was well stated six decades ago. Person A's choice of person B is not independent of A's choice of C, or of B's choice of A. 'One part of the structure is interdependent with another part; a change in position of one individual may affect the whole structure' (Moreno and Jennings, 1938: 343). Supposing each pair of people nonetheless to be independent of the other pairs, in order to establish benchmarks for assessing structure, Paul Lazarsfeld formulated a simple binomial model (reported in Moreno and Jennings, 1938) for the expected number of choices received, the expected number of mutual choices in a network, and related quantities. Due to the interdependence of social ties in observed networks, models of dyadic independence fit the data notoriously poorly, with researchers (such as Moreno and Jennings, 1938: 354–5) discovering much higher probabilities that an actor was an isolate (chosen by no one) or highly popular than expected by 'chance', and much higher levels of reciprocity in network ties than predicted from the binomial model.

A major line of investigation by Holland, Leinhardt, and Davis – see, e.g., Holland and Leinhardt (1975) and the summary by Davis (1979) – sought network inferences from a more realistic embedding of non-independent relationships within triads of social actors. There is a relatively small number of possible configurations on three actors that are possible for directed relations (i.e., ties from one actor to another where the tie may or may not be reciprocated). Davis, Holland, and Leinhardt computed a 'triad census' of the empirical distribution of three-actor configurations in an observed network. They formulated probability models for triads by conditioning on two-person configurations for the network as a whole; the possible two-person configurations are mutual (M), asymmetric (A), or null (N), indicating pairs of actors who either do (M) or do not (A)

reciprocate choices to each other, as well as pairs neither of whom has a tie to the other (N). The result was the random distribution $U|MAN$, the uniform distribution of all labeled directed graphs having a given number of actors and given values of M, A, and N (Holland and Leinhardt, 1975: 23). These authors noted the desirability of conditioning as well on the total numbers of choices each actor sent and received, but that 'no simple way seems to be known for generating random graphs with this exact distribution' (p. 40).

In a major breakthrough, however, Holland and Leinhardt (1981) reported an exponential family of models (which they termed the p_1 distribution) that did just that: provided an assessment of an observed network against a random one conditioning on the numbers of ties sent and received by each actor and the network's overall density and, simultaneously, on two-person configurations (M, A, and N). Moreover, Fienberg and Wasserman (1981) demonstrated that the model parameters are easily estimated by log-linear modeling techniques, thus allowing the Holland and Leinhardt p_1 model to be widely implemented on network data. Application of the model led to substantively important research, for example, Galaskiewicz and Wasserman (1989) on decision-making in organizational fields. (On the question of enumeration and simulation methods for 0–1 matrices with given marginals, the state of the art remains Snijders, 1991.)

Three problems with the p_1 model were to motivate further work. First, the advances of Holland and Leinhardt's (1981) model entailed a return to the assumption of dyadic independence (e.g., the assumption that person A's choice of B is independent of A's choice of C). This assumption was surely unrealistic (see Lincoln, 1984, on appropriate techniques for analyzing relations in dyads), leading to the second problem with the p_1 model: because it was essentially a null model, its ability to characterize actual network data was found to be poor. Third, degrees of freedom for assessing the overall fit of the model often depended on the number of actors in the network, thus violating the usual assumptions about asymptotics in maximum likelihood estimation.

Recent work constituting fully a new breakthrough, however, has allowed the assumption of dyadic independence to be surpassed by families of more realistic assumptions (susceptible to empirical test)

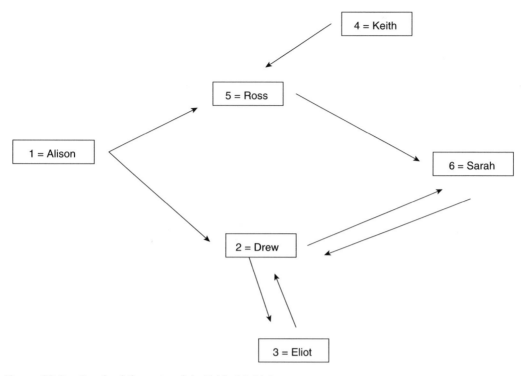

Figure 22.2   *Graph of the network in Table 22.2(a)*

about the precise nature of network dependencies. Analysts (Wasserman and Pattison, 1996; Pattison and Wasserman, 1999; and Robins et al., 1999) have formulated an exponential family of models p^* based on the pathbreaking Markov spatial interaction models for random graphs of Frank and Strauss (1986) and Strauss and Ikeda (1990). Markov graphs permit dependencies among any ties that share a node. One example of network dependence is the structure hypothesized in a blockmodel. Other examples include a set of ties such that person A chooses both B and C (in which case A is termed a '2-out-star'), and a set of ties such that A is chosen by both persons B and C (in which case A is a '2-in-star').

Specific forms of dependence may be hypothesized a priori (i.e., prior to data analysis) in a p^* model and tested against network data. A *dependence graph* is an a priori statement about how the number of configurations of a specific kind (such as mutual dyads or 2-in-stars) depends on whether or not a particular directed tie in the data is 0 or 1. Each entry in a dependence graph is calculated under the assumption that *all other* directed ties in the graph are as observed.

Estimation of p^* models is by means of pseudolikelihood estimation, a generalization of maximum likelihood. Specifically, the tie from every actor to every other is estimated conditioning on the rest of the data, which allows any interdependencies in the data to be directly modeled. An important practical consequence of this point (Wasserman and Pattison, 1996: 404) is that logistic regression computer programs can be used to fit p^* models, thus making this family of network statistical models easily available to researchers.

Statistical references (the series of papers authored by Wasserman, Pattison, and Robbins) and a didactic guide (Anderson et al., 1999) are available for p^* models. Rather than repeat these treatments, I will suggest a non-technical, intuitive approach for understanding how dependence is modeled within the p^* framework. My example will use illustrative data on six second-grade children, data that Wasserman and Faust (1994: 610) employed to illustrate computation of the

Table 22.2 *Sociomatrix and matrix representation of four dependence graphs*

(a) Sociomatrix for six second-grade children (from Wasserman and Faust, 1994: 610)

	1	2	3	4	5	6
1. Alison	–	1	0	0	1	0
2. Drew	0	–	1	0	0	1
3. Eliot	0	1	–	0	0	0
4. Keith	0	0	0	–	1	0
5. Ross	0	0	0	0	–	1
6. Sarah	0	1	0	0	0	–

(b) Dependence graph for mutuality

	1	2	3	4	5	6
1. Alison	–	0	0	0	0	0
2. Drew	1	–	1	0	0	1
3. Eliot	0	1	–	0	0	0
4. Keith	0	0	0	–	0	0
5. Ross	1	0	0	1	–	0
6. Sarah	0	1	0	0	1	–

(c) Dependence graph for 2-in-stars

	1	2	3	4	5	6
1. Alison	–	2	1	0	1	2
2. Drew	0	–	0	0	2	1
3. Eliot	0	2	–	0	2	2
4. Keith	0	3	1	–	1	2
5. Ross	0	3	1	0	–	1
6. Sarah	0	2	1	0	2	–

(d) Dependence graph for 2-out-stars

	1	2	3	4	5	6
1. Alison	–	1	2	2	1	2
2. Drew	2	–	1	2	2	1
3. Eliot	1	0	–	1	1	1
4. Keith	1	1	1	–	0	1
5. Ross	1	1	1	1	–	0
6. Sarah	1	0	1	1	1	–

(e) Dependence graph for transitivity

	1	2	3	4	5	6
1. Alison	–	0	2	1	0	3
2. Drew	0	–	0	0	2	0
3. Eliot	1	0	–	0	0	3
4. Keith	1	0	0	–	0	1
5. Ross	0	3	0	0	–	0
6. Sarah	1	0	3	0	0	–

older p_1 model. The illustrative sociomatrix is given in Table 22.2(a), and the network is shown graphically in Figure 22.2.

Consider the matrix representation of the dependence graph for mutuality (Table 22.2(b). This reports a 1 for the tie from Drew to Alison. This is because, if Drew *were* to choose Alison, the Drew → Alison tie would complete a 'mutual' dyad. (Notice from Figure 22.2 that Alison chooses Drew.) This example illustrates an important feature of p^* models: each possible tie from one person to another is considered *conditioning* on all the other structures in the model. Similarly, Table 22.2(b) reports a 1 for the tie from Drew to Sarah. We notice that, according to the observed data (Table 22.2(a), or equivalently Figure 22.2), Drew really *does* choose Sarah. For purposes of modeling the Drew → Sarah tie, however, we bracket this knowledge and we consider that a tie from Drew to Sarah would complete a mutual relation (as Sarah is seen to choose Drew). Because the Drew → Sarah tie completes one mutual dyad, there is a 1 from Drew to Sarah in the dependence graph for mutuality (Table 22.2(b)).

Consider now the matrix representation of the dependence graph for 2-in-stars (Table 22.2(c)). An example of a 2-in-star is the relation Alison → Drew ← Sarah, an indication of the popularity of (in this case) Drew. Notice that, if we focus on the tie from Alison to Drew while keeping all other observed ties fixed, the Alison → Drew tie actually completes two 2-in-stars (namely, Alison → Drew ← Eliot, in addition to the one mentioned directly above; see Figure 22.2). Because a tie from Alison to Drew completes two 2-in-stars, a 2 is entered in (row 1, column 2) of Table 22.2(c). Considering as another example a possible tie from Keith to Drew, this tie would complete three 2-in-stars (Keith → Drew ← Alison, Keith → Drew ← Eliot, and Keith → Drew ← Sarah); therefore, a 3 appears at the intersection of (row 4, column 2) of Table 22.2(c).

The dependence graph for the other configurations has been constructed in the same sort of way (according to explicit computing formulas given in Wasserman and Pattison, 1996: 415). To take one illustration from the dependence graph for transitivity (Table 22.2(e)), there is a '2' in Alison's row and Eliot's column. This is because a tie from Alison to Eliot would result in two transitive configurations (one of which is

Alison → Drew → Eliot and Alison → Eliot; the other being Alison → Eliot → Drew and Alison → Drew).

On the a priori assumption that the dependencies within the network in Table 22.2(a) are given by mutuality, 2-in-stars, 2-out-stars, and transitivity, we may estimate the p^* model for these data by running a (relatively) straightforward logistic regression model, using any standard logistic regression program. This model considers the observed data (Table 22.2(a)), represented as a single vector of size 30×1, as the 'dependent' variable. The dependence graph for each of the configurations (Tables 22.2(b)–(e)), each represented as a single vector of size 30×1, are taken as the 'independent' variables in the logit regression model. Parameters from the regression may be interpreted in terms of their contribution to the 'likelihood' of occurrence of a network with the relevant feature of interest. For instance, a large positive value of a parameter corresponding to transitivity means that ties completing transitive configurations are more likely to occur, controlling for all other effects in the model (Wasserman and Pattison, 1996: 415). In this manner assumptions about various forms of interdependence among network actors are brought to bear in specifying a statistical model. Information on computer programs is given at the end of this chapter.

Strategies for statistical network modeling

It is of substantive interest that a model for the probability of an interpersonal attachment that seems to lie within the p^* family was formulated independently by Noah Friedkin (see Friedkin, 1998: 73–7) as part of his elaboration of a comprehensive structural theory of social influence. For Friedkin (1998: 83), interpersonal attachments causally govern the distribution of interpersonal influences. If two actors are situated in a structural environment in which an attachment from actor i to actor j is probable (as estimated by the logit regression model defined above), then actor i is likely to monitor and consider salient the opinions of actor j. The probabilities estimated from the logit regression equation that Friedkin defines are a basic pillar of the estimation of concepts (such as interpersonal influences and equilibrium outcomes) in his overarching theory (see the summary of the modeling steps in Friedkin, 1998:

60–1). Friedkin and Johnsen (1997) relate types of equivalence (both structural and automorphic) in influence network to homogeneity of actor opinion at equilibrium.

Although p^* modeling is still a very recent development, Lazega and Pattison (1999) provide a rich empirical research application to network relations in a corporate law firm. Three types of relation are queried (coworkers' goodwill, advice, and friendship). The authors (p. 81) develop specific dependence configurations that may be seen as hypotheses about how the three networks interpenetrate with respect to triads of lawyers in a firm where 'status competition' is strong. Statistical analysis leads Lazega and Pattison (1999: 84) to conclude, for example, that a dependence configuration containing two paths comprising one advice and one cowork tie appears to be likely to coincide with a cowork tie, but not with an advice tie, suggesting that advice is a 'strong' tie and coworking is a 'weak' tie in the sense of Granovetter (1973).

New extensions and areas of application for the p^* model continue to be developed. For example, Skvoretz and Faust (1999) extend the model to affiliation networks (networks relating, for example, the chief executive officers of corporations and the clubs they belong to, indicating the membership of executives in clubs), developing the relevance of dependence configurations such as 2-in-stars for modeling (in this case) two different executives who are both connected by a membership tie to the same club. Skvoretz and Faust apply a blockmodel version of p^* to the affiliation data of executives with corporate boards and clubs collected by Galaskiewicz (1985) in a major metropolitan area. This work provides foundations for making inferences about the significance of ties in a network based on affiliations of persons with groups. Gulati and Gargiulo (1999: 1482–6) develop an innovative model akin to p^* that incorporates a random-effects panel design to deal with unobserved heterogeneity in a study of factors influencing the formation of new ties between organizations. Iacobucci and Hopkins (1992; see also Iacobucci, 1996) illustrate applications of the Holland–Leinhardt p_1 model in substantive areas of market research, such as coalition formation in buying centers, identification of opinion leaders in word-of-mouth networks, and the management of expectations in service encounters. Moreover, in distinguishing dyad-independent and full-network properties of relations, Iacobucci and Hopkins (1992: 5–6) in a sense anticipate possible substantive applications of p^*-style statistical models.

Stochastic models, some of them related to p^*, have been developed for the statistical analysis of blockmodels. An extensive review is Wasserman and Faust (1994: 692–719). Snijders and Nowicki (1997) propose an estimation procedure for the probabilities of edges and for predicting the block structure based on Gibbs sampling. An associated computer program, BLOCKS, is available (see Table 22.3).

Models such as p_1 and p^* apply to network data of a binary (0–1) nature (although extensions to ordinal relationships have been developed). Networks may also consist of counted data, such as the number of members of each of a set of religious denominations who marry a partner in the same or another denomination. Marsden (1981, 1988) pioneered the use of log-linear models for cross-classification tables as means of analyzing the structuring of networks such as these. Marsden is particularly interested in capturing the substantive concepts of social distance and homophily (the tendency of similar types of actors to relate to one another), areas in which Yamaguchi (1990) has elaborated the relevance of a highly refined log-linear modeling framework.

Breiger and Ennis (1997) have applied a log-linear model to the counted data underlying a blockmodel density table (reporting the tendency of one set of actors to send network ties to and receive them from other sets) as a means of assessing the hypothesis that a given partition of actors results in a meaningful reduced-form representation of the full network. Their application is to data from the study of Anheier et al. (1995), reviewed above, on multiple networks among writers in a major German city. Breiger and Roberts (1998) argued that a similar model represents hierarchy, mutual relations, and a concept akin to betweenness centrality (Freeman, 1977) when applied to data on the proportion of times that US Supreme Court justices vote together in their written opinions. Han and Breiger (1999) apply this log-linear framework to counted data on the tendency of major New York banks to join together in forming syndicates to underwrite securities issues, arguing that the modeling uncovers

dimensions which may be seen to compose the network. In all these cases networks of counted data are seen to be promising sites for substantive applications and statistical assessment of models.

Strategies for dynamic modeling of social networks are receiving increasing attention. The volume on network evolution edited by Doreian and Stokman (1997) includes a range of statistical models, including a proposal for combining autocorrelation models with models of continuous-time Markov processes (Leenders, 1997); a proposed class of models for network dynamics based on individually optimizing social actors (under constraints), with parameters estimated from simulation models from empirical data (Snijders, 1997); and a set of models, with associated tests, each of which follow directly from a sociocognitive theory about how individuals alter the colleagues with whom they are likely to interact (Banks and Carley, 1997).

Structural research is not always centered on analysis of who-to-whom matrices, notwithstanding the impression that may have been conveyed in this review of statistical approaches. Van Duijn et al. (1999) apply multilevel methods (hierarchical linear modeling) to analyze changes in personal networks. McPherson and colleagues have developed an evolutionary model of the dynamics of voluntary organizations that is rooted in Blau's (1977) idea that social groups exist in a multidimensional space of sociodemographic dimensions in which social differentiation occurs. McPherson's model, in which processes of membership recruitment and loss are linked to social networks connecting individuals, generates hypotheses about the time path of organizations in sociodemographic dimensions (McPherson and Ranger-Moore, 1991) that are tested with reference to life-history data on the group affiliations of a thousand individuals (McPherson and Rotolo, 1996).

CULTURE AND COGNITION

The emphasis of network analysis on formal aspects of social structure often seems the opposite of a concern for culture and cognition; indeed, in the early work on structural equivalence 'the cultural and social-psychological meanings of actual ties are largely bypassed ... We focus instead on interpreting the patterns among types of tie' (White et al., 1976: 734). However, over the past decade a fusion of concern across structural modeling and problems of culture, cognition, action, and agency has been among the most important developments for an influential segment of the community of networks researchers.

An important spur to network thinking about culture and cognition was White's (1992) rethinking of network theory in *Identity and Control*. He now wrote of agency as 'the dynamic face of networks', as motivating 'ways of ... upend[ing] institution[s] and ... initiat[ing] fresh action' (White, 1992: 315, 245). He considered discursive 'narratives' and 'stories' to be fundamental to structural pursuits, writing that 'stories describe the ties in networks' and that 'a social network is a network of meanings' (White, 1992: 65, 67). Emirbayer and Goodwin (1994), who characterized *Identity and Control* in exactly this way (p. 1437), went on to prod network analysts to conceptualize more clearly the role of 'ideals, beliefs, and values, and of the actors that strive to realize them' (p. 1446).

A second spur (reviewed in Pattison, 1994) can be identified for reconsidering the boundary between network research and cognitive studies: developments arising internally within the networks paradigm as presented in this chapter's first two sections. Networks researchers (Bernard et al., 1984) demonstrated substantial discrepancies between records of social interactions and participants' reports of those interactions, with Freeman et al. (1987) arguing that the discrepancies could be explained in part by appealing to cognitive biases favoring longer-term patterns of social interactions. Carley (e.g., 1986) developed an influential 'constructuralist' model of knowledge acquisition according to which individuals' cognitive structures, their propensity to interact with others, the social structures they form, and the social consensus to which they give rise are all continuously constructed in a reflexive and recursive fashion as individuals interact with those around them. And Krackhardt (1987) launched the study of 'cognitive social structure' by suggesting that the usual who-to-whom matrices be replaced by a three-way design in which each actor is asked to provide perceptions on all the who-to-whom interactions. Thus, it is possible to ascertain empirically the 'fit' between, for example, a

manager's view of her own centrality to an organization and the average or weighted perceptions of her colleagues – or, for that matter, of the vice president for marketing (see Krackhardt, 1987: 123). This formulation allowed Krackhardt to raise such questions as how the position of an individual in an organizational network affects his or her perception of the network (see also Kumbasar et al., 1994).

A third motivation for fresh work on networks and culture was Ann Swidler's formation of a working group on 'meaning and measurement' within the American Sociological Association's section on culture, resulting in the publication of new research on networks, culture, and measurement (see DiMaggio, 1994; Jepperson and Swidler, 1994). In reviewing recent work on culture and cognition, DiMaggio (1997: 283) conceives of networks as crucial environments for the activation of schemata, logics, and frames. He points, for example, to the role of political protest networks in activating pre-existing identities (Gould, 1995), to the correlation between the social network complexity of an occupational group and the diversity of its conversational interests (Erickson, 1996), and to the relation between questioning marriage and the altering of social relations in order to create new, independent identities as a prologue to separation (Vaughn, 1986).

Culture, cognition, and networks: Research strategies

I will emphasize network analysis of three topics that DiMaggio (1997) touches on in his review of cognition and culture: logics of action, switching dynamics, and the mapping of meaning structures.

Logics of action Friedland and Alford (1991: 248–9) define institutional logics as sets of 'material practices and symbolic constructions' that constitute an institutional order's 'organizing principles' and are 'available to organizations and individuals to elaborate'. DiMaggio (1997: 277) describes the concept as 'immensely appealing', in part because it recognizes culture as rooted in rather fragmented sets of local practices without, however, 'surrendering the notion of limited coherence, which thematization of clusters of rituals and schemata around institutions provides'.

Mohr (1994) provided an empirical framework for uncovering such logics with reference to poor relief efforts in New York City a century ago. Using a charity directory for 1907, Mohr constructed a blockmodel reporting relations among categorical descriptors of eligible clients – 'tramps (male)', 'unwed mothers', 'widows', and so on – grouped together on the basis of similarity in the patterns of treatment provided (vocational school, domestic training, farm colony, etc.). Mohr (1994: 333) suggested the concept of 'discourse role' to shift attention from 'how particular individuals are connected to one another by way of specific types of relationship' and toward the question of 'how particular social identities are connected to one another by virtue of having the same types of social welfare treatments applied to them'.

In subsequent work Mohr and Duquenne (1997) employ a different structural technique, Galois lattice analysis (see Freeman and White, 1993), in order to model more directly the relations between two different kinds of social nodes: the categories of clients and the categories of treatment provided by agencies for poor relief. The authors develop a specific research context for viewing lattice analysis and analysis of affiliation networks as operationalizing a form of 'practice theory' according to which the material world (the world of action) and the cultural world (the world of symbols) interpenetrate 'and are built up through the immediate association of each with the other' (Mohr and Duquenne, 1997: 309). There are some interesting relations between the kind of lattice analysis that these authors apply and the dimension of social and cultural 'fields' uncovered by the practice theorist Pierre Bourdieu (on which see Breiger, 2000).

Switching dynamics DiMaggio (1997: 278) argues that the notion of institutional logics can be interpreted as an effort to thematize cognitive schemata and link them to social structure. Exploitation of this insight requires (among other things) an understanding of cultural change, which in turn requires an 'understanding of the way in which actors switch among institutional logics' (DiMaggio 1997: 278). An outstanding study of such dynamics was Padgett and Ansell's (1993) analysis of Cosimo de' Medici's deployment of multiple identities and 'robust discretion' to gain power in fifteenth-century Florence; see also Padgett (2001). Traditional social network analysis does not deal

well with the disruption of structure, for example with the disruption of the career paths of elite social engineers in the former USSR produced by glasnost (White, 1992: 257). A central problem for White is 'getting action' by reaching 'through' existing social structures. Mische and White (1998: 711) observe that a given set of multiple-network ties within a self-consistent domain (e.g., an interlock of colleague and friendship ties among graduate students) implies a continual juggling of the set of possible stories consistent with the structure. Switchings between network domains (e.g., when a graduate student works at night as a self-employed head of a small corporation designing corporate web pages) are discontinuities in sociocultural processes, and may open up opportunities for entrepreneurs to seize action in more projective and practically evaluative ways (Emirbayer and Mische, 1998) than would be routine within a domain (perhaps, in the example given, showing up as efforts to decrease the tension of identities between students and earners of large but erratic incomes). An example of switching dynamics that is receiving the attention of a formal modeler consists of topic changes in group conversations (such as among management team members in a large corporation) and their relation to sequences of the order in which the participants take the floor (Gibson, 2000).

Mapping structures of meaning By 'structure mapping' DiMaggio (1997: 281) refers to 'the existence of some form of content-related domain-specificity'. Structure exists not only as ties among actors but also as networks among cognitive and cultural content that is more or less meaningful to the actors. Carley (1994), for example, uses network analysis techniques to map the structure of relations between conceptual terms used in narratives (30 science-fiction novels written at different times) and then uses these structural representations of meaning to compare cultural phenomena (specifically, changes in the portrayal of robots – from menacing to clever – from the 1950s to the 1980s). Martin (2000) maps relations between occupations and animal species in a well-known children's book, as part of a larger effort to understand how children are instructed in realities of social class prior to experiencing those realities themselves. Mohr (1998) elaborates a framework for the uncovering of meaning structures that emphasizes relations among lexical or semantic terms in a classification system and the application of

Table 22.3   *Selected computer programs for network analysis*

Program	Type	Author or vendor	Internet site
UCINET 6	Comprehensive suite of network analysis and selected visualization programs	Analytic Technologies, Inc.	http://www.analytictech.com/
Pajek	Many programs, with emphasis on large networks and visualization	Vladimir Batagelj	http://vlado.fmf.uni-lj.si/pub/networks/pajek/
KrackPlot 3.0	A widely used network visualization program	Analytic Technologies, Inc.	http://www.contrib.andrew.cmu.edu/~krack/
p*	Programs for creation of a dependence graph for running p^* models	Stanley Wasserman et al.	http://kentucky.psych.uiuc.edu/pstar/index.html
PSPAR (p* for sparse networks)	Sparse matrix version of p^* models	Andrew Seary	http://www.sfu.ca/~richards/Pages/pspar.html
SIENA, BLOCKS, Z0	Programs for dynamic network modeling and network simulation studies	Tom Snijders	http://stat.gamma.rug.nl/
Other network analysis programs	Links to many programs for network analysis; new listings to be expected	A listing maintained by the International Network for Social Network Analysis	http://www.heinz.cmu.edu/project/INSNA/

formal network models or pattern-matching techniques. Mohr and Lee (2000) take as their data a massive compendium of 765 different programs that the University of California system maintains with 'pre-collegiate' institutions. These authors provide and employ a set of procedures for mapping 'the implicit meanings of a system of identity discourses' (Mohr and Lee, 2000: 47) and thus they investigate recent changes in the university system's diversity policies.

The implication of the lines of research reviewed in this section is to link network analysis with 'understanding of the relationship between culture and social structure built upon careful integration of micro and macro, and of cognitive and material, perspectives' (DiMaggio, 1997).

COMPUTER PROGRAMS AND FURTHER STUDY

Table 22.3 is a selective listing of computer programs available to accomplish many of the analyses reviewed in this chapter, along with internet addresses at which the programs can be obtained or ordered. UCINET (Borgatti et al., 1999) is, I believe, the most widely used suite of network analysis programs. Wasserman and Faust's (1994) text, although it does much more, may be seen as a comprehensive guide to the many programs and algorithms contained in UCINET. PAJEK (the word is Slovenian for 'spider') is a set of highly innovative analysis and visualization programs written by Vladimir Batagelj. The KRACKPLOT program of David Krackhardt provides a useful and convenient way to plot a visual image of a social network (see Krackhardt, 1992, for a research application). A comprehensive set of resources for network visualization is provided on Linton Freeman's web page. Also listed are two different programs that aid in computation of p^* models. A comprehensive set of resources for the p^* model as well as a set of programs allowing p^* models to be run in SAS or SPSS may be downloaded from the site maintained by Stanley Wasserman. A less comprehensive but remarkably convenient program to run many of the p^* models is Andrew Seary's PSPAR program. Innovative programs of Tom Snijders for analysis of network dynamics and simulation studies are also included in Table 22.3.

For further study, Wellman and Berkowitz (1988) provide a wide-ranging set of research applications that have proven influential to the field. Texts by Degenne and Forsé (1999), Knoke and Kuklinski (1982), Scott (1991), and Wasserman and Faust (1994) contain comprehensive introductions to a wide range of technical issues, models, and algorithms. The journal *Social Networks* is a major source of new developments in the area. The *Journal of Social Structure* is an on-line journal featuring articles on social network analysis (available on the internet at http://www. heinz.cmu.edu/project/INSNA/joss/). The International Network for Social Network Analysis (INSNA) is the international professional organization of networks researchers. INSNA maintains a highly informative web page (listing, for example, links to journals and computer programs), the address of which is given in Table 22.3.

ACKNOWLEDGMENT

I am grateful for detailed comments from Melissa Hardy and from two anonymous reviewers, and for discussions with Joseph Galaskiewicz, Paul McLean, Miller McPherson, John Padgett, and Stacy Wolski.

REFERENCES

Abbott, Andrew D. (1999) *Department and Discipline: Chicago Sociology at One Hundred*. Chicago: University of Chicago Press.

Anderson, Carolyn J., Wasserman, Stanley and Crouch, Bradley (1999) 'A p^* primer: Logit models for social networks', *Social Networks*, 21: 37–66.

Anheier, Helmut K., Gerhards, Jurgen and Romo, Frank P. (1995) 'Forms of capital and social structure in cultural fields: Examining Bourdieu's social topography', *American Journal of Sociology*, 100: 859–903.

Arabie, Phipps, Boorman, Scott A. and Levitt, Paul R. (1978) 'Constructing blockmodels: How and why', *Journal of Mathematical Psychology*, 17: 21–63.

Banks, David L. and Carley, Kathleen M. (1997) 'Models for network evolution', in Patrick Doreian and Frans N. Stokman (eds), *Evolution of Social Networks*. Amsterdam: Gordon and Breach, pp. 209–32.

Barton, Allen H. (1968) 'Bringing society back in: Survey research and macro-methodology', *American Behavioral Scientist*, 12(2): 1–9.

Batagelj, Vladimir, Doreian, Patrick and Ferligoj, Anuška (1992) 'An optimizational approach to regular equivalence', *Social Networks*, 14: 121–35.

Bearman, Peter S. (1991) 'The social structure of suicide', *Sociological Forum*, 6: 501–24.

Bearman, Peter S. and Stovel, Katherine (2000) 'Becoming a Nazi: A model for narrative networks', *Poetics*, 27: 69–90.

Bernard, H. Russell, Kilworth, Peter D., Kronenfeld, D. and Sailer, Lee (1984) 'The problem of informant accuracy: The validity of retrospective data', *Annual Review of Anthropology*, 13: 495–517.

Blau, Peter M. (1977) *Inequality and Heterogeneity: A Primitive Theory of Social Structure*. New York: Free Press.

Boorman, Scott A. and White, Harrison C. (1976) 'Social structure from multiple networks: II. Role structures', *American Journal of Sociology*, 81: 1384–446.

Borgatti, Stephen P. and Everett, Martin G. (1992) 'The notion of position in social network analysis', in Peter V. Marsden (ed.), *Sociological Methodology 1992*. London: Basil Blackwell, pp. 1–35.

Borgatti, Stephen P., Boyd, John P. and Everett, Martin G. (1989) 'Iterated roles: Mathematics and application', *Social Networks*, 11: 159–72.

Borgatti, Stephen P., Everett, Martin G. and Freeman, Linton C. (1999) *UCINET 5 for Windows: Software for Social Network Analysis*. Harvard, MA: Analytic Technologies.

Boyd, John Paul (1969) 'The algebra of group kinship', *Journal of Mathematical Psychology*, 6: 139–67.

Boyd, John Paul (1991) *Social Semigroups: A Unified Theory of Scaling and Blockmodeling as Applied to Social Networks*. Fairfax, VA: George Mason University Press.

Breiger, Ronald L. (1974) 'The duality of persons and groups', *Social Forces*, 53: 181–90.

Breiger, Ronald L. (1990) 'Social control and social networks: A model from Georg Simmel', in Craig Calhoun, Marshall W. Meyer and W. Richard Scott (eds), *Structures of Power and Constraint: Essays in Honor of Peter M. Blau*. Cambridge: Cambridge University Press, pp. 453–76.

Breiger, Ronald L. (2000) 'A tool kit for practice theory', *Poetics*, 27: 91–115.

Breiger, Ronald L. and Ennis, James G. (1997) 'Generalized exchange in social networks: Statistics and structure', *L'Année Sociologique*, 47: 73–88.

Breiger, Ronald L. and Pattison, Philippa E. (1978) 'The joint role structure of two communities' elites', *Sociological Methods and Research*, 7: 213–26.

Breiger, Ronald L. and Roberts, John M., Jr. (1998) 'Solidarity and social networks', in Patrick Doreian and Thomas J. Fararo (eds), *The Problem of Solidarity: Theories and Methods*. New York: Gordon and Breach, pp. 239–62.

Breiger, Ronald L., Boorman, Scott A. and Arabie, Phipps (1975) 'An algorithm for clustering relational data, with applications to social network analysis and comparison with multidimensional scaling', *Journal of Mathematical Psychology*, 12: 328–83.

Burt, Ronald S. (1976) 'Positions in networks', *Social Forces*, 55: 93–122.

Burt, Ronald S. (1984) 'Network items and the General Social Survey', *Social Networks*, 6: 293–339.

Burt, Ronald S. (1990) 'Kinds of relations in American discussion networks', in Craig Calhoun, Marshall W. Meyer and W. Richard Scott (eds), *Structures of Power and Constraint: Essays in Honor of Peter M. Blau*, Cambridge: Cambridge University Press, pp. 411–51.

Carley, Kathleen M. (1986) 'An approach for relating social structure to cognitive structure', *Journal of Mathematical Sociology*, 12: 137–89.

Carley, Kathleen M. (1994) 'Extracting culture through textual analysis', *Poetics*, 22: 291–312.

Cook, Karen S., Emerson, R.M., Gillmore, M.R. and Yamagishi, T. (1983) 'The distribution of power in exchange networks: Theory and experimental results', *American Sociological Review*, 43: 721–39.

Cooley, Charles Horton (1964) *Human Nature and the Social Order*. New York: Schocken. First published in 1902.

Davis, James A. (1979) 'The Davis/Holland/Leinhardt studies: An overview', in Paul W. Holland and Samuel Leinhardt (eds), *Perspectives on Social Network Research*. New York: Academic Press, pp. 51–62.

Degenne, Alain and Michel Forsé (1999) *Introducing Social Networks*. London: Sage.

DiMaggio, Paul (1994) 'Introduction [to special issue on measurement and meaning in the sociology of culture]', *Poetics*, 22: 263–7.

DiMaggio, Paul (1997) 'Culture and cognition', *Annual Review of Sociology*, 23: 263–87.

Doreian, Patrick (1999) 'An intuitive introduction to blockmodeling with examples', *Bulletin de Méthodologie Sociologique*, 61(January): 5–34.

Doreian, Patrick and Stokman, Frans N. (eds) (1997) *Evolution of Social Networks*. Amsterdam: Gordon and Breach.

Durkheim, Emile (1965) *Montesquieu and Rousseau, Forerunners of Sociology*. Ann Arbor: University of Michigan Press.

Emirbayer, Mustafa (1997) 'Manifesto for a relational sociology', *American Journal of Sociology*, 103: 281–317.

Emirbayer, Mustafa and Goodwin, Jeff (1994) 'Network analysis, culture, and agency', *American Journal of Sociology*, 99: 1411–53.

Emirbayer, Mustafa and Mische, Ann (1998). 'What is agency?', *American Journal of Sociology*, 103: 962–1023.

Epstein, A.L. (1969) 'The network and urban social organization', in J. Clyde Mitchell (ed.), *Social Networks in Urban Situations: Analyses of Personal Relationships in Central African Towns*. Manchester: Manchester University Press.

Erickson, Bonnie (1996) 'Culture, class and connections', *American Journal of Sociology*, 102: 217–51.

Faulkner, Robert R. (1983) *Music on Demand: Composers and Careers in the Hollywood Film Industry*. New Brunswick, NJ: Transaction Books.

Faust, Katherine and Wasserman, Stanley (1992) 'Blockmodels: Interpretation and evaluation', *Social Networks*, 14: 5–61.

Festinger, Leon (1949) 'The analysis of sociograms using matrix algebra', *Human Relations*, 2: 153–8.

Fienberg, Stephen E. and Wasserman, Stanley (1981) 'Categorical data analysis of single sociometric relations', in Samuel Leinhardt (ed.), *Sociological Methodology 1981*. San Francisco: Jossey-Bass, pp. 156–92.

Forsyth, E. and Katz, L. (1946) 'A matrix approach to the analysis of sociometric data: Preliminary report', *Sociometry*, 9: 340–7.

Frank, Ove and Strauss, David (1986) 'Markov graphs', *Journal of the American Statistical Association*, 81: 832–42.

Freeman, Linton C. (1977) 'A set of measures of centrality based on betweenness', *Sociometry*, 40: 35–41.

Freeman, Linton C. (1989) 'Social networks and the structure experiment', in Linton C. Freeman, Douglas R. White and A. Kimball Romney (eds), *Research Methods in Social Network Analysis*. Fairfax, VA: George Mason University Press, pp. 11–40.

Freeman, Linton C. (2000) 'Visualizing social networks', *Journal of Social Structure* 1(1). http://www.heinz.cmu.edu/project/INSNA/joss/vsn.html

Freeman, Linton C. and White, Douglas R. (1993) 'Using Galois lattices to represent network data', in Peter V. Marsden (ed.), *Sociological Methodology 1993*. Cambridge, MA: Blackwell, pp. 127–46.

Freeman, Linton C., Romney, A. Kimball and Freeman, Sue C. (1987) 'Cognitive structure and informant accuracy', *American Anthropologist*, 89: 310–25.

Friedkin, Noah E. (1998) *A Structural Theory of Social Influence*. Cambridge: Cambridge University Press.

Friedkin, Noah E. and Johnsen, Eugene C. (1997) 'Social positions in influence networks', *Social Networks*, 19: 209–22.

Friedland, Roger and Alford, Robert (1991) 'Bringing society back in: Symbols, practices, and institutional contradictions', in Walter W. Powell and Paul DiMaggio (eds), *The New Institutionalism in Organizational Analysis*. Chicago: University of Chicago Press, pp. 223–62.

Galaskiewicz, Joseph (1985) *Social Organization of an Urban Grants Economy*. New York: Academic Press.

Galaskiewicz, Joseph and Wasserman, Stanley (1989) 'Mimetic and normative processes within an inter-organizational field: An empirical test', *Administrative Science Quarterly*, 34: 454–79.

Gerlach, Michael L. (1992) 'The Japanese corporate network: A blockmodel analysis', *Administrative Science Quarterly*, 37:105–39.

Gibson, David (2000) 'Seizing the moment: The problem of conversational agency', *Sociological Theory*, 18: 369–82.

Goffman, Erving (1971) *Relations in Public: Microstudies of the Public Order*. New York: Harper & Row.

Gould, Roger (1995) *Insurgent Identities: Class, Community and Protest in Paris from 1848 to the Commune*. Chicago: University of Chicago Press.

Granovetter, Mark S. (1973) 'The strength of weak ties', *American Journal of Sociology* 81: 1287–303.

Gulati, Ranjay and Gargiulo, Martin (1999) 'Where do interorganizational networks come from?', *American Journal of Sociology*, 104: 1439–93.

Hage, Per and Harary, Frank (1996) *Island Networks: Communication, Kinship, and Classification Structures in Oceania*. Cambridge: Cambridge University Press.

Han, Shin-Kap and Breiger, Ronald L. (1999) 'Dimensions of corporate social capital: Toward models and measures', in Roger Th. A. J. Leenders and Shaul M. Gabbay (eds), *Corporate Social Capital and Liability*. Boston: Kluwer, pp. 118–33.

Holland, Paul W. and Leinhardt, Samuel (1975) 'Local structure in social networks', in David R. Heise (ed.), *Sociological Methodology 1976*. San Francisco: Jossey-Bass, pp. 1–45.

Holland, Paul W. and Leinhardt, Samuel (1981) 'An exponential family of probability distributions for directed graphs', *Journal of the American Statistical Association*, 76: 33–65.

Iacobucci, Dawn (1996). *Networks in Marketing*. Thousand Oaks, CA: Sage.

Iacobucci, Dawn and Hopkins, Nigel (1992) 'Modeling dyadic interactions and networks in marketing', *Journal of Marketing Research*, 29: 5–17.

Jepperson, Ronald L. and Swidler, Ann (1994) 'What properties of culture should we measure?', *Poetics*, 22: 359–71.

Joas, Hans (1993) *Pragmatism and Social Theory*. Chicago: University of Chicago Press.

Kim, K.H. and Roush, F.W. (1983) *Applied Abstract Algebra*. New York: Wiley.

Knoke, David and Kuklinski, James H. (1982) *Network Analysis*. Newbury Park, CA: Sage.

Krackhardt, David (1987) 'Cognitive social structures', *Social Networks*, 9: 109–34.

Krackhardt, David (1992) 'The strength of strong ties: The importance of *philos* in organizations', in Nitin Nohria and Robert G. Eccles (eds), *Networks and Organizations*. Boston: Harvard Business School, pp. 216–39.

Kumbasar, Ece, Romney, A. Kimball and Batchelder, William H. (1994) 'Systematic biases in social perception', *American Journal of Sociology*, 100: 477–505.

Latour, Bruno (1988) *The Pasteurization of France*. Cambridge, MA: Harvard University Press. First published in 1984.

Laumann, Edward O., Marsden, Peter V. and Prensky, David (1983) 'The boundary specification problem in network analysis', in Ronald S. Burt and Michael J. Minor (eds), *Applied Network Analysis: A Methodological Introduction*. Beverly Hills, CA: Sage, pp. 18–34.

Law, John (1999) 'After ANT: Complexity, naming and topology', in John Law and John Hassard (eds), *Actor Network Theory and After*. Oxford: Blackwell, pp. 1–14.

Lazega, Emmanuel and Pattison, Philippa E. (1999) 'Multiplexity, generalized exchange and coopera-tion in organizations: A case study', *Social Networks*, 21: 67–90.

Leenders, Roger Th.A.J. (1997) 'Longitudinal behav-ior of network structure and actor attributes: Modeling interdependence of contagion and selec-tion', in Patrick Doreian and Frans N. Stokman (eds), *Evolution of Social Networks*. Amsterdam: Gordon and Breach, pp. 165–84.

Levine, Joel H. (1999) 'We can count, but what do the numbers mean?', in Janet L. Abu-Lughod (ed.), *Sociology for the Twenty-First Century: Continuities and Cutting Edges*. Chicago: University of Chicago Press, pp. 83–93.

Lidl, Rudolf and Pilz, Günter (1998) *Applied Abstract Algebra* (2nd edition). New York: Springer.

Lin, Nan (1982) 'Social resources and instrumental action', in Peter V. Marsden and Nan Lin (eds), *Social Structure and Network Analysis*. Beverly Hills, CA: Sage, pp. 131–45.

Lincoln, James R. (1984) 'Analyzing relations in dyads', *Sociological Methods and Research*, 13: 45–76.

Lonkila, Markku (1997) 'Informal exchange relations in post-Soviet Russia: A comparative perspective', *Sociological Research Online* 2(2) http://www.socresonline.org.uk/socresonline/2/2/9.html

Lorrain, François P. and White, Harrison C. (1971) 'Structural equivalence of individuals in social networks', *Journal of Mathematical Sociology*, 1: 49–80.

Luce, R. Duncan and Perry, A.D. (1949) 'A method of matrix analysis of group structure', *Psychometrika*, 14: 95–116.

Markovsky, B., Willer, D. and Patton, T. (1988) 'Power relations in exchange networks', *American Sociological Review*, 53: 220–36.

Marsden, Peter V. (1981) 'Models and methods for characterizing the structural parameters of groups', *Social Networks*, 3: 1–27.

Marsden, Peter V. (1988) 'Homogeneity in confiding relations', *Social Networks*, 10: 57–76.

Marsden, Peter V. (1990) 'Network data and measurement', *Annual Review of Sociology*, 16: 435–63.

Martin, John Levi (2000) 'What do animals do all day? The division of labor, class bodies, and totemic thinking in the popular imagination', *Poetics*, 27: 195–231.

Marx, Karl (1956). *Karl Marx: Selected Writings in Sociology & Social Philosophy* tr. T.B. Bottomore. New York: McGraw-Hill.

McLean, Paul (1998) 'A frame analysis of favor seeking in the Renaissance: Agency, networks, and political culture', *American Journal of Sociology*, 104: 51–91.

McPherson, J. Miller (1982) 'Hypernetwork sampling: Duality and differentiation among voluntary organizations', *Social Networks*, 3: 225–50.

McPherson, J. Miller (2001) 'Sampling strategies for the arts: A hypernetwork approach', *Poetics*, 28: 291–306.

McPherson, J. Miller and Ranger-Moore, James R. (1991) 'Evolution on a dancing landscape: Organizations and networks in dynamic Blau space', *Social Forces*, 70: 19–42.

McPherson, J. Miller and Rotolo, Thomas (1996) 'Testing a dynamic model of social composition: Diversity and change in voluntary groups', *American Sociological Review*, 61: 179–202.

Mische, Ann (2003) 'Cross-talk in movements: Reconceiving the culture–network link', in Mario Diani and Doug McAdam (eds), *Social Movements and Networks: Relational Approaches to Collective Action*. Oxford: Oxford University Press.

Mische, Ann and Pattison, Philippa E. (2000) 'Composing a civic arena: Publics, projects, and social settings', *Poetics*, 27: 163–94.

Mische, Ann and White, Harrison (1998) 'Between conversation and situation: Public switching dynamics across network-domains', *Social Research*, 65: 695–724.

Mohr, John W. (1994) 'Soldiers, mothers, tramps, and others: Discourse roles in the 1907 New York City charity directory', *Poetics*, 22: 327–57.

Mohr, John W. (1998) 'Measuring meaning structures', *Annual Review of Sociology*, 24: 345–70.

Mohr, John W. (2003) 'Implicit terrains: Meaning, measurement, and spatial metaphors in organizational theory', in Joseph Porac and Marc Ventresca (eds), *Constructing Industries and Markets*. New York: Elsevier.

Mohr, John W. and Duquenne, Vincent (1997) 'The duality of culture and practice: Poverty relief in New York City, 1888–1917', *Theory and Society*, 26: 305–56.

Mohr, John W. and Lee, Helene K. (2000) 'From affirmative action to outreach: Discourse shifts at the University of California', *Poetics*, 28: 47–71.

Molm, Linda D. and Cook, Karen S. (1995) 'Social exchange and exchange networks', in Karen S. Cook, Gary Alan Fine, and James S. House (eds), *Sociological Perspectives on Social Psychology*. Boston: Allyn and Bacon, pp. 209–35.

Moreno, Jacob L. and Jennings, Helen H. (1938) 'Statistics of social configurations', *Sociometry*, 1: 342–74.

Padgett, John F. (2001) 'Organizational genesis, identity, and control: The transformation of banking in Renaissance Florence', in James E. Rauch and Alessandra Casella (eds), *Networks and Markets*. New York: Russell Sage Foundation, pp. 211–57.

Padgett, John F. and Ansell, Christopher K. (1993) 'Robust action and the rise of the Medici, 1400–1434', *American Journal of Sociology*, 98: 1259–319.

Pattison, Philippa E. (1980) 'An algebraic analysis for multiple social networks'. PhD dissertation, University of Melbourne.

Pattison, Philippa (1993) *Algebraic Models for Social Networks*. Cambridge: Cambridge University Press.

Pattison, Philippa (1994) 'Social cognition in context: Some applications of social network analysis' in Stanley Wasserman and Joseph Galaskiewicz (eds), *Advances in Social Network Analysis*. Thousand Oaks, CA: Sage, pp. 79–109.

Pattison, Philippa and Wasserman, Stanley (1999) 'Logit models and logistic regressions for social networks: II. Multivariate relations', *British Journal of Mathematical and Statistical Psychology*, 52: 169–93.

Radcliffe-Brown, A.R. (1940) 'On social structure', *Journal of the Royal Anthropological Institute of Great Britain and Ireland*, 70: 1–12.

Ragin, Charles C. and Becker, Howard S. (eds) (1992) *What Is a Case? Exploring the Foundations of Social Inquiry*. Cambridge: Cambridge University Press.

Robins, Gary, Pattison, Philippa and Wasserman, Stanley (1999) 'Logit models and logistic regressions for social networks, III: Valued relations', *Psychometrika*, 64: 371–94.

Scott, John (1991) *Social Network Analysis: A Handbook*. London: Sage.

Skvoretz, John and Faust, Katherine (1999) 'Logit models for affiliation networks', in Mark P. Becker and Michael E. Sobel (eds), *Sociological Methodology 1999*. Washington, DC: American Sociological Association, pp. 253–80.

Smith, David A. and White, Douglas R. (1992) 'Structure and dynamics of the global economy: Network analysis of international trade 1965–1980', *Social Forces*, 70: 857–93.

Smith-Lovin, Lynn and McPherson, J. Miller (1993) 'You are who you know: A network approach to gender', in Paula England (ed.), *Theory on Gender/ Feminism on Theory*. New York: Aldine de Gruyter, pp. 223–51.

Snijders, T.A.B. (1991) 'Enumeration and simulation methods for 0–1 matrices with given marginals', *Psychometrika*, 56: 397–417.

Snijders, T.A.B. (1997) 'Stochastic actor-oriented models for network change', in Patrick Doreian and Frans N. Stokman (eds), *Evolution of Scoial Networks*. Amsterdam: Gordon and Breach, pp. 185–208.

Snijders, T.A.B. and Nowicki, Krzysztof (1997) 'Estimation and prediction for stochastic block-models for graphs with latent block structure', *Journal of Classification*, 14: 75–100.

Snow, David A. and Benford, Robert D. (1988) 'Ideology, frame resonance, and movement participation', *International Social Movement Research*, 1: 197–217.

Stark, David (1996) 'Recombinant property in East European capitalism', *American Journal of Sociology*, 101: 993–1027.

Steiber, Steven R. (1979) 'The world system and world trade: An empirical exploration of conceptual conflicts', *Sociological Quarterly*, 20: 23–36.

Steinberg, Marc W. (1999) 'The talk and back talk of collective action: A dialogic analysis of repertoires of discourse among nineteenth-century English cotton spinners', *American Journal of Sociology*, 105: 736–80.

Strauss, D. and Ikeda, M. (1990) 'Pseudo-likelihood estimation for social networks', *Journal of the American Statistical Association*, 85: 204–12.

Turner, Jonathan H. (1991) *The Structure of Sociological Theory* (5th edition). Belmont, CA: Wadsworth.

van Duijn, Marijtje A.J., van Busschbach, Jooske T. and Snijders, Tom A.B. (1999) 'Multilevel analysis of personal networks as dependent variables', *Social Networks*, 21: 187–209.

Vaughn, Diane (1986) *Uncoupling: Turning Points in Intimate Relationships*. New York: Oxford University Press.

von Wiese, Leopold (1941) *Sociology*, ed. Fritz Mueller. New York: Oskar Piest.

Wasserman, Stanley and Faust, Katherine (1994) *Social Network Analysis: Methods and Applications*. Cambridge: Cambridge University Press.

Wasserman, Stanley and Pattison, Philippa (1996) 'Logit models and logistic regressions for social networks: I. An introduction to Markov graphs and p^*', *Psychometrika*, 61: 401–25.

Weil, André (1969) 'On the algebraic study of certain types of marriage laws (Murngin's system)', in Claude Lévi-Strauss, *Elementary Structures of Kinship*. Boston: Beacon Press.

Wellman, Barry (1988) 'Structural analysis: From method and metaphor to theory and substance', in Barry Wellman and S.D. Berkowitz (eds), *Social Structures: A Network Approach*. Cambridge: Cambridge University Press, pp. 19–61.

Wellman, Barry (ed.) (1999) *Networks in the Global Village: Life in Contemporary Communities*. Boulder, CO: Westview Press.

Wellman, Barry and S.D. Berkowitz (eds) (1988) *Social Structures: A Network Approach*. Cambridge: Cambridge University Press.

White, Douglas R. and Reitz, Karl P. (1983) 'Graph and semigroup homomorphisms on networks of relations', *Social Networks*, 5: 193–234.

White, Douglas R. and Reitz, Karl P. (1989) 'Re-thinking the role concept: Homomorphisms on social networks', in Linton C. Freeman, Douglas R. White and A. Kimball Romney (eds), *Research Methods in Social Network Analysis*. Fairfax, VA: George Mason University Press, pp. 429–88.

White, Harrison C. (1963) *An Anatomy of Kinship*. Englewood Cliffs, NJ: Prentice Hall.

White, Harrison C. (1992) *Identity and Control: A Structural Theory of Social Action*. Princeton, NJ: Princeton University Press.

White, Harrison C., Boorman, Scott A. and Breiger, Ronald L. (1976) 'Social structure from multiple networks: I. Blockmodels of roles and positions', *American Journal of Sociology*, 81: 730–80.

Winship, Christopher (1988) 'Thoughts about roles and relations: An old document revisited', *Social Networks*, 10: 209–31.

Yamaguchi, Kazuo (1990) 'Homophily and social distance in the choice of multiple friends: An analysis based on conditionally symmetric log-bilinear association models', *Journal of the American Statistical Association*, 85: 356–66.

PART V

Analyzing Qualitative Data

23

Tools for Qualitative Data Analysis

RAYMOND M. LEE AND NIGEL G. FIELDING

This chapter profiles approaches to the analysis of qualitative data, with an emphasis on resources and tools. In contrast to the quantitative tradition, this emphasis has only lately become a focus of the qualitative literature. The use of quantitative approaches became increasingly common in mainstream American sociology in the decades following World War II (Platt, 1996: 123–7). There were three main responses to this growing dominance. Some writers engaged in a debate about the relative merits and demerits of different methods (Becker and Geer, 1957, 1958; Trow, 1957). A second response stressed the importance of first-person accounts of fieldwork experience, emphasizing the messy character of field research as opposed to what was seen as the sterile codification of survey procedures. A third response was the attempt by some writers to provide explicit accounts of analytic strategies for handling data from field research (Becker and Geer, 1960; Glaser and Strauss, 1967). As Platt (1996) points out, however, the reception of methodological innovation often occurs in a haphazard and contingent way. Despite the availability of explicit analytic models, analytic issues remained somewhat slighted within the literature on qualitative research relative to discussions of issues to do with, for example, access, field relations, and ethics (Miles, 1983). Of course, information about analytic methods is likely to have been transmitted in other ways. Qualitative researchers often learn their craft in apprentice-like relations with a more experienced mentor. How far

such channels served as vehicles for the transmission of analytic approaches remains unclear. Jackson (1990), writing about anthropology, points to the prevalence of 'sink-or-swim' approaches, and a conviction that fieldwork is so particularized, or the character of the discipline so contested, that general advice seems impossible or undesirable. The situation has changed, however, in recent years. Although one can hardly speak of 'codification' in the Lazarsfeldian manner, analytic issues have attained a greater degree of transparency and accessibility within the qualitative tradition. The growing popularity of qualitative methods has encouraged a pedagogically driven elaboration of analytic procedures by writers such as Strauss (Strauss, 1987; Strauss and Corbin, 1990). Texts specifically concerned with qualitative analysis began to appear (e.g. Miles and Huberman, 1994; Dey, 1993; Bryman and Burgess, 1994), and a growing interest in analytic procedures can be traced in successive editions of popular textbooks on qualitative research – compare, for example, Lofland and Lofland (1984) with Lofland and Lofland (1995). Meanwhile, the advent of computer-assisted qualitative data analysis software (Lee and Fielding, 1991), focused attention on procedural aspects of qualitative data analysis, invited the comparison of approaches, and raised conceptual questions, for example, about the nature of 'coding' as an analytic procedure (Fielding and Lee, 1998; Dey, 1999).

Holmes (1992) makes a useful distinction between conceptual tools, operative tools and literal tools. A literal tool takes the form of a 'concrete physical apparatus' (Holmes, 1992: 153). At one time in qualitative research, such apparatus might be very simple, different coloured pencils, say, punched cards or multiple copies of segments of fieldnotes. Today, the computer has become, literally, a major tool for the analysis of qualitative data. Conceptual tools can be thought of as theoretical and methodological approaches routinely developed to solve analytic problems. Such approaches do not need to be extensively elaborated. Indeed, in some cases they might be little more than heuristics or 'tricks of the trade' (Becker, 1998). Even where they have been elaborated, as in the case of grounded theory, there might still be considerable disagreement over the character, scope and applicability of the approach (Fielding and Lee, 1998). Operative tools can be thought of as the specific procedures used as part of the analytic process. Procedures for segmenting, coding, retrieving, indexing, cross-referencing and abstracting (Levine, 1985; MacQueen and Milstein, 1999) are examples. In this chapter, we address the use by qualitative researchers of tools in each of these senses by exploring a variety of common approaches, procedures and software programs. We begin with an overview of software tools for qualitative research. This follows in broad outline the content of the chapters following this one, focusing on lexical analysis, code-based approaches, case-based approaches, and discursive methods. For each, we note salient features of the approach together with relevant aspects of software implementation, introducing wider analytic and methodological issues as appropriate.

SOFTWARE TOOLS FOR QUALITATIVE ANALYSIS

As we have observed elsewhere (Fielding and Lee, 1998: 3), qualitative research is a broad church represented in many disciplines. It contains many schools of thought and has many uses, many audiences, and many sponsors. Some approaches seek a systematic, rigorous consideration of usually text-based data in order to identify themes and concepts that will contribute to our understanding of social life. Themes and concepts that are identified and coded in one data source are then compared and contrasted with (any) similar material in other sources. New themes

that emerge necessitate further consideration and analysis of previously coded data. The analytical challenge is the identification of thematically similar segments of text across the data available. The practical counterparts are the labelling and subsequent retrieval of similarly coded segments, together with a reference to their original location. Other approaches involve a commitment to the interpretive and hermeneutic understanding of social life through the analysis of narratives, sign systems or the properties of talk. The manifest content of texts is sometimes analysed in an enumerative way by listing, counting and categorizing the words within a text, while a rather old tradition that has found new life seeks to analyse cases either as individual entities or as conjunctions of logical relations.

We start by looking at tools for lexical analysis and for text retrieval. We then discuss the use of dedicated computer packages that have lately become available for the analysis of qualitative data (Weitzman and Miles, 1995), particularly so-called 'code-and-retrieve' and 'theory-building' packages. After a brief discussion of software tools for making diagrams of various sorts, we look at software support for important aspects of the analytic process that are often treated in a marginal way: transcription and data management. Finally, we note the computer's ability to support analytic approaches impossible or difficult using traditional 'manual' methods of analysis.

Analysing textual data

Content analysis was one of the earliest approaches to the analysis of text. Lists of words are an important tool in this tradition. One familiar kind of word list, the *index*, shows not only which words appear in a text but also the *position* of each. A *concordance* lists the words in a text, showing for each the immediate *context* within which it appears. Concordances are often generated by computer in a key-words-in-context format. This shows each word, usually centred on a page, surrounded by the words appearing immediately before and after it in the text. The analysis of collocated words (i.e., co-locates) looks at how words in a text are associated with one another, such as the range of words which appear within some specified distance of words having analytic interest. An example can be found in Hansen's (1995) account of how British newspapers covered 'mad cow disease'. Hansen found that words such as 'scientist' or 'expert' were typically accompanied by terms like 'top', 'senior' and 'leading' – words used by the newspapers, in his view, to buttress the authority and legitimacy of one set of commentators on the disease.

Almost anyone who has used a word processor has encountered a 'find' or a 'search' command that allows the user to quickly locate a particular word or phrase. This is an example of simple string searching. The computer is used to find a specific sequence or 'string' of characters. 'Text retrievers', packages such as Metamorph, WordCruncher, ZyINDEX and Sonar Professional, are stand-alone programs that extend the ability to find text in complex ways. (Increasingly, fairly sophisticated search routines are also being built into dedicated qualitative data analysis packages of the kind further discussed below.) The scope of a search can be widened by using so-called 'wild cards', a term taken from poker and referring to situations where one card, the joker say, can substitute for another. Thus, if a particular program uses the asterisk as a wild card, it is possible to enter laug* in order to find the terms 'laugh', 'laughs', 'laughter', and so on. Boolean searches allow the analyst to find combinations of search terms defined by the Boolean operators AND, OR, NOT. Proximity searches find instances where one search term appears within a given distance of another, distance usually being measured in terms of words, lines, sentences and the like. Pattern searching involves the matching of a pattern of characters to a search request, for example, a search for all words beginning with a capital letter followed by a vowel and ending in 'ing'. Retrievals can also be made of things that sound alike, are synonyms, or display patterns like the sequences of letters and numbers in social security records. Retrieved text can be collected into new files, and analytic memos can be linked to the data. Some text retrievers can perform content analysis procedures and include facilities to handle quantitative data.

The main value of text retrievers is information management where similar data are held on many people. Some researchers relish the speed and flexibility that text retrieval methods allow (Wellman, 1990). For others, the use of string searching is primarily a filtering and focusing device. Fisher (1995) suggests that text retrievers are ideally suited

for making an 'aerial reconnaissance' of textual data. Text retrieval can be improved through the use of a 'textbase manager' package, which stands some way between dedicated text retrieval packages and database software. (For details of textbase managers, see Rubinstein, 1991; Fischer, 1994; Weitzman and Miles, 1995.) Conventional databases are organized into records and fields. For example, in a bibliographic database each record might refer to a book, article or other work. Within each record would be found fields for author, title and so on. In a conventional database there are usually restrictions on the length of records and fields, and the information stored in the database tends to have a relatively structured form. Textbase managers are free of some of these constraints. They typically accept free text of varying length but allow the definition of fields which can be associated with the text. A textbase manager will usually support complex search procedures which will return both structured and unstructured records. Textbase managers deal readily with the mixture of structured, semi-structured and unstructured information typically generated by field research but do have some disadvantages (Fischer, 1994). Some take up large volumes of disk storage and some can be slow in searching through large volumes of material.

Code-and-retrieve packages, including HyperQual, Kwalitan, maxQDA and The Ethnograph, focus on attaching codes to data segments and retrieving segments by code (or code combinations). To manage the range of data used by qualitative researchers, software has to be able to store data in different formats and enable their annotation. Since analysis involves moving around the corpus looking at how particular analytic ideas relate to different segments, a means is needed to 'navigate' the database, and it is helpful if researchers can retrace their steps. To this end the corpus has to be divided into segments, and codes must be assigned to them which relate to the analytic themes being developed. Codes try to express what is judged to be some inherent quality of the segment, and codes are usually chosen which apply to more than one segment. Researchers sometimes must revise codes, either globally or as they apply to particular segments. When data are coded they can be retrieved using various analytic strategies.

Code-and-retrieve software allows users quickly and easily to: assign codes to data segments; allow recoding either globally or selectively; provide facilities to write, store and view memos; allow Boolean retrievals, retrievals using other kinds of set logic, proximity retrievals (recovering data within some user-defined 'distance' from the head search term), and semantic retrievals (recovering data whose meaning is similar to that expressed by the head search term); support various other manipulations of retrieved data, such as quantitative content analysis, presentation in matrices, tables or lists; allow data to be exported to and imported from websites; and support various forms of graphical representation of data and/or analysis, for example, tree diagrams representing a coding hierarchy, or 'network views' representing the links between different codes in terms of a causal network, chronological process or implementation cycle. It is increasingly common to provide for 'autocoding', where one can request a search pattern and automatically assign a code to the string(s) found. In some cases a certain amount of context can be attached to each 'hit'. Some packages allow users to retrieve online sound, picture or video files so that codes are assigned directly to recorded material, which is played back when retrieved, accompanied by a diagram of pitch and intonation in the dialogue.

Code-and-retrieve software focuses analysis on relationships between codes and data. What has been called 'theory-building software', such as ATLAS.ti, HyperRESEARCH, NUD*IST, and NVivo, emphasizes relationships between the codes, while still supporting code-and-retrieve work. The idea is to develop higher-order classifications than those derived directly from data, formulate propositions which fit the data and test how well they apply, and/or visualize connections between codes as a stimulus to conceptualization. Boolean searching, and features to assist hypotheses to be tested, may be offered. Some can show codes (or other objects, such as memos) as nodes in a graphic display and allow the nodes to be linked by specified relationships like 'leads to', 'is a kind of' and so on, or by user-defined relationships, which can be helpful in thinking about conceptualization at a more abstract level than when examining the 'raw' data. These procedures rely on the data supporting these relationships being comparable and coding having been done in a commensurate fashion, because they work 'one level up' from the data. Since the comparability of qualitative data can never be assumed (e.g., rapport may vary among respondents) the activity of theory-building may be as controversial at the level of techniques and tools as it is in other respects.

One development aided by software is the trend towards more visually-based analytic strategies. Quantitative researchers have long been interested in how visual means can be used to make complex data more readily understandable, and visualization is becoming more important in qualitative analysis too. This is apparent in the tree diagrams of NUD*IST and the conceptual network views of ATLAS.ti, but some software specializes in facilitating visualization, an example being the package called Inspiration™. Software from the allied field of psychology can also be useful. The program called Decision Explorer was originally developed to aid cognitive mapping – the representation of thought processes involved in mental activities such as reaching a decision – but can be useful to qualitative researchers. Using software is not the only means to visualize qualitative data. Diagrams and tables can be used to display text. At its simplest, a display matrix consists of a table with rows and columns into which, rather than putting numbers, the researcher enters code names, extracts from the data or other textual information. This helps in both managing the data and thinking about them analytically, beginning as it does the process of data reduction and comparison. A researcher studying the impact of a new resource centre in a school system might design a matrix with columns headed 'early users', 'later users' and 'administrators', and with rows for interview extracts from individuals representing those categories. Miles and Huberman (1994) describe several kinds of matrix, including 'event history matrices' which capture the chronology of some process, such as the progress of a cohort through a training programme, and another variant which is directed to tracing causal relationships. Sophisticated graphical representations, such as the 'site dynamics matrix', can be used to represent in diagrammatic form key agents and agencies in some social process and their relationships. Miles and Huberman make the point that such diagrams are efficient devices by the telling observation that the half-page diagram they offer as an example summarizes 300 pages of field data.

Managing data

Qualitative data from field sources such as interviews are usually rendered into a textual form by transcription. What one chooses to transcribe, how the transcription is actually done, and what is included or left out all depend on the investigator's purposes, resources and assumptions (Kvale, 1996). The choice of a particular transcription method usually involves a trade-off between time and cost constraints and the demands of theory development. While full verbatim transcription has become common, transcription is a major bottleneck. Estimates of the transcribing time needed for every hour of recorded tape vary from approximately 4 hours (McCracken, 1988: 70–1) to around 8 (Arber, 1993). The amount of time, and therefore the cost, of transcription, depends on several factors: the nature of the data, how detailed the transcript is to be, the quality of the original recording, the equipment used to transcribe, and the keyboarding skills of the transcriber. Voice-recognition software can help but it does not easily recognize recorded speech. What is heard on the tape must be spoken into the software, and the software itself needs to be 'trained' to recognize the user's voice. Even then, the output is likely to contain a high proportion of errors. Some researchers have bypassed transcription altogether by working directly with digitized audio or video. When a search results in a hit the researcher can listen or look at the original data. It seems likely that recourse might still be made to text for detailed analysis, so working directly with audio or video might chiefly be useful for relatively superficial or narrow analytic work, like making a first high-level 'pass' through the data as a preliminary to coding them, or for detailed work involving the fine-grained examination of paralinguistic features of speech. Both voice transcription software and packages supporting work with audio, video and graphic files impose substantial hardware requirements. So far, too, the benefits and challenges of working directly with audio and video materials have received little discussion in the literature.

Qualitative research is characterized by a 'fluid, interactive relationship' between data collection and data analysis (Denzin, 1970). One aspect of that relationship is the need for a data management regime. Huberman and Miles (1994: 428) define data management as 'the operations needed for a systematic, coherent process of data collection, storage and retrieval'. Levine (1985) gives four reasons for paying explicit attention to data management issues. These relate to (a) the problems for data management of working with large data volumes, (b) the tension that emerges in the analytic process between data collected on a chronological basis and the need to analyse data by topic, (c) the extent to which qualitative analysis is procedurally transparent, and (d) the importance of foresight in the analytic process if one is to avoid drowning in data. We will now look at each of these in turn.

Qualitative researchers typically generate large volumes of (often variegated) material, producing in effect an 'assemblage' of data (Lee, 1993). Typically, this assemblage is multi-stranded, derives from multiple sources, and frequently has multiple forms: transcripts, fieldnotes, documents and so on. Further, as Miles and Huberman (1994: 262) point out, when human beings process information they are likely to give undue emphasis to the vivid over the pallid, to the views of the articulate over the ill-informed and to those standing in a close rather than a distant relation to the observer. The ability to counter these tendencies can be inhibited if data volumes are large and data cannot be managed in an efficient way. In qualitative research, data are usually chronologically acquired, often as the result of progressive immersion in the field. Analysis, however, is for the most part topic-oriented, with the analyst trying to identify themes emerging from the data (see also Fischer, 1994). A well-organized data management system allows for rapid and effective movement back and forth between chronologically and topically organized data. This in turn can improve the quality of ongoing data collection. An explicit data management regime enhances the transparency of research procedures, which can vitiate concerns about the veracity of research (Miles and Huberman, 1994: 287), facilitate the secondary use of qualitative data, and open up qualitative analysis to audit, meta-analysis, meta-evaluation (the evaluation of evaluation studies) and replication (Schwandt and Halpern, 1988).

Because data collection and data analysis are intertwined in qualitative research, early decisions or non-decisions about how to handle data can have longer-term analytic consequences. Data management systems need to be designed before or soon after data collection begins but should not be complex or rigid. What is important is to think about one's likely information needs as an overall system, working out a broad schema which avoids problems of information overload and omission. MacQueen and Milstein (1999) identify four elements that form a basis for organizing a qualitative data analysis system: information about sources of data; data collected from these sources; interpretations generated from data sources; and information about those involved in the analysis process and their procedures. Each element has associated with it a 'data structure', a set of files describing the form, content and location of the components comprising each of the four elements. Outputs from data structures serve as inputs to later typically more complex data structures. MacQueen and Milstein's conceptualization has influenced the development of the software program AnSWR. Other packages have their own procedures for maintaining and interrelating data structures. Whatever the specifics, using software for data management has advantages compared with non-computer-based methods because of the convenience of digital over paper storage, tailored procedures for data storage and the ability to maintain audit trails.

From one perspective the computer has so far mostly provided what might be thought of as 'enhancing technologies' for qualitative research. By providing more efficient methods of handling qualitative data, computer-based methods promise a better or at least an easier way of doing things. The computer can also be seen, however, as making available 'transformative technologies' (Lee, 1995) that provide ways of doing things *differently* rather than simply better. As we describe later, examples might include approaches based around the comparative analysis of cases, and forms of non-linear representation associated with discourse-based approaches to qualitative analysis difficult or impossible with traditional methods.

LEXICAL ANALYSIS

Content-analytic methods stress quantification, systematicity, procedural transparency and theoretical relevance (Holsti, 1969; Krippendorf, 1980). Content analysis is quantitative in the sense that it is based on procedures that permit categorized data to be translated into nominal, ordinal or interval scales. Once produced, scales can be transformed into multidimensional classifications, or can be used to develop quantitative indices. The analysis is made systematic and transparent through the use of explicitly formulated rules and procedures. Content analysis is usually not a descriptive method (Holsti, 1969); it seeks theoretical relevance through hypothesis and theory testing. Aided in part by software developments, newer approaches to content analysis have begun to appear. Popping (2000) distinguishes 'semantic' and 'network' approaches from the traditional 'thematic' approach. In the semantic approach a text to be analysed is parsed into clauses having a subject–verb–object form. This uses much more of the information already present in the text, permitting one to code not only the presence or absence of themes but also the relations between underlying concepts. The network approach goes further by constructing networks of semantically linked concepts. Carley (1988), for example, has developed a two-stage process for explicating the network of concepts and conceptual relationships within a verbal protocol. Coding a large number of protocols is tedious, time-consuming and prone to error. However, providing knowledge of the definitions, connections and implications found within a protocol can be made explicit for at least some of the data, it can be embodied within an expert system. In the first stage of the procedure Carley describes, assistants code protocols with the aid of a coding program, CODEF. An expert system, SKI, is then used to diagnose and correct errors and omissions in the initial coding produced by CODEF.

The content analysis of text often proceeds from a count of the number of times each word appears within the text on the assumption that the frequency with which words appear is a reflection of their salience. This statement needs immediately to be qualified; the words that appear most frequently in a text, like 'a' and 'the', are usually of little interest to social scientists. Weber (1985: 53) notes that word frequencies can be misleading if context is ignored. Because words have different meanings or vary in their meaning across context, a simple count can overestimate the salience of a particular word.

Conversely, if one pays no attention to synonyms or words such as pronouns that can be substituted for other words, word frequencies can underestimate salience. Weber (1985: 48) also points out that, since a concordance is usually many times longer than the text which produced it, content analysis involves 'data expanding rather than data reducing techniques'. In addition, it might be necessary to go through several iterations in order to focus on relevant data. An alternative and rather common way of analysing both textual and graphical content is to code data on the basis of a user-generated category system. Categories should be exhaustive, mutually exclusive, independent and 'derived from a single classification principle' as Holsti (1969: 95) puts it, that is, should be governed by a process of conceptual ordering.

Content analysts mostly work with 'found' texts such as newspaper articles or political speeches. Indeed, as Hansen (1995) points out, the increasing availability of such sources in electronic form is set to transform areas such as the study of newspaper content. Although those who work with found media will often move back and forth between quantitative and qualitative analysis of the text, content-analytic techniques are relatively seldom used to analyse data from, say, interview transcripts. This is because counting and listing techniques have some serious drawbacks as far as qualitative researchers are concerned. Although concordances display words in context, usually that context is fixed – a certain number of words, of lines or whatever. While this poses few problems in strictly lexically-oriented studies, a qualitative researcher would rarely want to be constrained in this way. The context for an utterance in an interview, say, may well be a word, a few lines or several paragraphs. Qualitative researchers, in other words, often want to work with user-defined 'chunks' of text.

Against this, content-analysis techniques have some advantages for qualitative researchers. Computer packages for indexing and concordancing are widely used in the humanities. As a result, and in contrast to the situation in many institutions as far as qualitative data analysis software is concerned, they are often widely available in, and supported by, university computer centres. Moreover, a number of concordance packages are in the public domain or are quite modestly priced. A second possible advantage of using content-analysis techniques, according

to Werner (1989), is that they can be heuristically useful in situations where material is piling up and analysis time is short. Werner routinely generates word frequency counts from transcripts as a way of judging how adequately particular interview topics are being covered, and as an indicator of possible lines of inquiry. Interestingly, he suggests inspecting not only words that appear recurrently, but also those that only occur once. Rare but seemingly salient words may reflect areas not covered in sufficient detail in the interview and which may need to be probed in subsequent fieldwork.

CODE-BASED ANALYSIS

Handbooks, like methodology courses, are premised on anticipation and preparation. We can see some of the qualities of code-based analysis if we imagine an alternative scenario, one which is not all that fanciful. An undergraduate has as part of her degree to produce an empirically-based dissertation. Several of her relatives have connections with the police. She decides she will research 'police attitudes to recent social change'. With little more than this in mind she interviews three people – a close relative who has recently retired from the rank of inspector, an acquaintance of his who is a police dog handler, and a policewoman currently suspended while she brings a sexual harassment case against her commanding officer. The student tapes the interviews and transcribes them over the summer vacation.

In September the student spends half an hour with her university dissertation advisor. He tells her to read three references – a textbook on the politics of the police, a government report on Total Quality Management in policing, and an article he has written on police communications equipment. He tells her she should decide what aspects of 'recent social change' to ask her respondents about, that she can regard her initial interviews as pilot fieldwork but still use the data from them as part of her analysis, and that she needs to do 15 interviews to satisfy the examiners that she has 'done enough fieldwork'. He gives her the name of a police friend who can provide access to more respondents, and discusses the number of questions she should have on her interview guide. He leaves to her the final choice of questions. In the following three months she conducts the interviews and transcribes the data.

At the beginning of January she calls on her advisor again, with 300 pages of neatly formatted transcripts. She read the textbook the advisor recommended but could not find the report on TQM and did not understand how she could bring police equipment into her topic. She has three months to complete the dissertation, and she has a simple question for her advisor: 'What do I do now?' In the course of a sometimes agitated hour-long discussion, the advisor establishes that: the student has had no clear rationale for drawing her sample, simply interviewing those referred by the advisor's police friend and the people in her social network with police connections; the student has not asked the same questions of every respondent, and has added some questions to the last five interviews relating to a recently published official report on police corruption; one of the respondents has told the student that he planted drugs on a suspected dealer in order to 'get him off the street', to which she has responded by writing a note on fieldwork ethics.

We expect that some readers may recognize scenarios of the sort we have described. But what has it got to do with a particular approach to analysis? One interesting thing about the scenario is that, for a code-based analysis, this (all too common) travesty of a research design is not necessarily a disaster. By drawing on principles of hermeneutic analysis which have been established over several centuries of interpretive work, but which are also the cultural endowment of anyone who has sought evidence to support and discount interpretations of any substantial narrative, our student may be able to extract a compelling analysis, with a few basic tools and a lot of concentrated attention. In short, to produce a 'code-based analysis' one does not have to do everything 'just so'. The secret of carrying one's readers with one's interpretation lies in making apparent at every stage the basis of one's interpretation, recognizing and identifying the constraints applicable to given interpretations. Certain tools and procedures provide especially strong or efficient support for such work. We are not saying that a code-based analysis *will* enable a satisfactory analysis to be achieved, only that it *may* do. Code-based analysis is a flexible and forgiving procedure, and the electronic resources to maximize these qualities are both substantial and readily available.

Since time-honoured methods remain at the heart of these resources, despite the sophisticated things they can do, they are also quite accessible.

Recall that we established that our student had no clear rationale for drawing her sample. In the kind of code-based analysis we posit here, whether this is a problem depends on how systematic our interpretation aims to be. We may simply wish to document a body of opinion, or to examine the structure of argument respondents employ on a given topic. Analytic mileage can be extracted from this regardless of any skew (or in this case, ad-hocery) in sampling. Our student might identify several rhetorical strategies and a couple of narrative forms which apply across cases, so that the 'case' is not the consideration but the occurrence of a particular rhetorical form. These occurrences are the subject of a 'code', a label in the form of a word or short phrase which in some way captures the particular form and distinguishes it from others. Characteristics of the rhetorical form become the focus of her analysis. Extracting all the instances of rhetorical forms which have been given the same code allows the student to compare and contrast instances. Comparing instances uttered by female and male respondents would move the analysis back to a topic where sample design becomes important (e.g., were there equal numbers of males and females in the sample?), so this line of analysis may not have a sufficiently secure basis to succeed. Thus, the adequacy of the code-based analysis much depends on what analysis one wants to develop. The more the analysis is built around treating respondents as instances of a category, a classifiable type ('female', 'manager', 'corrupt detective'), the more the research design needs to adhere to basic sampling assumptions (even in work where generalization cannot be pursued because of constraints on representativeness).

Our student also neglected to ask the same questions of every respondent, and her later interviews focussed on a topic likely to dominate any interview in which it was raised, the official report on police corruption. But in unstructured (or 'non-standardized') interviews it is acceptable to adjust the interview guide to the specifics of the respondent's knowledge, comprehension, experience and interests. Provided restraint is shown in claiming generalizability, on similar grounds to those operating in respect of sample selection, the variation in questions can be countenanced. To take again the example of an analysis based on rhetorical form, it is likely that responses will display differences in rhetorical strategy, even where the topic has been developed at different lengths by different respondents. The analysis can evaluate or describe the way, for example, respondents use evidence to support their opinions, but cannot purport to survey opinion on the topic because sampling has not adhered to conventions for representing views of the population.

The code-based approach allows benefit to be gained from the inclusion with some respondents of questions relating to the report on police corruption; the student might consider the presence and nature of any discussion of corruption by 'pre-report' respondents as compared to respondents aware of the inquiry report. The theme will also allow the student to bring into her account the confession of planting evidence by one respondent. Such unexpected contingencies often happen in fieldwork and a code-based analysis can seek for connections between fieldwork contingencies and the themes developed in the analysis, whereas other approaches to analysis having a less post hoc character would merely regard the contingency as 'noise'. This characteristic also permits researchers to incorporate points developed independently of the data at hand; for instance, many practise what Becker (1985) tags the writing of 'modules', self-contained considerations of a topic which are 'stored up' ready for use when the occasion arises. The flexibility of code-based analysis allows such material to be incorporated because its scope is not bounded by a corpus containing a set number of words and no more, as with the lexical analysis of a document, and because its procedures are not predetermined by the manipulation of outcomes, as in the analysis of a set of cases.

ANALYTIC STRATEGIES

Previous generations of researchers have recognized the essential procedure of code-based analysis as 'cut and paste', and the basic tools as scissors, paper and multiple copies of transcripts, fieldnotes and/or documents. Researchers kept one set of the data as a complete record and literally cut up the copies so that all (or a subset of) the data on a given

theme could be put together. To get to this stage, data had to be segmented according to topic. Some do without the 'cut and paste' procedure by marking data with the index terms or numbers from an outline, the outline itself being marked with identifiers for each data extract (e.g., 'page 5, line 10'). The outline is then used to guide the writing up. These processes are usually iterative, with several revisions of the outline. Code assignments may also need to be revised; the code labels may change, and/or their assignment to a particular segment of the data. Either the thickness of the stack of paper relating to a given theme, or the extent of data references on the outline, indicates how well evidenced a given topic may be, and thus whether more fieldwork is needed or the topic should be dropped.

There is a further practice often associated with the work of Glaser and Strauss (1967) but which is useful more generally, that of writing 'analytic memos'. These are *aides mémoires* from the researcher to herself (or other team members in a group project). One frequent use is to guide code assignment by defining the code, another is to explain why a particular code has been assigned to a particular datum. Sometimes the researcher changes heart about a code and has to selectively or globally change the data to which it is assigned, a significant move which merits careful memoing. Other memos may be more expansive and less closely tied to the data; the process of reading and rereading field data often sparks new thinking. Memos are seldom polished or precise (except where a memo defines a code); they are the researcher's equivalent of that vital category 'miscellaneous', a collection of things one knows may be useful, when one's thinking becomes clearer. Some fieldworkers commend a special kind of memo, the fieldwork log or diary, in which researchers keep an account of their subjective experience of the fieldwork; this is where our student might have filed her note on the ethics of fieldwork. Memoing is not always a background activity; some memos are drawn into the foreground by being coded as data (e.g., to support methodological discussion of the fieldwork) or as the basis of a passage of the write-up.

These tools and procedures have long supported hermeneutic (interpretive) work. This does not mean they are uncontroversial. For example, the advent of computer support for qualitative research, and debates over the status of qualitative data, revealed disagreement over the very use of the term 'code', which to some bore unfortunate resonances of survey-type research (Dey, 1995). To them, the meaning of qualitative data was more complicated and unstable than the things which could be captured in a code; unlike 'age' or 'sex', qualitative data could mean more than one thing at once. Note that an orientation to multiple meanings cannot comfortably be accommodated by manual code-based procedures (it requires much duplication of data); as we shall see, it can straightforwardly be handled by using software. This is one respect in which new technologies affect research procedures, and we should not assume this is a mark only of the computer age. For example, hermeneutic analysis began with the interpretation of sacred texts by theologians, and the presentation of their arguments became more richly detailed with the introduction of printing technologies which enabled footnotes and marginalia to be typeset. Closer to our era, fieldwork was transformed by the invention of recording devices, especially the advent of the cassette recorder, a device which eventually became small enough to fuel ethical arguments over covert recording of research subjects in the field.

When we specify the tools for the job, then, we need to be alert to the effect that the 'tools' have on 'the job'. Unfortunately, because the innovation quickly becomes the essential commonplace, we tend to look past those things which transform our practice. Nowadays we only remark the indispensable nature of word-processing software when there is a power cut. But the word processor is not just an essential tool for writers, it is an important device in code-based analysis. The ability to create an electronic file structure without organizing and, worse, constantly reorganizing, a physical filing system is a major aid to the mundane but crucial business of data management. The conventional term, 'clerical data management', suggests a perception that such concerns are trivial. It is worth noting, then, that when qualitative data are held in a word processor they can be: sorted and re-sorted almost instantaneously; copied as required and revised as necessary; sent as files to the computers of other researchers and/or posted to websites; extracted and retrieved, i.e., cut and pasted, by using editing features and user-written 'macros' to create subsets and enable selective retrievals. To do this latter

procedure, which we refer to as 'embedding and retrieving', a code (or other typed symbol) has to be added to the data segment, which the software can then search for and 'retrieve'; a macro (a processing instruction) can be written to retrieve and write to a separate file the marked segments (see Fischer 1994: Chapter 4; Ryan, 1993a, 1993b).

While these applications of word processors emerged in the 1980s, more sophisticated developments were also taking place: the design of software intended from the outset to support qualitative data analysis, opening new possibilities for code-based analysis. Packages supported retrievals which allowed the user to find all of the data pertaining to a given code. A number of packages also let users retrieve data in which material to which one code has been applied also relates to material to which another code has been assigned, for example, all instances where there is talk about the relationship between 'gender' and 'social class'. Elaborately specified retrievals could be constructed – 'interview data about police corruption by female respondents with less than five years' service', for instance. Boolean search strategies gave users both greater control over the retrieval process, and the ability to handle larger data sets. None of these practices is impossible without a computer. But to attempt them manually may be so time-consuming as to place them outside the realistic scope of most researchers.

Of the kinds of qualitative software noted earlier, the types most suited to code-based analysis are the 'code-and-retrieve package' and the 'theory builder' (Weitzman and Miles, 1995). Code-based analysis dominated the thinking of the social scientists who worked with software developers designing the first generation of qualitative software. Nor should the 'code-and-retrieve' and 'theory-builder' distinction be seen as terribly important. Following the first generation, there has been a substantial convergence of features between the two types and most qualitative software now available will provide good support for code-based work and more conceptual work.

Concerns about being distanced from data has prompted some wariness about the use of 'code-and-retrieve' software. Coffey et al. (1996) point out that qualitative data analysis packages commonly incorporate facilities for coding and retrieving segments of text from fieldnotes or interview transcripts. For them, the injunction to code data implied by the software combined with 'methodological perspectives claimed to be associated with "grounded theory"' implicitly drives an 'orthodoxy that is being adopted in a large number of research sites around the world' (Coffey et al., 1996: §1.4). Using bibliometric methods Fielding and Lee (1998) have challenged this view, arguing that the influence of grounded theory on software-driven practice is far from hegemonic. They conclude that grounded theory is 'an important, but by no means ubiquitous, influence on studies where there is a strong likelihood that computer-based analysis has been used' (Fielding and Lee, 1998: 179).

Dey (1995, 1999) points out that a problem with code-and-retrieve procedures is that text segments bearing the same code bear an apparent conceptual relationship to one another. Once retrieved, however, each segment appears divorced from the context in which it originally appeared. Thus is compromised the ability to understand human action in an explicitly contextual way. One response to this concern is to explore a little further what might be meant by 'context'. The idea of context implies a notion of boundedness; if it did not the only context it would be possible to have for a segment of text from an interview transcript, say, would be the entire transcript. Presumably, however, analysts work in fact with a notion of *local* context, and it is this which determines where the boundaries of a given segment are located. Thus, in classical grounded theory open coding is based on an indicator-concept model (Glaser, 1978). Presumably, the boundaries of coded segments are determined in this case by how far the degree of fit between concept and indicator is compromised by extending the segment. In the kind of 'loose, inclusive coding' advocated by Becker and Geer (1960), segment boundaries are left deliberately wide, but subject to revision, presumably based on an understanding of context, as the analytic model is pieced together.

A further point to make here is that *different kinds of data* might imply different analytic strategies. Code-and-retrieve is a *synoptic* strategy. It might therefore be appropriately used in situations where it makes sense to compare and contrast *across* cases. Studies based primarily on interviewing are an obvious example. Code-and-retrieve might be less appropriate, however, where, as in participant observation, data are organized chronologically and one wishes to build up a multi-stranded analysis that is only partly thematic in character. Having said this, even within interview-based studies, concerns about fragmentation are clearly relevant whenever sequence is a consideration in data analysis. When something of interest is embedded within a narrative, refers back to something said or observed at an earlier juncture, or where one is interested in transitions from one topic to another, fragmentation *is* a problem. One solution to this problem might be in developing more complex coding approaches (Riessman, 1993). On the technical side, developers have experimented both with proximity searching (Drass, 1989), which allows the recovery of sequences of coded text, and the use of hyperlinking techniques (Dey, 1995), the non-linear and associative character of which readily permits the recovery of context.

CASE-BASED ANALYSIS

Within the early Chicago tradition in sociology, analytic induction was an important approach to the analysis of case materials referring to individual research subjects (usually belonging to deviant, unconventional or marginal groups). The development of causal theory is a relatively uncommon aim of contemporary qualitative research studies. Causal analysis came to be associated with quantitative research, where statistical methods can be seen as providing an approximation to experimental controls. Analytic induction is analogous to the use of the experimental method and aims to produce universal statements about social phenomena. Such statements seek to identify the essential features of a social phenomenon by identifying conditions always associated with that phenomenon. In other words, a universal statement asserts that the phenomenon only occurs in the presence of these conditions. If they are absent, it does not occur.

A good example of a universal statement is seen in the theory of opiate addiction developed by Lindesmith using analytic inductive methods. Briefly, Lindesmith argues that individuals become addicted when the following conditions are present: they (a) use an opiate; (b) experience distress due to withdrawal of the drug; (c) identify or recognize the symptoms of withdrawal distress; (d) recognize that these symptoms will be alleviated if they use the drug; and (e) take the drug and experience relief. The important point for the present discussion is that Lindesmith (1968: 4) is quite unequivocal about the universality of this theory:

> The theory that is developed is a general one; its applicability is not limited to American addicts, to lower-class users, to twentieth century addiction, to any restricted segment of the problem, to any specific historical period. Consequently, the focus of theoretical attention must be on those aspects of addiction which may reasonably be regarded as basic or essential in the sense that they are invariably manifested by all types of addicts regardless of place, time, method of use, social class, and other similar variable circumstances.

Because explanations produced by analytic induction aim to be complete and universal, negative cases are important (Manning, 1982). Such cases, when they occur, point to the need to modify the existing formulation of a supposedly universal statement. This means that analytic induction is a stepwise procedure. Cressey (1953), who studied instances where those placed in positions of financial trust violated that trust by embezzling funds, describes the steps involved in the method as follows:

1. Identify the phenomenon you want to explain.
2. Formulate a rough definition of that phenomenon.
3. Formulate a working hypothesis to explain the phenomenon.
4. Study one case.
5. Ask whether the facts of this case fit your initial hypothesis.
6. If the answer is 'yes', go on to study the next case. If the answer is 'no', *either* redefine the phenomenon to exclude the case, *or* reformulate your working hypothesis.
7. Continue step 6 until you have a 'universal solution', that is, until there is 'practical certainty' that the emerging theory has accounted for all of the cases which have been considered. However, the occurrence of any negative case must lead to either redefinition or reformulation.

Robinson (1951) commended analytic induction for formalizing and systematizing the process of generating a causal theory from an initial working hypothesis. He also saw as a strength the insistence implicit in the method that negative evidence should prompt redefinition of the phenomenon. In this way the analyst limits the scope of the theory or the range of situations to which it is applicable. However, in a robust and sustained critique, Robinson points to a logical difficulty with analytic induction. As already indicated, the analyst working by analytic induction looks at instances where the phenomenon of interest is present. The argument, it will be remembered, is that the phenomenon only occurs when particular conditions are present. It does not occur in their absence. Robinson points out, however, that this implies the need to look at cases where the phenomenon is *not* present. In this way, the analyst can be sure that there are no cases where the supposedly universal conditions under which the phenomenon occurs are actually in some cases associated with its absence.

Citing the examples of both Lindesmith and Cressey, Robinson points out that this is precisely what researchers who use analytic induction do *in practice*. Lindesmith systematically studied hospital patients who received drugs over a long period of time but who had not become addicted, and compared them with the addicts he had studied. Cressey did not study a sample of non-violators. He did, however, study the personal histories of his informants to see whether the conditions he had identified as producing trust violations had been present earlier in their lives in situations where they had not violated the financial trust placed in them. For Robinson, the difference between analytic induction *as described* and the method as used *in practice* undermines claims for analytic induction as a method of proof, as a means, that is, for isolating the essential conditions determining a phenomenon. 'The success of analytic induction in producing its complete explanations is due to its procedure, to its systematisation of the method of the working hypothesis, and not to its logical structure' (Robinson, 1951: 816).

Despite at least one spirited defence of the method (Manning, 1982), subsequent commentaries on analytic induction, while often sympathetic, have generally acknowledged the force of Robinson's criticisms (Denzin, 1970; Bloor, 1978; Hammersley and Atkinson, 1983; Hammersley, 1989). Compromised by its logical flaws, analytic induction also suffered from a wider shift of orientation in qualitative research, the movement away from procedures based on the analysis of cases and the increasing popularity of analytic approaches involving data directly captured from interviewing or field observation.

Qualitative comparative analysis (QCA) provides a simple, compact, if somewhat restricted, way of analysing patterns of causation in a small to moderate number of cases; the method is also known as qualitative configuration analysis (Huber and García, 1991). QCA looks at combinations of conditions and outcomes found across a given set of cases. An analytic method proposed by Ragin (1987), QCA is based on Boolean algebra, the algebra of sets and logic. QCA proceeds by means of 'Boolean minimization'. While this procedure can be carried out by hand, it rapidly becomes tedious for anything other than a small number of cases. Computer programs, such as QCA and AQUAD, are now available which implement the necessary procedures (Drass, 1992; Huber and García, 1991). The first step in the process is to produce a 'truth table'. This lists 'the various combinations of independent variables that appear in a data set along with their corresponding values [*sic*] on the dependent variable. Configurations appear only once in a truth table, regardless of their frequency of occurrence in the data' (Drass, 1992). A truth table having been constructed, the configurations within it are then simplified. (A full exposition of the principles involved is given in Ragin, 1987; see also Ragin, 1994: Chapter 5.)

Briefly, and non-technically, the computer systematically compares each configuration in the truth table with all the other configurations. The aim of this procedure is to simplify the truth table by removing configurations through combination. The rule for doing this is as follows (Ragin, 1994: 125):

> If two rows of a truth table differ on only one causal condition yet result in the same outcome, then the causal condition that distinguishes the two rows can be considered irrelevant and can be removed to create a simpler combination of causal conditions (a simpler term).

Using the procedure outlined above, one attempts to combine together as many rows of the truth table as possible. These can be simplified further in an additional process of minimization. This produces a Boolean expression which contains only the logically essential 'prime implicants'. By contrast, QCA seeks to recover the complexity of particular situations by recognizing the conjunctural and context-specific character of causation. Unlike much qualitative analysis, the method forces researchers to select cases and variables in a systematic manner. This reduces the likelihood that 'inconvenient' cases will be dropped from the analysis or data forced into inappropriate theoretical moulds.

QCA has been subjected to a number of criticisms. One problem is how to choose candidates for inclusion as input conditions (i.e., independent variables). A second problem relating to the selection of input conditions is how they are to be defined and measured. QCA requires dichotomous input variables. Latterly, Ragin (2000) has extended the method to work with fuzzy sets. If the original data sources are qualitative in character – interviews, documents and the like – what kinds of prior data reduction need to be carried out in order to select relevant input conditions? If source data are quantitative, how are ordinal- or interval-level data to be handled? Moreover, the method assumes that the way in which input variables are defined has no impact on the overall configuration of conditions and outputs produced by the analysis (Coverdill et al., 1994). QCA is also potentially at some disadvantage when judged against more conventional qualitative approaches. Firestone (1993) notes that the method does not easily handle process. Indeed, some may see this extremely formal approach as antithetical to the traditional virtues of qualitative research. Hicks (1994) suggests that QCA has affinities with what he calls 'neo-analytic induction'. In using this term, Hicks recasts Robinson's distinction between analytic induction *as described* and analytic induction *in practice* as a distinction between 'classical analytic induction' and 'neo-analytical induction'. Neo-analytical induction extends classical analytic induction in three ways. First, like analytic induction in practice, neo-analytic induction does not look simply at cases where the phenomenon to be described is present; cases having negative configurational outcome values as well as positive ones are examined. Second, rather than working with a succession of single cases, successive multiple-case comparisons are made. Finally, while neo-analytic induction aspires, like classical analytic induction, to universal solutions, it is willing to accept 'reasonable' theoretical closure some way short of that goal. Its aims are directed to the development of theory rather than theory-testing.

DISCOURSE ANALYSIS STRATEGIES

Discourse analysis, with roots variously in hermeneutics, structuralism, poststructuralism, and conversation analysis, is an increasingly important approach. Its focus is largely on 'found text', that is, discourse created for some other purpose than social research, although its techniques can be applied to field data too. Analysis involves the interpretation of cultural representations treated as text. As a relative newcomer, discourse analysis is less codified than earlier approaches such as grounded theory, but its orientation to the *construction* of written and spoken 'texts' means that hypertext tools developed to aid 'navigation' around textual corpora serve it well.

Hypertext allows information to be organized and linked in an associative non-linear way. Users can move rapidly and flexibly between information sources of various kinds and can organize and order text in multiple ways. In qualitative analysis, reading and writing are dialectically related since the assimilation and interpretation of field data are typically accomplished through the writing of an analytic commentary, usually in memo form (Weaver and Atkinson, 1994: 117). Using hypertext, these processes take place online, facilitating movement between data and the analytic commentary. Hypertext tools allow commentary to be added to data as that commentary is formulated but in a way that ensures that the original context is not lost. Data can easily be re-examined and existing interpretations modified as analysis proceeds. Unlike other strategies, the use of a hypertext approach does not depend on extensive prior familiarity with the data. Preliminary browsing of the data produces initial ideas and hypotheses, the identification and recording of which forms a basis for analytic development.

Weaver and Atkinson (1994) identify several difficulties researchers might encounter in using hypertext. Establishing hypertext links can be a time-consuming process. Second, a hypertext consists of many objects linked in complicated ways. Because of this, 'cognitive overheads are high' (Cordingley, 1991: 175). It might not always be easy to remember relevant analytic categories when linking data to memos. It can also be difficult to remember what links are available or might be relevant. Users can become side-tracked in the analytic process precisely because of the associative character of the links. In addition, only some kinds of information within a hypertext transfer easily to hard copy; it is hard to produce the trails between documents or the information in 'pop-up' windows in printed form (Weaver and Atkinson, 1994).

CRITERIA OF VALIDITY IN QUALITATIVE ANALYSIS

Criteria for assessing the validity of conclusions arising from qualitative analysis have always been contested. The intrinsic nature of lexical and case-based analysis offers a partial means to assess validity. Challenges to the validity of a lexical analysis can be addressed in part by reference to the original document. Provided researchers indicate the procedures used to manipulate the text, validity can be weighed. Due to its affinity to modelling and interest in causation, the validity of a case-based analysis can sometimes be resolved by assessing the value of predictions based on analysing the outcomes of cases. Resolving the validity of code-based analysis poses more serious difficulties. Perhaps the price of the approach's flexibility is lack of agreement over how such analyses should be validated. There are several contending positions. The most straightforward might be called 'quality of fieldwork'. This attempts to validate the adequacy of an analysis by reference to factors such as the extent of fieldwork, the rapport achieved with participants, the effort devoted to coding, the proportion of data accounted for by the most prominent analytic themes, and so on. At the extreme, there is recourse to what Hammersley and Atkinson (1983) call 'ethnographic authority', the assertion that because the researcher was there (in the field), unlike her critics, the researcher's interpretation should prevail. The trouble with this criterion is that the claim is non-reviewable, because even if critics have field experience of a similar setting, it will not literally be of exactly the same setting. This is surely the least satisfactory way to establish validity. The vital word is 'establish': a criterion of validity must make available to critics some oversight of the fieldwork and analytic procedures (in the same way that an experimental result must be capable of confirmation in other laboratories). The

The

components of the 'quality of fieldwork' criterion are an element in establishing validity but insufficient on their own. They also primarily validate fieldwork rather than analysis, although qualitative software can help here because it allows researchers to retrace the analytic process (e.g., through inspection of the coding schemes or program records of the composition of searches/retrievals).

An alternative to appeals to ethnographic authority can be called 'analytic-procedural adequacy'. This assumes that validity can be derived from adherence to a systematic analytic procedure. A prominent example is grounded theory (Glaser and Strauss, 1967). Full adherence to this approach may be less common than is claimed, but grounded theory does offer a series of widely accepted steps. If researchers document their conduct of each stage, the adequacy of their procedures can be evaluated and the analysis validated, assuming acceptance of the precepts of grounded theory. The procedures for 'micro-analysis' commended by Agar and Hobbs (1982) are another example. Developed primarily in application to interview data, this involves assigning one of a small number of semantic relations to adjacent segments of text, for example, statement B may be 'background' to statement A, or it may 'contrast' with statement A. The analyst can then identify where, for example, a statement would normally be expected to be followed by some 'background' as explanation; its absence suggests unreliable data and a poor basis for an interpretation.

Latterly postmodernism has contributed to the debate over validating qualitative research. One prominent postmodern approach recognizes validity in analyses which 'empower' research subjects, provoke political action and social change, and disrupt conventional understandings of social reality (Altheide and Johnson, 1994), although, unless they wish to encourage racists, criminals and other disliked groups, the approach presumably restricts research to those whom researchers feel should be 'empowered'. Postmodernism has often been criticized for declaring that, since knowledge is relative and subjective, validity is an inappropriate criterion of the quality of qualitative analysis (see the editorial essays in Denzin and Lincoln, 1994). What is often neglected in the debate between postmodernism and its critics is that both sides agree on the impossibility of absolute objectivity in the study of the social. But this need not mean we have no standards at all.

In the debate over validation, there is an increasing acceptance that what counts in establishing 'validity' is the operation of the research community itself. By the nature of our subject of study we are never going to achieve criteria of validity which convince everyone. But in the process of debate all schools of qualitative thought have made more explicit their conception of validity and deepened their understanding of other positions. As Seale (1999) argues, no one approach can satisfy every criticism that can be mounted on epistemological grounds; indeed, some are so intrinsic that they are inescapable by any approach. We need to stop feeling that we have to find a 'complete' philosophical justification before we can do useful research. We know that, to the extent that such judgments are possible, research is accepted as 'good' or 'valid' through the operation of the core conventions of the research community: publication and grant refereeing, debate in the literature and at conferences, citation by others, and, most importantly, an understanding (implicitly modest) of what qualitative research can rightly claim. For these things to operate researchers have to be explicit and open about what they have done in the field, in data management, coding, and analysis.

The matter is not purely one of philosophy but of tools as well. New technologies allow us better than before to capture and preserve the ambivalence of social meaning. We can use software features which display 'audit trails' of code construction, definition and application to reveal our thinking at key stages of the analytic process, making more of our work 'transparent' to oversight. We can use hypertext to organize our data in a way which avoids 'reducing' highly nuanced data to oversimplified codes. We can post our data and analyses to closed-access websites so team members and/or supervisors can co-work on the data, or to open-access websites to allow research subjects, sponsors and others to review and respond to our thinking. We can publish our research in electronic journals so that others can append their own commentaries or links to online work of their own. By these means we get closer than before to community criteria of validity truly sensitive to the qualities of qualitative research.

CONCLUSION

Developments in information technology have greatly expanded the support available for qualitative data analysis, and this will no doubt continue. Designing new tools always involves an effort to better understand the work which the tools are to support. Further, the potential of new tools and techniques takes time to establish. There is more than one way in which the tools available affect the work which is to be done. Technologies can be transformative, but not always in the ways that are expected. Changes in disciplinary practice come about not because of the simple availability of technical means, but because there is a well-informed community with the imagination to see how new technologies can be applied.

REFERENCES

Agar, M. and Hobbs, J. (1982) 'Interpreting discourse coherence and the analysis of ethnographic interviews', *Discourse Processes*, 5: 1–32.

Altheide, D. and Johnson, J. (1994) 'Criteria for assessing interpretive validity in qualitative research', in N. Denzin and Y. Lincoln (eds), *Handbook of Qualitative Research*. London: Sage.

Arber, S. (1993) 'The research process', in N.G. Gilbert (ed.), *Researching Social Life*. London: Sage.

Becker, H. (1985) *Writing for Social Scientists*. Chicago: University of Chicago Press.

Becker, H.S. (1998) *Tricks of the Trade: How to Think about Your Research While You're Doing It*. Chicago: Chicago University Press.

Becker, H.S. and Geer, B. (1957) 'Participant observation and interviewing: A comparison', *Human Organization*, 16(3): 28–32.

Becker, H.S. and Geer, B. (1958) 'Participant observation and interviewing: A rejoinder', *Human Organization*, 17(2): 39–40.

Becker, H.S. and Geer, B. (1960) 'Participant observation: The analysis of qualitative field data', in R.N. Adams and J.J. Preiss (eds), *Human Organization Research*. Homewood, IL: Dorsey Press.

Bloor, M.J. (1978) 'On the analysis of observational data: A discussion of the worth and uses of inductive techniques and respondent validation', *Sociology*, 12: 545–52.

Bryman, A. and Burgess, R.G. (1994) *Analyzing Qualitative Data*. London: Routledge.

Carley, K. (1988) 'Formalizing the social expert's knowledge', *Sociological Methods and Research*, 17: 165–232.

Coffey, A., Holbrook, B. and Atkinson, P. (1996) 'Qualitative data analysis: technologies and representations', *Sociological Research Online* 1. http://www.socresonline.org.uk/socresonline/1/1/4.html

Cordingley, E.B.S. (1991) 'The upside and downside of hypertext tools: The KANT example', in N.G. Fielding and R.M. Lee (eds), *Using Computers in Qualitative Research*. London: Sage.

Coverdill, J.E., Finlay, W. and Martin, J.K. (1994) 'Labor management in the Southern textile industry: Comparing qualitative, quantitative and qualitative comparative analysis', *Sociological Methods and Research*, 23(1): 54–85.

Cressey, D.R. (1953) *Other People's Money*. New York: Free Press.

Denzin, N. (1970) *The Research Act in Sociology: The Theoretical Introduction to Sociological Methods*. London: Butterworth.

Denzin, N. and Lincoln, Y. (1994) *Handbook of Qualitative Research*. Thousand Oaks, CA: Sage.

Dey, I. (1993) *Qualitative Data Analysis: A User-Friendly Guide for Social Scientists*. London: Routledge.

Dey, I. (1995) 'Reducing fragmentation in qualitative research', in U. Kelle (ed.), *Computer-Aided Qualitative Data Analysis: Theory, Methods and Practice*. London: Sage.

Dey, I. (1999) *Grounding Grounded Theory: Guidelines for Qualitative Inquiry*. San Diego, CA: Academic Press.

Drass, K. (1989) 'Text-analysis and text-analysis software: A comparison of assumptions', in G. Blank, J.L. McCartney and E. Brent (eds), *New Technology in Sociology: Practical Applications in Research and Work*. New Brunswick, NJ: Transaction.

Drass, K.A. (1992) *QCA3: Qualitative Comparative Analysis*. Evanston, IL: Center for Urban Affairs and Policy Research.

Fielding, N.G. and Lee, R.M. (1998) *Computer Analysis and Qualitative Research*. London: Sage.

Firestone, W.A. (1993) 'Alternative arguments for generalizing from data as applied to qualitative research', *Educational Researcher*, 22(4): 16–23.

Fischer, M.D. (1994) *Applications in Computing for Social Anthropologists*. London: Routledge.

Fischer, M. (1995) 'Desktop tools for the social scientist', in R.M. Lee (ed.), *Information Technology for the Social Scientist*. London: UCL Press.

Glaser, B. (1978) *Theoretical Sensitivity*. Mills Valley, CA: Sociology Press.

Glaser, B. and Strauss, A. (1967) *The Discovery of Grounded Theory*. Chicago: Aldine.

Hammersley, M. (1989) *The Dilemma of Qualitative Method: Herbert Blumer and the Chicago Tradition*. London: Routledge.

Hammersley, M. and Atkinson, P. (1983) *Ethnography: Principles in Practice*. London: Tavistock.

Hansen, A. (1995) 'Using information technology to analyze newspaper content', in R.M. Lee (ed.), *Information Technology for the Social Scientist*. London: UCL Press.

Hicks, A. (1994) 'Qualitative comparative analysis and analytical induction: The case for the emergence of the social security state', *Sociological Methods and Research*, 23(1): 86–113.

Holmes, F.L. (1992) 'Manometers, tissue slices, and intermediary metabolism', in A.E. Clarke and J.H. Fujimura (eds), *The Right Tools for the Job: At Work in the Twentieth-Century Life Sciences*. Princeton, NJ: Princeton University Press.

Holsti, O.R. (1969) *Content Analysis for the Social Sciences and Humanities*. Reading, MA: Addison-Wesley.

Huber, G.L. and García, C.M. (1991) 'Computer assistance for testing hypotheses about qualitative data: The software package AQUAD 3.0', *Qualitative Sociology*, 14: 325–48.

Huberman, A.M. and Miles, M.B. (1994) 'Data management and analysis methods', in N. Denzin and Y. Lincoln (eds), *Handbook of Qualitative Research*. Thousand Oaks, CA: Sage.

Jackson, J.E. (1990) '"I am a fieldnote": Fieldnotes as a symbol of professional identity', in R. Sanjek (ed.), *Fieldnotes: The Makings of Anthropology*. Ithaca, NY: Cornell University Press.

Krippendorf, K. (1980) *Content Analysis: An Introduction to its Methodology*. Beverly Hills, CA: Sage.

Kvale, S. (1996) *InterViews: An Introduction to Qualitative Research Interviewing*. Thousand Oaks, CA: Sage.

Lee, R.M. (1993) *Doing Research on Sensitive Topics*. London: Sage.

Lee, R.M. (1995) 'Introduction', in R.M. Lee (ed.), *Information Technology for the Social Scientist*. London: UCL Press.

Lee, R.M. and Fielding, N.G. (1991) 'Computing for qualitative research: Options, problems, potential', in N.G. Fielding and R.M. Lee (eds), *Using Computers in Qualitative Research*. London: Sage.

Levine, H.G. (1985) 'Principles of data storage and retrieval for use in qualitative evaluations', *Educational Evaluation and Policy Analysis*, 7(2): 169–86.

Lindesmith, A. (1968) *Addiction and Opiates*. Chicago: Aldine.

Lofland, J. and Lofland, L.H. (1984) *Analyzing Social Settings: A Guide to Qualitative Observation and Analysis* (2nd edition). Belmont, CA: Wadsworth.

Lofland, J. and Lofland, L.H. (1995) *Analyzing Social Settings: A Guide to Qualitative Observation and Analysis* (3rd edition). Belmont, CA: Wadsworth.

MacQueen, K.M. and Milstein, B. (1999) 'A systems approach to qualitative data management and analysis', *Field Methods*, 11(1): 27–39.

Manning, P.K. (1982) 'Analytic induction', in R.B. Smith and P.K. Manning (eds), *A Handbook of Social Science Methods, Volume 2: Qualitative Methods*. Cambridge, MA: Ballinger.

McCracken, G. (1988) *The Long Interview*. Newbury Park, CA: Sage.

Miles, M.B. (1983) 'Qualitative data as an attractive nuisance: the problem of analysis', in J. Van Maanen (ed.), *Qualitative Methodology*. Beverly Hills, CA: Sage.

Miles, M. and Huberman, A. (1984) *Qualitative Data Analysis: A Sourcebook of New Methods*. Beverly Hills, CA: Sage.

Miles, M.B. and Huberman, A.M. (1994) *Qualitative Data Analysis: An Expanded Sourcebook*. Thousand Oaks, CA: Sage.

Platt, J. (1996) *A History of Sociological Research Methods in America, 1920–1960*. Cambridge: Cambridge University Press.

Popping, R. (2000) *Computer-Aided Text Analysis*. London: Sage.

Ragin, C.C. (1987) *The Comparative Method: Moving Beyond Qualitative and Quantitative Strategies*. Berkeley: University of California Press.

Ragin, C.C. (1994) *Constructing Social Research*. Thousand Oaks, CA: Pine Forge Press.

Ragin, C.C. (2000) *Fuzzy-set Social Science*. Chicago: University of Chicago Press.

Riessman, C.K. (1993) *Narrative Analysis*. Newbury Park, CA: Sage.

Robinson, W.S. (1951) 'The logical structure of analytical induction', *American Sociological Review*, 16: 812–18.

Rubinstein, R.A. (1991) 'Managing ethnographic data with askSam', *Cultural Anthropology Methods*, 3(2): 4–8.

Ryan, G.W. (1993a) 'Using styles in WordPerfect as a template for your fieldnotes', *Cultural Anthropology Methods*, 5(3): 8–9.

Ryan, G.W. (1993b) 'Using WordPerfect macros to handle fieldnotes', *Cultural Anthropology Methods*, 5(1): 10–11.

Schwandt, T.A. and Halpern, E.S. (1988) *Linking Auditing and Metaevaluation: Enhancing Quality in Applied Research*. Newbury Park, CA: Sage.

Seale, C. (1999) *The Quality of Qualitative Research*. London: Sage.

Strauss, A.L. (1987) *Qualitative Analysis for Social Scientists*. Cambridge: Cambridge University Press.

Strauss, A.L. and Corbin, J. (1990) *Basics of Qualitative Research: Grounded Theory Procedures and Techniques*. Newbury Park, CA: Sage.

Trow, M. (1957) 'Comment on "Participant observation and interviewing: a comparison"', *Human Organization*, 16(3): 33–5.

Weaver, A. and Atkinson, P. (1994) *Microcomputing and Qualitative Data Analysis*. Aldershot: Avebury.

Weber, R.P. (1985). *Basic Content Analysis*. Beverly Hills, CA: Sage.

Weitzman, E.A. and Miles, M.B. (1995) *Computer Programs for Qualitative Data Analysis*. Thousand Oaks, CA: Sage.

Wellman, B. (1990) 'Integrating textual and statistical methods in the social sciences', *Cultural Anthropology Methods*, 2: 1–5.

Werner, O. (1989) Short takes: Keeping track of your interviews II. *CAM Newsletter*, 1: 8.

24

Content Analysis

ROBERTO P. FRANZOSI

Wallace E. Lambert was a social psychologist at McGill University who did a great deal of work on language – enough to warrant a conference in his honor upon his retirement from McGill (Reynolds and Lambert, 1991). In one of his early papers, Lambert toyed with the methodology of content analysis. Approaching content analysis from the perspective of a social psychologist, Lambert thought well of adopting Pareto's complex theory of motives to interpret the linguistic representations of the *same* event by *different* newspapers, in particular, newspapers of different ideological persuasion. The event is the trial of Madame Paule Schlumpf, the wife of a very wealthy Swiss citizen who was living in Alsace during the Nazi occupation and who was suspected of having been a Nazi-party member. Madame Schlumpf, in 1946, had murdered her lover, Mr Raoul Simha, 'an Oriental, possibly a Jew'. Here are two of the accounts studied by Lambert. The first is from *L'Humanité*:

> The second session of the trial of the depraved Mme Schlumpf was, if possible, still more fashionable than the preceding one. Even more jewels, more feathers, and more fur coats were on display than the day before, to the point that at one o'clock, newsmen could hardly get through the crowd of fashionable females palpitating with anticipation while they munched little cakes ... The accused forgets, this time, to hide her tearless eyes behind a handkerchief. She displays her true face, cold, calculating and ill-tempered. There is a great silence when her husband enters, the billionaire *col-laborateur* whose complaisance makes him virtually an accessory to the crime. Quite self-possessed, this

singular Helvetian blushes a little when Attorney General Turland refers to his conduct – worthy of a Teuton – during the Occupation, and shows him the oath of allegiance to Hitler he signed in 1944. By what maneuvers was this traitor able to have the damning evidence against him quashed? Nobody has the curiosity to ask him. But one witness, Mr. Diffort, who upon the orders of the resistance had simply kept a record of Mr. Schl.'s actions, was discharged from his factory job and threatened. For 16 months, he was unemployed. Think, he had had the courage to tell of the Nazi galas and receptions for S.S. colonels given by the husband of the criminal ... A witness casts a clear light upon the nature of the accused: 'If you quit me, I'll turn you over to the Gestapo,' Paule said to her lover in 1940 ... And this is what Simha told a friend: 'Look, here's a pistol I took from her yesterday. She gets new ones all the time.' Fifteen minutes after midnight, Judge Loser reads the sentence: 'eight years in prison,' which the murderer greets with faked sobs for the benefit of her 'chic' girl friends. All the same, eight years for a murder is getting away with murder!

The second is from *L'Aurore:*

> There is, incontestably, love involved in this affair that Attorney General Turland, with all his skill, wishes to present as a drama of sordid selfishness. It remains certain that a great tourney of the flesh impelled Paule Schlumpf and her victim, Raoul Simha, to fight, to insult each other, to separate, to reconcile. For me, what pleaded for the woman condemned yesterday was not her declarations, her tears, but the testimony of her husband. I know nothing of what this Swiss citizen, living in a provisionally annexed Alsace, may have done, considered from a French national point of view. What I remain sure of, per contra, is that from a human point of

view, I will always remember him as a gentleman, for the literally unheard-of way he defended his cruel and unfaithful wife. I take my hat off to him for having launched these words at his detractors in open court: 'One does not put a *Parisienne* in a cage, even a golden cage. To love a woman does not mean to try to keep her to oneself alone.'

The brilliant orator of the state prosecution flung himself with dialectal felicity upon this neutral industrialist and, if I understood him correctly, even insinuated that he had shot the unfortunate Simha in the back of the neck, and even implied that it was doubtless because the victim knew too much about the suicide of a former mistress of the gentleman whom I so admire that the Oriental (Simha was a Jew) met his death. He did not persuade me.

Should one set down exactly what one thinks? I almost regret now to have written the qualification that I just attached to the name of the victim in this story. A voyage in the heart of a long, amorous adventure, that is what I should have liked to entitle my impressions of this enthralling trial whose slightest developments were followed yesterday by so many pretty women.

Maître Charpentier of the prosecution was astonishing, in moderation and logic. He told us that the heroine of this drama had had a weakness for the green-uniformed invaders. That, of course, is deplorable. The defence, later, swore to the contrary. But that has only a distant relation to the case.

One word now about the jurors. I sat next to them. I observed them with passionate attention. They are probably decent people, but incapable 'socially,' intellectually, of weighing all the factors in the problem submitted to them. There is, then, something limping, imperfect, in the present organization of our criminal courts ... Is it my fault if the procession of prosecution witnesses left me cold? I wasn't even moved much by the star witnesses for the defence. And nevertheless, Maître Floriot, the defence attorney, was always there to shove with his index finger – a marvelous sharpshooter who defends his clients by attacking when the opportunity offers. His pleading seemed to me to give off sparks. We saw him, turn by turn, comical, logical, sensitive – serious, too – and always relaxed. I find no words to express the satisfaction, the joy, that he produces when he really lets himself go. You say to yourself, 'It is a pleasure, all the same, to know there exist in our country men so brilliant, so blessed by the gods.' Paule Schlumpf was lucky that he consented to take her case on August 8, 1946.

CONTENT ANALYSIS

Lambert's (1972: 49) declared ambition is 'to develop and illustrate a new method of content analysis by making use of Pareto's residue-derivation scheme'. But what is content analysis? Early definitions are clear enough (e.g., Shapiro and Markoff, 1997):

> The technique known as content analysis ... attempts to characterize the meanings in a given body of discourse in a systematic and quantitative fashion. (Kaplan, 1943: 230)

> Content analysis is a research technique for the objective, systematic, and quantitative description of the manifest content of communication. (Berelson, 1952: 18)

> 'Content analysis' ... refer[s] to the objective, systematic, and quantitative description of any symbolic behavior. (Cartwright, 1953: 424)

One thing seems clear: content analysis was born as a tool of quantitative analysis. But why be surprised? After all, it was Harold D. Lasswell who played a crucial role in the development of the technique. Madge (1953) tells us how Lasswell took one of the first steps in the direction of standardization, systematization, and quantification of meaning as early as 1937 in his work on psychoanalytical interviews.[1] The very label 'content analysis', according to Kaplan (1943), originated among the researchers involved in the Experimental Division for the Study of War Time Communications[2] directed by Lasswell from 1941 to 1945. For sure, the first printed use of that label is found in the title of one of Lasswell's own documents (Lasswell, 1941). And it was Lasswell who in 1949 wrote a famous article titled 'Why be quantitative?'. In that paper, Lasswell forcefully argued the case for a quantitative approach in the study of politics. The call to arms came after a careful investigation of several major qualitative works, all plagued, according to Lasswell, by imprecision in the definitions and concepts adopted and arbitrariness in the selection of the material reported. Lasswell (1949: 52) concluded: 'Why, then, be quantitative about communication? Because of the scientific and policy gains that can come of it.'

The 'archaeology of knowledge', advocated by Foucault as the best method for digging up lost traces of struggles over meaning and definitions, reveals unequivocally that content analysis was born as a quantitative technique under the aegis of science. Later definitions abandoned the strict requirement of quantification, shifting the emphasis to 'inference', 'objectivity', and 'systematization'. In one of the early textbooks, Holsti (1969: 14) specifically wrote: 'Content analysis is any technique for making inferences by objectively and systematically identifying specified characteristics of messages. ... Our definition does not include any reference to quantification'. Stone, the developer of *The General Inquirer*, one of the early attempts at computer understanding of natural languages, similarly wrote: 'Content analysis is any research technique for making inferences by systematically and objectively identifying specified characteristics within text' (in Stone et al., 1966: 5). And Krippendorf's classic textbook, *Content Analysis: An Introduction to Its Methodology*, defines content analysis as 'a research technique for making replicable and valid inferences from data to their context' (Krippendorf, 1980: 21). As Shapiro and Markoff (1997) point out,

the designation of any work as content analysis as distinguished from the ordinary reading of text makes an implicit claim that the researcher is participating in a scientific enterprise. Such a claim must be based on something on the order of systematic or methodical procedures ... [with] rules (as opposed to some feelings or intuitions) ... [and a] standard set of coding decisions.

But, of course, scientific enterprises and inference are loaded terms. We do not talk about linguistic inference but statistical inference. And that is quantitative.

Whether the emphasis is on quantification or simply on such characteristics as inference, objectivity, or systematization agreement is strong enough on the general features of content analysis as a research technique. But what about specifics? Agreement, here, vanishes. Unlike, say, regression analysis in statistics, content analysis does not refer to a unique tool of analysis, but rather to a wide range of tools and approaches unified, perhaps, by that common goal of quantification, standardization, and systematization – in other words, of doing science. That is why, perhaps, Lambert (1972: 49) can claim 'to develop and illustrate a new method of content analysis by making use of Pareto's residue-derivation scheme'. A new method indeed – one of many. Krippendorf (1980: 60–3) provides a list of these possible methods: from the word counts of the most elementary syntactical analysis, to referential analysis, prepositional analysis, and thematic analysis.

VARIETIES OF CONTENT ANALYSIS

Even the most elementary form of syntactical analysis – word count (or a count of words in context) – can provide valuable information about a text (Weber, 1990: 44–52). The word 'I', for instance, appears 13 times in the article by *L'Aurore* (and not at all in *L'Humanité*, other than in quoted matter). This emphasis on the 'I' – this index of individuality, indeed, a celebration of the individual – is not accidental. It is consistent with other characteristics of the *L'Aurore* article. Together, these characteristics reinforce one another cumulatively, offering precious markers of the ideological orientation of the two newspapers: the 'I', the individual versus the masses. 'Unhappy the land that has no heroes!' screams Andrea, Galileo's pupil, in Brecht's play *Life of Galileo*. 'No. Unhappy the land that needs a hero' replies Galileo. Heroes or not heroes? Supermen or ordinary people? 'It is a pleasure', concludes the journalist of *L'Aurore* in talking about the defense attorney, 'to know there exist in our country men so brilliant, so blessed by the gods.' One concluding sentence brilliantly fuses this Nietzschean celebration of the individual *and* the country, the superman-god. Paule Schlumpf fades away into the background, just a 'lucky' woman, lucky to have met one such man, closer to the gods than to the rest of humanity (in fact, two such men – her husband and her defense attorney – how lucky can one get?). *L'Humanité*'s own heroes with ordinary factory jobs (or unemployed as they may be), who follow rather than lead, taking orders from others (and the Resistance at that!) have no place in this world of supermen. *L'Humanité*'s heroes – Mr. Diffort – have no name and no place in history as written by *L'Aurore*.

Yet, as revealing as simple word counts can be of underlying meaning structures, syntax can have far more profound effects on meaning. Consider the sentence 'Police shot dead Africans' (see Trew, 1979a). The sentence foregrounds responsibility: syntactic subject and semantic agent of the sentence coincide (police). Now, consider the same sentence in passive form: 'Africans were shot dead by the police.' In this sentence, agency is backgrounded. And while agency cannot be omitted in active sentences, because the agent is also the subject of the sentence,[3] in passive sentences it syntactically *can* (e.g., 'Africans were shot dead'). In analyzing newspaper articles, Trew shows that the process of linguistic change through deletions and rewordings is part and parcel of the process of ideological production of news. These linguistic processes point to the subtle ways in which preferred readings can be imparted on information through the same basic material (see also Kress and Hodge, 1979; van Dijk, 1983). Social science writing similarly underscores its 'noble dream' of objectivity through passive sentence construction. Typical sentences as 'In this essay it will be shown' take the emphasis away from the 'I', from the personal and the subjective ('In this essay I will show') (see Franzosi, 2004: Chapter 5, for an analysis of this example).

Content analysts, of course, do not typically pay such close attention to the subtleties of language. After all, quantity is the name of the game, rather than quality. Analysts rely on computers or on undergraduate students – hardly experts in linguistics – as instruments for the systematic extraction of a specific set of characteristics from a set of texts. Rather, in content analysis each characteristic of interest is typically formalized as a 'coding category'. The set of all coding categories to be applied to a set of texts is known as a 'coding scheme'. The scheme is then systematically applied to all selected texts of interest for the purpose of extracting uniform and standardized information: if a text contains information on any of the coding categories of the coding scheme, the relevant coding category is 'ticked off' (a process known as 'coding' in content analysis).

One of the most common approaches to content analysis is *thematic analysis*, where the coding scheme is based on categories designed to capture the dominant themes present in a text. And which themes could we look for in the newspaper articles reproduced above and other similar articles? There is of course no single answer to that question. Different investigators could be looking for different things. We could be interested in temporal changes in standards of morality or in media portrayal of the judicial system, or of female criminals, or of class or nation. We would ask our coding scheme to provide empirical evidence on these broad research issues. Our coding scheme design would have to reflect that imperative.

Indeed, it is coding scheme design that reveals both the richness and the fundamental limitation of the technique. Paradoxically, the limitation of the technique lies in the very richness in the variety of coding scheme designs. There is no single way of capturing the meaning of a text (or of all types of texts). Content analysis resorts to designing different coding schemes for different research questions applied to different types of text. Despite decades of efforts (starting with Lasswell) to standardize and systematize the variety of issues and themes found in different text genres and different texts, content analysis has failed, by and large, to reduce the bewildering variety of language texts to simple invariant structures. It has failed, in other words, in its 'noble dream' of achieving scientific status.

But in the name of exegesis, let us focus on morality as the topic of our investigation: we may wish to code the specific *type of violation* of the moral order (e.g., adultery, murder), the *type of justification* provided (e.g., love), the *punishment demanded and/or given* (8 years in prison). The coding scheme (our measurement instrument) would have to be sensitive enough to pick up the moral outrage expressed by *L'Humanité*: not only is murder or adultery morally wrong, but so is dismissing a factory worker from his job simply because he is carrying out his patriotic duties. And maneuvering 'to have … damning evidence … quashed' in a court of law is morally wrong; 'sign[ing] the oath of allegiance to Hitler' and throwing galas and receptions for a war enemy – the SS colonels – is morally wrong; threatening a lover is morally wrong ('If you quit me, I'll turn you over to the Gestapo'); getting 'eight years [in prison] for a murder is getting away with murder!' and is morally wrong.

Contrary to *L'Humanité*, *L'Aurore* places very little emphasis on issues of morality. If anything, *L'Aurore* provides justifications for violations of accepted standards of morality (at least by some individuals). Is Ms Schlumpf an adulterer? Yes, no doubt (even for *L'Aurore*). But rather than 'a drama of sordid selfishness' there is 'love' behind this story and 'a great tourney of the flesh'. So much so that the journalist of *L'Aurore* acknowledges that he should have entitled his article: 'a voyage in the heart of a long, amorous adventure'. And in the name of love one *must* justify even the most hideous of crimes, particularly in France. One of the most compelling French love stories, that of Abelard and Eloise, as told by Abelard himself in his moving *Stories of Abelard's Adversities*, started with the seduction of a young girl by her tutor/monk. In any case, who are we to judge when even the woman's husband recognizes that you simply cannot 'put a *Parisienne* in a cage, even a golden cage.

To love a woman does not mean to try to keep her to oneself alone'? Did Ms Schlumpf have a weakness for the green-uniformed invaders? Yes, perhaps; and 'that, of course, is deplorable'. *But* 'that has only a distant relation to the case'. Furthermore, we have the prosecution's word against the defense's. After all, 'the defense ... swore to the contrary'. And what about Mr Schlumpf? Is he a *collaborateur*, a collaborator with the German enemy? First, we don't know: 'I know nothing of what [he] ... may have done', writes the journalist. Second, even if this were true, it is so strictly from 'a French national point of view'. And this 'gentleman' (in the journalist's words) is a 'Swiss citizen, living in a provisionally annexed Alsace'. Would Mr Schlumpf still be considered a collaborator from a non-French point of view? And there is the 'human point of view', and from that perspective Mr Schlumpf certainly deserves the journalist's admiration ('I take my hat off to him'; 'the gentleman whom I so admire') for 'the literally unheard-of way he defended his cruel and unfaithful wife'. No – Mr Schlumpf is definitely not a collaborator, but a 'neutral industrialist'.

There is no room in *L'Aurore*'s article for *L'Humanité*'s world of moral certainties – certainties that should apply only to ordinary people. The journalist of *L'Aurore* skillfully weaves the relativism of different points of view into the narrative, providing a curious mixture of certainties and uncertainties ('For me', 'I know nothing', 'What I remain sure of', 'Is it my fault', 'it remains certain', 'seemed to me'). The journalist sows a seed of reasonable doubt in the reader's mind – doubt reinforced by the final attack against the judicial system as a whole. 'There is something limping, imperfect, in the present organization of our criminal courts'. Why? Because the jurors, although 'probably decent people' – but only 'probably' – are 'incapable "socially", intellectually, of weighing all the factors in the problem submitted to them'.

REFERENTIAL CONTENT ANALYSIS

Once more these games with words push us back to language and its relation to meaning. One way to express different meanings is no doubt to simply focus on different things, on different aspects of the same social reality, that same trial described in terms of different social actors, actions, and issues. Thematic content analysis is well equipped to deal with the themes expressed in a text. But meaning is also the result of other kinds of language games, of different ways of describing the same thing. Referential content analysis, in this sense, may be better suited than thematic analysis to capturing the complexity of language in the production of meaning. Referential analysis, Krippendorf (1980: 62) tells us, is used when 'the task is to ascertain how an existing phenomenon is portrayed'. And the way *L'Humanité* and *L'Aurore* portray the same events and people could not be more strikingly different. *L'Humanité* refers to Mme Schlumpf as 'depraved', 'the accused', 'the criminal', 'the murderer', 'Paule', as having 'tearless eyes', a 'true face, cold, calculating and ill-tempered'. Her actions are not exactly noble: 'greets with faked sobs', 'forgets, this time, to hide her tearless eyes behind a handkerchief', 'If you quit me, I'll turn you over to the Gestapo', 'here's a pistol I took from her yesterday. She gets new ones all the time.' Compared to this wealth of negative references, *L'Aurore*'s portrayal of Paule Schlumpf is both less central and less negative: 'the heroine of this drama', 'the woman condemned yesterday', the 'cruel and unfaithful wife' (but cruel, not because she killed a man – a fact never explicitly acknowledged by the journalist – but because she was unfaithful to a gentleman the journalist so admires).

L'Humanité's references to Mr Schlumpf are also negative – 'billionaire', '*collaborateur*', 'complaisant', 'accessory to the crime', 'singular Helvetian', 'traitor', 'worthy of a Teuton' – and his actions, again, are far from noble: he 'maneuvers ... to have the damning evidence against him quashed', he 'signs the oath of allegiance to Hitler'. In sharp contrast to this, for *L'Aurore*, Mr Schlumpf is an 'industrialist' (the focus here is on someone who creates jobs and wealth rather than dismisses workers); he is a 'Swiss citizen', 'neutral' (by definition, not a *collaborateur*) who happens to be 'living in a provisionally annexed Alsace' (thus clearly not French and to whom French standards should perhaps not apply). He nobly and unselfishly 'defended ... his wife' even when she had been so 'cruel and unfaithful' to him.

Both papers are not kind to women, albeit perhaps for different reasons. In the masculine world of supermen embraced by *L'Aurore*, women are mostly a matter of décor: there are 'many' of them and they are 'pretty'. In the class world of rich and poor of *L'Humanité*, the upper-class women present at the trial are described as 'a crowd', 'females', 'fashionable', 'palpitating with anticipation', '"chic" girl friends', as 'munching little cakes'. This frenzy of palpitating females – like so many maggots in a fisherman's box – contributes to a negative class-loaded view of the trial, on its second day with 'even more jewels, more feathers, and more fur coats … on display than the day before'.

No doubt, referential analysis goes a long way in bringing to the fore the ideological biases of the two newspapers. There is a great deal of evidence in the media literature of these biasing practices. The media typically label left-wing groups as 'terrorists' (rather than 'freedom fighters' or, in more recent times, 'martyrs'). Their actions are labeled as 'disruptive' and 'violent' (Hartley, 1982: 63–74). The reasons for their existence, the ideas for which they stand (their manifesto) are never made clear. There is an overall negative connotation in the media description of these groups (Murdock, 1973). Yet, the different references only begin to tell the story of ideological bias. Bias in media representation (in any type of representation, in fact) is also constructed through the differential weight that different events, actions, people, and circumstances get in the overall text. Bias operates like a spotlight: some things come under a flood of light, some things are left in darkness. But in Brecht's words, 'things left in the darkness will soon be forgotten'.

Light and shadow, background and foreground, silence and emphasis: these are the main mechanisms of ideological bias. Again, the two articles are quite different in what and whom they focus on. *L'Humanité* focuses on the murder, on class, on the war between France and Germany. *L'Aurore* never even mentions the word 'murder'. The only reference comes in the sentence 'the Oriental (Simha was a Jew) met his death'. Given the right-wing ideological position of the newspaper, the qualification that 'Simha was a Jew' serves to discount the gravity of Mme Schlumpf's action. 'Should one set down exactly what one thinks?' asks *L'Aurore*'s journalist, 'I almost regret now to have written the qualification that I just attached to the name of the victim in this story.' Regret or not, what the journalist thinks of Simha, the 'Jew', is clear enough, without setting it 'down exactly'. Second, Mme Schlumpf has

nothing to do with this. There is no agency on her part. The only agent is Simha. He simply 'met his death'. Most unfortunate.

One actor plays a central role in *L'Humanité*'s story – an actor with no role in *L'Aurore*'s drama: Mr Diffort, one of the witnesses. *L'Humanité* dedicates to him as many lines of text as to Mme Schlumpf or her husband. There are no adjectives in the text to characterize Mr Diffort. But his actions and the actions of others towards him clearly describe him as a brave man (he 'had the courage to tell'), a patriotic man (he works for the Resistance; he tells of the Nazi galas and receptions; compare his character to that of the traitor Mr Schlumpf!), and a victim (who endures unemployment 'for 16 months', after being unjustly 'discharged from his factory job' and 'threatened'). Mr Diffort's character is introduced by the newspaper in sharp contrast to all other characters, as highlighted by the use of 'but' in the sentence: 'Nobody has the curiosity to ask him. *But* one witness' (emphasis added).

Contrary to *L'Humanité*'s emphasis upon Mme Schlumpf, her husband, and Mr Diffort, *L'Aurore*'s attention is focused on Mme Schlumpf's husband, on the defense attorney, Maître Floriot, and, to highlight the contrast, on the jurors. The defense attorney is described 'a marvelous sharpshooter', 'comical', 'logical', 'sensitive', 'serious, too', 'always relaxed', 'brilliant', 'blessed by the gods'. This is a man who does not miss a thing: 'he is always there to shove with his index finger', 'defends his clients by attacking when the opportunity offers', he 'give[s] off sparks', he gives 'satisfaction', 'joy', 'pleasure'. By contrast, and to stress this world of supermen and heroes, the jurors are described as inferior beings: 'incapable "socially", intellectually'; the only compliment the journalist pays to them ('decent people') is attenuated by the qualifier 'probably'.

Both papers seem to agree on one thing: they both ignore the victim, Mr Simha. His name comes up only in the final lines of *L'Humanité*'s article. *L'Aurore* is hardly more generous, although it does provide the full name, Raoul Simha, right at the beginning of the article. It also tells us that he was an 'Oriental (Simha was a Jew)'. Whose lives count? Right or Left, clearly not the life of a Jew in 1946 France. For both papers, Mr Simha's death – the entire legal case of Mr Simha vs. Mme Schlumpf – is just a pretext for more important dichotomies: lower-class vs. upper class, France vs. Germany, supermen vs. ordinary men (and, perhaps, men vs. women).

This dichotomous view of the world is typical of the organization of news. It characterizes both the narrative of individual newspaper stories (Russians vs. British, Tories vs. Labour, Mr Foot vs. Mr Rodgers within the Labour Party, etc.) and even the overall layout of specific pages (peace, stability, freedom, welfare stories, associated with 'us', on one side of a page and war, violence, racism, poverty, associated with 'them', on the opposite side) (Laclau, 1980; Trew, 1979a, 1979b; Hartley and Montgomery, 1985). The oppositional framework of news, regardless of the topic treated, provides a supratextual unity among newspaper articles and a master key to the reading of *any* article (Hartley, 1982: 116; Trew, 1979a, 1979b).

'FRAMING' MEANING

Absorbed in its drive to quantify and to deal with large volumes of data, content analysis has typically had little taste and patience for the subtleties of language. But the emphasis of referential content analysis on the way actors, actions, and events are portrayed (or referred to) in a text gets content analysis closer to qualitative forms of textual analysis more attentive to language and more prominent in current sociology: from frame analysis to discourse analysis and narrative analysis (e.g., Snow et al., 1986; Fairclough, 1995; Franzosi, 1998a). Narratively, our two articles tell a similar story of the murder trial of a Parisian upper-class woman in World War II France. But the two articles differ in terms of the number of purely narrative sentences (i.e., sentences characterized by actors doing something for or against other actors): nearly all the sentences in *L'Humanité*'s article are characterized by a narrative structure, while *L'Aurore*'s article contains several descriptive and evaluative sentences. The language of *L'Humanité*'s article is more metonymic (i.e., concrete), with its many references to objects (e.g., furs, pistols); *L'Aurore*'s article is more metaphorical (in such images as an attorney as a sharpshooter, pleading that gives off sparks, a love affair described as a tourney of the flesh). Finally, they tell their basic story using different ideological frames: the injustice of a class society (for *L'Humanité*) and the superiority of

the elite and of the white race (for *L'Aurore*) (and perhaps the inferiority of women, for both papers). Indeed, class, race, gender, and nation are the main framing devices.

Both papers appeal to their audiences on the basis of an emotional, rather than logical-rational, rhetorical discourse. The frames these articles use are largely uncritically shared with their audiences; they are preset as part of wider ideological discourses (e.g., the elitism of the Right, the struggle for equality of the Left, the subtle anti-women tones shared by both Left and Right in the context of a fundamentally patriarchal society). Interestingly, it is the Left-wing *L'Humanité* that frames its overall discourse in patriotic terms. We typically associate the Right with patriotism, yet the *L'Humanité* article abounds with references to such collective actors as the Resistance, the SS colonels, and the Gestapo, and to such events as the occupation, the oath of allegiance to Hitler, the Nazi galas and receptions, the adjectival reference to Mr Schlumpf as a 'Teuton'. By contrast, from *L'Aurore* you would hardly know that the crime occurred in a Nazi-occupied France.

On the one hand, the journalist of the right-wing *L'Aurore* has to perform a balancing act to deal with the role the Right played in France during the war (with the authoritarian and collaborationist Vichy government that imprisoned tens of thousands of political dissidents and sent to Germany hundreds of thousands of Jews and French workers). The best way to deal with this unsettling past, no doubt, is silence, mixed with a bit of doubt. On the other hand, the journalist of *L'Humanité* is playing a tune that was to become familiar in decades to come in both France and Italy: the role played during the war by the Communists against the Nazi invaders. The Left appropriated the Resistance as a mechanism of legitimation.

'STORY GRAMMARS' AND THE STRUCTURE OF NARRATIVE

The emphasis of referential content analysis on social actors, their actions, and the social relations in which they are involved brings us closer to yet other recent developments in the analysis of narrative text. Markoff et al. (1975) regretted that content analysis had made little use of advances in the field of linguistics. Following up on their plea, Franzosi (1989, 1994, 2004) has argued that narrative texts (indeed, the kind of text encountered in the two newspaper articles analyzed here, where someone does something for or against someone else) are characterized by an invariant linguistic structure known as 'story grammar', 'semantic grammar' or 'text grammar' (to distinguish it from syntax grammar). A story grammar is nothing but the simple structure subject–action–object (or, better, agent–action–patient/beneficiary) and their modifiers (e.g., type and number of subjects and objects; time and space, reasons and outcomes of actions). This structure can be rigorously formalized as follows:

⟨event⟩	→	{⟨event type⟩} {⟨semantic triplet⟩}
⟨event type⟩	→	trial
⟨semantic triplet⟩	→	{⟨subject⟩} {⟨action⟩} [{⟨object⟩}]
⟨subject⟩	→	{⟨actor⟩} [{⟨actor modifiers⟩}]
⟨actor⟩	→	the accused, the husband, the victim, the defense lawyer, the jurors, …
⟨actor modifiers⟩	→	{⟨type of actor⟩} {⟨number of actors⟩} {⟨organization to which actor belongs⟩} …
⟨action⟩	→	{⟨action phrase⟩} [{⟨action modifiers⟩}]
⟨action phrase⟩	→	kill, fight, insult, love, testify, …
⟨action modifiers⟩	→	{⟨time⟩} {⟨space⟩} {⟨type of action⟩} {⟨reason⟩} {⟨outcome⟩} …
⟨object⟩	→	{⟨actor⟩} {⟨inanimate object⟩} {⟨implicit targets⟩} {⟨infinitive clauses⟩}
⟨inanimate object⟩	→	jewels, feathers, pistol, …
⟨implicit target⟩	→	⟨actor⟩
⟨infinitive clauses⟩	→	⟨semantic triplet⟩

where the symbol → refers to a rewrite rule (or production), that is, it 'rewrites' the element to its left in terms of the element(s) to its right; the symbol ⟨ ⟩ indicates that the element enclosed within it is a non-terminal entity, that is, it can be further rewritten in terms of other elements; terminal entities that cannot be further rewritten appear in the grammar without the angle brackets; the symbol { } indicates that the element enclosed within it can be repeated several times; the symbol [ ] indicates that the element enclosed within it is optional. What the grammar says is that events are made up of (rewritten as) semantic triplets; semantic triplets are made up of the set {⟨subject⟩ ⟨action⟩ [object]}. A ⟨subject⟩ is made up of at least one ⟨actor⟩, such as the accused, the husband, the victim, the defense lawyer, and so on.

A story grammar provides the basic template for structuring narrative text, a sort of coding scheme no different from other types of content analysis scheme. Where it is different, however, is in the fact that this coding scheme is based on linguistic properties of the text, rather than on the substantive or theoretical interests of an investigator. It captures intrinsic properties of *narrative* texts: the subject, the verb, the time and space, etc. And this is a fundamental difference advocated by Markoff et al. (1975), where the set of semantically defined categories of a story grammar are of general applicability (namely, to all texts of narrative type) and where the relationships between coding categories are explicitly specified (e.g., ⟨actors⟩ related to ⟨actions⟩ and both to their respective ⟨modifiers⟩). Coding narrative information within the categories of a story grammar has the further advantage that coded output preserves the narrative characteristics of the input text. Consider the sentence 'On the evening of April 20, 1772, several village men came down to Mrs Alice Watts's house, a shrew, and dragged her out of the village'. This could be coded as:

⟨subject⟩ village men (⟨number⟩ several)
⟨action⟩ came down to (⟨when⟩ evening of April 20, 1772 (⟨where⟩ Mrs Alice Watts's house)
⟨action⟩ dragged (⟨where⟩ out of the village)
⟨object⟩ Mrs Alice Watts (⟨type⟩ shrew).

As the example shows, the output data have the 'look and feel' of the input text. Coded output makes narrative sense to any competent user of the language. Coding errors can be easily detected, yielding far more reliable data than data collected via traditional coding schemes (Franzosi, 1987). Finally, the *relational* nature of story grammars makes it possible to implement such complex coding schemes based on story grammars in a computer environment using *relational* database management systems. This in turn makes possible the collection of large quantities of data (Franzosi, 1990b).

For all their advantages, coding schemes based on a story grammar do have limitations: they apply only to narrative texts. Other types of texts do not conform to the simple structure of the five Ws (who, what, where, when, and why; someone doing something, for or against someone else, in time and space). Furthermore, even narrative texts often mix purely narrative clauses (of the five Ws type) with descriptive, evaluative, or analytical clauses. The information provided in these types of clauses could not be captured by a story grammar. There are some advantages to the *ad hoc* nature of traditional coding schemes: you can pull them and push them in any way you want!

VISITORS FROM MARS

More or less sophisticated 'story grammars' of the kind described above have been used extensively in the social movement literature as templates of data collection. Paige (1975) used a similar scheme in his study of agrarian revolutions. Tilly (1995) coded thousands of documents from several centuries to draw the social map of contention in Great Britain. Shapiro and Markoff (1998) coded the narratives of the *cahiers de doléances*, the set of documents produced in 1789 on the eve of the French Revolution by some 40 000 corporate and territorial entities of the old regime. Tarrow (1989) coded thousands of narratives of protest that occurred during the cycle centered around the 1969 *hot autumn* in Italy. I have coded some 15 000 protest narratives on a tumultuous period of Italian history, the revolutionary mobilization of the 'red years' (1919–20) and the counter-mobilization of the 'black years' (1921–2) which led to Mussolini's rise to power (Franzosi, 1997a). I have also coded another 15 000 documents on labour disputes in Italy during the 1986–7 period to study the

differences between industrial and service sector strikes (Franzosi, 1997b).

The narratives typically used as sources of data in these projects have come from newspaper articles and, to a lesser extent, police reports (Franzosi, 1987). In light of the clear distortion in the information provided by *L'Aurore* and *L'Humanité* illustrated in these pages, it may seem foolhardy to rely on newspapers as sources of socio-historical data or as mirrors of 'reality'. Yet, for all their striking differences, there is some agreement among the two papers: there was a trial; this trial happened in France soon after World War II; the trial was about a woman who had allegedly killed her lover; the trial (suppose we are visitors from Mars, knowing nothing about the French judicial system of the mid-twentieth century) involved defense and prosecution attorneys, judge, jurors, witnesses; the accused woman was rich; she was married to a rich Swiss man. The trial was attended by many journalists and many women (and both papers agree that these women were 'pretty' or 'chic'). The trial ended with a guilty sentence for the accused. Both papers seem to agree that the sentence was light. *L'Humanité* expresses outrage that the accused was condemned to only 8 years ('eight years for a murder is getting away with murder!'). *L'Aurore* does not give us the details of the sentence but does acknowledge that Mme Schlumpf was lucky to be defended by a brilliant defense attorney, implying that the sentence could have been far stiffer. Of many of the social actors involved in the narratives we have first names and last names (which are not disputed). The two papers also separately provide other 'factual' information. While this information would have to be validated against other sources, there is no a priori reason to believe it to be false. It does appear that some types of information are 'harder' than others.[5] The analysis of the two articles by *L'Aurore* and *L'Humanité* clearly supports the view of Capecchi and Livolsi (1971: 264) that:

> The distortion of news does not operate so much through an obvious alteration of an event (for example: the news that 'A loves B' reported by a right-wing newspaper, which appears as 'A hates B' in a left-wing newspaper), as much as through the downplay or the insistence on some particular features of an event.

The media manipulate information through the use of adjectives, the frequency of certain nouns, the use of synonyms and paraphrases, of comments and editorials, of titles and subtitles, the emphasis on some aspects of an event to the exclusion of others, the break-up of information and its recomposition in such a way as to suggest precise causal relations.[6]

SAMPLING

I have chosen the two articles from *L'Aurore* and *L'Humanité* for heuristic and didactic purposes, taking them from a published paper on content analysis. But in a real research project (whether on morality, media bias, women and the law, cultural indicators, social movements or other) both the newspapers to be used as sources and the articles to be coded would have to be chosen on the basis of rigorous criteria. More generally, both data sources and documents would have to be appropriately selected. Should you use police records as sources of socio-historical data, or newspapers? Should you use television, magazines, or newspapers to study cultural trends or media bias? And having selected the most appropriate source(s), should you look at *all* the documents produced by the source(s)?

Ideally, of course, you would like to use all the documents from all the available sources. But realism will tell you otherwise. We never have enough resources to carry out our ideal projects. So you must be prepared to compromise. One type of compromise that perhaps does not require sacrificing scientific integrity on the altar of (always too limited) resources is based on sampling. Rather than work with all the possible sources and documents, sample an appropriate number of sources and an appropriate number of documents. The same statistical sampling rules applied in survey research would guarantee in content analysis the statistical relationship between universe and sampled coded data.[7] Sampling may be particularly appealing in content analysis since content analysis is a very labor-intensive, and therefore expensive, methodology.[8] By sampling, you may focus on just a handful of newspapers; you may read one or more days a week of a newspaper's output, one or more weeks a month, one or more months a year.

Sampling, to be effective (rather than just efficient), requires informed knowledge of the characteristics of each data source. And the best way to gather that knowledge is through systematic comparisons of different sources. These comparative analyses could be based on simple and rough counts of available documents on the research issues of interest (e.g., number of articles on morality reported by newspapers). Or they could be based on the result of more extensive information collected using the coding scheme to be applied to the final sample of documents.

Effective sampling also requires a sound knowledge of the relationship between source characteristics and investigator's research questions. Even the best sampling frame cannot guarantee error-free data. Thus investigators involved in social movement research have often sampled newspapers by day of the week or months of the year (e.g., coding every issue published on Monday). The drawback is that the sample of coded events would be not only left- and right-censored (after all, events attracted media attention some time after they started and typically lose media attention before they have run their full course) but also censored in the middle: by skipping intermediate days of the week or weeks of the month we may skip events that form an integral part of longer events (e.g., police breaking through the picket line in an ongoing strike); the internal historical logic of these longer events would become incomprehensible in light of missing information.

In sum: sample, by all means. But do so in light of rigorous systematic comparative analyses of available sources and of informed knowledge of the relationship between your sources and your research questions and between sampling frame and coded output.

WHERE ARE THE NUMBERS?

Content analysis, as we have seen, is a technique for the quantitative analysis of communication messages. But if so, where are the numbers? Several sections into this chapter, the numbers are still nowhere to be seen. All we have seen is a detailed analysis of two brief texts.

The numbers, in content analysis, are the result of counting: counting words (13 instances of 'I', remember?), counting themes, counting references, counting actors and their actions, depending upon the type of content analysis. But always counting. To make the steps involved in counting easier to understand, let us start by summarizing the actors, events, and objects cited in the two articles

Table 24.1   *List of actors, events, and objects*

	L'Humanité	L'Aurore
Individual actors	Mme Schlumpf	Paule Schlumpf
	Mr Schlumpf	Mr Schlumpf
	Simha	Simha
	Simha's friend	
		Defense attorney (Maître Floriot)
		State prosecutor (Maître Charpentier)
		Mr Schlumpf's former mistress
	Attorney General Turland	Attorney General Turland
	Mr Diffort (witness)	Witnesses
	Nameless witness	
	Judge Loser	
Collective actors	Crowd of females	Many pretty women
	Newsmen	Jurors
	Resistance	
	SS colonels	Green-uniformed invaders
	Gestapo	
Events	Trial	Trial
	Crime	Love story
	Occupation	Suicide of Mr Schlumpf's mistress
	Oath of allegiance to Hitler	
	Nazi galas and receptions	
Objects	Jewels	
	Feathers	
	Fur coats	
	Cakes	
	Handkerchief	
	Pistol	

(Table 24.1) and the references used for the main actors, whether through adjectives, verbs, or other more complex linguistic forms (Table 24.2). Table 24.2 also reports whether the reference is negative (−), positive (+), or neutral (~), in terms of the point of view of the journalist as inferred from the context.

We can now count the number of positive, negative, and neutral references of Table 24.2 to produce the results of Table 24.3. What do these numbers mean? By themselves, of course, numbers mean nothing, a disappointing result after so much effort. Numbers, no less than words, need to be analysed (and, oddly enough, converted back into words to make them intelligible). Even simple column totals and ratios would reveal some basic patterns in our data (the ultimate goal of data analysis, whether qualitative or quantitative). The column totals in Table 24.3 are 32, 4, 6, 10, 9, and 21, respectively. Thus, *L'Humanité* is three times as likely (32/10 = 3.2) to use

negative references as is *L'Aurore*. *L'Aurore*, on the other hand, is more than three times as likely to use positive references (21/6 = 3.5) and twice as likely to use neutral references (9/4 = 2.25). The numbers, then, confirm that the two newspapers stand on polar-opposite positions. Closer inspection of the numbers would provide further insights: *L'Humanité*'s villains are *L'Aurore*'s heroes (and vice versa), in particular Mme and Mr Schlumpf (with 12 to 1 and 14 to 0 negative references and 0 to 2 and 0 to 6 positive ones) and, less importantly, Mr Diffort (6 to 0 positive references). By and large, the quantitative data succinctly confirm the patterns revealed by the previous in-depth qualitative analyses.

MORE TO THE POINT, WHERE IS SOCIOLOGY?

In the end content analysis did deliver what it promised: the numbers. And I could have

Table 24.2   *List of main actors, with type of reference**

Actor	References	
	L'Humanité	*L'Aurore*
Mme Schlumpf	Depraved –	The woman condemned ~
	Accused –	Her tears ~
	Tearless eyes –	Cruel and unfaithful wife –
	Forgets to hide her true face –	Heroine of this drama +
	Cold –	Lucky +
	Calculating –	
	Ill-tempered –	
	I'll turn you over to the Gestapo –	
	She has pistols –	
	Greets with faked sobs –	
	The criminal –	
	The murderer –	
Mr Schlumpf	Husband ~	Husband ~
	Billionaire –	
	Collaborateur –	Neutral industrialist +
	Complaisance –	Living in the provisionally annexed Alsace ~
	Singular Helvetian ~	Swiss citizen +
	Teuton –	Gentleman +
	Accessory to the crime –	The gentleman I so admire +
	Self-possessed –	I take off my hat +
	Blushes a little –	Unheard-of way he defended his cruel and unfaithful wife +
	Signs oath of allegiance to Hitler –	
	Traitor –	
	Maneuvers –	
	Quashes damning evidence –	
	Discharges Mr Diffort from his factory –	
	Threatens Mr Diffort –	
	Throws Nazi galas and receptions for SS colonels –	
Raoul Simha	Her lover ~	Her victim ~
	Simha ~	Meets his death ~
		The Oriental –
		A Jew –
		Unfortunate +
		The victim in this story ~
Women at the trial	Crowd of fashionable females –	Many pretty women ~
	Jewels –	
	Feathers –	
	Fur coats –	
	Palpitating with anticipation –	
	Munched little cakes –	
	Chic girl friends –	
State prosecution		Maître Charpentier ~
		Astonishing in moderation and logic +
		Brilliant orator +
		Flung himself –
		Dialectical felicity +
		Insinuates –
		Implies –
		Did not persuade me –

(Continued)

Table 24.2 (*Continued*)

Actor	References L'Humanité	L'Aurore
Defense attorney		Maître Floriot ~
		Always there +
		To shove with his index finger +
		A marvellous sharpshooter +
		Defends his clients by attacking +
		His pleading gives off sparks +
		Comical, logical, sensitive … +
		The satisfaction, the joy … +
		Men so brilliant +
		Men so blessed by the gods +
Jurors		Probably decent people –
		Incapable socially –
		Incapable intellectually –
Mr Diffort	Follows orders from the Resistance +	
	Keeps record of Mr Schlumpf's actions +	
	Was discharged from his factory job +	
	Was threatened +	
	Suffered 16 months of unemployment +	
	Had the courage to tell +	

*The symbols –, + and ~ refer to negative, positive and neutral references, respectively.

Table 24.3 *Summary table of referential content analysis*

Actor	Reference L'Humanité			L'Aurore		
	–	~	+	–	~	+
Paule Schlumpf	12	0	0	1	2	2
Mr Schlumpf	14	2	0	0	2	6
Simha	0	2	0	2	2	1
Women at the trial	6	0	0	0	1	0
Jurors	0	0	0	3	0	0
Defense attorney	0	0	0	0	1	9
Prosecution attorney	0	0	0	4	1	3
Mr Diffort	0	0	6	0	0	0

produced more numbers, measuring different things. By using a story grammar as a basic content analysis scheme we could then count the number of different types of social relations (e.g., love, threat, violence) in which the various social actors are involved. To analyse these numbers we could then use novel tools of data analysis as network models (Franzosi, 1998b; for an overall view of the process of going 'from words to numbers', see Franzosi, 2004).

Only one question remains: where is sociology in all this? Neither the detailed linguistic analyses of the first few sections nor the numbers of the previous section seem to have

pulled sociology out of the conjurer's hat. Perhaps referential content analysis, with its emphasis on the relationship between actors, events, objects, and their representation (e.g., positive or negative, metaphorical or metonymical, emotional or rational) and the type of content analysis based on story grammars, with its emphasis on social actors and their actions – on who does what, when, where, and why – may point to a way out of both language and number games and back to sociology, indeed back to the very heart of sociology as originally laid out by our 'father' founders from Comte to Marx, Weber and Simmel: sociology as social relations (Franzosi, 2004). It was von Wiese who explored the full implications of a view of sociology as social relations. The last sentence of his *Systematic Sociology* reads: '*The sole task of the systematic sociologist is the scientific study of interhuman behavior as such*' (von Wiese, 1932: 713; emphasis in original). And as he explains elsewhere (von Wiese, 1941:25), 'the specifically "social" or interhuman consists in an involved and entangled network of relations between men; each social relation is the product of one or more social processes'. But the variety of social processes all lead to only two fundamental types of social relations: relations of association and relations of dissociation. There are no other types of social relations for von Wiese. Indeed, the task of sociology is that of systematizing 'all the relations of association and dissociation ... nothing more and nothing less than this is the object-matter of sociology' (von Wiese, 1932: 49–50). And since processes are basically actions, and actions fundamentally express themselves in verbal form – 'the fundamental categories of systematic sociology are *verbal* in nature' (von Wiese, 1932: 131) – von Wiese spent much of his life as a professor of sociology at the University of Cologne classifying words (and not just verbs).

Thus, the relational view implicit in referential content analysis and explicit in story grammars takes us far from methodology and closer to theory, to this rich sociological tradition of sociology as social relations and social processes, to a sociology of action to which Weber and Simmel were early contributors, followed by von Wiese, Vierkandt, Park, Ross, Burgess in the 1920s and 1930s, and later yet by Parsons and Coleman, down to the contemporary revival of social networks. With the mostly forgotten work of von Wiese, the relationship between content analysis (with its goal of classifying and counting words) and sociology (conceived as social relations) is restored.

But if the social is the relational, which kinds of relations can a text reveal? If a text belongs to the narrative genre, it will no doubt reveal relations among the social actors and their actions as narrated in the story. It is indeed by exploiting the structural properties of narrative texts that social movement scholars have been able to map the network of social interactions involved in protest events. But narratives will also invariably tell us something about the narrator. In that sense, all narratives are positional, from a perspective, from a particular point of view. How can an investigator tease out those points of view? And would those points of view tell us anything about the social relations in which the narrators are embedded? What is the relation of those points of view, of those perspectives and wider networks of social relations? Referential content analysis goes a long way in teasing out fundamental differences in points of view. But to fully understand those differences the investigator would have to embed the different meanings in wider ideological spaces (the 'Left', the 'Right'), in wider social relations of production (e.g., the media industry).

Respondents' answers to investigators' questions during ethnographic work or in-depth interviews may similarly reveal complex networks of social relations in which actors are embedded. But they may also reveal the relation between self and culture in the construction of identity, the networks of concepts and images people put side by side in telling stories (think of the Schlumpf trial for murder conceptually linked to the war and the patriotic resistance against the invaders versus a trial narratively constructed as a love story and in terms of the godlike qualities of the elite), the way certain social categories are constructed in language through the images they invoke (e.g., the category of gender – 'pretty women', 'chic', 'munching little cakes', 'palpitating', not to mention Mme Schlumpf, this *Parisienne*, this *femme fatale*, quite literally, whom one cannot keep 'in a cage, even a golden cage' – or of racism – 'Simha was a Jew ... Should one set down exactly what one thinks?').

Like von Wiese, content analysts should be concerned with the relational, the relation among narrated actors, events, and concepts, images, and the relation of the narrator to what is being narrated and between the narrator and the social relations in which the narrator is involved (for whom is the narrator writing? For what purpose? Under what conditions?).

CONFESSION

Toward the end of his paper, Lambert (1972: 49) assures us that 'the editorial materials analyzed were *easily* placed into Pareto's classifications' (emphasis added). No doubt Lambert was a better content analyst than I am. For I stared at the two newspaper articles for weeks. I turned them over in my head. I used them as examples in a course I taught on content analysis. All in all, I played with this handful of lines of text for over a year. There was nothing *easy* about doing content analysis. For one thing, the content analysis scheme Lambert proposes – based on Pareto's theory of residues and derivations – has all the negative characteristics of obscure, abstract, and theoretical categories pointed out by Markoff et al. (1975) in their critique of content analysis. All the more so, since Pareto's categories are themselves obscure and abstract. Under these conditions, coders come to play a major (yet unknown) role in the process of converting text into code. Clear coding rules and clear definitions of coding categories help to reduce coders' discretion, but do not suffice. Abstract coding categories invariably result in the contamination of measurement, with each coder playing surrogate scientist. In the coding process, the coder's mind is a *black box*.

This is no different from survey research, where respondents' cognitive processes involved in producing a given answer remain largely unknown (see Mishler, 1986: 72). Indeed, there is much in common between these two distinctively sociological tools of quantitative research: content analysis and survey research. After all, a coding scheme is like a standard questionnaire in survey research, where the different coding categories correspond to different questions and where the questionnaire/coding scheme is administered to a set of written texts, rather than human respondents. And like survey research, content analysis is preoccupied with the validity of the questionnaire/coding scheme design and with the reliability of the coding process (a problem more specifically known as 'inter-coder reliability' in content analysis: would different coders, confronted with the same text and using the same coding scheme, 'tick off' the same coding categories?). Even a cursory look at the table of contents of any standard textbook in content analysis (indeed, a quick exercise in content analysis ...) will reveal the central role that these themes occupy in the methodological literature on content analysis in its attempt to achieve scientific status.[9]

Yet, for all its *emphasis* on sampling and on mathematical formulae of inter-coder reliability, content analysis is quite *silent* about the coder's black box. And it is just as silent about the trick behind counting: classification. We count after having assigned verbal items to a given category. But ... Why did I classify 'billionaire' as negative? And should 'heroine of this drama' be positive? No doubt, Cicourel is right when he writes (in a wonderful book on measurement which includes a devastating critique of content analysis) (1964, p. 18):

Our often arbitrary classifications of data become the basis for establishing some form of quantification. Since the classification is after the fact, the validity of our measurement is relative to the arbitrary classification and makes replication and the possibility of rigorously obtained knowledge remote

at this time. The most serious problems of measurement, then, arise when we deal with qualitative 'variables'.

The same mechanisms of silence and emphasis, background and foreground, light and darkness that operate in media production of news, operate also in the production of all texts, including scientific texts on content analysis (Franzosi, 2004: Chapter 5). We foreground strengths, we background weaknesses. Indeed, there is much that is 'sociological' to be learned from the application of any of the content analysis techniques illustrated in this chapter. And that includes the 'sociology of sociology', the sociology of how we produce knowledge as sociologists. To conclude with Cicourel (1964: 35):

Thus, science and scientific method as means of viewing and obtaining knowledge about the world around us provide those who accept its tenets with a grammar that is not merely a reproducing instrument for describing what the world is all about, but also shapes our ideas of what the world is like, often to the exclusion of other ways of looking at the world. Language, then, and the cultural meanings it signifies, distorts, and obliterates, acts as a filter or grid for what will pass as knowledge in a given era.

ALCHEMIST'S RECOMMENDATIONS TO THE NOVICE

It was the practice of the alchemists of old to dispense advice to the novice in this dangerous art. Let me – a practitioner of this alchemic transformation of words into numbers – also part with some advice to the reader (Franzosi, 2004).

If you are a sociologist, remember your calling: the study of social relations. It is neither that of the linguist nor that of the statistician. If the sociologist's fascination with numbers in the 1960s and 1970s has turned us all into third-rate statisticians (to be generous ... read Freedman, 1991), the 'linguistic turn' of the 1980s and 1990s may have fared no better for us, turning us all into third-rate linguists. Remember this: as a sociologist, neither the words nor the numbers as such are your goals, but the social relations. Use the words or the numbers to lead you to the social relations.

As a content analyst, you work with language. Do not forget one thing: language is the most powerful cultural tool for denying cognitive access to alternatives. Beware of the rhetoric of the science of content analysis (and all other science). Do not fall victim to the lure of the sirens' songs of science. When you get to the numbers, do not forget how you got there. For all the emphasis of content analysis on formulae of inter-coder reliability and sampling frames, when coding text with the use of a coding scheme, when classifying coded items into broader analytical categories, you may be closer to performing an alchemic transformation than a scientific operation under the total control of the investigator. Acknowledge with humility the limits of your art and be thankful if it helps you to disclose patterns in the social relations of interest to you.

Do not, however, forget what science can do for you. While you do want to be well aware of the rhetoric of science, there is no need to cut off your nose to spite your face. Issues of research design, sampling frame, validity, and reliability are fundamental in any scientific project. A rhetorical approach to content analysis will not, by itself, necessarily produce better content analysis.

Content analysis is typically a tool of quantitative analysis of textual material. Beware of the dangers of taking the easy road to the numbers. Become familiar with the types of text you want to quantify. Turn in your head as many of these texts as you can and for as long as you can. Develop your coding scheme in an iterative process where familiarity with your texts plays as important a role as your theory. As in survey research, pre-testing of both the coding scheme and the input material sampled is key to a successful research outcome. Read the input material extensively and keep refining the coding scheme (modern computer software, such as NUD*IST and ATLAS.ti – will help you in this; most software for the analysis of qualitative data will allow you to refine coding categories without having to throw away the work already done).

Beware of easy numbers; but do not succumb to 'dialectical felicity' either. Start by constructing tables where you systematically work your way through the actors, events, and objects and all their references. This will give you something concrete to stare at. Since I do not seem to have followed my own advice and started out instead on the path of 'dialectical felicity', do as I say, not as I do! *Mea culpa.*

In fact, you should start neither from tables nor from 'dialectical felicity'. Rather, start from research questions and then decide which technique is better suited to answering those questions. That should be your point of departure.

If you are still wondering 'what's in it for me?', consider this. If you are a social scientist (or a historian for that matter), you likely deal with data that are basically words: archival documents of all sorts (produced by the police, governments, firms, universities, the media, …), notes you yourself have taken in long months in the field, stories that interviewees have told you. If all you have is a handful of documents, a few pages of fieldnotes or people's stories, you can probably safely juggle the information in your head and, sooner or later, you will (hopefully) find basic patterns in the data. In this case, there may not be much for you in content analysis (although even then it can help; it certainly helped me in analysing just two newspaper articles!). The strength of content analysis is in processing large volumes of qualitative data. The parsimony of numbers will make it easier to discover patterns in the data.

Bear in mind that content analysis represents not just one but several different techniques for dealing with text in quantitative ways. Each specific technique (e.g., thematic analysis, referential analysis, frame analysis, structural analysis of narrative) has its strengths and weaknesses, its field of applicability. The advantage of a structural analysis of narrative is that the coding scheme follows closely the characteristics of the input text, reducing (although by no means eliminating) 'the role of the reader'. Unfortunately, it only works with narrative text, in fact with narrative clauses. And not all texts belong to the narrative genre. Even in narrative, not all clauses are strictly narrative in nature (many are descriptive or evaluative). No doubt, thematic analysis, referential, and frame analysis are of more general applicability. But generality comes at a cost: the coder has to struggle to fit concrete and specific text into typically abstract coding categories designed on the basis of the investigator's substantive and theoretical interests, rather than the intrinsic linguistic properties of the text.

The different techniques also serve different purposes. Thematic analysis is ideally suited to getting a clear picture of the basic content of a text. It allows you to answer such questions as: What's in the mind of your interviewees? What's in your fieldnotes? Which issues do managers worry about during boom and bust times, as found in company documents? Can you get insights into national identity by focusing on the themes dealt with in the newspaper editorials of different countries? Referential analysis is more concerned with *form* than *content*, with *how* than *what*, how an object, a situation, an event, a social actor is portrayed in a text (e.g., positively or negatively). Frame analysis goes one step further in understanding how meaning is constructed by focusing on the broad images conjured up in a text (e.g., the class, gender, race, love frames of our articles). Finally, structural narrative analysis is an ideal tool in the study of social movements and protest events, concerned as these are with social action and interaction. But it may also help those scholars working with in-depth interviews and people's stories to map out the network of social relations in which a respondent is involved.

Do not fail to ask yourself: Do I really need to process large volumes of data? (To put it another way: am I using a sledgehammer to kill an ant?) How else can I approach my research questions? Other types of textual analysis, such as narrative analysis or discourse analysis, deal with words in the words' own terrain (see Franzosi, 1998a). Perhaps you can use a quantitative content analysis to map patterns and use more qualitative linguistic or semiotic analyses (e.g., frame analysis or discourse analysis) to reveal specific *mechanisms* concerning how certain social (or causal) relations actually work.

In short, content analysis is just a tool (in fact, several different tools) of sociological investigation. As a sociologist, use it in your search for the social relations. Do not abuse it. Beware of its limitations, of the shortcuts you take. Keep your gaze on the shadows as much as on the light. It is one tool among many, not a passe-partout. With the realism and humility of a skilled artisan, reach in your toolbag for a hammer if you need to pound a nail, a screwdriver to set a screw, and a wrench to tighten a nut. Keep this advice constantly before you and this ancient art of content analysis will serve you safely and well. *Vale!*

ACKNOWLEDGMENTS

I would like to thank Alan Bryman, John Markoff, Francesca Polletta, and another anonymous referee for the helpful comments provided on an earlier draft.

NOTES

1 Lasswell systematically classified the themes referred to in these interviews and found that the same system of categories could be used in a variety of other contexts ... On that basis he worked out and standardized an elaborate code of analysis (Madge, 1953: 112–13).

2 The Experimental Division had been set up at the beginning of the war in the basement of the Library of Congress in Washington, DC. The Division was part of the War Communications Research Project sponsored by the Rockefeller Foundation (Lasswell, 1941; Lasswell et al., 1949: v; Berelson, 1952: 23).

3 There cannot be syntactically well-formed sentences without a subject.

4 US television coverage of the Iran hostage crisis shows a similar dichotomous format: interviews with the grieving families of hostages became the symbol of the American perspective, while shots of Iranian crowds (both in Iran and inside the United States) chanting anti-American slogans vividly portrayed the other side (Altheide, 1982, 1985).

5 On the use of newspapers as sources of socio-historical data, see Franzosi (1987; 2004: Chapter 4).

6 On these practices, see Franzosi (1987).

7 In these cases, if sampling is required in order to reduce data collection costs, it is better to first collate all the articles into macro-events and then sample on the events (rather than articles). Although this procedure requires a two-pass coding (having to read the same material twice, once to collate articles into events, and a second time to code the selected articles) it produces much more reliable data (see Franzosi, 1990a, 1990b).

8 Sampling can be profitably used not only in input but also in output. A randomly drawn sample of all coded output to be inspected for errors can ensure high data quality at reduced cost, using acceptance sampling schemes (on these issues see Franzosi, 1990a, 1990b).

9 See Berelson (1952), Krippendorf (1980), and Weber (1990). No one, of course, would dispute that these are, indeed, important issues that need addressing. What is at issue here is the fact that content analysis, no different from any of the texts it studies, foregrounds certain types of information and backgrounds others. And among the issues it backgrounds is the fundamental question of how meaning is constructed in the coder's mind. Thus, the same mechanisms of silence and emphasis work in the production of scientific texts. On these issues, see Franzosi (2004).

REFERENCES

Altheide, David L. (1982) 'Three-in-one news: Network coverage of Iran', *Journalism Quarterly*, 48: 476–90.

Altheide, David L. (1985) 'Format and ideology in TV news coverage of Iran', *Journalism Quarterly*, 62: 346–51.

Berelson, Bernard (1952) *Content Analysis in Communication Research*. New York: Free Press.

Capecchi, Vittorio and Livolsi, Marino (1971) *La Stampa Quotidiana in Italia*. Milan: Bompiani.

Cartwright, D. (1953) 'Analysis of qualitative material', in L. Festinger and D. Katz (eds), *Research Methods in the Behavioral Sciences*. Niles, IL: Dryden, pp. 421–70.

Cicourel, Aaron (1964) *Method and Measurement in Sociology*. New York: Free Press.

Fairclough, Norman (1995) *Critical Discourse Analysis. The Critical Study of Language*. London: Longman.

Franzosi, Roberto (1987) 'The press as a source of socio-historical data: Issues in the methodology of data collection from newspapers', *Historical Methods*, 20(1): 5–16.

Franzosi, Roberto (1989) 'From words to numbers: A generalized and linguistics-based coding procedure for collecting event-data from newspapers', in Clifford Clogg (ed.), *Sociological Methodology*, Vol. 19. Oxford: Basil Blackwell, pp. 263–98.

Franzosi, Roberto (1990a) 'Strategies for the prevention, detection and correction of measurement error in data collected from textual sources', *Sociological Methods and Research*, 18: 442–72.

Franzosi, Roberto (1990b) 'Computer-assisted coding of textual data using semantic text grammars', *Sociological Methods and Research*, 19: 225–57.

Franzosi, Roberto (1994) 'From words to numbers: A set theory framework for the collection, organization, and analysis of narrative data', in Peter Marsden (ed.), *Sociological Methodology*, Vol. 24. Oxford: Basil Blackwell, pp. 105–36.

Franzosi, Roberto (1997a) 'Mobilization and counter-mobilization processes: From the 'red years' (1919–20) to the 'black years' (1921–22) in Italy', *Theory and Society*, 26: 275–304.

Franzosi, Roberto (1997b) 'Labor unrest in the Italian service sector: An application of semantic grammars', in Carl W. Roberts (ed.), *Text Analysis for the Social Sciences: Methods for Drawing Statistical Inferences from Texts and Transcripts*. Hillsdale, NJ: Lawrence Erlbaum Associates, pp. 131–45.

Franzosi, Roberto (1998a) 'Narrative analysis, or ... why (and how) sociologists should be interested in narrative', in John Hagan (ed.), *Annual Review of Sociology*, Vol. 24. Palo Alto, CA: Annual Reviews Inc.

Franzosi, Roberto (1998b) 'Narrative as data. Linguistic and statistical tools for the quantitative study of historical events', in Marcel van der Linden and Larry Griffin (eds), *New Methods in Historical Sociology/Social History*. Cambridge: Cambridge University Press, pp. 81–104.

Franzosi, Roberto (2004) *From Words to Numbers: Narrative, Data, and Social Science*. Cambridge: Cambridge University Press.

Freedman, David (1991) 'Statistical models and shoe leather', in Peter V. Marsden (ed.), *Sociological Methodology, 1991*. Oxford: Basil Blackwell, pp. 291–313.

Hartley, John (1982) *Understanding News*. London: Methuen.

Hartley, John and Montgomery, Martin (1985) 'Representations and relations: Ideology and power in press and TV news', in Teun van Dijk (ed.), *Discourse and Communication*, Berlin: Walter de Gruyter, pp. 233–69.

Holsti, O.R. (1969) *Content Analysis for the Social Sciences and Humanities*. Reading, MA: Addison-Wesley.

Kaplan, Abraham (1943) 'Content analysis and the theory of signs', *Philosophy of Science*, 10: 230–47.

Kress, Gunther and Hodge, Robert (1979) *Language as Ideology*. London: Routledge & Kegan Paul.

Krippendorf, Klaus (1980) *Content Analysis: An Introduction to Its Methodology*. Beverly Hills, CA: Sage.

Laclau, Ernest (1980) 'Populist rupture and discourse', *Screen Education*, 34: 87–93.

Lambert, Wallace E. (1972) 'The use of Pareto's residue-derivation classification as a method of content analysis', in: Wallace E. Lambert, *Language, Psychology, and Culture*. Stanford, CA: Stanford University Press. First published in 1956.

Lasswell, Harold D. (1941) 'The technique of symbol analysis (content analysis)', *Experimental Division for the Study of War Time Communications*. Washington, DC: Library of Congress.

Lasswell, Harold D. (1949) 'Why be quantitative?', in Harold D. Lasswell, Nathan Leites, et al. (eds), *Language of Politics: Studies in Quantitative Semantics*. New York: George W. Stewart, pp. 40–52.

Lasswell, Harold D., Leites, Nathan, et al. (eds) (1949) *Language of Politics: Studies in Quantitative Semantics*. New York: George W. Stewart.

Madge, John (1953) *The Tools of Social Science*. London: Longmans, Green and Co.

Markoff, John, Shapiro, Gilbert and Weitman, Sasha (1975) 'Toward the integration of content analysis and general methodology', in David R. Heise (ed.), *Sociological Methodology*, Vol. 5. San Francisco: Jossey-Bass, pp. 1–58.

Mishler, Elliot (1986) *Research Interviewing, Context and Narrative*. Cambridge, MA: Harvard University Press.

Murdock, Graham (1973) 'Political deviance: The press presentation of a militant mass demonstration', in Stanley Cohen and Jock Young (eds), *The Manufacture of News: Deviance, Social Problems and the Mass Media*, London: Constable, pp. 156–76.

Paige, Jeffrey (1975) *Agrarian Revolution*. New York: Free Press.

Reynolds, Allan G. and Lambert, Wallace E. (1991) *Bilingualism, Multiculturalism, and Second Language Learning: The McGill Conference in Honour of Wallace E. Lambert*. Hillsdale, NJ: Lawrence Erlbaum Associates.

Shapiro, Gilbert and Markoff, John (1997) 'A matter of definition', in Carl W. Roberts (ed.), *Text Analysis for the Social Sciences: Methods for Drawing Statistical Inferences from Texts and Transcripts*. Mahwah, NJ: Lawrence Erlbaum Associates, pp. 9–34.

Shapiro, Gilbert and Markoff, John (1998) *Revolutionary Demands: A Content Analysis of the Cahier de Doléances of 1789*. Stanford, CA: Stanford University Press.

Snow, David A., Rochford, E. Burke, Worden, Steven K. and Benford, Robert D. (1986) 'Frame alignment and processes, micromobilization, and movement participation', *American Sociological Review*, 51: 464–81.

Stone, P.J., Dunphy, D.C., Smith, M.S. and Ogilvie, D.M. (1966) *The General Inquirer: A Computer Approach to Content Analysis*. Cambridge, MA: MIT Press.

Tarrow, Sidney (1989) *Democracy and Disorder. Protest and Politics in Italy, 1965–1975*. Oxford: Clarendon Press.

Tilly, Charles (1995) *Popular Contention in Great Britain, 1758–1834*. Cambridge, MA: Harvard University Press.

Trew, Anthony (1979a) 'Theory and ideology at work', in Roger Fowler, Bob Hodge, Gunther Kress and Anthony Trew (eds), *Language and Control*. London: Routledge & Kegan Paul, pp. 94–116.

Trew, Anthony, (1979b) 'What the papers say: Linguistic variation and ideological difference', in Roger Fowler, Bob Hodge, Gunther Kress and Anthony Trew (eds), *Language and Control*. London: Routledge & Kegan Paul, pp. 117–56.

van Dijk, Teun A. (1983) 'Discourse analysis: Its development and application to the structure of news', *Journal of Communication*, 33(2): 20–43.

von Wiese, Leopold (1932) *Systematic Sociology, on the Basis of the Beziehungslehre and Gebildelehre of Leopold von Wiese* (edited by Howard P. Becker). New York: Wiley.

von Wiese, Leopold (1941) *Sociology*. New York: O. Piest.

Weber, Robert Philip (1990) *Basic Content Analysis*. Newbury Park: Sage.

## 25

Semiotics and Data Analysis

PETER K. MANNING

Semiotics, the science of signs, is an object language that refers to itself and its workings as well as serving as a metalanguage by which other systems of signs can be analyzed. A sign, we can begin by stating, is something that makes sense in the mind of some person, but may be seen usefully as the connection between an expression and a content (Hjemslev, 1961). Semiotics takes itself as an object as well as a subject. Semiotics can be used to analyze any system of signs, including language, the pre-eminent communicational system. Semiotics is a formal and logical framework that resembles mathematics since it contains the tools to execute logical operations on itself (as a sign system) as well as using these tools to analyze motion, change, or disruption in other systems. However, the term 'semiotics' remains a 'sponge concept' (Noth, 1990), soaking up diverse meanings, and precise definitions are avoided. In part because Saussure, who originated the term, had grandiose aims, semiotics facilitates semantic, syntactical and grammatical analyses, as well as serving a subject of *semiology* (Barthes, 1970).[1] Thomas Sebeok (1994: 4–5), the most important American practitioner of semiotics, argues that semiotics includes the study of at least five elements: the real world; complimentary or actual models of the real world; semiosis, or 'sign action', concerning how matters are communicated; how abstractions from the real world circumscribe what we can know about it; and how the interplay of models, readings of the real world, illuminate experience. The question

of this chapter is: how does one undertake this kind of analysis?

Semiotics seeks to understand the structure of *representation* and its functions. While the field was defined as a search for law-like statements that might govern communicational systems, including language, distinguishing actual speech from Saussure's forms of speech by Saussure, most current theories of symbolization and representation accept the ultimately context-bound nature of meaning (Ogden and Richards, 1923; Searle, 2002). The complexity of 'context', of the logics of systems of representation, muddles many uses of semiotics. Since all representations, including words, are selective and combinatory, they may well stimulate associations, fantasies, dreams, wishes, and confabulations, and contain within themselves the potential for counterintuitive, miraculous, and even phantasmagoric formulations. Meaning is use-based and therefore any representation partakes of the meaning that context provides. These may be grounded in cultures, group experiences, or even other symbols. Pure representation is confounded also, made more complex, by the irreducible emotive, phatic, and subjective or 'emotional' aspect of speech. That is, the subjective meaning, or association between a message and an idea, always exists. 'Language games', as we might call them, following Wittgenstein (1953), include questioning, commanding, ordering, asking, exhorting, promising, and these games alter the meaning-use of any representation. Furthermore, strings of representations, such as texts, poems, essays, novels, sonnets, and academic chapters, produce changes in meaning that unfold as every sign points to another and so on, moving away from an (often arbitrary) starting point. Context, or what is brought to the communicative encounter, is a resource, often unreflective, that allows sense-making to proceed. Context is a very powerful guide to words in action when a collective situation, such as producing work in a kitchen or bar, playing a sport, or making love, requires cooperation. People do not so much 'understand' as they communicate (Lévi-Strauss, 1981). The question persists of how mutual understanding (or intersubjective realities) arises.

Semiotics elevates the question of how we make sense of each other's communications, even in spite of our inability to 'understand' in depth any other person. Signification is arbitrary in origin and therefore ambiguous. A system of signifiers is composed of elements that at the same time (intrinsically or essentially) signify nothing (Jakobson, 1981: 66–7) – they allow meaning to arise, while being invisible tools. Semiotics is a means for unpacking and managing the ambiguities inherent in human communication.[2] From ambiguity emerges the idea of truth and its variants or opposites. Animals, other than humankind, so far as we know, cannot and do not lie for they can only signal – their displays are consistent in their meaning, not arbitrary or contextual. Human communication includes all manner of representation, including misrepresentation, in part because in conflict situations misleading and misrepresentation can benefit the liar. Semiotics powerfully uncovers and plays on the potential in communication for fabrication or lying. That is, the ambiguity inherent in abstract communication can never fully eliminate the problematics of interpretation and context. Umberto Eco (1979: 7), a philosopher and semiotician, states flatly:

> Semiotics is in principle the discipline studying everything which can be used in order to lie. If something cannot be used to tell a lie, conversely, it cannot be used to tell the truth: it cannot in fact be used to 'tell' at all. (Emphasis in original)

Social science research is an attempt to reveal, to tell something of the underlying structure of social life, more than its descriptive or surface features. Eco (1979: 7) continues:

> One cannot do theoretical research without having the courage to put forward a theory, and, therefore, an elementary model as a guide for discourse; all theoretical research must however have the courage to specify its own contradictions, and should make them obvious where they are not apparent.

The task of data gathering is not a random walk, a sensual search, or the bemused collectings of a beachcomber. Semiotics makes central the question of what *underlying model of social processes* guides data gathering, analytic techniques, and descriptions of meaningful possible social worlds. As with methods, it rests initially on an intuitive understanding that is made visible to others by means of some 'tools'. The conventions guiding statistical analysis that are widely shared or at least can be debated within a shared vocabulary in the social sciences, are absent in semiotics. Semiotics can only reveal partially what is known in other ways, intuitively and commonsensically, but its strength lies in that it formalizes these insights into more than epigrams and mottoes.[3] It provides maps of partially known territories (Bateson, 1980: 32–3), but its fruits must be explained in words, translated and back-translated, and thus it is a reflective exercise. There are several quite vexing reasons for the limits of the method and technique to be taken up below. They include: questions of how to establish a domain of meaning and its 'head term' (an ordering, central idea); how to eliminate or substantiate alternative interpretations of a configuration; discovering the referential basis of an inference (usage, style and grammar, interviews or questionnaires); and connecting these matters to theoretical frameworks.

This chapter concerns data analysis, and sets aside questions of data gathering and the intriguing matter of the stylistics or poetics of presentation (a presentation is always a representation, or a representation of something).[4] While it is often difficult to separate data gathering, which often entails an implicit encoding of materials, and analysis, I intend to focus rather tightly on semiotic analysis. Data analysis using semiotics encompasses semiotics as *method* (or set of rules for dealing with already encoded data) and as a *technique* (tools and tactics for approaching uncoded data). The aim in each case is to display their relationships, specify and elaborate the conditions under which the generalizations hold, and identify exceptions or anomalous materials. In this chapter, semiotics is used as *method* to analyze crime mapping and

McDonald's menus, and as a *technique* to analyze recent displays (in late 2001 and early 2002) in America of the American flag.

SEMIOTICS

Saussure

Ferdinand de Saussure was a brilliant innovator who described semiotics, taken from the Greek *semeion*, as the study of signs and the laws that govern their constitution and operation.[5] Saussure sought a master taxonomy of the sciences, and argued for the dominance of the science of signs over all other abstract systems (Noth, 1990: 59). The sign is the combination of a signifier (a sound) and a signified (concept), linked mentally. Saussure (1966: 16) saw language holistically, as a closed system of elements that operated through differences. These differences may be surface phonetic ones, such as the sound that distinguishes 'crime' from 'dime', or 'cat' from 'hat', but they are made possible by structure, grammar and syntax, and enable speakers to talk without reflection upon these matters. Saussure separated language as a system of signs from speech as performance. It is only by knowing the system, language, that we know and can identify speech and its variants – ungrammatical statements, mispronunciations, and awkward, scrambled syntactical constructions.

Let us begin with Saussure's main arguments (Culler, 1977). The first is that sound and object are one and the same. The sound 'cow' stimulates a thought or image in the mind, and this process produces the sign. This might also be called the *dyadic view of the sign* – sound and concept, signifier and signified, comprising the sign, are both 'mentalistic'. Sign-production is a closed system based on thought. The second is that the 'material world', while extant, is secondary, and not the primary object of sign work, because the sign unites sound and concept, not sound and objects. The third is the assumption that nothing exists prior to language as a system of relations. A sign is a form, independent to some degree of the content it contains. A signifier 'speaks' through what it excludes and includes, and thus it selectively points. Language as a system precedes meaning – no 'raw reality' or unprocessed stimuli exist; through language, a constitutive mechanism, society is possible. The fourth is the 'arbitrary'

or motivated nature of signs. Signs represent concepts or ideas, and are culturally embedded. Cultural understandings reveal the conventions that govern the 'arbitrariness' of the sign; the externality and objectivity of language (much as Durkheim emphasized this as the facticity of social realities); and their 'productivity', or the unending range of units that can be strung together. The fifth idea is the binary structure of relations within a system of signs. Present/absent contrasts that may not be a product of awareness produce the differential value of a given sign. The sixth idea is that language works in two ways simultaneously: synchronically, or as a structure of relations (e.g., grammar and syntax – the ordering and elements of a sentence), and diachronically, or over time as the signs 'unfold'.

These six ideas are linked in complicated fashion. Consider a series of names or signifiers. The connection between them is dual. Both signifiers and signifieds symbolize mutually. What is taken to be a signifier shades the way the signified is seen and vice versa – 'beverage', 'drink' or 'libation' all might suggest a cup of water. The impact of the signified, what is pointed to, refers back to the signifier, 'colors' it, and gives it texture as well. 'Beverage', the signifier, can refer to any number of liquid refreshments. The mental link between sound and concept may be more problematic than Saussure had anticipated. The associational links between a string of signs can also influence thinking. Think of the difference between seeing a series of mathematical signs, pictures of cattle slaughtered as a result of foot and mouth disease, and 'ice cream has no bones'. When strings of signs are considered, they are 'double articulated' in speech. Words and sounds, although they flow and in some sense are continuous, are heard as units or phonemes (including the silences and pauses) as well as creating signs.

Consider further the relationships between signifiers and other signifiers as well as those between a signified and other signifieds. *Signifiers* can be grouped as words that rhyme (moon, June, swoon, tune), homonyms, and those with similar prefixes or suffices (pre-, post-, un-). *Signifieds* also can be grouped as synonyms (words meaning the same), and antonyms (oppositions), and one can explore similarities that link *both* (these are rare) (Silverman, 1983: 10). The relations of a given sign to other signs in a system work either by *association* or by *substitution*. Consider first associations. Some are *metonymic* (associated by proximity) and some *metaphoric* (based on association or shared features that convert a 'this' into a 'that'). A list of American baseball teams, the Red Sox, Yankees, and Orioles, or of English football clubs, Liverpool, Chelsea, and Manchester United, will be heard both as a series of words and as a set of major league baseball teams or Premier League clubs. The sounds, or the phonemes, the sequence of signs in a sentence, is conventionally called the 'horizontal dimension', while the 'vertical dimension' is associational or paradigmatic. Both dimensions 'work' as we hear or see communication, and they tend to be cumulative over the course of a narrative. Associations may be conveyed by many *sign vehicles* (things that carry a signifier or signified, such as a building, neon sign, automobile, or a text), which themselves may communicate, and may take stylized forms. Narratives, such as the novel, poem, sonnet, or short story, are rather longer versions of texts with characteristic governing rules. Poetry is a play with and against formal rules of association and substitution, but these effects are brought about by known techniques. Within texts, dominant tropes or stylistic modes can prevail, such as poetic associations and irony, and point of view, voice, and so on can also vary. Now, consider substitution. Metonymy (sequence) and synecdoche (part–whole relations) work by substitution. There are many instances of *metonymy* (a series, a list) and proximity, formal or informal, obtaining among items. These patterns, signs meshed with other signs, as in a sequence on a menu (a concrete instance of signification), a grocery or laundry list, or a set of instructions on how to work a VCR, are frequently encountered. In the case of *synecdoche*, a part can stand for the other as in 'Buckingham Palace (or the Crown) announced today...', meaning the Queen; or in metonymy, each piece makes up a component of a list such as 1,2,3,4,5,9 or 1,2,3,4,5,10. We can predict the next number in a sequence such as this, but we may not be able to explain why – that is semiotics at work.

Such 'substitutional lists' have immediate and strong associations as well, such as excitement, taste, competence, or historical associations, and they suggest the importance of *connotation* as well as *denotation* in social analysis. While a series of announcements from the Palace denotes 'news', it also connotes power, authority and perhaps mystery and tradition. A list of cars, such as Jaguar, Mercedes-Benz, BMW, Lexis and Infiniti, will have denotations such as their country of origin (nominally, UK, Germany, Japan) as well as connotations such as expensive, fast, luxurious, elegant, and reliable. As one moves into combinations of denotation and connotation, the signs tend to 'pile up' and move attention away from the starting point.[6]

Charles Sanders Peirce

Charles Sanders Peirce (1839–1914), an eccentric American philosopher, considered that pragmatism, the doctrine that meaning arises though interaction, pointing, doing, and reflecting, was closely linked to semiotics (Peirce, 1965; Brent, 1988). Recall that in Saussure's argument, the signifier–signified link is assumed as a kind of common-sense knowledge. Peirce's semiotics explicitly designated as a concern the source of a 'working' representation, the interpretant. His was a *triadic system* that included an object, the sign (still a two-part construction), and the *interpretant*. The functions and meaning of the concept of an interpretant is key because it calls out for specification of a context (Eco, 1979: 70). Defining and explicating context, or what is brought to the message, is the foundational idea of all interpretive work in social science.

Let us begin with Peirce's key concepts, the sign and the interpretant. Sebeok (1994: 13–14) writes concerning Peirce's concept of the sign that 'a sign is anything "which determines something else (its interpretant) to refer to an object to which it itself refers (its *object*) in the same way, the sign becoming in turn a sign, and so on *ad infinitum*"'. For Peirce, the object could be anything in the natural or social world, or the world of representations or secondary signs (signs about signs). The sign had a social location and meaning for Peirce: a sign was something that stood for something in the eyes of someone, and in a sense, completing the sign, connecting it to the interpretant, was social activity. How this 'standing for' was accomplished depended on the source of interpretation. This, the Peircian interpretant, could be a body of knowledge, a formalized code book, or an abstract statement of principles, but it was not a person or an 'interpreter'.

From this conceptual base, Peirce created an elaborate complex system of subsigns, which he continued to modify, and introduced the idea of context and the fundamental incompleteness of the sign. In his view, four levels of signs existed – those with firstness and secondness are the most relevant distinctions and the most consistent in his massive corpus of writing (1935–66). The idea of firstness referred to signs pertaining to things with a natural quality or property such as hardness, softness, light, and water. Those with secondness include the *icon* (and varieties thereof), or visual image; the *index*, narrowly conceived as connected without much question, as smoke is to fire, or as a footprint is to a person; and the *symbol*, something that has an arbitrary meaning determined by 'culture' or social relations. His elaborate system of classification has never been accepted, in part because of the complexity of the process and in part because in order to make sense of signification, one has to consider time and change as well as uncertainty in the communicative event itself.

Peirce recognized the unfolding aspect of signification, and emphasized semiosis, the interactional–indicative sequences by which messages, or groups of signs, took on significance. Each sign was considered something of a stimulus, producing meaning 'backward' as well as 'forward' in a communicative encounter. As Mead emphasized, there is no 'knife edge present', but the past and future, both as imagined and recalled, flow together in the imagery of the moment.[7]

Umberto Eco

Umberto Eco is perhaps the most important systematic thinker in the field of semiotics at present because his work has the potential to shape further social science research and data analysis. His book, *The Theory of Semiotics* (1979), although immodestly titled, is a comprehensive overview of the theory of codes and coding, and issues in semantics and semiotics. Eco takes from Saussure the elemental system assumption and the prior determinancy of language over individual speakers. That is, we come into a world of speakers and are socialized to a language and its conventions. We do not invent it. However, Eco elaborates Peircian ideas, sets aside the arbitrary distinction between levels and complex named subtypes of signs, accepts the incompleteness of the sign and develops this idea, in the form of the notion of 'open text', in quite elaborate detail. Eco takes Peirce's idea of semiosis as critical, referring to the idea of 'unlimited semiosis'. This nomenclature highlights the active, sense-making processes, the interpretive and referential process rather than the posited internal or mental process that grounds the signifier–signified nomenclature of Saussure. The links between expression and content are various, as noted above. Saussure, in many respects, was developing a theory of the code, absent consideration of the matter encoded, the coders, or the encoding process. The issues of the role of the coder (how the messages are heard, read, seen); the code (what rules are used to interpret the messages) and sign–object relations, all of which bear on the relationship between the message and its sender and receiver, are aspects of the theory of *coding* (Eco, 1979). In the empirically oriented social sciences, data analysis requires an articulation of code, coder and encoded. This leads to questions of context and analysis of an extant system of expressions and the sign vehicles by which they are conveyed.

ANALYSIS

With this background, we can now address some of the standard problems that are taken up in semiotic analyses. Signs differ in their 'level of abstraction' regardless of the vocabulary of terms used. Music is the classic non-referential mode – it has no referent except other music. At the other level, one can imagine abstractions of a simple sort such as an emblem, a personal name, or a picture of a person. The modern world now has the capacity to copy anything, from the human voice to classic paintings – we live in an age of copies. Signs differ in the degree to which they are internally tight or loose as a system. Any system of signs, Morse code, etiquette, street signs, language, chemical formulae, ranges in the extent of its *internal coherence* and interpretive possibilities. The system may 'work' through different relations among the expressions and content, as well as between the signs and other signs, for example, by analogy, homology, or phonetic similarities (Guiraud, 1975). These relationships, as Silverman (1983) argues, can obtain between expressions, between contents, between expression and content of a given sign. The same complexity can be found in strings of signs called messages. A *tightly linked code* permits deductions and induction from it, for example chemical or algebraic formulae, or the sequential notations and extrapolations of computer programs. A closed system is logically insulated from the associations of everyday life and exists independent of it. A *loosely linked code*, on the other hand, like etiquette, or the system of concepts called 'social science', is shaped by its concrete realizations. Its internal structure tends to be inconsistent or loosely coupled, and internal relations quite complex and subject to subjective interpretations. Think of the differences between the concept of 'role' in an organization, a family, or a team; or the variations possible within a system of greetings ('hi', 'hello', 'how's it goin'?', 'how ya doin'?', 'good morning', 'good day') or the leaving set ('goodbye', 'ciao', 'adios', 'have a nice day', 'have a good one', 'see ya'). While a closed system is theoretically independent of its concrete manifestations, an open system is embedded in everyday life and, as a result, the 'shadings' of the expressions 'rub off' or affect the meaning of the contents. Further, the role of register (the degree of formality of language, from casual to highly formal), honorifics (how people are addressed, whether with titles or implicit regard to degrading terms), and time and place (often critical in non-literate systems) are often critical to message transmission (Levinson, 1985).

Eco, Morris, and Sebeok, among others, have argued convincingly for the importance of the pragmatic and referential aspects of semiotics and their link to the social sciences, especially what might be called cultural studies (the social and social psychological connection between history, values, norms, and beliefs in the holistic study of ways of life). Eco also implicitly addresses the fundamental issue of aesthetics, that of the impact of the object (and/or the sign vehicle that carries the message) on the audience. When notions like audience are connected to interpretant and context, sociological issues, those of perspective, social role, values and beliefs, must be addressed. None of these writers, nor the French structuralists, employ the self as a central idea.[8] Introducing the concept of a self as both transmitting and processing information complicates analyses, as seen below when semiotic association is addressed.

ELABORATION AND INTERPOLATIONS

The ideas of Saussure were converted in a very powerful fashion to apply the model of language to other social systems – kinship, manners, myths, colors, and everyday processes in diverse cultures. Beginning with Lévi-Strauss (1963), structuralism in its various forms swept the intellectual world in France for the best part of thirty years.[9]

The work of Roland Barthes, touched on above, has been seminal in the flow of semiotic ideas into cultural studies. His writings, even in translation, are elegant, lucid, and at times quite brilliant. His view is that semiotics is a sub-category of semiology, his own version of the language-structure model. His work has ranged from the masterful discussions of style and structures in *S/Z* (1974) and *The Fashion System* (1984), to light and witty essays on wrestling, French patriotism, and topical subjects. In many respects the power of his writing results from the exploitation of a point within a context that is overlooked on merely cursory examination. In many respects, both Barthes and Derrida were arguing against the Saussurian notion (also found in Lévi-Strauss) that signifier and signified were always linked in a few and very limited ways. The context and ambiguity of signs, especially to a reader, should be explored.

Debates about the nature of knowledge, science, and society, distorted by translation, lack of knowledge of the French cultural and political context, and works seen through the eyes of American empiricism, toppled over into the United States in the late 1970s and 1980s. The resultant contemporaneous discussion, moribund, if not dead, in France, is multifaceted and abiding and concerns 'structuralism', 'the linguistic turn', 'semiotics', and 'postmodernism', all of which are products of the politicized intellectual scene in Paris in the 1970s. When the pragmatism of Peirce, Mead and Morris, enhanced by the efforts of Sebeok,[10] MacCannell and MacCannell (1982), and Eco, reached American social science, it was too late.[11] The dominance of the Foucault version of structuralism, drawing on his readings of historical facts and using the *semiotic analogy*, had been established.

However, the importance of culture and representation in sign work was emphasized by structuralists and post-structuralists. The argument goes as follows: if expressions or *signifiers* point, indicate or arbitrarily symbolize something social, rather than merely being a logical connection as in Saussure, that is, become representational, and are linked to content, or *signifieds*, the connection, the linkage, is cultural and derives largely from context. These modes of perception-interpretation, in turn, may be institutionalized and become unexamined connections. Second, the divisions between earlier versions (Lévi-Straussian) and later versions of structuralism can be calibrated precisely with respect to how much attention was given to active, situated sense-making. In many respects, nevertheless, phenomenology is reduced in Bourdieu (1977), for example, to a question of agency, *habitus* and other structural glosses, and the relevance of the self is denied. This is true in versions of structuralism including those as diverse as Baudrillard, Lyotard, and Deleuze. These latter are modified and stylized versions of cultural Marxism in which exchange of meaning and exchange of symbols are parallel, analogous ideas which can be understood in the same way as the exchange of money. The irrational, the semi-conscious, and the traditional pattern these exchanges in a mysterious and mystifying fashion, and they work through overtly richly elaborated symbols and institutions. In this process, institutionalized versions of the true, the real, and the human become accepted as unquestioned 'common sense'.

One cannot easily combine *formalism* via structuralism, which denies the transcendence of the self or ego, and *existential meaning*, with a critique that rests on an interpretive, aesthetically grounded existentialism. This formulation now drives American discussions of the crisis of representation, especially in cultural studies (Denzin and Lincoln, 1994). The peculiar and eccentric merging of structuralism, a response to phenomenology, and existentialism in France emerged as an attack on all forms of structural-functionalism and interpretive sociology in America, and became most powerful as a dismissive, anarchistic anti-theory. The idea that standpoint and deep unconscious forces shaped perception, feeling, and interpretation was honed to a fine edge in writings that critiqued the dominant patriarchy in social sciences.[12]

USES OF SEMIOTICS

Recent variations on semiotic research

The uses of semiotics in social science, outside anthropology, have been largely descriptive.

Tightly reasoned analyses, based on rather narrow assumptions about meaning generated within the taxonomies developed (Bouissac, 1976), because they obviate the question of framing or perspective (standpoint), are dubious. In other words, the question of who frames the meaning of a sign, or sequence of gestures or postures, is unanswered by generalized cultural descriptions. The abstractions produced concerning sets of oppositions themselves are questioned by some, not only their surface features, but also their deeper significance (Needham, 1981, 1983). These questions have been extended in quite masterful and detailed fashion by the neo-Freudian analyst, Jacques Lacan (1968), who uses the linguistic metaphor to articulate stages of development and signification (mirror stage, and two levels of symbolization, the imaginary and the real), and the connections between 'symptoms' and metaphor and signs and desire. In this move, the overt or 'stimulus model' of Peirce is converted into the Freudian model of symbolic interpretation of the sign and includes the powerful notion that the unconscious is itself structured by language.[13] Some intense work has been done on what might be called the commodification of experience, studies of the social construction and reconstruction via signs of 'excitement', of 'culture', of new experience (D. MacCannell, 1986). Both Dorst (1992), writing of the creation of a tourist place from Chadd's Ford, Delaware, and MacCannell, writing on the touristic experience, have shown how selective revealing and concealing via signs, in museums, displays, exhibits, talking and lived history (e.g., Williamsburg), simulates the real, and induces an amnesia for historical contingencies and social structure. In a *tour de force essay*, Eco (1981) traces copies and simulation across the United States, showing how the experience of the real is produced by the false and the deceptive. He includes a variety of 'Last Suppers' that he views in Southern California, some painted on wood, some in stone, some elegant, others crude, and dismisses them as vulgar. Arguably, the notion of the 'real', or non-copy originals, should perhaps now be restricted to the world of fine art (Eco, 1981).[14] On the other hand, Eco finds the robotic Mickey Mouses (Mickey Mice?) and other fantasy figures in Disneyland charming and beguiling (my words). These exercises in ethnography locate *context*, showing how the references of the expression shift from the 'original' to versions of it that are far removed from the original form, yet are viable, commercially exchanged and desired objects.

The social sciences are best at explaining decline or growth, the steady erosion of social organization, but inept in identifying the beginnings of any social process or institution. The issue of deriving a head term, or the bases by which the denotations and connotations are arrayed (discussed below), remains a question whenever one is using semiotics as a technique, or in an open system analysis; as opposed to reanalyzing data from a closed system. One of the trickiest issues in the inductive case is how to establish the range of connotations associated with a given term, or set of terms. As is implied, the focus of semiotics on signs, rather than on narratives, makes the connection of the system of signs used with the 'concrete instantiations' studied a translation activity, rather than a deductive exercise. The intervals used in the taxonomies derived may not, strictly speaking, be comparable – they may variously be nominal, cardinal, ordinal or interval, thus the 'space' between the sign categories has meaning as well. As Derrida (1979) has argued, the link between the expression and content is always lagged or deferred, such that other signs are activated and other associations touched off – one sign has as its interpretant another sign or set of signs and so on. Thus, narrow and acontextual analyses tend to be not only unsatisfying aesthetically, but also rather unrewardingly thin. Denzin (1986) notes that semiotics tends to be rigidly insensitive to the code–coder–encoded processes, as well as to history. While the idea of 'constant semiosis' is appealing, it is difficult to reconcile with fieldwork-based analysis, because most fieldwork is done over brief periods of time and rarely includes the historical precursors of the present scenes.

Perhaps the most subtle applications of semiotics have been in the performative or poetics area, and anthropological work has addressed some of the aesthetics of performances and rituals. The classic study of ritual, arguably, is that of Rappaport (1971, 2000) which defines ritual in terms of its redundancy, self-referential character and wholly non-referential content and form. His argument is that the rise of the symbol culturally precipitates uncertainty, ambiguity, and ambivalence in human relations. Symbolic repertoire, whether pictures, texts, maps, or words, moves away from the present, the known and the experienced. The question of trust cannot be foresworn. Ritual asserts the ahistorical, formulaic, unswerving, repetition that is taken as true. It is the base for other communications. Even works like Rosaldo's (1989) and Gossen's (1974) on metaphors tend to be rooted in the here-and-now context of their tribal studies. In large part, however, this work focuses on narrative and poetic language rather than on the referential aspects of speech. We do not have a conventionalized language for analyzing prose meanings, as is the case for poetry (Culler, 2000: 66–77), and attempts to analyze social science prose styles have been ingenious, but have had little influence (Cushman and Marcus, 1977; Gusfield, 1989; McCloskey, 1985; Richardson, 1997). Such work is closer to ritual and ceremonial studies than to semiotic analysis. Furthermore, attention given to writing and representation without connection to the social world has diverted attention from the task of connecting the expression with the content as embedded in a described context (Van Maanen, 1995). The study of writing *per se*, discourse and its forms, is marginal to the semiotic analysis of referential language that is the focus of this chapter.

Qualifications and subtleties

While pragmatism emphasized the doing of communication, how meaning was created over time, and was profoundly anti-reductionist, it was the phenomenological formalist, Erving Goffman, who stated flatly that there is no communication that is not situated. Goffman (1983) argued that there are many levels of interlaced orderings, but they are based in and validated against the primary reality – face-to-face co-presence. When this 'base' of face-to-face interaction is lacking, it is nevertheless created and brought to that which is experienced. Hence the complicated nature of communication on the internet – it tends to be ungrounded. The endlessly iterative algorithm of interpretation exists only in theory, for time, energy, and patience, not to speak of memory, are limited. As Goffman (1974) wrote, people do not long tolerate meaninglessness, and the question is how they bring closure to complex communicative displays. Ironically, Goffman, like Charles Morris, had no interest in 'inner states' or 'thoughts' but remained an observer of all that is offered up and taken to be real.

Semiotics concerns all forms of signs; however, the most studied sign is certainly the symbol. A symbol is a type of sign in which the expression refers to something else in an arbitrary fashion, or is embedded in cultural context such that without this context it has either richly ambiguous meaning or is merely a nonce symbol signifying nothing. Dean MacCannell usefully distinguishes sign and symbol. He writes that a symbol is a SIGN that lacks a syntactical component so that its meaning seems constant (1979: 102). It seems to reference the same thing for 'respondents', but floats in order to do this work. In other words, the absence of syntax is a determinant of slippery meaning because the rules for combining symbols are unclear or are manipulated. Sign work, for precision, requires rules as constraining and predictable as grammar and syntax rules governing sentence construction. Advertising plays with desire, and manipulates ambiguous and absent features of communication. Think of such ideas as 'Toyota, I love what you do to me', '[you should] drive excitement' or an iconic representation of two Mercedes cars being driven side by side into an ark with pairs of exotic animals as rains begin (these are all televised ads for automobiles). They produce associations that are produced by the absent thing, the car, emotional states.

A sign is a kind of SIGN, according to MacCannell (1979: 104), that lacks the *semantic* component so that the meaning it conveys seems *restricted to the situation in which it occurs*. Poetry plays on ambiguity of this type. In Eco's terms, signification based on symbols (used as MacCannell does) is 'overcoded' in that instances and examples all are generalized and stabilized by the vague referential component (e.g., desire, fun, patriotism, thrift, religiosity, sin, or morality), while the latter, based on signs (in MacCannell's terms), is 'undercoded'. The possible range of inference is insufficiently generalized. Reference is, as Eco writes, a matter of cultural interpretation and the extent to which the reference of a statement is understood to be a token of a general instance or type. The fact that reference is related to a code and its many meanings does not mean that all complex messages are inexplicably ideological (Denzin, 1986), or that their connotations are a matter of open-ended desire. An ideological reading is in effect a 'metareading', which adds connotations to the stated. Put in another fashion, the study of signs, or the patterning of communication, must be used with the study of signs about signs, or social organization.

This raises questions of the role of the *simulacrum*, or a false representation, and of the ever-present question of copies. Baudrillard (1988) argues that although signs operate at several levels, the mythological has become dominant, and that signs about signs are fetishized – that we become attached to the emotional meaning of the sign beyond its instrumental use or other symbolic value. As a result, the sign is embroiled in emotional attachments and the use no longer dominates (this is an echo, of course, of Marx's view of ideology and consumption). He states that the produced is the real, or conversely that anything that can be reproduced is seen as real. Baudrillard's writing conveys the unseen; there is a lurking sense in Baudrillard that the real exists somewhere. For example, he writes that 'Disneyland', a fetishized symbol, conceals the real fantasyland of consumption that is America. Disneyland is a simulacrum, engaged in a play with other signs and symbols. Like Walter Benjamin's *Arcades Project* (1999), fascination with the play of signs easily diverts one from the constraints of the material world. It is clear that copies and copies of copies dominate modern consciousness, something one might call the power of the icon.

THE OPERATION CALLED SEMIOTICS

The operational

Semiotic analysis can be seen in time terms as a series of operations. Semiotics requires (a) a rich description of the phenomenon (a police communications system, a circus, a famous tourist venue, a ritual such as a wedding or an African tribal court), and (b) identification of the key features of the phenomena or process; and (c) it isolates domains of particular interest to the investigator (see Manning, 1989). These domains, in turn, may be (d) theoretically derived, as when medical taxonomies are laid onto native categories, or arise from the eliciting process itself. These identified stages precede (e) the presentation of taxonomy or several taxonomies that combine a created classification, categories, items, and some specialized relationships within the described system of notation. What is suppressed in such a description of operations are those assumptive matters that connect. This common-sense knowledge, often unverbalized in a culture, and therefore more difficult to draw upon in an analysis, must be employed to 'reinsert' the semiotically treated material into a broader, yet specified cultural context.

Each expression is linked in some way to a content, and each sign to another sign and so on, and each of these connections or links is based on a meaning that may be unrecognized. These connections are culture, or the ways we read off others' readings of the world. In some ways, semiotics is in danger of being readings of other's minds, a tricky and often distorted operation.

In doing fieldwork, it is often very difficult to define context because it is often unspoken, or unrecognized, even by one's informants. Thus, one is not attempting to reproduce the native's culture, or the native point of view (Geertz, 1970). The perspective is not theirs, cognitively or emotionally. Even when an anthropologist is working with a translation from the indigenous language, the context of use that makes words, pictures or music meaningful cannot be reproduced. We return then to the critical point of all forms of cognitive analysis, including semiotics: one must know the context in order to discern subtleties in meaning. One of the most luminous of these examples is how Malinowski's (1923) description of fishing, canoeing, competition, and geography amongst the Trobriand islanders makes sensible three fragments, hardly a sentence, and thereby supplies cultural context. 'Fishing' glosses this horrendously. By positing system and elements, semiotics cries out for pragmatics, which in turn hinges on various ways into context, either linguistically, non-verbally, or culturally legitimated forms.

The importance of context brings up a penultimate point in the social science approach to data analysis. Whereas the *literati* seek to explicate uncertainties, anomalies, fragments of experience that are evocative, if not true, social science tries to pin down meanings and reduce ambiguities. Perhaps the most difficult of these maneuvers in social science is the proper use of the great trope, irony. Irony contrasts that which is with that which might be or should be; it plays on the contradiction of surface and reality, past and present, life and ideals, and so on.

Since all social science is an attempt to understand how things work elegantly or simply or parsimoniously, following at least the guidelines of a science, research soon discovers that rules are not followed, that people lie and betray each other, that the law is an umbrella that hides a variety of things, few of which are 'fair' or 'just'. Ways of explaining the differences between ideal and real are the real tools of the craft.

Semiotics and poetic meaning

In some ways a poem is a verbal icon, or a sketch resembling the things or matters drawn about. Think of Gertrude Stein's epigram, 'A rose is a rose is a rose'. She is playing on the idea of an expression 'rose' that can be associated with a number of contents such as a flower with a botanical name, the name of a person, an ornament, a decoration on a dress, an actual person, a symbol standing for a company as a logo, and finally, a pun on 'eros', 'arose', or 'rows'. The ways in which one hears such an expression gives it a context, or frames it as a literalism, a symbol, a pun or literary maxim. Iconically:

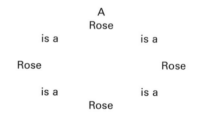

This arrangement is an iconic suggestion that this is to be read as a circular poem of some kind, and as such the interconnections of the meanings are shown figuratively as well as by the repeated sounds and rhythm of the words if read. The spaces communicate as expressions. Each rose is a different rose indicated by its position, but what do the positions mean other than relative to each other?

Eco notes that any semantic outline of associations would be a 'regulatory hypothesis' (an inference about how associations would be formed by the reader), eroded in part by being subjected to analysis. In effect, it is a testable hypothesis. He advances what might be called a methodological principle of semantic/semiotic research: a semantic field can only be described if one studies the conditions of signification of the message

(Eco, 1979: 128). The case for social semiotics lies in this requirement. Identification and analysis of 'the conditions of the signification of the message' must rely heavily on working out the social context in which the 'message' (which can be as diverse as a single word or an entire text) is sent (produced in whatever fashion *and* sent) and received (gathered in, made sense of, read, interpreted).

McDonald's menus

A well-known matter that can be worked over using semiotics are McDonald's menus, a series of variously colored distinctive placards listing items available for each of the three meals served, a representation seen throughout the world.[15]

Notice first that it is center stage, high and visible at first glance inside the business. The menus stand above and behind the servers in a well-lit place and in front of the partially seen (through slits) kitchen. They are immediately visible when one walks into any McDonald's anywhere. It is therefore timeless and in a sense a cultural icon that stands for itself as well as its many copies. It has resonance. McDonald's is represented mentally and in advertisements synedochecally – as 'golden arches'. The icon stands as a symbol of many things. The source of integration at a metaphoric level across all items within the menus is phonetic, the repetitive pun on the sound of 'Mc', as in 'Egg McMuffin', 'Big Mac', 'Chicken McNuggets', and the 'McChicken sandwich'. The menus are the target – the to-be-explained representational matter. As *sign vehicles*, they are bright, colorful, readable, and set out prominently. They are square and positioned straight ahead. The menus are divided into four sections – more or less, breakfast, lunch and dinner and a menu with sub-categories (drinks, desserts and extras). A recent addition is 'value meals' which combine items into ensembles that are less expensive than each item bought *à la carte*. Within each menu the items are arranged from hot to cold and from more expensive to less expensive. By any standard, the constitutive items are cheap, high-carbohydrate 'fast food', easily and quickly consumed on foot, in a car or standing. We can see immediately that the *domains of meaning* around which the items are clustered are the conventional three daily meals in the Anglo-American world (and 'snacks'). These three are contrasting categories, but not mutually exclusive, as some items, especially drinks, can be eaten at any of the meals. The items are *metaphorically* related because they make up in total an organic unity, 'a meal'. Each one connotes the meal in which it is located – for example, an Egg McMuffin is composed of two common breakfast staples, eggs and muffins. Within each value meal is a constant coupling of main item, fries and a drink, a contrast of hot, warm and cold. The three meals make up a total, or 'daily bread'. This idea is part of the *belief* in Anglo-American society that one needs 'three squares' a day. The items, of course can in theory be assembled in many ways at any time, but operations (time of day), marketing, and advertising in fact limit them.[16]

This set of propositions can be further illustrated. Consider the color and visibility of the menu, its organization into familiar, well-understood and named domains, its items that are familiar from 'normal meals' and other menus. The menus are ordered from left to right, a representation of the time progression of the day (from morning to night and back again). The menus are the same in every McDonald's, hence predictable, efficient in conveying coded and abstracted information (and known by children from age 3). Time limits selection from the items as breakfast is only cooked until 11 a.m., but the rest of the menu is available from 11 a.m. until closing. The menus are located above the eye-line so that one can ponder and still be in line (people are encouraged to queue immediately and asked 'Can I help the next person in line?'). Customers are prompted by queries that increase profits: 'Would you like fries with that?' Conversely, the employees can make and remake the items without thinking, can memorize the menu (reproduced in the cash registers), can easily cluster the items for entering them, and can assemble and fill the cardboard containers needed for any list of items. Whether one works from the theorizing to the items, constructing a kind of ideal type of 'McDonaldization', or elicits the menu and items from speaker-hearers, the same configuration results. In this sense, although McDonald's is only part of the material work, the symbolization of meals, items (named commodities), their placement in the kitchen and dispensation provide a reproduction of a kind of social ordering over and over again. If one takes this display further, it indicates culture. Soon, the routines of standing in line, ordering from the menu, recognizing and knowing the items in a 'value meal', speaking of them in shorthand terms ('Big Mac with fries') become habitual. We can read off other's readings of these symbols to orient and reorient our own behavior. We can thus imagine in advance what is wanted, how to order it, what it will cost, what it will weigh or what will be required to carry it, and even how long it takes to eat it! Finally, note that the key head terms, the meals, and the menus, seem 'obvious' ways of ordering the data, but are not based on 'theory'.

FURTHER EXAMPLES OF
SEMIOTIC DATA ANALYSIS

Semiotics permits various kinds of methodological 'translations'. The McDonald's menu analysis uses semiotics as a *method*.[17] The following example works from a closed to an open system (crime mapping). The second example illustrates semiotics as a *technique* and uses flag display as material.

Semiotic method

Police in the Anglo-American world (North America, the UK, and the Antipodes) have begun to use geocoded data for analyzing crime patterns. The data are collected, and organized on the basis of the address from which the call was made, which units were dispatched to the call, and include formation on what, if any, arrests or stops were made as a result of the dispatch. They are then mapped by computer to create multicolored maps. They are ornamented with signifiers (see, for example, Braga et al., 1998). These maps are attractive polysemantic displays that have all but replaced the old pin map means of plotting (mostly) reported and recorded crimes. They are engaging, and rather easy to produce, given the software and the extent database.

Many things are symbolized by the maps' signs. The map itself is an icon, a kind of abstract representation of socially defined matters in spatial terms. A map suggests or bears a resemblance to the subject of the map. As an icon, however, it also contains other signification. It may contain or display, often at the side, indexes or lists of places shown on the map, such as streets, parks, or

interstate freeways. In the Windows operating system on a computer, the screen on which a map can be displayed is surrounded by visible and invisible menus with lists and icons (sometimes combined) that can be 'clicked' into visibility by pointing to an icon or a word. On the map itself are signifiers, or quasi-symbols, requiring the active presence of an interpretant to make an interpretation (Culler, 1977: 129). As noted above, any signifier is incomplete, requires an interpretant and a signified. No sign 'speaks for itself'. To be heard, it must speak to someone. All representations, such as tables, figures, graphs, or models (with arrows and directions), expressions require interpretation with reference to the content(s) they stand for. A map, like a picture, is an iconic sign, displaying other signs.

In what follows, I use the nomenclature of Peirce and Morris, speaking of signs and their subdivisions – icons, indexes, and symbols. For each one has a visible indicator, a *designata*, and something to which it 'points' in a general way, a *designatum*. The two are linked by means of an intepretant in a context.

Crime maps, as currently used, employ four types of signs. *Symbols* are those signs with an arbitrary or motivated cultural link between the expression and content that is problematic. *Icons* resemble the thing represented, as noted above. *Indices* represent a place or thing in conventional terms, for example a hand print denoting a person's presence. *Marks* are rather arbitrary, perhaps personalized or idiosyncratic, denoting a reminder of something to which one wants to return, like a bookmark.

A map with crimes shown on it, or a crime map (Figure 25.1), is a miniaturized, stylized, conventional representation of a very complex reality. To what does it point and in what context? Let us make the first and rather obvious point that the display conventions of maps, how they are shown in what place and time and to what audience, can themselves enhance or detract from the effects of a map. The variations in maps are sometimes shown, sometimes explained in an accompanying text, and sometimes merely assumed. Among these variations are the following:

- The scale of the map.
- The colors used to represent and which are conferred on given signs, e.g., hot colors in Western society such as red and yellow, neutral colors such as gray, brown,

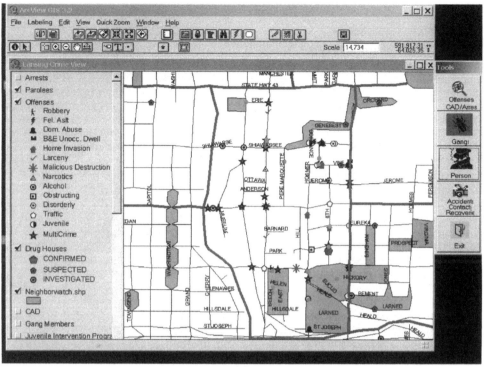

(a)

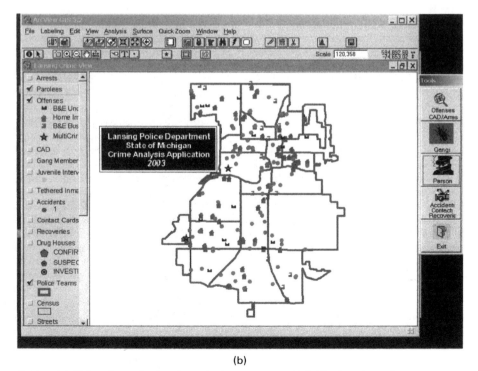

(b)

Figure 25.1 *(a) Thirty days of crime in a single team area. Neighborhood watch areas are shaded – these areas stay far more crime-free than those with no neighborhood watch. (b) Thirty days of burglaries city-wide. Note the presence of some parolees near the actual crimes.*

green or blue, and cold colors such as black, make a different impact on viewers.

- The time dimension included in the map, e.g., a month, a year, several years, a series (roughly the number of data points registered).
- The processing of the data prior to their display on the map: have they been treated statistically, e.g., using log-linear standardization of a time series?
- The signs selected for inclusion and those omitted, e.g., crimes, names of offenders, victims, ethnic composition of the area.
- The size of the map as displayed.
- The number and kinds of signs shown on the map at one time, e.g., a few scattered instances such as homicides in the last month as opposed to auto thefts.
- The material on which the map is displayed, e.g., on a large or small screen, on a printer with various sizes that can be adjusted, on a pasteboard or wall (related to the previous point about size, but an independent dimension in any case).
- Any descriptive material included on or around the map: texts, numbers, tables, etc.

Given that these vary, the question is how are they 'known' and used, rather than simply what constitutes their configuration. The crime maps in use by police are *occasioned*, or developed, printed and displayed for a reason – to inform a meeting, meet a citizen's request, fill an officer's request, or for a crime analysis (McDonald, 2002; Silverman, 2000). Police are pragmatists, and produce maps to do something, intervene, even if that 'something' is unclear, vague or unimagined. Crime mapping has flowered in police departments for several reasons. The advent of cheap, reliable geocoded databases produced by commercial vendors such as ArcInfo means that it is possible to map CAD data (computerized calls for service) and combine them with other data compiled such as home ownership, suicides, hospital and trauma data, social services data and so on. The current fashion to urge police to become closer to neighborhoods and their publics, manifested in the community policing rhetoric, has generated interest in supplying the public with data on crime in their neighborhood in simple, vivid and portable (even electronic) form (Dungworth, 2000). This same set of forces has led the police to adopt a 'problem solving' approach (how widely this is used is not known – the literature enthuses about it but gives few examples of it in action). Problem solving, in which a call for service is set into a broader socio-economic pattern to discern what the call (literally) signifies other than an immediate request for service, moves to more abstract levels of reasoning. Finally, there is increased interest in crime prevention rather than merely reacting to extant and known problems indicated by calls for service and the vicissitudes of random patrol. This means in police terms that the maps should be used to anticipate and solve problems in advance, using 'intelligence'. Such maps might indicate where police actions might reduce, prevent or mollify crime or the effects of crime.

Crime maps can include any or all of the types of signs noted above, even on the same map. Consider these: marks (street locations), indices (the location of gangs, drug dealing or crack houses), and symbols (large blurs, the size of which connotes several crimes in an approximate location, called 'hot spots'). Each of the *designata* shown points somewhere, but has to be linked or interpreted on some basis to a content or reference. Notice also that what is represented is itself quite different in its material reality – gangs are groups, crimes are endpoints of processes; street addresses are static, and calls for service are surrogates for a very complex set of processes, both organizational and at the household level. There is similarity in the *designata* level in that they all refer to some sort of 'disorder'. But the *designatum* is very different. What, for example, do the indexes showing traffic accidents represent? They could be some or all of the following: drunk driving, speeding; poor road design, construction, or maintenance; road conditions and/or bad weather; children crossing at unexpected times; poor signposting. What about icons of gangs? Do they refer to people, crimes, meeting places, graffiti, residences, and to what other of these does any given one point? While the range of meaning is relatively restricted for indexes and marks, symbols reach out beyond their narrow denotations to touch off other associations (connotations). Some of the interpretants are known and accepted – the uniform crime report and the typology of crimes have a long history of about 75 years as a code for organizing incidents of reported crime and their significance to the police and the public. They are roughly ordered by level of severity and impact on victims, from homicide to auto theft.

Although a given instance may violate the category's rank, they are grouped together as a collection category. Likewise, arson figures are linked conventionally to costs of insurance, damage and repair or rebuilding. Then others – traffic, gangs, accidents – cannot be understood without deep cultural knowledge of neighborhoods, police activities, local politics, ethnic residential patterns and past crimes. Descriptions, such as the number of gangs in a city, or areas of intense dealing, can be produced by officers who know an area. These are the background against which the signs have meaning.

Looking now at the maps as aesthetic spatial representations, what is the relationship between the three kinds of *designata* found on maps? Marks and indexes can be read off with some common-sense understanding of an area: gang territories, the prevalence of stolen cars, and the past history of traffic stops in an area. These are connected synecdoche-like, as are the signs they create, and they 'add up to' the local level of disorder. When placed side by side in substitutable fashion, they are metonymical – they are a list. If they are to be seen as part of a problem-solving complex or exercise, they must be elevated into symbols with an arbitrary yet known meaning, and a readily accessible interpretant.[19] Recall that 'hot spots' could be created from a cluster of any number or kind of incidents, from slips by the elderly on icy sidewalks to homicides. The idea or the label rubs off on the connection between the *designata* and the *designatum* – the connection itself is hot! Similarly, the short-circuiting of disorders into 'broken windows' – including everything from jaywalking, pornographic book stores and squeegee men washing windows to high levels of drug dealing on the streets with related crimes of robbery and assault – is a distortion and conflation of types of problems without a proper code.

The modes of combination of signs run from mere listing to metaphor or even myth with connotations consistent with police ideology – 'something about which something should be done or it will get worse' (Bittner, 1972). While the expressions collected and labeled may have a variety of causes, possible points of intervention (primary, secondary, or tertiary prevention), offenders, and social consequences, they are selectively and dramatically pointed to and spotlighted as an aspect of reality.

In part because they do not think 'metaphorically', and in part because police databases (fingerprints, photos of those arrested, prior arrests, etc.), with a few exceptions, are not connected so that they can be aggregated, the police have short horizons.[20] The police when using geocoded data have mounted a set of severely limited interventions that replicate their usual tactics. These interventions include saturation patrols, special squads to make arrests in high-crime areas, and sweeps to clean up street dealing areas. Crime mapping has been used to reify already known 'problems' and to intervene in conventional reactive fashion (Braga et al., 1998; Greene-Mazerolle and Terrill, 1997). A map alone, a set of representations, does not make a 'problem' visible. Nor does it display alternative approaches to the apparent problem, options such as crime-prevention efforts, problem solving, or co-production with local groups, nor non-interventionist approaches. Crime maps (and other analytic models), while often colorful, fascinating, and provocative, have no intrinsic actionable meaning. A picture may need a thousand words to explain it. Maps combine diverse types of information, bearing on many aspects of social organization, often with complex linkages, and use dramatic size, color, and dynamics to command attention.

What is not shown on a map? Crime maps reveal information, but many underlying social processes, e.g., social disorganization (Sampson and Bartusch, 1998), are not shown on them but read off or into them. The world represented on the map is not composed totally of ideas, or conceptions, but has a material, physical reality. The constraints of railroad tracks, parks, vacant lots, and high-rise public housing projects are real and visible, whereas the constraints of gang memberships, co-offending, networks of victims and their 'at risk' status are not visible, nor so easily comprehended.

What is the relationship between that which is represented or seen on the map and what is brought to it, matters unseen? It is clear that the figurative and the metonymic outperform the metaphoric. Maps certainly dramatize selected indices of the selected offenses. Maps have vivid texture, variable size and flexibility, and can be easily manipulated in public presentations using graphics software, allowing the presenter to zoom in, bring up details of a particular crime by clicking on an address, and add layers of information while speaking. Graphics packages produce beautiful multicolored and coded maps of various sizes and detail, and can easily distract the viewer from considering what underlies the display, animates the changes, and what they indicate and symbolize. The rarer the crime, the more dramatic the iconic presentation. When a serious crime, serial murder or rape is symbolized by huge, mountainous red blurs (created by amplifying each crime in an arbitrarily designated area) rising in the middle of large cities, when a number of years are collapsed into a location on a map, they are excessively dramatic. These displays are very eye-catching *and* misleading because the color and size of the sign are mistaken, via resemblance, not decoding, for the seriousness or pervasiveness of the underlying problem or process or criminal act.

Semiotics as a technique

As noted above, a semiotic analysis begins with a description, some points about which to muse, and then proceeds to identify units and their relationships. Semiotics can be useful as a technique to reformulate flags featured post September 11, 2001. The flag is a sign (it represents something to somebody but, as Peirce writes, it is 'incomplete') and a sign vehicle (it displays other signs), a *designata* whose *designatums* are many and complex and set off semiotic chains. An American flag is a multisonorous sign about signs, an iconic symbol (an icon that also has signifying properties because it raises culturally grounded meanings), and thus speaks to social organization, on the one hand, and about feelings and deep emotions, on the other. In many respects, a flag is a powerful stimulus or summating sign, that works because by displaying it one does not have to verbalize, explain, enunciate, rationalize or grapple with what 'terrorism', a 'war' against 'terrorism', or what differences between al-Qaeda, the Taliban and the Northern Alliance mean. Let us begin with a narrative of points, a compendium of associations that have arisen (I write this in March 2002). Think of these associations:

1. Who wears the flag has significance, and the flag has significance as identity and as identification. The firefighters and police of New York City who died in the disaster are heroes, celebrated with flag-draped coffins, and by association other firefighter are heroes (brothers of Patriots footballer Chris Andruzzi). The sign rubs off on the signer or person who bears it. Mariah Carey wears it on her dress, and is thus a patriot. Similarly, the addition of a small flag to the uniforms of postal employees, firefighters, and police associates them with the values that the flag connotes.[21] The Vice President visiting the scene wears a hardhat with a flag on the right-hand side.

2. The flag refers to itself and to other more abstract ideas and beliefs, some quasi-religious in the sense that patriotism is a kind of 'civil religion' in America. As an iconic sign conveying rich and complex associations, a flag is easily taken as a metasign, a source of ideological meanings – stabilized, exaggerated and simple summated feelings and beliefs not subject to empirical demonstration. These ideas – unity, God, bless and blessing, our country, America – have mythological associations with past battles, heroes, and victimization. It elevates the standing of the country over other matters – individual lives lost, personal differences, the complexities of international politics, history, and of religion. It also elevates the American nation over others.

3. The violations of the past display conventions regarding the flying of the flag suggest that this time is an exceptional one. The content and manner of flag display are governed by code, flag-related etiquette, which conflicts with primitive, virtually spontaneous displays of patriotism. The sign vehicle, the cloth and staff, has sacred aspects. For example, an American flag is not to be displayed at night without proper lighting, must be displayed only on the front fenders of a car, and is to be burned ceremoniously when it shows signs of wear, ragged edges, fading, or discoloration. Driving with ragged flags flowing from a bent aerial, or staff mounted in the back of a pickup at night without lighting on the flag itself, and when it is ragged, dishonors the flag. Yet its display is honorific.[22]

4. The banalization and comodification of the flag-as-sign took place rapidly. The *Boston Globe* published a story including a half-page display (October 25, 2001) showing fingernails painted with the flag; a wedding dress in ghastly combinations

of red, white and blue (highlighted by a blue veil with a little flag perched on top of the bride's head); a backless, sideless evening dress in primarily blue stars with a sweeping red and white stripe ensemble sweeping across the back and down to the ankles; stars-and-stripes boots by an Italian designer for $485, and Mariah Carey's beflagged dress. T-shirts, lapel pins, bumper stickers, and running shoes permit the sign to be embedded in the everyday, in shopping, display, conspicuous consumption, and the circulation of symbols that indicate further modes of differentiation of style, class and taste. The unfolding of flags chronologically is ongoing.[23]

It appears that there are at least four *domains or connotative clusters* of meaning which organize the denotative meanings of the flag as displayed post September 11. The first is *patriotism*, including active notions such as loyalty, patriotism, chauvinism, honor, and passive ones such as the good citizen, or merely being a citizen, and contrasting with disloyalty, betrayal, low support for country and dishonor. The second is *sport* in which American competitiveness and aggression are represented at second remove. Thus, within days of September 11, football, baseball and eventually basketball teams sported small flags on their caps, helmets, jerseys, and outer jackets. The third domain is that of *entertainment*, in which the flag is now more than merely on display for opening ceremonies, and at games and occasions, but is flaunted, paraded around before games by honor guards (Marines in dress uniforms), held high after games by the visitors, and displayed as the ragged flag from the World Trade Center firefighters. The fourth domain might be called *vulgar fashion*, as seen in pictures showing the flag on the front of Mariah Carey's formal dress, and on the breasts of men and women wearing designer sweatshirts. These domains, in some sense, can be ranked from 'honorable' or quasi-sacred to the most secular or profane. The admixture of these elements creates a dissonant response – is this sacred, and honorable, or the profane and disgusting vulgarizing of a national symbol?

The flag, regardless of domain as a symbol, has denotative meanings. Denotatively, the flag shows the stars as states, the stripes as the original 13 colonies, and the colors stand for courage (red), purity (white), and tenacity (blue). The flag is the *designatum* and indirect symbol associated with the pledge of allegiance, with its references to one nation, 'under God', and 'indivisible', as well as with several songs, including the 'Star Spangled Banner' and the hyper-patriotic 'God Bless America'.

CONCLUSION

In many respects, semiotics has flowered and yet remains underutilized in the social sciences. Ethnography must now address the sources of experience and context, rather than focusing on the abstract questions such as: how to represent this. The presentation and representation of imagery is problematic, as is the fact that the social world is changing radically, and nineteenth-century social psychology no longer suffices. Inferences from general statements about the functions of a sign, the objective or subjective aspects of meaning that reduce these to formulaic statements, cannot be sustained ethnographically (e.g., Denzin, 1986). As a method and technique, it remains on the edge of utility if linked with the major innovations in qualitative software. Like content and narrative analysis, it remains marginal to the positivistic statistically based, inductive social science paradigm that predominates.

ACKNOWLEDGMENT

I am grateful to Steve Barley for helpful comments as well as a history lesson.

NOTES

1 Barthes claims, as will be explained below, that language is the system by which thought is expressed, and that semiotics, a science of signs, is a sub-category of semiology, the study of meaning.

2 I personally am devoted to the writings of Kierkegaard, Hamann, Lichtenberg and modern others such as Richard Rorty who doubt the possibility of validation of the external world, or true representation, and opt for a profound and deep absurdity in the world overcome only by counterintuitive belief in something.

3 This formulation is analogous to the Chomskian view that a surface collection can be understood only in terms of an underlying code or set of 'deep rules'

which allows translation of the possible alternatives suggested by the surface features (see Searle, 2002).

4 On representation in texts, see Atkinson (1990, 1992) and Van Maanen (1995). For a succinct treatment, see Culler (2000).

5 His lectures, like those of Mead, were transcribed and edited by his students and then translated into an English version published by McGraw-Hill.

6 This is a critical aspect of Marxian thinking. Sophisticated Marxists like Raymond Williams and Terry Eagleton note that such piling up, called 'ideology', obscures life chances, suffering and exploitation in the material world. Another way of saying this is that social realities are really signs about signs in multiple and complex relations, and the more powerful the expression's evocative power, the less one is able to discern its contradictions and flaws. Style is power.

7 The implications of this behavioristic theme were expanded by Morris (1934, 1961) and Sebeok (1991, 1994). The sign points somewhere else; thus the 'pointing' is a stimulus, an invitation to look for something out of sight, and leads to a series of signs, each indicating itself, others previously noted and those yet to come.

8 See Norbert Wiley's (1994) failed but systematic analysis of the 'semiotic self' in which he tries to unravel the semiotics of Peirce, especially his reading of the self as a collective object, and connect it to democratic theory.

9 The discontent and fragmentation within the social sciences is symbolized by the responses of European intellectuals to the death of Marxism after World War II, and challenges to conventional French rationalism-existentialism, structuralism(s), and psychoanalysis. These ideas were loosely derived from surrealism, semiotics, and the role of the irrational and the unconscious, and contained residues of Heideggerian and Hegelian phenomenology. The overt point of crystallization and differentiation was the May 1968 explosion in Paris. The failure of French thought to accommodate new guises of old irrationalities stimulated major debates in the Haute Ecole and the College de France. Classic primers include: Culler (1975, 2000), Leach (1976), Hawkes (1977), Sturrock (1977), Kurzweil (1980), and Dosse (1991a, 1991b).

10 Thomas Sebeok was a student of Charles Morris, who was in turn a student of Mead. All studied at the University of Chicago. His activities are many, and include sponsorship of many other scholars, beginning a journal, *Semiotics*, publishing a series of influential books in a series with the University of Indiana Press, organizing numerous international conferences on semiotics, and publishing an impressive list of monographs, essays, and even textbooks on the subject himself.

11 Distinctions between semiotics, phenomenology, and symbolic interactionism, well discussed in the prescient work of Dean MacCannell (1976, 1979), Charles Lemert (1977) and Norman Denzin (1986), vanished into the maw of postmodernism.

12 European writers such as Cixous, Irigaray, Mol, and Kristeva address these issues as well as do Judith Butler, Juliet Flower MacCannell (1986) and Kaja Silverman (1983) in the United States.

13 The tension noted here between surface and underlying structure is a fabulously useful insight but beyond this chapter's scope.

14 The recent history of semiotics does not suggest a burgeoning of its popularity. The development of semiotics and its impact in the social sciences came via France, from the explosion of new ideas there in the 1960s, and their introduction to American anthropology via Lévi-Strauss, rather than through renewed interest in the complex and powerful semiotics of the American, Charles S. Peirce, although the assiduous work of Charles Morris and his student Thomas Sebeok, kept the hope alive. Charles Lemert's (1977) paper introduced many American scholars to the ideas of semiotics, especially Eco's rendition thereof, as did the work of the MacCannells on semiotics generally. The word became woven into the rhetoric of postmodernism, often without much close attention to the method, the technique or utility of the ideas. The introduction in the UK of the *International Journal of Semiotics and Law*, edited by Bernard Jackson and later by Dragan Milovanovic, and Jackson's work on the semiology of law introduced semiotics to another international audience.

15 I draw on previously published work I have done with Betsy Cullum-Swan (Manning and Cullum-Swan, 1994).

16 The sociologist, George Ritzer (1996), argues that the strategy of McDonald's is based on American beliefs. It asserts that Americans believe, in connection with fast food and perhaps other services, that everything can be quantified and calculated (a good deal, cheap, bigger is better ...), life is predictable (the Big Mac is the same in London, England, London, Ontario, and New London, Connecticut), and food service should be fast, cheap, and efficient. He notes that what is on the surface a representation of Americanism, an icon of modern, fast, efficient life, is also a plan for technological control that increases profits, management ease, and the manipulation of customers to consume consistently, regularly, and unreflectively (Schlosser, 2001).

17 Coding, encoding, and decoding, within a close system to another one, is a very complex matter, the details of which need not concern us here, other than the logic of the process. Similar work is done in the social sciences when a set of categories, such as native firewood, wedding requirements, or native botanical systems are translated from one language (native) to another (English). These exercises are guided by rules

of thumb about translation and back-translation, questions of equivalence of terms within and across the taxonomies, and the question of head terms (Tyler, 1969). Furthermore, since the aim is primarily cognitive, the subjective context is often unexplored. Code-breaking has existed even prior to written languages in the form of hieroglyphics and other icon languages that are used to convey messages to some groups while excluding others.

18 My work in this area is part of a larger project on the rationalizing of policing. The crime mapping and intelligence-led aspects of rationalization have been a key interest of mine. I have not until now done extensive and in-depth work in any one site, but work in a number of sites. I have done fieldwork in a large Canadian city over a month in 1999 (assisted by two undergraduates at York University, Amanda Rigby and Jenny Young); two days in a northern constabulary that had just introduced a crime-mapping center; Western City (a month in the fall of 1999); and previously (see Manning, 2001a, 2001b). I am presently working on crime mapping in a large southern city, and spent over a month in 2000 and early 2001 in fieldwork and interviews.

There are also technical problems concerning the meaning of 'blocks', 'block faces', clusters of addresses that are incorrectly recorded or spelled; the notional location of many kinds of disorder, the fact that high-rise apartments may have multiple calls and complaints all at the same street address. The scale of the map affects the size of a cluster, making it easy to inflate a handful of incidents into a 'hot spot' or to make a large number of incidents appear rather small or unimportant. The databases are also important. Some departments map calls for service, while others use reported crime, or crimes known to the police. These two databases, taken as examples, represent quite distinctive samples of activities.

19 Ironically, this reflects the long history of sociological research in the 'social disorganization' tradition beginning with Thrasher, Mowrer, Park and Burgess and continuing in the work of Bursik, Sampson, and associates. Clusters of signs such as 'hot spots' stand in part–whole relationship to the crime or disorders named. Designating the cluster, giving the cluster an active label, 'hot', a metaphoric dramatization, suggests the need for intervention, the potential for further 'flaming' and spread, and the need for active intervention.

20 Police gather far too much information for which they have no identified purpose. Data are kept in case, or because they have always been kept. Statements about the number of files, record-keeping forms, or databases in themselves do not indicate useful information. Databases are not coordinated in the departments I have studied. There are many standard and some new types of data being gathered in policing,

some of which can be combined, but others that are not and cannot be. In addition to CAD data, criminal records, vehicles and registration, current and outstanding warrants, and traffic stops, the present arrested or jailed population, stolen/returned property, other functions are being automated and digitalized such as fingerprint files, mugshots, and other forensic evidence. Some detectives are using expert systems and/or computerized files (Harper, 1991). For many years, major incidents in England have been organized using the HOLMES system which can be used for a major investigation, and the current VICLAS system in Canada and the National Crime faculty at Bramshill, England, aim to computerize serious crime nationally to enable further pattern analysis.

21 In the wake of the September 11 crash, and before play was resumed, small flags were sewn on the uniforms of footballers and on the uniforms and caps of baseball players. To extend this analogy further, recall that the discourse of sport, especially American football, is freighted with violent war metaphors – long bombs, smash mouth play, long campaigns or drives into enemy territory, blitzing the passer, and sacking him (originally referring to the ravaging of a town after a conquest). These suggest the violent celebrity role of athletes in the culture and their surrogate status as warriors.

22 The flag's meanings are shaped by the broader surround, or politics and high politics of the day. Flags were last seen on public display by large numbers of people as a part of anti-government peace demonstrations in the 1970s in the United States. 'Hippies' of the 1970s used flags (wearing them, burning them, desecrating them in public) as means to mock and ironicize patriotism and show their distance from American values (unspecified and unnamed). Subsequently, laws were passed against public flag burning in several states. They were subsequently reversed by the Supreme Court (by etiquette, less than perfect flags were required to be burned in private). However, a change in context changes meaning. In the context of a national crisis, post September 11, wearing a flag T-shirt, flag-bearing shoes or flag boots, or draping it across your behind, connotes loyalty and closeness to American values (unnamed and unspecified).

23 Think first in time terms, or chronologically, about the appearance of flags. After September 11, American flags began to appear. First, they flapped from car aerials, hung in shop windows, sprouted on people's lapels in the form of little pins, then waved from front porches of houses, and at half staff on flagpoles. Then flags were produced and sold en masse and appeared hanging from windows, as the façade on key chains, reproduced on T-shirts, sweat shirts and on uniforms. Tommy Hilfiger and Ralph Lauren created special fashionable sweaters with bright flags

ensconced horizontally across the breast. Bumper stickers with 'United we stand', 'God bless America', and 'These colors do not run' were displayed. Newspapers, magazines and television showed images of flags in various places, including at the scene, where a firefighter raised a flag shortly after the disaster, resembling the Iwo Jima flag-raising that was a memorial symbol in World War II. In this brief early list, we see a flag as a symbol representing the nation, the society, the government, in its 'firstness' or as a material thing; as a copy or icon, on clothes and sold items, on pictures of the shredded flag that was flown at the World Trade Center.

REFERENCES

Atkinson, Paul (1990) *The Ethnographic Imagination*. London: Routledge.

Atkinson, Paul (1992) *Understanding Ethnographic Texts*. Thousand Oaks, CA: Sage.

Barthes, R. (1970) *Mythologies*. New York: Hill and Wang.

Barthes, R. (1974) *S/Z*. New York: Hill and Wang.

Barthes, R. (1984) *The Fashion System*. New York: Hill and Wang.

Bateson, Gregory (1980) *Man and Nature*. New York: Signet.

Baudrillard, J.P. (1988) *Selected Writings* (ed. Mark Poster). Stanford, CA: Stanford University Press.

Benjamin, Walter (1999) *The Arcades Project*. Cambridge, MA: Belknap Press.

Bittner, Egon (1972) *The Functions of Police in Modern Society*. Washington DC: National Institutes of Mental Health.

Bouissac, Paul (1976) *Circus and Culture: A Semiotic Approach*. Bloomington: Indiana University Press.

Bourdieu, Pierre (1977) *Outline of a Theory of Practice*. Cambridge: Cambridge University Press.

Braga, Anthony et al. (1998) 'Problem-oriented policing in violent crime places', *Criminology*, 37: 541–80.

Brent, Joseph (1988) *Charles Sanders Peirce*. Bloomington: Indiana University Press.

Culler, Jonathan (1975) *Structuralist Poetics*. Ithaca, NY: Cornell University Press.

Culler, Jonathan (1977) *Saussure*. Harmondsworth: Penguin.

Culler, Jonathan (2000) *Literary Theory*. Oxford: Oxford University Press.

Cushman, M. and Marcus, G. (eds) (1977) *Writing Culture*. Chicago: University of Chicago Press.

Denzin, Norman (1986) 'Postmodern social theory', *Sociological Theory*, 4: 194–206.

Denzin, Norman and Lincoln, Yvonne (eds) (1994) *Handbook of Qualitative Research*. Thousand Oaks, CA: Sage.

Derrida, Jacques (1979) *On Grammatology*. Baltimore, MD: Johns Hopkins University Press.

Dorst, Jonathan (1992) *The Written Suburb*. Philadelphia: University of Pennsylvania Press.

Dosse, Frederick (1991a) *History of Structuralism*, Vol. I. Minneapolis: University of Minnesota Press.

Dosse, Frederick (1991b) *History of Structuralism*, Vol. II. Minneapolis: University of Minnesota Press.

Dungworth, T. (2000) 'Criminal justice and the information technology revolution', in *Policies, Processes and Decisions of the Criminal Justice System*, Vol. 3. Washington, DC: National Institute of Justice.

Eco, Umberto (1979) *The Theory of Semiotics*. Bloomington: University of Indiana Press.

Eco, Umberto (1981) *Travels in Hyperreality*. New York: Harcourt, Brace, Jovanovich.

Geertz, Clifford (1970) *The Interpretation of Cultures*. New York: Basic Books.

Goffman, Erving (1974) *Frame Analysis*. Cambridge, MA: Harvard University Press.

Goffman, Erving (1983) 'The interaction order', *American Sociological Review*, 48: 1–17.

Gossen, Gary (1974) *Chamulas in the World of the Sun*. Cambridge, MA: Harvard University Press.

Greene-Mazerolle, L. and Terrill, W. (1997) 'Problem-oriented policing in public housing', *Policing*, 20: 235–55.

Guiraud, Pierre (1975) *Semiology*. London: Routledge & Kegan Paul.

Gusfield, Joseph (1989) *The Culture of Public Problems*. Chicago: University of Chicago Press.

Harper, R.H.R. (1991) 'The computer game: Detectives, suspects and technology', *British Journal of Criminology*, 31: 292–307.

Hawkes, Terrence (1977) *Structuralism and Semiotics*. Berkeley: University of California Press.

Hjelmslev, Louis (1961) *Prolegomena to a Theory of Language*. Madison: University of Wisconsin Press.

Jakobson, R. (1981) *Six Lectures on Sound and Meaning*. Cambridge, MA: MIT Press.

Kurzweil, E. (1980) *The Age of Structuralism*. New York: Columbia University Press.

Lacan, J. (1968) *The Language of the Self*. Baltimore, MD: Johns Hopkins University Press.

Leach, Edmund (1976) *Culture and Communication*. Cambridge: Cambridge University Press.

Lemert, Charles (1977) 'Language, structure and measurement', *American Journal of Sociology*, 84: 929–57.

Lévi-Strauss, C. (1963) *Structural Anthropology*. Garden City, NY: Doubleday Anchor.

Lévi-Strauss, C. (1981) 'Preface' in R. Jakobson, *Six Lectures on Sound and Meaning*. Cambridge, MA: MIT Press.

Levinson, Daniel (1985) *Pragmatics*. Cambridge: Cambridge University Press.

MacCannell, Dean (1976) 'The past and future of symbolic interactionism', *Semiotica*, 16: 99–114.

MacCannell, Dean (1979) *The Tourist*. New York: Schocken Books.

MacCannell, Dean (1986) 'Semiotics and sociology', *Semiotica*, 61: 193–200.

MacCannell, Dean and MacCannell, Juliet Flower (1982) *The Time of the Sign*. Bloomington: University of Indiana Press.

MacCannell, Juliet Flower (1986) *Figuring Lacan*. Beckenham: Croom-Helm.

Malinowski, B. (1923) 'Supplement I', in C. Ogden and A. Richards (eds), *The Meaning of Meaning*. New York: Harvest Books.

Manning, Peter K. (1989) *Semiotics and Fieldwork*. Thousand Oaks, CA: Sage.

Manning, Peter K. (2001a) 'Technology's ways', *Criminal Justice*, 1: 83–103.

Manning, Peter K. (2001b) 'Theorizing policing', *Theoretical Criminology*, 5: 315–44.

Manning, Peter K. and Cullum-Swan, Betsy (1994) 'Narrative, content and semiotic analysis', in Norman K. Denzin and Y. Lincoln (eds), *Handbook of Qualitative Research*. Thousand Oaks, CA: Sage.

McCloskey, Donald (1985) *The Rhetoric of Economics*. Madison: University of Wisconsin Press.

McDonald, P.P. (2002) *Managing Police Operations*. Belmont, CA: Wadsworth.

Mead, G.H. (1934) *Mind, Self and Society*. Chicago: University of Chicago Press.

Morris, Charles (1934) *Foundations of a Theory of Signs*. Chicago: University of Chicago Press.

Morris, Charles (1961) *Signs and Signification*. Chicago: University of Chicago Press.

Needham, Rodney (1981) *Circumstantial Deliveries*. Berkeley: University of California Press.

Needham, Rodney (1983) *Against the Tranquility of Axioms*. Berkeley: University of California Press.

Noth, Winifried (ed.) (1990) *Handbook of Semiotics*. Bloomington: University of Indiana Press.

Ogden, C. and Richards, A. (1923) *The Meaning of Meaning*. New York: Harvest Books.

Peirce C.S. (1965) *Collected Papers of Charles Sanders Peirce* C. Hartshorne and P. Weiss (eds). Cambridge, MA: Belknap Press.

Rappaport, R. (1971) 'Ritual, sanctity and cybernetics', *American Anthropologist*, 73: 59–76.

Rappaport, R. (2000) *Ritual and Religion in the Making of Humanity*. New York: Cambridge University Press.

Richardson, L. (1997) *Fields of Play*. New Brunswick, NJ: Rutgers University Press.

Ritzer, George (1996) *The McDonaldization of Society* (revised edition). Thousand Oaks, CA: Pine Forge Press.

Rosaldo, Renato (1989) *Culture and Truth*. Boston: Beacon Press.

Sampson, R. and Bartusch, D.J. (1998) 'Legal cynicism and (subcultural?) tolerance of deviance', *Law and Society Review*, 32: 777–804.

Saussure, Ferdinand de (1996) *Course in General Linguistics*. New York: McGraw-Hill.

Schlosser, E. (2001) *Fast Food Nation*. New York: Harper/Collins.

Searle, John (2002) 'End of the revolution', *New York Review of Books* (Feb. 28): 33–6.

Sebeok, Thomas (1991) *Semiotics in the United States*. Bloomington: University of Indiana Press.

Sebeok, Thomas (1994) *Signs: An Introduction to Semiotics*. Toronto: University of Toronto Press.

Silverman, Eli (2000) *The NYPD Battles Crime*. Boston: Northeastern University Press.

Silverman, Kaja (1983) *The Subject of Semiotics*. New York: Oxford University Press.

Sturrock, John (ed.) (1977) *Structuralism*. Oxford: Oxford University Press.

Tyler, S. (ed.) (1969) *Cognitive Anthropology*. New York: Holt, Rinehart and Winston.

Van Maanen, John (1995) *Representation in Ethnography*. Thousand Oaks, CA: Sage.

Wiley, Norbert (1994) *The Semiotic Self*. Chicago: University of Chicago Press.

Wittgenstein, L. (1953) *Philosophical Investigations*. New York: MacMillan.

26

Conversation Analysis

STEVEN E. CLAYMAN AND
VIRGINIA TEAS GILL

Human interaction lies at the very heart of social life. It is primarily through interaction that children are socialized, culture is transmitted, language is put to use, identities are affirmed, institutions are activated, and social structures of all kinds are reproduced. Moreover, as Schegloff (1987) has observed, talk-in-interaction is the primordial site of human sociality and a fundamental locus of social organization in its own right. It is thus ironic that the study of interaction was long overlooked. This was due in part to an erroneous assumption that interactional conduct is either an epiphenomenon of social structure or inherently disorderly (Sacks, 1984), coupled with the lack of an approach that would expose its organizational principles. Conversation analysis (CA) has begun to rectify this state of affairs. It offers a rigorous methodology of data collection and analysis that is uniquely suited to addressing the problems and exploiting the opportunities posed by human interaction as an object of inquiry.

CA was developed by Harvey Sacks in collaboration with Emanuel Schegloff and Gail Jefferson. It emerged within sociology in the late 1960s, a time when the discipline was dominated by abstract theorizing about large-scale structural phenomena. However, certain intellectual cross-currents had begun to run counter to the sociological mainstream, devoting new attention to the specifics of social conduct in everyday life, and this would provide a foundation for the eventual development of CA. Erving Goffman (1963, 1964, 1967) began to explore what he would later call 'the interaction order' (Goffman, 1983), the domain of direct interaction between persons. Goffman repeatedly argued that this domain is a type of social institution in its own right, one that intersects with other more familiar societal institutions but is organized by its own distinctive imperatives such as the preservation of 'face'. In a related but distinct development that would come to be known as ethnomethodology, Harold Garfinkel (1967) began to examine the procedures of common-sense reasoning that people use to make sense of their circumstances and to navigate through everyday life. Garfinkel challenged the mainstream view that social conduct is regulated by internalized norms, arguing instead that all norms – including those identified by Goffman – rest upon an unexplicated foundation of practical reasoning through which norms are implemented and action is produced and rendered intelligible in normative terms.

Harvey Sacks was a student of Goffman and an associate of Garfinkel, and his development of CA can be understood as a partial synthesis of these twin concerns with the institution of interaction and the procedures of common-sense reasoning used to produce and recognize interactional conduct (Heritage, 2001). The research enterprise that emerged from this synthesis has generated a substantial and cumulative body of empirical findings. In a relatively short span of time the field has grown and diversified to encompass a variety of distinguishable variants. Some researchers work with data drawn primarily from ordinary conversation and seek to describe highly general interactional practices and systems of practice such as those governing the organization of turn-taking, the sequencing of action, the repair of misunderstandings, the relationship between vocal and nonvocal behaviors, and so on (Atkinson and Heritage, 1984; Button and Lee, 1987; Psathas, 1990). Others focus on data drawn from institutional settings – doctor–patient interactions, news interviews, trial examinations, etc. – with the aim of exploring how generic practices of talk get mobilized and adapted for the accomplishment of specific institutional tasks (Boden and Zimmerman, 1991; Drew and Heritage, 1992b; and Heritage and Maynard, forthcoming). Gender differences at the level of interaction have also been explored (West and Zimmerman, 1983; Goodwin, 1990). Still others have used CA methods and findings to address practical questions that extend beyond the organization of interaction *per se* – questions such as how speaking practices bear on bureaucratic and professional decision-making (Boyd, 1998; Clayman and Reisner, 1998; Maynard, 1984; Heritage and Stivers, 1999; Heritage et al., 2001; Peräkylä, 1998), affect the conduct and results of survey research (Maynard et al., 2002), shed light on speech disorders (Goodwin, 1995; Heeschen and Schegloff, 1999) and processes of cognition and cognitive development (Goodwin, 1994; Maynard and Schaeffer, 1996; Schegloff, 1991; Wootton, 1997), and illuminate large-scale cultural differences (Houtkoop-Steenstra, 1991; Lindström, 1994) and processes of historical change (Clayman and Heritage, 2002).

If the empirical productivity of CA exceeds that of its intellectual forebears, this is mainly due to the methodology that underlies it. While the substance of CA owes much to Goffman and Garfinkel, its methodology bears little resemblance to either the ethnographic methods employed by Goffman or the quasi-experimental demonstrations favored by Garfinkel in his early work. By utilizing naturalistic observation – the direct observation of naturally occurring conduct – CA is broadly congruent with the ethnographic tradition of social science research. However, within CA observation is always directed toward conduct as it has been preserved in audio and video recordings, and this facilitates a highly disciplined mode of analysis marked by standards of evidence and analytic precision that are distinctive.

Indeed, the CA approach is difficult to categorize in terms that usually dominate discussions of social science methodology. On the one hand, the enterprise has a strong qualitative dimension involving the close analysis of single instances of conduct; on the other hand, it has an informally 'quantitative' dimension in that practitioners typically assemble and systematically examine numerous instances of a given phenomenon. It is both an interpretive enterprise seeking to capture the understandings and orientations displayed by the participants themselves, and at the same time it enforces rigorous standards of evidence made possible by the use of recorded data. It is a predominantly data-driven or inductive enterprise, but it is guided by a well-developed conceptual foundation grounded in empirical findings from past research. Given the natural tendency to process novel stimuli in terms of familiar conceptual categories, it is perhaps not surprising that CA has in the past been incorrectly pigeonholed in relation to extant social science methods.

Accordingly, in the spirit of clarification and as a guide to those wishing to work with interactional materials, we offer a brief introduction to the methods of CA.[1]

GENERATING DATA: RECORDING AND TRANSCRIBING

Conversation analysts work almost exclusively with naturally occurring interaction as it has been captured in audio and video recordings and rendered into detailed transcripts. Both the subject matter and its rendering into usable data require some discussion.

Naturally occurring interaction

Naturally occurring interaction is perhaps best understood by contrast to what it is not. It does not include hypothetical or invented examples of interaction, nor role-playing or experimentally induced interactions. There are compelling reasons for excluding these forms of data. Invented or contrived interaction is necessarily conditioned by the researcher's ungrounded intuitions about how talk normally unfolds. Past research has demonstrated that intuition, no matter how plausible it might seem, simply is not a reliable guide in this area. As Zimmerman (1988: 421) has observed:

> Indeed, if the analysis of conversation is to be anything more than an intuitive, interpretive exercise carried on through artfully posed opinions about what is going on in some segment of talk, or what is possible or plausible in interaction, then intuition and its offspring, interpretation, must be disciplined by reference to the details of actual episodes of conversational interaction. (Zimmerman 1988:421)

Working with actual interaction can yield astonishing discoveries that, in Sacks's (1984: 25) words, 'we could not, by imagination, assert were there'. Any detailed transcript of everyday recorded interaction reveals a richness and complexity that could not be invented or contrived.

What constitutes 'natural' interaction is, however, by no means straightforward. Because of the 'observer's paradox' (Labov, 1972) a researcher can never know whether the interaction is unfolding as it would have were it not being externally observed (ten Have, 1999). In addition, the recording equipment itself may become a topic of conversation for participants, such that the content of the talk becomes 'researcher-produced' (ten Have, 1999: 49).

However, such observer effects are much less significant than they might seem at first glance. Sensitivity to being observed is a highly general and hence 'natural' feature of interaction. As Goodwin (1981: 44) notes, 'within conversation, participants never behave as if they were unobserved; it is clear that they organize their behavior in terms of the observation it will receive from their coparticipants'. Thus, while people may indeed avoid discussing sensitive topics on tape, as a general practice of interaction they may also avoid mentioning such topics before strangers.

Moreover, these effects tend to be limited to the surface content of the interaction; they do not affect the underlying structure of interaction, which is the primary focus of CA research. When the participants refer to the presence of the recording machine, they do so via processes – ways of taking turns, building actions, and organizing them into sequences – that are not markedly different from the rest of their talk (ten Have, 1999).

In any case, hyperconsciousness about the recording machine tends to be short-lived. It recedes into the background as the participants become enmeshed in the practical demands of the interaction in which they find themselves.

Under the rubric 'naturally occurring interaction' falls a wide range of interactional events. It encompasses everything from casual encounters between family and friends, to interaction that takes place in institutional and workplace contexts, to interaction that is produced in the course of scientific research itself. Underlying this range of events are various organizations for taking turns – that is, various speech exchange systems (Sacks et al., 1974) – ranging from ordinary conversation (where the length, order, and content of turns are free to vary) to highly formal and constrained speech exchange systems such as debates, interviews, and business meetings.

A note on sampling

Unlike most social science disciplines, CA addresses a largely unexplored domain of phenomena whose components are not yet fully known or understood. Sacks (1984: 21) called this domain 'the methods people use in doing social life', and it has been demonstrated that these methods have a describable order of their own. Until these methods are formally described and analyzed, it is premature to ask how prevalent they are within some larger 'population' of interactions, or how they are distributed in relation to exogenous psychological or social variables. Such questions cannot be answered without formal quantification, and this cannot proceed in a valid way until the complex phenomena of interaction have been identified and thoroughly understood (Schegloff, 1993).

Because the object of CA analysis is to describe the endogenous organization rather than the exogenous distribution of interactional phenomena, the issue of sampling is approached rather differently in CA than in other fields. Conversation analysts typically follow the naturalist's strategy of gathering 'specimens' of particular phenomena from as many settings of interaction as possible for the purposes of systematic analysis and comparison (Heritage, 1988: 131; ten Have, 1999: 51).

As sources of interactional data, not all settings are created equal. Ordinary conversation among acquaintances and family members appears to represent the richest and most varied source of interactional phenomena, while interactions in bureaucratic, occupational, and other institutional contexts tend to contain a markedly narrower range of practices that may differ from their counterparts in ordinary conversation (Drew and Heritage, 1992a). Underlying these differences is the fact that ordinary conversation appears to be the primordial form of interaction, the original source of interactional practices that get specialized and adapted in task-oriented institutional contexts. It is thus important to bear in mind the social context from which data are drawn. Moreover, although the researcher's substantive interests may favor focused data-gathering from a specialized type of setting, it is generally useful to use ordinary conversation as a comparative frame of reference (Schegloff, 1987).

While the naturalistic approach remains primary within CA, conversation analysts do not necessarily dismiss the possibility ofconducting formally quantitative/distributional analyses of interactional phenomena (Zimmerman, 1988; Heritage, 1999). Indeed, once such phenomena have been carefully mapped, this can provide a rigorous empirical basis for distributional studies, replacing vague concepts with well-defined categories that are firmly anchored in interactional reality.

Audio and video recording

The emphasis on talk-in-interaction was originally a practical decision for Harvey Sacks, whose main concern as a sociologist was to formally describe the structure of real social events as they actually occurred (Sacks, 1984). The availability of audio recording technology in the early 1960s made it possible to capture and preserve a particular type of social event, conversational interaction. Given the centrality of interaction in the life of society, Sacks's ostensibly practical decision turned out to be a fortuitous one.

Technological advances over the years have made it possible to make video as well as audio recordings, and thus to record nonvocal behaviors that unfold in conjunction with the stream of speech. However, recordings still offer the same basic service as they did for Sacks in the 1960s – recordings provide access to social interaction at a level of detail that approaches what is available to the interactional participants themselves. This encompasses not only what was said but also how it was said, including vocal behaviors such as silences, audible breathing, and laughter, and (in the case of video recordings) nonvocal behaviors such as gaze direction, gestural displays, and body positioning. Since recordings can be replayed, segments of interaction can be examined repeatedly, slowed down for frame-by-frame scrutiny, and re-examined as new information becomes available.

The importance of recordings in CA can be likened to that of slow-motion 'instant replay' during televised sporting events (Atkinson, 1984). While spectators in the stands may have only a vague grasp of the fleeting events within a particular play, television viewers can – by virtue of the instant replay – achieve a more detailed and precise understanding of the specific sequence of behaviors that led to the play's outcome. Similar benefits accrue to the academic study of interaction when it has been preserved in recorded form.[2]

Recordings also provide reliable evidence. Recordings provide a more accurate record of interactional events than do other data-gathering methods such as writing fieldnotes, and thus serve as more convincing evidence upon which to base findings about detailed interactional patterns. On-site observations, fieldnotes, and interviews suit the purposes of and questions posed within ethnographic and other studies, but the purposes of and questions posed within CA investigations cannot be addressed without tape-recorded evidence (see Heritage, 1984b: 236). Moreover, there is a strong tradition within CA of including such evidence – as rendered in transcript excerpts and video 'frame grabs' – in published work. This practice exposes the researcher's processes of inference and interpretation to public scrutiny, enabling readers to independently assess the validity of analytic claims by reference to key data excerpts on which they are based.

Many researchers will face the choice of whether to use audio or video recording technology. In general, video is preferable to audio when recording face-to-face interactions. This is because nonvocal activities such as facial expressions, gaze direction, and gestural displays serve – along with vocal activities – as communicative and interpretive resources for participants in interaction. Only video recordings give researchers access to both vocal and nonvocal resources. For telephone encounters, by contrast, only the speech stream is available to the participants, hence audiotaping will often suffice. However, if the participants are engaged in additional embodied work that the researcher would like to explore, video recordings are again necessary. For example, while survey interviewers and emergency call takers are talking on the phone, they may be simultaneously engaged in reading a computer screen, entering information via a keyboard, and at times communicating with nearby co-workers. All of this can have a significant impact on the ongoing telephone talk, which might not be apparent without a video record of the full range of embodied conduct (Maynard and Schaeffer, 2000; Whalen, 1995).

Transcribing data

Once the interaction of interest has been recorded, the rationale for transcribing it is straightforward. Transcripts make features of the recording more transparent and accessible, enabling one to 'see' the vocal and nonvocal activities that unfold on the tape. A good transcript helps the analyst get a purchase on the organization of the interaction, including its fleeting and momentary features. A transcript is not a substitute for the recording, but rather is an essential analytical tool to be used along with the recording. Moreover, as noted previously, transcripts also serve as a resource in CA publications and presentations, allowing others to independently assess analytic claims by reference to excerpts from the data themselves.

Gail Jefferson originated the transcription system commonly used within CA (Jefferson, 1974). It was designed as a compromise between two objectives: to preserve the details of talk as it is actually produced, while at the same time remaining simple enough to yield transcripts that are accessible to a general audience. Thus, a full phonological system was avoided in favor of one that uses standard orthography supplemented with additional symbols to capture articulatory elements such as overlapping speech, silences, various forms of stress, and so on. At first exposure the system can seem unfamiliar, but skill in applying it increases rapidly with practice. Over the years, other investigators have built upon Jefferson's system, most notably Goodwin (1981) who developed symbols to represent nonvocal activities, such as gaze and gesture, on a transcript. A brief outline of the transcription system appears in the Appendix to this chapter; for a more thorough guide, see Atkinson and Heritage (1984: ix–xvi).

The transcription process is itself part of the analytical process. For this reason, it is generally recommended that researchers do at least some of their own transcribing rather than delegating the entire task to research assistants. Transcribing a large corpus of data does represent a major time commitment, however, so many researchers follow a two-step process in which assistants make initial 'rough' transcripts of a data corpus, which the researcher then refines in whole or in part.

Ten Have's (1999: 75–98) discussion of the actual process of transcribing is comprehensive and his advice is exceptionally practical. Here, we will briefly note some the main issues involved.

Audio transcribing has traditionally been done with the aid of a transcribing machine, essentially a stenographer's audio tape playback machine with a foot pedal for starting, stopping, and rewinding the tape. If the data are on videotape, nonvocal details can be added by viewing the video after the audio transcription is complete. More recently, technological advances have made it possible to digitize audio and video tapes and to store the data files on CD, DVD, or hard drive. A computer can now serve as a 'transcribing machine'; computer software programs let the researcher work with a split screen and transcribe in a word-processing program while watching the video on the same screen. Some programs can also automatically time silences, although at the time of writing we know of no voice recognition software that can transcribe real-time multiparty conversation. Still, the future of data is undoubtedly digital. It is much easier to access individual segments on a digitized recording than on an analog tape, and digitization also eliminates the problem of wear and tear on analog tapes and the resulting deterioration of data. However, analog equipment remains adequate to the task, provided transcription is done from copies of the original tapes rather than the originals themselves.

The level of detail in a CA transcript often strikes non-CA researchers as superfluous and unnecessary. However, if the objective is to understand the resources through which interactants build mutually intelligible courses of action, then anything that is available to the interactants is potentially relevant as an interactional resource. For instance, Jefferson (1985) demonstrates the importance of seemingly trivial behavioral details surrounding the articulation of laughter (see also Glenn, 2003). In excerpt 1, Louise laughs during the utterance, 'playing with his organ' (at the arrow, line 7). This transcript has been simplified in various ways, most relevantly by

(1) [Jefferson, 1985: 28, simplified transcript]

```
 1    Ken:      And he came home and decided he was gonna play with
 2              his orchids from then on in.
 3    Roger:    With his what?
 4    Louise:   heh heh heh heh
 5    Ken:      With his orchids. [He has an orchid-
 6    Roger:                      [Oh heh hehheh
 7  → Louise    Playing with his organ yeah I thought the same thing!
 8              ((spoken through laughter))
 9    Ken:      Because he's got a great big [glass house-
10  → Roger:                                 [I can see him playing with
11  →           his organ ((laughing))
```

summarizing the laughter (line 8) rather than transcribing it beat by beat.

Such simplification obscures the way laughter is employed as an interactional resource. In the more detailed excerpt 2, the laughter is fully transcribed. With the added detail, it becomes apparent that Louise precisely places her laughter within the utterance, 'PLAYN(h)W(h)IZ O(h)R'N' (line 8), stopping abruptly when she moves on to the next utterance ('ya:h I thought the same'). Roger subsequently laughs in a strikingly similar way within essentially the same phrase (second arrow, line 14). Deployed in this way, laughter displays recognition of an alternate 'obscene' hearing of the phrase 'playing with his orchids', even as it partially but not totally obscures its articulation.

Accordingly, researchers should strive to preserve as much detail as possible. However, because transcribing is extremely labor-intensive and time-consuming, the practicalities of the research process mandate transcripts that fall short of perfection. The amount of time invested in a transcript will inevitably vary with the interests of the researcher and the level of detail deemed necessary for the research task at hand. One practical strategy is to transcribe in varying amounts of detail, reserving the highest level of detail for segments that will receive the most analytic attention.

The placement of silences is another illuminating detail, one that also highlights the connection between transcription and analysis. When transcribing a silence, the transcriptionist must decide whether to place the silence within a line of talk, or have it be free-standing on its own line. This decision is predicated on an analysis of whom, if anyone, the silence 'belongs' to, and hence whether turn transition is relevant at that point (Psathas and Anderson, 1990: 89). To illustrate, in excerpt 3 all of the silences are placed within B's lines of talk, and are thus treated as hesitations within an ongoing turn. However, two of the silences (0.7 and 1.5) actually occur at the end of a possibly complete unit of talk. It would be more analytically helpful to give these silences their own lines (see below), thus acknowledging them as places where the floor is open and other parties could come in

(2) [Jefferson, 1985: 29, detailed transcript]

```
 1    Ken:      An'e came hom'n decided'e wz gonna play with his o:rchids.
 2              from then on i:n.
 3    Roger:    With iz what?
 4    Louise:   mh hih hih [huh
 5    Ken:                 [With iz orchids. =
 6    Ken:      =Ee[z got an orch [id-
 7    Roger:       [Oh:.         [ hehh [ h a h .he:h ]   .heh
 8  → Louise:                          [heh huh .hh ] PLAYN(h)W(h)IZ O(h)R'N
 9              ya:h I[thought the [same
10    Roger:          [uh::        [.hunhh. hh.hh
11    Ken:                         [Cz eez gotta great big [gla:ss  house]
12    Roger:                                               [I c'n s(h) e e ]=
13    Ken:      = [(         )
14  → Roger:      [im pl(h)ay with iz o(h)r(h)g.(h)n.uh
```

(3) [Psathas and Anderson, 1990: 89]

```
1  B:  … all of which were no:rmal. (0.7) So:: I was pegged, (0.5) as a
2      person with (.) more than a back problem. (1.5) Or at least that's
3      what I …
```

if they choose. Transcript 4 makes it much easier to see that others were declining the opportunity to respond at a place where they had the option to do so.

A final note on the transcription of silences. Conversation analysts are divided about whether silences should be timed with the aid of a mechanical device such as a stopwatch or computer, or whether they should be gauged by simply counting beats ('*one* one thousand, *two* one thousand …'). The latter method may be less reliable, but is arguably more sensitive to local variations in the tempo of interaction. Whichever method is chosen, it should be used systematically throughout a corpus (see ten Have, 1999: 85; Psathas and Anderson, 1990: 87).

ANALYZING DATA

Getting started

Once data have been gathered and prepared, how should analysis begin? A geographic analogy is useful here. The domain of interaction may be likened to an uncharted territory whose topography remains only partially understood. Conversation analysts seek to map this territory with the aid of recordings and transcripts, which make specimens of its contours available to repeated scrutiny. At this point the analogy breaks down, for conversation analysts then go on to analyze how the participants jointly produce and reproduce the topography of interaction as they deal with one another in real time. Analysis is thus a type of mapping exercise, albeit one that maps not only interactional patterns but also the underlying methods and procedures

through which participants produce them and render them intelligible.

This type of analysis requires holding in abeyance premature questions about *why* a social activity is organized in a particular way, focusing instead on *what* is being done and *how* it is accomplished. That is, the analyst should put aside theoretical considerations about the possible intersections between the interaction and other aspects of the social world (e.g., social structural variables such as status, race, and gender, as well as psychological variables such as motivations, emotions, and personality traits) in order to understand the endogenous organization of the interaction. This means being willing to accept that order is neither wholly external to interaction nor automatically present despite what the participants do. It entails being attentive to the ways the participants themselves produce the orderly features of the interaction and display their understanding and appreciation of those features to one another – and by implication for professional analysts as well. As Schegloff and Sacks (1973: 290) observe:

> We have proceeded under the assumption (an assumption borne out by our research) that insofar as the materials we worked with exhibited orderliness, they did so not only for us … but for the co-participants who had produced them. If the materials … were orderly, they were so because they had been methodically produced by members of the society for one another, and it was a feature of the conversations that we treated as data that they were produced so as to … allow the participants to display to each other their analysis, appreciation and use of that orderliness.

Interactional activities can be investigated at several different levels. Conversations have

(4) [Psathas and Anderson, 1990: 89]

```
1  B:  … all of which were no:rmal.
2  →  (0.7)
3  B:  So:: I was pegged, (0.5) as a person with (.) more than a back problem.
4  →  (1.5)
5  B:  Or at least that's what I …
```

nested layers of activity, any one of which may be analyzed in terms of the underlying procedures through which it is accomplished (Drew and Heritage, 1992a: 29–45). At the most macroscopic level are overarching activity frameworks that organize lengthy stretches of interaction, such as 'getting acquainted' or 'talking about personal problems' or 'seeing a doctor for medical help' or 'cross-examining a witness'. One step below this are discrete sequences of action, which may be analyzed for their relatively generic sequential properties (e.g., paired actions, story-telling sequences) or for type-specific characteristics (e.g., as question– answer sequences, invitation sequences, news delivery sequences). Next come the singular actions that comprise sequences, actions normally accomplished through a single turn at talk such as questions, requests, news announcements, or ways of responding to these various actions. Finally, at the most microscopic level are the specific lexical choices, intonation contours, nonvocal behaviors, and other turn components that are mobilized within turns at talk.

As should be apparent from the preceding list, virtually everything that happens in interaction is fair game for analysis. While there is a natural tendency to dismiss the seemingly small and all too familiar details of interactional conduct as varying randomly or as insignificant 'manners of speaking', conversation analysts proceed from the assumption that all elements of interaction are orderly and meaningful (Sacks, 1984), analyzable in terms of the underlying methods participants use to produce and understand them. This attitude opens up a wealth of possibilities for analysis, but it can be daunting for the novice. Where to begin? While there is no simple recipe for getting started or for locating phenomena for analysis, drawing on Schegloff (1996: 172), we suggest two pathways into the data.

Begin with a 'noticing' One pathway begins with relatively unmotivated observation. The analyst simply notices something about the way a speaker says or does something at a given point within interaction, something that strikes the analyst as in some way interesting. Of course, purely unmotivated observation is an unattainable ideal. Experienced conversation analysts approach data with a well-developed empirically-based conceptual/theoretical foundation that affects what analysts are inclined to notice in the data and what strikes them as 'interesting'. Nevertheless, it is possible to approach data without a specific agenda in mind at the outset, and thus remain open to previously unexplored practices of interaction. Having noticed a given practice, the analyst can then proceed to analyze it in terms of what it might be 'doing' – the action(s) that it accomplishes, and how it figures within and contributes to an ongoing course of interaction.

For example, Sacks (1992: 256–7) observed that when children speak to adults, they commonly begin by asking a question such as 'You know what, Daddy?' Anyone who has been around children for any length of time will be familiar with this recurrent feature of children's talk. What is going on with this practice? One clue can be gleaned from the response it elicits. Adults typically respond to the 'You know what' question with another question – 'What?' This type of response not only invites the child to speak again and say what motivated the original question, but in so doing it simultaneously aligns the adult as one who is prepared to listen to the ensuing talk. Thus, the original 'You know what' query sets in motion a chain of events that gives the child a ratified speaking 'slot' and an attentive recipient. The fact that children use this practice disproportionately displays their orientation to having somewhat diminished rights to talk, for the practice

(5) [Heritage, 1998]

```
 1    Act:  ....hhhh and some of thuh- (0.3) some of my students
 2          translated Eliot into Chine::se. I think thuh very
 3          first.
 4          (0.2)
 5    Har:  Did you learn to speak (.) Chine[:se.
 6  → Act:                                  [.hh Oh yes.
 7          (0.7)
 8    Act:  .hhhh You ca::n't live in thuh country without speaking
 9          thuh lang[uage it's impossible .hhhhh=
10    Har:           [Not no: cour:se
```

can be understood as a methodical solution to the problem of how to get the floor in conversation despite such diminished rights.

A similar course of reasoning underlies Heritage's (1998) analysis of a particular way of designing answers to questions. Heritage initially observed that some answers to questions are prefaced with 'Oh', as in excerpt 5 example (line 6, arrowed), taken from a radio interview with Sir Harold Acton, a noted British aesthete.

This practice, far from being random or insignificant, turns out to have a systematic interactional import. By prefacing an answer with 'Oh', the answerer implies that the prior question 'came from left field' and is thus of questionable relevance. In this particular case, the prior discussion concerned Acton's experience teaching modern poetry at Beijing University, and it is in the context of that discussion that he is asked (at line 5) if he learned to speak Chinese. He plainly finds this question to be obvious or self-evident – he expresses that view explicitly at lines 8–9, but he also conveys it implicitly in his initial response to the question (line 6) via the 'Oh'-prefaced affirmative answer.

With this pathway into the data, an initial noticing is 'pursued by asking what – if anything – such a practice of talking has as its outcome' (Schegloff, 1996: 172). Of course, not every observed practice will turn out to have a systematic import. Nonetheless, many core findings of CA have their origins in noticings of previously unnoticed and unexplored practices of interaction.

Begin with a vernacular action Another pathway is to focus on a particular type of action that is already known as part of the vernacular culture – asking questions, giving advice, delivering news announcements, etc. Here the challenge for the analyst is to transcend what competent members of the culture intuitively know about the action in question. This can be accomplished by exploring the ways a given action can be designed and implemented and the ramifications of such alternatives, identifying the sequential environments in which the action occurs, and exploring how it is consequential for subsequent talk.

For example, using the delivery of bad news as a starting point, Maynard (1992, 1996, 1997, 2003) has examined a wide range of practices that bearers of bad news use to manage this difficult interpersonal task. Such practices serve to minimize recipient resistance and thus maximize the likelihood that recipients will be adequately prepared to register and accept the news. In a similar vein, various studies have explicated familiar aspects of doctor–patient interaction with surprising results. Halkowski (forthcoming) has examined how patients initially present their symptoms to doctors. As it turns out, patients employ a range of practices that serve to display their competence as observers of their own bodies. Gill (1998) and Gill and Maynard (forthcoming), focusing on diagnostic explanations in doctor–patient encounters, have explored how patients offer explanations for their own illnesses. As it turns out, they do so normally with marked caution and in ways that reflect their orientation to the structure of the medical interview, where getting information about symptoms normally precedes diagnosis (see also Gill et al., 2001). In each case, a familiar type of action – delivering bad news, describing symptoms, offering medical explanations – is explicated in terms of previously unexamined design features and sequential properties.

Grounding an analysis

Once a possible phenomenon has been located, how should analysis proceed? In the broad tradition of interpretive sociology that extends back through Alfred Schutz and Max Weber, and *emic* analysis in social anthropology, CA seeks analyses that are grounded in the understandings and orientations of the participants themselves. From a CA perspective these understandings cannot be adequately assessed either by interviewing the participants after the fact or by asking informants about the import of the practice in question. The problem with such retrospective accounts is not only that they may be misguided – they are also conditioned by the immediate interactional context in which they are produced, and are couched in vernacular terms that are generally inadequate to the technical demands of social scientific inquiry. In the domain of interaction, the understandings that matter are those that are incarnate in the interaction being examined – understandings that participants act on within interaction and thus render consequential for its subsequent development (Schegloff and Sacks, 1973).

The response as an analytic resource For tapping into such understandings, one crucial resource centers on how recipients respond to the practice in question. Consider that interactions ordinarily unfold as a series of turns or 'moves', each one of which is to some extent sensitive to and conditioned by the move that preceded it (even as it shapes

(6) [Whalen and Zimmerman, 1987: 174]

1	Dispatcher:	Midcity Emergency
2	Caller:	Um yeah (.) somebody jus' vandalized my car,
3	→ Dispatcher:	What's your address.
4	Caller:	Sixteen seventy Redland Road.

and constrains what comes next). Given the general responsiveness of contributions to interaction, each contribution will normally display that speaker's understanding of what came before (Sacks et al., 1974). Interactants themselves rely on such retrospective displays of understanding to ascertain whether and how they were understood, and this 'architecture of intersubjectivity' (Heritage, 1984b: 254) can also be a resource for conversation analysts.

To illustrate, consider the utterance 'Somebody just vandalized my car'. As Whalen and Zimmerman (1987) have observed, while the lexical meaning of this utterance is transparent and unambiguous, the type of action that it implements – what it is 'doing' from the standpoint of the interactants themselves – is less obvious and cannot be determined by considering the utterance in isolation. It could in principle be a straightforward *announcement of news*, with no agenda other than that of conveying information to an uninformed recipient. If this were the case, one would expect it to generate an initial response along the lines of 'Oh' or 'Oh really' or 'My goodness' – that is, a response that attends to it as new and perhaps surprising information (Jefferson, 1981; Heritage, 1984b). Alternatively, the news announcement could be subsidiary to the task of *requesting help* or assistance of some sort, in which case one would expect a response that either accepts or rejects the request, or at least proceeds in that direction. In reality, the utterance was produced by a caller to an emergency service, and it was responded to as shown in excerpt 6. Notice that the dispatcher's response – a query about the caller's address (arrowed) – is a purely instrumental query, a necessary prerequisite for sending assistance that clearly treats the prior utterance as a request for help rather than a mere news announcement. The dispatcher's impetus to hear this as a request is undoubtedly conditioned by the local institutional environment. In this context, while not everything a caller says will be understood as a request for help, descriptions of trouble are

routinely heard and treated this way (Whalen and Zimmerman, 1987). But the crucial point is that such understandings are displayed publicly in the subsequent response and are thus available as an analytic resource.

Responses can also be informative in more subtle ways. Beyond revealing participant understandings of the basic type of action embodied in a prior utterance, they can also shed light on more detailed aspects of the action, such as its level of intensity or its valence. For instance, an announcement of news may be regarded not only as an announcement generically but as embodying either good or bad news, and this too is displayed through subsequent talk (Maynard, 1997). Thus, the birth announcement in excerpt 7 is receipted (arrowed) not just as news ('Oh') but specifically as good news via the inclusion of a favorable assessment ('how lovely').

In other cases, the proper valence of a given news announcement may be unclear to the recipient, resulting in a more cautious mode of receipt. Contrast the birth announcement sequence in excerpt 7 with a similar announcement in excerpt 8. This time the announcement (line 1) generates an initial response ('Oh my goodness' at arrow 1) that registers it as surprising, but specifically avoids evaluating the news in an explicit way. This non-evaluative response is intelligible under the circumstances – the announcement is being issued by the expecting mother (Andi) whose husband (Bob) had previously had a vasectomy, raising the spectre of an unplanned pregnancy. Moreover, the recipient of the news (Betty) is clearly aware of this fact, as evidenced by her subsequent query about a reversal (line 3). Only when subsequent talk reveals that the husband's vasectomy had indeed been reversed and that the pregnancy was fully planned does Betty receipt it unequivocally as good news ('Oh I'm so happy' at arrow 2).

At a still more subtle level, responses can even shed light on the meaning and import of a momentary silence in interaction

(7) [Maynard, 1997: 111]

1	Carrie:	I: <u>thought</u> you'd l<u>i</u>ke to know I've g<u>o</u>t <u>a</u> little gran'daughter
2	→ Leslie:	thlk <u>Oh: how</u> l<u>o</u>vely.

(8) [Maynard, 1997: 116, simplified]

```
1       Andi:  hhhh! Bob and I are going to have a baby.
2   1→ Betty:  Oh my goodness hhow- (1.0)
3              did you have a reversal- he have a reversal?
4       Andi:  Yea:h.
             .
             .
             .
5       Andi:  It was [very successful,] [very quickly] hh::h. hhh
6   2→ Betty:         [OH I'M  SO  ] [HAPPY.    ]
```

(Davidson, 1984; Pomerantz, 1984). In excerpt 9, C invites B (and a third party) to stay with him at the beach (line 1). This invitation launches a particular type of sequence, one that establishes the relevance of a response that either accepts or declines the invitation. However, what initially follows is silence (line 2). A silence in this sequential context would ordinarily be understood as 'belonging' to the recipient of the invitation (Sacks et al., 1974), and it could in principle result from a number of causes. B may have a basic problem hearing or understanding the invitation, or B may have heard/understood but is intending to reject it and is presenting herself as hesitant in order to do so. The problem, in short, could be either the intelligibility or the acceptability of the invitation. C's response to the silence (arrowed, line 3) clearly treats it as indicating the latter type of problem. Instead of repeating or rewording the invitation – which would be the usual way of handling a problem of intelligibility (Schegloff et al., 1977) – C offers an argument for accepting the invitation. This move presupposes the intelligibility of the invitation and seems designed to overcome what C infers is resistance on B's part. Moreover, the substance of C's argument displays his analysis of B's reason for resisting (concern about insufficient room and the inconvenience that this might entail), a reason that he counters in an effort to nudge her toward an acceptance.

At varying levels of detail, then, successive contributions to interaction can shed light on the meaning and import for the participants of the events to which they are responsive. Of course, it is entirely possible for a respondent to misunderstand what a speaker originally intended, but such errors are typically revealed through repair efforts undertaken in subsequent turns at talk (Schegloff, 1992). More often, subsequent talk by the speaker implicitly confirms the respondent's understanding (see example 9, line 6, above). In any event, the sequential organization of interaction provides a running index of how the participants understand and orient to one another's conduct.

Deployment as an analytic resource The response to a practice is an extremely useful resource, but it is not always a sufficient basis on which to build an analysis. Subsequent talk does not always reveal a wholly transparent understanding of prior talk, and it may at times be designedly opaque (as in example 8, arrow 1, above). Moreover, subsequent talk is most useful for analyzing utterances that initiate sequences (e.g., news announcements, requests, invitations) and thus generate responses that are closely geared to their particulars of the talk in question; subsequent talk is less useful for analyzing talk that is itself primarily responsive and hence generates less attentive sequelae.

Fortunately, other analytic resources are available that center not on the *recipient* but on the *producer* of the talk in question. Examining in detail how speakers recurrently deploy a given practice – in particular sequential environments, in particular positions inside the speaker's own turn, and in conjunction with other practices – can provide important clues as to the meaning and import of that practice for those who use it.

(9) [Davidson, 1984: 105, simplified]

```
1     C:  Well you can both sta:y.
2         (0.4)
3   →C:  [Got plenty a' roo:m, hh[hh
4     B:  [Oh I-              [Oh(h)o(h)o,
5         (.)
6     B:  Please don't tempt me,
```

(10) [Jefferson, 1984: 205]

```
1       M: and she's been very thrifty.
2   →   B: Mm hm,
3       M: .hhhhh So: (.) I said it- it a:dds up to one thing
4           money somepla:ce
5   →   B: Mm hm,
6       M: .hhhh=
7   →   B: Mm [hm,
8       M:     [But ish (.) she tn- transacts all her business in
9           Lo:s Angeles you know and people like this are so secretive
10          it's a(m) really it's almost a mental state
11  →   B: Yeah .hh Well .hh uh:m (0.9) y- there's something wrong too
12          if she doesn't pay her bills....
```

To illustrate, consider the various bits of talk that are used to receipt prior talk – items such as 'mm hm', 'yeah', 'oh', and 'okay'. These were long assumed to comprise an undifferentiated set of 'acknowledgement tokens' or 'backchannel' displays of understanding. However, it has been demonstrated – largely on the basis of the highly selective manner in which these tokens are deployed – that each performs a somewhat distinct interactional function (Beach, 1993; Heritage, 1984a; Jefferson, 1984). The contrast between 'mm hm' and 'yeah' provides a useful case in point (Jefferson, 1984). In excerpt 10, notice how B deploys these receipt tokens (arrowed) in the course of M's extended telling. Although B uses both forms of receipt, she deploys them in discriminably different ways. One point of difference is the prior sequential environment; the 'mm hm' tokens appear in the midst of M's extended telling as it unfolds, while the 'yeah' token appears at what is constructed as the completion of the telling. Correspondingly,

there are differences in what B does next – each 'mm hm' token stands alone within B's turn at talk, while the 'yeah' token is followed by further talk as B assumes the role of speaker and produces a more substantial response to M's telling. It turns out that some speakers do not discriminate in their use of these tokens, but those that do discriminate systematically in precisely this way. Accordingly, these tokens embody different stances toward the talk to which they are responding; 'mm hm' displays a stance of 'passive recipiency' while 'yeah' displays 'incipient speakership'. This conclusion is based on the systematic manner in which they are deployed in interaction.

The distinct functions of these tokens are perhaps most apparent when the tokens are used in sequentially incongruous ways. Thus, in excerpt 11, when speaker G finishes an extended telling and clearly marks it as finished via an explicit assertion to that effect ('So that's the story' in line 10), B receipts the story with 'Mm hm' (arrowed).

(11) [Jefferson, 1984: 209]

```
1       G: I'd li:ke to have the mirrors. But if she wants them? (.)
2           .hh why that's: I-th-tha:t's fi::ne.
3       B: Mm hm,
4       G: If she's going to use them you kno:w.
5       B: Mm [hm,
6       G:     [.hhhhhh I'm not going to uh,hh maybe queer the dea:l
7           just by wanting this that and the othe[r (you know),
8       B:                                        [NO:.
9           (0.2)
10      G: .hhhh s:So: uhm,h (.) tha:t's the story.
11  →   B: Mm hm,
12          (0.2)
13 G:      An:d uh (0.6) uhm,hhh (1.0) .hhhh u-Then I have a ma:n
14          coming Tue:sday...
```

If this is a display of passive recipiency, it is strikingly misfitted to such an obvious story completion, which might be expected to generate a more substantial response. And yet, it seems to have been produced and understood as embodying just such a passive stance – subsequent to this token, B falls silent and offers no further talk (line 12), whereas G searches for and eventually finds something further to say (lines 13–14). Here then, an interactant exploits the passivity of 'mm hm' as a resource for resisting the impending speakership role by prompting the prior speaker to continue.

The preceding discussion does not by any means exhaust the analytic resources that are available to the researcher, but it does illustrate at least some of the resources that may be exploited in the service of developing an analysis that is properly grounded in the displayed understandings and orientations of the participants themselves. These resources include both how speakers deploy the practice in question, and how it is subsequently dealt with by other participants. Given such resources, the analyst need not speculate about the endogenous meaning and import of a given practice, because such understandings are continually being displayed by the participants as they use and respond to the practice in question. Exploiting these resources as thoroughly as possible is a hallmark of the CA approach.

Working through collections

The primary objective of CA is to elucidate generic mechanisms that recurrently organize interaction. Although analysis often begins by examining a single fragment of interaction, this is normally the first step in a deeper analysis that transcends that particular fragment and sheds light on practices and organizations of practice that appear within and are consequential for numerous interactions. As Sacks (1984: 26–7) has observed:

> Thus it is not any particular conversation, as an object, that we are primarily interested in. Our aim is to get into a position to transform … our view of 'what happened', from a matter of a particular interaction done by particular people, to a matter of interactions as products of a machinery. We are trying to find the machinery. In order to do so we have to get access to its products.

Such organizations of practice can be observed in operation within single specimens of talk, but a full understanding of how they work usually requires the systematic analysis of numerous examples that instantiate the phenomenon in question. This is the informally quantitative aspect of CA alluded to earlier. In a variety of ways, working with collections can flesh out and enrich an analysis initially arrived at through a single case. It enables the researcher to begin to specify the scope of the phenomenon being examined, and in particular the conditions under which it does or does not hold. Collections also enable one to specify the strength and normativity of the practice – whether it is merely an empirical regularity evident only to the analyst, or a social convention that the participants themselves recognize and orient to, or a normative practice that the participants enforce on one another such that noncompliance is sanctionable.

When building a collection of candidate instances of a given phenomenon (e.g., news announcements, receipt tokens, follow-up questions in news interviews, symptom descriptions in doctor–patient interactions), it is useful to begin the search by casting a wide net. One should include not only what appear to be clear instances of the phenomenon in question, but also less clear boundary cases in which the phenomenon is present in a partial or imperfect form, as well as negative or 'deviant' cases where the phenomenon simply did not occur as expected. When a phenomenon has not yet been analytically specified, such cases are necessary to clarify the phenomenon's boundaries and to illuminate some of its more elusive properties.

Once a collection is assembled, analysis proceeds on a case-by-case basis with the ultimate objective of developing an account of the phenomenon that will be comprehensive, encompassing all relevant instances in the collection. In this respect, the methodology of CA is formally similar to what has elsewhere been termed 'analytic induction', a qualitative method that can be traced to Znaniecki (1934) and which seeks to produce a relationship of perfect correspondence between an empirical phenomenon and the analytic apparatus postulated to explain its various manifestations within a corpus of data (Katz, 1983). Beyond this the similarity ends, for analytic induction has traditionally been concerned with the formulation of causal laws, while CA seeks to explicate the endogenous principles that interactants use to organize their conduct.

Central to this process is the analysis of deviant cases – that is, cases that run contrary to the researcher's developing sense of how

(12) [Schegloff, 1968: 1079]

1   ((ring))
2   ((receiver is lifted, and there is a one-second silence))
3   Caller: Hello.
4   Answerer: American Red Cross.
5   Caller: Hello, this is police headquarters....

the phenomenon is organized. Rather than dismissing such cases or chalking them up to random error, such cases should be aggressively sought and incorporated into the analysis. Almost invariably, confronting such cases is an analytically fruitful endeavor.

Some deviant cases are shown, upon analysis, to result from interactants' orientation to the same considerations that produce the 'regular' cases. These cases are, in effect, 'exceptions that prove the rule', providing powerful evidence for the original analytic formulation. We have already seen an illustration of this in the discussion of excerpt 11 above, in which an 'mm hm' token was placed in an unusual sequential environment, but was nevertheless shown to function much like other such tokens as a display of passive recipiency. For another illustration, consider the phenomenon known as an adjacency pair – a pair of actions (e.g., question–answer, request– response, greeting–greeting) whose sequential co-occurrence is explained by the property of conditional relevance, which stipulates that the production of a first action makes a corresponding response both relevant and expectable (Schegloff, 1968, 1972; Schegloff and Sacks, 1973). How, then, do we account for instances where the relevant response was not immediately produced? In many cases it can be shown that even though the response item was not produced then and there, the interactants nonetheless acted in accordance with the assumption that it should properly be forthcoming. For instance, the recipient may provide an account to explain and justify the nonproduction of a relevant response; alternatively, if no account is forthcoming, the initiator of the sequence may, after a pause, attempt to elicit the relevant item and thereby complete the unfinished sequence (see excerpt 9, line 3, above). In any case, through such actions the parties display an orientation to the very same principles that are postulated to underpin the production of 'normal' adjacency pair sequences (Heritage, 1984b: 248–53). This line of reasoning not only confirms the initial analysis regarding conditional relevance; it also enriches it by showing how the same principles can generate a nonstandard course of action.

In other instances, deviant cases can prompt the researcher to revise the initial analysis in favor of a more general formulation, one that can encompass both the regular cases and the anomalous departure. Perhaps the clearest statement of this process can be found in Schegloff's (1968) analysis of telephone call openings. In a corpus of 500 telephone calls, Schegloff found that a straightforward rule – 'answerer speaks first' – adequately described all but one of the call openings (excerpt 12). In that one unusual case, the caller speaks first (line 3): Rather than ignoring this instance or explaining it away in an *ad hoc* fashion, Schegloff returned to the drawing board and developed a more general analytic apparatus that could account for all 500 cases. This apparatus involved what would later be termed adjacency pairs, and the recognition that the ringing of the telephone launches a special kind of adjacency pair sequence – a summons–answer sequence – and thus establishes the relevance of an appropriate response to the summons. Against this backdrop, the rule that 'answerer speaks first' actually reflects the more general principle that once a summons (here a ringing phone) has been issued, an appropriate response is due. The deviant case can also be explained in light of the summons and its sequential implications. In that case the ring (line 1 above) was followed by silence (line 2), during which the relevant response was heard by the caller to be absent. This in turn prompted the caller to speak first as a way of reissuing the summons to solicit a response and thereby 'repair' the unfinished sequence. In this way, deviant cases can encourage the development of a more general and analytically powerful account that can encompass both the regular cases and the atypical variant.

Finally, some deviant cases may, upon analysis, turn out to fall beyond the parameters of the core phenomenon being investigated, and are thus not genuinely 'deviant' at all. Here the impetus is to clarify as precisely as possible what distinguishes the apparent departure from the other cases, and thus constitutes it as an alternate interactional phenomenon. For instance, consider how personal troubles are discussed in conversation

(Jefferson, 1988; Jefferson and Lee, 1981). When speakers disclose their troubles, recipients commonly respond with affiliative displays of understanding. However, in contrast to this typical pattern, recipients may instead offer advice and thereby transform the situation from a 'troubles-telling' to a 'service encounter', implicating different discourse identities and situated activities. This line of analysis, unlike the previous two, does not result in a single analytic formulation which can account for both the 'regular' and 'deviant' cases. Rather, it recognizes differences between alternate courses of action, and in so doing it clarifies the boundaries of the core phenomenon.

However deviant cases are handled, it is almost always productive to consider such cases carefully in pursuit of a comprehensive analysis of the available data. Whether they provide compelling evidence for the original analysis, or prompt the development of a more powerful analysis, or clarify the scope of the phenomenon being investigated, such cases ensure that the result will be firmly anchored to interactional reality.

RETROSPECT AND PROSPECT

Because CA is addressed to a domain of phenomena that did not previously have a disciplinary home within the social sciences, its significance has not always been recognized by those in other social science sectors. The sustained focus on the endogenous organization of talk-in-interaction has nonetheless proven to be both productive and illuminating, enabling researchers to begin to map what is an exceedingly complex domain of social phenomena. Much has been learned about the basic objects that comprise this domain and the principles in terms of which they are organized.

Progress on this front has made it possible for researchers to begin applying CA methods and findings to address questions that extend beyond the organization of interaction *per se*, questions involving how this domain intersects with and can thus illuminate other aspects of the social world. As we noted at the beginning of this chapter, some researchers have examined the impact of interactional practices on bureaucratic and professional decision-making (e.g., in medicine, journalism, and social science research). Others have done comparative analyses of interactional practices to illuminate large-scale processes of cultural variation and historical change. Still others have explored how interaction can illuminate processes of cognition and cognitive development. Some of this work involves formal quantification, correlating interactional practices with other variables of interest. The utility of CA in this context is that the growing body of past interactional research identifies previously unknown practices, establishes and validates the meaning and import of those practices, and thus provides a solid foundation for quantitative and distributional studies.

As progress is made in these various 'applied' areas, it is important to keep in mind that such work would not be possible without the 'pure' research on which it is based. The domain of talk-in-interaction remains a rich and compelling topic in its own right, one in which agency is exercised, intersubjectivity is achieved, and various contexts of the social world are brought to life. Notwithstanding what has already been accomplished, much remains to be discovered about how human interaction actually works.

APPENDIX

Transcript notational conventions

The transcription conventions developed by Gail Jefferson (1974) are designed to capture the details of talk and interaction as it naturally occurs. This is a brief guide to the symbols – for a more detailed exposition, see Atkinson and Heritage (1984, pp. ix–xvi).

A:	That's <u>my</u> <u>view</u>.	<u>Underlined items</u> were markedly stessed.
A:	That's my:: view.	<u>Colon(s)</u> indicate the prior sound was prolonged.
A:	That's MY view.	<u>Capital letters</u> indicate increased volume.
A:	That's my- my view.	<u>A hyphen</u> denotes a glottal stop or 'cut-off' of sound.

A:	hhh That's my view.	<u>Strings of 'hhh'</u> mark audible outbreath. The longer the string, the longer the outbreath.
A:	.hhh That's my view.	<u>Strings of '.hhh'</u> mark audible inbreath. (Note the preceding period.) Again the longer the string, the longer the inbreath.
A:	That's (.) my view.	<u>Numbers in parentheses</u> denote elapsed silence in seconds.
	(1.3)	A period denotes a
B:	But should it be.	micropause of less than 0.2 seconds.
A:	That's my view .=	<u>Equals signs</u> indicate that one sound followed the other with no
B:	= But should it be.	intervening silence.
A:	Tha[t's my view]	<u>Brackets</u> mark the onset and termination of simultaneous speech.
B:	[But should it] be.	
A:	That's my view,	<u>Punctuation marks</u> denote intonation rather than grammar at turn
B:	But should it be.	constructional unit boundaries. Periods indicate fallingintonation,
A:	I think so?	question marks indicate rising intonation, and commas indicate 'continuing' or slightly rising intonation.
A:	That's my ( )	<u>Open parentheses</u> indicate transcriber's uncertainty as to what was said.
B:	But (should it) be.	<u>Words in parentheses</u> represent a best guess as to what was said.

NOTES

1 For a much more elaborate discussion of CA methods, see ten Have (1999).

2 This is not to imply that recordings can capture every interactional feature that was available to the participants. A recording is always a version of reality, and will reflect such choices as how cameras are positioned and how much of the interaction is recorded. Although for simplicity's sake we will refer to recordings as 'the data', it is with the understanding that any recording is unavoidably a rendering of the data, the actual events that were recorded (see Psathas and Anderson, 1990).

REFERENCES

Atkinson, Max (1984) *Our Masters' Voices: The Language and Body Language of Politics.* London: Methuen.

Atkinson, Maxwell and Heritage, John (eds) (1984) *Structures of Social Action: Studies in Conversation Analysis.* Cambridge: Cambridge University Press.

Beach, Wayne A. (1993) 'Transitional regularities for casual "okay" usages', *Journal of Pragmatics,* 19: 325–52.

Boden, Deirdre and Zimmerman, Don H. (eds) (1991) *Talk and Social Structure.* Cambridge: Polity Press.

Boyd, Elizabeth (1998) 'Bureaucratic authority in the "company of equals": Initiating discussion during medical peer review', *American Sociological Review,* 63: 200–24.

Button, Graham and Lee, J.R.E. (eds) (1987) *Talk and Social Organisation.* Clevedon: Multilingual Matters.

Clayman, Steven E. and Heritage, John (2002) 'Questioning presidents: Journalistic deference and adversarialness in the press conferences of U.S. President's Eisenhower and Reagan', *Journal of Communication,* 52: 749–75.

Clayman, Steven E. and Reisner, Anne (1998) 'Gatekeeping in action: Editorial conferences and assessments of newsworthiness', *American Sociological Review,* 63: 178–99.

Davidson, Judy (1984) 'Subsequent versions of invitations, offers, requests, and proposals dealing with potential or actual rejection', in J.M. Atkinson and J. Heritage (eds), *Structures of Social Action.* Cambridge: Cambridge University Press, pp. 102–28.

Drew, Paul and Heritage, John (1992a) 'Analyzing talk at work: An introduction', in Paul Drew and John Heritage (eds), *Talk at Work.* Cambridge: Cambridge University Press, pp. 3–65.

Drew, Paul and Heritage, John (eds) (1992b) *Talk at Work.* Cambridge: Cambridge University Press.

Garfinkel, Harold (1967) *Studies in Ethnomethodology.* Englewood Cliffs, NJ: Prentice Hall.

Gill, Virginia Teas (1998) 'Doing attributions in medical interaction: Patients' explanations for illness and doctors' responses', *Social Psychology Quarterly* 61: 342–60.

Gill, Virginia Teas and Maynard, Douglas W. (forthcoming) 'Patients' explanations for health problems and physicians' responsiveness in the medical interview', in J. Heritage and D.W. Maynard (eds), *Practicing Medicine: Structure and Process in Primary Care Encounters.* Cambridge: Cambridge University Press.

Gill, Virginia Teas, Halkowski, Timothy and Roberts, Felkia (2001) 'Accomplishing a request without making one: A single case analysis of a primary care visit', *Text*, 21(1/2): 55–81.

Glenn, Philip J. (2003) *Laughter in Interaction.* Cambridge: Cambridge University Press.

Goffman, Erving (1963) *Behavior in Public Places.* New York: Free Press.

Goffman, Erving (1964) 'The neglected situation', *American Anthropologist* 66(6 Pt. II): 133–6.

Goffman, Erving (1967) *Interaction Ritual: Essays in Face to Face Behavior.* Garden City, NY: Doubleday.

Goffman, Erving (1983) 'The interaction order', *American Sociological Review*, 48: 1–17.

Goodwin, Charles (1981) *Conversational Organization: Interaction between Speakers and Hearers.* New York: Academic Press.

Goodwin, Charles (1994) 'Professional vision', *American Anthropologist* 96(3): 606–33.

Goodwin, Charles (1995) 'Co-constructing meaning in conversations with an aphasic man', *Research on Language and Social Interaction*, 28(3): 233–60.

Goodwin, Marjorie (1990) *He-Said-She-Said: Talk as Social Organization among Black Children.* Bloomington: Indiana University Press.

Halkowski, Timothy (forthcoming) 'Realizing the illness: Patients' reports of symptom discovery in primary care visits', in J. Heritage and D.W. Maynard (eds), *Practicing Medicine: Structure and Process in Primary Care Encounters.* Cambridge: Cambridge University Press.

Heeschen, Claus and Schegloff, Emanuel A. (1999) 'Agrammatism, adaptation theory, and conversation analysis: On the role of the so-called telegraphic style in talk-in-interaction', *Aphasiology*, 13: 365–405.

Heritage, John (1984a) 'A change-of-state token and aspects of its sequential placement', in J.M. Atkinson and J. Heritage (eds), *Structures of Social Action.* Cambridge: Cambridge University Press, pp. 299–345.

Heritage, John (1984b) *Garfinkel and Ethnomethodology.* Cambridge: Polity Press.

Heritage, John (1988) 'Explanations as accounts: A conversation analytic perspective', in C. Antaki (ed.), *Analyzing Everyday Explanation: A Casebook of Methods.* London: Sage, pp. 127–44.

Heritage, John (1998) 'Oh-prefaced responses to inquiry', *Language in Society*, 27(3): 291–334.

Heritage, John (1999) 'CA at century's end: Practices of talk-in-interaction, their distributions and their outcomes', *Research on Language and Social Interaction*, 32(1–2): 69–76.

Heritage, John (2001) 'Goffman, Garfinkel, and conversation analysis', in M. Wetherell, S.J. Taylor and S.J. Yates (eds), *Discourse Theory and Practice: A Reader.* London: Sage.

Heritage, John and Maynard, Douglas W. (eds) (forthcoming) *Practicing Medicine: Structure and Process in Primary Care Encounters.* Cambridge: Cambridge University Press.

Heritage, John and Stivers, Tanya (1999) 'Online commentary in acute medical visits: A method of shaping patient expectations', *Social Science and Medicine*, 49(11): 1501–17.

Heritage, John, Boyd, Elizabeth and Kleinman, Lawrence (2001) 'Subverting criteria: The role of precedent in decisions to finance surgery', *Sociology of Health and Illness*, 23(5): 701–28.

Houtkoop-Steenstra, Hanneke (1991) 'Opening sequences in Dutch telephone conversations', in D. Boden and D.H. Zimmerman (eds), *Talk and Social Structure.* Berkeley: University of California Press, pp. 232–50.

Jefferson, Gail (1974) 'Error correction as an interactional resource', *Language in Society*, 2: 181–199.

Jefferson, Gail (1981) 'Caveat speaker: A preliminary exploration of shift implicative recipiency in the articulation of topic'. End of grant report to the Social Science Research Council, Great Britain.

Jefferson, Gail (1984) 'Notes on a systematic deployment of the acknowledgement tokens "Yeah" and "Mm hm"', *Papers in Linguistics*, 17: 197–216.

Jefferson, Gail (1985) 'An exercise in the transcription and analysis of laughter', in T.A. van Dijk (ed.), *Handbook of Discourse Analysis Volume 3.* New York: Academic Press, pp. 25–34.

Jefferson, Gail (1988) 'On the sequential organization of troubles-talk in ordinary conversation', *Social Problems*, 35(4): 418–41.

Jefferson, Gail and J.R.E. Lee (1981) 'The rejection of advice: Managing the problematic convergence of a "Troubles-telling" and a "Service Encounter"', *Journal of Pragmatics*, 5: 399–422.

Katz, Jack (1983) 'A theory of qualitative methodology: The social system of analytic fieldwork', in R.M. Emerson (ed.), *Contemporary Field Research.* Boston: Little, Brown, pp. 127–148.

Labov, William (1972) *Language in the Inner City: Studies in the Black English Vernacular.* Philadelphia: University of Pennsylvania Press.

Lindström, Anna (1994) 'Identification and recognition in Swedish telephone conversation openings', *Language in Society*, 23(2): 231–52.

Maynard, Douglas W. (1984) *Inside Plea Bargaining: The Language of Negotiation.* New York: Plenum.

Maynard, Douglas W. (2003) *Bad News, Good News: Conversational Order in Everyday Talk and Clinical Settings.* Chicago: University of Chicago Press.

Maynard, Douglas W. (1992) 'On clinicians co-implicating recipients' perspectives in the delivery of diagnostic news', in P. Drew and J. Heritage (eds), *Talk at Work.* Cambridge: Cambridge University Press, pp. 331–58.

Maynard, Douglas W. (1996) 'On "realization" in everyday life: The forecasting of bad news as a social relation', *American Sociological Review*, 61(1): 109–31.

Maynard, Douglas W. (1997) 'The news delivery sequence: Bad news and good news in conversational interaction', *Research on Language and Social Interaction*, 30(2): 93–130.

Maynard, Douglas W. and Schaeffer, Nora Cate (1996) 'From paradigm to prototype and back again: Interactive aspects of "cognitive processing" in standardized survey interviews', in N. Schwarz and S. Sudman (eds), *Answering Questions: Methodology for Determining Cognitive and Communicating Processes in Survey Research*. San Francisco: Jossey Bass. pp. 65–88.

Maynard Douglas W. and Schaeffer, Nora Cate (2000) 'Toward a sociology of social scientific knowledge: Survey research and ethnomethodology's asymmetric alternates', *Social Studies of Science*, 30: 265–312.

Maynard, Douglas W., Houtkoop-Steenstra, Hanneke, Schaeffer, Nora Cate and van der Zouwen, Johannes (eds) (2002) *Standardization and Tacit Knowledge: Interaction and Practice in the Survey Interview*. New York: Wiley Interscience.

Peräkylä, Anssi (1998) 'Authority and accountability: The delivery of diagnosis in primary health care', *Social Psychology Quarterly*, 61: 301–20.

Pomerantz, Anita (1984) 'Agreeing and disagreeing with assessments: Some features of preferred/dispreferred turn shapes', in J.M. Atkinson and J. Heritage (eds), *Structures of Social Action: Studies in Conversation Analysis*. Cambridge: Cambridge University Press, pp. 57–101.

Psathas, George (ed.) (1990) *Interaction Competence*. Washington, DC: University Press of America.

Psathas, George and Anderson, Timothy (1990) 'The "practices" of transcription in conversation analysis', *Semiotica*, 78: 75–99.

Sacks, Harvey (1984) 'Notes on methodology', in J.M. Atkinson and J. Heritage (eds), *Structures of Social Action*. Cambridge: Cambridge University Press, pp. 21–7.

Sacks, Harvey (1992) *Lectures on Conversation*. Oxford: Blackwell.

Sacks, Harvey, Schegloff, Emanuel A. and Jefferson, Gail (1974) 'A simplest systematics for the organization of turn-taking for conversation', *Language*, 50: 696–735.

Schegloff, Emanuel A. (1968) 'Sequencing in conversational openings', *American Anthropologist*, 70: 1075–95.

Schegloff, Emanuel A. (1972) 'Notes on a conversational practice: Formulating place', in D. Sudnow (ed.), *Studies in Social Interaction*. New York: Free Press, pp. 75–119.

Schegloff, Emanuel A. (1987) 'Between macro and micro: Contexts and other connections', in J.C. Alexander, B. Giesen, R. Münch and N.J. Smelser (eds), *The Micro-Macro Link*. Berkeley: University of California Press. pp. 207–234.

Schegloff, Emanuel A. (1991) 'Conversation analysis and socially shared cognition', in Lauren B. Resnick, John M. Levine and S.D. Teasley (eds), *Perspectives on Socially Shared Cognition*. Washington, DC: American Psychological Association, pp. 150–71.

Schegloff, Emanuel A. (1992) 'Repair after next turn: The last structurally provided for place for the defence of intersubjectivity in conversation', *American Journal of Sociology*, 95(5): 1295–345.

Schegloff, Emanuel A. (1993) 'Reflections on quantification in the study of conversation', *Research on Language and Social Interaction*, 26: 99–128.

Schegloff, Emanuel A. (1996) 'Confirming allusions: Toward an empirical account of action', *American Journal of Sociology*, 102(1): 161–216.

Schegloff, Emanuel A. and Sacks, Harvey (1973) 'Opening up closings', *Semiotica*, 8: 289–327.

Schegloff, Emanuel A., Jefferson, Gail and Sacks, Harvey (1977) 'The preference for self-correction in the organization of repair in conversation', *Language*, 53: 361–82.

ten Have, Paul (1999) *Doing Conversation Analysis: A Practical Guide*. London: Sage.

West, Candace and Zimmerman, Don H. (1983) 'Small insults: A study of interruptions in cross-sex conversations with unacquainted persons', in B. Thorne, C. Kramarae and N. Henley (eds), *Language, Gender and Society*. Rowley, MA: Newbury House, pp. 102–17.

Whalen, Jack (1995) 'A technology of order production: Computer-aided dispatch in public safety communications', in P. ten Have and G. Psathas (eds), *Situated Order: Studies in the Social Organization of Talk and Embodied Activities*. Washington, DC: University Press of America, pp. 187–230.

Whalen, Marilyn and Zimmerman, Don H. (1987) 'Sequential and institutional contexts in calls for help', *Social Psychology Quarterly*, 50: 172–85.

Wootton, Anthony J. (1997) *Interaction and the Development of Mind*. Cambridge: Cambridge University Press.

Zimmerman, Don H. (1988) 'On conversation: The conversation analytic perspective', *Communication Yearbook*, 11: 406–32.

Znaniecki, Florian (1934) *The Method of Sociology*. New York: Farrar & Rinehart.

27

Discourse Analysis

JONATHAN POTTER

Discourse is a central part of our lives. Much of what we do with others we do by way of conversation, phone calls, letters and instructions. Learning to talk is fundamental to learning a culture, and language provides the categories and terms for understanding self and others. Our work places are imbued with talk and texts, whether they are part of the job itself or all the ancillary features of living that surround it. And while we can watch television with the sound turned down, and flick through the daily newspaper looking just at the pictures, our entertainment and cultural life is massively dependent on what the actors are saying and what the newspaper stories tell.

It is not surprising, then, that analysing discourse is a central task for social science. Yet despite the fact that virtually all social science depends on a range of (largely implicit) judgements about discourse and what it is doing, these judgements have often been hidden behind various more formal procedures of experimentation, polling and so on. Typically in studies involving experimentation, surveys, questionnaires, opinion polls, some styles of grounded theory, common strands of ethnography, and most content analysis, discourse is treated as a relatively transparent medium: a predominantly direct pathway to what the researcher is most interested in, be it events, cognitive structures, causal relations or whatever. So there is a curious paradox that for the majority of social science methods discourse is simultaneously pervasive and invisible.

VARIETIES OF DISCOURSE ANALYSIS

Discourse analysis is understood in a range of different ways across the social sciences. One of the reasons for this is that analytic and theoretical approaches have been developed in a range of different disciplines – notably linguistics, sociology, psychology, social psychology, philosophy, communication, literary theory and cultural studies. While some concerns are shared, disciplinary home typically inflects method and research questions in significant ways. Sometimes discourse analysis is a convenient name for a practice of analysing discourse which can include a variety of different approaches such as speech act theory, narrative analysis, conversation analysis and so on; while at other times discourse analysis is treated as a fully-fledged analytic position. Sometimes 'discourse' is treated simply as a word for language in use; at other times a 'discourse' is theorized as a linguistic object that can be counted and described. Sometimes discourse analysis is further specified as continental or critical. In the mid-1980s it was possible to find different books called 'Discourse Analysis' with almost no overlap in subject matter; the situation at the start of the 2000s is, if anything, even more fragmented. This is not the appropriate place for a general survey; however, it is worth sketching some of the major varieties of discourse analysis.

One of the first approaches to use something explicitly called discourse analysis was developed in linguistics by Sinclair and Coulthard (1975) in a study of classroom interaction. Their aim was to build a systematic model of interaction in classroom teaching, and they identified a pattern of 'initiation–response–feedback' as fundamental. This has the following form:

Teacher: Why are plants
                   green?   (*Initiation*)
Pupil: It's the stuff in
                   the leaves.   (*Response*)
Teacher: Yes, but what is it?
                   Anyone?   (*Feedback*)

Although developed with classroom material, their goal was a model that could capture interaction structures in different institutional settings (Coulthard and Montgomery, 1981). Despite limitations in their analysis, the aim of capturing the way institutional practices are organized is characteristic of much more recent discourse work. In analytic terms, this work performed broadly linguistic analyses of simplified transcripts of actual interaction. This was a departure from much of linguistics that had focused on invented or idealized materials.

A separate tradition in linguistics focused on the way sentences are linked together into coherent discourse. Part of this involved considering the use of terms such as 'however' and 'but' (Brown and Yule, 1983). Linguistic work of this kind spawned a psychological tradition of discourse processes that attempted to relate textual and cognitive concerns. This asked, for example, about the way psychological experiences become transformed when they are reconstructed into narrative and, conversely, how mental scripts are used to understand narrative organizations (Labov, 1972; Kinstch and van Dijk, 1978). Such work has increasingly become a part of modern cognitive psychology. In its research practice the work on linguistic coherence typically used standard linguistic methods, drawing on invented examples and considering whether they were 'well formed' or 'anomalous'. The more psychological work has drawn on a range of approaches – sometimes records of interaction are coded for statistical regularities and contrasts; sometimes experimental manipulations are used.

Another very different tradition of discourse analysis comes out of post-structuralism and particularly the work of Michel Foucault. His work rarely considered discourse in terms of specific interaction. Rather its focus was on how a discourse, or a 'set of statements', comes to constitute objects and subjects. For instance, the discourse of medicine may produce objects such as 'vapours' or 'HIV+' as distinct and factual at the same time as producing the doctor as an individual with knowledge and authority. In Foucault's own work analysis tends to involve broad-brush historical reinterpretations of topics such as criminology, medicine or sexuality. Some discourse workers have tried to combine Foucauldian ideas with other theoretical notions and apply them to specific interactional materials (see, for example, Fairclough, 1992; Prior, 1997; Wetherell and Potter, 1992).

The complexities here are formidable. Indeed, discourse analysis can be seen as a contested disciplinary terrain where a range of different theoretical notions and analytic practices compete (Potter, 1996a). Luckily, there are now a number of excellent introductions. In addition to Schiffrin (1994), which is idiosyncratic in its coverage, three collections provide breadth and depth in discourse studies. Van Dijk (1996) is particularly good on the more linguistically influenced traditions, on conversation analysis, and on cognitive psychological approaches. Jaworski and Coupland (1999) have collected together a set of classic papers in discourse work, and emphasize some of the sociolinguistic, social theory and post-structuralist themes that are less well covered in the van Dijk volumes. Wetherell et al. (2001) combines classic papers with especially commissioned pieces and has particularly good coverage of Foucauldian work and the style of discourse analysis that has come out of social psychology and sociology which will be discussed in more detail below. There are three books that take methods of discourse analysis as their main topic. Titscher et al. (2000) covers a range of approaches but has a particular emphasis on the application of ideas from critical discourse analysis. Wood and Kroger (2000) is an integrated introduction emphasizing social psychological themes. Yates et al. (2001) is probably the best book-length source covering the different varieties of discourse analysis.

It would not be helpful to try and survey all of the different styles of data analysis involved in these different approaches in the current chapter. The result would be superficial and probably deeply confusing. Instead the focus will be on one strand of discourse analysis that has its origins in social psychology and sociology, but is now commonplace in communication and other social science disciplines. In this form of discourse analysis the aim is to make visible the ways in which discourse is central to action, the ways it is used to constitute events, settings and identities, and the various discursive resources that are drawn on to build plausible descriptions. For analysts of talk and texts using this approach, discourse is not just one further topic of study but the key to understanding interaction and social life. Furthermore, it has paid particular attention to analytic practice and to the role of evidence (texts and recordings of interaction) in supporting claims.

THEORETICAL PRINCIPLES OF DISCOURSE ANALYSIS

There are a number of different ways of understanding the nature of discourse that reflect the different disciplinary concerns of psychology, linguistics, literary studies and social history. The approach that will be overviewed here has more of a general social science orientation; that is, it is concerned with practices and organizations rather than with abstract textual structures. At times it complements core disciplinary concerns; but at other times it provides a sharply conflicting account. It can be introduced by way of three fundamental principles: discourse is *action-oriented*, *situated* and *constructed*.

Discourse is action-oriented

Discourse analysis is concerned with actions and practices. In one sense this is simply its topic. Yet in another sense it has a more profound role as a metatheoretical axiom. Discourse analysts assume a world in motion; a world where getting things done is the paramount concern. This reflects the basic discourse-analytic questions:

- What is this discourse doing?
- How is this discourse constructed to make this happen?
- What resources are available to perform this activity?

This action-oriented focus contrasts with the cognitive psychological approach common in much discourse processes work where a major issue is how discourse organization is related to a putative underlying cognitive organization. And it contrasts with more linguistic approaches where the major issue is abstract discourse structure.

Discourse is put together to perform actions as parts of broader practices. Some of these actions have a generic character and appear across a wide range of formal and informal settings. Examples would be greetings, invitations, criticisms, and displays of neutrality. More specialized actions may be found in specific institutional settings such as counselling, air traffic control, or political interviewing. Such specialized actions are often seen as modifications and elaborations of actions that are common in more mundane settings (Drew and Heritage, 1992; although see Bogen, 1999, for an alternative position).

The notion of *action orientation* is taken from conversation analysis. It is meant to head off the expectation that there will be discrete acts that are performed by discrete action verbs (compliment, challenge, or whatever). Often in discourse research the business being done in talk or texts does not have a single speech act term to characterize it. Indeed, a central research theme is activity that is done indirectly, often through ostensibly factual, descriptive language.

In terms of analysis, then, a crucial concern is activity, what discourse is doing. It is about unpacking and rendering visible the business of talk.

Discourse is situated

Discourse analysis treats discourse as situated in two principal ways. The first way involves treating discourse as *occasioned* in the manner of conversation analysis (see Chapter 26). That is, talk and texts are embedded in sequences of interaction. The concern with the occasioning of talk follows from the concern with action; actions do not hang in space, but are responses to other actions, and they in turn set the environment for new actions. Greetings follow greetings; acceptances follow invitations; minimizations follow complaints. However, the occasioned nature of discourse is not a contextual determinism. Sequential positioning sets the conditions for what happens next, but does not force it. Thus an accusation sets up the conditions for a range of actions (a denial, minimization, confession, apology), but such actions may be deferred while other business is sorted out, or may be withheld altogether.

Much discourse analysis also follows conversation analysis in avoiding a broader contextual determinism which treats interaction as governed by the setting in which it takes place. When analysing talk that takes place in a doctor's surgery or a school classroom, the researcher will not assume that the talk is therefore *necessarily* medical or pedagogic (Heritage, 1984). This approach to analysis moves away from assuming contextual relevance by analytic fiat. Instead it considers the way participants make institutional activities and identities relevant to themselves, by invoking them, orienting to them or, sometimes, subverting and ignoring them (Schegloff, 1997). Two people interacting in a surgery, say, may do so as doctor and patient, or as friends, or as lovers, or as old religious white man and irresponsible adolescent. This point has been highly controversial within discourse work, and some take a very different view (Fairclough, 1992).

The second way in which discourse is situated is in terms of rhetoric (Antaki, 1994; Billig, 1991, 1996). This is one of the features that sets discourse analysis apart from conversation analysis. The way a description is put together in talk is often in a manner that counters an actual or potential alternative and, conversely, in a manner that resists an actual or potential attempt to undermine it as partial or interested (Edwards and Potter, 1992). Put another way, accounts and descriptions can have both an *offensive* and a *defensive* rhetoric (Potter, 1996b).

Analysis will consider the way that talk and texts are embedded in sequences of interaction, are oriented to institutional settings and identities, and are put together rhetorically. Many of the abstract issues in debates about social structure and the role of cognition become more straightforward when they are tackled in the context of actual analysis.

Discourse is constructed

Discourse analysis works with two levels of discourse construction. The first level concerns the way discourse is constructed out of words, idioms, rhetorical devices and so on. The second level concerns the way discourse constructs and stabilizes versions of the world. In particular situations descriptions are often assembled as neutral and disinterested to do particular actions. A person may construct a version of their feelings, or setting they are in, or the history of that setting, to perform some business. Discourse analysis treats discourse as both construc*ted* and construc*tive* (Potter, 1996b).

This *discursive* constructionism is distinct from a range of *cognitive* constructionisms that consider the way images of the world are mentally put together through processes of information processing. And it is distinct from a range of *social* constructionisms that attempt to understand the production of particular individual persons through the internalization of social relations. In discourse analysis, the way versions are constructed and stabilized as independent of the speaker is treated as an analysable feature of the production of discourse. Whereas cognitive constructionisms tend to focus on purported mental entities and processes, and social constructionists tend to focus on social relationships and social perception, discourse constructionists focus on people's practices.

In its most thoroughgoing form this discourse construction leads to a very different picture than other approaches. Rather than treating persons as acting in, and responding to, social settings on the basis of various psychological entities – beliefs, feelings, intentions, etc. – both the setting and the psychological entities are treated as *products* of discourse. This may seem rather perverse when considered in the abstract, but it becomes a powerful heuristic for producing coherent research. Its value is shown by studies that highlight the confusions in the research practice of approaches that take a more mix-and-match form of constructionism (see Edwards and Potter, 1992, for examples).

QUESTIONS THAT DISCOURSE ANALYSTS ASK

Discourse analysis in some form or other is spread across different social sciences. Substantial numbers of discourse studies have been published in psychology, sociology, communication, anthropology, medicine, geography and economics. The burgeoning number of studies is specifically catered for in journals such as *Discourse Studies*, *Discourse Processes*, *Discourse and Society*, *Journal of Pragmatics*, *Research on Language and Social Interaction*, and *Text*. Discourse research covers an enormous variety of topics and asks a wide range of different questions (as well as displaying wide variation in analytic adequacy!). Some of them stretch the notion of discourse analysis well beyond breaking point. What is clear is that, when done well, discourse analytic studies work with very different questions than those which are commonplace in other strands of research. In particular, the emphasis on action, rhetoric and construction in discourse analysis runs counter to the factors and outcomes logic that underlies many other areas of social science. To attempt to ask a question formulated in more traditional terms ('what are the factors that lead to condom use amongst HIV+ gay males') and then use discourse analytic methods to answer it is a recipe for incoherence.

Discourse analytic questions can be broken up into a range of themes. The following give an indication of just some of the kinds of work that has been done, as well as showing the sorts of questions that are involved. In practice, these themes often overlap.

Actions and practices in settings

The basic question here is: how is this done? There is a huge range of such studies, each trying to describe and explicate actions in everyday and institutional settings. How does a speaker (indirectly) display their investment in a claim or position by formulating it in an extreme manner (Edwards, 2000)? How does a speaker use an identity ascription to disqualify a rival's version as a product of their stake or interest (Antaki and Horowitz, 2000)? How does a schoolteacher present violent acts toward pupils as an unsurprising and accountable feature of doing the job (Hepburn, 2000)?

Fact construction

One of the major themes in discourse work has been concerned with the way versions are constructed and made (to seem) objective and factual or, conversely, the way (apparently) factual versions are undermined as partial, distorted or interested. For example, how does a clairvoyant establish that information they are providing is derived from a paranormal source rather than being made up on the spot (Wooffitt, 2000)? What procedures do news interviewees use to present their

claims as disinterested (Dickerson, 1997)? How do relationship partners construct versions of their infidelity to present it as a discrete one-off, as externally caused, or simply not to exist at all (Lawes, 1999)?

Psychology in practice

An increasingly central strand of discourse work has been involved with discursive psychology, the respecification of psychological notions in terms of their role in talk and texts (Potter and Edwards, 2001). For example, how did President Clinton use emotion descriptions to provide a range of indirect justifications and blamings in his grand jury testimony (Locke and Edwards, 2003)? What resources are used to construct and identify 'delusional' speech in psychiatric practice (Georgaca, 2000)? How can the psychoanalytic notion of repression be respecified in conversational terms (Billig, 1999a)?

Exploitation, prejudice and ideology

One of the enduring interests in discourse work has been in the way racism, sexism and related forms of oppression are obscured or legitimated. For example, one of the classic studies asked how white New Zealanders constructed descriptions of their society and its organization to present Maori protests as ill founded or politically motivated (Wetherell and Potter, 1992). How are the available discursive resources used to justify certain consumption practices that have ecological risks (Phillips, 2000)? How are particular descriptions of racism developed that help perpetuate certain social relations (Ahmed et al., 2000). This is a complex topic where the challenge is to provide analyses that avoid merely reiterating analysts' prior political values – see Potter et al. (1999) and Speer and Potter (2000) for discussions of some of these issues.

These themes give just an indication of the types of question that have been asked. It is worth stressing that the initial motor for much discourse work is often the result of taking categories from a traditional perspective and then considering them in terms of practices performed in talk or texts. This means that much discourse research develops as a rhetorical contrast to existing theory.

ANALYTIC MATERIALS

Discourse-analytic research can be conducted on virtually any set of materials that involve talk and texts. However, it is worth emphasizing two points to start with. First, the fact that any materials can be studied does not mean that any study will be equally easy. Some material offers sleepless nights; other material offers an embarrassment of rich analytic possibilities. Second, the focus on discourse is often taken contrastively, to be study of the talk as opposed to the embodied actions, the objects or settings. However, one of the features of people's interaction is that these things enter decisively into interaction through being formulated and oriented to in talk. Although their discursive formulation and orientation is not all there is, it makes a productive analytic start point. For example, it is possible to take something taken to be quintessentially material and physiological (eating and hunger), or irreducibly psychological (visual perception), and consider the way it is constituted through talk-in-interaction (Goodwin and Goodwin, 1996; Wiggins et al., 2001).

The main sources of material used in discourse analytic studies are naturalistic materials, interviews, focus groups, and texts. Each has positive and negative features.

Naturalistic interactional materials

Naturalistic materials involve talk and interaction that would happen whether the researcher is involved or not. It passes the 'dead social scientist test' – if the researcher got run over on the way to the university that morning, would the interaction nevertheless have taken place, and in the way that it did? Typically such materials are audio or video tapes of talk from everyday or work settings; everyday conversation over the telephone or during family mealtimes; counselling or therapy sessions; work groups; flight crew conversation; social worker assessment interviews; classroom talk. That is, anywhere that talk is happening.

This kind of material has a number of advantages over other materials, and is increasingly the data of choice for discourse researchers. Some would never touch anything else! The advantages of naturalistic materials are:

1. Most obviously, they document the thing itself. If you are interested in counselling, say, then studying the practices of counselling as it happens makes a lot of sense. It minimizes the difficulty of extrapolating from descriptions in interviews, experiments or questionnaires to the phenomena of interest.

2. They most easily retain the action-oriented and situated nature of talk. Actions are embedded in sequences of interaction, and any particular turn of talk is occasioned by what came before and occasions what comes next. However subtle the analysis, disruption of this organization in interviews and focus groups is likely to lead to analytic difficulties.

3. They show how participants orient to settings and institutions. They directly provide the sorts of institutional specifics that social researchers are often concerned with, avoiding the indirect and sometimes problematic route via the abstractions of sociological theorizations of institutions or via the conventionalizations of ethnographic notes.

4. They avoid flooding the research interaction with the researcher's categories and assumptions. This has the enormous virtue of starting with what is there rather than theoretical derived assumptions about what should be there, or the researcher wishes was there.

5. The research becomes more easily centred on situated practices rather than persons or institutions, avoiding the cognitive reifications of the former and the structural reifications of the latter.

Against these advantages can be set potential disadvantages:

1. Certain topics or phenomena present a challenge to naturalistic recording because they are particularly infrequent or particularly delicate or particularly private. This challenge has often led researchers to interviews or focus groups. However, it should be noted that judicious selection of settings, combined with extensive recording periods, can often capture infrequent events. And assiduous negotiation has often gained research access to settings involving surprisingly delicate or fraught issues

(gender reassignment clinics, abuse helplines, adolescent girls' playground arguments).

2. A related point is the potential for reactivity. There is general agreement that surreptitious recording is ethically wrong. This means that potential reactivity issues must be managed in one or more ways: through acclimatization and eliminating unacclimatized material from consideration; through using materials where reactivity will make little difference (because they are being recorded anyway, because they are so important and/or practically oriented); or through attending to, or even topicalizing, reactivity in the course of analysis.

Interviews and focus groups

For much of the 1980s and early 1990s, particularly within social psychology and sociology, analysing interviews became almost the exclusive approach of discourse researchers. This is partly a consequence of highly influential work on science discourse and, in particular, Gilbert and Mulkay (1984). Interviews in discourse work have a rather different role than in other research areas. They are not designed to neutrally access information beyond the interview, but to provide an arena for certain practices to take place and for participants to draw on discursive resources. This means that interviews tend to be active and sometimes argumentative to facilitate analysis. Such interactive features of interviews can be heightened in social science focus groups, where participants can argue with one another, in effect performing their own interviewing.

The advantages of interviews and focus groups are:

1. They allow the researcher to focus on particular topics or themes in a concentrated manner. Questions can be designed to provoke the use of different interpretative resources related to the same topic. They can attempt to draw out tacit knowledge so that it can be addressed explicitly.
2. They allow a degree of standardization across a sample of interviewees, with the same issues being addressed in each case.
3. They allow a degree of control of sampling of participants.

Against these are the following disadvantages:

1. As noted above, the interaction in interviews and focus groups is flooded by the expectations and categories of social science agendas. However much the analytic focus is on practices, it will have to deal with the participants' orientation to the interview organization or focus group orientation and their speaking position as expert informant or representative of a class or group. At best such orientations can become part of the analysis to illuminating effect (Widdicombe and Wooffitt, 1995). More common, however, is an uncomfortable ambivalence about whether the interview is an activity in itself or a pathway to something else. Focus groups present an additional complexity in that the participants may mix an orientation to a social science agenda and issues that arise in interacting with other participants.
2. These methods typically abstract participants from their location in settings where they have a particular stake and interest in what is going on, and encourage them to theorize about those settings as if disinterested.
3. Most importantly, given that access can be obtained, and high-class records can be made, why interview people about their relationship counselling, say, rather than use relationship counselling talk itself?

Texts

Texts are a pervasive and naturally occurring feature of everyday and institutional life. From diaries to newspapers, medical records and e-mail discussions, they present a rich source of material for analysis. In many ways they present special analytic issues, and there is not space to go into these in detail here (for illuminating discussion, see Atkinson and Coffey, 1997; Prior, 1997; Titscher et al., 2000; Watson, 1997).

The advantages of textual analysis can be summarized as follows:

1. Texts are naturally occurring and by their very nature tend to be available. Texts are, after all, designed for reproduction, storage and circulation.
2. Texts come already turned into words on the page, which is the central currency of

analysis. They do not require recording or lengthy processes of transcription.

3. Some phenomena only exist in this form – novels, newspapers and social work case notes offer no choice. Studying them will involve studying texts.

There are, however, two main problems:

1. One of the difficulties in dealing with texts is their designed mobility encourages the analyst to treat them in a decontextualized manner which is inattentive to the practices that they are part of. At the same time, working with decontextualized texts provides a temptation to speculate about their abstract relation to structures posited by social or psychological theory.
2. A related temptation is to attempt to consider texts in terms of their (putative) relation to what they describe, as if what they describe can be simply and independently captured by the research. This can generate all sorts of confusions (described in detail in Potter, 1996b).

It is likely that in future studies of naturalistic materials, possibly supplemented by studies of texts, will become more central, and interviews and focus groups will be mainly an adjunct to those naturalistic studies. Of course, materials will continue to be chosen in the first instance in relation to the specific research topic.

ANALYTIC PRELIMINARIES

There are a number of characteristic issues that arise when dealing with materials used in discourse analysis. Although they can be split into different headings, it is important to remember that they blur together in practice.

Recording

Recording technology has improved steadily over the period in which discourse analysis has developed. Nevertheless, one basic question usually arises at the start of research: should the recording be audio or video? This has theoretical aspects – what emphasis should be placed on embodied actions, and how relevant are they to the interaction being considered? And it has practical aspects – video

is considerably more difficult to manage in a range of ways. Video also tends to be more intrusive and has therefore more potential to disrupt what is going on. It is more expensive.

There is a lot of judgement involved in this choice, but my suggestion is that video materials are now relatively easily managed in digital form on a computer using a program such as Adobe Premier. This allows editing and the use of various anonymizing procedures for ethics purposes. This program also offers easy access to different parts of the recording. Even if the researcher works primarily with the audio record, there are often analytic issues where inspection of the video can assist understanding of what is going on. Adobe Premier can be purchased on the Internet at www.adobe.com.

For audio recording, a minidisc recorder connected to a flat microphone can record over 2 hours of very high-quality mono. This is an enormous advantage over C90 cassette tapes that almost invariably end just at the point where what you want to record gets interesting (how many recordings of fascinating therapy sessions miss the last five minutes?). The flat microphone (e.g., the cheap one sold by Sony) is particularly good for recording in rooms where air conditioning and background noises buzz away. Minidisc recorders are small and silent, and thus unobtrusive. The recording can then be copied into a sound editing programme such as Cool Edit on a computer (doing this into the optical port of a Creative Soundblaster Live! card avoids translating into analogue and back. Copying the recording in five-minute chunks means that the files that are produced will be relatively small and manageable. Converting them to MP3 format (which Cool Edit does easily) compresses them to about a tenth of their original size, and they are still perfectly usable for transcription and analysis.

For this kind of work recording quality is paramount. A poor recording can double transcription time, and means that all the work is going into making out the words rather than starting to understand what they are conveying.

Transcription

Transcription has been a source of some dispute in discourse work. There have been arguments over the best system of transcription, the level of transcription that is most valuable, and the status of transcripts as evidence. Transcription systems are related to research questions and theoretical judgements about what is important (Ochs, 1979). For instance, linguists interested in speech disorders may need to use a phonetic system that captures a very wide range of speech sounds. In discourse analysis the transcription scheme developed by Gail Jefferson in the 1960s and 1970s has increasingly become standard – see Hutchby and Wooffitt (1988) and ten Have (1998) for excellent overviews. This system emphasizes features of talk that are a part of its practical business. That is, it emphasizes features that are interactionally important for participants such as emphasis, while giving less importance to, for example, regional accent.

For much early discourse work transcription was done in a less careful and detailed manner, and was often treated as a simple secretarial job of transposing talk into a written form with the addition of some pauses and 'ums'. The inadequacy of such 'Jefferson Lite' transcripts (with most of the information taken out) for many analytic tasks has become clearer as discourse researchers have taken more seriously the findings and insights of conversation analysis.

The simplest way to transcribe is to work with two windows on a computer screen, one with Cool Edit running the sound file, the other with the word-processing program. Cool Edit allows a stepwise movement through the file which is ideal for transcription, selecting segments for replaying. The sound is represented by a waveform that allows extremely easy and accurate timing of pauses. It also allows proper names and identifying features to be easily selected and transformed (e.g., by reversing them) to retain anonymity. Cool Edit can be purchased on the net at www.syntrillium.com.

Producing high-quality transcript is very demanding and time-consuming. It is hard to give a standard figure for how long it takes because much depends on the quality of the recording (fuzzy, quiet recordings can quadruple the time needed) and the type of interaction (a one-to-one phone call presents much less of a challenge than a lively social work case conference with a lot of overlapping talk and extraneous noise); nevertheless, a ratio of 1 hour of tape to 20 hours of transcription time is not unreasonable.

The main features of the Jefferson scheme are reproduced in the Appendix to Chapter 26.

Listening and reading

One of the most important parts of discourse work is carefully listening to the material. This may seem obvious, but in much research there is an impetus to move to something more refined as soon as possible. For this reason it is recommended that researchers do at least a proportion of the transcription themselves. Often some of the most revealing analytic insights come during transcription as a consequence of the profound engagement with the material needed to produce a good transcript. It is generally useful to make analytic notes in parallel to the actual transcription.

Whatever interests motivated the research, it is inevitably productive to try and loosen up with the materials, listen to recordings and read transcripts for things that seem odd, or interesting, or confusing. Often prior expectations are surprisingly out of line with what is captured on video tape or minidisc. Group sessions where a number of researchers listen to a segment of interaction and explore different ways of understanding what is going on are invaluable for generating ideas to guide analysis.

Coding

In discourse research the principal task of coding is to make the task of analysis more straightforward by sifting relevant materials from a large body of recording and transcript. In this feature it differs from other approaches such as grounded theory and traditional content analysis where coding is intrinsic to the analysis. Here coding is more of a preliminary task that facilitates analysis. Indeed, the term 'coding' is perhaps unfortunate because of the positivist baggage that it brings with it. Coding is not a discrete stage of research, but a process that is ongoing from the point where materials start to arrive to the point where academic writing is completed.

Typically coding will involve sifting through materials for instances of a phenomenon of interest and copying them into an archive. It is often useful to accompany these codings with preliminary notes as to their nature and interest. At this stage selection should be inclusive – it is better to include material that can turn out to be irrelevant at a later stage than exclude it for ill-formulated reasons early on. Coding is a cyclical process. Full analysis of a corpus of materials can often take the researcher back to the originals as a better understanding of the phenomenon reveals new examples. Often initially disparate topics merge together in the course of analysis while topics that seemed distinctive are subsequently separated. For this reason, coding is inclusive rather than exclusive. Doubtful instances are included and, as will be discussed below, deviant cases can be some of the most analytically revealing.

In the past the sheer inconvenience of working with audio tape encouraged people to generate collections of transcribed examples without the recorded versions. However, programmes such as Adobe Premier and Cool Edit allow almost as much ease and flexibility in coding and sorting the digitized audio and video records. It should be straightforward to produce a set of transcripts along with a parallel set of audiovisual extracts.

Qualitative researchers have often looked to analytic programs such as NVivo or Ethnograph to organize their coding (see Chapter 23). Such programs can certainly provide supportive ways of sorting and comparing materials and have proved useful elsewhere. However, from a discourse-analytic perspective they sometimes encourage the researcher to focus on coding (which is what the programs are designed to deal with after all) at the expense of sequential organization. That is, they may downplay the situated nature of the discourse that is fundamental to discourse analysis. Nevertheless, discourse analysis is facilitated by good word-processing software which allows fluid editing, searching and pasting without the temptations to move beyond the complexity of the original materials to listing of codings and cross-tabulations.

ANALYSIS

There is no single recipe for doing discourse analysis. Different kinds of studies involve different procedures, sometimes working intensively with a single transcript, at other times drawing on a large corpus. Analysis is a craft that can be developed with different degrees of skill. It can be thought of as the development of sensitivity to the occasioned and action-oriented, situated, and constructed nature of discourse. Nevertheless, there are a number of ingredients which, when combined together, are likely to produce something satisfying. This is not an exclusive list,

but the majority of discourse work will focus on some combination of: variation, detail, rhetoric, orientation to context identity, accountability, stake and interest, and will build on prior analyses.

Variation

Variation in and between participants' discourse is a major analytic lever. All kinds of variations are potentially relevant – differences in descriptions of objects and events, stylistic shifts, the choice of different words, and so on. Variation is important because it can be used to help identify and explicate activities being performed by talk and texts. This is because the discourse is constructed in the specific ways that it is *precisely* to perform these actions. For example, a husband and wife in couple counselling may assemble very different descriptions of the state of their marriage to assign blame and the responsibility for change to the other (Edwards, 1995). Turned around, these differences are a major clue to the nature of the activities being performed. The researcher will benefit from attending to variations: in the discourse of single individuals (on one occasion or different occasions); between different individuals; and between what is said and what might have been said.

Detail

Discourse researchers have increasingly found that attending to the specifics of what is said and how it is said is essential for producing high-quality analysis. Conversation analysts such as Sacks (1992) have shown that detailed features of discourse – hesitations, lexical choice, repair, and so on – are commonly part of the performance of some act or are consequential in some way for the outcome of the interaction. Attending to the detail of interaction, particularly in transcript, is often one of the most difficult tasks for social scientists, particularly when they have spent years of academic training attempting to read through the apparently messy detail for the gist of what is going on. Analysis depends on a discipline of close reading.

Rhetoric

Analysis will often benefit from close attention to the rhetorical organization of discourse.

This involves inspecting discourse both for the way it is organized to make argumentative cases and for the way it is designed to undermine alternative cases (Billig, 1996). The focus on rhetoric directs attention from issues of how descriptions relate to the objects, events and so on that they are (putatively) describing, and focuses attention on how that description relates to competing alternatives.

Accountability

The focus on rhetoric is closely linked to an analytic concern with accountability. Accountability is involved where there is a concern with displaying one's activities as rational, sensible and justifiable. Indeed, ethnomethodologists have argued that accountability is an essential and pervasive character of the design and understanding of human conduct generally (Garfinkel, 1967; Heritage, 1984). As with variability, analytic attention to the way actions are made accountable helps understand precisely what those actions are.

Stake and interest

Discursive psychologists have highlighted the pervasiveness of a concern with stake and interest in interaction. These notions are closely related to rhetoric and accountability. People attend to their own and others' interests, displaying the basis on which they are talking or constructing positions of neutrality. The appearance of both evaluations, on the one hand, and factual versions, on the other, is typically bound up with concerns about stake and interest.

Building on prior studies

Successful analyses of discourse will typically build on prior analytic studies. Most research will benefit from a familiarity with research on mundane talk as well as an understanding of how the patterning of turn taking and activities changes in different institutional settings. For example, understanding of the organization of extreme case formulations in talk, and some of the activities that they are used to perform, can aid analysis of the talk of family therapists, say, when it includes extreme case formulations (Edwards, 2000).

These are not specific rules for research. They are not that easily codified. And they will have different degrees of importance in different studies. Rather they should be thought of as elements in an analytic mentality needed for research of this kind. Note that they are quite different from the procedures in many styles of quantitative research where following the procedures fully and correctly is a major warrant for the validity of the findings.

ANALYTIC VALIDATION

In the case of discourse research validation is provided by four main considerations. In practice, they inevitably overlap with analytic procedures, but for clarity of exposition they will be dealt with separately.

Participants' orientations

One of the basic principles in ensuring the validity of discourse work is that analytic claims are supported by detailed evidence that the participants in an interaction orient to what is claimed. This is provided in the most basic way by the turn organization of conversation. Any turn of talk is orientated to both what came before and what comes next, and that orientation typically displays the sense that the participant makes of the prior turn. Thus, at its simplest, when someone provides an answer they thereby display an orientation to the prior turn as a question. If the analyst is going to claim that some element of talk is making an indirect accusation, then it should be possible to identify some orientation to this in what happens next. Close attention to this turn-by-turn display of understanding provides one important check on analytic interpretations (see Heritage, 1997).

Although this consideration is discussed here in terms of its role validating research, a focus on participants' orientations is fundamental at all stages of analysis. This is a topic of some controversy in discourse work (see the sometimes heated but illuminating debate between Schegloff, 1997, 1998, 1999a, 1999b; Billig, 1999b, 1999c; and Wetherell, 1998); but there is broad agreement that orientations can be analytically powerful.

Deviant cases

As with other kinds of research, deviant cases can be some of the most informative in assessing claims. Most simply, deviant cases can show that analytic generalizations that are being advanced have broken down and need revising. However, deviant cases can also provide powerful support for claims in the detail of their organization. This principle is illustrated in studies of television and radio news interviews, where participants routinely avoid treating interviewers as accountable for views expressed in questions. This normative pattern is supported rather than refuted by studying deviant cases in which interviewees treat their interviewer as expressing personal views, whereupon considerable interactional trouble ensues (Heritage and Greatbatch, 1991; Potter, 1996b).

Coherence

The accumulation of empirical findings and analytic studies allows new studies to be compared for their *coherence*. For example, work on fact construction builds on the insights about accountability from earlier studies, and its success provides further confirmation of the validity of those studies (Edwards and Potter, 1993). Put another way, a study that clashed with some of those basic findings would be treated more cautiously – although if it stood up to scrutiny it would be more consequential.

Reader's evaluations

In discourse analysis claims are made accountable to the detail of empirical materials, and these are presented in a form that allows readers to make their own checks and judgements. This form of validation contrasts with much traditional experimental and content-analytic work, where it is rare for anything close to 'raw data' to be included, or for more than one or two illustrative codings to be provided. Sacks's (1992) ideal was to put the reader as far as possible into the same position as the researcher with respect to the materials. Such an ideal is unrealizable, but discourse work is closer than most other analytic approaches.

Whether they appear singly or together in a study none of these procedures guarantees the validity of an analysis. But they are all important features of improved quality control. A study that is not able to show participants' orientations to phenomena, that cannot account for deviant cases, that clashes with established findings and makes important claims on the basis of material that is not reproduced in the paper is unlikely to be worth spending time on.

ANALYTIC EXAMPLES

These various principles of analysis and validation are best illustrated through concrete examples. Given the heterogeneity of discourse research no one example would clearly indicate how these principles operate. The two examples discussed below are indicative of broad strands of discourse research. The first is an interview study concerned with the organized discursive resources people draw on to justify particular versions of marriage and marriage breakdown. The second is a study of the pragmatics of question asking in market research focus groups.

Discourses of marriage and marriage breakdown

This study by Rachel Lawes (1999) asked how people draw on organized discursive resources – interpretative repertoires – to variably construct the nature of marriage in the course of different activities (for more on the analysis of repertoires, see Potter and Wetherell, 1995). Apart from its intrinsic interest, this study has implications for a range of survey and questionnaire studies of marriage that are predicated on the idea that there is a unitary notion that is being drawn on by researcher and participant alike. The study aimed to make better sense of the highly contradictory research findings on this topic. In terms of the broad theoretical principles of discourse analysis and discursive psychology, Lawes is treating marriage talk to be *constructed* in particular *settings* and oriented to specific *actions*.

To capture these features of marriage accounts being assembled to do things, she recruited a heterogeneous sample of members of 'Generation X', white Anglo-Saxons born between 1961 and 1971. Her sample deliberately selected from a group much researched by sociologists and associated with marriage breakdown and new approaches to relationships.

All participants were interviewed in an active, conversational manner. Lawes was playful, challenging, and sometimes supportive – an interview style that would be anathema to more positivistic approaches that treat interviews as instruments for the neutral harvesting of responses. The different topics and issues that were raised led the participants through different conversational tasks. The interview was guided by a schedule of topics, which helped provide some points of comparison across the different interviews (Lawes, 1999: 4–5):

Is there anything that all marriages have in common?

How is marriage different to other kinds of 'couple' relationships?

How would you feel about never marrying?

What is a good enough reason for getting married?

Have you experienced pressure from other people to get married?

Whose responsibility is it to ensure that a married person is 'happy enough'?

What is a 'good wife' or 'good husband'? Would you want to be one?

What are you actually promising to do when you get married?

What is a good enough reason for getting divorced?

These questions were developed in pilot interviews and were found to present participants with a range of different concerns. These interviews were fully transcribed, but in the cut-down form of Jefferson Lite.

Lawes's analysis started by sifting *variations* in the way marriage was talked about into different coding files and considering the way the different constructions of marriage were suited, in their *detail*, to different *rhetorical* tasks and how they provided the speaker with different kinds of *accountability*. She found that much of the variation in the material could be understood by treating participants as working with two contradictory interpretative repertoires for constructing marriage. One was a 'romantic repertoire' based around the idea of 'commitment' to 'the right person'. For example, Lawes quotes the following from a participant on commitment:

Rachel: See, in some ways, marriage is a much simpler issue than living together. People have got a clearer idea of what being married involves. You know?

Catherine: Well, yeah, well, I think once you're married you know exactly how the other partner feels about you. I *think*. As opposed to living together, that other person, you might, you might not know what that other person is thinking in the long term. Maybe they're going to be comfortable for years or maybe they're not thinking about living together with you, so if you, you're giving your all to that person and then they just leave you because there's no commitment for the rest of your life. I don't know. That could be really (laughs) horrible for the person [who's] left behind. And if, if someone is committed to marrying you, in a way, it's a guarantee, I mean, I don't know, you know that you can trust that person.

For both interviewer and interviewee (Rachel and Catherine) cohabiting is characterized by uncertainty that the commitment of marriage removes. Within this repertoire, staying together is treated as a success and separating as a failure. The romantic repertoire makes available particular accounts for the failure and success of the marriage; most fundamentally, a successful marriage is 'with the right person' and an unsuccessful one is not. (Note that the purpose of analysis is to consider the organization of discourse, not evaluate people's coherence or sophistication when producing it.)

The other repertoire was a 'realist repertoire' of marriage. This characterized marriage more pessimistically as something liable to wear out and to be an institution characterised by debt, infidelity, staying together for the children and stress-related illnesses. A central point from the study was that the same interviewees would draw on the different repertoires to perform different tasks (justifying their married/unmarried status, criticizing others, and so on).

In terms of validation, the interview analysis focused on *participants' own orientations* to these different constructions of marriage. It focused particularly on potentially *deviant cases* where the two repertoires were drawn on together. Such cases were analytically interesting as we would expect trouble to arise if these are genuinely contradictory repertoires. Indeed, Lawes found such trouble and noted that participants used a range of rhetorical devices for managing it. Although there are no closely related studies to check its *coherence*, Lawes's study meshes in with studies of interpretative repertoires in other realms. Finally, extended extracts from interviews were quoted to allow *readers* to make their own assessment of the adequacy of the claims.

Elaborate questions in focus groups

Although Lawes's study is characteristic of much discourse work, and is an excellent illustration of what can be done with interviews, discourse analysts and discursive psychologists have tended to move on to naturalistic materials which are transcribed in more detail than the Jefferson Lite used in that study. And they have found the notion of interpretative repertoire does not do justice to the detailed and flexible organization of people's discourse. The risk with repertoires is in seeing coherence as a product of an abstract set of linguistic relations prior to interaction, when the coherence may actually be a consequence of the practical tasks that the talk is being used to perform (see Wooffitt, 1992, and Potter, 1996b, for critical comments on the repertoire notion).

The second analytic illustration is Puchta and Potter's (1999) study of the construction of questions in market research focus groups. The aim of this study was to explicate the way questions are asked in focus groups, and what the different elements of the questions were designed to do. The study was motivated in part by the observation that actual focus groups tended to contain many questions that were much more complex than those recommended in focus group manuals. The study used a set of videotapes of German market research focus groups, although it has been replicated and developed with a UK sample (Puchta and Potter, 2004; see also Puchta and Potter, 2002). A corpus of question sequences was built by transcribing 30-minute segments from a range of focus groups run by different moderators.

The study found that questions, particularly questions that start new topics, tended to be rather complex, with a range of different elements performing different tasks. Take the following extract, for example:

Moderator	E::m, (1.0) this <u>type</u> of fabric. (0.2) okay here, (.) these are little vinyl swatches. (0.6) notice in most of the vehicles you have (0.2) > <u>p</u>arts of (the) fabric and then there's vinyl (accenting) throughout, < (0.4) .hh e:m, so these are different, (0.4) e::h, (0.2) types of things that could be available, (0.4) You look at <u>the:</u>se. (0.2) Look at <u>patterns</u>, (0.2) > I mean you look < at the colours, (.) e:m, (.) your feeling is <u>what</u>. = what, (1.2) > what < <u>i</u>mage would this give you of the vehicle. (1.2)
Part. 1	°Cheap.°
Part. 2	hm. (1.0)
Part. 3	°They're too loud aren't they.°
Part. 4	too loud [and over the top
Part. 5	[yeah
Part. 6	You get tired of them very quickly. (1.0) (Etc.)

Elaborate questions, such as the one delivered by the moderator of a motor vehicle group at the start of this extract, were used to guide participants and head off trouble, particularly when the questions were different from the sorts of mundane questions that participants would be likely to be familiar with in other settings. Such questions helped secure participation by providing an array of alternative items to respond to. They also guided participants to produce a range of responses in the form of, or relevant to, opinions. More generally, they helped manage a dilemma between the requirement that the talk should be highly focused on predefined topics and issues, but at the same time spontaneous and conversational. It is important to remember here that this study took market research focus group talk as its topic; it is a study *of* focus group talk, not a study *using* focus groups.

In terms of the analytic principles outlined above, the emphasis is on the focus group talk as *situated*, *action-oriented* and *constructed*. That is, the focus group questions were studied in the settings in which they were used. The research considered these questions in terms of how they were *situated* in sequences of interaction, occasioned by what came before and occasioning what came after. The questions were studied for how they were *oriented to action*. What business did they perform in the focus group? Obviously they asked questions (although this is a rather more complex thing than it might appear). They also managed the kind of response, illustrating kinds of answer that were appropriate. In addition, they were designed to display informality, generating a relaxed and friendly environment for answering. The questions were also studied for how they were *constructed*. Different elements were introduced for different tasks.

This study considered focus group interaction at a level of *detail* that is relevant to the participants. In this case, various features of intonation and brief pauses were shown to be consequential for the interaction. The study attended to *variation*, particularly between topic-initial questions such as the one above, which were almost invariably elaborate, and follow-up questions, which tended to take a simpler form.

The analytic practice involved developing ideas about how the questions were operating, and testing them by considering other features of the corpus of materials. For example, one possibility was that question elaboration was a consequence of moderators adding new question components as they pursued a response from initially reluctant participants. However, this initially plausible alternative did not fit with other aspects of the material. For instance, the intonational contours at the point where different parts of the questions were joined indicated that the moderator was going to continue. Also, there were no examples of moderators completing at these points, and then restarting in the face of silent responses.

The validation of the study involved the principles outlined above. Thus, the analysis drew closely on the participants' orientations to the questions to ground claims about the activity the questions were performing. The analysis considered all deviant cases in the corpus, and their implications for the conclusions. The analysis drew on, and developed, other studies in conversation analysis and discursive psychology. It reproduced sufficient material from the corpus to allow readers to make a detailed judgement about the adequacy of its claims.

(1996c, 2004), Wood & Kroger (2000) and Wooffitt (1993). Potter and Wetherell (1994) work through the process of analysis with a specific example. Billig (1997) and Potter and Wetherell (1995) discuss the analysis of broad themes and interpretative repertoires drawn on in interview talk. Potter (1998) compares grounded theory, ethnography and discourse analysis in the analysis of clinical materials. Edwards and Potter (2001) discuss discursive psychological analysis of the role of psychological talk in institutions. Yates et al. (2001) introduce and compare a range of different approaches to analysing discourse.

Styles of analysis are developing under three kinds of pressures. First, technological developments in minidisc, digital video, and packages for audio and video manipulation have facilitated new analytic techniques. Researchers are only now beginning to exploit these new possibilities. The main consequence is that managing audio and video becomes nearly as simple as managing paper transcripts used to be. This will encourage work that addresses issues to do with features of vocal delivery and integrates non-vocal activities with vocal ones.

Second, there is an increasing crossover between work in conversation and discourse analysis. Indeed, at the boundaries these perspectives blur into one another. Discourse work has picked up on some of the robust findings of conversation analysis, as well as its rigorous analytic approach. This is a lively area of discussion, although some discourse researchers are more doubtful about the virtues of conversation analysis (Billig, 1999b; Fairclough, 1992).

Third, analysis of discourse has been hampered by confusions about the status of cognition in analysis. Some analysts see a fundamental task to be the connection of broad social phenomena to underlying cognitions via discursive organization (van Dijk, 1998). However, strong arguments as to the incoherence of this task, at least as it is currently formulated, have recently been developed (Edwards, 1997; te Molder and Potter, in press). This is likely to be a point of theoretical and analytic development in the next few years.

RESOURCES AND DEVELOPMENTS

There are a range of introductions to discourse analysis and discursive psychology. General overviews can be found in Coyle (2000), Gill (1996), Potter and Wetherell (1987), Potter

ACKNOWLEDGEMENT

I would like to thank the editors and two anonymous referees for making helpful comments on an earlier draft of this chapter.

REFERENCES

Ahmed, B., Nicolson, P. and Spencer, C. (2000) 'The social construction of racism: The case of second generation Bangladeshis', *Journal of Community & Applied Social Psychology*, 10: 33–48.

Antaki, C. (1994) *Explaining and Arguing: The Social Organization of Accounts*. London: Sage.

Antaki, C. and Horowitz, A. (2000) 'Using identity ascription to disqualify a rival version of events as "interested"', *Research on Language and Social Interaction*, 33: 155–77.

Atkinson, P. and Coffey, A. (1997) 'Analysing documentary realities', in D. Silverman (ed.), *Qualitative Research: Theory, Method and Practice*. London: Sage, pp. 45–62.

Billig, M. (1991) *Ideologies and Beliefs*. London: Sage.

Billig, M. (1996) *Arguing and Thinking: A Rhetorical Approach to Social Psychology* (2nd edition). Cambridge: Cambridge University Press.

Billig, M. (1997) 'Rhetorical and discursive analysis: How families talk about the royal family', in N. Hayes (ed.), *Doing Qualitative Analysis in Psychology*. Hove: Psychology Press.

Billig, M. (1999a) *Freudian Repression: Conversation Creating the Unconscious*. Cambridge: Cambridge University Press.

Billig, M. (1999b) 'Whose terms? Whose ordinariness? Rhetoric and ideology in conversation analysis', *Discourse and Society*, 10: 543–58.

Billig, M. (1999c) 'Conversation analysis and the claims of naivety', *Discourse and Society*, 10: 572–6.

Bogen, D. (1999) *Order without Rules: Critical Theory and the Logic of Conversation*. New York: State University of New York Press.

Brown, G. and Yule, G. (1983) *Discourse Analysis*. Cambridge: Cambridge University Press.

Coulthard, M. and Montgomery, M. (eds) (1981) *Studies in Discourse Analysis*. London: Routledge & Kegan Paul.

Coyle, A. (2000) 'Discourse analysis', in G.M. Breakwell, S. Hammond, and C. Fife-Schaw (eds), *Research Methods in Psychology* (2nd edn). London: Sage.

Dickerson, P. (1997) '"It's not just me who's saying this …". The deployment of cited others in television political discourse', *British Journal of Social Psychology*, 36: 33–48.

Drew, P. and Heritage, J.C. (1992) 'Analyzing talk at work: An introduction', in P. Drew and J. Heritage (eds), *Talk at Work: Interaction in Institutional Settings*. Cambridge: Cambridge University Press, pp. 8–65.

Edwards, D. (1995) 'Two to tango: Script formulations, dispositions, and rhetorical symmetry in relationship troubles talk', *Research on Language and Social Interaction*, 28: 319–50.

Edwards, D. (1997) *Discourse and Cognition*. London: Sage.

Edwards, D. (2000) 'Extreme case formulations: Softeners, investments and doing nonliteral', *Research on Language and Social Interaction*, 33: 347–73.

Edwards, D. and Potter, J. (1992) *Discursive Psychology*. London: Sage.

Edwards, D. and Potter, J. (1993) 'Language and causation: A discursive action model of description and attribution', *Psychological Review*, 100: 23–41.

Edwards, D. and Potter, J. (2001) 'Discursive psychology', in A.W. McHoul and M. Rapley (eds), *How to Analyse Talk in Institutional Settings: A Casebook of Methods*. London: Continuum International.

Fairclough, N. (1992) *Discourse and Social Change*. Cambridge: Polity.

Garfinkel, H. (1967) *Studies in Ethnomethodology*. Englewood Cliffs, NJ: Prentice Hall.

Georgaca, E. (2000) 'Reality and discourse: A critical analysis of the category of "delusions"', *British Journal of Medical Psychology*, 73: 227–42.

Gilbert, G.N. and Mulkay, M. (1984) *Opening Pandora's Box: A Sociological Analysis of Scientists' Discourse*. Cambridge: Cambridge University Press.

Gill, R. (1996) 'Discourse analysis: Methodological aspects', in J.E. Richardson (ed.), *Handbook of Qualitative Research Methods for Psychology and the Social Sciences*. Leicester: British Psychological Society.

Goodwin, C. and Goodwin, M.H. (1996) 'Seeing as situated activity: Formulating planes', in Y. Engeström and D. Middleton (eds), *Cognition and Communication at Work*. Cambridge: Cambridge University Press, pp. 61–95.

Hepburn, A. (2000) 'Power lines: Derrida, discursive psychology and the management of accusations of teacher bullying', *British Journal of Social Psychology*, 39: 609–28.

Heritage, J.C. (1984) *Garfinkel and Ethnomethodology*. Cambridge: Polity.

Heritage, J.C. (1997) 'Conversation analysis and institutional talk: Analysing data', in D. Silverman (ed.), *Qualitative Research: Theory, Method and Practice*. London: Sage, pp. 161–82.

Heritage, J.C. and Greatbatch, D.L. (1991) 'On the institutional character of institutional talk: The case of news interviews', in D. Boden and D.H. Zimmerman (eds), *Talk and Social Structure: Studies in Ethnomethodology and Conversation Analysis*. Oxford: Polity, pp. 93–137.

Hutchby, I. and Wooffitt, R. (1998) *Conversation Analysis: Principles, Practices and Applications*. Cambridge: Polity.

Jaworski, A. and Coupland, N. (eds) (1999) *The Discourse Reader*. London: Routledge.

Kintsch, W. and van Dijk, T.A. (1978) 'Toward a model of text comprehension and production', *Psychological Review*, 85: 363–94.

Labov, W. (1972) *Language in the Inner City*. Philadelphia: Philadelphia University Press.

Lawes, R. (1999) 'Marriage: An analysis of discourse', *British Journal of Social Psychology*, 38: 1–20.

Locke, A. and Edwards, D. (2003) 'Bill and Monica: Memory, emotion and normativity in Clinton's Grand Jury testimony', *British Journal of Social Psychology*, 42: 241–56.

Ochs, E. (1979) 'Transcription as theory', in E. Ochs and B. Schieffelin (eds), *Developmental Pragmatics*. New York: Academic Press, pp. 43–72.

Phillips, L. (2000) 'Mediated communication and the privatization of public problems: Discourse and ecological risks and political action', *European Journal of Communication*, 15: 171–207.

Potter, J. (1996a) 'Discourse analysis', in A. Cupar (ed.), *Encyclopedia of the Social Sciences*. London: Routledge, pp. 188–9.

Potter, J. (1996b) *Representing Reality: Discourse, Rhetoric and Social Construction*. London: Sage.

Potter, J. (1996c) 'Discourse analysis and constructionist approaches: Theoretical background', in J.E. Richardson (ed.), *Handbook of Qualitative Research Methods for Psychology and the Social Sciences*. Leicester: British Psychological Society.

Potter, J. (1998) 'Qualitative and discourse analysis', in A.S. Bellack and M. Hersen (eds), *Comprehensive Clinical Psychology*, Vol. 3. Oxford: Pergamon, pp. 117–44.

Potter, J. (2004) 'Discourse analysis as a way of analysing naturally occurring talk', in D. Silverman (ed.), *Qualitative Research: Theory, Method and Practice*. London: Sage.

Potter, J. and Edwards, D. (2001) 'Discursive social psychology', in W.P. Robinson and H. Giles (eds), *The New Handbook of Language and Social Psychology*. Chichester: Wiley, pp. 103–18.

Potter, J. and Wetherell, M. (1987) *Discourse and Social Psychology: Beyond Attitudes and Behaviour*. London: Sage.

Potter, J. and Wetherell, M. (1994) 'Analyzing discourse', in A. Bryman and B. Burgess (eds), *Analyzing Qualitative Data*. London: Routledge.

Potter, J. and Wetherell, M. (1995) 'Discourse analysis', in J. Smith, R. Harré and L. van Langenhove (eds), *Rethinking Methods in Psychology*. London: Sage.

Potter, J., Edwards, D. and Ashmore, M. (1999) 'Regulating criticism: some comments on an argumentative complex', *History of the Human Sciences*, 12: 79–88.

Prior, L. (1997) 'Following in Foucault's footsteps: Text and context in qualitative research', in D. Silverman (ed.), *Qualitative Research: Theory, Method and Practice*. London: Sage, pp. 63–79.

Puchta, C. and Potter, J. (1999) 'Asking elaborate questions: Focus groups and the management of spontaneity', *Journal of Sociolinguistics*, 3: 314–35.

Puchta, C. and Potter, J. (2002) 'Manufacturing individual opinions: Market research focus groups and the discussive psychology of attitudes', *British Journal of Social Psychology*, 41: 345–63.

Puchta, C. and Potter, J. (2004) *Focus Group Practice*. London: Sage.

Sacks, H. (1992) *Lectures on Conversation* (2 vols), edited by G. Jefferson. Oxford: Basil Blackwell.

Schegloff, E.A. (1997) 'Whose text? Whose context?', *Discourse and Society*, 8: 165–87.

Schegloff, E.A. (1998) 'Reply to Wetherell', *Discourse and Society*, 9: 413–16.

Schegloff, E.A. (1999a) '"Schegloff's texts" as "Billig's data": A critical reply', *Discourse and Society*, 10: 558–72.

Schegloff, E.A. (1999b) 'Naïveté vs sophistication or discipline vs self-indulgence: A rejoinder to Billig', *Discourse and Society*, 10: 577–82.

Schiffrin, D. (1994) *Approaches to Discourse*. Oxford: Blackwell.

Sinclair, J.McH. and Coulthard, R.M. (1975) *Towards an Analysis of Discourse: The English Used by Teachers and Pupils*. London: Oxford University Press.

Speer, S. and Potter, J. (2000) 'The management of heterosexist talk: Conversational resources and prejudiced claims', *Discourse and Society*, 11: 543–72.

te Molder, H. and Potter, J. (eds) (in press) *Talk and Cognition: Discourse and Social Interaction*. Cambridge: Cambridge University Press.

ten Have, P. (1998) *Doing Conversation Analysis*. London: Sage.

Titscher, S., Meyer, M., Wodak, R. and Vetter, E. (2000) *Methods of Text and Discourse Analysis*. London: Sage.

van Dijk, T.A. (1996) *Discourse Studies: A Multidisciplinary Introduction* (2 vols). London: Sage.

van Dijk, T.A. (1998) *Ideology – A Multidisciplinary Approach*. London: Sage.

Watson, D.R. (1997) 'Ethnomethodology and textual analysis', in D. Silverman (ed.), *Qualitative Research: Theory, Method and Practice*. London: Sage, pp. 80–98.

Wetherell, M. (1998) 'Positioning and interpretative repertoires: Conversation analysis and post-structuralism in dialogue', *Discourse and Society*, 9: 387–412.

Wetherell, M. and Potter, J. (1992) *Mapping the Language of Racism: Discourse and the Legitimation of Exploitation*. Brighton: Harvester/Wheatsheaf.

Wetherell, M., Taylor, S. and Yates, S. (2001). *Discourse Theory and Practice: A Reader*. London: Sage.

Widdicombe, S. and Wooffitt, R. (1995) *The Language of Youth Subcultures: Social Identity in Action*. Hemel Hempstead: Harvester/Wheatsheaf.

Wiggins, S., Potter, J. and Wildsmith, A.V. (2001) 'Eating your words: Discursive psychology and the reconstruction of eating practices', *Journal of Health Psychology*, 6: 5–15.

Wood, L.A. and Kroger, R.O. (2000) *Doing Discourse Analysis: Methods for Studying Action in Talk and Text.* London: Sage.

Wooffitt, R. (1992) *Telling Tales of the Unexpected: The Organization of Factual Discourse.* London: Harvester/Wheatsheaf.

Wooffitt, R. (1993) 'Analysing accounts', in N. Gilbert (ed.), *Researching Social Life.* London and Beverly Hills, CA: Sage, pp. 287–305.

Wooffitt, R. (2000) 'Some properties of the interactional organization of displays of paranormal cognition in psychic–sitter interaction', *Sociology*, 34: 457–79.

Yates, S., Taylor, S. and Wetherell, M. (2001) *Discourse as Data: A Guide for Analysis.* London: Sage.

28

Grounded Theory

NICK PIDGEON AND
KAREN HENWOOD

When Glaser and Strauss wrote their original treatise, *The Discovery of Grounded Theory* (1967), one of their main aims was to 'liberate' sociological analysis from the limitations imposed by a preoccupation with repeatedly testing a few speculative, 'grand', or large-scale theories. Glaser and Strauss were influenced by writers, such as Blumer (1954) and Merton (1957), who had raised the problem of lack of relationship between sociological theory and empirical research, arguing in favour of the development of 'middle-range' accounts that are neither so abstract that they lack empirical relevance nor so concrete that they lack explanatory scope and significance. Building upon elements present in a range of earlier empirical studies, primarily from ethnography and qualitative sociology, *The Discovery of Grounded Theory* explicitly codified the ways in which such accounts could be developed through the close and detailed inspection and analysis of data derived *in situ*, and so that they held a clear relevance to problems and phenomena identified in the course of study.

It is debatable to what extent the methods and procedures codified by Glaser and Strauss are distinctive to grounded theory. Indeed, one of the major reasons why the methodological approach has gained widespread contemporary appeal, going beyond the discipline of sociology, is that it is often read as describing one part of a core, generic set of techniques for conducting, and gaining

credibility for, qualitative inquiry and theory-building from qualitative data. In historical terms, as noted by Charmaz (2000: 509):

> grounded theory served at the forefront of 'the qualitative revolution' ... [and] at a critical point in social science history ... defended qualitative research and countered the dominant view that quantitative studies provide the only form of systematic social scientific inquiry.

This consideration remains important for many social scientists and research-practitioners today, for whom a depth of training in qualitative research is increasingly expected to mirror that which is routinely provided in more structured, quantitative and statistical methods classes. And many researchers new to qualitative interpretive inquiry, and especially analysis, find the provision of such explicit techniques both reassuring and genuinely useful.

Conceptually, grounded theory has an especially long-standing association with the pragmatist and symbolic interactionist philosophical traditions (see Blumer, 1969; Dewey, 1922; Mead, 1934; Thomas, 1966). These served to frame several generations of researchers' theorizing, questions and inquiries, initially within sociology (especially social psychological or micro-sociology) but increasingly within the wider range of health, practitioner and social science disciplines. The American interactionist tradition holds an important historical place in the development of qualitative research practice as it is today, providing an early and coherent alternative to studies that measured reified, essential properties of events, objects and people's perceptions of them. Symbolic interactionism presented a theorized case for (and practical examples of) studies that both explored the activities and interactions involved in the interpretive and symbolic production of meaning, and used these as a platform to account for interactional processes and illuminate complex social worlds.

Surveying the literature some 35 years on from the publication of *Discovery*, it is clear that both extensive methodological debates, and substantive examples of studies that self-label as grounded theory, are in plentiful supply. These contemporary examples reach beyond symbolic interactionist sociology to concern, amongst other things:

1. The meaningful patterns and processes of action, interaction and identity within many different time, space and culturally bounded settings, organizations and other kinds of 'social worlds' (including those of health and illness, adults and children, and public and private spheres). The sociologically oriented among these studies may also show an appropriate level of concern for the interrelationship between 'action and structure', thereby touching upon the more macro-social structures that can constrain socio-political processes and change (see Brown and Stetz, 1999; Charmaz, 1990, 1997; Lempert, 1997; Sarlio-Lähteenkorva, 2000; Turner and Pidgeon, 1997).

2. Actors', participants', patients' and professionals' understandings, phenomenological points of view or perspectives – to characterize either detailed 'structures of experience' (Bolger, 1999; see also Rennie, 1992) or (more frequently) taken-for-granted, routine or skilled knowledges and practices, and to investigate and provide guidance on socio-technical interventions, service and policy developments (see Baszanger, 1997; Michie, McDonald and Marteau, 1996; Orona, 1990; Tuler and Thomas, 1999; Weiner, 1975).

3. The complexity, fluidity and multiplicity of situated meanings and accounts either in relatively focused (e.g., therapeutic) or more spatially, temporally and culturally diffuse (e.g., consumer-oriented or

politically devolving) contexts and settings, in order to bring the micro-social, symbolically, textually or discursively organized character of roles, identities, cultures and power relations into view (Davis, 1988; Henwood and Pidgeon, 2001; Costain Schou and Hewison, 1996).

Such diversity in use suggests that 'grounded theory' today is best viewed not as a unitary method but as a node, nexus or focal point for discussions that can and should intersect with far more wide-ranging ones about the strategies and methods of qualitative inquiry (see also Alvesson and Sköldberg, 2000). In this respect, it is significant that even the recent collection of exemplars of grounded theory in practice (Strauss and Corbin, 1997) displays a considerable variety of methodological tactics within the broad approach. However, like Rennie (2000), we view most core methodological writings on grounded theory as rather insular, placing too little emphasis on making connections with other traditions of qualitative inquiry and ways of conceptualizing, justifying and practising social science research. In part this insularity comes as an inevitable by-product of a recent series of vigorous debates amongst grounded theorists themselves (see Stern, 1994), which we touch upon at various points in the chapter, about the 'true' nature of grounded theory, and in particular the relative merits of and demarcation between Glaser's approach (e.g., 1978, 1992) and that developed in Strauss (1987) and Strauss and Corbin (1994, 1998).

Current developments in qualitative inquiry are directed towards: identifying diversity of concerns and practices across the broad spectrum of qualitative methods (Denzin and Lincoln, 2000); exploring ways of 'mixing', combining or triangulating different variants of qualitative and quantitative methods (Brannen, 1992; Fielding and Fielding, 1986; Maynard and Purvis, 1994; Todd et al., 2004); and taking research epistemology and methodology beyond polarized views of the so-called quality–quantity debate (see Atkinson, 1995; Bryman, 1988; Seale, 1999), without minimizing the constructive challenges that quantitative and qualitative research can pose to one another. Within this changing intellectual landscape, allegiance to methodological school seems less important than devising manageable and worthwhile research projects (Bryman, 1988;

Coffey and Atkinson, 1996; Marshall and Rossman, 1999; Mason, 1996). As such we view grounded theory as exemplifying some of the core 'strategies' of qualitative inquiry that foreground the interplay of theory and method during the integrated processes of social research (Lincoln and Guba, 1985; Bryman and Burgess, 1994; Hammersley and Atkinson, 1983). In particular, it continues to offer important guidance on techniques for theoretical sampling and for comparative analysis of unstructured qualitative data. It is less well recognized that the approach was originally intended to explicitly include theory-building from quantitative data too, as in some forms of exploratory statistical data analysis (e.g., Tukey, 1977). Glaser brought his background in statistics to the writing of *Discovery*, and Chapter VIII of the monograph is devoted solely to the use of quantitative survey data for the inductive generation of theory. Although that chapter has subsequently puzzled many qualitative researchers who read the book, and as a result has received very little attention, it too represents a considerable break with mainstream (in this case statistical) research practice.

Our aim in this chapter is to present the core ideas of Glaser and Strauss's original work, commenting in places on how it has been followed up and developed by the individual authors and their co-workers (Glaser, 1978, 1992; Strauss, 1987; Strauss and Corbin, 1994, 1998). But we also go beyond this core literature, since qualitative researchers vary tremendously in the extent to which they depict their own studies as following the original approach (drawing on grounded theory methodology to justify their research design decisions) and in how far they select and integrate from a wider pool of practices and ideas. This suggests to us that a range of spaces – rather than a single one – is being opened up by the grounded theory vision of research design and research practices. We are aware that such an approach may invite criticism for detracting from the specificity of grounded theory's original definition and meaning.[1] In part, our efforts to be inclusive and less normalizing about what counts as grounded theory reflect the critical debates that are now occurring among grounded theorists, and the potential benefits that may follow from addressing the tensions these express. In so doing, we focus, in particular, on influences from more recent constructivist thinking within qualitative social

sciences (see Charmaz, 1990, 2000; Henwood and Pidgeon, 1994, 1995a, 1995b).

GROUNDED THEORY WITHIN CONTEMPORARY METHODOLOGICAL DEBATE: THE DILEMMA OF QUALITATIVE METHOD AND CONSTRUCTIVISM

In the same way that the practical uses of grounded theory have diversified over time, so has the complexity of its epistemological positioning within contemporary debates about qualitative inquiry. In particular, with hindsight it is clear that symbolic interactionism poses a challenge to the qualitative researcher by assuming tacit and subjective qualities, and context specificity, of the meanings which constitute the building blocks of its research 'objects'. *The Discovery of Grounded Theory*, however, rests upon a positivist empiricist philosophy: specifically, adoption of an inductive process of 'discovering' theory from data. This implies that a set of social or psychological relationships and processes exist relatively unproblematically and objectively in the world, can be reflected in appropriate qualitative data, and hence are there to be 'captured' by any sufficiently skilled grounded theory researcher who should happen to pass by.

Hammersley (1989) argues that many accounts of qualitative research founded upon symbolic interactionism tend to gloss over a fundamental tension, which he labels the *dilemma of qualitative method*. Put simply, this arises from a simultaneous commitment on the one hand to science and realism (by claiming to reflect objectively the 'data', in this case common-sense understandings, including participants' own accounts of their social and psychological life worlds), and on the other to a form of constructivism (through recognition of multiple meanings and subjectivities inherent in both a symbolic interactionist worldview and in the engagement of the researcher in generating new understandings and theory).

Accordingly, it is no surprise to find the dilemma of qualitative method writ large in many contemporary accounts of grounded theory, which often appeal simultaneously to inductivist-empiricist and to phenomenological-constructionist themes. Philosophically speaking, theory cannot simply 'emerge' from data, because interpretation and analysis are always conducted within some pre-existing conceptual framework brought to the task by the analyst. Alvesson and Sköldberg (2000) go further, arguing that grounded theorists cannot simply assume that the raw 'data' of analysis are themselves unproblematic or uncontested. This then raises the thorny question of what grounds grounded theory (Henwood and Pidgeon, 1992, 1995a).

For some analytic purposes it might be simplest just to ignore Hammersley's dilemma. However, the risk here is that grounded theory might then be followed as if it were a standardized procedure for guaranteeing 'truth'. Glaser and Strauss (1967) appear to effectively sidestep this dilemma by emphasizing induction rather than symbolic interaction. However, if their stated objective of articulating the complexity of the substantive social world is to be achieved, the challenges posed by symbolic interactionism have to be met. Our own preferred response is to argue for a constructivist revision of grounded theory, as this captures more nearly its characteristic combination of systematic rigour in analysis with the essentially creative and dynamic character of the interpretive research process. A constructivist revision alerts the researcher to the fact that data should *guide* but certainly should not *limit* theorizing (Layder, 1993). For this reason the term *generation of theory*, rather than discovery, seems more accurately to describe both the epistemological and practical realities of the approach (Henwood and Pidgeon, 1992). Similarly, Bulmer (1979) has commented that, rather than theory being discovered or emerging from a purely inductive process, grounded theory involves a constant two-way dialectical process or 'flip-flop' between data and the researcher's conceptualizations (see also Bailyn, 1977).

Of course, the classic writings on grounded theory do recognize that in order to be able to 'discover' or 'generate' questions, meaning, insights and theory, researchers must be able to retain their disciplinary knowledges and utilize their 'theoretical sensitivities' (Bulmer, 1979; Charmaz, 1990; Glaser, 1978; Hammersley, 1989). Rather than equating advances in knowledge with attempts at empirical falsification of theoretical constructs, theoretical sensitivities are seen as *tools* that can be vision-creating or blinkering[2] depending upon a complex mix of individual, structural and cultural conditions.

We would argue that use of theoretical sensitivity necessarily involves researchers in hermeneutic and constructivist practices,

rather than purely abstract, rational and logical ones.[3] Hermeneutic and constructivist-interpretivist practice requires that researchers remain aware that knowing always involves seeing or hearing from within particular individually, institutionally and other socio-culturally embedded perspectives and locations (a point raised vigorously by feminist epistemologists, amongst others: e.g., Smith, 1974; Haraway, 1991; Harding, 1991). Also taken into account are other complexities associated with the multiple, fragmented and shifting character of discursively patterned or 'ordered' frameworks of meaning (Denzin, 1997; Gubrium and Holstein, 2000; Schwandt, 2000). Otherwise one will simply lack awareness of the preconditions which inevitably structure understanding and which would remain hidden under the guise of 'emergent' ideas and theory. Charmaz (2000: 511) comments:

> Diverse researchers can use grounded theory methods to develop constructivist studies derived from interpretive approaches. Grounded theorists need not subscribe to positivist or objectivist assumptions. Rather they may still study empirical worlds without presupposing narrow objectivist methods and without assuming the truth of their subsequent analyses ... constructivist grounded theory studies of subjective experience can bridge Blumer's (1969) call for the empirical study of meanings with current postmodernist critiques.

Postmodernism is singled out by Charmaz as the historical moment of criticism that crystallized for her the need to explicate a different framing of grounded theory methods from Glaser, Strauss and Corbin as (i) assuming the existence of multiple realities, (ii) involving the mutual creation of knowledge by viewer and viewed and (iii) aiming towards interpretive understandings of participants' meanings. It could be argued that none of these three ways of framing a revised, 'constructivist' version of grounded theory is distinctively associated with postmodernism, given that the latter is renowned for promoting a good deal of intellectual scepticism regarding truth claims associated with empirical investigations (Woolgar, 1988; Edwards et al., 1995). Charmaz (2000: 528) sees her commitment to the flexible, non-formulaic use of grounded theory methods as a way for postmodernism to 'inform realist study of experience rather than simply serve as a justification for abandoning it'.

Also writing about the relationship between grounded theory and social constructionism,

Costain Schou and Hewison (1996) simultaneously turn attention back to grounded theory's roots in symbolic interactionism while paying special attention to the role of 'text and talk' in constructing experiences, knowledge and meanings. They advocate studying 'discourse' (Potter and Wetherell, 1987) along with the use of a textual metaphor to guide research thinking and practice itself (Game, 1991; Burman and Parker, 1993). Within the 'turn to text' the suggestion is sometimes made that it is necessary to guard against the overuse of method in conducting interpretive inquiries (e.g., Reicher, 2000), since this might prevent sufficient concern being shown for the role played by discursive and textual orderings of 'reality' in human agency, social processes, cultural events and psychological meanings. One of the implications of the textual variant of social constructionist thinking for grounded theory is that it highlights not only (de)construction of local understandings, actors' 'points of view', actions, interactions and meanings *in situ*, but also of necessity *the products* of grounded theory analyses.

If it is perplexing to find such complex, multiple and divergent ways of presenting the philosophical positions associated with grounded theory, this is no less than should be expected in circumstances where qualitative researchers are having to juggle with many epistemological tensions. Denzin and Lincoln (2000: 2) have described these as existing within a 'complex historical field' where modernism and postmodernism are two of seven 'crosscutting historical moments' that overlap and simultaneously 'operate in the present'. As grounded theory has become subjected to exegetical, critical and revisionist theorizing it becomes no longer possible to classify it in all respects as a modernist, as opposed to a postmodern, methodological endeavour. In the remainder of this chapter we seek to go beyond such simple classifications to provide a contemporary account of the uses that are made of its principles and practices.

STRATEGIES FOR CONDUCTING GROUNDED THEORY RESEARCH

The flow of work: 'emergence', flexibility, and cycles of inquiry/iteration

The monograph *Discovery* should be read primarily as a manifesto for a distinctive methodological *approach* to qualitative research design and data analysis. In subsequent writings Glaser (1978, 1992) and Strauss (1987; Strauss and Corbin, 1994, 1998) have explicated more detailed *strategies* for generating grounded theory. It is through their differences in practical detail that fundamental philosophical fractures have subsequently appeared. Our discussion of the strategies of grounded theory work also draws upon that of the late Barry Turner, who was one of the first European sociologists to make extensive use of the approach in substantive domains of organizational sociology (see Turner, 1976, 1978; Reeves and Turner, 1972), and subsequently to reflect in writing upon his experience of doing this (Turner, 1981, 1988; Martin and Turner, 1986; Gherardi and Turner, 1999).

In highlighting the current dispute over the 'true' legacy of *Discovery*, it is easy to forget that there is much that remains as common ground to all accounts of the method. The term 'grounded theory' has, over time, come to stand for a core set of analytic strategies for the generation of theory, specifically:

1. developing open-coding schemes to capture the detail, variation and complexity of observations and other material obtained;
2. sampling data and cases on theoretical grounds, and as analysis progresses, to extend the emergent theory ('theoretical sampling');
3. constantly comparing data instances, cases and categories for conceptual similarities and differences (the method of 'constant comparison');
4. writing theoretical memoranda to explore emerging concepts and links to existing theory;
5. continuing to make comparisons and use of theoretical sampling until no new or further relevant insights are being reached ('saturation');
6. engaging in more focused coding of selected core categories;
7. tactics to force analysis from descriptive to more theoretical levels (such as writing definitions of core categories and building conceptual models).

In the early stages of generating grounded theory the researcher must adopt a stance of maximum flexibility in generating new categories from data. This is a creative process, which taxes fully the interpretive powers of the researcher, who is nevertheless disciplined by the requirement that codes and categories generated should *fit* (provide a recognizable description of) the data. Success in generating theory that is well grounded in data depends upon maintaining a balance throughout between full use of the researcher's own imagination and theoretical sensitivity against this basic requirement of fit.

Figure 28.1 illustrates the interrelationships between the core stages. The flow of intellectual work is, in very broad terms, a linear one. The analyst works from an initial topic or set of research questions, to data gathering, through initial treatment of unstructured materials (using varied analytic operations, of which open coding is only one), and on to a set of theoretical categories, interpretations, models, and written accounts of theory. This flow is accompanied by a gradual development of the level of analysis away from the local descriptions inherent to (initially ill-structured) data towards more ordered analytic (theoretical) concepts and categories. However, in its detailed execution the flow of work is also *flexible and iterative*, reflecting the ongoing 'flip-flop' between data and conceptualization that we have noted earlier.

Hence, Figure 28.1 indicates pathways through which the researcher will move from later back to earlier operations as necessary, and as the analysis proceeds. For example, the research question itself, which Turner (1981) points out may only be tacitly understood at the outset of inquiry, is often sharpened and refined – sometimes changed entirely – by the process of data analysis. In a similar way, a recategorization of codes can follow the development of the emerging theoretical analysis, or a realization by the analyst that initial terms and concepts used do not in fact fit the data in the ways originally assumed. And data analysis may prompt a new round of data collection, in order to check out emerging ideas or to extend the richness and scope of the emergent theory. Indeed, the importance placed by Glaser and Strauss upon the close interplay of data analysis and data collection in the search for 'theoretical saturation' (unlike most other accounts of social science research methods which maintain, in published versions at least, a separation between the two)[4] is a characteristic feature of the grounded theory approach, and one which has a very wide appeal to qualitative researchers more generally. All of these

iterative processes are concrete manifestations of the flip-flop process we noted earlier.

Figure 28.1 is, at one level, merely a heuristic device with which to contrast the grounded theory process with more traditional forms of hypothetico-deductive research method. At another level, it represents a set of anticipated practices that will help to frame the design decisions the grounded theory researcher must make. Taken *too* literally (i.e. as a series of self-contained, albeit iteratively interrelated, operations or stages) it risks presenting what Silverman (1993, 1997) describes as a 'dead', or 'cookbook' recipe approach to the principles and practices of research design – that is, a recipe with no guarantee that researchers making design choices will do so in ways that result in a sound or workable design for their particular study. One means of meeting such criticism is to use the diagram (e.g., when teaching graduate students) in concert with exemplars of the ways in which researchers have successfully negotiated aspects of grounded theory design (e.g., to collect different kinds of data for different questions, or to sample particular groups or settings as appropriately relevant to the topic under investigation). Silverman's own resolution is to urge the researcher not to lose sight of the 'aesthetics' of research (meaning the appearance or shape of what is worthwhile practice; see also Turner, 1988) as seen by wider social science, community and practitioner audiences.

Figure 28.1 also depicts what is, in some ways, an unremarkable design dilemma: envisaging a set of clearly planned choices while simultaneously acknowledging that, because grounded theory research has a contingent and unfolding character, some of those decisions at least are likely to change. Emphasizing the latter aspect, Strauss and Corbin (1998: 33) explicitly link the principles of emergent design with their goal of theory-building.

> Because our approach to theory building is one of *emergence* … the design, like the concepts, must be allowed to emerge during the research process. As concepts and relationships emerge from data through qualitative analysis, the researcher can use that information to decide where and how to go about gathering additional data that will further the evolution of the theory. (emphasis in original)

In our view, presenting the dilemma of linearity and non-linearity in grounded theory design

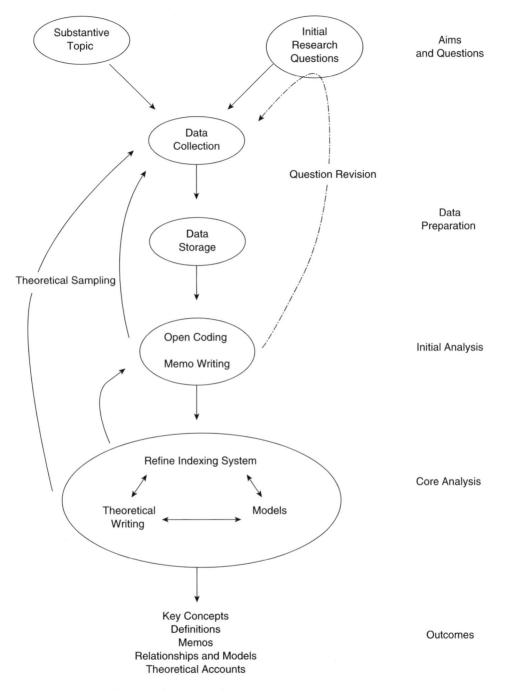

Figure 28.1 *Steps in the grounded approach*

has the additional aesthetic appeal of inviting a non-didactic view of the principle of flexibility, emergence, and iterativeness in relation also to a defined origin to inquiry and to qualitative research design. Although this suggestion might appear heretical to some advocates of grounded theory research, we would maintain that *all* research projects inevitably have to start from somewhere: and this will probably involve developing some form of guide, plan or protocol of how the study is 'designed' at the outset. The researchers' chances of being able to arrive at a successful set of results, interpretations or conclusions are maximized by this approach.

How, then, do research protocols for grounded theory come to be written? How are basic research design decisions made? How do the proposals made by advocates and users of grounded theory aid efforts at formulating or designing a qualitative study? Without at least some consideration of design issues, it is difficult to see how any but the most narrow of grounded theory studies (e.g., where a genuinely new field of inquiry, which also serendipitously suggests its own location and method for commencing data collection, is chanced upon by an experienced qualitative researcher) could even get off the ground. Our own experience of teaching grounded theory to students is that new researchers often struggle to put into practice the ideal (which they readily and enthusiastically glean from the classic writings on the topic) that they should approach fieldwork without any prior preconceptions or reference to prior literature. Equally, it can be difficult to convince grant-awarding bodies of the value of such a methodological approach without at least some justification of the intellectual origins to the issue at hand, and the plans made for initial fieldwork.

It would be fair to say that many writings in the grounded theory tradition are less than helpful on, and in some instances muddle, the issues surrounding study origin and (at least initial) research design. Two areas of design decision-making seem particularly problematic. First, the tension between keeping to a general statement of initial substantive interests/problems and formulating more specific research questions (including the use of the theoretical literature to sharpen initial focus). Second, what it means in practice to implement a flexible, 'emergent' or 'inductive' sampling strategy (and, in particular, the relationship between Glaser and Strauss's notion of theoretical sampling and other forms of 'purposive' sampling). We discuss these issues in the next two subsections, drawing in particular upon Cutliffe (2000), who attends to the differences of opinion that have emerged between Glaser and Strauss, but does not criticize other writings (as do Baker et al., 1992; Stern, 1994) for deviating from the tenets of 'true' grounded theory. We would also recommend Marshall

and Rossman (1999) as an aid to designing any grounded theory study. Their comprehensive account elucidates a number of initial design choices that are often left unstated in written accounts of grounded theory.

Initial problems and research questions (including how to use the research literature)

> Whereas traditional research starts from specific research questions (usually phrased in tightly defined terms, and often articulated in the form of testable hypotheses), research to generate grounded theory deliberately avoids defining the research focus too tightly. (Taber, 2000: 473)

This statement by Taber illustrates the rhetorical contrast frequently made between hypothesis-testing and the rather different goals of grounded theory development, exploration and generation. While clear as a statement of principle, in practice it conceals a significant tension. In particular, without a clear specification of what is meant by (avoiding) defining the research focus 'too tightly', it leaves open the issue of the appropriate level of prior conceptualization for commencing a grounded theory study. In practice, of course, this will differ enormously, study by study and researcher by researcher.

Many studies that report adopting a grounded theory methodology are often prompted by quite general research interests at the outset. Initial research goals might be: to identify actors' perspectives on a topic; to investigate social processes or phenomena of interest within their local contexts and settings; to devise explanatory schemes relevant to locally situated, 'real-world' problems; or to explore an unresearched topic. Examples are Kumar and Gantley's (1999) study which set out to explore general practitioners' views of their role in implementing genetic technology, and Tuler and Thomas's (1999) attempt to determine principles that are important in participatory decision-making about local forestry and land use. Michie et al. (1996) depict their own study as seeking to map how families attending a clinic for genetically inherited bowel cancer viewed the illness and its treatment. Turner was motivated to develop his pioneering account of the human and organizational preconditions to major technological accidents (*disaster incubation* theory: Turner, 1978; Turner and Pidgeon, 1997) because of a clear gap in existing knowledge, coupled with his realization that there was a potential store of (untapped) information about administrative failures and shortcomings in reports of public inquiries into large-scale accidents.

Glaser (1992) argues strongly for this kind of initially 'generalist position' when defending the logic of grounded theory as he sees it, thereby continuing the theme of qualitative researchers' refusal to subordinate open-ended, exploratory research activities to theory verification. Hence:

> The research question in a grounded theory study is not a statement that identifies the phenomenon to be studied. The problem emerges and questions regarding the problem emerge ... Out of open coding, collection by theoretical sampling, and analysing by constant comparison emerge the focus for the research. (Glaser, 1992: 25)

Strauss and Corbin (1998), however, argue for enhancing the early focus of grounded theory studies by making explicit the questions guiding a researcher's choice of topic or interest in investigating a particular setting, and then using these to direct attention to specific phenomena and the types of data to be gathered. For example:

> A researcher who is studying organizations, such as a laboratory that makes use of illegal drugs when doing some of its experiments, might ask a question such as the following: 'What are the procedures or policies (written and implied) for handling the illegal drugs in the organization?' The focus of data collection and analysis will be on the broader organizational processes of monitoring and accounting for the amounts and types of drugs used. Data will be gathered not only through interviews but also by studying written policies and then observing how these are carried out. Not all organizational policies will be studied; rather only those related to the handling of the illegal drugs will be studied. (Strauss and Corbin, 1998: 42)

The suggestion that *questions* must be developed early on to guide the subsequent course of an investigation is at variance with Glaser's position, but in so doing brings grounded theory more closely into line with other sociological accounts of qualitative research design (Kelly, 1998; Mason, 1996) and widely read resource-books on qualitative methods (Marshall and Rossman, 1999; Miles and Huberman, 1994; Robson, 1998). All of these caution against the dangers of too loose initial research designs, so as to avoid researchers becoming personally overwhelmed by 'too much data' and studies becoming conceptually diffuse. Novice researchers, in particular, may be unable to focus sufficiently to provide insights, accounts or explanations of important or relevant issues (or commence effective data gathering) if they do not make explicit what interests them about their chosen topic area, and state these interests as research questions fairly early on in their investigations.

The priority that Strauss and Corbin give to question formation in study design goes beyond the practical issue of asking manageable and answerable questions in order to avoid being overwhelmed by a wealth of detailed, but potentially distracting data. Rather their treatment begins to delimit the conceptual scope of subsequent analysis. Whether this then forecloses upon possible creative insights about the data is the main point of issue that Glaser (1992) raises in his critique of their development of the approach. Strauss and Corbin's apparent openness about the kinds of research questions and investigative pathways that researchers might actually take is, in fact, significantly counteracted by their explicit prioritizing of research questions that aim to identify the conceptual properties, dimensions, antecedents and consequences of actions and interactions. Embedding their concern for symbolic interactionism within a more socio-structural framework (see also Layder, 1982, 1993), a particular device that they advocate as a guide is the condition/consequence matrix. This indicates possible constraints (e.g., the context of 'family') on any specific social interaction (say, the process of 'divorce' between individual family members) as well as the site of possible consequences of that interaction (the impacts of persistent family breakdown on the 'family' again, but also on the wider 'community'). Cutliffe (2000) argues that this inevitably lends emphasis to asking 'what if' questions, in contrast to Glaser's (1978) 'what is actually happening in the data' orientation.

By thinking ahead to what is likely to be relevant in a particular topic and investigation, researchers will also be able to deploy their background or disciplinary knowledges so as to refine their research questions, avoid merely repeating studies that have been done before, move knowledge and theorizing about a problem or issue forward, and build into projects the capacity to benefit fully from the exercise of theoretical sensitivity.

Embedding projects in background and disciplinary knowledges in order to formulate not just workable but maximally useful research questions early on when designing a study, as in Strauss and Corbin's account, brings the role of the theoretical literature into question. The principle that people new to grounded theory often read into descriptions of the approach – of completely setting aside the literature at the start of the project so as to maintain sensitivity to relevance in the data[5] – is displaced by a more discriminating strategy of using the literature early on in specific ways. Cutliff (2000: 1481) emphasizes the importance, when investigating relationships between concepts (in his case between hope and bereavement counselling), of using the theoretical literature prior to entering the study to promote clarity in thinking about concepts as it 'helps the researcher to reach conceptual density, enhance the richness of concept development, and subsequently the process of theory development'. Others (e.g., Smith and Biley, 1997) have advocated an early skimming of the literature to provide what Glaser and Strauss described in *Discovery* as a partial framework of local concepts that identify a few main features of the situations that will be studied (actors, roles, organizational goals, etc.). This position reflects an awareness that researchers, far from approaching analysis as a *tabula rasa*, sometimes can use a first pass at the existing literature (necessary even if the objective is to address – as with Turner's organizational accidents study – a significant *gap* in that literature), alongside their own existing theoretical sensitivities, to support what might otherwise remain a tacit orientation towards the investigative process. The special counsel that remains within grounded theory is to avoid being so wedded to particular theoretical positions and key studies in the literature in ways that overly direct ways of looking and stymie the interactive process of engagement with the empirical world being studied. *Theoretical agnosticism* is a better watchword than theoretical ignorance to sum up the ways of using the literature at the early stages of the flow of work in grounded theory.

Charmaz (1990, 2000) clarifies how qualitative researchers must have a perspective from which they actively seek to build their analyses, but without merely 'applying' it to new data, problems or contexts. Researcher perspective, in her terms, includes substantive interests, a philosophical stance or school of thought which provides sensitizing concepts, together with one's personal experiences, priorities and values. Focusing upon the concepts provided by a school of thought in particular, her description of the grounded theory stance is that it 'implies a delicate balance between possessing a grounding in the discipline and pushing it further' (Charmaz, 1990: 1165). This emphasis upon the researcher's disciplinary knowledges and sensitivities in shaping research questions and taking research forward in original directions provides a logical reason to expect the kinds of synergies that are, indeed, now beginning to be found between grounded theory style investigations and frameworks of ideas that extend beyond symbolic interactionism. Familiarity with ideas from phenomenology can lead researchers to focus their research questions on exploring the complexity and structure of people's everyday and life experiences. An awareness of narrative theory can promote investigations into storytelling, and the possibility of linking together concepts about significant life events and aspects of life history. The importance of text to the context of people's activities, experiences and sense-making in discourse theory provides a rationale for investigating fissures, fractures and contestation over symbolism and meaning (rather than co-ordinated action and consensual meanings) and questions about the situated workings of agency and power.

Sampling: 'theoretical' and 'purposive'

Grounded theory shares with much qualitative research the use of non-probability sampling (i.e., sampling is not guided by the overriding need to militate against systematic 'errors' in the coverage of a population), and in particular the use of *theoretical sampling*. This involves collecting new data as the analysis proceeds, in order to elaborate and build up emerging insights and theory, a process which continues until nothing new is being said about the concepts and ways of theorizing being explored (theoretical saturation). Theoretical sampling is central to the successful prosecution of an iterative data–theory interaction, and hence theory emergence:

> Theoretical sampling is the process of data collection for generating theory whereby the analyst jointly collects, codes, and analyses his [sic] data and decides what data to collect next and where to find them, in order to develop his theory as it emerges. This process of data collection is *controlled* by the emerging theory. (Glaser and Strauss, 1967: 45)

This strategy is sometimes contrasted with purposive sampling, which involves making choices about cases or settings according to some initial prespecified criteria. Of course, there is a sense in which all sampling is purposive. Miles and Huberman (1994; also Patton, 1990; Curtis et al., 2000) list 16 purposive sampling strategies for qualitative research, most of which can be used within an emergent design where the aim is to extend theory iteratively through *analysis–sampling cycles*. Some of their most important examples for grounded theorists are:

1. *extreme or deviant cases* (which may prove to be troublesome, counter to, or enlightening in relation to emerging theory);
2. *theory-based selection* (elaborates and examines an important theoretical construct);
3. *typical cases* (to highlight what is average or 'normal', and to avoid claims that theory is grounded in atypical cases);
4. *maximum variation sampling* (to encompass the range of variations, or extremes, that emerge in relation to different conditions);
5. *critical cases* (which permit maximum application of findings to other cases);
6. *politically important or sensitive cases* (as a focus for drawing attention to the findings or study, perhaps for policy purposes);
7. *confirming and disconfirming cases* (elaborating initial analysis, seeking exceptions, looking for variation);
8. *stratified purposeful sampling* (illustrates subgroups, facilitates group comparisons);
9. *rich response sampling*[6] (to provide the richest or most explanatory data sources).

Grounded theorists would claim that one can only identify truly 'extreme', 'typical', 'sensitive' or 'subgroup' cases through the process of initial data analysis and conceptualization. Similarly, 'maximum variation' is bound up with the principle of theoretical saturation: only through comparative data analysis can the researcher judge whether maximum theoretical variation (or saturation) has been achieved, or alternatively whether new cases need to be sampled to build further theoretical density.

However, the question can also be raised: what guides sampling before the initial emergence of theory begins to prompt theoretical sampling? Cutliff (2000) argues that initial data collection does not differ from later selection in the need to be guided by relevance and appropriateness, implying at least some degree of purposive selection.[7] On the other hand, this needs to be balanced against the very real danger of becoming prematurely locked into a (possibly costly) data collection strategy that does not ultimately yield dense conceptualization. In pragmatic terms, it is often appropriate to commence data collection with a small number of 'rich response' cases or sources, such as a key 'gatekeeper' with the most experience of the topic (Morse, 1991). In other instances initial sampling can be prompted by an existing grounded theory (Strauss, 1970; Vaughan, 1992), or by a first pass at the available literature (albeit disciplined by theoretical agnosticism, and the need to develop a theoretical sampling strategy as data analysis proceeds). In practice, then, research using grounded theory commences inquiry from a number of starting points.

An important final consideration is that grounded theorists treat *any relevant medium* or combination of media as data (Fujimura, 1997; Horlick-Jones et al., 2003), such as documents, official records or reports, records of participant observation, focus group, interview, and, as noted earlier, possibly even statistical data. The a priori/emergent division is no longer so plain in differentiating between forms of sampling once it is realized that 'theoretical sampling' can be viewed more generically as the activity that treats 'everything as data'. Wuest (2000) has described coming belatedly to a more complex and sustainable view of the relationship between conceptual development, theoretical sampling and emergent design decisions. In her research on the relationship between healthcare systems and caregiving she had initially read the injunction not to use prior concepts, but to develop concepts from analysis of data gathered *in situ*, so literally that it prohibited her from making comparisons at a conceptual level 'to move beyond description to see theoretical possibilities in the data', which is in turn, of course, necessary if data is to be sampled appropriately to further extend the emerging theory. Her resolution was to view 'theoretical sampling' more generically as the activity that treats 'everything as data' (namely, other published studies and theoretical accounts, as well as new empirical data)[8] so as to maximize the possibilities of being able to make conceptual comparisons and developing theorizing through 'emergent fit'.

In this way the principle of emergent design through successive theoretical sampling becomes not just a feature of the grounded theory method but a recapitulation of a far more wide-reaching conceptualization of an analytical approach when engaging in qualitative inquiry more generally.

Storage: the research record

[T]he central principle of the process is tackling the cognitive problems of data analysis by bringing them into the open ... the research record makes it possible to manipulate and analyse the data collected, and to develop a theoretical understanding ... through this the researcher develops a gradually changing, abstract representation of the social world in a form which can be rearranged to let new aspects of its properties become evident. (Turner, 1981: 30)

For grounded theory work to proceed, the data must first be assembled in some form of permanent record that allows ready access during analysis. When working from documentary or archival data sources, photocopies have traditionally formed this permanent record (leaving sufficient in the margins for jotting the theoretical codes generated). Alternatively, with interview, observational or interactional (e.g., focus group) studies, tape recordings can be treated as the record (preserving a range of paralinguistic features of talk). More typically, though, the full data set (or a part thereof) from interviews and protocols is transcribed verbatim. Transcription itself is highly labour-intensive, taking at least 8–10 hours per hour of tape (and significantly longer if paralinguistic features are also transcribed).

A frequent next step in handling each discrete data set (from a single document, or interview, say) is to provide it with a label (e.g., indicating date, source and topic). A second is to allocate a numerical reference to segments of the text, typically numbering pages, paragraphs or sometimes lines in the record. The level of coarseness at which this initial segmentation is conducted is, in some respects, a matter of judgement. Our own preference when working manually has always been to segment text into naturally occurring paragraph breaks, or, where interaction is involved, into individual turns in talk. There is a sense in which very fine segmentation and subsequent coding (say, at the level of sentences or even individual words) runs

the danger of losing sight of overall context, or the contrasts and continuities in individual or group discourses, when text segments are subsequently accessed. Also, too fine a segmentation might restrict the possibility for potentially fruitful multiple codings on a single segment.[9] On the other hand, too large a segment (a page or above) will mean that a code's precise referent in the text may be hard to identify later. The aim here is to provide a systematic labelling system through which any particular segment of raw text can be quickly identified, accessed, compared to other segments, and interrogated on the basis of subsequent coding operations.[10]

Open coding (including the use of constant comparison)

Having collected and recorded a sufficient quantity of material, the next task is to build an indexing system for the data through 'open' (or 'substantive') coding, as soon as is practical after the first round of data collection (see Figure 28.1). The indexing system will subsequently allow the researcher to compare and reorder the data collected as interpretations develop, traditionally by highlighting, cutting, pasting and re-sorting photocopies of documents or transcripts. In the language of computer-aided qualitative data analysis software (CAQDAS) packages, the basic indexing amounts to a 'code-and-retrieve' paradigm (Kelle, 1995, 1997). Common packages such as NUD*IST, NVivo, ATLAS.ti, Ethnograph, and HyperResearch (see Weitzmann, 2000) are founded upon such a paradigm, and often explicitly reference grounded theory as their source of analytic logic. The technique we describe here involves building an indexing system on file cards. It is no surprise to find some CAQDAS programs, for example Hyper-Research, explicitly using the metaphor of file cards, in concert with hypertext links, as the basis for their electronic indexing system.[11] Here we use the term 'file card' interchangeably to represent both manual and virtual devices.

Open coding proceeds by means of the tentative development and labelling of concepts in the text that the researcher considers of potential relevance to the problem being studied.[12] To construct such a set of codes, Turner suggests starting with the first paragraph of the transcript and asking: 'what categories, concepts or labels do I need in order to account for what is of importance to me in this paragraph?' Clearly, the facets of the data that are coded will vary depending upon the aims of the study and the theoretical sensitivities of the researcher. Even when using CAQDAS programs, it is the researcher who must provide the difficult *interpretative* work which generates the label.

When a label is thought of it is recorded as the header on a file card. A précis of the data of interest, together with a reference for accessing the specific transcript and paragraph, is noted on the card, with the latter filed in a central record box. This initial entry then serves as the first *indicator* for the *concept* (or category) described by the card header. Open coding continues by checking whether further potentially significant aspects of the paragraph suggest different concepts (almost certainly they will), and continues in this way with subsequent paragraphs.

At this stage, the labels used may be long-winded, ungainly, or fanciful, and they may be formulated at any conceptual level that seems to be appropriate. Indeed, later success in moving the analysis from initial coding onto a greater level of abstraction will depend in part upon choosing an appropriate level of abstraction for the concepts in question. The use of highly particular terms ('member categories' or *in vivo* codes: see Strauss and Corbin, 1998) that are a direct précis of the data will tie the analysis to the specific context of that interview or document. Other terms ('researcher categories') may refer to more generalized theoretical ideas. A particularly difficult judgement for beginners to make here is the level of coding to be adopted: a common trap is to generate mainly member categories with few researcher categories.

When conducting open coding it is crucial that the terms should, to use Glaser and Strauss's (1967) term, 'fit' the data well, so that they provide a recognizable description of the item, activity or discourse under consideration. As coding continues, not only will the list of concepts (and hence store of file cards) rapidly expand, but also concepts will begin to recur in subsequent paragraphs or data segments. For the purposes of subsequent analysis, it is important to recognize that the aim is not principally to record *all* instances of a particular concept, but to record *different* instances which highlight significant variations on that concept. In this way the aim of open coding is to seek similarities and diversities, using the indexing to collect together a range of indicators that point to the multiple qualitative facets of a potentially significant concept. The active 'flip-flop' between the data and the researcher's developing conceptualizations also demands a dynamic process of changing, rechanging and adjustment of terms used where fit can be improved.

The exercise of coding to explore similarities and differences is basic to implementing the analytic method of *constant comparison*, upon which the generation of grounded theory is founded. The method of constant comparison involves continually sifting and comparing elements (basic data instances, emergent concepts, cases, or theoretical propositions) throughout the lifetime of the project. By making such comparisons the researcher is sensitized to similarities and nuances of difference as a part of the cognitive exploration of the full range and complexity of the data. In short, similarities and differences are central to promoting dense conceptual development. Thus, comparison of basic data instances in an emergent category

> very soon starts to generate theoretical properties of the category. The analyst starts thinking in terms of the full range of types or continua of the category, its dimensions, the conditions under which it is pronounced or minimized, its major consequences, its relation to other categories, and its other properties. (Glaser and Strauss, 1967: 106)

Taken together, the commitments of constant comparison and theoretical sampling define the analytic dynamic of the grounded theory process, which involves the researcher, as we have suggested, in a highly interactive and iterative process.

Theoretical memos

As the fund of codes builds up, some indexed to many incidents across the data corpus, some indexed to few, the analysis begins to involve other operations with the explicit aim of taking conceptual development forward. Theoretical memos, in particular, are often stimulated by the intellectual activity of coding, and many researchers build up a separate record system – or 'memo fund' (Glaser, 1978) – for them. Unlike categories (which have to 'fit' the data), the contents of memos are not constrained in any way and can include: hunches and insights; comments on new samples to be checked out later; deliberations about refinements of file cards; and explanations of modifications to categories. Memos serve both as a means of *stimulating* theoretical sensitivity and creativity, and as a vehicle for *making public* the researcher's emerging theoretical reflections. Indeed, Glaser (1978: 82) sets memoing at the heart of the whole process:

> The bedrock of theory generation, its true product is the writing of theoretical memos. If the analyst skips this stage by going directly from coding to sorting or to writing, he [sic] is *not* doing grounded theory. *Memos are the theorizing write-up of ideas about codes and their relationships as they strike the analyst.* Memos lead naturally to abstraction or ideation. (Emphasis in original)

Memos can subsequently be used: to discuss the emerging analysis with colleagues; as a part of a 'reflexive account' (Lincoln and Guba, 1985) charting the course of coding and analysis; as core material during the writing-up of the research; or to make connections to the existing literature. Conducting memoing and open coding as parallel cognitive operations allows sensitivity to existing literature and theory to be combined with a commitment to grounding in data.

Memo writing as an activity is, of course, only one of several ways in which grounded theorists raise the conceptual level, albeit one that is likely to continue throughout the lifetime of a project (as analysis develops, the content will shift from being 'memos on data' to 'memos on memos'). Also, there is no simple distinction one can make between memo writing and the assembly of a final account. The latter (as a first draft to, say, a thesis chapter, research report, or journal article) would expect to draw upon some earlier memos, but also to continue with the process of conceptual development started in these early memos. Grounded theories are always provisional and contingent, never 'complete'.

Core analysis: refining, renaming and defining concepts

Open coding leads to categorization through fragmentation of the data. However, over time the analysis increasingly involves other 'core' activities (Figure 28.1) designed to both raise the conceptual level and (re)construct an orderly theoretical account. Pidgeon et al. (1991) liken the early phases of grounded theory (open coding and initial

memoing) to stepping deeper into a maze, a place of uncertainty (and some anxiety), particularly for the new researcher. During the core analysis phase the researcher has to find suitable routes out of this maze. It is in the subsequent attempts to specify these routes that conceptual differences between Glaser and Strauss have most strongly emerged. We briefly discuss a number of strategies we have used for conceptual development, before going on to consider the axial coding debate between Glaser, Strauss and colleagues.

Alongside further analytic memo writing, core analysis typically involves a refinement of the indexing system through category splitting, renaming and integration, often as a direct product of the application of constant comparison at the level of data (i.e., with respect to instances collected under a single index card or category). For example, in a study of adult mother–daughter relationships, Henwood (1993) conducted 60 interviews with mother–daughter dyads. The initial coding led to the development of a long and varied, but highly unwieldy, list of instances under the label 'relational closeness'. The attributes that had been coded onto the card were initially glossed as attaching global value to the relationship. However, closer reading and comparison of the individual instances indicated a much more mixed view of the emotional intensity of the relationships, ranging from a welcome but painful sense of gratitude and debt to a stance of hypersensitivity and a desire to flee from a relationship which involved 'confinement' or 'smothering'. The inextricable link between the two concepts resulting from this subdivision was retained and coded through their respective labels 'closeness' and 'overcloseness'. This link then became a key stimulus and focus for conceptual development and reflection, in turn mediated by the writing of theoretical memos (for an example of the latter, see Pidgeon and Henwood, 1996).

Category integration, on the other hand, involves clarifying the relationships between emerging categories by linking, by reclassifying under higher-level concepts, and by conducting conceptual sorting exercises on both file cards *and* theoretical memos. This might eventually involve drawing up various forms of diagrammatic or tabular representation (see Miles and Huberman, 1994). Alternatively, even in this age of computer support, there may be no substitute to sorting paper memos, file cards and concepts into piles, often returning to re-sort, in order to develop understanding of basic classes and relationships.

Operations such as splitting categories, converting several categories into one, or relabelling categories to adjust fit are likely to occur repeatedly during the early phases of the core analysis. However, there comes a point at which the collection and coding of additional data no longer contribute further insights to a specific category or categories; that is, the researcher perceives nothing new – no more conceptual variation – as new data are coded. At this point a category may have become 'saturated', to use Glaser and Strauss's term.[13] The researcher's task then is to try to make the analysis more explicit by summarizing why all of the entries have been included under the same label. One way of doing this, recommended by Turner (1981; Martin and Turner, 1986), is to write a definition for the concept that explicitly states the qualities that were already recognized in an implicit manner when a new entry was classified. This is a demanding task (and typically comparative at the level of *both* data and concepts), but one which can nevertheless be crucial to the analysis. It often leads to a deeper and more precise understanding of central categories.

Finally, it should be noted that as the indexing system grows, many cards will hold only one or very few instances. This does not necessarily mean such a category is unimportant. However, tacit processes of 'forgetting' (about less relevant cases, instances or categories) are as much a part of the cognitive processes involved in generating grounded theory (Barry Turner, personal communication) as is the explicit narrowing of focus upon a set of core or particularly well-saturated categories.

Core analysis: theoretical coding and models

Perhaps the most critical stage of the whole analysis (and the path to escape the maze) comes at the point of theoretical saturation, where the researcher focuses on important core categories and on relationships between them and more formal theory. Glaser (1978: 72) elaborates this in terms of 'theoretical' coding:

> theoretical codes conceptualize how the substantive codes may relate to each other as hypotheses to

be integrated into the theory. They, like substantive codes, are emergent; they weave the fractured story back together again … theoretical codes give integrative scope, broad pictures, and a new perspective. This is why grounded theory is so often 'new' because of its *grounded integration*. (Emphasis in original)

In the spirit of theory generation, Glaser (1978: 73) advocates *maximum flexibility* in theoretical coding, because 'most theorists in sociology focus only upon their "pet" code – the code they were indoctrinated into – and no others!'. Glaser argues one should think in terms of families of theoretical codes expressing broader sociological and social-psychological constructs, at differing levels of analysis. A researcher could use any family or combination of such to integrate an account. He lists 18 generic families, 3 examples of which are: *the six Cs* (causes, contexts, contingencies, consequences, covariation, conditions); *process families* (stages, phases, progressions, passages); and *identity families* (self-concept, social worth, identity loss).

Integrating elements of generic social science concepts with those more directly derived from data is often achieved using models, serving as a way for grounded theory researchers to demonstrate that they have achieved a formal element to their substantive theorizing. The simplest of models are skeletal 'organizing schemata' that mainly serve to catalogue the features of codings and categories, and are more implicit in suggesting relationships between them. Many qualitative studies (within and beyond grounded theory) report their findings in this way, and so the usefulness of this simple representational device must not be understated. Models can also depict, explain or otherwise account for time-event sequences, patterns of action and interaction, or 'processes' of, for example, transition and change, typically by assuming some variant of a 'representational' theory of meaning. Visual displays of the relationships and conceptualizations specified in a model are frequently used as devices to immediately convey its particular kind of analytic message – for example, flow charts, concept maps, matrices, typologies, taxonomies and other sorts of ordering and pattern template diagrams (Miles and Huberman, 1994).

Models have a number of other useful features. They can be examined for their correspondence with pre-existing common sense, with theory, and with professional assumptions and understandings. They can also be referenced, navigated or searched – much as a resource-book or guidebook – in the quest to find answers to specific research questions. A study of health-care consumption patterns among communities of recent immigrants to the USA (Houston and Venkatesh, 1996) provides an illustration. The research findings suggested a three-part model comprising *cultural health beliefs* (culture-specific beliefs about health, illness and the body, all of which coexisted with ones discovered in the new cultural context), *cultural values* (which operate as emotionally charged preferences directing attention and selecting goals) and *relationships between consumers and providers* (social norms which meant that there were barriers in consumer relations and communication). The different parts of the framework suggested that there were many reasons why such communities were less likely to use the services available to them to treat sickness and promote health than other, comparably disadvantaged communities, while at the same time pointing towards the common idea that health-care services would be taken up only if they did not threaten the integrity of community members' prior cultural traditions. Use of the model to answer questions about the uptake of health services in relation to cultural beliefs, practices and values prompted further scepticism about attempts to account for contemporary socio-cultural patterns and relations through models of cultural assimilation, and supported the more recent emphasis on cultural hybridization.

Core analysis: axial coding

One important means to (re)assemble sub-stantive codes, developed by Strauss and Corbin (1998),[14] involves an intermediate process called *axial coding*. This is both a heuristic analytic device and a theoretical commitment, in that it is closely aligned with a concern for how socio-structural conditions inform interaction and meaning. In essence, they recommend the exhaustive coding of the intersecting properties of core conceptual categories along important dimensions or axes. For example:

> If we were to specify that 'degree of accessibility of drugs' is one of the causal conditions related to teen drug use in general, and we know that this concept can vary dimensionally from 'easy' to 'difficult', we might note that it is the 'easy' dimension of accessibility

that makes it one of the conditions for teens trying drugs (Strauss and Corbin, 1998: 132)

They also describe axial coding along multi-space typologies, whose axes are defined by the dimensions to important concepts, and the way in which axial coding can be fruit-fully used to link socio-structural conditions with contexts and consequences, as well as to elaborate emergent hypotheses.

For Glaser (1992), axial coding has led Strauss and Corbin down the path of verifi-cation and away from discovery, on the way displacing use of the method of constant comparison, and forcing data into preconcep-tions (particularly of cause and conse-quence)[15] rather than enabling researchers to hear what is relevant and meaningful in their data. He describes their approach as 'full con-ceptual description' (see also Stern, 1994) rather than grounded theory:

> if you torture the data enough it will give up! This is the underlying approach in the forcing precon-ceptions of full conceptual description. The data is not allowed to speak for itself, as in grounded the-ory, and to be heard from infrequently it has to scream. Forcing by preconception constantly derails it from relevance. (Glaser, 1992: 123)

The possibility exists that axial coding may fragment the data even *further*, becoming an exercise in ever finer logical elaboration, rather than a properly emergent *integration* of theory. For example, Judy Kendall (1999) recounts her research into families living with a child with attention deficit hyperactivity disorder – a chronic and stigmatizing behav-ioural condition. She describes how her study initially aimed to explain what helped or hin-dered families 'doing well' with such a condi-tion, but that adhering to the strictures of axial coding around an initial category of 'dis-ruption' (important to the families' own expressed experience of the condition) deflected her from the insight that most of her families were in fact doing well in a very difficult situation. She suggests that while axial coding provided depth of conceptual-ization, it nevertheless deflected her (for 2 years out of a 3-year project!) from rework-ing the data in ways that expanded her think-ing and using other organizing frameworks.[16] She provides two very contrasting diagram-matic models, one produced through axial coding, and a second developed later on.

Our own view is that axial coding is only one amongst many potential pathways to theoretical development, and, like any other path, is unlikely to *guarantee* a straightforward or simple route. There are many varied types and ways of utilizing models, and varying degrees of simplicity/complexity, hence Strauss and Corbin's approach is one very particular representational type – not the endpoint of analysis which all users of the grounded theory method must strive to achieve. The most appropriate way of displaying or modelling information, ideas, concepts, processes and events needs to be found for the particular stage the research has reached, for its targeted audience, and to reflect the researcher's varied interests in describing, explaining and understanding aspects of the human and social world.

DISCUSSION

Our purpose in this chapter has been to present the background to and contemporary place of grounded theory methodology as an approach to qualitative design and analysis, and to outline some of its core principles and practices, along with discussions of them. One final, interlinked set of considerations remains outstanding. How is the quality of research likely to be judged and by whom? How is it possible to foster informed appreciation and criticism of its credibility, quality or validity? What strategies are best used when presenting study outcomes or findings? While pertinent from the outset, these considerations tend to gain primacy as a project moves towards completion.

Some guidance on these issues can be found in the dedicated grounded theory literature, where they appear as integral to the task of building conceptual schemes and explanatory models out of the core grounded theory operations. Glaser and Strauss's discussion in *Discovery* embeds the 'credibility', 'plausibility' or 'trustworthiness' of qualitative analyses (as viewed both by researchers and readers) within their narratives of the ways in which grounded theory projects are brought to a close, and why discovery methods are as important in social inquiry as verificationist ones (rather than being a mere prerequisite to subsequent, more rigorous testing). At the point at which systematic efforts at coding data and constantly making conceptual comparisons no longer produce new insights (theoretical saturation), and when a high level of conceptual density and integration

has been reached, inquirers will deem it appropriate to disseminate their work based on a belief in their 'own knowledgeability and because they can see no reason to change that belief' (Glaser and Strauss, 1967: 224–5). Likewise, readers who find themselves in agreement with the researchers' judgement of the quality of the research output – and whose requirement is above all for a sufficient level of rigour to be convincing – would see no further benefit in further theory testing, as this would invite criticism of researchers seeking to undertake redundant, trivial work.[17]

Proposed sets of criteria for use in the evaluation of qualitative studies (e.g., Lincoln and Guba, 1985; Lincoln, 1995) now exist in a number of disciplines (each with slightly different emphases – for example, Elliott et al. (1999) and Yardley (2000) for psychology, and Blaxter (1996) for medical sociology – and these are a further source of guidance, together with discussions of the merits or otherwise of the 'criteriological' approach (Schwandt, 1996; Smith and Deemer, 2000; Henwood, 2004). The need for consistency in the various ontological, epistemological and logical claims that are being made in research is a major concern, alongside widespread criticism of post-positivist approaches for making 'naively realist' analytic claims.

Tensions still remain in some guidelines. It is not uncommon in some disciplines, for example, for users of grounded theory to interpret the proposal to eliminate 'researcher bias' as signalling the need for researchers to demonstrate credibility of coding schemes by having senior researchers check junior researchers' codes for their accuracy or by calculating inter-rater reliability scores (Bolger, 1999). This quantitative technique lacks consistency with the approach of grounded theory and other related forms of qualitative inquiry where quality concerns are met primarily by demonstrating links between data and conceptualization and, ultimately, the conceptual clarity of categories. As important as it may be to demonstrate credibility of categories and codes, this needs to be done without losing sight of the principle that they should capture the subtlety and complexity of contextual and/or experiential meanings. In some studies, where the stated goal of a study involves illuminating participants' phenomenological experiences and worlds, very tightly formulated conceptualization may be read as overwriting participants' meanings with externally imposed frameworks in overly controlling ways.[18] The technique of 'member validation' commonly exists in lists of quality criteria for qualitative studies, and can augment grounded theory research by addressing the risks attached to 'appropriating' differences in people's modes of expressing their concerns (Opie, 1992; Henwood and Pidgeon, 1995b; Bhavnani, 1993). Demonstrating that the categories derived from the research process are recognizable and acceptable to study participants represents a 'validity' criterion, however, only when there are grounds for believing that participants have special insights into the social worlds and issues under study. More typically such commentaries work best if they are also treated as data.

Two further techniques – external auditing and triangulation – are often also deemed to overlap with quality concerns within grounded theory. *External auditing* can be appropriate where projects attach special importance to the transparency of the definitions of categories or systems of meaning, for example in multi-site studies or in multi- or interprofessional working teams. *Triangulation* is feasible to use in studies using multiple sources of observation and data, and can be conceptualized so that practising it is consistent with 'subtle realism' (Altheide and Johnson, 1994) and even constructivist theories of meaning. It is possible to set aside the traditional navigational metaphor (where multiple measurements are taken because a single one would not determine an object's unique position in a dimensional space) and see triangulation as a way of opening up different facets of complex phenomena to view (for more explanation, see the account in Flick, 1998).

A different kind of input into discussions of research quality comes from accounts of specific connections between grounded theory and other qualitative inquiry traditions such as ethnography (Seale, 1999; Hammersley and Atkinson, 1983). For example, Seale (1999) views theoretical saturation as akin to thick description, based on (the following) contrast between thick and thin description (as discussed by Geertz, 1973). Thick description is a way of

> revealing and building a many layered interpretation of social life, so that a rich and detailed understanding of the several meanings available for particular events is made possible. Thin description

fails to engage with cultural meanings, and is both uninspired and uninspiring. (Seale, 1999: 94)

Seale also views literary devices (symbolism, metaphor) as important means of conveying analysis in both grounded theory and thick description.

There are a number of weaknesses in Seale's argument. When discussing commonalities it is as important not to neglect differences between thick description and theoretical saturation (the latter is a specific moment in research when conceptual comparisons of data no longer bring new insights in the exploration of richly contexted meanings). Nor does the argument resolve the problem of how it is possible for theoretical description to also be explanatory and vice versa. This problem is inherited by both grounded theory and ethnography from the dilemma of qualitative inquiry (as discussed at the beginning of this chapter: see also Hammersley, 1989). Nevertheless, the different ways in which some researchers have described escaping the maze of coding and appreciating the complexity of their data in the early stages of grounded theory does suggest that Seale's view merits some consideration.

In some of our own research exploring the personal and cultural significance of woods, forests and trees to people living in Wales (Henwood and Pidgeon, 2001), we arrived at a way out of the maze of initial codings by constantly comparing the different 'interpretive viewpoints' that could be brought to bear upon a subset of main themes.[19] By subjecting each of the themes to different interpretive possibilities in this way a detailed, multifaceted, context-sensitive – and hence, plausibly, thickly described – account was generated, effectively bringing out the many significant aspects of what were otherwise intangible forestry and cultural values.

In describing the process of development of their analysis of men talking about unemployment, Willott and Griffin (1999) discuss using the computer package ATLAS.ti to store transcripts and its grounded theory operations to chunk, develop categories, fit them to the data, link categories – 'constantly returning to the data while developing the theoretical story' (p. 448). Utilizing their theoretical sensitivities, they engaged in some prior as well as continued theorizing about the way discourses construct versions of self and reality in the later (explicitly theoretical) stages of the analysis. It would be possible to simply argue for the inconsistency of these authors' later analytic strategy with the grounded theory approach that was clearly used in the early phase of their research to disassemble and reassemble their data into categories. However, in terms of its substantive content and credibility, their analysis does also exemplify a well-grounded theory that has benefited fully from the researchers' systematic attention to (thick description of) the categories and local colour of the men's own discourse. In a manner that surpasses many other grounded theory studies, Willott and Griffin's (1999) study provides a particularly rich and vivid description of *in vivo* categories and metaphors used by men themselves (e.g., the need to build their own 'economic lifeboat'). Simultaneously an account is offered of the cultural meanings or themes drawn upon by participants to justify their self-beliefs and self-positioning within the social and moral order.

In a useful appraisal of the continuing legacy of grounded theory methodology to the theory and practice of qualitative inquiry, Alvesson and Sköldberg (2000: 9) suggest that it provides an important 'bottom line for research work' but that, in its focus on data collection and processing, it can occlude the 'fundamental hermeneutic element [that] permeates the research process from beginning to end'. Importance needs to be attached to the *interpretation* rather than the representation of meaning. Just as qualitative analysis is best when inspired, honed and disciplined by the unpredictabilities and idiosyncrasies of data, so it must refuse to be drawn into presenting an unproblematic replica of the 'reality' of social life. The extent to which exemplars of research deploying grounded theory methodology succeed in doing both depends not only upon their facility in moving from data description to conceptualization (operations that, as we have seen, are the core of grounded theory methods) but also on appropriately locating their analyses and interpretations within frameworks of intelligibility and practice – a matter that goes beyond Glaser and Strauss's strategies for maximizing the applicability and practical uses of theory. Questions do need to be asked about methods and models, but also about their interdependence with textual practices and embeddedness within webs of meaning. Accounts of qualitative empirical studies need to acknowledge their 'reflective and reflexive' (Alvesson and Sköldberg, 2000: 4) character. This is a further, important, quality issue for investigations of interactional processed complexities of meaning.

ACKNOWLEDGMENTS

We wish to thank Alan Bryman for his patient editing, together with three reviewers for their detailed comments on an earlier version. Thanks also to Sarah Pearce for her help with identifying contemporary literature. The authors shared many conversations on the topic of grounded theory with the late Barry Turner.

NOTES

1 A distinction has been drawn here (Benoliel-Quint, 1996) between 'grounded theory research' and 'research using grounded theory'. *Grounded theory research* can be characterized as setting out to *precisely* follow commitments and procedures depicted in the collected writings of Glaser, Strauss and colleagues, and *research using grounded theory* as indicating qualitative studies that are less purist about following all elements within a branded package. The latter view entertains two possible interpretations: either researchers are genuinely fuzzy or unclear about their understanding of how and why they are using elements of grounded theory, or they could alternatively be combining elements of grounded theory with other ideas and practices from within the social science and research methodology literature in novel and productive ways.

2 As Vaughan (1992: 195) puts it, 'the paradox of theory is that at the same time it tells us where to look it can keep us from seeing'.

3 Rennie (2000) suggests that grounded theory involves a 'double hermeneutic' in that both its processes (theory generation) and 'objects' of inquiry (the psycho-social world) inevitably involve pre-interpretation. His own solution to Hammersley's dilemma is that the grounded theory process has much in common with the logical strategy involving 'abduction' (Peirce, 1965).

4 In reality it is difficult to see any form of social science research – qualitative or quantitative – succeed without at least some element of such iteration. What Glaser and Strauss achieve is to make this explicit within the flow of research. Hammersley and Atkinson (1983: 206) argue, in similar vein, for the unification in ethnography of description and theorizing, development and testing of theory, and view the *non-separation* of elements in the research process as conveying the 'essence' of all social science – not some reified notion of method or direct appeal to getting in touch with reality.

5 Not so surprising when Glaser and Strauss (1967: 37) themselves state that 'An effective strategy is, at first, literally to ignore the literature of theory and fact on the area under study, in order to assure that the emergence of categories will not be contaminated by concepts more suited to different areas. Similarities and convergences with the literature can be established after the analytic core of categories has emerged.'

6 We wish to thank Ken Parry for drawing this final example to our attention.

7 This raises the difficult question of whether the purposive origin to a data sample places a subsequent 'bias' upon later theoretical sampling decisions. We see this as more of a problem if grounded theory is viewed as merely induced from (i.e., bounded by) the available data. In practice, the grounded theorist depends upon the disciplined use of theoretical sampling decisions, which transcend any origin point, in the search for theoretical saturation.

8 Hence one need not physically collect further empirical data to engage in theoretical sampling – another example where initial data analysis suggests that the subsequent focus should be a core set of 'critical' cases within those already collected.

9 Many computer-aided qualitative data analysis software (CAQDAS) packages overcome this by allowing multiple codings overlapping several segments.

10 It can also help in maintaining the anonymity of participants, so is a way of implementing one of the standard ethical practices in the conduct of qualitative research.

11 Such programs (see also Chapter 23, this volume) are clearly an invaluable aid where a grounded theory project involves large and complex data sets, which the analyst needs to organize, and in the later stages of analysis to efficiently sift and sort for comparisons and emergent relationships. However, what they will *not* do is carry out the hard creative intellectual work of analysis for the researcher.

12 Although 'open coding' (in Strauss and Corbin's terminology) and 'substantive coding' (Glaser's term) arguably involve a very similar practical process, Kendall (1999) notes there are subtle differences in definition. Strauss and Corbin emphasize 'breaking down' or 'fracturing' the data as the first step in analysis, Glaser that of 'emergence' of basic categories from the data. Other researchers also include surprising, interesting or puzzling data facets, which are retrieved or discarded depending upon their subsequent utility.

13 Saturation is, in one sense, both bound up with conceptual coverage of the available data, and simultaneously forever contingent upon possibly new and interesting data identified through further theoretical sampling.

14 It has close parallels to their colleague Leonard Schatzman's idea of dimensional analysis (Schatzman, 1991; Kools and McCarthy, 1996).

15 Although axial coding around condition–context–consequences aligns it closely with Glaser's code family the six C's, and this formulation clearly will be suitable for some researchers and particular research projects (Konecki, 1997; Wright, 1997).

16 We have also observed this happening to our own students.

17 The terms 'fit' and 'work', as coined by Glaser and Strauss, depict the charactistics of grounded theory analyses that signal such plausibility and credibility: conveying a strong *analytic logic*, its underpinnings in the systematic *use of data*, and a *meaningful* picture that can be grasped by people (because its theorizations remain grounded in the actions, interactions, symbolism, common-sense knowledge and human experience making up actual social worlds).

18 Although some commentators' major criticism of poor grounded theory studies is that they present only a descriptive and loosely connected set of themes, along with snippets of data providing no further indication of the way the researcher has conceptualized them (Silverman, 2000), it is also important to be aware of possible differences in people's views of what counts as an appropriate degree of conceptualization and theorization.

19 For example, the theme of 'stability and familiarity', read initially from some participants' remarks as indicating that woods and trees are valued for embodying the ideal of life in a rural idyll, was then explored in more depth and detail in two main ways. First, it seemed to be possible to interpret such claims differently, depending upon a speaker or hearer's status as cultural insider or outsider. Second, despite the obviousness of the idea that people are expressing 'cultural resistance to change', there seemed to be a more encompassing viewpoint – that desire for socio-economic progress and fear of cultural change and loss are both inextricably linked together in discussions of landscape values, social transformation and cultural identity within (and very possibly) beyond Wales. For full comment, see Henwood and Pidgeon (2003).

REFERENCES

Altheide, D.L. and Johnson, J.M. (1994) 'Criteria for assessing interpretive validity in qualitative research', in N.K. Denzin and Y.S. Lincoln (eds), *Handbook of Qualitative Research*. London: Sage, pp. 485–99.

Alvesson, M. and Sköldberg, K. (2000) *Reflexive Methodology: New Vistas for Qualitative Research*. London: Sage.

Atkinson, P. (1995) 'Some perils of paradigms', *Qualitative Health Research*, 5(1): 117–24.

Bailyn, L. (1977) 'Research as a cognitive process: Implications for data analysis', *Quality and Quantity*, 11: 97–117.

Baker, C., Wuest, J. and Stern, P.N. (1992) 'Method slurring: The grounded theory/phenomenology example', *Journal of Advanced Nursing*, 17: 1355–60.

Baszanger, I. (1997) 'Deciphering chronic pain', in A. Strauss and J. Corbin (eds), *Grounded Theory in Practice*. London: Sage, pp. 1–34.

Benoliel-Quint, J. (1996) 'Grounded theory and nursing knowledge', *Qualitative Health Research*, 6(3): 406–29.

Bhavnani, K.-K. (1993) 'Tracing the contours: Feminist research and feminist objectivity', *Women's Studies International Forum*, 16(2): 95–104.

Blaxter, M. (1996) 'Criteria for qualitative research', *Medical Sociology News*, 26(6): 34–7.

Blumer, H. (1954) 'What is wrong with social theory?', *American Sociological Review*, 19: 3–10.

Blumer, H. (1969) *Symbolic Interactionism*. Englewood Cliffs, NJ: Prentice Hall.

Bolger, E.A. (1999) 'Grounded theory analysis of emotional pain', *Psychotherapy Research* 9(3): 342–62.

Brannen, J. (ed.) (1992) *Mixing Methods: Theory and Practice in Combining Quantitative and Qualitative Research*. Aldershot: Avebury.

Brown, M.-A. and Stetz, K. (1999) 'The labour of caregiving: A theoretical model of caregiving during potentially fatal illness', *Qualitative Health Research*, 9(2): 182–97.

Bryman, A. (1988) *Quantity and Quality in Social Research*. London: Unwin Hyman.

Bryman, A. and Burgess, R.G. (1994) 'Developments in qualitative data analysis: An introduction', in A. Bryman and R.G. Burgess (eds), *Analyzing Qualitative Data*. London: Routledge, pp. 1–17.

Bulmer, M. (1979) 'Concepts in the analysis of qualitative data', in M. Bulmer (ed.), *Sociological Research Methods*. London: Macmillan, pp. 241–62.

Burman, E. and Parker, I. (eds) (1993) *Discourse Analytic Research: Repertoires and Readings of Texts in Action*. London: Routledge.

Charmaz, C. (1990) 'Discovering chronic illness: Using grounded theory', *Social Science and Medicine*, 30: 1161–72.

Charmaz, C. (1997) 'Identity dilemmas of chronically ill men', in A. Strauss and J. Corbin (eds) *Grounded Theory in Practice*. London: Sage, pp. 35–62.

Charmaz, K. (2000) 'Grounded theory: Objectivist and subjectivist methods', in N. Denzin and Y. Lincoln (eds), *Handbook of Qualitative Research* (2nd edition). London and Thousand Oaks, CA: Sage, pp. 509–35.

Coffey, A. and Atkinson, P. (1996) *Making Sense of Qualitative Data*. London: Sage.

Costain Schou, K. and Hewison, J. (1996) 'Health psychology and discourse: Personal accounts as social texts in grounded theory', *Journal of Health Psychology*, 3(3): 297–311.

Curtis, S., Gesler, W., Smith, G. and Washburn, S. (2000) 'Approaches to sampling and case selection in qualitative research: Examples in the geography of health', *Social Science and Medicine*, 50: 1001–14.

Cutliffe, J.R. (2000) 'Methodological issues in grounded theory', *Journal of Advanced Nursing*, 31(6): 1476–84.

Davis, K. (1988) *Power under the Microscope*. Dordrecht: Foris.

Denzin, N. (1997) *Interpretive Ethnography*. Thousand Oaks, CA: Sage.

Denzin, N. and Lincoln, Y. (2000) 'The discipline and practice of qualitative research', in N. Denzin and Y. Lincoln (eds), *Handbook of Qualitative Research* (2nd edition). London and Thousand Oaks, CA: Sage, pp. 1–28.

Dewey, J. (1922) *Human Nature and Conduct*. New York: Holt.

Edwards, D., Ashmore, M. and Potter, J. (1995) 'Death and furniture: The rhetoric, politics and theology of bottom line arguments against relativism', *History of the Human Sciences*, 8(2): 25–49.

Elliott, R., Fischer, C.T. and Rennie, D.L. (1999) 'Evolving guidelines for publication of qualitative research in psychology and related fields', *British Journal of Clinical Psychology*, 38: 215–29.

Fielding, N. and Fielding, J. (1986) *Linking Data*. Beverly Hills, CA: Sage.

Flick, U. (1998) *An Introduction to Qualitative Research*. London: Sage.

Fujimura, J. (1997) 'The molecular biology bandwagon in cancer research: Where social worlds meet', in A. Strauss and J. Corbin (eds), *Grounded Theory in Practice*. London: Sage, pp. 95–130.

Game, A. (1991) *Undoing the Social: Towards a Deconstructive Sociology*. Milton Keynes: Open University Press.

Geertz, C. (1973) *The Interpretation of Cultures*. New York: Basic Books.

Gherardi, S. and Turner, B.A. (1999) 'Real men don't collect soft data', in A. Bryman and R.G. Burgess (eds), *Qualitative Research*. London: Sage.

Glaser, B. (1978) *Theoretical Sensitivity: Advances in the Methodology of Grounded Theory*. Mill Valley, CA: Sociology Press.

Glaser, B. (1992) *Emergence versus Forcing: Basics of Grounded Theory Analysis*. Mill Valley, CA: Sociology Press.

Glaser, B. and Strauss, A. (1967) *The Discovery of Grounded Theory*. New York: Aldine.

Gubrium, J. and Holstein, J.A. (2000) 'Analysing interpretive practice', in N. Denzin and Y. Lincoln (eds), *Handbook of Qualitative Research* (2nd edition). London and Thousand Oaks, CA: Sage, pp. 487–508.

Hammersley, M. (1989) *The Dilemma of Qualitative Method: Herbert Blumer and the Chicago Tradition.* London: Routledge.

Hammersley, M. and Atkinson, P. (1983) *Ethnography: Principles in Practice.* London: Routledge.

Haraway, D. (1991) *Simians, Cyborgs and Women: The Reinvention of Nature.* New York: Routledge.

Harding, S. (1991) *Whose Science? Whose Knowledge? Thinking from Women's Lives.* Milton Keynes: Open University Press.

Henwood, K.L. (1993) 'Women and later life: The discursive construction of identities within family relationships', *Journal of Ageing Studies,* 7: 303–19.

Henwood, K.L. (2004) 'Reinventing validity: Reflections on principles from beyond the quality–quantity divide', in Z. Todd, B. Nerlich, S. Mckeown and D. Clarke (eds), *Mixing Methods in Psychology.* London: Routledge.

Henwood, K.L. and Pidgeon, N.F. (1992) 'Grounded theory and psychological theorising', *British Journal of Psychology,* 83: 97–111.

Henwood, K.L. and Pidgeon, N.F. (1994) 'Beyond the qualitative paradigm: A framework for introducing diversity in qualitative psychology', *Journal of Community and Applied Social Psychology,* 4(4): 225–38.

Henwood, K.L. and Pidgeon, N.F. (1995a) 'Grounded theory and psychological research', *Psychologist,* 8(3): 115–18.

Henwood, K.L. and Pidgeon, N.F. (1995b) 'Remaking the link: Qualitative research and feminist standpoint theory', *Feminism and Psychology,* 5(1): 7–30.

Henwood, K.L. and Pidgeon, N.F. (2001) 'Talk about woods and trees: Threat of urbanisation, stability and biodiversity', *Journal of Environmental Psychology,* 21: 125–47.

Henwood, K.L. and Pidgeon, N.F. (2003) 'Grounded theory in psychological research', in P. Camic, L. Yardley and J. Rhodes (eds), *Qualitative Research in Psychology.* Washington, DC: American Psychological Association.

Horlick-Jones, T., Sime, J. and Pidgeon, N.F. (2003) 'The social dynamics of environmental risk perception', in N.F. Pidgeon, R.K. Kasperson and P. Slovic, (eds), *The Social Amplification of Risk.* Cambridge: Cambridge University Press, pp. 262–85.

Houston, H.R. and Venkatesh, A. (1996) 'The health care consumption patterns of Asian immigrants: Grounded theory implications for consumer aculturation theory', *Advances in Consumer Research,* 23: 418–23.

Kelle, U. (1995) *Computer Aided Qualitative Data Analysis: Theory, Methods and Practice.* London: Sage.

Kelle, U. (1997) 'Theory building in qualitative research and computer programs for the management of textual data', *Sociological Research Online,* 2(2). http://www.socresonline.org.uk/socresonline/2/2/1.html.

Kelly, M. (1998) 'Writing a research proposal', in C. Seale (ed.), *Researching Society and Culture.* London: Sage, pp. 111–22.

Kendall, J. (1999) 'Axial coding and the grounded theory controversy', *Western Journal of Nursing Research,* 21(6): 743–57.

Konecki, K. (1997) 'Time in the recruiting search process by headhunting companies', in A. Strauss and J. Corbin (eds) (1997) *Grounded Theory in Practice.* London: Sage, pp. 131–45.

Kools, S. and McCarthy, M. (1996) 'Dimensional analysis: Broadening the conception of grounded theory', *Qualitative Health Research,* 6(3): 312–30.

Kumar, S. and Gantley, M. (1999) 'Tensions between policy makers and general practitioners in implementing new genetics: Grounded theory interview study', *British Medical Journal,* 319: 1410–13.

Layder, D. (1982) 'Grounded theory: A constructive critique', *Journal for the Theory of Social Behaviour,* 12(1): 103–23.

Layder, D. (1993) *New Strategies in Social Research.* Cambridge: Polity Press.

Lempert, L.B. (1997) 'The line in the sand: Definitional dialogues in abusive relationships', in A. Strauss and J. Corbin (eds), *Grounded Theory in Practice.* London: Sage, pp. 147–70.

Lincoln, Y.S. (1995) 'Emerging criteria for quality in qualitative and interpretive research', *Qualitative Inquiry,* 1(3): 275–89.

Lincoln, Y. and Guba, E. (1985) *Naturalistic Inquiry.* Beverly Hills, CA: Sage.

Marshall, C. and Rossman, G.B. (1999) *Designing Qualitative Research* (3rd edition). London: Sage.

Martin, P.Y. and Turner, B.A. (1986) 'Grounded theory and organizational research', *Journal of Applied Behavioral Science,* 22: 141–57.

Mason, J. (1996) *Qualitative Researching.* London: Sage.

Maynard, M. and Purvis, J. (1994) 'Doing feminist research', in M. Maynard and J. Purvis (eds), *Researching Women's Lives from a Feminist Perspective.* London: Taylor and Francis, pp. 1–9.

Mead, G.H. (1934) *Mind, Self and Society.* Chicago: University of Chicago Press.

Merton, R.K. (1957) *Social Theory and Social Structure.* Glencoe, IL: Free Press.

Michie, S., McDonald, V. and Marteau, T. (1996) 'Understanding responses to predictive genetic testing: A grounded theory approach', *Psychology and Health,* 11: 455–70.

Miles, M.B. and Huberman, A.M. (1994) *Qualitative Data Analysis* (2nd edition). Beverly Hills, CA: Sage.

Morse, J.M. (1991) 'Strategies for sampling', in J.M. Morse (ed.), *Qualitative Nursing Research.* London: Sage, pp. 126–45.

Opie, A. (1992) 'Qualitative research, appropriation of the other and empowerment', *Feminist Review*, 40: 52–69.

Orona, C.J. (1990) 'Temporality and identity loss due to Alzeimer's disease', *Social Science and Medicine*, 10: 1247–56.

Patton, M.Q. (1990) *Qualitative Evaluation and Research Methods* (2nd edition). London: Sage.

Peirce C.S. (1965) *Collected Papers of Charles Sanders Peirce* (C. Hartshorne and P. Weiss, eds). Cambridge, MA: Belknap Press.

Pidgeon, N.F and Henwood, K.L. (1996) 'Grounded theory: practical implementation', in J.T.E. Richardson (ed.), *Handbook of Qualitative Research Methods for Psychology and the Social Sciences*. Leicester: British Psychological Society Books, pp. 86–101.

Pidgeon, N.F., Turner, B.A. and Blockley, D.I. (1991) 'The use of grounded theory for conceptual analysis in knowledge elicitation', *International Journal of Man–Machine Studies*, 35: 151–73.

Potter, J. and Wetherell, M. (1987) *Discourse and Social Psychology*. London: Sage.

Reeves, T.K. and Turner, B.A. (1972) 'A theory of organisation in batch production factories', *Administrative Science Quarterly*, 17: 81–98.

Reicher, S. (2000) 'Against methodolatry: Some comments on Elliot, Fischer and Rennie', *British Journal of Clinical Psychology*, 39: 1–6.

Rennie, D. (1992) 'Qualitative analysis of the clients' experience of psychotherapy: The unfolding of reflexivity', in S. Toukmanian and D. Rennie (eds), *Psychotherapy Process Research: Paradigmatic and Narrative Approaches*. Newbury Park, CA: Sage, pp. 211–233.

Rennie, D. (2000) 'Grounded theory methodology as methodological hermeneutics: Reconciling realism and relativism', *Theory and Psychology*, 10(4): 481–502.

Robson, C. (1998) *Real World Research* (2nd edition). Oxford: Blackwell.

Sarlio-Lähteenkorva, S. (2000) '"The battle is not over after weight-loss": Stories of successful weight loss maintenance', *Health*, 4(1): 73–88.

Schatzman, L. (1991) 'Dimensional analysis: Notes on an alternative approach to the grounding of theory in qualitative research', in D.R. Maines (ed.), *Social Organization and Social Process*. New York: Aldine de Gruyter.

Schwandt, T. (1996) 'Farewell to criteriology', *Qualitative Inquiry*, 2(1): 58–72.

Schwandt, T. (2000) 'Three epistemological stances for qualitative inquiry: Interpretivism, hermeneutics and social constructionism', in N. Denzin and Y. Lincoln (eds), *Handbook of Qualitative Research* London: Sage, pp. 189–214.

Seale, C. (1999) *The Quality of Qualitative Research*. London: Sage.

Silverman, D. (1993) *Interpreting Qualitative Data: Methods for Analysing Talk, Text and Action*. London: Sage.

Silverman, D. (1997) 'Towards an aesthetics of research', *Qualitative Research: Theory, Method and Practice*. London: Sage, pp. 239–53.

Silverman, D. (2000) *Doing Qualitative Research: A Practical Handbook*. London: Sage.

Smith, D. (1974) 'Women's perspective as a radical critique of sociology', *Sociological Quarterly*, 44: 7–13.

Smith, J.K. and Deemer, D.K. (2000) 'The problem of criteria in an age of relativism', in N. Denzin and Y. Lincoln (eds), *Handbook of Qualitative Research* (2nd edition). London: Sage, pp. 877–96.

Smith, K. and Biley, F. (1997) 'Understanding grounded theory: Principles and evaluation', *Nursing Researcher*, 4: 17–30.

Stern, P. N. (1994) 'Eroding grounded theory', in J.M. Morse (ed.), *Critical Issues in Qualitative Research Methods*. Thousand Oaks, CA: Sage, pp. 212–23.

Strauss, A. (1970) 'Discovering new theory from previous theory', in T. Shibutani (ed.), *Human Nature and Collective Behavior*. Englewood Cliffs, NJ: Prentice Hall.

Strauss, A. (1987) *Qualitative Analysis for Social Scientists*. Cambridge: Cambridge University Press.

Strauss, A. and Corbin, J. (1994) 'Grounded theory methodology', in N. Denzin and Y. Lincon (eds), *Handbook of Qualitative Research* (1st edition). Thousand Oaks, CA: Sage.

Strauss, A. and Corbin, J. (eds) (1997) *Grounded Theory in Practice*. London: Sage.

Strauss, A. and Corbin, J. (1998) *Basics of Qualitative Research* (2nd edition). London: Sage.

Taber, K.S. (2000) 'Case studies and generalisability: Grounded theory and research in science education', *International Journal of Science Education*, 22(5): 469–87.

Thomas, W.I. (1966) *On Social Organisation and Personality* (ed. M. Janowitz). Chicago: University of Chicago Press.

Todd, Z., Nerlich, B., Mckeown, S. and Clarke, D. (eds) (2004) *Mixing Methods in Psychology*. London: Routledge.

Tukey, J.W. (1977) *Exploratory Data Analysis*. Reading, MA: Addison-Wesley.

Tuler, S. and Thomas, W. (1999) 'Voices from the forest: What participants expect of a public participation process', *Science and Natural Resources*, 12(5): 437–51.

Turner, B.A. (1976) 'The organizational and interorganizational development of disasters', *Administrative Science Quarterly*, 21: 378–97.

Turner, B.A. (1978) *Man Made Disasters*. London: Wykham Press.

Turner, B.A. (1981) 'Some practical aspects of qualitative data analysis: One way of organizing the cognitive processes associated with the generation of grounded theory', *Quality and Quantity*, 15: 225–47.

Turner, B.A. (1988) 'Connoisseurship in the study of organizational cultures', in A. Bryman (ed.), *Doing Research in Organizations*. London: Routledge, pp. 108–21.

Turner, B.A. and Pidgeon, N.F. (1997) *Man Made Disasters* (2nd edition). Oxford: Butterworth-Heinemann.

Vaughan, D. (1992) 'Theory elaboration: The heuristics of case analysis', in H. Becker and C. Ragin (eds), *What is a Case?* New York: Cambridge University Press, pp. 173–202.

Weiner, C.L. (1975) 'The burden of rheumatoid arthritis: Tolerating the uncertainty', *Social Science and Medicine*, 9(2): 97–104.

Weitzman, E. (2000) 'Software and qualitative research', in N. Denzin and Y. Lincoln (eds), *Handbook of Qualitative Research*. London: Sage, pp. 803–20.

Willott, S. and Griffin, C. (1999) 'Building your own lifeboat: Working class offenders talk about economic crime', *British Journal of Social Psychology*, 38(4): 445–60.

Woolgar, S. (1988) *Science: The Very Idea*. London: Tavistock.

Wright, K.B. (1997) 'Shared ideology in alcoholics anonymous: A grounded theory approach', *Journal of Health Communication*, 2(2): 83–100.

Wuest, J. (2000) 'Negotiating with helping systems: An example of grounded theory evolving through emergent fit', *Qualitative Health Research*, 10(1): 51–70.

Yardley, L. (2000) 'Dilemmas in qualitative health research', *Psychology and Health*, 15: 215–28.

## 29

The Uses of Narrative in Social Science Research

BARBARA CZARNIAWSKA

THE EVER-PRESENT NARRATIVE

The narratives of the world are numberless. Narrative is first and foremost a prodigious variety of genres, themselves distributed amongst different substances – as though any material were fit to receive man's stories. Able to be carried by articulated language, spoken or written, fixed or moving images, gestures, and the ordered mixture of all these substances; narrative is present in myth, legend, fable, tale, novella, epic, history, tragedy, drama, comedy, mime, painting ... stained glass windows, cinema, comics, news item, conversation. Moreover, under this almost infinite diversity of forms, narrative is present in every age, in every place, in every society; it begins with the very history of mankind and there nowhere is nor has been a people without narrative. All classes, all human groups, have their narratives ... Caring nothing for the division between good and bad literature, narrative is international, transhistorical, transcultural: it is simply there, like life itself. (Barthes, 1977: 79)

By this definition, practically all human forms of expression are narratives or at least can be treated as such. This by now classic statement of Barthes, at the time of its utterance, summarized a growing interest in narratives that had begun much earlier. The tales of origins are many and conflicting, as the beginnings of narrative analysis can be well placed in the hermeneutic studies of the Bible, Talmud and Koran, but it is usual to relate them to a work of the Russian formalist,

Vladimir Propp, who in 1928 published his *Morphology of the Folktale*, meticulously analyzing what he saw as the underlying structure of Russian folktales. Russian formalists and then post-formalists such as Mikhail Bakhtin continued to develop their approaches to narrative analysis, but it first received wider recognition in 1958 when Propp's book was translated into French and English, and it has been the second English edition, that of 1968, which has met with great attention within and outside literary theory.

The literary study of narrative, claims Donald E. Polkinghorne (1987) has its origins in four national traditions: Russian formalism, American new criticism, French structuralism and German hermeneutics. Much of contemporary linguistic and narrative analysis can be traced back to the disciples of two comparative linguists: the Pole Jan Niecislaw Baudoin de Courtenay (1845–1929) and the Swiss Ferdinand de Saussure (1857–1913).[1] The Russian revolution put an end to the cooperation between East and West, but émigrés such as Roman Jakobson (linguist), Tzvetan Todorov (literary theorist) and Algirdas Greimas (semiologist) continued to develop the eastern European tradition in France, while Mikhail Bakhtin and others persevered in their efforts behind the Iron Curtain.

What all these movements had in common, and contrary to traditional hermeneutics, was their interest in texts as such, not in the author's intentions or the circumstances of the text's production. Such was the main tenet of the new criticism, as represented by Northrop Frye and Robert Scholes, who looked for universal plots but also for the evolution of the narrative in history. The French narratologists such as Tzvetan Todorov and Roland Barthes were more under the influence of the structuralism of the anthropologist Claude Lévi-Strauss, who, along with Noam Chomsky, looked for the invariable structure of the universal human mind. Wolfgang Iser and Hans Robert Jauss have both extended and criticized Gadamer's hermeneutics (Gadamer, 1975) and created their own reception theory, where Iser especially puts emphasis on the interaction between the reader and the text (Iser, 1978). And, last but not least, there was, and is, the formidable presence of Paul Ricoeur, who took into consideration those aspects of various schools that related to his main interest: the relation between temporality and narrative (Ricoeur, 1984, 1986).

This interest in narrative spread beyond literary theory to the humanities and social sciences. Hayden White shocked his brethren by claiming that there can be no discipline of history, only of historiography, as the historians emplot the events into histories, instead of 'finding' them (White, 1973). William Labov and Joshua Waletzky espoused and improved on Propp's formalist analysis, suggesting that sociolinguistics should occupy itself with a syntagmatic analysis of simple narratives, which will eventually provide a key to the understanding of the structure and function of complex narratives (Labov and Waletzky, 1967: 12–13). Richard Harvey Brown, in a peculiar act of parallel invention, spoke of 'a poetics for sociology' (Brown, 1977), unaware that Mikhail Bakhtin had postulated it almost half of a century before him (Bakhtin and Medvedev, 1985).

By the end of the 1970s the trickle became a stream. Walter R. Fisher (1984) pointed out the central role of narrative in politics and of narrative analysis in political sciences, Donald E. Polkinghorne (1987) did the same for the humanities but especially psychology, and Deirdre McCloskey (1990) scrutinized the narrative of economic expertise. By the 1990s, narrative analysis had become a common approach in science studies (Curtis, 1994; Silvers, 1995).

This 'literary turn' in the social sciences has been legitimated by a claim that narrative knowledge, all modernist claims notwithstanding, is the main bearer of knowledge in our societies (Lyotard, 1984; Bruner, 1986, 1990). Although its main competitor, the logico-scientific kind of knowledge, has a higher legitimacy status in modern societies, the everyday use of the narrative form is all-pervasive. Graduate students read mountains of books on methods, like this one, but when they want to submit their first paper to a refereed journal, they ask a colleague who has already published: 'How did you go about it?' The method books are accompanied by growing numbers of biographies and autobiographies, and they themselves are richly illustrated with stories.

What is more, it is useful to think of an enacted narrative as the most typical form of social life, pointed out Alasdair MacIntyre (1981: 129). This is not an ontological claim; life might or might not be an enacted narrative, but conceiving of it as such provides a rich source of insight. This suggestion is at least as old as Shakespeare, and has been taken up and elaborated upon by Kenneth Burke (1969), Clifford Geertz (1980), Victor Turner (1982), Ian Mangham and Michael Overrington (1987), and many others.

Thirdly, but not least important, narratives are a common mode of communication (Fisher, 1984, 1987). People tell stories to entertain, to teach and to learn, to ask for an interpretation and to give one.

Therefore, a student of social life, no matter of which domain, needs to become interested in narrative as a form of knowledge, a form of social life, and a form of communication. This necessity was easily accepted by researchers into family life (Mishler, 1986) or life stories (Linde, 1993), but was not at all obvious in such domains as my own specialty, organization studies. Modern work organizations were seen as a site of production, of dominance, and of other forms of knowledge, such as technical knowledge and logico-scientific knowledge.

The presence of technical knowledge in the organizational context was taken for granted and seldom scrutinized before the sudden rise of studies of science and technology. In the meantime, the main pretenders for the form of knowledge most relevant to render the complexity of organizing were narrative knowledge and logico-scientific knowledge, technical knowledge often seen as a by-product of the latter.

Jerome Bruner (1986, 1990) has succinctly contrasted the two forms of knowledge, showing that narrative knowledge tells the story of human intentions and deeds, and situates them in time and space. It mixes the objective and the subjective aspects, relating the world as people see it, often substituting chronology for causality. In contrast, the logico-scientific knowledge looks for cause–effect connections to explain the world, attempts to formulate general laws from such connections, and contains procedures to verify/falsify its own results. In its style of presentation, it gives a preference to tables, typologies and lists (inventories), like the one here.

The contest between the two concerned both the kind of knowledge used in the field of practice, and the kind of knowledge to be produced by the field of theory for the benefit of this practice. In what follows, I shall be using examples mostly from the field of practice known as management, and from the field of theory known as organization theory. The reasons for this, apart from the obvious one that it is the field I know best, are twofold. First, I agree with Perrow's (1991) observation that modern societies are organized through and through. Children in a day-care center learn the rudiments of effective organizing, and churches rekindle their ancient knowledge of finance management. Managerialism, for good or bad, is swamping sectors and fields of life that before felt safely excluded from it: health care, culture production, universities (Power, 1997). Secondly, economic organizations were traditionally protected from cultural analysis – as sites 'outside culture', where neither art nor literary criticism could apply – by the claim of closeness to natural phenomena. This claim, most obviously formulated by economists who purport to be discovering the 'natural laws of economy', was forcefully contested by those economists who joined the 'literary turn' (e.g. McCloskey, 1986, 1990). Although there were always close ties between 'culture', in the sense of the arts, and economics, at present the ties are even closer and need to be recognized and taken into account.

It is not difficult to accept that narrative knowledge is ubiquitous in all social practices. Managers and their subordinates tell stories and write stories, to one another and to interviewers, be they researchers or journalists. So do doctors and patients, teachers and pupils, salespersons and customers, coaches and footballers. The genre of autobiography – personal and organizational – is steadily growing in popularity, while the older types of stories – folktales, myths and sagas – acquire new forms thanks to new technologies and new media.

A student of social practices retells narratives of a given practice and constructs them herself, first- and secondhand. Nevertheless, she cannot stop there, as by doing that she will be barely competing with the practitioners themselves, and from a disadvantaged position. She must go further and see how the narratives of practice unfold. This interest can lead her to a stance espousing the ideas of logico-scientific knowledge, as formalism and structuralism tended to do, but this is not a stance represented in this text. The analyses I intend to present are closer to the poststructuralist edge of the spectrum of narratology. Such an analysis does not look for chains of causes and effects but for frequent ('usual') connections between various elements of a narrative. It does not search for laws, but for patterns and regularities, which do not reveal a deep structure – either of the world or of the mind – but which are affixed to a text by the writer and the reader alike. The reader is able to see how a text was made not because she divines the writer's intentions, or comprehends universal human nature, but because reader and writer are both producers and consumers of the same set of human institutions.

But what, if any, is the relevance of the institution of narrating (e.g., literature) for the institution of organizing (e.g., management)? Narrating is organizing, and although organizing is more than narrating, even that part of it that is non-narrative can become a topic of a narration. One cannot repair a machine by telling how it was done, but one can always tell a story about the repair. This can also be restated in the terms used by Ricoeur (1981) when he claims that a text is a fitting analogy for an action just as an action is a proper analogy for a text.

Figure 29.1 depicts various uses of narrative and its analysis in social science studies, and summarizes the contents of the present chapter.

FIELD OF PRACTICE AS A SITE OF A NARRATIVE PRODUCTION, CIRCULATION AND CONSUMPTION

Watching how stories are made

The quote from Barthes with which this chapter opens represents the most inclusive definition of

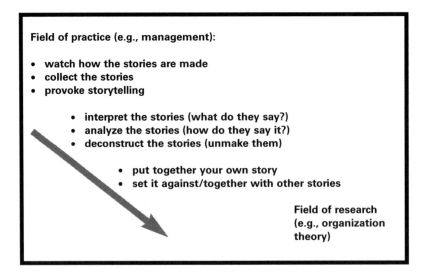

Figure 29.1   *Uses of narrative in social science studies*

narrative encountered in texts on narrative analysis. Such definitions are, and were, many, as signaled by the desperate tone of Richard Harvey Brown writing for a collection under the editorship of W.J.T. Mitchell, reprinted later as the book *On Narrative* (1981):

> What is narrative? To judge from the plethora of definitions, the lexical disparity and conflicting assumptions of the essays gathered here, one might conclude that the gods themselves disagree, that the literati do not share a clear conception of narrative. Such a judgment would be correct. For despite prescient efforts by our editor, there has not emerged a focused vision of narrative among those who are creating a new literary history (Brown, 1980: 545)

Usually, however, a narrative is understood as a spoken or written text giving an account of an event or series of events, chronologically connected. Indeed, it is easy to say what is not a narrative even if it is a text: a table, a list, a scheme, a typology (Goody, 1986). But Hayden White, who also contributed to Mitchell's (1981) anthology, convincingly demonstrated the advantages of a narrower definition of narrative, indeed of differentiating between a narrative and a story. He further developed his ideas in *The Content of the Form* (1987), describing how the way of writing history changed with time. Annals registered only some dates and events, not attempting to connect them. Chronicles presented causal connections, but were devoid of plot, or a meaningful structure. Only the

more modern way of writing history can earn recognition as a 'story' that is more than a chronological compilation. White (1987: 16) quotes the example of the 'Annals of Saint Gall' as most typical of early European historiography:

> 709. Hard winter. Duke Gottfried died.
> 710. Hard winter and deficient in crops.
> 711.
> 712. Flood everywhere.
> 713.
> 714. Pippin, mayor of the palace, died.
> 715.716.717.
> 718. Charles devastated the Saxons with great destruction.
> 719.
> 720. Charles fought against the Saxons.
> 721. Theudo drove the Saracens out of Aquitaine.
> 722. Great crops.
> 723.
> 724.
> 725. Saracens came for the first time.
> 726.727.728.729.730.
> 731. Blessed Bede, the presbyter, died.
> 732. Charles fought against the Saracens at Poitiers on Saturday.
> 733.
> 734.

If the monks of Saint Gall had decided to turn their annals into a chronicle, it could have looked like this:

> The year 709 was the beginning of harsh times for the land all around us. Two hard winters inevitably

led to bad crops, and people were dying like flies. Among them was Duke Gottfried, mourned by all his people. And while it seemed that nature became benevolent again, flood struck in 712.

After that, however, God took mercy on his people. For a good five years nothing much happened, apart from the fact that Pippin, mayor of the palace, died. The great leader, Charles, successfully combated the Saxons in 718 and in 720, while his ally, Theudo, drove the Saracens out of Aquitaine. Crops were great in 722, and the land enjoyed peace when, in 725, the Saracens came for the first time. They were defeated, but came again in 732, and reached as far as Poitiers. This happened almost immediately after Blessed Bede, our presbyter, died.

This is a narrative but, says White, it is still not a story as it lacks a plot. Or, to be more exact, this is how White (1987: 17) characterized the difference between a chronicle and a (hi)story, on the example of *History of France* by Richerus of Rheims (c. 998):

> We have no difficulty recognizing this text as a narrative. It has a central subject ...; a proper geographical center ... and a proper social center ...; and the proper beginning in time ... . But the work fails as proper history, at least according to the opinion of later commentators, by virtue of two considerations. First, the order of the discourse follows the order of chronology; it presents events in the order of their occurrence and cannot, therefore, offer the kind of meaning that a narratologically governed account can be said to provide. Second, probably owing to the 'annalistic' order of discourse, the account does not so much conclude as simply terminate; it merely breaks off ... and throws onto the reader the burden of retrospectively reflecting on the linkages between the beginning of the account and its ending.

How might one go about completing the chronicle of St. Gall into a proper story? Such stories, or histories, can be several, depending on who writes them. A contemporary historian, careful not to jump to conclusions, might write simply thus:

> As we can see, the early history of Europe was a constant fight against hostile nature and hostile invaders.

A monk of Saint Gall, having taken a course in narrative writing, would be more likely to write something along the following lines

> As we can see, the early history of France was the history of a people tried severely by their God who, however, was their only solace. When Blessed Bede died, Charles found it very difficult to lead his soldiers against the Saracens. But a great Mass was told on Sunday, after the victory.

(the added information about the Mass is a deduction from the fact that the battle was fought on Saturday). Finally, a theoretician of management who tends to exaggerate the import of leadership, could emplot it still differently:

> As we can see, the presence of a strong leader was crucial for the survival of the people. When Duke Gottfried died, hard winter, deficient crops and flood were felt painfully. When Charles took his place before his people, the hardship of nature ceased to occupy the minds of the people, who bravely fought at the side of their leader.

What prompted me to apply White's recipe for a chronicle and a history to the text of the 'Annals' was the analogy I saw between these three forms and the storymaking that I was able to watch during my study of the city of Stockholm (Czarniawska, 1999b). The register of my direct observation resembled annals, even if contemporary metrology permits a more detailed measure of time. Only an additional column, added by me in what was already an interpretative attempt, revealed that many of these seemingly disconnected events and actions were related to the common topic: the city administration was being divided into districts. Interviews with people engaged in carrying the reform through resembled chronicles: they reported the chronological and causal chains of events, but did not have a point, or a plot. After some time, however, complete stories begin to emerge.

One day at a city office (observation)

Time	Event/Action	Topic
08.00	Moving into the new office. People move up and down the corridor, carry boxes, arrange the coffee room.	Practical problems related to the DR
08.30	Conversation with the researcher in a car on the way to the training & development center	The role of research in municipal administration. DR
09.00	Coffee chat (a lengthy delay on the subway system prevented most of the course participants from arriving on time)	
09.45	Introduction to the course	The new management model and economic

		system resulting from DR
10.30	Return to the office. A tour around new offices, chats.	Practical aspects of DR: office and personnel
10.45	Work at the computer	?
11.10	A ventilation specialist comes in	Ventilation problems.
…	…	…

DR = district reform

District reform (interview with the project leader)
In the autumn of 1994 the mayor called to his office the head of one of the district social care centers, who was known for her positive attitude towards the idea of dividing the city administration into districts. She was informed that the majority had reached a decision to decentralize city administration and that she had been chosen to be responsible for the whole project.

After many earlier hesitations, this time all the political parties but one collaborated on formulation of guidelines for the reform and supported the nomination of the project leader. Her immediate task was to collect all the information necessary to implement the decision. Many practical details were still open for discussion, as the decision concerned the principle and only few issues were clear.

The project leader received extensive authority for her activity. Her first decision was to create a temporary network that would include all the municipal managers, rather than forming a new office for the reform. Her staff was very limited, consisting of three investigators who had extensive knowledge about most of the operations gathered under the municipal umbrella. As the reform required a new division of economic resources, the team was complemented with an economist, a person responsible for information, and a secretary. In time, a computer specialist was added. The team set to work on a detailed inventory of municipal activities. City managers were called to their first meeting with the reform team.

On January 1, 1997, the division of Stockholm's administration into 24 district offices and committees was a fact.

The story of the district reform *(interview with the head of the office, my attempt at discerning main elements that make up the story in the left-hand column)*

Move₁ It started as a political question: The conservatives were very doubtful, but the Social Democrats were always very interested. The other parties – center, liberals, and greens – were in favor, because they wanted to decentralize power away from the city hall. Thus when the Social Democrats came to power in 1994 they immediately ordered an investigation that was completed after 6 months, and of course gave a positive answer to the question.

Complication₁ They checked around and invited many researchers from Gothenburg, which had introduced this reform earlier on. Well, it is always possible to interpret research results in many ways. In my reading it was a total failure, but those who were responsible say that it was a great success. Politicians are always pleased with what they have done. They also say that they saved a lot of money, but I would like to point out that districts could show positive results because city hall ended with a deficit of a billion kronor every year. So I guess it depends how one counts. At any rate, we have Gothenburg as an ambiguous example, and then most other municipalities in Sweden who backed away from the district reform, deciding it was a failure. Big companies that want to save money reduce the number of their divisions and centralize, but we spend lavishly on decentralizing. For some reason Stockholm is always the last to catch the latest fad.

Complication₂ This year, 1996, the municipality invested 200 million kronor in reorganization, with the justification that it will bring in a billion in savings per year, due to resulting rationalization, synergy effects and increased effectiveness.

Equilibrium₂ As it is now, I think that we need to prove to the inhabitants that we really did save this billion and turned it to their advantage. But nobody listens to me. No wonder, as it is practically impossible to show. And if it is impossible to show it next year, the explanation will be that this billion vanished in quality improvement. And this could mean anything: free school lunches, more teaching hours, more care workers, more public transportation for the elderly. And so on year after year. Nobody would dare to ask: Do children enjoy school more? Do they learn more at school than in other European countries? Do we have the best or the worst schools in the world? But this is of course impossible to measure and to tie to money, spent or saved.

Moral So everything is as usual: politicians do everything they can to avoid measuring the actual quality.

The three excerpts above demonstrate *that* making sense is a retrospective process, requiring time, but they do not actually show *how* the narrative is woven from disparate events. This is difficult to evince because of the inevitable conflict between 'the prospective orientation of life with the retrospective orientation of narrative' (Ryan, 1993: 138). It is impossible to monitor the actors in order to capture the moments during which they elaborate their life experience into a story (in the example above, the minimum period of time would have been 3 years). Yet Marie-Laure Ryan (1993: 150) succeeded in locating what she calls 'a factory of plot': live radio broadcasts of sports events. There, 'the real life situation promotes a narrative tempo in which the delay between the time of occurrence of the narrated events and the time of their verbal representation strives toward zero, and the duration of the narration approximates the duration of the narrated' (Ryan, 1993: 138).

A broadcast is constructed around three dimensions: *the chronicle* (what is happening), *the mimesis* (how it looks, a dimension that allows the listener to construct a virtual picture of the events), and the emplotment (introducing structure which allows sense to be made of the events).

While emplotment is considered central for building a story (White, 1987), it is obviously the chronicle that is central to a sports broadcast. The necessity of matching the narrative time to a real time creates specific challenges and responses. One is 'empty time' (the 'missing years' in the annals), when 'nothing' is happening on the field, and the broadcasters fill it with past stories and general chat, at the risk of being caught in the middle of the story by a new event. Another is the congestion of events, a problem usually solved by quickening the pace of speech, sometimes to an impossible speed.

One way of filling empty time is to turn it to the service of the mimetic dimension of the broadcast. When there is a lull after a dramatic event, this event can be retold with an emphasis on how it happened.

The real challenge, however, is the emplotment of the broadcast. The broadcasters, says Ryan (1993: 141), perform it using three basic operations: *constructing characters*, that is, introducing legible differences between the actors (a hero and an opponent); *attributing a function* to single events; and *finding an interpretive theme* that subsumes the events and links them in a meaningful sequence ('near success', 'near failure', etc.).

The close analogy between sports events and organizational performance in contemporary societies has been extensively commented upon (Corvellec, 1997). Indeed, the spectators (e.g., the shareholders) insist on seeing the chronicle of the events, not least because they want to have an opportunity to make their own emplotment. Although the real interest concerns the plot ('why do you have losses?'), the loosely espoused principles of logico-scientific knowledge turn the attention away from the operation of emplotment. Plots are given (in the form of scientific laws), so the only activity required is to recognize their pattern in the chronicle. This hiding of the emplotment process results in the scarce interest in mimesis – on the part of the actors, spectators, and observers/researchers alike. And yet it is the mimesis, the how, that offers most clues as to the way events become connected with the help of an accessible repertoire of plots.

The Kalevala style of management

The chairman of a US university department told me that when newly appointed, he tried to draw the lines for the future development of the department. After being constantly rebuked by his colleagues, he changed tactics and went around collecting 'narratives of identity', just like the good Finnish doctor who is supposed to have collected his country's treasure of stories that became famous as the mythology of Kalevala. The chairman acquired a similar treasure – he could now tell the identity of the department better than any of his senior colleagues – and that earned him authority and respect (Seth Lerer, personal communication).

Not all managers have such a humble and understanding attitude toward their task – many fabricate and circulate stories with a clear ambition to manipulate. Nevertheless, each workplace has a contemporary and historical repertoire of stories, sometimes divided into 'internal stories' and 'external stories', sometimes stories spread abroad with a hope of their return in a more legitimate form, for example via mass media (Kunda, 1992). Any researcher who cares to spend some time in an organization, listening to what is told and reading some of its textual production, will encounter such narratives, and will sometimes be allowed to directly observe their practical use (see Boje, 1991, for a study of narrative performances).

Sabine Helmers and Regina Buhr (1994) carried out a field study in a large German company producing typewriters. They spent three weeks in the company, conducting interviews and observing. During their stay several interlocutors, all men, told them the following story:

The Tactful Typewriter Mechanic

The new secretary had called in the mechanic many times because her electric typewriter kept making spaces where they didn't belong. After trying unsuccessfully to find the cause, the mechanic decided to observe the secretary at work for a while. He soon discovered the problem. The girl, generously endowed with feminine attractions, kept hitting the space key involuntarily every time she bent forward. The mechanic showed that he was capable of dealing with this rather delicate situation. He found the excuse to send her out of the office and raised her swivel-chair four centimeters. Since then she has had no problems with her machine and has nothing but praise for the excellent mechanic. (Helmers and Buhr, 1994: 176)

At first, say Helmers and Buhr, they did not pay much attention to the story, but its repetitions made them curious. The story was told as if the event had taken place the day before, but the attempt to trace it led them to an Austrian in-house publication for a typewriter dealer dated 2 June 1963 (the excerpt is quoted from that source). Thus a practically ancient story was kept alive by retelling it, and was given relevance by situating it contemporarily and in the narrators' own company. The tale had its 'sisters' in other companies, industries, countries, and times. Helmers and Buhr were able to show that such stereotyping of women as 'dumb blondes' actually hampered the technological developments in the typewriter industry. Stories of the kind they encountered redefined many technically solvable machine errors as 'users' problems'.

Joanne Martin (1990) attended a conference sponsored by a major US university, dedicated to the ways that individuals and businesses might help to solve societal problems. One of the participants, the chief executive of a large transnational, told the conference participants the following story:

We have a young woman who is extraordinarily important to the launching of a major new (product). We will be talking about it next Tuesday in its first worldwide introduction. She has arranged to have her Caesarian yesterday in order to be prepared for this event, so you – We have insisted that she stay home and this is going to be televised in a closed circuit television, so we're having this done by TV for her, and she is staying home three months and we are finding ways of filling in to create this void for us because we think it's an important thing for her to do. (Martin, 1990: 339)

Unlike the Helmers and Buhr story, this one was found disembedded from its original context, recontextualized into the space of the conference. Accordingly, instead of following its connections through time and space, Martin decided to deconstruct and reconstruct the story from a feminist standpoint. The deconstruction revealed evidence of a suppressed gender conflict in work organizations, illuminating blind spots of management practice and theory that fueled the conflict and kept it out of view.

Boland and Tankasi (1995) took a critical view of 'collecting' organizational narratives, as if they were artifacts forever petrified in organizational reality waiting to be 'discovered' by a researcher. Yet every narrative becomes new with each retelling, and the 'petrification' of narratives is not the result of the myopia of the researcher, but of intensive stabilizing work by the narrators. Long-lived narratives are sediments of norms and practices, and as such deserve careful attention.

How to prompt for narratives in an interview situation

'Telling stories is far from unusual in everyday conversation and it is apparently no more unusual for interviewees to respond to questions with narratives if they are given some room to speak' (Mishler, 1986: 69). An interview situation can thus easily become a micro-site for production of narratives, or just an opportunity to circulate them, where a researcher is allowed to partake in narratives previously produced. In many cases answers given in an interview are spontaneously formed into narratives. This is usually the case for interviews aiming at life histories, or, in an organizational context, at career descriptions, where a narrative is explicitly asked for and delivered. This is also the case for interviews aiming at a historical description of a certain process. When the topic of an interview is a reform, or reorganization, that is, a chain of events that unfold in time, there is nothing unusual in formulating a question that prompts a narrative: 'Could you tell me the story of the budget reform as you experienced it?' or 'Can you recall when you first started to talk about the necessity of reorganizing your department? And what happened next?'

This does not mean that research interviews always evoke narratives. Unlike spontaneous conversation, they may incite a conscious avoidance of narratives insofar as they are constructed as arenas where only logico-scientific knowledge can be legitimately produced. Both sides have to combat the shared conviction that 'true knowledge' is not made of narratives. 'What were the factors that made a reorganization necessary?' will be perceived as a more 'scientific' question, prompting analytic answers. It is thus a task of the interviewer to 'activate narrative production' (Holstein and Gubrium, 1997: 123).

How, then, to obtain narratives in a situation which prompts the use of the logic of representation and offers many possibilities of avoiding an account? The ethnomethodologist and founder of conversation analysis, Harvey Sacks (1992), put emphasis on the way 'membership categorization' is used in construction of meaningful narratives (see also Baker, 1997). Switching from the vocabulary of ethnomethodology to that of narratology, one could say that membership categories are descriptions of *characters*, one of the necessary elements of every narrative. 'I' is just a personal pronoun, 'a woman of 35' a statistical category, but 'a mother of a family of five' is already a beginning of a narrative. Introducing a tentative membership categorization is a ploy that often works. A character must know his or her lines, and deliver them accordingly, or protest the categorization and offer an alternative account.

The other necessary element of a useful narrative is a *plot*. Narratives based on sheer chronology are of little use in interpretation. The regular occurrence of Tuesdays after Mondays can hardly produce any profound insights into the nature of organizing, unless the construction of a calendar is being discussed. Although narratives always engage the *logic of succession* (albeit not always in a straightforward manner), stories also involve the *logic of transformation* (Todorov, 1990). The minimal plot, says Todorov (1977: 111),

consists in the passage from one equilibrium to another. An 'ideal' narrative begins with a stable situation, which is disturbed by some power or force. There results a state of disequilibrium; by the action of a force directed in the opposite direction, the equilibrium is re-established; the second equilibrium is similar to the first, but the two are never identical.

The second equilibrium may resemble the first or reverse it. A company in trouble may reorganize and become profitable again, or it may go into bankruptcy. The episode that describes the passage from one state to another can have one or many elements. There can be one single force that changes the state of affairs into another one ('a paradigm shift'), or a force and a counterforce; the two latter often consist of an event and an action (a flood and emergency management). Usually plots are complicated and contain chains of actions and events, oscillating states of affairs, apparent actions and wrongly interpreted events, as in suspense or mystery, but a minimal plot is enough to make sense of a narrative. Thus the other common way of invoking narratives is fishing for a missing element in the minimal plot. Even an apparently analytical question like 'What were the factors that made the reorganization necessary?' is but a way of asking for the first element of the plot, the original state of affairs.

Once characters and a plot are in place, a story has been constructed. Before I move to the possible ways of reading it, another comment on characters is due. Unlike membership categories, they do not have to be human. Many organizational narratives have as important characters a computer, the market, or an equality program. Also, the accounting aspect of a narrative does not have to be explicit: the very way of structuring the elements of the plot may serve as an explanation or justification. Narratives mix together humans with non-humans, causes with reasons, explanations with interpretations. This makes them difficult but also interesting to interpret.

HOW TO READ A NARRATIVE

As there are many ways of reading a narrative (before one even decides whether it is an 'interpretation' or an 'analysis' that takes place), the 'hermeneutic triad' formulated by Paul Hernadi (1987) might be helpful. It separates conceptually three ways of reading a text, usually present simultaneously and intertwined in practice. *Explication* corresponds to a stance that the Italian semiotician Umberto Eco (1990) calls that of *a naive or a semantic reader*. It is guided by an ambition to understand a text, and Hernadi uses Frye's insight (see Frye, 1990) showing that it implies a humility on the part of the reader: standing under the text. *Explanation* sets the reader above the text. The innocuous question 'What does the text say?' is replaced with an interruptive 'How does it say it?' (Silverman and Torode, 1980). This equals corresponds to a stance of *a critical or a semiotic reader* (Eco, 1990). Hernadi's triad is egalitarian in that it puts all explanatory efforts on the same plane: be it semiotics, criticism, structural or rhetorical analysis, deconstruction – they all attempt to disassemble the text to see how it was made. *Exploration*, or standing in for the author, might be seen as more sparingly used in scientific texts, a genre that does not encourage existential enactment, or the readers bringing their lives and preoccupations into the text. Yet it can be found in most readings: in the conclusion of a positivist scholar, in the confessional remarks of an ethnographer (Geertz, 1988; Van Maanen, 1988), in standpoint feminism (Smith, 1987; Martin, 1990; Calás and Smircich, 1991) and in the empowerment ambitions of a narrative analyst (Mishler, 1986).

As this text is dedicated to the analysis of narratives, I will focus on two initial operations, that of explication and explanation, or the habits of a semantic and a semiotic reader.

The difficulty of explication

The traditional rendering of this operation consists of the researcher writing 'the one true story' of what 'really happened' in a clear, authoritative voice. This procedure is nowadays considered anathema, but this is misleading. After all, there are many good reasons to make up a consistent narrative – out of many partly conflicting ones, or out of an incomplete, or fragmented one. The justice or injustice done to the original narrative depends on the attitude of the researcher and on the precautions he or she takes.

The main problem of rendering somebody else's story in one's own idiom is the political act of totalizing that it entails. This problem became acute in anthropology as literacy increased in previously oral societies (Lejeune, 1989). The Other, who before was just 'described', took on the task of self-description and of questioning the descriptions of the anthropologists. Yet when a field of practice under study is highly literate, the redescriptions undertaken by the researchers are open to practitioners' comments and questions. The status of science, especially the social sciences, does not stifle the protests and critiques any more. As I pointed out at some length in a different context (Czarniawska, 1998), the 'voices of the field' reported in organization studies are as literate and eloquent as those of the reporters, and often have greater political clout.

This does not release the researchers from the responsibility for what they write and the duty to respect their interlocutors. But this responsibility and respect do not have to be expressed in a literal repetition of what has been said. A researcher has a right, but also a professional duty, to do a 'novel reading', in an apt expression coined by Marjorie DeVault (1990): an interpretation by a person who is not socialized into the same system of meaning as the narrator, but is familiar enough with it to recognize it as such. At any given time and place, she continues, there are *dominant and marginal readings* of the same text and, I may add, there are a number of narratives reporting the same developments but plotting them in different ways. Some plots are dominant while others are considered marginal, but it is not necessary that the researcher subscribes to the dominant plot. Agreement is not always the best way of expressing respect. The researchers' duty is, however, to take the authorial responsibility for the narrative they concocted, and also to admit the existence of opposition from the interlocutors, if they are aware of it.

There are many other ways of paying respect to one's interlocutors. One is a multi-voiced story, recommended by many anthropologists (Marcus, 1992). There is then not one, but many narratives; as in a postmodern novel, all tell their story and the researcher does not have to take a stand on which is 'right' and which is 'wrong'. One example is to be found in the work of Yiannis Gabriel (1995) who quoted four accounts of an explosion of a fire extinguisher. One account was a chronicle that merely reported the sequence of the events, while the remaining three constructed three different stories with different heroes, victims, and plots.

One has to point out, however, that polyphony in a text is but a textual strategy (Czarniawska, 1999a). 'The voices of the field' do not speak for themselves; it is the author who makes them communicate on his or her conditions. Therefore it is more adequate to speak, in line with Bakhtin (Bakhtin and Medvedev, 1985), about 'variegated speech' of the field, about leaving traces of different dialects, different idioms, and different vocabularies, rather than homogenizing them into a 'scientific text'. Again, this textual strategy is not as drastically different from one authoritative story as it may seem. Even pasting together fragments of narratives taken straight from an interview protocol decontextualizes them but, in return, it also recontextualizes them (Rorty, 1991). It is not a question of 'quoting literally'; it is a question of recontextualization that is interesting ('novel'), credible and respectful.

Explanation 1: Interpretation and overinterpretation

Interpretation is often set in contrast to explanation, but here it is understood (indeed, interpreted) in a pragmatist way, in the sense of all inquiry, of recontextualization. It therefore combines explication with explanation, asking the question 'What does this text say? And how come?' But this redefinition does not solve all the practical problems encountered in its application.

> To interpret means to react to the text of the world or to the world of a text by producing other texts ... The problem is not to challenge the old idea that the world is a text which can be interpreted, but rather to decide whether it has a fixed meaning, many possible meanings, or none at all (Eco, 1990: 23).

In response to the recent wave of reader-oriented theories of interpretation, Eco (1992) pointed out that interpretations are indefinite but not infinite. They are negotiations between the intention of the reader (*intentio lectoris*) and the intention of the text (*intentio operis*). They can end with a first-level reading (typical of a semantic reader) or an overinterpretation, a reading that ignores the text (a tendency of a semiotic reader). Most readers live someplace between those two extremes, and different readers have different interpretation habits.

Rorty (1992) had difficulty in accepting this pragmatic interpretation model precisely because of his pragmatist position. Despite all repudiations, there is a clear hierarchy between Eco's two extreme readers: the semiotic reader is a clever one (presumably a researcher), whereas the semantic reader is a dupe (presumably an unreflective practitioner). Also, the difference proposed by Eco between an 'interpretation' (which respects *intentio operis*) and 'use' (e.g., lighting a fire with a text, but more generally just a disrespectful reading) is something that Rorty could not accept. For him, all readings are 'uses'. If a classification of uses – that is, readings – is required, Rorty suggested a distinction between a *methodical reading*, one that is controlled by the reader and the purpose at hand, and an *inspired reading*, which changes the reader and the purpose as much as it changes the text.

For me these issues have more significance than simply being part of an altercation between two theoreticians who otherwise stand very close to one another. In undertaking study of a social practice other than science we are joining a conversation on this topic that is not limited to researchers alone (Czarniawska, 1997). Social science as a soliloquy in many voices is not an attractive vision. It seems both exciting and gratifying (as well as frustrating and difficult) to try to speak to the Other, and among many Others, practitioners are one possible partner in such a conversation.

I do not mean, naively, that people from other fields of practice than our own read or ought to read everything we write: there exist issues of a self-reflective nature which are not of much interest to outsiders, like this present chapter. Nor do I intend to announce condescendingly that we have to 'adapt to practitioners' needs', by which is usually meant that we have to operate at the level of the *Reader's Digest*. I claim that practitioners are educated enough to understand what we write; they rarely read us because they do not find our texts interesting. I would also postulate that there is no such thing as 'practitioners' needs', at least not as a fixed entity.

This reasoning concerns the impossibility of carrying through the *intentio auctoris*, of foreseeing and successfully manipulating an audience. But is there no *intentio operis*? Can readers interpret as they please?

What is a 'reasonable interpretation' and what is an 'overinterpretation' is negotiated not so much between the text and the reader, as among readers. In that sense *intentio operis* seems an excellent device, to be treated pragmatically. It is impossible, however, to establish the *intentio operis* of a given text once and for all. Intentions are being read into the text each time a reader interprets it. Again, this does not mean there is an unlimited variety of an idiosyncratic interpretation. In a given time and place there will be dominant and marginal readings of the same text (DeVault, 1990), and this makes the notion of interpretive communities very useful (Fish, 1989).

Explanation 2: Structural analysis and deconstruction

One traditional way of analyzing a narrative is that of a structural analysis, an enterprise close to semiology and formalism (see Propp, 1968; Todorov, 1977, 1990; Barthes, 1977). Almost before this method acquired legitimacy in the social sciences, it was swept away by poststructuralism. It makes sense, however, to follow Selden's (1985: 72) suggestion that 'poststructuralists are structuralists who suddenly see the error of their ways'. This statement is especially convincing when we observe that the figures central to poststructuralim were, in fact, leading structuralists or formalists: Barthes, Bakhtin, Todorov. 'The most fundamental difference between the structuralist and poststructuralist enterprises can be seen in the shift from the problematic of the subject to the deconstruction of the concept of representation' (Harari, 1979: 29). This shift led to the problematization of the 'deep structure' concept. To quote a well-known French structuralist's definition, narrative structures, 'or, more accurately, semio-narrative structures, [were] to be understood in the sense of deep semiotic structures (which preside at the generating of meaning and bear general forms of discourse organization)' (Greimas and Courtés, 1982: 317). 'Deep structures are customarily opposed in semiotics to surface (or superficial) structures. While the latter ostensibly belong to the sphere of the observable, the former are considered as underlying the utterance' (ibid: 69).

Thus one could say that the move from structuralism to poststructuralism meant abandoning the depth for the surface: if deep structures are demonstrable, they are observable. Structures can no longer be 'found', as they are obviously put into the text by those who read the text, including the author (after all, reading is writing anew). This meant abandoning the ideas of the universal structure of language, or of mind, and accepting the idea of a common repertoire of textual strategies (Harari, 1979), which are recognizable to both the writer and the reader. This relaxation of basic assumptions leads also to the relaxation of the technique: as there is no one true deep structure to be discovered, various techniques can be applied to structure a text and therefore permit its novel reading.

> An extension of poststructuralism is deconstruction. (Derrida, 1976)

> To 'deconstruct' a text is to draw out conflicting logics of sense and implication, with the object of showing that the text never exactly means what it says or says what it means. (Norris, 1988: 7)

Deconstruction is a technique and a philosophy of reading, characterized by a preoccupation with desire and power. Used by Derrida (1987) for reading philosophical texts, it becomes a kind of philosophy itself (Rorty, 1989). Used by gender scholars, it becomes a tool of subversion (Johnson, 1980). Used by organization researchers, it becomes a technique of reading by estrangement (Feldman, 1995). As a technique of reading, it earns an excellent introduction in Martin's (1990) paper, where she composed a list of deconstructionist 'moves'. This list, apart from being a useful aid to anybody who would like to try their hand at deconstruction, also reveals the historical roots of deconstruction, or rather, its historical sediments. It contains elements of close reading, of rhetorical analysis, of dramatist analysis, of radical rewriting – it is a hybrid. Therefore, it does not make much sense to speak about 'proper deconstruction' or the 'correct use of structural analysis': the literary techniques should serve as a source of inspiration, not a prescription to be literally followed.

In my rendition, narrative analysis does not have a 'method'; neither does it have a 'paradigm', a set of procedures to check the correctness of its results.[2] It gives access to an ample bag of tricks – from traditional criticism through formalists to deconstruction – but it steers away from the idea that a 'rigorously' applied procedure would render 'testable' results. The ambition of narrative analysis in social sciences I wish to plead for is an inspired reading, as Rorty (1992) calls it, or a novel reading as Marjorie De Vault (1990) does.

NARRATIVE ANALYSIS PUT TO USE

Reading action/decision as a narrative

As I mentioned before, the obvious move – of retelling the story of the events that took place in the form of a well-constructed narrative – is often treated with suspicion by authors familiar with narrative analysis, who want to know how a text has been constructed. The choice is between analyzing one's own narrative, a procedure that might be tedious for readers from outside academia, or hiding the work put into the construction of the text, a procedure that might be criticized by colleagues in academia. Creative ways are searched for, and found, to circumvent this difficulty.

One such solution has been applied by Ellen O'Connor (1997) who told the story of a US employee who mobilized opposition against her company's policy that pushed people toward involuntary retirement. She presented the event as a sequence of narratives (letters, documents, but also excerpts from interviews and media comments), showing how various people conformed to or rebelled against the common repertoire of characters, functions and plots, in their roles both of storytellers and the interpreting audience. In organizational life, unlike in literature, she concludes, 'one may intervene directly in the text to determine the limits and possibilities of intertext' (O'Connor, 1997: 414).

Ellen O'Connor applied 'decision making' as her emplotment device, and this might explain why she has attributed so much freedom in shaping of the narrative, and the intertext, to her characters. Kaj Sköldberg (1994) used genre analysis in his reading of change programs in Swedish municipalities, and saw the local actors carried away by the dramatic genres they employed rather than empowered by them. Two competing genres – a tragedy and a romantic comedy – resulted in a mixture that presented itself to the audience, including the researcher, as closest to satire, an effect unintended by either the directors or the actors of the drama. Sköldberg's use of genre analysis is inspired by Hayden White (1973).

Dramatizing narratives

Yet another way of avoiding the accusation of an unreflective narrative construction in research is to incorporate the analysis into the narrative itself, to exploit 'the content of the form', in White's (1987) formulation. Sköldberg's way of treating his field material is halfway to this solution; a complete step often involves a dramatization of the narrative. Such an operation makes at least a part of the construction work visible to the reader, and the choice of a device is a major choice in the analysis.

The title of Michael Rosen's article, 'Breakfast at Spiro's: Dramaturgy and dominance' (1985), summarizes it well. Rosen picked up his observation of a business breakfast at an advertising agency, and decided to present it as a social drama, which was also a convention decided upon by the organizers of the event themselves. The paper therefore has the form of an annotated screenplay. As the events unfold, Rosen offers both a dramaturgical critique, a connection to the events outside the time and the place of the drama, and a commentary on the reactions of the audience.

Bengt Jacobsson goes even further, forming the results of the study of municipal decision-making into a script for a *commedia dell'arte* (Czarniawska-Joerges and Jacobsson, 1995). The choice of this form summarizes the final results of his analysis, revealing the theatricality and ritualism of the political organization, its skillful production of the improvisation effect based on routines and rehearsals, and its standard stock of characters.

Narratives of identity: Life stories, career stories, organizational biographies

While it may not be surprising that organizational narratives offer a conventional stock of characters, they also offer material for constructing subjectivity or personal identities (Gabriel, 1995). This focus of narrative analysis has the longest tradition in social sciences, far exceeding the ample field of organization studies. According to Mishler (1986), Labov and Waletzky (1967) were the first to use narrative analysis on interview material gathered from people telling stories from their life experience. Mishler's book has since become the standard text on narrative interviewing, which he sees as a means of empowerment of respondents, 'the aim being to recover and strengthen the voice of the lifeworld, that is, individuals' contextual understanding of their problems in their own terms' (Mishler, 1986:

142–3). Charlotte Linde (1993) combined the ethnomethodological tradition with Labovian linguistic analysis and psychological theories of the self, showing how coherence is achieved in life stories. Catherine Riessman (1993) took a more sociological approach to women's life stories, where 'culture "speaks itself" through an individual's story'. Her narrative analysis is also situated within the Labovian framework.

In the organizational context, life stories acquire two variations: career stories and organizational identity narratives. Career stories are most often analyzed within the framework of Foucauldian discourse analysis, situating the process of identity construction within, or against, the dominant discourse (Fournier, 1998; Peltonen, 1999). Organizational identity narratives are not only official historical documents, but all kinds of collective storytelling that attempt to create a quasi-subject, the Organization (Czarniawska, 1997).

Blurring genres, or, how wide is the field?

All the examples above concerned narratives produced in the field of practice, or in the encounter between the researchers and the field of practice. It has been pointed out, however, that there exist a great variety of narratives about various fields of practice in fiction (Phillips, 1995). Reading the text created by fiction writers, both in a research mode and in a teaching mode (Cohen, 1998), offers a variety of insights not always easily accessible in field studies. After all, claims Kundera (1988: 32): 'The novel dealt with the unconscious before Freud, the class struggle before Marx, it practised phenomenology ... before the phenomenologists'.

The use of fiction may raise protests in the context of science. It has been pointed out, however, that there are no structural differences between fictional and factual narratives are to be found, and their respective attraction is not determined by their claim to be fact or fiction. Paul Veyne (1988: 21), a French historian who studied the notion of truth in history, expressed the feelings of many a reader, saying that

> [a] world cannot be inherently fictional; it can be fictional only according to whether one believes in it or not. The difference between fiction and reality is not objective and does not pertain to the thing itself; it resides in us, according to whether or not we subjectively see in it a fiction.

The critique of fiction in scientific texts is often grounded in a confusion of two ways of understanding fiction: as that which does not exist, and that which is not true (Lamarque, 1990). If we separate these two, it becomes obvious that Kafka's *Castle* did not exist, and yet everything that was said about it may be true in the sense that it appears as insightful and credible in light of other texts on the absurdities of impersonal bureaucracy. This is why it has been suggested that the notion of 'validity' should be replaced by 'credibility', and that 'generalization' is an operation best performed by the reader, not by the writer.

The sociologist of science Karin Knorr Cetina (1994: 8) is even more radical in reminding her readers that facts are produced (a 'fact' long known to anyone who bothered to check the etymology of the word, she says, agreeing with Latour, 1993b). Also, modern institutions including science run on fictions, as all institutions always did, and the task of the scholar is to study how these fictions are constructed and sustained. A narrative approach will reveal how institutional classifications are made, and will thus render the works of science more comprehensible. 'If classificatory schemes provide a science of the concrete, narrative may provide a science of the imagination. At the very least, a reemphasis on temporality may enable us to deal more directly with change, and thereby to make structural and symbolic studies more dynamic' (Bruner, 1986: 141).

Reading together

The use of narratives, fictional or not, in the process of education (Phillips, 1995; Cohen, 1998) assumes a possibility of a collective reading. Such a possibility has also been exploited as a resource in research. Bronwyn Davies (1989) read the feminist versions of fairy-tales to four- and five-year-old children, only to find herself (or the stories) corrected by her listeners, who appeared to have a well-entrenched notion of gender roles. She came to the surprising conclusion that 'children struggle for quite a long time to learn the liberal humanist concept of the person as fixed and unitary, since this does not adequately capture their experience which is of multiple, diverse and contradictory ways of being' (Davies, 1989: 40). Once winners in this struggle, they are prompt to exhibit this hard-learned lesson in applying reified stereotypes that result from such a concept.

Quite in line with this reasoning were the results of a study where students of management in various countries were asked to interpret short narratives illustrating gender discrimination in workplaces (Czarniawska and Calás, 1997). Some interpretations redefined the event as non-discriminatory; others recognized it as discriminatory but localized it safely in 'another culture', usually outside the 'modern western world'. Collective reading reveals the repertoire of institutionalized interpretations and stereotypical classifications.

Narratives from one's own backyard

The last example of the uses of narrative analysis concerns its application to narratives from the writer's own field of practice, that is, the field of theory. Such an analysis, often combined with rhetorical analysis, starts from the early dramatist analysis of drinking driver research by Gusfield (1976) and extends to numerous examples of narrative analysis in science studies (Mulkay, 1985; Traweek, 1992; Curtis, 1994), and in field studies in general (Geertz, 1988; Van Maanen, 1988).

The narratives from one's own practice are analyzed like all others, possibly with more bravado (after all, the analyst is on safe ground, at least epistemologically, if not always politically) but also with special care due to the fact that the narrators cannot be anonymized. As in previous examples, different options are open. Thus I have analyzed *Organizations* (March and Simon, 1993) as an example of my thesis that research writings often contain a plot without a narrative (Czarniawska, 1999a). Martin Kilduff (1993) decided to deconstruct the same text, coming to the conclusion that it contains a simultaneous rejection and acceptance of the traditions the authors sought to surpass. Kilduff ended his deconstruction with yet another narrative – a confessional tale that analyzed his motives in undertaking such an enterprise, a creative exercise in exploration.

WHAT IS TO BE FOUND IN A NARRATIVE?

To paraphrase Barthes, the narratives of field studies are indeed numerous, and so are analytical approaches that might be used to make sense of them. By sampling as many as I managed to cram into the given format, I wanted to convey the growing richness of such approaches, and a firm conviction that there is no (and there must not be) 'one best method' of narrative analysis. Authors reach out to varied sources for inspiration: many combine narrative analysis with rhetorical analysis, dramatist analysis, semiotics, and discourse and conversation analysis. Deconstruction is a hybrid in itself. Thus, rather than evaluating the advantages of different approaches, I would like to consider the question of what the analysts hope to find at the end of the analysis.

Let me simplify this question by assuming that a narrative usually presents itself to its analyst in the form of a text. Thus narrative analysis can be treated as a type of textual analysis. What does one look for in a text?

There are at least three versions of the answer to this question. According to the first, conventional one, texts are but a reflection of reality. One has to overcome the text, as it were, to get at what is behind it, at the true story of events. This is consistent with a theory of language as medium between objective reality (the world as it is) and a person's subjective cognition. A writer communicates his or her subjective understanding of the world via a text.

In the second and more radical version, the text is all there is; the text is the world. This idea, in its recent formulation coined by the symbolist poet Stéphane Mallarmé and taken up by Roland Barthes and Jacques Derrida, is not new. There are well-known precedents of treating the Bible and the Koran as texts containing the world as created by God (Eco, 1995). In social sciences, ethnomethodology claims that the rules typical of a community can be found in any conversation between competent members of this community. This is why Latour (1993a: 131) sees semiotics as an ethnomethodology of texts.

The third version, the one I opt for, is close to the previous one, but attempts to widen the angle and therefore leads to a different procedure. Instead of looking at a text under a deconstructivist (or conversation-analytical) microscope, it proposes treating a text as belonging to other texts, as a material trace of a conversation that was or is taking place. The most obvious example of this approach could be seen in O'Connor (1997). It is a conversation analysis writ large: texts speaking to other texts, across times and places.

It is difficult to imagine a textual analysis in the context of field studies that makes a clear-cut choice among the three, however. Some kind of realism will always linger, either as a style in the texts that we are analyzing or as a stylization of our own texts, undertaken for legitimating purposes. After all, every one of us sits in his or her appropriate iron cage of institutions, or rather in a whole collection of iron cages fitting into one another like Russian dolls, decorated with institutional trimmings. Rather than striving for a rigorous narrative analysis or for purity of a genre, reading and writing of narratives will remain a creative activity, based on bisociations and hybridizing.

ACKNOWLEDGMENT

The author wishes to thank Alan Bryman, François Cooren, Richard Fisher and two anonymous reviewers.

NOTES

1 For a short description of their work, see *The New Encyclopædia Britannica*, 1990, Micropædia, vol. 1, p. 969 and vol. 10, p. 427.

2 Although there exist attempts to create one; see Watson (1973) for a formal model of narrative analysis based on the works of Burke and Labov.

REFERENCES

Baker, Carolyn (1997) 'Membership categorization and interview accounts', in David Silverman (ed.), *Qualitative Research. Theory, Method and Practice*, London: Sage, pp. 130–43.

Bakhtin, Michail M. and Medvedev, P.N. (1985) *The Formal Method in Literary Scholarship. A Critical Introduction to Sociological Poetics*. Cambridge, MA: Harvard University Press.

Barthes, Roland (1977) 'Introduction to the structural analysis of narratives', in Roland Barthes, *Image-Music-Text*. Glasgow: William Collins, pp. 79–124.

Boje, David (1991) 'The story-telling organization: A study of story performance in an office-supply firm', *Administrative Science Quarterly*, 36: 106–26.

Boland, Richard J., Jr. and Tankasi, Ramkrishnan V. (1995) 'Perspective making and perspective taking in communities of knowing', *Organization Science*, 6(3): 350–72.

Brown, Richard H. (1977) *A Poetic for Sociology. Toward a Discovery for the Human Sciences*. Cambridge: Cambridge University Press.

Brown, Richard H. (1980) 'The position of narrative in contemporary society'. *New Literacy History*, 11(3): 545–50.

Bruner, Jerome (1986). *Actual Minds, Possible Worlds*. Cambridge, MA: Harvard University Press.

Bruner, Jerome (1990) *Acts of Meaning*. Cambridge, MA: Harvard University Press.

Burke, Kenneth (1969) *A Grammar of Motives*. Berkeley: The University of California Press. First published in 1945.

Calás, Marta and Smircich, Linda (1991) 'Voicing seduction to silence leadership', *Organization Studies*, 12(4): 567–601.

Cohen, Claire (1998) 'Using narrative fiction within management education', *Management Learning*, 29(2): 165–82.

Corvellec, Hervé (1997) *Stories of Achievement. Narrative Features of Organizational Performance*. New Brunswick, NJ: Transaction.

Curtis, Ron (1994) 'Narrative form and normative force: Baconian story-telling in popular science', *Social Studies of Science*, 24: 419–61.

Czarniawska, Barbara (1997) *Narrating the Organization. Dramas of Institutional Identity*. Chicago: University of Chicago Press.

Czarniawska, Barbara (1998) *A Narrative Approach in Organization Studies*. Thousand Oaks, CA: Sage.

Czarniawska, Barbara (1999a) *Writing Management. Organization Theory as a Genre*. Oxford: Oxford University Press.

Czarniawska, Barbara (1999b) *Det var en gång en stad på vatten*. Stockholm: SNS.

Czarniawska, Barbara and Calás, Marta (1997) 'Another country: Explaining gender discrimination with "culture"', *Administrative Studies*, 4: 326–41.

Czarniawska-Joerges, Barbara and Jacobsson, Bengt (1995) 'Politics as *commedia dell'arte*', *Organization Studies*, 16(3): 375–94.

Davies, Bronwyn (1989) *Frogs and Snails and Feminist Tales*. Sydney: Allen & Unwin.

Derrida, Jacques (1976) *Of Grammatology*. Baltimore: John Hopkins University Press.

Derrida, Jacques (1987) *The Postcard. From Socrates to Freud and Beyond*. Chicago: University of Chicago Press.

DeVault, Marjorie L. (1990) 'Novel readings: The social organization of interpretation', *American Journal of Sociology*, 95(4): 887–921.

Eco, Umberto (1990) *The Limits of Interpretation*. Bloomington: Indiana University Press.

Eco, Umberto (1992) *Interpretation and Overinterpretation*. Cambridge: Cambridge University Press.

Eco, Umberto (1995) *In Search for the Perfect Language*. Oxford: Blackwell.

Feldman, Martha (1995) *Strategies for Interpreting Qualitative Data*. Newbury Park, CA: Sage.

Fish, Stanley (1989) *Doing What Comes Naturally: Change, Rhetoric, and the Practice of Theory in Literary and Legal Studies*. Durham, NC: Duke University Press.

Fisher, Walter R. (1984) 'Narration as a human communication paradigm: The case of public moral argument', *Communication Monographs*, 51: 1–22.

Fisher, Walter R. (1987) *Human Communication as Narration: Toward a Philosophy of Reason, Value, and Action*. Columbia: University of South Carolina Press.

Fournier, Valérie (1998) 'Stories of development and exploitation: Militant voices in an enterprise culture', *Organization*, 5(1): 55–80.

Frye, Northrop (1990) *The Anatomy of Criticism*. London: Penguin.First published in 1957.

Gabriel, Yiannis (1995) 'The unmanaged organization: Stories, fantasies and subjectivity', *Organization Studies*, 16(3): 477–502.

Gadamer, Hans-Georg (1975) *Truth and Method*. New York: Continuum.

Geertz, Clifford (1980) *Negara: The Theatre State in Nineteenth Century Bali*. Princeton, NJ: Princeton University Press.

Geertz, Clifford (1988) *Works and Lives: The Anthropologist as Author*. Stanford, CA: Stanford University Press.

Goody, Jack (1986) *The Logic of Writing and the Organization of Society*. Cambridge: Cambridge University Press.

Greimas, Algirdas Julien and Courtés, Joseph (1982) *Semiotics and Language. An Analytical Dictionary*. Bloomington: Indiana University Press.

Gusfield, Joseph (1976) 'The literary rhetoric of science: Comedy and pathos in drinking driver research', *American Sociological Review*, 41 (February): 16–34.

Harari, Jose V. (1979) 'Critical factions/critical fictions.' in Jose V. Harari (ed.), *Textual Strategies: Perspectives in Post-structuralist Criticism*. Ithaca, NY: Methuen, pp. 17–72.

Helmers, Sabine and Buhr, Regina (1994) 'Corporate story-telling: The buxomly secretary, a pyrrhic victory of the male mind', *Scandinavian Journal of Management*, 10(2): 175–92.

Hernadi, Paul (1987) 'Literary interpretation and the rhetoric of the human sciences', in John S. Nelson, Allan Megill, and D.N. McCloskey (eds), *The Rhetoric of the Human Sciences*. Madison: University of Wisconsin Press, pp. 263–75.

Holstein, James A. and Gubrium, Jaber F. (1997) 'Active interviewing', in David Silverman (ed.), *Qualitative Research. Theory, Method and Practice*, London: Sage, pp. 113–29.

Iser, Wolfgang (1978) *The Act of Reading: A Theory of Aesthetic Response*. Baltimore, MD: John Hopkins University Press.

Johnson, Barbara (1980) *The Critical Difference: Essays in the Contemporary Rhetoric of Reading*. Baltimore, MD: John Hopkins University Press.

Kilduff, Martin (1993) 'Deconstructing Organizations', *American Management Review*, 18(1): 13–31.

Knorr Cetina, Karin (1994) 'Primitive classifications and postmodernity: Towards a sociological notion of fiction', *Theory, Culture and Society*, 11: 1–22.

Kunda, Gideon (1992) *Engineering Culture: Control and Commitment in a High-Tech Organization*. Philadelphia: Temple University Press.

Kundera, Milan (1988) *The Art of the Novel*. London: Faber and Faber.

Labov, Willim and Waletzky, Joshua (1967) 'Narrative analysis: Oral versions of personal experience', in June Helms (ed.), *Essays on the Verbal and Visual Arts*. Seattle: University of Washington Press, pp. 12–44

Lamarque, Peter (1990) 'Narrative and invention: The limits of fictionality', in Christopher Nash (ed.), *Narrative in Culture: The Uses of Storytelling in the Sciences, Philosophy and Literature*. London: Routledge, 5–22.

Latour, Bruno (1993a) 'Pasteur on lactic acid yeast: A partial semiotic analysis', *Configurations*, 1(1): 129–46.

Latour, Bruno (1993b) *We Have Never Been Modern*. Cambridge, MA: Harvard University Press.

Lejeune, Philippe (1989) *On Autobiography*. Minneapolis: University of Minnesota Press.

Linde, Charlotte (1993) *Life Stories. The Creation of Coherence*. Oxford: Oxford University Press.

Lyotard, Jean-Françoise (1984) *The Postmodern Condition. A Report on Knowledge*. Manchester: Manchester University Press. First published in 1979.

MacIntyre, Alasdair (1981) *After Virtue*. London: Duckworth Press.

Mangham, Ian L. and Overington, Michael A. (1987) *Organizations as Theatre: A Social Psychology of Dramatic Appearances*. Chichester: Wiley.

March, James G. and Simon, Herbert A. (1993) *Organizations*. Oxford: Blackwell.

Marcus, George E. (1992) 'Past, present and emergent identities: Requirements for ethnographies of late twentieth-century modernity world-wide', in Scott Lash and Jonathan Friedman (eds), *Modernity & Identity*. Oxford: Blackwell, pp. 309–30.

Martin, Joanne (1990) 'Deconstructing organizational taboos: The suppression of gender conflict in organizations', *Organization Science*, 1(4): 339–59.

McCloskey, Deirdre N. (1986) *The Rhetoric of Economics*. Madison: University of Wisconsin Press.

McCloskey, Deirdre N. (1990). *If You're so Smart. The Narrative of Economic Expertise*. Chicago: University of Chicago Press.

Mishler, Elliot G. (1986). *Research Interviewing. Context and Narrative.* Cambridge, MA: Harvard University Press.

Mitchell, W.J.T. (ed.) (1981) *On Narrative.* Chicago: University of Chicago Press.

Mulkay, Michael (1985) *The Word and the World. Explorations in the Form of Sociological Analysis.* London: George Allen & Unwin.

Norris, Christopher (1988) 'Deconstruction, postmodernism and visual arts', in Norris, Christopher and Andrew Benjamin (eds), *What is deconstruction?* London: Academy Edition, pp. 7–55

O'Connor, Ellen S. (1997) 'Discourse at our disposal. stories in and around the garbage can', *Management Communication Quarterly*, 10(4): 395–432.

Peltonen, Tuomo (1999) 'Finnish engineers becoming expatriates: Biographical narratives and subjectivity', *Studies in Cultures, Organizations and Societies*, 5(2): 265–95.

Perrow, Charles (1991) 'A society of organizations', *Theory and Society*, 20: 725–62.

Phillips, Nelson (1995) 'Telling organizational tales: On the role of narrative fiction in the study of organizations', *Organization Studies*, 16(4): 625–49.

Polkinghorne, Donald E. (1987) *Narrative Knowing and the Human Sciences.* Albany, NY: State University of New York Press.

Power, Michael (1997) *The Audit Society: Rituals of Verification.* Oxford: Oxford University Press.

Propp, Vladimir (1968) *Morphology of the Folktale.* Austin: University of Texas Press.

Ricoeur, Paul (1981) 'The model of the text: Meaningful action considered as text', in John B. Thompson (ed.), *Hermeneutics and the Human Sciences.* Cambridge: Cambridge University Press, pp. 197–221.

Ricoeur, Paul (1984) *Time and Narrative Vol. 1.* Chicago: University of Chicago Press.

Ricoeur, Paul (1986) *Time and Narrative Vol. 2.* Chicago: University of Chicago Press.

Riessman, Catherine Kohler (1993) *Narrative Analysis.* Newbury Park, CA: Sage.

Rorty, Richard (1989) *Contingency, Irony and Solidarity.* Cambridge: Cambridge University Press.

Rorty, Richard (1991) 'Inquiry as recontextualization: An anti-dualist account of interpretation', in *Philosophical Papers 1. Objectivity, Relativism and Truth.* New York: Cambridge University Press, pp. 93–110.

Rorty, Richard (1992) 'The pragmatist's progress'. in Umberto Eco, *Interpretation and Overinterpretation.* Cambridge, UK: Cambridge University Press, pp. 89–108.

Rosen, Michael (1985) 'Breakfast at Spiro's: Dramaturgy and dominance', *Journal of Management*, 11(2): 31–48.

Ryan, Marie-Laure (1993) 'Narrative in real time: Chronicle, mimesis and plot in baseball broadcast', *Narrative*, 1(2): 138–55.

Sacks, Harvey (1992) *Lectures on Conversation.* Oxford: Blackwell.

Selden, Raman (1985) *A Reader's Guide to Contemporary Literary Theory.* Brighton: Harvester Press.

Silverman, David and Torode, Brian (1980) *The Material Word. Some Theories about Language and Their Limits.* London: Routledge & Kegan Paul.

Silvers, Robert B. (ed.) (1995) *Hidden Histories of Science.* New York: New York Review of Books.

Sköldberg, Kaj (1994) 'Tales of change: Public administration reform and narrative mode', *Organization Science*, 5(2): 219–38.

Smith, Dorothy (1987) *The Everyday World as Problematic: A Feminist Sociology.* Boston: Northeastern University Press.

Todorov, Tzvetan (1977) *The Poetics of Prose.* Oxford: Blackwell.

Todorov, Tzvetan (1990) *Genres in Discourse.* Cambridge: Cambridge University Press.

Traweek, Sharon (1992) 'Border crossings: Narrative strategies in science studies and among physicists in Tsukuba Science City, Japan', in Andrew Pickering (ed.), *Science as Practice and Culture.* Chicago: University Chicago Press, pp. 429–65.

Turner, Victor (1982) *From Ritual to Theatre.* New York: Performing Arts Journal Publications.

Van Maanen, John (1988) *Tales of the Field.* Chicago: University of Chicago Press.

Veyne, Paul (1988) *Did the Greeks Believe in Their Myths?* Chicago: University of Chicago Press.

Watson, Karen Ann (1973) 'A rhetorical and sociological model for the analysis of narrative', *American Anthropologist*, 75: 243–64.

White, Hayden (1973) *Metahistory. The Historical Imagination in Nineteenth Century Europe.* Baltimore, MD: Johns Hopkins University Press.

White, Hayden (1987) *The Content of the Form. Narrative Discourse and Historical Representation.* Baltimore, MD: Johns Hopkins University Press.

30

Qualitative Research and the Postmodern Turn

SARA DELAMONT AND PAUL ATKINSON

In the course of this chapter we shall review and discuss a number of recent currents in the conduct of qualitative research in sociology, anthropology and the cultural disciplines. Postmodernism has been invoked to account for and justify a variety of perspectives and strategies. They are not confined to the analysis of data. One cannot discern a circumscribed 'postmodern' approach to data analysis in the social sciences. The analytic implications are more generic, incorporating every aspect of qualitative research, its epistemological foundations, its strategies of data collection, its analytic styles, and its modes of representation. We must, therefore, treat the overall theme of 'data analysis' in a more inclusive way than is the case for other chapters in this volume. Indeed, one must really think of the topic in terms of social analysis and of social representation rather than 'data analysis' in a narrow sense. In the same vein, our discussion is restricted to qualitative research – broad though that designation is – for the appeal to postmodernism has not impinged on all varieties of social research with equal force.

At the outset we need to outline the fundamentals of our argument. We shall not attempt to encapsulate a definitive summary of what postmodernism amounts to in the social sciences. It would be tempting to do so, and then to apply that definitive perspective to contemporary trends in research and representation. It would prove a frustrating and unsatisfactory approach, however. For the field we confront is far messier than that would allow. There is no consistent version of 'postmodernism' to be found in the research literature or in the practices of social researchers. Rather, we have a number of appeals to postmodernism that justify diverse approaches. Moreover, those research strategies are also justified by appeals to other epistemological or critical inspirations – such as feminism, poststructuralism, postcolonialism, or critical theory. The 'postmodern' tendencies in research methods are not always tied closely to the tenets of postmodernism conceived of as a general theoretical movement. The relationship between allegedly postmodernist research practices and the broader tenets of postmodern theory is not always clear, and may be tenuous in some cases. Moreover, the relationships between postmodernism and other 'post' theories – such as poststructuralism and postindustrialism – are also not always clear. Several of the inspirations of postmodernism that are claimed by some qualitative researchers and methodologists are also attributable to poststructuralist theorists such as Foucault (Lyon, 1999). To confound things further, it must also be recognized that there is equal potential for confusion in tracing the relationships between 'postmodern' research and the supposed conditions of 'postmodern' society.

Lastly, there is very little consensus in this area: the ideas and their application to empirical research are virtually all contested.

In tracing out these complex and contested ideas, therefore, we shall not begin with a generalized characterization of postmodernism *per se*. Rather, the chapter deals with some of the key ways in which postmodernism has been used to inspire or to justify particular research styles and approaches, and examines a number of critical perspectives that are at least sceptical of the claims that have been made in postmodernism's name. We ourselves remain sceptical as to many of those claims and remain unconvinced that there is a coherent postmodernist position: many of the specific things that are claimed, endorsed and practised are not necessarily attributable to postmodernism's inspiration.

The years since about the mid-1980s have seen a bewildering variety of 'new' and 'alternative' approaches to qualitative research. There has been an exponential growth in the publication of methodological texts, handbooks, journals and autobiographical accounts devoted to it. In addition to establishing a substantial corpus of methodological work, this growth has made possible the appearance of various heterodox perspectives. There has grown a kind of avant-garde in the treatment of qualitative research. The various alternative approaches have, indeed, become so pervasive that they are enshrined in major works of reference, to an extent that means one might think that the alternatives constitute a new orthodoxy. These recent developments go under various guises and have attributed to them various labels: postmodern, postpositivist, postparadigm are among them. They all connote a transgressive or radical approach to research. Other influences are attributed to poststructuralist and deconstructive theory, feminism and other critical standpoints.

There is no single, unified approach, and it is too detailed a task to trace out all of the different emphases and nuances that characterize the field. It is, however, important to stress at this stage that methodological contestation is grounded in different disciplinary and national intellectual traditions. There are, for instance, distinctions between sociology and anthropology: notwithstanding many affinities, the disciplines have developed, relatively speaking, in mutual isolation. Likewise, there are differences between American and British approaches. While, of necessity, we stress the commonalities, that glosses over some potentially significant differences. We shall, therefore, outline a number of key features that are characteristic of the 'postmodern' turn.

The authors have in common a core set of family resemblances, but no single set of precepts to which they subscribe. We find ourselves confronted by a number of networks, groups and individuals who explicitly claim to be engaged in postmodern styles of ethnography. We do not ourselves wish to reify research traditions and schools too narrowly, but the self-identification of a range of contemporary scholars in qualitative research with a postmodern turn is undeniable. Their self-identification is itself coupled with particular versions of how qualitative research has developed and changed over the years. They tend to emphasize the novelty of their own approaches and insights. They stress – in an appropriately poststructuralist and postmodern way – the disjunctures and discontinuities in their genealogical accounts of ethnographic and other qualitative research. They therefore tend to stress radical differences between their own preferences and 'modernist' or even 'positivist' tendencies (see Lincoln and Denzin, 1994; Denzin, 1997).

APPROACHES TO ANALYSIS

While there is no single set of postmodernist research practices, it is possible to identify a number of key themes that run through the methodological literature and that characterize the outcomes of analysis.

Rethinking research criteria

The postmodern turn is widely taken to enshrine a rejection of previously taken-for-granted criteria for the adequacy of research practice, and the simultaneous promotion of competing criteria. This is the most general form of the rejection of so-called 'modernist' or even 'positivist' modes of inquiry and data analysis. It is claimed that previous approaches to qualitative research were restricted by unduly rigid strategies and applied inappropriate notions of validity and reliability. Denzin and Lincoln's (1994) manifesto, for instance, relegates to an outmoded period of research preoccupations of 'modernist' approaches. It is argued that modernist strategies were grounded in the assumption of an objective world of social phenomena that could be examined by equally objective – or objectifying – methods. From this perspective, therefore, it is claimed that a great deal of qualitative research is essentially positivist in character. Paradoxically, they are retrospectively accused of employing a 'scientistic' model of social research. This is paradoxical from a number of perspectives: generations of other researchers, after all, accused ethnographers and others of being 'soft' and 'unscientific'; practitioners of social research themselves were often at pains to suggest that the criteria of adequacy were essentially different from those deployed by researchers that *they* regarded as improperly positivist.

The rhetorical contrast between modernist and postmodern social research is used, nevertheless, to reject any appeals to validity or reliability, while invoking different criteria for the conduct and evaluation of research. Prior to formulations of 'alternative' sets of criteria explicitly associated with postmodernism were those proposed by Lincoln and Guba (1985) for what they termed 'naturalistic' inquiry. Rather than the conventional appeal to the 'internal validity' of research, they propose to substitute the criterion of 'credibility'. This is guaranteed primarily through the checking of the analyst's accounts by members or informants. Likewise, the external validity, or generalizabilty, of research is replaced with the test of its 'transferability'. The latter does not depend on procedural criteria such as establishing the representativeness of a sample, but on providing sufficiently rich and recognizable accounts of social settings so that readers can discern their *transferability* to other social contexts. The conventional preoccupation with reliability was also replaced with the notion of *dependability*. This is warranted by the possibility that researchers' activities are available to be audited: the requirement is that the processes of data collection and analysis should be transparently available to the scrutiny of other researchers. Finally, the conventional criterion of objectivity is replaced by one of *confirmability*. The latter is represented in more open-ended, negotiable terms than conventional notions of objectivity, Lincoln and Guba claim. It is clear that Lincoln and Guba intend to insert interpretative judgments concerning the adequacy of research in place of objectivist accounts that

depend on impersonal and decontextualized criteria of objective science. This is an approach to inquiry that stresses the active and engaged role of the researcher, and lays emphasis on the principle of reflexivity.

Since Lincoln and Guba there has been a proliferation of criteria proposed in place of the so-called conventional protocols of modernist or positivist inquiry. Indeed, they have been bewildering in their variety. They have continued the trend, established by authors like Guba and Lincoln, in the preference for interpersonal judgments, and for the overt implication of both researcher and researched in the processes of inquiry and analysis. Arguably, their criteria represent a modification of conventional notions of adequacy in that they reframe them into more overtly interpretative frameworks. More thoroughgoing are the formulations of authors such as Lather (1993) or Altheide and Johnson (1994) who identify diverse goals for social inquiry that do not even implicitly endorse conventional criteria for the conduct and evaluation of research. Altheide and Johnson provide one summary of such perspectives. They identify, for instance, *validity-as-culture*, *validity-as-ideology* and *validity-as-gender*. These are not alternative versions of conventional notions of validity. Rather, they are radical alternatives to them. All stress the culturally and socially specific notions of validity. They stress that validity is always constructed within specific interpretative traditions, ideological positions and with reference to competing interests. From such critical perspectives, then, the adequacy of research is inescapably framed from within the constraints of language, prevailing notions of authority, and conventions of writing and other forms of representation.

The postmodern version of research adequacy, therefore, reflects a very different set of ideas from those enshrined in standard works on methodology. When not abandoned altogether, notions of adequacy are explicitly rendered in interpretative or constructivist terms themselves. Rather than furnishing universalistic benchmarks for the conduct and evaluation of research, postmodern criteria are themselves reflexively tied to specific standpoints, ideological positions and political purposes. They reflect a thoroughgoing scepticism concerning the authority and legitimacy of more conventional social research epistemology and methodology. This is in turn closely linked to the 'crisis of representation'.

The crisis of representation and the rhetorical turn

One of the major issues associated with post-modern standpoints concerns the so-called 'crisis of representation' that was especially prominent among social and cultural anthropologists in the 1980s, and permeated other social sciences too in subsequent years. This supposed crisis could readily (though not necessarily) be seen to threaten the foundations of social inquiry that for generations had been relatively taken for granted. It is in part a reflection of the literary or textual turn taken by the human disciplines, and in part reflects wider aspects of cultural and intellectual critique.

From within anthropology, the crisis of representation was centred on the appropriate modes of cultural representation or reconstruction. It was, and is, widely recognized that 'the ethnography' has for many decades referred to twin aspects of research – the conduct of fieldwork in all its aspects, and the written product of that research such as the research monograph. The anthropologist is thus recognizably engaged in a double process of engagement with the field. First, she or he is engaged in a protracted series of transactions and explorations in 'the field'. In and of themselves, these engagements are far from innocent. The cultures and social realities that are reported in the course of fieldwork are dependent on active explorations, and the joint negotiations that the anthropologist undertakes in conjunction with her or his hosts and informants. Secondly, there are further acts of interpretation when the anthropologist acts as author. The texts of anthropology craft reconstructions of the social world and the social actors in question. There is, therefore, a profound sense that the discoveries of a discipline like anthropology are not the revelations of an independent social reality, but are *fictions* – in the sense that they are created and crafted products.

This general perspective was articulated and widely publicized by the collection of papers *Writing Culture* (Clifford and Marcus, 1986). There a number of authors explored the textual conventions of cultural anthropology, and through their textual explorations raised more profound questions concerning the ethnographic project. Their reflections included the recognition that ethnographic representation is grounded in conventional modes of representation. These include textual devices and models associated with genres of fiction, as well as styles of non-fiction text, such as travel writing. Their concerns were not confined to the purely textual aspects of ethnographic monographs, however. They also focused on the direct relationship between the *authority* of the ethnographic text and the *authorship* of that selfsame text. The conventional ethnographic monograph, it was argued, was a depersonalized document, in which the ethnographer was an invisible but privileged implied narrator. The social world is surveyed and reported from the single, dominant perspective of the ethnographic author, who is elided from the text itself.

In other words, the stability of the ethnographic enterprise – an especially enduring characteristic of anthropology for many decades – was held up to question. Anthropologists had been able to withstand the ripples of theoretical and epistemological disputes (functionalism, structuralism, Marxism, or whatever) which were always contained within a relatively stable domain of ethnographies. The authority of the ethnography – as opposed to its subsequent interpretation at the meta-level of comparative ethnology and anthropological theory – had remained relatively stable. The crisis of representation in many ways seemed to offer a more profound challenge than the comings and goings of fashionable theories and debates. It seemed to strike at the very legitimacy of the conventional ethnographic mode of representation.

The 'crisis of representation' was by no means confined to the realms of cultural anthropology in the United States. In their surveys of the fields of qualitative research, Denzin and Lincoln (1994, 2000) have on several occasions referred to the crisis of representation as a key phase or 'moment' in the recent history of qualitative research. In and of itself, of course, this 'crisis' did not lead to complete stasis. The critiques of textual and other practices of representation did not halt the production of ethnographies. Indeed, as we shall argue shortly, the various supposed 'crises' have proved extremely productive (for good or ill) in legitimating a plethora of new, alternative, experimental or otherwise reformed ethnographic practices and representations. Clifford and Marcus (1986) is now seen as the landmark volume, but there had been precursors such as Boon (1982), Edmondson (1984) and Fabian (1983). Since the Clifford and Marcus book there has been a steady growth of analyses of all aspects of sociological and anthropological texts from fieldnotes (Sanjek, 1990; Jackson 1990; Emerson et al., 1995) to publications (Behar and Gordon, 1995; James et al., 1997; Denuvo, 1992; Atkinson, 1990, 1992, 1996; Atkinson and Coffey, 1995). Although some of the issues differed, the anthropological interests paralleled a more general exploration of the 'rhetoric of inquiry'. A number of scholars, with backgrounds in diverse academic disciplines, embarked on a series of intellectual projects – some consciously linked, others quite independently derived – on the textual practices that characterized specific disciplines and their historical and cultural specificities. This was partly fuelled by the so-called rediscovery of rhetoric.

Since the Enlightenment, rhetoric – once a respected and canonical discipline in classical and medieval scholarship – had been relegated to the margins of intellectual life. With the rise of modern science, rhetoric was a marginalized, even despised activity. It contrasted with the rational and factual status ascribed to science, having connotations of sophistry and persuasion. In recent years, however, there has been a growing movement to recuperate rhetoric, not least in the recognition that the 'sciences' and other factual enterprises are themselves inescapably rhetorical in character. The natural sciences, economics, history, among many other domains, have been shown to deploy their own rhetorical conventions – not least in their characteristic literary conventions. Such analyses have the consequence of demystifying those conventions. For instance, they can show how scholars convey their own authoritative status; how they persuade their readers through the use of metaphors and other figures of speech; how they use examples and other illustrative materials to build plausible arguments.

One of the consequences of the literary and rhetorical turn is an enhanced awareness of the social processes involved in analysis. In the collection edited by Sanjek (1990) anthropologists reflected upon fieldnotes – how they are constructed, used and managed. We come to understand that fieldnotes are not a closed, completed, final text: rather they are indeterminate, subject to reading, rereading, coding, recoding, interpreting, reinterpreting. The literary turn has encouraged (or insisted on) the revisiting, or reopening, of ethnographer's accounts and analyses

of her or his fieldwork. Wolf (1992), for example, revisited her fieldnotes, her journal, and a short story she had written doing fieldwork in a Taiwanese village.

Reflexive analysis of textual conventions coincides with the crisis of representation: 'The erosion of classic norms in anthropology (objectivism, complicity with colonialism, social life structured by mixed rituals and customs, ethnographies as monuments to a culture) was complete' (Denzin and Lincoln, 1994: 10). The crises put in hazard not only the products of ethnographers' work, but the moral and intellectual authority of ethnographers themselves. The 'crisis' was not founded merely in ethnographers' growing self-consciousness concerning their own literary work and its conventional forms. More fundamentally, it grew out of the growing contestation of (especially mainstream Western) ethnographers' implicit claims to a privileged and totalizing gaze. It leads to increasingly urgent claims to legitimacy on the part of so-called 'indigenous' ethnographers, and for increasingly complex relationships between ethnographers' selves, the selves of 'others' and the texts they both engage in (cf. Reed-Danahay, 1997).

Writing as analysis

It would be wrong to imply that the textual turn in qualitative research has been exclusively a matter of critique or ideological dispute. For better or worse, it has had its productive side. In other words, it has led to a self-conscious attempt on the part of some authors to deploy and develop a variety of textual conventions, to transgress the taken-for-granted boundaries between genres, and thus to match literary styles to analytic interests. Richardson (1990, 1994), for instance, makes a case for writing as a mode of analysis in its own right. There are, metaphorically speaking, two kinds of response to the 'crisis of representation' and its associated ideas. The pessimistic view might lead one to regard the ethnographic enterprise as all but impossible. One might lapse into silence. The crisis could easily result in an intellectualized form of writer's block. The more optimistic response would be to recognize literary and rhetorical conventions for what they are, and resolve to use and explore them creatively. In practice, many contemporary scholars have taken the optimistic path. (Not everyone regards their products with optimism, it must be acknowledged.) If one starts from the recognition that there is no such thing as a perfectly innocent or transparent mode of representation, then it is possible to explore the possibilities of written text – and other representations – in a creative way. One can use them to construct particular kinds of analysis, and to evoke particular kinds of response in one's audience.

As a consequence, we now have research monographs, journals, papers and book series that actively pursue and encourage textual experimentation in the pursuit of sociological or anthropological analysis. Indeed, within this genre of work, writing is stressed as a major analytic resource. As Goodall (2000: 10) puts it, in a book specifically addressed to the 'new ethnography': 'New ethnographers are not researchers who learn to "write it up", but *writers* who learn how to use their research and how they write to "get it down"'. Writing that reflects such a stance can become highly personalized. It conforms closely to a mix of what Van Maanen (1988) referred to as 'impressionistic' and 'confessional' writing: in the context of the 'new' ethnography, these literary styles do not contrast with 'realist' writing – conventionally used to convey the main thrust of the ethnography itself. Rather, the text as a whole is impressionistic and confessional. There are numerous recent examples. They include Jones's (1998) monograph on the setting and the performance of women's music. She mingles vividly impressionistic accounts of the setting – a music club – and some of the performers with autobiographical reflections on the conduct of the research and her own emotional responses to the setting and the music. The text itself is further interspersed with lyrics of the songs being performed. Moreover, the whole text is framed in a context of anxiety about the examination of the dissertation on which the monograph is based. The examination itself is dramatized in a surreal episode that includes Reliability and Validity as actors. Ellis and Bochner (1996) bring together an important series of exemplars that display a variety of literary devices and styles for cultural representation. They include an account by Folz and Griffin (1996) on their personal transformations through their immersion in feminist witchcraft and magic. Fox (1996), in the same anthology, constructs a three-person account of child sexual abuse, in which the edited

words of a perpetrator and his victim are juxtaposed, while the author's own words – as researcher and as a former victim herself – are interposed between the two. Textually, therefore, the bulk of the chapter consists of three columns of speech, in which the three actors' words are reconstructed as if to construct a three-way confrontation and exploration of their experiences. It echoes Ronai's (1995) 'layered account' of the experience of abuse in which a fragmentary text is used to evoke and convey its subject-matter.

Voice and polyvocality

The representational practices and devices we have alluded to relate closely to the analytic strategy of evoking multiple 'voices' in the reconstruction of social realities. If research dissolves the privilege of the observer/author, then it also implies that there should be multiple voices identifiable in the analysis. This goes well beyond the perfectly ordinary practice of quoting informants or including extracts from fieldnotes in order to illustrate ethnographic texts. The polyvocal text – and hence the analytic strategy that underlies it – does not subordinate the voices and press them into the service of a single narrative. Rather, there are multiple and shifting narratives. The point of view of the 'analysis' is a shifting one. There is no single implied narrator occupying a privileged interpretative position. A relatively early example of such a text is Krieger's (1983) account of a lesbian community. Krieger, as author/analyst, constructs a collage or palimpsest of narratives, juxtaposed in the style of stream-of-consciousness literary work. Her analysis of the community is implicit in those textual arrangements, which are not superseded or supplemented by a dominant authorial commentary. The expression of voices has become a major preoccupation of many qualitative researchers in recent years, and to some extent the force of polyvocality has become blunted: in some contexts it can seem to mean little more than 'letting the informants speak for themselves', with little or no theoretical sophistication. On the other hand, it can give rise to complex and dense representations (see Atkinson, 1999, for a review of different kinds of recent contribution). Equally, the celebration of voices can allow the author to find her or his 'voice' in a way that differs from the canons of conventional academic writing: it provides permission for first-person narratives that insert the author in her or his texts, rather than suppressing the personal in the analytic.

Reflexivity and autoethnography

Many of the texts we have referred to include a strong element of autobiographical writing on the part of the ethnographers. This leads us to a discussion of the principle of reflexivity in the conduct and representation of ethnographic work. Reflexivity is a term that has been applied widely and with differing connotations in the discussion of social research. At its most general, it implies the recognition that social researchers – especially but not exclusively qualitative researchers – are always implicated and engaged in the process of inquiry. All research is, in that sense, reactive. In the context of ethnography and other qualitative research, the principle of reflexivity means that the social reality that is reported is – to some degree – constructed through the explorations and transactions undertaken by the researcher. The 'field' of ethnographic fieldwork is not a preordained entity, but is actively generated through the ethnographer's own presence and is a negotiated outcome of the field research itself. In the same vein, interviews do not merely elicit preformed information or recollected experiences. They are thought of as a dialogue between the interviewer and the informant, while the content of the interview is also a jointly produced outcome of the encounter.

In the course of conducting the ethnography, or the interviews, therefore, the researcher will not seek simply to distance herself or himself. Reflexive practice calls for the careful documentation of how the researcher is implicated in the setting. This will not be seen, moreover, in purely cognitive terms. The principle of reflexivity is also taken by many contemporary researchers to include the affective aspects of the research process. The construction and reconstruction of a social reality – and hence the analytic process – is not, from this point of view, a matter of disengaged data collection and dispassionate data classification. Rather, the researcher's own emotional work is an integral part of the research enterprise. Ellis (1991), for instance, argues that the researcher's own experiences and responses

are part of the primary data: they are not gratuitous epiphenomena. Reflexive research practice thus deals with the observer and the observed simultaneously, in the belief that they are mutually constructed in the course of research. Coffey (1999) has documented how contemporary ethnographers conceptualize the personal transformations in their own identities in the course of ethnographic field research. One cannot analyse the social world in terms of process, changing definitions of the situation, and shifting or fragmented social identities while treating the self of the ethnographer as a static entity, separate from the research setting and one's research hosts. For some commentators, this kind of reflexivity is also a reflection of feminist analysis. The dissolution of authority and the celebration of polyvocal representations is congruent with feminist epistemological and ethical commitments. The emphasis on co-operation between researcher and researched, the radical questioning of authorial privilege, and the polyvocality of representations are often felt to be congruent with feminist goals.

Reflexivity and first-person narratives lead directly to the possibilities of autoethnography. The term itself has several connotations. Here we shall focus briefly on analyses that are based substantially or even exclusively on the writer's personal experiences, memories and actions. This, therefore, moves the personal from the marginal notes of the confessional tale to occupy the central place of sociological or anthropological analysis. Autoethnography and autobiography can be virtually indistinguishable. The resulting accounts can be highly charged emotionally for the author and reader alike. Tillmann-Healy (1996), for instance, has written a highly personalized account of her own experience of bulimia, while in the same anthology Ronai (1996) writes a moving account of her 'mentally retarded' mother. Reed-Danahay (1997) explores a range of usages of the term 'autoethnography', which – in anthropological circles at least – can range from the anthropology of one's own cultural setting – which is not novel – to treating oneself and one's immediate social circle as the object of scrutiny and reflection. Autoethnography at its most autobiographical, then, can treat the 'ethnographer' as the sole topic of study. In other words, the introspective or reflective account is not grounded in research about someone or something else, but is the sole topic of the 'research'.

The practice of autoethnography thus brings us full circle to the postmodern critiques of so-called positivist research. The latter, it is claimed, is grounded in a view of the researcher that effaces her or his presence in the research process and in the texts of social reporting. The goal of objectivity requires an impersonal mode of inquiry and an equally disengaged and impersonal mode of writing. Postmodern approaches, by contrast, reflect intensely personal engagement. Reflexivity dissolves the radical distinctions between the researcher and the researched, to the extent that the two may become indistinguishable in the practices of autobiographical reflection.

AMBIGUITIES OF POSTMODERNISM

Hitherto we have deliberately refrained from offering a definition of 'postmodernism' itself. We have provided a selective account of how postmodernism is invoked to justify recent 'alternative' positions concerning social inquiry itself. We have done so for one major reason. Postmodernism in social theory does not lend itself to simple definition. One cannot derive a simple set of propositions or maxims that constitute a single postmodernist epistemology or methodology, and then proceed to apply them to social research. Moreover, it is not perfectly clear how the recent debates in qualitative research relate to the general tenets of such postmodern thought. Here, therefore, we shall review a number of key themes in postmodernism and use them to reflect on the methodological debates. We shall then go on to suggest that the identification of current methodological perspectives as postmodern entails a number of ambiguities.

The denial of foundations

The key congruence between the research perspectives and the general theories lies in the rejection of foundational claims for knowledge and the claims for conventional science and scholarship. The latter are associated with the intellectual legacy of the Enlightenment, and the social forms of modernity. Modern society and modern social thought are grounded in faith in the possibility of objective knowledge of the natural and social world, in the commitment to progress as an ideal and as a possibility. The former is

guided by universal principles of reason, the latter by the universal principles of science.

The postmodern turn, on the other hand, denies such foundational principles. Major protagonists like Lyotard (1984) insist that the grand narratives of science and progress are no longer tenable. Far from a unity of progressive science, postmodernity identifies a proliferation of cultures of experience and knowledge. There is no single neutral standpoint from which objective truth may be derived. A unified canon of knowledge is thus replaced with a diverse array of cultural processes. The proliferation of information and representations in contemporary society leads to variegated domains of discourse, producing culturally specific and localized versions of reality. Postmodernism argues that there are no universal truths to be discovered, because all human investigators are grounded in human society and can only produce partial locally and historically specific insights. Because postmodernism denies that there are any universal truths, it also denies the possibility of generalized, universalistic theories. Patti Lather (1991: 21) summarizes postmodernism as follows:

> The essence of the postmodern argument is that the dualisms which continue to dominate Western thought are inadequate for understanding a world of multiple causes and effects interacting in complex and non-linear ways, all of which are rooted in a limitless array of historical and cultural specificities.

Similarly, Jane Flax (1990: 41) argues that 'Postmodern philosophers seek to throw into radical doubt beliefs … derived from the Enlightenment' (see also Flax, 1993). She lists among the beliefs thrown into doubt: the existence of a stable self, reason, an objective foundation for knowledge, and universalism. As she forcefully expresses this (Flax, 1993: 450): 'The meanings – or even existence – of concepts essential to all forms of Enlightenment metanarrative (reason, history, science, self, knowledge, power, gender, and the inherent superiority of Western culture) have been subjected to increasingly corrosive attacks.'

Now it is clear that the inspirations of qualitative research in sociology and other disciplines are not currently grounded in appeals to positivistic science. But it is equally unclear that they rest on a rejection of previous modernist and positivist epistemologies. It is quite wrong to imply that all of sociological or anthropological analysis of earlier generations was grounded in a commitment to positivist science. The imputation is, indeed, quite ironic. Generations of researchers were castigated for being 'unscientific' in their commitment to qualitative research and cultural interpretation. Among sociologists in particular the tradition of 'interpretative' scholarship is grounded in a radical distinction between the natural and cultural disciplines, rather than a unity of the sciences. This is a central tenet of European *verstehende* sociology from Dilthey and Weber onwards. Equally, it is far from clear that the philosophical roots of American symbolic interactionism in pragmatist philosophy can be equated with a positivist tradition. The symbolic interactionist tradition that has informed a great deal of ethnographic and other qualitative research has consistently stressed perspectival knowledge. It has certainly not endorsed a strongly 'objectivist' and 'scientistic' approach to research. It would be more accurate to recognize the complexities of research and its historical development (see Atkinson et al., 1999, and Delamont et al., 2000, for expansions of this point). Qualitative research has never been monolithically modern.

Modern society has been dissolved

The postmodern position is not just about transformation in how we understand the social, it also proposes a radical transformation in the social world itself. Modernity was, it is claimed, grounded in industrial production. The postmodern, by contrast, is predicated on consumption. Baudrillard's (1997) emphasis on symbolic exchange and consumer society is a major point of departure here. Postmodern society is characterized by a proliferation of lifestyles. The tourist, the spectator and the shopper are among the types of postmodern consumer (Lash and Urry, 1994; Urry, 1990).

It is far from clear that this is a transformation that has actually resulted in major changes in the everyday lives of most of the people with whom sociologists and anthropologists conduct field research. Indeed, it is not altogether certain that they have all experienced 'modernity'. Modernity is at least uneven. Even in modern European and American societies, the persistence of peasant cultures, practical religion and religious fundamentalism, and the uneven penetration of state bureaucracy, mean that modernity does

not uniquely define everyday experience for all their members. The anthropology of contemporary Europe is ample testimony to the persistence of the pre-modern (Delamont, 1994). Latour (1993) points out that 'we have never been modern', in the sense that postmodernism takes literally the claims of modernity in assuming that the social world has been uniformly secularized and disenchanted. This point was made forcibly in a letter to the *London Review of Books*, from K.W.C. Sinclair-Loutit, recounting a conversation with a proud Orthodox Serb in 1994: 'My friend, a good Serbian Orthodox Christian, was of a culture continuous with that of the Byzantine Empire. The Renaissance, the Reformation, the Enlightenment and the Industrial Revolution had not touched him.' (*London Review of Books*, 16 April 1998: 4). To that extent, the Enlightenment seems to have been the preserve of an intellectual minority with access to particular forms of knowledge: it constitutes the habitus of the intelligentsia (Bourdieu, 1996).

There is, therefore, little justification in the claim that postmodern research is predicated on the distinctive emergence of a postmodern society. On the contrary, social research confronts and explores a wide variety of social forms and types. It does little service to the social sciences to treat them uncritically in terms of their all being 'pre-modern', or 'modern' or 'postmodern'. Neither modernity nor postmodernity uniquely defines the everyday lives of the deviant, the marginalized, the impoverished or many other groups that have long been among the subject-matter of ethnographic and other qualitative research.

Indeed, there is a strong sense in which the topics claimed for postmodern analysis have been central to social research virtually since the early years of the twentieth century. Consider, for instance, the identification of the postmodern urban experience. The *flâneur* is identified as the archetype of the explorer and consumer of a postmodern urban experience, with its labyrinthine, splintered array of physical and symbolic representations. Yet this mode of experience and interpretation was identified and practised in Berlin by Simmel – whose sociology should be central to the ethnographic, qualitative tradition. Indeed, as Frisby (1985) documents, the project of 'modernity' explored by Baudelaire, Simmel, Benjamin and Kracauer prefigured key themes in the supposed 'postmodern' programme. Benjamin's 'arcades project', for instance, identifies the modern metropolitan experience in Paris in terms that could be applied to a 'postmodern' programme (cf. Buck-Morss, 1989). It is neither necessary nor accurate to impose spurious distinctions between the sociology of the modern and a postmodernist programme.

Texts and representations

The centrality of representations to postmodern theory is clear. The rejection of a simple correspondence between the social world and the texts that report it necessarily places renewed emphasis on the texts of social reportage. But it is not necessary to imply a radical break with past practices, or to invoke a distinctively postmodern slant. There is, for instance, little need to appeal only to recent developments in ethnographic writing and commentary as evidence of 'blurred genres'. Relationships between the aesthetic and the scientific, or between the positive and interpretivist have been detectable for many years – indeed, throughout the development of ethnographic research over the past hundred years. (Admittedly, they have not been equally remarked on, nor taken the same form at all times.) It is a well-known aspect of the history of sociology – but it bears repetition in this context – that the early period of urban ethnography in Chicago drew on aesthetic and literary models as much as on models of 'scientific' research. In her excellent book on the subject Cappetti (1993) traces the linkages between the sociological imagination that flourished among members of the Chicago School, and the contemporaneous literary traditions. The sociological perspective was fuelled by the textual conventions of realist fiction. The sociological celebration of the 'life story' – through the life-history and the ethnographic approach – was influenced by the novel of development. Equally, some of the literary inspirations drew broadly speaking on a sociological perspective. More generally still, the ethnographic tradition and literary genres in the United States have displayed intertextual relationships over many decades. The styles of urban realism, the literary creation of characters and types in the city, and the narrative of modern fiction – these all contributed to the styles of ethnographic representation (see Krieger, 1983, for an exemplar).

Furthermore, it is unnecessary to equate an awareness of textual conventions with a crisis of legitimation or with radical critique. Van Maanen's (1988) account of the conventions of ethnographic writing identifies different styles or genres of writing, but is clearly not intended to be a radical critique of the entire ethnographic enterprise. Atkinson (1982) wrote about the symbolic interactionist tradition in ethnographic fieldwork and its characteristic literary formats. In doing so he drew on aspects of literary theory. But he justified the exercise in terms of a continuation of symbolic interactionism's preoccupation with language rather than as an assault on that particular tradition of research. These analyses were certainly not intended to be postmodern. The application of literary theory to the texts of sociology or anthropology does not need to be understood in terms of a postmodern assault on the authority of such accounts.

Reflexive postmodernism

Advocates of postmodernism reject dualistic discriminations between the researcher and the researched. They stress the degree to which the researcher is implicated in the research process, and reject the myth of the disengaged researcher. Yet one does not have to appeal to postmodernism and invoke major epistemological ruptures to take seriously the notion of reflexivity. Indeed, Hammersley and Atkinson (1983, 1995) suggested that reflexivity was the major principle to guide our understanding of the ethnographic enterprise, avoiding the pitfalls of positivism and naturalism. They did so without recourse to appeals to postmodernism, however. Indeed, they saw the principle of reflexivity as embedded in the ethnographic tradition itself. In particular, symbolic interactionism suggested a direct homology between the researcher as a social actor and the social actors he or she is observing and talking to. Reflexive self-awareness is fundamental to symbolic interactionism's view of the social world. So too is the idea that the researcher is actively constructing the world under observation, through practical transactions and engagements with it. One is not dependent on the insights afforded by postmodernism to pay attention to the ethnographer's own presence and engagement with the research process and its products.

Feminist postmodernism

There are some serious paradoxes in the invocation of postmodernism and the alignment with feminist and other critical or emancipatory movements. Indeed, some feminist scholars themselves have not been slow to point out that the leading exponents of postmodernism were men. Many of the scholars who have argued that postmodernism renders extant research outdated, outmoded and passé are middle-class white men in secure jobs in industrialized countries. Thus Fox-Genovese (1986: 134) has commented: 'Surely it is no coincidence that the Western white male elite proclaimed the death of the subject at precisely the moment at which it might have had to share that status with the women and peoples of other races and classes who were beginning to challenge its supremacy'. A similar point is made by Somer Brodribb (1992: 7–8) when she asserts that 'postmodernism is the cultural capital of late patriarchy'. For those feminists hostile to postmodernism, its intellectual origins are inherently anti-women: 'Post-modern theory's misogynist and very specific historical origins among post World War II Parisian intellectuals – from Lévi-Strauss and Lacan to Foucault and Derrida – require excessive intellectual modification and machinations to include women' (Hoff, 1994: 151).

Feminists have been deeply divided in their responses to postmodernism, and Olesen (2000) provides a thorough and even-handed review of the substantial and varied literature. Feminist scholarship on science is a case in point. Feminists have proposed 'standpoint' epistemology in place of appeals to universalistic and neutral inquiry. Authors such as Haraway (1991) have drawn on feminist and poststructuralist themes in exploring the culture of scientific discourse and its appropriation of women's lives. Yet the direct assault on 'science' from these quarters also takes us to the paradox of feminist postmodernism. As Flax (1993: 447) points out, much feminist scholarship has been 'critical of the contents' of the Enlightenment dream, yet simultaneously 'unable to abandon them', and she argues (Flax, 1993: 448) that postmodernism is particularly threatening for feminism because 'Three of the discourses feminists have attempted to adapt to our own purposes, liberal political theory, Marxism, and empirical social science, express some

form of this Enlightenment dream'. Because the Enlightenment was a *male* cosmology, she argues, feminists must abandon it, to create their own. Flax is confident that the insights of postmodernism will set women free from a childlike state in which they wait for 'higher authorities' to rescue them, clinging to a naive myth of 'sisterhood'. For every Flax welcoming postmodernism (e.g., Flax, 1990) there are other women anxious that it will destroy feminism, or mounting a vigorous attack (e.g., Brodribb, 1992). The debate is highly polemicized, and Brodribb, in particular, reaches rhetorical heights which leave the majority of us gasping. Her opponents – those feminists who wish to become postmodernists, or adapt postmodernism to their own ends – are called 'ragpickers in the bins of male ideas' (Brodribb, 1992: xxiii). The violence of the controversy, and hence the anxieties underlying it, can be seen in a highly charged debate in *Women's History Review* between Hoff (1994, 1996) Kent (1996) and Ramazanoğlu (1996). Dorothy Smith – hardly a positivist by any conceivable stretch of the imagination – has reaffirmed the problematic relationship between feminism and postmodernist analysis (Smith, 1999).

Voices and identities

The ambiguities of postmodernism and social research are also detectable in the treatment of persons and voices. There is a deep ambiguity as to whether postmodern qualitative inquiry is concerned with individuals as persons, or with voices and discourse that displace or decentre the human subject. The treatments of persons and voices in contemporary social research are highly differentiated. The extent of biographical, autobiographical, narrative and cognate analytic strategies is voluminous (see Plummer, 2001, for an authoritative review). Within these diverse approaches there is a manifest tension. Much of what passes for contemporary 'postmodern' qualitative research can be attributed to an essentially romantic tradition of thought (Silverman, 1989; Atkinson, 1999; Atkinson and Silverman, 1997; Strong and Dingwall, 1989), privileging the personal, the interior, the emotional and the experiential. Researching 'lived experience' is celebrated as the goal of such inquiry. In itself this emphasis is ironic, for the romantic spirit it evokes has historically been antipathetic to the positivist and – in that sense – modernist spirit that the post modernists repeatedly assault.

The failure to see this irony is itself a reflection of the collective amnesia that too often lies behind the celebration of the new and the avant-garde by postmodernism's spokespeople. It is, however, antipathetic to postmodernism's indifference to the personal. The treatment of 'voice' that is derived from poststructuralist philosophy dissolves the human subject, whereas much contemporary qualitative research stresses the biographical and the centrality of personal experience. The perspectives of theorists such as Baudrillard, Lyotard and Derrida are not grounded in a humanist preoccupation with individual experience. Sociologists and others who commit themselves to the evocation of 'lived experience' and the celebration of social actors as heroes or heroines of their own life stories are in many ways at odds with the guiding metatheoretical preoccupations of post modernism and poststructuralism. Equally, as Plummer (2001) points out, it is not necessary to invoke those theoretical commitments in order to explore the biographical and the narrative. For those interests are grounded in a tradition of interpretative research that pre-dates recent theoretical enthusiasms. A similar tension can be identified with respect to the 'voice' of the author in her or his texts. The postmodern – certainly the poststructuralist – position announces the 'death of the author', in the sense that it rejects essentially romantic views of the creative subject. Textual practices rather than authorial inspiration are the topic of critical analysis. Postmodern social scientists have embraced the textual turn, emphasizing and exploring the textual production of social inquiry (Richardson, 1994). In doing so, however, many have written themselves in as romantic authors – as 'poets', 'playwrights' or 'screen-writers'. There is another profound irony here, which is but one manifestation of a recurrent tension between the humanist, interpretative tendency and its antithesis in poststructuralism and critical theory – postmodernism is invoked in order to gloss over these antinomies, but it cannot resolve them in its own terms.

CONCLUSION

Within the compass of a single chapter it is not possible to do full justice to the full range of themes and their implications. Much less is it possible to illustrate the diverse applications of such perspectives to empirical research. We have identified and discussed a small selection from among the many possible themes. It should be clear, however, that postmodern thought has been used to inspire and to justify a variety of research perspectives. Qualitative research has expanded exponentially throughout the social sciences, as has methodological commentary. Within this burgeoning literature, there have flourished a number of 'alternative' perspectives. In evaluating this contemporary avant-garde, one should be cautious in assessing the claims for postmodern research approaches.

As we hope to have made clear, we regard postmodernism as more of a rhetoric of justification in this context than a coherent set of theoretical and methodological precepts. Moreover, in order to identify contemporary versions as inherently postmodern it is necessary for its proponents to do some violence to the history of social research. They inappropriately lump together research traditions under the rubric of a monolithic modernist and positivist paradigm. In doing so they do symbolic violence to the tradition. They overlook the contributions of pragmatism and symbolic interactionism, and of various forms of interpretative social thought. The significant influence of phenomenology and existentialism is all but ignored. The tradition of *verstehen* is distorted. The long tradition of life-history and other biographical research can be overlooked and distorted (Plummer, 2001).

Further, under the influence of postmodern excesses, social research can be strangely transformed – or even deformed. Taken to their logical extremes, reflexivity and autoethnography can result in solipsistic exercises. The self-absorption of some autobiographical and introspective accounts contributes nothing to systematic understanding of social processes or institutions. Some of the exercises in literary experimentation, including 'poetry', can be embarrassingly clumsy, self-congratulatory texts. Hammersley (1999: 580) asks 'what justification is there for ethnographers trying to compete directly with Virginia Wolf or even with Tom Wolfe?'. In fact, few, if any of the experimental texts to be found in recent monographs, journal papers and book chapters come anywhere near 'competing' with the major works of literature or even of the new journalism.

Equally, there are dangers in the extreme relativization of social research. It is too easy to take a position that abandons altogether the normal criteria of truth and relevance. There are too many sharp dichotomies invoked. One may recognize the inescapably reflexive nature of social research without a complete denial of authority, or completely abandoning the aim of generating research texts that are faithful representations of the social world. Hammersley (e.g., 1992, 1995, 1999), amongst others, for instance, has consistently argued against the extremes of postmodernist claims in this area. Like ourselves, Hammersley has argued that advocates of postmodernism exaggerate their differences from previous generations. Social and cultural anthropologists, and interpretative sociologists of various persuasions, have certainly not been consistently 'positivist'; they have certainly not all endorsed a natural-science model of inquiry. Indeed, it would be odd indeed had the majority of ethnographers thought that they were mirroring 'science' when they themselves often made a clear differentiation between the cultural and natural sciences, and when their critics so consistently criticized them for *not* adhering to 'scientific' criteria. As Seale (1999) has cogently argued, one can learn much from the critical perspectives of recent years. But in doing so, it is not necessarily altogether to lose sight of the broad criteria of adequate method that have characterized qualitative research for many decades.

It would also be quite wrong to be seduced by the rhetoric that suggests that postmodern research has become the new orthodoxy, or that we have entered into a period of permanent revolution that transcends any cumulative traditions. As Lofland (1995) has pointed out, many practitioners of ethnographic research have continued to pursue their inquiries in the interests of generic knowledge. By no means all qualitative research is conducted under the auspices of post-paradigmatic or postmodernist perspectives (cf. Delamont et al., 2000). Experimental texts and other expressions of the postmodern tend to be clustered in particular journals, book series, conferences and the like, and to be celebrated by high-profile commentators like Denzin and Lincoln – tending to concentrate the work for particular audiences and to amplify its significance.

In general, therefore, we appreciate the lively variety of approaches to the analysis and representation of social phenomena that currently characterizes qualitative research. We think that there are some ideas that are to be welcomed. We endorse the recognition of reflexivity as a principle of fieldwork and of analysis. We approve of a renewed self-conscious awareness of how we construct arguments and written representations. But we do not think that these insights are necessarily derived from postmodernism *per se*. We do not think that it is necessary to invoke radical disjunctures between contemporary ideas and those of previous decades. Indeed, a reflexive research practice and a concern for language and representation are entirely congruent with the core preoccupations of interpretative sociology and cultural anthropology. In other words, our view of postmodernist research parallels the famous politician's verdict of an opposing political party: 'They have many sound and novel ideas; unfortunately none of their novel ideas are sound and none of their sound ideas are novel'.

ACKNOWLEDGMENTS

We are grateful to Amanda Coffey for useful discussions on these and related issues, and to Rosemary Jones for typing an early draft.

REFERENCES

Altheide, D.L. and Johnson J.M. (1994) 'Criteria for assessing interpretive validity in qualitative research', in N.K. Denzin and Y.S. Lincoln (eds), *Handbook of Qualitative Research*. Thousand Oaks: Sage, pp. 485–99.

Atkinson, P.A. (1982) 'Writing ethnography', in H.J. Helle (ed.), *Kultur und Institution*. Berlin: Duncker und Humblot, pp. 77–105.

Atkinson, P.A. (1990). *The Ethnographic Imagination*. London: Routledge.

Atkinson, P.A. (1992). *Understanding Ethnographic Texts*. Thousand Oaks, CA: Sage.

Atkinson, P.A. (1996). *Sociological Readings and Re-readings*. Aldershot: Gower.

Atkinson, P.A. (1999) 'Voiced and unvoiced' (review essay), *Sociology* 33(1): 191–6.

Atkinson, P.A. and Coffey, A. (1995). 'Realism and its discontents: The crisis of cultural representation in ethnographic texts', in B. Adam and S. Allen (eds), *Theorising Culture*. London: UCL Press, pp. 103–39.

Atkinson, P.A. and Silverman, D. (1997). 'Kundera's *Immortality*: The interview society and the invention of the self', *Qualitative Inquiry*, 3: 304–25.

Atkinson, P.A., Delamont, S. and Coffey, A. (1999) 'Ethnography: post, past and present', *Journal of Contemporary Ethnography*, 28 (5): 460–71.

Baudrillard, J. (1997) *The Consumer Society: Myths and Structures*. London: Sage.

Behar, R. and Gordon, D. (eds) (1995) *Women Writing Culture*. Berkeley: University of California Press.

Boon, J.A. (1982). *Other Tribes, Other Scribes: Symbolic Anthropology in the Comparative Study of Authors, Histories, Religions and Texts*. Cambridge: Cambridge University Press.

Bourdieu, P. (1996) *The State Nobility*. Cambridge: Polity.

Brodribb, S. (1992) *Nothing Mat(t)ers*. Melbourne: Spinifex Press.

Buck-Morss, S. (1989) *The Dialectics of Seeing: Walter Benjamin and the Arcades Project*. Cambridge, MA: MIT Press.

Cappetti, P. (1993) *Writing Chicago*. New York: Columbia University Press.

Clifford, J. and Marcus, G.E. (eds) (1986). *Writing Culture*. Berkeley: University of California Press.

Coffey, A. (1999) *The Ethnographic Self*. London: Sage.

Delamont, S. (1994) *Appetites and Identities: An Introduction to the Social Anthropology of Western Europe*. London: Routledge.

Delamont, S., Coffey, A. and Atkinson, P.A. (2000) 'The twilight years?', *Qualitative Studies in Education*, 13(3): 223–38.

Denuvo, R (1992) 'No anthro-apologies, or Der(r)id(a) a discipline', in R.H. Brown (ed.), *Writing the Social Text: Poetics and Politics in Social Science Discourse*. New York: de Gruyter.

Denzin, N.K. (1997) *Interpretive Ethnography: Ethnographic Practices for the 21st Century*. Thousand Oaks, CA: Sage.

Denzin, N.K. and Lincoln, Y.S. (eds) (1994). *Handbook of Qualitative Research*. Thousand Oaks, CA: Sage.

Denzin, N.K. and Lincoln, Y.S. (2000) *Handbook of Qualitative Research* (2nd edition). Thousand Oaks, CA: Sage.

Edmondson, R. (1984) *Rhetoric in Sociology*. London: Macmillian.

Ellis, C. (1991) 'Sociological introspection and emotional experience', *Symbolic Interaction*, 14: 23–50.

Ellis, C. and Bochner, A. (eds) (1996) *Composing Ethnography*. Walnut Creek, CA: AltaMira.

Emerson, R.M., Fretz, R.I. and Strauss, L.L (1995) *Writing Ethnographic Fieldnotes*. Chicago: University of Chicago Press.

Fabian, J. (1983). *Time and the Other: How Anthropology Makes Its Subject*. New York: Columbia University Press.

Flax, J. (1990) 'Postmodernism and gender relations in feminist theory', in L.J. Nicholson (ed.), *Feminism/Postmodernism*. London: Routledge.

Flax, J. (1993) 'The end of innocence', in J. Butler and J.W. Scott (eds), *Feminists Theorise the Political*. New York: Routledge.

Foltz, T.G. and Griffin, W. (1996) '"She changes everything she touches": ethnographic journeys of self-discovery', in C. Ellis and A. Bochner (eds), *Composing Ethnography: Alternative Forms of Qualitative Writing*. Walnut Creek, CA: AltaMira, pp. 301–29.

Fox, K.V. (1996) 'Silent voices: A subversive reading of child sexual abuse', in C. Ellis and A. Bochner (eds), *Composing Ethnography: Alternative Forms of Qualitative Writing*. Walnut Creek, CA: AltaMira, pp. 330–56.

Fox-Genovese, E. (1986) 'The claims of a common culture', *Salmagundi*, 72(Fall): 134–51.

Frisby, D. (1985) *Fragments of modernity*. Cambridge: Polity.

Goodall, H.L. (2000) *Writing the New Ethnography*. Walnut Creek, CA: AltaMira.

Hammersley, M. (1992) *What's Wrong with Ethnography: Methodological Explorations*. London: Routledge.

Hammersley, M. (1995) 'Theory and evidence in qualitative research', *Quality and Quantity*, 29(1): 55–66.

Hammersley, M. (1999) 'Not bricolage but boatbuilding', *Journal of Contemporary Ethnography*, 28(5): 574–85.

Hammersley, M. and Atkinson, P.A. (1983). *Ethnography: Principles in Practice*. London: Tavistock.

Hammersley, M. and Atkinson, P.A. (1995) *Ethnography: Principles in Practice* (2nd edition). London: Routledge.

Haraway, D. (1991) *Simians, Cyborgs and Women: The Reinvention of Nature*. London: Routledge.

Hoff, J. (1994) 'Gender as a postmodern category of paralysis', *Women's History Review*, 3(2): 149–68.

Hoff, J. (1996) 'A reply to my critics', *Women's History Review*, 5(1): 25–34.

Jackson, J.E. (1990) 'Déjà entendu: the liminal qualities of anthropological fieldnotes', *Journal of Contemporary Ethnography*, 19: 8–43.

James, A., Hockey, J. and Dawson, A. (eds) (1997) *After Writing Culture*. London: Routledge.

Jones, S.H. (1998) *Kaleidoscope Notes*. Walnut Creek, CA: AltaMira.

Kent, S.K. (1996) 'Mistrials and diatribulations', *Women's History Review*, 5(1): 9–18.

Krieger, S. (1983) *The Mirror Dance: Identity in a Women's Community*. Philadelphia: Temple University Press.

Lash, S. and Urry, J. (1994) *Economies of Signs and Space*. London: Sage.

Lather, P. (1991) *Getting Smart: Feminist Research with/in the Postmodern*. London: Routledge.

Lather, P. (1993) 'Fertile obsession: Validity after poststructuralism', *Sociological Quarterly*, 34: 673–93.

Latour, B. (1993) *We Have Never Been Modern*. London: Harvester-Wheatsheaf.

Lincoln, Y.S. and Denzin, N.K. (1994) 'The fifth moment', in N.K. Denzin and Y.S. Lincoln (eds), *Handbook of Qualitative Research*. Thousand Oaks, CA: Sage, pp. 575–86.

Lincoln Y.S. and Guba, E. (1985) *Naturalistic Inquiry*. Beverly Hills, CA: Sage.

Lofland, J. (1995) 'Analytic ethnography', *Journal of Contemporary Ethnography*, 24(1): 30–67.

Lyon, D. (1999) *Postmodernity* (2nd edition). Buckingham: Open University Press.

Lyotard, J.F. (1984) *The Postmodern Condition*. Manchester: Manchester University Press.

Olesen, V.L. (2000) 'Feminisms and qualitative research at and into the millennium', in N.K. Denzin and Y.S. Lincoln (eds), *Handbook of Qualitative Research* (2nd edition). Thousand Oaks, CA: Sage, pp. 215–55.

Plummer, K. (2001) *Documents of Life 2*. London: Sage.

Ramazanoğlu, C. (1996) 'Unravelling postmodern paralysis', *Women's History Review*, 5(1): 19–24.

Reed-Danahay, D. (ed.) (1997) *Auto/ethnography*. Oxford: Berg.

Richardson, L. (1990) *Writing Strategies: Reaching Diverse Audiences*. Newbury Park, CA: Sage.

Richardson, L. (1994) 'Writing: a method of inquiry', in N.K. Denzin and Y.S. Lincoln (eds), *Handbook of Qualitative Research*, Thousand Oaks, CA: Sage, pp. 516–29.

Ronai, C.R. (1995) 'Multiple reflections of child sex abuse', *Journal of Contemporary Ethnography*, 23: 395–426.

Ronai, C.R. (1996) 'My mother is mentally retarded', in C. Ellis and A. Bochner (eds), *Composing Ethnography*. Walnut Creek, CA: AltaMira, pp. 109–31.

Sanjek, R. (ed.) (1990) *Fieldnotes: the making of anthropology*. Ithaca, NY: Cornell University Press.

Seale, C. (1999) *The Quality of Qualitative Research*. London: Sage.

Silverman, D. (1989) 'The impossible dreams of romanticism and reformism', in J.F. Gubrium and D. Silverman (eds), *The Politics of Field Research: Sociology beyond Enlightenment*. London: Sage, pp. 30–48.

Smith, D. (1999) *Writing the Social: Critique, Theory, and Investigations*. Toronto: University of Toronto Press.

Strong, P. and Dingwall, R. (1989) 'Romantics and stoics', in J.F. Gubrium and D. Silverman (eds), *The Politics of Field Research: Sociology beyond Enlightenment*. London: Sage, pp. 49–69.

Tillmann-Healy, L.M. (1996) 'A secret life in a culture of thinness', in C. Ellis and A. Bochner (eds), *Composing Ethnography*. Walnut Creek, CA: AltaMira, pp. 76–108.

Urry, J. (1990) *The Tourist Gaze*. London: Sage.

Van Maanen, J. (1988) *Tales of the Field: On Writing Ethnography*. Chicago: University of Chicago Press.

Wolf, M. (1992) *The Thrice Told Tale*, Berkeley: University of California Press.

Appendix

Areas of the Standard Normal Distribution

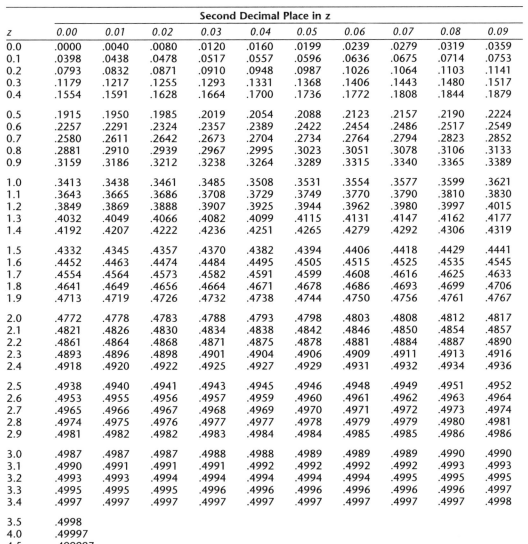

The entries in this table are the probabilities that a standard normal random variable is between 0 and Z (the shaded area).

	Second Decimal Place in z									
z	0.00	0.01	0.02	0.03	0.04	0.05	0.06	0.07	0.08	0.09
0.0	.0000	.0040	.0080	.0120	.0160	.0199	.0239	.0279	.0319	.0359
0.1	.0398	.0438	.0478	.0517	.0557	.0596	.0636	.0675	.0714	.0753
0.2	.0793	.0832	.0871	.0910	.0948	.0987	.1026	.1064	.1103	.1141
0.3	.1179	.1217	.1255	.1293	.1331	.1368	.1406	.1443	.1480	.1517
0.4	.1554	.1591	.1628	.1664	.1700	.1736	.1772	.1808	.1844	.1879
0.5	.1915	.1950	.1985	.2019	.2054	.2088	.2123	.2157	.2190	.2224
0.6	.2257	.2291	.2324	.2357	.2389	.2422	.2454	.2486	.2517	.2549
0.7	.2580	.2611	.2642	.2673	.2704	.2734	.2764	.2794	.2823	.2852
0.8	.2881	.2910	.2939	.2967	.2995	.3023	.3051	.3078	.3106	.3133
0.9	.3159	.3186	.3212	.3238	.3264	.3289	.3315	.3340	.3365	.3389
1.0	.3413	.3438	.3461	.3485	.3508	.3531	.3554	.3577	.3599	.3621
1.1	.3643	.3665	.3686	.3708	.3729	.3749	.3770	.3790	.3810	.3830
1.2	.3849	.3869	.3888	.3907	.3925	.3944	.3962	.3980	.3997	.4015
1.3	.4032	.4049	.4066	.4082	.4099	.4115	.4131	.4147	.4162	.4177
1.4	.4192	.4207	.4222	.4236	.4251	.4265	.4279	.4292	.4306	.4319
1.5	.4332	.4345	.4357	.4370	.4382	.4394	.4406	.4418	.4429	.4441
1.6	.4452	.4463	.4474	.4484	.4495	.4505	.4515	.4525	.4535	.4545
1.7	.4554	.4564	.4573	.4582	.4591	.4599	.4608	.4616	.4625	.4633
1.8	.4641	.4649	.4656	.4664	.4671	.4678	.4686	.4693	.4699	.4706
1.9	.4713	.4719	.4726	.4732	.4738	.4744	.4750	.4756	.4761	.4767
2.0	.4772	.4778	.4783	.4788	.4793	.4798	.4803	.4808	.4812	.4817
2.1	.4821	.4826	.4830	.4834	.4838	.4842	.4846	.4850	.4854	.4857
2.2	.4861	.4864	.4868	.4871	.4875	.4878	.4881	.4884	.4887	.4890
2.3	.4893	.4896	.4898	.4901	.4904	.4906	.4909	.4911	.4913	.4916
2.4	.4918	.4920	.4922	.4925	.4927	.4929	.4931	.4932	.4934	.4936
2.5	.4938	.4940	.4941	.4943	.4945	.4946	.4948	.4949	.4951	.4952
2.6	.4953	.4955	.4956	.4957	.4959	.4960	.4961	.4962	.4963	.4964
2.7	.4965	.4966	.4967	.4968	.4969	.4970	.4971	.4972	.4973	.4974
2.8	.4974	.4975	.4976	.4977	.4977	.4978	.4979	.4979	.4980	.4981
2.9	.4981	.4982	.4982	.4983	.4984	.4984	.4985	.4985	.4986	.4986
3.0	.4987	.4987	.4987	.4988	.4988	.4989	.4989	.4989	.4990	.4990
3.1	.4990	.4991	.4991	.4991	.4992	.4992	.4992	.4992	.4993	.4993
3.2	.4993	.4993	.4994	.4994	.4994	.4994	.4994	.4995	.4995	.4995
3.3	.4995	.4995	.4995	.4996	.4996	.4996	.4996	.4996	.4996	.4997
3.4	.4997	.4997	.4997	.4997	.4997	.4997	.4997	.4997	.4997	.4998
3.5	.4998									
4.0	.49997									
4.5	.499997									
5.0	.4999997									

Reprinted with permission from *CRC Standard Mathematical Tables* (27th edition). © CRC Press, Inc., Boca Raton, FL.

Index